Modern Industrial Organization

Dennis W. Carlton
University of Chicago

Jeffrey M. Perloff
University of California, Berkeley

1990 FIRST EDITION

SCOTT, FORESMAN/LITTLE, BROWN HIGHER EDUCATION
A Division of Scott, Foresman and Company
Glenview, Illinois   London, England

To Janie and Jackie

Library of Congress Cataloging-in-Publication Data
Carlton, Dennis W.
    Modern industrial organization / Dennis Carlton, Jeffrey Perloff.
        p.   cm.
    Bibliography: p.
    Includes indexes.
    ISBN 0-673-18062-X
    1.   Industrial organization (Economic theory)   I.   Perloff,
Jeffrey.   II.   Title.
HD2326.C376   1989
338.6—dc20   89-35096
                                                              CIP

1 2 3 4 5 6-KPF-94 93 92 91 90 89

PREFACE

Modern Industrial Organization combines the latest theories with empirical evidence about the organization of firms and industries. It compares the traditional structure-conduct-performance approach with the latest advances based on microeconomic theory including transaction-cost analysis, game theory, contestability, and information theory. Practical examples illustrate the role of each theory in current policy debates, such as whether mergers promote economic efficiency (Chapter 7), whether predatory pricing is likely to be a serious problem (Chapter 12), whether preventing manufacturers from restricting distributors' prices would benefit consumers (Chapter 16), whether providing consumers with more information about prices or products would increase welfare (Chapter 17), whether advertising is harmful (Chapter 18), whether joint ventures are the best means of encouraging research (Chapter 20), whether current antitrust laws promote competition and increase welfare (Chapters 9, 16, and 22), and whether government regulation does more harm or more good (Chapter 23).

Modern Industrial Organization is designed for both undergraduate and graduate students. The theories presented in the chapters require only a microeconomics course as a prerequisite and do not involve calculus. However, technical appendixes supplement selected chapters and provide a rigorous foundation for graduate students. We have used this book in both undergraduate and graduate courses. In our undergraduate courses, we rely on the chapters and skip the technical appendixes. In graduate courses, we use the chapters and technical appendixes along with supplementary readings based on selected articles from each chapter's bibliography.

The first half of the book covers the basics of competition, monopoly, oligopoly, and monopolistic competition. Chapter 1 discusses the basic paradigms used in this book. Chapter 2 discusses why firms exist. Chapters 3 through 6 develop the basics of micro-economic theory—costs, competition, monopoly, and competition and monopoly with externalities—that are used throughout the remainder of the book. Chapters 7 through 12 emphasize empirical applications and explain the recent developments in the theory of oligopoly and monopolistic competition. Chapter 7 covers market structure, merger activity, and barriers to entry. Chapter 8 deals with dominant firms that have a fringe of competitive firms. Chapters 9 and 10 cover oligopoly behavior ranging from cooperative behavior (cartels) to noncooperative behavior based on game theory. Chapter 11 focuses on monopolistic competition and product differentiation. Chapter 12 concludes the first half of the book with a thorough review and assessment of empirical work on market structure.

The second half of the book covers topics often missing from traditional texts: topics concerning the "new industrial organization." These topics, essential for applying the theories of industrial organization to everyday problems, are at the heart of many public policy debates and are the focus of considerable recent research. Chapter 13 examines strategic behavior where firms determine the best ways to do battle with their rivals. Chapters 14 and 15 examine common pricing strategies, such as price discrimination through quantity discounts and tie-in sales. Chapter 16 discusses common business practices between manufacturers and distributors (vertical integration and vertical restrictions) and the dramatic change in public policy in recent years toward these practices. The next two chapters, Chapters 17 and 18, address the problems that arise when consumers are not perfectly informed and when firms must advertise their products. Chapters 19 and 20 analyze how the durability of a product affects the market and how innovation can be encouraged. Chapter 21 examines evidence on the ways markets operate and explores how modern microeconomic models of industrial organization may effect the macroeconomic economy. The two concluding chapters, Chapters 22 and 23, analyze antitrust policy and government regulation.

Although we believe that *Modern Industrial Organization* contains innovative ideas, we recognize that any textbook must borrow from existing research. We have tried to indicate when we have relied on the insights of others. However, it is probably unavoidable that we have occasionally omitted a reference to some author whose ideas predated ours. We apologize in advance for any such oversights.[1]

■ ALTERNATIVE COURSE OUTLINES

To cover the entire book adequately will take two quarters or semesters. The book is designed, however, so that shorter courses can be constructed easily by choosing selected chapters, as shown in the following proposed reading lists. Chapters 2 through 6 review and extend the basic material that is often covered in an intermediate microeconomics course: the theory of the firm, costs, the theory of competition, the theory of monopoly, and externalities.

These chapters can be reviewed quickly for students with extensive preparation in microeconomics. Chapters 7 through 12 are the core chapters. Depending on the interests of the students and the instructor, a one quarter or semester course could then sample a few of the chapters in the second part of the book to obtain a flavor of the ways industrial organization can be used to study real world problems.

---

[1] Sometimes commonly used words have special meanings in the law that differ from the standard usage by economists and the general public. We have tried to use clear language to express economic rather than legal principles. For example, we might say that the "price of wheat in the market in Chicago affects the price of wheat in the market in Kansas City." Although such a statement uses the word "market" loosely, the point of the statement—that the prices of wheat in Chicago and Kansas City are related—is clear. In an antitrust trial or merger case, however, a specific legal definition of a market (studied in Chapter 22) is used and whether there are two separate markets or a single combined market is often of central interest. Our statement should not be interpreted to mean that there are necessarily two distinct wheat markets in Chicago and Kansas City for legal purposes.

All courses:

Carefully cover Chapters 2 and 7 to 12, the core theory.

For courses that do not assume a strong background in microeconomic theory:

Cover Chapters 3 to 6.

For courses that assume a strong background in microeconomic theory:

Review quickly Chapters 3 to 6.

For courses that require calculus:

Include the technical appendixes.

For policy-oriented courses:

Cover antitrust and regulation (Chapters 22 and 23). As time allows, include strategic behavior (Chapter 13), price discrimination (Chapter 14), vertical relationships (Chapter 16), and limited information, advertising, and disclosure (Chapters 17 and 18), government policies towards innovation (Chapter 20), and macroeconomics (Chapter 21).

For regulation courses:

Regulations are dealt with throughout the book. Cover, in particular, externalities (Chapter 6), vertical relations (Chapter 16), limited information, advertising and disclosure (Chapters 17 and 18), government policies toward innovation (Chapter 20), and government regulation (Chapter 23).

For business courses:

Include strategic behavior (Chapter 13), price discrimination (Chapter 14), (optionally, nonlinear pricing [Chapter 15]), vertical relations (Chapter 16), and information and advertising (Chapters 17 and 18).

For courses that stress the latest theories:

Include strategic behavior (Chapter 13), vertical relations (Chapter 16), information and advertising (Chapters 17 and 18), government policies towards innovation (Chapter 20), and market operation (Chapter 21).

For advanced courses:

Add chapters on nonlinear pricing (Chapter 15) and durability (Chapter 19).

■ ACKNOWLEDGMENTS

Finally, we would like to thank the many people who helped us in planning, researching, writing, revising, and editing this book. People who helped in the planning, writing, and revising include:

Mark Bagnoli, University of Michigan

Kyle Bagwell, Northwestern University

Ralph Bradburd, Williams College
Reuven Brenner, University of Montreal
Timothy Bresnahan, Stanford University
David Butz, University of California, Los Angeles
Richard Clarke, AT&T Bell Laboratories
Ron Cotterill, University of Connecticut
Keith Crocker, Pennsylvania State University
Frank Easterbrook, University of Chicago, and Judge, Federal Court of Appeals
Daniel Fischel, University of Chicago
Drew Fudenberg, Massachusetts Institute of Technology
Anita Garten, Lexecon, Inc.
Robert Gertner, University of Chicago
Richard Gilbert, University of California, Berkeley
Luis Guash, University of California, San Diego
Jonathan Hamilton, University of Florida, Gainesville
Charles Holt, University of Virginia
Adam Jaffe, Harvard University
Theodore Keeler, University of California, Berkeley
John Kwoka, George Washington University
William Landes, University of Chicago
Bart Lipman, Carnegie-Mellon University
Nancy Lutz, Yale University
William Lynk, Lexecon, Inc.
Marty Perry, Bell Communications Research
Russell Pittman, Justice Department
Richard Posner, University of Chicago, and Judge, Federal Court of Appeals
Stanley Reynolds, University of Arizona
Richard Rogers, University of Massachusetts
Andrew Rosenfield, Lexecon, Inc.
Thomas Ross, Carleton University
Stephen Salant, University of Michigan
Garth Saloner, Massachusetts Institute of Technology
Steve Salop, Georgetown University
Richard Schmalensee, Massachusetts Institute of Technology
Suzanne Scotchmer, University of California, Berkeley
Robert Sherwin, Lexecon, Inc.
Ted Snyder, University of Michigan
Pablo Spiller, University of Illinois, Urbana-Champaign
Mark Stegman, University of North Carolina

George Stigler, University of Chicago

Stephen Stigler, University of Chicago

Joseph Stiglitz, Stanford University

Valerie Suslow, University of Michigan

Lien Tran, University of California, Berkeley

John Vernon, Duke University

Roger Ware, University of Toronto

Leonard Weiss, University of Wisconsin

Lawrence White, New York University

Oliver Williamson, University of California, Berkeley

Robert Willig, Princeton University

Brian Wright, University of California, Berkeley

Edwin Zimmerman, Covington & Burling

We also thank David Buschena, Gary Casterline, George Frisvold, Carolyn Harper, Dave Mitchell, and Margaret Sheridan for excellent research assistance. Carlton gratefully acknowledges the typing assistance of Nila Davis, Tara Marin, and Joy Riggio. We received extensive editorial help on early drafts from Carole Nuckton and Jacqueline Persons. We thank Claire Friedland for proofreading the galleys. We are particularly grateful to George Lobell who helped us extensively in designing and planning the book and to Deborah Samyn, our developmental editor at Scott, Foresman/Little, Brown who helped us improve the organization and presentation of our book substantially. Our designer, Julie Anderson, and our project editor Colleen McCauley Shannon helped produce a well-designed book in a timely fashion. We are extremely grateful to Nicholas Murray and Mary Espenschied for superior copyediting. This book has benefited extensively from the comments of our students who cheerfully served as "guinea pigs," reading and using earlier drafts of this book. Most importantly, we thank our families for their support.

In any jointly authored work, readers often want to know how the book was written. Each of us took primary responsibility for different chapters. Each author blames the other for all remaining mistakes. Each takes credit for any good jokes.

Dennis W. Carlton
Jeffrey M. Perloff

Contents

PART 8
GOVERNMENT POLICIES AND THEIR EFFECTS   729

22 ANTITRUST LAWS AND POLICY   730

23 REGULATION   780

PART 1

INTRODUCTION

1 OVERVIEW

CHAPTER 1

OVERVIEW

Leave all hope, ye that enter.

DANTE ALIGHIERI

This text presents both traditional and new theories of **industrial organization:** the study of the ways firms and markets are organized and of their interactions. Introductory microeconomics analyzes idealized models of firms and markets; this text takes a closer, more realistic look at them, warts and all. In introductory physics, one first disregards gravity and friction in studying the movement of bodies, and then adds these complications to the analysis. The study of industrial organization adds to the perfectly competitive model real-world frictions, such as limited information, transaction costs, costs of adjusting prices, government actions, and barriers to entry by new firms into a market. It then considers how firms are organized and how they compete in such a world.

This chapter describes some of the paradigms that help to organize the study of industrial organization and gives an overview of the material in later chapters. Finally it describes some of the analytic tools that are used.

■ PARADIGMS

Buddy, can you spare a pair of dimes?

There are at least two major approaches to the study of industrial organization, and since they are compatible as organizing principles, this text uses both of them. The first, the structure-conduct-performance paradigm, is highly descriptive and provides an overview of the entire field. The second, the price theory paradigm uses microeconomic models to explain firm behavior and market structures.

Structure-Conduct-Performance

The **structure-conduct-performance** paradigm provides an overview of industrial organization.[1] According to this view, an industry's performance depends on the conduct

---

[1] The structure-conduct-performance approach was developed at Harvard by Edward S. Mason (1939, 1949) and his colleagues and students, such as Joe S. Bain (1959).

of sellers and buyers, which depends on the structure of the industry.[2] The structure, in turn, depends on basic conditions, such as technology and demand for a product. For example, in an industry with a technology such that the average cost of production falls as output increases, the industry tends to have only one firm, or possibly a small number of firms. When the single firm in an industry conducts its business so as to maximize profits, it is using monopoly pricing. If the basic conditions make the demand for the monopoly's product relatively inelastic (people are relatively insensitive to price), then the price in that market is higher than if the demand is relatively elastic (people are price sensitive).

Figure 1.1 illustrates the relationships among structure, conduct, and performance and shows how basic conditions and government policy interact. The relationships among the five boxes are complex; for example, government regulations affect the number of sellers in an industry, and firms may influence government policy to achieve higher profits. Similarly, if entry barriers lead to monopoly and monopoly profits, new industries may develop new, substitute products that affect the demand for the original product. Empirical researchers who rely on this paradigm typically use data at the industry level. They ask, for example, if industries with certain structural features (for example, few firms) have high prices.

The structure-conduct-performance paradigm is a very general way to organize the study of industrial organization, and can be used to organize the material in the rest of this book. The second major approach, the price theory paradigm, can also be used to organize and interpret this material.

Price Theory

In contrast to the structure-conduct-performance paradigm, **price theory** models analyze the economic incentives facing individuals and firms to explain market phenomena. George J. Stigler (1968) was an early proponent of this analytical approach. Stigler believes that a course in industrial organization should concentrate on using microeconomic theory to design empirical studies of markets and of the causes and effects of public policy. This approach has been extremely successful in attracting followers in recent years, and today, most industrial organization research and courses are well grounded in formal economic theory. One reason for the recent shift to this approach is the availability of data at a more micro level and advances in price theory. In recent years, three specific theoretical applications of price theory have won substantial support—transaction cost analysis, game theory, and contestable market analysis—and help to explain structure, conduct, and performance.

Transaction Costs

Transaction cost analysis emphasizes that firms incur costs in transacting business, such as the cost of writing and enforcing contracts. Using formal price theory analysis, this

---

[2] In this chapter, the terms "market" and "industry" are used loosely and interchangeably. In antitrust cases, important distinctions are made between these terms. These distinctions are discussed in later chapters.

FIGURE 1.1   Structure, Conduct, and Performance

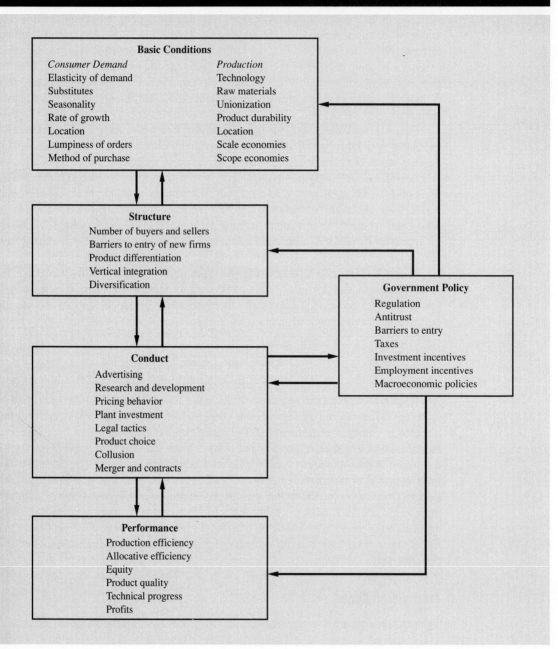

approach uses differences in transaction costs to explain why structure, conduct, and performance vary across industries.

Over 50 years ago, Ronald H. Coase (1937) explained that a firm and a market are substitute means of organizing economic activity. Coase emphasized the error in assuming that the use of the marketplace involves no cost. These costs help to determine market structure, for example. Where the cost of buying from other firms is relatively low, a firm is more likely to buy supplies from others than produce the supplies itself.

Oliver Williamson (1975, 8-10), one of the major proponents of the transaction cost approach, says that four basic concepts underlie this analysis:

1. Markets and firms are alternative means for completing related sets of transactions. For example, a firm can either buy a product or a service or produce it.

2. The relative cost of using markets or a firm's own resources should determine the choice.

3. The transaction costs of writing and executing complex contracts across a market "vary with the characteristics of the human decision makers who are involved with the transaction on the one hand, and the objective properties of the market on the other" (p. 8).

4. These human and environmental factors affect the transaction costs across markets and within firms.

This approach aims to identify a set of environmental factors and human factors that explain both internal firm and industrial organization. The key environmental factors are *uncertainty* and the *small number* of firms; the key human factors are *bounded rationality* and *opportunism*. Problems arise when uncertainty is combined with bounded rationality, or where the managers of the few firms in an industry behave opportunistically.

Bounded rationality refers to the limited human capacity to solve or anticipate complex problems. Thus, in a world of great uncertainty, it may be too difficult or costly to negotiate contracts that deal with all possible contingencies. As a result, firms may produce internally even though, otherwise, it would be cost-effective to rely on markets.

When the number of firms is small and individuals may behave opportunistically, firms may not want long-term contracts for fear of being victimized in the future. For example, a firm that relies on another to supply a factor that is essential to its production process may be vulnerable to blackmail because it cannot produce if the supply is cut off. This problem is likely to be important if there are few alternative suppliers.

Thus, reliance on markets is more likely when (1) there is little uncertainty and (2) there are many firms (competition) and limited opportunities for opportunistic behavior. When these conditions are reversed, firms are more likely to produce for themselves than to rely on markets. The transaction cost approach has been very successful because of its broad explanatory power.

Game Theory

Another approach that is increasingly important to economic theorists is **game theory,** which models competition among firms as a game of *strategies,* or battle plans, that describe the behavior of each firm.[3] A firm's strategy determines, for example, its output, price, and advertising level. In the game, firms compete for profits. Game theory describes how firms form their strategies and how these strategies determine the profits.

Game theory provides the most insights in games in which there are relatively few firms. Much of this text concerns such markets, and many of the models it presents are examples of game theory.

Contestable Markets

The importance of entry to the competitive process has been recognized for a long time. Demsetz (1968) and Baumol, Panzar, and Willig (1982) emphasize that industries with only a few firms (or just one) can be very competitive if there is a threat of entry by other firms. Markets in which there are few firms, but many firms will enter rapidly if prices exceed costs are called **contestable markets.** Baumol, Panzar, and Willig emphasize the importance of exit as well as entry: Firms are reluctant to enter an industry if it is very costly to exit. If entry or exit are difficult, a market is not contestable and the strategic behavior studied by game theorists is relevant. If entry and exit are easy, a market is contestable and can have the properties of a competitive market: price equals marginal cost and strategic behavior is irrelevant.

■ ORGANIZATION OF THIS TEXT

> *Where I am not understood, it shall be concluded that something very useful and profound is couched underneath.* —JONATHAN SWIFT

The main objective of this text is to provide a systematic presentation of the basic theories—both traditional and new—of how firms and markets are organized and how they behave. Rather than treating structure and conduct as given, the text explains them as the outcome of individuals' maximizing behaviors. That is, it shows how the price theory models provide the underpinnings for the structure-conduct-performance paradigm. The paradigms complement each other, and both are useful for developing an understanding of industrial organization.

Basic Theory

Part 2 (Chapters 2 and 3) reviews and extends basic microeconomic theory about costs and introduces the theory of the firm. Special attention is paid to costs, since they are crucial in explaining market structure. For example, costs (especially *transaction costs*) are crucial in determining whether a firm should produce a factor of production or buy it in a market. When a firm produces a factor itself, the firm is said to be *vertical integrated*. Thus, costs help to determine whether the firm vertically integrates or not. Chapter 2 on the theory of the firm introduces vertical integration, which is discussed in more detail in Chapter 16. In addition, Chapter 2 covers the internal organization and ownership of

---

[3] The first clear presentation of game theory was made by John von Neumann and Oskar Morgenstern (1944).

TABLE 1.1	Some Basic Market Structures				
	Sellers			Buyers	
Market Structure	Entry Barriers	Number		Entry Barriers	Number
Competition	no	many		no	many
Monopoly	yes	one		no	many
Monopsony	no	many		yes	one
Bilateral monopoly	yes	one		yes	one
Oligopoly	yes	few		no	many
Oligopsony	no	many		yes	few
Monopolistic competition	no	many		no	many

firms, pointing out that the division between firms and markets is not always clear and that the structure of an industry may change rapidly as costs shift. Chapter 3 analyzes several cost concepts and provides empirical evidence on costs.

Market Structures

Parts 3 and 4 (Chapters 4 through 12) introduce the most important market structures and provide (in chapter 12) an empirical overview of market structure and performance. The factors that determine market structures, such as cost and government intervention, are discussed at length.

Table 1.1 shows the basic taxonomy used in this text to describe several structures. The number of firms in a market and the ease of entry by new firms determine the type of structure. Chapter 7 discusses in detail *barriers to entry,* but for the moment, view an entry barrier as something that prevents new firms from entering a market. For example, a new airline company cannot offer service between New York and London without permission from both the United States and Great Britain. Such permission is usually not granted unless a company currently flying ceases operation; thus, a government-created entry barrier exists in this market.

When a market includes many potential buyers and sellers and has no entry or exit barriers, the market structure is that of **competition.** When one firm sells to many buyers, and no new sellers can enter, the firm is a **monopoly.** Conversely, a firm that buys from many sellers, is a **monopsony.** If sellers can influence price even though they face competition from other firms, the market structure is either **oligopoly** or **monopolistic competition.** It is oligopolistic if substantial barriers prevent new sellers from entering the market. If there are no barriers to entry or exit, then the market is monopolistically competitive.

Competition and Monopoly.   Chapters 4 through 6 review and extend the theory of competition and monopoly. Chapter 4 discusses the basic theory of competition. Competitive firms are too small to affect the market price, so they take that price as given and choose how many units of output to produce. As a result, competitive firms are *price takers*. The chapter shows that such behavior has desirable consequences for social welfare. It is the market structure to which all other structures are compared. Because there are no barriers to entry, firms enter competitive markets whenever positive profits can be made. This influx of sellers drives profits to zero for all firms in the market in the long run.

In contrast, monopolists (discussed in Chapter 5) are *price setters*. A monopolist, as the only firm in the market, can set the price it wants and prices above the level of a competitive market. The ability to price above the competitive level is referred to as *market power,* and such conduct leads to welfare losses by society. Because of entry barriers, the monopolist can earn positive economic profits in the long run. Analogously, monopsony results in a lower price than a competitive market would set, which also has undesirable welfare implications.

Chapter 6 extends the basic theories of competition and monopoly to discuss *externalities,* which are failures of the pricing mechanism that cause desirable or undesirable products (or byproducts) to have a price of zero. Pollution is an example of a negative externality. People produce too much pollution because they are not charged when they pollute (the price is zero). Competition does not maximize social well-being in the presence of externalities, and may not be better than monopoly.

Other Market Structures.   Chapter 7 discusses the structure of the U.S. economy and introduces the concept of an entry barrier. When a barrier prevents new firms from entering an industry, existing firms are often able to exercise market power.

Chapter 8 introduces a new structure, which does not easily lend itself to being described in Table 1.1. It is a hybrid of the competitive and monopolistic structures, in which there is a *dominant firm* and a *competitive fringe*. The dominant firm has some market power so that it can set prices and the other (fringe) firms are price takers. One cause of such a structure is that the dominant firm has substantially lower costs than do the other firms.

Chapter 9 shows how monopoly-like conduct may occur in a market with more than one firm: the firms may form a *cartel,* agreeing to coordinate their behavior so that they imitate a monopoly. If they all restrict output and raise the industry price above the competitive level, they can increase their profits. Government antitrust laws may be used to prevent explicit cartels from forming. The chapter considers why cartels only form in some industries and why they fall apart. Members of cartels are shown to have an incentive to cheat on one another. The theory of cartel behavior is used to study the behavior of markets with only a few competitors, called *oligopolists*.

Chapter 10 also examines oligopolists' behavior. Unlike competitive and monopolistic firms, oligopolistic firms expect their rivals to react to their behavior or strategies. We start by considering some older (but still used) models of how firms form expectations about the reactions of other firms to their behavior. An expected reaction is called a *conjectural variation*. For example, firm 1 may assume a conjectural variation in the output of firm 2 in response to a small change in its own output.

One criticism of the conjectural variation approach is that it fails to explain how firms arrive at their conjectures about other firms' behaviors. An alternative approach to oligopoly behavior, based on cartel theory, holds that all firms recognize the benefits of behaving collectively like a cartel, but each firm also recognizes it can benefit from cheating. Game theory formalizes and elaborates on this theory by considering that incentives to cooperate or cheat are based on rational beliefs about economic incentives. Chapter 10 also presents experimental and empirical evidence on oligopolistic behavior.

Chapter 11 modifies the oligopoly model of Chapter 10 by allowing entry. In monopolistic competition, unlike in an oligopoly, entry by new firms drives economic profits to zero. Thus, other things being equal, removing entry barriers typically increases output.

Chapter 11 also considers the implications of product differentiation on social welfare and the effect of government interventions in these markets. For example, consumers presumably prefer low prices and many choices of differentiated products. Thus, government intervention that results in fewer firms and products but lower average prices may be a mixed blessing. Whether consumers prefer slightly higher prices with more variety becomes an empirical question for each market.

Chapter 12 surveys a great deal of empirical evidence on profits and market structure in the United States and other economies. Thus, Chapters 4 through 12 cover both traditional and new (game) theories on the structure and performance of market economies.

Business Practices: Strategies and Conduct

Part 5 (Chapters 13 through 16) deals with general business practices and covers some of the latest research using game theory and transaction cost theory. The chapters on basic market structures concentrate on only a few strategies: firms only vary price, output levels, or the degree of differentiation of their products, usually on a once-only basis. Chapter 13 considers other, more complex strategies in dynamic models. For example, a firm may set such a low price that it drives its competitors out of business and then raise its price. Similarly, a firm may engage in behavior designed to raise its rivals' costs, so they cannot compete as effectively. Other more complex strategies involve exchanging (or not exchanging) information with competitors.

Chapters 14 and 15 concentrate on complex pricing behavior. Chapter 14 deals with *price discrimination*. Firms with market power can maximize profits by charging some consumers a higher price than others for identical products. For example, some consumers are more price sensitive than others. Chapter 15 deals with pricing schemes that are related to price discrimination. For example, an electrical utility may engage in *two-part pricing,* charging one price to be connected to the system and another for each kilowatt consumed. Another important example is *tie-in sales:* for example, a firm might sell you one of its products only if you agreed to buy another.

Chapter 16 examines the reasons for *vertical integration.* As mentioned earlier, firms may buy supplies in markets or produce them. The chapter explains why some industries are vertically integrated and others are not. It also examines the welfare implications of vertical integration.

Some firms, instead of vertically integrating, use *vertical restraints.* For example, an automobile manufacturer may require that its dealers, which are independent firms, agree in contracts about the way they will conduct their business. Thus, the manufacturer uses contractual restrictions to approximate vertical integration. The recent change in public policy towards vertical restraints is also discussed.

Information, Advertising, and Disclosure

Part 6 (Chapters 17 and 18) examines the effects of limited information on markets and how strategic behavior by firms can alter information. Chapter 17 discusses the effect of information on quality and prices in a market and shows that many typical properties of a competitive market disappear if information is limited. Limits on consumer information often give firms market power; thus, better information may reduce market power and increase competition.

Chapter 18 examines advertising and how it may either increase or decrease welfare. The chapter also explains how laws designed to limit lying or to require disclosure of important facts to consumers may have paradoxical effects.

Dynamic Models and Market Clearing

Virtually all the models discussed through chapter 18 are **static models:** like snapshots, they tell us what happens at a point in time.[4] Typically, static models are used for long-term analysis. In contrast, **dynamic models** describe the evolution of markets through time: they show how firms adjust their behavior. Dynamic models are more difficult to use than static ones, but they provide additional insights.

Part 7 (Chapters 19, 20, and 21) deals with models in which current actions affect future profits. Chapter 19 examines the issue of *durability;* for example, would a car that lasted 15 years produce higher or lower profits for the manufacturer than one that lasts 10 years? One surprising result of this investigation is that a durable goods monopolist may have more market power if it rents its product than if it sells it.

Chapter 20 considers how laws on patents affect technological change. New discoveries that reduce production costs or create new products are obviously highly desirable. Unfortunately, for reasons explained in Chapter 6 on externalities, a competitive industry produces too few inventions. Governments grant patents that allow inventors to be monopoly sellers of new products. These monopoly profits encourage greater inventive activity. Alternative incentives, such as prizes and government research contracts, are also studied.

Chapter 21 is the only chapter to deal explicitly with macroeconomic issues. As in the other chapters, however, the focus is on price theory. This chapter is particularly concerned with the way markets actually adjust over time as a function of their structure. Other means of *clearing a market* (having quantity demanded equal to quantity supplied) besides price adjustments are also discussed.

Government Policies and Their Effects

Part 8 deals with government actions that increase or decrease welfare. Chapter 22 examines the *antitrust* laws. These laws are intended to prevent conduct that adversely affects welfare, such as the formation of cartels that set prices above competitive levels

---

[4] A few exceptions are the dynamic (nonstatic) models discussed in Chapters 8 (dominant firm and competitive fringe) and 13 (strategic behavior).

or mergers or combinations of several firms that might lead to substantial market power. The chapter points out, however, that antitrust laws sometimes have been used to prevent rather than encourage competitive behavior.

Finally, Chapter 23 discusses various government laws that *regulate* business conduct and market structure. The chapter examines the effects of the recent trend towards deregulating markets. One theme of this chapter is that government intervention in markets may lead to inefficiency and that many laws proposed with the noblest objectives may benefit special interest groups at the expense of the general population.

■ TOOLS AND TECHNIQUES FOR ANALYSIS

Civilization aims at making all good things . . . accessible even to cowards.
— NIETZSCHE

This text minimizes the use of mathematical tools and jargon; when they appear, they serve to speed communications. The chapters use tables and graphs freely to illustrate models without formal mathematics. Many chapters include footnotes and technical appendixes that present rigorous mathematical models for those who are mathematically inclined. The presentation does make repeated use of certain key concepts and tools that economists commonly use to analyze the behavior of firms and the structure of markets.

Fundamental approaches underlie most analytic work in any discipline, including economics. Chemists often say that the answer to most questions is "It's the electrons and how they are arranged in space." In microeconomics, the answers "Supply equals demand" and "Marginal benefit equals marginal cost" work for most questions (assuming the axes are labeled appropriately). Most of the models in this text are about **maximizing behavior** and most of the questions can be answered with the phrase "Marginal benefit equals marginal cost." For example, a firm maximizes its profits when it sets its output level so that its marginal benefit (marginal revenue) equals its marginal cost. Maximizing is a basic tool used in all the chapters. Throughout the text, empirical evidence is presented to support many of the models, and statistical techniques are briefly discussed as needed. Most other tools and concepts appear in only some chapters, and they build on each other; tools introduced early provide a foundation for those introduced later.

■ Key Terms

bounded rationality
competition
contestable markets
dynamic models
game theory
industrial organization
maximizing behavior
monopolistic competition

monopoly
monopsony
oligopoly
price theory
static models
structure-conduct-performance
transaction cost

■ References

Bain, Joe S. 1959. *Industrial Organization*. New York: John Wiley and Sons.

Baumol, W., J. Panzar, and R. Willig. 1982. *Contestable Markets and the Theory of Industry Structure*. New York: Harcourt Brace Jovanovich.

Coase, Ronald H. 1937. "The Nature of the Firm." *Economica*, n.s. 4:386-405.

Demsetz, Harold. 1968. "Why Regulate Utilities?" *Journal of Law and Economics* 11:55-65.

Mason, Edward S. 1939. "Price and Production Policies of Large-Scale Enterprise." *American Economic Review*, supp. 29:61-74.

Mason, Edward S. 1949. "The Current State of the Monopoly Problem in the United States." *Harvard Law Review* 62:1265–85.

Stigler, George J. 1968. *The Organization of Industry*. Homewood, Ill.: Richard D. Irwin.

Von Neumann, John, and Oskar Morgenstern. 1944. *Theory of Games and Economic Behavior*. Princeton, N.J.: Princeton University Press.

Williamson, Oliver E. 1975. *Markets and Hierarchies: Analysis and Antitrust Implications*. New York: The Free Press.

CHAPTER **2**

THEORY OF THE FIRM

It is better to know some of the questions than all of the answers.

JAMES THURBER

Industrial organization is the study of the actions of a firm and the effect of those actions on industry behavior and performance. But what is a firm and what does it try to do? How is it organized and how has the organization of the typical firm changed over time? This chapter answers these questions.

This chapter first discusses why markets and firms can be viewed as alternative means to accomplish the same goals, and then explains when firms are likely to be more efficient than the market in performing certain tasks and when they are likely to be less efficient. It also analyzes the internal structure of firms and documents how multiproduct firms are organized. It shows how workers can be motivated to perform and how the chain of command within a firm can be structured. The chapter discusses the common forms of ownership and analyzes the importance of debt and equity (stock) in understanding how firms operate. Finally, there is a discussion of the difficulty of controlling managers' actions in a large firm and whether it is reasonable to suppose that such large firms maximize profits.

■ DEFINITION OF THE FIRM

A *firm* allocates resources that it has purchased in order to produce and sell valued product; it earns the difference between what it receives as revenue and what it spends for the resources. For example, a steel firm builds a plant, hires workers, purchases raw materials, and then produces and sells steel. The firm decides how much to pay for its resources and how to combine them to make steel. It makes a profit if the price at which it sells its steel exceeds the costs of producing it.

This definition of a firm immediately raises a question. As all students of economics learn, the marketplace can use prices to produce an **efficient allocation** of resources. An efficient allocation is one in which no reallocation of resources can make at least one person better off without making someone else worse off. If resources are efficiently allocated, the only way for society to increase production of one product is to produce less of other products and use some of the released inputs in the production of the one product. If the marketplace can allocate resources efficiently, why then is it advantageous for a firm to perform some activities itself when it could rely on the marketplace? For example, why does General Motors now produce its own car bodies rather than purchase them from someone else as it did before 1926? The answer is that internal production is sometimes less costly and hence more efficient than relying on the marketplace. A more sophisticated way of saying the same thing is that the incentive structure (the incentives facing managers and production workers) is different for markets than for internal production. Because of this difference, firms sometimes find it better to do things internally. When a firm performs a task itself rather than relying on another firm, it is said to have *vertically integrated*. Chapter 16 covers vertical integration in more detail.

Transaction Costs and Opportunistic Behavior

One major difference between producing internally and relying on the marketplace has to do with **transaction costs.**[1] Transaction costs are the costs of doing business with another firm. Transaction costs refer to the initial cost of negotiating an agreement as well as to the ongoing costs of ensuring that the agreement does what the firm desires. Since no agreement can specify all possible contingencies, modifying agreements in light of unforeseen events is an important component of these costs. For example, suppose a piece of equipment can be manufactured out of either aluminum or copper. A supplier agrees to manufacture it out of aluminum. If the price of aluminum suddenly rises, the supplier might want to manufacture the equipment out of copper instead. The renegotiation involved in adding new delivery schedules, new prices, and new quality controls to the contract is time-consuming, and the buyer can use it as an opportunity to take advantage of the seller by threatening to enforce the original contract unless the seller offers favorable terms. Anytime two unrelated parties agree to transact in the marketplace, such **opportunistic behavior** is possible. Each side may try to interpret the terms of the contract to its advantage, especially when terms are vague or even missing.

If contracts are simple (for example, a transaction involving 1 bushel of a specific variety of corn in Chicago on a particular date), then opportunistic behavior is unlikely. In complicated contracts, it may be too difficult to specify all possible contingencies, and a signed contract may contain provisions that turn out to be undesirable to one of the parties. For example, in 1919 General Motors (GM) contracted with Fisher Auto Body for exclusive production of GM auto bodies. Since Fisher had to develop specialized production devices that could be used only for GM cars, it was reluctant to sign a short-term contract because at renegotiation time Fisher would be at the mercy of GM. On the other hand, GM was reluctant to depend so heavily on one supplier, fearing that, with a short-term contract, at renegotiation time GM would be at the mercy of Fisher. Because

---

[1] This point was first made by Coase (1937) and was further developed and significantly expanded by Williamson (1975, 1985). Alchian and Demsetz (1972) and Klein, Crawford, and Alchian (1978) also contain excellent discussions of the issues. The recent resurgence of interest in the theory of the firm is primarily due to the extensive work of Williamson (1975, 1985). This chapter relies heavily on his insights.

each party feared that a short-term contract would allow it to be taken advantage of, they signed a long-term contract for ten years, with price being set according to a specified formula. However, demand conditions changed greatly after 1919, and GM found that the prices according to the formula in the contract were too high. GM finally merged with Fisher in 1926, thereby removing the costs associated with transacting in the marketplace. GM's experience illustrates one difficulty with any long-term contract: it is difficult to foresee all possible changes that could occur over the term of the contract and to specify how the contractual terms, especially price, should adapt to changed circumstances (Klein, Crawford, and Alchian 1978, 309–10).

In summary, the incentive for opportunistic behavior changes if activities are organized within a firm rather than between firms in the marketplace.[2] In a single firm, if one division can behave opportunistically toward another division, the overall supervisor tries to ensure that such behavior does not occur unless overall profitability increases—an arrangement that may be difficult to achieve in a market setting. Also, conflicts are often easier to resolve when they develop within a firm than when they develop between firms. Legal and other remedies may be inadequate and expensive compared to a manager's orders; thus, the **dispute resolution mechanism** can be different within a firm than between firms (Williamson, 1979).

Situations with High Transaction Costs

A firm will perform activities itself rather than rely on the market when transaction costs are likely to be high. Such costs tend to rise when it is difficult to specify a contract that eliminates opportunistic behavior. Transaction costs are likely to be especially high when products are specialized, market conditions are changing, and information is sold.

Specialized Products.   When a product is specialized or custom-made, a buyer who signs a contract with a single supplier has only one source for immediate supply. Similarly, the supplier would find it hard to sell the specialized product to another buyer. In addition, specialized products (for example, GM auto bodies) often require specialized machinery (for example, special molds) that may be worthless to the supplier except for making the specialized product. Both the buyer and seller, because of their limited options, are vulnerable after the contract is signed. In such a situation of **asset specificity,** both may benefit if the buyer owns the specialized production equipment that the seller uses (Williamson 1975). Ownership by the buyer diminishes the incentive for opportunistic behavior; neither side can now be harmed as badly as before. For example, automobile manufacturers that rely on outside suppliers for custom-made components often own the specialized dies needed to make them. Monteverde and Teece (1982) found that the more specialized the die, the more likely an automobile company is to own the die.[3]

There are numerous examples of the way ownership of specialized products solves

---

[2] Incentives change when all assets are owned by one, rather than two firms, but, as discussed later, incentives do not always improve if activities are organized within the firm.

[3] See also Masten (1984), who shows that asset specificity influences asset ownership in the aircraft industry, and Anderson and Schmittlein (1984), who examine asset specificity and the decision of a firm to have its own sales force.

EXAMPLE 2.1

ASSET SPECIFICITY AND LONG-TERM CONTRACTS

When a firm develops assets that are custom-made for a particular transaction, it may be exploited by the firm for whom it developed the particular assets. A firm may deal with the problem by conducting transactions internally. As an alternative, it may write detailed contracts that protect it from being exploited. Presumably, the greater the risk of exploitation—that is, the more specialized the asset—the longer the term of the contract and the more detailed it will be.

Paul Joskow (1987) investigates the length of contracts that electric utilities sign with coal mines. Some electric utilities are located right beside coal mines and have few alternatives for obtaining coal. Such utilities are called "mine mouths." Similarly, the mines may have nowhere else to sell their coal, other than to the neighboring electric utilities. This is an extreme example of asset specificity. In such a situation, one might expect a coal mine and an electric utility to merge and thereby avoid bargaining problems. However, federal and state regulations often discourage such arrangements because regulators do not want the added burden of watching over a utility that has activities other than electricity generation and sale. Instead, Joskow finds that long-term contracts are often used. He shows that the length of the contract is directly related to whether the utility is a "mine mouth," and whether there are alternative buyers or sellers of coal in the region. He finds, for example, that a "mine mouth" utility has a coal contract that lasts for about 16 years longer than contracts do for other electric utilities.

the problem of opportunistic bargaining. For instance, a resort hotel typically owns its swimming pool. If it did not, both the hotel and pool company could contract with each other, but possibilities for future opportunistic bargaining would occur. Similarly, chemical plants often own specialized railcars, rather than negotiating with railroads. In situations where ownership is not used to solve the problem of opportunistic bargaining, one expects to see detailed long-term contracts. See Example 2.1.

Changing Market Conditions. The more unpredictable the future, the harder it is to specify contractual terms. People have a limited ability to enumerate and understand all future possibilities, so no contract can spell out every contingency. This limited ability is sometimes called **bounded rationality.** Failure to specify how terms should adjust over time puts both buyer and seller at risk each time the terms are renegotiated. Rigid price formulas are unlikely to allow the flexibility required for efficient responses to changed circumstances. If costs are changing, it may be hard to specify how price should change in response to cost for at least two reasons. First, a buyer will not accept a supplier's word for its costs, especially if they are hard to observe. Many contracts avoid this problem by allowing price to change according to publicly available cost information (for example, the Producer Price Index published by the Bureau of Labor Statistics). Second, a buyer may be reluctant to sign a contract at unknown prices, even if they are to be determined by a known formula.

Information as a Product.   Transactions involving information create special difficulties. Suppose a firm hires a consultant to discover a new cost-reducing production process for a fixed fee, and the consultant returns several months later to report that there is no better way to produce the product. The firm does not know how hard the consultant has worked and pays the fixed fee. Next year, the firm hires the same consultant for a similar project, but this time the fee is set at 1 percent of the increased profits attributable to any suggestion. The consultant returns with a suggestion, and the firm implements it in a new plant that earns $100 more profit than the firm's other plants. When it comes time to calculate the consultant's fee, the firm sends a check for 1 percent of $50, reasoning that the new manager at the new plant is responsible for at least half of the superior profits. In both situations, each side may be acting honestly, yet the other side may feel distrustful; on the other hand, each side may be acting dishonestly, yet there is nothing the other side can do. Enforcing such contracts is costly, which suggests why product development and engineering development are often done internally.

Monitoring Costs

If transaction costs are lower for a firm that allocates its own resources instead of using the market, why not eliminate the marketplace and have one big firm? The answer is that sometimes the allocation of resources in a firm can cost more than in a market.[4] A firm may hire its outside accountant, but that does not mean that the accountant will follow instructions any better. Maybe the accountant will work less hard at a steady job. A firm must check on its employees to make sure its resources are used efficiently, and the costs of doing so are called **monitoring costs.**

An employee on a fixed wage whose output is hard to observe may be able to take it easy on the job. For example, a person who makes and sells furniture strives to be efficient because lower production costs mean higher profits. If this person works on an assembly line with fifty other workers, the person will not have the same incentive to work hard or minimize cost. If workers' efforts cannot be easily distinguished from those of their co-workers, they are unlikely to be rewarded for their extra hard work, and hence will work less. Firms therefore must spend resources (for instance, on supervision) to maintain internal efficiency.

The larger the firm, the greater the potential for nonmarket transactions and the greater the monitoring resources required. Three individuals each performing separate tasks would require three transactions between the various pairings of individuals. With four individuals, there can be six such transactions. If there are N individuals, there can be $N(N - 1)/2$ transactions. As the scale of the firm increases, the number of nonmarket transactions increases, as does the cost of monitoring them. As the firm grows, these costs will eventually outweigh the benefits of allocating resources within the firm; thus, it would not be efficient to have one giant firm.

A good example of the difficulty of monitoring arises in car sales. Most auto makers do not own their dealerships; their dealers are independent individuals who buy cars at wholesale from auto makers and sell them to the public. Dealers who sell cars at too low

---

[4] Grossman and Hart (1986) examine this problem in detail.

a price suffer the loss. If dealers were employees on fixed salaries, they might not be as careful in selecting retail prices, since their salaries are unaffected. If they select low prices, it is hard for the employer to figure out whether they are being lax, or are actually setting the price needed to sell the car to a particular buyer. For that reason, Alfred Sloan, the former chairman of General Motors, said:

> Automobile manufacturers could not without great difficulty have undertaken to merchandise their own product. When the used car came in to the picture in a big way in the 1920s as a trade-in on a new car, the merchandising of automobiles became more a trading proposition than an ordinary selling proposition. Organizing and supervising the necessary thousands of complex trading institutions would have been difficult for the manufacturer; trading is a knack not easily fit into the conventional type of a managerially controlled scheme of organization. So the retail automobile business grew up with the franchised-dealer type of organization (1963, 282).

Firms choose to perform activities internally rather than purchasing them when the costs of monitoring internal efficiency are less than the transaction costs of using markets. However, it is far too simple to think of a market as using prices exclusively to allocate resources and a firm as making exclusive use of managerial command and internal monitoring. Many contracts in the market contain detailed monitoring provisions, and many large firms use internal prices, called **transfer prices,** to allocate goods among their divisions.

In some cases, it is easy to explain why a firm does not rely on a market, as in the GM-Fisher Auto Body example. In other cases, it is harder to explain. For example, whether a firm employs a full-time janitor or hires a cleaning service seems immaterial in economic effect.

Motivating Workers

Copy Mat founder Terry Fairbanks found that by giving his workers a percentage cut of the business they do, a lot more gets done. For example, operators who are alone on the graveyard shift used to run a single Xerox machine. With the incentives, they run several machines at once.[5]

Microeconomics can be used to determine the best incentives to encourage efficient behavior so as to minimize internal monitoring costs. Wage increases over time, vested pension funds, piece rates (payment for each piece produced), bonuses and contests, and stock ownership can all be used to improve internal efficiency by providing incentives for employees to work harder. As the incentive structure changes, so as to create incentive for workers to be efficient, the monitoring cost of internalizing activities decreases, and it is optimal for firms to become larger.

To see the advantages of a piece-rate system, suppose that in a shoe factory, all workers own their machines and are paid a set price for each pair of shoes. The more shoes a worker makes, the more money that worker earns. In contrast, if all workers

---

[5] *San Francisco Chronicle. 1987.* October 26, C1.

receive the same wage regardless of the number of shoes they make, they will have little incentive to work hard. In this case, the piece rate is superior.

Suppose now that the ability to make shoes depends on how well maintained the machines are, as well as on the skill of the workers. Each day the firm maintains the machines by lubricating them with a special oil, but the oil's effectiveness varies from day to day, perhaps because of temperature. On any given day, each worker's output is equally affected by the oil's effectiveness. The firm cannot really monitor how effective the lubrication is except by looking at how many shoes get produced. One way to distinguish hard-working workers is to compare their output to that of their co-workers. The firm can then reward those workers whose relative output is greatest. By holding a contest, the firm can try to reward only hard effort and not the good luck of maintenance, which affects all workers equally. In fact, firms frequently use prizes and contests to motivate their employees to work hard.

One of the best examples of a contest is the race to enter top management. The salary structure in large companies typically rewards the very top management at a much higher level than middle management, from whom top managers are frequently chosen. Even at the highest levels, wide differences in salary can exist. For example, the chairperson at Bank America earned $1,500,000 in salary and bonus in 1988, while the vice-chairperson earned the far lower salary of $975,000.[6] The prize of a high salary motivates managers to work hard so as to distinguish themselves. Even if the large prize has no relation to a manager's worth, it may be economically justified because it motivates all managers to work hard and strive for the top prize.

The longer employees are with a firm, the more management knows about their abilities. Therefore, even if they are unchanged, they become more valuable because the firm knows exactly which tasks they do best. In order to reduce turnover, firms often have skewed wage profiles: they pay low wages initially and high wages later on. Early in life, workers choose not to leave because of the anticipation of higher payment, which could come in the form of higher wages or a pension that workers forfeit if they leave within a specified time period (Becker and Stigler 1974; Lazear 1979).

Another common motivational tool is stock ownership. Workers or managers who own stock in a firm prosper when the firm does well. This creates an incentive for hard work even when their superiors can't observe them. Demsetz (1983) shows that top management in medium-to-small manufacturing firms in the Fortune 500 held about 20 percent of their firm's shares. Demsetz and Lehn (1985) find that stock ownership by key employees did vary in accordance with economic theory: it increased with the difficulty and need that outsiders would have in monitoring employee performance.[7]

■ ORGANIZATION WITHIN FIRMS

Given that a firm should perform several tasks, how should the tasks be organized? Should each worker perform several different tasks or concentrate on only a few? For example,

---

[6] *Business Week.* 1989. May 1, 56.

[7] Demsetz (1983) also shows that for the largest manufacturing firms in the Fortune 500, stock ownership by top management is much lower, around 2 percent.

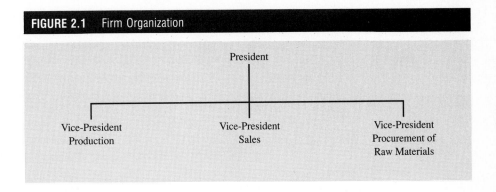

FIGURE 2.1   Firm Organization

President

Vice-President
Production

Vice-President
Sales

Vice-President
Procurement of
Raw Materials

in a company that makes shoes, someone must buy raw material to have on hand for production. The number of shoes to produce depends upon the pricing of the shoes, which in turn depends upon demand and production costs. Once the number is determined, the shoes must be produced. Someone must oversee production costs and keep management informed of any cost changes.

Hierarchies

Should one manager be responsible for pricing, another for monitoring production costs, and another for purchasing raw materials? Or should each of three people be responsible for certain phases of all three functions? A **hierarchy** is the chain of control in an organization. Figure 2.1 shows the hierarchy of a typical organization: three divisions report to one individual who coordinates the various pieces of information. Because people have limited information processing ability, it is impossible for each division vice-president to convey all information to the president. Instead, every time information gets transferred, some is lost. The gain in transferring information up the hierarchy is the desirability of having one individual (the president in our example) put together information from the individual divisions and make a **coordinated decision**—one that recognizes the important costs and benefits to *all* divisions. Within any hierarchy, there is a trade-off between the amount of information from each division and the need for coordinated decisions.[8] The more detailed the information from each division, the less able is one person to absorb information from several divisions and hence the less coordinated the decision making becomes.

The president of any company typically knows much less about how a particular market works than a buying agent and much less about how a particular machine works than the production engineer. The president's role is to assimilate information from all sources and to make the most important coordinated decisions—those that cannot be undone quickly. For example, a president is more likely to be involved in a decision to build a highly specialized plant than to purchase a large machine that can readily be resold.

---

[8] See Williamson (1967, 1975) for a detailed analysis of hierarchies within firms.

Internal Organization of Large Firms

Large firms that produce several related products may be organized in several ways, two of which are discussed here.[9] One way is to create a separate unit for each function. So, for example, if GM makes Oldsmobiles and Cadillacs, there could be a common purchasing agent and common manufacturing, accounting, and marketing divisions that could handle both models. This form of organization, known as **functional separation,** yields the advantages of specialization of labor and other efficiencies that occur as many tasks are handled by one economic unit.

An alternative organizational form is the multidivision form (the **M-form**), in which there are two divisions, Oldsmobile and Cadillac. Each division is responsible for its own input purchasing, manufacturing, accounting, and marketing. GM's top management makes only the most important decisions regarding the strategy each division should follow.

Although all the functions must ultimately be the same in the two forms, the hierarchy of command is different, and hence the cost of organizing (monitoring efficiency) can be different. In particular, it is difficult to keep the functional divisions focused on the goal of maximizing overall profits. The reason is that it is hard to calculate the profits for the accounting, manufacturing or marketing division separately. It is much easier to calculate profits for a division that sells a product than for a functional division. Although it allows less specialization, the multidivision form stresses profit maximization for each division and holds the managers of each division accountable for any shortfalls.

Until the 1920s, large firms that produced many products used the functional separation mode of organization. A few large firms, notably DuPont, General Motors, Standard Oil of New Jersey, and Sears, Roebuck, devised the multidivisional organizational form in response to their increasing size and diversity. Chandler (1962, 48–49) notes that "the multidivisional type of administrative structure, which hardly existed in 1920, had by 1960 become the accepted form of management for the most complex and diverse of American industrial enterprises." (See Example 2.2.)

In the United States, the M-form became prevalent in the 1950s (Williamson and Bhargava 1972), while in other countries its adoption was slower. For example, its widespread diffusion in the United Kingdom did not occur until the 1960s (Steer 1978; Marginson 1985). In the early 1970s, it appeared that the M-form was used in 70 percent of the major firms in the United Kingdom, 50 percent in Germany and 42 percent in Japan (Cable and Yasuki 1985).

■ OWNERSHIP AND CONTROL

Firms can be owned and controlled in a variety of ways. A firm must raise money to finance itself, decide how its business is to be managed, and distribute its revenues to those who have contributed to its activity.

---

[9] For an excellent detailed analysis of the internal structure of firms, see Williamson (1975, Chapter 8).

EXAMPLE 2.2

EFFICIENCY OF THE M-FORM

Armour and Teece (1978) test Williamson's (1975) predictions that adoption of the M-form should lead to higher profits. Using a sample of petroleum companies, they compare the profitability of those firms that adopted the M-form to those that did not during the period 1955–1973 and find that the percentage of firms that adopted the M-form rose from 16 percent to 78 percent. Firms that adopted the M-form had much better initial profit performance (about 30 percent improvement in profit) than other firms. By the end of the period, there was no difference between those few firms not adopting the M-form and the others. This result may show that only a few firms had special reasons for not adopting the M-form.

Forms of Ownership

Typical business forms in the United States are sole proprietorships, partnerships (multiple owners), and corporations. Before the twentieth century, sole proprietorships and partnerships accounted for the bulk of economic activity. Both sole proprietors and partners are personally liable for the debts of the business. *All* the owner's assets, not just those invested in the business, are at risk. For example, a partner bears full personal liability for the debts of a failed business if the other partners have no assets, even if the business fails through no fault of the partner with the assets. If one member of a partnership leaves, the entire partnership is automatically dissolved. If the business is to continue, a new partnership must be formed.

Sole proprietorships and partnerships are usually small, and many such businesses start (and fail) each year. By number, about 83 percent of businesses are sole proprietorships or partnerships. However, only about 10 percent of sales comes from such organizations (*Statistical Abstract of the U.S.* 1985, 516).

Most sales in the United States are made by **corporations.** Large corporations whose stock is publicly traded account for the bulk of economic activity and own a large percentage of all assets. For example, in 1980, the top 200 manufacturing corporations accounted for about 60 percent of all manufacturing assets (Weiss, 1983). A corporation raises money by selling shares of stock. Its shareholders elect a board of directors to run the corporation. In practice, the board of directors of a large corporation rarely becomes involved in day-to-day affairs; it delegates that responsibility to officers of the company. In large corporations, after the stock is issued, the stock is typically traded publicly (for example, IBM stock is traded on the New York Stock Exchange) and is not necessarily concentrated in the hands of a few key employees. Once stock is issued, the corporation receives nothing when individuals buy or sell its shares on a stock market.

A shareholder is entitled to receive dividend payments, which come out of the corporation's profits. Dividends are one way stockholders earn returns on their investments, but even if a corporation pays no dividends, shareholders can earn returns. If the price

EXAMPLE 2.3

VALUE OF LIMITED LIABILITY

The rise of limited liability coincides with an increase in the size of firms. If it is efficient for firms to become large, and limited liability is the best structure for large firms to have, then a group of firms can limit competition if they can get a law passed that grants limited liability protection to them alone. In Scotland until 1879, limited liability was granted to only three Edinborough banks; all other competing banks had to accept unlimited liability.

We would expect that the limited-liability banks were larger than the others and more successful. In fact, even though over 50 banks with unlimited liability failed between 1845 and 1879, none of the three limited-liability banks failed. Furthermore, data from 1825 indicate that the three limited-liability banks averaged about 10 times the assets of the average bank with unlimited liability. After 1879, laws were changed, and all banks effectively became protected by limited liability.

SOURCE: Carr and Mathewson 1986.

of the stock rises above the price that the shareholder paid, the shareholder can sell it and make a profit.

The benefit of a corporation is that shareholders have **limited liability.** This means that if a corporation fails—it is unable to pay its bills—the stockholders are not liable for the shortfall. A stockholder's losses are limited to the price paid for the stock. The worst situation that a stockholder could face is that the stock becomes worthless. The value of limited liability is that it makes individuals more willing to buy shares than they would be if they could lose more than they paid initially to acquire the shares.

The rise of the corporation coincided with the need to increase the size of firms. See Example 2.3. The money needed to finance large enterprises could be efficiently raised only through the corporate form of organization. Otherwise, investors were not willing to accept the potential liabilities arising from the actions of managers whom they neither knew nor had the ability to monitor. The increase in the importance of the corporation and the coincident rise in stock trading is a relatively recent phenomenon of the last 100 years. In 1900 only 113 companies were listed on the New York Stock Exchange, while in 1920 the number had more than doubled to 391, and today, over 1500 companies are listed.[10]

Corporations also raise money by issuing debt: they promise to pay those who lend them money *(debt holders)* a stipulated amount of interest plus repayment of the loan.

---

[10] *Wall Street Journal,* 24 Dec. 1900, 1920, and telephone communication with the New York Stock Exchange 1985. The number of companies is calculated as the number listed in the table entitled New York Stock Exchange "Closing Bid and Asked Prices," which appears daily in the *Wall Street Journal.* Some companies may not appear if their stock was not traded.

TABLE 2.1	An Example of the Returns to Debt Holders and Equity Owners			
Outcome of Project		*Probability*	*Payoff Received by Debt Holders*	*Payoff Received by Equity Owners*
Success		.5	$600,000	$1,400,000
Failure		.5	500,000	0
Expected payoff			550,000	700,000
Initial investment			500,000	500,000
Expected payoff minus initial investment			50,000	200,000
Expected return			10%	40%

For example, General Electric might sell a *note* for $1 million in which it promises to pay 10 percent or $100,000 per year for three years and at the end of three years repay the $1 million. Debt holders are paid first; the stockholders are paid from what remains.

An example will clarify the distinction between the claims of debt holders and shareholders (also called *equity owners*). Suppose that Corporation X raises $1 million by borrowing $500,000 at 20 percent interest and selling 500,000 shares at $1 each. Corporation X invests in one project that has a 50-50 chance of succeeding. If the project succeeds, Corporation X will earn $2 million, of which $100,000 will be used to pay interest and $500,000 to repay the loan; the remainder will go to shareholders as dividends. If the project fails, the corporation will go out of business and sell its machines for $500,000, which will go to the debt holders. Table 2.1 summarizes this information.

If the project succeeds, the firm will distribute the $2 million dollars in such a way that debt holders receive $600,000 and equity owners $1,400,000. If the project fails, the firm will distribute the entire $500,000 to debt holders. On average, debt holders expect to receive a payoff of $550,000 ($\frac{1}{2} \times \$600,000 + \frac{1}{2} \times \$500,000$), and equity owners expect to receive a payoff of $700,000 ($\frac{1}{2} \times \$1,400,000 + \frac{1}{2} \times 0$). The expected return on an investment is the expected payoff above the initial investment divided by the initial investment, which the table shows is 10 percent for debt holders and 40 percent for equity owners.

The example shows that the expected return is higher for equity owners than for debt holders and that the payoff is not as variable for debt holders as for equity owners. In general, because debt holders get paid before equity owners, it is safer to hold debt. But, because debt is less risky, the expected return tends to be lower than for equity owners—if it were not, no one would hold equity. As the firm becomes more *highly leveraged* (that is, increases its ratio of debt to equity), the returns to the equity holders become riskier. That is why stock prices fluctuate more for companies with high debt-equity ratios than for companies with low debt-equity ratios, all other things equal.

The tax treatment of corporations and single proprietorships or partnerships is significantly different. For example, corporate income is taxed before it is distributed to a shareholder, who then pays personal income taxes. In contrast, income from proprietorships and partnerships is not directly taxed; it flows untaxed to the owner(s), who then pays personal income taxes.

Separation of Ownership and Control

> *Corporation, n. An ingenious device for obtaining individual profit without individual responsibility.* — AMBROSE BIERCE

The dramatic rise in the importance of the corporation caused quite a clamor in the 1930s. The clamor was in part precipitated by *The Modern Corporation and Private Property*, by Berle and Means (1932), who argued that the corporation had separated ownership from control. **Separation of ownership and control** means that the owners of a corporation, the shareholders, are typically not the same as the managers, who are employees of the corporation. This separation, which does not exist in single proprietorships and partnerships, means that managers may no longer have an incentive to be efficient. Rather than maximize profits, managers can pursue other objectives, like not working too hard or having plush offices. In many corporations, there is often no single shareholder with the incentive to monitor managers' actions. Therefore, according to Berle and Means, the actions of corporations cannot be predicted by a traditional economic analysis based on profit maximization. Their implication was that the severity of the Great Depression was at least in part attributable to the rise of this new and inefficient form of business. Their book had an immediate impact that persists to this day.[11]

The board of directors elected by stockholders acts to minimize the conflicts that arise because of the separation of ownership and control. Its primary function is to act as an agent for the shareholders and oversee the efficient management of the company. But, who monitors the board of directors? If they do a bad job, how will they be punished? One way is that they may not be reelected and may acquire bad reputations that make it difficult for them to get other good jobs. Another way is that a wise investor may recognize a company that is poorly managed, buy it up on the stock market at a price reflecting its inefficient management, fire the board of directors, and proceed to manage it efficiently (such takeovers are discussed in detail in Chapter 7).

Aside from the conflict that Berle and Means pointed out between equity owners and managers, conflicts arise between debt holders and equity owners. For example, suppose the firm in Table 2.1 has already raised its $500,000 from debt holders and $500,000 from equity holders and is deciding between two projects: the one described in Table 2.1 or one that pays $600,000 if it fails and $1,900,000 if it succeeds. The total expected payoff to the latter project is $1,250,000, as before. Yet the division of the payoff between equity owners and debt holders is different: debt holders now receive $600,000 for sure, while the equity owners can expect to receive $650,000. The payoffs of the new project are summarized in Table 2.2.

The debt holders prefer this new project, but the equity owners prefer the original one. Because debt holders recognize that their interests may diverge from those of equity owners, debt holders often insist on **bond covenants** which are restrictions on the corporation's choices of investment projects or further financing.

---

[11] Related works include Leibenstein (1966). See also The Symposium on Berle and Means in *Journal of Law and Economics*, June 26, 1983.

TABLE 2.2	Returns from Alternative Project			
Outcome of Project		*Probability*	*Payoff Received by Debt Holders*	*Payoff Received by Equity Owners*
Success		.5	$600,000	$1,300,000
Failure		.5	600,000	0
Expected payoff			600,000	650,000
Initial investment			500,000	500,000
Expected payoff minus initial investment			100,000	150,000
Expected return			20%	30%

One interpretation of Berle and Means is that they were focusing attention on the monitoring problems and conflicts that arise as a firm grows. These are exactly the issues discussed earlier. There is nothing inefficient about incurring costs as long as they are offset by benefits. It is incorrect to suggest that large corporations are inefficient just because they entail monitoring costs. These costs can be offset by the benefits of larger size and the ability to raise money cheaply.

■ THE OBJECTIVE OF A FIRM

The standard assumption in economics is that the primary objective of a firm is to maximize profits. The preceding discussion shows that it is generally impossible to achieve the level of profits that would result if monitoring were costless and perfect; operating a firm requires expending resources to monitor internal efficiency. However, most of the economic models in this text do not explicitly consider monitoring costs but implicitly assume them to be zero. Firms in these models maximize profits with monitoring costs ignored.

If monitoring costs are very high, firms may pursue policies that look different than simple profit maximization.[12] For example, if managers value having many employees, and if the board of directors finds it hard to monitor managers, then managers may maximize sales (which leads to many employees) rather than profits.

There are good reasons to believe that managers do not have unchecked ability to deviate from goals of simple profit maximization. Competition with other firms provides a check against inefficiency: an unusually inefficient firm cannot survive in a competitive market. The market for managers provides another check: managers who are fired for inefficiency or laziness find it difficult to get new jobs. Incentives, such as stock and other bonuses, also motivate managers to maximize profit. As long as large deviations from simple profit maximization are unlikely to persist in equilibrium, it makes sense to use simple profit maximization as a first step in understanding a firm's objectives.

---

[12] See, for example, Cyert and March (1963), March and Simon (1958), Marris (1964), and Williamson (1964).

■ SUMMARY

This chapter has analyzed in detail how and why firms are organized. Some activities can be performed more efficiently within a firm than in the marketplace, and the explicit recognition that using the market (and its price system) is not costless helps one to understand why firms form. A firm must make many decisions about how to organize itself internally to prevent employees from shirking and managers from making bad decisions. The multidivisional structure evolved because firms need to monitor and control their employees' actions efficiently. The most significant firms in the United States (and elsewhere) are organized as corporations with limited liability. Corporations typically raise money by issuing debt and equity (stock). The corporation must make sure that its managers operate to maximize profits and do not pursue different goals that would adversely affect other concerned parties, such as debt holders or shareholders.

■ Key Terms

asset specificity	efficient allocation	monitoring cost
bond covenant	functional specialization	opportunistic behavior
bounded rationality	hierarchy	separation of ownership and control
corporation	limited liability	transaction cost
coordinated decision	M-form	transfer prices
dispute resolution mechanism		

■ Discussion Questions

1. Do limited liability laws take advantage of creditors?
2. Corporations should not be allowed to donate to charity. Instead, shareholders should receive dividends that they can donate to charity if they wish. Discuss.
3. To help monitor the conflict between shareholders and management, there should be a wage cap on the highest salary a corporation can pay. Discuss.
4. Suppose employees of a corporation know more about the firm than outsiders. Should they be allowed to trade in the stock? If not, should the ban apply to all employees?
5. In what ways is the monitoring problem related to the corporate form? In what ways is it unrelated?

■ Problems

1. If firms have monitoring problems, what causes the problems?
2. Firms can raise money by issuing debt: pieces of paper that are IOUs. Why didn't firms issue debt in the 1920s and remain as either single proprietorships or partnerships?
3. For each situation on the following page discuss how two separate firms could carry out the activities. Identify those areas in which transaction costs are highest and you would expect to see only one firm.

Answers to the odd numbered problems are given at the back of the book.

a. Oil pipelines, once built, cannot be moved. A pipeline ends at electric power facility, which buys oil.
b. A golf course locates beside a hotel.
c. A postcard manufacturer wants a readily available supply of custom-made paper.
d. A candy manufacturer needs to purchase sugar daily.
4. Suppose a law is passed that forbids a firm from performing certain activities internally and requires it to

hire other firms to perform these activities. Analyze the effect of such a law.
5. Which of the following decisions is the president of a company most likely to make and why?
a. Where to build a new specialized plant;
b. Where to buy raw materials;
c. What price to set for a product.

References

Alchian, Armen A., and Harold Demsetz. 1972. "Production, Information Costs and Economic Organization." *American Economic Review* 62:777–95.

Anderson, Erin, and David C. Schmittlein. 1984. "Integration of the Sales Force: An Empirical Examination." *Rand Journal of Economics* 15:385–95.

Armour, Henry O., and David J. Teece. 1978. "Organization Structure and Economic Performance: A Test of the Multidivisional Hypothesis." *Bell Journal of Economics* 9:106–22.

Becker, Gary S., and George J. Stigler. 1974. "Law Enforcement, Malfeasance, and Compensation of Enforcement." *Journal of Legal Studies* 3:1–18.

Berle, Adolph A., Jr., and Gardiner C. Means. 1932. *The Modern Corporation and Private Property*. New York: Macmillan.

Cable, John, and Hirohiko Yasuki. 1985. "The Empirical Test of Multidivisional Hypothesis." *International Journal of Industrial Organization* 3:401–20.

Carr, Jack L., and G. Frank Mathewson. 1988. "Unlimited Liability as a Barrier to Entry." *Journal of Political Economy* 96:766–84.

Chandler, Alfred D., Jr. 1962. *Strategy and Structure: Chapters in the History of the American Industrial Experience*. Cambridge, Mass.: The MIT Press.

Coase, Ronald H. 1937. "The Nature of the Firm." *Economica*, 4 n.s.:386–405.

Cyert, Richard M., and James G. March, eds. 1963. *Behavioral Theory of the Firm*. Englewood Cliffs, N.J.: Prentice-Hall.

Demsetz, Harold. 1983. "The Structure of Ownership and the Theory of the Firm." *Journal of Law and Economics* 26:375–90.

Demsetz, Harold, and Kenneth Lehn. 1985. "The Structure of Corporate Ownership: Causes and Consequences." *Journal of Political Economy* 93:1155–77.

Grossman, Sanford J., and Oliver D. Hart. 1986. "The Costs and Benefits of Ownership: A Theory of Vertical Integration." *Journal of Political Economy* 94:691–719.

Joskow, Paul L. 1987. "Contract Duration and Relationship-Specific Investments: Empirical Evidence from Coal Markets." *American Economic Review* 77:168–85.

Klein, Benjamin, Robert G. Crawford, and Armen A. Alchian. 1978. "Vertical Integration, Appropriable Rents, and the Competitive Contracting Process." *Journal of Law and Economics* 21:297–326.

Lazear, Edward P. 1978. "Why is There Mandatory Retirement?" *Journal of Political Economy* 87:1261–84.

Leibenstein, Harvey. 1966. "Allocative Efficiency vs. X-Efficiency." *American Economic Review* 56:392–412.

March, James G., and Herbert A. Simon. 1958. *Organizations*. New York: John Wiley & Sons.

Marginson, Paul. 1985. "The Multidivisional Firm and Control over the Work Process." *International Journal of Industrial Organization* 3:37–56.

Masten, Scott E. 1984. "The Organization of Production: Evidence from the Aerospace Industry." *Journal of Law and Economics* 27:403–17.

Marris, Robin. 1964. *The Economic Theory of Managerial Capitalism*. Glencoe, Ill.: Free Press of Glencoe.

Monteverde, Kirk, and David J. Teece. 1982. "Supplier-Switching Costs and Vertical Integration in the Automobile Industry." *Bell Journal of Economics* 13:206–13.

Sloan, Alfred P., Jr. 1963. *My Years with General Motors*. New York: Doubleday.

Steer, Peter S., and John R. Cable. 1978. "Internal Organization and Profit: An Empirical Analysis of Large

UK Companies." *Journal of Industrial Economics* 27:13–20.

Weiss, Leonard W. 1983. "The Extent and Effects of Aggregate Concentration." *Journal of Law and Economics* 26:429–55.

Williamson, Oliver E. 1985. *The Economic Institutions of Capitalism: Firms, Markets, Relational Contracting.* New York: The Free Press.

———. 1979. "Transaction-Cost Economics: The Governance of Contractual Relations." *Journal of Law and Economics* 22(October):233–61. Reprinted in Williamson (1985).

———. 1975. *Markets and Hierarchies—Analysis and Antitrust Implications: A Study in the Economics of Internal Organization.* New York: The Free Press.

———. 1967. "Hierarchical Control and Optimum Firm Size." *Journal of Political Economy,* 75:123–38.

———. 1964. *The Economics of Discretionary Behavior: Managerial Objectives in a Theory of the Firm.* Englewood Cliffs, N.J.: Prentice-Hall.

———, and N. Bhargava. 1972. "Assessing and Classifying the Internal Structure and Control Apparatus of the Modern Corporation," in *Market Structure and Corporate Behavior: Theory and Empirical Analysis of the Firm,* ed. K. Cowling. London: Gray-Mills Publishing Ltd.

CHAPTER 3 Costs

> **F**ew have heard of Fra Luca Parioli, the inventor of double-entry bookkeeping; but he has probably had much more influence on human life than has Dante or Michelangelo.
>
> HERBERT J. MULLER

To understand industrial organization, an understanding of costs is necessary for several reasons. First, many of the predictions of economic theory, such as those involving price and firm size, revolve around concepts like marginal costs and profits. Without a knowledge of cost concepts, one cannot understand or empirically test these predictions. Second, recent theoretical work has emphasized that oligopoly behavior depends crucially on certain types of fixed cost. (Baumol, Willig, Panzar 1982. Third, regulatory intervention often occurs in industries called *natural monopolies,* in which competition leads to excessive costs. Knowing how to regulate these industries requires an intimate familiarity with cost concepts (see Chapter 23).

This chapter introduces the concepts of marginal, average, and variable costs, and then discusses some subtleties associated with economic costs. It analyzes the theory and evidence concerning economies of scale and concludes with a discussion of costs for a multiproduct firm. Appendix 3A shows how to treat the costs of a durable investment, Appendix 3B analyzes in detail the relevant cost concepts for a multiproduct firm, and Appendix 3C considers adjustment costs.

■ COST CONCEPTS

Every firm needs to know what it costs to produce its products if it is to make sensible business decisions. There are a variety of ways to measure costs, and some cost concepts are more appropriate for certain problems than others. This section explores these different cost concepts and some subtleties in understanding them.

Types of Costs

Every firm incurs a variety of costs to stay in business and produce and sell its product. Some costs are **fixed costs**—they do not vary with the level of output. A good example of a fixed cost is the fee a state charges for a firm to incorporate and conduct business. Whether the firm produces a lot or a little, it must pay the fee. Another example is the monthly rent that a lawyer must pay for an office after signing a one-year lease. The monthly rent must be paid regardless of how much business the lawyer does.

If the firm and the lawyer decide to go out of business, they would not renew their incorporation or rental agreement for the next year. But what if they decide to go out of business just one month after they began? Are they still stuck paying their fee or monthly rental? If they have paid in advance, can they get a refund? The answer depends on the particular situation. For the corporation, it is probably true that the entire incorporation fee has been prepaid and is not refundable. The lawyer, although obligated to pay a monthly rent, may be able to rent to someone else and recoup some if not all of the cost. The portion of fixed costs that is not recoverable is a **sunk cost.** A sunk cost is like spilt milk: once it is sunk, there is no use worrying about it, and it should not affect any subsequent decisions. In contrast, a fixed cost that is not sunk *should* influence decisions. For example, whether or not the lawyer should go out of business depends in part on how costly it is to get out of the lease (that is, the financial penalty for breaking the lease). Costs, including fixed costs, that can be avoided if operations cease are sometimes called **avoidable costs.**

In addition to fixed costs, a firm incurs **variable costs.** As their name suggests, such costs vary with the level of output: as output increases, so does the need for labor, electricity, and materials, so variable costs depend on the prevailing wages and prices that a firm must pay. The sum of fixed costs and variable costs is equal to **total costs.**

Associated with the concepts of total cost and variable cost is **marginal cost (MC),** which is the *increment,* or addition, to cost that results from producing one more unit of output.[1] Since fixed cost does not change as output increases, the increase in total cost when output increases is identical to the increase in variable cost. Hence, marginal cost is the same whether total costs or variable costs are used to define it.

It is important to distinguish between the concept of marginal cost and the various concepts of average cost. There are three common types of average cost: **average total cost** (sometimes simply called *average cost*), **average variable cost,** and **average fixed cost.** *Average total cost (ATC)* equals total cost divided by output. *Average variable cost (AVC)* equals variable cost *(VC)* divided by output *(q)*. *Average fixed cost (AFC)* equals fixed cost *(FC)* divided by output *(q)*. Since *ATC* equals the sum of *AVC* and *AFC*, it immediately follows that *AVC* and *AFC* are each less than *ATC*.

Summarizing these relationships, we see that

$$ATC = \frac{VC + FC}{q} = \frac{VC}{q} + \frac{FC}{q} = AVC + AFC$$

It is a common error to think that marginal cost is less than average total cost, because marginal cost ignores fixed cost, and average total cost does not. But that confusion is avoided by remembering that marginal cost refers to *changes* in cost, not to levels.

Imagine going into a supermarket to buy fruit. You carry a basket and put in some

---

[1] More precisely, if *C(q)* is total cost of producing *q* units, *MC* equals *dC(q)/dq*.

			TABLE 3.1 An Example of Cost Concepts				
Output	Fixed Cost	Average Fixed Cost	Total Variable Cost	Average Variable Cost	Total Cost	Average Total Cost	Marginal Cost
0	100		0		100		
1	100	100	10	10	110	110	10
2	100	50	19	9.5	119	59.5	9
3	100	33.3	25	8.3	125	41.7	6
4	100	25	32	8.0	132	33	7
5	100	20	40	8.0	140	28	8
6	100	16.7	49	8.2	149	24.8	9
7	100	14.2	60	8.6	160	22.9	11
8	100	12.5	73	9.1	173	21.6	13
9	100	11.1	88	9.8	188	20.9	15
10	100	10	108	10.8	208	20.8	20

apples, which naturally differ in weight. The total weight of the basket and the associated average weight per apple are easily determined (for simplicity assume the basket weighs nothing). Suppose you *add* a very small apple. The weight of that apple is the increment to the weight of the basket (marginal weight). But the weight of the small apple is less than the average weight of the basket, which contains mostly larger apples. Suppose you add a very large apple. This time the marginal weight will exceed the average weight of the basket. The marginal weight is totally determined by the *one* additional apple. The average weight (after the additional apple) is determined in large part by the apples that were already there. Thus, like the marginal weight in this example, marginal cost can be either above or below average cost.

To illustrate further the relationship between marginal cost, average cost, and average variable cost, Table 3.1 shows how the various elements of cost vary as output increases. The fixed cost is $100 regardless of whether production occurs or not and is assumed to be an obligation that cannot be avoided by going out of business (that is, the fixed cost is all sunk, or nonrecoverable). If part of the fixed cost is recoverable, as when a license fee is refundable, then the relevant cost for output of zero would be only the sunk cost. For example, a firm that goes out of business but obtains a $60 refund on its $100 state license fee, has costs of $40 for producing nothing.

The variable cost rises from 0 to 108 as output expands from 0 to 10. Total cost— the sum of fixed plus variable costs—rises from 100 to 208 as output expands to 10. Marginal cost equals the increase in total costs that results from producing an additional unit of output. Note that it initially falls, reaches a minimum of 6, and then rises.

Average variable cost equals total variable cost divided by output, and average total cost equals total cost divided by output. Average total cost always exceeds average variable cost, but as you can see, marginal cost may be less than, equal to, or greater than average total or average variable cost. In fact, there is a clear geometric relationship between *MC, AVC,* and *AC* as depicted in Figure 3.1: *When MC is below AVC, the AVC curve is falling. When MC is above AVC, the AVC curve is rising. When MC equals AVC, the AVC is at its minimum.* A similar relationship exists between *MC* and *AC.* Figure 3.1 also shows

FIGURE 3.1   Cost Curves

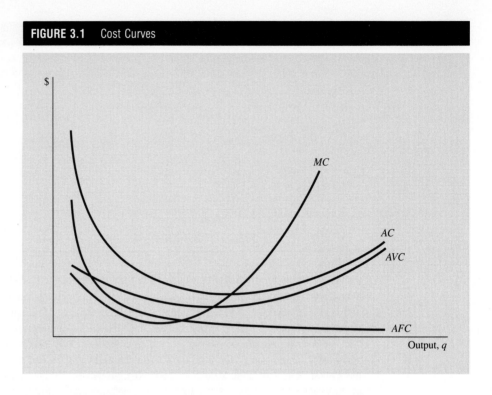

that as output increases average fixed cost *(AFC)* approaches zero and that *AVC* and *AC* get closer together.

To understand why *AC* rises if *MC* exceeds it or falls if *MC* is below it, go back to the grocery example. If you add an apple that is heavier than the average apple, the average weight of the basket will increase. Conversely, if you add a lighter-than-average apple, the average weight will fall.

In general, total costs depend on the amount of output produced as well as the costs of using the factors of production (for example, wages of workers, cost of raw materials). Figure 3.1 illustrates how a typical average cost curve varies as a function of output; it eventually rises in the short run as output expands. The reason is that it becomes harder and harder to produce more output within a given plant. The curves are based on the assumption that the prices of the factors of production (for example, wages of employees) are held constant. If, for example, wages were to rise, then the entire average cost curve would shift up. It is *not* necessarily true that the curve would shift straight upward because the minimum-cost output may well change. That is, the size of a firm that yields minimum average cost depends on the wages of labor and costs of all other factors of production.

A cost curve contains a great deal of information. For instance, knowing how the cost curve changes as wages (and other factor costs) change, one can figure out the **production technology** (that is, the relation of output to inputs) of a firm. In other words, knowing the cost function of a firm and knowing its technology are equivalent.[2] For example, suppose the wage rate is $10 per hour, and workers are the only input used to produce corn (seeds are free). To plant 1 bushel of corn costs $10, 2 bushels cost $20, and so on. From this information on costs and wages, we can infer that the production technology is that one worker can plant 1 bushel of corn per hour.

Subtleties in Understanding Cost

Although the definitions of the various cost concepts may seem straightforward, there are several complicated issues associated with them. The following sections explore the most important ones.

Cost Factors in Addition to Output.   The firm's costs depend, in the preceding example, on how much it produces for any given set of input prices. But that is generally not the only influence on cost (Alchian 1959). The costs of production depend not only on how much is produced but also on *how fast;* producing something quickly is more costly than producing it slowly. Moreover, variation in the rate of production over time matters. For example, steady production of 60 units/hour for 10 hours might involve lower costs than 100 units/hour for 2 hours plus 50 units/hour for 8 hours, even though total production is 600 units in either case (see Appendix 3C).

It might make sense for a firm to spend money to make its plant highly adaptable to different levels of production. If a business is seasonal (for example, New Year's cards), the relevant cost is not the cost of producing a specific output but rather the cost of producing the range of outputs experienced during the year. If output fluctuates between 25 and 100 units per month, then a plant with a cost curve like AC_1 in Figure 3.2 might well be more efficient (that is, have lower total cost) than one with the curve AC_2.

The Short Run versus the Long Run.   Economists distinguish between the **short run** and **long run.** In the short run, there are some factors of production whose use cannot be costlessly varied. For example, returning to the lawyer, at the end of the year, he or she is free to renew the lease or lease a new space. During the course of the year, however, the lease may not be broken without cost (that is, there are sunk costs). In this example, the short run is less than one year, while the long run is one year or longer.

Another example illustrating the difference between short and long run has to do with installed machinery, which is costly to move and reinstall. If machines last for one year and must then be replaced, the number of machines can be regarded as predetermined in the short run of one year, though not the long run. More generally, the short run is that time period during which the number of machines and physical space (the plant) is

---

[2] Let x = inputs (for example, labor, raw materials), q = output, w = wage rate (and other unit prices for inputs), f = production function (that is, $f(x)$ = output if x are the inputs). The cost function $C(q,w)$ solves the following problem: Minimize the cost of producing q units subject to the constraint that q units are produced according to the engineering relationship between q and x. Knowledge of $C(q,w)$ allows one to infer $f(x)$ under reasonable assumptions. (This is called "duality theory.") See Varian (1984, Ch. 4) for details.

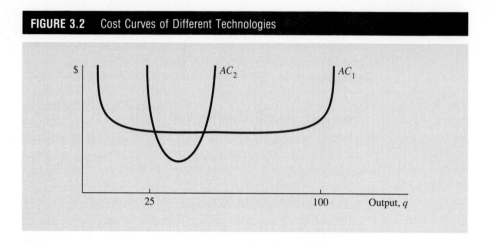

FIGURE 3.2 Cost Curves of Different Technologies

fixed and cannot be varied except at so substantial a cost that it is never profitable. In the short run, the firm must make do with its current plant and stock of machines. In the long run, the firm can alter its capital: it can buy new machines, discard old ones, and even move into a different plant designed to allow production of any given level of output at minimum cost.

Obviously, the distinction between short and long run is not precise. In fact, there is a continuum of runs, with increasingly more adjustment possible as the length of the run increases. The firm must incur greater costs as it increases the speed at which it adjusts its operations. The cost of adjusting its operations is called a **cost of adjustment.** See Appendix 3C.

Long-Run Costs. A firm can configure itself in any way it wants to in the long run, but in the short run its choices are constrained. Therefore the long-run average cost is always at least as low as the short-run average cost. This relationship between long-run and short-run costs implies that the long-run curve is the *envelope* of the short-run curves; that is, the long-run curve *(LRAC)* is traced out by the best part of each of the short-run curves, as shown in Figure 3.3. Notice that the best part is not always the minimum point of a short-run average cost curve. Figure 3.3 shows that the least expensive way to produce 100 units is to use Plant 2, even though that is not the output that minimizes average cost in Plant 2 but *is* the output that minimizes average cost in Plant 3.

It is typical to draw the long-run average cost curve so that it eventually rises as output expands, which means that the firm's efficient size (output that minimizes average cost) is finite. Firms have a maximum efficient size if monitoring costs rise significantly as they get larger.

Opportunity Cost. "The real price of everything is the toil and trouble of acquiring it" (Adam Smith). Economists want costs to reflect the value of the resources used when those resources are employed in their most productive use, other than the current one. This is the concept of **opportunity cost,** which sometimes appears just as common sense

FIGURE 3.3   Long-Run Cost Curve

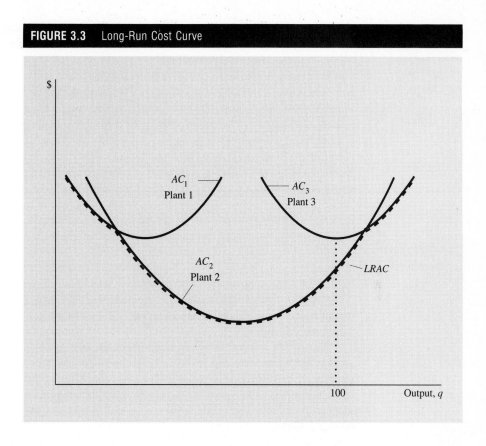

would suggest. For example, if a firm hires three workers at the going wage of $10 per hour, then its labor cost is $30 per hour. If the firm did not use the labor, some other firm would be willing to pay $30 per hour for these workers. But what if one of the three workers is the firm's owner who does not receive a wage. The economist would still say that the labor cost is $30 per hour; that is, the labor used by the firm is worth $30 because another firm would value the labor at that amount.

Opportunity cost has the advantage of revealing at a glance whether an activity should continue. To return to the example, suppose that each worker produces 1 unit of output per hour, and the price is $9. The owner calculates the profits earned in one hour as the revenue of $27 minus the cost (using opportunity cost as the measure) of $30 for a net loss of $3. The presence of a loss shows that the owner should cease production and consider working for someone else at $10 per hour. Clearly, the owner is better off earning $10 per hour than earning $7 ($27 − $20 in wages).

A more important example of the usefulness of opportunity cost arises when a firm owns an asset that could be readily sold or rented. For example, suppose a firm owns the building that it occupies. If the building could be rented to another tenant for $1000 per month, then the firm should count that amount as its cost of occupying the building. It is the foregone earnings of not renting out the building. If the firm cannot afford to pay itself rent (because doing so would result in a negative profit), then the firm should realize that its use of the building is not the most profitable—it would be better to go out of its current business and rent the building.

If all costs are valued at their opportunity cost, then profits need only be *zero* to make remaining in business worthwhile. This sounds odd at first, but it is actually straightforward. Opportunity cost values *all* resources used at the highest value they could receive elsewhere. If revenues just cover costs, then all resources (for example, the owner's time, the firm's building) are being used in an efficient manner and would not be worth more if used elsewhere. Because opportunity cost values each resource at its most profitable alternative use, economists sometimes say that opportunity cost attributes a **normal profit** (profit achievable elsewhere) to all of the firm's resources.

Expensing versus Amortization.   Suppose that a firm rents a machine by the month for $100, and then decides to purchase the machine outright for its market price of $10,000. Should it count all $10,000 as a fixed cost incurred in its month of purchase, or should it spread the cost over the months the machine will be used? When costs are counted as they are incurred, they are said to be **expensed;** when they are spread out over the useful life of the machine, they are said to be **amortized.** If the firm amortizes the cost of the machine, how much should it charge itself? The answer clearly affects how the firm judges its performance.

The simple answer to any question about the appropriate cost to assign a durable asset is that the relevant cost is the *rent* that the owner could earn by renting the asset to someone else. This calculation is often easy—when a firm owns an office building and uses only some of the space for its own needs, the appropriate market rent is easy to discover. In other cases, the appropriate rent may not be available; for example, there is no rental market for blast furnaces. How should the cost of such assets be treated? One answer is to calculate the cost of owning an asset as the lost interest on its value (if it were sold for $100, that $100 could be earning interest) plus the depreciation on the asset. Economic **depreciation** is the value of that part of an asset that is consumed during the year (using a machine causes it to wear out and lose value). Even when assets, once installed, cannot be resold, one can still use this method to calculate a rent. The resulting profit calculation reveals whether the firm's decision to install the machine was a good one, and whether further investment would be profitable. (See Appendix 3A for more details.)

■ ECONOMIES OF SCALE

A firm's average costs may remain constant, rise, or fall as its output expands. If average cost remains constant as output expands, the firm is said to have **constant returns to scale.** If average cost falls as output increases, the firm is said to have **economies of scale,** and if average cost rises with output, the firm is said to have **diseconomies of scale.** For the typical cost curve (Figure 3.1), the firm first enjoys economies of scale, then (at least for an instant) has constant returns, and then diseconomies. If a firm enjoys economies of scale at all output levels, then it is efficient for one firm to produce the entire industry output. When it is efficient for only one firm to produce, a **natural monopoly** exists. Natural monopoly is examined in Chapters 5 and 23.

Reasons for Economies of Scale

There are many reasons to expect a firm's average costs to decline, at least initially, as its output expands. One is that fixed setup costs do not vary with the level of output. For example, a publishing company typically incurs substantial costs to have a book written. The authors must be paid, the book edited, and the plates for printing made. If 100 rather than 50 books are produced, the average cost does not rise by a factor of 2 because the additional books require few additional costs. Another example is an automobile stamping facility. Typically, special dies must be made to press the parts into their unique shapes. The more parts produced with each die, the lower the average total cost of production.

As output expands, a firm can use its labor in more specialized tasks. For example, at low levels of business, one lawyer may handle both divorce and bankruptcy cases. As the law firm expands, one lawyer may specialize in divorce, while another specializes in bankruptcy, and each one can develop unique expertise. If a training cost is associated with developing expertise in each task, only a firm that required frequent repetition of each task would find it worthwhile to train separate workers for each task (see Example 3.1).

If a firm produces several products in one production facility, the length of the production run could increase as output expands. Imagine a paper manufacturer that sells three grades of paper. To produce each grade requires a separate setup of the production line. If the firm is small and has only one production line, then two switchovers are needed to produce the three grades daily. But if the firm triples in size, it can have one production line for each grade and will never incur switching costs.

Certain physical laws generate scale economies; the best known concerns the relationship between volume and surface area. Suppose a chemical firm plans to make a certain liquid in a spherical container. The volume of the sphere is $(4\pi r^3)/3$ where r is the sphere's radius. The cost of the sphere depends upon how much steel it takes to make it. That cost is related, not to volume, but to the surface area of the sphere, which equals $4\pi r^2$. Doubling the radius raises volume (and output) by a factor of 8, but raises surface area by only a factor of 4.

There is a natural economy of scale in the holding of inventories and replacement parts. This is a result of the statistical law of large numbers that explains how random events tend to cancel out if there are enough of them. For example, suppose that each consumer has a random demand for bread and demands either 1 or 2 loaves per day. Suppose one firm has only two customers and that it must produce at the beginning of each day. Unsold goods are thrown out. The probabilities of the customers' demands and firm's supply are given in Table 3.2.

Suppose that customers get upset if they are refused bread more than 15 percent of the time. If our firm holds 3 loaves of bread, then ¼ of the time, one of the two customers will be refused bread, so that each customer will be refused bread ⅛ (12.5 percent) of

EXAMPLE 3.1

SPECIALIZATION OF LABOR

Why doesn't everyone work individually and sell finished products to each other as needed? One answer is that it can be more efficient to break down production processes into several small steps in which workers specialize. Two examples illustrate the advantages of breaking production into several tasks.

Adam Smith (1937, 4–5) offers an example to show that the division of labor can have important advantages in the "very trifling manufacture" of pin-making:

> [A] workman not educated to this business . . . nor acquainted with the use of machinery employed in it . . . could scarce, perhaps, with his utmost industry, make one pin a day, and certainly could not make twenty. But in the way in which this business is now carried on, not only the whole work is a peculiar trade, but it is divided into a number of branches, of which the greater part are likewise peculiar trades. One man draws out the wire, another straightens it, a third cuts it, a fourth points it, a fifth grinds it to the top for receiving the head; to make the head requires two or three distinct operations; to put it on, is a peculiar business, to whiten the pins is another; it is even a trade by itself to put them into the paper; and the important business of making a pin is, in this manner, divided into about eighteen distinct operations, which, in some manufactories, are all performed by distinct hands, though in others the same man will sometimes perform two or three of them. I have seen a small manufactory of this kind where ten men only were employed, and where some of them consequently performed two or three distinct operations. . . . [T]hey could, when they exerted themselves, make among them about twelve pounds of pins in a day [or] upward of forty-eight thousand pins in a day."

Similarly, Henry Ford became the largest automobile manufacturer in the early 1900s, and probably the most profitable, by developing mass production. He adapted the conveyor belt and assembly line so that he could produce a standardized and inexpensive car in a series of tasks in which individual workers specialized. He achieved cost savings despite paying wages that were considerably above average. Indeed, in 1914, he created a profit-sharing plan that would distribute up to $30 million annually among his employees.

the time. Hence customers are not dissatisfied more than 15 percent of the time. The firm sells on average 2.75 loaves of bread. Hence the firm holds 0.25/2.75, or 1/11 (9 percent) more than its average sales as inventory to satisfy the demand for reliability.

Suppose now that the firm has four customers. The demand possibilities are listed in Table 3.3. If the firm holds 6 loaves of bread, two of the four customers will be unable to buy 1/16 of the time, and one of the four will be unable to buy 1/4 of the time.[3] Therefore, any one customer will be unable to buy about 10 percent of the time, (1/16

---

[3] For simplicity, assume that the firm always supplies at least 1 loaf to each consumer.

TABLE 3.2   An Example of Random Demand

Probability	Demand of Customer 1	Demand of Customer 2	Total Demanded	Supplied
.25	1	1	2	3
.25	1	2	3	3
.25	2	1	3	3
.25	2	2	4	3

TABLE 3.3   An Example of Random Demand

Probability	Demand of Customer 1	Demand of Customer 2	Demand of Customer 3	Demand of Customer 4	Total Demand
1/16	1	1	1	1	4
1/4	1	1	1	2	5
	1	1	2	1	5
	1	2	1	1	5
	2	1	1	1	5
3/8	2	2	1	1	6
	2	1	2	1	6
	2	1	1	2	6
	1	2	1	2	6
	1	2	2	1	6
	1	1	2	2	6
1/4	2	2	2	1	7
	1	2	2	2	7
	2	1	2	2	7
	2	2	1	2	7
1/16	2	2	2	2	8

$\times$ 2/4 + 1/4 $\times$ 1/4 = 3/32). Hence no customers will be upset, since none are disappointed more than 15 percent of the time. Average sales are about 5.6 (1/16 $\times$ 4 + 1/4 $\times$ 5 + 3/8 $\times$ 6 + 1/4 $\times$ 6 + 1/16 $\times$ 6 = 90/16). Hence, by holding 6 loaves or just 6 percent (not 9 percent as before) more than average sales, the inventory problem is solved. The reason is that when there are many customers, one customer's high demand will often be offset by another's low demand, so that total demand is less volatile (in percentage terms). This makes it easier to satisfy customers with a relatively low inventory.

Total Costs Determine Scale Economies

Even if economies of scale characterize some functions of a firm, diseconomies of scale may characterize other functions. Whether the firm experiences economies of scale overall

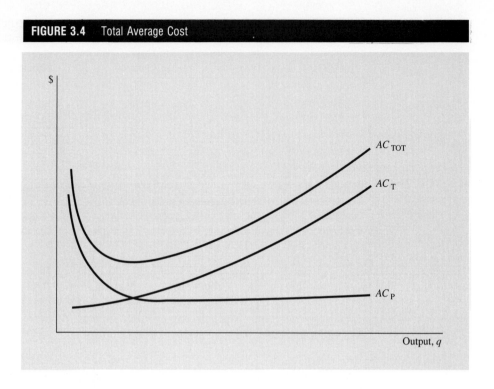

FIGURE 3.4   Total Average Cost

depends on the contribution of each function to overall cost. One common error is to observe that an individual plant has economies of scale in production and conclude that it is most efficient to have only one plant producing. The error comes from ignoring other types of costs, such as monitoring costs or transportation costs.

Suppose that a firm produces pasteurized milk and delivers it to grocery stores. The fewer the plants, the farther, on average, the milk has to be shipped, and the higher the transportation costs. Even if economies of scale characterize production, it is not efficient to have one plant if transportation costs are very high. In such a case, the relevant average cost curve is the sum of the cost of producing the milk and the cost of transporting it to customers.

Figure 3.4 shows the AC curve of production, AC_P. It slopes downward initially, indicating economies of scale in production. The curve, AC_T, is the average cost of transporting raw materials to the plant and transporting the milk to customers. As more milk is produced in one location, it must be shipped farther, and so average transport costs rise. The sum of these two curves is the overall average total cost, AC_{TOT}, which is the relevant curve for determining the cost of operation. The output at the minimum AC_{TOT} point becomes smaller as transportation costs increase. That means, all else equal, that the optimal size of the plant becomes smaller as transportation costs become more important. Many plants of small size are common in industries characterized by high transportation costs.

The location of a plant is influenced by the relative costs of transporting raw materials to the plant compared to transporting the output from the plant to customers. The higher the cost of transporting raw materials, the closer the plant will be to their source. For example, it is expensive (and dangerous) to ship bromine compared to the cost of shipping bromide fluids (which are made from bromine). Therefore, bromide fluid plants tend to be located close to facilities that make bromine. Conversely, if numerous raw materials come from many different locations, or if they are readily available in many locations, the differences across locations in the transportation costs for obtaining raw materials may be insignificant. In such a case, the plant tends to locate close to its customers. For example, cement is costly to transport, and the main raw material, limestone, is widely available. Therefore, cement plants tend to locate close to their customers.

The decision of how many plants a firm should have depends on both the cost of transporting raw materials and finished products and the economies of scale in production.[4] The more important the economies of scale in production, the more likely it is to see production concentrated in only a few plants. The greater the transportation costs (and dispersion of customer locations), the more likely it is to decentralize production in several plants (see Example 3.2).

Technical Definition of Scale Economies

The previous section shows that scale economies exist if average cost falls as output expands. As long as marginal cost is below average cost, economies of scale exist, while if marginal cost exceeds average cost, there are diseconomies of scale. This relationship suggests that a natural measure of scale economies is the ratio of average to marginal cost. If $S = AC/MC$, then economies of scale exist if $S > 1$, constant returns to scale exist if $S = 1$, and diseconomies of scale exist if $S < 1$. If a firm sets price equal to marginal cost, then S measures the ratio of costs to revenues.

We have defined economies of scale using concepts based on the cost function, which answers the question: What is the minimum cost of producing a given amount of output? We could instead have chosen to use concepts based on the production function, which answers the question: How much output is produced with given amounts of labor and raw materials? In fact, a common definition of scale economies is based on the production function: Economies of scale exist if an equal percentage increase in the use of all factors of production results in a proportionately greater expansion of output. So, for example, if a firm increases its use of its two inputs, labor and raw materials, by 10 percent, economies of scale exist if output rises by more than 10 percent. A natural measure of scale economies, therefore, is the percentage of output expansion generated by an increase of 1 percent in the use of all inputs.

Suppose output q is produced according to a production function $F(x_1, x_2, \ldots, x_n)$, where $x_1, x_2, \ldots, x_n$ are the factors of production, and F is a function that reveals how much output the inputs create. If all inputs, $x_1, x_2, \ldots, x_n$ are expanded by 1 percent,

---

[4] See Scherer et al. (1975) for an extended analysis.

EXAMPLE 3.2

OPTIMAL PLANT SIZE: A CASE STUDY

The carbon black industry provides an interesting case study of how plant sizes have changed over time. Although carbon black has several uses, its primary use is as an ingredient in the making of rubber tires. The figure on the opposite page indicates the 1983 (or latest available year prior to 1983 for which data were available) annual capacity of each carbon black plant in existence in 1976 and whether it still operated as of 1983. As the figure indicates, the smallest plants have been closing. There are several reasons for this.

First, in response to the energy crisis, firms developed new, energy-saving technologies for producing carbon black that are more efficient at higher volume plants. In other words, production economies of scale have increased relative to transportation costs, and this leads to larger plants.

Second, the industry has shifted away from using natural gas to using oil. Natural gas prices do not vary regionally as much as current oil prices. Therefore, the shift to oil has favored location near the Gulf of Mexico, where oil is available at relatively low cost.

Third, the tire companies that purchase carbon black have become less dispersed throughout the United States. Whenever the locations of buyers become less dispersed, the transportation-cost disadvantage of centralization can decline, which creates an incentive for further centralization.

then the additional output is equal to $.01 \, (x_1 \, MP_1 + x_2 \, MP_2 + \ldots X_n \, MP_n)$ where $.01x_i$ = the amount of increased usage of factor i from a 1 percent increase in use, and MP_i = the marginal product of factor i, which equals the extra output from use of one more unit of factor i. The ratio, R, of this extra output to the original level of output, is

$$R = \frac{x_1 \, MP_1 + x_2 \, MP_2 + \ldots + x_n \, MP_n}{q}$$

There is clearly a close relationship between the cost function and the production function. A close relationship is therefore expected between the measure of scale economies, S, based on the cost function and the measure R, based on the production function. In fact, it is possible to show that under competition $R = S$.[5] In other words, the measure of scale economies is identical whether one uses the definition based on costs or on production.

Capacity of Carbon Black Plants, Ranked by Size (1983)

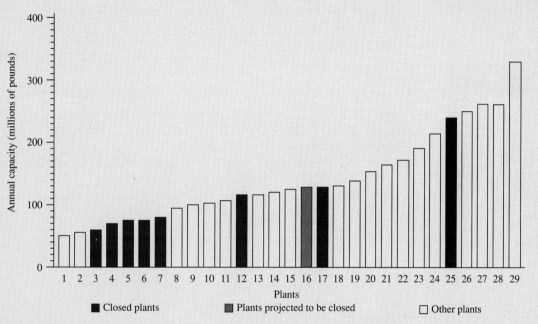

SOURCE: Industry data.

■ EMPIRICAL STUDIES OF COST CURVES

Numerous empirical studies have attempted to discover what a firm's cost curves look like and to identify the importance of economies of scale. Since economies of scale refer to cost savings that arise as output increases, it is important in any study of economies

---

[5] Let $q = F(x_1, \ldots, x_n)$, and $R = \Sigma x_i F_i / q$, where $F_i = \partial F / \partial x_i$. Under competition $F_i / F_1 = W_i / W_1$, or $F_i = F_1 (W_i / W_1)$ where $W_i =$ wage of factor i. Therefore,

$$R = \frac{x_1 F_1 + \dfrac{F_1}{W_1} \sum_{2}^{n} x_i W_i}{q} = \frac{F_1}{W_1} \frac{\Sigma x_i W_i}{q} = \frac{1}{MC} AC = S$$

TABLE 3.4   Estimates of Economy of Scale in the Purchase of New Equipment

Value of b	Percentage of Products
0–.49	24.4
.50–.79	56.8
.8 –.99	13.4
1.0 and above	5.4

SOURCE: Haldi and Whitcomb (1967, 376).

of scale to verify that output is the *only* variable accounting for cost differences among firms (or for the same firm over time). Large firms may differ from small firms in many ways; for example, they may produce more products or perform different functions, such as marketing. To show that cost differences between firms are due to economies of scale, one must make sure that the two firms produce the same products and perform the same functions. If one firm markets its product itself, while another, smaller firm does not, any analysis that failed to account for this difference would find diseconomies of scale: average costs would appear to rise as output expands, when in fact the opposite may be the case.

Some studies have focused on whether economies of scale characterize certain specific functions, such as purchase of equipment or operating costs. Other studies have asked the more general question of whether economies of scale characterize the entire operations of a firm.

Purchase of New Equipment

Haldi and Whitcomb (1967) estimate one aspect of scale economies by examining the relationship between the cost of new equipment and its capacity. If cost rises less than proportionately as capacity increases, then economies of scale are present in the purchase of new equipment. They estimate separate cost relationships for 687 different types of common industrial equipment and find that costs do not increase proportionately to capacity, even at very large capacities. In other words, their data "support the conclusion that there are increasing returns in equipment up to and including the largest sizes built." (p. 377). This does not mean that all aspects of a firm's average costs decline with output; only the cost of new equipment does.

Haldi and Whitcomb estimate the following relationship: Cost $= a K^b$, where $K =$ capacity. If b equals 1, then costs rise proportionately with output. If b is below 1, then costs rise less than proportionately with output. In fact, b can be interpreted as the percentage increase in costs that results when capacity expands by 1 percent. Their results, summarized in Table 3.4, show that for most products (about 95 percent), the value of b is below 1, indicating economies of scale in the purchase of new equipment.

Haldi and Whitcomb also estimate economies of scale in operating cost. They define operating cost as in-plant production cost less taxes and capital costs, and they base their analysis upon engineering cost estimates. They estimate the same type of relationship as they did for Table 3.4, and their results, summarized in Table 3.5, show that the values

TABLE 3.5   Economies of Scale in Operating Cost

Value of b	Percentage of Estimates
0– .49	15.1
.5– .79	56.3
.8–1.0	28.1

SOURCE: Haldi and Whitcomb (1967, 382).

for *b* are well below 1 for a large percentage of products, again indicating strong scale economies. For example, for over 70 percent of the products, a 10 percent increase in output leads to less than an 8 percent increase in operating cost.

Total Manufacturing Costs

Johnston (1960) estimates cost curves for a variety of different manufacturing firms and finds that they tend to be L-shaped. That is, initially there are large economies of scale, but eventually those economies are exhausted, and average costs remain constant. A typical diagram for an average cost curve is illustrated in Figure 3.5.

FIGURE 3.5   L-Shaped Average Cost Curve

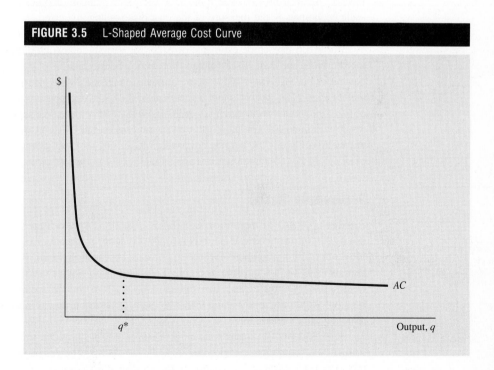

TABLE 3.6	Estimates of Minimum Efficient Size *(MES)*		
Product	*MES (physical output per year)*	*MES as Percent of U.K. Market*	*Percent Increase in Unit Cost Incurred by a Plant of 50% MES*
Oil	10 million tons	10	5
Chemicals			
Ethylene	300,000 tons	9	25
Dye	large	100	22
Sulfuric acid	1 million tons	30	1
Beer (brewery)	at least 1 million barrels	3	9
Steel production	9 million tons	33	5–10

SOURCE: Silberston (1972, 380) reported in Pratten (1971).

If long-run cost curves look like those in Figure 3.5, it is clear that the output, q^*, above which average costs do not significantly change is a point of particular interest. A plant that produces the lowest output that attains its minimum average cost is called the **minimum efficient scale (MES)** plant. The size of the MES plant, especially in relation to the overall market, is useful for judging how many firms could possibly operate in a market. Aside from knowing how large the MES plant is, another useful description of scale economies is the measure of the cost disadvantage incurred by a plant less than the MES. If this disadvantage is small, then economies of scale are unimportant.

Table 3.6 lists some estimates of MES for various industries in the United Kingdom together with the cost disadvantage that would be incurred if plants equal in size to 50 percent of the MES were built. These numbers are based on engineering estimates. Pratten (1971) shows that in only about 25 percent of the cases examined is the cost disadvantage of producing in the suboptimal size plant more than 10 percent. Weiss (1976) uses Pratten's results to show that for most industries, the size of the MES plant is typically a small percentage of total U.S. output. This work implies that for most industries, plant economies of scale are not so significant as to preclude having numerous firms in an industry.

Survivorship Studies

Another approach to measuring economies of scale is due to Stigler (1968), who makes use of the following simple but powerful observation: If a particular plant size is efficient, then eventually all plants in the industry should approach that size. Any plant or firm size that survives for a long time is efficient. According to Stigler (1968), it is instructive to classify the fraction of industry output coming from the different-sized plants. If the fraction of output from a particular size class is declining over time, then it must be a relatively inefficient size.

It is important to understand what a survivorship study can reveal. If all firms face similar cost conditions, a survivorship study reveals the efficient plant size as the industry replaces its obsolete plants. If firms face *different* costs or produce *different* products, their optimal scales will vary, and a survivorship study can only identify the *range* of

TABLE 3.7 Distribution of Petroleum Refining

Plant Size (percent of industry total)	Percent of Industry Capacity		
	1947	1950	1954
under .1	8.22	7.39	6.06
.1– .2	9.06	7.60	7.13
.2– .3	5.45	4.99	7.28
1.5–2.5	17.39	23.64	22.45
2.5–4.0	21.08	16.96	15.54

SOURCE: Stigler (1968,69).

TABLE 3.8 Number of Plants in the Beer Industry

Year	No. of Plants
1947	465
1954	310
1958	252
1963	211
1967	154
1974	108
1978	96
1983	80

SOURCE: Adapted from Breweries Authorized to Operate, Department of the Treasury, Bureau of Alcohol, Tobacco, and Firearms, Washington D.C. U.S. Government Printing Office, various years; Modern Brewery Age, Blue Book, Stamford Ct.; Modern Brewery Age Pub., various years; and The Brewery Industry, Staff Report of the Federal Trade Commission, Bureau of Economics, Washington D.C., U.S. Government Printing Office, 1978.

efficient plant sizes. In other words, economies of scale measure how costs fall as output expands, holding *all else constant*. If other factors are not constant across plants, a survivorship study does not reveal the efficient plant size but merely describes the range of efficient plant sizes.

Stigler analyzes the distribution of output in petroleum refining by plant size; his results are reported in Table 3.7. Stigler uses these data to conclude that the very smallest and the very largest plants are inefficient, because their share of industry output is declining.

Since Stigler's initial study, there have been numerous applications of his survivorship method to other industries. One product that has attracted economists' attention is beer. The beer industry has undergone major changes since 1947; Table 3.8 illustrates the dramatic decline in the number of plants over time.

Table 3.9 illustrates the composition of plants by size (annual capacity). It shows that, until 1979, the smallest plants are diminishing in importance, and the largest are increasing. The data suggest that in the beer industry, economies of scale at the plant level have become increasingly important. (However, during the 1980's, there has been growth in the number of very small breweries.)

TABLE 3.9 Number of Plants			
Annual Capacity (thousands of barrels)	1959	1971	1979
0– 25	11	2	2
26– 100	57	19	8
101– 250	51	19	6
251–2000	88	67	26
2001–3000	5	9	6
3001–4000	3	3	7
4000+	2	7	20

SOURCE: Elzinga (1986, 215).

■ COST CONCEPTS FOR MULTIPRODUCT FIRMS

Most firms do not produce a single product; it is far more typical for a firm to produce several different, though perhaps related, products. For example, a doughnut shop produces filled doughnuts and plain doughnuts, a doctor treats sore throats and skin rashes, and a plumber fixes sinks and bathtubs. When a firm produces many different products, it is a *multiproduct firm*.[6] The multiproduct nature of firms does not materially affect the analyses in most of this text. However, it is important to remember that treating firms as multiproduct is more realistic than not and that, in some cases, ignoring the multiproduct characteristics of firms can lead to improper conclusions.

Adaptation of Traditional Cost Concepts for a Multiproduct Firm

If a firm produces two or more products, it is no longer possible to speak of *the* average cost or *the* marginal cost because there is no one measure of output. However, it is straightforward to define total cost and then to define the relevant cost concepts analogous to those in a single-product environment. For example, if q_1 units of Product 1 and q_2 units of Product 2 are being produced, then the marginal cost of producing Product 1 is the additional cost incurred by increasing output of Product 1 from q_1 to $q_1 + 1$ *holding the output of Product 2 constant at q_2*. Notice that the marginal cost of Product 1 depends not only on the level of output for Product 1 but also depends on the level of output for Product 2 (q_2). Marginal cost for Product 2 is defined analogously.

Unlike marginal cost, average costs are not as easy to define in a multiproduct context. The problem arises in trying to decide whether to divide total cost by the output of Product 1, q_1, or Product 2, q_2. Perhaps total cost should be divided by the sum, $q_1 + q_2$. In fact, there is no single right answer, and several relevant average cost concepts are reasonable to use. These and other cost concepts that arise for a multiproduct firm are described in detail in Appendix 3B.

---

[6] See Baumol, Panzar, and Willig (1982) for a detailed study of multiproduct firms.

Aside from the extrapolation of the concepts of marginal and average cost to a multiproduct environment, there are some cost concepts that arise only in a multiproduct setting. The most important such cost concept is economies of scope. Appendix 3B discusses some other ones.

Economies of Scope

When it is cheaper to produce two products together (joint production) rather than separately, an **economy of scope** exists. (See Baumol, Panzar and Willig 1982; Panzar and Willig 1977). For example, a steer produces beef and hide. Although it is possible to use some steers just for hide and others just for beef, it would be inefficient with current technology.

Economies of scope imply that it is efficient to produce two or more products together; they do not necessarily imply that these products should be produced by a single firm. For example, consider how steel is made. First, iron ore is melted down into pig iron in a blast furnace; the molten pig iron is then run into a steel-making furnace. It is possible to conceive of two separate firms, side by side, one of which makes pig iron and the other steel, with a pipe carrying the molten pig iron between the two firms.[7] Recall from Chapter 2 that this is a situation that leads to high transaction costs and exposes each firm to exploitation by the other because each depends so heavily on the other. High transaction costs explain why only a single firm typically produces all the products for which economies of scope exist.

Many possible factors contribute to economies of scope, and one of the most important is the use of common inputs. In the example of producing beef and hide, given earlier, it is easy to see why it might be best to produce both simultaneously rather than using one steer for beef and another for hide.[8]

Knowledge is one of the most important common inputs for producing and selling related products. Information about one product is likely to be relevant for another closely related product. For example, knowing how to market steel bars efficiently (for example, knowing where the customers are) might help in marketing steel sheets. Or knowing how to manufacture steel bars efficiently (for example, knowing where the low-price iron ore is) might help in the efficient manufacture of steel sheets. In such situations, products are expected to be produced and sold together, because it is efficient to do so. Otherwise,

---

[7] The student should not dismiss as unrealistic the possibility of a pipe connecting two separate firms. For example, when leaded gasoline is made, a lead additive must be added to prevent engine knock. In the early 1980s, an Exxon refinery that makes gasoline in Louisiana was located beside a plant owned by the Ethyl Corporation that made the lead additive and delivered it by pipe to Exxon.

---

[8] Another example of multiproduct production involves sheep that simultaneously produce mutton and wool. Mutton spoils unless refrigerated. Before refrigeration, it was efficient sometimes not to use the sheep to produce both mutton and wool. It is believed that in the twelfth century, the sheep in Flanders, a sheep-raising center in the United Kingdom, were used exclusively for wool. The optimal shearing location was so far from the population centers that the mutton would spoil by the time it arrived, and the alternative of shipping the sheep and slaughtering closer to the population center was not cost-effective. Mutton was provided by sheep raised near the population centers (Bailey and Friedlaender 1982, 1026).

resources like information would have to be wastefully duplicated. Moreover, because it is difficult to transact in information, a single firm often produces related products.

A final example of using common input arises when a person's physical presence is required for certain services. Consider a plumber who handles a wide variety of plumbing problems and can fix sinks as well as bathtubs. It might be that a plumber who repairs only sinks could service them better than a more versatile plumber. For that matter, there might be gains from specializing further and having one plumber repair sink washers and another repair sink stoppers. But a homeowner would have to call several plumbers to diagnose the problem before finding the right specialist. In other words, because of the *indivisibility* involved in diagnosing a problem (you need one person physically present to do it), it would be inefficient if that person was unable to fix a wide range of plumbing problems. If the gains from specialization in plumbing were great, it might be worth having specialists—perhaps even a specialist at diagnosing problems. But as long as the gains are small, such specialization is unlikely.

Economies of Scale and Economies of Scope

Firms often produce many products to gain economies of scope in marketing and distribution. A salesperson who sells white bread to a store can also sell rolls. A store may prefer to deal with one person who can satisfy all its needs rather than with several different salespeople. A firm that produces and sells many products can specialize production by plant, which allows economies of scale in production and maintains a full product line. The disadvantage of such specialization is that transportation costs may rise as individual products must be shipped farther.[9] See Example 3.3.

An Example of an Industry with Economies of Scope

Friedlaender, Winston, and Wang (1983) estimate a multiproduct cost function for each of the four U.S. auto makers. They postulate that costs depend on prices of various inputs (for example, wages, raw materials) and various outputs (for example, small cars, large cars, and trucks). Their statistical procedure also adjusts for the differing physical specifications of small and large cars and trucks.

The measure of economies of scale (see Equation 3B.1 in Appendix 3B) equals 1.23 for General Motors at a typical point, suggesting that economies of scale characterize GM. This means that if GM expanded output of small cars, large cars, and trucks by 10 percent, costs would rise by about 8 percent (10/1.23).

They are also able to measure the degree of economies of scope (see Equation 3B.2 in Appendix 3B), which depends on the group of outputs being considered. For example,

---

[9] Suppose that there are no transaction cost difficulties so that it is not necessary for the marketing and production to be done by the same firm. Will a competitive market consisting of individual specialized plants adopt the optimal plant locations? The answer is generally no (Koopmans and Beckmann 1957).

EXAMPLE 3.3

THE BAKING INDUSTRY

The baking industry provides an excellent example of multiplant specialization. Until recently, bakeries typically produced a wide range of products (breads, rolls, cakes) and served relatively small geographic areas. Since the product is perishable, shipping distances were limited. The development of improved preservatives extended the shelf life of baked goods with the result that shipping distances could be increased. Bakeries began to acquire nearby bakeries and use the concept of *reciprocal baking* to produce their products. Reciprocal baking means that plants become specialized in particular products and then ship their products to each other, so that each geographic area is served by a full line. Reciprocal baking has allowed bakery firms to take advantage of scale economies and still preserve the economies of scope in marketing that come from having a full product line.

the economy of scope, *SC,* of producing large cars together with small cars and trucks is defined as

$$SC = \frac{C(\text{large cars alone}) + C(\text{small cars} + \text{trucks}) - C(\text{large} + \text{small cars} + \text{trucks})}{C(\text{large} + \text{small cars} + \text{trucks})}$$

where *C* stands for the total cost of producing the indicated outputs. *SC* indicates the percentage increase in costs that would occur if large cars were produced separately from small cars plus trucks. For GM, this number equals 25 percent, which indicates substantial benefit from combining the production of large cars with small cars plus trucks. Surprisingly, no economies of scope arise from producing trucks together with small and large cars; it appears that truck production could occur in a separate firm with no loss of efficiency.

■ SUMMARY

A firm's costs are described by its cost function. An economist's definition of cost relies on the concept of opportunity cost and automatically builds a normal profit into the cost calculation. A cost function reveals how much it costs the firm to produce various amounts of output, or, in the case of a multiproduct firm, various combinations of different outputs. A cost function depends not only on the output(s) produced, but also on the cost of the factors of production, like wages of workers and the cost of raw materials.

There are many different types of costs: sunk costs, fixed costs, variable costs, avoidable costs, marginal costs, average variable costs, and average total cost. Some cost functions exhibit economies of scale, while others do not. A typical manufacturing process exhibits economies of scale at least initially. But the other functions of the typical firm, such as administration, monitoring, marketing, and delivery entail costs that eventually exhaust all scale economies and lead to an optimal firm size.

When a firm produces several different products, an analysis of costs requires the development of cost concepts analogous to those used with a single-product firm, and the development of new cost concepts, like economies of scope. Cost concepts for a multi-product firm explicitly recognize that the cost of producing one product depends on the amount of other products that are produced.

■ Key Terms

amortized	diseconomies of scale	natural monopoly
average fixed cost	economies of scale	normal profit
average variable cost	economy of scope	opportunity cost
average total cost	expensed	production technology
avoidable cost	fixed cost	short run
constant returns to scale	long run	sunk cost
cost of adjustment	marginal cost	total cost
depreciation	minimum efficient scale	variable cost

■ Discussion Questions

1. Economies of scope imply that it is efficient to have only one firm producing in an industry. Discuss.
2. A fractional unit of output is a reasonable concept if output is really a rate of output per unit of time. Discuss.
3. Explain why the price of a machine is not the correct price to compare to the wage rate if a firm is trying to figure out how many machines and how much labor to hire.
4. The footnote in the section on economies of scope discusses the pipeline between Ethyl and Exxon. Based on the discussion in Chapter 2 of opportunistic behavior, is it likely that Exxon formed a large component of demand for this Ethyl plant? Is it likely that the cost of the lead additive was a large component of Exxon's costs?
5. If there are no sunk costs, and if costless and instantaneous entry and exit are possible, then constant returns to scale prevail since the optimal size plant can keep jumping in and out of the industry. Discuss.

■ Problems

1. In the very short run, practically all costs are fixed. Does that mean that marginal cost is zero?
2. If there are economies of scope and if the price for each product equals marginal cost, is it possible for a firm to cover all its costs? If the firm's average cost of production declines the more it produces, can a price equal to marginal cost ever cover all its costs?
3. Suppose the cost of producing q_1 cars and q_2 trucks is $10,000 + 70\,q_1 + 80\,q_2$. Calculate the marginal cost of producing cars and the measure of scope economies when $q_1 = 100$ and $q_2 = 200$.
4. Why can the measure of economies of scope not exceed one as long as marginal costs are always positive?
5. Suppose there are a wide range of plant sizes in an industry. What do you conclude about the shape of the average cost curve if the plants are in the same area? (Hint: Plants in the same area probably face similar costs). How does your answer change if the plants are located in different countries?

Answers to the odd numbered problems are given at the back of the book.

■ References

Alchian, Armen A. 1959. "Costs and Outputs," in *The Allocation of Economic Resources*, ed. M. Abromovitz. Stanford: Stanford Univ. Press.

Bailey, Elizabeth E., and Ann F. Friedlaender, 1982. "Market Structure and Multi-product Industries." *Journal of Economic Literature* 20:1024-1048.

Baumol, William J., John C. Panzar, and Robert D. Willig. 1982. *Contestable Markets and The Theory of Industry Structure*. New York: Harcourt Brace Jovanovich.

Elzinga, Kenneth G. 1986. "The Beer Industry," in *The Structure of American Industry*. ed. Walter Adams. New York: Macmillan 203–238.

Friedlaender, Ann F., Clifford Winston, and Kung Wang. 1983. "Costs, Technology, and Productivity in the U.S. Automobile Industry." *Bell Journal of Economics* 14:1–20.

Haldi, John, and David Whitcomb. 1967. "Economies of Scale in Industrial Plants." *Journal of Political Economy* 75:373–85.

Johnston, John. 1960. *Statistical Cost Analysis*. New York: McGraw-Hill.

Koopmans, Tjalling, and Martin Beckmann. 1957. "Assignment Problems and the Location of Economic Activities." *Econometrica* 25:53–76.

Lucas, Robert. 1967. "Adjustment Cost and the Theory of Supply." *Journal of Political Economy* 75:321–34.

Panzar, John C., and Robert D. Willig. 1977. "Economies of Scale in Multi-Output Production." *Quarterly Journal of Economics* 91:481–93.

Pratten, C. F. 1971. "Economies of Scale in Manufacturing Industry." Occasional Paper, no. 28. Cambridge: Cambridge University Press (Department of Applied Economics).

Scherer, Frederic M., Alan Beckenstein, Erich Kaufer, and R. Dennis Murphy. 1975. *The Economics of Multi-Plant Operation: An International Comparison Study*. Cambridge: Harvard University Press.

Silberston, Aubrey. 1972. "Economies of Scale in Theory and Practice." *Economic Journal* 82:369–91.

Smith, Adam. 1937. *The Wealth of Nations*. New York: The Modern Library, 4–5.

Stigler, George. 1968. "Economies of Scale." *Journal of Law and Economics* 1, 54–71. Reprinted in *The Organization of Industry*. Chicago: University of Chicago Press, 1968.

Varian, Hal. 1984. *Microeconomic Analysis*. New York: W. W. Norton.

Weiss, Leonard W. 1976. "Optimal Plant Size and the Extent of Suboptimal Capacity," in *Essays on Industrial Organization in Honor of Joe S. Bain*, ed. Masson and Qualls. Cambridge, Mass.: Ballinger.

TURNING AN ASSET PRICE INTO A RENTAL RATE

The appropriate cost concept to apply to capital (anything that lasts, for example, a piece of equipment, knowledge) is the rental price. So, for example, the relevant cost to a firm that has purchased its own truck is the rental rate it could earn on that truck. The analyst imagines the firm paying that rent to itself. The problem is that, although some equipment can be rented (and so data exist on the rental rate), for other equipment only a purchase price may be available. This appendix shows how to convert a purchase price to a rental price.

Let $R(t)$ = rental price for 1 unit of capital at time t,

$p(t)$ = purchase price for 1 unit of capital at time t,

$K(t)$ = amount of capital remaining at time t, if 1 unit was purchased at time 0,

r = interest rate,

δ = rate of depreciation; the rate at which capital declines in its productive capacity ($\delta = -\dot{K}/K$, where a dot indicates differentiation with respect to time).

Assume that $p(t)$ is observable and you wish to calculate $R(t)$. It is a fundamental law of capital theory that the price of an asset equals the discounted present value of the rentals one could obtain from the asset. If the rental rate at time t is $R(t)$ and if $K(t)$ units of capital remain at time t, then total rental at time t is $R(t) K(t)$. Therefore,

$$p(0) = \int_0^\infty R(t) K(t) e^{-rt} dt, \qquad \text{[3A.1]}$$

where $K(0) = 1$.

This formula for the asset price applies not just at time, 0, but at any time, y. Hence,

$$K(y)\ p(y)\ =\ \int_{y}^{\infty} R(t)\ K(t)\ e^{-r(t-y)}\ dt. \qquad [3A.2]$$

By taking the derivative of Equation 3A.2 with respect to y, one obtains

$$\dot{K}(y)\,p(y) + K(y)\ \dot{p}(y)\ =\ -R(y)\ K(y) + r\int_{y}^{\infty} R(t)\ K(t)\ e^{-r(t-y)}\ dt$$

$$=\ -R(y)\ K(y)\ +\ r\ p(y)\ K(y),$$

or

$$R(y)\ =\ r\ p(y) - \frac{\dot{K}(y)\ p(y)}{K(y)} - \dot{p}(y),$$

or

$$R(y)\ =\ (r\ +\ \delta\ -\ \frac{\dot{p}}{p})\ p(y). \qquad [3A.3]$$

In summary, the rental rate equals forgone interest plus depreciation minus any price appreciation (or decline).

COST CONCEPTS FOR A MULTIPRODUCT FIRM

When moving from a single-product to a multiproduct environment, one must adapt some of the definitions of cost and develop some new concepts to characterize cost.[1]

Definitions

Suppose that $C(q_1,q_2)$ represents the cost of a firm that produces q_1 units of Product 1 and q_2 units of Product 2. The marginal cost of producing Product 1 at any given output level is defined, as in the single-product case, as the incremental cost of producing one more unit of Product 1—except now it is necessary to specify not only how much of Product 1 is being produced but also how much of Product 2. In mathematical terms, the marginal cost of Product 1 is just the (partial) derivative of $C(q_1,q_2)$ with respect to q_1.

What meaning can be given to the concept of average cost? The answer is that there is no unambiguous measure of average cost. Although total cost is well defined, there is no one unique output level to choose when two products are produced. One could define total output as $q_1 + q_2$, but that literally would be akin to adding up apples and oranges. In fact, there is no reason why any linear combination of output, $a_1 q_1 + a_1 q_1$, is better than any other, where a_1 and a_2 are any two numbers.

If one specifies the proportions in which Products 1 and 2 are produced, it is possible to define an average cost concept, called *ray average costs (RAC)*. Let λ_1 and λ_2 be the proportions in which Products 1 and 2 are produced. Then, *RAC* are defined as total costs divided by a scale of output measure. That is,

$$RAC(q) = C(\lambda_1 q, \lambda_2 q)/q.$$

---

[1] See Baumol, Panzar, Willig (1982, Ch. 3, 4) for a detailed treatment of these topics.

By investigating how *RAC(q)* behaves as *q* increases, one can define increasing ray average costs, constant ray average costs, and decreasing ray average costs. *RAC(q)* will depend on the values of λ_1 and λ_2.

Arbitrarily choosing λ_1 and λ_2 reduces the multiproduct case to a single-product case. For any given value of λ_1 and λ_2, we can calculate *RAC* and then find the scale, *q*, that minimizes *RAC*—just as in the single-product case. However, the scale at which RAC is minimized along different rays (different combinations of λ_1 and λ_2) generally differs. For example, consider an automobile company that makes small and large cars. If it is required to have a 50 percent mix, its average production cost may be minimized at 1 million units of each type of car. However, if the mix is 25:75 percent, its average production costs may be minimized at 1 million small cars, and 3 million large cars.

It is possible to show that *RAC(q)* will be falling or rising or constant as *q* increases depending on whether *S* (*S* stands for scale economy) is above, below, or equal to 1, where

$$S = \frac{C(q)}{q^1 \frac{\partial C}{\partial q^1} + q^2 \frac{\partial C}{\partial q^2}}. \quad {}^2 \tag{3B.1}$$

S is simply the multiproduct analogue of the ratio of average to marginal cost. As in the single-product case, if firms are pricing at marginal cost, then *S* is the ratio of costs to revenues. In the single-product case, if *S* exceeds 1 so that *AC* exceeds *MC*, *AC* will be falling, while if *S* is below 1 so that *AC* is less than *MC*, *AC* will be rising. Similarly, in the multiproduct case, if *S* exceeds 1, *RAC* will be falling, while if *S* is below 1, *RAC*

---

[2] *Proof:*

$$\begin{aligned}
\frac{d\,RAC(q)}{dq} &= (1/q)\frac{\lambda_1 \partial C}{\partial q_1} + \frac{\lambda_2 \partial C}{\partial q_2} - C(q)\frac{1}{q^2} \\
&= \frac{1}{q}\left[\lambda_1 q \frac{\partial C}{\partial q_1} + \lambda_2 q \frac{\partial C}{\partial q_2} - C(q) \right] \\
&= \frac{1}{q^2}\left[q_1 \frac{\partial C}{\partial q_1} + q_2 \frac{\partial C}{\partial q_2} - C(q) \right].
\end{aligned}$$

Hence, $d\,RAC(q)/dq > 0$ if

$$\Sigma q_i\, \partial C/\partial q_i > C(q), \text{ or if}$$

$$1 > \frac{C(q)}{\Sigma q_i \dfrac{\partial C}{\partial q_i}}$$

or $1 > S$, where

$$S = \frac{C(q)}{\Sigma q_i \dfrac{\partial C}{\partial q_i}}.$$

will be rising. S can be viewed as measuring the proportionate increase in total costs from a percentage increase in the amount of *all* outputs. If S exceeds 1, it means that costs increase by less than the percentage increase in output.[3]

In addition to the concept of RAC, there are several cost concepts that do not have a clear analogy to the single-product case. Consider the cost of producing q_2 units of Product 2. *Incremental costs (IC)* are defined as the difference between $C(q_1,q_2)$ and $C(q_1,0)$. *Average incremental costs (AIC)* are defined as $[C(q_1,q_2) - C(q_1,0)]/q_2$. Notice that the incremental cost of producing q_2 units of Product 2 includes any fixed cost associated with the production of q_2 and depends on the assumed production of q_1. The AIC function for q_2 can be analyzed as q_2 varies, holding q_1 fixed. This gives rise to the notion of *product-specific economies of scale (PS)* of q_2 given q_1. PS_i can be defined as follows:

$$PS_i \equiv AIC_i / MC_i$$

PS_i is the same as S, defined earlier, for the particular case where all outputs except q_i are held fixed. The AIC cost function is like a typical single-product average cost function. The multiproduct cost function is made into a single-product one by fixing the level of all outputs except that of the product under analysis.

As already discussed, most firms produce more than one product because it is cheaper to produce them together rather than separately. The term *economy of scope* refers to the savings that result from doing so. Consider the production of q_1 units of Product 1 and q_2 units of Product 2. The cost of producing each separately is $C(q_1,0) + C(0,q_2)$; the cost of producing them together is $C(q_1,q_2)$. Economies of scope, SC, are measured as

$$SC = \frac{[C(q_1,0) + C(0,q_2) - C(q_1,q_2)]}{C(q_1,q_2)} \qquad \text{[3B.2]}$$

SC measures the relative increase in cost that would result if the products were produced separately. If SC is everywhere positive, it is cheaper to produce the products together. As long as marginal costs are positive, SC cannot exceed 1.[4]

When a firm increases its output of several products, it can take advantage of both economies of scope and economies of scale. It is possible for these two types of economies

---

[3] It is also possible to express the measure of scale economies, S, in terms of a production function. Let $F(x_1 \ldots x_m, q_1, \ldots q_n) = 0$ describe the relation between the inputs of $x_1, x_2, \ldots x_m$, and the outputs $q_1 \ldots q_n$. Then it can be shown that $S = \Sigma x_i F_{xi} / \Sigma q_i F_{qi}$, where a subscript on F indicates (partial) differentiation. Notice that this definition of S is the multiproduct analogue to the definition of S given in the section in the chapter entitled "Technical Definition of Scale Economies."

[4] *Proof:* Suppose $SC > 1$. That implies that $C(q_1, 0) + C(0,q_2) - C(q_1, q_2) > C(q_1, q_2)$ or $[C(q_1, 0) - C(q_1, q_2)] + [C(0, q_2) - C(q_1, q_2)] > 0$. But each term in parenthesis must be negative as long as marginal cost of additional production is positive. Therefore, the inequality cannot hold, and SC cannot exceed 1.

to pull in opposite directions. A cost function is *trans-ray convex* at a given point if the cost of producing a linear combination of any two appropriately chosen output vectors is less than the weighted cost of producing the outputs separately.[5]

An Example

Suppose that it costs $100 to rent a machine that can produce either red balloons or blue balloons. Let q_1 be the number of red balloons and q_2 the number of blue balloons. Suppose the cost function is $C(q_1,q_2) = 100 + q_1 + 2q_2$.

The cost function shows that it costs $1 to produce an additional red balloon but $2 to produce an additional blue balloon, after the machine is purchased. Now several of the cost concepts that have been discussed can be illustrated.

Marginal Cost.　The marginal cost of Product 1 is the derivative of $C(q_1,q_2)$ with respect to q_1. In this case, the marginal cost of Product 1 is constant and equals 1. The marginal cost of Product 2 is also constant and equals 2.

Ray Average Cost.　Consider the particular case of $\lambda_1 = .5$, $\lambda_2 = .5$. Then

$$C(.5q,.5q) = 100 + .5q + 2 \times .5q$$
$$= 100 + 1.5q.$$

Hence

$$RAC(q) = (100 + 1.5q)/q$$
$$= \frac{100}{q} + 1.5$$

In this example, *RAC* always falls as q increases.

Overall Economies of Scale.　The measure of scale economies, S, is easily calculated.

$$S = C(q_1,q_2)/\left(q_1 \frac{\partial C}{\partial q_1} + q_2 \frac{\partial C}{\partial q_2} \right)$$
$$= \frac{100 + q_1 + 2q_2}{q_1 + 2q_2} = \frac{100}{q_1 + 2q_2} + 1.$$

---

[5] The technical definition of trans-ray convexity is as follows. "A cost function $C(q)$ is trans-ray convex through some point $q^* = (q_1^*, \ldots, q_n^*)$ if there exists any vector of positive constants $w_1, \ldots, w_n$ such that for every two output vectors $q^a = (q_1^a, \ldots, q_n^a)$ and $q^b = (q_1^b, \ldots, q_n^b)$ that lie on the hyperplane $\Sigma w_i q_i = w_0$ through point q^* (so that they satisfy $\Sigma w_i q_i^a = \Sigma w_i q_i^b = \Sigma w_1 q_1^*$), for any k such that $0 < k < 1$ we have
$$C[kq^a + (1 - k)q^b] \leq kC(q^a) + (1 - k)C(q^b)."$$
See Baumol, Panzar, and Willig (1982, Ch. 4, Def. 4D1).

Notice that the measure of scale economies always exceeds 1, which shows that for this particular example, scale economies are always present.

Economies of Scope. If q_1 were produced separately, the cost would be $C(q_1,0) = 100 + q_1$. Similarly, if q_2 were produced separately, the cost would be $C(0,q_2) = 100 + 2q_2$. The cost of producing q_1 and q_2 separately is

$$C(q_1,0) + C(0,q_2) = 200 + q_1 + 2q_2.$$

This is clearly higher than the cost of producing them together, $C(q_1,q_2)$. Using equation (3B.2), we can calculate economies of scope as

$$
\begin{aligned}
SC &= [C(q_1,0) + C(0,q_2) - C(q_1,q_2)]/C(q_1,q_2) \\
&= [200 + q_1 + 2q_2 - (100 + q_1 + 2q_2)]/[100 + q_1 + 2q_2] \\
&= \frac{100}{100 + q_1 + 2q_2}.
\end{aligned}
$$

Since SC always exceeds zero, it is always cheaper to produce the two goods together rather than separately.

Product-Specific Economies. By fixing the level of output of one of the products, say q_2, we can calculate $AIC\ (q_1)$ as $[C(q_1,q_2) - C(0,q_2)]/q_1$, or

$$
\begin{aligned}
AIC(q_1) &= [(100 + q_1 + 2q_2) - (100 + 2q_2)]/q_1 \\
&= q_1/q_1 = 1.
\end{aligned}
$$

That is, AIC is always constant and equals 1. Notice that marginal cost of Product 1 is always constant and equals 1. Since AIC is constant, there are no product-specific economies for q_1 (nor for q_2), yet recall that there are overall scale economies.

ADJUSTMENT COST

No firm can instantly change its level of production without incurring some adjustment costs. One way to account for adjustment costs is to allow a firm's costs to depend on its current rate of output, q, and the change in its rate of output, $\dot{q}$. A competitive firm that faces a price at time t of $p(t)$ chooses its output at time t, $q(t)$, to maximize the present discounted value of its profits. The firm decides whether an increase in production today is desirable based not only on how costs rise because of a higher level of output but also on how adjustment costs are affected.

The competitive firm chooses $q(t)$ to maximize

$$\int \{p(t)\, q(t) - C[q(t),\dot{q}]\}\, e^{-rt}dt.$$

This is a problem in the calculus of variations, and the interested reader is referred to Lucas (1967). Lucas shows how capital investment can allow the firm to expand over time and how the rate of capital investment depends on adjustment costs.

The essential features of the adjustment problem can be illustrated in a simple model involving two periods. Let q_1 and q_2 be output in Periods 1 and 2. Let the cost, $C(q_1,q_2)$, of producing q_1 in Period 1 and q_2 in Period 2 equal $C(q_1,q_2) = q_1^2 + q_2^2 + (q_1 - q_2)^2$.

Notice that cost depends, in part, upon the change in production, $(q_1 - q_2)$, between the two periods and rises the greater the difference between q_1 and q_2. In Chapter 4 we will learn that competitive firms equate price to marginal cost. Let p_1 and p_2 be the prices in Periods 1 and 2, respectively. If $p_1 = 2$ and $p_2 = 4$, then the firm chooses q_1 and q_2 so that price is equated to marginal cost in each period. Hence

$$2 = \frac{\partial C}{\partial q_1}(q_1,q_2) \quad \text{and} \quad 4 = \frac{\partial C}{\partial q_2}(q_1,q_2),$$

or

$$2 = 2q_1 + 2(q_1 - q_2) \quad \text{and} \quad 4 = 2q_2 - 2(q_1 - q_2),$$

or $q_1 = 1.33$ and $q_2 = 1.66$.

CHAPTER 4

COMPETITION

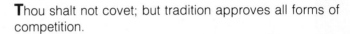

Thou shalt not covet; but tradition approves all forms of competition.

ARTHUR HUGH CLOUGH

This chapter reviews the key features of competition. It first examines perfect competition. This model, though unrealistic in many of its assumptions, provides a framework for analyzing more realistic models. It reveals the desirable features of competition as well as its shortcomings. The chapter goes on to discuss more realistic models of competition and concludes with examples of industries that most economists would characterize as competitive.

■ PERFECT COMPETITION

Perfect competition provides a benchmark against which the behavior of markets is judged. Even though perfect competition is rarely, if ever, encountered in the real world, it can be valuable to see in what respects actual markets deviate from perfectly competitive ones and to determine the circumstances under which the deviations are likely to be greatest. However, a deviation from perfectly competitive behavior does not necessarily mean that the performance of a market can be improved. In order to understand this point, it is first necessary to understand what is meant by perfect competition and how firms behave in perfect competition.

Assumptions

The desirable properties of a perfectly competitive economy explain why economists generally favor competition. The main assumptions of **perfect competition** follow:

- **Perfect Information.** Buyers and sellers each know the price and quality of the product.
- **Price Taking.** Buyers and sellers each take the price at which the product can be purchased or sold as given. Price is determined by the market and no one buyer or seller can influence it. Using the market entails no transaction costs.

FIGURE 4.1 Cost Curves and Profit Maximization

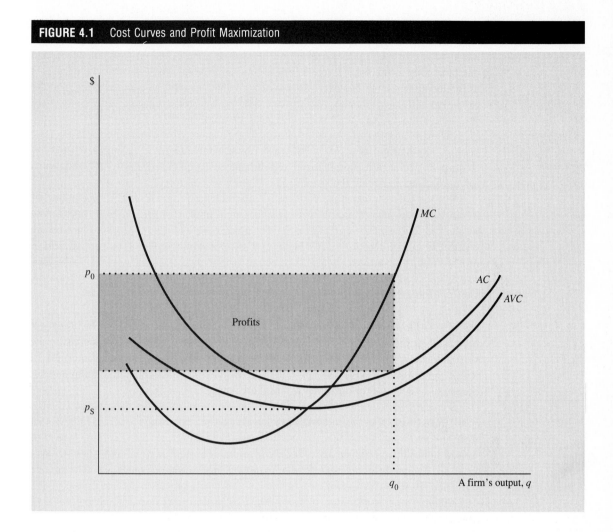

- **Many Buyers and Sellers.** There are many potential or actual buyers and sellers who can enter and exit the market costlessly in the long run.
- **Perfect Divisibility of Output.** The amount of output demanded or supplied varies continuously with price. This assumption avoids problems caused by large discrete changes in either supply or demand in response to small price changes.

The Behavior of a Single Firm

Let us first examine the incentives of a typical firm. Suppose a firm has the short-run cost curves shown in Figure 4.1. How should it decide how much to produce, if indeed it should produce anything at all?

Profit Maximization.   A competitive firm's objective is to maximize its profits (or, equivalently, minimize its losses), which equal $pq - C(q)$ where p is price, q is output and $C(q)$ is cost. A firm that can sell all it wants at price p finds it profitable to expand output as long as the extra revenue from selling an additional unit exceeds the extra cost of producing that unit. The extra revenue from selling an additional unit is *price,* and the extra cost is the *marginal cost.* Therefore, the optimal production rule for a competitive firm is to expand output until price, p, equals marginal cost, *MC.*

Figure 4.1 illustrates the profit-maximizing decisions of a competitive firm facing a price p_0. To the right of q_0, $p_0 < MC$, and it is profitable to cut back output. To the left of q_0, $p_0 > MC$, and it is profitable to expand output. At output q_0, $p_0 = MC$, and profits are maximized and equal the shaded area of the box in Figure 4.1.

If price, p, rises above p_0, the firm will earn higher profits at its current output, but it will earn even higher profits if it expands output until $p = MC$. If price falls below p_0, the firm will earn lower profits at q_0, but it can raise its lowered profits somewhat by contracting output until $p = MC$. In short, it is most profitable for a competitive firm to produce at that output level where price equals marginal cost. As the price rises, the firm moves up its marginal cost curve, and its profits rise. Increases and decreases in profits signal a firm either to expand or contract output, respectively.

Shutdown Decision.   A firm produces only if doing so is more profitable than not producing. It produces only if the revenues from producing exceed **avoidable costs:** the costs that are not incurred if a firm ceases production. The revenues earned in excess of avoidable cost are called **quasi-rents:** they are the payments above the minimum amount necessary to keep a firm operating in the short run.

For simplicity, assume that all fixed costs are sunk (recall the example in Chapter 3: the firm loses its entire incorporation fee if it ceases operating). Then it follows that avoidable costs are variable costs, and this leads to a simple rule for deciding whether to remain in business: Produce and sell only if revenues exceed or equal total variable cost. Equivalently, produce and sell at price p, only if p exceeds or equals average variable cost *(AVC).*

An important implication of this rule is that a firm may find it more profitable to produce than to shut down even though price is below average cost ($p < AC$). As long as price is above average variable cost ($p > AVC$), it is better to produce and earn some revenue in excess of variable cost than to shut down and earn no revenue to offset the fixed costs. The firm chooses to produce even though it is losing money when all costs are considered. An example will clarify this apparent contradiction.

Suppose a firm's fixed cost is $200 and sunk. It's marginal cost *(MC)* is $10 up to 100 units. At more than 100 units, *MC* is extremely high. Suppose the price is $10, and the firm produces and sells 100 units. The firm just covers its production cost and makes no contribution to the $200 fixed cost: it has lost $200. If the price were $9, the firm would be better off not producing at all, because it would lose an additional $1 for every unit it produced and would lose $300 if it produced 100 units. It is better to lose only $200 than to produce and lose more. Now suppose the price is $11. By producing 100 units, the firm now more than covers variable cost—in fact it earns $100 above variable cost. It still loses money overall ($-200 + 100 = -100$) because of the fixed cost of

$200, but it is better to lose $100 than $200. The point of the example is that the decision to produce or not is *independent* of the fixed sunk cost. As long as the obligation to pay the fixed costs exists with or without production, these sunk costs should be ignored in deciding whether to produce.

Because a firm operates if $p > AVC$, but not if $p < AVC$, the point at which $p = AVC$ is called the **shutdown point** (indicated by p_S in Figure 4.1). That is, as long as price exceeds *AVC*, the firm operates along its *MC* curve. Therefore, *the portion of the MC curve above the AVC curve is the firm's supply curve.* It reveals how much the firm is willing to supply at any given price.

If a firm has losses in the short run (the period in which costs remain sunk), will it continue to operate and remain unprofitable in the future?[1] The answer is that in the long run, a firm that is losing money will not reinvest—will not continue to sink costs in its industry. Short-run losses are a signal for a firm to curtail investments to replace plant and equipment. In the long-run, no rational firm ever continues to experience losses; it prefers to cease production rather than invest in new facilities and lose even more.

When a firm "makes losses" in the short-run, its revenue is below the opportunity cost of its resources. Since opportunity cost includes a normal profit, a firm that is making a loss may not literally be paying out more money than it is taking in; it is simply earning less than it could have earned had it invested its (already) sunk costs elsewhere.

Chapter 3 points out that some fixed costs are not sunk. The shutdown decision, however, depends on whether revenues exceed *avoidable* costs. If some fixed costs are avoidable (as when the lawyer in Chapter 3 can pay a penalty to break a lease), a price equal to *AVC* is not high enough to prevent the firm from shutting down. In the earlier example, suppose the fixed cost of $200 represents a yearly rental payment and that for a $100 penalty fee, the landlord will release the firm from the obligation to pay $200 (the landlord finds this profitable because the space can be rented). The firm compares losing $100 for sure (the penalty fee) with producing and earning revenues minus production costs minus the $200 rental payment. If price is $10, the firm earns $0 per sale and is stuck paying the $200 of fixed cost; therefore, it prefers to pay the $100 penalty and go out of business. Even if price were $10.50 so that the firm would make 50¢ on each of its 100 units sold, it would still be better to pay the $100 penalty and go out of business.

The shutdown point (the price at which a firm shuts down) moves above average variable cost and closer to average cost as fixed costs include greater proportions of avoidable costs. In the extreme, when all fixed costs are avoidable, the shutdown point coincides with the minimum point on the *AC* curve. Thus, if it has no sunk costs, a firm shuts down before it ever loses money.

The Short-Run Supply Curve for the Industry.   Suppose in the short run there are *n* identical firms and that all fixed costs are sunk. The short-run **industry supply curve** is the horizontal sum of the supply curves of each firm, as shown in Figure 4.2. The

---

[1] As described in Chapter 3, especially Appendix 3C, the short run and long run are useful abstractions, but in reality adjustment costs determine how fast an industry can adjust to change. The time needed to adjust to any change depends on the current state of the industry and the size of the needed adjustment.

FIGURE 4.2   Short-Run Equilibrium

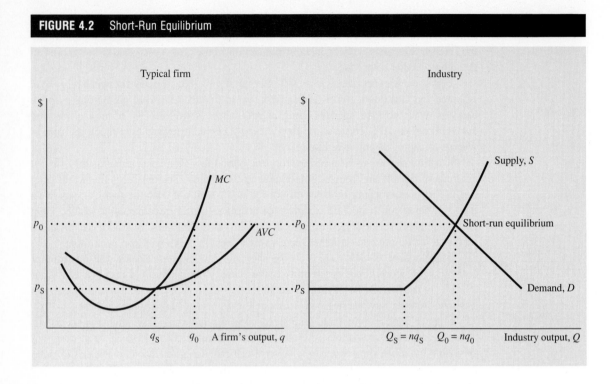

horizontal portion of the industry supply curve reflects that no output is forthcoming if price is below the shutdown point and that at a price slightly above the shutdown point, all firms produce. The intersection of the demand curve with the short-run industry supply curve determines the **short-run equilibrium,** price, p_0, and quantity, Q_0, as depicted in Figure 4.2.

In the equilibrium in Figure 4.2, firms earn a profit, which provides an incentive for other firms to enter the industry. In the long run, firms can enter at the optimal scale (the one that minimizes long-run average cost) indicated by output q^* in Figure 4.3. If each firm's long-run average cost is as shown in Figure 4.3, then firms will find it profitable to enter as long as price exceeds C^*. This means that in the long run, when firms can enter or exit with no sunk costs, the supply curve facing the industry is perfectly horizontal at C^*, the minimum average cost of production.

The Long-Run Equilibrium.   Short-run profits or losses induce firms to enter or leave the industry until price gets driven to C^*. The **long-run equilibrium** is determined by the intersection of the demand curve and the industry long-run supply curve. In the long-run equilibrium, the number of firms in the industry, n^*, is such that the industry is in short-run *and* long-run equilibrium, as shown in Figure 4.4 (on page 72).

Notice that in long-run equilibrium the demand curve, D, intersects both the long-run supply curve and the short-run supply curve corresponding to the equilibrium number of firms, n^*, at the equilibrium price C^*, and equilibrium output Q^*. From Figure 4.4,

FIGURE 4.3   Long-Run Average Costs

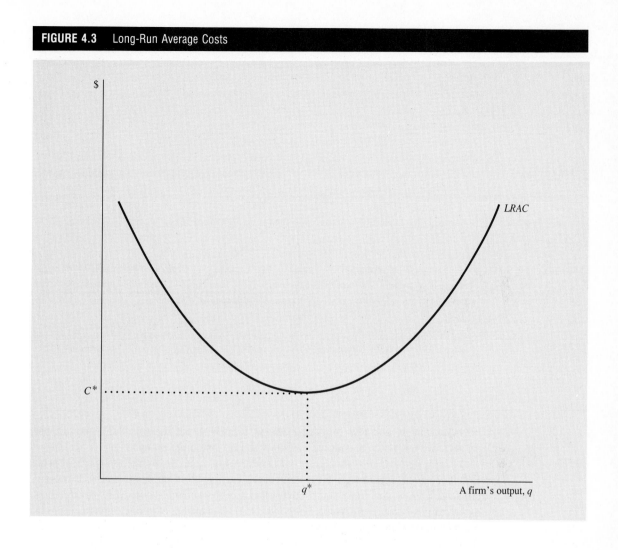

we see that $Q^* = n^*q^*$. In long-run equilibrium, economic profits equal zero; firms receive just enough to induce them to remain in the industry and no more.

Properties of Competitive Equilibrium

The competitive equilibrium of price and quantity has a number of desirable properties. The most important are described here:

Efficiency in Production.   Production is efficient. That is, all products are produced at the minimum possible cost. There is no possible rearrangement of resources (such as

FIGURE 4.4 Long-Run Equilibrium

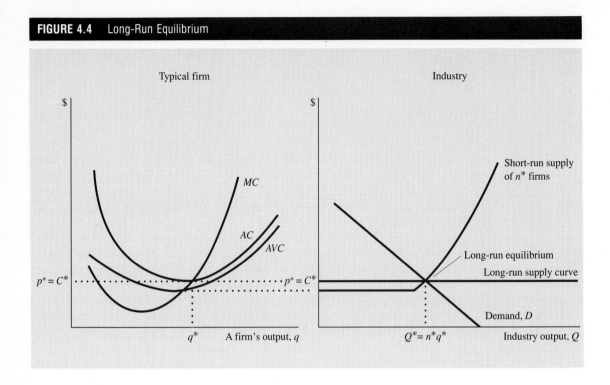

labor, machines, and raw materials) among firms that can increase the output of one product without also reducing the output of at least one other product.

Efficiency in Consumption. The amount of each product produced and consumed is efficient. That is, the value that a buyer places on consuming the good is exactly equal to the marginal cost of producing that good. No rearrangement of goods among consumers can benefit one consumer without harming at least one other.

Zero Economic Profit. Long-run profits for each of the identical firms are zero.[2] Suppliers receive just enough to pay for their costs of production and no more. Short-run profits can be positive or negative. Positive short-run profits attract new firms and encourage existing firms to expand their capacities. The resulting increase in supply drives price down until profit opportunities are eliminated in the long-run. Conversely, short-run losses induce firms to leave the industry and reduce output until price rises again to yield normal profit levels.

---

[2] If additional identical firms are unable to enter, then profits could be positive, but firms in the industry would still produce where price equals marginal cost.

FIGURE 4.5   Long-Run Supply

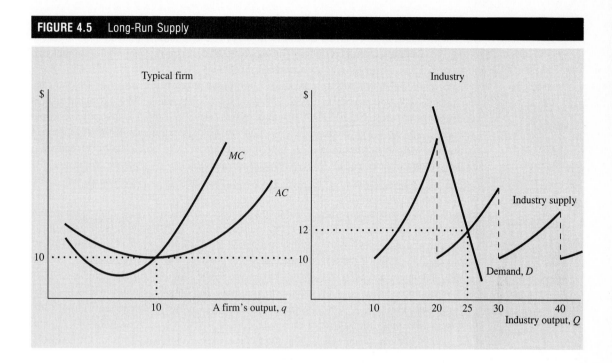

Supply Equals Demand.   There is a single price at which the amount that firms want to supply equals the amount that consumers demand. There are no unsatisfied buyers and no unsatisfied sellers; all buyers pay, and all sellers receive the same price.

Extensions of the Competitive Model

The previous discussion showed that the long-run supply curve is perfectly flat. We now explore in more detail the shape of the long-run supply curve and the effect of its shape on the competitive equilibrium.

Shape of the Long-Run Supply Curve.   The previous discussion claimed that the long-run supply curve for the industry is horizontal at C^*, the minimum average cost of production. This claim is not always correct, especially for small amounts of industry output. When firms have U-shaped average cost curves, the long-run supply curve is not horizontal, as shown in Figure 4.4.

Imagine two identical firms with the cost curve as shown in Figure 4.5. Each of the identical firms has a minimum average cost of $10 when 10 units are produced. Therefore, the minimum efficient scale of a firm is 10 units. If the industry consists of only these two firms, then the average cost of producing less than 10 units exceeds $10. Similarly, the average cost of producing more than 10 units also always exceeds $10 as long as the amount produced is less than 20 units. However, once the amount produced in the industry is 20, the average cost of producing can again be $10, since that amount of output can support two firms operating at their minimum efficient scale.

As more and more output is produced, more and more firms can enter the industry at their efficient scale. Therefore, the average cost of producing industry output that is an integer multiple of 10 (10, 20, 30) is $10. When a level of output that is not a multiple of 10 has to be produced, the average cost cannot be $10, because each firm has to operate at an output slightly different than its minimum. But this extra cost penalty of producing industry output that is not an integer multiple of ten declines as industry output and the number of firms increase because each one of *many* firms can be operated at very close to its efficient output. For example, if only 11 units are to be produced in the industry, there must be one firm producing 11 units (producing at 10 percent higher than its minimum efficient scale). On the other hand, if the industry output is 101, and there are ten firms in the industry, then each firm only has to operate at slightly above its minimum efficient scale (10.1) to produce the 101 output units in aggregate, and therefore the average cost is not much above the $10.[3] As a result the bumps in the long-run supply curve eventually die out as output increases, and hence, *in the limit,* the long-run supply curve becomes perfectly flat. Figure 4.5 shows the industry supply responses. There is no supply forthcoming in the long-run if price is below $10. The supply curve is a series of scallops, each corresponding to the sum of the marginal cost curves of all firms in the industry. Notice how the scallops flatten out as they reflect the summation of the marginal cost curves of more and more firms. The following discussion explains why a "bumpy" supply can create serious problems for the establishment of an equilibrium.[4]

Nonexistence of Competitive Equilibrium. A requirement of a competitive equilibrium is that no group of buyers or sellers has an incentive to break off from the market and strike their own deal. Indeed, it can be proven that the competitive equilibrium is the only price-quantity pair such that no coalition of buyers and sellers can better itself by avoiding the market and striking a separate deal. The study of the incentives to form coalitions is referred to as the **theory of the core** (Telser 1978).

Suppose all firms have the U-shaped average cost curve drawn for the typical firm in Figure 4.5 and that there is free entry. The long-run industry supply curve has bumps in it, as illustrated. Suppose that the demand curve cuts the supply curve where price equals $12 and output equals $25. Since firms of efficient size produce 10 units, it is not possible to produce the demanded output at the minimum average cost of $10. But is the price of $12 and quantity of 25 really a competitive equilibrium? Suppose that some

---

[3] Notice that the assumption of divisibility of output is being used. Chapter 3 defined output as a rate of output per unit time, assuming that fractional rates of output production are possible.

[4] This section raises some subtle issues regarding ease of entry and exit in the long run. If entry and exit are costless, then firms could produce at the optimal rate of output but keep jumping in and out of the industry. If this is possible, then cost curves will be flat. See Weitzman (1983).

| EXAMPLE 4.1 | # WHAT HAPPENS WHEN EQUILIBRIUM DOES NOT EXIST? |

Sometimes it may be impossible for a competitive equilibrium to exist. In such situations, "the core is empty": there is no coalition of buyers and sellers who can reach agreement with each other. Any price can be overturned by another, and chaos results. Some economists (Clark 1923) have described such situations as destructive competition. An industry that is prone to such instability is likely to foster rules, laws, institutions, or associations that are designed to create stability.

Pirrong (1987) has studied the stability of the industry of ocean shipping. He shows that because of its cost and demand characteristics, ocean shipping for small cargo (less than a boatload) is characterized by destructive competition, while ocean shipping for boat-sized cargo is not. The supply curve for small cargo is bumpy; for large loads it is smooth. Pirrong finds that there have been several instances of destructive competition in small cargo and that numerous international regulations and cartels have been formed to control ocean shipping for small cargo. The cartels have often controlled price and allocated demand among suppliers. Buyers often sign loyalty agreements under which they agree to use only one cartel's ships. In contrast, the shipping of large, boat-sized cargo has behaved as a typically competitive industry.

buyers form a group that collectively buys 10 units and that the group negotiates a separate deal with one of many potential supplying firms. The group is able to obtain their 10 units at the minimum average cost of $10 a piece. They have an incentive to contract with a potential supplier, because they can do better than if they rely on the market, and their incentive increases as the supply curve becomes bumpier (as it would if fixed costs increased). When this incentive induces buyers to split off and negotiate separately with a supplier, then the competitive equilibrium does not exist.

Another way to see that the competitive equilibrium may be hard to establish is to note that long-run profits are positive, yet entry is free: free entry and positive long-run profits are inconsistent with each other. Furthermore, when only a few firms can fit into an industry, the price-taking assumption of perfect competition is likely to fail, and other models of industry behavior (like those studied in later chapters) are appropriate. Example 4.1 analyzes what happens in situations that yield a bumpy supply curve.

The possibility of the nonexistence of competitive equilibrium could be substantially avoided if the industry supply curve were perfectly flat at finite output levels rather than only in the limit. A simple case in which this can occur provides a compelling justification for expecting equilibrium to exist as long as demand is large enough. If each average cost curve has a flat bottom for some range of output, then the long-run supply curve becomes perfectly flat at some *finite* output level. For example, if an individual firm's average cost curve in Figure 4.5 is flat and equal to $10 for outputs between 9 and 11 units, then the long-run supply curve for the industry is perfectly flat for outputs equal to or greater than 45 units.[5] As long as the demand curve intersects the industry supply curve in the perfectly flat portion, equilibrium will exist.

A Rising Long-Run Supply Curve.   An expansion of output sometimes causes the prices of some key inputs to rise. For example, as the output of wheat increases, farmland becomes more valuable, and the land rents (or the opportunity cost of owning the land) increase. As rents increase, the average cost curve of each farmer rises; in particular, the minimum average cost point rises. This means that the long-run supply curve for the industry (whose height is traced out by the minimum average cost points) rises as output expands.[6] Whenever some factors of production (such as fertile land) are in fixed supply, their price gets bid up as industry output expands. The long-run supply curve of an industry tends to be flat as long as the industry accounts for only a small fraction of any one factor's total employment.

Figure 4.6 illustrates a rising long-run supply curve. At output Q_1 the minimum average cost is C_1, which occurs when each of the n_1 firms produces at output Q_1/n_1. As industry output expands from Q_1 to Q_2, the number of firms increases to n_2, the prices of various factors of production rise, and these price increases cause the entire average cost curve of an individual firm to rise. If there are n_2 firms in the industry, the minimum average cost is C_2 when each firm produces output of Q_2/n_2. Although minimum average cost must increase as the prices of production factors increase, so that C_2 exceeds C_1, the efficient output for the firm could either increase or decrease. (Figure 4.6 illustrates the case in which efficient output of a firm increases as output expands in the industry.)

The Theory of Contestability

The total output of some industries may be small relative to the efficient size of a firm. In other words, the economies of scale in production are so important that perhaps only one or a few firms can efficiently produce in the industry—a situation that appears to violate the earlier assumption that there are many firms in an industry.

Even in such a setting, it is possible for competition to work, although the process would be different from the one just described.[7] In the extreme example, only one efficient producer can exist in the industry. This would result, for example, from economies of scale in the production and sale of a product at all levels of output. As long as many firms are capable of production, no firm is able, in the long run, to earn more than the

---

[5] If there are five firms in the industry, they can produce outputs of 45 through 55 at the minimum average cost. Six firms can produce outputs between 54 and 66 at minimum average cost.

[6] Prices of key inputs may also fall as output expands. This can occur, for example, if economies of scale exist in the production of some inputs. In such a case, the long-run industry supply curve could slope downward.

[7] See Demsetz (1968) and Baumol, Panzar, and Willig (1982) for more details.

FIGURE 4.6   Rising Supply Curve

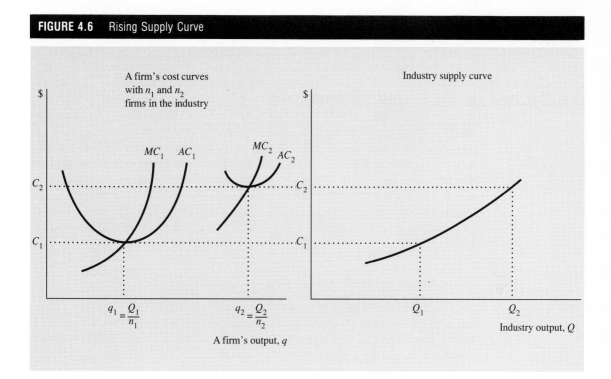

A firm's cost curves with n_1 and n_2 firms in the industry

Industry supply curve

normal level of profits. That is, as long as there is free entry into and exit from an industry (no sunk costs), firms have an incentive to enter whenever price exceeds average cost. Industries with free entry and exit are called **perfectly contestable** (Baumol, Panzar, and Willig 1982).[8]

One way to think about how a contestable industry operates is to imagine that buyers are solicited by firms that wish to enter the industry. Each firm offers a long-term contract that commits a buyer to purchase from the seller at a fixed price. If buyers collectively agree to choose only one seller, they will never have to pay a price higher than average cost. For example, there are economies of scale in providing residential garbage collection in a single town (see Example 23.4). It would be inefficient for more than one firm to traverse the same route to pick up garbage. A town can solicit bids from garbage collection

---

[8] Weitzman (1983) has explained that if instantaneous entry and exit (no sunk costs) are possible, then cost curves will be flat. Therefore, the theory of contestability requires some sunk costs for some time period in order to be an interesting theory.

firms and choose the lowest bidder. Competition among bidders ensures that the town will be served at the lowest possible cost, even though only one firm actually provides the service.[9]

■ ELASTICITIES AND THE RESIDUAL DEMAND CURVE

This text makes repeated use of two related concepts to analyze both competitive and noncompetitive industries: (1) price elasticity of demand or supply and (2) the demand curve facing a single firm, the residual demand curve. The price elasticity of supply or demand aids in understanding how an industry responds to changes in either demand or supply. The residual demand facing a single firm allows an analyst to comprehend the behavior of a single firm. The following discussion explains how the elasticity of the residual demand curve is related to the assumption that a competitive firm cannot affect price.

Elasticities of Demand and Supply

If either the demand or supply curve shifts, the competitive equilibrium changes, and the shapes of the demand and supply curves influence how the new equilibrium compares to the old. For example, if the demand curve is perfectly flat, the competitive price remains unchanged, even if the supply curve shifts radically.

One concept used to characterize the shape of demand or supply curves is the **price elasticity** of demand or supply (often the word *price* is omitted). The elasticity of demand equals (approximately) the percentage change in quantity demanded in response to a 1 percent change in price. Similarly, the elasticity of supply equals (approximately) the percentage change in quantity supplied in response to a 1 percent change in price.[10] The elasticity of demand is a negative number, and the elasticity of supply is usually (but not always) positive. If the absolute value of the elasticity of demand is above 1, the demand curve is called **elastic.** (The absolute values of 5 and -5 are both 5.) In that case, a 1 percent increase in price causes more than a 1 percent reduction in the quantity demanded,

---

[9] A complication arises when economies of scale exist. If the bidding competition drives profits to zero so that price equals average cost, then as long as there are economies of scale, price will *exceed* marginal cost. When price does not equal marginal cost, the allocation of resources is less efficient than when price equals marginal cost. Therefore, it turns out that a more efficient way to finance garbage collection service is to charge a fee per pick up that reflects marginal cost, and to charge a separate fee for the right to have garbage picked up at all. Under this scheme, if residents want garbage picked up twice a week, they would pay the fixed fee plus twice the fee per pick up. These complicated, two-part pricing schemes are studied in Chapter 15.

[10] The price elasticity of demand equals $(p/Q)(dQ/dp)$, where Q = quantity demanded, and p is price. If Q instead equals the quantity supplied, then the preceding definition yields the elasticity of supply. The elasticity is invariant to changes in scale of either price or quantity (it is a *pure* number—without scale itself). For example, if price is measured in cents rather than dollars, the elasticity is unchanged even though the slope of the demand curve does change.

and the total amount paid in the market falls. When the absolute value of the elasticity of demand is 1, the demand curve is of **unitary elasticity.** In that case, a 1 percent change in price causes a 1 percent change in the quantity demanded, and the total amount paid remains unchanged. If the absolute value of the elasticity of demand is less than 1, the demand curve is **inelastic;** a 1 percent increase in price causes less than a 1 percent decline in the quantity demanded, and the total amount paid rises.[11]

In general, the elasticities of demand and supply depend upon many economic factors, such as the level of output, the availability of substitute products, and the ease with which suppliers can alter production. For example, as more substitute products are available, consumers find it easier to substitute for a product whose price has risen, which makes the demand curve more elastic. Similarly, the more flexible the production process of a firm, the more likely it is that the firm will greatly increase production in response to a price increase, which tends to increase the elasticity of supply.

Price Taking among Competitive Firms and the Residual Demand Curve

Competitive firms are often described as *price-takers;* they believe that they cannot affect the market price and must accept, or take, it as given.

Three equivalent statements occur throughout this chapter:

- A competitive firm is a price-taker.
- The demand curve facing a competitive firm is horizontal at the market price.
- The elasticity of demand facing a competitive firm is infinite.

A firm is a price-taker if it faces a horizontal demand curve, since such a demand curve has an infinite price elasticity of demand. If a firm facing an infinite price elasticity raises its price even slightly, it loses all its sales. Alternatively stated, by lowering its quantity, the firm cannot cause the price to rise. In contrast, a firm facing a downward sloping demand curve can raise its price by decreasing its output.

When the number of firms in an industry gets large, the demand curve facing one of them *is* nearly horizontal; hence, it faces a nearly infinite price elasticity. In an industry with a large number of firms, the elasticity of demand facing any one firm is nearly infinite, even though the demand curve facing the industry is downward sloping and its elasticity is relatively small. Indeed, in most cases, there do not have to be very many firms in an industry for the elasticity of demand facing a particular firm to be large.

To show this result, it is necessary to determine the demand curve facing a particular firm: the **residual demand curve.** A firm can sell to people whose demands are not met by the other firms in the industry. The residual demand $R(p)$ is the market demand, $D(p)$, minus the supply of other firms, $S_0(p)$, or

$$R(p) = D(p) - S_0(p).$$

---

[11] It is common to omit the phrase *the absolute value of* when discussing the price elasticity of demand. The statement, "The price elasticity of demand is 2," is interpreted to mean that the price elasticity is -2.

FIGURE 4.7   Derivation of Residual Demand Curve

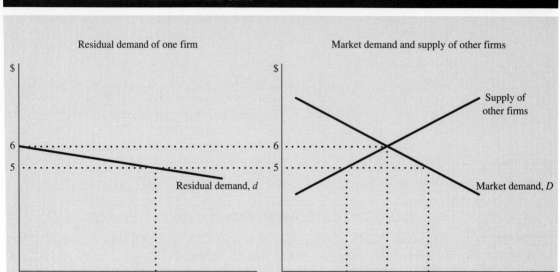

Figure 4.7 shows the market demand curve and the supply of the other firms. The horizontal difference between the market demand curve and the supply of the other firms is the residual demand facing a particular firm, shown on the left in Figure 4.7. Taking a horizontal difference means that price is held constant, so that the market demand at that price minus the supply of other firms at that price is the residual quantity the firm can sell at that price.

For example, in Figure 4.7, supply of the other firms equals market demand at $6 at 10,000 units. Thus, at any price greater than or equal to $6, the firm represented on the left will sell no units; its residual demand curve equals zero at $6. At $5, however, other firms are willing to supply only 9,950 units, while the market demand is 10,050 units. Thus, at $5, the firm's residual demand is 100 units.

As Figure 4.7 shows, the residual demand curve facing the firm is much flatter than that facing the market demand curve. In fact, the single firm's demand elasticity is much higher than the market elasticity. As drawn, the elasticity of demand[12] for the individual

---

[12] The elasticities are arc elasticities of demand, which are sometimes used to estimate the demand elasticity from actual discrete data. The arc elasticity of demand between two observation points is

$$\frac{\Delta q / 0.5(q_1 + q_2)}{\Delta p / 0.5(p_1 + p_2)},$$

where $\Delta q = q_2 - q_1$ is the change in quantity and $\Delta p = p_2 - p_1$ is the change in price. Notice that as Δp becomes small, the arc elasticity reduces to the definition of price elasticity given previously as $(dq/dp)(p/q)$.

TABLE 4.1	Price Elasticity For a Single Firm		
	Market Elasticity		
Number of Firms (n)	*Inelastic* ($\epsilon = 0.5$)	*Unitary* ($\epsilon = 1$)	*Elastic* ($\epsilon = 5$)
10	-5	-10	-50
25	-12.5	-25	-125
50	-25	-50	-250
100	-50	-100	-500
500	-250	-500	-2500
1000	-500	-1000	-5000

NOTE: These calculations assume that the elasticity of supply of the other identical firms is inelastic ($\eta_c = 0$), so that the elasticity of demand facing a particular firm is $\epsilon_i = n\epsilon$.

firm, from \$5 to \$6, is -11, whereas the corresponding market elasticity of demand is -0.025. In other words, the firm's residual demand elasticity is 440 times as elastic as the market elasticity.

More generally, if there are n identical firms in the industry, then the elasticity of demand facing any one firm i is

$$\epsilon_i = \epsilon n - \eta_0 n/(n - 1), \qquad (4.1)$$

where ϵ is the market elasticity of demand (a negative number) and η_0 is the elasticity of supply of the other firms (a positive number).[13] Thus, as n grows large, for a given market elasticity, ϵ_i grows large in absolute value (more negative). Similarly, the larger the elasticity of supply of the other firms, the larger in absolute value (more negative) is the firm's elasticity of demand.

Table 4.1 illustrates the effects of changes in the number of firms and the market elasticities, given that the elasticity of supply of other firms is completely inelastic ($\eta = 0$).

---

[13] The residual demand curve facing any one firm, $R(p)$, is $R(p) = D(p) - S_0(p)$. Differentiating this expression with respect to p, we obtain $dR/dp = dD/dp \; ; \; dS_0/dp$. By multiplying both sides by p/q and multiplying and dividing the first term on the right-hand side by Q/Q and the second term by Q_0/Q_0, this expression becomes

$$\frac{dR}{dp}\frac{p}{q} = \frac{dD}{dp}\frac{p}{Q}\frac{Q}{q} - \frac{dS_0}{dp}\frac{p}{Q_0}\frac{Q_0}{q}$$

where q, Q, and Q_0 equal $R(p)$, $D(p)$, and $Q_0(p)$ respectively. This expression can also be written as $\epsilon_i = \epsilon/s - \eta/s_0 = \epsilon n - \eta_0 n/(n - 1)$, where $s = Q/q = n$ and $s_0 = Q_0/q = (n - 1)/n$. That is, the elasticity of demand facing one firm, ϵ_i, equals the market demand elasticity, ϵ, times n, minus the elasticity of supply of the other firms times $n/(n - 1)$.

EXAMPLE 4.2

ARE FARMERS PRICE-TAKERS?

Most agricultural markets include a large number of farms, and no farm has even as much as 1 percent of total sales. As a result, the elasticity of demand facing each farm is nearly infinite: farms are price-takers.

We can roughly calculate the residual demand price elasticity facing an individual farm. For simplicity, assume that other farms have an inelastic supply ($\eta = 0$), which is probably a reasonable assumption in the short run. Less accurately, assume that all farms are approximately the same size, so that each farm's share of the market is equal to 1 divided by the number of farms.

The following table shows the approximate elasticity of demand facing each farm. The table conservatively uses the lowest estimated market price elasticity in the literature for various fruits and vegetables.

Crop	Lowest Estimated Market-Demand Elasticity	Number of Farms	Each Farm's Residual Demand Elasticity
Fruits			
apples	−.21	41,187	−8,649
sweet cherries	−.77	14,078	−10,840
grapes	−.16	24,982	−3,997
peaches	−.24	24,121	−5,813
pears	−1.64	13,244	−21,711
plums/prunes	−.63	11,186	−7,047
Vegetables			
snap beans	−.94	12,260	−11,544
sweet corn	−1.06	29,260	−31,353
cucumbers	−.57	9,935	−5,663
lettuce	−.33	2,452	−809
dry onions	−.59	3,516	−2,074
peas	−.68	8,204	−5,579
tomatoes	−.16	17,290	−2,766

SOURCES: Number of Farms: U.S. Department of Commerce, Bureau of the Census, *1982 Census of Agriculture;* Survey of Elasticities: Nuckton (1978, 1980).

Thus, each farm faces a gigantic price elasticity. For example, were a sweet-corn farm to increase its price by as little as 0.001 percent (one thousandth of one percent), the quantity demanded from the farm would fall by 31 percent. Thus, each farm is a price-taker.

For example, if the market elasticity is unitary ($\epsilon = 1$), and there are 50 firms, then $\epsilon_i = -50$. That is, if one firm were to increase its price by 1 percent, the quantity it sold would fall by about 50 percent. See Example 4.2.

■ A SHORT COURSE IN WELFARE ECONOMICS

The welfare of the people is the chief law. — CICERO

The study of the cost of a departure from perfect competition is called **welfare economics.** This section briefly describes and applies some of the concepts from that branch of economics. Welfare economics is used extensively in industrial organization to study a range of issues that includes optimal product diversity, cost of monopoly, and optimal regulation.

Consumer Surplus

A demand curve reflects the valuation that consumers place upon consuming additional units of a good. For example, the demand curve in Figure 4.8 indicates that consumers would pay $10 for 1 unit of the good, $8 for the second unit, and $6 for the third unit. **Consumer surplus** is defined as the amount above the amount paid that a consumer would willingly pay if necessary to consume the units purchased. In Figure 4.8, consumers pay a price of $6 for each of the 3 units and therefore enjoy a consumer surplus of $4 on the first unit, $2 on the second, and $0 on the last. Therefore, the demand curve in Figure 4.8 tells us that consumers would willingly pay $6 more for the goods. If the market requires them to pay only $6 per unit, then they are enjoying $6 in consumer surplus. The area above the price and bounded by the demand curve in Figure 4.8 measures consumer surplus.[14]

Producer Surplus

A supply curve represents the marginal cost of producing output. **Producer surplus** is analogous to consumer surplus: it is the largest amount that could be subtracted from a supplier's revenue that would still induce the supplier to produce the product. For example, Figure 4.8 shows that it costs $2 to produce the first unit, $4 to produce the second unit, and $6 to produce the third unit. If the market price is $6 for each item, the firm earns a producer surplus of $4 on the first unit, $2 on the second unit, and $0 on the third. The producing firm would be willing to pay $6 for the right to sell its three units of the good at $6 rather than selling none at all. The area below the price and bounded by the supply curve in Figure 4.8 measures producer surplus.

---

[14] Consumer surplus assumes these are no income effects affecting the demand curve. (A change in a consumer's income leaves demand unchanged.) Even when there are income effects, consumer surplus can provide a close approximation to a correct measure of welfare (Willig 1976). Consumer surplus, as measured in Figure 4.8, also ignores the fact that the area illustrated in Figure 4.8 only approximates consumer surplus; the demand curve is not really a smooth line because fractional units are not purchased in the example.

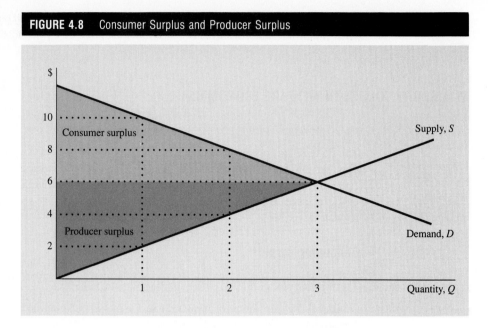

FIGURE 4.8   Consumer Surplus and Producer Surplus

Deadweight Loss

Deadweight loss is the cost to society that results when markets do not operate optimally. It represents the lost consumer plus producer surplus caused by a deviation from the competitive equilibrium. In Figure 4.9, the competitive equilibrium is at price p_0 and quantity Q_0. At quantity Q_0, the value that a consumer places on additional consumption is precisely equal to the marginal cost of producing the good. If, for some reason, consumers could consume only Q^*, then the value that they place on consuming an additional unit, p^*, would exceed the marginal cost C^* of producing an additional unit. There is a lost gap between the demand curve and the supply curve, which represents a lost opportunity to create value for the society. The area of the shaded deadweight loss triangle in Figure 4.9 represents the total value that society loses when output does not expand from Q^* to Q_0.

The Effects of a Tax on Competitive Equilibrium

Governments impose taxes on the sale of goods in order to raise revenues, and many policies that firms pursue can be analyzed in exactly the same way as a tax. For example, a monopolist can be regarded as placing a tax on a competitive industry. Let us trace through the effects of a tax placed on a good sold in a competitive market. Suppose the

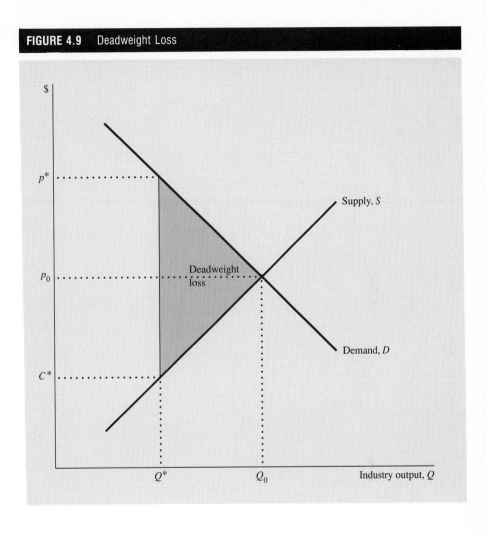

FIGURE 4.9 Deadweight Loss

government places a tax of T dollars per unit of output on a good whose supply and demand curves are shown in Figure 4.10.

The original competitive equilibrium is at output Q_0 and price p_0. When there is a tax, the price that the customer pays (p^*) must include the tax (T) plus the amount that the supplier receives ($p^* - T$). Therefore, the tax, T, inserts a wedge between the value that the (marginal) demander places on the good (as revealed by the demand curve) and the cost that the marginal supplier is willing to incur in order to provide the good (as revealed by the supply curve). The difference between the two is the tax, T, that goes to the government. In Figure 4.10, the imposition of the tax reduces the quantity produced from Q_0 to Q^*, raises the price to consumers to p^*, and lowers the price that suppliers receive to $p^* - T$. In other words, the tax creates a gap between the value of the last unit to demanders, p^*, and the cost at which suppliers supply the good, $p^* - T$. The

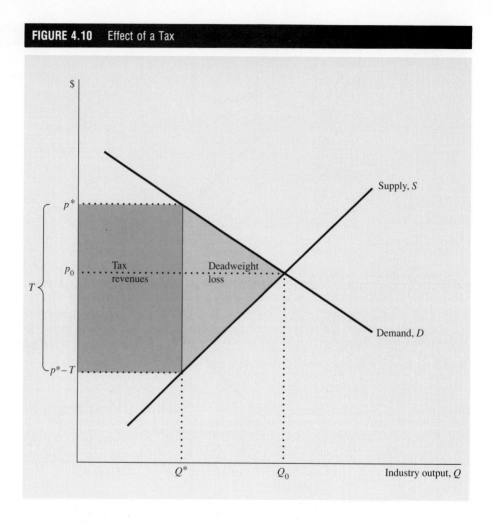

FIGURE 4.10   Effect of a Tax

clear effect of the tax is to reduce the quantity supplied, raise the price consumers pay, and lower the price that suppliers receive. The government receives in tax revenues an amount equal to TQ^*, the shaded box in Figure 4.10, which represents a transfer of money from consumers and producers to the government. As long as the government makes efficient use of this money, the transfer does not represent an inefficiency, although it does affect the distribution of income.

An inefficiency occurs whenever the marginal cost of producing a good is less than the marginal willingness of consumers to pay for it. In the competitive equilibrium at price p_0 and output Q_0, the value of additional consumption precisely equals the marginal cost of production. However, in Figure 4.10, a tax has inserted a wedge between the value, p^*, a consumer places on the last unit of the good consumed and the marginal cost to society, $p^* - T$. Since the demand curve represents the willingness of consumers to pay for a good, and the supply curve represents the marginal cost of the goods produced, it is clear that the production of 1 additional unit of the good at Q^* would benefit society. The value that consumers place on the extra unit is p^*, yet it would cost society only $p^* - T$ to produce it. In general, since the demand curve lies above the supply curve between the outputs Q^* and Q_0, expansion of output from Q^* to Q_0 produces a net benefit to the consuming public. At all outputs between Q^* and Q_0, the good is valued at more than the cost its production would impose on society. The deadweight loss triangle in Figure 4.10 represents the benefits from producing additional units of the good beyond Q^* until output Q_0 is reached. The deadweight loss is a measure of the inefficiency that the tax creates; it measures the cost that a tax policy imposes on society by reducing the amount of output of the taxed product.[15] Notice that consumers pay a higher price than p_0 and that suppliers receive a price lower than p_0. The tax has therefore affected the price that each pays or receives. The **incidence of a tax** is the effect of the tax on the price paid or received, using p_0 as a benchmark.

The amount by which p^* exceeds the competitive price, p_0, depends upon the relative shapes of the supply and demand curves. Figure 4.11 illustrates a case in which the supply curve is perfectly elastic. In that case, the tax serves to increase the price that consumers pay by precisely the amount of the tax. In this case, the effect, or incidence, of the tax is fully borne by consumers, in the sense that their purchase price rises by the exact amount of the tax.

Figure 4.12 (on page 89) portrays the opposite extreme—a case in which the demand curve is perfectly elastic, but the supply curve is not. Imposing a tax does not affect the final price that consumers pay and lowers the net price received by sellers by the full amount of the tax. In this case the incidence of the tax falls entirely upon the supplier.

Figures 4.10, 4.11, and 4.12 show that a tax tends to raise the price that consumers pay as the supply curve is more elastic, and tends to lower the net price received by suppliers as the demand curve is more elastic. The previous chapter showed that in the short run the supply curve tends to be less elastic than in the long run. This suggests that the incidence of any tax tends to shift towards consumers and away from producers in the long-run.[16]

---

[15] It is possible to express the deadweight loss triangle, in Figure 4.10 in terms of the price elasticities of supply and demand. Take the simple case in which the supply curve is perfectly horizontal (infinitely elastic). The deadweight loss triangle $= -\frac{1}{2}\Delta p\Delta Q$, where $\Delta p = p^* - p_0$ and $\Delta Q = Q^* - Q_0$. The elasticity of demand, ϵ is (approximately) equal to $\dfrac{\Delta Q}{Q_0} \bigg/ \dfrac{\Delta p}{p_0}$.

Let $t = \Delta p/p_0$, then the deadweight loss triangle $= -\frac{1}{2} \Delta p \, \Delta Q$, or

$$\cong -\frac{1}{2} \frac{\Delta p}{p_0}(P_0 Q_0)\left(\frac{\Delta Q}{Q_0} \bigg/ \frac{\Delta p}{p_0}\right)\frac{\Delta p}{p_0} \cong -\frac{1}{2} t^2 \, V\epsilon,$$

where $V =$ value of output ($p_0 Q_0$), and $\cong$ means *approximately equals*. This simple formula emphasizes that deadweight loss depends on the size of the market, V, in addition to t and ϵ.

[16] However, it can also be true that long-run demand curves are more elastic than short-run demand curves. Consumers may be able to substitute away from a product more in the long-run, when they have a longer time to adjust. For example, in response to increases in apartment rents, renters will shift their demand more in the long run than in the short run because it takes time to arrange to move. The incidence of a tax shifts away from consumers and toward producers in the long run in such a case.

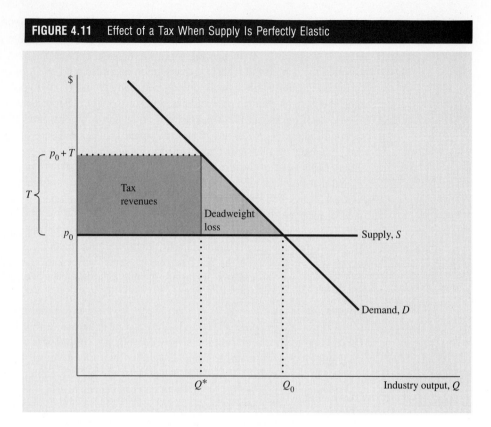

FIGURE 4.11   Effect of a Tax When Supply Is Perfectly Elastic

The effect of a tax on society's welfare depends upon its effect on output. If either the demand curve or the supply curve is perfectly inelastic for some output (Figure 4.13 on page 90), then the equilibrium output with and without a tax is identical. If the quantity consumed is independent of whether or not a tax is imposed, then the tax by itself introduces no economic inefficiency and creates no deadweight loss. For this special case, producing more output is not desirable when there is a tax. It is true that the tax transfers money from consumers and producers to the government, but as long as the government spends the money efficiently, the tax affects only the income distribution (which consumers have the money), but not efficiency (whether the appropriate amount of output gets produced).

A government may trade off the deadweight loss from the tax against the need to raise revenues. The government presumably prefers to raise revenues in a way that creates the lowest possible deadweight loss to society. Figure 4.13 suggests that the government should prefer to tax those items with inelastic supplies (or demands). This intuition is indeed correct and forms the basis for optimal taxation (Ramsey 1927).

The effect of a tax can also be analyzed in terms of the lost producer and consumer surplus. Figure 4.14 (on page 91) shows the effect on both consumers and producers of

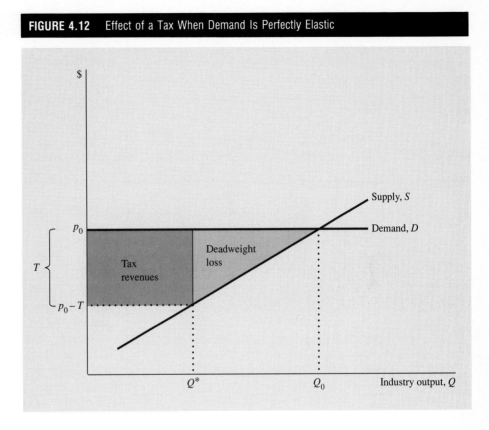

FIGURE 4.12   Effect of a Tax When Demand Is Perfectly Elastic

imposing a tax. Consumers lose consumer surplus equal to *ABCD*, and producers lose producer surplus equal to *ADEF*. The government gains tax revenues equal to *BCEF*. The sum of the consumer and producer surplus minus the transfer to the government of *BCEF* equals the triangle *ABF*, the deadweight loss triangle. The reason for subtracting the transfer to the government of the tax revenues is that transfers of wealth by themselves do not necessarily affect the efficiency of resource allocation. Presumably the government spends the money on valuable resources that it distributes back to (perhaps different) consumers; therefore, the tax revenue should not necessarily be considered a loss to society.

Restrictions on Entry

In many industries, governments or groups of firms that collectively set licensing requirements impose restrictions on entry. An example of an entry restriction is the limit on the number of taxicabs allowed in a city. Such entry restrictions elevate prices above competitive levels.

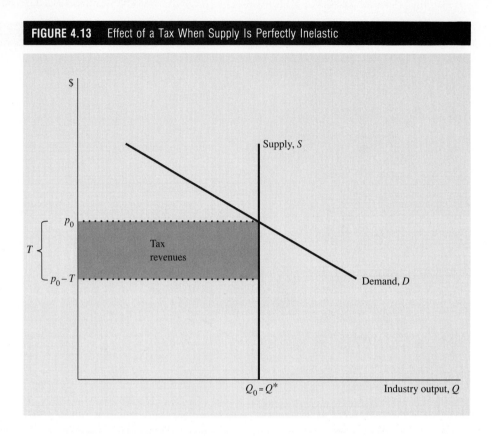

FIGURE 4.13 Effect of a Tax When Supply Is Perfectly Inelastic

Figure 4.15 illustrates how a restriction on entry can generate a price above the long-run competitive equilibrium. Figure 4.15b shows two supply curves for an industry—one with 100 firms (restriction on entry) and the other with 150 (the number with free entry).[17] When the industry is limited to 100 firms, the competitive equilibrium is at price p^*. If free entry is allowed, there are 150 identical firms in the industry, and the equilibrium price is p_0, which is the minimum average cost point on the firm's average cost curve. If all firms are identical, the long-run supply curve to the industry is horizontal at p_0. The entry restriction, therefore, results in consumers paying a price, p^*, higher than p_0 and consuming a quantity, Q^*, less than the quantity, Q_0, that would have been consumed in a competitive equilibrium with no entry restrictions.

An entry restriction causes a deadweight loss similar to that caused by a tax and represents the inefficiency of restricting output from Q_0 to Q^* (see Figure 4.15b). A firm that is among the 100 firms allowed into the industry is better off than one in an industry with no entry restrictions. The elevated price raises the profits of each firm above the

---

[17] The long-run supply curves indicate that no firm will produce in the long run if price is below p_0, which is the minimum average cost.

FIGURE 4.14   Re-Examination of a Tax

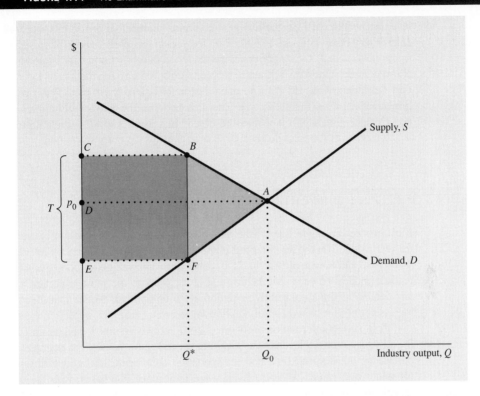

FIGURE 4.15   Long-Run Equilibrium with an Entry Restriction

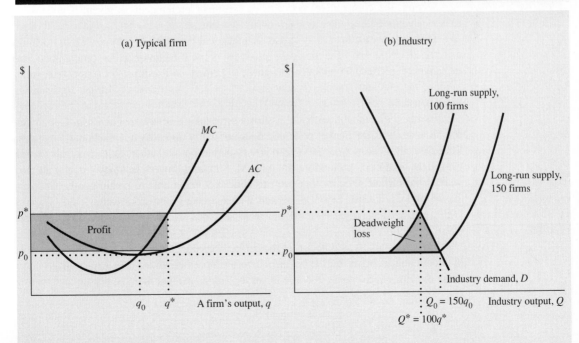

level that would have existed had the equilibrium number of firms, 150, been allowed to enter. Entry restrictions are like a tax on the consumption of a good, but instead of going to the government, the tax revenues go to the producers who are fortunate enough to be allowed in the industry. The entry restriction also causes production of the Q^* units to cost more than it would with no entry restrictions since the typical firm operates at q^* instead of q_0. (See Figure 4.15a). The area between the two supply curves between 0 and Q^* in Figure 4.15b is a measure of this increased cost. The shaded area in Figure 4.15b represents the total deadweight loss caused by the entry restriction.

■ LIMITATIONS OF PERFECT COMPETITION

Most economists agree that all the assumptions of perfect competition are rarely met in the real world. The model of perfect competition is therefore not directly relevant to many industries, and much of this book is devoted to analyzing the consequences of more realistic models of economic behavior. Let us examine the most important assumptions and conditions for a competitive equilibrium to be optimal. Notice that they differ from the assumptions required for an equilibrium to exist.

First, perfect information about prices and quality is assumed. This assumption ignores the difficulty many buyers have in acquiring valuable information. For example, consumers purchasing autos spend time and transportation costs searching among different dealers for prices and valued features. Even when they make purchases, they are unsure how reliable the cars are or whether they have hidden defects. There is no role in the perfectly competitive model for advertising or sales effort to inform consumers about price or quality. Chapters 16–18, and 21 discuss these issues in more detail.

Second, the competitive model takes consumer preferences as given; it assigns no role to advertising designed to alter consumers' tastes.

Third, the competitive model takes technology as given; it assigns no role to innovation and the development of either new products or new techniques for production. The incentive to produce knowledge is ignored. Perfect competition does not necessarily produce the efficient amount of new products or new discoveries. Chapter 20 discusses these issues.

Fourth, the competitive model assumes price-taking behavior. Each firm feels it can sell all it wants at the market price and does not worry about rivals' reactions to its sales. Therefore, firms do not need to spend any resources on marketing. Salesmen, advertising campaigns, and price promotions are ignored. Similarly, buyers feel they can buy all they want at the market price; no one worries about not being able to obtain goods. Chapters 16–18 and 21 discuss issues associated with marketing and information, and Chapters 8–11, and 13–15 analyze issues that arise when firms are not price takers. (See Example 4.3.)

Fifth, an implicit assumption of the perfectly competitive model is that the entire cost of production is borne by the seller. There are no externalities. An **externality** occurs when the cost of an activity is borne in part by someone other than the person undertaking

EXPERIMENTAL ECONOMICS

It is often difficult to predict theoretically the effect of a departure from the assumptions of perfect competition. One approach has been to conduct experiments in which participants are given incentives to behave according to the competitive model. For example, Plott (1982) reports experiments in which students are given incentives to behave in accordance with known supply and demand curves. To investigate the effect of relaxing the price-taking assumption, buyers and sellers are allowed to call out prices at which they are willing to buy or sell. These experiments show that with only a handful of participants, the price that typically emerges is very close to that predicted by the perfectly competitive model. Therefore, the predictions of the perfectly competitive model seem robust to at least some changes in the model's underlying assumptions.

the activity. For example, a chemical plant discards its chemical waste in a river, where the pollution kills the fish and destroys the fishing industry. The chemical plant has imposed a cost (loss of the fishing industry) on others that it does not bear. In the presence of externalities (see Chapter 6), perfect competition does not produce efficient results.

Sixth, the distribution of income may be unjust (according to some people's opinions) in a competitive equilibrium. Individual wealth depends on assets (for example, money, machines) and skills. Competition does not necessarily reward the deserving. It rewards those who are the most productive and those who own productive assets.

If the distribution of income is not just, why does anyone care about efficiency? After all, efficiency only means that one person cannot be made better off without another being made worse off. If there are only $10,000 to distribute and Debbie gets $9,999 and Rebecca gets $1, that is efficient. But so is $1 for Debbie and $9,999 for Rebecca. There are many efficient points; in fact, *any* division of the $10,000 between Debbie and Rebecca is efficient. The particular efficient point that the competitive equilibrium produces depends on the initial ownership of assets. Public policy may assert that it is unjust for either Debbie or Rebecca to receive only $1 while the other receives $9,999, and might prefer $5,000 to Debbie and $5,000 to Rebecca. It might even find $4,999 to Debbie and $4,999 to Rebecca preferable to the policy of $9,999 for one and $1 for the other. That means that an *inefficient* policy may be preferred to an efficient one! Why then do economists seem to stress efficiency?

One answer is that the morally just (however defined) distribution of income can be achieved by competition plus a system of appropriate income redistribution. That is, ask the government to assign wealth initially according to society's moral values, and then competition will lead society to the efficient optimal outcome. One interpretation of this result is that it is up to the government to achieve the moral distribution of wealth through nondistorting taxation, and it is up to the competitive process to achieve efficiency.

Economists can objectively discuss whether economic efficiency is achieved, but they are no better equipped than others to discuss the best or most moral income distribution. They may analyze how the distribution of income changes as a result of certain policies, but they cannot scientifically determine whether one distribution is ethically superior to another.

■ THE MANY MEANINGS OF COMPETITION

The preceding discussion has focused on the assumptions required for perfect competition to prevail and have desirable properties. Some industries do come close to satisfying most of the assumptions. For example, the New York Stock Exchange is a place where people buy and sell shares of stock of individual firms, like IBM. Individuals who own the stock but want to sell it ask their brokers to sell, and those who want to buy ask their brokers to buy. There are many well-informed participants in the stock market, and the price of a particular stock is determined by the forces of supply and demand. Most individuals correctly feel that they have no effect on the price of the stock. Although some markets do come close to satisfying the assumptions required for perfect competition, most do not. Certain of these markets nevertheless are sometimes described as competitive or as characterized by competition. This can and has led to confusion.

Some use the term *competition* to refer to a situation in which a few firms in an industry compete vigorously for sales—each firm trying to get customers for itself at the expense of its rivals. Notice how this meaning contrasts with the price-taking assumption of the perfectly competitive firm, which assumes that it can sell all it wants at the market price. The value of stressing rivalry in defining competition is that it emphasizes the independent actions of firms and explains their incentive to outdo other firms through, for example, the development of innovative products and the creation of new technologies. Firms succeed by satisfying consumer wants better than other firms.

Even though few industries fit the requirements of perfect competition, economists often speak of certain types of industries as being *reasonably competitive* if they have certain characteristics. Independent price setting, many firms, and free entry and exit are often used as criteria to judge the competitiveness of an industry. Free entry and exit guarantee that firms will eventually earn zero profits. For example, in some states, it is very easy to become a barber, and there are often many independent barber shops in an area. Even though barbers are not identical in either quality or prices, and all consumers are not aware of all barber shops, most economists would describe the provision of haircuts by barber shops as a reasonably competitive industry.

Another example of a reasonably competitive industry is steel scrap. Firms in that industry collect used steel, process it, and sell it to steel firms. Entry into the steel-scrap industry is easy and quick, the product sold is fairly homogenous, and there are published quotations of prices. Even though transaction prices undoubtedly vary from firm to firm, the large number of sellers acting independently would cause most economists to label this industry as reasonably competitive.

Some discussions involving public policy use the term *competitive* in a still different way: A competitive industry is one that requires no intervention to improve its performance; a noncompetitive industry is one that has some defect that can be corrected. This usage of the terms *competitive* and *noncompetitive* can be confusing. The confusion arises because intervention can sometimes improve the performance of industries that satisfy all the assumptions of perfect competition—as can occur, for example, when the government encourages inventive activity. Conversely, the failure of an industry to satisfy all the assumptions of perfect competition does not necessarily mean that some intervention can improve market performance.

■ SUMMARY

Under certain circumstances, competition leads to an efficient use of resources. Firms that maximize their profits benefit consumers by their actions. In such cases, any interference with competitive markets leads to inefficiencies. The assumptions of perfect competition are unlikely to apply to many industries. Subsequent chapters explore the implications of departures from perfect competition.

■ Key Terms

avoidable cost
consumer surplus
deadweight loss
elastic
externality
firm's supply curve
incidence of a tax
inelastic
industry supply curve
perfect competition

perfectly contestable
price elasticity
producer surplus
quasi-rents
residual demand curve
short-run and long-run equilibrium
shutdown point
theory of the core
unitary elasticity
welfare economics

■ Discussion Questions

1. Perfect competition, if attainable, leads to social optimality. Discuss.
2. Perfect competition is a useless notion because its assumptions apply to few industries. Discuss.
3. The long run is never attainable because industries are always undergoing change. Therefore, the concept of long-run equilibrium is not valuable. Discuss.

4. How can there be a deadweight loss from taxation when the demand curve is infinitely elastic since the price consumers pay is unaffected by the tax?
5. A competitive firm cannot earn positive profits in the long-run. Discuss.

■ Problems

1. Will a tax of $1 per unit of output change the optimal scale of a competitive firm if all firms are identical and any firm can enter the industry?

2. Suppose the government imposes a fixed fee per year on each firm that operates in a competitive industry. What will happen to output, the optimal scale of a firm, and price in the short run and in the long run? Discuss the differential effect of the fee on new entrants that tend to be smaller than established firms.

3. Suppose a competitive industry consists of identical firms with a constant long-run marginal cost of $10. (There are no fixed costs in the long run.) Suppose the demand curve at any price, p, is given by $Q = 1000 - p$.
   a. What are the price and quantity consumed in the long-run competitive equilibrium?
   b. Suppose one new firm enters that is different from the existing firms. The new firm has a constant marginal cost of $9 and no fixed costs but can only produce 10 units (or less). What are the price and the quantity consumed in long-run competitive equilibrium? Are these the same as in a? Explain.

c. Are positive economic profits inconsistent with a long-run competitive equilibrium?
d. Identify the marginal cost of the last unit sold in b. Is it $10 or $9? That is, if demand fell by 1 unit, would the new entrant or the other firms reduce output?
e. What is the profitability of the less efficient firms in b?
f. Do you agree that in long-run competitive equilibrium the profit of the marginal entrant (the next firm to enter the industry if demand expands or, alternatively, the next firm to leave the industry if demand contracts) must be zero?

4. If $Q = 100 - p$ is the market demand curve, what is the market price elasticity of demand? If the supply curve of individual firms is $q = p$ and there are 50 identical firms in the industry, draw the residual demand facing any one firm. What is the residual demand elasticity facing one firm at the competitive equilibrium?

5. When is a firm's shutdown point equal to the minimum point on its average cost curve?

Answers to odd-numbered problems are given at the back of the book.

■ References

Baumol, William, John C. Panzar, and Robert D. Willig. 1982. *Contestable Markets and the Theory of Industry Structure.* New York: Harcourt Brace Jovanovich.

Clark, James M. 1923. *Studies in the Economics of Overhead Costs.* Chicago: University of Chicago Press.

Demsetz, Harold. 1968. "Why Regulate Utilities?" *Journal of Law and Economics* 11:55–65.

Nuckton, Carole F. 1978. *Demand Relationships for California Tree Fruits, Grapes, and Nuts: A Review of Past Studies.* Giannini Foundation of Agricultural Economics, Special Report 3247. University of California at Berkeley.

——. 1980. *Demand Relationships for Vegetables: A Review of Past Studies.* Giannini Foundation of Agricultural Economics, Special Report 80-1. University of California at Berkeley.

Pirrong, Stephen C. 1987. "An Application of Core Theory to the Study of Ocean Shipping Markets." Ph. D. diss., University of Chicago.

Plott, Charles. 1982. "Industrial Organization, Theory, and Experimental Economics." *Journal of Economic Literature* 20, no. 4 (December).

Ramsey, Frank P. 1927. "A Contribution to the Theory of Taxation." *Economic Journal* 37:47–61.

Telser, Lester. 1978. *Economic Theory and the Core.* Chicago: University of Chicago Press.

U.S. Department of Commerce, Bureau of the Census. 1984. *1982 Census of Agriculture: U.S. Summary and State Data,* vol 1, part 51.

Weitzman, Martin. 1983. "Contestable Markets: An Uprising in the Theory of Industry Structure: Comment." *American Economic Review* 73:486–487.

Willig, Robert D. 1976. "Consumer's Surplus without Apology." *American Economic Review* 66:589–97.

CHAPTER 5 | # MONOPOLY

The earnings of many in the hands of one.

EUGENE DEBS

Chapter 4 discussed the desirable properties of perfect competition. This chapter examines what happens if competition does not prevail, and only one firm, a monopolist, exists in a particular market. The chapter analyzes the monopolist's behavior and the consequences of that behavior; it explains what a monopoly is and what inefficiencies it creates. It also discusses how a monopoly is maintained and addresses the important question of whether monopoly is always bad. Finally, it examines monopsony, which is a monopoly on the buying side of the market.

■ THE DEFINITION OF MONOPOLY AND MONOPOLY BEHAVIOR

Unlike a competitive firm, a monopolist can set price and earn a profit without worrying that other firms will enter and drive down price. The consequences of monopoly are that price is higher and output lower than under competition.

Monopoly Power

A **monopoly** is a situation in which a single firm faces a downward sloping industry demand curve and is insulated from the competition of rivals, whereas most firms face competition from firms that produce identical or similar products. In contrast to a firm in a perfectly competitive market, a monopolist is a price setter, not a price taker. (Subsequent chapters analyze cases where firms face some competition but do not behave as pure price takers.) The monopolist recognizes that the quantity it sells is affected by the price it sets. Whenever a firm can influence the price it receives for its product, the firm is said to have **monopoly power** (sometimes called **market power**).

The terms *monopoly power* and *market power* typically are used interchangeably to mean the ability to profitably set price above competitive levels (that is, above marginal

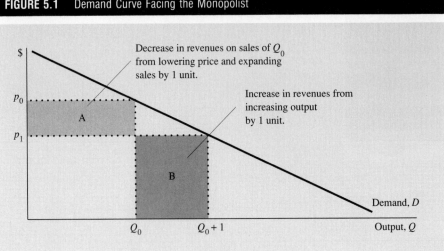

FIGURE 5.1   Demand Curve Facing the Monopolist

cost). Of course, prices may exceed marginal cost even though profits are not above competitive levels. For example, if there are large enough fixed costs, profits may be zero even if price exceeds marginal cost. One could usefully distinguish the two terms by using *monopoly power* for cases in which price exceeds marginal cost and profits are above competitive levels, and using *market power* for cases in which price exceeds marginal costs, but profits are not above competitive levels. This distinction, however, is not commonly made.

Profit Maximization

A monopolist faces a downward sloping demand curve and must decide how much of its product to sell to maximize its profits: the more it sells, the lower the price at which it has to sell if the firm must charge the same price to each buyer, as we assume for now. The demand curve in Figure 5.1 shows that if the firm wishes to sell Q_0 units, it has to charge a price p_0, and if it wishes to sell one more unit, it has to charge a lower price, p_1, to induce consumers to purchase the additional unit.[1]

Like a competitive firm, a monopolist recognizes that as its production expands, additional costs (marginal costs) arise. The monopolist earns additional revenue (p_1) on the additional unit sold. This additional revenue equals area B in Figure 5.1. However,

---

[1] The discussion is phrased so that the monopolist chooses price and consumers choose how much to buy. The discussion could also be phrased so that the monopolist chooses quantity and consumers decide what price to pay. There is a subtle, implicit assumption about timing. The discussion assumes that the monopolist chooses the price, and then individual consumers decide whether to purchase, not that customers first announce the price at which they are willing to purchase, and then the monopolist decides whether to sell. The party who gets to go first and design the allocation mechanism usually has an advantage. For more on this complicated topic, see Harris and Townsend (1981).

the firm's total revenues decrease to the extent that the firm has to lower price from p_0 to p_1 in Figure 5.1 on the Q_0 units that can be sold at price p_0 in order to sell the additional unit. This decrease in revenue equals area A in Figure 5.1. This decrease in revenue was completely absent from our examination of a competitive firm's behavior in Chapter 4. The change in revenues $[p_1(Q_0 + 1) - p_0Q_0]$ that a firm receives when it produces one more unit of the product is called **marginal revenue.**[2] Hence, marginal revenue equals area B minus area A in Figure 5.1. If the monopolist did not have to lower its price to sell the additional unit, then the increment to revenues from selling an additional unit would simply be the initial price, p_0. But as long as the demand curve is downward sloping, the monopolist must always lower its price to sell more units; therefore, marginal revenue is always *less* than price for a monopolist. For a firm in a perfectly competitive industry, marginal revenue equals price.

As one would expect, there is a close relationship between marginal revenue and total revenue: when marginal revenue is positive, total revenue increases as output expands, but when marginal revenue is negative, total revenue falls as output expands. Total revenue is maximized when marginal revenue equals zero. Figure 5.2 illustrates these relationships.

A monopolist maximizes profits when the extra revenue from selling one more unit just equals the extra cost that production entails, that is, when *marginal revenue (MR) equals marginal cost (MC),* or

$$MR = MC \tag{5.1}$$

That profit-maximizing relationship is illustrated in Figure 5.3 (on page 101), which uses the subscripts c and m to distinguish between competition and monopoly. Notice that the profit-maximizing output (Q_m) is lower than the competitive output (Q_c) determined by the intersection of the demand curve with the marginal cost curve (taken, for simplicity, to be a constant, p_c).

The profit-maximizing behavior of a monopolist requires it to choose output such that marginal revenue equals marginal cost. Therefore, a monopolist's output can be determined only if marginal revenue is known, and because marginal revenue depends only on the demand curve, it is necessary to describe the demand curve facing a monopolist before its output can be determined. There is no such thing as a supply curve for a

---

[2] Marginal revenue *(MR)* is defined as the change in revenue from selling an additional unit. If pQ is revenue, then marginal revenue is equal to $p + Q (\Delta p/\Delta Q)$, where $(\Delta p/\Delta Q)$ is the decline in price necessary to sell the additional unit. Since $\epsilon = \Delta Q/Q \div \Delta p/p$, the expression for *MR* can be rewritten as

$$p\left(1 + \frac{\Delta p}{p}\frac{Q}{\Delta Q}\right),$$

or as $p\left(1 + \dfrac{1}{\epsilon}\right)$. Using calculus,

$$MR = \frac{d(pQ)}{dQ} = p + \frac{dp}{dQ}Q = p\left(1 + \frac{1}{\epsilon}\right)$$

where $\quad \epsilon = \dfrac{dQ}{dp}\dfrac{p}{Q}.$

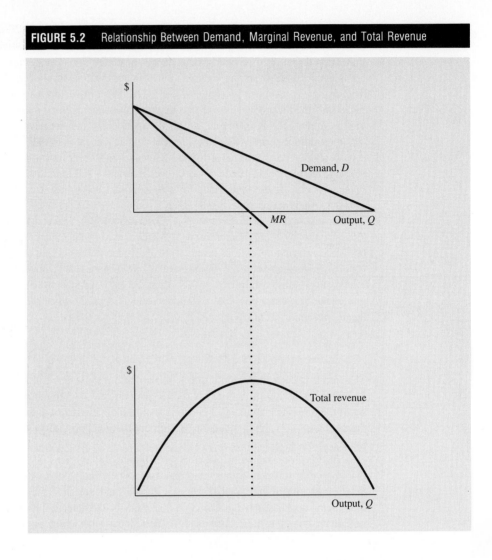

FIGURE 5.2 Relationship Between Demand, Marginal Revenue, and Total Revenue

monopolist that can be specified solely as a function of price, since the monopolist's output depends upon marginal revenue and marginal cost.

The properties of the demand curve determine the monopoly *overcharge:* the amount by which the monopoly price, p_m, exceeds the competitive price, p_c, in Figure 5.3. A simple relationship exists between the monopoly overcharge and the price elasticity of demand, which was defined in the previous chapter. Recall that the elasticity of demand is a characteristic of the demand curve and is defined as the percentage change in quantity that results from a 1 percent change in price. If the elasticity of demand is very high (a large negative number), then the curve is said to be *elastic.* In such a case, a small price change induces a very large change in the quantity demanded. If the elasticity is low (a

FIGURE 5.3   Monopoly Profit Maximization

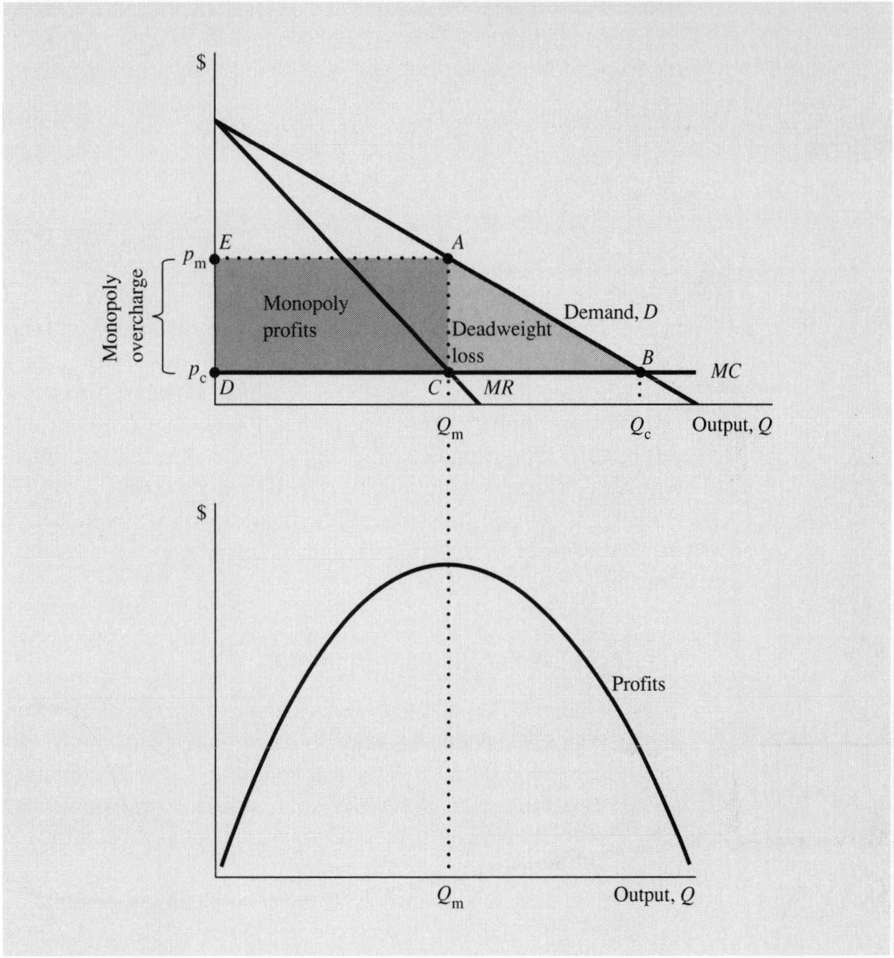

number between -1 and 0), then the demand curve is said to be *inelastic*. In that case, a price change of 1 percent has relatively little effect on the quantity demanded.

Marginal revenue can be rewritten as follows:

$$MR = p(1 + \frac{1}{\epsilon}), \qquad (5.2)$$

where MR = marginal revenue,
            p = price, and
            ϵ = elasticity of demand.

This relationship says that marginal revenue is positive as long as the demand curve is elastic ($\epsilon < -1$). It is negative when the demand curve is inelastic ($-1 < \epsilon < 0$). The elasticity of demand, in general, depends not only on the particular demand curve, but also the point (that is, price and quantity) on the particular demand curve under examination. For example, the elasticity of demand could decrease as price becomes lower.

When Equation 5.2 is substituted for *MR* in Equation 5.1, the profit-maximizing condition for the monopolist is written as follows:[3]

$$\frac{p - MC}{p} = -\frac{1}{\epsilon}.$$ (5.3)

Equation 5.3 is a very useful summary of the optimal pricing policy for a monopolist. It shows that the markup (the difference between price and marginal cost as a fraction of price) that a monopolist can charge depends only on the elasticity of demand the monopolist faces. The markup, which is the quantity on the left-hand side of Equation 5.3, is sometimes called the *Lerner index* (Lerner 1934).

When the elasticity of demand is very high, Equation 5.3 implies that the monopolist's price is close to *MC*. Conversely, when the elasticity of demand is very low, price far exceeds *MC*. For example, if the elasticity of demand is -2, price equals twice marginal cost. In contrast, if the elasticity is -100, price equals $1.01MC$. Thus, the higher the elasticity of demand, the closer is the monopoly price to the competitive one. Therefore, the key element in any investigation of market power must be the price elasticity of demand.

The Incentive for Efficient Operation

It is a common belief that monopolists may not operate as efficiently as competitors. The argument is that monopolists have so much money already that they do not worry about cutting corners in the same way that competitors do. This simple argument turns out to be incorrect. However, a reasonable and logical explanation may be given for why a monopolist may behave less efficiently than a competitive firm. Let us first examine why the simple argument is logically wrong.

Monopolists, like competitors, want to maximize profits, and the only way a firm can do so is to minimize its costs at its chosen output level. Therefore, to postulate that monopolists want to maximize profits is to assume implicitly that they also minimize their costs. No firm—monopolist or competitor—wants to throw money away. If improving the efficiency of operations will increase profits, the firm should do it, whether it is a monopolist or a competitor. For that reason, the simple argument that monopolists do not have the same incentive as competitive firms to minimize costs is incorrect.

A monopolist, however, may not have the same *ability* to produce as efficiently as a competitive firm. After all, a firm in an industry with many other firms can observe what those other firms are doing; it can observe, for example, whether its own costs of production are above or below the market price. Because the market price reflects the

---

[3] Another condition for profit maximization is that the marginal revenue curve cut the marginal cost curve from above, as in Figure 5.3.

efficiency of the other firms in the industry, a competitive firm knows that it can improve its production efficiency if its costs of production are high relative to the market price. In contrast, a monopolist has no other firms to look at and may have no other standard by which to judge how efficiently it is operating. Therefore, because it is more difficult for a monopolist to monitor internal efficiency than it is for a competitive firm, it may be the case that a competitive firm operates more efficiently than does a monopolist. Notice that this means that a competitive market creates benefits to all firms in the market.

The consequences of inefficient behavior are different, however, for monopolists and competitors. An inefficient competitor may not be able to remain in business because it is unprofitable, but an inefficient monopolist can profitably remain in business. This observation has led some to conclude that the monopolist strives less hard to be efficient (sometimes called **x-inefficiency;** see Leibenstein 1966) than a competitor does.

Monopoly Behavior Over Time

If demand is inelastic (that is, ϵ is below 1 in absolute value), then it is not possible to satisfy Equation 5.3. Therefore, a common observation is that monopolists never operate on the inelastic portion of their demand curve. That is, monopolists always profit more by changing prices until they reach the elastic portion of their demand curve. In the inelastic portion of the demand curve, a 1 percent increase in the monopolist's price causes the quantity sold to fall by less than 1 percent, so that revenues increase. With reduced output, however, the monopolist's costs must fall, so that total profits must rise. Thus, if the monopolist is operating in the inelastic portion of the demand curve, it should keep increasing its price, getting ever more profits, until it is in the elastic portion of the demand curve.[4] Although technically true, this observation applies only in the context of a simple, timeless model. In fact, demand curves have a time dimension, and the monopolist's pricing policy must take this into account.

Consumers typically have a more inelastic demand curve in the short run than in the long run. In the short run there are limitations on how fast consumers can substitute away from a product in the face of a price increase. Therefore, monopolists who take advantage of an inelastic short-run demand curve increase the possibility that consumers will arrange to substitute away from their products in subsequent periods. This reasoning leads to the conclusion that monopolists may well operate in the inelastic portion of their short-run demand curve to avoid making their long-run demand curve too elastic.

An excellent example of the time it takes to substitute away from a product is provided by the consumption of energy. When OPEC raised the price of oil in the early 1970s, total consumption of energy changed very little in the first year. However, over the next several years as consumers adjusted to the increased price and began to take energy-saving measures, the demand for oil fell precipitously.

---

[4] What if there were no elastic portion of the demand curve? In that case, the monopolist should produce just a small amount of output and charge an enormous price. This unrealistic solution underscores the empirical irrelevance of the case of a monopolist whose relevant demand curve is always inelastic.

■ THE COSTS AND BENEFITS OF MONOPOLY

A monopoly is socially reprehensible in the hands of others.

A monopolist has an incentive to restrict output and raise price compared to a competitive industry, and this behavior results in a deadweight loss. An investigation of how monopolies arise will produce a better understanding of deadweight loss and also show how monopolists may create benefits. Indeed, in certain situations, monopoly may be preferable to competition.

The Deadweight Loss of Monopoly

As Figure 5.3 shows, the profit-maximizing output of a monopolist occurs at the intersection of the marginal revenue and the marginal cost curves. The gap between the monopolist's price and marginal cost represents the difference between the value (price) that buyers place on the product and the marginal cost of producing it. This gap is similar to the one, studied in Chapter 4, that is caused by a tax in a competitive industry. In both cases, price and output differ from their competitive levels, and there is a deviation between the demand price (as given by the demand curve) and the supply price (as given by the marginal cost curve). Using the same reasoning as in the previous chapter, we can calculate that the deadweight loss (DWL) caused by the monopolist equals the area of the triangle *ABC* in Figure 5.3, which can be approximately expressed as follows:

$$\text{area of } ABC = -\tfrac{1}{2}\, t^2\, V\epsilon \qquad (5.4)$$

where $V = p_c Q_c$ (the value of the competitive output),

   $t = \dfrac{p_m - p_c}{p_c}$ (the monopoly markup above the competitive price),

   $\epsilon =$ elasticity of demand.

Equation 5.4 illustrates that the deadweight loss from monopoly depends on the elasticity of demand.[5] See Example 5.1.

One difference between the monopoly case and the tax case in Chapter 4 is in who gets to keep the revenues: tax revenue goes to the government, and monopoly profit goes to the monopolist. Aside from this difference, the welfare analysis is similar. Many researchers have used a formula like Equation 5.4 to estimate the deadweight loss that monopoly imposes on the U.S. economy. The pioneering paper in this area is by Harberger (1954), who found that this deadweight loss is quite small, less than 0.1 percent

---

[5] A common error made in interpreting Equation 5.4 is to state that the DWL rises as the absolute value of ϵ increases so that the deadweight loss from monopoly rises as the elasticity increases. That observation is correct only if t were to remain fixed as ϵ increased. But t does not remain fixed because it depends on ϵ. Moreover, it is unclear why such a comparison between demand curves with different elasticities is interesting without trying to keep the output produced constant. See Example 5.1. Since t is inversely related to ϵ, it follows that, holding V constant, the deadweight loss, as measured by Equation 5.4, declines as the absolute value of ϵ rises. We also stress that Equation 5.4 is only an approximation that becomes increasingly accurate as the absolute value of ϵ increases.

EXAMPLE 5.1

Monopoly Profits and Deadweight Loss Vary with the Price Elasticity of Demand

To illustrate how monopoly profits and deadweight loss vary with the elasticity of demand, we use an example of a linear demand curve,

$$p = a - bQ,$$

and a constant marginal cost (MC = $10). As shown in the figure below, we rotate the demand curve so as to change the elasticity of demand at the profit-maximizing monopoly equilibrium.

The demand curve is rotated around the point where it crosses the MC line, at 100 units. That is, for all the demand curves examined, if price were set efficiently at MC = $10, consumers would buy 100 units. Since the demand curve is linear, the marginal revenue curve is also linear, and crosses the horizontal MC line at half the distance that the demand curve does. Thus, the profit-maximizing monopoly equilibrium quantity is 50 units, for all the demand curves examined.

As the demand curve is rotated, its intercept with the price axis increases (from $60 to $90 in the figure below), and the demand curve becomes less elastic at the (100 units, $10) point.

Monopoly Profits and Deadweight Loss Vary with the Elasticity of Demand

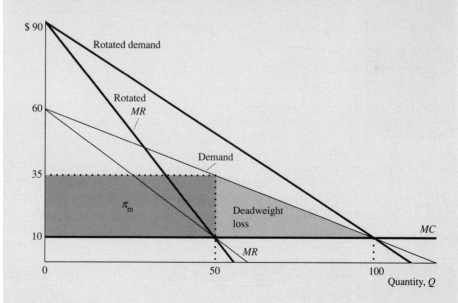

Continued

EXAMPLE 5.1

MONOPOLY PROFITS AND DEADWEIGHT LOSS VARY WITH THE PRICE ELASTICITY OF DEMAND continued

As shown in the table below, when the demand curve intercepts the price axis at $60, at the monopoly equilibrium quantity of 50 units, the elasticity of demand is −1.4. When the demand curve is rotated so that the intercept is at $90, the price elasticity is −1.25 at the quantity of 50.

As the demand curve becomes less elastic (elasticity approaches 0), monopoly profits and deadweight loss become larger. When the elasticity is −1.4, monopoly profits are $1,250 and deadweight loss is $625; when the elasticity is −1.25, profits are $2,000 and deadweight loss is $1,000.

As the demand curve becomes more inelastic at the monopoly equilibrium, people are less willing to do without this good: an increase in price causes the quantity they purchase to fall by less than if demand were more elastic. The monopolist, realizing this opportunity exists, increases the equilibrium price, and monopoly profits rise. As the demand curve becomes steeper (demand is more inelastic), the deadweight loss increases.

Monopoly Profits and Deadweight Loss Vary with the Demand Elasticity

Intercept of Demand[a] with Price Axis	Elasticity of Demand[a]	Monopoly Price	Deadweight Loss	Monopoly Profit
$ 30	−2.00	$20	$ 250	$ 500
60	−1.40	35	625	1250
90	−1.25	50	1000	2000
120	−1.18	65	1375	2750
150	−1.14	80	1750	3500

[a]At the profit-maximizing monopoly equilibrium, where $Q = 50$.

of the gross national product.[6] Several subsequent researchers have redone the calculation using different assumptions. Many estimates (for example, Worcester's (1973) estimate of 0.5 percent) tend to support Harberger's initial finding, although some estimates are larger (for example, Kamerschen's (1966) estimate of 6 percent). The next section investigates whether Equation 5.4 really measures the complete deadweight loss from monopoly.

---

[6] Gross national product, or GNP, is a measure of the value of all goods and services.

Rent-Seeking Behavior

The gods help them that help themselves—AESOP

Monopoly profits can be regarded as a transfer from consumers to the monopolist, just as tax revenues are a transfer of income from consumers to the government. By itself, a transfer of income does not affect efficiency. Only if the monopoly restricts output below competitive levels is there an efficiency effect.

Consider again the effects of a monopolist in Figure 5.3. Consumers lose consumer surplus of area *ABDE* when they are forced to pay a monopoly price, p_m, instead of the competitive price p_c. However, the monopolist gains in profits an area equal to *ACDE*. Subtracting the monopolist's gains from the consumers' losses leaves us with the deadweight loss from monopoly of area *ABC*.

Posner (1975) argues that the area of monopoly profit, *ACDE*, might also represent an inefficiency to the extent that it creates incentives for a firm to use real resources to become a monopolist. For example, suppose that a firm can become a monopolist by persuading the government to pass a law that restricts entry into the industry. (Government regulation through legislation is one of the important ways in which monopolies are created.) The use of a firm's resources to hire lobbyists, lawyers, and economists to argue its case before legislators is a cost to society, because these resources could have been productively employed elsewhere.

If monopoly profits of *ACDE* are possible, a firm would be willing to spend an amount up to *ACDE* in order to become a monopolist. Of course, the firm would like to spend as little as possible, but the opportunity to earn monopoly profit could create the incentive to use valuable resources up to the amount of monopoly profits in order to secure the monopoly.[7] Because firms will compete to earn the "rent" of *ACDE,* the expenditure of resources to attain a monopoly is called **rent seeking.**

If this reasoning is correct, the calculation of the deadweight loss from monopoly must include that part of the transfer that is dissipated by the firm seeking to become the monopolist. This will raise the cost of monopoly in the United States, because the loss will no longer be just *ABC;* it will include at least part of *ACDE*. Posner recalculates the deadweight loss from regulated and unregulated monopoly on the assumption that the entire amount of monopoly profit is dissipated in rent-seeking activities. His estimates of deadweight loss as a percent of revenues exceed previous estimates. For example, Posner finds deadweight losses of up to 30 percent of revenues for some of the industries he examines (such as motor carriers, physician services, and oil). His insight is that a great part of the loss to the economy from monopoly (or, more generally, noncompetitive pricing) is directly traceable to the existence of government institutions that insulate some firms from competition. The recent trends toward dismantling government regulation (examined in Chapter 23) could therefore provide sizable benefits to society.

---

[7] Whether the firm would dissipate the entire monopoly profit will depend on the details of how the monopoly can be acquired (Fisher 1985).

EXAMPLE 5.2

PREVENTING IMITATION—CAT GOT YOUR TONGUE?

Why are violin strings called *catgut* when they are really made of sheep intestines? An old Roman named Erasmo (c. A.D. 130) started making strings for musical instruments out of sheep intestine. The demand grew. Since it was considered extremely bad luck to kill a cat, Erasmo identified his product as *catgut* so nobody would imitate it and ruin his monopoly.

SOURCE: Boyd (1984), p. 35.

Creating and Maintaining a Monopoly

No one can earn a million dollars honestly.—WILLIAM JENNINGS BRYAN

Among the means by which a firm may become and remain a monopolist, some of the most important are the following:

1. A firm may have special knowledge that enables it to produce a new or better product that others cannot imitate. The firm may try to keep secret its special knowledge so as to prevent rivals from imitating it. See Example 5.2. In such a case, the firm faces a downward sloping demand curve for its product and need not fear the entry of rival firms or the introduction of products that are close substitutes.

2. In addition to new or improved products, a firm may have special knowledge about production techniques that enable it to produce at lower cost than other firms, which may be unable to discover the production technique of the efficient firm. Suppose, for example, that a competitive industry is in equilibrium at price C_1, and quantity, Q_1, as illustrated in Figure 5.4.

   Suppose a firm discovers a new production technique that it can keep secret and that lowers its marginal costs from C_1 to C_0. It faces a demand curve that is horizontal at a price equal to C_1, because many firms can produce and sell at price C_1. The curve coincides with the industry demand curve for the product for prices below C_1, because below C_1 no other firm can profitably produce. If C_0 is quite close to C_1, the firm may maximize profits by selling at a price equal to C_1. However, if C_0 is far below C_1, the profit maximizing monopoly price may be somewhere below C_1 but above C_0. In such a case, no firms would remain in the industry other than the low-cost, efficient firm, because none could afford to compete. The price would be above C_0, the marginal cost of the efficient firm, but below C_1, and output would exceed Q_1. Figure 5.5 (on page 110) shows that the marginal revenue curve is discontinuous at the output where the firm's demand curve is kinked and that the marginal revenue curve intersects the new cost curve at output Q_0, leading to a price of p_0, which is below C_1. (See Chapter 20.)

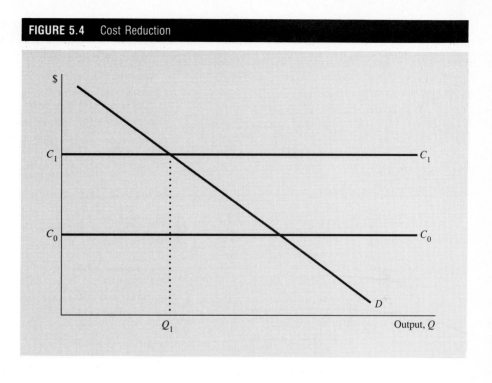

FIGURE 5.4   Cost Reduction

3. The previous two points have assumed that imitation of the new product or technique was impossible. When imitation *is* possible, an innovating firm may rely on legal protection to prevent entry. The law on intellectual property, in particular the patent law, grants a legal monopoly to any firm that has discovered a new product or technique. A firm can obtain a **patent** on a new product that prevents any other firm from copying its product and competing with it for a period of seventeen years. (Chapter 20 discusses patents in detail.)

4. Aside from the patent laws, other types of government restrictions on entry can serve to create and maintain monopolies. For example, taxicab owners must usually purchase medallions, whose supply is fixed by local authorities, in order to operate. As another example, any firm that wishes to produce a narcotic substance must obtain the approval of the Drug Enforcement Agency. In most instances, government restrictions on entry allow at least a few firms to produce but still prevent the normal competitive forces from driving price and profits down to competitive levels (see Examples 5.3 and 5.4).

5. New firms may have no incentive or ability to enter, even if a monopolist is earning high profits. The monopolist may be able to prevent other firms from entering through a variety of strategic decisions (discussed in Chapter 13), such as controlling essential inputs. Alternatively, the existing firm may be so large in relation to the overall market that there is room for only one firm. This tends to occur most when markets are geographically local. Chapter 13 examines behavior that deters entry in markets that have room for only one or a few firms.

FIGURE 5.5 Monopolization Through Efficiency

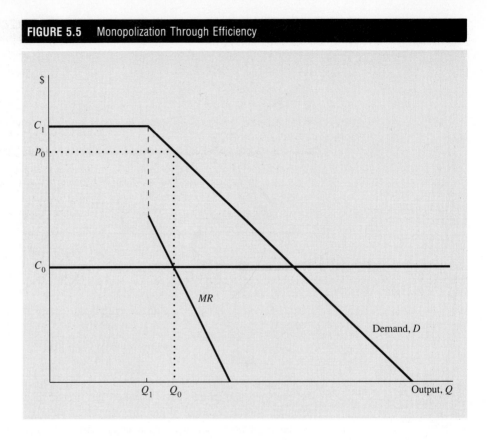

The Benefits of Monopoly

The welfare calculations in the previous sections have shown how to measure the dead-weight loss that monopoly imposes upon an economy. However, offsetting efficiencies may often result from the creation of a monopoly—efficiencies that are ignored in the static theory upon which the previous calculations of deadweight loss were based. For example, the prospect of receiving monopoly profits may motivate firms to develop new products, improve products, or find lower cost methods of manufacturing. Were it not for the incentive of monopoly profits, firms might innovate less and not strive as hard to improve their efficiency. It makes no sense to condemn monopoly unless one can be sure that removal of monopoly profits would not alter socially desirable behavior of firms.

The benefit of monopoly is most clearly recognized in research and development, which Chapter 20 covers in more detail. If a firm succeeds in developing a new product, it can obtain a patent that prohibits other firms from using the patented technology for seventeen years. Were it not for the patent, the innovative firm might discover that, within a matter of weeks, other firms had copied the new product. The innovative firm would then receive no more than the competitive level of profits and would not recover its

EXAMPLE 5.3

The Number of Doctors

The restriction of entry is one effective method for existing firms to raise their profits and protect themselves from competition. The American Medical Association (AMA) has exerted control over the number of doctors in the United States for several decades. During the 1960s, the AMA's control of the number of domestic graduates weakened. At the same time, the immigration laws were changed; as a result, many more foreign doctors were able to practice in the United States and the percentage of new doctors who were foreign rose from roughly 15 percent in the 1960s to about 40 percent in the early 1970s. With these two sources of increased supply, the number of doctors per capita rose by almost 50 percent between 1965 and the early 1980s. One estimate is that the increased supply reduced the annual income of doctors by about $23,000 in 1981 dollars.

SOURCE: Noether (1986).

EXAMPLE 5.4

A Monopoly on Insanity

Many monopolies are created by governments. A young venture capitalist discovered a way to profit from government-created local monopolies in psychiatric hospitals.

Robert L. Green bought a psychiatric hospital south of San Francisco intending to use the site for an office complex. After a study, however, he discovered that a psychiatric hospital could be a gold mine.

His company, Community Psychiatric Centers (CPC), went public in 1969 and through 1985, has had annual earnings growth of 15 to 30 percent. It is the most profitable psychiatric hospital chain in the country, owning hospitals across the United States and in Britain.

Much of this phenomenal growth and profitability is due to a law in every state that requires someone wishing to build an in-patient facility to obtain a certificate of need by demonstrating that a new facility is needed. By setting up operations before anyone else in several California suburbs, CPC has obtained virtual local monopolies and has kept its before-tax profit margins near 40 percent.

Unfortunately for CPC, the government programs that preserve these local monopolies have been eliminated in several states. Thus, in the future, CPC may only be able to earn competitive rates of return on its hospitals.

SOURCE: Fisher (1985).

expenditures on research and development. The firms that copied the product would have no research and development expenditure to recover. The ability of other firms to copy a new product removes a firm's incentive to invest in research and development. The patent system attempts to deal with this problem by granting the innovating firm the sole property right to commercially exploit its innovation.

Naturally, if monopoly had no offsetting benefits, competition would be preferable. For example, if all firms in a competitive industry decide to merge, and if the merger does not lead to a more efficient industry, then the only result is the creation of a monopoly. As long as new entry takes time, the firms could price above their marginal cost. By assumption, there is no benefit from this action, and such behavior should be discouraged. One responsibility of the Department of Justice and Federal Trade Commission is to scrutinize each merger carefully to make sure that its effect is not simply to raise prices to consumers.

■ THE RELATIONSHIP BETWEEN PROFITS AND MONOPOLY

Many people casually associate high profits with monopoly or too little competition, normal profits with competition, and losses with too much competition. Although each of these beliefs has some element of truth, none are correct. Moreover, they often lead to erroneous answers to three important economic questions considered in the following sections.

Is Anyone Who Earns Positive Profits a Monopolist?

Although it is true that a monopolist may earn positive profits (that is, more than the normal rate of return), it is not true that any firm that earns positive profits is a monopolist. The previous chapter discusses the possibility that certain scarce resources, such as land, can earn rents. For example, a wheat farmer who owns particularly productive land will presumably earn a large profit. This profit is attributable to the land that is owned and should properly be called a rent. The farmer behaves as a competitor, taking price as given and operating at the point where price equals marginal cost. As long as a firm is operating at that point, it is behaving as a competitive firm. The rents that it may earn on factors of production that it owns do not change the fact that it is a competitive firm; rents on factors of production do not indicate a monopoly. As long as output is not restricted, and supply and demand determine price, there is no market power. Scarce resources can command very high prices and those who own those resources benefit.

Does the Monopolist Always Earn Positive Profits?

Although a monopolist earns higher profits than a competitive firm would, it is not true that a monopolist always earns positive profits. In the short run, a monopolist can make losses, just as a competitive firm can. A monopolist that faces a sudden decline in demand may well continue to operate even though its profits are lower than the competitive rate of return on its sunk investment; that is, it earns losses in an economic sense. In the long-run, when there are no sunk costs, no firm will continue to operate if there are only losses in the industry, but the mere fact of losses in an industry does not mean that it can be characterized as competitive.

The length of time that losses will be earned in an industry depends, in the case of monopoly, on exactly the same things that it does in the case of competition, namely, how long the short run is. That is, how long does it take for plant and equipment to wear out, forcing a decision on whether to replace them? In some industries the short run may be very long. For example, railroad tracks can last for several years, making the short run quite long for the railroad industry. Therefore, one might expect that a railroad could earn negative profits on its investments for a long time before deciding to exit the industry.

In summary, monopoly behavior is characterized by a firm operating where price exceeds marginal cost. In the long run, a competitive firm makes normal (that is, zero) economic profits, while a monopolist makes at least this amount. In the short run, both competitive firms and monopolists may make losses or profits.

Should the Government Allow Mergers That Create Monopoly in an Industry Suffering Short-Run Losses?

The previous section shows that a monopolist, just like a competitor, may earn losses in the short run. When firms are earning losses, a merger of the firms can eliminate competition and allow the merged firm to exercise market power and raise price so that the losses are eliminated. This motivation for merger has a certain logical appeal—if the merger eliminates the losses, perhaps it is efficient for the merger to occur. In fact this is not true at all!

If a merger enables firms in the short run to price above the level at which they would have priced had they remained competitive, then the merger imposes a deadweight loss on society. The existence of sunk costs in the short run (which are, after all, responsible for the losses) cannot be changed by merging firms together. The merger only changes the amount of competition that firms face. If the amount of sunk costs must remain unchanged by the merger, as it must, then it is clearly inefficient to allow firms to merge solely to eliminate competition and allow the price to rise.

■ NATURAL MONOPOLY

In some industries, it is most efficient for only one firm to produce all of the output. When total production costs would rise if two or more firms produced instead of one, the situation is called a **natural monopoly,** which is discussed briefly here and covered in more detail in Chapter 23.[8]

---

[8] We consider only single-product firms in this section. Chapter 23 considers natural monopoly in a multiproduct setting.

If production is characterized by economies of scale everywhere, then average cost is declining with output, and it is always less costly for one firm to produce any given output than to split the output up among several firms. Therefore, when average cost falls with output, there is a natural monopoly. A natural monopoly can occur even if average cost is not declining everywhere with output. For example, a U-shaped average cost curve with the minimum average cost occurring at output of 100 means that it may be most efficient for only one firm to produce if output is 101, even though average cost is rising at that output. Therefore, economies of scale are a sufficient but not a necessary condition for natural monopoly.

One difficulty that natural monopoly creates is that competition of *actual* competitors cannot guarantee efficiency, because the efficient arrangement allows for no other competitors. Competition of potential entrants may provide a check on a firm's behavior, but even here there can be problems. Suppose that each potential entrant competes by announcing the price it would charge if it were the sole firm. Suppose that average cost declines everywhere with output. But if the average cost curve is falling, then marginal cost must be below average cost, and setting price equal to marginal cost will yield losses. In this case, there is no way to set price equal to marginal cost and earn zero profits. One possible solution is to have each firm announce a *two-part price* consisting of a fixed charge plus a usage charge. The usage charge could be based on marginal cost, and the fixed fee could be chosen to yield zero profits. Another solution is to have the firm charge an average cost that is above marginal cost—but this results in the usual deadweight loss from the gap between price and marginal cost.

Even if it were possible to determine what pricing scheme to use to earn zero profits, a related problem is that no monopolist is content to earn zero profits if greater profits are possible. Once a firm has been established as the natural monopolist, it is likely to develop advantages over potential entrants who can then no longer adequately constrain prices. Therefore regulation of the natural monopolist's profits may be necessary to protect consumers from excessive pricing, even though it is often difficult and creates its own problems. The issues associated with natural monopoly and regulation are considered in more detail in Chapter 23.

■ MONOPSONY

Monopsony refers to a situation in which a single buyer faces an upward sloping supply curve for a product.[9] For example, if there is only one firm that hires workers in a local area, that firm must recognize that its decision on how many workers to hire affects the wage rate that it must pay, just as the monopolist realizes that its output level affects the price it can receive. Monopsony is simply the flip side of monopoly. In both situations, a single firm recognizes that its actions affect the market price.

---

[9] In contrast, in a *monopoly*, a single seller faces a downward sloping demand curve for its product.

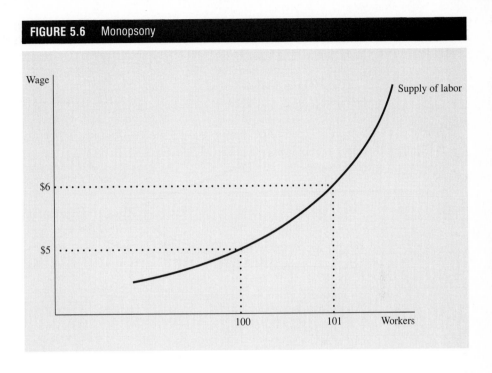

FIGURE 5.6   Monopsony

A monopsonist—the sole buyer of a product—determines how much to buy in much the same way that a monopolist determines how much to produce: a monopsonist expands its consumption of the good as long as the value of the extra consumption as given by its demand curve equals or exceeds its marginal cost of consuming one more unit.

In a competitive market where each firm takes the wage rate as given, the marginal cost of hiring one more worker is simply the wage rate. In a monopsonized market, the monopsonist recognizes that hiring one more worker forces it not only to pay that worker a slightly higher wage rate but also to pay *all* workers a slightly higher wage rate, because only by raising the wage can extra labor be induced into the marketplace. Figure 5.6 illustrates this point: in order to increase the number of workers hired from 100 to 101, the wage rate must rise from $5 to $6 per hour. (Each worker works one hour.)

Notice that the extra cost of hiring the additional worker is not just $6; it is $6 plus the $1 increase in wages that must be passed along to each of the 100 original workers. The total wage bill rises from $500 to $606, for an increase of $106. The monopsonist recognizes that its marginal cost of hiring the additional worker is $106 rather than $6 and takes that into account in deciding whether to hire the additional worker. The monopsonist continues to hire as long as the marginal benefit as given by the demand curve exceeds the marginal cost of hiring an additional worker.

The marginal cost to a monopsonist of hiring an additional worker is sometimes called the **marginal outlay schedule,** which is exactly analogous to the marginal revenue curve studied earlier. A monopsonist equates marginal benefits, as given by the demand

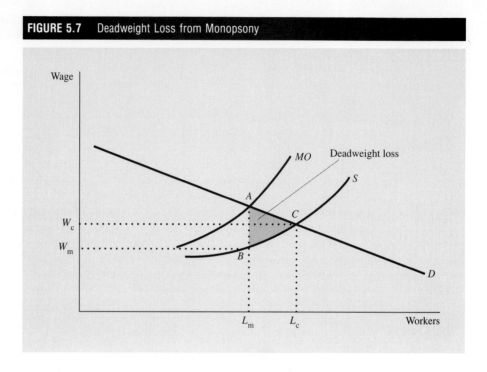

FIGURE 5.7   Deadweight Loss from Monopsony

curve, to the marginal outlay. Because the marginal outlay curve lies above the supply curve, the monopsonist always purchases less than the output represented by the intersection of the demand curve and the supply curve. In other words, monopsony results in a restriction of output just as monopoly does. Figure 5.7 illustrates the restriction of output, which is reduced from the competitive level of L_c to the monopsonized level of L_m.

Notice that the wage rate, W_m, associated with the monopsonized output is below the wage rate, W_c, that would prevail in competition. Therefore monopsony has two effects: it restricts the amount of output below the competitive level, and it lowers the wage rate below that of a competitive market. Using a definition analogous to the one for market power, we can define *monopsony power* as the ability to profitably set wages (or any input prices) below competitive levels.

At the monopsonized solution of (Q_m, W_m) in Figure 5.7, there is a gap between the demand curve and the supply curve. Any gap between the demand curve (which represents the benefits to society of consumption) and the supply curve (which represents the marginal cost to society) represents an inefficiency. In Figure 5.7, the inefficiency creates a deadweight loss that equals the area of the triangle *ABC* and is analogous to the deadweight loss that results from monopoly.

Most labor economists believe that monopsony in the labor market is limited because many firms compete for the available workers. The most frequent examples given of monopsony in the labor market concern single-company towns, local employment markets, and sports leagues. For example, someone who wishes to play major league baseball in the United States can only play in either the American League or National League. Collectively, the teams in those two leagues are the sole buyer for the services of this baseball player. If all the teams reach an agreement not to compete for players, they could act as a monopsonist in hiring. (Of course, if baseball players form a union, they acquire their own bargaining leverage.)

In markets other than labor, monopsony is also considered to be rare; it is likely only when resources are specialized to a few uses. See Example 5.5. Moreover, even if resources are initially specialized to one use, as with a piece of custom-designed machinery (or a plant in a specific location serving a single buyer), monopsony may not persist in the long run. The reason is that no one will make new custom-designed machinery (or new investments in a plant) for a specific buyer if they earn a depressed return compared to what they can earn from making other machines (or building a plant elsewhere). In other words, few resources are specialized in the long run, and therefore it is unlikely that monopsony can persist in the long run.

Another way to explain the preceding point is as follows. If resources are not specialized to a particular industry in the long run, then the long-run supply curve tends to be flat. As Chapter 3 shows, a flat long-run supply curve is most likely to occur when the industry in question uses only a relatively small fraction of the total consumption of its inputs. Long-run monopsony power is impossible if the long-run supply curve is flat, because then price cannot be lowered below the competitive price.

If the long-run supply curve is flat, there may not be any monopsony power even in the short run. Suppose that before a firm enters an industry, it has many alternative uses for the resources it owns. After it enters the industry, it specializes its machines so that it has very few alternative uses for its assets. Suppose that it will only enter a particular industry if it receives $10 per unit of output (which is the long-run average cost). The sole buyer, the monopsonist, agrees to pay $10. After the firm enters, it is committed, at least for some time, in the sense that its machines are specialized to this particular industry. If the monopsonist suddenly lowers the price to $9, it may not pay for the firm to exit immediately. But the firm will not replace the worn-out specialized machines when the time comes, and the buyer may eventually have no one willing to supply the product. Even if the buyer again promises $10 per unit to induce a supplier to enter, no firm would believe the buyer in light of the previous behavior. So, for a buyer that is concerned about a long-run source of supply, it may not pay to exercise short-run monopsony power.

■ SUMMARY

Monopoly or market power is the ability to price above marginal cost. Monopoly leads to less output and higher prices than arise under perfect competition, with a resulting inefficiency in the economy. Many estimates of the cost, or deadweight loss, of monopoly are at most a few percent of GNP. However, monopoly is not always bad; the incentive of monopoly profits can spur a firm to benefit society by developing new products or more efficient production techniques.

EXAMPLE 5.5

IDENTIFYING MONOPSONY POWER IN TOMATOES

Do firms that process tomatoes collectively have monopsony power? That is, do they pay too little (less than the competitive price) to farmers? It is hard to tell just by looking at the price paid and the quantity sold. To see why, consider the following example.

Suppose an analyst observes that the price is p_0 and the quantity bought is Q_0 and even knows the supply curve S for the tomato farmers. One possibility is that competition prevails and the equilibrium of (p_0, Q_0) is determined by the intersection of S with some demand curve, like D_0, in the figure on the opposite page. Another possibility is that the processors have monopsony power and that the equilibrium of (p_0, Q_0) is determined by the intersection of the marginal outlay (MO) curve, which depends on the shape of S, with a demand curve like D. The analyst who observes only prices and quantities cannot distinguish competition from monopsony.

Just and Chern (1980) reason that if the shape of the supply curve changed, but not its level (that is, the supply curve still goes through (p_0, Q_0) but with a different slope), then the equilibrium would be unchanged if competition prevailed but not if monopsony prevailed. The competitive equilibrium would be unchanged because supply and demand would still intersect at (p_0, Q_0). The monopsony equilibrium would change because the MO curve would shift when the shape of the supply curve changed and would intersect the demand curve at a new point. Just and Chern also show how to apply their insight to more general types of shifts in supply. Changes in the shape of supply should affect the monopsony equilibrium but not the competitive one, after adjusting for the levels of supply and demand.

Just and Chern apply their method to tomato processors. After the invention of the mechanical harvester and the development of new "hardball" tomatoes that could be machine-harvested, virtually all California farmers adopted the use of the harvester between 1963 and 1967. As a result, the variable costs of harvesting (associated with labor) fell substantially, and the fixed costs (harvesters) rose, so that the short-run supply became more inelastic. Just and Chern find that the new equilibrium did depend on the shape of the supply curve—a finding consistent with monopsony and not competition.

Just and Chern also apply their insight in a different way. If the supply curve shifts out over time *and* becomes more inelastic, then the quantity must increase if the market is competitive. The new supply curve intersects demand at a greater quantity than

Monopsony in Tomato Harvesting

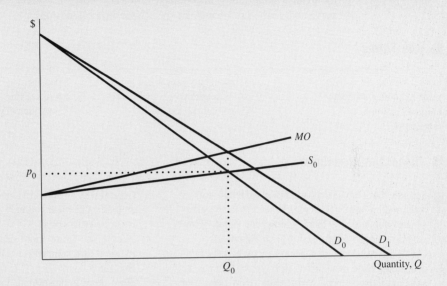

before. However, this increase in quantity need not occur for a monopsony since the new *MO* curve (which depends on the shape of the new supply curve) could intersect demand at a lower quantity than before. According to Just and Chern, the supply curve for tomato harvesting shifted out and became more inelastic over time. In half the countries that grew tomatoes, the quantity sold fell, again consistent with the monopsony hypothesis and inconsistent with the competitive one.

There has been some confusion over the relationships of profits and monopoly. Just like a competitive firm, a monopolist can earn either profits or losses in the short run. Profits do not imply monopoly. However, unlike a competitive firm, a monopolist can earn positive profits in the long run.

Monopsony is monopoly on the buying side. A firm with monopsony power sets lower prices and employs fewer resources than would prevail under competition. Like monopoly, monopsony imposes an efficiency cost on society. Monopsony power can persist only when resources are specialized in the long run.

■ Key Terms

market power
marginal outlay schedule
marginal revenue
monopoly

monopoly power
monopsony
natural monopoly

patents
rent seeking
x-inefficiency

■ Discussion Questions

1. Suppose that a firm is a monopolist in the output market and a monopsonist in the input market. (To keep matters simple, suppose that there is only one input.) How would output be determined in such a market?

2. Discuss: Since inefficient behavior raises costs for a competitor and a monopolist, each type of firm has the same incentive to behave efficiently. How does your discussion change if the possibility of inefficient behavior would result in the competitive firm's going bankrupt (and incurring related extra legal expenses)?

3. Explain why a natural monopoly cannot avoid creating an inefficiency if it can only charge a single price and must cover its costs?

4. Does a tax create more deadweight loss when it is imposed in a competitive industry or in a monopoly? Explain.

5. Since there is deadweight loss from monopoly, governments should always intervene to prevent the loss. Discuss.

■ Problems

1. Suppose that the demand curve is $Q(p) = 10 - p$. If marginal cost is constant and equals 4, what is the monopoly price and output? What is the price elasticity at the monopoly price and output?

2. Suppose that the supply of football players is elastic at the lowest salary levels paid. Would a monopsonist of football players restrict output?

3. Suppose that the demand curve is given by $Q(p) = 5/p$. What is the elasticity of demand? What is total revenue when $p = \$1$ and when $p = \$30$? If production

costs \$1 per unit, and the smallest production level is 1 unit, how much should the monopolist produce?

4. Suppose the demand curve is given by $Q(p) = p^{-\epsilon}$. What is the elasticity of demand? If marginal cost is \$1 and $\epsilon = -2$, what is the profit-maximizing price?

5. Suppose the demand curve for oil is $Q(p) = 10 - p$. Suppose that one firm owns all the oil in the world and that there are 5 units of it. Will the monopolist restrict output compared to the competitive case in which 100 firms each owns 0.05 units of oil?

Answers to the odd-numbered problems are given at the back of the book.

■ References

Boyd, L. 1984. "Grab Bag." *San Francisco Chronicle,* October 27, p. 35.

Fisher, Franklin M. 1985. "The Social Costs of Monopoly and Regulation: Posner Reconsidered." *Journal of Political Economy* 93:410–16.

Fisher, Lawrence M. 1985. "Strains on Psychiatric Centers," *New York Times,* December 30, D1 and D10.

Harberger, Arnold. 1954. "Monopoly and Resource Allocation." *American Economic Review* 44:77–79.

Harris, Milton and Robert M. Townsend. 1981. "Resource Allocation Under Asymmetric Information." *Econometrica* 49:33–64.

Just, Richard E. and Win S. Chern. 1980. "Tomatoes, Technology, and Oligopsony." *The Bell Journal of Economics* 11:584–602.

Kamerschen, David R. 1966. "An Estimation of the Welfare Losses for Monopoly in the American Economy." *Western Economic Journal* 4:221–36.

Lerner, Abba P. 1934. "The Concept of Monopoly and the Measurement of Monopoly Power." *Review of Economic Studies* 1:157–75.

Leibenstein, Harvey. 1966. "Allocative Inefficiency vs. X-Inefficiency." *American Economic Review* 56:392–415.

Noether, Monica. 1986. "The Effect of Government Policy Changes on the Supply of Physicians: Expansion of a Competitive Fringe." *Journal of Law and Economics* 29:231–62.

Posner, Richard A. 1975. "The Social Costs of Monopoly and Regulation." *Journal of Political Economy* 83:807–27.

Worcester, Dean A., Jr. 1973. "New Estimates of the Welfare Loss to Monopoly, United States: 1956–1969." *Southern Economic Journal* 40:234–45.

CHAPTER 6 | COMPETITION AND MONOPOLY IN MARKETS WITH EXTERNALITIES

I durst not laugh, for fear of opening my lips and receiving the bad air.

SHAKESPEARE

Not all goods (such as information or fresh air) or "bads" (such as pollution or garbage) are priced in our economy. Goods that are not priced are referred to as **externalities.** Whenever a good has no price—or the wrong price—distortions occur. For example, in the absence of government regulations, manufacturing firms do not have to pay for the pollution they create, so they ignore the cost to society of pollution in deciding how much output to produce. Such distortions, or inefficient production due to improper pricing, are referred to as **market failures.**

Although in most markets competition is superior to monopoly, *when a market failure occurs, monopoly may be socially preferable to competition.*[1] For example, if pollution is a byproduct of a manufacturing process, a competitive industry produces more output *and* more pollution than would a monopoly. Whether more output and pollution are better than less of both is an empirical question. An optimally regulated industry, however, with the optimal levels of output and pollution, is superior to both unregulated competition and monopoly. This chapter uses examples of market failures due to externalities to compare competition, monopoly, and an optimally regulated industry.

---

[1] When all goods have prices set in the market, competition produces the socially optimal output level because the price (marginal benefit) of each good equals its marginal cost of production (as shown in Chapter 4). In contrast, a monopoly sells too little output because it sets price above marginal cost (Chapter 5).

■ EXTERNALITIES

When a firm does not bear the full cost of the harm it does to others, the damage is called a **negative externality.** Pollution is one of the most important examples; for example, the toxic chemicals that a manufacturing plant adds to the water supply damage the fishing industry and may directly harm individuals. Similarly, exhaust fumes from cars injure others' health.

In contrast, an uncompensated action by a firm that benefits others is a **positive externality.** For example, if you benefit from the shade tree planted by your neighbor, but do not help pay for it, you receive a positive externality.[2] Information and scientific discoveries, which can benefit many people at once, also provide positive externalities. When Henry Ford developed the assembly line, other firms benefited from his innovation without compensating him. If you consume a hot dog, no one else can consume it, so there is no externality. In contrast, you can purchase and "consume" a newspaper without preventing others from consuming it also. The information in that newspaper provides a positive externality for which the publisher is not fully compensated—not everyone who reads the paper pays for it. Information is also described as a **public good:** if it is supplied to one person, it can be made available to others at no extra cost.

Some externalities are negative for some people and positive for others. Your neighbor's tree is a benefit if you like shade, but an annoyance if you prefer sunlight or dislike raking leaves.

Externalities arise because property rights are not clearly defined. You have **property rights** when you own or have exclusive rights to use some property. For example, you may have property rights to a particular car, but no clearly defined area of a highway belongs to you alone: you share the highway with others. Each driver claims a temporary property right in a portion of the highway by occupying it (thereby preventing others from occupying the same space). Competition for space on the highway can lead to congestion (a negative externality), which slows up every driver on a highway. See Example 6.1.

In the competitive and monopolistic markets discussed in Chapters 4 and 5, property rights were clearly defined so that externalities did not arise. For example, growing wheat does not affect a farmer's neighbors or anyone else, but cars emit harmful pollution into the air (which no one owns). Similarly, if a software company cannot protect its property right to its computer programs by preventing purchasers from providing copies to friends, these programs provide a positive externality (Chapter 20 discusses this issue in detail).

Externalities are extremely common in all economies. Externalities produce market failure when the competitive price system fails to produce the socially optimal quantity of goods. Since externalities have no price, people ignore them in their private calculations, which causes a market failure. To illustrate how externalities affect the way markets function, this chapter considers two important cases in more detail: pollution (a negative externality) and fisheries (common access to public property).

---

[2] Analogously, the old saying, "When it happens to you, it's a tragedy; when it happens to the other guy, it's funny," could be restated, "When it happens to the other guy, it's a positive externality.".

EXAMPLE 6.1

THERE AUTO BE A SOLUTION

Hong Kong's traffic problems are spectacular, but a program has been designed to reduce congestion. Under the plan, a device will be installed in each car to allow the government to bill people according to the amount of traveling they do on city streets. According to Hong Kong's secretary of transport, "If we don't try it, the city will grind to a halt, full stop."

A pilot program will equip 5000 government vehicles with electronic identification plates. At 30 of the city's busiest intersections, electronic devices will record the passage of each vehicle over an electronic transmitter buried in the road. If the system works, all automobiles will be equipped with a plate, and 300 sensors will be installed at intersections. Charges will vary with the time of day, and each vehicle will be billed monthly. Such a system would help in the United States, where it is estimated that 4 percent of gasoline consumption occurs during traffic jams, and a great deal of time and gasoline are wasted by congestion on city streets.

SOURCES: "Pay-As-You-Go Gridlock." 1983. *San Francisco Examiner*, November 13: *This World*, 3.
"Harper's Index." 1988. *San Francisco Examiner*, October 2: *This World*, 6.

■ POLLUTION

> *Approximately 80% of our air pollution stems from hydrocarbons released by vegetation, so let's not go overboard in setting and enforcing tough emission standards from man-made sources.* —RONALD REAGAN[3]

Consider the example of an industry that produces automobile tires and air pollution. The air pollution is a byproduct of the production process and increases with production.[4] Consumers value the tires but are harmed by the pollution—a thick, noxious smoke that damages health, destroys plants, and soils clothing and houses.

Since competitive manufacturing firms do not have to pay the costs associated with the pollution, they underestimate the true costs of production and charge too little for their product, resulting in large tire sales and too much pollution.

---

[3] *Sierra*. 1980. September 10. In Green, Mark, and Gail MacColl. 1983. *There He Goes Again: Ronald Reagan's Reign of Error*. New York: Pantheon Books, 99-100. The authors note that trees decay into nitrous oxide which is not an immediate threat to human health, unlike man-made oxides of nitrogen, which are harmful. Moreover, according to Dr. Michael Oppenheimer of the Environmental Defense Fund, industrial sources are responsible for at least 65% and possibly as much as 90% of the oxides of nitrogen in the United States.

[4] For simplicity, assume that the only way to reduce pollution is to reduce production. Smokestack scrubbers and other pollution control devices are assumed to be prohibitively expensive. Relaxing this assumption would complicate the analysis without changing the basic point.

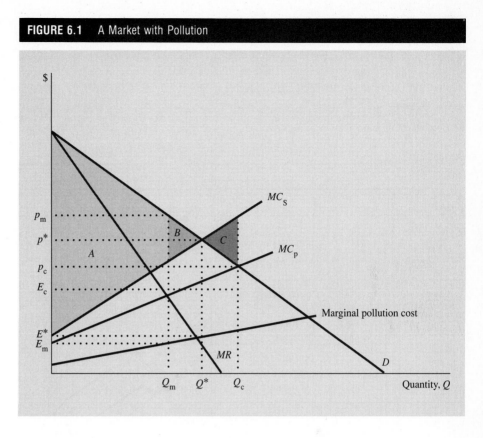

FIGURE 6.1   A Market with Pollution

A monopolist, which produces less output than a competitive industry, might produce closer to the optimal combination of tires and pollution than a competitive industry. If a monopolist reduces its output too much, however, society may prefer excessive pollution and many tires to less pollution and few tires.

Graphic Analysis

These points can be illustrated graphically. In Figure 6.1, the demand curve, D, shows how much consumers will pay for tires. The MC_p curve is the horizontal sum of the **private marginal cost** curves of all the manufacturing plants in the industry. This curve represents only the costs of producing tires (labor, capital, equipment, materials) paid by the manufacturers and does not include the full social costs (the harm done by the air pollution). If the industry is competitive, this curve is the industry supply curve. With only one firm in the industry, this curve is the (multiplant) monopoly's marginal cost curve.

In the absence of government intervention, a competitive industry ignores the pollution damage and produces where supply, MC_p, equals demand, D. As shown in the figure, it produces Q_c tires at a price of p_c. A monopolist also ignores the pollution damages and produces where marginal revenue, MR, equals its private marginal cost of production, MC_p. The monopolist sells Q_m units at a price of p_m. As always, a competitive industry produces more output at a lower price than does a monopoly.

Both types of industry ignore the damage done by the air pollution they create. The dollar value of the marginal damage it causes (health harms, property damage, reduced agricultural output, and so forth) is also shown in Figure 6.1. This curve reflects the amount of money that pollution victims would have to receive to be indifferent between tolerating the pollution and being compensated and not having to face the pollution caused by the last unit of production. The pollution damage is greater at the competitive equilibrium, E_c, than at the monopolistic one, E_m, since the competitive output (and hence amount of pollution) is greater.

The full cost of a tire to society, the **social marginal cost,** is the cost of manufacturing the tires (the height on the MC_p curve) plus the marginal damage due to pollution. The full marginal cost to society, MC_s, is shown in the figure as the vertical sum of the MC_p and the marginal pollution cost curves.

The socially optimal solution includes some pollution—the only way to eliminate pollution is to shut down the tire manufacturing industry altogether. Because consumers value tires (as shown by their consumer surplus), shutting down the industry would do more harm than good. Optimality occurs where the marginal social benefit (value of the last tire) equals the social marginal cost (the marginal manufacturing and pollution costs).

The optimal solution for society is to produce Q^* tires at price p^*, as determined by the intersection of the social marginal cost, MC_s, and demand, D, curves. At that point, welfare (consumer plus producer surplus) is maximized: the area below the demand curve and above the MC_s curve is greatest. In order to calculate social welfare, we must use the MC_s rather than the MC_p curve so as to capture the full costs of production.[5]

Regulation of Pollution

England's first smoke abatement law, passed in 1273, was seriously enforced. In 1306, a manufacturer was convicted for burning coal and beheaded.

Two methods are commonly proposed to achieve the social optimum, and both involve optimal government intervention.[6] First, the government could restrict output to Q^*. Second, it could impose a tax equal to the marginal pollution cost on manufacturing

---

[5] Some of the cost of production, damage due to pollution, may fall on individuals who do not purchase tires. To consider only the demand and the MC_p curve would be to ignore the bystanders' interests altogether. People who live near a manufacturing plant in Akron may be harmed by pollution, whereas purchasers of tires in, say, Miami are unaffected by it. The tire consumers in Miami prefer to ignore the costs of pollution in Akron and to buy low-price tires.

[6] In most of the following analysis, government regulation is assumed to be optimal and costless, which is not always true in the real world. Chapter 23 discusses nonoptimal and costly regulation in more detail.

firms.[7] This taxation method is referred to as **internalizing the externality,** because the firms now bear the full social costs of production. An optimally taxed competitive industry produces the socially optimal level of output, but if the government does not have enough information to determine all the curves in Figure 6.1, it cannot determine the optimal regulations.

We have just argued that an unregulated competitive industry produces too much pollution and that an optimally taxed one produces the socially optimal outcome. What about a monopoly? As shown in Figure 6.1, the monopoly produces even less output (and pollution) than is socially optimal when pollution is taken into account, however, it could produce the socially optimal output at the socially optimal price if the MC_s curve happened to hit the demand curve at p_m. Income is distributed differently, however: if the government taxes a competitive industry in order to regulate it, part of the price goes to the government (and perhaps back to consumers), whereas an unregulated monopoly keeps the entire amount. Theory alone can only say that both a monopoly and an optimally regulated industry produce less output than a competitive industry; it cannot determine if the monopoly output is larger, smaller, or equal to the optimal amount.

In the absence of optimal pollution regulation, it is not clear whether society is better off with monopoly or competition. Although monopoly produces too little output at too high a price, it does produce less pollution. The particular curves shown in Figure 6.1 indicate which equilibrium is associated with a higher level of social welfare.

Under monopoly, social welfare is Area A in the diagram (the area above the social marginal cost curve and below the demand curve). Area A is the sum of consumer and producer surpluses, net of the pollution damage.[8] Under an optimally regulated competitive industry, social welfare (Areas A and B) is maximized. Under an unregulated competitive industry, social welfare is Areas A plus B minus C. Compared to monopoly, the unregulated competitive industry produces extra output at a lower price, which leads to an increase in consumer plus producer surplus equal to Areas B and C. The extra social cost not offset by consumer payments or consumer surplus is Area C.[9] Thus, in this example, social welfare is greater under monopoly than under an unregulated competitive industry if Area B is less than Area C. See Example 6.2.

---

[7] A tax does not always lead to optimality if the regulator wants to control the size of each firm (Carlton and Loury 1980, 1986).

[8] At the monopoly output, the consumer surplus is the area below the demand curve and above p_m. The producer or monopolist's surplus is the area below p_m and above MC_p to the left of Q_m. The pollution damage can be measured in two ways: (1) it is the area below the marginal pollution cost curve to the left of Q_m, or (2) it is the area between the MC_s and the MC_p curves to the left of Q_m (since the difference between MC_s and MC_p is the marginal pollution cost).

[9] The extra benefit to consumers of tires from expanding output from Q_m to Q_c is the area below the demand curve and above p_c between Q_m and Q_c. The extra benefit to manufacturers is the area below p_c and above MC_p between Q_m and Q_c. The extra pollution damage is the area between MC_s and MC_p between Q_m and Q_c. The sum of the extra consumer surplus and producer surplus minus the extra pollution damage simplifies to Area B minus Area C.

EXAMPLE 6.2

COSTS OF POLLUTION CONTROL BY INDUSTRY

Pollution controls raise costs within industries, and the change in the relative costs of various products causes polluting industries to shrink relative to nonpolluting industries.

Although no accurate, detailed estimates exist of the increase in costs that optimal pollution controls would cause, some estimates have been made of the costs of stringent waste controls. The lower numbers are thought to represent the most likely estimates, while the upper limits represent the worst that could happen to an industry or to a few firms in that industry.

One estimate of the effects of pollution controls on the entire economy is that the Gross National Product would fall by about 1.3 percent if air pollution controls were put on industry and automobiles. All of these estimates should be viewed as quite tentative.

Estimated Costs of Stringent Pollution Control as a Percentage of Current Costs of Production

Industry Group	Percentage
Foods and live animals	1–5%
Beverages and tobacco	1–5
Crude materials	1–10
Cotton, soybeans, hemp, etc.	1–5
Metal ores, paper base stocks, textile fibers, rubber, concentrates	5–10
Mineral fuels, petroleum products	5–10
Oils, fats, waxes	5–10
Manufactured goods	
Textiles, iron and steel, nonferrous metals	5–10
Machinery and transport equipment	5–10

SOURCE: Stahr (1971).

In short, the optimal solution is to properly regulate a competitive industry. In the absence of optimal pollution controls, whether society is better off with a competitive or with a monopolistic industry organization depends on the exact shape of the relevant curves. Regulating a polluting industry causes it to produce less; thus, were the United States to properly regulate pollution, there would be fewer manufacturing and other pollution-causing activities and more service and other relatively nonpolluting activities.

TABLE 6.1	Benefits by Category of the Improvement in Air and Water Quality from 1970 to 1978 (in billions of 1978 dollars)		
	Air	*Water*	*Total*
Gross National Product Increases			
Cost reductions	$ 0.5	$0.8	$ 1.3
Output increases	0.5	0.4	0.9
Total	1.0	1.2	2.2
Utility increases	20.7	3.6	24.3
Total	$21.7	$4.8	$26.5

NOTE: These figures are based on an extensive survey of the available empirical studies.
SOURCE: Freeman (1982, 174-78).

The Net Social Cost of Pollution

New York City 100 years ago was pretty near buried in garbage, sewer spillover, and, most particularly, horse manure. Editorialists called it a "nasal disaster." They wrote that they doubted it ever could be reclaimed for human habitation, but they held some hope the automobile might rescue them from such pollution.[10]

Given the historical failure to regulate pollution (especially before 1970), there is little doubt that society would benefit from better regulation of competitive industries. The passage of the Clean Air Act of 1970, which required a substantial reduction in the emissions of particulate matter from fuel combustion and industrial processes, has resulted in lower pollution levels.

According to the Environmental Protection Agency (EPA), the total suspended particulates (annual national composite average) fell by 13.4 percent from 1970 to 1977, and sulfur dioxide levels fell by 15.7 percent (Freeman 1982, 29–33). Another study by National Economic Research Associates (NERA) in 1980 concluded that federal policy was responsible for a 27 percent reduction in suspended particulates and an 18 percent reduction in sulfur dioxide concentration (Freeman 1982, 29–33).

Table 6.1 shows some rough estimates of the benefits of reducing pollution to the Clean Air Act standards, based on a survey of the literature (Freeman 1982, 173–78). The gains from cost reductions and increased output are probably small compared to the increase in utility or well-being of individuals (including recreation). Of these benefits from air pollution control, fewer deaths and less illness represent 73 percent of the gains;

---

[10] Boyd, L.M. 1984. "Grab Bag." *San Francisco Chronicle,* June 30, 33.

EXAMPLE 6.3

THE COSTLIEST WAY TO CONTROL POLLUTION

Current regulations to control pollution cost more than is necessary to meet environmental quality standards. A dramatic example is provided by a study of various approaches to meeting a short-term standard for nitrogen dioxide from stationary sources of nitrogen oxide emissions in the Chicago Air Quality Control Region. Three approaches are considered that vary greatly in cost. In each case, firms are charged for exceeding the pollution standard. See the table on the opposite page.

Uniform Standard. The traditional approach to pollution control applies a single standard of emission control to all sources of pollution. That is, no firm in a region may produce more than a specified amount of emissions in a given time period. Because the same standard must apply to all sources, it may not be the ideal one in some locations, and very low levels of emissions are allowed. To monitor firms, many monitoring devices are required throughout the region. In the Chicago region, the uniform charge necessary to achieve the standard set is $15,800 per year per pound (of pollutants) per hour.

Source-Category Emission Controls. Tailoring controls to various sources of pollution achieves lower costs than the uniform approach. Depending on location and type of emission, some firms contribute more to the pollution problem than others. Differential standards allow stricter controls to be placed on major contributors to the problem; lower standards can be set for others. In the Chicago region, the overall standard could be achieved if coal-fired boilers are charged $15,800 per year per pound per hour, oil- and gas-fired boilers are charged $15,300, and industrial process units are charged $3,500.

Least-Cost Controls. Because sources of the pollution vary in location and type, the least costly way to achieve a given standard requires different standards at each location. By controlling only the worst sources (where the benefit-cost ratio from controls is highest), costs can be kept relatively low. Here, only the very worst offenders are controlled and each of these may have to meet a different standard. This approach has more diversity in the standards set for firms than either of the other two, and because fewer firms are regulated, fewer monitoring devices are needed.

reduced costs of cleaning and reduced damage to vegetation, 1.3 percent; reduced costs of materials, 3 percent; and increased property values, 9.9 percent. According to the Council on Environmental Quality, the cost incurred in achieving improved air quality benefits in 1978 was approximately $16.6 billion, which is substantially less than the estimated total benefits of $21.7 billion (Freeman 1982, 130–31).

Nearly half (48.9 percent) the benefits from reduced water pollution are in recreation. Improvements in aesthetics, ecology, and property values represent 12.8 percent of the benefits; gains from commercial fisheries, 8.5 percent; and health gains related to drink-

The Annual Effects and Costs of Alternative Pollution Control Approaches

Plan	Number of Sources Controlled	Reduction of Pollution (percent)	Monitoring Costs (in millions)	Payments by Firms (in millions)	Monitoring Costs + Payments by Firms (in millions)
Uniform Standard	534	84%	$305	$414	$719
Source-Category	472	18	66	89	155
Least-Cost	100	3	9	4	13

SOURCE: Seskin, Eugene P, Robert J Anderson, Jr, and Robert O Reid. 1983. "An Empirical Analysis of Economic Strategies for Controlling Air Pollution." *Journal of Environmental Economics and Management* 10:112–24.

With the least-cost approach, the cost of achieving a given emission standard is 1.8 percent as great as the traditional, uniform approach. If individually tailored controls are considered politically infeasible, the compromise source-category controls could be used at only 21.6 percent of the uniform standard costs. The uniform standard achieves reductions in estimated nitrogen oxide emissions rates that are more than 80 percent below the levels of the least-cost approach. This overcontrol is not cost-effective, however.

The administration, monitoring, and enforcement costs are probably lower under a charge system than under the current quantity-control regulatory system. These costs are estimated to range between $0.921 and $2.602 million for an explicit regulatory system and between $0.758 and $1.327 million for the least-cost charge system. Effective regulation currently requires substantial investigation, negotiation with firms, and litigation.

ing water, lower municipal treatment costs, household gains, and reduced industrial supplies costs, 29.8 percent. The Council of Environmental Quality estimates a total benefit of $9.4 billion, which is less than its estimate of annual cost of $10.2 billion. Although the costs appear to outweigh the benefits, both estimates are uncertain, and the benefits do not include gains to human health, recreation or the ecology that may be realized by control of toxic substances and metals (Freeman 1982, 169–71). Moreover, the costs could be substantially reduced if more efficient programs were used (see Example 6.3).

Property Rights

A competitive market produces too much pollution when property rights are not clearly defined. If property rights to air are clearly defined (that is, one has the right to pollute or to be free from pollution), and certain other conditions are met, the **Coase Theorem** (Coase 1960) shows that the optimal levels of pollution and output may be obtained through competitive bargaining. According to this theorem, if the government clearly defines property rights, it may not have to regulate pollution directly to achieve the social optimum.

To illustrate the Coase Theorem, consider two firms that share a small lake. One firm dumps the waste byproducts of its manufacturing process into the lake, causing the other firm to lose boat rentals because many potential customers dislike the smell. Until property rights are clearly defined, the firms may hesitate to negotiate with each other. After all, why should the boat rental firm consider compensating the manufacturer not to pollute if the courts may declare that it has a right to be free from pollution?

If the manufacturing firm has the right to pollute clearly conferred on it by the government or the courts, the boat rental firm can negotiate with it to reduce the amount of pollution dumped into the lake. The boat rental firm is willing to pay to reduce pollution to the point where the marginal benefit it receives (additional rentals) equals the marginal cost to the manufacturing firm (alternate waste disposal costs). If the firms can bargain amicably, the socially optimal level of pollution (where marginal benefit equals marginal cost) is achieved, and income is transferred from the boat rental firm to the manufacturing firm.

Alternatively, if the boat rental firm is given the property rights to the lake so that it can forbid pollution, it is in the manufacturing firm's best interest to purchase the right to pollute up to the point where its marginal benefit equals the marginal cost to the boat rental firm. The level of pollution is optimal as before, but income is transferred from the manufacturer to the boat rental firm. In other words, the level of pollution is not affected by the determination of property rights, but the income distribution is.[11]

This solution does not always work, however, even when property rights are clearly defined. To achieve the optimal outcome, the two sides must be able to bargain successfully with each other. There are at least three important reasons why firms may not be able to do so (Polinsky 1979). First, if transaction costs are very high, it may not pay for the two sides to meet. For example, if a manufacturing plant pollutes the air, thousands, if not millions, of people may be affected. The cost of getting them all together to bargain is generally prohibitive. Second, if firms engage in strategic bargaining behavior (for example, extortion), an agreement may not be reached. Third, if either side lacks information about the costs or benefits of reducing pollution, a nonoptimal outcome may occur.

---

[11] If the income effects are large enough, this redistribution of income can alter the outcome. For example, if being free of pollution is a superior good, then as people become poorer, they will not pay as much to remove pollution.

■ THE COMMONS: A FISHERY

Fisheries are another example of an important market that involves externalities. The lack of properly defined property rights leads to overfishing. As a result, monopolizing a competitive fishery may increase efficiency.

If anyone can fish in a particular area, then no one has property rights to the fish until they are caught. As a result, fishermen have an incentive to catch more fish than if access to a fishery were restricted. Alternatively stated, as in the pollution example, competitive firms look only at their private costs (the cost of catching fish today) and not true social costs (the private costs plus the effect of fishing today on reducing the fish population in the future).

Before studying the economics of fisheries further, it is necessary to examine the biological issues. A mathematical presentation of both biological and economic models appears in Appendix 6A.

Fishery Biology

Consider an ocean-dwelling fish that is initially not caught by humans. The *stock* of fish in the ocean today (the current population) determines the stock of fish next period. The change in the stock of fish between the current period and next period is the *net births:* the fish born this period minus the fish that die this period from natural causes (age, disease, lack of food, and natural predators).[12] Thus, if net births are positive, the stock of fish next period will be larger than it is this period.[13]

Figure 6.2 shows the relationship between the stock of fish, N, and net births (the *flow,* or change, in fish from one period to the next), b, for a typical fish population. The curve shown has a single peak, indicating that when the stock of fish is low, net births are positive but small. As the population grows, fish find each other more easily, and births increase relative to deaths, causing net births to rise. When the stock gets larger, though, deaths increase relative to births, and net births fall. The largest stock of fish that can survive in the long run is called the *carrying capacity* of the ocean. If the stock exceeds the carrying capacity (N^* in Figure 6.2), there is not enough food; deaths exceed births, and net births are negative.

---

[12] For some species, the age distribution of the population may matter (Clark 1976). For others, such as halibut, net births are largely a function of population alone. Age distribution is ignored in the following example.

[13] A bathtub is a physical analogy to such a fish population. Consider a tub that is partially full of water. The amount of water in the tub is the stock of water (and corresponds to the number of fish in the ocean). The flow of water into the tub from the faucet corresponds to new births, and the flow out through the open drain corresponds to natural deaths. The change (flow) in the water level (stock) from one time period to another corresponds to the net births. If more water is flowing into the tub (births) than is flowing out (deaths), then the stock of water (fish) will rise over time.

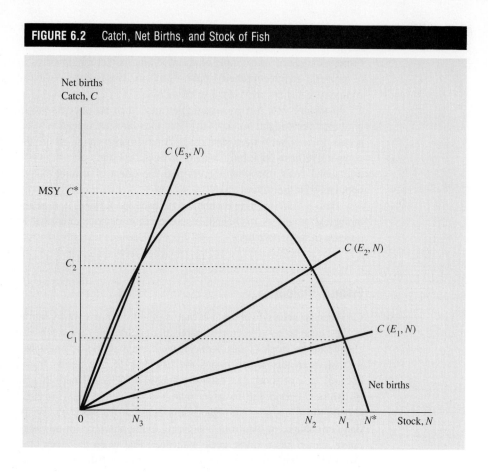

FIGURE 6.2   Catch, Net Births, and Stock of Fish

In the absence of fishing, there are two long-run possibilities: either the number of fish in the sea is zero or N^*. If the population ever falls to zero, this fish will be extinct.[14] If the population starts at any small, positive stock of fish, net births are positive, so the stock grows each period until it reaches N^*. The population cannot grow larger than N^*

---

[14] Two types of ocean fish are caught for commercial purposes. The *demersal* are bottom-feeding fish, which tend to remain confined to a certain area (for example, scallops), while the *pelagic* are not similarly confined (for example, swordfish and whales) and roam the seas. Because the demersals stay in a small area, virtually the only way to make them extinct is to kill them all. The net birth curve hits the horizontal axis when the stock is zero (and at N^*), as shown in Figure 6.2. On the other hand, if the number of pelagic fish drops below some critical level, they may become extinct because fish of reproductive age may have trouble finding each other. The corresponding figure for pelagic fish would show the quadratic curve shifted to the right so that extinction could take place at a positive stock.

because net births would become negative (deaths would outnumber births as the population exceeded the carrying capacity of the ocean). Thus, in the long run, net births equal zero.[15]

Effect of Fishing

In Knoxville, Tennessee, it is illegal to lasso a fish. In California, shooting any animal, except a whale, from an automobile violates the penal code.[16]

Now, let fishermen enter the picture. The number of fish that are caught, C, in a given time period depends on the stock of fish in the ocean, N, and the effort (for example, boats and labor), E, of fishermen. Holding effort constant, the more fish in the sea, the higher the catch; holding the stock of fish constant, the more effort, the higher the catch.

These relationships between catch, effort, and stock of fish are shown in Figure 6.2. The line through the origin labeled $C(E_1,N)$ shows how the catch (shown on the vertical axis) increases, holding effort constant at E_1, as the stock of fish increases (the line is higher as we move to the right). This line starts at the origin because if there are no fish in the sea, none will be caught. The second line through the origin, labeled $C(E_2,N)$, shows what happens as effort is increased from E_1 to E_2. For any given stock of fish, the catch with effort E_2 is greater than with effort E_1.

If fishermen put forth effort E_1 and maintain that effort forever, then season after season, they would catch C_1 fish, which is determined by the intersection of the $C(E_1,N)$ line and the net births curve shown in Figure 6.2. At this point, the catch exactly equals the net births, so that the stock of fish in the ocean remains constant: births exactly equal deaths from natural causes plus deaths from fishing, so that the total population is unchanged.[17]

Maximum Sustainable Yield

Notice that the catch that could be maintained in the long run would be higher, C_2, if effort were raised to E_2. If effort were raised even further to E_3, however, the catch would remain at C_2, as shown in Figure 6.2. At that point, the fishermen are clearly overfishing. They could have the same long-run catch with less effort.

---

[15] In technical jargon, the two population levels, zero and N^*, that can be maintained in the long run are called *stable equilibria*. A stable equilibrium can be illustrated using a bathtub analogy. Suppose that a tub is partially filled with water (corresponding to the stock of fish), water is flowing in through the faucet (births) at a rate equal to that at which it is flowing out through the drain (deaths) so that the net change (net births) in the water level is zero. Then the level of water in the tub (stock of fish) will remain constant over time (in stable equilibrium).

[16] Seuling, Barbara. 1976. *You Can't Eat Peanuts in Church and Other Little-known Laws.* Garden City, N.Y.: Dolphin Books, 57-58.

[17] Where effort is E_1, the stable equilibrium occurs at a population of N_1. If the population were to fall slightly below N_1, net births would exceed the catch, so that the population would grow until it reached N_1. If the population were slightly larger than N_1, net births would be less than C_1, so that the population would shrink until it reached N_1. Thus, in the long run, the population would settle at N_1.

Catch may not rise as effort increases because the stock of fish falls. At E_2 in the figure, the stock of fish is N_2; at E_3, the stock of fish is N_3. When there are relatively many fish in the sea, they can be caught with less effort than when there are relatively few. Notice that if the catch line hits the net birth curve to the left of its peak, further effort reduces the catch. Thus, the largest possible catch is C^*, which corresponds to the peak of the net birth curve and is called the *maximum sustainable yield (MSY)* by biologists.

The *MSY* or *biological optimum* is not the social (or economic) optimum, however. The *MSY,* as the name implies, is merely the largest catch that could be sustained over time. It is a function of only biological factors (just as the production function in the analysis of a manufacturing firm depends only on technological factors). The *MSY* does not take into account the *costs* and *benefits* of the catch. For example, suppose the cost of catching a trout were $100,000 per fish. Although the MSY might be large, society would probably choose not to catch any fish at that cost. Thus, the social (or economic) optimum must take into account the costs and benefits of the catch. As the following discussion shows, social well-being is maximized when the *net social benefits* (social benefits minus social costs) are maximized.

Fishery Economics: Private Versus Social Costs

In their calculation of costs, fishermen include the cost of renting (or owning) a boat, wages for the crew, equipment, materials, and other factors having to do with catching fish in the present. They do not include the cost they impose on future generations by reducing the stock of fish today. If the stock is reduced, fewer fish will be in the sea next season, so the cost of catching a fish will be higher. Thus, by fishing intensively now, fishermen impose costs (externalities) on future generations.

Since society wants fish in the future, the private cost of fishing is less than the social cost, which results in excessive fishing in each time period. Thus, in many fisheries, the annual catch could be increased by *reducing* effort from the competitive level.

To see the intuition behind this conclusion, suppose that each of the fishermen has a private lake. In that case, each one would be careful not to overfish in any one year so as to maintain the supply of fish in future years. In contrast, with equal access to an ocean fishery, fishermen realize that only by catching a fish first can they prevent others from catching it. As a result, they pay no attention to leaving fish for the future. The distinction in these two cases is that in the first, property rights are clearly defined (lakes are owned by individuals), so that there is no externality; in the second, property rights are not clearly defined, so that one can obtain property only by grabbing quickly, thereby imposing an externality (reduced stock of fish) on others.

Static Analysis

Determining the effects of market structure on a fishery begins with a static analysis that compares long-run levels of catch that can be maintained indefinitely. Such an analysis is useful in comparing the optimal catch to a competitive industry's or a monopoly's catch. Assuming that demand and biological factors remain constant, these catch levels (once reached) are steady or constant.

FIGURE 6.3 Fishing Industry

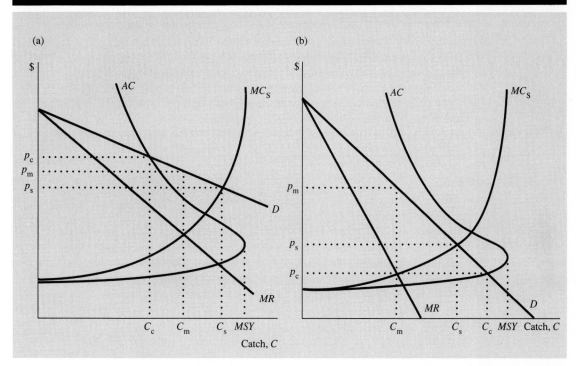

The alternative to the static approach is a dynamic analysis, which studies the sequence of adjustments that fisheries and fishermen make over time. Appendix B describes how the dynamic analysis differs from the simpler static analysis discussed here. When a new policy (or a change in the market structure) occurs, there is an *adjustment period,* during which the catch is different from the static level. If this adjustment period lasts a long time, a comparison of only the static catch levels is misleading.

A Competitive Fishery.   A competitive (or *open-access*) fishery is open to entry by any firm (boat). As in any industry, competitive firms enter a fishery so long as expected economic profits are positive and stop entering when profits are zero, where the private average cost of catching a fish equals the price. If firms enter until profits are driven to zero, each firm operates at the minimum of its average cost curve, where the private marginal and average costs are equal. Thus, the competitive supply curve is the average cost, AC, (and private marginal cost, MC_p) of catching fish.

The private cost of catching fish depends on the cost of factors (boat rentals, wages, material prices) and the ease of catching fish, which is a function of the number of fish in the sea. Even assuming that factor costs remain constant, the private average cost of catching fish rises as the stock of fish falls.

Figure 6.3a shows the private average cost, AC, curve (which is also the private marginal cost curve). As fishing effort increases, the catch, C, increases, in turn raising

EXAMPLE 6.4	# THE END OF ANCHOVY PIZZA AS WE KNOW IT?

Overfishing can cause extinction. An important example of a fishery in danger of being destroyed is that of the Peruvian anchovy, which became the world's largest fishery during the 1960s due to the rapidly increasing demand for fish meal. Its annual catch of approximately 10 million tons was about 15 percent of the total global catch of marine fisheries, including mammals and crustaceans.

As shown in the table on the opposite page, the number of boats increased rapidly in the early 1960s. To offset the increase in boats, Peruvian authorities imposed ever-shorter fishing seasons. By 1972, the fleet's capacity was estimated to be at least twice that necessary to achieve the maximum sustainable yield *(MSY)*.

Biologists warned that this large fleet posed a substantial danger of causing extinction, because every few years an incursion of warm tropical waters (called *El Niño*— the Child—because of its occurrence during the Christmas period) greatly reduces the anchovy population. The prediction was nearly realized in 1973. In spite of the arrival of El Niño and biologists' warnings, the fishery was opened. By March, virtually all the anchovies had disappeared from Peruvian waters. No more fishing was allowed that year, and the government expropriated and nationalized all 100 fishmeal factories and 1,400 boats and established a state company, Pescaperu, to run the industry.

Reportedly, the fleet size has been reduced substantially since then. The catch was 4 million tons in 1974, although it may have included undersized young fish. In 1978 the catch was only 500,000 tons, and the Peruvian authorities had to ban fishing again. By then, Pescaperu ran only 15 factories, having sold equipment from the remainder to other countries. The boats were sold back to the fishermen at reduced prices.

Peru's approach to regulating the fishery was extremely expensive—and probably too little, too late. The government's buying and selling of boats and equipment was done at a loss. Further, restricting the number of fishing days per season was very wasteful, since the large capital expenditure tied up in boats sat idle for much of the year. It is substantially more efficient to limit the number of boats directly.

the cost of catching additional fish. Thus, the average cost curve at first rises as catch rises. Eventually, however, so much effort is put forth (any effort level beyond that associated with the *MSY*) that the stock of fish falls, and additional effort reduces the long-run sustainable catch while driving up costs. As a result, the *AC* curve starts bending back on itself.

A competitive industry's catch, C_c, and price, p_c, are determined by the intersection of supply (the *AC* curve) and demand, *D*. Figures 6.3a and 6.3b show two possible demand curves: one (Figure 6.3b) crosses the supply in the upward sloping section, and the other crosses the supply curve in the backward bending portion.

Even though the demand is greater at every price in Figure 6.3a than in 6.3b, the

	Peruvian Anchovy Fishery		
Year	Number of Boats	Number of Fishing Days	Catch (million tons)
1959	414	294	1.91
1960	667	279	2.93
1961	756	298	4.58
1962	1069	294	6.27
1963	1655	269	6.42
1964	1744	297	8.86
1965	1623	265	7.23
1966	1650	190	8.53
1967	1569	170	9.82
1968	1490	167	10.26
1969	1455	162	8.96
1970	1499	180	12.27
1971	1473	89	10.28
1972	1399	89	4.45
1973	1256	27	1.78
1974	NA	NA	4.00
1975	NA	NA	3.30
1976	NA	NA	4.30
1977	NA	NA	0.80
1978	NA	42	0.50

SOURCE: Clark, Colin W. 1981. "Bioeconomics of the Ocean," *BioScience* 31:231–37 (and especially Table 2, 231). Copyright © 1981 by the American Institute of Biological Sciences.

competitive industry produces less output at a higher price in 6.3a. As demand shifts out, a competitive fishery responds by increasing effort. In the upward sloping section of the supply curve, an increase in demand leads to higher prices and higher output (as happens in most competitive industries). When the demand curve shifts far enough out that the industry is in the backward bending section, a further increase in demand causes price to rise but catch to fall (due to excessive fishing). The Peruvian anchovy industry provides a dramatic example of such behavior. See Example 6.4.

Socially Optimal Fishery.   Figure 6.3a also shows the socially optimal output, C_s, and price, p_s, which are determined by the intersection of demand and the social marginal cost, MC_s.[18] Because the marginal benefit to consumers is equal to the price as shown on the demand curve, social marginal benefit equals social marginal cost at the point where these two curves intersect. If the catch were larger (smaller), the social marginal cost would exceed (be less than) the marginal benefit, and hence society would benefit by reducing (increasing) the catch to C_s. Using the argument from the preceding pollution case, welfare is maximized at C_s as measured by the sum of consumer and producer surplus (taking into account true social costs).

In Figures 6.3a and b, the effort corresponding to the social optimum is less than that of the competitive industry. In Figure 6.3b, where the competitive equilibrium is in the upward sloping section of the supply curve, C_s is less than C_c. In Figure 6.3a, where the competitive equilibrium is in the backward bending section, C_s is greater than C_c, because the greater effort by the competitive industry merely reduces the catch.

Monopoly Fishery. Figure 6.3 also shows the monopoly equilibrium, which is determined by the intersection of the social marginal cost curve, MC_s, and the marginal revenue, MR, curve. The monopolist uses the social marginal cost curve (rather than the private marginal cost curve, AC) because the monopolist takes into account the effect of fishing today on future catch. In contrast to most industries, here the monopolistic output can exceed the competitive output when the competitive equilibrium is in the backward bending section of the supply curve, as shown in Figure 6.3a. In this case, the monopolistic equilibrium is closer to the social optimum than is the competitive equilibrium.[19]

Regulation of Fisheries

Overwork n. *A dangerous disorder affecting high public functionaries who want to go fishing.* — AMBROSE BIERCE

A number of studies find substantial overfishing in many open-access, competitive fisheries, to the extent that some fisheries operate in the backward bending section of the supply curve (less effort would produce more output). For example, the 1973 harvests of groundfish (11.84 million tons), halibut (0.12), and mackerel (3.01) exceeded their respective estimated *MSY*s of 11.73, 0.06, and 2.74 (Bell 1978, 127).

The competitive catch could be obtained with less effort (and capital) in most fisheries. The savings would be substantial: $50 million in the United States and Canadian Pacific salmon fishery, $50 million in Peru's Pacific fishery; and between $50 and $100 million in the North Atlantic cod fishery (Howe 1979, 270–71). Reducing effort to the optimal level would result in even greater savings.

---

[18] The MC_s curve is marginal to the upward sloping section of the AC (private marginal cost) curve. As a result, it lies above the AC curve (in the upward sloping section). The backward bending section of the AC curve represents inefficient production, so no meaningful MC curve corresponds to it (see Appendix 6A). The "optimal" solution discussed here assumes the social discount rate is zero. Appendix B relaxes this assumption.

[19] The monopolistic equilibrium must be less than the social optimum because C_m is determined by the intersection of MR with MC_s, while C_s is determined by the intersection of D with MC_s, MR lies below D, and MC_s is upward sloping.

Most countries, however, have not optimally regulated fishing. In the United States, fishermen are often in charge of regulating their own fisheries (Dewar 1983). Many fisheries overlap state and national boundaries, so that regulating them is particularly complicated. Border clashes have often occurred between countries, such as those concerning Icelandic cod in the North Sea. After the adoption of the 200-mile territorial limits for fishing in 1979, Canada and the United States argued over jurisdictions in four areas: Georges Bank off New England, the Juan de Fuca Strait between Vancouver Island and Washington, waters off the Alaskan Panhandle, and the Beaufort Sea off northeastern Alaska. At one point, Canada banned U.S. commercial fishermen from its waters, and the United States reciprocated.[20] Much of the struggle concerns different attitudes toward conservation (with the United States generally regulating less stringently).

There are many ways to reduce overfishing. Assigning property rights could eliminate the externality problem, but unfortunately, this solution is not viewed as practical in most ocean fisheries. The government can control a competitive fishery by taxing or direct quantity controls.

Taxing fishermen per fish would cause the demand curve—as perceived by the fishermen—to shift down by the amount of the tax. If the tax were set optimally, the perceived demand curve would intersect the AC curve at the socially optimal catch, C_s, so that the taxed competitive fishery would produce the optimal output. The average excess cost from overfishing is estimated, at a minimum, to be 20 percent on about 60 percent of the world's marine fishing. As a result, the optimal tax on international marine fisheries would generate annual revenues on the order of $2.5 billion.[21] The government could also tax boats, so that fishermen would internalize the externality. Again, an appropriately set tax could reduce the problem.

Alternatively, the government could directly regulate the number of boats, thereby preventing overfishing. Any of these approaches is superior to restrictions on the length of the fishing season or on the catch, which may result in a large number of boats sitting idle for much of the year (excessive capital investment). Unfortunately, many governments rely on such inefficient regulations (see Example 6.4).

An Example: Lobsters.   The American lobster is overfished in both the United States and Canada because of common property (externality) problems. The social returns to regulating would be large relative to the value of the catch.

Three types of externalities arise in lobstering (Wilson 1977):

1. Crowding: fishermen competing in a small area cause congestion, getting in each others' way.

2. Age or size of harvest: in an attempt to catch lobsters before others, fishermen catch lobsters below the optimal size (age).

3. Size of stock: the stock is reduced below the optimal level (a problem made worse by catching females bearing roe).

---

[20] "Fish Fuss: A Falling-Out Between Friends." 1978. *Time*, June 19.

[21] These numbers are based on the work of Cooper as summarized in Dasgupta (1982, 137–38).

Only comparatively recently has the externality problem become obvious to all. At the end of World War II, there was concern that postwar prices for lobsters would decline, and lobstermen would lose money unless new technology were introduced (Dewar 1983, 11–12). Instead, the industry thrived, and the number of fishermen grew. From World War II through the mid-1960s, fishermen in New England (where 91 percent of all American lobsters in the United States are landed) depended heavily on lobsters. In 1946, 4200 lobstermen used 356,000 traps to catch 23 million tons of lobsters in New England. By 1960 there were 6600 lobstermen, using 710,000 traps to catch 29 million tons. By 1965 the number of lobstermen fell (5800), but the number of traps increased (790,000), while the total catch remained at 29 million tons. In 1982 the catch reached 37 million tons.

The Fish and Wildlife Act of 1956 provided loans for financing the operation, maintenance, replacement, and repair of fishing vessels and gear for owners unable to obtain loans elsewhere. A majority of the loans under the program (from 1957–1973) went to small boats, especially for Maine lobstermen. In other words, instead of restricting entry, the federal government encouraged it (Dewar 1983, 66–67). While the states acted to regulate the lobster fisheries (including the use of licenses), the federal government did little until 1973, when it started to protect U.S. fishermen from foreign competition for offshore lobsters (a relatively minor share of all lobsters). In any case, the 200-mile limit (1976) and other protection for U.S. fishermen hardly solves the common-property problem—it merely causes the excess fishing to be entirely domestic.

Empirical Evidence of Overfishing.   A number of studies show that the rewards of optimal regulation would be large. Table 6.2 summarizes the results of three studies of the period (1961–1971) when the severity of the overfishing problem became obvious. These studies conclude that the actual catch was substantially more than the optimal catch in both Canada and New England. The competitive catch is nearly 50 percent too large in New England and 79 percent too large in Port Maitland, Canada. In New England, the competitive catch was close to *MSY*: 98 percent according to Bell (1972). In contrast, the competitive catch in Port Maitland was well below *MSY,* as shown in Figure 6.4 (on page 144). Nonetheless, in both cases society could gain substantially by reducing effort (and catch). The three studies show that between two and eight times too much effort (too many pots) is used (see Table 6.2).

In Port Maitland, the annual resource savings (value of savings on effort less value of reduced catch) would be 62 percent of the total value. The optimal tax per lobster would be about 56 percent of the price in Port Maitland and 47 percent in Maine, indicating substantial distortions in the absence of the tax. The alternative optimal tax per pot would be 1.26 times the private cost in Port Maitland and 0.83 times that cost in Maine, showing that the private costs grossly underestimate the true social costs. In Maine, the total taxes raised at the optimum would have been $8.9 million in 1971.

One reassuring finding is that the lobster population apparently can grow rapidly, so that if controls were introduced, the population would quickly reach the optimal level. As the Port Maitland study shows, in the free-access, competitive equilibrium, the catch (which equals net births) is 53 percent of the stock. In other words, if fishing were banned for one year, the population would increase by over 50 percent.

TABLE 6.2   Optimal and Competitive Lobstering

Location	Port Maitland, Canada	New England	Maine
Year of comparison	1961	1965	1971
Interest rate	6	0	5
Ratio (competitive to optimal)			
Stock	0.82	—	—
Catch	1.79	1.45	1.48
Effort (pots)	4.05	2.06	8.17
Catch/effort (competition)	2.93	2.81	1.80
Catch/effort (optimal)	6.65	3.97	4.95
Optimal Tax as a ratio of the			
Price of fish	0.56	—	0.47[a]
Private cost of a pot	1.26[a]	—	0.83

NOTES: All three studies find that yield depends on water temperature and possibly other factors (for example, season, length). The numbers above are based on average values for these variables. The optimal taxes in Reddy are based on an interest rate of zero. The annual resource savings in Henderson and Tugwell (value of trap savings less value of reduced catch) is $202,173 (62 percent of the total value). Henderson and Tugwell find that the actual average stock (2,467 thousand pounds) and catch (1,183 thousand pounds) for 1959–1963 were very close to the estimated competitive stock (2,490) and catch (1,330). Reddy, similarly, finds that the estimated catch (26.5 million pounds) was virtually identical to actual (regulated) landings (26.5).

[a]Calculation based on numbers in the article.

SOURCES: Bell (1972), Reddy (1974), and Henderson and Tugwell (1979).

Private versus Common Property

Overfishing of lobsters results from the externality caused by the lack of clearly defined property rights. If property rights were clearly allocated, individual fishermen would take the true social costs (including the effect of today's catch on future supply) into account, thereby eliminating the excessive fishing problem. A test of this assertion is possible using data from inshore lobster fisheries in Maine (Wilson 1977).

Certain small areas (typically harbors) of Maine have been effectively appropriated by groups of fishermen for their sole use. By preventing fishermen from other areas from "poaching," group property rights are created. In some cases, they have also limited the growth of the group, thereby creating a large partnership.

A comparison of behavior in private-access fisheries with limits on the size of the group and public-access fisheries shows that externalities are reduced by establishing property rights, as shown in Table 6.3 (on page 145).[22]

---

[22] The private and public ownership areas were adjacent, so temperature and other variables were unlikely to vary greatly between the two types of areas.

FIGURE 6.4   Lobsters

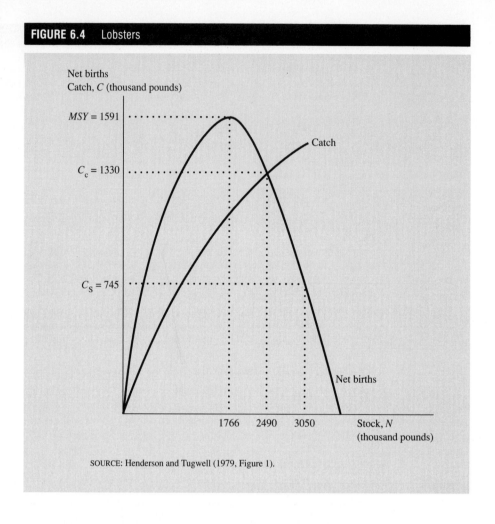

SOURCE: Henderson and Tugwell (1979, Figure 1).

- More lobsters are caught per trap haul in the controlled-access (private-ownership) fishery than in the public-access fishery (0.98 versus 0.61), because of the frequent, nonoptimal placement of traps (to establish limited property rights) and lower stock in the latter.

- The average weight produced per trap haul is greater with controlled access (0.54) than with uncontrolled access (0.32) because undersized lobsters are not caught in the controlled areas.

- The greater age of the lobsters in the controlled area is also shown by their slightly greater length (89.98 versus 87.89 mm). As a result, the probability of females reaching mature age or size is slightly greater in the controlled area.

TABLE 6.3	Private Versus Common Property in Maine Lobster Fisheries	
	Ownership	
	Private	*Common*
Weight per trap haul (kgm)	0.54	0.32
Number of lobsters per trap haul	0.98	0.61
Weight per lobster (kgm)	0.55	0.53
Length of lobster (mm)	89.98	87.89
Average gross income of fishers ($)	22,929[a]	16,449

NOTE: All differences between the two types of ownership are statistically significant at the .05 level.

[a] Income of fishers in privately controlled areas was adjusted to remove the effect of higher prices in seasons in which their output remained high (while it fell off in the commons).

SOURCE: Wilson (1977, especially Table 12.1).

- The controlled-access fisheries exhibit less seasonality than those with uncontrolled access. The sudden increase in the number of legal-sized lobsters at molting time produces massive entry by fishermen in the uncontrolled areas. During the molting season (August 1 to December 31), a relatively small but statistically significant difference appears in the catch per trap haul in the controlled (0.98) versus uncontrolled areas (0.70). During the other two seasons (January 1 to April 30 and May 1 to July 31), catch per trap haul falls off drastically in the uncontrolled areas (0.59 and 0.41), but not in the controlled areas (0.91 and 0.86).

- As a result of large stocks and less wasted effort due to crowding, fishermen in the controlled areas have higher incomes than those in the uncontrolled areas (where rents are dissipated): $22,929 versus $16,449. Apparently they can control within-group externalities.

Thus, by at least partially limiting entry to a fishery, fishermen can gain substantially; they have a clear incentive to limit fishing rights. Another approach, with clearly defined property rights, that may be viable in the future is farming lobsters, either in the ocean or in tanks on land.[23]

■ OTHER INDUSTRIES WITH COMMON PROPERTY

The common property problems that arise in fishing also occur in many other industries, among them the following (Weitzman 1974):

- *Gathering natural harvests:* hunting, grazing, and primitive agriculture.
- *Shared resources from common pools:* petroleum, water, or other fluids or gases extracted from common pools. Owners of wells drawing from a common pool

---

[23] "In a Pinch: Ranches for Lobster Next?" 1979. *Philadelphia Inquirer,* March 27, 3-B.

compete to remove the substance most rapidly, thereby gaining ownership. This competition lowers fluid pressure, making further removal more difficult.

- *Research:* the stock of potential results in a specific research area (pool of knowledge) is less than directly proportional to the research effort being applied, due to decreasing returns. Too many firms may be trying to make the same discovery, because the pool of knowledge is similar to a common-access fishery. This effect may lead to overinvestment in research. Alternatively, because it is often not possible to maintain property rights in information, there may be underinvestment in research. Which effect dominates is an empirical question, as discussed in Chapter 19.

- *Commercial transportation lines:* freight, communications routes, pipelines, and so forth. Where property rights are not clearly defined, many firms may compete (excessively) for these lines.

- *Queueing:* commuter congestion and job search. The presence of others creates externalities. Indeed, the analysis of highway congestion is very similar to the fishery analysis above. Figure 6.3 could be relabeled with the number of people using the highway at a particular time on the horizontal axis and the total number of cars to complete the trip on the vertical axis. The backward bending supply curve shows that at first, as the number of drivers increases, the total number of people completing the trip in a given time increases. Eventually, however, extra drivers get into each others' way, causing fewer trips to be completed.

■ SUMMARY

Where property rights are not clearly defined, negative externalities usually cause a competitive industry to produce at excessive levels. Since monopolies produce at lower levels than competitive industries, their output may be closer to the optimal level if there are externalities. This chapter considers two important examples of markets with externalities.

Where property rights are not clearly established or high transaction costs prevent negotiated solutions, polluting firms do not pay for the damage they cause. Since competitive firms can ignore the cost to others, they produce too much pollution. Each competitive firm produces where price equals its private marginal cost, which is less than the social marginal cost. The latter includes the costs of pollution damage, and the gap between social and private marginal costs is a measure of the externality.

A monopoly, on the other hand, charges a price above private marginal cost. Thus, it is possible—but not certain—that a monopoly produces closer to the socially optimal level of output and pollution than an unregulated competitive industry.

A government with enough information and the desire to regulate appropriately can induce a competitive industry to produce the socially optimal level of output. For example, if the government sets a tax equal to the marginal cost of pollution, so that the competitive firms' after-tax private marginal cost equals the social marginal cost, the taxed competitive industry produces the socially optimal level of output and pollution: the externality has been internalized.

Where negotiation costs are low, if the government assigns clear property rights, the social optimum is obtained through bargaining without the need for further government intervention. Negotiation costs are high, however, if many people are harmed by pollution.

Where property rights are not clearly defined and the government does not optimally regulate, resources are misallocated. Too much of society's resources goes to polluting industries and not enough to nonpolluting industries.

A lack of clearly defined property rights also causes problems in markets with commons, such as fisheries. Overfishing occurs as fishermen try to appropriate property rights by catching fish before anyone else. As in the pollution case, each fisherman's private marginal cost is less than the social marginal cost. It is possible that a monopolistic fishery produces closer to the social optimum than a competitive fishery.

If a government has enough information and the will, it can regulate a competitive fishery to obtain the socially optimal catch. One approach is to tax fishermen so that their private marginal costs equal the social marginal cost. This approach causes fishermen to internalize the externality. Another approach is to assign or sell property rights by creating private fishing areas.

■ Key Terms

Coase Theorem
externalities
internalizing the externality

market failures
negative externality
positive externality
private marginal cost

property rights
public good
social marginal cost

■ Discussion questions

1. Reducing pollution reduces manufacturing output relative to that of the service sector. Should we regulate pollution given this change in output mix?
2. If government does not know enough to regulate pollution optimally, what should it do?
3. Can there be too little pollution? Why or why not?
4. What are the pros and cons of using regulations or taxes to control pollution? Describe a cost-effective method to deal with auto pollution. What desirable properties would your program have?
5. Can pollution problems be solved by bargaining between polluters and victims? If so, under what conditions?
6. Is there too little or too much commercial fishing? Why? What regulations would you propose to deal with this problem?

■ Problems

1. Suppose, in Figure 6.1, the monopolist is taxed at a rate equal to the marginal social cost of pollution. What happens to output, price, and social welfare? Does the deadweight loss from monopoly increase or decrease? Can you suggest a better way to regulate a monopoly?
2. Redraw Figure 6.1, and directly below draw another diagram with $ on the vertical axis and Q on the horizontal axis (draw the diagrams so that the horizontal axes line up). On the new graph, draw the profits of the monopoly (remember it reaches its peak where $MR = MC_p$). Now add the total cost of pollution curve and the monopolist's profit curve if it must pay a pollution tax. What is the relationship between the three curves in your bottom diagram?

Answers to odd-numbered problems are given at the back of the book.

3. Draw a backward bending competitive supply curve for a fishery (see Figure 6.3). Now add a demand curve that intersects the supply curve more than once (that is, it crosses in both the upward sloping and backward bending sections). Where does the industry operate? Are all the equilibria stable?

4. Suppose that only one firm (a monopsonist) buys the catch from all boats. Compare the long-run monopsony equilibrium to the social, competitive, and monopolistic equilibria, using a diagram similar to Figure 6.3.

5. Can a per-fish tax in a competitive industry increase output and reduce consumer cost? Illustrate using a graph, and explain.

6. Suppose one firm has a monopoly on selling boats for use in a competitive fishery. How would this equilibrium compare to the competitive, socially optimal, and monopolistic equilibria described in the chapter?

■ References

Bell, Frederick W. 1972. "Technological Externalities and Common Property Resources." *Journal of Political Economy* 80:148–58.

———. 1978. *Food from the Sea: The Economics and Politics of Ocean Fisheries.* Boulder, Colo.: Westview Press.

Berck, Peter, and Jeffrey M. Perloff. 1984. "An Open-Access Fishery with Rational Expectations." *Econometrica* 52:489–506.

Carlton, Dennis W., and Glenn C. Loury. 1980. "The Limitation of Pigovian Taxes as a Long-Run Remedy for Externalities." *Quarterly Journal of Economics* 95:559–66.

———. 1986. "The Limitation of Pigovian Taxes as a Long-Run Remedy for Externalities: An Extension of Results." *Quarterly Journal of Economics* 101:631–34.

Clark, Colin W. 1976. *Mathematical Bioeconomics.* New York: John Wiley and Sons.

———. 1981. "Bioeconomics of the Ocean." *BioScience* 31:231-37.

Coase, Ronald H. 1960. "The Problem of Social Cost." *The Journal of Law and Economics* 3:1–44.

Dasgupta, Partha. 1982. *The Control of Resources.* Cambridge: Harvard University Press.

Dewar, Margaret E. 1983. *Industry in Trouble: The Federal Government and New England Fisheries.* Philadelphia: Temple University Press.

Freeman, A. Myrick, III. 1982. *Air and Water Pollution Control: A Benefit-Cost Assessment.* New York: John Wiley and Sons.

Henderson, J.V., and M. Tugwell. 1979. "Exploitation of the Lobster Fishery: Some Empirical Results." *Journal of Environmental Economics and Management* 6:287-96.

Howe, Charles W. 1979. *Natural Resource Economics (Issues, Analysis, and Policy).* New York: John Wiley and Sons.

Polinsky, A. Mitchell. 1979. "Controlling Externalities and Protecting Entitlements: Property Right, Liability Rule, and Tax-Subsidy Approaches." *Journal of Legal Studies* 8:1–48.

Reddy, Bernard J. 1974. "The New England Lobster Pot Fishery: An Empirical Study." Department of Economics, Massachusetts Institute of Technology.

Seskin, Eugene P., Robert J. Anderson, Jr., and Robert O. Reid. 1983. "An Empirical Analysis of Economic Strategies for Controlling Air Pollution." *Journal of Environmental Economics and Management* 10:112-24.

Spence, A. Michael. 1973. "Blue Whales and Applied Control Theory," in H. W. Gottinger, ed. *Systems Approaches and Environmental Problems.* Gottingen: Vandehoeck and Ruprecht.

Stahr, Elvis J. 1971. "Antipollution Policies, Their Nature and Their Impact on Corporate Profits," in Kenneth E. Boulding, Elvis J. Stahr, Solomon Fabricant, and Martin R. Gainsbrugh, eds., *Economics of Pollution.* New York: New York University Press.

Weitzman, Martin L. 1974. "Free Access vs. Private Ownership as Alternative Systems for Managing Common Property." *Journal of Economic Theory* 8:225—34.

Wilson, James A. 1977. "A Test of the Tragedy of the Commons," in Garrett Hardin and John Baden, eds., *Managing the Commons.* San Francisco: W. H. Freeman, 96–111.

A MATHEMATICAL MODEL OF FISHERIES ECONOMICS

A well-known model of fishing, created by the biologist M. B. Schaefer, has been used to describe the net births of halibut, lobsters, and other fish populations (Clark 1976, 15f). This model assumes that the fish population follows a simple logistic growth curve, which implies that net births, b, are a quadratic function of the stock of fish, N.[24] Thus,

$$b = gN\left(1 - \frac{N}{K}\right),$$ (6A.1)

where g is the intrinsic growth rate of the population (the rate at which the population grows if it is initially nearly zero) and K is the environmental carrying capacity or *saturation level*. If the stock of fish, N, exceeds K, net births become negative (deaths outnumber births). Thus, K is the largest sustainable population. This function has the quadratic shape shown in Figure 6.2. It intersects the horizontal (stock of fish) axis at zero and at K.

As discussed in the chapter, the catch, C, is an increasing function of both effort, E, and the stock of fish in the sea. For simplicity, assume that the catch relationship is linear in both E and N:

$$C(E,N) = \alpha EN,$$ (6A.2)

where α is a positive constant. Figure 6.2 shows that the catch for a given level of effort, E_1, starts at the origin and rises as N increases. This line has a slope of $\partial C / \partial N = kE_1$.

If the level of effort E_1 is put forth every season, then C_1 fish are always caught, and the fish population is N_1, where this equilibrium (N_1, C_1) is determined by the equality between the catch, Equation 6A.2, and the net births, Equation 6.1. In general, equating

---

[24] This specific formulation was first proposed as a population model by P. F. Verhulst in 1838 (see Clark 1976, 11).

the left-hand sides of these equations allows a solution for the equilibrium (long-run) population N as a function of E:

$$N = K\left(1 - \frac{\alpha}{g}E\right). \qquad (6A.3)$$

Since α, K, and g are constants, N is a linear function of E (in (N,E) space). The slope of this line $(\partial N / \partial E)$ is $-\alpha K / g$, which shows that as effort rises, the stock of fish in the ocean falls. To derive this relationship graphically, imagine increasing the slope of the straight catch line in Figure 6.2 (that is, increasing effort), causing the intersection between that line and the net birth curve to move to the left, implying a lower population.

To determine the equilibrium (long-run) catch as a function of effort, substitute the long-run population relationship determined by Equation 6A.3 into the catch Equation 6A.2:

$$C = \alpha K E\left(1 - \frac{\alpha}{g}E\right). \qquad (6A.4)$$

That is, the long-run catch is a quadratic function of effort and this relationship could be plotted in (C,E) space.

Now differentiate Equation 6A.4 with respect to E, set that derivative equal to zero, and solve for the level of effort, E^*, which maximizes the long-run catch:

$$E^* = \frac{g}{2\alpha}. \qquad (6A.5)$$

Substituting E^* into Equation 6A.4, gives the maximum sustainable yield (MSY):

$$C^* = \frac{gK}{4}. \qquad (6A.6)$$

Figure 6.2 shows C^*. Substituting E^* into Equation 6A.3, shows that the stock of fish corresponding to C^* is $K/2$.

If the cost of a unit of effort is a constant, w, then the total cost of effort is wE. Calculating the marginal cost requires knowing how much extra effort is needed to catch one more fish permanently. Totally differentiating Equation 6A.4 with respect to C and E reveals the following:

$$\frac{dE}{dC} = \frac{g}{\alpha K(g - 2\alpha E)}. \qquad (6A.7)$$

Thus, the social marginal cost is $w(dE/dC) = wg/[\alpha K(g - 2\alpha E)]$.

The average cost is total cost divided by output, or wE/C. Again, Equation 6A.4 shows that average cost $= wg/[\alpha K(g - \alpha E)]$. As discussed in the chapter, the average cost curve is also the private marginal cost curve; that is, it includes the out-of-pocket costs (the direct costs of effort) but ignores the effect of effort today on stock and catch tomorrow. Thus, the private marginal cost curve is less than the social marginal cost curve, because it ignores the externality that extra fishing today creates in the future.

To show that the private marginal cost is the same as the average cost curve, use Equation 6A.2 to obtain $E = C/\alpha N$. Thus, the private marginal cost, which ignores the indirect effect of effort on the stock of fish, is $w(\partial E/\partial C) = w/\alpha N = wg/[\alpha K(g - \alpha E)]$ (using Equation 6A.3), which is the same as the average cost curve.

The social and private marginal cost curves are shown in Figures 6.3a and 6.3b. The private marginal cost curve (or average cost curve) is the competitive supply curve.[25] The competitive supply curve may be derived more simply, however.

In a competitive environment, fishermen enter the industry until profits are driven to zero. Each fisherman catches C/E fish (if E is the number of fishermen) and sells the fish at price p, so that in competitive equilibrium, $pC/E = w$ (total revenues equal the total cost of effort). From Equation 6A.2, $C/E = \alpha N$, so this zero-profit condition can be rewritten as $N = w/\alpha p$. From Equations 6.1 and 6.2 and this zero-profit condition, the supply curve is

$$C = \frac{gw}{\alpha p}\left(1 - \frac{w}{\alpha pK}\right).\qquad (6A.8)$$

The supply curve is zero for $p < w/K$, then increases to the maximum sustainable yield at $p = 2w/K$, and then is backward bending (the catch falls as the price rises) for $p \geq 2w/K$, as shown in Figures 6.3a and 6.3b.

---

[25] The social marginal cost curve is marginal to the private marginal cost *(AC)* curve. Average cost is wE/C, so total cost is wE. Social marginal cost is the partial derivative of wE with respect to C.

DYNAMIC ANALYSIS OF A FISHERY

APPENDIX 6B

The chapter's analysis of a fishery concentrates on maximizing sustainable economic rent (net economic revenue); that is, it seeks the policy that could be maintained forever and that would maximize social benefit less social cost. That analysis ignores the opportunity cost of capital—it implies that the future counts as much as the present.

The weight that society puts on the future compared to the present is called the *social discount rate*. It is like an interest rate: it tells us how much more a dollar is worth today compared to its worth in the future.[26] Thus, the static analysis of the chapter is appropriate when the social discount rate is zero. Some social philosophers contend that using a social discount rate of zero is appropriate: we should leave as many resources for our children's children as we have. It is not possible, however, for individuals and firms to borrow at zero interest rates.

Intuitively, the higher the interest rate, the less likely is a conservation policy. If you knew with certainty that you would be dead next year from an illness, you would put a very low value on consumption next year. Your personal discount rate (interest rate) would be nearly infinite; you would be unwilling to loan money for repayment in a year at any finite rate of interest and would prefer to consume all your wealth this year, saving none for the future. Thus, as the social discount rate rises (the future is valued less), the socially optimal catch rises.

To see the logic behind a dynamic analysis, consider the following experiment. Suppose society was fishing at level E_A and was considering reducing effort to level E_B. At first, the reduction in effort causes the catch to fall. Eventually, however, if society has been overfishing, the catch rises as the stock grows. Thus, in the short run, society has a smaller catch, but in the long run the catch is greater (Spence 1973). Whether it pays for society to reduce effort in this fashion depends on how it values goods today relative to goods in the future.

---

[26] If you were asked to loan a bank money for a year with a government guarantee that the same amount of money would be returned at that time, you would probably be unwilling to make such a loan. Unless the bank will return more money next year than it borrows, you would prefer to use the money yourself this year. If the bank will return $1.05 for every $1 it borrows, the annual interest rate is 5 percent. If society values resources tomorrow the same as it does today, the social discount rate is zero.

Dynamic Fishing Model

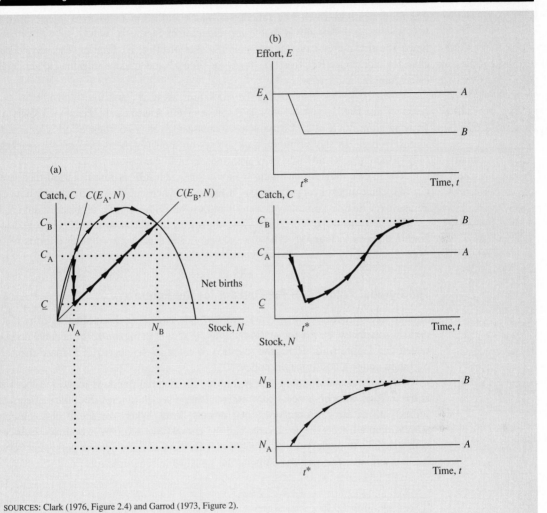

(b)

Effort, E

(a)

Catch, C $C(E_A, N)$ $C(E_B, N)$

Net births

Catch, C

Stock, N

Stock, N

SOURCES: Clark (1976, Figure 2.4) and Garrod (1973, Figure 2).

Graphic Analysis

In Figure a, the long-run catch and stock at effort levels E_A and E_B are shown in a diagram that illustrates how catch is a function of stock and effort (similar to Figure 6.3). The two policies are also shown in the top diagram in Figure b, which plots effort versus time. The first policy calls for maintaining level of effort E_A forever. The second policy calls for reducing effort from E_A to E_B at time t^* and maintaining that lower level of effort forever.

When effort first falls to E_B, the stock remains at N_A and the catch falls to $\underline{C}$ (the point on line $C(E_B, N)$ at $N = N_A$). Because of this lower catch, the stock slowly starts growing from N_A to N_B. As the stock increases, given a constant effort, E_B, the catch gradually rises (as shown by the dark arrows on the $C(E_B, N)$ curve) until it reaches C_B (where the $C(E_B, N)$ line intersects with the net birth curve).

The middle diagram in Figure b shows that catch falls at first to $\underline{C}$ and then rises to C_B. The same adjustment path shown in Figure a, where the dark arrows show how catch adjusts over time, is also shown using dark arrows in the middle diagram of Figure b.

The adjustment path of the stock is shown using light arrows in Figure a and in the bottom diagram in Figure b. The stock steadily rises from N_A to N_B after effort is reduced from E_A to E_B.

The Optimal Tradeoff of the Present for the Future

Should society reduce effort from E_A to E_B? The preceding discussion suggests that the optimal solution when the social discount rate is zero is to maximize sustainable economic rent (C_s in Figure 6.3). Here, the sacrifice of catch in the short run is more than offset by future gains: a conservation policy.

When the social discount rate is infinite, the optimal policy is to exploit the fishery at the level of an open-access, competitive fishery, which ignores the future effects of its actions, taking into account only their current costs. When the social discount rate is infinite, future effects are irrelevant, and the competitive solution is optimal. In societies with a positive (though typically small) social discount rate, the optimal policy lies between the competitive effort and maximizing the sustainable economic rent.[27]

---

[27] See Clark (1976) and the articles he cites for analyses of optimal policies for finite social discount rates. See Berck and Perloff (1984) for a model of competitive fisheries where firms discount the future using finite interest rates and the cost of entry depends on the rate of entry. Both the competitive and socially optimal solutions differ from the steady states discussed in the chapter when the interest rate or social discount rate is greater than zero.

PART 4

OTHER MARKET STRUCTURES

CHAPTER 7

U.S. MARKET STRUCTURE, MERGER ACTIVITY, AND ENTRY BARRIERS

Science, at bottom, is really anti-intellectual. It always distrusts pure reason, and demands the production of objective facts.

—H. L. MENCKEN

So far, the primary focus has been on theory—for example, the forces that influence how firms form and how they behave in a perfectly competitive or monopolistic environment have been described. This chapter's focus is on facts about the structure of the U.S. economy. The chapter serves as an empirical background for subsequent chapters, which explore theoretical models of market structure in which the level of competition lies between perfect competition and monopoly. To understand the relevance of these models, it is necessary to have some idea of the degree of competition in the various sectors of the U.S. economy. Most empirical studies in industrial organization focus on manufacturing, and this chapter examines manufacturing in some detail.

One of the key determinants of market structure in most models is the ease with which new firms can be created. New firms can come into existence in two ways. First, they can result from the amalgamation or dismemberment of existing firms. For example, two firms can join together through merger or, conversely, one firm can split itself into two or more separate firms. Second, a group of investors can raise money and start a new firm. Both ways of creating firms are important, although they have different implications for market behavior. At least until recently, neither way has received much study. The recent merger wave has raised policy questions about the desirability of massive consolidations among existing firms and has stimulated study of mergers.

The chapter is organized as follows. First, it provides a brief overview of the U.S. economy, describes its most important sectors, and provides evidence on the degree of competition in various sectors of the economy. Neither perfect competition nor monopoly describes most industries. Instead, a typical firm has some market power and at the same time does respond to competition from rivals. Next the chapter examines how firms are formed. First, mergers of existing firms are analyzed. The chapter documents the historical trends in merger activity and explains how such activity can promote cost minimization and reduce the internal conflicts of interests that were discussed in Chapter 2. Second, the creation or loss of firms through the process of entry and exit is analyzed. The models of competition and monopoly assume the extremes of zero entry cost and prohibitive entry cost respectively. A discussion of entry barriers and their measurement and importance prepares for subsequent chapters, which examine more realistic models of competition that rely heavily on the concept of entry barriers.

■ DESCRIPTION OF THE U.S. ECONOMY

The U.S. economy is composed of many different sectors. Table 7.1 reports the composition of gross national product (GNP), which measures the total value of goods and services produced in the economy, since 1950. The table indicates that manufacturing is the largest sector, comprising about 20 percent of GNP, and also that the relative importance of the various sectors has not changed dramatically in the last 30 to 40 years. Still, some trends are evident. Agriculture, forestry, and fisheries have declined, as has mining. Services have grown (especially recently), as has finance, real estate, and insurance. Although the sector shares of output value do not show enormous changes over time, there have been sizable shifts in employment. Because machines have become more productive, manufacturing output is now produced with fewer employees. For example,

TABLE 7.1   Composition of GNP by Industry Sector

	Percent				
Industry Sector	*1950*	*1960*	*1970*	*1980*	*1987*
Agriculture, forestry, fishery	5	4	3	2	2
Mining	6	6	6	4	3
Construction	8	10	7	5	5
Manufacturing	21	20	21	21	22
Transportation and public utilities	8	8	8	9	9
Wholesale and retail trade	15	15	15	16	17
Finance, real estate and insurance	10	12	13	15	15
Services	11	11	12	14	16
Government	14	14	14	12	11

NOTE: Column totals do not add to 100 because of rounding and omission of miscellaneous industry categories.

SOURCE: *Economic Report of the President* (1989, Table B-11).

TABLE 7.2   Distribution of Establishments and Eployees By Enterprise Size

Enterprise Size (number of employees)	Percent of Establisments	Percent of Employees
0–19	83.4	25.2
20–99	9.9	19.8
100–499	3.2	16.7
500–4,999	1.9	18.3
5,000 or more	1.5	19.8
TOTAL	100.0	100.0

SOURCE: Reprinted with permission of The Free Press, a division of Macmillan Inc., from Job Creation in America by David L. Birch, © 1987 by The Free Press.

the fraction of the nonagricultural labor force in manufacturing declined from about 34 percent in 1950 to about 18 percent by the end of 1988 (*Economic Report of the President*, 1989, Table B-43).

Overall Market Structure

The industry sectors differ considerably in their market structures. The most detailed data available are for manufacturing, but some generalizations can be made about the other sectors. Agriculture and construction are generally regarded as being composed of numerous firms, and entry is generally considered easy. Mining is affected by the availability of natural resources, which may limit the location of competing firms. Transportation has become more competitive since government regulation of railroads, trucks, and airlines has been relaxed. Wholesale and retail trade is generally competitive, and entry is relatively easy. Sometimes, however, geographic areas may be characterized by the presence of only a few large wholesalers or retailers. In such cases, one should investigate whether the threat of entry or expansion by competitors is sufficient to make the industry behave competitively in those areas.

The entire economy is also affected by various government regulations that influence price: agriculture has price-control and entry-restriction programs, construction is affected by restrictive building codes that raise costs, public utilities are directly regulated, and services are affected by numerous laws that require licensing or otherwise limit entry. The stated reason for much regulation is to protect consumers, but in fact regulations may often harm consumers and protect the regulated industry. This point is developed more fully in Chapter 23.

Aggregate Concentration

The U.S. economy as a whole comprises about 7 million companies, roughly 90 percent of which employ fewer than 20 people (Birch 1987, 7). Even though they are numerous, these small companies account for a relatively small share of total employment, as Table 7.2 indicates.

Table 7.3 shows that the top 200 firms (in terms of shipments) accounted for 21 percent of nonfarm employment and 34 percent of the assets of nonfinancial corporations

TABLE 7.3	Aggregate Concentration in the Private Sector by Employment and Assets			
	Share of Nonfarm, Private Sector Employment (%)			
Top Firms	*1970*	*1975*	*1980*	*1984*
25	10	10	9	7
100	19	18	17	15
200	25	23	22	21
	Share of Assets of Nonfinancial Corporations (%)			
25	17	17	16	13
100	29	29	28	27
200	38	38	36	34

SOURCE: Golbe and White (1988, Table 9.4) in Alan J. Auerbach, ed. *Corporate Takeovers.* Copyright 1988 by the National Bureau of Economic Research. All rights reserved.

in 1984. These figures reflect the relative importance of the largest firms and are called concentration measures. The aggregate measures of concentration indicate a trend toward decreasing concentration that undoubtedly reflects the growth of industry sectors (for example, service) in which large firms are less important.

Manufacturing

Let us now take a more detailed look at the largest industry sector, manufacturing. The Bureau of the Census, a statistical agency of the U.S. government, classifies each manufacturing industry using standard industrial classification (SIC) codes. The 20 major industries in manufacturing are identified by the two-digit SIC codes 20–39. For example, SIC 28 is the chemical industry. About 450 more narrowly defined industries are identified by four-digit SIC codes. For example, SIC 2812 includes alkalies and chlorine. The Bureau of the Census also provides detailed product classifications at four-digit, five-digit, and seven-digit levels of detail. For example, product 28133 is carbon dioxide. The Bureau of the Census publishes several reports, such as the *Annual Survey of Manufactures* and the *Census of Manufactures,* which provide detailed information about manufacturing.

Concentration in Manufacturing.   The *Census of Manufactures* reports for each industry (and also for each product) measures of concentration such as the **four-firm concentration ratio** (CR4), which measures the share of industry sales generated by the top four firms. These concentration ratios can be used as rough guides to judge competitiveness. However, there are five major limitations to using four-firm concentration ratios[1]:

1. The criterion used by the Census to group products by industry are not based on demand substitution, but on similarity of production processes. If glass containers and plastic containers are perfect substitutes in use, then they compete, and the

[1] See also the discussion in Chapter 12.

price of one constrains the price of the other. The Census, however, treats them as separate industries. Therefore, even if glass containers did have a high four-firm concentration ratio, it would be incorrect to conclude that manufacturers of glass containers face little competition.

2. The Census reports national statistics for the United States. If imports are currently or potentially important, then Census concentration ratios understate the degree of competition. For example, the 1982 four-firm concentration ratio in autos was 92 percent. This provides a misleading impression of the auto industry, in which over 25 percent of 1982 sales were from imports. Conversely, if transportation costs are high, regional markets may not compete with each other. In such a case, the concentration ratio could overstate the degree of competition.

3. Firms classified in one industry may be able to modify their equipment and produce products in another industry. Such potential suppliers may influence current pricing but not affect the four-firm concentration ratio.

4. The choice of the top *four* firms is arbitrary; the share of the top three or top six firms might be more relevant. Alternative relevant measures of concentration could depend on each firm's market share, as does the **Herfindahl-Hirschman Index (HHI)**, which is defined as the sum of the squared shares of each firm. For example, the HHI equals 5000 in an industry consisting of two firms, each with a share of 50 percent.

5. Other factors, such as regulatory barriers preventing entry or restrictions on imports, could be more important than concentration in explaining whether price is elevated above competitive levels.

With these caveats, let us now turn to the Census data. Table 7.4 reports the four-firm concentration ratios for several different product groupings. A tabulation by Scherer (1980, 68) using 1972 data indicates that industries with a CR4 in excess of 80 percent accounted for only about 7 percent of the value contributed to GNP by manufacturing, industries with CR4 below 40 accounted for 55 percent, and industries with a CR4 between 40 and 80 percent accounted for 37 percent. These tabulations suggest that the bulk of manufacturing is carried out in industries with several small competitors, a significant fraction of it is carried out in industries with several large competitors, and a much smaller fraction in industries dominated by only a few firms. Moreover, examination of the historical importance of industries with a CR4 in excess of 50 percent indicate that since 1947 there has been only a slight drift upward in their importance (Scherer 1980, 70).[2] One interesting finding is that concentration ratios are correlated across different countries; that is, if an industry is of above average concentration in the United States, it tends to be of above average concentration in other countries (Pryor 1972).

Aside from concentration in individual industries, one can examine concentration in manufacturing in general. Table 7.5 shows that there has not been a trend toward increasing aggregate concentration in the manufacturing sector. The table measures the *value added*

---

[2] Imports, which obviously increase competition, are not reflected in these concentration ratios and have been increasing over time.

TABLE 7.4	Concentration Ratios	
SIC	Product Grouping	Four-Firm Concentration Ratio (%)
2011	Meat packing plant products	27
2043	Cereal breakfast foods	81
2067	Chewing gum and chewing gum base	87
2085	Liquor, distilled (exc. brandy)	46
2111	Cigarettes	90
2311	Men's and boy's suits and coats	25
2335	Women's and misses' dresses	6
2434	Kitchen cabinets	13
2519	Household furniture (exc. wood and metal)	33
2631	Paperboard mill products	27
2648	Stationery products	28
2731	Book publishing	16
2812	Alkalies and chlorines	44
2911	Petroleum refining	28
3011	Tires and inner tubes	67
3144	Women's footwear (exc. athletic)	36
3211	Flat glass	78
3331	Primary copper	92
3353	Aluminum sheet, plate, and foil	73
3411	Metal cans	50
3523	Farm machinery and equipment	54
3632	Household refrigerators and freezers	90
3651	Radio and TV receiving sets	47
3711	Motor vehicles and car bodies	92
3873	Watches, clocks, and watch cases	46
3944	Games, toys, and children's vehicles	39

SOURCE: *Census of Manufactures*, "Concentration Ratios in Manufacturing" (1982, Table 6).

TABLE 7.5	Percent Aggregate Concentration in the Manufacturing Sector (measured by value added)						
Top Firms	1947	1954	1963	1967	1972	1977	1982
50	17	23	23	25	25	24	24
100	23	30	30	33	33	33	33
200	30	37	38	41	42	43	44

SOURCE: *Census of Manufactures* "Concentration Ratios in Manufacturing" (1982, Table 1).

(measured as revenues minus the cost of fuel, power, and raw materials) accounted for by the largest firms (measured by value of shipments). The table shows that aggregate domestic concentration has increased since 1947, though very little since 1967. (These domestic concentration statistics overstate concentration because they ignore imports, which have grown in importance.)

Specialization in Manufacturing.   Firms often produce different products in the same plant. The Census publishes a measure of how specialized each plant's output is for each industry. The **specialization ratio** for an industry equals shipments of products in the particular industry divided by total shipments of all products for all plants listed as being in the industry. For example, suppose there is only one plant that makes steel bars and the plant also makes steel wire. If the plant sells $100 worth of steel bars and $50 worth of steel wire, it is classified as producing in the steel bar industry. The specialization ratio for this industry is 2/3, or 66.7 percent. The specialization ratio for an industry is typically in excess of 80 percent. This high share indicates that individual manufacturing plants (not necessarily firms) are relatively specialized.

A tabulation of the number of different four-digit SIC industries in which one firm operates indicates that 146 of the top 200 manufacturing firms (in terms of shipments) operated in 11 or more different industries in 1968 (Scherer 1980, 76). Dunne, Roberts, and Samuelson (1988) study all manufacturing firms (which numerically are dominated by very small firms) and find that in 1982, firms on average produced between one and two separate four-digit products. Multiplant firms on average produced between two and three separate products.

■ CREATION OF FIRMS

A new firm can be formed by the merger of two or more firms. This method of creating firms can attract national attention, especially when the two firms are large. Related ways of creating new firms include the acquisition of one firm by another or the sale of a part of a firm. These transactions all involve a reshuffling of property interests among existing firms. A completely separate method of creating a firm is for investors to buy equipment and start from the beginning. These two different methods of firm creation are examined in detail in the following sections.

Merger Activity in the U.S. Economy

Our ignorance of history makes us libel our own times. People have always been like this. —Gustave Flaubert

The structures of firms and industries can change as firms enter, exit, or combine. Recently, numerous large firms have merged with other large firms. Some of these transactions occur between competitors **(horizontal mergers),** others between firms that could produce for each other **(vertical mergers),** and others between firms in unrelated businesses **(conglomerate mergers).** Merger transactions (which we will use broadly to include acquisitions) often involve billions of dollars, generate national news headlines, and can involve battles between the acquiring firm and the acquired firm, whose management may resist the takeover. Before examining the reasons for mergers, let us first examine the historical evidence.

FIGURE 7.1   Annual Number of Mergers and Acquisitions

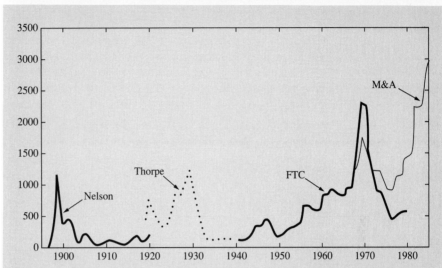

Nelson: Data derived by Nelson (1959) for manufacturing and mining. Thorpe: Data derived by W. Thorpe, reported in Nelson (1959, 166) for manufacturing and mining. FTC: Continuation of Thorpe series by Federal Trade Commission. M&A: Data from *Mergers and Acquisitions*, domestic series (includes all sectors of economy).

SOURCE: Golbe and White (1988), Figure 9.6, in Alan J. Auerbach, ed. *Corporate Takeovers*. Copyright © 1988 by the National Bureau of Economic Research. All rights reserved.

Evidence.   Surprisingly, it is difficult to obtain consistent data on merger activity over time.[3] Most early data concentrate on manufacturing and mining, which have declined in relative importance in the U.S. economy. The data sources report transactions only if they are "large enough." Because this eliminates small firms, any measure of merger activity is biased, especially in earlier periods when firms tended to be smaller, as measured by sales unadjusted for inflation.

Figure 7.1 presents the available data from various sources on the number of mergers since 1900. The figure indicates four large spurts of activity: one is near the turn of the century, a second is in the late 1920s, a third is in the late 1960s, and the fourth is in the 1980s. George Stigler (1950) has called the first wave the *merger to monopoly* movement. During this period, the U.S. economy was undergoing widespread changes in response to the development of railroads and communications. The stock market became a more important source of capital, and this period witnessed the creation of firms that, to this day, remain large and successful—firms like General Electric and U.S. Steel. The end of the first merger wave in the early 1900s coincided with a downturn in economic activity and with the Supreme Court's 1904 decision in the Northern Securities case, in

---

[3] This section is based on evidence reported in Golbe and White (1988).

FIGURE 7.2   Annual Number of Mergers and Acquisitions per Billion Dollars of Real GNP

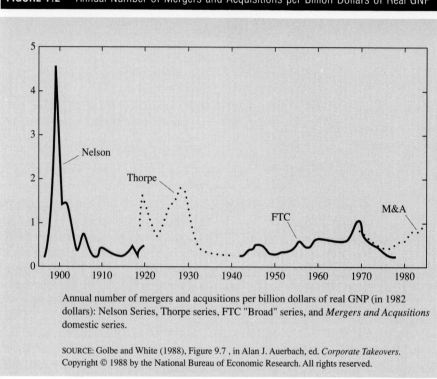

Annual number of mergers and acqusitions per billion dollars of real GNP (in 1982 dollars): Nelson Series, Thorpe series, FTC "Broad" series, and *Mergers and Acqusitions* domestic series.

which the Court found that certain (horizontal) mergers violated the antitrust law of the Sherman Act, which was passed in 1890.[4] Stigler (1950) calls the second wave in the 1920s the *merger to oligopoly* movement. The third wave in the 1960s is called the conglomerate movement since it represents the creation of many *conglomerate* firms. A conglomerate firm is one that produces in different industries. There is no common name for the fourth and most recent wave.

Current news reports proclaim that the 1980s are unparalleled in terms of both the number and value of mergers. Judged by absolute numbers or inflation-adjusted value, that statement is true. However, the current economy is much larger than in previous years. Figures 7.2 and 7.3 correct for the size of the economy by reporting the number of transactions per billion dollars of inflation-adjusted, or real, GNP and the value of the assets acquired by merging firms per billion dollars of GNP.

The results are surprising: the merger activity around the turn of the century exceeds all subsequent merger activity after adjusting for the size of the U.S. economy. The recent activity of the 1980s has been decidedly great, but its levels are not unprecedented.

There have been numerous attempts to explain the level of merger activity. By and large, the attempts have not been successful. One puzzling finding that emerges from this

---

[4] *Northern Securities Co. vs. U.S.,* 193 U.S. 197 (1904).

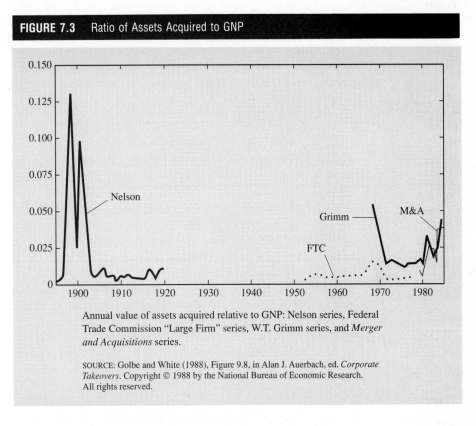

FIGURE 7.3   Ratio of Assets Acquired to GNP

Annual value of assets acquired relative to GNP: Nelson series, Federal Trade Commission "Large Firm" series, W.T. Grimm series, and *Merger and Acquisitions* series.

SOURCE: Golbe and White (1988), Figure 9.8, in Alan J. Auerbach, ed. *Corporate Takeovers*. Copyright © 1988 by the National Bureau of Economic Research. All rights reserved.

research is that bursts of merger activity seem to coincide with booms in the stock market. The following section examines some possible reasons for mergers.

Economic Reasons for Mergers and Acquisitions.   There are several reasons why it may make economic sense for two firms to consolidate into one or for one firm to purchase another. The following sections present the most important of them.

Increase in Optimal Scale.   As the costs of factors of production change, the optimal size of a firm (that is, the output at which average cost is minimized) may increase. In the late 1800s the cost of transportation fell because of the development of railroads, and the cost of communication fell because of the development of the telegraph and telephone. Further, the development of financial markets (for example, bond and stock markets) lowered the cost of raising large sums of money. These developments probably caused the optimal size of a firm to increase, and led to the importance of the large corporation as the major organizational form in the U.S. economy.

Synergies.   Firms that engage in different but complementary activities may benefit from mergers because of economies of scope. (Recall from Chapter 3 that an economy of scope exists when it is less costly for one firm to perform two activities than for two specialized firms to perform them separately.) If Firm A excels at designing fast cars and Firm B excels at designing attractive cars, the two firms may gain by merging. Similarly, reduced transaction costs (recall Chapter 2) could explain why two firms that engage in different activities might prefer to merge. Bittlingmayer (1985) has argued that the Sherman Act of 1890 created uncertainty about the legality of contracts between direct competitors and thereby created an incentive for firms that had been cooperating with each other through contracts to merge.

Creation of Efficiencies in Management. Suppose that the managers of Firm X are doing a poor job. Firm X generates a large amount of cash, but the managers keep investing the money in unprofitable projects and raising their salaries, so that stockholders see little if any of the cash as a dividend. Stockholders could urge the board of directors to control management, but that may be difficult, especially if some members of the board are managers. An alternative way to discipline managers is to allow shrewd investors to discover inefficiently run firms. Such investors could then "take over" (that is, acquire or gain control of) the inefficient firm at a low price, improve it, and either resell it or pass along the increased dividends to shareholders. Imagine that the stock of Firm X is worth $100 per share, based on the low dividends that current management is paying shareholders. If Mr. Smart can fire the current management, improve the firm's operations, and double dividends, he could double the value of the company's stock to $200 per share. Mr. Smart would be willing to buy shares for $101 and thereby make a $99 profit per share. The threat that someone like Mr. Smart could come along and buy enough shares to gain control of the company might so scare the managers of Firm X that they would perform efficiently to avoid losing their jobs.

To gain control of Firm X, Mr. Smart would offer to buy shares of Firm X from shareholders. Shareholders stand to gain if (a) they keep their stock, Mr. Smart takes over Firm X, improves its performance, and raises dividends; (b) they sell to Mr. Smart at a price above $100; or (c) they hold onto their stock, Mr. Smart fails to gain control of the firm, but his attempt motivates current managers to improve their performance. Of course, the managers of Firm X may not care at all about the shareholders, and they may fight the attempted takeover in order to protect their comfortable jobs. Such **hostile takeovers** have resulted in spectacular battles, and managers often use clever tactics to prevent takeovers by people like Mr. Smart. We will return to these issues in the next section.

It is also possible that the managers of Firm X believe they could significantly improve profits if only the Board of Directors would allow them to fire employees, sell off parts of the business, and embark on new projects. Such radical changes in operation might not appeal to either shareholders or the board, so the managers themselves might decide to buy out the firm. This is called *going private,* because there are no longer any outside stockholders to whom management must answer. But how could a group of managers afford to buy out a firm? One way is to use a **leveraged buyout (LBO),** in which bonds are sold in order to raise a tremendous amount of money. These bonds are backed by the firm's assets and are sometimes called **junk bonds,** because they are usually considered riskier than typical corporate bonds. Junk bonds are a recent financial innovation that have made it easier for anyone to raise money to acquire control of a firm.

Tax Effects.   Because of the complexities of the U.S. tax code, firms may have an incentive to merge even if there is no fundamental economic efficiency involved. Suppose Firm A has $100 in accounting profits while Firm B shows $100 in accounting losses. If the corporate tax rate is 50 percent, Firm A must pay $50 in taxes, and Firm B pays nothing. If Firms A and B combine, their accounting profit is zero. The profits of Firm A are exactly offset by the losses of Firm B, and the combined firm owes no taxes. The U.S. government gets $50 less, but the new firm has $50 more than the two previously had together. No economic efficiencies are created, but the merger is privately profitable.

Exploitive Reasons.   Suppose a firm has implicitly agreed to keep loyal workers even in slack times. As a result of this arrangement, workers receive lower wages in return for steadier employment. If management reneged on its arrangement and fired workers during slack times, workers would never trust management again. If Mr. Smart buys Firm X and gets rid of surplus labor in slack times, he can make a short-run gain. Workers will soon demand higher wages to compensate them for less steady employment, but in the meantime, Mr. Smart can run Firm X more profitably than the previous management. Mr. Smart's action might harm the firm in the long run as the wage payments rise. Still, the short-run gain to the firm could offset the long-run loss[5] (Shleifer and Summers 1988).

Creation of Additional Market or Political Power.   If a sufficient number of firms in one industry all merge, the resulting firm would face less competition and acquire additional market power. (Recall that *market power* is the ability to set price above competitive levels.) The elimination of competitors through merging could therefore lead to higher prices for consumers. Some economists have pointed to the relaxation of antitrust scrutiny as a reason for the merger wave of the 1980s. Even if firms are in different industries, so that there are no concerns about a reduction in competition, their amalgamation may create a potent political force that could influence legislation to their benefit at the expense of the rest of society.

Manager Ego.   Some managers desire to control large firms because they enjoy power, and they may pursue a policy of acquisition, not because it is profitable, but because it appeals to their ego, which may bias their judgments about value (Roll 1986).

Defensive Tactics of Management.   When Mr. Smart discovers that the poorly run Firm X, which is worth only $100 per share, could be worth $200 per share if run properly, he must figure out how to obtain control. He could approach the management of Firm X, negotiate the terms on which he would obtain control, and have management rec-

---

[5] Even if the firm's actions are inefficient, the firm's long-run losses from the higher wages could be offset by the firm's short-term gains.

ommend that shareholders accept the terms of the offer. Alternatively, he could make a **tender offer** in which he deals directly with the shareholders of Firm X and offers to purchase their shares at stipulated prices. Finally, he could wage a **proxy contest,** in which he asks stockholders to vote to give him control of the board of directors so that he can alter how Firm X is run. As mentioned, inefficient managers may not want him to succeed, and they may resort to a variety of techniques, called **defensive tactics,** to thwart his attempt at a hostile takeover. Even if management wants Mr. Smart to succeed, it may thwart him temporarily to make him raise his bid. Management's defensive tactics may include the following:

Make Firm X Undesirable to Acquire.   If Mr. Smart succeeds in controlling Firm X, the managers legally obligate the firm to sell off valuable assets **(scorched earth policy),** pay very high severance pay **(golden parachutes)** to key employees, or make available stock at bargain prices to original shareholders **(poison pill),** with the effect of diluting the value of Mr. Smart's ownership.

Find Another Buyer.   The managers can try to find a friendly firm, known as a **white knight,** to come to the rescue, obtain control of Firm X, and leave current management in place.

Require More than 50 Percent Vote to Change Control.   Managers (who often own some stock) can try to enact a shareholder agreement under which anyone, like Mr. Smart, who seeks to gain control of the firm must obtain the approval of a supermajority (a percentage higher than a 50 percent majority) of the firm's shareholders.

Harass Mr. Smart.   By bringing lawsuits alleging fraud or antitrust objections, managers can raise the cost of trying to gain control of Firm X.

Make Assets Less Liquid.   Mr. Smart will probably not have enough capital himself to buy the firm; he will most likely borrow (for example, by issuing junk bonds) to raise the money, using the assets and earning potential of Firm X as security to guarantee bond payments. If Firm X has a large amount of cash—a *liquid* (easy to sell quickly) asset—the buyers of bonds will regard it as good security for the bonds. If Firm X invests its cash in real estate, which takes time to resell and whose future value may be hard to predict, a lender will be less inclined to lend unless Mr. Smart raises the interest payments on the bonds. By making it more costly for Mr. Smart to gain control of Firm X, managers reduce his incentive to try.

Urge Shareholders to Side with Management.   Managers can advertise to convince stockholders that their long-run interests are better served by refusing to sell to Mr. Smart (at a price above the current share price) and trusting that the current management will make the company even more profitable than Mr. Smart can. Such a claim must have a hollow ring to it; after all, the current share price reflects the market's valuation of the firm's stock with current management in place. If Mr. Smart can outbid that price, then management's claim makes sense only if the market incorrectly perceives the profit potential of the current management.

Difficulty in Gaining Control.   Takeover specialists like Mr. Smart spend large amounts of time and money looking for firms whose performance they can improve. By improving a firm's performance, Mr. Smart can reap large rewards, but he faces a difficult problem: having spent his time discovering an underperforming firm, he must gain control of it. Suppose Mr. Smart tries to gain control of Firm X by purchasing 51 percent of its stock. Once shareholders realize that Mr. Smart wants to control the firm, they may decide that it would be better to hold on to their shares rather than sell them to Mr. Smart—but if no one sells to Mr. Smart, he cannot gain control of the company (Grossman and Hart, 1980). To deal with this problem, Mr. Smart might make a **two-tiered offer,** paying $120 per share until he has acquired 51 percent of the shares and paying $100 for the remainder. This creates an incentive to tender shares to Mr. Smart. If he does not obtain 51 percent of the shares, Mr. Smart can cancel the offer and return all shares to their original owners. If he does obtain 51 percent of the shares, he can then pay $100 to the remaining shareholders.

Mr. Smart still runs the risk that other take-over entrepreneurs like himself will observe what he is doing and bid for control for themselves. Mr. Smart would be justifiably annoyed by a bidding war because it was his initial hard work that identified Firm X as a hot prospect. The greater the roadblocks that Mr. Smart must face in acquiring control, the lower is his initial incentive to engage in the costly activity of uncovering underperforming firms.

If Mr. Smart could swoop in quickly and buy up all the shares of Firm X, he would avoid the problem of having other investors benefit from his discovery that Firm X is an underperforming firm. Hostile takeover battles were rare prior to 1968 and are, in part, a result of recent government legislation. Unfortunately for Mr. Smart, the U.S. government has legislation (such as the Williams Act of 1968) that requires him to reveal his intentions about Firm X before he can acquire a controlling interest in the firm. The legislation also imposes certain delays on Mr. Smart that give managers time to thwart his attempt to gain control. The result is that Mr. Smart must often share a large part of his expected gains with the stockholders of the firms he acquires, which reduces his incentive to engage in such activities.

The Social Desirability of Mergers and Acquisitions.   There has been much debate about whether the recent wave of mergers and acquisitions benefits the economy. One view is that mergers and acquisitions involve a reshuffling of ownership that produces short-run stock gains for financial manipulators who are not interested in the long-term health of the firm. Another view is that mergers and acquisitions transfer control of assets to those who can manage them most efficiently. Evidence on mergers and acquisitions analyzed by Bradley, Desai, and Kim (1988), Jarrell, Brickley, and Netter (1988), Jarrell and Poulsen (1987), Jensen (1988), Jensen and Ruback (1983), Romano (1985), Scherer (1988), and Shleifer and Vishny (1988) indicates the following:

1. Shareholders of an acquired firm receive a large premium above the prevailing stock price prior to the acquisition. Typical estimates of the premium are in the range of 16 to 35 percent. The premium did rise significantly as a result of the Williams Act, and the gains to shareholders of acquired firms have been increasing over time.

2. Much of the increase in the share price of an acquired firm occurs *before* public announcement of the transaction.

3. The shareholders of an acquiring firm do not earn substantial, above-average rates of return as a result of the acquisition. They do slightly better in hostile takeovers than in friendly mergers. The return to stockholders of acquiring firms has declined over time from about 4 percent in the 1960s to −3 percent in the early 1980s. White knights, on average, overpay for the firms they acquire.

4. Overall, total shareholder value of the combined companies rises about 7.5 percent after the consolidation.

5. Management tactics to thwart takeovers reduce the probability of a takeover but raise the acquisition price, if the takeover is successful. The evidence is mixed on the effect of defensive provisions on stock prices. For example, adoption of supermajority amendments lowers a firm's stock price, presumably because of the reduced likelihood of takeover. **Greenmail,** in which management of Firm X buys back Mr. Smart's shares (and only his) at a premium, has a negative effect on a firm's stock price. A firm that changes its state of incorporation to take advantage of the new state's strong antitakeover laws enjoys a slight increase (though not a statistically significant one) in its share price. Poison-pill arrangements, in which the original shareholders of Firm X (but not Mr. Smart) have the legal right to engage in favorably priced stock transactions (for example, buy additional stock of Firm X at half-price) if the firm has been acquired, have been found to significantly lower the stock price of Firm X. Poison pills lower Mr. Smart's share of the firm and hence raise his costs of acquisition, reducing his incentive to acquire the firm.

6. If Mr. Smart (or a subsequent bidder) fails to gain control of Firm X, the huge increase in its stock price caused by Mr. Smart's bidding is completely eliminated, and price returns to its previous level.

7. The increased value of a consolidated firm is not typically due to the creation of market power. If the new firm acquires market power, then the price consumers face will rise. This benefits the rivals of the combined firm, and hence their stock price should rise. If the transaction is motivated by efficiencies, the combined firm will be a more efficient competitor, and the stock price of its rivals should decline in anticipation of the increased competition. Stillman (1983) and Eckbo (1983) indicate that the second explanation is more consistent with the evidence.

8. Merger activity has not increased the aggregate level of concentration of economic activity in either manufacturing or in the overall economy. Tables 7.3 and 7.5 show that there has been little, if any, increase in concentration since 1970.

Evidence from the 1970s indicates that less than 20 percent of merger activity among large manufacturing and mining firms was horizontal (Scherer 1980, 124).

9. There is no evidence that consolidated firms are "myopic," and cut back on research and development (R&D). Hall (1988) finds that R&D spending is not influenced by the change in control.

10. Targets of takeovers have performed poorly in the stock market prior to takeover. Firms in declining industries are prime targets for takeovers.

11. The evidence on low profitability for acquiring firms is somewhat disturbing. Is it possible that acquiring firms are overpaying? Instead of using stock-price data, some researchers look directly at accounting data from the consolidated firm to see if efficiency has improved. This is much more difficult than looking at stock prices. Moreover, the efficiency gains for the *firm* are likely to be smaller than the previously mentioned 7.5 percent increase because that figure applies to the increase in the *equity* value (not total value, which includes debt) that results from acquisition. Scherer (1988) and Ravenscraft and Scherer (1987) are unable to detect any improvement in profits after acquisition based on their examination of profit data by line of business. In contrast, Lichtenberg and Siegel (1987) examine the productivity of individual plants and detect significant improvements in efficiency in plants whose ownership had changed. Moreover, they find that the plants most likely to undergo an ownership change were those that were performing poorly.

12. Tax reasons alone do not account for much merger activity (Auerbach and Reishus 1988).

In summary, considerable evidence from the stock market supports the view that merger activity improves efficiency and creates value. Shareholders of target firms are the primary beneficiaries of this increased value. As legislation and management have made it more difficult for acquiring firms to gain control of targets, the returns to shareholders of target firms have increased and those to shareholders of acquiring firms have decreased. Additional research on profits subsequent to consolidation, not stock prices, is needed to confirm the efficiency gains. Without such research, some may argue that mergers and takeovers create illusory value that represents either the unjustified transfer of wealth from those dependent on the acquired firm (for example, employees) to its shareholders, or judgmental errors by the management of the acquiring firm.

Entry and Exit

Although the study of industry concentration is informative in a descriptive way, the economist seeks to explain why industries become and remain concentrated and to see what consequences concentration brings. A central determinant of the structure of an industry and its subsequent performance is the ability of equally efficient firms to enter and exit. Industries in which entry and exit can occur costlessly are called perfectly *contestable* (Baumol, Panzar, Willig 1982). In such industries, consumers are protected from exploitation by any one firm or group of firms. In contrast, industries that are protected from entry can maintain elevated prices because no new firm can easily enter to drive prices down. Economists have spent much time trying to understand and identify barriers to entry. By doing so, they are singling out those conditions that could lead to concentrated markets and elevated pricing.

The Definition of Barriers to Entry. A discussion about measuring whether barriers to entry exist requires a precise definition of the term. Unfortunately, the term *barriers to entry* has been used with a variety of meanings. This has led to some confusion in the literature, even though the authors proposing the different definitions may not disagree about the economic implications of certain economic facts.

The literal definition of a **barrier to entry** is simply anything that prevents instantaneous entry. However, this definition is inadequate; it would mean, for example, that the cost of hiring labor or the cost of building a plant could be considered an entry barrier. Moreover, it would imply that any industry in which entry takes time would be characterized as having a barrier to entry. In any industry, there is a difference between the short run and long run. Because it is only in the long run that economic theories predict the erosion of profits by entry, one reasonable approach is to focus on **long-run barriers to entry** that allow a firm to earn long-run profits without inducing entry.

If there are many firms that can enter with identical cost curves and face identical prices, then no one firm can succeed in the long run at earning profits that exceed competitive rates of return without inducing additional entry. Only by having some advantage over new entrants could a firm persistently earn higher than competitive profits. Since long-run profits can only persist if a firm has an advantage over potential entrants, a logical definition of a long-run barrier to entry is a cost that must be incurred by a new entrant that incumbents do not (or have not had to) bear.[6]

A good example of a long-run barrier to entry is a patent. The U.S. government grants an inventor the monopoly right to sell the invention for a period of 17 years. A patent therefore creates a legal monopoly. Suppose an incumbent firm has been granted a patent. To compete against this firm, a potential entrant would either have to invent around the patent or license it from the incumbent firm. Because the incumbent firm has the right to exclude anyone from using the patent, it can prevent entry. If it is costly to invent around the patent, or if there is a license fee, the potential entrant faces a higher cost than the incumbent currently faces. Of course, the incumbent probably had to invest in research and development in order to acquire the patent.[7] The same avenue of research and development may not be available once a patent has already been granted, and thus the patent may raise the cost to the potential entrant. If the original firm is deprived of its ability to benefit from its patent, it may cease doing research and development, and society may be worse off even though there would no longer be a barrier to entry.

---

[6] This definition is adapted from Stigler (1968). See also von Weizsäcker (1980), who adds the condition that an entry barrier must lower consumer welfare.

[7] A patent creates a monopoly after the discovery. However, there may be competition to obtain the patent, so that on average expected profits for innovating firms may be zero (see Chapter 20).

An incumbent may use a variety of strategies designed to raise the cost of entry, all of which require the incumbent to exploit some asymmetry between it and a potential entrant in order to raise the cost to a potential entrant above its own. When it is successful, the incumbent firm can create a long-run barrier to entry. Chapter 13 examines these strategic responses in detail.

An important consideration in understanding a firm's incentive to enter an industry is, paradoxically, the firm's ability to exit the industry. If it is costly to exit an industry, the incentives to enter are reduced. It is costly to exit an industry if there are sunk costs that cannot be recovered. For example, suppose that a firm in Industry X must have very specialized equipment that is difficult to resell. A firm contemplating entry into Industry X will realize that if the unusual profit opportunities in the industry are short lived, it may not pay to enter. In contrast, if there are no costs to entry or exit, then instantaneous entry and subsequent exit, sometimes called **hit-and-run** entry, by outside firms guarantees that only competitive profits can be earned at each instant.[8] Therefore, understanding the costs of exit is essential to understanding barriers to entry.

Identifying Barriers to Entry.   Pioneering theoretical work on barriers to entry began with Bain (1956), who identified three barriers to entry: (1) absolute cost advantage, (2) economies of large-scale production that requires large capital expenditures, and (3) **product differentiation,** which refers to differences among related products. It is obvious that an absolute cost advantage can allow an incumbent firm to earn excess profits without fearing entry. For example, if Firm A can produce at a constant marginal cost of $2, while all other firms produce at a cost of $5, then Firm A can set price at $4, earn higher than competitive profits (price is above marginal cost) and not fear entry. Because it is less clear that the other two barriers fit our definition of long-run entry barriers, let us examine them in more detail.

If both an incumbent and a new entrant can enjoy the same benefits of economies of scale, why should an incumbent be able to earn excess profits? Some argue that a new entrant would have difficulty raising money (or be unwilling to invest its own) to finance a large expenditure. It is not correct to argue that it is difficult to obtain financing for large projects; as long as capital markets work, raising capital should be no more difficult for a profitable large-scale project than for a profitable small-scale project. There are lots of investors for good projects. But, is it reasonable that the scale of a firm has no effect on the incentives to enter? If large *sunk* costs are associated with entry and if entry is unsuccessful, the entrant's losses are large. In such a setting threats of strategic behavior (for example, vigorous price competition) may prevent new entry. The greater the risk of encountering strategic behavior and the greater the potential loss, the more potent is the threat of strategic entry deterrence. In such a case, the need for large-scale investment that involves large sunk costs could well provide a disincentive for a potential entrant because it would have so much to lose. (Strategic entry deterrence is covered in more detail in Chapter 13.)

---

[8] Baumol, Panzar, and Willig (1982) have emphasized this point and are responsible for popularizing the concept of hit-and-run entry. See also Eaton and Lipsey (1980).

TABLE 7.6   Bain's Barriers to Entry

Industry	Scale Economy	Product Differentiation	Absolute Cost	Capital Requirement
Automobiles	3	3	1	3
Cigarettes	1	3	1	3
Liquor	1	3	1	2
Shoes	2	1–2	1	0
Soap	2	2	1	2
Steel	2	1	3	3
Tractors	3	3	1	3
Tires and tubes	1	2	1	2
Meat packing	2	2	2	0 or 1
Cement	2	1	1	2
Flour	1	1–2	1	0

NOTE: Higher scores indicate greater entry barriers.

SOURCE: Bain (1956, 169).

Is product differentiation a long-run barrier to entry? Could a new entrant with its own differentiated product compete against the differentiated product of the incumbent? The answer is yes, but an advantage can accrue to the first firm to introduce a new product, called the **first-mover advantage.** The first firm to enter incurs lower marketing costs because it faces no rivals. The second firm to enter, however, faces higher marketing costs because it must compete against the first.[9] If the presence of the incumbent raises the marketing costs of the second firm to enter, then the first firm will have a permanent advantage and will be able to maintain high prices. For example, the first firm in the market may gain a familiarity among customers, who then become reluctant to switch (Schmalensee 1982). Such a first-mover advantage can create a permanent long-run barrier to entry.[10] (First-mover advantages are covered in more detail in Chapter 13.)

Evidence on the Size of Entry Barriers.   Economists have attempted to measure the size of long-run barriers to entry in a number of ways. One way is to use subjective methods of determining how difficult it would be for a new firm to enter an industry. These estimates can be based on how frequently entry has occurred in the past. Other measures of barriers to entry could be based on the answers to questions like the following: What would be the cost disadvantage if a new entrant came in at a scale 50 percent smaller than the incumbent's? How much higher are the entrant's costs because of the

---

[9] Sometimes the reverse is true and the second firm to enter can incur lower marketing costs than the first, which may have spent money convincing consumers of the desirability of the new type of product.

[10] Caves and Porter (1977) have stressed the importance of *mobility barriers* that prevent firms in an industry from moving into different segments of that industry.

TABLE 7.7   Bain's Overall Barriers to Entry

Industry	Overall Barrier
Automobiles	Very high
Cigarettes	Very high
Liquor	Very high
Soaps	Substantial
Steel	Substantial
Tractors	Very high
Flour	Moderate to low
Cement	Moderate to low
Meat packing	Moderate to low
Tires	Moderate to low
Rayon	Moderate to low

NOTE: Industries with very high barriers could elevate price 10 percent or more above competitive levels. Substantial and moderate-to-low entry barriers allow prices to be in excess of competitive levels by 7 percent and 4 percent respectively.

SOURCE: Bain (1956, 170.)

incumbent's patents or acquired expertise? Tables 7.6 and 7.7 reproduce Bain's characterization of the extent of barriers to entry in certain industries.[11]

In the long run, only long-run barriers to entry can prevent profits from falling to competitive levels as new firms enter. From a practical point of view, if the long run is very long, knowing that excess rates of return will eventually be driven to zero may not matter much to firms that are earning large profits. A more relevant concept is how long it takes for entry to expand output enough to eliminate profits that exceed competitive levels. Both competitive and noncompetitive industries can differ in the rates at which entry can occur. Some research has been done on the speed with which entry into various industries erodes profits. A typical finding is that profit erosion takes longer in concentrated industries (Stigler 1963) and in high-profit industries (Connolly and Schwartz 1985). Unfortunately, the term *barrier to entry* is commonly used to refer to both long-run barriers to entry and the time it takes for entry to occur.

Evidence on Entry and Exit.   Few attempts have been made to measure directly the process by which firms enter and exit an industry because of the difficulty of finding adequate data. Early studies used Dun and Bradstreet data,[12] but recently the Census has created a new, more expanded data set that enables researchers to observe the detailed activities of new manufacturing firms over several years.

Analysis of this data has already produced several interesting results (Dunne, Roberts, and Samuelson 1988). Some of the most noteworthy are the following:

---

[11] Harris (1976) examines the rate of entry into those industries that Bain and later Mann (1966) considered difficult to enter and finds that several industries have had significant entry. The entry barriers identified by Bain and Mann that did seem to restrict entry were those having to do with product differentiation.

[12] See, for example, James and Struyk (1975).

- The rate of entry and exit in an industry are highly related. Industries with high rates of entry also have high rates of exit.

- Differences in entry and exit rates across industries persist over time. Some industries have persistently higher entry and exit rates than others.

- There is considerable dispersion in entry and exit rates across industries. In roughly half the manufacturing industries, entrants account for 7–25 percent of industry value, and exiting firms account for 8–25 percent of value.

- Existing firms that choose to enter a new business enter at a larger scale than do newly created firms.

- Small, new firms have the highest failure rate. The probability of survival and the size of surviving firms are highest for entrants that are diversifying into new lines of business.

- On average, 40 percent of all firms and about 60 percent of new entrants vanish after five years.

- Entrants are much smaller than the average firm in an industry; they produce at 17 percent of the output level of existing firms and account for about 11 percent of industry output on average.

- Exiting firms account for about 11 percent of output in any year. Exiting firms produce on average at 20 percent of the output of the average firm.

- Existing firms that enter a new industry through new plant construction are larger and have better survival probabilities than other entrants.[13]

Birch (1987) uses Dun and Bradstreet data to investigate entry and exit in all sectors (not just manufacturing) of the U.S. economy. He finds that about half of all new entrants fail within five years and that despite their high rate of failure, entrants over a period of a few years are a significant source for the creation of (net) new jobs.

The most interesting findings in the relatively new research on entry and exit are the high rates of entry and exit in many industries and the high rates of failure of new firms. This area of research is an important one that should provide valuable evidence about one of the key determinants of industry structure.

---

[13] There are not many economic models about how new firms enter and grow in an industry. Simple application of the models of Chapter 4 would suggest no difference between a new entrant and existing firm. More realistic models based on differences in knowledge can generate specific growth processes for new firms (Jovanovic 1982).

■ SUMMARY

The U.S. economy is comprised of several sectors. The largest sectors are manufacturing (22 percent), wholesale and retail trade (17 percent), and services (15 percent). Most businesses in the United States have less than 20 employees, but these small businesses do not collectively comprise the bulk of output. The top 200 nonfinancial corporations account for about one third of all assets in the economy. Statistics on concentration in individual manufacturing industries indicate that a relatively small amount of value is created in industries with four-firm concentration ratios in excess of 80 percent.

There are two important ways that new firms are created. One way involves creating firms through mergers of existing firms. There have been several merger waves in the last 100 years. Merger activity has been at high levels recently. After adjusting for the size of the economy, it turns out that the merger wave around 1900 was the largest. Mergers can generate efficiencies, but they can also create market power. The recent merger wave has involved hostile takeovers in which the target of the takeover resorts to numerous defensive tactics to preserve its independence. The threat of takeovers can keep management on their toes. The evidence indicates that takeovers create economic value and that shareholders of companies that are acquired capture the lion's share of the gains.

A second method by which new firms are created is through entry. Considerable work has been expended on defining barrier to entry. A long-run barrier to entry allows a firm to permanently earn a return above competitive levels. In addition to knowing whether entry will eventually erode monopoly profits, it is valuable to know how long entry will take. There have been relatively few empirical studies of entry. The available evidence indicates that new firms fail at a high rate and that industries with a high rate of entry also have a high rate of exit.

■ Key Terms

barrier to entry
conglomerate merger
defensive tactics
first-mover advantage
four-firm concentration ratio
golden parachute
greenmail
Herfindahl-Hirschman Index (HHI)
hit-and-run entry
horizontal merger
hostile takeover
junk bonds

leveraged buyout (LBO)
long-run barriers to entry
poison pill
product differentiation
proxy contest
scorched-earth policy
specialization ratio
tender offer
two-tiered offer
vertical merger
white knight

■ Discussion Questions

1. Suppose that the (national domestic) four-firm concentration ratio of Industry X is much higher today than it was 50 years ago. Explain why Industry X may be more competitive today. Consider transportation cost, advertising cost, and imports in your answer.

2. Who would benefit if a law were passed that prevented the use of junk bonds?

3. Explain how value can be created if a firm is acquired and then its businesses are sold off separately.

4. Would it make sense to forbid mergers whose profitability depends only upon tax consequences? Would the denial by the Internal Revenue Service of merger-related tax benefits be one way to accomplish this?

5. Are entry barriers ever desirable?

■ Problems

1. Firm A spends money on research and development (R&D) and succeeds in lowering its marginal cost from $10 to $5. Does a new entrant with a marginal cost of $10 face a barrier to entry because of its cost disadvantage? Does it face a barrier to entry if the R&D is highly specialized?

2. Explain when the four-firm concentration ratio is likely to (a) overstate the amount of competition, and (b) understate the amount of competition.

3. Explain why the data on entry are not consistent with the simple competitive model of Chapter 4.

4. (Difficult) The managers of Firm A recommend that Firm A purchase Firm B because the purchase will diversify the business of Firm A. Diversification of risks is a desirable strategy for individual shareholders, but if shareholders can diversify their risks by holding stock in Firm B, is there any reason for Firm A to purchase Firm B? Suppose labor turnover is costly; could that provide an efficiency saving to support the proposed purchase? (*Hint:* If output is less variable, labor employment can be steadier).

5. Suppose that each manufacturing industry undergoes no change in its concentration. How can aggregate concentration in manufacturing change?

Answers to odd-numbered problems are given at the back of the book.

■ References

Auerbach, Alan J., ed. 1988. *Corporate Takeovers: Causes and Consequences*. Chicago: University of Chicago Press.

Auerbach, Alan J., and D. Reishus. 1988. "The Effects of Taxation on the Merger Decision," in Auerbach, 1988.

Baumol, William, J. Panzar, and Robert D. Willig. 1982. *Contestable Markets and the Theory of Industry Structure*. San Diego, Calif.: Harcourt Brace Jovanovich, 1982.

Bain, Joe S. 1956. *Barriers to New Competition*. Cambridge: Harvard University Press.

Birch, David. 1987. *Job Creation in America: How Our Smallest Companies Put the Most People to Work*. New York: The Free Press.

Bittlingmayer, George. 1985. "Did Antitrust Policy Cause the Great Merger Wave?" *Journal of Law and Economics* 28:77–118.

Bradley, Michael, Amand Desai, and E. Han Kim. 1988. "Synergistic Gains from Corporate Acquisitions and Their Division Between the Stockholders of Target and Acquiring Firms." *Journal of Financial Economics* 21:3–40.

Caves, Richard E., and Michael E. Porter. 1977. "From Entry Barriers to Mobility Barriers: Conjectural Decisions and Contrived Deterrence to New Competition." *Quarterly Journal of Economics* 91:241–61.

Connolly, Robert, A., and Stephen Schwartz. 1985. "The Intertemporal Behavior of Economic Profits." *International Journal of Industrial Organization* 3:379–400.

Dunne, Timothy, Mark Roberts, and Larry Samuelson. 1988. "Patterns of Firm Entry and Exit in U.S. Manufacturing Industries." Mimeo.

Eaton, B. Curtis, and Richard G. Lipsey. 1980. "Exit Barriers Are Entry Barriers." *Bell Journal of Economics and Management Science* 11:721–29.

Eckbo, Espen B. 1983. "Horizontal Mergers, Collusion, and Stockholder Wealth." *Journal of Financial Economics* 11:241–73.

Golbe, Devra L., and Lawrence J. White. 1988. "A Time Series Analysis of Mergers and Acquisitions in the U.S. Economy" in Auerbach, 1988.

Grossman, Sanford J., and Oliver D. Hart. 1980. "Takeover Bids, the Free Rider Problem, and the Theory of the Corporation." *The Bell Journal of Economics* 11:42–64.

Hall, Bronwyn H. 1988. "The Effect of Takeover Activity on Corporate Research and Development," in Auerbach, 1988.

Harris, Maury N., "Entry and Barriers to Entry." 1976. *Industrial Organization Review* 4:165–74.

James, Franklin J., and Raymond J. Struyk. 1975. *Intrametropolitan Industrial Location*. Lexington, Mass: Lexington Books.

Jarrell, Gregg A., and Annette B. Poulsen. 1987. "Shark Repellents and Stock Prices: The Effects of Antitakeover Amendments Since 1980." *Journal of Financial Economics* 19:127–68.

Jarrell, Gregg A., James A. Brickley, and Jeffrey N. Netter. 1988. "The Market for Corporation Control: The Empirical Evidence Since 1980." *Journal of Economic Perspectives* 2:49–68.

Jensen, Michael C. 1988. "Takeovers: Their Causes and Consequences." *Journal of Economic Perspectives* 2:21–48.

Jensen, Michael C., and Richard S. Ruback. 1983. "The Market for Corporate Control: The Scientific Evidence." *Journal of Financial Economics* 11:5–50.

Jovanovic, Boyan. 1982. "Selection and Evolution of Industry." *Econometrica* 50:649–70.

Lichtenberg, Frank R., and Donald Siegel. 1987. "Productivity and Changes in Ownership of Manufacturing Plants." *Brookings Papers on Economic Activity* 3:643–83.

Mann, Michael. 1966. "Seller Concentration, Barriers to Entry, and the Rates of Return in Thirty Industries, 1950–1960." *The Review of Economics and Statistics* 48:290–307.

Nelson, Ralph L. 1959. *Merger Movements in American Industry, 1895–1956*. Princeton, N.J.: Princeton University Press.

Pryor, Frederic L. 1972. "An International Comparison of Concentration Ratios." *Review of Economics and Statistics* 54:130–40.

Ravenscraft, David J., and F. M. Scherer. 1987. *Mergers, Sell-offs and Economic Efficiency*. Washington: Brookings Institution.

Roll, Richard, 1986. "The Hubris Hypothesis of Corporate Takeovers." *Journal of Business* 59:197–216.

Romano, Roberta. 1985. "Law as a Product: Some Pieces of the Incorporation Puzzle." *Journal of Law Economics and Organization* 1:225–83.

Scherer, Frederic M. 1980. *Industrial Market Structure and Economic Performance*. Boston: Houghton Mifflin.

———. 1988. "Corporate Takeovers: The Efficiency Arguments." *Journal of Economic Perspectives* 2:69–82.

Schmalensee, Richard. 1982. "Product Differentiation Advantages of Pioneering Brands." *American Economic Review* 72:346–65.

Shleifer, Andrei, and Lawrence Summers. 1988. "Hostile Takeovers as Breaches of Trust," in Auerbach, 1988.

Shleifer, Andrei, and Robert W. Vishny. 1988. "Value Maximization and the Acquisition Process." *Journal of Economic Perspectives* 2:7–20.

Stigler, George. 1950. "Monopoly and Oligopoly by Merger." *American Economic Review* 40:23–34.

———. 1963. *Capital and Rates of Return in Manufacturing Industries*, Princeton, N. J.: Princeton University Press.

———. 1968. "Barriers to Entry, Economies of Scale, and Firm Size," in Stigler *The Organization of Industry*. Homewood, Ill.: Richard D. Irwin.

Stillman, Robert S. 1983. "Examining Antitrust Policy Toward Horizontal Mergers." *Journal of Financial Economics* 11:225–40.

von Weizsäcker, C. C. 1980. "A Welfare Analysis of Barriers to Entry." *The Bell Journal of Economics* 11:399–420.

CHAPTER **8**

A DOMINANT FIRM WITH A COMPETITIVE FRINGE

Where does the gorilla sleep?
Anywhere the gorilla wants to sleep.

Some industries consist of a **dominant firm**—one with a large share of the market—and many **fringe,** or smaller, firms, each with a trivial share of the market. A dominant firm can affect market price by varying its output—it is a price setter rather than a price taker. A firm that can affect the industry price in this way is said to have *market power*.

Industries in which one firm has a large share of the market are common in developed economies; Example 8.5 on page 201 gives estimates of industry shares for 13 dominant firms. For example, Kodak's share of the photographic film business is estimated at 65 percent, and International Business Machines' share of the mainframe computer business is estimated to be 68 percent.[1] It is also common, however, for dominant firms to lose some of their market share over time. When U.S. Steel was created in 1901, its share of the steel ingot market was thought to be 66 percent (see Example 8.4 on page 200), but by 1982 its share had fallen to 19 percent.

How firms become dominant and why they lose market share over time are the key issues examined in this chapter, which begins by discussing what makes a firm dominant and how size allows a dominant firm to exercise a leadership role. It then analyzes how entry limits a dominant firm's market power. We consider three situations in which (1) entry by other firms is impossible, (2) entry by competing fringe firms occurs instantaneously, and (3) entry by fringe firms occurs only gradually over time. The analysis shows how a dominant firm's price-setting behavior depends on the ease of entry by fringe firms.

---

[1] A firm's share of sales in an industry depends crucially on how the industry is defined, and hence is highly debatable, especially in court proceedings. For example, Fisher, McGowan, and Greenwood (1983) argue that IBM's market power and market share are more limited than the federal government alleged in its recent antitrust suit against IBM.

Two main points are made in this chapter: (1) it is generally not in a profit-maximizing dominant firm's best interest to set its price so low that it drives all competitive-fringe firms out of the market; (2) nonetheless, the presence of competitive-fringe firms or the threat of entry by additional firms does keep a dominant firm's price lower than the price a monopoly would set.

Although a dominant firm may be able to set an extremely high price and maintain it in the short run, it may not choose to do so. A very high price attracts additional fringe firms, which causes the market price to fall. On the other hand, if a dominant firm keeps its price very low to prevent entry, it has very low profits in both the short and long run. Thus, a dominant firm that faces the threat of entry must trade off high profits in the short run against the entry of more competition and lower profits in the future. If the rate of entry is slow, a dominant firm sets a relatively high price in the short run and lowers it as necessary to compete with any new entrants. If many firms can enter very quickly, a dominant firm may not be able to charge a very high price even in the short run.

After a large number of firms have entered, a dominant firm cannot continue to charge a price higher than the minimum average cost of these new firms because the new firms would sell at a lower price and take away the dominant firm's sales. Indeed, if potential entrants' costs are as low as the dominant firm's, the dominant firm eventually has no more market power than any other firm.

■ WHY SOME FIRMS ARE DOMINANT

All animals are equal, but some animals are more equal than others.
GEORGE ORWELL

Why do some firms gain substantial market power, while others do not? At least three possible reasons are sufficient to create this market structure.

The first reason is that *dominant firms may have lower costs than fringe firms*. The following are three major causes of lower costs:

- A firm may be more efficient than its rivals. For example, it may have better management or better technology that allows it to produce at lower costs. (A technological advantage may be protected by a patent).

- An early entrant to an industry may have lower costs from having learned by experience how to produce more efficiently: "learning by doing."

- An early entrant may have had time to grow large optimally (in the presence of adjustment costs) so as to benefit from economies of scale. By spreading fixed costs over more units of output, it may have lower average costs of production than a new entrant could instantaneously achieve.

A second important factor is that *a dominant firm may have a superior product* in a market where each firm produces a differentiated product. This superiority may be due to a reputation achieved through advertising or through goodwill generated by its having been in the market longer.

A third cause is that *a group of firms may collectively act as a dominant firm*. As the next chapter shows, groups of firms in an industry have an incentive to coordinate

EXAMPLE 8.1

PRICE UMBRELLA

It is often asserted that a dominant firm provides a *pricing umbrella* for smaller firms; that is, as long as competing firms price at or below the level of the dominant firm, they will be able to find buyers. Obviously, if their products are inferior, they will have to set their prices substantially below the dominant firm's.

Just prior to the breakup of AT&T, several firms competed with AT&T to provide long-distance phone services. Their prices per minute of connect time averaged several cents less than AT&T price, but unlike AT&T, they required a fixed-cost monthly charge (and in some cases minimum monthly expenditure or an initial set-up fee). As a result, their prices were lower only for heavy users. For example, at the end of 1983, night (11:00 P.M. to 8:00 A.M.) and weekend rates for calls of 100–3000 miles were as shown in the following table:

Company and Plan	Range of Costs (cents per minute)	Average Cost of 9 Sample Calls
AT&T	14–19	$9.49
Combined Network Allnet	12–15	6.26
GTE Home Sprint	12–16	7.06
ITT Consumer Service	11–15	6.53
MCI SuperSaver	13–17	7.41
Western Union 24-hour MetroFone	12–16	6.86

SOURCE: Consumers Union. 1983. "Update: Cut-Rate Phone Services," *Consumer Reports,* November, pp. 618–20. Copyright 1983 by Consumers Union of the United States Inc., Mount Vernon, New York 10553. Excerpted by permission from *Consumer Reports,* November 1983.

Many users viewed non-AT&T services as inferior; they required a user to have a touch-tone phone, push more buttons, and suffer more service outages and often lower quality transmissions than with AT&T. Under the court-mandated divestiture agreement, however, local phone companies were required to give all long-distance companies equal access. Because of equal access and technological improvements, the quality of AT&T's competitors improved over time.

Prior to divestiture, AT&T announced plans to cut long-distance rates by roughly 10 percent at the time of the breakup, creating uncertainty about relative prices after divestiture. AT&T's competitors tried to eliminate this uncertainty about pricing in the minds of potential customers. A spokesman for MCI (AT&T's largest competitor) told one publication: "We're going to stay below them; that's how we made our market, and that's how we'll continue to do it." They announced in their advertising: "Though no one knows what the specific outcome of divestiture will be on every score, one thing that is certain is that *MCI's rates will still be lower than AT&T's.*"

Indeed, AT&T's long-distance pricing has fallen over time, and all its competitors have lowered their prices accordingly. The differential between the firms' prices has shrunk, however. By April 1986, the rates were as shown in the following table:

EXAMPLE 8.1

PRICE UMBRELLA *continued*

Company and Plan	Average Cost of 9 Sample Calls		
	Day Rate	Evening Rate	Night/Weekend Rate
AT&T (direct dial)	$20.95	$12.54	$8.36
Allnet	19.66	11.92	7.89
GTE Home Sprint	19.70	12.18	8.17
ITT Consumer Service	19.68	11.81	7.86
MCI	20.00	11.88	7.86
US Telecom	18.60	11.25	7.41
Western Union	19.56	11.98	8.13

SOURCE: Consumers Union. 1986. "Long-Distance Phoning: Time to Get Fickle." *Consumer Reports*, May, pp. 302–4. Copyright 1986 by Consumers Union of United States Inc., Mount Vernon, New York 10553. Excerpted by permission from *Consumer Reports*, May, 1986.

Thus, over time, AT&T's price umbrella has offered its competitors less protection. Chapter 23 provides more extensive discussion of the effects of deregulation on this industry.

their activities to increase their profits. A group of firms that explicitly acts collectively to promote its best interests is called a **cartel.** If all the firms in an industry coordinate their activities, then the cartel is effectively a monopoly; if only some of them do so, then the group acts as a dominant firm facing a competitive fringe of noncooperating firms.

■ PRICE LEADERSHIP

Competitive-fringe firms follow the price leadership of the dominant firm (see Examples 8.1 and 8.2).[2] If all firms produce identical products, the dominant firm sets a price, and the others take it as given. So long as the dominant firm lets the fringe firms sell as much as they want at that price, they have no incentive to charge lower prices. Were they to charge a higher price than the dominant firm, they would be unable to sell their products.

___
[2] It is possible for a firm to have a price leadership role in markets without a single large firm. Markham (1951) describes three types of price leadership: (1) dominant-firm price leadership, (2) collusive price leadership, and (3) barometric price leadership. We discuss the first type in this chapter. Collusive price leadership occurs when firms coordinate their pricing to achieve monopoly-level pricing and is discussed in Chapter 9. Barometric price leadership occurs when one (typically large) firm is thought by other firms to have superior information, so they attempt to duplicate its behavior. Thus, price leadership occurs in markets with dominant firms, in markets with collusion, or in markets that are very competitive—it does not automatically imply a monopolistic price.

EXAMPLE 8.2

PRICE RIGIDITY WITH DOMINANT FIRMS

Stigler (1947) finds that in an industry in which there is a dominant firm that exercises price leadership, prices are relatively rigid; that is, there are fewer changes in prices. In his classification, an industry has price leadership if there is a relatively large firm, "producing, say, 40 per cent of the output of the industry at a minimum, and more if the second largest firm is large . . ." (p. 228).

Nineteen industries with a small number of firms and two monopolies were studied. The criteria for inclusion in this study were that Stigler was able to obtain "a fairly precise knowledge of the industry structure" (p. 222) and that a continuous price and output series existed for the period of June 1929 through May 1937. Of the 19 nonmonopolies, seven had leaders. The following table summarizes the key facts about them.

In the table, the first coefficient of variation is a measure of the variability of monthly prices; the larger this measure, the greater the fluctuation in prices. Comparing the 7 price-leader industries to the other 12 nonmonopolies, Stigler concludes: "Except for the number of price changes of two-firm industries (where bananas dominate the result), the prices of industries with price leaders are less flexible than those of industries without price leaders, despite the larger fluctuations of output of the former group." (p. 228). As the table shows, the average coefficient of variation for the price leader group was 6.7 compared to 16.9 for the other group.

For example, if the producer of a popular brand of antacids lowers its price, producers of less popular antacids must accept it and lower their prices or be driven out of business. After all, most consumers will not pay as much or more for an unknown product as they will for a well-known one.

Whether a dominant firm can exercise market power in the long run depends crucially on the number of firms that can enter the industry, how their production costs compare to those of the dominant firm, and how fast they can enter. The following sections examine three versions of the dominant-competitive fringe model under alternative assumptions about entry.

	Number of Firms in Industry	Price Flexibility		Coefficient of Variation of Output
		Number of Price Changes	Coefficient of Variation	
Price-Leader Industries				
Bananas	2	46	16	17
Cans	4	6	5	27
Grain-binder	2	5	3	63
Plaster	3	4	5	29
Starch	4	20	12	13
Sulfur	2	0	0	24
Tractors	4	6	6	76
Averages	3.0	12.4	6.7	35.6
Non-Price-Leader Industries				
Boric acid	3	7	17	16
Cement	12	14	11	41
Copper	4	63	37	43
Gasoline*	11	84	22	16
Linoleum	2	12	9	30
Newsprint	9	6	16	16
Plate glass	2	8	13	34
Plows	6	25	6	50
Rayon	8	26	30	34
Soap	3	9	12	7
Tires	8	36	9	16
Window glass	3	20	21	24
Averages	5.9	25.8	16.9	27.3
Monopolies				
Aluminum	1	2	6	47
Nickle	1	0	0	35

*In Pennsylvania and Delaware

■ THE NO-ENTRY MODEL

Consider an industry with a dominant firm and a competitive fringe in which no additional fringe firms can enter. Two key results emerge from an analysis of this model: (1) it is more profitable to be the *gorilla* of an industry than a mere fringe firm, and (2) the existence of the fringe limits the dominant firm's market power—that is, it is more profitable to be the only firm in an industry (a monopolist) than merely a dominant firm.

Assumptions

Five crucial assumptions underlie this simple, no-entry model:

1. *There is one firm that is much larger than any other firm because of its lower production costs.*[3]

2. *All firms except the dominant firm are price-takers*, determining their output levels by setting marginal cost equal to the industry price (p).

3. *The number of firms (n) in the competitive fringe is fixed: no new entry can occur.* That is, the dominant firm knows that it can raise the industry's price without causing new firms to enter the market or existing firms to build additional plants.

4. *The dominant firm knows the industry's demand curve, D(p).* Each firm produces a homogeneous product, so that there is a single price in this market.

5. *The dominant firm can predict how much output the competitive fringe will produce at any given price;* that is, it knows the competitive fringe's supply curve, $S(p)$.[4]

The Dominant Firm's Reasoning

Suppose you ran the dominant firm. How would you choose your output level? Given your firm's large size, you could drive up the market's price by restricting your output. Unfortunately for you, as your dominant firm lowers its output and price rises, the competitive fringe increases its output because it is moving up its supply curve, $S(p)$. As a result, industry output falls less than you would like, and the industry price does not rise as high as it would if your firm had a monopoly.

Thus, your dominant firm's problem is much more complex than that of a simple monopolist, which merely needs to consider the market demand curve (with its corresponding marginal revenue curve) and its marginal cost curve to determine its profit-maximizing output. Your dominant firm, in contrast, must consider not only those factors, but also how the competitive fringe responds to your actions.

To maximize your profits, you must take the competitive fringe's actions into account when setting your policy. A convenient way to calculate your optimal price level is to do the following thought experiment. For lack of an ability to stop them, let the fringe firms sell as much as they want at the market price: the price you set. Except at the very highest prices, the competitive fringe does not produce enough to meet all of the market's demand. Your dominant firm, then, is in a monopoly position with respect to this residual demand. Thus, you can determine your optimal output by a two-step procedure. First, determine your firm's residual demand curve; then, act like a monopolist with respect to the residual demand. This two-step procedure can be illustrated with the use of graphs.

---

[3] Although an industry may be characterized by a small group of relatively large firms rather than a single dominant firm, we concentrate on the case of the single dominant firm for simplicity.

[4] Since the dominant firm knows its own output, Q_d, it calculates the quantity supplied by the fringe as $Q_f = Q - Q_d$, where Q is total industry output. Thus, if the dominant firm knows the industry's demand curve, it can vary its own output to infer the fringe's supply curve.

FIGURE 8.1   The Dominant Firm and the Competitive Fringe

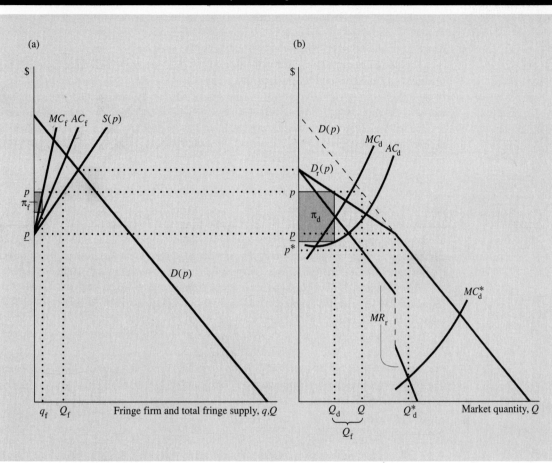

A Graphic Analysis of Dominant Firm Behavior

The first step is to determine the long-run residual demand curve facing the dominant firm. Figure 8.1 shows two graphs: (a) one for a representative competitive-fringe firm and for the entire competitive fringe, and (b) one for the dominant firm.

The graph on the left, Figure 8.1a, shows the long-run supply curve of a typical, price-taking, competitive-fringe firm, which is its marginal cost curve above the minimum of its average cost curve ($\underline{p}$). The fringe firm's shutdown price is $\underline{p}$. The market price is in one of two price ranges: at or above $\underline{p}$ or below $\underline{p}$. Above $\underline{p}$, each fringe firm earns positive economic profits. At $\underline{p}$, each fringe firm makes zero profits and is indifferent between operating and shutting down.[5] Below $\underline{p}$, each fringe firm shuts down, and the dominant firm is a monopoly. Also shown is the competitive fringe's supply curve, $S(p)$, which is the horizontal summation of the individual fringe firm's supply curves. That is, $S(p) = nq_f(p)$, where n is the number of firms and q_f is the output of a typical fringe firm. The market demand curve, $D(p)$, is also shown.

The dominant firm's residual demand curve is the horizontal difference between the market demand curve and the competitive fringe's supply curve: $D_r(p) = D(p) - S(p)$. In the graph on the right, Figure 8.1b, the market demand curve (dotted line) is above the residual demand curve (solid line) at prices above $\underline{p}$ and equal to it at prices below $\underline{p}$. That is, the fringe firms meet some or all of the market demand if price is above $\underline{p}$, but they drop out of the market and leave all of the demand to the dominant firm if price falls below $\underline{p}$.

Any firm, regardless of market structure, maximizes its profits by picking a price (or equivalently, an output level) so that its marginal cost equals its marginal revenue. The dominant firm's marginal revenue curve (MR_r) corresponds to its residual demand curve and has two distinct sections. If the competitive fringe produces positive levels of output, the dominant firm's residual demand curve lies below (and is flatter than) the market demand curve. The marginal revenue curve, MR_r, in this region is flatter than the marginal revenue curve in the region where the residual demand curve and the market demand curve are identical.[6] There is a discrete jump between the two sections of the marginal revenue curve at the point where the residual demand curve and the market demand curve meet.

The dominant firm behaves as a monopolist would with respect to the residual demand; it sets its price (or output) so that its marginal cost equals marginal revenue. Because the marginal revenue curve has two sections, there are two possible types of equilibria; which one occurs depends on the dominant firm's cost curves.

The following sections consider two types of markets:

1. The dominant firm charges a high price, so that it makes economic profits and the fringe firms also make profits or break even.

2. The dominant firm sets a price so low that the fringe firms shut down to avoid making losses. The dominant firm is now a monopoly.

---

[5] As drawn, each fringe firm produces essentially no output at $\underline{p}$. If the firms had the usual U-shaped average cost curves, however, they would produce a positive amount of output at that price.

[6] The marginal revenue curve is more steeply sloped than the corresponding residual demand curve, however. In the graphs, we have used straight lines for simplicity. An easy way to draw marginal revenue curves is to recognize that if a straight-line demand curve hits a horizontal line at Q, the corresponding marginal revenue curve is also a straight line and hits the horizontal line at $Q/2$. This relationship can be proved using calculus. Let the straight-line demand curve be $p = a - bq$. Then total revenues are $R \equiv pq = aq - bq^2$. The marginal revenue curve is obtained by differentiating R with respect to q: $MR = a - 2bq$. At $p = 0$, the demand curve hits the horizontal axis at output $Q = a/b$. At $MR = 0$, the marginal revenue curve hits the horizontal axis at output $Q/2 = a/(2b)$.

The Dominant Firm–Competitive Fringe Equilibrium. The first type of equilibrium occurs if the dominant firm's costs are not substantially less than those of the fringe firms (a mathematical analysis of this case is presented in Appendix 8A). The dominant firm's marginal cost curve, MC_d, crosses the first downward sloping segment of the marginal revenue curve, MR_r, in Figure 8.1b.

The dominant firm chooses to produce Q_d level of output at price p (the height of the residual demand curve at the output level Q_d). At the price level p, the difference between the market demand, Q, and the dominant firm's output, Q_d, is the competitive fringe's supply, Q_f (which is shown in Figures 8.1a and 8.1b). If the dominant firm's costs are this high, it does not drive the competitive fringe out of business. Its own profits are maximized at a price so high that the fringe firms make positive profits.

In most markets, positive economic profits would attract new entrants. In this market, however, no new firms can enter (by assumption), so both the dominant firm and the competitive fringe firms can make positive profits forever. In Figure 8.1b, the dominant firm's profits are labeled π_d.[7] The profits of a typical fringe firm are positive as well (since $p > \underline{p}$), and a typical fringe firm's profits are shown as π_f in Figure 8.1a. Because the dominant firm's average cost is lower than the fringe firms' (minimum $AC_d < \underline{p}$), the dominant firm makes more profits per unit (average profits), and it also sells more units than an individual fringe firm, so it must make more total profits as well.

Thus, the dominant firm maximizes its profits by charging a price so high that it loses some of its market share to the competitive fringe. It does not make sense for the dominant firm to set its price so low that it drives the fringe out of business, even though that would increase the number of units of output the dominant firm could sell. After all, few good businesspeople accept the argument: "I lose a little on every sale, but make up for it in volume."

The dominant firm makes lower profits than it would if it were a monopolist and the fringe did not exist. The fringe can only hurt the dominant firm. Figure 8.2 compares the dominant firm to the monopolist by showing both equilibria on the same graph.

A monopolist sets its output where its marginal cost curve, MC, intersects its marginal revenue curve, MR_m,—the curve that is marginal to the market demand curve, $D(p)$. The monopoly output is labeled Q_m in Figure 8.2. The corresponding price is p_m (the height of the market demand curve at output level Q_m).

In the figure, the dominant firm's marginal revenue curve, MR_r, intersects the marginal cost curve at a smaller quantity, Q_d, than the monopolist's Q_m (see Appendix 8A). The dominant firm's corresponding price is p. Not surprisingly, the monopolist charges more (p_m is greater than p). The monopolist produces less than does the industry with a dominant

---

[7] A firm's profits are total revenue minus total cost: $\pi = pq - C$, where pq (price times quantity) = total revenues. A firm's average revenue is the price (the amount of revenue the firm receives per unit of output). Its average cost is $C/q = AC$. Thus, we can rewrite the definition of a firm's profits as $\pi = (p - AC)q$. That is, profits equal average profits per unit (average revenue, p, minus average cost, $AC = C/q$) times the number of units sold (q). Thus, profits can be shown graphically as a box with a height equal to average profits per unit and a length equal to the number of units the firm sells.

FIGURE 8.2 Dominant Firm Compared to Monopoly

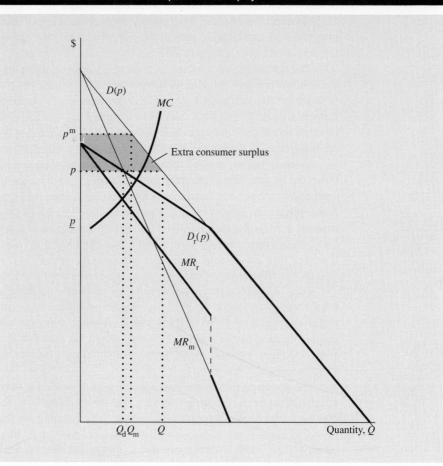

firm and a competitive fringe (Q_m is less than $Q = Q_d + Q_f$). Because the monopolist can pick any output level it wants and chooses a smaller output level than does a dominant firm with a competitive fringe ($Q_m < Q$), the dominant firm must earn lower profits than the monopolist.

Consumers are obviously better off with a dominant firm and a competitive fringe than with a monopolist: a monopolist charges them a higher price (and hence they buy fewer units of output). Consumer surplus is the area under the demand curve and above the price, and there is more consumer surplus with a dominant firm and a competitive fringe than with a monopolist. This extra consumer surplus is shown as the shaded area in Figure 8.2.

The Dominant Firm as Monopolist. Now, suppose that the dominant firm has extremely low costs compared to the fringe firms, so that its marginal cost curve is MC_d

in Figure 8.1b. Notice that MC_d^* crosses MR_r in the lower part of its two downward sloping sections. The dominant firm chooses to produce Q_d^* level of output at price p^* (the height of the residual demand curve at output level Q_d^*). Since p^* is below the fringe firms' shutdown point (p = their minimum average cost), the fringe firms produce nothing ($Q_f^* = 0$). As a result, industry output, Q^*, equals the dominant firm's output, Q_d^*.

In this case, the dominant firm sets a monopoly price, and no competitive-fringe firm enters. The dominant firm meets all the demand of the market, unchecked by the fringe and is thus a monopolist. The reason it is a monopolist is that $MC_d^* = MR_r$ along the segment of MR_r that is same as the marginal revenue curve associated with the market demand curve. As Dr. Hunter S. Thompson said, "Stand aside. Let the big dog eat."[8]

■ A MODEL WITH FREE, INSTANTANEOUS ENTRY

If unlimited entry is possible, a dominant firm cannot set as high a price as it can if entry is limited or prevented. This section retains all the assumptions made in the preceding section except that now an unlimited number of competitive-fringe firms may enter the market. Firms enter if they can make positive profits.

In this situation, fringe firms cannot make profits in the long run; they either break even or are driven out of business. If fringe firms produce at all, the market price can go no higher than a fringe firm's minimum average cost, so that fringe firms always just break even. After all, if they made positive profits, more firms would flood into the industry and drive price down to the level where each earns zero economic profits. Since the dominant firm has lower costs than fringe firms, it makes positive profits, but its profits are lower than if entry did not occur.

Even with unlimited entry, the dominant firm can gain and hold indefinitely a large share of the market if it has some cost or other advantage. For example, the Cheerleader Supply Co. accounts for 60 percent of cheerleading uniforms and equipment sold in this country.[9] This is an industry with easy entry, and yet one firm has the lion's share of the market, presumably because it has superior products, a superior sales force, or has generated goodwill with buyers.

Graphic Analysis of Unlimited Entry

The competitive-fringe firms' cost curves are the same as before, but because unlimited entry is possible, the fringe's supply curve is horizontal (Figure 8.3a).[10] That is, as long

---

[8] *Rolling Stone.* 1983. July 21/August 4.

[9] According to its chief executive officer, Lawrence Herkimer, in Applebome, Peter. 1984. "The World's Oldest and Fatest Cheerleader." *San Francisco Chronicle,* January 12, 24.

[10] As more and more firms enter (n rises), the slope of the competitive-fringe supply curve becomes flatter and flatter (it is n times the slope of a typical firm's supply, or MC, curve). Eventually, the fringe's supply curve becomes essentially horizontal.

FIGURE 8.3 Dominant Firm with Free, Instantaneous Entry by Fringe Firms

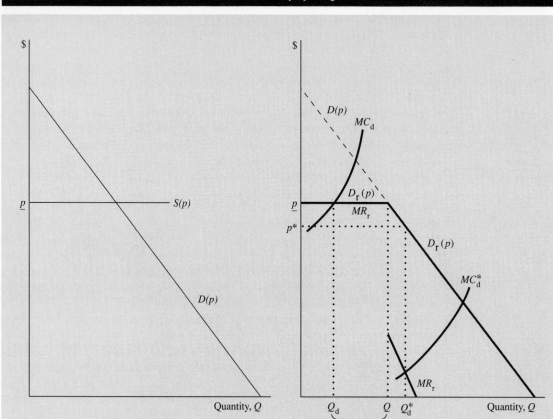

as price is at least $\underline{p}$, the competitive fringe is capable of and is willing to supply any quantity that the market demands.

As shown in Figure 8.3b, the residual demand curve facing the dominant firm is horizontal at $\underline{p}$, so the corresponding marginal revenue curve is also flat (remember that in a competitive market a firm faces a horizontal demand curve, and hence its marginal revenue curve is identical to its demand curve at the market price). Below $\underline{p}$, the residual demand curve is the market demand, which slopes downward, so that the corresponding marginal revenue curve also slopes downward. Again, the marginal revenue curve corresponding to the residual demand curve jumps at the quantity where the kink in the residual demand curve occurs.

There are two possible equilibria. First, if the dominant firm's marginal cost is relatively high (MC_d in Figure 8.3b), so that it intersects the horizontal portion of the MR_r

curve, the price is $\underline{p}$, and the competitive fringe meets some of the market's demand. At this price, each fringe firm makes zero economic profits (since its average cost equals $\underline{p}$) and is indifferent between staying in business and leaving the industry. How much is produced by the competitive fringe depends on the dominant firm's cost structure (that is, where MC_d intersects the horizontal marginal revenue curve), which determines the dominant firm's output, Q_d. Collectively, the fringe firms produce an output level $Q_f = Q - Q_d$, as shown in Figure 8.3b.[11]

Thus, if fringe firms flood into a market whenever positive profits can be made, the dominant firm cannot charge a price above the minimum average cost of a fringe firm. Although a dominant firm can make positive profits, competitive-fringe firms just break even. If the dominant firm's price would be above $\underline{p}$ in the absence of entry, consumers are better off if entry is possible because it results in lower prices.

The second type of equilibrium occurs if the dominant firm's marginal cost is lower (MC_d^* in Figure 8.3b), so that it hits the marginal revenue curve in the downward sloping portion. Here, the price is so low that no fringe firm stays in the industry when the dominant firm's costs are lower than fringe firm's costs. This equilibrium ($Q = Q_d, p^*$) is the same as discussed previously in the second no-entry equilibrium and is shown in Figures 8.1b and 8.3b. The dominant firm is a monopolist, and the potential supply of fringe firms is irrelevant.

■ A MODEL WITH GRADUAL ENTRY AND PRICE ADJUSTMENT

In most industries, firms cannot enter instantaneously. It takes time to build new plants, design new products, order special parts, inform consumers of new products, and so forth. As a result, a dominant firm may be able to charge very high prices for an extended period of time before having to deal with new competitors. Then, as entry gradually occurs, the dominant firm must lower its price.

Suppose an industry is dominated by a large firm that charges a very high price, and another firm can profitably produce in that industry at that price. Should it enter the industry? The answer is yes, unless it has a still better opportunity elsewhere. How quickly should it enter the industry? The answer to this question is more difficult.

Suppose, for example, a producer of floppy disk drives for personal computers notices that Apple is charging a very high price for the floppy disk drives used on its personal computer. If the firm is already producing disk drives that are compatible with Apple's computer, and it could profitably produce at Apple's price, it could compete with Apple

---

[11] Why don't fringe firms meet the entire demand at $\underline{p}$, instead of splitting it with the dominant firm? The answer is that the dominant firm has lower costs and can force some of the fringe firms out of the industry. Suppose that the dominant firm is producing its desired output of Q_d, and n fringe firms are producing $Q_f = Q - Q_d$. Now, if additional fringe firms enter this market, output exceeds market demand at $\underline{p}$. For the market to clear, the price must fall. Since the dominant firm is making positive profits, it stays in the industry. The fringe firms, however, start making losses (since they just break even at $\underline{p}$). Thus, some of the fringe firms must drop out of the industry until the price again rises to $\underline{p}$. Alternatively stated, the dominant firm can always charge slightly below $\underline{p}$ to sell as much as it wants.

immediately. Even if its disk drives must be modified slightly to make them compatible, if this firm can do so quickly and inexpensively, it can enter the Apple-compatible market almost immediately. In contrast, suppose the firm has the technical knowledge to produce compatible floppy disk drives but is not already producing them or anything like them at the time Apple's pricing creates an opportunity for entry. In this case, its entry time is longer.

The cost of entering a new market is likely to be higher the faster a firm tries to enter, because of adjustment costs. For example, if it tries to begin production in six months rather than one year, it might not have time to get multiple bids for new construction, it may have to pay workers at overtime rates during the conversion period, it may not have time to test its new equipment and products fully, and so forth.

Because it is more costly to enter immediately, entry into even very profitable industries occurs slowly. As a result, a dominant firm may decide to set a high price at first, when it has few competitors, and then lower its price as new firms enter. That is, where entry occurs slowly, a dominant firm does not equate its short-run marginal cost with the marginal revenue curve corresponding to the current demand curve; it realizes that the higher its price today, the faster new firms will enter the market. Thus, in early periods, the dominant firm sets a lower price than it would if it ignored the future. In most cases, it is in the dominant firm's best interest to set a high price at first and then slowly lower it as entry occurs. Although the high price increases the rate of future entry, profits today are worth more to the dominant firm than are profits in the future (given positive interest rates).

There are several alternative models of a dominant firm's behavior when potential competitors enter gradually in response to prices and predicted profitability. Two well-known models will be discussed: the first assumes a continuous flow of entrants and a rate of entry that is known with certainty by all concerned; the second assumes "lumpy entry" (all new firms enter at once) and uncertainty about when entry will occur.

Dynamic Limit Pricing with Continuous Entry

One of the best-known models of a dominant firm's pricing behavior in the face of certain entry is that of Gaskins (1971).[12] In Gaskins' model, the dominant firm takes into account the gradual but continuous entry of competitors in determining its optimal pricing behavior.

The model assumes that new fringe firms enter at a rate that is proportional to expected profits: the higher the expected profits, the faster they enter. In other words, the higher the dominant firm sets its price (which raises potential entrants' expected profits), the faster fringe firms enter. The fringe firms have **myopic expectations:** they think profits in the future will equal profits today. Thus, an increase in the dominant firm's price proportionally raises the rate of entry.

The dominant firm takes this threat of gradual entry into account in determining the price that maximizes profits. As discussed in the case of instantaneous entry, the dominant firm wants to maximize its own profits, not merely to prevent other firms from entering.

---

[12] See Baron (1973) for a similar story. For an earlier, intuitive explanation, see Stigler (1965).

FIGURE 8.4   Dynamic Limit Pricing

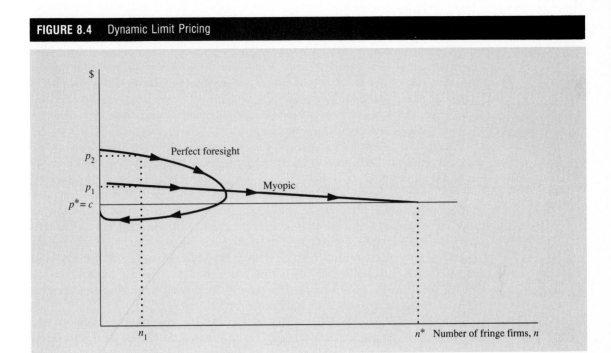

After all, if the dominant firm discourages entry by keeping its price very low, it reduces both the expected profits of potential entrants and its own as well.

As before, the dominant firm is assumed to have a lower cost of production than potential entrants do. For simplicity, the model assumes that firms have constant average and marginal cost and that fringe firms can produce one unit of output at a given cost, c. Such a firm enters the industry if the industry price, p, is at least as high as c. As a result, as long as the dominant firm picks a price greater than c, fringe firms gradually enter; if it sets a price less than c, fringe firms gradually leave the industry.

Given his assumptions, Gaskins shows that the dominant firm's optimal pricing policy depends on the initial number of fringe firms in the industry. The curve in Figure 8.4 labeled *myopic* illustrates the dominant firm's pricing behavior. In the figure, the vertical axis shows the price set by the dominant firm at time t, $p(t)$, and the horizontal axis shows the number of fringe firms at time t, $n(t)$.

If there are initially very few fringe firms in the industry, say n_1, the dominant firm starts with a relatively high price, say p_1, and then lowers the price gradually to $p^* = c$. In Figure 8.4, the myopic line that falls from p_1 to p^* shows that the dominant firm lowers its price over time. The arrows on this price-adjustment path indicate the direction of movement.

At p^*, there are n^* fringe firms that are exactly breaking even, so they have no further incentive to enter or leave the industry. The dominant firm then continues to price at p^* forever, and no further entry occurs. Since the dominant firm's costs are less than c, it makes positive profits even at p^*.[13]

The price p^* is often referred to as a **limit price** because it is a price that, if maintained forever, prevents further entry (it *limits* entry). The dominant firm in the Gaskins model may set a price above or below the limit price in the short run, but in the long run it sets a limit price and maintains it. If a firm sets a limit price in the long run, even if it sets other prices in the short run, it is said to be using **dynamic limit pricing.**

The assumption that the dominant firm has a cost advantage is crucial: if it does not, its market share will ultimately shrink to that of any fringe firm. Thus, *where there is no cost advantage, the dominant firm's market power melts away over time*, and it ceases to be a dominant firm.

There are many examples of new industries in which a product is introduced at a high price that soon falls to a competitive level (see Example 8.3). When an industry is new, one or a few firms have large market shares and face relatively few competitors. Only over time do new entrants drive down the price. A particularly striking example from the early days of the ball-point pen industry is given in Example 8.3. A more recent example is the pocket calculator. When simple models that only added, subtracted, multiplied, and divided were introduced in the early 1970s, they often sold for prices in excess of \$100. Today, such a calculator generally sells for less than \$10.[14]

This model of dynamic limit pricing (as do all models) deviates from reality in three ways. First, in this model, the dominant firm's strategic activities are limited to setting price.[15] Second, because fringe firms have no sunk costs, exit and entry take place at the same rate. Finally, and most importantly, fringe firms have myopic expectations about profits: they implicitly assume that future profits will equal current profits.

One conclusion this model leads to is surprising, because it is inconsistent with the model of instantaneous entry. In Gaskins' model, a low-cost dominant firm does not drive out the fringe in the long run. In contrast, in the static model (with a flat fringe supply curve), a low-cost dominant firm drives out the fringe. After all, the dominant firm could price slightly below the fringe's cost of production (any price less than p^*) and grab all the industry's business for itself. This difference is especially surprising because the instantaneous-entry model appears to be a special case of Gaskins' model. If the proportional rate of increase is made very large, entry of fringe firms approaches being instantaneous.

---

[13] Figure 8.4 only shows the myopic adjustment path to the left of n^*. The straight-line adjustment path continues and crosses the $p^* = c$ line, although it is not shown in the figure. If there are initially a relatively large number of fringe firms in the industry, the dominant firm should start with a price below p^*. Where the price is below p^*, fringe firms lose money, so some of them leave the industry. As the fringe firms exit, the dominant firm raises its price until it reaches $p^* = c$, where the number of fringe firms is n^*. It then continues to charge p^* forever. Thus, in the long run, the price, p^*, and the number of fringe firms, n^*, are the same, regardless of whether the initial number of fringe firms was large or small.

[14] Other factors that contributed to the fall in the cost of calculators included entry in silicon chip manufacturing (an industry that creates inputs for the calculator manufacturers), learning by doing, technological change (Chapter 20), and possibly intertemporal price discrimination (Chapter 14).

[15] Strategic behavior (including varying output or price from period to period, threats, and advertising) is discussed at length in later chapters, especially Chapters 10 and 13.

EXAMPLE 8.3

AND ONLY A SMILE REMAINED

[The Cheshire Cat] vanished quite slowly, beginning with the end of the tail, and ending with the grin, which remained some time after the rest of it had gone.
—LEWIS CARROLL

Laszlo Jozsef Biro took out a patent on a ball-point pen in Paris in 1939. During World War II, he moved to Argentina where his company, Eterpen S. A., started producing and selling the pens in 1943. Unlike a conventional fountain pen, it had a miniature socket that held a ball bearing, it used a special ink that dried almost instantly, and it held enough of this unconventional ink to work for months without refilling.

Unlike fountain pens, this pen could work at high altitudes without the risk of leakage. As a result, the U.S. Air Force was interested. It sent pens to various American manufacturers, saying it might be interested in buying ten thousand or so of them. The big three pen manufacturers—Parker, Sheaffer, and Eversharp—looked into the patent rights and discovered that Eberhard Faber, a pencil manufacturer, had obtained them but had run into difficulties producing them. Eversharp obtained the rights in 1945.

Eversharp started redesigning the pen for mass production and instituted an advertising campaign to prepare the public for this new "miracle pen." This advertising greatly benefited Milton Reynolds, who beat Eversharp to the market.

Reynolds had seen the pen in South America. When he found he was too late to buy the rights from Biro, he developed ways around Biro's patent. What was unique about the Biro pen was its pressure-feed system that regulated the ink supply. Reynolds developed a different system that used gravity.

The Reynolds International Pen Company started production on October 6, 1945. A major New York department store, Gimbel's, advertised extensively that the pen was guaranteed to write for two years without refilling, to write under water and at stratospheric altitudes, and to make a clear impression on from six to eight carbons. These claims made Gimbel's price of $12.50 (the maximum price allowed by the wartime Office of Price Administration) seem, if not a bargain, at least not the most staggering extravagance of all times.

Since the initial cost of production was estimated to be around 80¢ per pen, healthy profits were realized when Gimbel's sold 10,000 pens (worth about a third of the store's average total daily sales volume) on the first day of sale, October 29, 1945. This success encouraged Reynolds to expand production; by early 1946, his 800 employees were producing 30,000 pens per day.

Production could not keep up with orders, and gift certificates were printed. By March 1946, Reynolds had banked a cool $3 million. During one 10 day period, he deposited $1.5 million from orders of pens yet to be made. By February 1946, Reynolds had an after-tax profit of $1,558,607.81.

These enormous profits encouraged entry. Gimbel's rival department store, Macy's, sold the Biro pen for $19.98. It too did well, encouraging still more entry. Late in April, Eversharp finally entered the market with a $15 pen. The July 1946 *Fortune* magazine reported that Sheaffer was going to sell a pen at $15. Eversharp then announced plans to sell a retractable pen at $25.

Continued

EXAMPLE 8.3

AND ONLY A SMILE REMAINED *continued*

Meanwhile, Reynolds introduced a new model with a retractable point protector that cost 60¢ per pen to produce but sold at the original price of $12.50. By late in the summer of 1946, his pens were being sold in 37 other countries (with prices in Hong Kong reaching $75). As profits remained high, still others entered.

The Ball Point Pen Company of Hollywood ignored a patent infringement suit and sold a $9.95 version. Another manufacturer, David Kahn, announced plans to sell a pen for less than $3. In October, Reynolds introduced a new pen that cost 30¢ to produce and sold for $3.85.

Approximately 100 manufacturers were producing pens by Christmas 1946, some selling for as little as $2.98. Reynolds again introduced a new model priced at $1.69, but Gimbel's sold for 88¢ in a price war with Macy's. At one point, Gimbel's changed prices five times during shopping hours. Again Reynolds introduced a new, two-color model priced at 98¢ that was still highly profitable.

By mid-1948, some ball-point pens were selling for 39¢ and cost between 8¢ and 10¢ to produce. The price of some pens fell to 25¢ by 1951, and soon after pens were available at 19¢. By this time, the large number of firms in the industry had driven the price down to the point where no unusual economic profits were being earned. Reynolds' market share went to zero and the firm stopped producing new pens in the United States.

This example shows that if a firm has no cost or other advantage, it cannot maintain a large share of the market in the long run. Nonetheless, even a short-lived period of dominance can be highly lucrative. It is estimated that in a single month, Reynolds earned profits as high as $500,000, which was about 20 times his original investment of $26,000.

SOURCES: Lipsey and Steiner (1981) and Whiteside (1951).

The two models reach different conclusions because of the way fringe firms form expectations about future profits. In the instantaneous-entry model (static model) fringe firms know their present and future profits, which are the same, but in Gaskins' model fringe firms have myopic expectations about profits: they *incorrectly* assume that future profits will be the same as current ones.

Suppose, instead, that fringe firms **perfect foresight,** so that they perfectly forecast future prices and profits. Now, the dynamic model has the same long-run result as the instantaneous-entry model. As shown by the curve labeled *perfect foresight* in Figure 8.4, the dominant firm initially sets a very high price to make extraordinary short-run profits, and as fringe firms enter, it lowers its price. Eventually, since it sets its price below $p^* = c$, all the fringe firms leave the industry, whereupon the dominant firm raises its price to p^* to keep them out in the future. That is, where fringe firms have perfect foresight and enter slowly, the dominant firm charges p^* in the long run and makes all the sales, just as in the instantaneous-entry model when the dominant firm has lower costs.[16]

A dominant firm can achieve this result by credibly committing itself to a particular price path. Although it is difficult to be certain about a firm's motives, in 1988 IBM announced its price plans for the next couple of years. While it charged between $7000 and $13,500 for an 80386 computer in 1987, it said it would charge between $3600 and $13,500 in 1988, and between $1350 and $13,500 in 1989.[17] That is, IBM announced to smaller firms that produced similar computers that it intended to lower the price on its low-end machines to less than 20 percent of their initial levels. High-cost manufacturers that believed IBM would stick to this policy may have been deterred by this announcement from entering the market.

These gradual-entry models abstract from reality, but they serve the useful purpose of illustrating the basic trade-off a dominant firm must face between short-run and long-run profits. Notice that it is inefficient for fringe firms to be in such an industry: they produce at higher cost than does the dominant firm. Nonetheless, their presence may be socially useful because they keep the dominant firm's price lower than it would otherwise be, at the limit price. Thus there is a social trade-off between efficiency in production (low costs) and efficiency in pricing.

Dynamic Limit Pricing with Lumpy Entry

Several models have been developed in which a dominant firm's potential rivals enter at the same time.[18] Entry does not happen gradually over time as in the Gaskins model; hence it is called *lumpy entry*. In these models, the dominant firm knows that the higher it sets its price, the sooner other firms enter *as a group*.

A well-known model by Kamien and Schwartz (1971) looks at two periods: period one is the time interval from the dominant firm's initial pricing decision until the appearance of one or more entrants; period two is the rest of time. Since the dominant firm earns lower profits after other firms enter, all else the same, it is in its interest to delay entry

---

[16] The perfect foresight curve in Figure 8.4 is based on Berck and Perloff (1988). In the perfect foresight model, fringe firms can perfectly predict their profits, because the dominant firm commits itself to a price path from the first day. Karp (1988) shows that when the dominant firm cannot commit to a price path, but may revise its policy in the future, it cannot convince rational fringe firms that it will maintain such a low price that they should leave the industry. In the absence of commitment, the dominant firm sets its short-run profit-maximizing price at every moment. Thus, in the long run, fringe firms remain in the industry. Flaherty (1980) and Judd and Petersen (1986) also present models in which entrants have nonmyopic expectations, but they differ from the Gaskins model in several ways.

[17] LaPlante, Alice, and Paula S. Stone. 1988. "IBM's Pricing Strategy Puts Pressure on Rivals." *InfoWorld*, February 29, 1 and 81. Brownstein, Mark. 1988. "IBM Manufacturing Edge Makes Price Cuts Viable." *InfoWorld*, March 14, 5, argues that IBM is the low-cost producer, so that such a policy of undercutting clone manufacturers' prices is possible.

[18] In most of these models (such as those described here), the exact time of entry is unknown by the dominant firm. This description ignores the uncertainty issue.

EXAMPLE 8.4

THE STEEL OF A LIFETIME

United States Steel was formed in 1901 by merger, when its share of the output of steel ingots was 66 percent. This share fell gradually over the next two decades, reaching 46 percent in 1920 and 42 percent in 1925. The book value of the assets of the constituent firms was approximately $700 million just before the merger, while the book value of U.S. Steel was listed as $1.4 billion.

Stigler (1965) has contrasted two theories that are consistent with the fall in market share and the initial markup of book value:

1. The purpose of the merger was to sell securities to "untutored investors," who bought stock based on the inflated book value of the underlying assets. Over time, since U.S. Steel had no advantage stemming from the merger, the higher prices it may have set would provide an umbrella under which more efficient rivals would flourish, and their shares would gradually increase. As a result, the value of U.S. Steel's stock would fall.

2. The merger created a dominant firm that achieved some economies of scale (its operating costs fell). In setting its price, a profit-maximizing dominant firm (Stigler argues) will take account of the rate at which other firms will enter, and will usually find it profitable to set higher prices and expect to lose some of its market share. Book value would be marked up to reflect increased efficiency and market (monopoly) power. In this case, the value of its stock need not fall over time.

An obvious test of these contrasting views is whether the financial returns to the original investors in U.S. Steel common stock were as great as those of other steel stocks over the next several decades. Under the dominant firm theory, the U.S. Steel stock should have done as well as that of other companies; under the other theory, it should have done substantially worse. If the return to U.S. Steel stock exceeded that of other firms, the original investors got a bargain.

The return on U.S. Steel's stocks was about the same as that of Bethlehem Steel and much better than that of the other major firms (Colorado, Crucible, Lackawanna, Republic, and Sloss-Sheffield). If $10,000 of U.S. Steel's stock had been purchased at the time of the merger and any earnings reinvested, by 1924 the assets would have been worth $101,039. In contrast, if $10,000 had been similarly invested in the average of the other firms, by 1924 this investment would have been worth only $53,514. The average return to investments in the other companies was below that of U.S. Steel in 16 of the 18 years after 1905.

Thus, it appears that all the potential monopoly profits were not captured by those individuals who created U.S. Steel through merger and sold the original stock. Apparently, either U.S. Steel grew more efficient than the other firms, or it was able to increase its market power over time.

As Stigler concludes, "The formation of United States Steel Corporation must therefore be viewed as a master stroke of monopoly promotion, and it is churlish of the literature to complain at the $62 million of stock given to the Morgan syndicate for bringing it about."

EXAMPLE 8.5

The Shrinking Share of Dominant Firms

Generally, a dominant firm's share of an industry's sales shrinks over time. Consider 13 unregulated, major industries in which firms compete on a national or international basis. Using the *Fortune* 500 rankings to determine the leading firm in each industry, Pascale (1984) has traced these firms' shares of industry sales over a 20-year period:

Industry Share Trends in 13 Key Industries

Leading Firm	Industry	Industry Share 1962	Industry Share 1982	Percent Change
Sears	Mass-market retailing	5	5	0
International Harvester	Farm tractors	24	18	−25
U.S. Steel	Finished steel	26	19	−27
Goodyear	OEM tires	29	27	−7
General Electric	Electrical appliances (refrigerators)	40	53	+33
RCA	Color TVs	49	20	−59
Boeing	Commercial wide-body jet aircraft	51	60	+18
General Motors	Passenger cars	52	46	−12
General Electric	Generators	59	61	+3
IBM	Mainframe computers	60	68	+13
Kodak	Photographic film	85	65	−24
Harley-Davidson	Motorcycles	100	36	−64
Xerox	Plain copiers	100	42	−58

Of these 13 leading firms, eight lost share, and one firm's share remained unchanged over the period. Three firms lost over half of their share of industry sales (RCA, Xerox, and Harley-Davidson), including both the firms that made essentially all their industry sales in 1962.

as long as the cost of doing so is not excessive. The dominant firm has a choice: it can earn very high profits for a short period of time before competitors flood into the market, or it can earn lower profits for a longer period of time before they enter. Thus, the dominant firm must trade off high profits in the short run versus the lower, long-run profits associated with the later entry of other firms. Given the assumptions of this model, the optimal pre-entry pricing policy of the dominant firm is to set a price below the short-run monopoly price but above the limit price.[19]

Again, this model deviates from reality by assuming that all competing firms enter at once and that there is limited strategic behavior by the dominant firm. This abstraction from reality is useful in illustrating that even before entry can take place, the dominant firm prices below the monopoly level so as to delay entry. The Gaskins and the Kamien and Schwartz models describe different types of entry behavior, but their basic conclusion—that the threat of entry reduces prices even before entry occurs—is the same. See Examples 8.4 and 8.5.

■ SUMMARY

A dominant firm has such a large share of the market that it has some market (monopoly) power even though it must compete with other firms. A profit-maximizing dominant firm does not attempt to prevent entry at all costs. Its behavior depends on how great its cost (or other) advantages over entrants are and on how quickly other firms can enter.

If the dominant firm has no cost or other advantages, its dominance is short-lived. If it has an advantage, it may be able to earn positive economic profits forever.

A dominant firm with a great cost advantage may find it profitable to price low enough to prevent any other firm from entering. Although it is then a monopoly (in the sense that it is the only firm in the industry), the threat of potential entry can keep its price below the monopolist's short-run profit-maximizing price. Only if costs are so high for potential entrants that they can profitably produce only at a price above the monopoly price does the threat of potential entry have no limiting effect on the dominant firm's price. In this case, the dominant firm is a monopolist and need not fear entry.

If the dominant firm's cost advantage is smaller, it maximizes profits by giving up some of its market share to competitive fringe firms in order to charge a higher price for awhile. If competitive firms can enter the market only gradually, the dominant firm may set a very high price initially and then slowly lower it over time, possibly low enough to drive the fringe out of the market.

If a large number of price-taking firms can enter the industry whenever a profit opportunity occurs, and if they can produce at costs not much above those of the dominant firm, the dominant firm is unable to charge prices substantially above the competitive price. Entry of comparable firms is the ultimate check on the monopoly power of a dominant firm.

---

[19] De Bondt (1976) extends this model to examine how the pricing policy changes if there is a lag between a rival's decision to enter and its appearance as a viable firm.

■ Key Terms

cartel
dominant firm
dynamic limit pricing
fringe (firm)

limit price
myopic expectations
perfect foresight

■ Discussion Questions

1. Are dominant firms socially harmful? If so, under what conditions?
2. Would you recommend regulating a dominant firm? If so, how and under what conditions?
3. How could one distinguish between dynamic limit pricing and reductions in prices due to reductions in costs?

4. Does the competitive fringe control the dominant firm, or does the dominant firm control the fringe?
5. Suppose a foreign, dominant, low-cost firm is competing with our domestic fringe for sales in our country. Should we feel differently about the dominant firm because it is foreign and should we regulate it differently?

■ Problems

1. Using one or more graphs, show that the profits of a monopolist are greater than the profits of a dominant firm in the no-entry equilibrium (MC_d). *Hint:* A firm's variable costs are the area under its marginal cost curve up to the relevant output.
2. Suppose the Environmental Protection Agency sets new requirements that raise the (fixed) costs of reporting compliance with pollution control rules (Pashigian 1984). How would this change affect (a) the market price, (b) the number of fringe firms, (c) total output, and (d) the dominant firm's share of the market? *Hint:* What does an increase in fixed costs do to the average cost curve of a fringe firm?
3. How would the no-entry model diagrams (Figure 8.1) change if fringe firms had the usual U-shaped average and marginal cost curves? Assume that because of a barrier to entry, there are only n fringe firms. Describe the types of possible equilibria.

4. In the case described in problem 8.3, is it possible for the dominant firm's marginal cost curve to intersect its marginal revenue curve at more than one point? Draw a diagram showing such a marginal cost curve and the multiple intersections. If multiple intersections occur, what output should the dominant firm produce to maximize its profits?
5. Are there cases in which a dominant firm would produce more than it would if it were a monopolist? *Hint:* What happens if the marginal cost curve is shifted in Figure 8.2?
6. How could a government agency that knew all the relevant cost and demand curves best regulate a dominant firm to maximize welfare? Using a graph, show a price regulation that would increase welfare (the sum of consumer and producer surplus). Would a restriction on the dominant firm's market share necessarily increase welfare? Why or why not?

Answers to odd-numbered problems are given at the back of the book.

■ Recommended Reading

Stigler (1965) provides a good, nontechnical introduction to this area. Fisher, McGowan, and Greenwood (1983) is a very readable (albeit controversial) discussion of the recent important IBM case.

■ References

Baron, David P. 1973. "Limit Pricing, Potential Entry, and Barriers to Entry." *American Economic Review* 63:666–74.

Berck, Peter, and Jeffrey M. Perloff. 1988. "The Dynamic Annihilation of a Rational Competitive Fringe by a Low-Cost Dominant Firm." *Journal of Economic Dynamics and Control* 12:659–78.

De Bondt, Raymond R. 1976. "Limit Pricing, Uncertain Entry, and the Entry Lag." *Econometrica* 44:939–46.

Fisher, Franklin M., John J. McGowan, and Joen E. Greenwood. 1983. *Folded, Spindled, and Mutilated: Economic Analysis and U.S. v. IBM*. Cambridge, Mass. The MIT Press.

Flaherty, M. Therese. 1980. "Dynamic Limit Pricing, Barriers to Entry, and Rational Firms." *Journal of Economic Theory* 23:160–82.

Gaskins, Darius, Jr. 1971. "Dynamic Limit Pricing: Optimal Pricing Under Threat of Entry." *Journal of Economic Theory* 3:306–22.

Judd, Kenneth L., and Bruce C. Petersen. 1986. "Dynamic Limit Pricing and Internal Finance." *Journal of Economic Theory* 39:368–99.

Karp, Larry S. 1988. "Consistent Policy Rules and the Benefits of Market Power." Working Paper, Department of Agricultural & Resource Economics, University of California at Berkeley.

Kamien, Morton I., and Nancy L. Schwartz. 1971. "Limit Pricing and Uncertain Entry." *Econometrica* 398 (May):441–54.

Lipsey, Richard G., and Peter O. Steiner. 1981. Economics, 6th ed. New York: Harper & Row, 281–22.

Markham, Jesse W. 1951. "The Nature and Significance of Price Leadership." *American Economic Review* 41:891–905.

Pascale, Richard T. 1984. "Perspectives on Strategy: The Real Story Behind Honda's Success." *California Management Review* 26:47–72.

Pashigian, Peter B. 1984. "The Effect of Environmental Regulation on Optimal Plant Size and Factor Shares." *Journal of Law and Economics* 27:1–28.

Stigler, George J. 1947. "The Kinky Demand Curve and Rigid Prices." *Journal of Political Economy* 55; reprinted in Stigler, George J. 1968. *The Organization of Industry*. Homewood, Ill.: Richard D. Irwin, Ch. 18, 208–34.

———. 1965. "The Dominant Firm and the Inverted Umbrella." *Journal of Law and Economics* 8; reprinted in Stigler, George J. 1968. *The Organization of Industry*. Homewood, Ill.: Richard D. Irwin, Ch. 9, 108–22.

Whiteside, Thomas. 1951. "Where Are They Now?" *New Yorker*, February 17, 39–58.

ANALYSIS USING CALCULUS

The behavior of a dominant firm with a competitive fringe can be analyzed using mathematical tools instead of graphic ones. This appendix illustrates such an analysis with the no-entry model, using more general demand and cost functions than were (implicitly) assumed in Figure 8.1 and concentrating on a long-run analysis in which average variable costs and average costs are equal.

Let the cost function of a fringe firm be $C(q_f)$ with average $(AC = C(q_f)/q_f)$ and marginal cost $(MC = C'(q_f)$, where primes indicate differentiation). The fringe firm's objective is to maximize its profits, π, through its choice of output level, q_f. This firm believes it is a price-taker that can sell as much as it wants at the going price and that it cannot affect the price through its own actions. Mathematically, the fringe firm's problem is

$$\max_{q_f} \pi = pq_f - C(q_f), \tag{8A.1}$$

where pq_f is total revenue and the difference between total revenue and total cost $[c(q_f)]$ is profits, π.

The first-order condition for profit maximization is

$$p = C'(q_f). \tag{8A.2}$$

This condition requires that the firm set its output at the point where price (the firm's marginal revenue) equals its marginal cost. The second-order condition requires $C''(q_f) > 0$; that is, the marginal cost curve must be upward sloping at the equilibrium quantity for profits to be maximized.[1]

While the individual fringe firms are price-takers, their combined output added to that of the dominant firm determines the market price. That is, the inverse demand curve

---

[1] The theory of the competitive firm requires that, in addition to meeting the first- and second-order conditions, a firm must make sure that its profits are positive (or else it should go out of business). Profits will be positive if market price is above minimum average cost ($\underline{p}$ in Figure 8.1a).

can be written as $p(Q) = p(Q_f + Q_d) = p(nq_f + Q_d)$, because there are n fringe firms. Thus, Equation 8A.2 can be rewritten as

$$p(nq_f + Q_d) = C'(q_f). \qquad (8A.2')$$

Totally differentiating Equation 8A.2', $p'ndq_f + p'dQ_d = c''dq_f$, and rearranging, yields

$$\frac{dq_f}{dQ_d} = \frac{-p'}{np' - C''} < 0, \qquad (8A.3)$$

since $np' < 0$ and $-c'' < 0$ (by the second-order condition). That is, the quantity supplied by a fringe firm falls as Q_d rises. This inverse relationship between outputs of the two firm types can be illustrated using the previous graphs. As Q_d rises, all else the same, price must fall, and as price falls, the quantity supplied by a fringe firm falls (see Figure 8.1).

We can write $Q_f(Q_d)$ to show that Q_f is a function of Q_d. From Equation 8A.3, we know that $dQ_f/dQ_d = ndq_f/dQ_d = -np'/(np' - C'') < 0$, which says Q_f falls as Q_d rises.

The dominant firm must take this relationship into account when trying to maximize its profits through its choice of output level:

$$\max_{Q_d} Q_d p[Q_d + Q_f(Q_d)] - C_d(Q_d), \qquad (8A.4)$$

where $C_d(Q_d)$ is the dominant firm's cost function. The first-order condition for a profit maximization is

$$p(Q_d + Q_f) + Q_d p'(Q_d + Q_f)\left(1 + \frac{dQ_f}{dQ_d}\right) = C_d'(Q_d). \qquad (8A.5)$$

Equation 8A.5 states that profits are maximized if the dominant firm sets its output so that its marginal revenue (conditional on the response of the competitive fringe), the left-hand side of the equation, equals its marginal cost, the right-hand side of the equation. Since, from Equation 8A.3, $dQ_f/dQ_d = -np'/(np' - C'')$, the term in brackets in Equation 8A.5 can be rewritten as $-C''/(np' - C'')$. This ratio is positive but less than 1.

If $Q_f \equiv 0$ and $dQ_f/dQ_d \equiv 0$ (the dominant firm is a monopolist), then Equation 8A.5 is the monopolist's profit maximization condition: Marginal revenue equals marginal cost. In the monopoly case, p is a function of only the monopolist's output, and $Q_d p'(Q_d)$ is multiplied by 1; whereas in the dominant firm model, price is a function of the dominant firm and the competitive fringe's output, and $Q_d p'(Q_d + Q_f)$ is multiplied by a term that is less than 1.

We can also express the effect of the fringe's supply on the dominant firm using elasticities. The fringe's supply affects the elasticity of demand that the dominant firm faces and hence helps determine the dominant firm's price. Using slightly different notation, the dominant firm's residual demand, $Q_d = D_r(p)$, can be written as the market demand, $D(p)$, minus the supply, $S(p)$, of the fringe:

$$D_r(p) = D(p) - S(p) \tag{8A.6}$$

The dominant firm's marginal revenue corresponding to this residual demand curve is obtained by differentiating Equation 8A.6 with respect to p:

$$\frac{dD_r}{dp} = \frac{dD}{dp} - \frac{dS}{dp} \tag{8A.7}$$

Equation 8A.7 can be expressed in terms of elasticities by multiplying both sides of the equation by p/Q, multiplying the left-side by Q_d/Q_d, and multiplying the last term on the right side by Q_f/Q_f:

$$\left(\frac{Q_d}{Q}\right)\epsilon_r = \epsilon_d - \left(\frac{Q_f}{Q}\right)\eta_f, \tag{8A.7'}$$

where $\epsilon_r = [(\partial D_r/\partial p)(p/Q_r)]$ is the residual demand elasticity, ϵ_d is the elasticity of the market demand curve, η_f is the fringe's supply elasticity, Q_d/Q is the dominant firm's share of output, and Q_f/Q is the fringe's share. This expression may be rewritten as

$$\epsilon_R = \epsilon_d \cdot \frac{1}{S_D} - \frac{1-S_D}{S_D}\,\eta_f$$

$$\epsilon_r = \frac{Q}{Q_d}\epsilon_d - \frac{Q_f}{Q_d}\eta_f, \tag{8A.7''}$$

where Q/Q_d is the ratio of total industry output to that of the dominant firm and Q_f/Q_d is the ratio of the fringe's output to that of the dominant firm. Thus, all else the same, the higher the absolute value of the elasticity of the residual demand facing the dominant firm (and hence the lower the price it charges), the higher the supply elasticity of the fringe, the higher the fringe's relative share of the market (Q_f/Q_d), and the higher the industry elasticity of demand. If the fringe does not exist, the dominant firm's residual demand elasticity equals the industry demand elasticity (so it charges the same price as a monopolist).

$$\frac{Q_f}{Q_d} = \frac{\frac{Q_f}{Q}}{\frac{Q_d}{Q}} = \frac{1-S_D}{S_D} =$$

CHAPTER 9

CARTELS: OLIGOPOLY JOINT DECISION MAKING

People of the same trade seldom meet together, even for merriment and diversion, but the conversation ends in a conspiracy against the public, or in some contrivance to raise prices. It is impossible indeed to prevent such meetings, by any law which either could be executed, or would be consistent with liberty and justice. But though the law cannot hinder people of the same trade from sometimes assembling together, it ought to do nothing to facilitate such assemblies; much less to render them necessary.

ADAM SMITH

In any market, firms have an incentive to coordinate their production and pricing activities to increase their collective and individual profits by restricting market output and raising the market price. An association of firms that explicitly agree to coordinate its activities is called a **cartel.** A cartel that includes all firms in an industry is in effect a monopoly, and the member firms share the monopoly profits.

Fortunately for consumers, although firms have an incentive to coordinate activities to restrict market output and raise prices, each member of the cartel has an incentive to "cheat" on the cartel agreement. That is, each firm wants to produce more output than is best for the cartel collectively. As a result, most cartels tend to break apart without government intervention.

When a cartel partially breaks apart so that some firms act independently or not all firms in the industry join the cartel in the first place, the cartel may act like a dominant firm facing a competitive fringe of nonmember firms. As discussed in Chapter 8, the rapid entry of new fringe firms into an industry can destroy the market power of a dominant firm or a cartel. Thus, only cartels that do not fall apart through lack of cooperation and that exist in industries in which entry is difficult can maintain market power for substantial lengths of time.

This chapter examines four key questions:

1. Why do cartels form?
2. What factors cause some cartels to last and others to break up, even without government intervention?
3. How harmful are cartels?
4. What have governments done about cartels?

Cartels are more likely when there are only a few firms, or oligopoly. In this chapter we concentrate on **cooperative oligopolies,** in which firms coordinate their actions to maximize joint profits. Even without an explicit agreement, firms in a cooperative oligopoly may coordinate their actions to maximize joint profits. The theory of cooperative oligopoly is based on the theory of cartels. (See Chapter 10.) The next chapter turns to *noncooperative oligopolies,* in which firms act as rivals.

■ WHY CARTELS FORM

> *United we stand, divided we fall. Union gives strength.* —AESOP

Why is Adam Smith correct that firms want to form cartels? The answer is that each individual firm wants to increase its own profits. But why should a firm's profits go up when it joins a cartel? After all, competitive firms "maximize their profits." How can they do better by forming a cartel if they are already maximizing their profits?

There is a subtle trick in this argument. In the competitive case, each firm considers how much a reduction in its own output benefits it and ignores the gains to other firms, which benefit from a reduction in total industry output by the amount that reduction raises the price. In contrast, a cartel takes into account the benefits to all its members of the reduction in each firm's output. Thus, a competitive industry (in which each firm ignores the collective gain from output reduction) produces more output than a cartel.

To illustrate the nature of this collective gain, consider two polar cases. First, suppose that an industry is made up of many identical, competitive firms, each of which is a price taker. In contrast, suppose that all the firms join together to form a cartel and act as a monopoly. Figure 9.1a shows a typical firm's marginal cost curve. The sum of the individual firms' marginal cost curves is the industry supply curve, which is shown in Figure 9.1b (labeled *MC*) along with the industry demand curve. The competitive output, Q^*, is determined by the intersection of this supply curve with the industry demand curve, with each firm producing q^* units of output (as shown in Figure 9.1a). The cartel (monopoly) reduces industry output in order to drive up the price and its profits. Since the cartel is made up of many small, identical firms, it requires each firm to reduce its output in proportion; as a result, they share in the profits equally.

Why does it pay for the cartel to reduce output from the competitive level?[1] At the competitive output, the cartel's marginal cost is greater than its marginal revenue, so it pays the cartel to reduce its output, as shown in Figure 9.1b. The horizontal sum of the

---

[1] As with any monopoly, the cartel can restrict output and let the demand curve determine price, or raise price and let the demand curve determine output. The two approaches are equivalent. This section concentrates on output reductions for ease of exposition.

FIGURE 9.1 Cartel

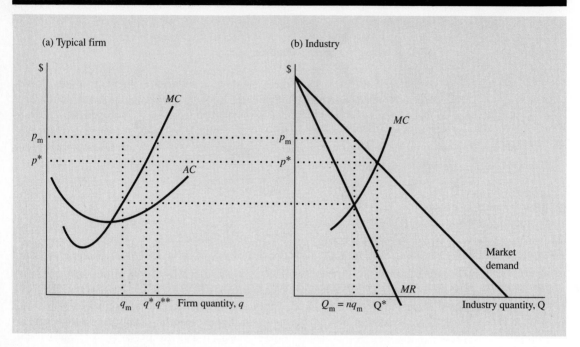

individual firms' marginal cost curves is the cartel's marginal cost curve. Because the demand curve slopes downward, the marginal revenue curve lies below the demand curve, and marginal revenue is less than marginal cost at the competitive output Q^*. Thus, it pays for the cartel to reduce output from the competitive level—but by how much? It should lower output until its marginal revenue equals marginal cost, which guarantees that profits are maximized. The cartel increases its profits by lowering the aggregate cartel output to Q_c in Figure 9.1b. The corresponding individual firm's output is q_c in Figure 9.1a.

Why doesn't each competitive firm on its own reduce its output below the competitive level? At the competitive equilibrium, each competitive firm sets its marginal revenue equal to its marginal cost and has no incentive to further lower its output.[2] If it were to reduce its output by one unit, it would lose profits because the marginal revenue on the last unit produced (the price) would exceed its marginal cost. Thus, each competitive firm is maximizing its profits at the competitive output.

The gain in collective activity comes from the very slight slope to the competitive firm's demand curve. Although economists often say that each competitive firm acts as

---

[2] A competitive firm is a price taker: it acts as though it faces a horizontal demand curve. Since its demand curve is horizontal, its marginal revenue curve is also horizontal (and identical to the demand curve). Thus, the competitive firm's *MR* curve is horizontal at the competitive price p^* (where the industry supply, or *MC*, curve hits the industry demand curve in Figure 9.1b).

though it faces a horizontal demand curve—that it cannot raise its price by lowering its output—that is not absolutely correct. The demand curve does have a slight slope: a competitive firm that stops producing might raise the industry price by a small amount.[3] That small slope can be ignored when talking about a single firm, but it cannot properly be ignored when talking about all firms collectively.

If all firms cut back by, say, 10 percent, the industry price definitely rises; however, if only one firm cuts back by 10 percent, there is no measurable effect on price. Each competitive firm decides that it doesn't pay to reduce significantly its output because its gain is less than its cost. If it reduces its output by one unit, its gain is the trivial amount by which price rises, whereas its loss is the price it would have received for this last unit.

A competitive firm ignores the good it does other firms by reducing its output and increasing the market price; it places no value on the gains of other firms. This gain by others is referred to as an *externality*.[4] Working cooperatively, the cartel members gain from the output reductions of each firm. When all firms belong to the cartel, all the gains from reducing output go to the cartel. Here, the externality created by each firm in reducing its output has been internalized by the cartel. As a result, it pays the cartel to reduce total output below the competitive level, even though it does not pay any competitive firm to reduce its output individually.

■ CREATING AND ENFORCING THE CARTEL

> Socrates: *[Tell] me whether you think that a city, or an army, or a band of robbers or thieves, or any other company which pursue some unjust end in common, would be able to effect anything if they were unjust to one another?*
> Thrasymachus: *Of course not. . . .*
> Socrates: *[When] we say that any vigorous joint action is the work of unjust men, our language is not altogether accurate. If they had been thoroughly unjust, they could not have kept their hands off one another. Clearly they must have possessed justice of a sort, enough to keep them from exercising their injustice on each other at the same time as on their victims. For the thorough villains who are perfectly unjust, are also perfectly incapable of action.*[5]

---

[3] The residual demand curve facing an individual firm is the industry demand curve minus the supply of other firms, as discussed in Chapter 4. If there are n identical firms in an industry, the residual demand curve's elasticity for a single firm is $n\epsilon - (n - 1)\eta$, where ϵ is the elasticity of the industry's demand curve (a negative number), and η is the elasticity of supply (typically a positive number) of the other firms. Thus, if other firms' elasticity of supply is zero, or *inelastic* (they supply the same output regardless of the price), a firm's elasticity of demand is n times as great as the industry elasticity of demand. For example, if the industry's demand elasticity were -2, and there were 50 firms, an individual firm would face an elasticity of -100 (a high elasticity). The larger the elasticity of supply of other firms, the larger (in absolute terms) the elasticity facing the individual firm, since a positive number is being subtracted from a negative number, making the total a larger negative number.

[4] An externality is a good (or bad) which is not priced by the market, as explained in Chapter 6.

[5] Based on Plato, *The Republic of Plato*, trans. A. D. Lindsay (New York: E. P. Dutton 1957), 37–38. The names of the speakers have been added and some material has been dropped.

Would you join a cartel if all the other firms in your industry were forming one? Such behavior is blatantly illegal in the United States and many other capitalist countries, and you might think twice on either moral or legal grounds. Suppose it was not a moral person like you who was being asked this question—suppose it was your slightly shady cousin. Would your cousin join an illegal cartel conspiracy?

Well, it depends. Your cousin's first thought is likely to be: "What's in it for me?" It should be obvious to him that it is in his best interest to let all the other firms in the industry form a cartel that does not include his firm. Then the cartel would restrict output, driving up the price, while his firm could produce as much as it wanted. Of course, every other firm in the industry makes the same calculation. Now suppose the other firms tell him that unless his firm agrees, none of the others will join the cartel and restrict output. Your cousin now realizes that he can't have his cartel and produce as much output as he wants too. He can only obtain the higher price if his firm agrees to a reduction in output. Your cousin then thinks: "What do I have to lose? If the cartel is caught by the government and convicted, my firm will have to pay a fine. But if the chance of being caught is small or the fine is low, it may be worth it to me." That is, if the expected loss from such a fine is low enough, your cousin joins the cartel.[6]

But your cousin is always looking for an edge. Once he's joined the cartel, he says to himself: "Why shouldn't I cheat and produce more output than the cartel's agreement permits? After all, the cartel probably won't know who's producing the extra output." Of course, if all firms in the cartel think this way, the cartel will fall apart. The success of the cartel, then, turns on its ability to enforce its agreement.

Figure 9.1 illustrates why a firm has an incentive to cheat on the cartel's agreement. As explained above, the cartel members agree to restrict output to Q_m, which drives the price to p_m, the monopoly price. Figure 9.1a shows the cost curves of your cousin's firm, which is one of n identical firms in the industry (and in the cartel). The cartel wants your cousin to produce $q_m = Q_m/n$ output (the output corresponding to his firm's share of the cartel output). But at the cartel's price, p_m, your cousin's firm can maximize its profits by producing q^{**} units of output (where its marginal cost curve equals p_m). Thus, although it is in the cartel's best interest for every firm to restrict output, it is in your cousin's best interest for every firm except his own to restrict output.

Cartels have little effect on prices if members do not cooperate. For example, at a recent meeting in Kuala Lumpur, representatives of four pepper-producing countries decided that they would set a minimum export price for black pepper, which is called a form of price-fixing. Even though the pepper cartel (Brazil, India, Indonesia, and Malaysia) produces more than 95 percent of the world's pepper and could raise the price, it has never been able to do so because its members keep undercutting the cartel's minimum set price.[7]

---

[6] The expected loss is the probability of being caught times the fine. Thus, if there is a 1 in 10 chance of being caught and the fine is $100,000, the expected loss is $10,000 (= 1/10 × $100,000). If your cousin were risk-averse (hates facing risk) or very law-abiding, he might calculate the costs and benefits of joining the cartel differently.

[7] "Chaos in the Cartel: Pepper Producers Pick a Purchasers' Price." *San Francisco Chronicle*, August 8, 1983, 49.

EXAMPLE 9.1

AN ELECTRIFYING CONSPIRACY

On a steamy Saturday, May 9, 1959, at 2:30 PM, reporter Julian Granger of the Knoxville *New-Sentinel* sat at his desk reading routine handouts from local publicity sources. The usual weekly newsletter from the Tennessee Valley Authority (TVA) announced that several contracts had been awarded. Pretty dull stuff.

But then Granger read that one contract had been awarded to Westinghouse for transformers for $96,760. The newsletter went on to note that "Allis-Chalmers, General Electric, and Pennsylvania Transformer quoted identical prices of $112,712." How could three companies bid prices that were identical to the penny under a system of secret, sealed bids?

Further on in the release, he read that two other companies had quoted identical prices on a $273,200 contract. On yet another contract for conductor cable, there were seven identical bids of $198,438.24. Identical down to the 24¢.

His story, which appeared on page 1 of the second section of the Knoxville *News-Sentinel* on May 13, 1959, drew little reaction. The lead of his second story on May 17, 1959, stated, "TVA purchasing records revealed today that at least 47 large and small American manufacturers have taken part in identical bidding on a wide variety of items in the past three years." He noted that the TVA had no choice in many cases but to award the contract on a chance drawing from a hat.

Could these identical bids have happened by accident? Oh come now. Granger showed that some identical bids quoted the same delivered prices even though distances from delivery points varied by hundreds or thousands of miles for equipment you couldn't exactly weigh on a bathroom scale.

Moreover, General Electric and Westinghouse, the two biggest electrical equipment manufacturers, turned up more frequently than any others in the equal bidding. Further, between 1946 and 1957, these firms raised prices 10 times on switching-gear in a parallel pattern: the announcements of these increases came within a few days of each other.

After the second story, Granger went to local suppliers and got nowhere—they seemed afraid to talk. Granger did learn, however, that the Knoxville Utility Board had received a long series of identical bids from the electrical equipment manufacturers: up to 11 at one time. Their purchasing agent, Karl Strange, told Granger that he had noticed an increase in the practice since the end of World War II.

The Scripps-Howard papers reprinted the first two articles nationwide. On May 19, Senator Kefauver inserted Granger's second story verbatim in the *Congressional Record* of the hearings before the Subcommittee on Antitrust and Monopoly.

Eight days before Granger's first story broke, Ralph J. Cordiner, Chairman of the Board of General Electric (GE), testified before the subcommittee on a bill to promote more vigorous competition in a variety of industries. He asked, "Is it assumed that companies in industries affected by this bill have the ability to 'administer' prices in a manner not responsive to market supply and demand?" He responded to his own question: "If so, the assumption is false, because these companies are just as much subject to competitive market conditions as any others." He continued, "In all instances

Continued

EXAMPLE 9.1

AN ELECTRIFYING CONSPIRACY continued

the price is completely subject to the force of competition in the marketplace and the value the customer believes he is receiving." He concluded that the then-current antitrust laws were "well enforced."

Exactly six months before Cordiner testified so sanctimoniously about competition, seven of his top executives met with their competitors in the Hotel Traymore in Atlantic City, New Jersey to jack up the price of power switchgear assembly ($125 million in annual sales). Up until that time, the firms had an agreement that their sealed government bids would be divided by each of the conspiring companies in the ratios:

General Electric	42% of the market
Westinghouse	38% of the market
Allis-Chalmers	11% of the market
I-T-E	9% of the market

Apparently, the initial conspirators made room for a major new entrant at this meeting. Federal Pacific, the newcomer to the cartel, was given permission to quote prices slightly lower than the others for a brief period in order to establish its assigned share of the market. GE and Westinghouse agreed to lower their shares to 39% and 35%, respectively, giving Federal Pacific 7% of the market. Over the next twelve months, at least 35 such meetings were held, with GE playing a prominent and active leadership role.

Senator Kefauver, the chairman of the Subcommittee on Antitrust and Monopoly, moved the hearings to Knoxville in September 1959. The hearings demonstrated that the prices of heavy industrial electrical equipment had increased 50 percent since 1951.

At the hearings many examples of identical bids were presented. Even when the bids were not identical, the companies followed a rotation pattern. For example, on April 18, 1957, the TVA received the following bids for an oil circuit breaker:

General Electric	$7,440 (Low)
Westinghouse	7,455 (Middle)
Allis-Chalmers	7,455 (Middle)
Federal Pacific	7,610 (High)

One bid was low, one high, and the other two identical. The next time around, the order of the firms might change, but there would be one low, one high, and two equal bids. Presumably, the firms took turns winning the bidding in the proportions agreed to earlier.

The Philadelphia Antitrust Office spent 18 months tracking down evidence used to indict 29 manufacturers (practically the entire heavy electric industry) and 44 of their top executives. Attorney General William P. Rogers issued the first official announcement of the indictments on February 16, 1960.

According to the first indictments returned by a federal grand jury sitting in Philadelphia, Westinghouse, Allis-Chalmers, Federal Pacific Electric Company, GE, I-T-E, and many of these firms' top executives had engaged in a conspiracy since at least 1956. The defendants were accused of fixing and maintaining high prices, allocating the business among themselves, submitting noncompetitive, rigged bids, refusing to sell equipment to other manufacturers of electrical equipment, or raising prices to them so that they could not effectively compete.

Apparently the firms agreed to take turns winning the bidding according to a *phase of the moon* formula: the firm to give the low bid was determined by the fullness of the moon. One set of contraband lyrics circulated at GE shortly after the indictments (to be sung to the tune of "Moonglow"):

It must have been Moonglow
Way up in the blue
It must have been Moonglow
That brought that bid to you.

I still hear them saying
As they rigged the price
The customer's paying
Too much, but it's so nice!

We've fixed the prices in the air
All of our schemes sock the buyer everywhere

If we play it cozy
And build our cartel
Our life will be rosy
Who cares and what the hell? . . .

Conspiracy in this industry was facilitated by the relatively small number of firms and the large market shares of the largest firms. Electrical manufacturing had a four-firm concentration ratio (sum of sales by the four largest firms divided by total industry sales) of over 50 percent compared to about 25 percent in all manufacturing. The concentration ratios were above 75 percent in all specific product areas involved and over 95 percent for turbogenerators, power transformers, power switchgear assemblies, distribution transformers, low-voltage distribution equipment, meters, insulators, power capacitors, instrument transformers, low-voltage power circuit breakers, isolated phase buses, bushings, and lightning arresters.

Eventually 45 executives and 29 corporations were indicted. Most of them made no defense in the face of this overwhelming evidence. Generally, vice-presidents and division managers took the fall. The seven men with the highest positions received jail sentences, but those were typically only on the order of 30 days. In addition, 24 people received suspended sentences. Total fines to firms were nearly $2 million, while individual fines were $137,500.

In addition to the government suits, nearly 2000 private suits were filed. General Electric settled its lawsuits for over $200 million (including $6.74 million to the TVA and $1 million to other federal agencies), and Westinghouse for over $100 million. Total damages paid by all companies were over $400 million.

Many articles and books presented this story as a triumph of the system over evil conspirators, but this conclusion is hard to understand. Many if not most of the top directors of these firms were not personally indicted or punished, and the total fines were a small fraction of the monopoly profits the cartel earned over its life span. (Sultan

Continued

EXAMPLE 9.1

An Electrifying Conspiracy continued

[1974, 1975] argues that the conspiracy did not significantly raise prices; however, Bane [1973] and Lean, Ogur, and Rogers [1982] find that prices did rise.) According to a U.S. Congress report, this long-lasting conspiracy may have raised prices by nearly 10 percent. Other estimates have been over twice that for specific products. Electrical manufacturing accounts for about one-twelfth of total manufacturing and about 3 percent of all economic activity. About 30 percent of this manufacturing was electrical apparatus, which had $5 billion in shipments in 1958. The indictments only referred to about $1.75 billion of these annual sales (about 10 percent of all electrical manufacturing sales). Even assuming that prices were only 10 percent too high on only $1.75 billion worth of annual sales, purchasers paid roughly $175 million too much during each year of the conspiracy, which apparently lasted decades. From the viewpoint of the firms involved, this experiment in cartel behavior probably looked like a great success, even after they were caught and punished.

The threat of penalties for illegal price-fixing was apparently not viewed as sufficiently high by G.E. and Westinghouse to deter price-fixing. These same firms have been charged and punished repeatedly since the Sherman Antitrust Act first went into effect in 1890. There were 13 U.S. Department of Justice antitrust cases and 3 Federal Trade Commission cases against GE and Westinghouse between 1911 and 1952. The government essentially "won" all of these cases, obtaining convictions, *nolo contendere* pleas, or consent decrees in each (Walton and Cleveland 1964, 16-20).

Presumably, potential conspirators learned to be more subtle as a by-product of the publicity, if not the fines, in the 1960s cases. Indeed, GE and Westinghouse were accused of tacitly conspiring to fix prices on turbogenerators, starting with a new pricing policy GE announced in May 1963, just two and one-half years after they were found guilty in this bid-rigging case.

SOURCES: Fuller (1962); Walton and Cleveland (1964); and U.S. Congress, Joint Committee on Internal Revenue Taxation, *Staff Study of Income Tax Treatment of Treble Damage Payments under the Antitrust Laws* (Washington, D.C.: Government Printing Office, 1965), 39 (cited by Posner [1975]).

Factors that Facilitate the Formation of Price-Fixing Conspiracies

Once a cartel forms, the firms must agree to fix price (or equivalently, reduce output) if it is to be successful.[8] Why are there successful cartels in some industries but not in others? Unfortunately, we know a great deal about cartels that get caught, but very little about those that escape detection. As a result, it is not known whether the cartels that

---

[8] Generally, price-fixing is discussed rather than output reductions because it is apparently more common. In a study of antitrust cases from 1890 through 1969, Posner (1970, especially p. 400) found that only 1.6 percent of the cases had explicit production or sales quotas.

find themselves in court are unsuccessful or merely unlucky. Some evidence suggests that cartels that end up in court are actually unprofitable and hence, presumably, atypical (Asch and Seneca 1976).

Many characteristics of industries and firms that contribute to successful price-fixing conspiracies have been identified using studies of cartels that have ended up in court (Stigler 1964; Hay and Kelley 1974). These characteristics may be roughly divided into those that allow a cartel to raise the industry price in the first place and those that prevent the cartel agreement from breaking apart due to cheating by members. The following sections describe some of the major factors that facilitate the formation of cartels. Factors that lead to their survival are discussed in the next section. See Example 9.1.

Three major factors are necessary to establish a cartel. First, a cartel must be able to raise price without inducing increased competition from nonmember firms. Second, the expected punishment for forming a cartel must be low relative to the expected gains. Third, the cost of establishing and enforcing an agreement must be low relative to the expected gains.

The Ability to Raise the Industry Price.   Only if a cartel is expected to raise the price and keep it high do firms join. The more inelastic the demand curve facing a cartel, the higher the price the cartel can set and the greater its profits. If the cartel's demand curve is inelastic (relatively vertical), raising price can significantly raise revenues (that is, quantity demanded falls by a smaller percentage than price rises) and profits. In contrast, if a potential cartel faces an elastic demand curve (relatively horizontal), raising price causes revenues to fall (since quantity would fall by more than price increases, and profits may rise only slightly). See Example 9.2.

Entry by nonmember firms or the existence of close substitutes produced in other industries prevents a cartel from raising price. If the cartel only controls a small share of the relevant market, which includes all close substitutes, noncooperating firms undercut the cartel and prevent it from raising the industry price; that is, the demand curve facing the cartel is relatively elastic. Even if all firms initially in an industry form a cartel and raise the price, the higher price may induce enough new firms to enter that the cartel is unable to keep the price high in the long run (see the following discussion of entry and the one in Chapter 8). That is, the long-run elasticity of demand facing the cartel is very high (especially relative to the short-run elasticity). Obviously, the longer the cartel can expect to keep the price high, the greater the current value of creating a cartel.

Low Expectation of Severe Punishment.   Cartels only form if members do not expect the government to catch and severely punish them. Large expected penalties reduce the expected value of forming a cartel in the first place. Before they were made illegal in the United States, explicit cartels were much more common. During periods when the Department of Justice has been relatively lax in enforcing the laws, price-fixing conspiracies have been more prevalent (Posner 1970). Internationally, where cartels are legal (see the discussion of OPEC in Appendix 9A), they have been more common than in the United States. In some cases, governments arrange cartels; some European examples are discussed later in this chapter.

EXAMPLE 9.2

THE VIABILITY OF COMMODITY CARTELS

Attempts have been made to cartelize the market for many of the major internationally traded commodities, according to Eckbo (1976). Most of these attempts failed, however, as the cartels fell apart quickly or were unable to raise prices substantially.

Eckbo studied 51 formal international cartel organizations in 18 industries, with the earliest agreement in 1819 and the latest in 1964. He defined a cartel as successful if it raised the price at least three times the marginal production cost of the member with the highest cost. Only 19 (37 percent) were successful by this criterion. One of them, the iodine cartel, lasted 61 years. The remaining successful cartels had formal agreements that lasted from 2 to 18 years, with a median lifetime of 5 years and a mean of 6.6 years Only 5 of the 19 lasted 10 years or longer.

Of these successful cartels, 3 (out of 9 for which there is information) broke down for nonmarket reasons such as government intervention or war. Of those that broke down for market-related reasons, 7 out of 16 (44 percent) had internal conflicts among cartel members, whereas 9 (56 percent) ended because of external forces such as competition from nonmembers (the usual case) or retaliation by buyers.

For a cartel to persist and raise prices, it must (1) be able to detect and prevent cheating by members, (2) have a substantial share of the resource, and (3) face a relatively inelastic supply response from nonmembers. The longest lived cartel in Eckbo's survey, iodine (1878–1939), made all sales through a central cartel office in London, which prevented members from cheating. Maintaining a cartel is not sufficient for success, however, if it cannot raise prices.

The Organization of Petroleum Exporting Countries (OPEC), the International Bauxite Association (IBA), and the Conseil Intergouvernemental des Pays Exportateurs de Cuivre ("International Council of Copper Exporting Countries," or CIPEC) differ in their market powers because of their different market shares and the residual demand elasticities they face. OPEC was able to quadruple the world oil price initially; IBA was able to triple the price of bauxite; but CIPEC has been unable to raise copper prices significantly.

When OPEC was formed, it had approximately two-thirds of the world's oil reserves and a similar fraction of the noncommunist world's oil production. By 1975, IBA accounted for 85 percent of total noncommunist world bauxite production. In contrast, CIPEC accounts for only about one-third of the noncommunist world's copper production.

Of Eckbo's successful cartels, 15 out of 19 (79 percent) had four-firm concentration ratios over 50 percent. In 14 of them (74 percent), the cartels' share of total production was over 75 percent. Of the 9 successful cartels about which we have enough information, 7 faced inelastic demand curves (elasticities less than 1 in absolute value). In

8 of the 9 cases, no short-term substitutes for the commodity were available outside the cartel, although for 7 cartels there were long-term substitutes—which may be why they eventually ended.

Pindyck (1977, 1979) shows that dynamic, long-run adjustments in commodity markets are also important. OPEC faces a relatively inelastic fringe supply. Despite major price increases, non-OPEC petroleum producers have not substantially increased their supply in the short to medium run. Similarly, the world demand for bauxite is extremely inelastic (up to a limit price), even in the long run.

In contrast, in the short run and even more so in the long run, secondary copper, which is produced from scrap, is very responsive to price. As a result, CIPEC faces a much larger long-run elasticity than short-run elasticity. If CIPEC were to raise its price very much, others would merely increase their production from scrap.

Given these differences, it is little wonder that OPEC and IBA were able to raise prices while CIPEC was not. These factors may also explain why still other natural resources have not been successfully cartelized. Pindyck holds that other minerals, such as iron ore, manganese ore, lead, tin, zinc, and nickel, would also face high long-run residual demand elasticities due to secondary supplies from scrap. Recently IBA has suffered setbacks because Brazil and other producers have not restricted output. It continues as a research group.

Indonesia and Grenada produce 98 percent of the world's nutmeg and agreed to form a nutmeg cartel in 1987. For the 15 months before the formal agreement, however, Grenada operated informally under an Indonesian guideline. They claim they do not intend to force prices higher but merely want to insure that there is "no price cutting"— presumably from the informal cartel level. They are not worried about the impact of the cartel on demand. Nutmeg has no close substitutes; it has a distinctive taste, so bakers are unlikely to change their recipes appreciably.

One continuously successful cartel is the de Beers diamond cartel, which, throughout this century, has been the single largest selling agent of most of the world's diamonds. Even the Soviet Union, the second largest diamond exporter after South Africa, has sold all its diamonds through the de Beers cartel for the last quarter-century. As new mines are developed, de Beers gives them sufficient market share that they agree to sell through de Beers and accept its production control system. When Tanzania decided to act independently, de Beers depressed the price for the quality of stones sold by Tanzania, forcing it to rejoin the syndicate.

SOURCES: Fisher, Cootner, Baily (1972), Ekbo (1976), Pindyck (1977, 1979); Fisher (1981), Alan J. Wax, "Spicy New Cartel Sets Nutmeg Prices," *San Francisco Chronicle*, May 25, 1987, p 20; and Clyde H. Farnsworth, "OPEC Isn't the Only Cartel That Couldn't," *New York Times*, April 24, 1988, p 3.

So long as coordinating firms did not use unlawful acts of violence, intimidation, or fraud, British courts did not stop price-fixing in modern times until 1956.[9] A survey of industrial trade associations carried out by the Political and Economic Planning agency in 1953–56 found that 243 of the 1300 associations (19 percent) attempted to fix prices (Phillips 1972).

Low Organizational Costs. Even if a potential cartel could raise prices in the long run and not be discovered, it will not form if the cost of initial organization is too high. The more complex the negotiations, the greater the cost of creating a cartel. Four factors keep the cost low, facilitating the creation of a cartel: few firms are involved, the industry is highly concentrated, a good of uniform quality is produced, and there is a trade association.

Only a Few Firms are Involved in the Cartel. Setting up a secret meeting without the government's knowledge is relatively easy when there are few firms involved. Even if there are many firms in an industry, the largest firms may meet and establish a cartel (dominant firm) that does not explicitly include the smaller fringe firms. Of the 606 Department of Justice price-fixing cases (1910–1972) examined by Fraas and Greer (1977), the average number of firms involved in each case was 16.7, whereas the median was 8, and the mode was 4.[10] A few cases involving a large number of firms raised the average, but the most common type of case involved 4 firms, and half the cases involved 8 or fewer firms.[11]

Of the Department of Justice price-fixing cases (January 1963–December 1972) studied by Hay and Kelley (1974), only 6.5 percent involved 50 or more conspirators.[12] The average number of firms in the remaining cases was 7.25. Although only 26 percent of the cases involved 4 or fewer firms, nearly half (48 percent) involved 6 or fewer firms, and 79 percent involved 10 or fewer firms.

---

[9] The Restrictive Trade Practices Act (passed by Parliament in 1956) required that all contracts or agreements among suppliers in restraint of trade be reported to the Registrar of Restrictive Practices. This law has been modified substantially since then; in 1973 the Office of Fair Trading took over this responsibility, and agreements among service industries had to be reported as well. This agency was empowered to challenge agreements that were contrary to the public interest. A special Restrictive Practices Court decides whether such agreements are prohibited. In contrast to U.S. practice, this court can accept the argument that benefits outweigh damages and allow price-fixing.

[10] If the number of firms involved in each case is arranged in ascending order, then the middle number is the median number of firms. Thus, if there were 5 cases with 2, 4, 5, 8, and 9 firms involved, the median number of firms would be 5. Consider a graph that plots the 606 cases so that the horizontal axis shows the number of firms involved and the vertical axis shows the number of cases involving a given number of conspiring firms. The mode is the highest point on the plot. Loosely speaking, it is the most common number of conspirators.

[11] The median number of firms involved varied by industry. In natural resources markets, the median number of firms was 13. The corresponding numbers were 7 in manufacturing, 11 in distribution, 15 in construction, 4 in financial institutions, 4 in transportation, and 8 in services.

[12] Hay and Kelley (1974) studied horizontal price-fixing conspiracies that were prosecuted by the U.S. Department of Justice Antitrust Division. Their study excluded price-fixing by various professional groups (because they were not covert), but included virtually all other cases that were filed and won in trial or settled by *nolo contendere* ("no contest") pleas, which is equivalent to a plea of guilty for the purposes of sentencing but is not an admission of guilt by the defendant. When such a plea is accepted by the court a trial is not necessary. Occasionally, courts accept such pleas over the objection of the Department of Justice.

Even where cartels are legal, as are many international cartels not involving U.S. firms, the number of firms is crucial. For example, a long period (1928–72) of successful cartelization by two countries of the world mercury market was followed by years of unsuccessful attempts at price-fixing by a larger group of countries (MacKie-Mason and Pindyck 1986).

The Industry Is Highly Concentrated.   If a few large firms make most of the sales in an industry, and if they coordinate their activities, they can raise price without involving all the other (smaller) firms in the industry. For example, Spain and Italy, which controlled 80 percent of the world's production of mercury, formed a successful cartel that did not formally involve five other producers (MacKie-Mason and Pindyck 1986).

Indeed, large firms may decide independently to behave as though they had a cartel arrangement without a formal meeting; that is, each one can cut its output and hope that the others will do likewise, thereby creating an informal cartel. Inevitably, in oligopolies, firms take their rivals' actions into account (as discussed in more detail in Chapter 10). When firms in an oligopoly coordinate their actions as if they were a cartel without an explicit arrangement, the resulting coordination is sometimes referred to as **tacit collusion or conscious parallelism.**[13]

Empirical evidence supports the view that cartels are more likely in concentrated industries. In 42 percent of the Department of Justice price-fixing cases studied by Hay and Kelley (1974), the four-firm concentration ratio (the sum of the market shares of the four biggest firms) was over 75 percent; in another 34 percent of the cases, the ratios were between 51 and 75 percent. Thus, in 76 percent of the cases, the concentration ratio was greater than 50 percent. Only 6 percent of the cases had concentration ratios less than 25 percent. The overall average was 67.7 percent.[14] See Example 9.3.

Similarly, the existing evidence shows that cartels are often found in smaller geographic areas. In the U.S. Justice Department price-fixing and other antitrust cases from the passage of the Sherman Act (1890) through 1969 studied by Posner (1970), nearly half (47.4 percent) the conspiracies were in local or regional markets, 37.6 percent were nationwide, and 8.7 percent involved foreign trade. The smaller the geographical area of a market, the more likely it is that a few firms have a large share of the business.

A Homogeneous Good Is Produced.   Firms have more difficulty agreeing on relative prices when each firm's product has different qualities or properties. Each time a product is modified, a new relative price must be established. It is easier for a cartel to spot cheating when all it has to examine is a single price. It is relatively difficult to detect

---

[13] The use of these terms has led to some confusion in legal disputes. They are used here only to mean that firms are attempting to act as a cartel without explicitly communicating.

[14] To minimize the systematic bias from excluding cases for which the concentration measure could not be determined directly, if the number of firms was known, Hay and Kelley (1974) calculated minimum concentration ratios by assuming each firm had an equal share. These minimum concentration ratios are for the relevant product markets. Based on Bureau of the Census data at the industry level, the average concentration was only 28.6 percent. Thus, the conclusion that the industries were highly concentrated would change if the Census industry data were used.

EXAMPLE 9.3

CAR WARS

In 1955, American passenger automobile production was 45 percent greater than it was in 1954 or 1956. Why?

Based on sophisticated econometric tests, Bresnahan (1987) contends that American automobile manufacturers' successful tacit collusion fell apart in 1955 but was reestablished in 1956. During the 1950s, major entry by foreign manufacturers had not yet occurred; thus, American manufacturers could collectively reduce output and increase price.

A casual perusal of automobile output for this period certainly indicates that 1955 was an unusual year. American automobile production from 1953 through 1959 was 6.13 million, 5.51, 7.94, 5.80, 6.12, 4.24, and 5.60 million cars. Thus, the 7.94 million cars produced in 1955 not only were substantially more than were produced in the adjacent years, 1954 and 1956, but also were substantially more than were produced in any year for the rest of that decade.

Not surprisingly, the large output in 1955 drove down the price of cars. Adjusting for quality, the price in 1955 was approximately 6 percent lower than in the adjacent years. The price fell by a smaller percentage than quantity increased, so that total expenditures rose. Automobile expenditures were (in billions of 1957 dollars) $13.9 in 1954, $18.4 in 1955, and $15.7 in 1956. In other words, consumers spent 32 percent more in 1955 than in 1954 and 17 percent more in 1955 than in 1956.

price-cutting that is achieved by an increase in quality; a firm could increase its quality and hold its price constant if it wanted to increase sales without explicitly violating the pricing agreement.

In virtually all the price-fixing cases studied by Hay and Kelley (1974), the product was homogeneous across firms. In the few exceptions, complicated products or services were allocated on a job-by-job basis that facilitated coordination, or a single factor was isolated for the agreement. For example, a group of swimsuit manufacturers agreed to delay end-of-season discounts.

A Trade Association Exists.   Trade associations, by lowering the costs of meeting and coordinating activities among firms in an industry, facilitate the establishment and enforcement of cartels. Most industries have trade associations that meet regularly. As Adam Smith observed, such meetings are conducive to price-fixing agreements, and trade associations are often the mechanism by which large groups coordinate activities. In the Hay and Kelley (1974) study of Department of Justice price-fixing cases, trade associations were involved in 7 out of 8 cases in which more than 15 firms conspired, and in all cases involving more than 25 firms. Overall, 29 percent of the cases involved trade associations. Fraas and Greer (1977) found that 36 percent of all price-fixing cases involved trade associations. Moreover, the median number of firms involved was 16 when there was a trade association, compared to 8 for all cases. Posner (1970) found that 43.6 percent of all antitrust cases involved trade associations.

Enforcing a Cartel Agreement

Never trust a friend who deserts you at a pinch. — AESOP

Even if an industry consists of a small number of firms producing a homogeneous good with no close substitutes, has an inelastic demand curve, and faces no threat of entry, a cartel cannot succeed if members can and want to cheat on the agreement. Some of the factors that lead to the formation of a cartel also help it to detect cheating and enforce its agreement.

Detecting Cheating.   Cartel agreements are easier to enforce if detecting violations is easy. Four factors aid in the detection of cheating: (1) there are few firms in the industry, (2) prices do not fluctuate independently, (3) prices are widely known, and (4) all cartel members sell identical products at the same point in the distribution chain.

With relatively few firms, the cartel may more easily monitor each one, and increases in one firm's share of the market (an indication of price-cutting) are easier to detect. Further, moral (or immoral) suasion may be easier when there are only a few conspirators. See Example 9.4.

Hay and Kelley (1974) found that most of the price-fixing conspiracies lasting 10 or more years were in markets in which there were few firms and the largest firms made most of the sales. When a large number of firms was involved, conspiracies were generally discovered very quickly, especially since details about some of the large-group organizational meetings often were printed in local newspapers. In contrast, Posner (1970) found that, of the detected cartels, large ones had lasted as long as smaller ones. He found that 52 percent of conspiracies involving 10 or fewer firms had lasted for 6 or more years, whereas 64 percent of larger conspiracies persisted that long. Presumably, the more firms involved in a conspiracy, the more likely is discovery by the government. In general, conspiracies are uncovered through information provided by outsiders rather than by Department of Justice investigations.[15]

If an industry has frequent shifts in demand, input costs, or other factors, prices in that industry have to adjust often. In that case, cheating on a cartel arrangement may be difficult to detect, because it cannot be distinguished easily from other factors that cause price fluctuations. Cheating is easier to detect if prices are known. Some cartels have

---

[15] Of the cases studied by Hay and Kelley (1974), detection was due to Grand Jury investigation of another case in 24 percent; to complaint by a competitor in 20 percent; to complaint by a customer in 14 percent; to complaint by local, state, or federal agencies in 12 percent; and to complaint by current or former employees in 6 percent. Each of the following methods was responsible for detection in 4 percent of the cases: complaint by a trade association official, investigation of conduct or of performance by the Antitrust Division, report of a newspaper, and referral to the Antitrust Division by the Federal Trade Commission. Each of the following methods was responsible for 2 percent of the cases: complaint by an anonymous informant, merger investigation, and private suit.

EXAMPLE 9.4

LARGE NUMBER OF CONSPIRATORS

All professions are conspiracies against the laity. —GEORGE BERNARD SHAW

Economists normally argue that cartel agreements are only feasible when there are relatively few firms in an industry. It is difficult for a large number of firms to meet and agree on a cartel arrangement without being caught by the government. Moreover, it would seem even harder for a large number of firms to implicitly or tacitly agree to set prices without formally talking to each other.

Many economists and federal regulators were surprised when Owen and Grunfest found that 75 percent of all residential real estate transactions in California involved a commission to the realtors of exactly 6 percent. Indeed, casual empiricism indicates that around the country virtually all realtors charge the same rate, which is 5, 6, or 7 percent depending on the community. Could these realtors have been conspiring implicitly? If they were not, why did virtually every firm charge the same rate?

In the 1940s and 1950s, the National Association of Realtors and local associations enforced an agreement. Local associations required all members to sell at a fixed commission rate and also established barriers to entry by allowing only full-time realtors to join—unless one had a large enough customer base to earn one's living as a realtor, one could not become a realtor. Failure to become a member of a local association effectively prevented one from selling homes because only members had access to the association's Multiple Listing Service (MLS) that listed all houses for sale in an area. Similarly, loss of membership, the punishment for price-cutting, was a strong deterrent.

Either the costs of doing business rose or cartel power increased over time. In the 1920s, commission rates were 2 to 3 percent; by the 1950s, they were 5 percent; and by the 1960s, they were 6 or 7 percent.

Moreover, the practice of charging a fixed percent of sales may be a form of price discrimination (charging different prices to different customers for the same service). It is hard to believe that it costs substantially more to sell houses that cost $100,000 than houses that cost $50,000. Rather, wealthier people are made to pay more. Price discrimination is a sign of market power (see Chapters 14 and 15).

From the 1960s to 1980, a series of private suits and Supreme Court decisions brought an end to the formal cartel agreement (explicitly fixed rates and formal entry barriers) and left individuals and associations open to treble damages suits for antitrust violations. Moreover, licensed brokers or agents can no longer be barred from using the MLS.

The end to formal barriers led to a great deal of entry, implying that the former barriers had been effective. The number of brokers in California quickly rose from 150,000 to 400,000 by the end of the 1970s (although it has declined slightly since then). At that point, 1 in 50 adults in the state was a realtor. (Were that rate of increase to continue, pretty soon there would be more realtors than people!) Despite the end of formal rate agreements, there has been no pronounced tendency for the rates to fall, although casual evidence indicates that sales by individuals and secret rebates by realtors may have increased over time.

An alternative to the cartel explanation is that the current rate is competitive. If the rate is not competitive, it is hard to see how this large group maintains a tacit or explicit agreement.

SOURCES: Owen and Grunfest (1977) and Wachter, Susan. "Residential Real Estate Brokerage: Cartel Without Entry Barriers." public lecture, University of California, Berkeley, February 10, 1984.

arranged for firms to inspect each other's books. In Posner's (1970) study of antitrust cases, at least 6.2 percent of the cases involved exchange of information, whereas 4.3 percent involved policing, fines, and audits. Of course, books can be faked, so such inspections cannot prevent all violations of the cartel agreement.

In some cases, governments help. For example, they often report the outcome of bidding on government contracts, so that cheating is instantly observable by the cartel. A quarter of the cases Hay and Kelley (1974) examined involved some form of bid rigging.[16]

Example 9.1 describes a *phases of the moon* scheme used by manufacturers of electrical products to rotate the winning of sealed bids. No firm could hope to win out of turn because its treachery against the cartel would be instantly exposed when the government announced the winner.

Vincent (The Fish) Cafaro, a former member of the Genovese organized crime family, told senators the mob rigged bids in New York City, controlling the concrete industry and construction unions.[17] He said the contractors and unions that won construction jobs through bid rigging were required to kick back 2 percent to the "2 Percent Club," an organization run by the Genovese, Gambino, Lucchese, and Colombo families of New York City. He estimated that at least 50 percent of the highrise construction in New York had a mob connection and added, "Legitimate guys ain't got a chance" to win contracts for those buildings. According to Mr. Cafaro, the 2 Percent Club split up all of the jobs worth over $2 million. Contracts worth over $5 million went to mob-run companies. When smaller contractors complained about the arrangement, they were given the right to split all jobs worth over $3 million. He said the Genovese family was "a very disciplined organization," with strict rules and capital punishment for serious violations.

Because it is illegal for firms to exchange confidential pricing or other information, public availability of such information can greatly simplify cartel enforcement. Publicly announcing price changes well in advance is one method of making price information available to all interested parties. An extreme, special case of sharing information occurs when a single sales agent or pool is used by all firms for all their sales, as was the case in 3 percent of the cases Fraas and Greer (1977) examined and in 6 percent of the cases studied by Posner (1970). Sales agents are commonly used in European cartels.

If some firms are *vertically integrated* (the same firm produces inputs, manufactures the product, and sells at the retail level), it may be difficult for the cartel to determine at what point in the distribution chain cheating occurs. In contrast, if all firms sell to the same type of customer (for example, at the retail level), cheating is easier to detect.

Cartels with Little Incentive to Cheat.   A cartel may find enforcement easy under certain circumstances. Members have no incentive to cheat on the cartel agreement if

---

[16] Hay and Kelley (1974) found some cases in which government agencies were explictly excluded from the agreement. Apparently cartel members believed that price-fixing was more likely to be detected and prosecuted if directed against the federal government. In other cases, some market segments were excluded from agreements in order to reduce potential friction among cartel members. Fraas and Greer (1977) found that 19 percent of all cases over a longer period involved bid rigging. Posner (1970) determined that 7.4 percent of all cases involved sales to the government, and 6.7 percent involved other bidding cases.

[17] "Witness Says Mob Is into Highrises," *San Francisco Chronicle,* April 30, 1988, A7.

their marginal cost curves are relatively inelastic, their fixed costs are low relative to total costs, their customers place small, frequent orders, or when they have a single sales agent.

If a firm's marginal cost curve is nearly vertical, it has little to gain by cheating on the cartel agreement because it costs too much to substantially increase its output. In Figure 9.1a, if the marginal cost curve were nearly vertical, q^{**} would be close to q_c. Marginal cost curves are likely to be nearly vertical if firms are operating near their full capacities. Indeed, cartels may force their marginal cost curves to be more vertical by signing union contracts that require double wages for overtime work or using similar techniques (Maloney, McCormick, and Tollison 1979).[18]

Firms with low fixed costs are more likely to reduce output when demand falls (for example, during a recession) than to reduce their prices. In contrast, a capital-intensive firm with highly underutilized capacity (such as one with large fixed costs due to a large plant) may decide to charge a price below the cartel's price to stimulate sales so that its plant does not sit idle. Price cutting by one firm can set off price wars that can destroy a cartel—an issue covered in more detail in the following discussion.

Firms with many customers have no incentive to lower prices below the cartel level unless they can advertise the reduction (which would be instantly known to the cartel). In contrast, when only a few customers place large, infrequent orders, a cartel has trouble detecting and preventing cheating.[19] Firms have an incentive to grant price reductions to large buyers to keep them as customers.

Legal cartels can prevent cheating by allowing a single agent or organization to sell all their output. For example, the iodine cartel, one of the longest-lived international cartels (61 years: 1878–1939), made all its sales through a central office in London (Eckbo 1976).

Methods of Preventing Cheating.   Unless a cartel can detect violations of its price-fixing agreement and prevent reoccurrences, member firms engage in secret price-cutting (or output expansions) that destroys the cartel. Although economists and lawyers understand a number of mechanisms that aid cartels in enforcing their agreements, the most successful cartel agreements and their enforcement mechanisms may be unknown.

Control More than Price.   To prevent cheating, successful cartels must agree on more than just a price. Posner (1970, 400) finds that at least 14 percent of all Department of Justice antitrust cases involved collusion on terms besides basic price (and this figure apparently does not include explicit rules on dividing the market, exchanging information, or sales quotas).[20]

---

[18] So long as a cartel raises its marginal cost curve by more than its average cost curve, such actions increase profits (Salop, Scheffman, and Scwartz, 1984).

[19] Hay and Kelley (1974) argued that bid rigging or allocation of jobs among cartel members occur in industries in which orders are relatively large ("lumpy") compared to total sales.

[20] Posner (1976, 39) notes, "The machinery of cartelization includes sales quotas, exclusive sales agencies, price-fixing committees, the levying of penalties for infractions, provisions for arbitration of disputes, investigative apparatus, customer allocation, geographical-market division, and the like."

Divide the Market.   Some cartels succeed in preventing cheating by assigning each firm certain buyers or geographic areas, which allows cheating to be easily detected. Fraas and Greer (1977) found that 26 percent of price-fixing cases involved market allocation schemes. Posner (1970) found that 7.8 percent of the antitrust cases involved an allocation of customers, 14.6 percent involved a division of territories, and 1.8 percent involved a division of product markets (or 24 percent overall). The two-country mercury cartel used a geographic division of markets: Spain supplied the United States, and Italy supplied Europe.

Fix Market Shares.   Another effective technique is for members of a cartel to agree to fix market shares (say, at their precartel levels). As long as market shares are easily observable, no firm has an incentive to cut its price. If it lowered its price, its share would increase, and other firms would retaliate. For example, cartel members who detected changes in the output levels of other firms could adjust their own output to maintain their proportionate shares of industry output (Osborne 1976; Spence 1978a, 1978b). All firms expect this reaction, so no firm has an incentive to increase its own output only to earn lower profits after retaliation. As the next chapter shows, fixing market shares results in the cartel price.

Use Most-Favored-Nation Clauses.   A **most-favored-nation clause** in a sales contract provides the buyer with a guarantee that the seller is not selling at a lower price to another buyer (Salop 1986). A variant of such clauses was used in sales of large steam-turbine generators. The two major sellers, General Electric and Westinghouse (see Example 9.1), each used clauses in their contracts stating that the seller would not offer a lower price to any other buyer, current or future, without offering the same price decrease to the initial buyer. This rebate mechanism created a penalty for cheating on the cartel: if either company deviated from the agreement by cutting its price, it would have to cut prices to all previous buyers as well.

Use Meeting-Competition Clauses.   A **meeting-competition clause** in a long-term supply contract or in an advertisement guarantees the buyer that if another firm offers a lower price, the seller will match it or release the buyer from the contract (Salop 1986). Such a clause makes it difficult for a firm to cheat, because buyers will bring news of lower prices to the cartel. Thus, surprisingly, these clauses could be associated with high cartel prices rather than the low ones they seem to guarantee.

Establish Trigger Prices.   Alternatively, all cartel members could agree that if the market price drops below a certain level (called a **trigger price**), each firm will expand its output to the precartel level (Friedman 1971); that is, all firms will abandon the cartel agreement. In this case, a firm that cut its price might gain in the extremely short run, but would lose in the end due to the destruction of the cartel by this predetermined punishment mechanism.

Random fluctuations in price due to fluctuations in demand or supply costs could make cheating hard to detect. It is possible, however, for cartels to modify their punishment methods to prevent cheating even when random shocks occur (Green and Porter 1984). If firms were to permanently revert to the competitive level of output whenever they detected a fall in price, the cartel could be destroyed by a random fluctuation in price (rather than price-cutting by one firm). Instead, if the firms agreed to produce their precartel levels of output only for a predetermined length of time and then to revert to the cartel level of output, a random fluctuation in price would not destroy the cartel permanently.[21] One attraction of this scheme is that even if the agreement temporarily breaks down, it can be reestablished without further meetings. In a market in which random price fluctuations can obscure price-cutting by particular firms, such an agreement could lead to recurrent sharp declines in price and cartel profit levels. When a random drop in price occurred, cartel members punish themselves unnecessarily.

Nonetheless, this mechanism may be attractive to the cartel because if the punishment period (when all firms produce large levels of output) is long enough, it is never in a firm's best long-run interest to cut its price. Thus, cartel members realize that the price only falls below the trigger price because of random fluctuations (because no firm ever engages in price cutting). The cartel must keep punishing itself, however; if it stopped, price-cutting would occur. Example 9.5 provides an example of the American rail-freight industry in the 1880s that may illustrate such behavior.

Cartels and Price Wars

Many observers, seeing large price fluctuations in a market, have argued that the firms in that industry were trying to form a cartel that kept breaking apart. They then concluded that no government intervention was required because competitive forces keep destroying the cartel. Instead, these fluctuations could be part of a rational, long-run cartel policy involving trigger prices, as discussed in the preceding section. This trigger-price argument holds that price wars are more likely during business cycle downturns (recessions and depressions) when price is likely to decline in response to lowered demand. Thus, we expect that cartels would terminate during such conditions. Other economists have argued that price wars should occur in periods of high demand (Rotemberg and Saloner 1986). They reason that the benefit from undercutting the cartel price is greatest during booms.

To see whether either or both theories are realistic, Valerie Y. Suslow (1988) investigated the stability of cartels over the business cycle by examining 72 international cartel agreements covering 47 industries during the period 1920–39. Table 9.1 on pages 230 and 231 shows the history of these cartels.

Because major European countries had no systematic antitrust legislation prior to World War II, these cartels were legal and had formal written contracts. As of 1927, cartels were legal in Switzerland, while Belgium, France, Spain, Italy, and the Netherlands did not explicitly prohibit them. Under German law, cartels were legal; however, Germany passed antitrust legislation in 1923 that was designed to guard against abuses of economic power. In 1930, Great Britain adopted a resolution recognizing cartels as a fact of economic

---

[21] If the firms revert to their precartel output level, the price falls to the precartel level as well. A more severe punishment, a price below the precartel level, may be used instead: with a lower price, it may be possible to shorten the punishment period. Setting prices is obviously a key issue. For an illustration of how prices might be set, see Davidson and Martin (1985). Where members of a cartel disagree on how to behave, some kind of voting mechanism may be used; see, for example, Cave and Salant (1987).

EXAMPLE 9.5

HOW CONSUMERS WERE RAILROADED

During the 1880s, a cartel of railroads openly operated as the Joint Executive Committee (JEC). Prior to the Sherman Act in 1890, there was no law prohibiting such a cartel. As Porter explains, the JEC appears to have used a trigger-price strategy (Green and Porter [1984]).

The JEC agreement allocated market shares rather than the absolute quantities shipped. Each railroad set its rates individually, and the JEC office reported weekly accounts, so that each railroad could see the total amount transported. Since total demand was quite variable, each firm's market share depended on both the prices charged by all firms and unpredictable market fluctuations.

Entry occurred twice between 1880 and 1886 (the period Porter [1983] studies). In each case, the cartel passively accepted the entrants, allocated them market shares, and thereby allowed the collusive agreement to persist.

On a number of occasions, however, when the cartel thought that cheating had occurred, it cut prices for a time, and then returned to the collusive price. Porter finds that noncooperative periods averaged about ten weeks in duration and occurred in 1881, 1884, and 1885. The 1881 and 1884 incidents each occurred about 40 weeks after a new firm entered. He notes, however, that these price wars were not triggered by an unexpected tapering off of demand.

Porter also finds that price was 66 percent higher and quantity was 33 percent lower in cooperative periods. As a result, the cartel as a whole earned about 11 percent more revenues in cooperative periods.

SOURCES: MacAvoy (1965), Ulen (1980), and Porter (1983).

life, but called for the *principle of publicity,* which required compulsory notification, registration, and publication of the cartel agreements. Other European countries followed Great Britain's policy in the mid-1930s. It was not until after World War II that France passed legislation to control cartel activity.

It should have been easier for these cartels to survive than for illegal ones in the United States. Indeed, German, French, or British firms were participants in roughly half the cartels, and U.S. firms were involved in one-third of them. In the 1940s U.S. firms were indicted for their participation in 10 of these international cartels.

According to Suslow, the median cartel lasted slightly more than 5 years; 75 percent lasted more than 2 years, and 20 percent lasted more than 10 years. As Table 9.1 shows, there is an industry pattern. Of the single-episode cartels, 40 percent involved chemicals, with only 6 percent in metals. In contrast, 46 percent of the multiple-episode cartels involved metals, with only 17 percent in chemicals.

In the 42 cartel episodes in which the number of firms is known, 83 percent had 10 or fewer firms, 64 percent had 5 or fewer, and 39 percent had 3 or fewer. Of the 74 percent of the 39 cartels for which there is market-share information, each had a world

TABLE 9.1   Pre–World War II International Cartels

Industry	Dates of Cartel Operation[1]
Aluminum	2/23–?/26; 9/11/26–1/31; 7/3/31–1/39
Acetic acid #1	10/17/24–WWII
Acetic acid #2	?/24–?/32
Alkalis	?/24–3/16/44[2]
Calcium carbide	2/29/24–10/37
Citric acid	1/35–WWII
Coal	1/1/35–WWII
Copper	12/18–1/24; 10/26–4/30; 9/31–6/32; 3/28/35–WWII
Dyes	?/27–?/29; 2/26/31–WWII (indicted 1941)
Ferrosilicon	?/29–WWII
Firearms	?/20–1/6/44[2]
Heavy electrical equip.	12/13/30–WWII
Hormones	5/26/37–12/41[2]
Incandescent electrical lamps	?/21–2/24; 12/24/24–WWII
Lead	5/1/31–3/32; 11/1/38–WWII
Linen thread	10/28/25–12/30/40
Magnesium	10/23/31–4/15/42[3]
Matches	?/20–5/1/44[2]
Mechanical wood pulp	?/27–end of 1941
Nitrate of soda (synthetic)	?/26–WWII
Nitrogen	6/26/29–6/26/30; 8/9/30–7/14/31; 7/21/32–WWII
Optical goods	4/29/21–7/9/40[2]
Pharmaceutical chemicals	11/17/32–10/28/43[2]
Phosphate rock	?/33–WWII
Pins & snap fasteners	?/27–at least 1945
Plate glass	3/24/21–no end

market share of over 50 percent. Thus, as with U.S cartels, these international cartels involved relatively few firms with large collective market shares.

Suslow estimated the probability that a cartel will fall apart at a specific time, given that it survives until that time. Controlling for other factors, she found that cartels are relatively more likely to fail during business cycle downturns (recessions and depressions).[22] Moreover, cartels that were alive during periods of growth in the United States or the United Kingdom were less likely to end than others. In general, greater volatility in aggregate economic activity over the lifetime of the cartel (frequent upswings and downturns) increases the probability of cartel breakdowns.

---

[22] Based on data on a railroad cartel in the United States, 1880–1886, Hajivassiliou (1989) also rejects Rotemberg and Saloner's (1986) prediction.

TABLE 9.1	Pre–World War II International Cartels continued
Industry	*Dates of Cartel Operation*[1]
Platinum	?/18–?/27; 10/21/31–?/33
Potash	8/15/24–5/7/26; 12/29/26–9/39[2]
Quebracho extract	?/19–?/22; ?/26–?/31; 5/34–?/42[2]
Rayon	2/27–WWII
Rubber	?/20–?/21; 11/1/22–?/26; 6/1/34–4/30/44
Saccharine	?/30–?/45
Sheet glass	?/32–?/34
Sodium chlorate	?/31–WWII
Sodium sulphate	?/26–WWII
Steel	10/1/26–5/1/29; 3/13/30–1/31; 6/1/33–WWII
Sugar	5/31–9/1/35; 5/6/37–WWII
Sulfur	3/14/23–?/33; 8/1/34–WWII
Synthetic rubber	11/9/29–extended past 9/39
Tea	1/30–12/30; 4/1/33–WWII
Timber	11/15/35–WWII
Tin	2/21–12/24; 3/1/31–12/41
Titanium compounds	7/30/20–?/27; 1/1/33–6/28/43
Tungsten carbide	?/28–?/40
Wire and cable	?/28–WWII
Wood pulp (sulphite pulp)	?/30–Summer 1939
Zinc	1/1/29–12/29; 8/31–1/33; 3/33–12/34

[1]The beginning date refers to the date the agreement went into effect. The ending date is inclusive.
[2]The date the Department of Justice filed an antitrust complaint.
[3]The date a consent decree was signed.
SOURCE: Suslow (1988, Appendix A)

■ CONSUMERS GAIN AS CARTELS FAIL

Men who know the same things are not long the best company for each other. —EMERSON

Obviously, firms that follow a cartel's rules look with disfavor on firms that produce more than it says they should. Violators of the cartel's rules may be called "cheaters" or "chiselers" or worse by the firms that obey them. Yet one should remember that consumers benefit from such noncartel behavior; the violators of the cartel agreement produce more than the cartel wants, which lowers the market price.

A simple linear example illustrates the effects of noncompliance by some firms.[23] The industry in this example includes 50 firms with identical cost functions. Assume that no more firms can enter this industry.

---

[23] See Appendix 9A for the derivation of the equations used in this example.

FIGURE 9.2   Imperfect Cartel

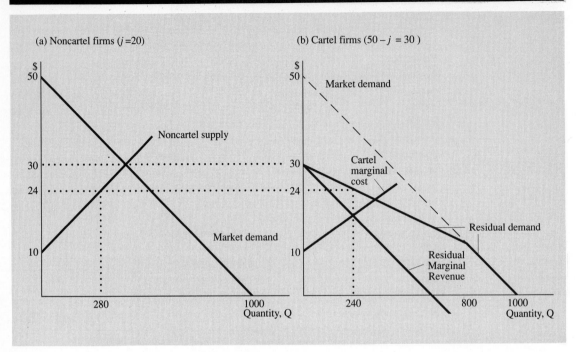

(a) Noncartel firms (j =20)

(b) Cartel firms ($50 - j = 30$)

Of the 50 firms, j firms do not follow the cartel's agreement to restrict output; they sell as much as they want. These firms are price-takers. For specificity, assume that each firm's marginal cost is linear in the quantity (q), $MC = 10 + q$. If the industry price, p, is greater than 10, each firm produces $q = p - 10$ units of output (the output at which its marginal cost equals p). As a result, the j noncartel firms produce $Q_{nc} = jq = j(p - 10)$ units of output.

Figure 9.2a shows both the market demand curve, $Q = 1000 - 20p$, and the supply by 20 competitive (noncartel) firms. Because not all firms in the industry belong to the cartel, *the cartel is a dominant firm facing a competitive fringe,* and its decision making can be analyzed as in Chapter 8, using a residual demand curve.

The residual demand facing the cartel can be determined by subtracting the fringe supply from the market demand. Figure 9.2b shows the residual demand curve (solid line) that lies below the market demand curve (dashed line) at prices above the competitive firms' shutdown level ($p = 10$).[24] The residual demand curve has a kink in it at $p = 10$. Because cartel firms have the same cost functions as noncartel firms, the cartel cannot afford to produce below $p = 10$ either, so the lower portion of the residual demand curve

---

[24] Each competitive firm's supply curve is $q = 10 - p$, so it would lose money by producing positive levels of output if the price were below 10.

is not of interest. The profit-maximizing cartel chooses its output, 240, by setting its marginal revenue (the curve marginal to its residual demand curve) equal to its marginal cost, as shown in Figure 9.2b. This output determines the cartel price, 24. At that price, the noncartel firms' output is 280, as shown in Figure 9.2a.

Table 9.2 presents the details for the case of $m = 20$ and also shows what happens as the number of firms belonging to the cartel changes. The industry is in competitive equilibrium if all 50 firms refuse to belong to the cartel. The market price is $21.43 and 571 units of output are produced by the industry. Each firm produces 11.43 units and earns $65.31 in profits. Consumer surplus and total welfare are maximized if the market is competitive.

At the other extreme, if all the firms join the cartel ($m = 0$), the cartel is a monopoly. The monopolistic price is $33.33, or 56 percent higher than the competitive price. The price markup [(price − marginal cost)/price] is 50 percent.[25] Only 333 units of output are produced by the industry, or 58 percent as much as the competitive quantity. Individual firms produce only 6.66 units of output. Each firm's profits of $133.33, however, are more than double those of the competitive level. Consumer surplus is only about a third as great, and total welfare is only 83 percent as great as under competition; that is, consumer losses are greater than the cartel gains. This loss to society is referred to as the *deadweight loss* to monopoly (discussed in Chapter 5). The deadweight loss is 18 percent of sales and 71 percent of consumer surplus (at the monopoly price).

Table 9.2 shows that as the number of noncartel firms rises, the price to consumers falls, the quantity produced by the industry rises, the quantity produced by a cartel firm rises, but the quantity produced by a noncartel firm falls (since price is lower), and profits fall for both types of firms. The table shows why firms would want to cheat by producing more than the cartel says they should: at every output, nonmembers earn more than cartel members, because they produce more and sell at the same price. If even one firm refuses to abide by the cartel rules and is a price-taker, industry price is about 3 percent lower than the monopoly price. Similarly, the deadweight loss is 10 percent lower, consumer surplus is 10 percent higher, and total profits are 2 percent lower.

Table 9.2 also shows that it hardly pays for one firm to try to act as a price-setter by itself. If one firm forms a "cartel" consisting only of itself (so that there are 49 noncartel firms), it faces a residual demand curve with only a slight slope. It can reduce its output from the competitive level of 11.429 to 11.27 units, thereby maximizing its profits, which rise by 1¢ from $65.31 to $65.32. The 49 noncartel firms, seeing the higher price and acting as price-takers, increase their output to 11.431 units, causing profits to rise by a phenomenal 2¢ to $65.33—each noncartel firm's profits rise by more than those of the single-firm cartel. All firms' profits rise in this case because the expansion of output by the 49 noncartel firms does not completely offset the reduction in output by the single firm. Total industry output falls from 571.43 to 571.38 units, causing the price to rise from $21.429 to $21.431. The welfare losses from such a limited cartel are minimal.

---

[25] Although the competitive industry operates in the inelastic portion of the industry demand curve (the elasticity of demand is -0.75), the monopolistic cartel operates in the elastic portion (the elasticity of demand is -2.00).

TABLE 9.2   Market Variables Under Various Degrees of Cartelization

	Noncartel Firms (number)	Price (p)	Market Elasticity	Market Output	Industry Profits (π)	Consumer Surplus (CS)	Welfare (CS + π)	DWL as a % of Sales	Cartel's Market Share (%)	Cartel Firms Price Markup (%)	Cartel Firms Output	Cartel Firms Profits	Noncartel Firms Output	Noncartel Firms Profits
monopoly	0	33.33	−2.00	333.33	6666.67	2778.33	9445.00	17.85	100.0	50.0	6.66	133.33	—	—
	1	32.41	−1.84	351.82	6524.08	3094.26	9618.34	15.88	93.6	48.4	6.72	128.02	22.41	251.10
	10	26.97	−1.17	460.61	5317.72	5303.92	10621.64	6.50	63.2	36.0	7.27	96.95	16.97	143.99
	20	24.00	−0.92	520.00	4360.00	6760.00	11120.00	2.47	46.2	25.0	8.00	80.00	14.00	98.00
	30	22.44	−0.81	551.11	3742.82	7594.30	11337.12	0.74	32.3	15.8	8.89	71.08	12.44	77.38
	40	21.67	−0.76	566.67	3390.78	8026.88	11417.66	0.09	17.6	8.4	10.00	66.70	11.67	68.09
	49	21.431	−0.75	571.38	3266.62	8161.88	11428.38	0.00	2.0	0.8	11.27	65.32	11.431	65.33
competition	50	21.429	−0.75	571.43	3265.31	8163.16	11428.66	—	0.0	—	—	—	11.429	65.31

CS = Consumer Surplus is the triangle with area $(1000 - 20p)^2/40$.

Cartel's Market Share as a percent is 100 times the cartel's sales divided by total sales.

DWL = Deadweight Loss (competitive welfare − actual welfare).

Price Markup = $100 \, (p - MC)/p$ (that is, it is expressed as a percent markup).

EXAMPLE 9.6

THE SOCIAL COSTS OF CARTELIZATION

Posner (1976) estimates the social cost of several (mainly international) well-organized, overt cartels using his theory, discussed in Chapter 5, that all cartel profits are dissipated in rent-seeking activity. His results are shown in the table:

Industry	Cartel Price Increase (%)	Elasticity	Social Costs (as a % of industry's sales)
Nitrogen	75%	2.33	62%
Sugar	30	4.33	36
Aluminum	100	2.00	75
Aluminum	38	3.63	42
Rubber	100	2.00	75
Electric bulbs	37	3.70	42
Copper	31	4.25	36
Cast-iron pipe	39	3.56	42

NOTE: These figures are based on the updated table in Posner's book. Apparently, two figures are given for aluminum because he has two estimates of the cartel price increase.

The elasticities are based on the cartels' price-increase data, on the assumption that the industry is charging the profit-maximizing monopoly price and that the demand curve is linear. Because of these restrictive assumptions, Posner warns that these results should be viewed with some caution. Nonetheless, if these figures are anywhere near accurate, the social costs of these cartels are enormous.

SOURCE: Posner R.A.: *Antitrust Law,* © 1976 by The University of Chicago. All Rights Reserved.

The larger the market share of the cartel, the greater the efficiency cost. In competition, price equals marginal cost, so that consumers pay what it costs to manufacture the product. Table 9.2 shows (in the price markup column) that the greater the number of cartel members, the higher the price relative to their marginal cost. In this example, when all firms are members of the cartel, so that the cartel is a monopoly, the price markup is 50 percent. If 20 firms refuse to join the cartel, the price markup is only 25 percent, but if 30 firms refuse to join, the markup is just 15.8 percent. Consumer surplus, total welfare, and deadweight loss all move similarly. See also Example 9.6.

To summarize, if entry is limited, the greater the proportion of firms in a cartel, the higher the price and the smaller the industry output. Consumers lose as the cartel becomes more powerful. In the example, the equilibrium output and price range from competitive to monopolistic as the cartel's share of the market goes from zero to 100 percent. Firms that do not belong to the cartel always earn more than cartel members, and the discrepancy and hence the incentive to cheat are greatest when the cartel is successful. This result shows that it does not always pay to be a price-setter rather than a price-taker.

■ THE LAWS ON PRICE-FIXING

Nothing is illegal if a hundred businessmen decide to do it.—ANDREW YOUNG

In the late nineteenth century, cartelization was extremely common in the United States. There were major trusts in oil, powder, railroads, sugar, and tobacco. The Sherman Antitrust Act of 1890 was passed in response to this activity "to protect trade and commerce against unlawful restraints and monopolies."[26] In 1914, the Federal Trade Commission Act established the Federal Trade Commission (FTC), and its Section 5 holds that "unfair methods of competition are hereby declared illegal." This act is still used by the FTC, as is the Sherman Act by the U.S. Department of Justice, in prosecuting antitrust violations.

As discussed in detail in Chapter 22, the Sherman Act makes conspiracies whose sole purpose is to raise price illegal. For example, in the *Addyston Pipe and Steel* case in 1899, outright bid rigging and the dividing of the market into regional monopolies were found illegal.[27]

The *Trenton Potteries* case of 1927 and *Socony-Vacuum Oil Co.* case of 1940 determined that price-fixing was a **per se** violation (the action by itself is illegal), regardless of whether the price set was above the competitive price.[28] These cases established that the violation is the *attempt* to charge the monopoly price; the government does not have to show that the defendants succeeded in their attempt (Posner 1976, 25).

This approach to preventing price fixing is based on evidence of conspiracy rather than the economic effects of monopoly. The government can try a price-fixing case based on evidence of conspiracy (for example, secret meetings in a smoke-filled room) rather than economic evidence. Cases involving tacit collusion (without formal meetings) may not be actionable under antitrust laws.[29] Cartels formed solely to raise prices are strictly prohibited.

---

[26] The Sherman Act, which is concerned with the price and output consequences of monopolies and cartels, has a different objective than the common law that was used in the United States and Great Britain prior to the passage of explicit antitrust laws. The common law had a variety of objectives, such as to assert the supremacy of Parliament over the Crown, to interfere with unionization, to limit competition in the distribution of goods, and to protect individuals from making improvident contracts. See Bork (1966), Posner (1976, Chaps. 3 and 4), and Chapter 22 for a discussion of this and other topics discussed in this section.

[27] *Addyston Pipe and Steel Co. v. United States,* 175 U.S. 211 (1899). This citation is from the U.S. Reporter volume 175 and starts on page 211. The case was decided by the U.S. Supreme Court in 1899.

[28] *United States v. Trenton Potteries Co.,* 273 U.S. 392 (1927) established a per se rule. A later case, *Appalachian Coals, Inc. v. United States,* 288 U.S. 344 (1933), however, appeared to deviate from this per se rule. *United States v. Socony-Vacuum Oil Co.,* 310 U.S. 150 (1940) firmly established the per se rule.

[29] Lawyers refer to needing to prove "conscious parallelism plus" some evidence of conspiracy to win a tacit collusion case. Additional evidence that could be used includes circumstantial evidence of a conspiracy (as opposed to proof of actual meetings) or concerted (that is, exclusionary or predatory) actions.

The Use of U.S. Antitrust Laws

U.S. antitrust laws have been increasingly used to prosecute price-fixers, and penalties have increased.[30] From 1890 through 1974, the Justice Department brought 1000 civil and 723 criminal cases (Posner 1976, 25). The penalty in a criminal case can be a jail sentence, but the penalty in a civil case cannot. Since World War II, Democratic and Republican administrations have brought cases at roughly the same rate (Posner 1970, 411–12). The Department of Justice wins most of the cases it brings. In every five-year period since 1910 studied by Posner (1970, 381–82), the Department won at least 64 percent of all its cases; since 1925 it has won at least 78 percent; and since 1955 it has won at least 85 percent.[31]

The Department of Justice has won a very high percent of its criminal cases (Posner 1970). Since 1890, 57 percent of the cases have been disposed of on *nolo contendere* ("no contest") pleas, 21 percent on other convictions, and only 22 percent resulted in acquittals and dismissals. This high success rate may indicate that the Department only tries sure cases or that it wins many of its cases because defendants plead *nolo contendere* and pay small fines (avoiding the costs of long court battles and the risks of losing). One advantage of a *nolo contendere* plea for a defendant in a government case is that it does not provide evidence of collusion that can be used subsequently in a private antitrust action seeking treble damages.

The penalties imposed by these antitrust laws have always been relatively small. The FTC's only remedy is an injunction called a **cease-and-desist order,** which prohibits the behavior but does not penalize the firm for engaging in it. The maximum fine under the original Sherman Act was $5000 and the maximum prison sentence was one year. The Department of Justice or a private individual or firm injured by a violation of this law, however, could seek relief that not only prohibited the violation from continuing but also provided for treble damages plus a reasonable attorney's fee.[32] The fines were increased to $50,000 in 1955 and to $100,000 for individuals and $1 million for corporations in 1974, which were not large increases when adjusted for inflation. In the 1950–59 period, the fines in the Justice Department's cases averaged $40,000 (0.08 percent of the sales involved in the conspiracy); whereas from 1960 to 1969 they averaged $131,000 (0.21 percent of the sales involved in the conspiracy) (Posner 1970, 1976).

Prison sentences are rare in federal antitrust cases. There were none during the period from 1890 to 1909. From 1910 to 1974, there were 33 cases in which a prison sentence was imposed, roughly one every other year (Posner 1976, 33). Prior to 1925, most of those jailed were union organizers and officers. Until after World War II, most prison sentences for price-fixing involved violence. The maximum jail sentence was increased to three years in 1974.

---

[30] Cases brought by states under their own antitrust laws were extremely infrequent prior to the 1970s. In recent years, a few states have made increasing use of their antitrust laws, but state cases are still uncommon.

[31] Posner (1970, 384) also shows that the Department of Justice has won 74 percent of its cases before the Supreme Court, the Federal Trade Commission has won 75 percent, and private claimants have won 63 percent. Averaged across the three groups, 70 percent of these cases before the Supreme Court were won by the plaintiffs.

[32] Treble damages means that the guilty defendant must pay the victim three times the actual damages.

Private Litigation

Private actions brought by individuals or firms harmed by anticompetitive behavior were rare for price-fixing cases until the electrical conspiracy of the early 1960s (see Example 9.1). In the next two decades, private actions, including class-action suits, increased substantially. These private actions, which often follow federal suits, can substantially increase the cost of conspiracy, because treble damages may be collected.[33] For the period 1937–54, there was an average of 104 private cases per year; for the period 1955–59, the average increased to 229 cases per year. From 1960 to 1964, 1919 cases were filed concerning electrical equipment, causing the yearly average to rise to 671 cases. In 1974, 1162 private suits were filed (Posner 1976, 34).

Success of Antitrust Laws

The current laws have been successful in eliminating overt collusion. As Posner (1976, 39) observes, "The elimination of the formal cartel . . . is an impressive, and remains the major, achievement of American antitrust law." As discussed in Chapter 22, the laws have not been used successfully to prevent firms from coordinating their activities through conscious parallelism (tacit collusion).

■ SUMMARY

Firms have incentives both to form cartels and to cheat on them. Firms want to form cartels when they are capable of raising prices for sustained periods of time. Prices are more likely to be significantly elevated above the competitive level when the cartel controls a substantial share of the market's output, faces a relatively inelastic demand curve, and entry is limited. The expected rewards of forming illegal cartels are greater when detection appears less likely and the fines for firms that are caught are low.

Individual firms have an incentive to cheat on a cartel agreement because they can make higher profits by increasing output (or undercutting the cartel's price). A cartel can maintain its agreement only if cheating can be detected and adequately punished. Cartels have developed a number of techniques, including division of the market, complex contract clauses, and trigger-price policies, in order to enforce their agreements.

When cartels succeed in raising prices, there is a loss of consumer surplus. The gain to the cartel is less than the loss to consumers: the difference is a deadweight (efficiency) loss. The fewer the firms that go along with the cartel agreement, the less monopoly power the cartel has, and hence the less it harms consumers and society.

---

[33] According to Posner (1970, 372), in the period 1956–60, at least 278 private cases were preceded by a Department of Justice judgment, while in 1961–63, 880 cases followed such judgments.

■ Key Terms

cartel
cease-and-desist order
conscious parallelism
cooperative oligopoly
meeting-competition clause

most-favored-nation clause
per se
tacit collusion
trigger price

■ Discussion Questions

1. What domestic economic policies could the United States or other Western countries use to weaken international cartels like OPEC?
2. Are there any reasons why a government would want to promote or actively create cartels? For example, if a domestic industry mostly sold abroad, would the government be justified in encouraging the formation of a cartel?
3. Why do you think that the United States has stricter anticartel laws than other countries?
4. Would you expect strictly enforced antitrust laws to have adverse effects on innovative companies that want to cooperate in research and development projects?
5. (Question based on Appendix 9B) What evidence beyond that given in the chapter would be useful in distinguishing among the four hypotheses about OPEC?

■ Problems

1. Suppose cartel members have lower (average and marginal) costs than noncartel firms. Draw the residual demand curve facing the cartel. (What assumptions are you making about entry?) Show on the graph the cartel's profit-maximizing output and price. Could the cartel drive the other firms out of business and still make a profit? Under what conditions?
2. Using the data in Example 9.3, calculate the market demand elasticity for automobiles in the mid-1950s. For large changes in price and quantity, an *arc elasticity* is used. One common method of calculating an arc elasticity is to use the midway point between the two price-quantity pairs: (p,q) and (p^*, q^*). Thus, the formula for an arc elasticity is

$$\epsilon = \frac{(q - q^*)/(q + q^*)}{(p - p^*)/(p + p^*)}.$$

Is that number consistent with the theory that there was a profit-maximizing cartel in 1954? Why or why not?
3. Use a graph to show why an increase in the market demand elasticity reduces a cartel's monopoly power. Show how an increase in the market demand elasticity affects the elasticity of the residual demand curve.
4. (Problem based on Appendix 9.1) Show that a cartel's output plus the output of noncartel firms are less than the competitive output and that the corresponding price is higher than the competitive price.
5. (Problem based on Appendix 9.1) Show that a cartel's price falls as the number of noncartel firms *(m)* increases.

Answers to odd-numbered problems are given at the back of the book.

■ References

Adelman, Morris A. 1982. "OPEC as a Cartel," in James M. Griffin and David J. Teece, eds. *OPEC Behavior and World Oil Prices*. London: George Allen & Unwin.

Asch, Peter, and J. J. Seneca. 1976. "Is Collusion Profitable?" *Review of Economics and Statistics* 68:1–12.

Bane, Charles A. 1973. *The Electrical Equipment Conspiracies: The Treble-Damages Actions*. New York: Federal Legal Publications.

Bork, Robert H. 1966. "Legislative Intent and the Policy of the Sherman Act." *Journal of Law and Economics* 9:7–48.

Bresnahan, Timothy F. 1987. "Competition and Collusion in the American Automobile Industry: The 1955 Price War." *The Journal of Industrial Economics* 35:457–82.

Castle, Emery N., and K. Price. 1983. *U.S. Interests and Global Natural Resources*. Washington, D.C.: Johns Hopkins University Press.

Cave, Jonathan, and Stephen W. Salant. 1987. "Cartels That Vote: Agricultural Marketing Boards and Induced Voting Behavior," in Elizabeth Bailey, ed., *Regulation at the Crossroads*. Cambridge, Mass.: MIT Press.

Crémer, Jacques, and Djavad Salehi-Isfahani. 1980. "Competitive Pricing in the Oil Market: How Important is OPEC?" CARESS Working Paper 80-4, University of Pennsylvania.

Davidson, Carl, and Lawrence W. Martin. 1985. "General Equilibrium Tax Incidence Under Imperfect Competition: A Quantity-setting Supergame Analysis." *Journal of Political Economy* 93:1212–23.

Eckbo, Paul L. 1976. *The Future of World Oil*. Cambridge, Mass.: Ballinger.

Fisher, Anthony C. 1981. *Resource and Environmental Economics*. Cambridge: Cambridge University Press.

Fisher, Franklin M., P.H. Cootners, and Martin N. Bailey. 1972. "An Econometric Model of the World Copper Industry." *Bell Journal of Economics and Management* 3:568–609.

Fraas, Arthur G., and Douglas F. Greer. 1977. "Market Structure and Price Collusion: An Empirical Analysis." *Journal of Industrial Economics* 26:21–44.

Friedman, James W. 1971. "A Noncooperative Equilibrium for Supergames." *Review of Economic Studies*. 28:1–12.

Fuller, John G. 1962. *The Gentlemen Conspirators: The Story of the Price-Fixers in the Electrical Industry*. New York: Grove Press.

Green, Edward J., and Robert H. Porter. 1984. "Noncooperative Collusion Under Imperfect Price Information." *Econometrica* 52:87–100.

Griffin, James M. 1985. "OPEC Behavior: A Test of Alternative Hypotheses." *American Economic Review*. 75:954–63.

Griffin, James M., and David J. Teece. 1982. "Introduction," in James M. Griffin and David J. Teece, eds., *OPEC Behavior and World Oil Prices*. London: George Allen & Unwin.

Hay, George A., and Daniel Kelley. 1974. "An Empirical Survey of Price-Fixing Conspiracies." *Journal of Law and Economics* 17:13–38.

Hajivassiliou, Vassilis A. 1989. "Measurement Errors in Switching Regressions Models: With Applications to Price-Fixing Behavior." Cowles Foundation for Research in Economics Working Paper.

Hnyilicza, Esteban, and Robert S. Pindyck. 1976. "Pricing Policies for a Two-Part Exhaustible Resource Cartel: The Case of OPEC." *European Economic Review* 8:139–54.

Lean, David F., Jonathan D. Ogur, Robert P. Rogers. 1982. *Competition and Collusion in Electrical Equipment Markets: An Economic Assessment*. Washington D.C.: Federal Trade Commission.

McAvoy, Paul W. 1965. *The Economic Effects of Regulation*. Cambridge, Mass.: MIT Press.

MacAvoy, Paul. 1982. *Crude Oil Prices as Determined by OPEC and Market Fundamentals*. Cambridge, Mass.: Ballinger.

MacKie-Mason, Jeffrey K., and Robert S. Pindyck. 1986. "Cartel Theory and Cartel Experience in International Minerals Markets," in R. L. Gordon, H. D. Jacoby, and M. B. Zimmerman, eds., *Energy: Markets & Regulation: Essays in Honor of M. A. Adelman*. Cambridge, Mass.: MIT Press.

Maloney, Michael T., Robert E. McCormick, and Robert D. Tollison. 1979. "Achieving Cartel Profits Through Unionization." *Southern Economic Journal* 46:628–34.

Mead, Walter J. 1979. "The Performance of Government Energy Regulation." *American Economic Review* 69:352–56.

Osborne, D. K. 1976. "Cartel Problems." *American Economic Review* 66:835–44.

Owen, Bruce M. and Joseph Grunfest. 1977. "Kickbacks, Specialization, Price-Fixing, and Efficiency in Residential Real Estate Markets." Stanford Law Review 29:931–67.

Phillips, Almarin. 1972. "An Econometric Study of Price-Fixing, Market Structure, and Performance in British Industry in the Early 1950s," in Keith Cowling, ed., *Market Structure and Corporate Behaviour: Theory and Empirical Analysis of the Firm*. London: Gray-Mills Publishing, 177–92.

Pindyck, Robert S. 1977. "Cartel Pricing and the Structure of the World Bauxite Market." *Bell Journal of Economics and Management* 8:343–60.

———. 1978. "Gains to Producers from the Cartelization of Exhaustible Resources." *Review of Economics and Statistics* 60:238–51.

———. 1979. "The Cartelization of World Commodity Markets." *American Economic Review*. 69:154–58.

Porter, Robert H. 1983. "A Study of Cartel Stability: The Joint Executive Committee, 1880–1886." *Bell Journal of Economics and Management* 14:301–14.

Posner, Richard A. 1970. "A Statistical Study of Antitrust Enforcement." *Journal of Law and Economics* 13:365–419.

———. 1975. "The Social Cost of Monopoly and Regulation." *Journal of Political Economy*. 83:807–27.

———. 1976. *Antitrust Law: An Economic Perspective*. Chicago: The University of Chicago Press.

Rosenstein-Rodan, P. N. 1961. "International Aid for Underdeveloped Countries." *Review of Economics and Statistics* 43:107–38.

Rotemberg, Julio J., and Garth Saloner. 1986. "A Supergame-Theoretic Model of Price Wars During Booms." *American Economic Review* 76:390–407.

Salop, Steven C. 1986. "Practices that (Credibly) Facilitate Oligopoly Coordination," in Joseph E. Stiglitz and G. Frank Mathewson, eds., *New Developments in the Analysis of Market Structure*. Cambridge, Mass.: The MIT Press, Chap. 9, 265–90.

Salop, Steven C., David T. Scheffman, and Warren Scwartz. 1984. "A Bidding Analysis of Special Interest Regulation: Raising Rivals' Costs in a Rent-Seeking Society." *Political Economy of Regulation: Private Interests in the Regulatory Process*. Washington D.C.: Federal Trade Commission.

Smith, Adam. (n.d.) *An Inquiry into the Nature and Causes of the Wealth of Nations*. New York: Random House.

Spence, Michael. 1978a. "Tacit Coordination and Imperfect Information." *Canadian Journal of Economics* 11:490–505.

———. 1978b. "Efficient Collusion and Reaction Functions." *Canadian Journal of Economics* 11:527–33.

Stigler, George J. 1964. "A Theory of Oligopoly." *Journal of Political Economy* 72. Reprinted as Chap. 5 in *The Organization of Industry*. Homewood, Ill.: Richard D. Irwin, 1968, 39–63.

Sultan, Ralph G. M. 1974, 1975. *Pricing in the Electrical Oligopoly*. Boston: Harvard Business School, vols. I and II.

Suslow, Valerie Y. 1988. "Stability in International Cartels: An Empirical Survey." Hoover Institution Working Paper No. E-88-7.

Teece, David J. 1982. "OPEC Behavior: An Alternative View," in James M. Griffin and David J. Teece, eds., *OPEC Behavior and World Oil Prices*. London: George Allen & Unwin.

Ulen, Thomas S. 1980. "The Market for Regulation: The ICC From 1887 to 1920." *American Economic Review* 70:306–10.

Verleger, Philip K., Jr. 1982. "The Determinants of Official OPEC Crude Prices" *Review of Economics and Statistics* 64:177–83.

Walton, Clarence C. and Frederick W. Cleveland. 1964. *Corporations on Trial: The Electric Cases*. Belmont, Calif.: Wadsworth.

The Effects of Cartel Size

This appendix shows the derivation of the equations used to calculate the linear example in the chapter that demonstrates the effects on price and output of varying inclusiveness of cartel membership. The number of firms is assumed to be fixed at n—no further entry is possible.

The market demand curve is assumed to be linear:

$$Q = a - bp, \tag{9A.1}$$

where a and b are positive constants, Q is market output, and p is the price. The elasticity of demand is

$$\epsilon = \frac{dQ}{dp} \frac{p}{Q} = 1 - \frac{a}{Q} = \frac{-bp}{a - bp}. \tag{9A.2}$$

Each firm has a linear marginal cost *(MC)* of

$$MC = d + eq, \tag{9A.3}$$

where q is the output of one of the n firms and d and e are positive constants. As a result, the competitive supply (the output produced at the point where marginal cost equals price) is

$$Q = nq = \frac{n(p - d)}{e}. \tag{9A.4}$$

Competitive equilibrium is determined by setting the right-hand sides of the quantity-demanded equation (9A.1) and the quantity-supplied equation (9A.4) equal, and solving for p^* (the equilibrium price). The equilibrium quantity, Q^*, can be found by substituting p^* into Equation 9A.1 or 9A.4. The equilibrium values are

$$p^* = \frac{ae + nd}{be + n}, \tag{9A.5}$$

$$Q^* = n\left(\frac{a - bd}{be + n}\right). \tag{9A.6}$$

Now suppose that $n - j$ firms in the industry form a cartel and the remaining j firms ($j < n$) do not. As shown in Figure 9.2b, the residual demand, Q_r, is the market demand minus the noncartel supply, $Q_{nc} = jq$:

$$Q_r = Q - jq = a - bp - \frac{j(p - d)}{e}. \qquad (9A.7)$$

The cartel acts as a monopolist with respect to its residual demand and sets its marginal revenue, MR_m, equal to its marginal cost. The cartel's revenues, R_m, may be found by solving Equation 9A.7 for p as a function of Q_r and multiplying that by Q_r to obtain

$$R_m = pQ_r = \left(\frac{ae + jd - eQ_r}{be + j}\right)Q_r. \qquad (9A.8)$$

By differentiating R_m with respect to Q_r, the cartel's marginal revenue can be shown to be

$$MR_m = \frac{ae + jd}{be + j} - \left(\frac{2e}{be + j}\right)Q_r. \qquad (9A.9)$$

The cartel's marginal cost is

$$MC_m = d + \left(\frac{e}{n - j}\right)Q_m. \qquad (9A.10)$$

The quantity the cartel chooses to produce, Q_m ($= Q_r$), is determined by equating the cartel's marginal revenue, Equation 9A.9, and marginal cost, Equation 9A.10:

$$Q_m = \frac{(n - j)(a - bd)}{be + 2n - j}. \qquad (9A.11)$$

By differentiating Q_m with respect to j, it can be shown that the cartel's output falls as the number of nonmember firms rises.

APPENDIX 9B OPEC: AN EXAMPLE

For years it was fashionable to use the Organization of Petroleum Exporting Countries (OPEC) as an example of a successful cartel. OPEC greatly raised the price consumers pay for oil products, made a fantastic amount of money, and has survived for years. Today, however, its returns are much smaller than in its heyday. It is not clear that OPEC was or is a profit-maximizing cartel.

Table 9B.1 presents a chronology of major events in the history of OPEC, which was formed by five major oil exporters in September 1960. Some economists believe that prior to the formation of OPEC and for several years thereafter, the seven major oil companies *(the Seven Sisters)* kept the price of oil above the competitive level by restricting output. According to these economists, the price of oil declined throughout the 1960s and early 1970s because the entry of independent oil companies increased the competitiveness of the market. In 1986 dollars, the real price of crude oil fell from $10 per barrel in 1964 to $8.60 in 1972, as shown in Figure 9B.1 on page 247.

From 1970 to 1973 exporting countries increased their control over supply (through agreements and nationalizing production). As a result, their revenues from crude oil became more linked to the actual market price for refined oil. In October 1973, six Persian Gulf members of OPEC met and raised the amount they charged the oil companies. Also in October, in response to the fourth Arab-Israeli war, the Arab governments ordered oil production cutbacks and placed an embargo on oil shipments to the United States and the Netherlands. The price of oil shot up: the 1974 real price was triple that of the year before, as shown in Figure 9B.1. The price held steady or slightly declined in real terms for the next several years. Then, in 1979–1980, it again increased substantially, to more than five times the price in 1973. Since then, the price has declined in real terms. By 1986, the real price of gasoline was only 10 percent above the 1964 level.

After OPEC's first large price increase at the end of 1973, many economists, political scientists, journalists, and other self-proclaimed seers turned out article after article on OPEC. Each explained why OPEC was or was not a cartel, why it was or was not about to self-destruct, why or why not oil prices would continue to rise, and why or why not the earth was going to come to an end because of the increase in the oil price. Unfortunately, this spate of articles seems to have abated at about the time OPEC had existed for long enough to provide sufficient data to test the various theories.

We wish to thank George Frisvold, David Mitchell, and David Buschena for help in preparing this appendix.

TABLE 9B.1   An OPEC Chronology

1960 September	Five major oil exporters—Iran, Iraq, Kuwait, Saudi Arabia, and Venezuela—form the Organization for Petroleum Exporting Countries (OPEC). The OPEC nations' export taxes are based on 50 percent of the profits of the major international oil companies.
1965	Annual growth rates for each OPEC member's oil exports are set. This unsuccessful program ends in 1967.
1967 June	Third Arab-Israeli war closes Suez Canal.
1968	OPEC issues a declaration of goals including the maximization of oil revenues and the ultimate achievement of effective control of oil company operations.
1971 February	OPEC's Teheran Agreement signals that OPEC will take an active role in setting oil prices. OPEC raises its excise tax (which replaced the profits tax) rate from 50 to 55 percent and bases it on a tax reference price that exceeds the market price and does not decline with oil prices.
1973	The world price of oil rises after the Teheran Agreement so that by early 1973 it surpasses the posted tax reference price.
1973 September	Libya nationalizes 51 percent of all oil properties.
1973 October	The representatives of the six Persian Gulf states of OPEC meet and raise the reference price. The fourth Arab-Israeli war leads Arab governments to order oil production cutbacks and to place an embargo on oil shipments to the United States and the Netherlands. Panic buying of oil sends prices in special auctions over $15 per barrel.
1974 January 1	OPEC raises prices from $2 per barrel ($2/b) to over $7/b (both spot and contract prices are increased) and restricts output.
1974 March–June	Kuwait Oil Company is nationalized. Several governments acquire 60 percent interest in oil production.
1974 July	Saudi Arabia's Oil Minister, Yamani, announces a 1.5 MMB/D (million barrels per day) auction on the open market. This announcement is strongly criticized by the rest of OPEC and creates dissension within the Saudi royal family.
1974 August	Saudi Arabia cancels the auction. Political tensions between the Saudis and the Shah of Iran increase. The Shah wants high prices to pay for arms.
1974 December	Price of Saudi Arabian oil increases 65¢ per barrel. Other countries follow the Saudi lead. Saudi Arabia absorbs the largest share of the resulting reduction in total OPEC exports.
1975	World economy at the bottom of a major recession. Industrial activity is down 3 percent while inflation is up 14 percent.
1975 Jan.–August	OPEC production is down 17 percent from 1974 levels. There is widespread price discounting by Abu Dhabi, Libya, Nigeria, Iraq, Algeria, and Ecuador. In June, the Suez Canal reopens.
1975 Sept.–Oct.	Saudis push for a price reduction in real terms, but the Shah of Iran, facing a $4 billion trade deficit, pushes for a large price increase. The Saudis call for a 5 percent nominal price increase, while the Shah advocates a 15 percent increase. The Saudis threaten to freeze prices and produce at near full capacity. The price of oil rises 10 percent.
1976	Industrial activity in the world economy is up 8 percent over 1975 levels, increasing the demand for oil. Algeria and Libya undersell Nigerian high-grade oil.
1976 December	Saudis propose a price freeze. Iraq calls for a 25 percent increase and Iran for a 15 percent increase in price. Saudi Arabia lifts its 8.5 MMB/D production ceiling.
1977 February	Iranian production rises from 5.1 to 6.2 MMB/D. Saudi production rises from 8.5 to 8.9 MMB/D.
1977 July	OPEC nations agree to set price at $12.70. Saudi Arabia returns to 8.5 MMB/D ceiling.
1978	Widespread strikes in Iranian oil fields and political unrest lead to sharp reductions and then suspension of Iranian exports. Saudi Arabia's production increases from 8.4 to 10.4 MMB/D. OPEC's excess capacity is three times greater than Iran's reduction in oil exports.
1979 January	Shah of Iran is overthrown. Saudi Arabia's production falls from 10.4 to 9.5 MMB/D. The spot price rises.
1979 February	Uncertainty about supply creates a "buyer panic." The price of oil rises to $31/b.
1979 March	The new Iranian government resumes production at a lower (than historical) rate. All but a few OPEC countries increase production. The spot price falls from $31/b to $24/b.
1979 April	Saudi officials meet with those of the new Iranian regime. Saudi Arabia cuts production to 8.5 MMB/D.

Continued

TABLE 9B.1	An OPEC Chronology continued
1979 Summer	OPEC decides to make export determinations on a monthly rather than quarterly basis, which increases uncertainty. Western nations stockpile oil. Saudi Arabia keeps its price $2/b below the rest of OPEC and increases production back up to 9.5 MMB/D.
1979 October	Oil glut forces prices lower again. OPEC countries ignore an agreement to cut production 10 percent.
1979 Nov.–Dec.	The spot price reaches $35/b. Arab Light raised to $24/b after disruption of OPEC price unity and a series of individual member price increases.
1980 May	Saudi Arabia sets the price of Arab Light oil at $28/b.
1980 September	Start of the Iran-Iraq war. Arab Light oil price is set at $34/b.
1981	Production is 2 MMB/D above actual consumption despite low production by Iraq and Iran. OPEC members jointly agree to production cuts.
1981 Feb.–March	Total OPEC production falls 15 percent from 1980. Official government selling prices fall for every OPEC nation except Saudi Arabia, which raised the price of Arab Light to $34, and Indonesia, which kept price constant.
1982 January	Saudi Arabia holds price of Arab Light at $34 and cuts price of lower grade crude. Rest of OPEC cuts or holds official price. Total OPEC production falls 17 percent and Saudi production falls 34 percent from 1981 levels.
1983 March	A world oil glut forces OPEC to make its first major price cut. Saudi Arabia lowers price of Arab Light from $34 to $29. OPEC official prices fall over 14 percent between January 1982 and March 1983.
1984 August	Saudi Arabia boosts output by 1 MMB/D beyond its voluntary quota of 4.5 MMB/D. This increase triggers a further slide in prices. It also signals to other OPEC countries that increasing output is acceptable.
1984 December	This year has been a difficult one for OPEC. Oil purchases by western industrial countries increased by less than 4 percent from the previous year, while OPEC's total output increased by 30 percent. OPEC's market share is down 16 points since 1979.
1985 March	Great Britain decides to price its North Sea oil at market prices rather than following OPEC's price structure. This "free market" policy puts OPEC under further pressure to lower its posted prices.
1985 June	Saudi Arabia cuts back production to 2.4 MMB/D, its lowest in nearly two decades and one-quarter of its 1981 high, in an effort to stabilize prices. Non-OPEC production is 33 percent higher than in 1979, undercutting OPEC's prices.
1985 September	Saudi oil minister Ahmed Zaki Yamani threatens a price war in an effort to pressure the rest of OPEC's 13 members into halting the now common practice of selling below official prices and exceeding their production quotas.
1985 October	Saudi Arabia announces that it will sell an additional 1 MMB/D at the discount price of $3/b, which is below the official rate. King Fahd threatens that Saudi Arabia may go further and start producing its full quota of oil.
1986 March	OPEC meets in Geneva and fails to reach a new agreement on limiting quotas.
1986 April	For the first time in seven years, gasoline is selling at U.S. pumps for less than $1 per gallon. Oil prices plummet to $12/b.
1986 Aug–Sept.	OPEC agrees to limit output. Production falls from 20 MMB/D in August to 15 MMB/D in September. Prices rise from $10/b to nearly $17/b, but then settle at $14/b. Dissension continues within OPEC. Saudi Arabia, Kuwait, and the United Arab Emirates demand larger national quotas after years of self-imposed restrictions designed to shore up prices. Lower prices result in increased demand and decreased U.S. production.
1986 November	Sheik Yamani, long time Saudi oil minister and unofficial leader of OPEC, is fired by King Fahd for allowing prices to plummet for the past several years.

TABLE 9B.1   An OPEC Chronology continued

1987 December	OPEC oil ministers debate how to arrest the price slide and their falling market share, down 11 points from 1980 through 1986. A special production committee will police members' output levels. OPEC votes to impose production quotas on all member countries, but Iraq and the UAE announce they will not comply. The UAE has a long history of noncompliance and Iraq is worried that higher prices will help Iran continue fighting. Iran is pushing hard for production cuts and higher prices so that it can increase revenues to buy arms for the war. Saudi Arabia, supporting Iraq, states it is unwilling to reduce output enough to boost prices.
1988 March	Open-market oil prices fall. OPEC hopes to put pressure on nonmember producers by abandoning its official price of $18/b and sustaining its present production levels. Fadhil al Chalabi, OPEC's deputy secretary general, calls on member nations to abandon fixed prices for a more flexible market price system that would let them compete with non-OPEC producers.
1989 January	Oil prices reach $15/b but then fall again. OPEC production is above quotas.
1989 March	The Soviet Union announces cuts in exports to cooperate with other producers to raise prices.
1989 April	Oil prices exceed $22/b due to an Alaskan oil spill, damage to the Alaskan pipe line, and an explosion on a North Sea platform.

SOURCES: Griffin and Teece (1982, especially 4–13, 37–48, 64–82, and 104–12); American Petroleum Institute, *Basic Petroleum Data Book* (1983); Crémer and Salehi-Isfahani (1980); *Business Week; Fortune; Maclean's; Newsweek; Time; U.S. News & World Report;* and the *New York Times*.

FIGURE 9B.1   Real Average Price of Crude Oil Imports (1986 dollars)

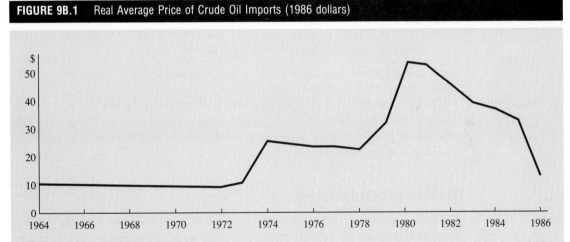

SOURCE: Nominal prices per barrel are from various issues, U.S. Department of Energy, *Monthly Energy Review.* Real prices are obtained by using the GNP Deflator.

This appendix will not end the delightful activity of speculating about the nature of OPEC by providing a definitive statement; rather, it summarizes four of the major theories put forth by economists and others in light of the available evidence.[1]

1. *OPEC is a profit-maximizing cartel.* The cartel agreement may break apart from time to time (countries produce too much output), but OPEC generally is able to meet and reestablish the cartel. A slight variant of this theory holds that OPEC countries have different discount rates and hence disagree on setting a price to maximize the present discounted value of profits.

2. *Saudi Arabia is a dominant firm.* Saudi Arabia by itself (or possibly in conjunction with a small core group within OPEC) acts as a dominant firm by restricting its own output. As the world's biggest producer, Saudi Arabia does not have to rely on the other more volatile countries within OPEC.

3. *OPEC is trying to achieve political objectives rather than maximize its profits.* Some writers believe that Arab members of OPEC are using oil as a weapon against Israel and the West. Others argue that oil money is used primarily for domestic investments by OPEC nations, so these countries try to raise only the money they need for these investments.

4. *The oil industry is competitive: OPEC is little more than a social club.* This theory holds that the oil industry is so competitive that OPEC has no monopoly power. The reason price increased so substantially in 1973 was that the competitive supply curve is backward bending, so that a slight shift in supply or demand can dramatically increase price and reduce output.

These theories are not necessarily completely inconsistent with each other; for example, OPEC's political and economic objectives might coincide.

The chronology, Table 9B.1, of major OPEC events and statements by OPEC leaders does not resolve the question as to which of the four theories is correct. After all, public explanations given by OPEC leaders as to the reasons for their activities may bear little resemblance to their true motives.

The Monopoly-Cartel Theory

Besides the two large price increases that occurred in the 1970s, other evidence supports the monopoly-cartel theory. For example, a large share of the market is a necessary condition for a cartel to exercise monopoly power. The first column of Table 9B.2 shows that in the 1970s OPEC sold two-thirds of total noncommunist oil production (see also Example 9.2). In 1981 and 1982, however, OPEC's share of world output fell significantly, in part because it was operating at less than its full capacity. Whether this drop was due to competition from other producers, wars in the Middle East (reduced production in Iran and Iraq), or other factors is not clear, but it might indicate the end of any substantial monopoly power.

---

[1] A fifth hypothesis holds that a number of unusual, random events are responsible for the price rises associated with OPEC. As this sort of atheoretical approach is hard to prove or disprove, it is ignored here.

TABLE 9B.2   OPEC Data

	Share of Noncommunist World Output (%)		Capacity Utilization (%)		Saudi Arabia		Price ($) of OPEC Crude Oil		
								Deflated Price (in 1973 $)	
								U.S. GNP	OPEC Import
					Output	Market Share	Nominal	Deflator	Deflator
	OPEC	Saudi Arabia	OPEC	Saudi Arabia	(% change)	(% change)	(% change)	(% change)	(% change)
1970	58.4	9.3							
1971	62.9	11.3					29.6	23.7	29.8
1972	63.7	13.7					8.6	4.1	8.6
1973	67.5	16.0					38.9	31.3	9.5
1974	67.8	18.1					262.1	233.0	204.2
1975	65.4	16.4	69.7	61.5			9.4	0.1	−1.4
1976	67.5	18.4	79.5	74.6	22.2	12.2	10.0	4.5	14.4
1977	67.0	19.2	77.6	72.1	8.0	4.3	11.9	5.8	2.3
1978	64.5	18.1	74.5	68.2	−5.4	−5.7	0.4	−6.6	−13.9
1979	63.2	18.9	74.7	74.0	8.5	4.4	44.4	32.9	27.8
1980	63.2	21.3	65.1	77.0	4.1	12.7	65.3	51.3	45.5
1981	59.5	23.1	58.4	77.0	−0.1	8.5	11.8	2.1	16.2
1982	48.6	16.3	45.4	50.5	−34.4	−29.4	−4.0	−9.5	0.5

SOURCES: Various issues of the U.S. Department of Energy, *Monthly Energy Review;* various issues of the U.S. CIA, *International Energy Statistical Review;* Castle and Price (1983, 14).

Because oil is a nonrenewable natural resource, the price of oil is expected to rise over time (as the supply runs out) regardless of the market structure. Typical models of a nonrenewable resource show that a monopolist sets a higher initial price than does a competitive industry.[2] Due to its relatively high price in early years, the monopolist sells oil slowly, so the resource is exhausted less rapidly than under competition. In both types of markets, the rate of increase of the price depends on the interest rate (discount rate); thus, a small change in the discount rate could have a substantial effect on the respective paths that prices would follow.

Pindyck (1978) contrasts a model in which OPEC behaves as a monopoly to one in which it behaves competitively. Pindyck modifies the standard monopoly model to take account of the slow rate at which consumers adjust to a rapid increase in price. For example, in the long run, consumers may buy smaller cars and put more insulation in their homes, allowing them to reduce their demand for oil; in the short run, they are not able to make such adjustments (that is, long-run demand elasticities are greater than short-run elasticities). In Pindyck's monopoly model, OPEC's profit-maximizing strategy was

[2] This result depends on how the elasticity of demand changes over time. If the elasticity of demand is constant and exceeds 1 in absolute value and the supply is fixed, then a monopoly and a competitive industry price the same.

to charge a high price initially (taking advantage of the slow rate of adjustment of net demand to higher prices), then to lower the price through the 1970s, and then to raise it as the oil reserves were depleted.

As Table 9B.2 shows, oil prices increased substantially (1973–74), were roughly constant in real terms for a few years (1975–78), shot up again (1979–1980), and then fell (1981–82). Apparently Pindyck's profit-maximizing strategy does not describe OPEC's plan.

The first two columns of Table 9B.3 show Pindyck's simulations of OPEC's output under monopolistic and competitive behavior respectively (assuming a discount rate of 5 percent). For the period shown, the competitive output is always greater than the monopoly output, while from 1976 to 1980 OPEC's actual output (column 6) lay between the simulated monopoly and competitive outputs. In 1981 and 1982 OPEC's actual output was very low—probably lower than the profit-maximizing monopoly level.

It seems reasonable to expect that if market power is being exercised, either OPEC as a whole or some substantial subset is restricting output to drive up price. As shown in Tables 9B.2 and 9B.3, OPEC's output and capacity utilization levels were high in the first few years following the substantial 1973–74 price increases. These levels did not fall until 1979–1980, when the second large price increase occurred. Both output and capacity levels have been falling since then (possibly for noneconomic reasons, such as wars).

How could OPEC have raised prices in the early 1970s and still have increased output? Apparently, the coordinated OPEC boycott of the United States and other Western nations in 1973 caused many to panic, and several countries built up large stockpiles for protection against future disruptions in the supply of OPEC oil.[3] Stockpiling kept demand high for several years. Substitution away from oil by firms and households, world-wide recessions, and an end to the policy of stockpiling has reduced the demand for oil in recent years. As a result, OPEC has reduced output each year since 1980, and it lowered its price in 1982.

This analysis suggests that OPEC's output has generally differed from the monopoly level. As Table 9B.1 shows, many debates have occurred within OPEC's ranks as to how to set price and output levels. Even if one believes that OPEC is a unified cartel some of the time, one must concede that its cartel agreement breaks apart often. Rather than viewing OPEC as a unified cartel, many economists use a dominant-firm model to describe its behavior.

The Cartel Core-Dominant Firm Model

Many people argue that Saudi Arabia acts as a dominant firm while many other OPEC countries are price takers. One problem with claiming that Saudi Arabia is a dominant

---

[3] According to the American Petroleum Institute's *Basic Petroleum Data Book,* vol. 3 (1983), U.S. petroleum imports went from 4741 million barrels per day (bb/day) in 1972 to 6256 in 1973. By 1979, imports reached 8389, but they fell in 1980 to 6865, in 1981 to 5740, and in 1982 to 4948 million bb/day. Total U.S. stocks rose 135,000 bb/day from 1972 to 1973. The year-to-year changes in stocks from 1974 through 1982 were 179, 32, −58, 529, −257, 81, 94, −176, and −497 million bb.

TABLE 9B.3 Predicted and Actual OPEC Production Levels (billions of barrels per year)

	Pindyck's Model (discount rate = 5%)		Hnyilicza & Pindyck's Model			Actual Output			Percent Change In OPEC Output
	Monopoly	Competition	Total OPEC	Spender Nations	Saver Nations	Total OPEC	Spender Nations	Saver Nations	
1975	9.94	11.92	9.65	3.38	6.27	9.93	4.43	5.50	
1976	9.23	12.29	8.85	3.08	5.77	11.15	4.84	6.32	12.29
1977	8.94	12.62	8.45	2.91	5.49	11.47	4.84	6.63	2.87
1978	8.87	12.90	8.34	2.92	5.42	12.30	4.59	6.50	7.24
1979	8.91	13.14	8.37	2.93	5.44	11.28	4.00	7.28	-8.29
1980	9.00	13.35	8.44	2.95	5.49	9.83	3.16	6.60	-12.85
1981			8.55	2.99	5.56	8.27	2.81	4.99	-15.87
1982			8.68	3.04	5.64	6.85	2.36	3.89	-17.17
1983						6.44	2.86	3.49	-5.96
1984						6.37	2.83	3.48	-1.09
1985	9.67	13.99	9.11	3.19	5.92	5.88	2.74	3.09	-7.69
1986						6.76	2.63	4.06	14.97

NOTES: Saver nations are Saudi Arabia, Libya, Iraq, Abu Dhabi, Bahrain, Kuwait, and Qatar.
Spender nations are Iran, Venezuela, Indonesia, Algeria, Nigeria, and Ecuador.
Gabon is not included in either group.
Bahrain is not reported separately in 1985.
SOURCES: Pindyck (1978); Hnyilicza and Pindyck (1976); Castle and Price (1983); American Petroleum Institute. *Basic Petroleum Data Book*, vol. 8 (1988).

firm is that its share of OPEC production rose from 23.98 percent in 1973 to 36.8 percent in 1980. Some of the increase in Saudi Arabia's share, however, may have been due to reduced output by warring OPEC nations.

A more sophisticated model holds that Saudi Arabia and a few other OPEC nations collectively act like a dominant firm and restrict output. While several OPEC countries have had substantial excess capacity in various years (see Table 9B.2), it is generally believed that non-OPEC producers have had little excess capacity since 1973 (Griffin and Teece 1982, 29). For example, Adelman (1982) contends that a cartel core within OPEC (Saudi Arabia, the United Arab Emirates [UAE], Kuwait, Qatar, and Libya) has acted as a profit-maximizing dominant firm, facing a competitive fringe composed of non-OPEC producers. Saudi Arabia has not reduced its output to the short-run profit-maximizing level since it fears that high prices speed the development of viable oil substitutes or induce consumers to make investments that allow them to purchase less oil, increasing the elasticity of demand for OPEC oil in the future.[4]

Adelman argues that when oil prices are high, the cartel partially breaks down: countries start to produce more and undersell each other. The resulting fall in the price of oil induces Saudi Arabia (and, in some cases, other countries) to cut back production. As shown in Table 9B.2, Saudi Arabia's output and market share fell in years when the real price of oil fell and rose in years when the real price increased.

Adelman implicitly divided demand for OPEC oil into two groups: oil for short-term use and oil for stockpiles (to ease the shock of future embargoes or other cutbacks). When Saudi Arabia cuts back production, importers' uncertainty increases their demand for stockpiles, so the total demand for oil increases. Thus, supply cutbacks cause short-term buyer panics, enabling OPEC to raise its prices without losing its share of the market. Each time, as uncertainty diminishes and prices peak, OPEC countries again increase production and undersell each other, starting the cycle over again.

In another variant of the dominant-firm model, Hnyilicza and Pindyck (1976) suggest that some OPEC nations have lower discount rates (interest rates) than others. One group of "saver" countries (Saudi Arabia, Libya, Iraq, Abu Dhabi, Kuwait, and Qatar) has relatively large oil reserves and little immediate need for cash, and thus uses a low discount rate in computing the present value of profits. The "spender" countries (Iran, Venezuela, Indonesia, Algeria, Nigeria, and Ecuador) have relatively small reserves and immediate cash needs, and so use a higher discount rate. The spender group wants high profits today, while the saver group wants high profits in the long run.

According to Hnyilicza and Pindyck, most of the debate among OPEC nations is about market shares. Table 9B.3 presents the simulation results for their model, assuming that the market share of the two groups of nations is fixed at the 1974 level. According to the simulations, saver countries initially cut back output more than spender countries (total output falls and then rises as in Pindyck's monopoly model). While saver countries

---

[4] Professor Adelman notes that the Saudis, despite talk of lowering prices for political or other reasons, have raised their prices overall. For example, the Saudis canceled an oil auction in 1974 that would have driven down oil prices. According to data from the American Petroleum Institute's *Basic Petroleum Data Book*, vol. 3 (1983), Saudi Arabia raised the official price of all its oil grades from 1974 through 1981. On January 1, 1982, it lowered the price on some grades, and in March 1983 it lowered the price on all grades.

may have reduced output more initially, as Table 9B.3 shows, the output of saver countries has been a larger percentage of the 1975 level in each successive year than has the output of the spender countries.

The Non-profit Maximizing Model

Many writers (including several economists) do not accept these monopoly and dominant-firm models, arguing instead that OPEC countries are not profit maximizers. For example, Teece (1982) argues that OPEC members make production decisions based on their national budget requirements, which are a function of their *absorptive capacities*—the ability to use oil revenues (profits) and capital productively.[5] Absorptive capacity is limited where the size of the economy is small relative to oil revenues or where a country's infrastructure (capital investments) cannot support more rapid economic development.

Teece cites cases in which OPEC countries choose less profitable domestic investment over more profitable foreign investment.[6] Even countries that did invest in the West, such as Saudi Arabia, reported that they felt compelled to keep prices low for political reasons.[7]

In Teece's target-revenue model, oil prices can rise above the competitive price path even if OPEC members do not collude: "The world price was elevated above competitive levels by good luck and special circumstances" (p. 86). If a political action, such as the 1973–74 embargo, brings oil production into the target-revenue range, individual members have no reason to cheat on the cartel and expand output. If demand curves shift down or OPEC countries' revenue needs increase, then OPEC members expand production to generate additional revenues.

Teece observes that OPEC countries set different official prices, which appears inconsistent with a cartel model. The Saudis usually sell their oil for less than other OPEC countries, which Teece argues is for political rather than economic reasons.

Adelman (1982) rejects this model because it does not explain how revenue needs change in the long run. He argues that OPEC wants to generate as much revenue as possible; how OPEC spends the revenues is a separate issue. Moreover, he notes, OPEC appears to have failed to achieve its political objectives (with respect to Israel and the Palestinians), and its price increases have hurt nominal allies in the Third World more than the industrialized nations.

Another noncollusive explanation for the increased price is that property rights changed (Mead 1979; Griffin 1985). In the 1970s there was a transfer of ownership and control of the oil concessions from the international oil companies to producing countries. The oil companies, foreseeing their loss of control over production were using a very high rate of time discount, whereas the countries used a much lower discount rate. The standard

---

[5] The concept of *absorptive capacity* is developed in Rosenstein-Rodan (1961).

[6] Teece notes, however, that some OPEC countries believe foreign investments are relatively risky, so domestic investments with lower expected rates of return may be consistent with expected profit-maximizing behavior.

[7] Teece cites Saudi Arabia's oil minister Sheik Yamani's explanations for pursuing a moderate path: "The Kingdom is very anxious to prevent any deterioration of the world economy because that would hurt us financially in view of the large investments we have in the Western countries. To increase oil price now would also expose us to certain political repercussions because we are bound to the West by clearly defined political interests." (*Middle East Economic Survey,* June 19, 1978.)

theoretical model of competitive oil extraction predicts that the real price of oil rises at the real discount rate; thus, as the discount rate falls, the price eventually falls, and production falls. In the short run, however, as production falls, price can increase dramatically. Only in the long run does the price rise more slowly.

The Competitive Model

A final theory holds that OPEC is an unsuccessful cartel and behaves in an essentially competitive fashion. After all, at one time or another every OPEC country has increased its output substantially. The first serious statement of this theory by economists was by Crémer and Salehi-Isfahani (1980).[8] Using a target-revenue model, they contend that the supply curve for oil is backward bending, as in the fishery model presented in Chapter 6. Exporting countries try to achieve a target revenue for internal investment purposes. A target revenue is set because the countries have limited capacity to absorb investment. For a given oil price, fixing revenues determines output: there is no incentive to produce more oil. OPEC, so this theory holds, is a disorganized body that does not impose output restrictions on its members; it only asks them to behave as price-takers. Thus, it is not surprising that market shares have not remained constant over time.

Figure 9B.2, which is based on Crémer and Salehi-Isfahani's diagram, shows a backward bending supply curve with a demand curve that intersects it three times. In their explanation, the oil industry in early 1973 was at the low-price, competitive equilibrium (p_1, Q_1). In two steps (October 1973 and January 1974), the six Persian Gulf OPEC members agreed to raise prices, which caused a shift to the high-price equilibrium (p_3, Q_3).[9] These price increases were supported by short-run reductions in output, possibly due to the Middle East War of October 1973. Thereafter, competitive equilibrium could be maintained at the high price. Even though each country could produce as much output as it wanted, countries voluntarily restricted output because they did not know what to do with all the revenues (limited absorptive capacity).

In real-price terms, the OPEC price took a large jump in 1973 and remained fairly constant at the higher level afterward. The only major price increase since then, in 1978–79, may have been due to special events that caused Iran and other countries to restrict output further. Extending this theory, the price fall in recent years is seen as due to shifts in demand.[10] This explanation apparently implies that demand fell for years.

---

[8] MacAvoy (1982) also argues that the long-run trend in oil prices can be explained by a competitive model.

[9] The equilibrium at (p_2, Q_2) is unstable. Were the quantity to fall slightly below Q_2, the price would be above p_2, but demand would be greater than supply. As a result, there would be upward pressure on the price, driving it towards p_3. A similar argument holds that if the price fell below p_2, it would continue to fall to p_1. In contrast, the (p_1, Q_1) and (p_3, Q_3) equilibria are stable.

[10] Verleger's (1982) empirical study indicates that OPEC countries set their official prices in response to shifts in demand. He concludes that attempts to persuade members of OPEC to exercise price restraint have no effect. All countries adjust their official prices as the price in the competitive spot market (market for immediate delivery) changes. The so-called price moderates with OPEC are not following moderate pricing strategies at all, but only adjusting prices at a slower rate.

FIGURE 9B.2   Competitive Theory about OPEC

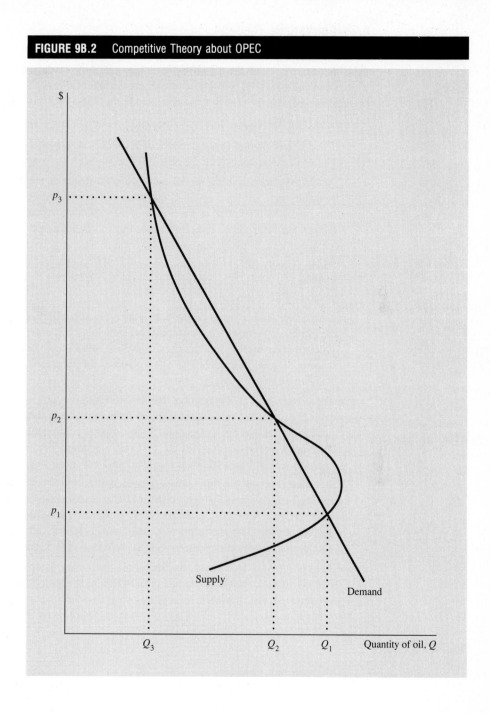

A Test of Various Theories

Griffin (1985) uses data from 1971 through the third quarter of 1983 to test a number of these theories for 11 of the 13 OPEC countries (for lack of data, Ecuador and Gabon were not included) and 11 non-OPEC countries. As interesting as his results are, it should be remembered that the data set did not include the mid-1980s price collapse. Some of his key results follow:

- The constant market-sharing model of a cartel is decisively rejected for 10 out of 11 OPEC countries and all 11 non-OPEC countries.

- A weaker market-sharing model, which allows shares to vary with price, appears plausible for 5 of the 11 OPEC countries (Qatar, United Arab Emirates, Libya, Iran, and Nigeria) and 2 of the 9 non-OPEC countries. Apparently Kuwait, Qatar, Libya, and Venezuela will accept lower market shares in a high-price regime.

- An even weaker, partial market-sharing model says that market-sharing considerations partially affect production decisions, but production cutbacks are not proportional to shares. This model is accepted for all 11 OPEC countries and 8 of the 11 non-OPEC countries.

- Even Saudi Arabia varies production along with other OPEC countries. As a result, the dominant-firm model, in which Saudi Arabia acts as a market leader and varies production inversely with the output level of other producers is wrong. Indeed a number of countries, including Saudi Arabia and Indonesia increase their market shares in response to rising prices.

- The property-rights explanation that oil-producing countries have lower discount rates than oil companies have can be indirectly tested. Under this explanation, production falls as the percentage of government-controlled production increases. This theory is rejected for 5 of the 11 OPEC countries. For example, in 1972, Iraq nationalized the Iraq Petroleum Company and expanded capacity by 235 percent.

- A strong form of the target-revenue models used by Crémer and Salehi-Isfahani and by Teece predicts that output should fall proportionately as real price increases. This model is rejected for all 10 OPEC countries for which it can be tested. A weaker version that says a price increase should lead to a fall in output (but less than proportionate) is consistent with the behavior of 9 of these 10 countries.

- A competitive model would, in part, imply that output is a positive function of the real oil price. Even this weak test of competition is rejected for 5 of the 11 OPEC countries. It was, however, rejected for only 1 of the 11 non-OPEC countries.

■ CONCLUSIONS

Oil's well that ends well.

OPEC has a large share of the market and entry by competitors is slow (see Example 9.2). Moreover, in some periods, price has increased substantially. These factors support a monopoly or dominant-firm model. On the other hand, the cartel agreement appears to break down regularly, resulting in prices below the profit-maximizing level. Possibly various countries vary their production for political rather than economic reasons. Alternatively, OPEC countries may have limited capacities to absorb revenues in making only domestic investments. Taking the argument for limited absorptive capacity to its limit, it is even possible that the price increase reflects a shift to a high-price, competitive equilibrium. There is relatively little support, however, for this last view.

While currently available empirical studies do not clearly confirm or reject any of the four hypotheses about OPEC's behavior, stronger conclusions may be reached in the near future. Since the peak in real prices in 1980–81, OPEC's real price has fallen substantially. Presumably this price drop reflects the destruction of a cartel, but more study is required to draw definitive conclusions.

CHAPTER 10

NONCOOPERATIVE OLIGOPOLY

> **T**he Puritan's idea of hell is a place where everybody has to mind his own business.
>
> WENDELL PHILLIPS (attributed)

This chapter presents models of an industry with a **noncooperative oligopoly:** a small number of firms acting independently but aware of one another's existence.[1] Unlike monopolistic and competitive firms, noncooperative oligopolists cannot blithely ignore other firms' actions.

As the only firm in an industry, a monopolist has no rivals. At the other extreme, individual competitive firms are too small to affect the industry's price, so each firm can reasonably ignore the actions of any other; only the industry's collective actions matter to a competitive firm. In contrast, because there are only a few firms in an oligopoly, each firm can affect market price and hence its rivals' profits: Ford cannot and does not ignore General Motors or Honda when making decisions. Thus, oligopoly differs from competition and monopoly in that a firm *must* consider rival firms' behavior to determine its own best policy. This interrelationship between firms is the key issue examined in this chapter.

As discussed in Chapter 7, some industries are highly concentrated: a few firms make virtually all the sales. For example, the top four cereal manufacturers sell 90 percent of all breakfast cereals, and the top eight sell 98 percent. Only a handful of manufacturers produce many consumer durables. Until foreign manufacturers entered the U.S. market, the Big Three auto manufacturers sold virtually all the automobiles.

Where transportation costs are so high that it is not cost-effective to sell a product outside a small geographic region, or local market, oligopolies are also common. In

---

[1] The distinction between cooperative and noncooperative oligopoly is not a sharp one. For example, at the time a cartel forms, firms could behave cooperatively, but later they may behave noncooperatively.

countries with smaller markets (fewer consumers), many industries are oligopolistic. Similarly, *oligopsonies* (few buyers) are frequently observed. For years, only two firms purchased most of the mussels caught in New England, and four firms bought most of the Pacific tuna.

Several models of noncooperative oligopolistic behavior have been developed that differ as to the ways firms expect their rivals to act. While there is extensive agreement among economists on the basic models of competition and monopoly, there is no consensus on a single noncooperative oligopoly model. One reason for the lack of agreement is that market characteristics of real-world oligopolies differ substantially, so that the assumptions of each model fit some markets better than others. The oligopoly models discussed here differ in their details, but in all of them, the equilibrium lies between competition and monopoly.

This chapter presents the best-known noncooperative oligopoly models. To keep the discussion as simple as possible, three strong assumptions are made:

1. Firms can only choose their price or output. Discussions of advertising, product quality, and other strategic behavior are deferred to later chapters.

2. All firms produce *homogeneous* (identical) products: consumers perceive no differences among them.

3. There is *no entry* into the industry, so the number of firms remains constant over time.

The next chapter extends the models to consider *heterogenous* (differentiated) products and entry of new firms. Advertising is discussed in Chapter 18, and Chapter 13 discusses other strategic actions.

In all of the oligopoly models in this chapter, each firm maximizes its own profits given its beliefs about how other firms behave: each firm's expected profits are maximized when its *expected marginal revenue equals its marginal cost*. The models differ in their assumptions about the methods firms use to predict their rivals' actions and thus to formulate expected marginal revenue.

The earliest and simplest models—*conjectural variations models*—have been developed over the last 150 years. In these models, each firm forms a **conjecture** (hypothesis or guess) about how a rival will react to a change in its behavior, and this belief about its reaction is called a **conjectural variation.** Each firm chooses its price or output to maximize its profits based on its conjectural variations.

The three best-known conjectural variations models are the Cournot, Bertrand, and Stackelberg models. In the **Cournot model,** each firm conjectures that if it varies its output level, other firms will continue to produce their *current levels of output*. In the **Bertrand model,** each firm assumes that if it changes its price, its rivals will continue to charge their *current prices*. In the **Stackelberg model,** a *leader* firm—realizing that all the other firms, or *followers,* maintain Cournot conjectures—is able to profit from its rivals' naive behavior.

These conjectural variations models are most appealing as *static* or *one-period* models: the firms compete only once for a brief period of time. For example, firms from all over the country may meet only once at a one-day crafts fair. Such firms do not observe how their rivals actually vary their outputs or prices over time; hence they cannot adjust their expectations accordingly. Indeed, conjectural variations models have serious failings if viewed as multiperiod models. Even when treated as one-period models, the conjectures used by firms are arbitrary and unexplained.

The major alternative to conjectural variations models is *game theory*.[2] In an oligopoly game theory model, **players** (firms) compete in a **game** (a competition) by formulating **strategies,** or battle plans, describing how they compete with rival firms. A firm's strategy determines its actions, such as its output or price level. Game theory models do not restrict the set of strategies as much as conjectural variations models do. For example, **multiperiod games** are considered in which markets last many periods, so that firms may adjust their beliefs about rivals' behavior over time and may use more complex strategies than in single-period models. In such a model, a firm's strategy might require it to set different output levels depending on how its rivals had behaved in previous periods. One possible outcome of such a model is that firms may collude in early periods and then produce at higher levels in the last period.

An even more important distinction between game theory and conjectural variations models concerns a firm's beliefs about its rivals' behavior. In game theory, only actions by a rival that are in the rival's best interests are considered **credible strategies.** Thus, in game theory, a firm does not believe that its rivals use arbitrary and unexplained strategies as in conjectural variations models. For example, in a Cournot conjectural variation model, a firm believes that its rival will produce the same level of output no matter how the firm changes its own level. In game theory, a firm only maintains such a belief if it is in the rival's best interests to keep its production level constant.

Given the advantages of game theory models, why are conjectural variations models used at all? There are three reasons. First, conjectural variations models are relatively easy to explain and serve as an introduction to the issues examined by game theorists. Second, the equilibria of the static conjectural variations models sometimes can be justified using game theory models. Third, unlike game theory models, the conjectural variations models are easy to apply in empirical research.

After discussing the conjectural variations and game theory models, the chapter concludes by presenting experimental and empirical tests of various oligopolistic models that support the predictions of some of these models.

■ CONJECTURAL VARIATION MODELS

No state sorrier than that of the man who . . . is curious in conjecture of what is in his neighbor's heart. —MARCUS AURELIUS ANTONINUS

An oligopolistic industry includes only a few firms, and each is large enough to affect the market's price. Each oligopolist therefore expects other firms to react to its behavior. When IBM drops the price on its personal computers, it expects Apple to change its price too.

---

[2] For an interesting history of how the conjectural variations and dynamic games theories evolved, see Shubik with Levitan (1980). Modern game theory was first clearly described in von Neuman and Morgenstern (1944).

The earliest models of oligopolistic behavior assumed that firms formed expectations about the reactions (or *variations*) of other firms, now called *conjectural variations*.[3] The three best-known are the Cournot, Bertrand, and Stackelberg models.[4] These conjectural variations models have three characteristics in common:

1. They are most appealing when viewed as single-period models.

2. The equilibrium in each model lies between the competitive and monopolistic solution: with a small number of firms, the Bertrand model predicts a competitive equilibrium, and the Cournot and Stackelberg models predict prices and quantities strictly between the competitive and monopoly levels. In all the models, if there is only one firm, there is a monopoly equilibrium, and if there are a large number of firms, the equilibrium is the same as in a competitive industry.

3. In each model, firms control only quantity or price. In the Cournot and Stackelberg models, firms choose their output levels, and the demand curve determines price; in the Bertrand model, firms choose prices and let demand determine output.

The Cournot Model

Who is so deafe or so blinde as is hee
That wilfully will neither heare nor see?—JOHN HAYWOOD

The first—and probably still one of the most widely cited—model of noncooperative oligopoly behavior was developed by the French mathematician Augustin Cournot (1963) in 1838. Cournot assumed that each firm acts independently and attempts to maximize its profits by choosing its output. A Cournot firm makes one of the simplest possible assumptions: other firms continue to produce the same level of output no matter how it behaves. That is, each firm assumes other firms are satisfied to continue selling their current quantity of output. This very parsimonious and strong assumption leads to clear behavioral implications, but it is arbitrary and may be incorrect.

The Cournot model is best viewed as a single-period model. For the purpose of simple exposition, however, we start by discussing this model as though it were a multiperiod model and conclude with a critique of the multiperiod Cournot model.

In the multiperiod version, each Cournot firm chooses an output level in an attempt to maximize its profits given its belief that other firms will continue to sell their original levels of output. All firms sell a homogeneous product, so each firm charges the same price because a firm charging a higher price would make no sales. Total output of all the firms determines the market price.

The Cournot model can be used to study an industry with any number of firms. The discussion starts with the *duopoly,* or two-firm, case and then considers what happens as the number of firms increases.

---

[3] Arthur L. Bowley first presented the concept in 1924; however, the term was coined by Ragnar Frisch in 1933 (Friedman 1983, 106).

[4] The "kinked demand curve" model is also well known. It is no longer as widely used as the other three and is discussed in Appendix 10B.

A Cournot Duopoly.   Consider an isolated town with the following market for melons:

- There are two firms and no entry by other firms is possible (these firms own the only good farm land anywhere in the area).
- The firms' output is homogeneous, so the sum of their outputs equals industry output: $Q = q_1 + q_2$, where Firm 1 produces q_1 and Firm 2 produces q_2.
- The melons *cannot be stored;* they must be sold as soon as produced or they spoil.
- The quantity demanded is a linear function of price;

$$Q(p) = 1000 - 1000\, p, \tag{10.1}$$

as shown in Figure 10.1, that is, the inverse demand curve is

$$p = 1 - 0.001\, Q. \tag{10.1'}$$

Thus, when $p = \$1.00$, $Q = 0$ melons; when $p = \$0.50$, $Q = 500$ melons; and when $p = 0$, $Q = 1000$ melons.

- Each firm has a *constant marginal cost* of production of 28¢ per melon and no fixed costs. Each firm can produce enough output to meet the entire market's demand, as shown in Figure 10.1.
- Each firm makes the *Cournot conjecture:* each firm believes that regardless of how much it produces, its rival's output remains constant.

Firm 1 believes that Firm 2 will sell q_2 units of output no matter how Firm 1 behaves. Thus, Firm 1 thinks it can sell all but q_2 units of the amount demanded by the market; that is, it faces the *residual demand curve,*

$$q_1(p) = Q(p) - q_2, \tag{10.2}$$

which is the market demand curve, $Q(p)$ from Equation 10.1, minus the expected output of Firm 2, q_2. As Figure 10.1 shows, the residual demand curve is obtained by shifting the market demand curve $q_2 = 240$ units to the left. Thus, the residual demand curve hits the horizontal axis at $1000 - q_2$.

Firm 1 acts as though it has a monopoly over those consumers whose demand is not met by Firm 2: it sets output where its marginal revenue curve based on the derived residual demand curve intersects its marginal cost curve. A partial tabulation of Firm 1's beliefs and its profit-maximizing quantity responses follows:

Firm 1's Belief About Firm 2's Output (q_2)	Firm 1's Profit-Maximizing Output (q_1)
100	310
200	260
240	240
300	210
400	160

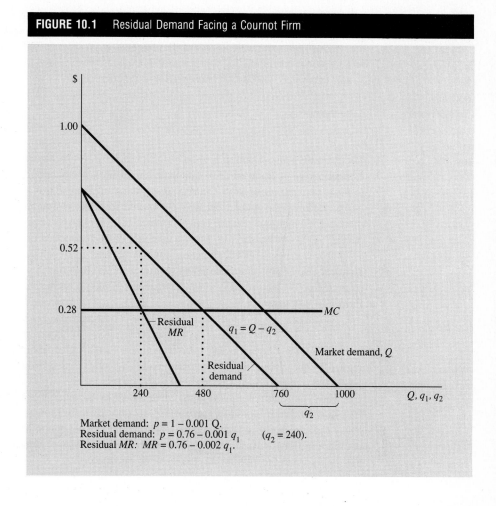

FIGURE 10.1   Residual Demand Facing a Cournot Firm

Market demand: $p = 1 - 0.001\ Q$.
Residual demand: $p = 0.76 - 0.001\ q_1$ ($q_2 = 240$).
Residual *MR*: $MR = 0.76 - 0.002\ q_1$.

The relationship between Firm 1's profit-maximizing quantity and its belief about Firm 2's quantity, $q_1 = R_1(q_2)$, is called a **best-response function.**[5] To derive the best-response function completely, rather than simply giving examples, it is necessary to express the intersection between the marginal revenue curve *(MR)* and the marginal cost curve *(MC)* algebraically (see Appendix 10A for a mathematical derivation).

Firm 1's residual demand curve is linear, so its marginal revenue curve, is also linear and has twice the slope of the residual demand curve: the *MR* curve hits the quantity axis

---

[5] Early writers (Bowley, 1924) on conjectural variations models called this relationship a *reaction function*. Most game theorists refer to it as a *best-response function*, the term used here.

at half the quantity of the demand curve.[6] In Figure 10.1, where q_2 equals 240, the residual demand curve intersects the horizontal MC curve at $q_1 = 480$. More generally, the residual demand curve intersects the marginal cost curve at $720 - q_2$. The marginal revenue curve corresponding to the residual demand curve crosses the marginal cost curve at half that value, so Firm 1's best-response function is

$$q_1 = R_1(q_2) = 360 - \frac{q_2}{2}. \qquad (10.2')$$

This best-response function is shown in Figure 10.2. As shown above, if $q_2 = 0$, Firm 1 produces $q_1 = R_1(0) = 360$, the same output level a monopolist would produce. The residual demand curve of a Cournot firm facing no competition is the market demand curve. Because the market demand curve intersects the marginal cost curve at 720, a monopolist's marginal revenue curve intersects the marginal cost curve at half that quantity, or 360. At the other extreme, Firm 1 does not cease production until $q_2 = 720$.

Firm 2's best-response function can be derived in a similar way. The firms are identical, so Firm 2's best-response function is the mirror image of Firm 1's: $q_2 = R_2(q_1) = 360 - q_1/2$. Firm 2's choice of output depends on the output it expects Firm 1 to produce.

As Figure 10.2 shows, the two firms' best-response functions cross once at $q_1 = q_2 = 240$.[7] The intersection of the best-response functions is a point of particular interest. At the corresponding quantities, each firm's belief about its rival's output is ratified by the output decision actually made. Indeed, the two firms' Cournot beliefs are confirmed only when each is producing 240 melons.

Thus, the Cournot equilibrium is determined by the intersection of the best-response functions. If Firm 1 produces any other quantity than 240, Firm 2 changes its output level, and vice versa: no other output combination can be an equilibrium. In the Cournot equilibrium, total market output is $240 + 240 = 480$. Using the market demand curve, that implies that the equilibrium price is 52¢ per melon.

---

[6] Where the inverse market demand curve is $p = a - bQ$, the total revenue curve is $R = pQ = aQ - bQ^2$. The marginal revenue curve is obtained by differentiating the total revenues with respect to quantity: $MR = dR/dQ = a - 2bQ$. That is, the marginal revenue curve is twice as steep as the demand curve. The demand curve hits the horizontal axis, where $p = 0$, at a/b. The marginal revenue curve hits the horizontal axis, where $MR = 0$, at $a/(2b)$. Similarly, where $p = MC \equiv m$ (a constant), the quantity demanded is $(a - m)/b$. If quantity is set so that $MR = MC \equiv m$, then quantity equals $(a - m)/(2b)$.

[7] The interesection can be determined algebraically by simultaneously solving the two best-response reaction function equations,

$$q_1 = 360 - q_2/2,$$

and

$$q_2 = 360 - q_1/2.$$

Substituting the second expression into the first,

$$q_1 = 360 - (360 - q_1/2)/2.$$

The solution to this last equation is $q_1 = 240$. Substituting 240 for q_1 in Firm 2's reaction function shows that q_2 also equals 240.

FIGURE 10.2   Cournot Best-Response Functions and the Market Adjustment Pattern

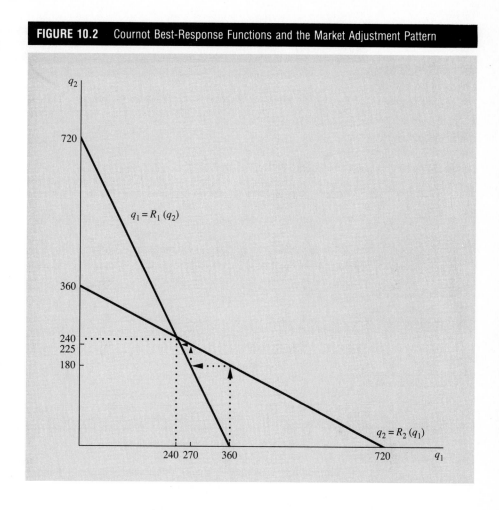

The Stability of a Cournot Equilibrium.   The Cournot equilibrium is stable in the sense that no firm has an incentive to alter its behavior if the industry is in equilibrium. But what if firms are not initially in equilibrium? Will they have an incentive to adjust their behavior?

Some economists have used Cournot's model to consider how firms adjust from a nonequilibrium to an equilibrium. When Cournot firms adjust their behavior over time, their output levels gradually approach the Cournot equilibrium level, and that at the equilibrium, no firm has an incentive to change its output level.

To illustrate this concept, suppose that the two melon-producing firms vary output at discrete time intervals (say, once a day, or once a week, or once a month). Each firm knows how much its rival produced in the previous period. Because the firms make Cournot conjectures, each one thinks its rival will choose the same output level in period t that it chose in period $t - 1$.

TABLE 10.1 A Comparison of Oligopoly Equilibria: A Linear Demand and Constant Marginal Cost Example

	Output		Price (Cents)	Profits ($)		Consumer Surplus
	Firm	Industry		Firm	Industry	
Monopoly	360	360	64	129.60	129.60	64.8
Cournot Duopoly	240	480	52	57.60	115.20	115.2
Stackelberg Duopoly		540	46		97.20	145.8
Leader	360			64.80		
Follower	180			32.40		
Competition*		720	28	0	0	259.2
Cournot: n firms	$\dfrac{720}{n+1}$	$\dfrac{720n}{n+1}$	$\dfrac{100+28n}{n+1}$	$\dfrac{518.4}{(n+1)^2}$	$\dfrac{518.4n}{(n+1)^2}$	$\dfrac{259.2n^2}{(n+1)^2}$
Stackelberg: n firms		$\dfrac{360(2n-1)}{n}$	$\dfrac{28n+36}{n}$		$\dfrac{129.6(2n-1)}{n^2}$	$\dfrac{64.8(2n-1)^2}{n^2}$
Leader		360			$\dfrac{129.6}{n}$	
Followers		$\dfrac{360(n-1)}{n}$			$\dfrac{129.6(n-1)}{n^2}$	

Specific functions used in this example:
  Market demand ($): $Q = 1000 - 1000p$
  Firm's cost function ($): $C(q) = 0.28q$
  (so, each firm's marginal cost is 28¢)
*Efficient point, Bertrand equilibrium, Cournot equilibrium with unlimited number of firms.

Suppose Firm 1 is initially the only firm producing, and then Firm 2 starts producing. As Firm 2 increases its output, Firm 1 decreases its output. The two firms alternate adjusting their output until they reach the equilibrium point, where neither has an incentive to adjust further. This adjustment path over time is shown in Figure 10.2 as the dotted line that forms a cobweb pattern. In the example, this adjustment pattern is stable in the sense that over time, each firm produces closer to the equilibrium level of output (there is no overshooting of the equilibrium).

A problem in this model is that a firm observes that its rival's output is varying over time, and hence is not fixed as the Cournot conjecture assumes. Why then does it maintain the Cournot conjecture in light of conflicting information? The answer is that this dynamic story does not make sense. It helps in explaining Cournot's idea, but the Cournot model should be viewed only as representing a static equilibrium, not as a reasonable dynamic model.

In the static equilibrium, each firm expects the other to produce its equilibrium quantity, and that is what occurs. Each firm's belief about the other's behavior is fulfilled; neither firm receives contradictory evidence. Thus, the inconsistencies in the multiperiod model, in which firms adjust their behavior over time, are avoided in the static model.

TABLE 10.2   Equilibrium Levels Relative to the Monopoly Levels For any Linear Demand Function and Constant Marginal Cost

	Output		Price − MC	Profits		Consumer Surplus
	Firm	Industry		Firm	Industry	
Monopoly	1.0	1.0	1.0	1.0	1.0	1.0
Cournot Duopoly	0.667	1.333	0.667	0.444	0.889	1.778
Stackelberg Duopoly		1.5	0.5		0.75	2.25
Leader	1.0			0.5		
Follower	0.5			0.25		
Competition	0.0	2.0	0.0	0.0	0.0	4.0
Cournot: n firms	$\dfrac{2}{n+1}$	$\dfrac{2n}{n+1}$	$\dfrac{2}{n+1}$	$\dfrac{4}{(n+1)^2}$	$\dfrac{4n}{(n+1)^2}$	$\dfrac{4n^2}{(n+1)^2}$
Stackelberg: n firms		$\dfrac{2n-1}{n}$	$\dfrac{1}{n}$		$\dfrac{2n-1}{n^2}$	$\dfrac{(2n-1)^2}{n^2}$
Leader	1			$\dfrac{1}{n}$		
Followers	$\dfrac{n-1}{n}$			$\dfrac{n-1}{n^2}$		

NOTE: These results are independent of the coefficients in the demand function and the size of the constant marginal cost.

A Comparison of the Cournot and Monopoly Equilibria.   The firms are worse off and the consumers are better off when the firms use Cournot conjectures than when they coordinate and act as a cartel (monopoly). In our example, the monopoly output is 360, so $p_m = 64¢$. Thus, the Cournot industry's output is a third larger, and the price is 19 percent less than the monopolist's (Table 10.1).

The price-cost margin, $(p - MC)/p$, is less for a Cournot industry than for a monopolist. The monopolist's price-cost margin is 56 percent, whereas the Cournot industry's margin is 46 percent—only 82 percent as large as the monopoly's. The price minus marginal cost of Cournot firms is only two-thirds as great as for a monopolist (Table 10.2).

Consumers are better off when they pay lower prices. The consumer surplus under the cartel is 64.8; the Cournot consumer surplus is 115.2 (Table 10.1). Thus, consumer surplus falls 44 percent if the Cournot firms form a cartel.

The Cournot firms have an incentive to form a cartel. Each Cournot firm's profits— $\pi_1 = (p - AC)q_i = (52¢ - 28¢)240$—are $57.60 (Table 10.1). The sum of the profits of the Cournot firms, $\pi_1 + \pi_2$, is $115.20, but the cartel's combined profits are $129.60. Thus, if the firms form a cartel, their profits will rise by 12.5 percent.

The maximum combined profits that the two firms can earn is $129.60, the monopoly level. There are many ways to divide these profits: Firm 1 could earn $0 and Firm 2 could earn $129.60; each could earn half, $64.80; Firm 1 could earn $129.60 and Firm 2

FIGURE 10.3   The Profit Possibility Frontier

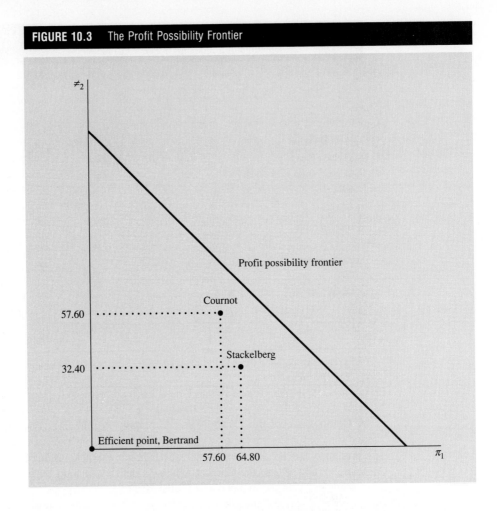

could earn \$0; and so forth for any combination in which the sum of profits is \$129.60. The highest profit one firm could earn, holding the profits of the other firm constant, is shown in the **profit possibility frontier,** $\pi_1 + \pi_2 = \$129.60$, in Figure 10.3.[8]

Figure 10.3 also shows the Cournot equilibrium profit level, where each firm earns \$57.60, so $\pi_1 + \pi_2 = \$115.20$. The Cournot equilibrium lies well inside the profit possibility frontier, giving the firms an incentive to collude and increase their profits to the levels on the profit possibility frontier.

---

[8] A profit possibility frontier is derived by holding Firm 1's profits constant at some level and then maximizing the profits of Firm 2 with respect to q_1 and q_2. In this example, the solution is

$$(q_1 - 1080)q_1 + (q_2 - 1080)q_2 - 2q_1q_2 + 259{,}200 = 0.$$

For any particular q_1, this equation simplifies into a quadratic in q_2. The relevant root is the smaller one. See Friedman (1983, 22–27).

A Comparison of the Cournot Equilibrium and the Social Optimum. How does the Cournot equilibrium compare to the competitive equilibrium? This question is not as straightforward as it might first appear. The problem is that competition requires a potentially unlimited number of firms, but here only two are assumed. Thus, a better comparison is of the Cournot equilibrium to the socially optimal equilibrium, at which the firms maximize profits subject to the constraint that price equals marginal cost (as in a competitive equilibrium).[9] Henceforth, the terms *social optimum* and *competitive equilibrium* are used interchangeably.

If both firms act as price takers at a price equal to marginal cost (28¢), they make zero profits per melon, so they are indifferent as to how many melons they produce. If the price is 28¢, total market demand is for 720 melons; if they split the output, each firm produces 360. This equilibrium is determined in Figure 10.1 by the intersection of the marginal cost curve and the demand curve. Consumer surplus is 259.2, as shown in Table 10.1.

Thus, in our linear example, a competitive industry produces twice as much as a monopoly and one-and-a-half times as much as a Cournot duopoly. The competitive price is only 44 percent of the monopoly price and 54 percent of the Cournot price, as Table 10.2 shows. Competitive consumer surplus is four times greater than under a monopoly and two-and-a-quarter times greater than under a Cournot duopoly. The Cournot duopoly equilibrium, then, lies between the competitive and monopolistic equilibria. In linear examples, it is closer to the monopolistic equilibrium, as shown in Table 10.2.

Three or More Cournot Firms. In general, when there are n identical Cournot firms, the same analysis can be used to derive the Cournot equilibrium, as shown in Appendix 10A. Suppose that Firm 1 believes that all the other $(n - 1)$ firms will produce the same output $q \equiv q_1 = q_2 = \ldots = q_n$. Firm 1's best-response function is $q_1 = R_1(q_2, \ldots, q_n) = 360 - q(n - 1)/2$. The other firms have identical best-response functions. As a result, the Cournot equilibrium quantity is $q = 720/(n + 1)$, and the equilibrium price is $p = (1 + 0.28n)/(n + 1)$.

Table 10.3 shows that as n gets large, output per firm and industry price fall, and industry output rises. The effect of additional rivals on quantity and price is initially very strong but tapers off as the number of firms increases. As the number of firms gets large, the output per firm, industry price, and industry output approach the competitive level, so that consumers are better off (lower prices, higher consumer surplus) and firms are worse off (lower profits).

As Table 10.3 shows, when there are only 2 identical firms, the price is 86 percent above the competitive price. With 10 firms, however, the price is only 23 percent above the competitive price, and with 50 firms it is only 5 percent above the competitive price. In summary, the Cournot model includes monopoly and competition as extreme cases, and the Cournot equilibrium approaches the competitive one as the number of firms increases. See Example 10.1 on p. 271.

---

[9] This equilibrium concept was introduced by Shubik (1959), who called it the *efficient point*. See Shubik with Levitan (1980) and Friedman (1983) for a discussion of the fixed costs consistent with the efficient point.

TABLE 10.3	Cournot Equilibrium with Few and Many Firms					
	Number of Firms	Price (Cents)	Firm		Industry	
			Output	Profits ($)	Output	Profits ($)
Monopoly	1	64	360	129.60	360	129.60
	2	52	240	57.60	480	115.20
	3	46	180	32.40	540	97.20
	4	42.4	144	20.74	576	82.94
	5	40	120	14.40	600	72.00
	6	38.3	102.9	10.58	617.1	63.48
	7	37	90	8.10	630	56.70
	8	36	80	6.40	640	51.20
	9	35.2	72	5.18	648	46.66
	10	34.5	65.5	4.28	654.5	42.84
	15	32.5	48	2.30	675	32.26
	20	31.4	34.3	1.18	685.7	23.51
	50	29.4	14.1	0.20	705.9	9.97
	100	28.7	7.1	0.05	712.9	5.08
	500	28.1	1.4	0.002	718.6	1.03
	1000	28.1	0.7	0.001	719.3	0.52
Competition	∞	28	~0	0.00	720	0.00

(handwritten margin notes:)
$when = dues = n.$
$HHI = \frac{n}{n^2} = \left(\frac{1}{n}\right)$
$P = \beta_0 + \beta_1 HHI$

Strengths of the Single-Period Cournot Model. In a one-period model in which firms must choose their output before observing their rivals' behavior, the Cournot assumption makes sense. Neither learning nor reactions can occur in a one-period model; hence assuming that a rival's output is predetermined is reasonable.

Indeed, the Cournot equilibrium is very appealing. In the equilibrium, each firm has chosen the output that maximizes its profits given the other firm's choice of output—the *best response* to the other firm's output level.

The output levels the firms choose represent an equilibrium that can be maintained because no firm has an incentive to change its output, hence the equilibrium is *self-enforcing*. In a single-period model in which firms only choose output levels, any output levels at which no firm believes it can increase its profits by increasing or decreasing its output is, by definition, a Cournot equilibrium, and no combination of outputs could be agreed upon by all firms except a Cournot equilibrium. Thus, in a single period model in which binding agreements are impossible and firms choose output levels, the Cournot equilibrium is not only realistic; it is the only one possible (Friedman 1983, 32–33).

Weaknesses of the Multiperiod Cournot Model. Two serious objections are raised to the Cournot multiperiod model. First, the firms' myopia in a multiperiod model is unreasonable. A firm can observe the response of its rivals to changes in its output and can verify that those changes *do* affect what its rivals do. In other words, although a firm sees that its Cournot conjecture about its rival's behavior is wrong, it continues to rely on this false conjecture. Alternatively stated, this equilibrium is not robust with respect

EXAMPLE 10.1

MERGERS IN A COURNOT ECONOMY

If all Cournot firms join together and behave as a monopolist, collective profits increase. Suppose only some of the Cournot firms merge (or coordinate actions as a cartel). If they maintain their Cournot beliefs that other firms will maintain constant output levels, this model has surprising (and disturbing) implications about the oligopolists' profits (given linear demand functions and constant marginal and average costs):

- In an industry with at least three firms (before mergers), if only two firms merge, their collective profits will fall.
- A merger of a larger number of firms *may* increase the size of the collective losses due to merger.
- For any given number of (premerger) firms, if a merger of k firms causes collective losses, a merger by a smaller number of firms also causes losses. Similarly, if a merger of k firms causes gains, a merger by a larger number of firms also causes gains.
- If less than 80 percent of the firms merge, mergers will be collectively unprofitable.
- If any given share (less than 100 percent) of the firms in an industry merge, there is an initial industry size (number of firms) such that the merger causes losses.

These results imply that if firms maintain Cournot beliefs, they will only merge or form a cartel if virtually all other firms in the industry join them. Alternatively, if they maintain Cournot beliefs, and only a few firms merge, their profits will fall. A final possibility is that only firms that do not maintain Cournot beliefs merge.

SOURCES: Salant, Switzer, and Reynolds (1983) and Patinkin (1947). Compare Aumann (1973) and Okuno, Postlewaite, and Roberts (1980).

to experimentation. Even at the equilibrium, if one firm varies its output slightly, as an experiment, and observes how the other firm behaves, it may learn how to increase its profits, as discussed below.

Second, it does not make sense for a firm to maximize its profits in the current period alone, as the multiperiod Cournot model implies. Rather, the firm should maximize the present discounted value of its future stream of profits.[10] A firm may be willing to

---

[10] Profits in later periods are worth less than profits in the first period. If the interest rate is 10 percent, $1 of profits in the first period is worth $1, but $1 of profits guaranteed in the second period is only worth 91¢ ≈ 1/(1.1) in the first period. That is, if you put 91¢ in the bank in the first year and received 10 percent interest per year, in the second year, the bank would return $1. The *present discounted value* of $1 of profits in both the first and second years, then, is $1.91.

trade large profits in the future for smaller profits today. Indeed, firms can increase profits by varying their behavior over time, using the trigger-price strategies described in Chapter 9 or other strategies discussed later in the section on multiperiod games.

These two objections only relate to the multiperiod version of the Cournot model, not the static Cournot model. In a one-period model, in which firms produce at the Cournot equilibrium without an adjustment period, each firm's belief about its rival's behavior *is* reasonable, experimentation is impossible, and future profits are irrelevant.

Whether or not the Cournot model is completely realistic, however, may be the wrong question; its ability to explain or predict phenomena in the real world is the important issue. This chapter presents some experimental and empirical evidence that the Cournot equilibrium often occurs.

The Bertrand Model

Cournot's work was well ahead of its time. Indeed, it was not until 1883, 45 years after his book was published, that it was even reviewed. In this first critique, Joseph Bertrand argued that it is hard to see who sets prices in oligopolistic markets if the firms do not set them. Cournot, by having firms choose output rather than price, fails to explain explicitly the mechanism by which prices are determined (but for that matter, so does a competitive model).

In Bertrand's model, firms set prices rather than output. If consumers have complete information and realize that firms produce identical products, they buy the one with the lowest price. In a Bertrand model, each firm believes its rival's price is predetermined; by a slight price cut, a firm is able to capture all its rival's business. In the Bertrand equilibrium discussed below, firms make zero profits and no firm can increase its profits by raising or lowering its price, which, when it exists, is equivalent to the social optimum (competitive equilibrium) discussed above.

An Example.   To illustrate the Bertrand equilibrium, let us make the same assumptions as in the Cournot example:

- The duopolists produce homogeneous products that cannot be stored.
- The market demand curve is Equation 10.1′, $p = 1 - 0.001\ Q$.
- Marginal cost is constant at 28¢, and there are no fixed costs. Both firms have essentially unlimited production capacities: either firm can produce enough to meet the market's entire demand.

The only change in the earlier model is the way in which firms form their conjectures. Instead of using the Cournot conjecture, they use the *Bertrand conjecture:* each firm believes that it can charge whatever price it wants, while the other firm continues to charge the same price as before. Whereas Cournot firms believe that rivals hold their quantities constant, Bertrand firms believe that they hold their prices constant. Now each firm chooses its price, not its quantity.

Suppose that Firm 1 is charging price p_1, which is greater than its marginal cost of 28¢. If Firm 1 makes any sales at all, it earns a positive profit. Because both firms produce

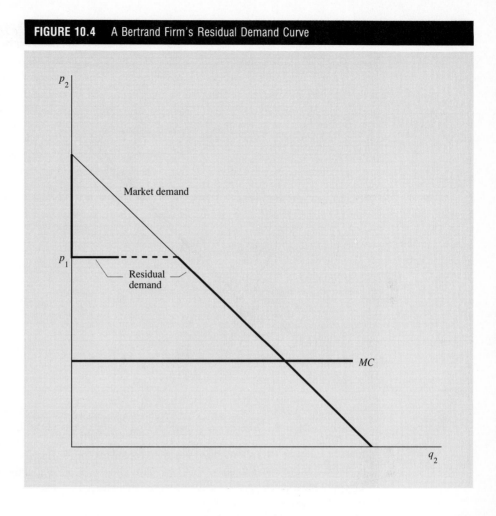

FIGURE 10.4   A Bertrand Firm's Residual Demand Curve

identical products, however, all consumers buy from Firm 2 if p_2 is even slightly below p_1; none buy from Firm 2 if p_2 is above p_1; and consumers are indifferent between the two firms when $p_2 = p_1$. Thus, as Figure 10.4 shows, the residual demand curve (heavy line) facing Firm 2 is zero when p_2 is above p_1, equals the market demand when p_2 is below p_1, and is horizontal at p_1. If both firms charge the same price, they split the total market demand. Thus, in Figure 10.4, where the demand facing Firm 1 is horizontal (where $p_2 = p_1$), half the horizontal line is dashed to indicate that Firm 1 sells only half the total amount demanded.

When both firms charge 28¢, neither firm profits by changing its price. If a firm lowers its price, it loses money (because price is then below marginal and average cost). If either firm raises its price, it makes no sales at all. Thus, $p = MC$ is the only possible Bertrand equilibrium. This example can be illustrated graphically using best-response

FIGURE 10.5   Bertrand Best-Response Functions

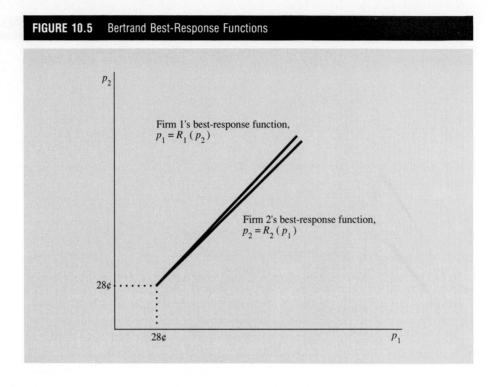

functions. Figure 10.5 shows these functions for the two firms. Each best-response function is slightly exaggerated to show that each firm chooses a price slightly below its rival's. The only intersection of these best-response functions occurs where price equals marginal cost, which is the only equilibrium.

In this equilibrium, both firms charge a price equal to marginal cost and earn zero profits; thus, it is the same as the social optimum (competitive equilibrium). As in the Cournot model, the single-period model has more appeal than the multiperiod version with best-response functions.

A Comparison of the Bertrand and Cournot Equilibrium Concepts.   In the absence of an auctioneer, it is difficult to imagine how prices are determined if firms set output rather than prices, as in Cournot's model. As a result, many economists find Bertrand's model more attractive than Cournot's, because it explains how prices are set.[11]

---

[11] A firm that must sell its product immediately and cannot store it, as in the melon example, must adjust its price rapidly, as necessary, or it will be stuck with useless output. On the other hand, a firm that cannot change prices quickly or can do so only at great cost—say, because it prints elaborate catalogs—may meet fluctuations in demand by varying output. See Chapter 21.

Because price rather than output is the decision variable, the Bertrand firm's residual demand curve differs substantially from a Cournot firm's. When goods are homogeneous and all firms charge the same price, a Bertrand firm's residual demand curve is kinked, as in Figure 10.4. By slightly lowering its price, a firm may increase sales from none of the market to all of the market. Such sudden shifts in sales are rarely observed, however, in most industries. Rather, demand curves appear to be smooth (nonkinked), as in the Cournot model, so that each firm's output only shifts slightly from period to period.

In summary, Bertrand's model of a homogeneous good may be more realistic in explaining who sets prices, but the nonkinked Cournot residual demand curve is more realistic. The assumptions and predictions of both models are more realistic when products are heterogeneous, as discussed in the next chapter.

Capacity Constraints in Bertrand's Model: Edgeworth's Model.   In 1897, Francis Edgeworth presented an important variant of Bertrand's model. The **Edgeworth model** shows that when firms have limited capacity to produce, there is no single-price, static Bertrand equilibrium (Shubik with Levitan 1980, 64–65). To illustrate Edgeworth's point, suppose the previous Bertrand example is modified so that firms no longer have unlimited capacity. Now each firm's maximum output capacity is 360, which is half the amount demanded at a price equal to marginal cost. That is, each firm's average and marginal cost curves are vertical at 360: the cost of the next unit of output is infinite.

If both firms initially charge prices equal to marginal cost, $p_1 = p_2 = 28¢$, their combined output can just satisfy the market's demand. If the first firm slightly raises its price while the second firm maintains its price at $p_2 = MC$, all consumers want to buy from the second firm. Half the market, however, is unable to buy at that price because of the second firm's limited capacity. The first firm faces a positive residual demand from frustrated consumers who are unable to buy from Firm 2, as shown in Figure 10.6. Its residual demand is the market demand minus the 360 units sold by the second firm (where only the portion above its marginal costs is of interest to the first firm).

Firm 1 can maximize its profits by acting like a monopolist with respect to its residual demand. Its marginal revenue equals its marginal cost at a price of 46¢, and it makes positive profits. The second firm's price equals its marginal cost (28¢), so it makes no profits in spite of its larger sales.

In the next period Firm 2 raises its prices to a level just below Firm 1's price of 46¢, so that all consumers want to buy from it. Given its limited capacity, however, Firm 2 meets only two-thirds of the market demand. Here, Firm 2 sells twice as much as Firm 1 at almost the same price, so its profits are double those of Firm 1. In subsequent periods the firms could take turns undercutting each other until the price reaches 37¢. At that point it again pays for one of them to raise its price to 46¢, and the price-cutting cycle is repeated.[12] Thus, there is no single-price, static equilibrium here. Firms that continue

---

[12] Each firm's owner makes the following calculation: If I drop my price to p, which is slightly below my rival's price, I can sell my maximum output, 360 melons. On the other hand, if I raise my price to 46¢, I can only sell 180 melons, but I make more per melon. At what price, p, are my profits the same as if I set my price at 46¢? To answer that question, I equate my profits at 46¢ to those at p and solve for p: $(46¢ - 28¢) \times 180 = (p - 28¢) 360$. That is, my profits are equal if I raise my price to 46¢ or lower it to $p = 37¢$.

FIGURE 10.6   Bertrand Residual Demand When Firms Have Limited Capacity

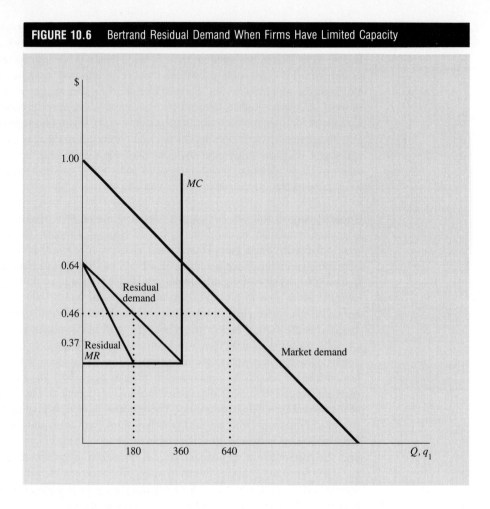

in this manner are locked in a perpetual price war, with prices rising and falling forever.[13]

   This example shows that there is no static equilibrium if firms have extremely limited capacity (or, equivalently, their average costs rise rapidly at some relatively low output level). If any firm can meet the entire market's demand, however, an equilibrium exists that is identical to the efficient solution.

---

[13] Having prices continuously adjusting under plausible circumstances such as capacity constraints is unsatisfactory, since we rarely observe such instability in the real world. Technically, Edgeworth showed that there is no equilibrium in "pure strategies." There is no simple rule of the sort discussed in the Cournot and Bertrand models for firms to follow at all times that leads to equilibrium. See, however, Dasguta and Maskin (1986), who show that a more complex type of equilibrium does exist. See also Allen and Hellwig (1986).

The Stackelberg Leader-Follower Model

In many ways the saying "Know thyself" is not well said. It were more practical to say "Know other people." —MENANDER.

The third important conjectural variations model was developed by Heinrich von Stackelberg (1952) in 1934, who assumed that one firm acts as a leader and the others follow like sheep.[14] The best way to see how this model works is to suppose that a follower firm uses naive Cournot conjectures, whereas the leader firm realizes how the followers are behaving and takes advantage of them.

The following example uses only one follower, but the model generalizes to any number of follower firms. The leader firm realizes that the follower firm has a Cournot best-response function; that is, the follower chooses its output on the assumption that the leader's output is fixed.

The leader, therefore, maximizes its profits subject to the constraint that the follower chooses a corresponding output on its Cournot best-response function. The Stackelberg leader is better off than if it were also a Cournot firm, while the follower is worse off. In short, being naive does not pay: knowing how its rival behaves allows a leader to profit at the follower's expense.

An Example.   To illustrate this model, assume there are two melon-producing firms with the same cost functions and the same market demand curve as in the Cournot example. Firm 1, the leader, knows the Cournot best-response function of Firm 2, the follower, $R_2 (q_1)$ in Figure 10.7b. Firm 1 maximizes its output, knowing Firm 2's corresponding output from its best-response function.

Because it knows the follower's best-response function, the leader knows how much the follower will produce at any level of output the leader chooses. The follower's output choice is its best response *given* the output level the leader chooses. Thus, the leader can calculate the *total* production corresponding to any output level it chooses, and it chooses the level that maximizes its profits.

By subtracting the follower's output (as summarized by the follower's best-response function in Figure 10.7b) from total demand, the leader can calculate its residual demand curve, shown in Figure 10.7a. The leader picks its output, q_1, where its marginal revenue (based on its residual demand curve) equals its marginal cost. As Figure 10.7a and Table 10.1 show, Firm 1 maximizes its profits by producing 360 melons. Firm 2 produces only 180 melons, which is determined by substituting 360 into Firm 2's best-response function, as shown in Figure 10.7b.

The leader produces more output than would a Cournot firm. Its naive (Cournot) rival produces less than the Cournot equilibrium output.[15]

---

[14] Economists long ago learned to buy sheep and sell deer.

[15] This model cannot be modified so that the follower uses a Bertrand reaction function. Where firms use Bertrand reaction functions, a knowledgeable firm cannot increase its profits because it cannot prevent the other firm from price-cutting. That is, a knowledgeable firm could do no better than maintain the Bertrand equilibrium price.

FIGURE 10.7 The Stackelberg Equilibrium

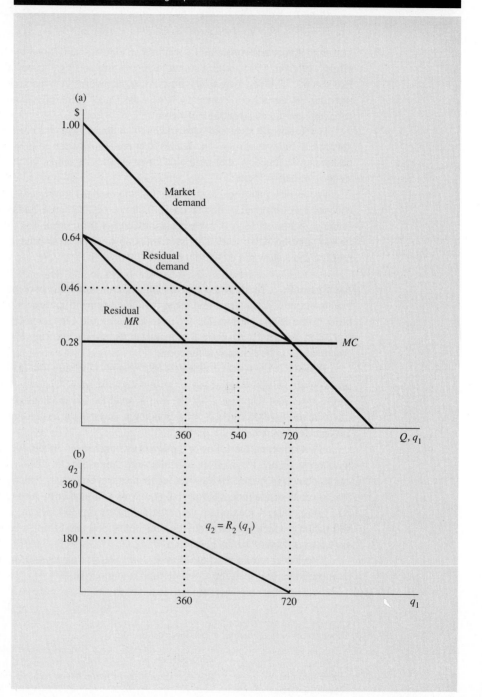

Stackelberg Equilibrium Compared to Other Equilibria.   The Stackelberg equilibrium lies inside the profit possibility frontier, as shown in Figure 10.3. The leader, Firm 1, makes $64.80 in profits, while the follower, Firm 2, only makes half that, or $32.40. Thus, industry profits, $97.20, are less than the combined profits in a Cournot equilibrium, $115.20, which also lies inside the profit possibility frontier. Stackelberg industry profits are lower because the Stackelberg industry output, 540 melons, is greater than the Cournot industry output, 480. Of course, the Stackelberg industry still produces less than the social optimum (competitive equilibrium) output of 720 melons.

The Stackelberg price, 46¢, is higher than the competitive price, 28¢, but less than the Cournot price, 52¢. As a result, consumer surplus is higher with a Stackelberg duopoly, 145.8, than with a Cournot duopoly, 115.2, but lower than the social optimum, 259.2. Tables 10.1 and 10.2 compare this equilibrium to others.

Problems with the Stackelberg Model.   There are two problems with the Stackelberg model: a static equilibrium may not exist, and the multiperiod version has the same flaws as the Cournot model. Stackelberg's analysis gives a clear, deterministic answer if one firm is a sophisticated leader and the other is a naive follower: the Stackelberg equilibrium. The analysis also gives a deterministic answer if both firms are naive: the Cournot equilibrium. If both firms are sophisticated, however, the outcome is unclear. Both firms may try to be leaders, and a price war (analogous to that in Edgeworth's model) may result. Unless at least one firm changes its behavior (for example, becomes a follower or forms a cartel with the other firm), there is no static equilibrium; Stackelberg's analysis does not explain why one firm becomes the leader and the other the follower.

As with the multiperiod Cournot model, one could also object that firms should be maximizing discounted profits rather than current profits and that the follower's expectations may prove to be wrong outside of equilibrium. Again, these objections do not apply to a static version of the Stackelberg model, because expectations are correct in equilibrium, and there is no important distinction between maximizing current profits and present discounted profits.

A Comparison of the Major Conjectural Variations Models

The three major conjectural variations, noncooperative oligopoly models make different assumptions about the ways firms expect rivals to behave. As a result, they predict very different firm and industry outputs, prices, profits, and consumer surpluses in equilibrium (see Tables 10.1 and 10.2).

If there is only one firm, all three conjectural variations models predict monopoly behavior. The more firms, n, in the industry, the closer the Cournot (Tables 10.1 and 10.3) and Stackelberg (Table 10.3) equilibria to the social optimum or competitive equilibrium.

The Bertrand equilibrium with homogeneous goods, however, is unaffected by the number of firms in the industry, as long as it includes at least two firms with unlimited capacity. The Bertrand oligopoly equilibrium is the same as the social optimum. With heterogeneous goods (discussed in the next chapter), the Bertrand equilibrium differs from the competitive equilibrium, and the number of firms in the industry affects prices.

The Attack on Conjectural Variations Models

Economists have long been aware of the weaknesses of the conjectural variations models, as discussed above. The three most important are

1. The conjectures that firms hold are arbitrary.

2. The multiperiod versions are implausible. Even granting that a firm holds a given arbitrary conjecture, why does it maintain that assumption in the face of contradictory evidence?

3. The conjectures are credible in the equilibrium, but not elsewhere. (This attack is related to the previous point.)[16]

In response to these problems, economists have developed alternative models. One of the most influential critics of the conjectural variations approach is Stigler (1964), who argues that oligopolists want to collude (at least tacitly) to maximize joint profits. Thus, according to Stigler, the cartel theory discussed in the previous chapter provides a good basis for explaining all oligopoly behavior. Oligopolists try to behave cooperatively as a monopolist would, but sometimes they cannot fully enforce the cartel. In particular, some firms behave noncooperatively and engage in secret price reductions that are undetected by other firms. This "cheating" keeps the average price below the monopoly level. If cheating is widespread at all prices above the competitive one, the cartel is completely unsuccessful in raising the price.

This approach has the advantage of avoiding arbitrary assumptions about firms' conjectures, but it makes many of the same predictions as the conjectural variations models. For example, it predicts that the more firms an industry includes, the harder it is to detect cheating by any one firm, so more cheating occurs, and the average price is lower. Similarly, both the Cournot and Stackelberg models predict lower prices with more firms in an industry.

Recently, game theory has been revived as a way to analyze successful and unsuccessful collusive behavior more formally. The trigger-price strategies discussed in the previous chapter illustrate the use of game theory to explain collusive behavior. The following section introduces game theory and suggests how it can be used to develop rigorous models of oligopoly behavior based on Stigler's insights into oligopoly behavior.

■ GAME THEORY

> *When the One Great Scorer comes to write against your name—He marks—*
> *not that you won or lost—but how you played the game.* —GRANTLAND RICE

Game theory analyzes the interactions between rational, decision-making individuals who may not be able to predict fully the outcomes of their decisions. Models of cooperative and noncooperative behavior can be viewed as *games* of *strategies* or *actions* (such as

---

[16] Recently, some economists have developed new conjectural models that purportedly avoid this problem. These *consistent conjecture* models are discussed in Appendix C. Unfortunately, they still suffer from the other weaknesses of conjectural variations models.

setting output, price, or advertising levels). Oligopolistic games have three common elements:

1. There are two or more firms, or players.
2. Each firm attempts to maximize its profits or **payoff.**
3. Each firm is aware that other firms' actions can affect its profits.

The third element is the crucial one. Oligopolistic markets differ from competitive and monopolistic markets because each firm's actions or strategies significantly affect its rivals. For example, oligopolists may form cartels for the purpose of mutually beneficial actions; yet, because each firm's interests are different from those of other firms, the best outcome for a particular firm is not always in the collective best interest.

In competitive and monopolistic markets, firms do not act as if the actions of rivals affect their payoffs or as if other firms may have different objectives. Indeed, the competitive model may be viewed as one of many intertwined games against nature rather than against other players with strategies.

This section first describes the types of oligopoly games and defines an oligopoly equilibrium. It then considers three determinants of the oligopoly equilibrium: the number of firms, the rules of the game, and the length of the game. After a brief discussion of why the number of firms and the rules of the game affect the equilibrium, it concentrates on the effects of the game's length on the equilibrium. Single-period, or static, games are discussed first, using the famous prisoner's dilemma example. Some single-period games that produce the same equilibrium as predicted by the conjectural variations models are discussed next, and then the focus shifts to multiperiod games of infinite and finite length. This section shows how the single-period prisoner's dilemma equilibrium changes if the game is repeated for more periods and concludes by describing some recent work on multiperiod games.

Oligopoly Games and Equilibria

Oligopolistic games may be categorized according to the degree of cooperation among players, the number of players, and the payoff structure. Oligopolistic players interact in one of two ways.[17] In a *cooperative game* firms make binding agreements to cooperate or form a cartel. In a *noncooperative game,* firms cannot make binding agreements, so they act independently; however, the cooperative outcome may be obtained.[18] This chapter concentrates on noncooperative games; cooperative games were discussed in the preceding chapter.

---

[17] Competitive and socialist firms engage in *mechanistic games,* in which each firm believes that it faces an impersonal mechanism—the price system or a socialist system—and has no influence on the market (Shubik with Levitan 1980, 33–34). That is, they are not engaged in a game of strategy. Thus, competitive and socialistic markets are mechanistic games; oligopolistic markets are games of strategies.

[18] For the current discussion, it is convenient to assume that it is costless to enforce agreements. There are, of course, other economic models, as discussed in Chapter 9 on cartels, in which the cost of enforcing agreements is positive. That is, limited cooperation may be possible. Limited cooperation is considered later.

Types of Payoffs. Games may be characterized in two ways according to their payoffs as constant-sum or variable-sum games. In *constant-sum games* the payoffs sum to a constant no matter what strategies are chosen. For example, in a *zero-sum game* any increase in one firm's profits must be offset by an equal loss by another firm. The only issue in constant-sum games is the division of payoffs among players. All possible outcomes are *Pareto optimal:* one player cannot be made better off without making another player worse off. In *variable-sum games* the sum of the payoffs may vary depending on the strategies played. Such games are typical of the real world; for example, if all firms charge high prices, industry profits may be higher than if all firms charge low prices.

As an example of a constant-sum (but not zero-sum) game, suppose your family has a pie to divide among all family members (perhaps in accordance with strategies such as whimpering or offering to help clean up afterwards). The size of the pie is fixed: only the relative shares are yet to be determined. In contrast, if the pie has not yet been made, both its size and the shares must be determined. In this variable-sum game, one family member can get a larger share without another one necessarily getting a smaller share.

Nash Equilibrium. This discussion of oligopoly models, such as game theory models, focuses primarily on the equilibrium strategies and payoffs—on who wins or loses. It is concerned with the profits of firms and the well-being of consumers.

In game theory, firms may have complex strategies, and new equilibrium concepts must be used. The best-known noncooperative equilibrium is a generalization of Cournot's equilibrium concept, in which an equilibrium occurs when no firm wants to change its output level. This generalization is the work of John F. Nash (1951). A set of strategies is called a **Nash equilibrium** if, holding the strategies of all other firms constant, no firm can obtain a higher payoff (profit) by choosing a different strategy.

This generalization is useful when strategies include choosing more than output levels, players include consumers or other nonfirms, and players maximize utility or some payoff other than profits. Example 10.2 describes a nonbusiness game in which the Nash generalization is apt.

Number of Firms, the Rules of the Game, and the Length of the Game

The rules of the game are what we call the laws of Nature.
—THOMAS HENRY HUXLEY

The equilibrium payoffs are dictated by the number of firms, the rules of the game, and the length of the game. First let us examine how the number of firms and the rules of the game affect the equilibrium payoffs.

For example, consider a two-player, constant-sum game in which the players split $90 (Friedman 1983, 210). The rules of the game are that if the two players sign a contract specifying how the money is to be divided, it is binding; if they cannot agree, the money is split equally. Although the rules allow for cooperation through signing a contract, the players cannot specify a contract that does more for each of them than they can achieve without a contract.

EXAMPLE 10.2

Do Birds of a Feather Cournot-Flock Together or How Do You Play the "Game" Game?

Flocking birds must look up (or *scan*) frequently while they are feeding to see an approaching predator in time. Frequent scanning, however, decreases the feeding rate of individual birds. Since any bird can give the warning of impending doom (which greatly reduces the probability of death), it is in an individual bird's best interest for another member of the flock to scan (incur costs) while it eats constantly (benefits). Not surprisingly, as the size of the flock increases, each bird spends less time scanning and more time feeding.

Using high-speed cameras with telephoto lenses and trained predators that fly over the flock from time to time, scientists determined how members of a flock of yellow-eyed juncos behave. The scientists compared two game-theoretical models as explanations for this behavior. In the cooperative model, the birds work together, whereas in the selfish solution (analogous to the Cournot-Nash model), they operate independently. The following table compares the observed and predicted scanning rates (as percentages of time) under the cooperative and selfish models (using the most likely parameter estimates for each model—which explains why the numbers are different in the two models when there is only one bird in the "flock"):

Number in Flock	Observed	Predicted	
		Cooperative Model	Selfish Model
1	13.9%	15.9%	18.6%
2	7.85	6.2	3.4
3	6.22	5.9	0.6
4	6.02	5.5	0.0
5	5.87	5.2	0.0
6	5.66	4.9	0.0
7	5.58	4.7	0.0
8	5.59	4.5	0.0
9	4.88	4.4	0.0
10	4.65	4.0	0.0

The predictions of the cooperative model do not differ in a statistically significant way from the observed values. A statistical test shows that the probability of the selfish (Nash) model is less than 0.005: it is virtually impossible that the observed scanning rates are the outcome of selfish behavior.

The scientists who conducted this study were surprised that birds behaved cooperatively. After all a "selfish" bird—one that did not cooperate by sharing scanning duty—should have an advantage over a "cooperative" bird. Thus, they expected selfishness to be an "evolutionarily stable strategy."

Continued

EXAMPLE 10.2

Do Birds of a Feather Cournot-Flock Together or How Do You Play the "Game" Game? *continued*

After a little more thought, however, they concluded that the results made sense when the same players in a "game" meet again and again: "the only strategy evolutionarily stable to invasion may be to reciprocate in kind." That is, it is optimal to cooperate only so long as other birds cooperate. They call a bird that follows this conditional cooperative strategy a *judge*. A judge behaves like a cooperative bird if others are cooperative and like a selfish bird if others are not cooperative.

They calculate the following "payoff" matrix for a flock of two birds with these three types of strategies, where the payoff (the numbers in the following table) is the probability that Player 1 survives predator attacks for a day under adverse conditions:

		Player 2		
		Cooperative	Selfish	Judge
Player 1	Cooperative	0.513	0.492	0.513
	Selfish	0.528	0.503	0.503
	Judge	0.513	0.503	0.513

Notice that a judge does as well as a cooperative bird with another cooperative bird and better than a cooperative bird when paired with a selfish bird. So long as the birds are all cooperative or judges, we would expect to see cooperative behavior.

SOURCE: Pulliam, Pyke, and Caraco. 1982.

To see that a contract is only valuable when there is mutual gain from its use, contrast the example above to a *majority* game involving three players: any contract signed by two or more players is binding; however, in the absence of a contract, the money is split equally. If two players form a coalition and agree to divide the money equally and leave nothing to the third player, they can split the $30 that would go to the third player; each receives $45.

We now consider the effects of the game's length on the equilibrium. Single-period games are examined first, and then single-period game equilibria are compared to multiperiod game equilibria.

Single-Period Games

Early work on oligopoly theory, using conjectural variations models or game theory models, concentrated on single-period, or static games. Such models are appropriate for markets that last for only brief periods of time, so that rival firms compete once, but

TABLE 10.4	Prisoners' Dilemma Game		

		Firm 1	
		Low Price	*High Price*
Firm 2	*Low Price*	0 0	−5 10
	High Price	10 −5	5 5

never again. In such models, complex, long-run strategies and reputations for hard-nosed competition are irrelevant. This section begins by discussing what is known about single-period games and then shows how multiperiod games differ from single-period games. The distinction between the single- and multiperiod models is illustrated by the prisoner's dilemma game.

Most of what is known about single-period games concerns zero-sum games. Von Neumann and Morgenstern (1944) derived solutions for zero-sum games given rational behavior by players. Unfortunately, most oligopoly games have variable-sum payoffs: one player's loss is not another player's gain. In variable-sum games, if players do not cooperate, all may be worse off; yet, in many cases, rational firms do not cooperate, as the prisoner's dilemma game illustrates.

Single-Period Prisoner's Dilemma Game.   Suppose the two firms in an industry have only two possible strategies: set a low price or set a high price. Their payoffs depend on the strategies both choose, as shown in Table 10.4, where the first firm's profits are shown in the upper right and the second firm's profits are in the lower left of each cell. If both firms set low prices, each earns zero profits; if both charge high prices, each earns profits of 5. If the first firm sets a low price and the second firm sets a high price, however, the first firm gains 10, while the other loses 5.

What strategy should Firm 1 choose? One approach is the *maxmin* strategy: a player maximizes the *minima,* or worst possible outcome. For example, the owner of Firm 1 could use the following reasoning:

- If Firm 2 chooses the low-price strategy, then if I choose it also, my profits are 0; if I use my high-price strategy, I lose 5. I prefer 0 to −5, so I'm better off with my low-price strategy.
- If Firm 2 chooses the high-price strategy, then if I use my low price strategy, my profits are 10; if I use my high price strategy, my profits are 5. Again, I'm better off with my low price strategy.
- Therefore, whatever strategy Firm 2 uses, I'm better off using my low-price strategy.

Since the payoff table is symmetric, Firm 2 should use the same reasoning and also decide to use its low price strategy.

Thus, since both firms use the low-price strategy, the competitive equilibrium is chosen. The set of strategies by which both firms charge the low, competitive price produces a Nash equilibrium. For example, as shown in Table 10.4, if Firm 2 charges the competitive price, Firm 1 would be worse off by charging the high price, which would yield profits of -5, than by charging the competitive price, which yields profits of 0. Similarly, if Firm 1 charges the low price, Firm 2 does not want to change its strategy. Thus, neither firm wants to change its strategy if its rival plays its equilibrium strategy.

This Nash equilibrium does not maximize the players' collective payoff. The two firms would be better off if they could cooperate and both use the high-price strategy. If the game is only played once, then its solution is nonoptimal from the players' viewpoint. This game is called a **prisoner's dilemma game** because each player has an incentive to play noncooperatively but would benefit if both played cooperatively.[19]

Single-Period Games with Cournot, Bertrand, and Stackelberg Equilibria.   The conjectural variations models have been criticized because firms make arbitrary assumptions about rivals' behavior. Game theorists have shown, however, that reasonable and rational strategies exist that can lead to the single-period Cournot, Bertrand, and Stackelberg equilibria. Moreover, these equilibria may be viewed as special cases of Nash equilibria.

Cournot-Nash Equilibrium.   The Cournot model can be reinterpreted in game theory terms to show that the Cournot equilibrium is a special type of Nash equilibrium. Game theory can then replace the Cournot conjectures and the Cournot equilibrium can be derived in a more satisfactory manner.

In the Cournot example, the two firms only use strategies for choosing output levels. Obviously, the strategy of a firm's rival affects a firm's profits, since each firm's profits are a function of the output of the other firm. A set of outputs is said to be a Cournot (Nash) equilibrium if, holding the output levels (strategies) of all other firms (players) constant, no firm (player) can obtain higher profits (payoff) by choosing a different output level (strategy). In our Cournot duopoly example, only one set of strategies has this property: $q_1 = q_2 = 240$.

Because the Cournot equilibrium is a special case of the Nash equilibrium, it is often referred to as a *Cournot-Nash equilibrium*. Because the only strategies are choosing output levels, the Cournot-Nash equilibrium is also referred to as *Nash in quantities*.

Merely redescribing the Cournot equilibrium as a Nash equilibrium using terms like *strategies* instead of *output levels* accomplishes little by itself. The more important aim is to avoid relying on the arbitrary Cournot conjectures and best-response functions in order to develop a better explanation of the choice of strategies—one that does not arbitrarily assume that rivals always choose a particular output level. A number of game

---

[19] The prisoner's dilemma game is attributed to A. W. Tucker in Luce and Raiffa (1957, 94). In the original version, two prisoners are accused of committing a crime. They are held in different rooms, so they are unable to communicate. Each prisoner has two strategies: talk or do not talk. If neither talk, each gets a one-year sentence on a minor charge. If both talk, each gets a five-year sentence. If one talks, but the other does not, the prisoner who confesses goes free, while the other gets a ten-year sentence. By the same reasoning as in the Table 10.4 example, both talk, even though they are obviously better off if both keep quiet. As Shakespeare said, "The game is up."

theoretic explanations have been offered for firms' strategies. The following paragraph describes a single-period model that avoids arbitrary assumptions about conjectures and derives each firm's belief about its rival in a reasonable manner (Daughety 1985).

Suppose Firm 1 chooses an output level to maximize its profits subject to its model of Firm 2's strategy. Firm 1's model of Firm 2 is subject to Firm 2's model of Firm 1's model, and so on. That is, Firm 1's manager thinks about what Firm 2's manager is thinking: "I think that she thinks that I think that she thinks that I think . . ." Based on this type of *infinite regress* reasoning, each firm chooses an output level. The game is static because there is only one move—output levels are chosen only once. Daughety shows that there is only one equilibrium in this game: the Cournot-Nash equilibrium. Although there is "conjecturing" in this model, the Cournot strategy is logically consistent, not arbitrary.[20]

Bertrand-Nash Equilibrium.   The Bertrand model can be similarly reinterpreted as a game in which the strategies of firms are the prices they choose. The Bertrand equilibrium is often referred to as *Nash in prices,* since it is a Nash equilibrium in which firms choose prices as their strategies.

A number of game theoretic models have been developed that lead to this equilibrium using a different model than Bertrand's. For example, Grossman (1981) shows that if a firm's strategy is a supply function (the quantity supplied as a function of price rather than just the price itself), under weak conditions the competitive, or Bertrand, equilibrium is a Nash equilibrium.[21]

Stackelberg-Nash Equilibrium.   The Stackelberg equilibrium can similarly be interpreted as a Nash equilibrium. Stackelberg described a game in which the firms' strategies (output levels) and the equilibrium concept are the same as in the Cournot model. By presenting the Stackelberg model as an explicit game with *sequential* moves (one firm moves first and then the other moves), the Stackelberg equilibrium is justifiably different from the static Cournot model.

Suppose Firm 1 is allowed to choose its output level first. Firm 1 does a thought experiment to determine what the best response of Firm 2 is, *given* the output level that Firm 1 chooses. Determining the best output level for Firm 2 is no problem, because Firm 2 will know Firm 1's output level by the time it chooses its own. Firm 2 does not have to use an arbitrary conjecture.

Firm 1 picks the output level that maximizes its profits, *given* the best response of Firm 2 to Firm 1's choice. Firm 1 picks the Stackelberg-leader's output level, to which Firm 2's best response is to pick the output level that maximizes its profits: the Stackelberg-follower's output level.[22]

Explicitly determining which firm moves first in this game eliminates the need to use arbitrary conjectures in Stackelberg's model. Of course the choice of the first mover

---

[20] Kreps and Scheinkman (1983) provide an alternative model justifying Cournot behavior.

[21] This outcome is the result of the threat of entry, however, which is not considered until the next chapter.

[22] Eaton and Ware (1987) examine multiple sequential entrants.

is still arbitrary, but in some industries historical, institutional, or legal factors determine which firm is the first mover. For example, the firm that discovers and develops a new product has a natural first-mover advantage.

Multiperiod Games

The wise may learn many things from their foes. — ARISTOPHANES

The most important recent development in game theory has been the analysis of repeated, or multiperiod, games. Consistent with Stigler's beliefs, this analysis shows that cartel theory is better suited to understanding oligopoly than most single-period models suggest. Repeated games are often referred to as **supergames** because a player can have a strategy over many single-period games.

The chief advantage of a multiperiod model is that it allows for more complex and realistic interactions between firms than a single-period model. For example, a firm can signal to another firm that it wants to play cooperatively by lowering its output for a few periods. If the other firm responds by lowering its output, both behave cooperatively and avoid competition. If either firm increases its output, the other can retaliate for a while by raising its output (and lowering price) to punish the transgressor. Thus, in multiperiod markets, firms that would produce at the Cournot-Nash level in a single-period model may further restrict output and make larger profits.

This result can be illustrated using a prisoner's dilemma game that is repeated an infinite number of times. The results of repeating the game only a finite number of times are also considered, and some other recent work on multiperiod games is discussed.

Infinitely Repeated Prisoner's Dilemma Game.   If a single-period prisoner's dilemma game is repeated forever, collusion is more likely. For example, at a special event such as the Super Bowl, a souvenir firm may compete with others for a short period and then never see its rivals again. Such firms are relatively unlikely to form a cartel, because each one knows it can cheat on any agreement with no fear of reprisal. In contrast, souvenir stands at popular tourist attractions face each other over long periods, and hence are more likely to collude.

In the single-period prisoner's dilemma game, each firm took its rival's strategy as given and assumed it could not influence it. If this game is repeated, however, each firm can influence its rival's behavior by *signaling* and *threatening to punish*.

Since both firms gain by collusion, they have an incentive to communicate to avoid the prisoner's dilemma problem, which stems from a lack of trust. Because antitrust laws make direct communications illegal, firms may try to communicate through their choice of strategy if (and only if) the game is repeated. For example, a firm can use a multiperiod strategy of setting a high price and taking losses for several periods to signal its willingness to collude.[23]

---

[23] Shapiro (1980) discusses how an equilibrium on a profit-possibility frontier might arise when firms cannot communicate and when they start with arbitrary initial prices.

Similarly, a firm can threaten to punish its rival if it does not collude. To illustrate how penalties can be used to insure collusion, a more general version of the single-period prisoner's dilemma game presented in Table 10.4 is considered. Each of the two firms in the industry can produce at different output levels in different periods. One possible strategy for a firm is to produce the Cournot-Nash level of output, q_n, each period. If the other firm does the same, each earns the Cournot-Nash profits, π_n, each period. Alternatively, each firm can produce q_m, which is half the monopoly output, and earn profits of π_m each period, which are greater than the Cournot-Nash profits.

Firm 1 considers using the following two-part strategy:

- Firm 1 produces q_m output each period so long as Firm 2 does the same.
- If Firm 2 produces a different level of output in any period, t, then in period $t + 1$ and thereafter, Firm 1 produces q_n.

If Firm 2 believes that Firm 1 will follow this strategy, Firm 2 should produce q_m. Firm 2 knows that it can make greater profits in period t by producing more than q_m in that period. If it does so, however, in the $t + 1$ period and every period thereafter, Firm 1 would produce q_n. As already demonstrated, when Firm 1 produces q_n, Firm 2 maximizes its profits by producing q_n also. Thus, Firm 2 can earn unusually high profits in period t, but then earns relatively low profits for the rest of the time. Unless Firm 2 does not care about future profits, it is in Firm 2's best interest to tacitly collude and produce q_m in each period.

In short, so long as the future matters, the one-period gains from deviating from the collusive output cannot possibly compensate for the losses from getting π_n forever instead of π_m. Indeed, Firm 1 need not punish Firm 2 forever to induce it to cooperate; all it needs to do is produce q_n for enough periods so that it does not pay for Firm 2 to ever deviate. Thus, because strategies can involve signals and threats of punishment, firms are more likely to collude in multiperiod than in single-period games. See Example 10.3.

Types of Equilibria in Multiperiod Games.   All repeated games do not result in collusion, however. The type of equilibrium in a repeated game depends on a player's ability to effectively threaten other players who are not cooperative.[24] The effectiveness of a threat depends on the discount rate, the length of the game, and the credibility of the threat.

At the beginning of a game, each firm chooses a strategy to maximize its present discounted profits. If discount rates are so high that profits in future periods are worth substantially less than profits in the current period, future punishment is inconsequential and hence has no effect on current behavior. Lower discount rates, therefore, make the threat of punishment more effective. The more periods left in the game, the larger the total punishment that can be inflicted on a transgressor, because the punishment can be inflicted for more periods. However, if the threat is not credible, in the sense that Firm 2 does not believe that Firm 1 will actually inflict the punishment in future periods, then Firm 2 ignores the threat altogether.

---

[24] See Tirole (1988), Friedman (1986), and Ulph (1987). This section may be skipped in an introductory course.

EXAMPLE 10.3

COPYING PRICING

As every student knows, the way to learn something is to xerox the relevant article and then absorb it through osmosis. As a result, copy shops often spring up near colleges. In the early 1970s, four firms in the Harvard Square area of Cambridge, Massachusetts satisfied a large portion of the copy business of students from Harvard, MIT, Tufts, and other colleges in the area.

Initially, the smallest of the "big four" firms, Copy Cat Educational Services, Inc. (located in the J. August Clothing Store) charged much higher prices than its larger competitors. Then Jimmy Jacobs, the owner of the clothing store and copying service, lowered his prices to a level that the other firms contended was too low to make profits.

One competitor, Gnomon Copy, posted a sign in its window on the "Xerox Price Story." Gnomon charged that Jacobs "had sent word to the other Xerox services in Harvard Square that he was going to drive them all out of business . . . if they did not raise their prices to match his, which were then substantially higher than the going rate. . . . Now, Jacobs has carried out his threat."

Gnomon said it was meeting Copy Cat's price in Harvard Square in order not to lose customers but that it would keep its prices at its other stores at their previous levels, which Gnomon considered "to be fair and reasonable." They urged customers to boycott Copy Cat, claiming, "You may pay a higher price today, but you will insure a viable competitive situation for the future."

Within hours of the posting of Gnomon's sign, according to Gnomon employees, Jacobs barged into their shop and said, "You call your boss and tell him he's got five minutes to take that down or I'll photograph it and use it in a libel suit." Upon reflection, Gnomon management decided it had not gone far enough and assigned an employee to hand out leaflets in front of Jacobs's clothing store/copy center. In turn, Jacobs filmed the leafleters in the presence of a reporter, while a Gnomon salesperson was frantically searching for her camera to photograph Jacobs photographing everyone else. According to the reporter, "When the Gnomon leafleter ran out of notices, he began modeling his clothes. Mr. Jacobs laughed and kept filming."

The other firms did not lower their prices at first, and their business suffered. These other firms supported Gnomon's charge that Jacobs tried to get them to fix their prices at a higher level and had threatened to punish them by undercutting their prices if they did not cooperate. Jacobs said he believed that all the firms had been charging too much and that he had decided to lower his prices, but only to a level where he could still make profits. He vigorously denied any attempt to fix prices.

Eventually, prices in Harvard Square settled at a lower level, but cost changes may have been partially responsible. While it is hard to tell what actually happened in this case, it does illustrate strategic reactions of firms to their rivals' behavior.

SOURCE: McLellan. 1971.

To illustrate these issues, we modify the multiperiod prisoner's dilemma example used before so that it only lasts a finite number of periods, say two periods. Suppose Firm 1 announces that it will produce the collusive quantity, q_m, in Period 1 and the Cournot-Nash quantity, q_n, in the second period if Firm 2 will produce the collusive quantity in the first period. Firm 1 also announces that if Firm 2 produces more than the collusive quantity in the first period, Firm 1 will punish it by producing a very large quantity (greater than q_n) in the second period. If Firm 2 believes that Firm 1 will carry out its threat, and the potential losses in the second period are large enough, it produces the collusive quantity in the first period.

Firm 2, however, probably believes that Firm 1's threat is not credible. Suppose Firm 2 does not produce q_m in the first period. There is now only one period left in the game. Firm 1 *can* punish Firm 2 in Period 2 by producing more than q_n, thereby lowering Firm 2's profits below the Cournot-Nash level. But will Firm 1 do that? Probably not, because it is not in Firm 1's best interests to do so in Period 2. Firm 1 can only harm Firm 2 by harming itself and lowering *each* firm's profits below π_n. In the second period, however, Firm 1 does not benefit from doing so. It is too late to affect Firm 2's behavior in the first period, and there are no future periods. Indeed, in Period 2 Firm 1 should act as though it is participating in a one-period game and produce q_n. Thus, Firm 2 should believe Firm 1's threat is not credible; to carry it out would be like locking the barn after the horse is stolen.

Collusion is possible, however, if Firm 1 can make its threat credible by precommitting itself to punish Firm 2 in the second period. Ignoring the legal issues, if Firm 1 writes a binding and enforceable contract in Period 1 that says it will forfeit an enormous sum of money if it does not punish Firm 2 in the second period, if necessary, then its threat is credible.

Much of the recent research in multiperiod games only considers equilibria that result from credible strategies. That is, this research places a **refinement** or restriction on the possible equilibria. One widely used refinement is to consider only *perfect Nash equilibria:* those Nash equilibria in which threats are credible (Selten 1975).

Which Nash equilibria are perfect? An equilibrium is perfect if the strategies of the firms are credible. For example, in the two-period game, Firm 1 threatens to punish Firm 2 in the second period if Firm 2 produces too much in the first period. That threat is only credible if the punishment is in Firm 1's best interest *in the second period.*

More generally, a strategy or threat is credible only if the firm will stick to that strategy in any *subgame* from period *t* forward. That is, if the original strategies would still be best responses in any game that started in period *t* and ignored what had happened in previous periods, then these strategies are called a *perfect Nash equilibrium,* or **subgame perfect Nash equilibrium.**

One way to obtain a subgame perfect Nash equilibrium is to solve the game backward; this technique is illustrated for the two-period game. In the last period (the only interesting subgame), the strategy of each firm must be its best response. That is, there is a Nash equilibrium in the second period in which the strategies are optimal in the sense that the players would have chosen them if there had been no Period 1 and the game was beginning in Period 2. In the second period, the Nash, or best-response, strategy for both firms is to produce q_n. Thus, Firm 1's only credible claim is that it will produce q_n in the second period. Because there is no credible threat, both firms also produce q_n in Period 1.

Now consider a game that lasts for a finite number of periods, T, greater than 2. To solve for a perfect equilibrium requires working backward from the last period. In the last period, the firms produce q_n, by the preceding reasoning. Thus, Firm 1 cannot credibly threaten to punish Firm 2 for noncollusive production in period $T - 1$. What happens in period $T - 1$? Effectively, it is now the last period. By the same reasoning, both firms produce q_n in that period. This reasoning can be repeated for $T - 2$, $T - 3$, and other earlier periods, with the conclusion that the firms produce q_n in each period. That is, the T-period game equilibrium simply repeats the single-period equilibrium T times (Selten 1978).

The intuition in this argument is that because the firms cheat in the last period by producing more than the collusive output, they will, in turn, cheat in earlier periods, so that any collusive agreement in earlier periods unravels. The entire argument, then, depends crucially on the firms' cheating in the last period. The argument implicitly assumes that there is a *known,* fixed number of periods, T. That is, all firms cheat in the last period, *if they know it is the last period.* If the period in which the game will end is not known until that period is over, a player is less likely to deviate from the collusive output level in that period. A game with a finite number of periods and an uncertain final period is therefore similar to a game with an infinite number of periods.

To summarize, the subgame perfect Nash equilibrium depends on the number of periods in a multiperiod game and whether that number is known. First, we argued that producing the collusive output, q_m, each period is a subgame perfect Nash equilibrium in a game with an infinite number of periods. Then we showed that in a game with a known, finite number of periods, producing the Cournot-Nash output, q_n, in each period is a subgame perfect equilibrium. Finally, we contended that if the number of periods is finite but firms do not know which period is last until after it is over, then collusion is a subgame perfect Nash equilibrium.

An infinite number of other subgame perfect Nash equilibria are possible in games with an infinite number of periods and little or no time discounting. The **folk theorem** describes this set of subgame perfect Nash equilibria in infinitely long games (Fudenberg and Maskin 1986). It says, loosely, that any combination of output levels could be infinitely repeated so long as each firm's profits at those levels are at least as great as the minimum each firm could earn in a one-period game, π_n. As a result, in addition to the collusive solution, another perfect equilibrium in the infinitely repeated game is for each firm to produce the Cournot-Nash output, q_n, each period. Much current research is directed at further refining these results to provide better explanations of which equilibria occur. Without further refinements almost any output level is a sustainable equilibrium, which makes this theory difficult to test.[25]

---

[25] With an additional refinement, one can estimate a perfect multiperiod game model (Karp and Perloff, forthcoming).

So far, this chapter has concentrated on games that assume no uncertainty about underlying economic conditions. Games in which firms are uncertain are even more complex. For example, consider a multiperiod model in which Firm 1 does not know Firm 2's costs. Firm 1's beliefs about Firm 2's costs may affect how it behaves. For example, Firm 1 may drop out of the market if it believes Firm 2's costs are much lower than its own. As a result, Firm 2 may attempt to convince Firm 1 that its costs are very low, perhaps by setting a very low price for several periods. Firm 1 uses the history of Firm 2's behavior in forming its beliefs about Firm 2's costs, taking into account Firm 2's attempts to mislead. Using the additional information about Firm 2's behavior that becomes available each successive period, Firm 1 updates its beliefs about Firm 2's costs.

Firm 1 can combine the information about Firm 2's actual behavior with its prior beliefs to form a new estimate of the probability that Firm 2's cost is low by using Bayes's law from probability theory. An equilibrium in which firms form their beliefs using Bayes's law and in which each strategy is subgame perfect is called a **Bayesian perfect equilibrium.** Because such games have so many possible outcomes, economists studying them often place further restrictions or refinements on the possible equilibria to eliminate some possibilities.[26] Much of the current research in game theory is focused on games with uncertainty.

■ TESTING OLIGOPOLY MODELS

The various conjectural variations and game-theoretic models predict different equilibrium outcomes because they make alternative assumptions about how firms behave or about the nature of the market or the game. Because all these models are mathematically correct, one cannot choose between them on purely theoretical grounds. A number of economists have tried to test whether the predictions of these models are true in the real world using two chief approaches: controlled experiments and empirical studies of particular industries.

In the controlled experiments, college students are asked to act like owners of firms. Depending on the business decisions they make, their profits vary, and the resulting equilibrium is compared to the various theoretically predicted equilibria. In the empirical studies of particular industries, statistical tests are used to determine how close the observed equilibrium comes to the various theoretically predicted outcomes.

Experimental Evidence

It is difficult to run natural experiments in the real world to determine how firms actually make decisions. As a result, some economists have conducted laboratory experiments to determine how college students behave under controlled conditions. The students are allowed to keep their profits, so they have an incentive to maximize profits in the ex-

---

[26] For more detail on this and related topics, such as sequential equilibrium, see Kreps and Wilson (1982a, 1982b) and Tirole (1988).

perimental market. Postexperiment interviews indicate that a few students try to win the game by maximizing the difference in their profits relative to other players, rather than maximizing their own profits. The vast majority, however, do try to maximize their own earnings.

A survey of these experiments (Plott 1982, 1523) concludes that "Three models do well in predicting market prices and quantity: the competitive equilibrium, the Cournot model, and the monopoly (joint maximization) model. Experiments help define the conditions under which each of these alternative models apply."

To give some idea of the results that have been obtained, we discuss four representative experiments using multiperiod games. Virtually all simulation experiments use linear demand curves and a constant marginal cost.

Lave (1962), in work that started as a B.A. thesis at Reed College, conducted an experiment with undergraduates who participated in a repeated two-person, two-strategy, multiperiod prisoner's dilemma game. The players were placed so they could not see each other, making explicit communications impossible. Nonetheless, the vast majority of players were apparently able to communicate indirectly and collude. In various versions of the experiment, 75 to 100 percent of the outcomes were collusive. As predicted theoretically, in the last period, when players knew the experiment was going to end, many deviated from the collusive agreement because there could be no retaliation at that point.

Fouraker and Siegel (1963) conducted duopoly and triopoly (three-firm) experiments. Each subject was given a payoff table showing that profits depended on a player's output choice (an integer between 8 and 32) and the output (between 8 and 64) of the rival(s). For a duopoly, the collusive industry output was 30 (15 per subject), the Cournot equilibrium was 40, and the competitive or Bertrand equilibrium was 60.[27]

Each of 16 pairs of undergraduates played the game 25 times. Fouraker and Siegel used the players' decisions in the 21st period to evaluate the equilibrium. The duopoly outputs were distributed fairly uniformly over the range from slightly less than the collusive level (25) to the competitive level (60). Five were closest to competition, 7 were closest to Cournot, 1 was between Cournot and cartel, and 3 were closest to the cartel equilibrium.[28] The mean output was 41.8 and the median was 40; that is, on average, the equilibrium output was Cournot.

On the other hand, the triopoly results were more consistent with competitive behavior. The Cournot equilibrium was either 45 or 48, and the competitive output was 60. The mean output of 54.4 and median output of 58 are close to the competitive result. In 5 cases the industry output was closest to Cournot, and in 6 it was closest to competition.

Fouraker and Siegel also conducted experiments in which subjects chose prices instead of output levels. According to the payoff table, a player who chose a price above a rival's

---

[27] Holt (1985) notes that because they rounded off their payoffs to the nearest half penny, there was another Nash (Cournot) equilibrium at 44 (as well as at 40).

[28] Holt (1985, 8) points out that the experiment's instructions may have kept players away from the competitive solution. The instructions stated that if a subject made "appropriate decisions," the subject "may earn an appreciable amount of money . . . but poor choices will result in small or no profit to you." The instructions also referred to the output of the "competition."

made no sales and suffered a small loss of profits. This framework is the same as in the Bertrand model with homogeneous goods, and the Bertrand equilibrium is the same as the competitive equilibrium.

When players had incomplete information (they knew whether their price was higher or lower than a rival's but did not know the rival's profits), the price converged to the competitive equilibrium (or just above it) within 14 periods in 17 out of 18 cases. When duopoly players had full information (each knew all past prices and all players' profits), the results were more varied. In 6 cases the market was at the competitive equilibrium by the 14th period, and in 3 more, the price was just above it. In 4 cases the price was exactly midway between the competitive and the collusive price; in the remaining 4, it was at or adjacent to the collusive price.

In the triopoly case, whether players had incomplete or complete information, the market converged to the competitive level virtually every time. Thus, with full information, competitive behavior seems likely in three-person price games, but not in two-person ones. With incomplete information, competitive equilibrium is also more likely with three-person games.

One possible reason that competitive behavior was not observed in full-information duopoly games is that profits were near zero at the competitive level, so players had little to lose by choosing other strategies. Holt (1985) conducted a similar experiment of repeated duopoly games, in which the profits at the competitive or Bertrand equilibrium were positive.[29] The collusive equilibrium was 12 units of output, the Cournot equilibrium was 16, and the competitive, or Bertrand, equilibrium was 24. Twenty-four subjects participated in the first experiment, and 16 of them were rematched in a second experiment to see if experience mattered. In both experiments, the mean and median outputs were between 14 and 16; that is, they were between collusive and Cournot, and closest to the Cournot outcome. Indeed, in no case did industry output exceed 21, which is less than the competitive output of 24.

Realizing that the repetition of the game favors collusive behavior, Holt then tried a single-period experiment, which he felt would favor the Cournot equilibrium or possibly even more competitive behavior. Twelve experienced subjects engaged in a series of single-period games (with no guarantee as to which players faced each other in a given game). In early games, the output choices were quite diverse, but eventually, virtually all the players chose the symmetric Cournot output of 8, resulting in an industry output of 16.

Holt concluded that in full-information duopoly games, whether or not there are multiperiod markets, the Cournot equilibrium is more likely than the competitive, or Bertrand, equilibrium. The only effect of experience and repeated games seems to be to encourage cooperation. In the single-period game, even with experienced players, there was no tendency toward cooperation.

---

[29] This experiment differs from the Fouraker and Siegel experiment in a number of ways, most importantly in that it was constructed so that no strategy was possible that ensured a profit that always exceeded the positive competitive payoff. Further, the end of the game was determined by the throw of a die, so as to avoid endgame effects.

Where explicit signaling is permitted, we would expect collusion to be more likely. In a series of experiments, Friedman (1967) allowed players to transmit two written messages before privately making a price decision. Collusive agreements were attained over 75 percent of the time. Further, 75 percent of these collusive agreements maximized each player's profits (with no side payments allowed). As should be expected, once the players succeeded in colluding, the probability of another collusive agreement was 96 percent.

Empirical Evidence

A number of statistical studies of particular industries test whether the observed equilibrium is the same as various theoretically predicted equilibria. This section focuses on two of the earliest and best-known studies. Chapter 12 presents a more complete survey.

Both studies assume that oligopolists choose quantities based on conjectural variations about their rivals' behavior. The studies estimate a conjectural variations parameter that can take on a range of values. The estimated parameter can then be compared to the cartel, Cournot, or Bertrand values:

- The collusive conjectural variation is 1 when the firms produce the same initial outputs. A firm believes that all other firms will change their output by the same amount as it does. Thus, a firm can affect total industry output, but not its market share, by varying its output. The firm cannot increase its profits at the expense of others, so it produces the cartel output.

- The Cournot conjectural variation is 0. That is, no matter what a firm does, its rivals do not change their output levels.

- The Bertrand (competitive) conjectural variation when firms choose quantities instead of prices is $-1/(n - 1)$, where n is the number of firms (Telser 1972). A Bertrand firm believes that any increase in its output is exactly offset by a decrease of its rivals' output, so that the market price remains unchanged.

When a firm's conjectural variation is negative, as in the Bertrand case, it expects its rivals to accommodate its actions in the sense that as it increases its output, its rivals' output falls, so that total output does not increase substantially.

Although these empirical studies say they are estimating a conjectural variations model, it would be wrong to conclude that they are inherently flawed in the same way that conjectural variations theoretical models are flawed (Bresnahan 1989). One can give their estimates an alternative interpretation that is consistent with Stigler's approach or the game theory approach. The estimated conjectural variations parameter is a function of the gap between price and marginal cost. Thus, if the parameter takes on the Bertrand value, the gap between price and marginal cost is zero. Similarly, if the parameter reflects collusion, the gap equals that of a monopolist.

Thus, this parameter can be interpreted as a measure of the degree of collusion in the market, as Stigler suggests. The higher the value, the greater the collusion. One would estimate the same types of equations whether one believed in a conjectural variations model or a game theory model. The only difference is in the interpretation of the estimated parameter.[30] For expositional simplicity, we discuss the estimated parameters as though they are conjectures, which is the term the authors of these studies use.

Japanese Flat-Glass Industry.   Iwata (1974) studies the behavior of the two major firms (Asahi and Nippon) in the Japanese flat-glass industry that produce nearly identical products.[31] He provides separate estimates for the window glass and polished plate-glass markets in Japan.

For each type of glass, he estimates each firm's conjectural variation about the other firm's behavior in each year. His estimate of Asahi's conjectural variation for window glass for Nippon is stable at about 0.2 for the entire period. Nippon's corresponding conjectural variation for Asahi fluctuates between 0.3 and 0.7 over the period. In other words, the conjectural variations for window glass lie between the Cournot, 0, and perfectly collusive, 1, levels. Based on statistical tests, his conclusion is that one cannot reject either the Cournot or the perfectly collusive model.

A different pattern is found for polished plate glass. Asahi's conjectures slowly decreased over time from -0.1 to -0.3 (with one positive value in the middle of the period). Nippon's conjectures varied greatly, starting negative, becoming positive, and then turning negative again. Since the conjectures are not constant over time, it is probably better to interpret this parameter neutrally as reflecting merely the market power of each firm or the gap between price and marginal cost.

---

[30] Given its beliefs about other firms, a typical firm, i, maximizes its profits when it chooses its output, q_i, so that

$$p(q_1 + \ldots + q_n) + q_i p'(q_1 + \ldots + q_n)\lambda - c'(q_i) = 0,$$

where $p(\bullet)$ is the inverse demand or price, c' is the marginal cost, $p'(\bullet)$ is the change in price with respect to the change in output, n is the number of oligopolists, and λ, which ranges between 0 and n, reflects the market power of the firm. If λ equals 0, then price, p, equals marginal cost, c', the competitive solution. If λ equals n, then industry marginal revenue, $p + nq_i p'$, equals marginal cost, the cartel solution. One can rewrite this equation as

$$\lambda = -(p - c')/q_i p'.$$

If one can observe or estimate p, p', q_i, and c', then one can calculate λ. The numerator of the right-hand-side of this last equation is the gap between the price and marginal cost, $p - c'$.

The authors of these empirical studies note that if a firm holds identical conjectural variations about each of its rivals, $v = dq_j/dq_i$, $j \neq i$, then $\lambda = 1 + (n - 1)v$, which follows from Equation 10A.2 in Appendix 10A. Given this assumption, one can use the estimate of λ to obtain an estimate of the conjectural variation, v, used by the firm. For example, if $\lambda = 1$, then firms hold Cournot conjectures, $v = 0$, and $p + q_i p' = c'$. It is not necessary, of course, to take this last step. One can interpret λ simply as a measure of the market power of the firm and not use it to discuss conjectural variations.

[31] Iwata assumes that the price elasticity of market demand, the marginal cost of each firm, and each firm's conjectural variation are constants. His study covers the period 1956–65. More recent data were not included because of a major technological innovation after 1966. A third firm, Central, entered the window glass market in 1959 and the polished plate glass market in 1964. Because it entered so late in the sample period, only the conjectural variations of the other two firms were studied. In 1965, the market shares of the three companies, Asahi, Nippon, and Central were 52.7 percent, 33.5 percent, and 13.8 percent for window glass and 46.2 percent, 30.2 percent, and 23.6 percent for polished plate glass.

Iwata speculates that the conjectural variations in the polished plate glass market differed because of competition from abroad. In the window glass market, the Japanese price was substantially lower than international prices, so that 20 percent of all production was exported, and there was essentially no international competition in Japan. The Japanese window glass market was an oligopoly with a small number of firms.

In contrast, the domestic price of polished plate glass was much higher than the international price, so that in spite of a high tariff and shipping costs, imports varied between 2 and 20 percent during the period. This outside competition makes a standard oligopoly model less tenable. The greater competition presumably contributed to the lower conjectural variations (that is, they were closer to the competitive level, -1).

U.S. Coffee-Roasting Industry. Gollop and Roberts (1979) study the U.S. coffee-roasting industry. This industry has over 160 firms, but as of 1972, the four largest firms accounted for 65 percent of the market.[32] Although firms advertise in this industry, the authors believe it is reasonable to treat the products as homogeneous because wholesale prices are generally uniform across firms.

Gollop and Roberts assume that a firm's conjectures varied according to its relative (output) size ranking.[33] The firms were divided into three mutually exclusive subgroups, with firms in each subgroup having identical conjectural variations. The first subgroup contained only the largest firm, with a market share of 40 percent, which was more than twice the size of the second largest one. The second subgroup contained the next five firms, each of which had a market share of more than 4 percent, while the group's market share was 35 percent. The firms in the remaining subgroup had market shares of less than 3.2 percent, while the group's market share was 25 percent.

Gollop and Roberts test a number of hypotheses. The first is that all the firms used Cournot conjectural variations. Their statistical test strongly rejects this hypothesis, implying that at least some firms assumed their rivals reacted to their own behavior. The second hypothesis is that all firms have identical (but nonzero) conjectural variations, which their statistical test also strongly rejects. These two hypotheses are also rejected for individual subgroups of firms. The tests indicate that none of the representative firms maintained Cournot conjectural variations with respect to all other firms. Moreover, they find that conjectural variations varied across firm sizes.

One possible explanation for these results is that firms viewed the largest firm differently than the others; for example, they may have believed that the largest firm was a dominant firm or Stackelberg leader. Gollop and Roberts find that firms maintained conjectural variations that differed by firm size. Each firm expected the medium-sized firms to partially accommodate its output expansions by reducing their output. Both the

---

[32] This study uses data for 1972, a year in which there were no unusual, large shocks to the market. Data for the 52 largest firms (those with 20 or more employees) are used. The other 100 or so plants in the industry account for less than 3.5 percent of industry employment and 2.5 percent of industry output.

[33] This approach may create a chicken-and-the-egg problem: do relatively large firms form different conjectures because they are large, or are they large because they form different conjectures?

second and fourth largest firms expected the largest firm to duplicate their actions: each believed that when it increased its output, the largest firm would increase its output by the same amount.

While the largest firm expected the smallest firms to follow its lead and expand their output levels when it did, other firms maintained Cournot conjectural variations with respect to the smallest firms. That is, both medium and small firms expected small firms' output to remain unchanged when they varied their own output levels. Thus, only the largest firm expected all others to change their output levels in response to its actions.

Statistical tests do not reject the hypothesis that all firms (except the largest) expected other firms to react identically to their actions. That is, nonleading firms expected all other nonleading firms to react the same way to their actions, but they expected the largest firm to react differently.

To summarize, these studies indicate that neither the Japanese window glass producers nor the American coffee roasters acted like competitive, or Bertrand, firms, though Japanese polished plate glass producers may have been price-takers. The best estimate is that Japanese window glass producers had a price markup above marginal cost, somewhere between the Cournot-Nash and the collusive levels. Not all American coffee roasters set quantities at the Cournot-Nash level, although some firms may have set quantities in this manner. It is possible that the largest coffee roaster acted like a Stackelberg leader.

■ SUMMARY

Although most economists agree about the basic characteristics of oligopolistic markets, they do not agree about the best way to model these markets. Many noncooperative oligopoly models make very different assumptions about how firms behave; as a result, they make very different predictions about the nature of the equilibrium. A few conclusions can be drawn, however.

First, collusive outcomes are more likely in markets that last indefinitely than those that exist for only a short period of time. Experimental evidence supports the conclusion that collusion is most likely to occur in repeated games. Explicit contact between the firms increases the probability of successful collusion.

Second, most models, except the Bertrand (single-period, Nash-in-prices) model, predict that the more firms in the industry, the more competitive is the equilibrium. The Bertrand model in which firms have constant marginal costs predicts the competitive equilibrium, regardless of the number of firms.

Third, although the conjectural variations version of the Cournot model makes arbitrary assumptions and is otherwise theoretically flawed, the Cournot-Nash equilibrium can be justified on the basis of more reasonable game-theoretic models. Moreover, existing experimental and empirical evidence indicates that the Cournot equilibrium is often (but not always) observed, especially in games lasting few periods. This evidence and the relative ease of using the model explain its continuing popularity.

Fourth, the reemergence of game theory has led to a better understanding of when strategies are credible to other firms. Research is ongoing to restrict the number of possible equilibria that can occur in multiperiod games with and without uncertainty.

All models in this chapter assume that firms maximize their profits by setting their expected marginal revenues equal to their marginal costs. The models differ only in the way in which firms calculate their expected marginal revenues. The next chapter extends these models to include product differentiation and the entry of new firms.

■ Key Terms

Bayesian perfect equilibrium
Bertrand model
best-response function
conjecture
conjectural variation
Cournot model
credible strategies (or threats)
Edgeworth model

folk theorem
game
multiperiod games
Nash equilibrium
noncooperative oligopoly
payoff
players
profit possibility frontier

prisoner's dilemma game
refinement
Stackelberg model
strategies
subgame perfect Nash equilibrium
supergames

■ Discussion Questions

1. What types of markets would you expect to be oligopolistic and why?
2. In what types of markets do oligopolists collude, and when do they act noncooperatively?
3. Under what circumstances does it *not* pay for a firm to try to collude with other firms in a repeated game? (*Hint:* consider the number of firms, interest rates, and the number of times the game will be repeated.)

4. What evidence from the real world would cause you to choose one of the oligopoly models over the others?
5. Should the government regulate noncooperative oligopoly to promote efficiency? If so, should it regulate price, number of firms, or something else?

■ Problems

1. Under what conditions are the Cournot and Bertrand equilibria the same?
2. In the examples in this chapter, fixed costs were assumed to be zero and marginal (average) costs were constant. What additional complications are raised in each of the conjectural variations models if the cost functions have the usual U-shape?
3. What are the best strategies for Players 1 and 2 if the payoffs in Table 10.4 are changed so that the payoff is zero for all combinations of strategies except that in which both firms charge the high price, when the payoff to each is 5?
4. What happens to price and output in each of the con-

jectural variations models if marginal costs increase by 10 percent?
5. For $n = 2, 5, 10, 50$, and 1000, add columns to Table 10.3 for:
   a. Market elasticity, ϵ, which equals $(dQ/dp)/(p/Q)$.
   b. Lerner's measure of market power, $(p - MC)/p$.
   c. Consumer surplus.
   d. Social welfare = consumer surplus + industry profits.
   e. Deadweight loss (the amount by which social welfare is less than the optimum).
   Confirm that Lerner's measure of market power, $(p - MC)/p$, equals $1/(n\epsilon)$.

Answers to the odd-numbered problems are given at the back of the book.

■ Suggested Readings

For a clear presentation of traditional oligopoly models and an introduction to game theory that is only slightly more technical than this textbook, see Shubik with Levitan (1980), Friedman (1983), and Ulph (1987). For a good, relatively nontechnical discussion of how to solve simple games, see Williams (1966). Two short surveys of dynamic game issues are Kreps and Spence (1984) and Fudenberg and Tirole (1986). Some of the more useful, relatively technical textbooks on game theory are Luce and Raiffa (1957), Shubik (1982 and 1984), Friedman (1977, 1986), and Tirole (1988). Some of the most important recent game theory papers that were not discussed in the chapter include Harsanyi (1967–1968), Bernheim (1984), and Pearce (1984). For a thorough survey of modern empirical evidence on oligopolistic behavior, see Bresnahan (1989).

■ References

Allen, Beth, and Martin Hellwig. 1986. "Bertrand-Edgeworth Oligopoly in Large Markets." *The Review of Economic Studies* 53:175–204.

Aumann, Robert. 1973. "Disadvantageous Monopolies." *Journal of Economic Theory* 6:1–11.

Bernheim, B. Douglas. 1984. "Rationalizable Strategic Behavior." *Econometrica* 52:1007–28.

Bowley, Arthur L. 1924. *The Mathematical Groundwork of Economics*. Oxford: Oxford University Press.

Bramness, Gunnar. 1979. "The General Conjectural Model of Oligopoly—Some Classical Points Revisited." Warwick Economic Research Paper Number 142.

Bresnahan, Timothy F. 1981. "Duopoly Models with Consistent Conjectures." *American Economic Review* 71:934–45.

———. 1989. "Empirical Studies of Industries with Market Power," in Richard Schmalensee and Robert Willig, eds., *Handbook of Industrial Organization*. New York: Elsevier Science Publishing Co., Inc.

Cournot, Augustin A. 1963. *Researches into the Mathematical Principles of the Theory of Wealth*. Trans. Nathaniel T. Bacon. Homewood, Ill.: Richard D. Irwin.

Dasguta, P., and Eric Maskin. 1986. "The Existence of Equilibrium in Discontinuous Economic Games, I: Theory, and II: Applications." *The Review of Economic Studies* 53:1–26 and 27–42.

Daughety, Andrew F. 1985. "Reconsidering Cournot: the Cournot equilibrium Is Consistent." *The Rand Journal of Economics* 16:368–79.

Eaton, B. Curtis, and Roger Ware. 1987. "A Theory of Market Structure with Sequential Entry." *Rand Journal of Economics* 18:1–16.

Fellner, William J. 1949. *Competition among the Few*. New York: Alfred A. Knopf.

Fouraker, Lawrence, and Signey Siegel. 1963. *Bargaining Behavior*. New York: McGraw-Hill.

Friedman, James W. 1967. "An Experimental Study of Cooperative Duopoly." *Econometrica* 35:1979–97.

———. 1977. *Oligopoly and the Theory of Games*. Amsterdam: North-Holland.

———. 1983. *Oligopoly Theory*, Cambridge: Cambridge University Press.

———. 1986. *Game Theory with Applications to Economics*. Oxford: Oxford University Press.

Fudenberg, Drew, and Eric Maskin. 1986. "The Folk Theorem in Repeated Games with Discounting and with Incomplete Information." *Econometrica* 54:533–54.

Fudenberg, Drew, and Jean Tirole. 1986. *Dynamic Models of Oligopoly*. London: Harwood Academic Publishers.

Gollop, Frank M., and Mark J. Roberts. 1979. "Firm Interdependence in Oligopolistic Markets." *Journal of Econometrics* 10:313–31.

Grossman, Sanford J. 1981. "Nash Equilibrium and the Industrial Organization of Markets with Large Fixed Costs." *Econometrica* 49:1149–72.

Hall, R.L., and C.J. Hitch. 1939. "Price Theory and Business Behavior." *Oxford Economic Papers* 2:12–45.

Harsanyi, John C. 1967–1968. "Games with Incomplete Information Played by Bayesian Players." *Management Science* 14:159–82, 320–34, and 486–502.

Holt, Charles A., Jr. 1985. "An Experimental Test of the Consistent-Conjectures Hypothesis." *American Economic Review* 75:314–25.

Iwata, Gyoichi. 1974. "Measurement of Conjectural Variations in Oligopoly." *Econometrica* 42:947–66.

Kamien, Morton I., and Nancy L. Schwartz. 1983. "Conjectural Variations." *The Canadian Journal of Economics* 41:191–211.

Karp, Larry S., and Jeffrey M. Perloff. 1988. "Open-Loop and Feedback Models of Dynamic Oligopoly." Giannini Foundation Working Paper No. 472, University of California at Berkeley.

———. Forthcoming. "Dynamic Oligopoly in the Rice Export Market." *Review of Economics and Statistics*.

Kreps, David M., and Robert Wilson. 1982a. "Reputation and Imperfect Information." *Journal of Economic Theory* 27: 253–79.

———. 1982b. "Sequential Equilibrium." *Econometrica* 50:863–94.

Kreps, David M., and José Scheinkman. 1983. "Quality Precommitment and Bertrand Competition Yield Cournot Outcomes." *Bell Journal of Economics* 14:326–37.

Kreps, David M., and A. Michael Spence. 1984. "Modelling the Role of History in Industrial Organization," in George Feiwel, ed., *Contemporary Issues in Modern Microeconomics*. London: Macmillan.

Laitner, John. 1980. "'Rational' Duopoly Equilibria." *Quarterly Journal of Economics* 95: 641–62.

Lave, Lester B. 1962. "An Empirical Approach to the Prisoners' Dilemma Game." *Quarterly Journal of Economics* 75:424–36.

Luce, R. Duncan, and Howard Raiffa. 1957. *Games and Decisions*. New York: John Wiley and Sons.

McLellan, Vin. 1971. "Harvard Square: War of the Xerox Machines." *The Phoenix*, February 9.

Nash, John F. 1951. "Non-Cooperative Games." *Annuals of Mathematics* 54:286–95.

Neuman, John von, and Oskar Morgenstern. 1944. *Theory of Games and Economic Behavior*. Princeton: Princeton University Press.

Okuno, Masahiro, Andrew Postlewaite, and John Roberts. 1980. "Oligopoly and Competition in Large Markets." *American Economic Review* 70:22–31.

Patinkin, Don. 1947. "Multiple-Plant Firms, Cartels, and Imperfect Competition." *Quarterly Journal of Economics* 61:173–205.

Pearce, David G. 1984. "Rationalizable Strategic Behavior and the Problem of Perfection." *Econometrica* 52:1029–50.

Perry, Martin K. 1982. "Oligopoly and Consistent Conjectural Variations." *Bell Journal of Economics and Management* 13:197–205.

Plott, Charles R. 1982. "Industrial Organization Theory and Experimental Economics." *Journal of Economic Literature* 20:1485–1527.

Pulliam, H. Ronald, Graham H. Pyke, and Thomas Caraco. 1982. "The Scanning Behavior of Juncos: A Game-theoretical Approach." *Journal of Theoretical Biology* 95:89–103.

Salant, Steve, Sheldon Switzer, and Robert Reynolds. 1983. "Losses from Horizontal Merger: The Effects of an Exogenous Change in Industry Structure on Cournot-Nash Equilibrium." *Quarterly Journal of Economics* 98:185–99.

Selten, Reinhard. 1975. "Reexamination of the Perfectness Concept for Equilibrium Points in Extensive Games." *International Journal of Game Theory* 4:25–55.

———. 1978. "The Chain Store Paradox." *Theory and Decisions* 9:127–159.

Shapiro, Leonard. 1980. "Decentralized Dynamics in Duopoly with Pareto Optimal Outcomes." *Bell Journal of Economics* 11:730–44.

Shubik, Martin. 1959. *Strategy and Market Structure*. New York: John Wiley and Sons.

———. 1982 (vol. 1), and 1984 (vol. 2). *A Game Theory in the Social Sciences*. Cambridge, Mass.: MIT Press.

Shubik, Martin, with Richard Levitan. 1980. *Market Structure and Behavior*. Cambridge, Mass.: Harvard University Press.

Stackelberg, Heinrich von. 1934. *Marktform und gleichgewicht*. Vienna: Julius Springer. Reprinted in *The Theory of the Market Economy*. Trans. A.T. Peacock. London: William Hodge, 1952.

Stigler, George J. 1947. "The Kinky Oligopoly Demand Curve and Rigid Prices." *Journal of Political Economy*. 55:432–49.

———. 1964. "A Theory of Oligopoly." *Journal of Political Economy* 72:55–59.

Sweezy, Paul M. 1939. "Demand under Conditions of Oligopoly." *Journal of Political Economy* 47:568–73.

Telser, Lester G. 1972. *Competition, Collusion and Game Theory*. Chicago: Aldine-Atherton.

Tirole, Jean. 1988. *The Theory of Industrial Organization*. Cambridge, Mass.: MIT Press.

Ulph, Alistair. 1987. "Recent Advances in Oligopoly Theory from a Game Theory Perspective." *Journal of Economic Surveys* 1:149–72.

Williams, J.D. 1966. *The Compleat Strategyst*. New York: McGraw-Hill.

A Mathematical Derivation of Cournot and Stackelberg Equilibria

This appendix uses calculus to derive the Cournot and Stackelberg equilibria prices and quantities. Both general functional forms and a linear example are used.

Assume that there are n firms, and the number of firms is exogenously determined. The output of the ith firm is q_i, while total output is the sum of the (homogeneous) output of each firm: $Q = \Sigma q_i$. The demand and cost functions appear in the following table:

	General Functional Form	Linear Example
Market demand	$P(Q)$	$p = a - (a/b)\,Q$
Firm's cost	$c(q_i)$	$c(q_i) = mq_i$

In the example, demand is linear and marginal cost is constant.

For the sake of comparison, the competitive and monopoly solutions are:

	General Functional Form	Linear Example
Competition	$c'(q_i) = p(Q)$	$m = p = a - (a/b)\,Q$
	$[MC = p]$	$Q = (b/a)\,(a - m)$
Monopoly	$c'(Q) = p'(Q)Q + p(Q)$	$m = a - (2a/b)\,Q$
	$[MC = MR]$	$Q = (b/[2a])\,(a - m)$
		$p = 0.5\,(a + m)$

To analyze a Cournot industry, one starts by examining the behavior of a representative firm. Firm 1 tries to maximize its profits through its choice of q_1:

$$\max_{q_1} \pi_i(q_1, q_2, \ldots, q_n) = q_1\, p(q_1 + \ldots + q_n) - c(q_1). \qquad (10A.1)$$

The first-order condition is $[MR = MC]$:

$$p(q_1 + \ldots + q_n) + q_1 p'(q_1 + \ldots + q_n) \times$$
$$\left(1 + \frac{\partial q_2}{\partial q_1} + \ldots + \frac{\partial q_n}{\partial q_1}\right) = c'(q_1), \qquad (10A.2)$$

where the $\partial q_i / \partial q_1$ terms in the brackets are the conjectural variations (how much the output of the ith firm changes as the first firm's output shifts). If Firm 1 forms Cournot conjectural variations, these partial derivatives are all zero: firm 1 believes that the output of the other firms will remain constant. Thus, the first-order condition may be rewritten as follows:

$$p(q_1 + \ldots + q_n) + q_1 p'(q_1 + \ldots + q_n) = c'(q_1). \qquad (10A.3)$$

Rearranging terms in Equation 10A.3, multiplying and dividing the right-hand side by n, and noting that $p' = dp/dQ$ and $Q = nq_1$ (given that all firms are identical), one obtains

$$\frac{p - c'}{p} = -\frac{1}{n} \frac{1}{dQ/dp} \frac{Q}{p} = \frac{1}{n\epsilon}, \qquad (10A.3')$$

where the second equality holds because the elasticity of market demand, ϵ, is defined as $-(dQ/dp)(p/Q)$. The left-hand-side of Equation 10A.3' is Lerner's measure of market power: the price markup over marginal cost as a fraction of price. If the market is competitive, then $p = c'$, and Lerner's measure is zero. The larger the measure, the greater the market power. With symmetric firms, the elasticity facing any one firm is $n\epsilon$. Notice that, holding market elasticity constant, as the number of firms increases, Lerner's measure must fall. As n approaches ∞, the elasticity facing any one firm approaches ∞, so Lerner's measure $= 0 = 1/\infty$, and the market is competitive.

Equation 10A.3 shows how the profit-maximizing q_1 depends upon $q_2, \ldots, q_n$. One can rearrange this expression, solving for q_1, to derive firm 1's best-response function:

$$q_1 = R_1(q_2, \ldots, q_n). \qquad (10A.3)$$

In the case of the linear example (and assuming $n = 2$), the first-order condition for profit maximization (10A.2) is:

$$a - \frac{a}{b}(2q_1 + q_2) = m. \qquad (10A.4)$$

Solving this expression for q_1, the best-response function (10A.3) is

$$q_1 = R_1(q_2) = \frac{b}{2a}(a - m) - \frac{1}{2}q_2. \qquad (10A.5)$$

More generally, with n firms, if all the other firms produce at the same output level ($q_i = q$), Firm 1's best-response function is:

$$q_1 = R_1(q_2, \ldots, q_n) = \frac{b}{2a}(a - m) - \frac{n-1}{2}q. \qquad (10A.6)$$

The Cournot equilibrium occurs where the best-response functions intersect. In the example, that occurs where $q_1 = q = q_i$ ($i = 2, \ldots, n$). Setting $q_1 = q$ in Equation

10A.6 and solving for the resulting q gives

$$q = \frac{b}{a}\frac{a-m}{n+1}.$$ (10A.7)

The corresponding price (substituting $Q = nq$ into the demand function) is

$$p = \frac{1}{n+1}(a + nm).$$ (10A.8)

Setting $n = 1$ in the last two equations yields the monopoly quantity and price. As n becomes extremely large, the quantity and price approach the competitive levels. That is, from Equation 10A.7, as n grows large, total output, nq, approaches $(a - m)b/a$; and from Equation 10A.8, price approaches m. Similarly, using Equation 10A.8, Lerner's measure of market power, $(p - c')/p$, may be written as $(a - m)/(a + nm)$. As n grows large, the denominator goes to ∞, so Lerner's measure goes to 0, and there is no market power.

A Stackelberg leader (say, Firm 1) takes the Cournot best-response functions of the follower firms as given. In the example, each follower's best-response function is analogous to Equation 10A.6:

$$q_i = \frac{b}{a}\frac{a-m}{n} - \frac{q_1}{n}, \quad i = 2, \ldots, n.$$ (10A.9)

The leader firm maximizes its profits, taking the best-response functions of the followers as given. The first-order condition for profit maximization is given in Equation 10A.2. We can determine the leader firm's (correct) conjectural variations by differentiating Equation 10A.9 with respect to q_1, to obtain $dq_i/dq_1 = -1/n$. That is, for every unit the leader firm's output rises, a typical follower firm's output falls by $1/n$, so the followers' collective output falls by $(n - 1)/n$. Substituting the conjectural variations and the linear demand curve expression for p into Equation 10A.2 and solving for q_1, one obtains

$$q_1 = \frac{b}{a}\frac{a-m}{2},$$ (10A.10)

while the output for the other firms ($i = 2, \ldots, n$) is

$$q_i = \frac{b}{a}\frac{a-m}{2n}.$$ (10A.11)

Thus, $q_1 > q_i$ for any number of firms.

The corresponding price is

$$p = \frac{a + m(2n - 1)}{2n}.$$ (10A.12)

Again, as the number of firms, n, grows large, price and total quantity approach the competitive levels.

THE KINKED DEMAND CURVE MODEL

One other well-known model of oligopoly behavior that can be viewed as a conjectural variations model is the *kinked demand curve model* (Bramness 1979). Two versions of the model were developed independently and virtually simultaneously by Hall and Hitch (1939) and by Sweezy (1939).

In Sweezy's version, an oligopolist believes its rivals quickly match price reductions but follow price increases only slowly and incompletely. The resulting residual demand curve, which has a kink in it at the current price, p_0, is shown in the figure on page 307. The corresponding marginal revenue curve is discontinuous at the quantity corresponding to the current price, q_0, as shown. Since marginal cost curves could shift substantially and yet still intersect this marginal revenue curve in its vertical region, only large fluctuations in marginal cost alter output and price. This model has been used to explain why prices and output remain unchanged in the face of changes in supply conditions.

There have been many attempts to test the implications of this theory empirically. Stigler (1947) finds no asymmetry in the reaction of oligopolists to price changes by rivals. The theory predicts that there will be no kink (the prices become more flexible) when the oligopolists explicitly collude. Stigler's evidence contradicts this hypothesis. The theory also predicts that very large shifts in costs will cause prices to change while small shifts will not. Again, Stigler finds no evidence to support this prediction.

The theory has other problems as well. Most importantly, it does not explain how the initial price, p_0, and output, q_0, are determined. It is much more an explanation of why the status quo will persist than of how it was determined. Thus, while this theory was very popular in the two decades following its introduction, it is of limited importance today.

Kinked Demand Curve Model

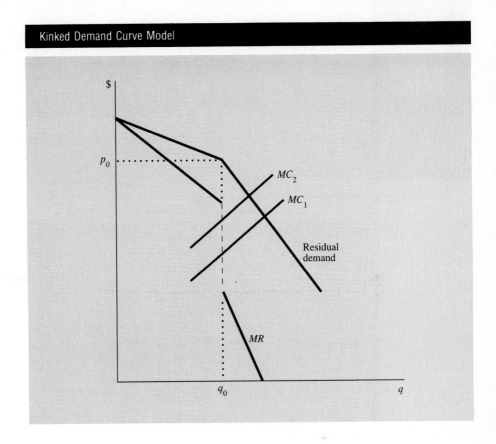

APPENDIX

10C

CONSISTENT CONJECTURES

One major objection to the conjectural variations models is that firms maintain false conjectures about their rivals' behavior during periods of adjustment. Recently, several economists have argued that if firms are to believe a given conjectural variation, it must be consistent with observed behavior (Laitner 1980, Bresnahan 1981, Perry 1982, and Kamien and Schwartz 1983). A firm's conjecture is consistent if a rival behaves as predicted at the equilibrium *and* near the equilibrium.[1]

In all the conjectural variations models, each firm's conjectures are correct at the equilibrium. For example, in equilibrium, a Cournot firm expects other firms to hold their output constant at the current level and, indeed, they produce at that level. A Bertrand firm expects its rivals to hold their prices constant, and in equilibrium they do so. In equilibrium each firm's beliefs about the *level* of all other firms' actions are correct.

Outside of equilibrium—when firms are adjusting their behavior while approaching equilibrium—their conjectures may be false. Why should a firm maintain a conjecture that is proven false repeatedly? Only if it is myopic and ignores all evidence that contradicts its beliefs will it maintain such conjectures. Thus, if firms are rational, their conjectures must be consistent with reality outside of equilibrium as well as at equilibrium. A model with consistent conjectures requires that a firm have correct beliefs about the *level* of other firms' actions and the *relationship of other firms' actions to its own*.

To illustrate this approach, one can formally derive a special case of a consistent-conjecture duopoly equilibrium and show, for that case, that the Bertrand equilibrium is a consistent-conjecture equilibrium. As in other conjectural variations models, Firm 1 has a conjecture, r_1, about how much Firm 2 will change its output in response to a small change in Firm 1's output, $r_1 = dq_2/dq_1$. Similarly, Firm 2 holds a conjecture about Firm 1, $r_2 = dq_1/dq_2$. This example makes three important assumptions:

1. The two firms produce homogeneous products.
2. Their marginal costs are constant at c.

---

[1] Most articles discuss the consistency of conjectures near the equilibrium. That is, they do not require that firms be able to predict how rivals would respond to large changes in behavior—just small ones. Thus, these articles normally only require that conjectures be consistent *locally* about the equilibrium.

3. The firms have identical, constant conjectures, $r_1 = r_2 = r$. That is, each firm's conjecture about the other firm's behavior, r, does not vary with the output levels, q_1 and q_2.

Suppose that the first firm's conjectural variation about the second firm's behavior is $r = -1$. That is, the first firm believes that if it raises its output by 1 unit, the second firm will reduce its output by 1 unit, so that total output to the industry stays constant. This conjecture is equivalent to the standard Bertrand conjecture, because if total output remains unchanged, price remains unchanged. That is, if the first firm believes that the second firm will not change its price, then it must also believe that the second firm will vary its output in a way that exactly offsets changes in the first firm's output.

If both firms hold these Bertrand expectations and both have marginal and average costs equal to c, then the resulting equilibrium is consistent. To show this consistency, one first calculates the best-response functions and shows that the slope of Firm 2's best-response function is identical to Firm 1's conjecture (and similarly for Firm 1's best-response function and Firm 2's conjecture).

Let $p(q_1 + q_2)$ be the inverse demand curve that tells us what the market price is for total output $q = q_1 + q_2$. Firm 1 must decide how much to produce given its conjecture about Firm 2. The problem facing Firm 1 is to choose q_1 so as to maximize its profits:

$$\pi = p(q_1 + q_2) q_1 - mq_1, \tag{10C.1}$$

where the first term on the right-hand-side is Firm 1's total revenues and the second term is its total costs. Maximizing 10C.1 with respect to q_1 shows that Firm 1's profit-maximizing output is determined by setting its marginal revenue equal to its marginal cost:

$$p'(q_1 + q_2) (1 + r) q_1 + p(q_1 + q_2) - m = 0, \tag{10C.2}$$

where $p'(q_1 + q_2)$ is the change in price as quantity changes and Firm 1 calculates its marginal revenue taking into account its conjecture, r. Given its Bertrand conjecture $(r = -1)$, its marginal revenue is just p, because $(1 + r)$, which multiplies the first term in Equation 10C.2, equals zero, so that Equation 10C.2 can be rewritten as:

$$p(q_1 + q_2) - m = 0 \tag{10C.3}$$

As shown earlier in this chapter, in the Bertrand equilibrium, price equals marginal cost.

Equation 10C.3 defines Firm 1's best-response function: For any given q_2, q_1 is chosen so that market price equals marginal cost, m. Totally differentiating this equation with respect to q_1 and q_2 shows that this rule implies that $dq_1/dq_2 = -1$. That is, the slope of Firm 1's best-response function is -1, which exactly equals Firm 2's conjecture $(r = -1)$. Thus, in this example, the Bertrand equilibrium is a consistent-conjecture equilibrium; each firm's conjecture equals the slope of the other firm's reaction function. In other words, each firm's prediction of the other firm's behavior is correct.

If, instead, the firms hold Cournot conjectures $(r = 0)$, Firm 1's marginal revenue would be $p'q_1 + p$, so that its profit-maximizing output is determined by (rewriting Equation 10C.2

$$p'(q_1 + q_2) q_1 + p(q_1 + q_2) - c = 0. \tag{10C.4}$$

Equation 10C.4 determines Firm 1's reaction function. By totally differentiating this equation, one finds that the slope of Firm 1's Cournot reaction function is

$$\frac{dq_1}{dq_2} = -\frac{p''(q_1 + q_2) \; q_1 + p'(q_1 + q_2)}{p''(q_1 + q_2) \; q_1 + 2p'(q_1 + q_2)}. \tag{10C.5}$$

For virtually any demand curve, the slope of Firm 1's reaction function does not equal zero. That is, the Cournot equilibrium is generally not a consistent-conjecture equilibrium. The Cournot example in the chapter shows that Firm 1 believes that Firm 2 will not change its output level as Firm 1 increases its output by 10 melons; yet Firm 2 will produce 5 fewer melons.

Thus, given that the number of firms is fixed, demand is linear, and conjectures do not vary with output:

- With constant marginal costs, competitive (Bertrand) behavior is consistent.[2]
- With rising marginal costs, the consistent conjectural variation equilibrium lies between competitive and Cournot behavior.

No constant conjectural variation is consistent for all demand and cost functions. Firms could maintain conjectural variations that vary, say, with total industry output. These consistent-conjecture functions depend on the shapes of the demand and cost curves (Kamien and Schwartz 1983, 198–201).

The appeal of the consistent-conjecture equilibrium is that firms' conjectures about how rivals will behave are correct (locally) and realized. Moreover, with linear demand and constant marginal cost, there is only one constant consistent conjecture (Bresnahan 1981). Without these conditions, many conjectural variation equilibria are possible (Kamien and Schwartz 1983).

Serious problems exist with this approach, however. Such an equilibrium does not exist for many simple models. For example, in the model just examined, if the cost curves of the duopolists are quadratic, no constant consistent-conjecture equilibrium exists. Further, the appeal of consistent conjectures is illusory. Consistent conjectures is an equilibrium concept for a static model, in which firms have no uncertainty about anything except their rivals' behavior. Yet, the justification for this model is that firms' beliefs are confirmed outside of equilibrium. For this justification to be attractive, the departures from equilibrium should be part of the model. One solution would be to make the model dynamic or have it involve uncertainty.[3]

---

[2] Perry (1982) shows that if free entry is allowed (as discussed in the next chapter), then only competitive behavior is consistent.

[3] A linear-quadratic dynamic model can partially justify the static consistent-conjecture model (Karp and Perloff 1988).

CHAPTER 11

PRODUCT DIFFERENTIATION AND MONOPOLISTIC COMPETITION

 Good taste is better than bad taste, but bad taste is better than no taste.[1]

In many markets, firms have *market power,* the ability to raise price above marginal cost, yet the firms make zero economic profits, as in a competitive industry. Such a market structure is called **monopolistic competition,** because it combines attributes of both monopoly and competition.

An industry is monopolistically competitive if there is *free entry* and each firm faces a *downward sloping demand.* If firms enter the industry whenever positive profits are available, each firm makes zero economic profits in the long run, as in a competitive industry. If a firm faces a downward sloping demand curve, it has some market power: its price is higher than its marginal cost.

The monopolistic competition models analyzed in this chapter differ from Chapter 10's oligopoly models in two ways. First, whereas the oligopoly models assume entry is impossible, firms are now free to enter and exit the market. Thus, in this chapter, the number of firms is determined within the model by entry behavior, rather than arbitrarily determined outside of the model as in the oligopoly chapter. Second, whereas the oligopoly models in Chapter 10 assume all firms produce identical products, now products may differ across firms.[2]

Product *heterogeneity,* or *differentiation,* has two important effects. First, product differentiation can lead to market power. When consumers view brands in an industry as imperfect substitutes, a firm may raise its price above that of its rivals without losing all its customers. That is, product differentiation causes a firm's residual demand curve to be downward sloping, rather than flat as for a competitive firm that produces

---

[1] Arnold Bennett. 1930. "Sayings of the Week." *Observer,* August 24.

[2] Most oligopolistic markets have heterogeneous products. This heterogeneity was ignored in the previous chapter for simplicity only. Most of the analysis of differentiation in this chapter may be applied to the oligopoly models directly.

a homogeneous good. Second, consumers value product differentiation. In the models of Chapter 10, in which firms produced homogeneous goods, an increase in the number of oligopolists benefited consumers because the additional competition led to lower prices. If firms produce differentiated products, the entry of a new firm helps consumers for two reasons: it lowers prices and increases the variety of products from which to choose.

Both these effects are illustrated in models of monopolistic competition. There are two major types of monopolistically competitive models with free entry and differentiated products. In one, the *representative consumer model,* all firms compete equally for all consumers. This model might be used to study the sporting goods market, in which firms produce differentiated products, but all compete for the same customers.

In the other, the spatial or location model, each consumer prefers products that have certain characteristics and is willing to pay more for them than for products that lack some or all of those characteristics. For example, a consumer whose favorite cereal is Kellogg's corn flakes is more sensitive to the relative price of Post's corn flakes than to the relative price of Nabisco's shreaded wheat. The other brand of corn flakes is a much better substitute than another type of cereal.

These models differ in the type of demand each firm faces. In the representative consumer model, a firm's demand varies continuously with the prices of all firms. A small change in any one firm's price causes a relatively small change in the demand facing a firm. In the location model, as the cereal example suggests, the demand for one brand may be independent of some other brands' prices because they are not close substitutes. Moreover, a firm may, at some very low price, gain a large number of extra consumers as it captures all the customers of another firm that produces a very similar product.

Either model can be used to study the welfare of consumers and firms, by comparing the monopolistically competitive equilibrium to the social optimum in terms of price and variety. The analysis in the oligopoly chapter has shown that, when firms face downward sloping demand curves, price is above marginal cost, so there is inefficiency in the amount produced. That is, total output is too low in a monopolistically competitive industry. This chapter, however, also asks whether there are too many or two few brands in the monopolistically competitive equilibrium.

The answer to this question depends on how much more consumers are willing to pay for more variety. Which would you prefer: a choice of three different soft drinks at 50¢ per drink or only one flavor at 25¢? The answers to such questions determine the optimal variety-price combination. Neither too much variety (with its associated high price) nor too little variety (with its associated low price) is desirable.

The first section of this chapter explains why product differentiation affects the residual demand curve facing a firm. Then the two most widely used models of monopolistic competition are discussed. Representative consumer models of a monopolistically competitive industry with both homogeneous and heterogeneous products are examined. The discussion shows how the homogeneous product, Cournot-Nash oligopoly model presented in the previous chapter changes when free entry is allowed and then describes how the equilibrium price in this model compares to the social optimum. Next, the model is modified to allow for product differentiation, and price and variety in the monopolistically competitive equilibrium are compared to the optimal combination.

The discussion then turns to a location model. Product differentiation is inherent in location models, so no homogeneous product model is presented. Again, the welfare implications are examined. Finally, hybrid models that have elements of both models are used to explain why these two types of models have different properties.

■ DIFFERENTIATED PRODUCTS

In previous chapters, we have concentrated on industries with **homogeneous** or **undifferentiated** goods. Consumers view the products of all the firms in these industries as identical; that is, the products are *perfect substitutes* for each other. In industries with small numbers of firms, however, products are typically **heterogeneous** or **differentiated.** Consumers consider different products or brands to be close but not perfect substitutes. For example, most consumers consider various wines to be imperfect substitutes for each other.

The study of an industry of differentiated products is based on two key concepts:

- Products are differentiated because consumers *think* they differ. That is, even though aspirin brands may be chemically identical, if consumers believe that the products differ and shop accordingly, then for all effects and purposes, the products are differentiated. Conversely, if consumers view chemically or physically different products as identical, then for economic purposes they are homogeneous. "The consumer is always right." See Examples 11.1 (page 314) and 11.2 (pages 316 and 317).

- Whether various products constrain each other's pricing or not depends on how close substitutes they are. For example, few would dispute that Pepsi and Coke are close substitutes, because they are both colas. Indeed, Canada Dry Ginger Ale may also compete with Coke and Pepsi, because they are all soft drinks with sugar. But are soft drinks without sugar close substitutes? What about noncarbonated drinks like milk?[3]

An example of a competitive market with homogeneous products is wheat: no consumer would ask which farm produced a particular bushel of wheat. It is harder to think of industries with a small number of firms whose products consumers view as perfectly identical, but there are a number of industries whose products consumers may view as nearly identical. For example, delivery firms or plumbing supply firms in a city may be viewed as quite similar. Typically, an industry has a relatively homogeneous product if consumers do not care about brand names.

---

[3] The definition of a market is often a crucial issue in antitrust and merger cases (see Chapters 7 and 22). Often, expert witnesses in these cases contend that if products are "close substitutes," they are part of the same *market*. Throughout this book, unless otherwise noted, the term *market* is used loosely, without reference to legal definitions. This chapter assumes each firm's product is in the market being discussed, in the sense that at least some consumers view it as a substitute for at least some other products in the market. That is, it assumes the products are "adequately close" substitutes without defining what "adequately close" means.

EXAMPLE 11.1

SPURIOUS PRODUCT DIFFERENTIATION: A DRUG ON THE MARKET

Consumers often believe that similar products differ in quality even when the products are physically identical. Some economists say such goods have *spurious product differentiation*. An example commonly offered is over-the-counter drugs.

For example, a consumer may form a false belief that one aspirin brand is superior to another after it relieves a mild headache and the (chemically identical) so-called inferior brand does not relieve a more serious one. Experiments show that even a placebo achieves a headache relief rate of about 45 percent compared to a relief rate of around 80 percent for actual aspirin. For some people, headaches go away by themselves, or the psychological effect of a placebo is sufficient to relieve their headaches. Of course, if a consumer believes that a product is more effective and that belief indeed makes the product work better (the placebo effect), then it is not appropriate to call this product differentiation "spurious."

Chemical tests of different aspirin brands indicate that they are virtually identical in aspirin content and rate of dissolution. Indeed, the judge in the Federal Trade Commission's case against the makers of Bayer aspirin who claimed that Bayer was the best aspirin (being faster and gentler) concluded that Bayer was neither qualitatively nor therapeutically superior. Yet consumers apparently believe Bayer's claims. Although there are more than 400 brands of plain aspirin, Bayer is the best selling, even though it is relatively expensive.

Similar examples exist for many drugs. The manufacturer of the well-known name brand claims that its drug is safer or more effective, perhaps because of better filler materials or stricter quality control. Comparative studies, however, often fail to find these quality differences. Nonetheless, the name brand sells at prices much higher than those of generic brands. For example, Consumers Union found that Tylenol No. 3 costs 2.2 times as much as generic acetaminophen with codeine. Valium sells for 3.2 times as much as its generic equivalent, diazepam. On the other hand, at least in the San Francisco area, Amoxil (an antibiotic for infections) sells for only 1 percent more than its generic substitute.

Experiments have been conducted to determine if consumers' buying decisions are based on name recognition and not the product itself. Blind tests of consumers' preferences after use do not replicate market shares. In addition, the experimental market shares vary according to whether products are labeled with brand names. That is, consumers cannot always tell similar products apart and would not buy one product instead of another in the absence of brand names.

SOURCES: Food and Drug Administration. 1977. "Proposed Monograph for OTC Internal Analgesic, Antipyretic, and Antirheumatic Products," *Federal Register* 42 (July 8): 353–82; Consumers Union. 1982. "Is Bayer Better?" *Consumer Reports* 47 (July): 347–49; Consumers Union. 1987. "The Big Lie About Generic Drugs," *Consumer Reports* 52 (August): 480–85; Center for the Study of Services. 1988. "Prescription Drugs," *Bay Area Consumers' Checkbook* 43 (Summer): 37–41; McConnell (1968); and Monroe (1976).

There are two approaches to analyzing differentiation. In the standard consumer theory of basic microeconomics books, consumers have preferences regarding commodities; they choose between ice cream and cake, or perhaps between brands of ice cream and cake. In the new consumer theory, discussed here, consumers have preferences regarding the attributes, or characteristics, of commodities. For example, some consumers love chocolate, a characteristic of some ice creams and cakes. These consumers prefer either chocolate ice cream or chocolate cake to vanilla ice cream or white cake.

The Effect of Differentiation on a Firm's Residual Demand Curve

A cynic is a man who knows the price of everything, and the value of nothing.
OSCAR WILDE

In industries with undifferentiated products, the residual demand facing a particular firm depends only on the total supply of its rivals, whereas in an industry with differentiated products, the residual demand facing a firm depends on the supply of each of its competitors separately. For industries with either differentiated or undifferentiated goods, we can write the inverse residual demand curve facing firm i as:

$$p_i = D(q_1, \ldots, q_n). \tag{11.1}$$

That is, the price, p_i, that firm i may charge depends on the quantity of its brand sold and the quantities of all other $n - 1$ firms. Where products are differentiated, this expression cannot be simplified.

If consumers view all products as identical, or perfect substitutes, however, the demand curve may be written more simply. Consumers are unwilling to pay more for one firm's product than another's. Thus, all firms must charge the same price, p, if all are to sell their products. With undifferentiated products, only total market output, $Q = q_1 + q_2 + \ldots + q_n$, matters in determining the price, p.[4] In this case, the inverse residual demand equation may be written as

$$p_i = p = D(q_1 + q_2 + \ldots + q_n) = D(Q). \tag{11.2}$$

---

[4] If two goods are perfect substitutes and sold in the same sizes, a consumer's indifference curve for the goods is a straight line with a slope of -1. That is, a consumer is indifferent between having 20 units of Good 1 and 0 units of Good 2, or 10 units of each, or 0 units of Good 1 and 20 units of Good 2. The consumer's utility, and hence the consumer's demand curve, depends only on the sum of the output of the two goods.

EXAMPLE 11.2

NATIONAL BRANDS VERSUS PRIVATE LABELS AND GENERICS

National brands generally sell for more than house brands (private labels, such as Safeway's Cragmont or Town House labels) or generics. Presumably consumers believe that the national name brands are of higher quality. Whether this belief is accurate or not is irrelevant as long as consumers believe it.

There is very little difference in quality between some national brands and store brands, such as aspirin and bleach; yet consumers pay substantially more for national brands. In other cases, such as some canned fruits and vegetables, there are substantial differences between national brands and generics that consumers can determine in blind taste tests.

It is often difficult to determine, without careful chemical analysis or blind taste tests, whether house brands or generics are equivalent to national name brands. There is good reason for uncertainty. For example, Wonder Bread produces many of the private-label breads. That does not imply, however, that private brands are necessarily of the same quality as the name brand. Wonder Bread may vary its formula when it produces private brands, and the private brands may not be as fresh.

Similarly, Falstaff, one of the largest brewers of beer in the United States under its own label, is also the largest supplier of private-label beer. Most private-label brands of bourbon, scotch, vodka, and gin are produced by well-known name-brand companies. Sears often induces major manufacturers of typewriters, water heaters, and other products to produce Sears (Kenmore) brand products to the same or higher standards than the manufacturer's own brand.

Consumers may be willing to pay more for national brands to avoid the risk of buying a low-quality product. As a result, if they can be induced to try the cheaper brands and can see that their quality is as good as the name brand's, they may switch.

A Gallup Poll found that nearly 80 percent of people who try a product with a store-brand label become repeat buyers. Typically the store-brand buyer is a better-educated, affluent person who reads and understands the labels.

Many consumers do study labels and prices. The Gallup Poll indicates that 40 percent of shoppers *cherry pick:* they do not just choose the national brand, but compare products on a variety of dimensions (quality, price, and special offers). Nonetheless, nationally, only 2 or 3 percent of store-brand sales are generics.

As an example, suppose there are two firms in an industry. If the two products are viewed by consumers as identical, the price each firm may charge ($p = p_1 = p_2$) might be written as

$$p = a - bQ = a - b(q_1 + q_2) = a - bq_1 - bq_2. \tag{11.3}$$

where a and b are positive constants. That is, an increase in either firm's output reduces the market price—and hence the price for each firm—by an equal amount.

Many, but not all, national-brand products are of a superior quality and hence sell for substantially higher prices than private labels. The Private Label Manufacturing Association had an independent research firm compile a "Market Basket List" for 17 staple items in June 1984 (shown below). The total cost for the private labels was $25.59 compared to $34.15 for the name brands. Thus, private-label shoppers pay $8.56 less or 25 percent, though not necessarily for comparable quality items.

	Size	Name Brand	Private Label
Corn flakes	18 oz.	$1.35	$1.12
Orange juice, concentrated	6 oz.	.76	.59
Coffee, regular grind	16 oz.	2.79	2.37
Margarine, stick	16 oz.	.72	.54
Bacon, sliced	16 oz.	2.61	1.81
Peanut butter, creamy	18 oz.	1.62	1.41
Grape jelly	18 oz.	1.32	1.06
Chili with beans	15 oz.	1.01	.82
Cut beans, frozen	9 oz.	.78	.57
Mashed potatoes, instant	16 oz.	1.41	1.17
Vegetable oil	48 oz.	3.24	2.07
Pineapple chunks	20 oz.	.90	.79
Aluminum foil	75 ft.	1.70	1.62
Plastic wrap	200 ft.	1.54	.79
Toilet tissue, 2-ply	4-pk.	1.33	1.02
Disposable diapers	48 ct.	9.01	6.73
Dish detergent	32 oz.	2.06	1.11

A market with a small number of name-brand products and generic products is said to consist of an oligopoly with a competitive fringe. See Chapter 8 for a discussion of the analogous market structure of a dominant firm with a competitive fringe.

SOURCE: Al Morch. 1984. "Off-the-Shelf Advice on Saving Money." *San Francisco Sunday Examiner and Chronicle,* August 5, "Scene," P 4.

In contrast, if consumers view the products as imperfect substitutes, Firm 1's demand curve may be:

$$p_1 = a - b_1 q_1 - b_2 q_2, \qquad (11.4)$$

where $a > 0$ and $b_1 > b_2 > 0$. That is, an increase in Firm 1's output has a greater effect on its price than an increase in Firm 2's output. Indeed, the more a firm succeeds in differentiating its product, the more insulated its demand is from the actions of other firms.

Oligopolistic or monopolistically competitive markets may have differentiated goods, but in a purely competitive market, products are not differentiated. If a firm's product is differentiated, it faces a downward sloping demand function, which is inconsistent with pure competition. Indeed, the more differentiated a firm's product, the greater the downward slope of its demand curve, and the closer it comes to being a monopolist.

Preferences for Characteristics of Products

In Lancaster's (1966, 1971, 1979) consumer theory, consumers have preferences over the characteristics of commodities.[5] Each commodity is a bundle of characteristics. For example, candy bars and ice cream vary in sweetness, temperature, texture, and so forth. Rather than comparing the products as such, consumers choose on the basis of the more fundamental characteristics.

To illustrate how products can be compared by examining their characteristics, suppose the only important characteristic of a soft drink is how sweet it is. Soft drinks are located in "sweetness" space:

Not sweet ⟵————————————————————————⟶ Sweet

In this space, Schwepps Club Soda is located to the left of Classic Coke, which is to the left of Pepsi; that is, products are sweeter, the further to the right they are located. Soft drinks, then, can be said to be located in a **characteristic space,** which shows the sweetness of each drink. Of course, a product may have many characteristics: cereal brands may differ by sweetness and "mouth feel." If those are the only important characteristics, then cereal brands could be shown located in a characteristic space that had sweetness on one axis and mouth feel (from soggy to crunchy) on the other.

The representative consumer model may use either the product or characteristic approach; location models inherently use a characteristic approach. We examine both models in turn.

■ THE REPRESENTATIVE CONSUMER MODEL

I alone am here the representative of the people. —Napoleon Bonaparte

The first monopolistic competition model was published by Edward Chamberlin in 1933. In his **representative consumer model,** the typical consumer views all brands as equally good substitutes for each other: the brands are treated symmetrically. The representative consumer model can be used to examine industries with either differentiated or undifferentiated products. We start by examining undifferentiated product markets and then extend

---

[5] A theory similar to Lancaster's was independently developed by Becker (1965). There is also a related empirical literature (for example, Griliches 1971 and Rosen 1974) that examines *hedonic* pricing, where the price of a product depends on its mix of characteristics.

TABLE 11.1	Comparison of Oligopoly and Monopolistic Competition Models	
Model	*Profit Maximization by Individual Firms*	*Number of Firms (n) Determined by Entry*
Noncooperative oligopoly	marginal revenue = marginal cost	No entry: number of firms is fixed at *n*
Monopolistic competition	marginal revenue = marginal cost	Free entry: firms enter until profits = 0, so *n* is endogenously determined.

the analysis to markets in which products are heterogeneous. The analysis shows that whether or not products are differentiated, the equilibrium prices and number (variety) of brands is not generally socially optimal.

A Representative Consumer Model with Undifferentiated Products

In the simplest version of the representative consumer model, the various brands are homogeneous: all brands have the same characteristics. This model differs from the oligopoly models of the previous chapter only in the way the number of firms in the industry is determined. Both the oligopoly model and the monopolistic competition model determine the output of each firm and the number of firms. In both models, profit-maximizing behavior determines the output of each firm. That is, each firm chooses its output so that its marginal revenue corresponding to its residual demand curve, MR_r, equals its marginal cost, MC.

Entry is treated differently in the two models. In the oligopoly model, the number of firms is arbitrarily determined outside the model: the existing firms, the government, or some other force prevents new entry. In Chamberlin's model, firms freely enter the industry so long as it is profitable for them to do so. This *entry condition* determines the number of firms in the industry within the model. The two conditions that determine the oligopolistic and monopolistically competitive equilibria, profit-maximization and entry, are shown in Table 11.1.

The monopolistically competitive model requires that firms face downward sloping residual demand curves. Although product differentiation leads to such demand curves, high fixed costs can have the same result by limiting the number of firms that enter the industry, as the following example shows.

A Cournot Example.   To illustrate how the monopolistic competition model with homogeneous goods differs from an oligopoly model, the Cournot-Nash model of a noncooperative oligopoly is modified to allow entry; otherwise the same assumptions are made as in the oligopoly example of Chapter 10:

- *Cournot equilibrium:* In equilibrium, no firm wants to change its output level, and each firm expects its rivals to produce at their actual level of output.

- *Homogeneity:* Output is homogeneous.
- *Demand:* Market demand is

$$q(p) = 1000 - 1000p. \tag{11.5}$$

- *Costs:* Each firm has a cost function of

$$C(q) = 0.28\, q + F, \tag{11.6}$$

F is the positive fixed cost. These are costs the firm must pay if it operates at all (that is, these costs are not sunk until the firm decides to produce a positive level of output). As in Chapter 10, marginal cost is constant at 28¢.

The assumption of the previous chapter of a fixed number of firms is replaced by the **entry condition:** firms enter the market when profits are positive and exit when profits are negative.

Based on the cost assumption, the marginal cost, MC, and average cost, AC, curves are drawn as shown in Figure 11.1. Marginal cost is a horizontal line at 28¢. The average cost may be calculated by dividing total cost (11.6), $C(q)$, by output: $AC = C(q)/q = 0.28 + F/q$. Thus, average cost is the sum of average variable costs ($28¢ = [0.28\, q]/q$) and average fixed cost (F/q). As output grows, fixed costs are spread over more and more units, so average fixed costs fall, and the average cost consists primarily of average variable costs. As a result, Figure 11.1 shows that AC is well above MC at low output levels and approaches MC (which is the same as average variable costs) as q gets large.

The entry condition says that in equilibrium, firms actually producing in the industry make zero economic profits:

$$\pi = pq - C(q) = 0. \tag{11.7}$$

If firms are making positive profits, others enter until further entry no longer pays.[6] In other words, in equilibrium each firm's average cost equals its price: $AC = p$. Where price (average revenue) equals average costs, firms are making zero profits per unit and hence zero profits overall.[7]

To determine the equilibrium number of firms, we use a two-step procedure. We first determine the Cournot equilibrium output for each possible number of firms, as shown

---

[6] The following discussion assumes that the profits of the last entrant are exactly zero. That condition does not always hold if there must be a whole number of firms. If there cannot be a fractional number of firms, profits may be positive in equilibrium, but if one more firm entered, all would make losses. Seade (1980) shows that the basic results discussed here hold when one carefully assumes that there must be a whole number of firms.

[7] If profits are zero, $\pi = 0$, then price must equal average cost:

$$\pi = pq - C(q) = [p - C(q)/q]\, q = (p - AC)\, q = 0.$$

Since output is positive, $q > 0$, for profits to equal zero, average profits, $p - AC$, must equal zero. In our particular example, average profits are zero if $p = AC = 0.28 + F/q$.

FIGURE 11.1   A Monopolistically Competitive Equilibrium

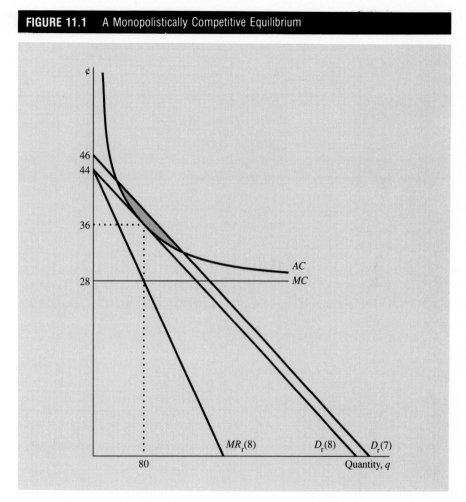

in Chapter 10. In the example, as the number of firms increases, their profits fall. Second, we determine the number of firms by examining these equilibria and picking the one in which firms make zero profits.

To illustrate how the number of firms is determined in a monopolistically competitive industry, suppose that each firm has a fixed cost of $6.40. Thus, a firm enters this industry if profits are positive or, equivalently, if price is greater than average cost, $AC = 0.28 + 6.40/q$.

Table 11.2 shows market price, firm output, and profits for various numbers of firms. If there are initially five firms in the industry, each produces 120 units of output, and the market price is 40¢. Each firm makes profits of $8.00, since it makes profits of 6.7¢ per unit ($= p - AC = \$0.40 - \$0.333$).

If another firm enters, profits per firm fall to $4.18, but profits are still positive, so more firms will want to enter. Entry continues until eight firms are in the industry, and

			F = $6.40		F = $1.60	F = $0.00
TABLE 11.2	Cournot Monopolistic Competition Example with Different Fixed Costs *(F)*					
Number of Firms	*Price (¢)*	*Firm Output*	*Average Costs (¢)*	*Firm Profits ($)*	*Firm Profits ($)*	*Firm Profits ($)*
1	64	360	29.8	123.20	128.00	129.60
2	52	240	30.7	51.20	56.00	57.60
3	46	180	31.6	26.00	30.80	32.40
4	42.4	144	32.4	14.34	19.14	20.74
5	40	120	33.3	8.00	12.80	14.40
6	38.3	102.9	34.2	4.18	8.98	10.58
7	37	90	35.1	1.70	6.50	8.10
8	36	80	36.0	0.00	4.80	6.40
9	35.2	72	36.9	−1.22	3.58	5.18
10	34.5	65.5	37.8		2.68	4.28
11	34	60	38.7		2.00	3.60
12	33.5	55.4	39.6		1.47	3.07
13	33.1	51.4	40.5		1.04	2.64
14	32.8	48	41.3		0.70	2.30
15	32.5	45	42.2		0.43	2.03
16	32.2	42.4	43.1		0.19	1.79
17	32	40	44.0		0.00	1.60
18	31.8	37.9	44.9		−0.16	1.44
20	31.4	34.3	46.7			1.18
100	28.7	7.1	118			0.05
500	38.1	1.4	485			0.002
1000	28.1	0.7	942			0.001
∞	28	~0	∞			0.00

NOTE: The negative profits shown in the table represent the profits that would occur if the number of firms indicated produced at their profit-maximizing (loss-minimizing) levels, given that exit was impossible and fixed costs were sunk. If exit is possible, these firms would shut down and incur zero rather than negative losses.

each of them exactly breaks even. Since no firm is losing money, none has an incentive to leave the industry. No additional firm has an incentive to enter. As Table 11.2 shows, if a ninth firm enters, all firms lose $1.22. Thus, eight firms is the equilibrium number in this industry.

Graphic Analysis. This equilibrium can also be shown graphically. Figure 11.1 shows the residual demand curve, $D_r(8)$, that each of the eight Cournot firms believes it faces, and the corresponding marginal revenue curve, $MR_r(8)$. The firm maximizes its profits by producing $q = 80$ units of output so that its $MR_r = MC$, as shown. It sells its output at the market price of 36¢. The firm's average cost curve is tangent to the demand curve where $q = 80$: $p = 36¢ = AC$. As a result, the firm makes zero profits.

Figure 11.1 shows that if only seven firms are in the industry, it pays for a firm to enter. The residual demand facing one of seven Cournot firms is shown as $D_r(7)$. This residual demand cuts the average cost curve, so that there is a shaded region where average costs are lower than the average revenues shown by the residual demand curve. A firm that operates at a point within this region makes positive profits, because its price is above its average cost. As Table 11.2 shows, each of the seven firms maximizes its profits at 90 units of output, so the market price is 37¢, which is greater than each firm's $AC = 35.1¢$.

Lower Fixed Costs.   How does this monopolistically competitive equilibrium change if each firm incurs lower fixed costs? Table 11.2 shows that the new equilibrium has 17 firms when fixed costs are $1.60, compared to 8 when fixed costs are $6.40.

Thus, the lower the fixed costs, the higher the equilibrium number of firms in a monopolistically competitive industry. The reason for the increase in the equilibrium number of firms is that the lower the fixed costs, the higher the profits for any given number of firms in an industry. Additional firms must enter the industry to drive profits to zero.

How do we know that each firm's profits are higher (holding the number of other firms constant) the lower are fixed costs? The reason is that a reduction in fixed costs does not affect total revenues but does lower total costs. Although fixed costs affect a firm's decision about whether to produce at all, they do not influence output levels if the firm actually produces, because each firm sets $MR_r = MC$ and neither MR_r nor MC are affected by fixed costs. The firm produces the same output regardless of the level of fixed costs, so its total revenues and total variable costs are not affected by a change in fixed costs. Total costs equal variable costs plus fixed costs, so holding variable costs constant and lowering fixed costs causes total costs to fall. Because total revenues remain constant as total costs fall, profits rise.

Graphically, with lower fixed costs, the average cost curve lies strictly below the one shown in Figure 11.1. For the new average cost curve to be tangent to a residual demand curve, the residual demand must be lower as well. The only way to get a lower residual demand curve is to have more firms in the industry.

It follows from this reasoning that if fixed costs fall to zero, then the number of firms becomes unlimited, and this Cournot monopolistic competition example becomes one of perfect competition. This result is shown in the last column of Table 11.2 where fixed costs equal zero.

To summarize: High fixed costs cause price to be above marginal cost. Where there are no fixed costs, enough firms enter the industry to drive price to marginal cost: the competitive solution.

Welfare with Undifferentiated Products.   How does this equilibrium compare to the social optimum in which social welfare is maximized by government regulation? Two welfare or efficiency problems arise with this monopolistic competition equilibrium.[8] First, because price is above marginal cost, the industry produces too little total output: an extra unit of this product is worth more to consumers than it costs firms to produce it. Second,

---

[8] The following results do not necessarily hold for all monopolistic competition models. These results are based on the assumptions of Cournot equilibrium, linear demand curves, sunk fixed costs, and each firm charging a single price.

the number of firms is excessive when marginal costs are nonincreasing (constant or falling with quantity). Each additional firm must pay a fixed cost, F, so too many firms cause society as a whole to pay excessive fixed costs.

The First-Best Solution. In the preceding example, each firm's cost function is $C(q) = mq + F$, where m is a firm's constant marginal cost. Here, society's optimal solution is to subsidize one firm to produce all the output and to require that the price be equal to marginal cost. This socially optimal solution is referred to as the **first-best optimum.**[9]

Figure 11.2 illustrates the first-best solution. It shows a single firm's marginal and average cost curves and the market demand curve, based on the preceding example with fixed costs of $6.40. In the proposed first-best equilibrium, the firm, which is regulated by the government, sets its price equal to marginal cost, $m = 28¢$, and consumers purchase $q^* = 720$ units of output. The socially optimal output is 80 units more than the monopolistically competitive output of 640, or 12.5 percent more.

At that price, the firm loses money because the price ($28¢$) is less than the average cost ($m + F/q^* = 0.28 + 6.40/720 = 28.89¢$). Thus, the government must subsidize the firm if it is to stay in business. The shaded area in Figure 11.2 represents the subsidized loss, which equals the loss per unit ($F / q^* = 0.89¢$) times the number of units ($q^* = 720$), or F ($6.40). The firm sells its product at its marginal cost or average variable cost, so it covers its out-of-pocket production expenses, but it does not recover its fixed costs.

The consumer surplus at the social optimum is $259.20.[10] If we define total welfare as the sum of consumer surplus plus profits (or minus losses), total welfare at the social optimum is $252.80. In contrast, in the monopolistically competitive equilibrium, consumer surplus and total welfare are $204.80. Thus, welfare at the social optimum is 23.4 percent higher than in the monopolistically competitive equilibrium.

If the government does not regulate the monopoly, it produces $q_m = 360$ units, where its marginal revenue equals its marginal cost. At the corresponding price, $p_m = 64¢$, which is above its average cost ($29.78¢$), it makes positive profits of $123.20. Here, consumer surplus is $64.80, and total welfare is $188. Thus, welfare in the monopolistically competitive equilibrium is 8.9 percent higher and welfare at the social optimum is 34.5 percent higher than in the monopolistic equilibrium.

When a single firm has a downward sloping average cost curve, it is called a *natural monopoly* because one firm could fulfill all consumers' demands more cheaply than could two or more firms (see Chapter 23). Each firm could produce at the same marginal cost,

---

[9] For expositional simplicity, the government is assumed to be able to costlessly and efficiently regulate so as to achieve a first-best equilibrium. That is, the government can raise tax revenues through nondistortionary, lump-sum taxes, determine the optimal output and price levels, and force the firms to operate at those levels. Government regulation, however, is typically costly to administer, and government agencies may lack the necessary information to set prices and output levels optimally. See Chapter 23 for a more extensive discussion of regulation. A mathematical version of the following welfare analysis is presented in Appendix 11A.

[10] Consumer surplus equals the triangle under the demand curve above $28¢$. If demand is $p = a - bq$, then consumer surplus at quantity q is $0.5 [a - p(q)]q = 0.5 [a - (a - bq)] q = 0.5 bq^2$. Here, consumer surplus is $0.0005q^2$.

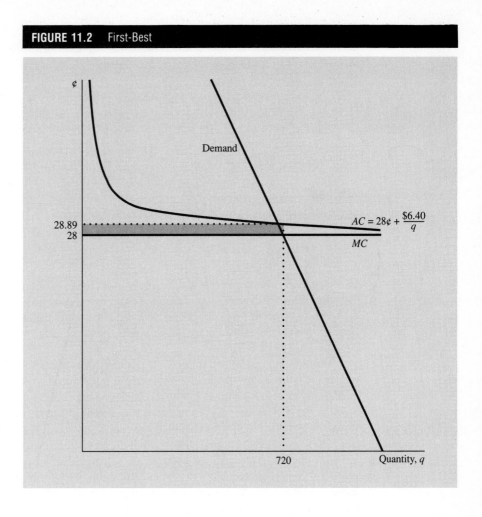

FIGURE 11.2   First-Best

$$AC = 28\text{¢} + \frac{\$6.40}{q}$$

but entry by an additional firm requires an additional expenditure of fixed costs, F. Thus, in the monopolistically competitive equilibrium, not only is price above marginal cost, but if there are eight firms, too much has been spent in fixed costs. That is, one firm could produce the total monopolistically competitive output for \$44.80 ($= 7F$) less than eight firms could because of the savings on fixed costs. In this example, unnecessary fixed costs represent 20 percent of total industry costs.

The Second-Best Solution.   Very often, the government cannot regulate an industry so as to achieve a first-best solution and maximize society's welfare. It may be politically infeasible to subsidize a monopolist such as a local electric company. In some industries, the government may be able to control the number of firms, but it may not be able to

TABLE 11.3	Second-Best Optimum				
Number of Firms	Price (¢)	Firm Output	Industry Profits ($)	Consumer Surplus ($)	Total Welfare ($)
1	64	360	123.20	64.8	188.00
2	52	240	102.40	115.20	217.60
3	46	180	78.00	145.80	223.80
4	42.4	144	57.34	165.89	223.25
5	40	120	40.00	180.00	220.00
6	38.3	102.9	25.08	190.34	215.42
7	37	90	11.90	198.45	210.35
8	36	80	0.00	204.80	204.80

NOTE: Parameters are the same as in Table 11.2, with fixed costs of $6.40

force them to produce more than the profit-maximizing quantity if it is unwilling to subsidize them.[11] Many cities control the number of taxicabs, for example. By choosing the optimal number of firms, the government hopes to achieve the **second-best optimum.**[12] That is, welfare is raised to the highest level possible given that the government is constrained (Spence 1976).

The government faces a tradeoff. If it allows more firms to enter, it can drive the market price down; yet additional firms increase total expenditures on fixed costs. It can be shown (see Appendix 11A) that under quite common conditions, there are too many firms in the monopolistically competitive equilibrium. That is, total welfare could be increased by restricting the number of firms.

The appropriately restricted equilibrium is the second-best optimum. Although welfare is not as high as in the first-best optimum, it is higher than in the unrestricted, monopolistically competitive equilibrium. Table 11.3 shows the sum of consumer surplus and industry profits from the first example in Table 11.2 ($F = \$6.40$). The monopolistically competitive equilibrium number of firms is eight, but the sum of consumer surplus and profits is maximized at three firms.[13]

A Representative Consumer Model with Differentiated Products

The essence of the monopolistic competition model just discussed remains unchanged if firms produce differentiated (heterogeneous) products. Profit maximization is still determined by $MR_r = MC$, and entry still occurs so long as profits are positive.[14] The only

[11] As discussed in Chapter 23, the government may regulate price so that it equals average cost. While this solution is not as efficient as setting price equal to marginal cost, no subsidies are required.

[12] Some might argue that the number of taxicabs is restricted to drive up the profits of those lucky enough to be allowed to operate (see the evidence in Chapter 23). That is, rather than trying to maximize social welfare, the government is merely trying to enrich existing cab companies.

[13] Based on the slightly different objective in Appendix 11A, the optimal number is closer to four.

modification to the model of the previous section caused by product differentiation is that a firm's residual demand curve (and hence its MR_r curve) depends on the individual quantities produced by each of its competitors rather than on just the total quantity.

Adding product differentiation complicates the model: each firm's demand curve may differ from another's, so that it is not sufficient to study a representative firm. Each firm in the industry must be considered separately. It is possible, of course, that although products are differentiated, the general form of the demand curves facing each firm is identical.

For example, all the firms in the industry could have demand curves of the form of Equation 11.4 where, due to product differentiation, a firm's price is more sensitive to changes in the quantity of its own product than to those of its competitors:

$$p_i = a - b_1 q_i - b_2 \sum_{j \neq i} q_j, \tag{11.8}$$

where $\sum_{j \neq i} q_j$ means the sum of the output of all firms except firm i.

The representative firm model with homogeneous products can be modified to handle this demand curve, and many of the qualitative results are the same as in the homogeneous model. For example, as each firm's fixed costs decrease, the number of firms in the industry increases, and price may fall.

As discussed, the primary impact of differentiation is that each firm faces a more steeply downward sloping demand curve than it does otherwise, because other products are less close substitutes. This greater slope gives the firm more market power—the power to set price above marginal cost.

Welfare with Differentiated Products. The optimal welfare solution changes when products are differentiated.[15] In general, a monopolistically competitive equilibrium with differentiated products has two problems: neither the price nor the *variety* (number of brands) is optimal. As before, price is above marginal cost. Where products are differentiated, however, there may be either too little or too much variety.

Two factors determine the variety in a monopolistically competitive equilibrium. One of them leads to too few brands, but the other may lead to too many brands. The first factor is that when firms face substantial fixed costs, some highly desirable products may not be produced if firms cannot make positive profits even though they cover variable costs. That is, substantial fixed costs tend to reduce the number of brands below the optimal level. The second factor, the effect on other firms, is a possibly offsetting force. When a firm introduces a new brand, it ignores the effect of its increased competition on the profits of other firms. When its product is a *substitute* for other brands, as Coke is

---

[14] In the differentiated products model, an entrant is assumed to produce a different product than those of existing firms.

[15] Perhaps the first, and certainly among the best studies of welfare with differentiated products are Spence (1976) and Dixit and Stiglitz (1977). These models have been critiqued by Pettingill (1979) and Koenker and Perry (1981), respectively. This section and the corresponding Appendix 11A are based, in part, on these articles and on unpublished lecture notes of Steven C. Salop, whom we thank.

FIGURE 11.3 When Does the Market Produce a Product?

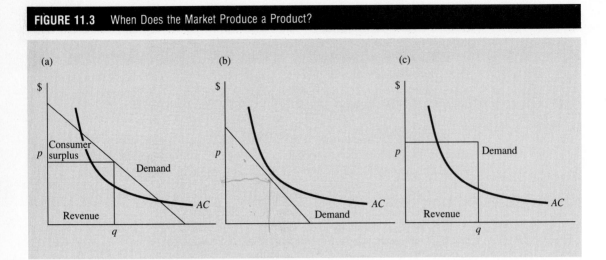

for Pepsi, part of its profits come from these other brands. Since firms ignore these effects on other firms, they have a tendency to produce too many products.[16]

The two factors do not operate in the same direction. Because each firm has fixed costs, there tend to be too few firms; however, because each firm ignores its effects on rivals, there tend to be too many firms. Thus, when goods are differentiated, there may be too many or too few brands.

In contrast, as discussed in the preceding example, if goods are homogeneous, there are definitely too many firms because there is no benefit to having more than one firm that is regulated to set price equal to marginal cost. With differentiated products, however, variety is desirable. Thus, regulating the markets so that there is only one firm charging marginal cost is unlikely to be optimal. The following section considers this analysis in more detail, first illustrating that fixed costs tend to result in underproduction of certain types of goods, and then discussing how the optimal number of brands is determined.

Fixed Costs Lead to Too Little Variety. When firms operate in the increasing-returns-to-scale section of their average cost curves, they tend to produce too few products. If a firm's marginal cost does not rise rapidly, and it has large fixed costs, it operates in the downward sloping, or increasing-returns, section of its average cost curve. Figure 11.3 illustrates why some desirable products are produced and others are not when the average cost curve is strictly falling.

In all the diagrams in Figure 11.3, society is better off if the products are produced: total social benefit, which equals the sum of consumer surplus and the producer's revenues, exceeds total social costs. In Figures 11.3a and 11.3c, the average cost crosses the demand

---

[16] If, however, products are *complements*, such as bread and butter, this factor results in too few brands or variety. Because in most (if not all) markets, brands are substitutes for each other rather than complements, we only consider cases where brands are substitutes.

curve, so it is profitable to produce. Profits are positive at quantity q, because the average cost per unit is less than average revenue or price.

In Figure 11.3b, however, the average cost curve is everywhere above the demand curve: total costs exceed total revenues at all output levels, so the product is not produced. The reason it is not produced, even though it is socially desirable to do so, is that the firm does not obtain the entire social benefit even though it pays the entire social cost. That is, the firm ignores the benefits to those consumers who enjoy surplus when it makes its decision whether or not to produce. Most consumers enjoy consumer surplus, whereas the firm's price is the value the marginal consumer (the one who has no consumer surplus) places on the good.[17]

To summarize, society benefits from the introduction of a new product if consumer surplus plus total revenues are greater than or equal to total costs. A firm, however, only introduces a product if total revenues are greater than or equal to total costs. As a result, firms may not find it profitable to produce all goods that are socially desirable.

The product that is most likely to be produced is one for which the demand curve is a right angle: consumers have an inelastic demand up to a cutoff price, p, at which their demand becomes perfectly elastic (see Figure 11.3c). In this case, there is no difference between total revenue and total social benefit, because there is no consumer surplus. The firm's decision to produce or not is identical to society's optimal criterion. Thus, all else the same, the smaller the ratio of consumer surplus to total revenues, the more likely is a firm to produce a socially desirable good.[18]

The crucial point is that this distortion—the underproduction of certain products— is due to the presence of fixed costs and the firm's inability to capture consumer surplus. Without the fixed costs, the average cost curve equals the marginal cost curve in our example. With constant marginal costs and no fixed costs, if it is socially optimal for a product to be produced, it pays for firms to produce it.

Optimal Diversity.   The key to determining the optimal equilibrium is the tradeoff between product *variety,* the number of brands, and the *quantity* of each brand produced,

---

[17] If a firm could perfectly price discriminate, it could capture the entire consumer surplus. That is, it would charge each consumer the maximum that consumer would pay for the product, so that there would be no consumer surplus. Because its revenues would be larger, the firm might find it profitable to produce in this case. Firms, however, can rarely perfectly price discriminate (see Chapter 14).

[18] For constant elasticity (ϵ) demand curves,

$$q = p^{-\epsilon} \ (\epsilon > 1),$$

the higher the elasticity, the smaller the ratio of consumer surplus to revenues. Here, revenues are,

$$R \equiv pq = p^{1-\epsilon},$$

and consumer surplus is

$$CS = \int_p^\infty s^{-\epsilon} ds = p^{1-\epsilon}/(\epsilon - 1).$$

Thus, the ratio of consumer surplus to revenues,

$$CS/R = 1/(\epsilon - 1),$$

is decreasing in ϵ.

TABLE 11.4 Variety and Quantity	
Number of Brands, n	*Quantity of Each,* q
1	95
2	45
3	28.33
4	20
5	15
6	11.67
7	9.29
8	7.5
9	6.11
10	5

which is determined by the price. For simplicity, assume that the number of brands, n, fully reflects the value of variety: all else the same, the more firms or brands, the better off are consumers. If all goods are produced with the same cost function and face the same demand curve, then the number of units of output, q, is the same for each brand in equilibrium. The essential facts about the equilibrium can be summarized by the number of brands, n, and the output per brand, q.

To illustrate the tradeoff between variety and quantity, suppose the economy has 100 units of input, each unit of output can be produced at a constant MC of 1, and the fixed costs are 5 units. Some possible combinations of number of brands and quantity *(n, q)* are shown in Table 11.4.

The **production possibility frontier (PPF)** in Figure 11.4 shows the feasible combinations of number of brands and quantity per brand that can be produced with society's total inputs. That is, the PPF graphs the type of information in Table 11.4.

Society's preferences concerning the choice between quantity and variety are summarized by the indifference curves shown in the figure. Point $O = (q^*, n^*)$, the tangency between the *PPF* and an indifference curve, represents society's optimal choice. At any point on any indifference curve that lies below the indifference curve through point O, society is worse off. Points on indifference curves that lie above point O are above the *PPF* and hence cannot be produced. The point A on the PPF represents a possible monopolistically competitive equilibrium. At that point, the industry is producing too few products, but more output per product than at the optimum. At point B on the PPF, the industry is producing more brands than at the optimum, but less output per brand.

Whether the monopolistically competitive equilibrium is at a point like A, B, or O depends on the preference of the economy and the production function. Appendix 11B discusses the factors that determine the relative position of the monopolistically competitive equilibrium. In general, any of these outcomes is possible.

Again, society might try to regulate the industry to increase welfare. If society is unable or unwilling to regulate all aspects of a firm's behavior and subsidize the firm if necessary, it may only be able to obtain a second-best optimum. Two such second-best regulatory policies have been studied. The first is a *structural policy,* which controls the number of firms in the industry. The second is a *behavioral regulation,* in which

FIGURE 11.4   Optimal *(O)* and Monopolistically Competitive *(A and B)* Equilibria

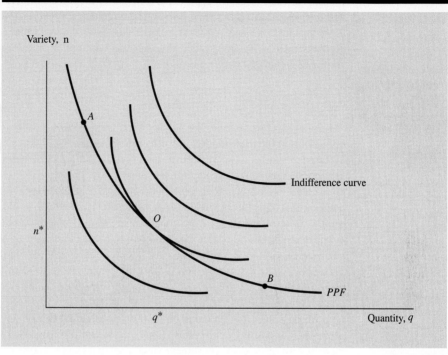

society controls output per firm but permits free entry and exit (Koenker and Perry 1981). The cost of administering such policies, which could be prohibitive, is again ignored.

Intuitively, the structural policy is most attractive when the unregulated monopolistically competitive equilibrium has more than the optimum number of firms; it is of little use when there are too few firms initially. Similarly, the behavioral approach is relatively useful when the unregulated equilibrium has too few firms producing large quantities of output. A formal analysis shows that the structural policy is most useful when product differentiation is strong relative to scale economies (there are relatively low fixed costs), whereas the behavioral policy does best when product differentiation is weak relative to the scale economies (Koenker and Perry 1981, 228).

Conclusions about Representative Consumer Models

In the Chamberlinian, representative consumer, monopolistic competition equilibrium, price is too high and the number of firms is nonoptimal. With undifferentiated products, there are almost certainly too many firms; with differentiated products, there may be too many or too few firms.

The representative consumer model assumes that all products are equally good substitutes for each other. To apply such a model to the ice cream market, for example, one must believe that Breyer's ice cream competes equally with Häagen-Dazs and with Baskin-Robbins. That is, one must not believe that Breyer's is a closer substitute to Baskin-Robbins than to Häagen-Dazs. Although this assumption is extremely strong, it makes the model relatively easy to use.

■ LOCATION MODELS

In a **location (spatial) model,** a firm views some brands as closer substitutes than others. A brand competes more vigorously with brands that are close substitutes than with those that consumers view as less close substitutes.

Location models make two key assumptions. First, each firm's product has a particular location in geographic or product (characteristic) space. That is, either the product is sold from a store that is located at a particular address, or the product is "located" at a particular point in characteristic space. The closer two products are to each other in geographic or characteristic space, the better substitutes they are. Second, consumers also have locations in geographic or product space. It costs consumers more to shop at stores further from home, or they receive less pleasure from products whose characteristics deviate from their ideal.

Because firms or products only compete directly with others near them, each has some market power, which stems from the preference of consumers to purchase from the nearest firm or product: consumers value proximity.

The following discussion first examines Hotelling's basic location model and then uses a location model to analyze the impact of increased competition on the market equilibrium. Finally, the welfare implications of this equilibrium are analyzed.

Hotelling's Location Model

Hotelling (1929) developed a model to explain the location and pricing behavior of firms.[19] Although he concentrated on geographic space, his model can be used to study monopolistic competition by viewing products as being located in product, or characteristic, space. In Hotelling's location (spatial) model, products differ in only one dimension, such as the location of the stores that sell them. Lancaster (1966, 1971, 1979) and others have shown, however, that this model can be extended to examine products that differ in more dimensions.

Consider a long, narrow, city with only one street, Main Street, that is L miles long. Consumers are uniformly distributed along this street, so that in any block there are an equal number. All consumers are identical except for location, and each consumer buys 1 quart of milk in each time period.

---

[19] See, also, Eaton (1976), D'Aspremont, Gabszewicz, and Thisse (1979), and Novshek (1980). Friedman (1983) has a good survey of this literature. In the literature most representative consumer models are Cournot and most location models are Bertrand, but any oligopoly concept is in either model.

FIGURE 11.5   Hotelling's Town

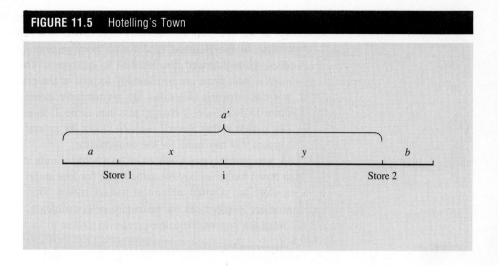

Two stores sell identical bottles of milk in this town. Store 1 is located a miles from one end of town, and Store 2 is located b miles from the other end of town, as shown in Figure 11.5. Consumers have no preference for either store, except that each consumer faces a transportation cost of c per mile. Each consumer buys from the least expensive store, taking transportation costs into account. Consider Consumer i who lives at the location shown in Figure 11.5. She lives x miles from Store 1, which is located a miles from the left edge of the city, and y miles from Store 2, which is located b miles from the right end of the city. Since x is less than y, she goes to Store 1 because her transportation costs are lower. Only someone who lived exactly halfway between the two stores is indifferent as to which store to patronize.

Suppose that the government sets the price of milk, so that stores choose only their locations. How should Store 1 choose its location to maximize its profits if Store 2 is already located b miles from the right end of the city, as shown in the figure, and cannot change its location? Because consumers only care about how far they must travel, Store 1 wants to be the nearest store for the greatest possible number of consumers. Store 1 maximizes its profits by locating just to the left of Store 2, a' miles from the left end of the city. There, it gets all the customers to its left, which is the majority.

If Firm 2 could costlessly relocate after Firm 1 locates, however, it would move slightly to the left of Firm 1's new location. This process would be repeated until both firms were in the middle of the town, with each firm having half the customers. You may have noticed the propensity of firms to locate near each other in a variety of markets. For example, several gas stations often locate on the corners of a busy intersection.

Thus, if price is given, the location of two firms can be determined. This spatial equilibrium is Nash (as discussed in Chapter 10); that is, the other firms are set at their equilibrium locations, and no firm wants to change its location. Similarly, by fixing location and letting the firms vary prices, a Nash equilibrium in prices can be determined (similar to the Bertrand equilibrium discussed in the previous chapter).

Hotellir...   ...of the Bertrand equilibrium disc... ...ms sell perfectly ho-
mogeneous ... ...roducts, if one firm
undercuts th... ...same thing happens
in Hotelling'... ...ter of town.

Suppose ... ...some distance apart
at a and b in... ...2 still gets a number
of customers... ...ustomers than Store
1, and some...

On occas... ...he local convenience
store rather th... ...ipermarket. That is,
the convenien... ...ower to raise prices
stems from c... ...he farther the convenience store... ...prices—the greater
its market pov...

Thus, Hotelling points out that the Bertrand equilibrium price equals the marginal cost only if the products are homogeneous (located at the same place in product or geographical space). In a more general model of differentiated products, firms with Bertrand expectations may charge different prices and all prices are above marginal cost.[20] In short, differentiation gives firms market power.

Unfortunately, it can be shown that when firms can costlessly change their prices *and* their locations (for example, reformulate their product), there is a *nonexistence of equilibrium* (D'Aspremont, Gabszewicz, and Thisse 1979). This result is analogous to the Edgeworth example in the previous chapter, in which the two firms continuously change their behavior, never settling down to a single price (and location). The existence of an equilibrium, however, can be shown in modified versions of this model. One modification allows for nonlinear transportation costs. Another, developed by Salop (1979), is studied next.

Salop's Circle Model

A circle is the longest distance to the same point. —TOM STOPPARD

A number of models modify Hotelling's basic model so that an equilibrium exists. One of the most interesting and best-known of these is Salop's (1979) circle model, which introduces two major changes in Hotelling's model.

First, in this model, firms are located around a circle instead of along a line. The reason for this change is that a circle has no end-points. That is, a circle is roughly equivalent to an infinitely long line in that neither has end-points. It turns out that a major cause of the nonexistence of equilibrium in Hotelling's model is the presence of end-points.

---

[20] Mergers of a subset of the firms in the industry have no effect in a Bertrand model with homogeneous goods but are profitable for the merging firms in a Bertrand model with heterogeneous goods (Deneckere and Davidson 1985). Compare this result to those in Example 10.1.

Second, Salop's model takes explicit account of a second, or outside, good. For example, the differentiated product might be brands (flavors) of ice cream (the products located around the circle), and the outside good might be chocolate cake, which is an undifferentiated product competitively supplied by another industry.

How Consumers Choose a Product.   Assume that customers are uniformly located around the circle that is of unit circumference. For simplicity, each customer buys exactly one scoop of ice cream. A customer's location, t^*, represents that customer's most preferred type of ice cream. For example, suppose one location on the circle is chocolate ice cream, another vanilla, and a point between chocolate and vanilla is chocolate-chip ice cream. Now suppose that each brand has only one flavor of ice cream and that brands are also located around the circle.

The pleasure a consumer gets from eating a scoop of ice cream located at t is:

$$U(t,t^*) = u - c\,|t - t^*|, \tag{11.9}$$

where u is the utility from the consumer's favorite flavor of ice cream (the flavor located at the same point, t^*, along the circle as the consumer); $|t - t^*|$ (the absolute value of the difference between t and t^*) is the distance brand t is from the customer's favorite flavor t^*; and c is the rate at which a deviation from the optimal brand lowers the consumer's pleasure. The consumer's utility function is shown in Figure 11.6, where a segment of the circle has been straightened out into a line. The figure shows that at a $t = t^* + u/c$, the consumer has a utility of zero.

The figure shows that the pleasure a consumer receives from a brand located to either the left or the right of the optimal brand is lower than from the optimal brand. (For simplicity, Figure 11.6 assumes that the utility function is symmetric.) For example, suppose the circle represents the sweetness of a soft drink. You like moderately sweet drinks. Your loss of pleasure from consuming a drink that is too sweet or not sweet enough may be roughly equal.

Each consumer attempts to maximize consumer surplus, which is the difference between the consumer's pleasure (utility) from eating a brand located at t and the price: $U(t,t^*) - p$. In other words, if your favorite flavor of ice cream is chocolate, but chocolate chip ice cream costs half as much, you might buy the chocolate chip because the loss in taste or utility is less than the gain from buying the cheaper product. Thus, you purchase the *best buy:* the product with the greatest surplus—the best combination of price and quality.

Instead of buying one of the brands of ice cream, however, the consumer may decide to buy the outside good, chocolate cake, if it is a *better buy* in the sense that it gives more pleasure for a given amount of money. Suppose the surplus from the cake (pleasure from eating it less the price) is $\underline{u}$. The consumer only buys a scoop of the best-buy brand, i, of ice cream if its surplus exceeds $\underline{u}$:

$$\max_{i}\ [U(t_i,t^*) - p_i] \geqq \underline{u}, \tag{11.10}$$

FIGURE 11.6   Consumer's Utility Function

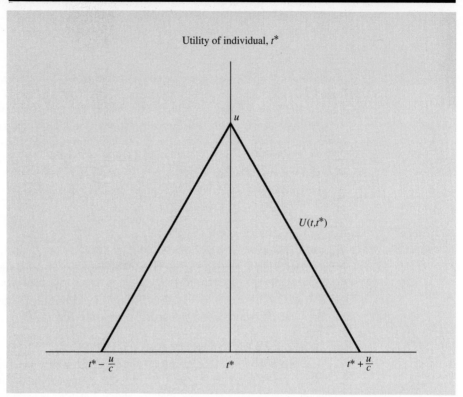

Utility of individual, t^*

u

$U(t,t^*)$

$t^* - \dfrac{u}{c}$ t^* $t^* + \dfrac{u}{c}$

where the expression on the left side of the equation is the surplus from the best-buy brand of ice cream (*max*imize the surplus through choice of brand *i*), and the right side is the surplus from cake. That is, the consumer should only buy ice cream if the surplus from the best-buy brand of ice cream is at least as great as the surplus from cake.

The greatest surplus the consumer can get from the best-buy ice cream is $u - p^*$, where p^* is the price of a brand located at t^*. The consumer is only willing to buy that brand if its surplus is greater than that from cake: $u - p^* \geqq \underline{u}$, or, rearranging terms, $u - \underline{u} \geqq p^*$. As a result, the consumer has a *reservation price*, $v = u - \underline{u}$, which is the highest price that the consumer is willing to pay for that brand of ice cream.

Alternatively stated, a consumer buys a scoop of ice cream only if the *net surplus* from the best-buy brand, the surplus from the best-buy brand minus the surplus from cake, is positive:

$$\max_{i} (v - c \, |t_i - t^*| - p_i) \geqq 0. \tag{11.11}$$

Equation 11.11 is obtained by subtracting $\underline{u}$ from both sides of Equation 11.10, substituting for $U(t,t^*)$ from Equation 11.9, and using $v = u - \underline{u}$.

FIGURE 11.7   Circular Market

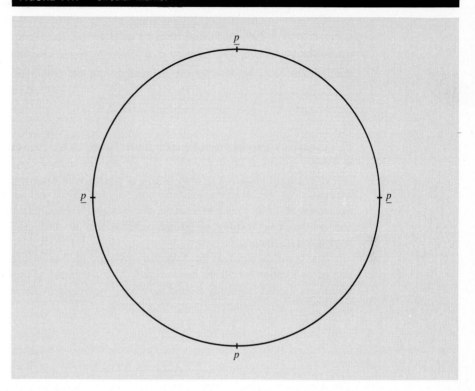

Firms' Behavior.   The symmetric equilibrium in this model depends on where firms are located and how they set price. All else the same, each firm wants to locate as far from its nearest competitors as possible. The further away other stores are from your store, the greater the market power you have with respect to the customers located near your store. As a result of trying to locate as far apart as possible, the stores locate equidistant from each other. If there are n ice cream brands located at equal distances around the circle, the distance between two brands is $1/n$ (because the circle is of unit circumference).

Salop starts his analysis by assuming that the stores are already located equidistant from each other and then asks what price each store charges. Suppose a typical brand (the one at the bottom of the circle) charges price p, and its two nearest competitors charge $\underline{p}$, as shown in Figure 11.7. How should the producer of the typical brand set p? Salop shows that the answer depends on how many brands there are. We first consider the case in which there are relatively few firms, and then consider a market with many more firms.

Monopoly Region.   If there are relatively few brands, they do not compete with each other for the same consumers. Each brand is a local monopolist and sells to all consumers living close enough so that their net surplus is positive. That is, each monopolist sells only to consumers who receive more surplus from that brand than they get from cake.

Consider a consumer located a distance $x = |t - t^*|$ from the brand at t with price p. Equation 11.9 shows that the consumer is willing to buy that brand only if the consumer's net surplus is positive: $v - cx - p \geq 0$. Thus, by rearranging this expression, the maximum distance, x_m, a consumer can be located from that brand and still buy it is

$$x_m = \frac{v - p}{c}. \tag{11.12}$$

This distance, x_m, is determined graphically in Figure 11.8a. The vertical axis in the figure is the net surplus from that brand. The greater the distance, x, a brand is from the consumer's most preferred product (which is labeled with the price, p), as shown on the horizontal axis, the lower the consumer's net surplus. When the brand is x_m distance from the consumer's most preferred location, the consumer's net surplus from that brand equals zero (where the net surplus line hits the x-axis) so that the consumer is indifferent between buying and not buying.

The brand captures all the consumers who are no further than x_m distance on each side of its location, or all the consumers in a $2x_m$ segment of the circle. If there are L consumers located uniformly around the circle, the monopoly demand facing this brand, q_m, is $2x_mL$, or, substituting for x_m from Equation 11.12:

$$q_m = \frac{2L}{c} (v - p). \tag{11.13}$$

The monopoly quantity demanded of the firm, as shown in Equation 11.13, falls by $-2L/c$ as its price rises by \$1. If the firm sets its price equal to the reservation price, v, of the customer who most prefers this product, its sales fall to zero.

Competitive Region. If there are more firms, so that they are located closer together and compete for the same consumers, then each firm must take into account the price its rivals charge in setting its own price as in the Bertrand model of Chapter 10. When firms compete with each other, a firm does not capture all the customers who prefer its ice cream to cake: it loses some to its two nearest rivals. Those customers located in the potential market of each of two brands buy from the one offering the highest net surplus.

Both of the typical brand's closest competitors are $1/n$ distance away and charge p. How many sales does this brand make if it sets its price at p? It captures all the consumers within a distance x_c, where x_c is the distance such that consumers get higher utility from this brand than from the other closest brand:

$$v - cx_c - p \geq v - c\left(\frac{1}{n} - x_c\right) - p. \tag{11.14}$$

The left side of Equation 11.14 is the net utility from this brand, and the right side is the net utility from the other closest brand (because a consumer who is x_c from this brand is

FIGURE 11.8   Two Market Structures

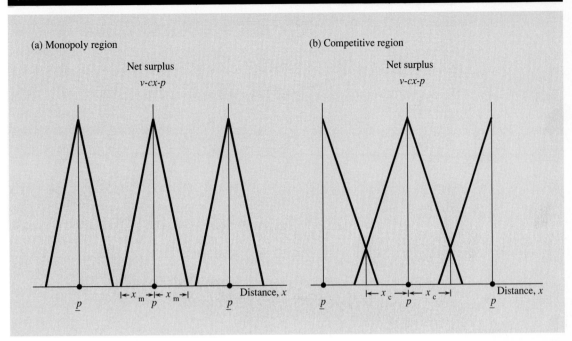

(a) Monopoly region

Net surplus

v-cx-p

(b) Competitive region

Net surplus

v-cx-p

$1/n - x_c$ distance from the other brand). Figure 11.8b shows how the limit of the competitive region, x_c, is determined by the point where a consumer is just indifferent between the two goods—where Equation 11.14 holds with equality. Where the net surplus lines from two rival brands intersect, a consumer is indifferent between buying either brand.

Solving Equation 11.14 for x_c, and noting that the quantity demanded of a competitive firm is $q_c = 2x_cL$:

$$q_c = \frac{L}{c}\left(\frac{c}{n} + \underline{p} - p\right). \tag{11.15}$$

In this case, the quantity demanded falls by $-L/c$ as p rises by \$1 (holding $\underline{p}$ constant). That is, the slope of the competitive demand curve is only half as steep as that of the monopolistic demand curve.

Types of Equilibria in the Circle Model.   At high prices, the demand regions of the firms do not overlap. Each firm is a local monopolist. As the price falls, so that more consumers are interested in ice cream, the regions overlap, and competition between the firms begins. The monopoly and competitive demand regions are shown in Figure 11.9.

FIGURE 11.9   Demand in Salop's Circle Model

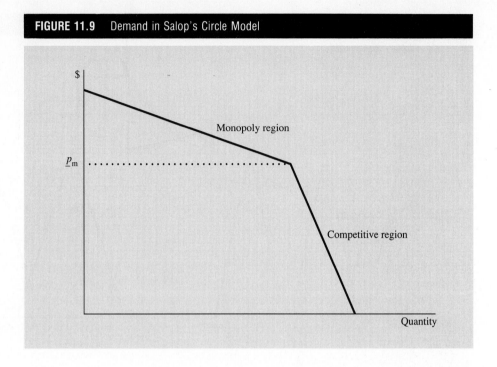

At prices above $\underline{p}_m$, the demand region is monopolistic: a brand's customers do not consider buying any other brand. Below $\underline{p}_m$ the brand competes with its nearest neighbors.[21]

Salop shows (in an argument analogous to the one used for the representative consumer models) that where firms have constant marginal and fixed costs, there exists a symmetric Nash equilibrium in which no firm wants to alter its price and no additional firms want to enter. That is, all firms charge the same price, say, $\underline{p}$, in equilibrium and are located $1/n$ distance from each other. Suppose that free entry is allowed and that firms can costlessly relocate so that they are equidistant from each other. Then, in a monopolistically competitive equilibrium, the entry of one more firm causes all firms' profits to be negative. Example 11.3 discusses what happens when firms cannot costlessly relocate as new entry occurs.

Changes in Costs and Welfare in the Circle Model.   Salop shows that, as in the representative consumer models, in the competitive region, as fixed costs rise, there are fewer firms or brands, so price rises and equilibrium variety falls. In that region, as the

---

[21] As shown in Equation 11.15, at prices below $\underline{p} - c/n$, *all* of the customers between a given firm and its neighbor prefer buying from the low-priced firm, even if they do not like that brand as much. Consider the consumer located at the same point as the neighbor firm: a distance of $1/n$ from the low-priced firm. That consumer loses c/n utility by consuming the low-priced brand rather than the preferred brand. But the price saving is greater than that loss. This type of behavior is extremely aggressive (or *supercompetitive* as Salop calls it), because the low-priced firm captures all of the neighbor brand's contested customers. For simplicity, such a region is not shown in Figure 11.9.

EXAMPLE 11.3

A SERIAL PROBLEM

In 1972, the U.S. Federal Trade Commission (FTC) charged the four largest U.S. manufacturers of ready-to-eat breakfast cereal (RTE cereal) with several antitrust violations including conspiring through brand proliferation and differentiating similar products to prevent entry into the industry. Although the FTC failed to win its case, this argument is theoretically interesting.

Schmalensee (1978) and Scherer (1979) use location models to explain the FTC's argument. In such models, consumers choose cereals based on their characteristics, such as sweetness and "mouth feel." Each brand is located in characteristic space. A given brand must compete with other nearby brands for customers located in that part of product space. If the company owning that brand can surround it with other similar brands of its own, then its brands compete with each other. For example, Kellogg's Corn Flakes and Sugar Frosted Flakes may be very close substitutes.

If a firm creates enough of these surrounding, or *defensive,* brands, there may not be enough customers left for any other firm to profitably establish a brand in that area of product space, according to this brand-proliferation theory. Similarly, several firms could conspire to establish a large number of brands (more brands than are profit-maximizing in the short run) in a given area of product space to prevent entry by new firms.

Whether the firms were conspiring or not, the top six firms had 95 percent of the sales of cereal. Moreover, between 1950 and 1972, the six leading producers introduced over 80 brands into distribution beyond test marketing.

In the early 1970s, however, "health" cereals started selling well. Since existing firms had not located in this new area of product space, new firms (which included such large firms as Colgate, International Multifoods, Pet, and Pillsbury) were able to enter. By mid-1974, these "natural" cereals had 10 percent of the market. Apparently, the previous positioning of these new firms did not prevent the established firms from entering this section of product space. The entry of the established firms and the decline in demand for that segment of the market from its 1974 height resulted in all but one of the new entrants (Pet) exiting from that area of product space by late 1977.

SOURCES: Schmalensee (1978), Scherer (1979), and (for a different view) Williamson (n.d.).

constant marginal cost rises, price rises by an equal amount (all increases in costs are shifted to consumers), but equilibrium variety remains unchanged.

At the kink in the demand curve at $\underline{p}_m$ in Figure 11.9, however, an increase in either fixed or marginal cost reduces the number of firms (variety) but, perversely, lowers price. Thus, if the economy is at such a point, a tax that raises firms' costs lowers prices and decreases variety. Salop shows, however, that welfare rises, even if the proceeds of the tax are ignored.

Indeed, welfare in this circle market can be studied in the same manner as in the representative consumer models. Salop shows that the first-best optimal variety is less than the variety in either the monopolistic or competitive equilibria. With fewer brands, the savings in fixed costs exceed the losses due to higher prices. Thus, in the circle model's monopolistically competitive equilibrium, there are unambiguously too many brands; whereas in the differentiated products, representative consumer model equilibrium there can be too many or too few brands.

Salop (1979) shows that the second-best optimum, given the government's only regulatory policy is to control entry, is either the market equilibrium or complete monopoly. That is, the optimal entry policy is either free entry or entry restricted so that each brand has a complete monopoly market.

■ HYBRID MODELS

We have drawn the distinction between representative consumer models and location models. Although the vast majority of all monopolistic competition models fall cleanly into one or the other of these two categories, increasing use is made of hybrid models that combine some of the properties of each model. Two hybrid models are discussed in Appendix 11C.

One of these hybrid models, Deneckere and Rothschild (1986), includes the circle model and a version of the representative consumer model as special cases.[22] It shows that prices are lower in a representative consumer model than in the circle model because there is more competition in a representative consumer model. The hybrid model also shows that in the circle model, adding another brand benefits relatively few consumers, whereas, in the representative consumer model, consumers always benefit substantially from the introduction of extra brands. It is for these reasons that there are too many brands in the equilibrium of the circle model, but there may be too many or too few brands in the equilibrium of the representative consumer model.

■ SUMMARY

This chapter examines product differentiation and monopolistic competition. Product differentiation may lead to greater market power for firms. The greater the perceived difference between two products, the more each producer can charge.

If free entry is allowed, firms enter markets until profits are driven to zero. A monopolistically competitive equilibrium is one in which firms face downward sloping demand curves (above marginal cost) and earn zero profits.

There are two basic types of monopolistically competitive models. In Chamberlin's representative consumer model, a typical consumer views all products as close but not

---

[22] Deneckere and Rothschild (1986) use Bertrand equilibria for both models.

necessarily perfect substitutes. Price is above marginal cost, and there may be too much or too little variety. Entry (due, for example, to a reduction in fixed costs) tends to reduce the prices of all firms.

Hotelling's location (spatial) model postulates that consumers' preferences and brands are located in product or geographic space. Consumers prefer brands near them. As a result, firms have some local market power. The pricing behavior of other firms has little effect if the consumers who buy from a given firm do not like those products. In the localized competition circle model, price is above marginal cost, and there is unambiguously too much variety. New entry does not lower the price a given consumer pays unless a firm enters near the firm that the consumer patronizes because consumers are uninterested in brands that are very dissimilar to the ones they like best.

In some markets, the representative consumer model may be more realistic; in others, the localized competition model may be more apt. Where competition is localized so that brands only compete with nearby brands, firms have market power. These markets have higher prices, all else the same, than markets in which all brands compete with each other.

■ Key Terms

characteristic space
entry condition
first-best optimum
heterogeneous (differentiated)
homogeneous (undifferentiated)

location (spatial) model
monopolistic competition
production possibility frontier (PPF)
representative consumer model
second-best optimum

■ Discussion Questions

1. Which types of markets do you think are monopolistically competitive and why? Identify several such markets.

2. Is the elasticity of demand facing a duopolist higher or lower if its product is differentiated from its competitor's product than if the products are identical? Always?

3. Which markets are better described by the representative consumer model and which by the spatial model? What characteristics distinguish these two models?

4. In what markets is there likely to be too little variety? In what markets is there likely to be too much variety? What characterizes these markets?

5. Should society intervene in monopolistically competitive markets? If so, in which markets and how? Do you think these interventions are likely to be politically feasible?

6. An overindulgent dad takes Daniel, Rebecca, and Debbie to the movies, buys each popcorn and a drink, and then takes them to a restaurant for dinner. For which of these transactions do you expect the price paid to be significantly above marginal cost? Which monopolistic competition model (if any) is likely to be most relevant for analyzing each of these transactions?

■ Problems

1. Compare the effect of a franchise tax (a lump-sum tax independent of the sales activity of the firm) on a monopolistically competitive industry to its effects on a monopolist or competitive industry.
2. In an oligopolistic industry with homogeneous products and firms with Cournot expectations, must profits fall when a new firm enters? Why or why not? (For an answer, see Seade [1980].)
3. Explain and illustrate the following claim: "In our example a monopolistically competitive industry with homogeneous products cannot be more than one firm away from the output sold at price equals marginal cost."

4. In Hotelling's town, if all firms are required to charge the same fixed price, describe the equilibrium location of three firms. Explain your answer. Now describe the equilibrium for four and for five firms.
5. What is the effect of a cost-saving technological change on a monopolistically competitive industry in which the cost curves facing each firm are $C(q) = mq + F$, where m is the constant marginal cost, and F is the fixed cost? *Hint*: a cost-saving technological change may be modeled as reducing m, reducing F, or reducing both.

Answers to the odd-numbered problems are given at the back of the book.

■ Suggested Readings

Friedman (1983) has a good survey and discussion of most of the models in this chapter. In the 1930s, there was a lively (and relatively nontechnical) debate between Chamberlin (1933) and Robinson (1934) and Kaldor (1935) concerning the necessary conditions for a firm to possess market power (the power to set price above marginal cost). A recent, more technical paper by Hart (1979) clarifies and resolves many of the issues of that debate.

■ References

Becker, Gary S. 1965. "A Theory of the Allocation of Time." *Economic Journal* 75:493–517.

Chamberlin, Edward H. 1933. *The Theory of Monopolistic Competition*. Cambridge, Mass.: Harvard University Press.

D'Aspremont, C., J. Jaskold Gabszewicz, and J. F. Thisse. 1979. "On Hotelling's 'Stability in Competition.'" *Econometrica* 47:1145–50.

Deneckere, Raymond, and Carl Davidson. 1985. "Incentives to Form Coalitions with Bertrand Competition." *Rand Journal of Economics* 16:473–86.

———and Michael Rothschild. 1986. "Monopolistic Competition and Preference Diversity." The Center for Mathematical Studies in Economics and Management Science, Discussion Paper no. 684, Northwestern University.

Dixit, Avinash K., and Joseph E. Stiglitz. 1977. "Monopolistic Competition and Optimum Product Diversity." *American Economic Review* 67:297–308.

Eaton, B. Curtis. 1976. "Free Entry in One-Dimensional Models: Pure Profits and Multiple Equilibria." *Journal of Regional Science* 16:21–33.

Friedman, James. 1983. *Oligopoly Theory*. New York: Cambridge University Press.

Griliches, Zvi, ed. 1971. *Price Indexes and Quality Change: Studies in New Methods of Measurement*. Cambridge, Mass.: Harvard University Press.

Hart, Oliver D. 1979. "Monopolistic Competition in a Large Economy with Differentiated Commodities." *The Review of Economic Studies* 46:1–30.

———. 1985. "Monopolistic Competition in the Spirit of Chamberlin: A General Model." *Review of Economic Studies* 52:529–46.

Hotelling, Harold. 1929. "Stability in Competition." *Economic Journal* 39:41–57.

Kaldor, Nicholas. 1935. "Market Imperfection and Excess Capacity." *Economica* 2:33–50.

Koenker, Roger W., and Martin K. Perry. 1981. "Product Differentiation, Monopolistic Competition, and Public Policy." *The Bell Journal of Economics* 12:217–31.

Lancaster, Kelvin J. 1966. "A New Approach to Consumer Theory." *Journal of Political Economy* 74:132–57.

——. 1979. *Consumer Demand: A New Approach.* New York: Columbia University Press.

——. 1971. *Variety, Equity and Efficiency.* New York: Columbia University Press.

McConnell, J. D. 1968. "The Development of Brand Loyalty: An Experimental Study." *Journal of Marketing Research* 5:13–19.

Monroe, Kent B. 1976. "The Influence of Price Differences and Brand Familiarity on Brand Preferences." *Journal of Consumer Research* 3:42–49.

Novshek, William. 1980. "Equilibrium in Simple Spatial (or Differentiated Product) Models." *Journal of Economic Theory* 22:313–26.

Perloff, Jeffrey M., and Steven C. Salop. 1985. "Equilibrium with Product Differentiation." *The Review of Economic Studies* 52:107–20.

Pettingill, John S. 1979. "Monopolistic Competition and Optimum Product Diversity: Comment," *American Economic Review* 69:957–60.

Robinson, Joan. 1934. "What Is Perfect Competition?" *Quarterly Journal of Economics* 49:104–20.

Rosen, Sherwin. 1974. "Hedonic Prices and Implicit Markets." *Journal of Political Economy* 82:34–55.

Salop, Steven C. 1979. "Monopolistic Competition with Outside Goods." *The Bell Journal of Economics* 10:141–56.

Sattinger, Michael. 1984. "Value of an Additional Firm in Monopolistic Competition." *Review of Economic Studies* 51:321–32.

Scherer, F. M. 1979. "The Welfare Economics of Product Variety: An Application to the Ready-to-Eat Cereals Industry." *The Journal of Industrial Economics* 28:113–34.

Schmalensee, Richard. 1978. "Entry Deterrence in the Ready-to-Eat Breakfast Cereal Industry." *The Bell Journal of Economics* 9:305–27.

Seade, Jesus. 1980. "On the Effects of Entry." *Econometrica* 48:479–89.

Spence, A. Michael. 1976. "Product Selection, Fixed Costs, and Monopolistic Competition." *The Review of Economic Studies* 43:217–36.

Williamson, Oliver E. n.d. "Entry Deterrence in the RTE Cereal Industry: A Comment." Working paper.

APPENDIX 11A

WELFARE WITH HOMOGENEOUS PRODUCTS

Why, a four-year-old child could understand this report. Run out and find me a four-year-old child. I can't make head or tail of it.

GROUCHO MARX

Two problems arise in a monopolistically competitive equilibrium with homogeneous goods:

1. Because price is greater than marginal cost, the industry produces too little output.
2. If marginal cost is constant, the industry bears excess fixed costs.

■ FIRST-BEST OPTIMUM

All is for the best in the best of possible worlds. — VOLTAIRE

Given constant marginal cost, m, the first-best optimum requires a single firm that charges a price equal to marginal cost, $p = m$, and a subsidy of the firm's losses. We illustrate this result using a simple, general equilibrium model.[1]

The representative consumer's utility function is:

$$U(Q,y) = u(Q) + y, \qquad (11A.1)$$

SOURCE: This appendix draws heavily on Steven C. Salop's unpublished lecture notes, Dixit and Stiglitz (1977), and Spence (1976).

[1] In this model, there is no important distinction between the partial and general equilibrium, because the general equilibrium's income effect is the same as in the partial equilibrium.

where Q is the output of the monopolistically competitive industry and y represents all other goods. Let y be produced at constant cost, and, by normalizing, let this constant cost equal 1, so that the competitive price is also 1.

The consumer maximizes his or her utility subject to the following constraint:

$$I = pQ + y, \tag{11A.2}$$

where I is the consumer's income and p is the price of a unit of Q. By substituting for y in the consumer's utility function (Equation 11A.1) and using Equation 11A.2, we may write the consumer's utility maximization problem as follows:

$$\max_Q u(Q) + I - pQ. \tag{11A.3}$$

The utility-maximizing first-order condition is

$$u'(Q) = p. \tag{11A.4}$$

That is, the consumer's demand function may be written as $p = p(Q) = u'(Q)$. Since marginal utility is positive, $p > 0$. Similarly, assuming diminishing marginal utility ($u'' < 0$), $p' < 0$.

If there are n identical firms in the Q-industry, each produces an equal amount of output, $q = Q/n$. The economy's resource constraint may be written as follows:

$$T = (nF + mQ) + y, \tag{11A.5}$$

where T is the total resources of the economy (maximum production), F is the fixed cost each firm must sink to be in business, $nF + mQ$ is the total cost of producing Q units of output, and each unit of y costs \$1 to produce. For example, if T is the total hours of labor available and y is leisure, then the total time spent producing output plus leisure equals T.

Society's problem is to maximize Equation 11A.1 subject to Equation 11A.5 through its choice of Q, y, and n. By substituting for y in Equation 11A.1 using Equation 11A.5, we may write this problem as follows[2]:

$$\max_{Q,n} u(Q) + T - nF - mQ \tag{11A.6}$$

subject to
$$n \geqq 1$$
$$Q > 0$$

---

[2] Equation 11A.6 says society should maximize the objective function $u(Q) + T - nF - mQ$, by choosing Q and n appropriately, subject to (s.t.) the restrictions that there is at least one firm and some positive amount of Q produced.

The problem assumes that there is at least one firm ($n \geq 1$) and that some positive amount of Q is produced ($Q > 0$).

The Kuhn-Tucker first-order conditions imply that

$$n = 1, \text{ since } -F < 0 \tag{11A.7}$$

$$Q > 0 \text{ and } u'(Q) = m. \tag{11A.8}$$

Thus, the first-best optimum requires (as shown in Figure 11.2) the following:

- One firm produces all the output: $n = 1$, from Equation 11A.7.
- If any of the monopolistically competitive good is produced ($Q > 0$), price equals marginal cost: $u' = p = m$, from Equations 11A.8 and 11A.4.
- The single firm's losses are subsidized to prevent it from shutting down. The subsidy is necessary since profits are negative, $\pi = -F$.

This solution is that of a regulated natural monopoly (see also Chapter 23). There are economies of scale everywhere; that is, the firm is always operating in the downward sloping portion of its average cost curve. For this solution to be optimal, funds for the subsidy must be raised in a nondistorting manner. Given a representative consumer, one efficient method of raising funds is a lump-sum tax.

■ SECOND-BEST OPTIMUM

Now assume that the government cannot achieve the first-best optimum because its actions are constrained:

- The government can control *only* the number of firms, n.
- The government cannot force the firms to produce more than the profit-maximizing quantity; that is, it may not subsidize firms.

In the second-best optimum, assuming Cournot conjectures, each firm chooses its (positive) output level such that marginal revenue equals marginal cost[3]:

$$\frac{Q}{n} p'(Q(n)) + p(Q(n)) = m, \tag{11A.9}$$

where $Q(n)$ is the amount of Q produced in equilibrium when there are n firms, and Q/n is the output of a single firm. Firms enter if the marginal firm earns nonnegative profits; that is, price is at least as great as average cost:

$$p(Q(n)) \geq m + \frac{F}{Q(n)/n}. \tag{11A.10}$$

---

[3] A single firm's revenue is $p(q^* + \underline{Q})q^*$, where q^* is its output and $\underline{Q}$ is the output of the $n - 1$ other firms. Differentiating revenue with respect to q^*, and noting that in equilibrium $q^* = \underline{Q}/(n - 1) = Q/n$, one obtains Equation 11A.9.

Equations 11A.9 and 11A.10 simultaneously determine $Q(n)$ and n.

To find out how much total output changes as the number of firms increases, we can totally differentiate Equation 11A.9 to solve for the slope of $Q(n)$:

$$\frac{dQ}{dn} = Q'(n) = \frac{Q(n)}{n}\left[\frac{p'}{(n+1)p' + Qp''}\right].\tag{11A.11}$$

That is, an extra firm increases output if the term in brackets in Equation 11A.11 is positive. A sufficient condition is $p'' \leq 0$. Since $p''(Q) = u'''(Q)$, we do not have any strong beliefs about this sign in general; however, we assume $p''(Q) \leq 0$ in what follows.[4]

As a result, increasing output through the market mechanism requires additional firms, and hence additional fixed costs. Thus, there is a trade off between the total cost of production (more firms) and lower price (more output).

Society's problem is

$$\max_{n} u(Q(n)) + T - nF - mQ(n),\tag{11A.12}$$

subject to Equations 11A.9 and 11A.10.

This problem differs from the problem in 11A.6 in that society is maximizing with respect to n and not with respect to Q and n. Thus, this second-best optimization is constrained in the sense that society can only control Q indirectly through its choice of n.

Ignoring the constraint of Equation 11A.10 for the moment, the first-order condition for a welfare-maximization is

$$(p - m)\, Q'(n) = F,\tag{11A.13}$$

using Equation 11A.4 to replace $u'(Q)$ with p. This condition states that the difference between price and marginal cost times the change in output as n increases by 1 $[Q(n + 1) - Q(n) \approx Q'(n)]$ equals fixed cost. The left side is the gain from more output from an extra firm, and the right side is the (fixed) cost from one more firm.

Equation 11A.13 is the appropriate maximizing condition if the constraint in 11A.10 is not binding. We can show that profits are positive in the solution represented by 11A.13 so that the constraint in 11A.10 does not bind. First, rewrite Equation 11A.13 as

$$p = m + \frac{F}{Q'(n)}.\tag{11A.13'}$$

For profits to be positive, we need $p = m + F/Q'(n) > m + F/(Q/n) = AC$, or

$$Q'(n) < \frac{Q(n)}{n} \quad \text{or} \quad \frac{nQ'(n)}{Q(n)} < 1.\tag{11A.14}$$

---

[4] See Seade (1980) for a discussion of how stability conditions rule out certain possibilities.

That is, the *elasticity of total output with respect to entry* is less than 1.
From Equation 11A.11,

$$\frac{nQ'(n)}{Q(n)} = \frac{p'}{(n+1)p' + Qp''},$$ (11A.15)

so, since $p'' \leqq 0$,

$$\frac{nQ'(n)}{Q(n)} \leqq \frac{p'}{(n+1)p'} = \frac{1}{n+1},$$

or

$$\frac{nQ'(n)}{Q(n)} < 1$$ (11A.16)

That is, if $p'' \leqq 0$, the constraint expressed in 11A.10 that p $\geqq$ AC is not binding. The free-entry equilibrium has too many firms (in the sense that the positive-profits constraint is not binding). Thus, society should restrict the number of firms.

APPENDIX

11B

WELFARE WITH DIFFERENTIATED PRODUCTS

The object of government is the welfare of the people.

THEODORE ROOSEVELT

We start by considering an economy with only one monopolistically competitive industry. We then extend the model to include an outside good.

■ AN ECONOMY WITH A SINGLE, MONOPOLISTICALLY COMPETITIVE INDUSTRY

Please all, and you will please none.—AESOP

Suppose that product variety is fully reflected in the number of different brands, *n*. If all firms have identical cost functions, in a symmetric equilibrium, each produces the same amount of output, *q*.

Each firm's cost function is $C = F + mq$, where C is total costs, F is fixed costs, and mq are the variable costs associated with output level q. Thus, both average variable and marginal costs equal m.

Society's production possibility frontier *(PPF)* is the set of points *(q,n)* that can be produced with society's total resources, *T:*

$$(F + mq)n = T, \qquad (11B.1)$$

where the left side of Equation 11B.1 is the total cost of *n* firms producing *q* units of output each. By rewriting Equation 11B.1, the *PPF* is $n = T/(F + mq)$, which is plotted

---

SOURCE: This appendix draws heavily on Steven C. Salop's unpublished lecture notes, Dixlit and Stiglitz (1977), and Spence (1976).

in Figure 11.4. Totally differentiating this equation, we find that the slope of the *PPF*, $dn/dq = -mT/(F + mq)^2$, is negative, as shown in Figure 11.4. Using the numerical example in Table 11.4, $dn/dq = -100/(5 + q)^2$. Further, as q rises, the slope becomes less negative, $d^2n/dq^2 = 2q^2T/(F + mq)^3$, so that the *PPF* is concave, as shown in the figure.

Consumers have preferences regarding quantity, q, and variety, n. That is, they are willing to trade off some output of each brand for more brands. For example, the utility function over all *potential* brands, $i = 1, 2, \ldots, \infty$ is:

$$U(q_1, q_2, \ldots, q_n, \ldots) = W(\sum_{i=1}^{\infty} u_i(q_i)) \qquad (11B.2)$$

In the symmetric case with n firms in the industry, $u_i(q) \equiv u(q)$, for all i; $q_i = q$, for $i = 1, 2, \ldots, n$; and $q_i = 0$, for $i > n$, so we can rewrite Equation 11B.2 as follows:

$$U(q, q, \ldots, q, 0, \ldots, 0) = W(nu(q)). \qquad (11B.3)$$

A consumer's indifference curve corresponding to utility level $\underline{w}$, then, is

$$W(nu(q)) = \underline{w}. \qquad (11B.4)$$

The optimum output-variety combination, $O = (q^*, n^*)$, is determined by the tangency of an indifference curve with the *PPF*, as shown in Figure 11.4. Points on lower indifferences curves are less desirable and points on higher indifference curves are unobtainable because they lie above the PPF.

Points A and B on the figure represent possible market equilibrium. That is, one does not know if the monopolistically competitive equilibrium lies to the left or the right of the optimum.

■ A SIMPLE GENERAL EQUILIBRIUM MODEL

What is algebra exactly; is it those three-cornered things?—J.M. BARRIE

To compare the market equilibrium to the optimum, an explicit general equilibrium model should be used. Figure 11.4 only considers the tradeoff between output and variety of a monopolistically competitive industry. If there is another good, y, one needs to consider the tradeoff between the two industries. The outside good, y, is produced at a constant cost equal to 1.

The Optimum

The utility function now is assumed to be additively separable in y, so that society's maximization problem is

$$\max_{q_i, y} W\left(\sum_{i=1}^{n} u(q_i)\right) + y \qquad (11\text{B}.5)$$

subject to

$$y = T - \sum_{i=1}^{n} (mq_i + F)$$

In the symmetric case where $q_i = q$, society's problem may be rewritten as maximizing surplus:

$$\max_{q, n} W(nu(q)) + T - n(mq + F). \qquad (11\text{B}.6)$$

There are two first-order conditions for a maximum. The first condition is obtained by differentiating 11B.6 with respect to n, setting the derivative equal to zero, and rewriting it as

$$W'u(q) = mq + F. \qquad (11\text{B}.7)$$

This condition says that brands should be added until the marginal gain in welfare from an extra brand, $W'u$, equals the opportunity cost of the outside good ($mq + F$ is the cost of one more firm in terms of foregone consumption of the outside good).

The other first-order condition is obtained by differentiating 11B.6 with respect to q, setting the derivative equal to zero, dividing through by n and rewriting it as

$$W'u'(q) = m \qquad (11\text{B}.8)$$

Equation 11B.8 says that each brand's output, q, should be increased until the marginal gain in utility from an extra unit of output, $W'u'(q)$, equals the marginal cost, m, of an additional unit of output. Using the same type of reasoning as in Appendix 11A, $p = W'u'(q)$. Thus, Equation 11B.8 says that price should equal marginal cost: $p = m$.

Equations 11B.7 and 11B.8 determine the optimal output per brand and number of brands (q^*, n^*). At the optimum, the ratio of the average to the marginal utility equals the ratio of the average to the marginal costs. Dividing 11B.7 by 11B.8 and multiplying by $1/q$, we obtain

$$\frac{u(q)/q}{u'(q)} = \frac{(mq + F)/q}{m} = \frac{AC}{MC}. \qquad (11\text{B}.9)$$

For a concave utility function ($u' > 0$, $u'' < 0$), average utility always exceeds marginal utility. Thus, Equation 11B.9 implies average cost is greater than marginal cost at the optimum. That is, the optimum lies on the downward sloping portion of the average cost curve. This condition is automatically met for the specific cost function we chose. It can be shown that this result holds even when average cost curves are U-shaped. Thus, firms should not produce at minimum average cost, as in a competitive industry. The optimum has more variety than would be the case if firms produced at full capacity (the bottom of a U-shaped average cost curve).

The Equilibrium

The equations that describe the Cournot monopolistically competitive equilibrium are different from those that describe the optimum, 11B.7 and 11B.8. We now present the corresponding equations for the equilibrium.

The profits of a representative firm are

$$\pi = qW'u'(q) - mq - F, \tag{11B.10}$$

since $W'u'(q) = p$. Ignoring the integer problem, firms enter until profits are zero ($\pi = 0$) or revenue equals cost:

$$qW'u'(q) = mq + F \tag{11B.11}$$

This equation differs from the corresponding condition for an optimum, Equation 11B.7, by having $qW'u'(q)$ instead of $W'u(q)$ on the left side.

By differentiating Equation 11B.10 with respect to q, we find that the Cournot firm maximizes profits where marginal revenue equals marginal cost, m:

$$W''(u'(q))^2 nq + W'(qu''(q) + u'(q)) = m. \tag{11B.12}$$

The left side of this equation is different from 11B.8, the condition for an optimum. Thus, since the conditions for an optimum (11B.7 and 11B.8) differ from those for the equilibrium (11B.11 and 11B.12), the optimum differs from the equilibrium.

The only situation in which the two sets of conditions are identical is when $W(\cdot)$ and $u(\cdot)$ are linear and $u' = u/q$. See Appendix 11A for this case. That case is uninteresting because each brand is a perfect substitute for every other brand. Demands are therefore perfectly elastic, and no market equilibrium even exists. That is, prices are driven to marginal cost and profits are negative (due to fixed costs).

In general, it can be shown that the equilibrium may lie on either the left or the right of the optimum (in Figure 11.4). To determine the exact relationship, more structure on the utility function is required. A number of articles (Spence 1976; Dixit and Stiglitz 1977; and Koenker and Perry 1981) have worked out the relationship for particular utility functions similar to the one used here. These articles have also shown that price regulation with a zero-profit constraint leads to the market equilibrium.

HYBRID MODELS

This appendix presents two hybrid models that combine elements of the representative consumer model and the spatial model. The first adds spatial elements to the representative consumer model. The second, more general model includes Salop's circle model and the first hybrid model as special cases.

■ A REPRESENTATIVE CONSUMER-SPATIAL MODEL

In one hybrid model, each consumer attaches a relative value, θ_i, to each brand, where θ_i is the pleasure the consumer receives from brand i.[1] In this model, as in a spatial model, a consumer does not view all brands as equally good substitutes (some products are ranked higher than others); however, as in a representative consumer model, a consumer considers all possible brands, because any brand may have a high value.

A representative consumer's net utility or surplus is

$$U_i = \theta_i - p_i, \tag{11C.1}$$

where p_i is the price of brand i. A consumer's best buy is the brand with the highest net surplus ($\max_i U_i$).[2]

Consider a symmetric example: preferences for the brands are such that an equal number of consumers like or dislike any given brand by any given amount. Suppose that consumers' preferences for Brand 1, θ_1, are uniformly distributed between $2a$ and $4a$.

---

[1] For reasons too obvious to mention, in the following we concentrate on Perloff and Salop (1985). The main reason we discuss it is that it, like Salop's circle model, is nested within the second hybrid model discussed later. Sattinger's (1984) model is similar to the Perloff and Salop model. A somewhat more general formulation has been used by Hart (1985).

[2] Of course, for some prices, even the best buy may provide less utility than that of an outside good, u. That is if $U_1 > U_i$ for any other i, then U_1 is a given consumers's best buy. The consumer will buy Brand 1 only if the net utility from that brand, U_1, is greater than $\underline{u}$. In the following, we assume $\underline{u}$ is so low that consumers always buy one of the differentiated brands.

That is, some consumers receive $\theta_1 = 2a$ pleasure from the first brand. Others receive $\theta_1 = 4a$ pleasure, and others receive intermediate amounts of pleasure. There are an equal number of consumers who have a θ_1 of any value between $2a$ and $4a$. Consumers' preferences are similar for all the other brands. Formally, $\theta_i \sim g(\theta_i) = 1/(4a - 2a) = 1/(2a)$, where $g(\cdot)$ is the uniform density of preferences for brand i.

Suppose there are only two brands. A consumer buys Brand 1 only if

$$U_1 = \theta_1 - p_1 > \theta_2 - p_2 = U_2. \tag{11C.2}$$

Rewriting Equation 11C.2, a consumer buys Brand 1 only if,

$$p_1 - p_2 < \theta_1 - \theta_2. \tag{11C.3}$$

That is, a consumer buys Brand 1 only if the price difference between 1 and 2 is less than the difference in value between the two brands ($\theta_1 - \theta_2$). The most any consumer might like Brand 1 is $4a$, and the least that consumer might like Brand 2 is $2a$, so if the price difference, $p_1 - p_2$, is greater than $4a - 2a = 2a$, that consumer does not buy Brand 1. The demand facing the first firm is shown in Figure 11C.1 as a function of the price difference between the two brands. Maximum demand for a good is arbitrarily scaled to equal 1, so when $p_1 = p_2$, Brand 1 receives half the total demand.

Stronger Preferences

Now, suppose that consumers have stronger differences in beliefs about the quality of the two brands. Preferences range from a to $5a$ instead of from $2a$ to $4a$, so the demand curve rotates in Figure 11C.1.

Both demand curves show that when prices are equal, half the consumers buy each of the brands. As differences in preferences increase—consumers feel stronger about the relative merits of the two brands—the demand curve becomes more steeply sloped. As a result, each brand faces a smaller elasticity of demand and has more market power. The larger the difference in preferences, the more one brand can charge than its competitor before it loses all its customers.[3]

One of the implications of this type of model is that if many people share the same preferences, there may be a multiprice equilibrium. For example, if many consumers think (rightly or wrongly) that Bayer aspirin is superior, Bayer may be able to charge more than generic brands. Thus, there may be a two-price equilibrium.

---

[3] This model may be reinterpreted to include *spurious product differentiation* as well as actual product differentiation. So far, it has been assumed that consumers accurately perceive true variations across brands. Differentiation is spurious when consumers mistakenly perceive that brands differ by more than they actually do (see Example 11.1). In the model, it does not matter why θ_i is high—only that it is high. In general, as spurious differentiation increases, equilibrium price may rise or fall (Perloff and Salop 1985). It will not necessarily rise, as in the example above.

11C.1   Effect of Product Differentiation on Demand

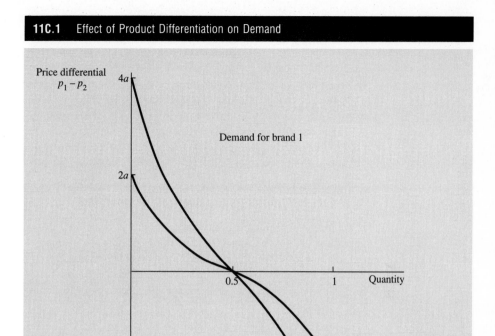

Lower Fixed Costs

If each Bertrand firm has the same type of cost curve as before, with constant marginal cost $= m$, then the price each firm charges, in equilibrium, is

$$p = m + \frac{2a}{n}, \qquad (11C.4)$$

where n is the number of firms, and preferences range between $2a$ and $4a$. As fixed costs fall, the number of firms increases, and as n rises, price falls to marginal cost. Thus, the more firms, the closer the equilibrium is to the competitive level.

The intuition behind this result is that as the number of firms increases, a consumer is more likely to find a close substitute for his or her current best buy. If there are two types of ice cream originally, butterscotch and chocolate, and the consumer does not like butterscotch, then the consumer is willing to pay substantially more for chocolate. If chocolate-chip ice cream is now introduced, the consumer is not willing to pay as great a premium for chocolate over chocolate-chip as the premium over butterscotch, because chocolate-chip is a better substitute for chocolate.

Thus, lowering fixed costs causes entry by new firms, which lowers the equilibrium price. When fixed costs are positive, there may be too many or too few firms (Sattinger 1984).

Imperfect Information and Localized Competition

If the model is changed slightly, however, so that firms only compete with those located near them, then as *n* increases, price does not fall. For example, some consumers may only be aware of firms located nearby, hence the prices of firms farther away do not influence their decisions. Here, unless consumers learn that there is a new firm across town, there is no extra competitive pressure on the firms that the consumer now patronizes.

■ A MORE GENERAL MODEL

Recently Deneckere and Rothschild (1986) have developed a more general hybrid model that includes the Salop circle model and the hybrid model just discussed as special cases. They use their model to explain why the circle model predicts that there are too many brands in monopolistically competitive equilibrium, while the symmetric hybrid model predicts there can be too many or too few.

Their explanation is that there is much more competition in the symmetric model than in the circle model (the point made above). As a result, all else the same, equilibrium prices and short-run profits are lower in the symmetric model than in the circle model. When short-run profits are lower, it is harder to cover fixed costs, so there are fewer stores or brands in the symmetric model's equilibrium than in the circle model's.

CHAPTER 12

INDUSTRY STRUCTURE AND PERFORMANCE

Merely corroborative detail, intended to give artistic verisimilitude to an otherwise bald and unconvincing narrative.

W.S. GILBERT

Preceding chapters have discussed how different market structures theoretically affect an industry's performance as measured by price, output, and profits. This chapter presents some of the ways in which economists have measured performance and discusses the relationship between the performance of markets and their structure. The main findings are that many industries seem to depart considerably from perfect competition, yet the degree of this departure does not seem to be strongly related to industry concentration. Most of the empirical studies discussed come from the manufacturing sector, primarily because of the availability of data. Bear in mind, however, that the manufacturing sector is only one of several sectors in the U.S. economy, comprising about 22 percent of the gross national product.[1]

The chapter first identifies what predictions the models studied so far make about the relationship between industry structure and some traditional measures of performance, like prices and profits. Next it presents a theoretical analysis of several measures of performance, such as rates of return, price-cost margins, and the ratio of a firm's replacement cost to its market value. Several measures of an industry's structure are then identified. The chapter analyzes the empirical relationship between an industry's measure of performance and its market structure. This type of analysis postulates implicitly that an industry's structure (for example, industry concentration) determines the conduct of firms (for example, their decisions on output), which in turn determines industry performance (for example, prices). Such analysis is sometimes called **structure-conduct-performance.** Although it is perhaps helpful as a way to organize one's thoughts, such analysis is shown to have several shortcomings. The chapter goes on to study more refined analyses of individual industries that build on many of the insights developed in Chapters 9, 10, and 11 to measure how far industry performance departs from the competitive norm.

---

[1] *Economic Report of The President,* 1989, Table B-11.

■ THEORETICAL PREDICTIONS OF THE RELATIONSHIP BETWEEN STRUCTURE AND PERFORMANCE

The economist can predict the relationship between price and marginal cost and the existence and persistence of economic profits depending on the market structure.

In a competitive industry composed of identical firms, price equals short-run marginal cost, profits in the short run can be either positive or negative, and profits in the long run must equal zero. However, each firm's profits equal zero in the long run only if each firm has equal access to the same technology and inputs. If a few firms have lower costs than others, their profits will not be completely eroded by entry. In that case, free entry guarantees that the profits of the last firm to enter equal zero.

In a monopoly, price exceeds marginal costs, profits in the short run can be either positive or negative, and long-run profits can be either zero or positive. In monopolistic competition, each firm faces a downward sloping demand curve and, like a monopolist, sets price above marginal cost. However, entry of additional firms lowers the *level* of demand facing each firm, so that profits in the long run equal zero. Therefore, in a monopolistically competitive industry, price is above short-run marginal cost, short-run profits can be either positive or negative, and profits in the long run must equal zero.

In an oligopoly, firms can set price above marginal cost, but their profits are not necessarily driven to zero in the long run because of some long-run barrier to the entry of new firms. Therefore, in an oligopoly, price tends to exceed short-run marginal cost, profits in the short run can be either positive or negative, and long-run profits can be either zero or positive.

Economists seek to verify these predictions by comparing various market structures. These relationships are summarized in Table 12.1.

Two important conclusions emerge from Table 12.1 without much analysis. First, testing whether long-run profits are positive is really a test of free entry, not of (perfect) competition. Free entry guarantees that long-run profits equal zero but not that price equals marginal cost; it is quite possible for a monopolistically competitive industry to earn zero profit, even if all prices are above marginal costs. To determine whether price exceeds marginal cost, one must examine price data, not profit data. Second, examining short-run profits actually reveals very little about the degree of competition in an industry, because in all market structures, short-run profits can be either positive or negative.

Before one can test the predictions of Table 12.1, a precise definition of market

TABLE 12.1 Predictions Based on Market Structure

	$p - MC$	π_{SR}	π_{LR}
Competition	0	+ or −	0
Monopolistic competition	+	+ or −	0
Monopoly	+	+ or −	+ (or 0)
Oligopoly	+	+ or −	+ (or 0)

p = price, MC = marginal cost (short run), π = profits (with subscripts indicating short run or long run).

structure is necessary. It is not true, as Table 12.1 suggests, that there are only four market structures. For example, some oligopolies have fewer firms than others and would be expected to behave differently. Think of all the possible market structures as special cases of one giant model in which price approaches marginal cost as the number of firms in an industry increases and as barriers to entry diminish in importance. By seeing whether the number of competitors and barriers to entry actually influence performance, one is testing the predictions of Table 12.1.

Researchers have taken two approaches in their study of industries. One of them, the structure-conduct-performance approach, tries to relate market characteristics to market performance. Do prices rise as the output of industries becomes more concentrated in the hands of a few firms or as entry barriers rise? The second approach seeks to use the insights of Chapters 9, 10, and 11 to estimate statistically the amount by which industry behavior deviates from competition. This approach is motivated by a concern that it is not easy to calculate measures of performance and that they must be estimated differently than is usually done in structure-conduct-performance studies. This approach has not yet explored in detail those industry characteristics that lead to the most significant deviations from competitive behavior.

This chapter reviews both approaches, beginning with the structure-conduct-performance approach. We first examine the measures of performance and then the measures of market structure that researchers have used.

■ MEASURES OF PERFORMANCE

Market performance refers to the success of a market in producing benefits for consumers, as occurs, for example, in the case of low prices. Three different measures have been commonly used to gauge how close an industry's performance is to the competitive benchmark. One measure, the rate of return, is based upon profits earned per dollar of investment. A second measure, the price-cost margin, is based upon the difference between price and marginal cost, although, in practice, researchers often use some form of average cost in place of marginal cost. A third measure, called Tobin's q, is based on a comparison between the stock-market value of a firm and its value based upon the replacement cost of its assets. Each of these measures focuses directly or indirectly on pricing in relation to costs, and each has some advantages and disadvantages.

Rates Of Return

A **rate of return** is a measure of how much is earned per dollar of investment. This section explains the relationship between economic profits and rates of return. The correct calculation of rates of return can be difficult, and sometimes compromises must be made that bias the final results. There are actually several different ways to calculate a rate of return, and we discuss some of them in detail.[2]

---

[2] Appendix 12A discusses another rate of return measure, the *internal rate of return*.

The Relationship Between Rates of Return and Economic Profits. Table 12.1 makes predictions about profits, and a rate of return is a measure of profits. Before exploring exactly how a rate of return measures profits, it is first necessary to understand that the predictions of Table 12.1 regarding profits apply only to *economic* profits, which equal revenues minus opportunity cost, not *accounting* profits (those measured by accountants, using standard accounting principles). Any empirical investigation must adjust accounting profits to reflect economic profits before calculating any rates of return to test the predictions of Table 12.1.

Chapter 3 presents several important distinctions between economic and accounting profits. The main distinction concerns long-lived capital assets, like plant and equipment. Economic profits equal revenues minus labor, material, and capital costs. Measuring revenues, labor costs, and material costs is generally easy. The problem is measuring **capital costs,** which are the total rental fees that the capital assets would bring if they were rented out. The total rental fees equal the rental rate per unit times the number of units of capital. Sometimes well-developed rental markets exist, as, for example, for used equipment, and it is easy to observe the relevant rental rate on capital. In such cases, it is straightforward to calculate economic profits. When rental rates are not readily available, the economist must implicitly calculate a rental rate before calculating economic profit.

After economic profits have been correctly calculated, researchers often express economic profits as an earned rate of return on capital in an attempt to standardize for firms of different size, but this procedure can lead to some peculiar results, as you will see. There is a close relationship between economic profits, the earned rate of return on capital, and rental rates on capital. To develop this relationship requires an understanding of what a rental rate on capital really is: a rental rate must provide an owner of capital with a certain rate of return *after* depreciation has been deducted on the equipment. **Depreciation** is the decline in economic value that results during the period the capital is used.[3] For example, if I rent my house annually for $1000, and the wear and tear on the house is, say, $300 a year, then depreciation is $300, and my net annual rental after the depreciation is $700. If the house is worth $10,000 initially, then my rate of return is 7 percent, and depreciation is 3 percent.[4] The return after depreciation has been deducted is what matters to the investor. For that reason, a rental rate (per dollar of capital) can be expressed as an earned rate of return, r, plus a rate of depreciation, δ.

In order to calculate the earned rate of return, notice that profits, π, can be written as follows:

$$\pi = \text{revenues} - \text{labor, material, and capital costs,}$$

where capital costs = rental rate $\times K$, and K is the value of capital. If rental rate = $(r + \delta)$, where r = earned rate of return, and δ = rate of depreciation, then we can rewrite π as follows:

---

[3] Accountants typically use a definition of depreciation based on a formula involving historical cost and age. The accounting definition of depreciation may or may not coincide with economic depreciation.

[4] For simplicity, we ignore some details regarding the timing of the receipts.

$$\pi = \text{revenues} - \text{labor and material costs} - (r + \delta) K. \qquad (12.1)$$

To calculate the earned rate of return, we solve for r such that economic profits are zero. Setting π equal to 0 and solving for r in (12.1) yields

$$r = (\text{revenues} - \text{labor and material cost} - \delta K) / K$$

If we define *net income* to equal revenues minus labor and material costs minus depreciation, then the earned rate of return equals net income divided by the value of assets.

For example, suppose a firm has 100 units of capital each worth $10, revenues are $110, labor and material costs are $10, and depreciation per unit is 2 percent, then the earned rate of return equals 8 percent [(110 − 10 − 20) / 1000]. Suppose that investments in competitive industries yield a 5 percent rate of return. Since 8 percent is higher than the rate earned in competitive industries, the firm is earning an *excess* rate of return. There is an equivalent way of coming to the same conclusion. If the rental rates on capital were based on the competitive rate of return of 5 percent, then the rental rate would equal 7 percent (5 percent plus depreciation of 2 percent). Calculating economic profits as revenues minus labor costs, material costs, and capital costs yields *positive* economic profits of $30 (110 − 10 − .07 × 1000 = 30). Thus, earning *positive* economic profits and earning *excess* rates of return (above the competitive level) are equivalent ways of expressing the same idea.

There are thus two equivalent ways of calculating excess economic profits. One way calculates economic profits directly by subtracting rental charges (using the competitive rate of return) and other costs from revenues. Excess profits exist if the result is positive. An alternative, more frequently used method, is to solve for the earned rate of return that equates revenues minus labor and material costs minus capital costs to zero and then compare that earned rate of return to the competitive rate of return. Excess economic profits exist if the earned rate of return exceeds the competitive rate.

In the calculation of economic profits, capital assets should be valued at **replacement cost,** which is the cost to purchase an asset of similar quality. If capital is valued at its replacement cost, then a low rate of return is a signal that no new capital should enter the industry. It does not mean that the firm should shut down or that it made an error in its past investment decisions. For example, a firm that bought machinery when it was cheap could earn a low rate of return on the current replacement value and still have enjoyed a huge profit on its initial purchase.

Notice that the earned rate of return is a **real rate of return** (adjusted for inflation), because one typically does not count as income in the numerator the price appreciation on assets that arises from inflation. If one did, the calculation would yield a *nominal* rate of return. For example, if capital is initially worth $100, annual income (before depreciation) is $20, and the annual depreciation rate is 10 percent (so depreciation is $10), then the earned rate of return is 10 percent [(20 − 10) / 100]. Now suppose that there is an inflation of 20 percent during the year. This means that the value of the capital at the end of the year equals $90 ($100 − 10 percent depreciation) times 1.2 (to adjust for inflation), or $108. The firm has incurred a "gain" of $18 on its capital, but it is illusory; it does not represent an increase in purchasing power because all prices have risen as a result of the inflation. A real rate of return ignores the gain in the value of capital caused by inflation. (If the increase in the value of the asset exceeds that due to general inflation, then it would represent a real gain and should be counted if one is describing how well the firm has done.)

Pitfalls in Calculating Rates of Return.   Several difficulties arise in calculating rates of return correctly. The following sections explain the most important ones.[5]

Valuing Capital and Depreciation.   Two key evaluations are required to calculate the earned rate of return: the value of capital, and the amount by which capital depreciated during the year. Both of these evaluations can be difficult to determine correctly and often accounting definitions are used instead of the economic definitions. The economic value of capital is the cost of replacing existing assets with comparable assets.[6] This number may have no relation at all to what it cost in the past to purchase the capital asset. Accountants typically account for the value of capital using the concept of *book value,* which is based on the historical cost of the capital combined with assumptions about depreciation. Because historical cost is often quite different from the actual replacement cost of the capital, using the book value of capital rather than the economic value can severely bias the measurement of rate of return.

Further difficulties arise in measuring depreciation. Accountants can use several fixed formulas to measure the depreciation of an asset. One common formula, called *straight-line depreciation,* assumes that the asset's value declines in equal annual amounts over some fixed period (the *useful life* of the asset). For example, a machine that costs $1000 and is assigned a useful life of 10 years would incur $100 of depreciation annually for its first 10 years of life. If it lasts more than 10 years, it incurs no additional depreciation. The fixed formula's predictions of the amount of depreciation may be unrelated to the asset's decline in economic value, which is the measure of its economic depreciation. The use of accounting concepts of depreciation and book value can lead to peculiar and biased results, especially in times when the value of capital is changing because of, for example, inflationary conditions (see Appendix 12B).

Capitalization of Monopoly Profits.   A special pitfall that arises in calculating rates of return on the basis of book value is that book value sometimes includes *(capitalizes)* monopoly profits. Consider the following example. Suppose a monopolist is earning a rate of return in excess of the competitive level. Suppose further that excess annual economic profits equal $100 and that the monopolist earns this $100 because of a government restriction on entry. Imagine that Daniel wants to purchase the firm in order to receive the flow of monopoly profits. If the interest rate is 10 percent, then Daniel is willing to pay $1000 for the firm above and beyond the cost of any assets. If the monopolist has no physical assets, and if Daniel purchases the monopoly for $1000, Daniel will

---

[5] See Fisher and McGowan (1983) for a critique of the use of rate of return.

[6] In all but a dying industry, this value depends on the cost of purchasing new facilities of comparable quality. In a dying industry, the value of capital will be below the cost of building new facilities. The low value of capital is a signal that the industry should not invest in new facilities.

receive a return of $100, or 10 percent a year, the competitive rate of return. Even though Daniel is receiving the competitive rate of return on *his* investment, it would be incorrect to say that pricing is at the competitive level. The reason is that the extra $1000 paid for the monopoly represents the capitalized value of the monopoly profits, *not* the cost to society of replacing the monopolist's capital. One must always be careful to determine that the reported value of capital does not include capitalized monopoly profits. Otherwise, the analyst could fail to detect excess economic returns. The replacement cost of the assets rather than Daniel's purchase price is the correct value to use in the denominator to calculate the rate of return earned by the firm's assets.

Valuing Advertising and Research and Development.   The problems that arise in valuing physical capital and depreciation also arise for other expenditures that have a lasting impact on either a firm's demand or costs. For example, the money a firm spends on advertising this year is likely to generate some benefit next year, just as a plant that is built this year provides a benefit next year. As explained in Chapter 3, it would provide a misleading picture of profits if a firm deducted its entire investment in a plant as a cost in the initial year and then made no deductions in subsequent years. It is more accurate to take the annual decline in the economic value of the plant as the annual cost. Similarly, one should not *expense* (that is, deduct in one year the entire cost of) annual advertising expenditures but should use the annual decline in the economic value of the firm's advertising. (Consumers forget about an ad. Hence, the ad's effect on demand declines over time. Other items that are more like investments than expenses for a firm include research and development. It is often difficult to determine the correct rates of depreciation to use for research and development expenses and for advertising expenses.

After-Tax Returns.   The relevant rate of return to measure excess profit is the after-tax rate of return. Corporations pay taxes to the government, and only what is left is of interest to individual investors. Competition among investors causes after-tax rates of return to be equated on different assets. If assets are taxed at different rates, the before-tax rate of return could vary widely even if all markets are competitive. For that reason, one should always try to use after-tax rates of return and after-tax measures of profit, especially when comparisons are made across industries that are subject to different tax rates.

Rate of Return on Assets.   As described earlier, economic profits are the relevant concept for testing the predictions of Table 12.1. Rates of return are related to economic profits as long as one is calculating the rate of return earned by *all* of a firm's assets. As described in Chapter 2, most firms issue debt in addition to equity, so that there are both debtholders and equity holders (stockholders) with claims on a firm's income. Some economists use the rate of return to the stockholders as a measure of the firm's profitability. Because the assets of the firm are paid for by both debtholders and stockholders, the rate of return on the firm's assets equals a weighted average of the rate of return to the debtholders and the stockholders. The rate of return to debtholders is typically lower than the rate of return to stockholders, because debt is less risky than stock. (Debtholders get paid before stockholders when a firm is in financial distress.) The rate of return to stockholders rises as the amount of debt in the firm increases.[7] This occurs because the income received by stockholders in a *highly leveraged* firm (one with a high ratio of debt to equity) is risky, so stockholders in such firms demand high rates of return. It is therefore improper to compare the rates of return to stockholders in two firms in order to measure differences in the degree of competition if the two firms have very different ratios of debt to equity.

A firm's debt-equity ratio influences the rate of return that stockholders earn. The debt-equity ratio has nothing to do with whether the firm is earning excess rates of return on its *assets*. For that reason, in order to test the predictions in Table 12.1, it is improper to use rates of return to *stockholders* unless one can establish that no serious biases are introduced. Differences among firms in their rates of return to stockholders could reflect differences in competition facing firms or differences in their debt-equity ratios.

Although the various measures of rates of return (for example, net income divided by assets, income to stockholders divided by the value of stockholder's equity) are different, one is not likely to obtain very different qualitative results by using one measure rather than another to test the predictions of Table 12.1. In fact, Liebowitz (1982) has shown that different measures of rates of return tend to be highly correlated.

Risk-Adjusted Rates of Return.   To determine whether a firm is earning an excess rate of return, the proper comparison is between the rate of return actually earned and the competitive **risk-adjusted rate of return,** which is defined as that rate of return earned by competitive firms engaged in projects with the same level of risk as that of the firm under analysis. Investors dislike risk and must be compensated for bearing it: the greater the risk, the higher the expected rate of return. To calculate a risk-adjusted rate of return, one must turn to methods of finance theory and calculate the rate of return that assets of any given risk are providing to investors. One measure that researchers in finance have devised to measure risk is called the *beta* of the returns on the asset. (Beta is the Greek letter, β). Beta is a measure of how closely the returns on one asset move with the returns on all other assets. An asset is considered risky if its return is sensitive to the movements of the general economy. A beta of 1 means the asset is as risky as the general economy. A beta below 1 means that the asset is less risky than the general economy, while a beta above 1 means that the asset is more risky. It is possible, but unusual, for an asset to have a negative beta. Such an asset generates returns that move in a direction opposite that of general economic conditions.

---

[7] The following example illustrates how debt can affect stockholders. Suppose that a firm has no debt and raises $1000 through sale of stock. The firm will earn next year either $100 or $200 with equal probability, plus it will receive back its $1000 investment. The stockholders therefore obtain a rate of return of either 10 percent or 20 percent for an average return of 15 percent. Suppose the firm instead raises the $1000 by issuing debt of $500 that pays 10 percent interest and selling stock worth $500. The debtholders must receive payment of interest before the stockholders receive any income. (This is the distinction between debt and equity.) Therefore, whether the firm earns $100 or $200, the debtholders receive their $500 plus $50 of interest. The stockholders receive their $500 plus either $50 or $150, so that the total amount paid to both debtholders and stockholders is $1000 plus either $100 or $200. The stockholders therefore earn either 10 percent (50 divided by 500) or 30 percent (150 divided by 500), for an average return of 20 percent. Notice that the stockholders now earn a higher average rate of return and face a wider range of outcomes, even though the income potential of the firm has remained unchanged.

Once beta is determined, there are well-known financial models that can be used to determine the rate of return required to compensate for risk as measured by beta.[8] The simplest form of one such model, the **Capital Asset Pricing Model,** predicts that the expected return on an asset equals the rate of return on risk-free investments (U.S. government treasury bills are an example of a relatively risk-free investment) plus beta times the difference between the market return (for example, return on the portfolio of all stocks) and the risk-free rate (Brealy and Myers 1984, Ch. 7–9).

Price-Cost Margins

In order to avoid the problems associated with calculating rates of return, several economists have instead turned to a different measure of performance, the **price-cost margin,** which equals

$$(\text{price} - \text{marginal cost})/\text{price} = (p - MC)/p.$$

The advantage of a price-cost margin is that it measures directly the prediction of the first column of Table 12.1 about the relationship of price to marginal costs.[9]

As shown in Chapter 5, economic theory predicts that under certain conditions the price-cost margin is related to the elasticity of demand facing the firm by the formula

$$\frac{p - MC}{p} = -\frac{1}{\epsilon}, \tag{12.2}$$

where ϵ = elasticity of demand. In a competitive industry, ϵ is infinite, hence $p = MC$.

Because it is often difficult to obtain an estimate of marginal cost, the typical measure of cost used to calculate a price-cost margin is *not* marginal cost. Instead, it is the more easily measured average variable cost with capital and advertising costs excluded. Price-cost margins are typically calculated as sales minus payroll minus materials cost divided by sales.[10] In order to see the complication that this calculation causes, suppose that marginal cost is constant and is given as

$$MC = V + (r + \delta)K/Q. \tag{12.3}$$

---

[8] Risks that are related to movements in the general economy ($\beta > 0$) must generate higher than the riskless rate of return in order to attract investors. Risks that are unrelated to the general economy ($\beta = 0$) can attract investors even if they offer only a riskless rate of return. The reason is that such risks can be diversified away, in the sense that if each investor holds only a small amount of many such independent risks, the law of averages guarantees that the resulting risk will be miniscule. Pooling independent risks is known as *diversification.* See Brealy and Myers (1984, ch. 7) for more details.

[9] Liebowitz (1982) has shown that the correlation between accounting rates of return and the price-cost margin can be relatively low. For this reason, it can make a difference which of the two types of performance measures is used.

[10] See Fisher (1987) for a critique of the typical price-cost margin.

Equation 12.3 describes a technology that requires K/Q units of capital to produce 1 unit of output. The competitive rate of return is r, the depreciation rate is δ, and the cost of the labor and materials needed to produce 1 unit of Q is V. Notice that V is the average variable cost of labor and materials. Many, if not most, studies of price-cost margins use V instead of marginal cost, because data on marginal cost are not readily available. Doing so can lead to serious bias, however, as can be seen by substituting (12.3) into (12.2) to obtain:

$$\frac{p - V}{p} - (r + \delta)\frac{K}{pQ} = -\frac{1}{\epsilon},$$

or

$$\frac{p - V}{p} = -\frac{1}{\epsilon} + (r + \delta)\frac{K}{pQ}. \qquad (12.4)$$

Equation 12.4 shows that if one uses $(p - V)/p$ instead of $(p - MC)/p$, one must recognize that an additional term, equal to the rental value of capital divided by the value of output, must be added to Equation 12.2.

It is also improper to use average total cost, rather than marginal cost, to calculate the price-cost margin. The reason is that average total cost does not generally equal marginal cost, which is the proper cost concept to use in Equation (12.2).

Tobin's *q*

Another measure of performance is the ratio of the market value of a firm (as measured by the market value of its outstanding stock and debt) to the replacement cost of the firm's assets. This measure of performance is not used as often as either rates of return or price-cost margins. It is sometimes referred to as **Tobin's *q*** because of work done by Tobin (1969) on investment theory. If a firm is valued at more than what it would cost (including a normal rate of return) to rebuild it, then excess profits are being earned. These profits are above and beyond the level that is necessary to keep the firm in the industry. The difficulty with this measure of performance is in constructing the replacement cost of the assets of the firm.

■ MEASURES OF MARKET STRUCTURE

Once a measure of performance is decided upon one must still determine the measure of market structure in order to check the predictions of Table 12.1. **Market structure** refers to those characteristics that influence the competitiveness of a market. A variety of measures are used, all of which are thought to have some relation to the degree of competitiveness. One difficulty with most measures of market structure is that they often depend on how profitable an industry is. That is, if an industry is extraordinarily profitable, it is likely to attract entry; by most measures, therefore, it appears competitive. Theoretically, the predicted relationships of Table 12.1 are between exogenous measures of market structure and economic performance. *Exogenous* means that the measures are unaffected by levels of profitability and, according to Table 12.1, determine profitability rather than vice versa. The problem with obtaining exogenous measures of market structure is usually ignored in studies of the relationship of performance to market structure, and this issue is discussed in more detail later. Let us now describe some of the most common variables that have been used to measure the market structure of an industry.

Industry Concentration

By far the most common variable used to measure the market structure of an industry is the four-firm concentration ratio, which measures the share of industry sales accounted for by the top four firms. If this share is large, the industry is said to be *concentrated* and is thought to be less competitive than an industry in which the four-firm concentration ratio is low. The following discussion considers whether this interpretation of concentration is appropriate.

The relevant *economic market* for Product A includes all products that significantly constrain the price of Product A. (This concept is discussed in Chapter 7 and again in Chapter 22.) In order for industry concentration to be a meaningful predictor of industry performance, it must be true that the industry comprises a relevant economic market. Otherwise, knowing that the industry is concentrated would have no implication at all for pricing. For example, in examining the price of Product A, for which Product B is a very good substitute, it would be improper to consider only the four-firm concentration ratio for Product A. If Products A and B are close substitutes, the relevant concentration measure should include firms producing Product A and also firms producing Product B.[11] Unfortunately, analysts are often constrained in their choice of concentration statistics by the available data. Concentration ratios are published by the government for specifically defined industries and products, and the definitions used do not necessarily coincide with relevant economic markets. If the concentration ratios are not based on an economically meaningful market definition, there is no reason to expect a relationship between the pricing or profits of a product and the concentration ratio.

It is, of course, arbitrary to focus attention on the top four firms in defining concentration ratios. Industry concentration has been measured in other ways. One can use the share of the top eight firms instead of the share of the top four. (The government also publishes statistics on eight-firm concentration ratios.) One could also use a *function* of all the individual firms' market shares to measure concentration. The most common function is the **Herfindahl-Hirschman index (HHI).** The HHI equals the sum of the squared market shares of each firm in the market, and statistics on industry HHIs are now published by the government. For example, if an industry has three firms with market shares of 50, 30, and 20 percent, then the HHI equals 3800 (2500 + 900 + 400). The use of the HHI has increased in recent years because of its use by the Department of Justice and Federal Trade Commission in evaluating mergers. Typically, though, empirical

---

[11] If the producers of some Product C could profitably switch production to Product A, then the producers of Product C should also be considered in the market for Product A. Product C is called a *supply substitute* for Product A.

results do not depend on whether one uses the HHI or a four-firm concentration index to measure industry concentration. The HHI can be theoretically derived as the right index of concentration to use to explain prices in a particular model of oligopoly behavior (see Appendix 12C).

Finally, one could separately examine the effects of the market shares of the first, second, third, fourth, etc. firms on industry performance. For example, one could determine whether increases in the market share of the second firm raise prices by as much as increases in the share of the leading firm.

Concentration measures are often based on aggregate national statistics. If the geographic extent of the market is local, as occurs, for example, when transport costs are very high, then use of national concentration statistics could provide a misleading description of the local market structures that determine prices. Some researchers use distance shipped to identify those situations in which use of national data could be misleading. The idea is that if distance shipped is short, then the concentration in the local market may be much different from the national market concentration.

Barriers to Entry

As discussed in Chapter 7, the most important variable determining industry performance is probably the ability of firms to enter the industry. Empirical measures of entry barriers that have been used include efficient firm size, advertising intensity, and capital intensity, as well as subjective estimates of the difficulty of entering specific industries. When long-run entry barriers are significant, prices can remain elevated above competitive levels.

In Chapter 7, a distinction was made between two concepts: a long-run barrier to entry and the speed with which entry can occur. Most researchers do not distinguish these two concepts, and so any measure they use for entry barrier typically reflects both concepts.

Buyer Concentration

For the same reason that seller concentration leads to higher prices, buyer concentration conversely leads to lower prices. When buyers are large and powerful, their concentration can offset the power of sellers. For that reason, several researchers have included buyer concentration as a market structure variable explaining industry performance.

Unionization

Several researchers use the degree of unionization to explain industry performance. If an industry is highly unionized, the union may be able to capture the industry profits by extracting them through higher wages. Moreover, the higher wages would drive prices up. Therefore, unionization may raise prices to final consumers even though profits to the firms in the industry are not excessive. It is also possible that unions could raise wages and prices and also raise profits to the industry. By making it costly to expand the labor force, unions can prevent industry competition from expanding output and driving profits down.

TABLE 12.2   Average Annual Returns, 1948–76

Industry	Nominal Rate of Return	Own Rate of Return*
Agriculture	.07	.04
Crude petroleum	.12	.08
Food	.10	.07
Tobacco	.14	.11
Textiles	.09	.06
Chemicals	.13	.10
Motor vehicles	.29	.25
All manufacturing-median industry	.11	.08
Railroads	.07	.03
Telephone and telegraph	.15	.11
Retail trade	.10	.07

*The own rate of return subtracts from income the effects of increases in the price of capital for each industry. If the price of capital changes only with inflation, the own rate of return is a real (inflation-adjusted) rate of return.

SOURCE: Fraumeni and Jorgenson (1980).

■ EMPIRICAL RESULTS RELATING STRUCTURE TO PERFORMANCE

This section presents the key empirical findings on the relationship between industry structure and performance for each of the three measures of performance that have been discussed. The section begins with a general description of the rates of return that different manufacturing industries have earned. After discussing the key empirical findings for each of the three performance measures, the section concludes with a critique of the results and their interpretation.

General Results on Rates of Return

Fraumeni and Jorgenson (1980) calculate the after-tax economic rate of return for a large sample of American industries over the period 1948–76. This study is careful to calculate an economic rate of return, taking into account many of the subtle points discussed earlier. They find that over this period, the median manufacturing industry earned a nominal (unadjusted for inflation) rate of return of approximately 11 percent. Over this same period, the average rate paid on high-grade, tax-free municipal bonds was roughly 3.8 percent, so the rate of return in manufacturing significantly exceeded the rate of return on municipal bonds, presumably to compensate for the increased risk.[12] Selected findings of Fraumeni and Jorgenson are presented in Table 12.2.

Fraumeni and Jorgenson reach two conclusions. First, rates of return differ greatly across industries. Second, their detailed investigation of rates of return by year reveal that

---

[12] *Economic Report of the President*, Table B–67 (1983).

TABLE 12.3	Rate of Return on Stockholder's Equity, 1948–76

Industry	Nominal Rate of Return
Food	.10
Tobacco	.13
Textiles	.08
Chemicals	.14
Motor vehicles	.15
Median—all mfg.	.11

SOURCE: Federal Trade Commission. *Quarterly Financial Reports, 1948–76.*

differences in rates of return across industries persist for many years. If there are no long-run barriers to entry or exit, rates of return across industries should tend to converge. Fraumeni and Jorgenson's results challenge this idea with what appear to be persistent differences across industries. Perhaps the rate of entry and exit is very slow, so that convergence in rates of return is slow across industries, or perhaps the different levels of risk in each industry help explain different returns.

Studies that calculate rates of return often differ in their methodologies and, because of data constraints, are often forced to calculate something other than economic rates of return. Nevertheless, they can still be valuable in investigating whether the rate of return in one industry is higher than that in another, as long as the biases in the calculated rates of return are similar across different industries. It is dangerous, however, to compare the absolute levels of rates of return from one study with the absolute levels of rates of return from another study if the studies follow different methodologies for calculating rates of return.

To illustrate the differences that can arise when different concepts are used to calculate rates of return, Table 12.3 presents the returns on the book value of stockholders' equity published by the Federal Trade Commission for some of the same industries reported in Table 12.2. (The book value of stockholder's equity is an accounting concept that equals the difference in the book values of assets and liabilities.) These rates of return are calculated as after-tax (corporate) income (which deducts interest payments on debt) divided by the stockholder's equity in the company. A comparison of Tables 12.2 and 12.3 shows how different methodologies can lead to different rates of return. For example, the nominal rate of return in motor vehicles is about 29 percent according to Fraumeni and Jorgenson (1980) but is 15 percent according to Table 12.3.[13] This difference illustrates the earlier warning about noncomparability of rates of return when they are calculated according to different methods. Notice, though, that relative rates of return between industries do match up pretty well for the two tables; for example, tobacco earns a higher rate of return than textiles in both tables.

---

[13] Certain industries are dropped from Table 12.3 because of the unavailability of data after 1973. The median for 1948–73 in manufacturing was also about 11 percent.

TABLE 12.4   Average Profit Rates (selected industries)

Eight-Firm Concentration Ratio over 70%		Eight-Firm Concentration Ratio below 70%	
Industry	*Profit Rate (%)*	*Industry*	*Profit Rate (%)*
Auto	15.5	Shoes	9.6
Cigarettes	11.6	Beer	10.9
Ethical drugs	17.9	Bituminous coal	8.8
Liquor	9.0	Canned fruits and vegetables	7.7
Steel	9.0	Average for all industries studied	9.0
Average for all industries studied	13.3		

SOURCE: Mann (1966, 299).

Rates of Return and Industry Structure

Joe Bain deserves the credit for pioneering work that has led to a voluminous literature investigating the relationship between rates of return and industry structure. Bain (1951) investigates 42 industries and separates them into two groups: those with an eight-firm concentration ratio in excess of 70 percent and those with an eight-firm concentration ratio below 70 percent. He finds that the rate of return (calculated roughly as income divided by the book value of stockholder's equity) for the more concentrated industries is 11.8 percent, while the corresponding rate for the less concentrated industries is 7.5 percent. Bain (1956) classifies industries by his subjective estimate as to the extent of barriers to entry, using factors discussed in Chapter 7. His hypothesis is that profits should be higher in industries with high concentration and high barriers to entry. The evidence that Bain presents confirms his hypothesis.

Brozen (1971) criticizes Bain's findings for two reasons. First, as Bain recognizes, the industries that Bain studies could be in disequilibrium. Brozen shows that the industries Bain identifies as highly profitable suffered a subsequent decline in their profits, while the industries of lower profitability enjoyed a subsequent increase in profits. In fact, for the 42 industries of Bain's initial 1951 study, the profit difference of 4.3 percent that he finds between the highly concentrated and less concentrated groups diminished to only 1.1 percent by the mid-1950s (Brozen 1971). Brozen also points out that Bain's use in some of his work of the profit rates of the leading firms, rather than the profit rate of the industry, could have skewed his results.

Using data over the 1950 to 1960 period, Mann (1966) is able to reproduce many of Bain's original findings. Using the same 70 percent concentration ratio as Bain used to divide his sample into two groups, Mann finds that the rate of return for the more highly concentrated group is 13.3 percent, while the rate of return for the less concentrated group is 9.0 percent. Table 12.4 presents a sampling of Mann's results.

Mann also investigates the relationship between profit and his own subjective estimates of barriers to entry. He finds that industries with "very high" barriers to entry enjoy higher profits than those with "substantial" barriers, which in turn earn higher profits than those with "moderate to low" barriers. He confirms Bain's predictions and earlier findings that

TABLE 12.5   Average Profit Rates in High-Concentration Industries by Mann's Barriers to Entry 1950–60

Industry	Profit Rate (%)
Very High Barrier	
Auto	15.5
Chewing gum	17.5
Cigarettes	11.6
Average	16.4
Substantial Barrier	
Steel	10.8
Soap	13.3
Average	11.1
Moderate to Low Barrier	
Glass containers	13.3
Razors	8.5
Average	11.9

SOURCE: Mann (1966, 300).

concentrated industries with very high barriers to entry have higher average profit rates than concentrated industries that do not have very high barriers to entry. Table 12.5 reports Mann's findings for highly concentrated industries.

An important question is what quantitative implications a high rate of return has for prices. For example, one can ask by how much price would have to fall in an industry in order for that industry to earn a normal rate of return. To see how excess rates of return translate into price overcharges, suppose that a firm earns a rate of return that is 5 percent higher than normal. This means that the firm's invested capital earns excess revenues of 5 percent times the value of its capital above what it would earn if it were in a competitive industry. If the firm's revenues were lower by exactly that amount, it would earn a normal rate of return. Therefore, calculating the amount by which revenues (R) must decline as a fraction of total revenues in order to yield normal returns to the firm is a measure of the amount by which price would have to decline in order to yield a normal rate of return. In other words, one calculates $(R - .05\,K)/R$, or $[1 - (.05\,K/R)]$, where K is the value of capital and K/R is the ratio of the value of capital to revenues. This number tells us the approximate percentage of revenue that the firm can keep if it is to earn a normal rate of return.

In many manufacturing industries, the ratio of the value of capital to the value of revenue is roughly 1. Therefore, if a firm is earning a real rate of return 5 percent higher than the normal rate of return (which was roughly between 5 percent and 10 percent over the period 1948–76), one can say that price would have to fall to roughly $1 - .05$ or about 95 percent of its current value. This means that industries that earn a rate of return 1.5 times higher than the return earned by competitive industries (that is, 15 percent instead of, say, 10 percent) have raised price by only 5 percent above the competitive level. This price overcharge is the same as would occur if a monopolist faced an elasticity of about 21.[14] In other words, even large differences in rates of return between concentrated and unconcentrated industries do not necessarily imply large price overcharges above a competitive level. In industries with very small amounts of capital, even large excess returns can translate into tiny price overcharges.

There have been numerous econometric estimates of the relation between rates of return, concentration, and a variety of other variables, such as those measuring barriers to entry.[15] Econometric studies attempt to measure the effects of several variables on rates of return. Such a study not only can provide an estimate of the effect of one variable upon another but also can reveal how reliable the estimate is. When the estimate is "statistically insignificant," that means that the data are consistent with the hypothesis that the true effect of a variable is zero. (More precisely, the data fail to reject the hypothesis that the true effect is zero.) Weiss (1974) concludes in his survey of several of these studies that there was indeed some relationship between profits, concentration, and barriers to entry. Recent work seems to indicate, at best, a weak relationship that often is not statistically significant. For example, Salinger (1984) estimates an effect that is close to being statistically significant for minimum efficient scale in concentrated industries but not for any of his other entry barrier variables (for example, advertising intensity). (As already discussed in Chapter 7, large capital requirements do not constitute a long-run barrier to entry unless other conditions, like imperfect capital markets or sunk costs, are present.)

Econometric studies linking profit to market structure often find that measured profitability is correlated with the advertising-to-sales ratio and with the ratio of research and development expenditures to sales. These studies also often find that high rates of return and industry growth are related.

Price-Cost Margins and Industry Structure

Beginning with the work of Collins and Preston (1969), it has become routine to use Census data to investigate econometrically the relationship in any one year between the variations in price-cost margins (based on average variable costs) across industries and various indicators of industry structure, such as the four-firm concentration ratio and the capital-output ratio. Such an estimated relationship is called a *regression*. A typical relationship that has been estimated in this literature is reproduced below for data from 1958 (Domowitz, Hubbard, and Petersen 1986, 7).

$$\frac{p - V}{p} = \frac{.16}{(.01)} + \frac{.10C4}{(.02)} + \frac{.08K/Q}{(.02)} + \text{other variables,}$$

---

[14] Since

$$\frac{p - MC}{p} = -\frac{1}{\epsilon},$$

then if $\epsilon = -21$, p equals $1.05MC$, or 2 percent above marginal cost.

[15] See Weiss (1974) for a survey of early studies and Schmalensee (1989) for a survey of more recent studies.

where $\dfrac{p - V}{p}$ = price-cost margin (V is a measure of average variable cost),

$C4$ = four-firm concentration ratio, and

K/Q = (book) value of capital to value of output.

The numbers in parentheses below each coefficient are standard errors, which are a measure of how accurately the coefficients are estimated. A commonly used method to express the confidence one has in a coefficient is to construct an interval (called a "95% confidence interval") for a coefficient that includes all values within roughly two standard errors of the estimated coefficient. So, for example, such a confidence interval for the coefficient on $C4$ would be (.06, .14).

Let us use this equation to investigate the sensitivity of price to increases in concentration. For a typical industry studied, the value of K/Q is roughly .4. The equation predicts that for such an industry, if the concentration ratio of the top four firms is 50 percent (.5) and if other variables equal zero, then the predicted price-cost margin would be as follows:

$$\frac{p - V}{p} = .16 + (.10)(.5) + .08(.4) = .24, \text{ or } p - V = .24p$$
$$.76\, p = V, \text{ or } p = 1.3V.$$

Hence price would be 1.3 times average variable cost, or roughly 30 percent above average variable cost.

Suppose now that this industry becomes so concentrated that its four-firm concentration ratio doubles from 50 percent (.5) to 100 percent (1). The equation then predicts the following price-cost margin:

$$\frac{p - V}{p} = .16 + .10(1) + .08(.4) = .29,$$

or price will be approximately 1.4 times average variable cost. That is, price goes up by only about 7 percent, even though concentration goes from 50 to 100 percent. This suggests that even very large differences in concentration serve to raise price by relatively modest amounts.

Domowitz, Hubbard, and Petersen (1986) carefully investigate the behavior of the price-cost margin over the time period 1958–81. Their results are striking. First, they find that the differential in price-cost margins among industries of high and low concentration has been greatly reduced over time, as has the differential between consumer- and producer-good industries. Second, they find when they estimate a price-cost equation with more recent data that the coefficient associated with the concentration ratio is much lower than its value in 1958. That is, the already small effect of concentration on price in 1958 is even smaller in later years. Furthermore, they find that the statistical significance of that coefficient vanishes during the later period. In general, they find that the relationship between price-cost margins and concentration is unstable, and to the extent that any relationship exists, it is quite weak, especially in recent times.

In addition to using Census data on industry price-cost margins to investigate the link between price-cost margins and industry structure, other investigators have used Federal Trade Commission (FTC) data to investigate price-cost margins at the individual firm level.[16] One of the most ambitious of these studies is by Kwoka and Ravenscraft (1985). They investigate the firm's price-cost margin as a function of the industry concentration ratio, the individual market shares of the largest firms in the industry, an estimate of the minimum efficient scale of the firm (that minimum size below which it is uneconomic to produce), the advertising sales ratio, and several other variables. The advantage of using the firm rather than the industry as the unit of observation is that the researcher can disentangle the effect of industry concentration on a firm's price-cost margin from the effect of the efficiency of that firm alone. For example, one firm's price-cost margin may be high either because the firm is particularly efficient (low cost relative to all other firms) or because all firms in the industry enjoy a high price-cost margin (lack of competition in the industry).

The results of studies such as Kwoka and Ravenscraft (1985) are somewhat difficult to summarize concisely, but basically they support the following proposition: In many cases the positive effect on price of industry concentration vanishes when one accounts for the market share of the individual firm. It is not true, however, that the effects of industry concentration are always nonexistent. It appears that for some industries greater concentration seems to raise prices. In other industries it appears that the high price-cost margins observed are due not to industry concentration but to the efficiency of the largest firms. The best summary of the studies using individual firm data is that the link between higher concentration and higher price-cost margins is ambiguous. In many cases the link, if it exists at all, is very weak, and in many other cases no link exists at all. Kwoka and Ravenscraft also include industry growth as an explanatory variable and find it to have a significant and positive effect on price-cost margins. They also find that the presence of a large second or third firm greatly reduces the price-cost margin that can be earned. This finding indicates that it can be a mistake to use only four-firm concentration ratios to measure market structure. Other common findings in the general literature[17] on price-cost margins are that increased buyer concentration sometimes lowers price-cost margins (Lustgarten 1975), that a higher advertising-sales ratio may raise the price-cost margin (Comanor and Wilson 1967), and that unions lower the price-cost margin (Freeman 1983).[18]

The Relationship Between Tobin's *q* and Industry Structure

Another measure of market power is Tobin's *q*, which is defined as the ratio between market valuation of assets and the replacement cost of assets (Tobin 1969). If *q* is above 1, it indicates that the firm is earning a rate of return higher than that justified by the cost

---

[16] See Benston (1985) for a criticism of studies that rely on the FTC data. Researchers using FTC data use a measure of average variable cost to construct a price-cost margin.

[17] There is voluminous literature investigating the relationship between measures of price-cost margins and structure. The interested reader is referred to the survey article of Schmalensee (1989).

[18] See Voos and Mishel (1986), whose analysis shows that although unions may depress the price-cost margin, they do not result in a significant elevation of price above that which would prevail in the absence of a union.

of its assets. Such a return could not persist in the absence of long-run entry barriers. The advantage of using Tobin's q is that the difficult problem of estimating rates of return or marginal costs are avoided. On the other hand, for q to be meaningful, one needs accurate measures of both the market value and replacement cost of a firm's assets.

It is usually possible to get an accurate estimate for the market value of a firm's assets by summing the values of the securities that a firm has issued, such as stocks and bonds. It is much more complicated to obtain an estimate of the replacement costs of its assets, unless markets for used equipment exist. Moreover, expenditures on advertising and research and development create intangible assets that may be hard to value. Typically, researchers who construct Tobin's q ignore the replacement costs of these intangible assets in their calculations. For that reason, q typically exceeds 1. Accordingly, it can be misleading to use q as a measure of market power without further adjustment.

If one believes that there is market power and that q is measured correctly, then it is possible to determine the monopoly overcharge once q has been correctly calculated. If q exceeds 1, the monopolist is charging a price higher than the competitive price. It is straightforward to calculate how much earnings (excluding the return to capital) would have to fall in order for q to equal 1. Let e_m be the annual earnings of the monopolist and let e_c be the annual earnings of a firm under competition. The ratio of the market value of assets to the replacement cost of assets then equals the ratio of e_m to e_c. Therefore, $e_m/e_c = q$. For example, if q equals 2, earnings must fall by one-half before the firm is charging a competitive price.

Table 12.6 reports some of the measured values of q for U.S. industries. Notice that the median value, 1.35, exceeds 1. Such a value of q implies that, barring measurement problems, price is typically above competitive levels.

There have been several investigations of the relationship of q to industry market structure, notably by Salinger (1984), Smirlock et al. (1984), Thomadakis (1977), and Lindenberg and Ross (1981). Lindenberg and Ross (1981) find that the q ratios of firms appear to be quite stable over time and that firms with high q ratios tend to have unique products and factors of production, all of which contribute to monopoly or *quasi-rents* (earnings in excess of the minimum necessary to induce the firm to produce). Firms with

---

TABLE 12.6   Average Tobin's q, 1960–76

Industry	q
Photo equipment	3.08
Chemicals	2.4
Food products	1.7
Tobacco	1.39
Apparel	1.13
Primary metals	.85
Median	1.35

SOURCE: Lindenberg E., and S. Ross. 1981. *Journal of Business* 54:1, © 1981 by The University of Chicago. All Rights Reserved.

low q ratios are typically in relatively competitive or tightly regulated industries. Lindenberg and Ross find a high correlation between price-cost margins and q, but a low correlation between q and concentration ratios. One interpretation of this result is that Census concentration ratios are not particularly useful for identifying relevant economic markets subject to market power.

Even if the level of q is not meaningful because of measurement errors, it may be possible to analyze the relationship between q and market structure in a regression, as long as one adjusts for the measurement problems by adding variables like the advertising/ sales ratio and research and development costs. This procedure is similar to that used in the price-cost regressions. Salinger (1984) has performed an econometric study relating q to barriers to entry, industry concentration, and unionization. Salinger makes several important methodological points. First, as Bain (1956) points out, without barriers to entry, there is no reason for market power to arise just because an industry is concentrated. Therefore, a relationship, arising from market power, between q and concentration should be present only when entry barriers exist. Second, if concentration arises because the most efficient firms get large, then there should be a negative effect on price from concentration. Finally, unions may capture any monopoly rents and would reduce the strength of the relationship between q and market power.

Salinger estimates the following equation:

$$q = b_0 + b_1(A/K) + b_2(R/K) + (1 - b_3U)C4[b_4M + b_5K + b_6(A/K)] + b_7C4 + b_8G,$$

where b_i's = coefficients to be estimated,

K = capital

A/K = advertising/capital ratio,

R/K = research and development/capital ratio,

U = unionization ratio (fraction of work force unionized),

$C4$ = four-firm concentration ratio,

M = minimum efficient sale, and

G = industry growth rate.

Salinger's empirical results are that b_4, b_5, b_6, b_7 are not statistically significant. Therefore, the data provide no statistically significant support for the views that entry barriers raise price or that efficient firms get large. Salinger finds that industries that are growing rapidly earn high returns. Salinger's results regarding unionization are discussed later.

Criticism of Results

There are several criticisms about the existing studies relating performance to market structure. The following sections discuss the most important ones.

High Profits and Efficiency.   As already indicated, one should not leap to the conclusion that high profits or margins indicate poor performance (that is, consumers paying excessively high prices). An alternative interpretation of a link between profit performance and concentration is that the largest firms tend to be the most efficient or innovative (Demsetz 1973; Peltzman 1977). Only when a firm is efficient or innovative is it profitable to expand in a market and make the market concentrated. In this interpretation, a successful firm attracts consumers, either through lower prices or better products. A firm's success, as measured both by its profits and its market share, is an indicator of consumer satisfaction, not an indicator of poor performance. One implication of this hypothesis is that a firm's success is explained by its own market share and not by industry concentration. Some empirical support for this hypothesis has already been discussed (Kwoka and Ravenscraft 1985).

Smirlock et al. (1984) use data on Tobin's q for individual firms and the market shares of individual firms as well as data on the industry concentration. They find that except at very high concentration levels, industry concentration is not a significant variable explaining a firm's q once one accounts for a firm's market share. The interpretation of this result is that a firm's financial success is almost entirely explained by its efficiency and not by industry concentration.

Cross-Sectional Studies.   Most of the studies discussed are cross-sectional studies that try to relate profits, price-cost margins, or Tobin's q across different industries to the differing levels of competition in those industries. This approach can lead to serious error.

Imagine that there are two industries. One has a high elasticity of demand, and the other has a low elasticity of demand. Suppose both industries are completely monopolized. Chapter 5 explains that the price-cost margin in the industry with the high elasticity of demand is much lower than the price-cost margin in the industry with the low elasticity of demand. The cross-sectional approach to estimating the relationship between performance and concentration assumes that the relationship between price and concentration is the *same* in every industry; thus, the approach implicitly assumes that different industries have similar elasticities of demand. To the extent that elasticities of demand differ, imposing such an assumption of homogeneity across different industries is likely to lead to error. A much more reliable method is to examine one industry over time as its degree of competition changes, for example, because of changes in government regulation. In such a study, changes in performance occur because of changes in concentration, not simply because of differences in the elasticity of demand among different industries.

Measurement Error.   The numerous pitfalls in calculating measures of performance (for example, rate of return, price-cost margin, Tobin's q) do not imply that relationships between performance measures and concentration are necessarily biased, although they can be. They do mean that one should always include variables in addition to concentration to control for such measurement problems. However, one must also recognize that inclusion of such variables may not always remove the bias. For example, as discussed, most price-cost margins ignore capital and advertising. Therefore, one should include those two variables in any statistical analysis of price-cost margins and concentration in order to control for the measurement error in the price-cost margin. However, if concentrated industries advertise a lot, it is not obvious that including advertising as a variable will allow for unbiased estimation of the relation between concentration and margins, especially if advertising has been changing over time. Remember also that the proper interpretation of the coefficients of variables such as advertising is that they reflect, in part, measurement error and not fundamental economic forces influencing "true" price-cost margins (based on marginal costs).

A serious problem arises when the *explanatory variables* (those used to explain the measure of performance) are measured with error. For example, the concentration ratio for an industry whose products compete closely with those of another industry may understate the amount of competition. If plastic bottles compete with glass bottles, for example, the concentration ratio in the glass-bottle industry may tell one very little about market power in that industry. Moreover, if imports of glass bottles are significant, a concentration ratio based on domestic sales is the wrong one to use (Census concentration ratios do not reflect imports). An improper concentration measure naturally makes a relationship between performance and concentration hard to find, and any relationship that is found will be inaccurately estimated.

Stability of Profits Over Time. It is important to remember that Table 12.1 says nothing about the relationship of short-run profits and market structure. For that reason, one must be careful to use a long-run measure of profits if profits are used to measure performance. Any relationships uncovered using short-run profits are likely to be unstable over time.

How long it takes to reach the long run will differ by industry. In the ordinary course of events, some industries are expected to be highly profitable while others are not. Over time, one expects exit from the low-profit industries and entry into the high-profit industries, which should tend to drive rates of return to a common level. These expectations suggest that a proper issue for study is the rate at which excess profits are eroded. Connolly and Schwartz (1985), Mueller (1985), and Stigler (1963) find that high profits often decline slowly in highly concentrated industries. It is only by analyzing both the level of profits (or other measures of performance) and the rate at which they change that the analyst can distinguish the two concepts, discussed in Chapter 7, of a long-run barrier to entry and the speed with which entry occurs.

Multiproduct Firms. Most firms do not make just one product; therefore, any estimate of profits or price-cost margins for a firm involves averages across different products. For a firm that makes products in many different industries, aggregate statistics can be misleading. For example, the Census assigns firms to industry categories based on the primary products produced and includes their total value of production under that industry category. The Census also tabulates statistics at the product level, based on data from individual plants. Because a plant is less likely than a firm to produce several products, product-level data are more accurate for performance studies than industry-level data and should be used.

Just as errors can be made if too aggregate statistics are used, so too can errors arise if too narrow categories are used. For example, suppose a firm performs research to discover new products and is successful about one time in ten. If the firm's expected profits are zero, then the profits on the successful product must be high enough to offset the losses on the nine failures. It would be misleading to conclude that there are excessively high profits based on an examination of the profits of the successful product.

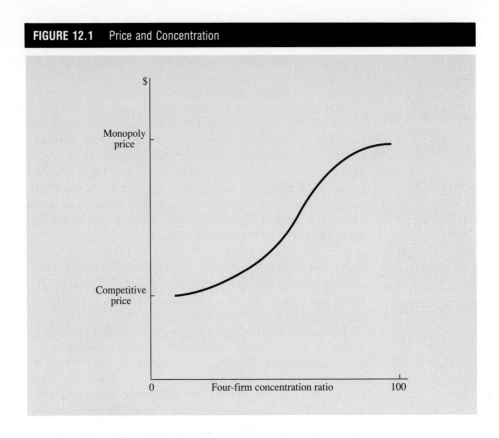

FIGURE 12.1 Price and Concentration

Functional Form. Many studies estimate linear relations between price (or other measures of performance) and concentration. Most analysts would expect very little relationship between price (or other measures of performance) and concentration at low levels of concentration, while at very high levels of concentration, it is unlikely that prices (or other measures of performance) increase at a constant rate as concentration increases.[19] Once a certain level of concentration has been achieved, additional increments of concentration are not likely to increase price at the same rate, which suggests an S-shaped curve (see Figure 12.1) for the relationship between price and concentration. Notice that an S-shaped curve can be approximated by a straight line as long as extremes of concentration at either the high end or the low end are not too prevalent. On the other hand, at very low levels of price or very high levels of concentration, a simple linear relationship would yield a misleading prediction of the effect of increasing concentration on price.

Some researchers (White 1976; Bradburd and Over 1982) have searched for critical levels of concentration below which price is less likely to increase as concentration

---

[19] An extension of this point is that the way in which each relevant variable influences price, or even which variables are relevant, may change as concentration changes.

increases, and threshold levels of concentration above which price is more likely to increase as concentration increases. They have been only partially successful: there does appear to be some evidence of an increase in profitability at four-firm concentration ratios above roughly 50–60 percent.[20]

Simultaneity Bias.   As already explained, it is improper to regard some of the measures of market structure as completely unaffected by levels of profits or prices. Presumably, high profits induce entry and thereby lower concentration. They also create incentives to overcome barriers to entry. Accordingly, the degree of concentration in an industry is not a proper variable with which to explain performance; rather, concentration and performance should be explained simultaneously. Weiss (1974) reestimates several equations using statistical techniques designed to deal with this simultaneity problem and find that the different estimation procedures make little difference.[21] Even if the results do not change, their interpretation does. It is incorrect to believe that industry structure as measured by concentration determines industry conduct and performance: they are interrelated.

STUDIES OF THE RELATIONSHIP BETWEEN MARKET STRUCTURE AND PERFORMANCE FOR INDIVIDUAL INDUSTRIES

The preceding section discusses a number of serious shortcomings in cross-sectional studies of the relationship between structure and performance across different industries. Two of the most serious concerns are that (1) it is unrealistic to expect the same relationship between structure and performance to hold across all industries, and (2) it is unlikely that the four-firm concentration ratios published in the Census necessarily correspond to the concentration ratios for relevant economic markets. If concentration ratios are not defined for the proper markets, one should not expect to find any correlation between performance and concentration. To remedy these two problems, several studies have focused, not on a cross-section of different industries, but on one industry over time or across different locations.[22] Three such industry studies are reviewed here.

Banking

The relationship of market structure and performance in banking is the subject of numerous studies. Part of the reason for this is that the Federal Reserve is charged with the responsibility under the Bank Merger Act of 1960 to consider the effects on competition

---

[20] Bradburd and Over (1982) present evidence that the effect of concentration on an industry's performance depends on levels of past concentration. As a highly concentrated industry becomes less concentrated, price remains higher than it would if the industry had never been highly concentrated.

[21] Weiss concluded that there was a link between concentration and profits.

[22] One should always ask why concentration is different over time or across locations. If concentration is responding to profits, then the same simultaneity problems arise as are present in cross-sectional studies.

when banks desire to merge. These studies analyze the effects of concentration on various measures of performance of banks, such as the prices they charge for providing certain services and the interest rates on loans.[23] A common finding of the best of these studies is that market concentration does indeed raise the prices of services or interest rates charged on loans to consumers. The effect of market concentration is statistically significant; however, as in aggregate studies, the magnitude of the effect is typically quite small. For example, Gilbert (1984, 644) concludes that "The studies that use the most appropriate measures of bank performance and the best estimation procedures find significant influences of market structure on bank performance. . . . The economic significance of the influence of market structure on bank performance is very small, however, in even the best studies."

Airlines

Since the airline industry has been deregulated, there have been several studies of the effects of concentration on fares between city pairs. The airline industry is interesting to study because it appears to have low costs of entry between city pairs for airlines already in operation. All that is needed is to fly a plane from wherever it is to the new origin and destination pair. In fact, airlines are often used in examples of contestable markets. Despite the apparent ease of entry, studies of the airline industry consistently show that concentration in a city pair market does influence fares.[24] Actual entry, not potential entry, is important in influencing airline fares. Studies by Call and Keeler (1985), Bailey, Graham, and Kaplan (1985) and Graham, Kaplan, and Sibley (1983) all show that fares rise as concentration increases. They typically find that fares rise by roughly 6 percent if the four-firm concentration ratio doubles from 50 to 100 percent between two cities (Bailey, Graham, Kaplan 1985, 165). Once again there is a statistically significant effect of concentration on performance, but it is of modest magnitude. Borenstein (1988) presents evidence that concentration at a city (rather than on a particular route between two cities) can also lead to modest increases in fares.

Railroads

A few studies have been done of the effects of competition on railroad rates. Railroads were deregulated under the Staggers Act of 1980 and given greater freedom to set fares. An advantage of studying railroads is that it is now so costly to build a railroad that no one is likely to enter with a new large rail system. Therefore, the number of competitors can be taken as a completely exogenous variable if one focuses on commodities that are

---

[23] See Gilbert (1984) for an extensive survey.

[24] One interpretation of this result is that it is not so easy to construct an optimal airline network that flies passengers to the appropriate hubs. Only in very dense markets with heavy end-to-end travel between city pairs (for example, Chicago–New York) with no interconnecting passengers (and hence no need for feeder traffic) are markets likely to be contestable. For more discussion on the economics of networks, see Carlton and Klamer (1983). The limited numbers of gates, landing slots, and take-off slots at congested airports also limit the ease of entry.

shipped only by rail and for which truck (or other) transportation is uneconomical. With such a focus, one can estimate an equation analyzing railroad rates as a function of distance, tons shipped, and concentration.

MacDonald (1987) estimates that with no competition, a railroad is able to charge rates for wheat that are 18 percent higher than when there is a competing railroad.[25] When three railroads compete, rates fall by another 2 percent. These results are statistically significant, yet they indicate that rates do not go up all that much even for dramatic increases in concentration. (Although 20 percent is not small, it is less than one might expect as the difference between monopoly and competition among these firms.)[26]

■ FOREIGN STUDIES OF MARKET STRUCTURE AND PERFORMANCE

There have been several attempts to relate market structure to performance for foreign countries. It is important to remember when examining foreign data that foreign markets are often much less isolated from international trade than American markets; therefore, concentration ratios based only on domestic concentration may not be economically meaningful as measures of market power. The relevant competition may well be from firms located outside the individual country. The results of studies using foreign data are generally similar to those using U.S. data, in that they have difficulty detecting an economically and statistically significant effect of concentration on performance (Hart and Morgan 1977; Geroski 1981). Encoau and Geroski (1984) find that the United States, the United Kingdom, and Japan tend to have slow rates of price adjustment in their most concentrated sectors.[27] One interesting finding that emerges from studies of foreign countries is that despite differences across countries in sizes of domestic markets, domestic concentration ratios are correlated across countries (Pryor 1972). That is, an industry that is concentrated in the United States is also likely to be concentrated in the United Kingdom.

■ OTHER APPROACHES TO MEASURING MARKET PERFORMANCE

So far this chapter has explored the relationship between measures of market structure, such as concentration, and measures of market performance, such as profits or price-cost margins. We have seen that accounting difficulties plague the calculation of rates of return and also of price-cost margins. Moreover, we have seen that unless markets are properly defined, a concentration ratio has no meaning. A number of authors have used other methods of estimating market performance, either directly or indirectly, which seek to

---

[25] In unpublished work, Carlton, Sherwin, and Weiss find smaller effects of competition on railroad rates. They find that the presence of a competing railroad lowered rates by 0–10 percent for commodities that depend primarily on rail for transportation.

[26] A 20 percent price overcharge is about what a monopolist would charge if it faced a demand elasticity of -6. The absolute value of the demand elasticity for rail transport of grain is believed to be considerably below 6.

[27] The reader interested in industrial organization in Japan should consult Caves and Uekasa (1976).

characterize the departure of an industry's performance from competitive performance. Some of these methods rely directly or indirectly on observations of marginal cost; others look at the behavior of output or price to see if it is consistent with the competitive model. Most of these methods have not yet been used for detailed study of the links between the degree of departure from competition and observable industry traits, like barriers to entry. The following sections discuss some of these methods.[28]

Measuring Marginal Costs Directly

The economist's interest in market power is to detect the difference between price and marginal cost. Presumably price is observable, but marginal cost is not. As long as information on total cost is available, however, an econometrician can estimate the relationship between observed total cost and observed total output and then calculate marginal cost. A simple comparison then shows by how much price exceeds marginal cost.[29] The problem with this approach is that accurate estimation of marginal cost can be difficult, especially when data are lacking on individual firms. There have been several attempts to estimate cost functions in regulated industries because of the availability of cost data. For example, Keeler (1983, 71) and Friedlaender and Spady (1980, ch. 4) find that price exceeded long-run marginal cost by about 22 percent for rail service for bulk commodities in the Northeast during the late 1960s and early 1970s.

Measuring Marginal Cost Indirectly

If a competitive industry expands its output by 1 unit, the value of the last unit produced equals the value of the resources consumed in producing it; that is, price equals marginal cost. If, when an industry expands output, the total value of its output increases by more than the increase in its total cost, then price is above marginal cost.[30] This relationship can be exploited to calculate the ratio of price to marginal cost for each industry.

Hall (1988) ingeniously applies this relationship to the major industry categories in manufacturing and other sectors and finds significant deviations between price and marginal cost, as a fraction of price, of roughly 60 percent on average. Domowitz, Hubbard, and Petersen (1988) apply Hall's methodology to a finer classification of manufacturing industries and also obtain significant deviations on average between price and marginal cost, as a fraction of price, of about 36 percent. Neither Hall nor Domowitz et al. find that concentration plays an important and statistically significant role in explaining the deviation

---

[28] See Bresnahan (1989) for a more extensive discussion.

[29] Hall and Hitch (1939) conducted a series of interviews with businessmen regarding pricing practices. Their conclusion was that businessmen generally believe they set price above marginal cost. One interpretation is that businessmen don't understand the concept of marginal cost. Another is that economists' models of perfect competition fail to explain business behavior.

[30] This statement assumes that today's output has no effect on future costs, as would occur with learning-by-doing.

between price and marginal cost. However, Shapiro (1987) applies a variant of Hall's method and does find a strong relation between margins and concentration.

Observing a Cartel

Imagine a cartel with occasional breakdowns in its discipline, as discussed by Stigler (1964). The differences between the prices charged during the periods of collusion and those charged during periods of noncollusion allow an estimate of the overcharge that results from the collusion. Applying this basic intuition in a more sophisticated way, Porter (1983) shows that the railroad cartels of the 1800s were able to increase their rates by over 60 percent during periods of successful collusion.[31]

Using Observed Behavior to Estimate Price-Cost Margins

In competition, firms believe that the industry price is beyond their control. If a firm believes that it can affect price by altering its output, then it does not set price equal to marginal cost. Let q be the firm's output and Q be the combined output of all its rivals. A profit-maximizing firm chooses q to maximize its profits, $[p(q + Q) - C] q$, where $p(\cdot)$ is the price of the product (which depends on the total amount produced) and C is the constant marginal (and average) cost. The firm will increase its output until its incremental profit is zero. The profit from increasing output by Δq is

$$(p - C) \Delta q + q\left(\frac{\Delta p}{\Delta q}\right) (\Delta q + \Delta Q)$$

where $\Delta p / \Delta q$ is the change in price that results from a unit change in q and ΔQ is the response of the rivals' output to Δq. Setting incremental profit equal to zero, one obtains

$$(p - C) + q\left(\frac{\Delta p}{\Delta q}\right)\left(1 + \frac{\Delta Q}{\Delta q}\right) = 0.$$

The incremental profit consists of two terms. The first is the gain in revenue from selling more at the current price. The second is the reduced revenue that results from the price decline caused by the expansion of the output of the firm and its rivals. If $\Delta Q / \Delta q = -1$, so that the second term equals 0, then $p = C$, as in competition. Rearranging the previous equation shows that the profit-maximizing firm sets output so that the gap between price and marginal cost is as follows:

$$\frac{p - C}{p} = -\frac{a(q)}{\epsilon}, \tag{12.5}$$

---

[31] See Bresnahan (1987) and Lee and Porter (1984) for related research.

where

$$a(q) = 1 + \frac{\Delta Q}{\Delta q}, \text{ and}$$

$$\epsilon = \frac{p}{Q} \frac{\Delta Q}{\Delta P}$$

The value of $a(q)$ measures the degree of competition in the industry. If $a(q)$ equals 0, price equals marginal cost, as under competition. If $a(q)$ equals 1, we obtain the monopoly outcome. Values of $a(q)$ between 0 and 1 therefore represent the intermediate cases between competition and monopoly. Therefore, $a(q)$ can be used to characterize the degree of competition in an industry.

Researchers attempt to estimate Equation 12.5 in a variety of ways. For example, suppose that marginal cost is known to be constant. Researchers obtain information on factors that influence marginal cost, such as wages. They then determine if the relationship between price and these proxies for marginal cost also depends on q, a firm's output. If it does, then $a(q)$ cannot equal 0, and the industry is not perfectly competitive.

Specifically, if p is price, w is wage, and q is output, these researchers estimate a relationship of the form

$$p = \beta_0 + \beta_1 w + \beta_2 q,$$

where the β_1's are statistically estimated coefficients. If a firm behaves as a perfect competitor, β_2 should equal 0. Notice that this method does *not* require an estimate of marginal cost; rather, it controls for cost factors and asks whether q affects price.[32]

Several econometric studies have used generalizations of the preceding approach to estimate the degree of competition.[33] Once $a(q)$ is estimated, it is straightforward to calculate the price-cost margin, $(p - mc)/p$. Table 12.7 summarizes the predicted price-cost margins for several industries that have been studied using the general methodology of this section.

Observing Price Responses to Changes in Costs

In a competitive industry, if the wages of all inputs go up by the same percentage, then price should rise by an equal percentage. This is not necessarily true for monopoly (or other noncompetitive market structures), because a monopolist equates marginal revenue to marginal cost, and a $1 increase in marginal cost (and hence marginal revenue) need not translate into a $1 increase in price. This predicted difference in price behavior in

---

[32] Another approach is based on the observation that Equation 12.5 implies that ϵ does not affect the price when $a(q) = 0$. Since $a(q) = 0$ under competition, it follows that changes in ϵ should leave the competitive price unchanged. If changes in ϵ affect price, then the industry is not perfectly competitive. See also Example 5.5.

[33] See, for example, Iwata (1974), Gollop and Roberts (1979), Spiller and Favaro (1984), Roberts (1984), and Applebaum (1979, 1982). See Bresnahan (1989) for a survey of these and related studies.

TABLE 12.7	Predicted Price-Cost Margins	
Study	*Industry*	*(p − mc)/ p*
Lopez (1984)	Food processing	.50
Roberts (1984)	Coffee roasting (largest firm)	.06
Appelbaum (1982)	Rubber	.05
	Textile	.07
	Electrical machinery	.20
	Tobacco	.65
Slade (1987)	Retail gasoline	.1
Bresnahan (1981)	Autos	.34–1
Suslow (1986)	Aluminum	.59
Spiller and Favaro (1984)	Large banks before deregulation	.88
	Large banks after deregulation	.4
Karp and Perloff (1989)	Small black-and-white TVs	.58
Karp and Perloff (forth-coming	Rice exports	.04-.11

SOURCE: Bresnahan (1989, Table 1) and Karp and Perloff (1989, forthcoming).

response to changes in input wages may be exploited in order to distinguish between competition and monopoly (Panzar and Rosse 1977). For example, if one assumes that demand curves are of the constant-elasticity variety and marginal costs are constant, then it is straightforward to determine if industries that are subject to taxes are competitive. One can simply look at what happens to price as taxes in the industry change. If a per-unit tax raises price by exactly the amount of the tax, then competition is suggested. A price change greater than the amount of the tax suggests that competition does not prevail (recall that a monopolist sets price equal to a multiple of a constant marginal cost if the demand elasticity is constant).

Sumner (1981) examines the effect of tax differences across states on the price of cigarettes. He reasons that if competition prevails, the retail prices of cigarettes should differ between states by the amount of the tax differences. He finds precisely that and concludes that competition is vigorous. Critics of Sumner (for example, Bulow and Pfleiderer 1983) point out that it is possible to construct demand curves for which a monopolist does pass on costs on a one-for-one basis. Sullivan (1985) uses a different method to avoid this criticism and confirms Sumner's finding of a significant degree of competition in cigarettes.

■ CONCENTRATION, CAPITAL INTENSITY, AND UNIONIZATION

So far, this chapter has focused on whether industries with high levels of concentration are characterized by high prices and profits. Aside from prices and profitability, other features distinguish highly concentrated industries from unconcentrated industries. This section examines the relationship between concentration and capital intensity and between concentration and unionization.

TABLE 12.8 Capital Output Ratios and Concentration (1963 manufacturing)	
Four-Firm Concentration Ratio	*Average K/Q ratio (in percent)*
0–10	26.5
11–20	26.9
21–30	32.7
31–40	34.5
41–50	37.7
51–60	37.9
61–70	44.2
71–80	49.8
81–90	51.8
91–100	57.7

SOURCE: Collins and Preston (1969, 272), based on book values of capital.

Concentration and Capital Intensity

Highly concentrated industries appear to have higher capital/output ratios than unconcentrated industries. Table 12.8 shows that capital/output ratios rise continuously with concentration.

One explanation for this result might be that the plant of minimally efficient scale (the smallest plant that can operate efficiently) is so large relative to industry size that when economies of scale are important, only a few of them can fit into the industry. However, as the discussion of minimum scale (Chapter 3) indicates, for most industries minimum efficient scale appears to be many times lower than total industry demand.

The precise reason for these high capital/output ratios in highly concentrated industries is not well understood. If highly concentrated industries are more capital intensive than less concentrated industries, that suggests that highly concentrated industries have relatively more specialized capital. Moreover, it suggests that their rates of adjustment are slower than those of less concentrated industries because it is typically harder to adjust the capital stock than it is to adjust the labor force. If highly concentrated industries, because of their greater capital intensity, adjust more slowly than unconcentrated industries, then high (or low) profits should persist longer in these industries. In fact, that is precisely what has been found—profit rates for highly concentrated industries seem to fall back to or rise to the industry average more slowly than those for unconcentrated industries (Connolly and Schwartz 1985, Mueller 1985, Stigler 1963).

Another test of the relative speeds of adjustment for concentrated and unconcentrated industries comes from the stock market. If concentrated industries take a long time to react to, say, demand changes, then, all else equal, good economic news should raise the value of a company in a concentrated industry more than the value of a company in an unconcentrated industry. The reason is that it takes a long time to adjust to the good news in the concentrated industry (that is, expand output to eliminate the profitable opportunities); therefore, because profits will last longer in the highly concentrated industry, the stock price should go up higher. Lustgarten and Thomadakis (1980) perform exactly such a study and confirm that good economic news raises the stock market values of companies in concentrated industries much more than those in unconcentrated industries, and bad economic news lowers their values more.

Concentration and Unionization

Concentrated industries are prime targets for unionization because organizing workers in them costs less than organizing workers in unconcentrated industries because there are fewer firms that the union has to go to. To the extent that concentration raises industry profits, the incentive to unionize is even greater because the union can capture some of the profits. In fact, studies of wages and concentration do show a positive relationship between the two. However, it also turns out that concentrated industries seem to hire more educated and better-trained workers. Once account is taken of these differing worker characteristics between concentrated and unconcentrated industries, some older studies claim that the wage differential disappears (Weiss 1966). Recent studies provide a contrary view and show that unionism has a significant negative effect on the profits of highly concentrated industries (Freeman 1983).[34] Salinger (1984) concludes that unions capture all of a firm's monopoly rents, and Ruback and Zimmerman (1984) find that unionization lowers the value of a firm's stock by about 4 percent.

■ SUMMARY

The departures of industry performance from competitive behavior and the relationship of performance to market structure are subjects of ongoing research. Although there have been numerous studies, there are still many unresolved issues. The following is a summary of the main findings to date.

Serious measurement problems plague studies relating measures of performance to industry concentration and entry barriers. Accounting measures of profit fail to measure economic profits correctly. Calculating economic profits in the presence of capital assets raises difficult issues regarding valuation of capital and depreciation rates. Similar measurement problems plague the two other common measures of performance, price-cost margins and Tobin's q. Concentration ratios for individual industries can be measured accurately but make sense only when the individual industries constitute a relevant economic market. Finally, the measurement of barriers to entry is often subjective and typically fails to distinguish between long-run barriers to entry and the speed with which entry can occur.

Many studies across industries have related measures of industry performance to concentration and barriers to entry. These cross-sectional studies suffer from several conceptual problems. The empirical results indicate either no effect or a small positive

---

[34] See also Voos and Mishel (1986).

effect of concentration and barriers to entry on, say, price, but this effect is often statistically insignificant. Similar results hold for studies of foreign competition.

There is evidence supporting the view that large firms become large precisely because they are the most efficient. This implies that within one industry the profits of the largest firms are higher than those of the smallest.

Highly concentrated industries have higher capital/labor ratios than other industries. Adjustment is slower in concentrated industries, and this probably accounts, in part, for the slow rate at which profits in concentrated industries are driven to competitive levels.

Studies of individual industries can avoid many, though not necessarily all, of the conceptual problems of cross-sectional studies. Such studies relate an industry's performance to its market structure and tend to find a small but statistically significant effect of concentration on industry measures of performance, such as price. Other methods that rely on sometimes sophisticated economic theory to detect market power in an industry have discovered substantial deviations from perfectly competitive behavior in numerous industries. These methods have not yet been used to explore in detail the relationship of industry structure to the degree of deviation from perfectly competitive behavior.

■ Key Terms

Capital Asset Pricing Model
capital costs
depreciation
Herfindahl-Hirschman index (HHI)
internal rate of return (Appendix 12A)
market performance
market structure

rate of return
real rate of return
replacement cost
risk-adjusted rates of return
price-cost margin
structure-conduct-performance
Tobin's *q*

■ Discussion Questions

1. Two firms are in the drug industry. Each firm makes large expenditures on research to discover a new drug. One firm succeeds, the other goes bankrupt. An economist calculates the rate of return for the successful firm and finds it to be very high. Discuss whether the successful firm has market power that government authorities should do something about.

2. Suppose that unions act as monopolists and completely extract all profits from a firm through high wages. What effect does this have on studies relating profit measures to concentration?

3. Discuss the difference between an industry with long-run barriers to entry and an industry with slow adjust-ment time but no long-run barriers to entry. Analyze the level of profits and prices over time in each type of industry. How would an analyst be able to distinguish the two types of industries?

4. How can the findings of substantial deviations of prices from marginal costs in many industries be consistent with a finding that rates of return are rarely elevated substantially for long periods?

5. Recall the discussion in Chapter 4 of the nonexistence of a stable equilibrium (*empty core*). Use the discussion to reinterpret the evidence during railroad pricing wars. As described in the chapter, Porter (1983) used this evidence to conclude that price substantially exceeded marginal cost.

■ Problems

1. Explain why researchers often include the advertising/sales and the capital/sales ratios in equations explaining performance.

2. Consider an industry whose price is p^* that earns a rate of return r^* on its capital. Suppose that the industry is characterized by a fixed-proportions production technology (a fixed amount of labor and capital is required to make each unit of output). Let p and r be the price and rate of return, respectively, that would emerge if the industry were competitive. What is the relationship between $p^* - p$, $r^* - r$, and the capital/output ratio?

3. If international trade becomes more important in the United States, what happens to the meaningfulness of a concentration ratio based on share of domestic production? Could this explain the vanishing of the price-concentration effect over time?

4. *(Difficult)* Evaluate the following argument: "There exist demand curves for which a monopolist would pass along cost increases in price on a one-for-one basis. Therefore, nothing can be inferred about the competitiveness of an industry by comparing price changes to cost changes." In your evaluation, see if you can derive a demand curve with the stated properties (see Bulow and Pfleiderer 1983).

5. Distinguish between zero profits and a price-cost margin that equals zero.

Answers to odd-numbered problems are given at the back of the book.

■ References

Appelbaum, Elie. 1979. "Testing Price-Taking Behavior." *Journal of Econometrics* 9:283–99.

_____. 1982. "The Estimation of the Degree of Oligopoly Power." *Journal of Econometrics* 19:287–99.

Bailey, Elizabeth E., David R. Graham, and Daniel P. Kaplan. 1985. *Deregulating The Airlines*. Cambridge: The MIT Press.

Bain, Joe S. 1951. "Relation of Profit Rate to Industry Concentration: American Manufacturing, 1936–1940." *Quarterly Journal of Economics* 65:293–324.

_____. 1956. *Barriers to New Competition*. Cambridge: Harvard University Press.

Benston, George J. 1985. "The Validity of Profits-Structure Studies with Particular Reference to the FTC's Line-of-Business Data." *American Economic Review,* 75: 37-67.

Borenstein, Severin. 1988. "Hubs and High Fares: Airport Dominance and Market Power in the U.S. Airline Industry." Institute of Public Policy Working Paper no. 278, University of Michigan.

Bradburd, Ralph M., and Mead A. Over, Jr. 1982. "Organizational Costs, 'Sticky Equilibria', and Critical Levels of Concentration." *Review of Economics and Statistics* 64:50–58.

Brealy, Richard A., and Stewart C. Myers. 1984. *Principles of Corporate Finance*. New York: McGraw Hill.

Bresnahan, Timothy F. 1981. "Departures from Marginal-Cost Pricing in the American Automobile Industry." *Journal of Econometrics* 17:201–27.

_____. 1987. "Competition and Collusion in the American Automobile Oligopoly: The 1955 Price War." *Journal of Industrial Economics* 35:457–82.

_____. 1989. "Studies of Industries with Market Power," in Richard Schmalensee and Robert Willig, eds., *Handbook of Industrial Organization*, New York: North Holland.

Brozen, Yale. 1971. "Bain's Concentration and Rates of Return Revisited." *Journal of Law and Economics* 14: 351–69.

Bulow, Jeremy I., and Paul Pfleiderer. 1983. "A Note on the Effect of Cost Changes on Prices." *Journal of Political Economy* 91:182–85.

Call, G., and Theodore Keeler. 1985. "Airline Deregulation, Fares, and Market Behavior: Some Empirical Evidence", in A. F. Daughety, ed., *Analytic Studies in Transport Economics*. Cambridge: Cambridge University Press.

Carlton, Dennis W., and Mark J. Klamer. 1983. "The Need for Coordination Among Firms, with Special Reference to Network Industries." *University of Chicago Law Review* 50:446–65.

Caves, Richard E., and Masu Uekasa. 1976. *Industrial Organization in Japan.* Washington, D.C.: Brookings Institution.

Collins, Norman R., and Lee E. Preston. 1969. "Price-Cost Margins and Industry Structure." *The Review of Economics and Statistics* 51:271–86.

Comanor, William S., and Thomas A. Wilson. 1967. "Advertising, Market Structure, and Performance." *The Review of Economics and Statistics* 49:423–40.

Connolly, Robert A., and Stephen Schwartz. 1985. "The Intertemporal Behavior of Economic Profits." *International Journal of Industrial Organization* 3:379–400.

Cowling, Keith, and Michael Waterson. 1976. "Price-Cost Margins and Market Structure." *Economica* 43: 267–74.

Demsetz, Harold. 1973. "Industry Structure, Market Rivalry, and Public Policy." *Journal of Law and Economics* 16:1–9.

Domowitz, Ian, Glenn R. Hubbard, and Bruce C. Petersen. 1986. "Business Cycles and the Relationship Between Concentration and Price-Cost Margins." *The Rand Journal of Economics* 17:1–17.

Encoau, David, and Paul A. Geroski. 1988. "Market Structure and Cyclical Fluctuations in U.S. Manufacturing." *Review of Economics and Statistics* 70:55–66.

———. 1984. "Price Dynamics and Competition in Five Countries." No. 8414, University of Southhampton.

Fisher, Franklin M. 1987. "On the Misuse of the Profit-Sales Ratio to Infer Monopoly Power." *The Rand Journal of Economics* 18:384–96.

Fisher, Franklin M., and John J. McGowan. 1983. "On the Misuse of Accounting Rates of Return to Infer Monopoly Profits." *American Economic Review* 73: 82–97.

Fraumeni, Barbara M., and Dale W. Jorgenson. 1980. "Rates of Return by Industrial Sector in the United States, 1948–1976." *American Economic Review* 70(May):326–30.

Freeman, Richard B. 1983. "Unionism, Price-Cost Margins and The Return on Capital." National Bureau of Economic Research Working Paper no. 1164.

Friedlaender, Ann F., and Richard H. Spady. 1980. "A Derived Demand Function for Freight Transportation." *Review of Economics and Statistics* 62:432–41.

Geroski, Paul A. 1981. "Specification and Testing the Profits-Concentration Relationship: Some Experiments for the United Kingdom." *Economica* 48:279–88.

Gilbert, R. Alton. 1984. "Bank Market Structure and Competition: A Survey." *Journal of Money, Credit and Banking* 16:617–45.

Gollop, Frank M., and Mark J. Roberts. 1979. "Firm Interdependence in Oligopolistic Markets." *Journal of Econometrics* 3:313–31.

Graham, David R., Daniel P. Kaplan, and David S. Sibley. 1983. "Efficiency and Competition in the Airline Industry." *Bell Journal of Economics* 14:118–38.

Hall, Robert E. 1988. "The Relationship Between Price and Marginal Cost in U.S. Industry." *Journal of Political Economy* 96:921–47.

Hall, R. L., and C. J. Hitch. 1939. "Price Theory and Business Behavior." *Oxford Economic Papers* 2: 12–45.

Hart, P. E., and Eleanor Morgan. 1977. "Market Structure and Economic Performance in the United Kingdom." *Journal of Industrial Economics* 25:177–93.

Iwata, Gyoichi. 1974. "Measurement of Conjectural Variations in Oligopoly." *Econometrica* 42:947–66.

Karp, Larry S., and Jeffrey M. Perloff. Forthcoming. "Oligopoly in the Rice Export Market." *The Review of Economics and Statistics.*

Karp, Larry S., and Jeffrey M. Perloff. 1989. "Estimating Market Structure and Tax Incidence: The Japanese Television Market." *The Journal of Industrial Economics* 37:225–39.

Keeler, Theodore E. 1983. *Railroads, Freight, and Public Policy.* Washington, D.C.: The Brookings Institution.

Kwoka, John E., Jr., and David Ravenscraft. 1985. "Cooperation vs. Rivalry: Price-Cost Margins by Line of Business." Working Paper no. 127, U.S. Federal Trade Commission.

Lee, Lung-Fei, and Robert H. Porter. 1984. "Switching Regression Models with Imperfect Sample Separation Information—with an Application on Cartel Stability." *Econometrica* 52:391–418.

Liebowitz, Stanley J. 1982. "What Do Census Price-Cost Margins Measure?" *Journal of Law and Economics* 25:231–46.

Lindenberg, Eric B., and Stephen A. Ross. 1981. "Tobin's q Ratio and Industrial Organization." *Journal of Business* 54:1–32.

Lustgarten, Steven H. 1975. "The Impact of Buyer Concentration in Manufacturing Industries." *Review of Economics and Statistics* 57:125–32.

Lustgarten, Steven H., and Stavros B. Thomadakis. 1980. "Valuation Response to New Information: A Test of

Resource Mobility and Market Structure." *Journal of Political Economy* 88:977–33.

MacDonald, James M. 1987. "Competition and Rail Rates for the Shipment of Corn, Soybeans, and Wheat." *The Rand Journal of Economics* 18:151–63.

Mann, Michael. 1966. "Seller Concentration, Barriers to Entry, and Rates of Return in Thirty Industries, 1950–1960." *The Review of Economics and Statistics* 48:290–07.

Mueller, Dennis C. 1985. *Profits in the Long Run*. Cambridge: Cambridge University Press.

Panzar, John, and James Rosse. 1977. "Structure, Conduct, and Comparative Statics." Mimeo.

Peltzman, Sam. 1977. "The Gains and Losses from Industrial Concentration." *Journal of Law and Economics* 20:229–63.

Porter, Robert H. 1983. "A Study of Cartel Stability: The Joint Executive Committee, 1880–1886." *The Bell Journal of Economics* 14:301–14.

Pryor, Frederic L. 1972. "An International Comparison of Concentration Ratios." *Review of Economics and Statistics* 54:130–40.

Roberts, Mark J. 1984. "Testing Oligopolistic Behavior." *International Journal of Industrial Organization* 2:367-83.

Ruback, Richard S., and Martin B. Zimmerman. 1984. "Unionization and Profitability: Evidence from the Capital Market." *Journal of Political Economy* 92:1134–57.

Salinger, Michael A. 1984. "Tobin's *q*, Unionization, and the Concentration-Profits Relationship." *The Rand Journal of Economics* 15:159–70.

Schmalensee, Richard. 1989. "Inter-Industry Studies of Structure and Performance," in Richard Schmalensee and Robert Willig eds., *Handbook of Industrial Organization*. New York: North Holland.

Shapiro, Matthew. 1987. "Measuring Market Power in U.S. Industry." National Bureau of Economic Research Working Paper no. 2212.

Slade, Margaret. 1987. "Conjectures, Firm Characteristics, and Market Structure: an Analysis of Vancouver's Gasoline Price Wars", Mimeo.

Smirlock, Michael, Thomas Gilligan and William Marshall. 1984. "Tobin's *q* and the Structure-Performance Relationship." *American Economic Review* 74:1051–60.

Spiller, Pablo T., and Edwardo Favaro. 1984. "The Effects of Entry Regulation or Oligopolistic Interaction: The Uruguayan Banking Sector." *The Rand Journal of Economics* 15:244-54.

Stigler, George, J. 1963. *Capital and Rates of Return in Manufacturing Industries*. Princeton: Princeton University Press.

———. 1964. "A Theory of Oligopoly." *Journal of Political Economy* 72:44–61.

Sullivan, Daniel. 1985. "Testing Hypotheses About Firm Behavior in the Cigarette Industry." *Journal of Political Economy* 93:586–98.

Sumner, Daniel A. 1981. "Measurement of Monopoly Behavior: An Application to the Cigarette Industry." *Journal of Political Economy* 89:1010–19.

Suslow, Valerie. 1986. "Estimating Monopoly Behavior with Competitive Recycling: an Application to Alcoa." *The Rand Journal of Economics* 17:389–403.

Thomadakis, Stavros B. 1977. "A Value-Based Test of Profitability and Market Structure." *Review of Economics and Statistics* 59:179–85.

Tobin, James. 1969. "A General Equilibrium Approach to Monetary Theory." *Journal of Money, Credit, and Banking* 1:15–29.

Voos, Paula B., and Lawrence R. Mishel. 1986. "The Union Impact on Profits: Evidence from Industry Price-Cost Margin Data." *Journal of Labor Economics* 4:105–33.

Weiss, Leonard W. 1974. "The Concentration-Profits Relationship and Antitrust," in Harvey J. Goldschmid, H. Michael Mann, and J. Fred Weston, eds., *Industrial Concentration: The New Learning*. Boston: Little, Brown.

———. 1966. "Concentration and Labor Earnings." *American Economic Review* 56:90–117.

White, Lawrence. 1976. "Searching for the Critical Industrial Concentration Ratio," in Stephen Goldfeld and Richard E. Quandt, *Studies in Non-Linear Estimation*. Cambridge, Mass.: Ballinger.

THE INTERNAL RATE OF RETURN

Another rate of return concept is the ***internal rate of return,*** which is a summary statistic that attempts to measure the return earned over several years. The internal rate of return is that interest rate such that the discounted present value of cash flows equals zero. The value of the internal rate of return is that it concisely summarizes the return earned by a project lasting several years. Because it is a summary statistic, it can sometimes be misleading. It is likely to be inaccurate when profitability is changing over time.

A typical calculation of the internal rate of return requires a time series on the cash flows of investment and profits that the firm has experienced in the business over a long period of time. The advantage of this approach is that it frees the economist from trying to calculate the value of capital each year; instead, the economist can simply use the observed cash flows. The only times at which the capital stock must be evaluated is at the beginning and end. The beginning value should be treated as an investment (cash inflow), and the ending value as a payout (cash outflow). The problems of calculating the initial and ending values of the capital stock are the same ones discussed in conjunction with calculating the value of a firm's capital.[1] It is a good idea to check the sensitivity of internal rates of return to different values for the initial and ending capital stock. It often happens, especially when long time periods are involved, that the internal rate of return is relatively insensitive to these beginning and ending values.

The advantage of the internal rate of return is that by focusing on a time series of unambiguous cash flows based on the pattern of actual receipts and expenditures, problems of evaluating long-lived capital items (like machines, R&D, and advertising) can be avoided. The disadvantage is that calculating an internal rate of return over a long period of time only makes sense if profitability is sufficiently constant so that using one internal rate of return to summarize profitability is reasonable.

---

[1] The beginning value of capital should be based on replacement costs, while the ending value of capital should be based on what a willing buyer would pay for the assets (including any monopoly premium). This procedure ensures that the analyst identifies any market power created during the period of analysis.

ACCOUNTING BIAS IN THE RATE OF RETURN

Suppose that a \$1 investment today yields profits of $\pi_0 e^{-\delta t}$ at time t. Therefore, true depreciation is δ, because that is the rate at which cash flows decline. Suppose that the true rate of return on this \$1 investment is r. Hence

$$\$1 = \int_0^\infty \pi_0 e^{-\delta t} e^{-rt} dt, \text{ or } 1 = \frac{\pi_0}{r + \delta}, \text{ or } r = \pi_0 - \delta$$

Suppose an analyst tries to calculate the rate of return using accounting concepts of book value and depreciation. A \$1 investment has a book value at time t of e^{-dt} where d is the rate of depreciation that the accountant uses. The amount of depreciation from this investment at time t is de^{-dt}. The analyst calculates the accounting rate of return, $r_{AC}(t)$, as accounting income at time t divided by the accounting (book) value of capital,

or
$$r_{AC}(t) = \frac{\text{Accounting income } (t)}{\text{Accounting book value } (t)}.$$

Accounting income equals revenues minus accounting depreciation minus other operating costs (which for simplicity, we take equal to zero). Therefore,

$$\text{Accounting income } (t) = \pi_0 e^{-\delta t} - de^{-dt}, \text{ and}$$
$$\text{Accounting book value } (t) = e^{-dt}.$$

Therefore,

$$r_{AC}(t) = \frac{\pi_0 e^{-\delta t} - de^{-dt}}{e^{-dt}}, \text{ or } r_{AC}(t) = \pi_0 e^{-(\delta - d)t} - d, \text{ or } r_{AC}(t)$$

$$= (r + \delta) e^{-(\delta - d)t} - d.$$

Notice that $r_{AC} = r$ if $\delta = d$. However, if d differs from δ, then r_{AC} is a biased measure of r. For example, if $r = .05$, $d = .2$ and $\delta = .1$, then even though the true r is constant and equals .05, the measured r_{AC} is $-.03$ in Year 1, .05 in Year 5, and .91 in Year 20.

RELATIONSHIP BETWEEN HERFINDAHL-HIRSHMAN INDEX (HHI) AND PRICE-COST MARGIN

Imagine an oligopoly consisting of n firms.[1] An individual firm, i, seeks to maximize profits, π_i, given as follows:

$$\pi_{i} = pq_i - Cq_i$$

where p is price, q_i is output of firm i, and C is constant marginal (and average) cost.

The price, p, depends upon total industry output, Q ($\Sigma_i q_i$). Firm i chooses q_i in order to maximize its profits. Suppose that firm i believes that its output q_i has no effect on the output of other firms (this is the Cournot model of oligopoly behavior). Differentiating the profit equation with respect to q_i and setting the results equal to zero, one obtains the following:

$$(p'q_i) + (p - C) = 0, \text{ or } \frac{(p'Q)}{p}\frac{q_i}{Q} + \frac{p - C}{p} = 0, \text{ or } \frac{p - C}{p} = -\frac{s_i}{\epsilon},$$

where $s_i = q_i/Q$, $1/\epsilon = (p'Q)/p$, and $p' = $ the derivative of price with respect to output.

Notice that s_i is the share of total output of firm i. Since the above equation holds for every firm, the weighted average price-cost margin for the industry equals

$$\Sigma s_i \frac{P_i - C}{P_i} = -\frac{\Sigma s_i^2}{\epsilon} = -\frac{\text{HHI}}{\epsilon}.$$

Therefore, the equation shows the relationship between the industry HHI and a weighted average of the firms' price-cost margins.

---

[1] This section is based on Cowling and Waterson (1976).

CHAPTER 13

STRATEGIC BEHAVIOR

All business sagacity reduces itself in the last analysis to a judicious use of sabotage.

THORSTEIN VEBLEN

This chapter analyzes how firms can act to reduce competition by actual and potential rivals. This behavior is loosely called *strategic* and can be more complicated than the relatively simple price- or quantity-setting behavior already studied. For example, a firm could rush into a market, expand capacity, and leave little room for new rivals. Although the early models of strategic behavior were proposed several decades ago, interest in strategic behavior waned until recently. In the past several years there has been an outpouring of literature analyzing strategic behavior, as economists have come to better understand and appreciate the importance of this phenomenon.[1]

This chapter first defines strategic behavior and then examines some early models of such behavior as well as the sharp criticism they received. The models presented in the subsequent sections eliminate the deficiencies of these early models and are consistent with profit maximization and rational behavior. We explore the differences between cooperative and noncooperative strategic behavior and discuss the legal treatment of strategic behavior under our antitrust laws.

■ STRATEGIC BEHAVIOR DEFINED

Strategic behavior consists of actions by a firm to influence the market environment within which it competes, so as to increase the profits of the firm. The **market environment** means all those factors that influence the market outcome, including the beliefs of customers and of rivals, the number of actual and potential rivals, the production technology of each firm, and the costs or speed with which a rival can enter the industry.[2] By

---

[1] Other overviews of strategic behavior include Porter (1980, 1985), Ordover and Saloner (1989), Spence (1981b), and Tirole (1988).

manipulating the market environment, a firm can sometimes increase its profits. As in the theory of oligopoly, the equilibrium in models of strategic behavior crucially depends on what one rival believes another rival will do in a particular situation. This chapter describes how a firm can influence the beliefs of its rivals and thereby affect the outcome of the rivalry.

We examine two types of strategic behavior: noncooperative and cooperative. **Noncooperative strategic behavior** refers to the actions of a firm that is trying to maximize its profits by improving its position relative to its rivals. The firms are not cooperating with each other; instead, each tries to maximize its own profits. Noncooperative strategic behavior generally improves the profits of one firm and lowers the profits of competing firms. **Cooperative strategic behavior** is designed to alter the market environment so as to make it easier for all firms to coordinate their actions and to limit their competitive responses.[3] This type of strategic behavior can raise the profits of all firms by reducing competition. Although the distinction between noncooperative and cooperative behavior is sometimes not a sharp one, for expositional purposes it is helpful to consider them separately. The simplest way to distinguish between noncooperative and cooperative behavior is to consider the following two examples.

A rival blowing up its competition is an example of noncooperative strategic behavior. On the other hand, two rivals, each distrustful of the other, sitting down in a room to work out a price-fixing agreement is an example of cooperative behavior. Their subsequent behavior (for example, attempts to cheat on the price-fixing agreement) may be noncooperative.

Our antitrust laws, which attempt to limit the undesirable acquisition of market power have been used to attack certain types of strategic behavior. The Sherman Act, passed in 1890, is one of the central pieces of legislation underlying our antitrust laws. Section I of the Sherman Act prohibits all contracts, combinations, and conspiracies in restraint of trade. Section I of the Sherman Act has been used to attack explicit cooperative behavior, like a price-fixing agreement, that leads to the creation of market power. Section II of the Sherman Act prohibits attempts to monopolize. Section II has been used to attack noncooperative strategic behavior, such as *predatory pricing* (pricing below cost to drive rivals out of business).

■ EARLY MODELS OF NONCOOPERATIVE STRATEGIC BEHAVIOR

Two of the earliest models of strategic behavior involve policies that are designed to make it unattractive for rivals to compete. In **predatory pricing,** a firm initially lowers its price to drive rivals out of business and scare off potential entrants. When rivals disappear, the firm raises its price. In **limit pricing,** a firm sets its price and output so that there is not enough demand left to support an additional firm. In both models, the firm succeeds in

---

[2] The term *market environment* is slightly more inclusive than the term market structure since the latter term, as commonly used, does not always include beliefs of market participants.

[3] The term *cooperative* is somewhat misleading. There need not be explicit agreement to undertake the behavior. The key point is that the behavior results in a higher price and profit for the firms than would otherwise emerge.

scaring off rivals because of their beliefs about the way the firm will compete. Recent models of strategic behavior pay greater attention than the early models to the formation of rivals' beliefs. Let us now examine how the two early models of strategic behavior work.

Predatory Pricing

A dead man can't bite. — PLUTARCH

This section presents and analyzes the early theory of predatory pricing. It then examines how to identify predatory pricing and concludes with a review of the evidence.

The Theory of Predatory Pricing. The theory of predatory pricing has been around for several decades and in its barest form is quite simple. An incumbent firm drives rival firms out of business by setting price below cost. Once all rivals have been driven out of business, the incumbent firm raises the price. If a firm enters the business to take advantage of the high price, the incumbent lowers price to drive that firm out too. Potential entrants soon realize that it does not pay to enter this business because of the incumbent's pricing behavior. As a result, no one enters, and the incumbent is free to raise price to the monopoly level with no fear of inducing entry.

Several important features of predatory pricing must be understood in order to assess its likelihood. During the period of predation the incumbent firm loses money, in fact, it loses much more money than an equally efficient rival. The incumbent firm must meet all demands at the low price in order to maintain the low price, but the rival is free to contract output in order to minimize its losses. To understand this point, consider Figure 13.1.

Suppose the incumbent firm wishes to set price at level p^* so as to inflict losses on a rival and drive it out of business. In order to do so it must be the case that a total of q^* units are produced in the marketplace because when q^* units are produced, consumers are willing to pay p^*. If the marginal and average cost curves of the incumbent and the rival are the same and are as drawn in Figure 13.1, then the rival produces only q_1 units if price is set at p^* and loses the amount *ABCD* indicated in the figure. In contrast, the incumbent must produce $q^* - q_1$ units so that total industry output will be q^* and price will remain at p^*. To produce $q^* - q_1$ units requires that the incumbent produce at a marginal and average cost higher than the price, p^*, as illustrated in the figure. The incumbent firm loses the amount *AEFG*. The incumbent's losses become greater (as industry demand becomes larger the industry demand curve shifts to the right). In summary, during the period of predation the incumbent loses more than its rival. Price predation is costly to the incumbent.

Consumers gain during the period of predation, because they are able to purchase the product at a price, p^*, which is below the price that would be likely to emerge if the incumbent and the rival were duopolists. If the predation is successful, consumers lose afterwards when the price rises to a higher level (monopoly level) than would emerge if the rival and the incumbent behaved as duopolists.

If the predator succeeds in forcing its rivals into bankruptcy, it must be sure that their assets are permanently withdrawn from the industry or at least controlled by the predator.

FIGURE 13.1   Predation

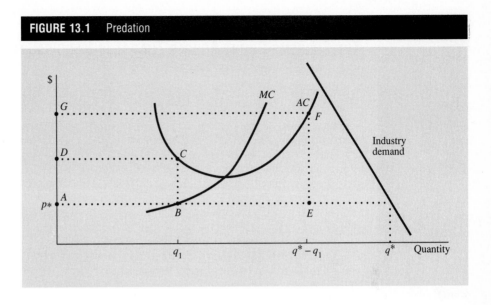

Otherwise, someone else could buy the assets and compete. Therefore, predation is most likely to succeed when rivals' assets exit permanently from the industry or become controlled by the predator. If a rival's assets are purchased by a firm in another industry, they could always be redeployed to compete against the predator. Thus, the most reliable strategy for successful predation is for the predator to drive (or threaten to drive) a rival into bankruptcy and buy up the rival's assets at a bargain price.

A serious criticism against the model of predatory pricing is that nothing in the description of the behavior distinguishes the incumbent from the rival. If both have identical costs, then from an economic point of view they are identical, and it would be just as reasonable to suppose that the rival can threaten the incumbent as to suppose the reverse. With no differences between the firms, it is difficult to see why one firm should believe that another firm is willing to suffer losses greater than those of its rival for as long as necessary to drive the rival from the industry. This behavior is not rational and is therefore not believable; it is not a **credible threat.** It may be more profitable for the two firms to behave as duopolists rather than for the incumbent to practice predatory pricing. Moreover, if for some reason an entrant does believe that an incumbent will drive it out of business by below-cost pricing, then it would pay for the two firms to merge, charge a high price immediately, and thus avoid the costly period of predation when consumers gain but the two firms in the industry suffer from low revenues. (Of course our antitrust laws prohibit merger to monopolize, but they also prohibit predatory pricing. See Example 13.1.)

If an entrant did fear that its entry would precipitate a price war and drive prices below cost, it could avoid this fear by agreeing with buyers to set the price in advance by contract. It would then be impossible for the new entrant to be affected by low prices, since its business would already be locked up at a fixed price. Notice that buyers should be willing to sign such fixed-price contracts because presumably the price the new entrant

EXAMPLE 13.1

THE SUPREME COURT AGREES THAT IT IS ILLOGICAL TO EARN LOSSES FOR LONG PERIODS OF TIME

In 1986 the Supreme Court reached an important decision regarding predatory pricing. In *Matsushita Electric Industrial Co., Ltd. v. Zenith Radio Corporation et al.*, 106 S. Ct. 1348 (1986), a group of United States manufacturers claimed that certain Japanese firms had conspired for twenty years to sell consumer electronic products in the United States at prices below cost in an effort to drive the U.S. producers out of business. The notion that any firm or group of firms would willingly inflict losses upon itself for twenty years in order to eventually drive firms out of business struck the Supreme Court as unlikely. Any firm that did behave in such a way would have made a very poor calculation of the discounted present value of the costs and benefits of the predatory strategy. The Supreme Court ruled that predation was not the reason for the low prices and other explanations, such as legitimate competition, better described the reasons why the Japanese were able to price below American producers.

offers would be less than the monopoly price that the incumbent is currently charging. Of course, it is not always possible to line up enough customers in advance on fixed-price contracts, especially when each customer is small. However, when there are large customers who realize that the new entrant will prevent the incumbent from exercising market power, the entrant should have an easier time signing up customers in advance.

As already mentioned, the rival can respond during the period of predation by cutting back output. In fact, if a rival can exit an industry costlessly and redeploy its assets, there can be no predation. During the predation period the rival simply redeploys its capital to another industry. When the incumbent raises its price, the rival re-enters the industry, and when the incumbent lowers its price, the rival can simply exit and redeploy its capital. For example, suppose that the incumbent produces desks. The rival enters the industry, and in response to its entry the incumbent lowers the price of desks below cost. Suppose that the capacity of the rival can be profitably redeployed to make tables instead of desks. As long as it is relatively inexpensive for the rival to switch between the manufacture of desks and the manufacture of tables, the incumbent cannot drive the rival out of business, or even threaten to do so. When the price of desks declines, the rival can switch to the production of tables, and whenever the incumbent tries to raise the price of desks to the monopoly level, the rival can switch back to the production of desks. In other words, the incumbent is unable to inflict any losses on the rival, and therefore the threat to sell below cost is not of serious concern to the rival.

Recall from Chapter 3 the discussion of sunk costs and contestable markets. *Sunk costs* are those costs that could not be recovered once a business had been entered. The preceding discussion indicates that in the absence of sunk costs, predatory strategies have no hope of succeeding. If the incumbent has no way to impose costs on rivals, then threats to price below cost are ineffective: pricing below cost would hurt only the incumbent. This means that in perfectly contestable markets—those in which instantaneous entry and exit are costless—predation can never succeed.

Descriptions of predatory pricing commonly describe the incumbent as a large firm and the new entrant or rival as a small firm and argue that large firms can afford the losses, while small firms cannot. Although this assumption itself may be questionable (why wouldn't somebody lend to a small firm if it is not believable that the large firm will continue to incur losses forever?), such a theory still does not explain why other large firms do not enter. For example, if small firms are at a disadvantage in competing with large firms, competition among large firms will ultimately dominate the economy. There are numerous large firms that can enter many industries, and if predation succeeds only when practiced by large firms against small ones, one would simply expect to see the replacement of small firms as entrants by large firms. Therefore, predation should not necessarily lead to monopoly profits even when small firms are ineffective competitors.

Standards for Determining Predatory Pricing.   An extensive economic and legal literature has developed on the standards for determining whether a firm is practicing predatory pricing. One of the most influential articles in this literature is by Areeda and Turner (1975), who suggest that a firm is practicing predatory pricing when its price is less than its short-run marginal cost. (They suggest using average variable cost as a proxy for short-run marginal cost if data difficulties prevent the determination of short-run marginal costs.) The logic behind this test is that no firm ever profitably chooses to operate where price is less than short-run marginal cost, unless it is motivated by strategic concerns. Therefore, if one ever discovers such a situation, the firm must have some aim other than traditional profit maximization. One possibility is that the firm is trying to drive rival firms out of business in order to eventually maximize profits. Pricing below short-run marginal costs would not make sense without some prospect of benefits in the future.

The article by Areeda and Turner generated an enormous outpouring of research suggesting modification of or alternatives to the Areeda and Turner test. Some authors suggest the use of long-run marginal cost, others suggest the use of average cost, and still others suggest observing price patterns over time or the amount produced over time in order to determine whether predation is actually occurring.[4]

The problem with all suggested tests for predation is that they can be difficult to implement. One reason is that the data needed to determine short-run marginal production costs or even average variable production costs are often difficult to obtain. A second reason is that other factors having nothing to do with price predation may explain the observations. For example, it is quite common for a new firm that enters an industry to attract consumer attention by running price promotions. During the start-up phase of business it is not unusual for a firm to give away its products. This appears to violate the Areeda-Turner test for predation. However, giving away a product may be a very effective promotional device to build business for the future; therefore, when properly interpreted, it might be a profit-maximizing decision. The reason price appears to be lower than short-

---

[4] Easterbrook (1981) discusses several of these alternative tests.

run marginal cost is that the economist has not treated the price cut as a promotional activity designed to attract future customers. Such promotional activities are an investment in the future, and it is wrong to ignore the promotional aspect of the price cut in calculating price. Just as investments in plant and equipment would not be expensed, but would instead be amortized over time, so too should price promotions. Unfortunately, such a calculation can be difficult to make.

Another instance in which price can appear to be lower than short-run marginal cost occurs where there is **learning by doing.** Learning by doing refers to the decrease in a firm's cost of production as it produces more, because it learns how to produce the product more efficiently. In such a situation, a firm's costs are initially high but decline over time. By setting a very low price initially, the firm makes many sales and thereby accumulates experience that will enable it to lower its costs in the future. Even if the current price is lower than its current production costs, the prospect of reducing costs in the future by accumulating knowledge today justifies the lower price as an important investment for the firm. Again, the problem arises because the low price today should be viewed as an investment for the future. The short-run marginal cost of production is not the relevant cost to look at when a firm is involved in dynamic learning over time. Instead, one should look at the marginal production cost today plus the (present discounted value of the) change in production cost in the future that results from increased production today.

Predation can be easily confused with competition. Most lawsuits involving predatory pricing are brought by a competitor against its rival, which suggests that the competitor is complaining not about prices below cost but about price competition from a more efficient firm. If one firm is more efficient than another, one would expect the efficient firm to charge lower prices and take over the market. Indeed, the price could be below the inefficient firm's cost but equal to or above that of the efficient firm. Predatory pricing suits could therefore be a strategy by which a less efficient firm attempts to protect its market position. The evidence in a predatory pricing case often involves a lowering of price that inflicts losses on rivals, which is precisely what one expects when a more efficient firm competes in an industry. If vigorous enforcement of predatory pricing cases prevents efficient firms from lowering their prices out of fear of a predatory pricing suit, consumers would be harmed rather than helped by vigorous enforcement. For this reason, some (for example, Easterbrook 1981) suggest that the courts should not consider a predatory pricing suit until after a firm has been driven from business *and* the alleged predator has raised its price. Only then could one be sure that it was predation and not vigorous competition that drove the rival out of business.[5]

---

[5] As discussed in Chapter 3, the concepts of cost become more complicated in a multiproduct setting. It is possible to adapt the definitions for predation to a multiproduct setting using the cost concepts of Appendix 3B. One relevant multiproduct cost concept is average incremental cost, which equals the change in total cost from producing q units of a product divided by q, holding output of all other products at some prespecified level. In a multiproduct setting one must form definitions that allow tests for predation involving only some of the many products that a firm produces. One standard, for example, could be that the price of one product could not be less than the average incremental cost that the product entails. (This standard was used in *MCI Communications Corp. vs. AT&T*, 708 F 2d 1081 [7th Circuit], cert. denied, 464 U.S. 891 [1983]). Notice that to apply such a standard one must make assumptions about the levels of the output of all the other products that are jointly produced with the product under discussion.

Evidence on predatory pricing.   Given all the problems with the theory of predatory pricing, it should not be surprising that economists have found it difficult to identify many instances of successful price predation in which rivals are driven out of business and prices then rise. Although there have been numerous alleged instances of price predation, careful examination of these cases indicates that predation in the sense of pricing below cost usually did not occur. For example, one of the most widely cited examples of price predation was the creation of Standard Oil. Supposedly, Rockefeller bought small, independent oil refineries after having lowered price to drive them out of business. In fact, in his careful examination of this historical period, McGee (1958) rejects that view and concludes that Rockefeller's rivals were bought out on rather favorable terms.

Koller (1971) reviews the available records in predatory pricing cases since 1890. Of the 26 cases for which adequate data existed, Koller finds evidence of below-cost pricing in 7 cases. Of these, only 4 represented successful predation, in that the rival vanished. Of these, 3 involved mergers. (Mergers that lead to significant increases in market power are illegal under our antitrust laws; thus, if successful predation requires merger to exercise market power, there is no need for a law aimed at predatory pricing, because merger policy will protect consumers.) Experiments in which students are given incentives to behave like firms confirm the difficulty of creating environments conducive to predatory pricing (Isaac and Smith 1985). A review of recent predation cases shows that the evidence for predation in most cases is very weak and that defendants win over 90 percent of the time (Hurwitz et al. 1981). The empirical evidence is consistent with the view that predatory pricing is rarely a profitable strategy and that claims of alleged predation often reflect the complaint of one rival about another's fierce (and socially desirable) competition. The lesson for managers is that price predation is unlikely to be a profitable strategy.

The theory of predatory pricing relies on the incumbent's creation of a reputation for being a fierce competitor. The criticism of that theory is that it is unclear how such a reputation can be established and why rivals should believe it. However, any theory that rests on a postulated set of beliefs cannot be logically *proven* wrong. Therefore, it is a mistake to think of price predation as inconceivable (see Example 13.2). Example 13.3 (p. 409) shows that the courts have occasionally found price predation when they failed to apply a standard of pricing below cost.

Limit Pricing

Another early model of strategic behavior is *limit pricing* and is associated primarily with the work of Bain (1956), Modigliani (1958), and Sylos-Labini (1962). This model was discussed in Chapter 8, but that discussion did not elaborate on the strategic issues. In the simple limit-pricing model the potential entrant believes that the incumbent firm will not change its output after the new firm enters. Therefore, the new firm contemplating entry believes that total industry output will equal its own output plus the current output of the incumbent. The extra output will cause price to fall. In this model, the incumbent firm chooses its output level and its associated price in such a way as to remove the incentive of a firm to enter.

The analysis that a potential entrant and incumbent go through in a limit-pricing model is illustrated in Figure 13.2 (p. 409).

EXAMPLE 13.2

EVIDENCE OF PREDATORY PRICING IN TOBACCO

One reason for a firm to practice predatory pricing is to force rivals to sell out to the firm at a low price. In this way, a firm can acquire its rivals cheaply and gain market power. The Tobacco Trust was alleged to have engaged in predatory pricing against its rivals around the turn of the century. During the period 1881–1906, the Tobacco Trust acquired over forty rivals and established large shares in plug tobacco, smoking tobacco, snuff, and fine cut. The Tobacco Trust would identify a rival that it wished to buy and then often introduce a competitive brand at a low price. The low profits would induce rivals to sell out to the Tobacco Trust at a low price.

For example, in 1901 the Tobacco Trust sold its American Beauty brand of cigarettes in North Carolina to compete with a similar product of its rival, Wells-Whitehead Tobacco Company of Winston, North Carolina. The price was $1.50 per thousand, which was exactly equal to the required tax; it was therefore definitely below production costs. The Tobacco Trust claimed that the low price was an introductory offer. In 1903, the Tobacco Trust purchased its rival.

A detailed analysis of the value paid for the rivals purchased by the Tobacco Trust between 1881 and 1906 shows that predatory pricing did indeed have a large negative effect on the purchase price paid: predation lowered the acquisition costs by about 25 percent.

SOURCE: Burns (1986) and Tenant (1950, 43).

The figure shows the industry demand curve as well as the average cost curve that both the incumbent and potential entrant face. If the incumbent firm produces q^* units (and will continue to do so in the face of entry), then the demand curve facing a new entrant equals the industry demand curve minus q^*. Figure 13.2 shows the entrant's demand curve as a leftward shift of the total demand curve by q^* units. If the potential entrant chooses not to enter, then the incumbent firm produces q^* units and receives a price of p^*. If instead the new firm enters the industry and produces q_1 units of output, then total industry output will equal $q_1 + q^*$, and the industry price will equal p_1. Notice that p_1 is just equal to the average cost for the potential entrant of producing q_1 units, which means that there is no incentive for entry into the industry. (We adopt the convention that no entry occurs if profits are zero.)

If q^* is chosen so that the residual demand curve facing the new entrant is just below (or equal to) its average cost curve, then no amount of production by the new entrant would enable it to earn a profit in the industry. By choosing a q^* that achieves this result, the incumbent firm is able to charge a ("limit") price, p^*, that is above its average cost of production, yet does not induce (that is, it limits) entry. (Actually, the incumbent does not have to produce q^* to deter entry; it needs only to *threaten* to produce q^* if entry occurs).

EXAMPLE 13.3

TOBACCO REVISITED

As a result of violations of the antitrust laws, the Tobacco Trust (see Example 13.2) was ordered in 1911 to be dissolved and was broken up into several firms (primarily American Tobacco, Liggett and Myers, and Lorillard.) By the 1920s, three firms dominated the cigarette industry, Reynolds (Camel brand), Liggett and Myers (Chesterfield brand) and American Tobacco (Lucky Strike brand). In a famous antitrust suit *(American Tobacco Co. v. United States*, 328 U.S. 781 [1946]), these three firms were charged with collusion and predatory pricing to drive rivals out of business. During the depression, the three major cigarette manufacturers increased their prices despite declining costs. This led to a profitable opportunity for entry, and new firms entered and sold the *10-cent brands*, which sold for roughly 5¢ less than the brands of the three major manufacturers. Between 1931 and 1932, the new brands increased their market share from below 1 to 23 percent. In early 1933, the three major manufacturers dropped their wholesale prices by about 20 percent so that their retail prices were only slightly higher than those of the 10-cent brands, whose share fell to around 6 percent. The evidence suggests that these prices were not below the average total costs of the major cigarette companies. The 10-cent brands maintained a significant market share until the 1940s, when they disappeared. Despite the fact that price exceeded average cost and that the 10-cent brands survived, the Court found that the companies had violated the antitrust laws by conspiring to lower prices with the intent to drive the 10-cent brands out of business.

SOURCE: Koller (1971) and *American Tobacco Co. v. U.S.*, 328 U.S. 781 (1946).

FIGURE 13.2   Limit Pricing

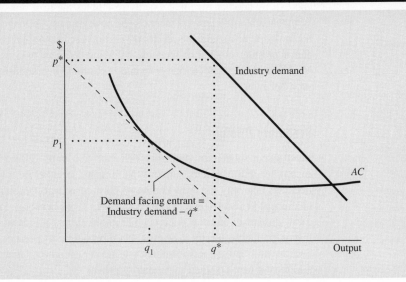

The main problem with this model of strategic behavior is the same as in the model of predatory pricing: why should an entrant believe that the incumbent will do what it says? Why would it make sense for an incumbent to continue to produce q^* units in the face of new entry regardless of the entrant's output? Moreover, as in the earlier model of predatory pricing, there is absolutely no difference between the incumbent and the entrant. Both have identical cost curves by assumption. If both have the same costs after entry, it is difficult to see how one firm could scare another based on assumed behavior after entry. Precisely because it is not profit maximizing for the incumbent to continue to produce q^* in the event of entry, its threat to do so is not credible. One might argue that a potential entrant might just as easily scare an incumbent into exiting by threatening to enter and produce q^*. Furthermore, as in the case of predatory pricing, a counterstrategy for the entrant would be to enter the industry with existing fixed-price contracts already in hand. Notice that a new entrant would easily attract customers as long as it offered to supply them at a price less than p^*, a price far above minimum average cost.

Models of limit pricing over time have also been developed, in which the rate of entry depends on the level of prices. The result is that the incumbent strategically chooses price and output in order to retard entry and maximize profits (Gaskins 1971; and Chapter 8).

■ RECENT MODELS OF NONCOOPERATIVE STRATEGIC BEHAVIOR

The recent models of strategic behavior correct the deficiencies of the early models. They take special care to insure that the beliefs of rivals are based on credible threats of the incumbent. Recent models all emphasize some existing asymmetry between firms and explain how a firm can exploit this asymmetry to its advantage. The asymmetry allows the incumbent to make a commitment that makes its threatened behavior believable. All of the recent models of strategic behavior rely upon the impossibility of costless entry and exit by another firm that exactly resembles the firm practicing the strategic behavior. Without these entry barriers there can be no asymmetry among firms, and strategic behavior has no hope of raising the profits of a firm. Let us now review some of the more recent and interesting models of strategic behavior. We can then assess the likely welfare implications of the strategic behavior and the attitude that antitrust policy should take toward such behavior.

Predatory Pricing

Most recent models of predatory behavior rely upon differences in firms' beliefs about each other. For example, suppose that a firm can either be a high-cost firm or a low-cost firm and that only the firm knows its own costs with certainty. In response to entry, an incumbent firm can lower its price for one of two reasons. First, the incumbent may be a low-cost firm, and the price decline might simply represent vigorous price competition that is profitable for the low-cost incumbent firm to pursue. Prices below the entrant's cost are still above the incumbent's cost. A second explanation is that the incumbent is a high-cost firm engaged in predatory pricing.

The difference between this model and the previous models of predation is that it provides a possible explanation of why it is profit-maximizing for a firm to drop its price in response to entry (that is, the firm is low-cost). A potential entrant that observes the incumbent's pricing behavior can learn whether the incumbent firm is likely to be high-cost or low-cost. The lower its cost, the more likely the incumbent firm is to meet entry with very low prices. An incumbent can therefore acquire a reputation of being a low-cost firm by responding to entry with very low prices, and its past pricing history can be used to infer whether the incumbent is low-cost or high-cost. Although its pricing history is not a perfect indicator as to whether the incumbent firm has high cost or low cost, it is an indicator. Because it is only a rough indicator, a high-cost firm could occasionally practice price predation and convince potential entrants that it is really a low-cost firm. (Pricing history can be an indicator of a firm's costs only if high-cost firms use low prices less frequently than low-cost firms do.)

Notice that an entrant with no associated pricing history cannot influence the incumbent's beliefs about its costs, and this creates the natural asymmetry in this model. The entrant comes with no prior history; the incumbent has a history, and because of that the rival's beliefs about the entrant can differ from the entrant's beliefs about the rival. It is possible to show in these models that predatory pricing occasionally makes sense. Pricing below cost for a high-cost firm turns out to be a rational strategy if it is able to create the illusion that it is a low-cost firm, and thereby deter entry.[6]

Although these recent models show that it is possible to construct believable models of predatory pricing, it is still true that the practice is costly to an incumbent firm. Moreover, the counterstrategy discussed earlier, in which entrants contract with customers at a fixed price in advance is still a viable strategy.

Finally, it is wrong to think that entrants never have a reputation. For example, a firm's reputation in one industry could carry over to a new industry that it chooses to enter. Thus entrants may have an associated history when they enter an industry, which tends to remove some of the asymmetry between the incumbent and the new entrant. Although theoretically consistent models exist under which price predation makes sense, from the evidence reviewed earlier, it is still correct to regard price predation as a rare phenomenon.

Limit Pricing

In order to make limit pricing believable and effective, an incumbent firm must pursue a strategy in which it is optimal for it to produce the q^* units discussed earlier in the face of entry. Certainly if two firms have identical average cost curves as in the earlier model, it is simply not believable that an incumbent would keep its output unchanged in the face of large-scale entry by another firm. The key to making limit pricing believable is for the incumbent firm to somehow manipulate the market environment when entry occurs so that the incumbent has the incentive to produce q^* units.

It is easy to create a model that creates the incentive to produce q^* units in the face of entry. Consider a simple model consisting of two periods. Firm 1 is the only firm in

---

[6] For additional analyses of predation, see Easterbrook (1981), Kreps et al. (1982), Kreps and Wilson (1982), Milgrom and Roberts (1982b), Selten (1978), Ordover and Willig (1981), and Williamson (1977).

Period 1. In Period 2 the possibility arises that another firm could enter. In Period 1, Firm 1 can invest to construct its manufacturing facility in such a way that in Period 2 the only output the firm can produce is q^* units. If the firm can construct its facility in this way, then if entry does indeed occur in Period 2, there is no doubt that Firm 1 will produce q^* units of output. But if Firm 1 has made that obvious, then no firm will enter in Period 2. Therefore, by investing in Period 1 in such a way as to make it optimal to produce q^* units in Period 2, Firm 1 can exclude entry in Period 2. In other words, Firm 1 has successfully practiced limit pricing: it has committed itself so that in Period 2 its previously unbelievable threat to produce q^* units becomes believable.[7] Notice the inherent asymmetry in this model between the incumbent and the new entrant. The incumbent is assumed to be able to make investments in Period 1 that commit it to certain production decisions in Period 2, but the new entrant is not able to do so. This is the fundamental asymmetry that can be exploited by Firm 1 and is what makes the strategic behavior on Firm 1's part believable.

An interesting feature associated with this simple model of strategic behavior is that Firm 1 spends money in Period 1 to limit its productive options in Period 2. That is, without any investing, Firm 1 would be able to produce a wider range of output than it can produce after it has invested to specifically construct its plant so that only q^* units of output can be produced. At first glance, this appears to worsen the options of Firm 1 and therefore should make the firm worse off. In fact, as demonstrated, just the opposite is true. Firm 1's investment makes believable its threat to produce q^* units in the face of entry in Period 2.

This notion of limiting options in order to precommit to certain actions turns out to be especially important in strategic behavior. By apparently worsening your options, you can actually make yourself better off! By reducing its flexibility of production, Firm 1 can convince a potential entrant that it should not enter and thereby earn higher profits than it would otherwise.[8] The point is that by making commitments that render its threats credible, a firm can improve its profit position even though it restricts its choices. In this example, Firm 1 manipulates the underlying environment, namely its ability to produce in Period 2, in such a way as to give itself an advantage over potential entrants.[9]

This example of limit pricing can be illustrated in a diagram, called an **extensive form game,** that lists the sequence of all the possible actions and outcomes for each firm (see Figure 13.3). Each line represents an action, and each box represents a decision

---

[7] Because the threat in Period 1 to produce q^* in Period 2 is credible, the model is sometimes called *subgame perfect*. See Chapter 10.

[8] Another way of making a commitment is for the firm to sign a contract that penalizes it if it fails to produce q^* in Period 2. One problem with such contracts is that they may not be legally enforceable.

[9] Committing to a fixed capacity in the future becomes more difficult if capital depreciates over time. If capital depreciates over time, it is unclear how the incumbent can maintain the natural asymmetry that arises from being able to go first. After entry, it appears that both the incumbent and new entrant are on equal footing in terms of their ability to precommit to replace capacity that is wearing out. Therefore, strategic behavior in models in which capital depreciates rapidly is unlikely to be achieved by precommitting to the building of capital by an incumbent. The incumbent's advantage should be eroded rapidly if depreciation is rapid. For additional analyses of limit pricing and entry deterrence, see Dixit (1979), Eaton and Ware (1987), Fudenberg and Tirole (1983), Gilbert and Lieberman (1987), Milgrom and Roberts (1982a), Salop (1979), Spence (1977; 1979), and Waldman (1987).

FIGURE 13.3   Extensive Form Game

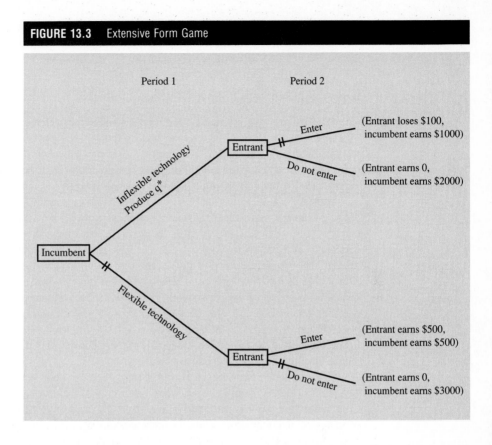

point. The outcomes of actions are shown in parentheses. To simplify the diagram, let us alter the example slightly so that the incumbent is choosing between two production technologies, a flexible one that allows a wide range of output to be produced, and an inflexible one that can produce only q^*, where q^* is an output level that deters entry.

Look at Figure 13.3 and work backward from the top right of the diagram. In Period 2, the entrant has a decision to make—whether to enter. Conditional on the incumbent having chosen the inflexible technology and producing q^*, the entrant can conclude that it is better not to enter in Period 2, since it is better to earn $0 than lose $100. The two lines across the *Enter* line of action rule it out. Now, look at the bottom right corner of the diagram. Conditional on the incumbent choosing the flexible technology, the entrant would decide to enter because by doing so, it would earn profits of $500, which exceeds $0 that is earned with no entry. Therefore, two lines block the action *Do not enter*.[10] We have now completely described how the entrant would behave in Period 2 conditional on the incumbent's behavior in Period 1.

Now look at the decision of the incumbent in Period 1: the incumbent must decide whether to produce with the flexible or inflexible technology. If the incumbent follows the upper branch in Period 1, it earns profits of $2000. If the incumbent follows the lower branch in Period 1, it earns profits of $500. Clearly, the upper branch dominates. Hence, the two lines across the lower branch in Period 1 block that line of action. We have now solved the model. The incumbent follows the upper branch in Period 1, and the entrant then follows the lower branch in Period 2. This model has the property that actions are always optimal and based on credible beliefs.

Investment Behavior to Lower Production Costs

Chapter 10 shows that no matter what model of oligopoly behavior is assumed to apply to an industry, the market outcome depends on the costs of the competing firms. In other words, the costs of each firm are part of the market environment that determines the outcome of the competition among the firms. In the following model, an incumbent firm manipulates the market environment to its own advantage.

Consider a model consisting of two time periods. In Period 1 the incumbent firm, Firm 1, is in the market and has the opportunity to invest in research and development that will lower its costs in Period 2. In Period 2, both the incumbent firm and a new entrant, Firm 2, compete. The costs of the new entrant are assumed to be identical to those of the incumbent in Period 1. We are interested in the incentives that the incumbent firm has to invest in research and development in order to lower its costs in Period 2 relative to the costs of the new entrant in Period 2. The asymmetry in this model results from the assumption that only the incumbent firm, not the new entrant, can invest in research and development to lower its costs. This asymmetry arises naturally when one firm is in a marketplace before another firm. To illustrate the strategic choices of the incumbent firm, consider a specific example.

Suppose that competition in Period 2 is governed by the Cournot model studied in Chapter 10. This is merely a simplifying assumption to facilitate some concrete results.[11] Suppose further that the incumbent firm's costs in Period 1 are $1 of fixed costs and $6 of (constant) marginal costs. If the incumbent firm makes no investments in research and development in Period 1, then its fixed and marginal costs in Period 2 will be identical to those in Period 1. Assume further that these cost conditions characterize the technology of the entrant in Period 2. Suppose the industry demand curve is $q = 12 - p$. Let us first work out the resulting equilibrium when no investment in research and development occur.

In Period 1, the incumbent firm, Firm 1, is a monopolist and equates marginal revenue to marginal cost. The incumbent charges a price of $9 and produces a quantity of 3 units in Period 1, which leads to a profit of $8 in Period 1.[12] In Period 2, Firm 1 and the entrant, Firm 2, are each governed by the same cost conditions and are assumed to behave as Cournot oligopolists. The resulting equilibrium in Period 2 is that each firm produces

---

[10] Notice that, but for the entrant, the incumbent prefers the flexible technology, since, in the absence of entry, the incumbent's profits are higher with the flexible technology ($3000 vs. $2000). However, as the example shows, the inflexible technology is better for the incumbent when entry can occur.

[11] None of the general insights depend upon the particular model of oligopoly behavior chosen in Period 2, though the quantitative results, of course, depend on the specific model. The key feature of the example is that Firm 1's behavior in Period 1 influences the equilibrium in Period 2.

[12] Profits in Period 1 equal total revenue minus total cost or $q_1 (12 - q_1) - (1 + 6q_1)$. Profits are maximized (and equal $8) when q_1 is 3 and p is $9.

TABLE 13.1A   Strategic R&D Investment: Monopoly in Period 1, Cournot Competition in Period 2

	Period 1	Period 2	Total Profit in Periods 1 and 2
No R&D investment	Profit of incumbent = $8	Profit of incumbent = $ 3 Profit of entrant = $ 3	$11
	Price = $9	Price = $ 8	$ 3
R&D investment	Profit of incumbent = $8 − $7.01 = $0.99	Profit of incumbent = $10.11 Profit of entrant = $ 0.63	11.10 $ 0.63
	Price = $9	Price = $ 7.33	

Optimal strategy is for incumbent to invest in R&D.

TABLE 13.1B   R&D Investment: Monopoly in Periods 1 and 2

	Period 1	Period 2	Total Profit in Periods 1 and 2
No R&D investment	Profit = $8 Price = $9	Profit = $ 8 Price = $ 9	$16
R&D Investment	Profit = $8−7.01 = $0.99 Price = $9	Profit = $15 Price = $ 8	$15.99

Optimal strategy is *no* R&D investment.

two units at a price of $8 and earns a profit in Period 2 of $3.[13] Therefore, the total profits of Firm 1 for both periods (for simplicity, ignore the fact that it is preferable to receive money in Period 1 since it is before Period 2) are $11. These results are summarized in Table 13.1A.

Suppose now that we give the incumbent firm the opportunity to invest in research and development in Period 1. Suppose that for an investment of $7.01, Firm 1 can lower its marginal cost next period by $2. Does it make sense for Firm 1 to undertake this investment when faced with competition in Period 2? If Firm 1 does make the investment, it earns less money in Period 1: before it was earning $8 in Period 1, and now it earns $8 − $7.01, or $.99. However, Firm 1 does better than before in Period 2, because its marginal cost is $4 instead of $6. In the Cournot equilibrium of Period 2, Firm 1 produces 3 1/3 units, Firm 2 produces 1 1/3 units, and the price equals $7.33.[14] Profit for Firm

---

[13] In Period 2, Firm 1 maximizes $q_1[12 − (q_1 + q_2)] − (1 + 6q_1)$. Firm 2 maximizes a similar expression. Solving for the intersection of the reaction (or best response) curves (discussed in Chapter 10) yields $q_1 = q_2 = 2$, which implies $p = 8$, and profits per firm equal $3.

[14] Firm 1 chooses q_1 to maximize $q_1(12 − q_1 − q_2) − (1 + 4q_1)$, while Firm 2 chooses q_2 to maximize $q_2(12 − q_1 − q_2) − (1 + q_1)$. The reaction (or best response) curves intersect at $q_1 = 3\ 1/3$, $q_2 = 1\ 1/3$.

1 in Period 2 equals $10.11. Combined with the profit of $.99 in Period 1, this yields a total profit of $11.10, which exceeds the $11 that it earns without investing in research and development. Thus it is clear that Firm 1 is better off making the research expense and earning less money than before in Period 1, because it makes more money than before in Period 2 (and more total profit). Notice also that consumers are better off when Firm 1 invests in R&D because the price in Period 2 is lower when R&D occurs. The example is summarized in the top half of Table 13.1. In this example the incumbent firm makes an investment early in Period 1 in order to alter the environment of Period 2 in its favor. This strategic behavior derives solely from the asymmetry that allows Firm 1 to act before Firm 2 to invest in research and development. Such asymmetry arises naturally when a firm is first in the industry.

Suppose Firm 1 did not have to worry about competition in Period 2: would it still be profitable to invest in research and development? If the firm makes no investment in either period, it earns its monopoly profit of $8 in each of the two periods, for a total profit of $16. If the firm invests in research and development, it is a monopolist in each period but earns $7.01 less than before in Period 1 and earns more in Period 2. If the firm makes the R&D investment, its monopoly profit in Period 2 is $15.[15] Its total profit therefore is $15 in Period 2 plus $8 in Period 1, minus the Period 1 investment of $7.01, which equals $15.99. Total profits are higher when the firm makes no investment in R&D, so it is optimal not to invest. Table 13.1B summarizes the results when Firm 1 is a monopolist. Table 13-1A and B shows how strategic behavior in a competitive environment can alter the incentive for undertaking various investments and how consumers benefit from this behavior.

A variant of this example relates to learning by doing, which, as mentioned, refers to the decline in the cost of producing an item as a firm gains experience in its production. In the context of the model just studied, this means that the more a firm produces in Period 1, the lower its costs are in Period 2. This creates an incentive for the firm to sell a lot in Period 1, gain experience, and be able to compete in Period 2 at a low cost relative to that of new entrants. To sell a lot in Period 1 may require a low price. Thus, profit is lower than it would be if production were lower in Period 1. Using the concept of learning by doing, however, the lowered profit in Period 1 can be thought of as an investment that enables the firm to earn more in subsequent periods.

In a learning-by-doing model the advantage of being able to go first depends on two things: the amount by which a firm can lower its cost relative to its rival's, and how long it takes to learn. Obviously, if the cost advantage is small, going first is not important. Moreover, if learning is either extremely rapid *or* extremely slow, the advantage of having a head start is not very great. The reason is that when learning is very rapid, rivals can quickly put themselves in the same position as the incumbent. Conversely, when learning is very slow, the head start a firm gets does not matter very much. It is in the intermediate cases in which learning is neither very rapid nor very slow that the strategic importance of learning by doing is greatest for increasing profits (see Spence 1981a). It is possible

---

[15] If the investment in R&D is made, monopoly profits in Period 2 equal $q(12 - q) - (1 + 4q)$. Equating marginal revenue to marginal cost yields q of 4, p of $8, and profits of $15.

that the learning so much improves the incumbent's cost advantage relative to the second firm that the second firm has no incentive to enter the industry.

Raising Rivals' Costs

Another type of strategic behavior involves raising rivals' costs. All the models of oligopoly predict that a firm's profit depends on its costs relative to those of its rivals. If a firm can costlessly raise its rivals' costs relative to its own, it can increase its profit at the expense of its rivals. In order to affect a rival's costs, a firm must usually start with some market (or political) power.

Direct Methods. Direct methods involve direct interference with rivals' production or selling methods. To take an extreme case, an unethical firm could behave criminally and blow up a rival's plant or sabotage a rival's production processes. Both actions would raise a rival's costs, reduce competition, and raise the profits of the unethical firm practicing the strategic behavior (assuming that the firm is not caught). Of course, if the unethical firm must spend money to raise a rival's costs, then this increased expenditure must be balanced against the competitive gain from raising the rival's cost.

Another example of a direct method involves making it difficult for a rival to gather information. A new entrant may have less information about the marketplace than an incumbent and may need to do some market research, perhaps research that the incumbent firm has already done. The incumbent's behavior can raise the cost of gathering the marketing information for the entrant. For example, if the entrant conducts a marketing experiment to see whether its product is liked in a certain location, the incumbent can counteract the experiment by conducting its own marketing experiment in an effort to "jam the signal," reducing the reliability of the entrant's experiment (Fudenberg and Tirole 1986). The incumbent firm could offer huge promotional discounts in cities where the entrant is trying to gain marketing information, making it more difficult for the entrant to judge consumer acceptance of its product relative to the incumbent's product. To further confuse the entrant about the demand for its product, the incumbent could run ads to make it more difficult for the entrant to gain consumers' attention in cities where the marketing experiment is being conducted. The incumbent could also buy the rival's product off the store shelves during periods of heavy advertising and then return it later on, depriving the entrant of sales it otherwise would have made. Some of these direct methods of raising a rival's costs could expose the firm to legal attack, a topic discussed in Chapter 22.

Interference Through Government Regulation. Another method of raising rivals' costs is to use government regulation. Many government regulations "grandfather" (exempt from regulation) existing firms and make it more onerous for new firms to operate in an industry. For example, some environmental regulations impose more onerous requirements on new equipment than on old equipment and thus favor existing firms over entrants. By supporting government regulation so that a new rival cannot adopt their production techniques, incumbent firms can often preserve and protect their market position and make it more costly for entrants to compete.

MUST A FIRM INFORM A COMPETITOR OF ITS PLANS?

In *Berkey Photo Inc. v. Eastman Kodak Co.*, Berkey brought a suit against Kodak.[1] Berkey was a photofinisher and a manufacturer of cameras. One of Berkey's claims was that Kodak should have informed Berkey of its intention to develop a new camera (the Kodak 110) and new film for it so that Berkey could have redesigned its cameras and participated in the sales of the 110 cameras. When the 110 was introduced in 1972, it was a big success for Kodak and a disaster for Berkey, which lost camera sales. The Court ruled that Kodak's failure to predisclose did not violate the antitrust laws. A firm has no duty to provide a competitor with advance information about improved products to enable the competitor to remain a viable future competitor.

[1] 602 F.2d 263, cert. denied, 444 U.S. 1093 (1980).

Production of Complements.   Sometimes an incumbent produces a variety of products, while a new entrant produces only one or two. To the extent that the products must be compatible, as with computers and peripheral devices, or cameras and film, an incumbent may be able to raise costs for entrants by making it more costly (through product design) for them to determine how to make their products compatible with the incumbent's. Even if a product's design reduces the amount consumers are willing to pay for it, the increased profits that come from hampering a rival may offset the loss (Farrell and Saloner 1986; Matutes and Regibeau 1988). See Example 13.4.

Raise Switching Costs.   An incumbent can make it difficult for consumers of its product to switch in the future to a new entrants' product (Schmalensee 1982). This can be thought of as raising the entrant's marketing costs to attract customers. For example, appropriate design may make it impossible to use computer programs written for one computer on another computer. Although the design may make the incumbent's product less desirable, it also serves to raise the switching costs to consumers. This causes the demand that a future entrant sees to be lower than it would otherwise be and reduces the incentive of rivals to enter.

Raising Wages or Other Input Prices.   Another illustration of the strategic value of raising rivals' costs occurs when production technology differs between an incumbent firm and a rival. Suppose the rival uses more labor per unit output then does the incumbent firm. Then the incumbent would suffer less from an increase in wage rates than the new entrant. Although each firm's costs go up if wages rise in an industry, the new entrant's costs go up by more than the incumbent's. This can actually lead an incumbent to prefer increasing wages, for example, by supporting union activities (Williamson 1968). Although total profits in the *industry* must go down when wages rise, the market share of the less labor-intensive firm can so increase that its profits rise. In other words, a smaller

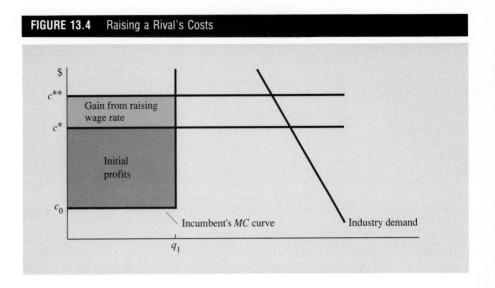

FIGURE 13.4   Raising a Rival's Costs

pie can be better for the firm that gets a larger slice. This strategic behavior takes advantage of the natural asymmetry in production and assumes that the incumbent can influence marketwide wages.

A variant of the above example occurs when the incumbent firm raises wages, not by encouraging unionization, but rather through direct market purchases. An incumbent that can purchase enough of the labor in a market to drive up the market wage has market power. It can strategically use that market power to increase the costs of other firms more than its own when other firms are more labor intensive than the incumbent.[17]

To illustrate how raising a rival's costs can raise an incumbent firm's profits even if its own costs go up, consider the case of an incumbent that uses less labor per unit output than does a rival. Suppose that the incumbent has a constant marginal (and average) cost, c_0, until its capacity, q_1, is reached. The incumbent's marginal cost curve is illustrated in Figure 13.4. Assume that there are many rivals, all with the same constant marginal cost, c^*, as shown in Figure 13.4.

In the absence of strategic behavior, the equilibrium price in the industry is c^*, and it is optimal for the incumbent to produce at capacity, q_1, where it earns profits equal to $(c^* - c_0)q_1$. Suppose now that the incumbent is able to raise the wage rate in the industry. Because the incumbent's technology is different from everyone else's, the wage increase will have a different effect on c^* than on the incumbent's marginal cost. Consider an extreme example in which the marginal cost of the incumbent firm does not change, while the marginal cost of rivals increases from c^* to c^{**}. The equilibrium price will rise from

---

[17] This discussion has explored only some of several different ways to raise rivals' costs. The interested reader is referred to Salop and Sheffman (1987), Krattenmaker and Salop (1986), and the papers in Salop (1981).

TABLE 13.2   Natural Advantage of An Incumbent

No Strategic Behavior

Incumbent profit with no entry	= $100
Incumbent profit with entry	= $ 40
Entrant profit	= $ 40

Result: Entry occurs and incumbent earns $40.

Strategic Behavior That Raises Incumbent's and Entrant's Cost by $50

Incumbent profit with no entry	= $100 − $50 = $ 50
Incumbent profit with entry	= $ 40 − $50 = $ − 10
Entrant profit	= $ 40 − $50 = $ − 10

Result: No entry occurs, and incumbent earns $50.
Overall Result: Optimal strategy is to pursue strategic behavior and earn $50.

c^* to c^{**}, the incumbent will still find it optimal to produce at capacity, and its profit will increase from its original level to the new level of $(c^{**} - c_0)q_1$. The increase in profits is illustrated in Figure 13.4. By behaving strategically and raising the costs of the competitive fringe (the rivals) from c^* to c^{**}, the incumbent is able to increase its profit. Moreover, even if the wage increase raises the incumbent's costs, it may still be profitable for the incumbent to raise wages as long as the cost increase is smaller than the gain shown in Figure 13.4.

The Natural Advantage of An Incumbent

A natural asymmetry often exists between an incumbent and entrants, in that the incumbent has already made expenditures (that is, sunk costs) that make it unlikely that it would exit the industry.[18] Having made these expenditures before anyone else, the incumbent is committed earlier than anyone else to remaining in the industry and derives a strategic advantage from this commitment. This strategic advantage creates incentives for the incumbent to spend more money to keep entrants out of an industry than they are willing to spend to get into it. The following example illustrates this point.

Suppose that when the incumbent is the only firm in the market, it earns monopoly profit of $100. Table 13.2 summarizes the example. If a second firm enters the industry, the combined profits of the two firms are likely to be less than $100, because perfect collusion, as shown in Chapters 9 and 10, is unlikely. Suppose that joint profits in the industry when the two firms compete are $80 and that each firm gets $40. Notice that the incumbent firm would pay up to $60 to prevent entry because without entry it earns $60 more than it earns with entry ($100 - $40). The entrant would only spend $40 to enter. If the incumbent could raise the entrant's costs as well as its own by the same amount, say, $50, then the incumbent's profit would be $50 without entry and − $10

---

[18] For an analysis of the strategic issues that arise in the context of exit in a declining industry, see Ghemawat and Nalebuff (1985).

with entry. However, with these increased costs the entrant's profits would be $-\$10$, and negative profits would provide no incentive for entry. Because profits of $50 exceed the $40 that the incumbent would earn with no strategic behavior, the incumbent has an incentive to raise costs for both its rival and itself by $50.[19]

One way the incumbent could raise costs would be to support government legislation that raises both its own and its rival's costs by $50, for example, legislation regarding pollution controls. Alternatively, the $50 could be spent on advertising. Suppose that advertising does not change total consumption, affecting only the market shares of firms within an industry. Suppose a rival must match the advertising expenditures of the incumbent if anyone is to purchase the rival's product. The assumed asymmetry in this example is that the incumbent can spend its advertising money first. As the example shows, this guarantees that the incumbent can gain by behaving strategically to raise both its own and its rival's costs.

Another implication of this natural asymmetry between an incumbent and a rival is that the incumbent is willing to bid more than an entrant for the right to a scarce resource that would enable entry. For example, suppose that only one distribution outlet is available to a new entrant to market a product. Returning to the preceding numerical example, the incumbent firm is willing to bid $60 in order to purchase that distribution channel. An entrant would be unwilling to bid that much. Moreover, notice that the incumbent, which presumably already has a channel of distribution, would simply be purchasing the additional distribution outlet in order to foreclose its use by the entrant—it might not actually use the outlet. This strategy would deter entry and guarantee that the incumbent's profit would be more than it would be if entry were allowed to occur. Notice that the scarcity of distribution channels is critical in this example. If distribution were easy to obtain, the incumbent could not profitably foreclose entrants by purchasing all distribution channels.[20]

Allegations that incumbent firms buy up industry supplies of scarce resources in an effort to prevent rivals from using them have appeared in antitrust cases. For example, in the Alcoa antitrust case,[21] it was alleged that Alcoa had signed contracts with power companies containing a provision that prevented the power companies from supplying power to any other firm for the purpose of making aluminum.

Strategic behavior analogous to that just described relates to **sleeping patents:** patents that, once obtained, are "put to sleep" and not used. The reason a firm acquires sleeping patents is to prevent rivals from obtaining and using them in competition (Gilbert 1981). Chapter 20 discusses strategic behavior related to patents in detail.

---

[19] The natural asymmetry can be seen as follows. Without entry the incumbent earns monopoly profit, π_m. With entry the incumbent and entrant together earn duopoly profits, π_d, which are less than π_m. If the incumbent and entrant equally share the duopoly profits, the entrant would pay $.5\,\pi_d$ to enter, while the incumbent would pay $\pi_m - .5\,\pi_d$ to keep the entrant out. Since π_m exceeds π_d, it is worth more to the monopolist to keep the entrant out than it is worth to the entrant to enter. See Salop (1979) and Gilbert (1989).

[20] For more on strategic purchasing behavior, see Salop and Sheffman (1987).

[21] *U.S. vs. Aluminum Co. of America*, 148 F.2d 416 (1945).

EXAMPLE 13.6

INFORMATION EXCHANGES: THE HARDWOOD CASE

In *American Column and Lumber Co. et al. v. United States*, 257 U.S. 377 (1921), known as the Hardwood case, a group of lumber mills exchanged price and production information through a central organization, the American Hardwood Manufacturers Association, run by the producers. The plan to collect and disseminate price information was called the *Open Competition Plan.* The number of mills in the industry was large—about 9000 mills in 20 states. Participation in the Open Competition Plan was voluntary, and 465 mills participated (representing 30 percent of output). Although monitoring output and prices can facilitate collusion, collusion can be difficult with such a large number of independent firms in the industry. Information sharing arrangements should be most suspect when the number of firms in the industry is small enough to make collusion likely. Despite this, the Supreme Court ruled that the information exchange violated Section I of the Sherman Act, and the information dissemination ceased.

An alternative explanation for why the mills went to the trouble to collect and disseminate information is that it was efficient. Information is costly for each firm to collect separately and knowledge of market conditions can benefit competition.

SOURCE: Alexander (no date).

as rivals believe that the shift was not motivated by a lowered price. There may also be legitimate efficiency reasons for industry members to exchange information. When a centralized market does not exist, disseminating price information can improve market efficiency. Moreover, firms can monitor their own efficiency better if they can compare their costs to those of other firms (see Example 13.6).

Prediction of a Rival's Reactions

Sometimes a firm can predict reactions to competition by analyzing its rival's incentives.[26] For example, if a rival has multiple locations that all charge the same price, and an entrant is trying to come into the market at just one location, it may be better for the rival to abandon the location than to lower prices everywhere in a geographic area. In such a case, the entrant has reason to believe that its entry will not be met by strong price competition. Similarly, a large firm may have more to lose than a smaller firm if price falls; thus, a large firm may prefer to let a small firm develop a small foothold rather than engage in a price war. Of course, if the large firm believed the small firm (or other entrants) would continue to expand, it might choose to fight vigorously. If the large firm

---

[26] Depending on the circumstances, this type of strategic behavior could be either cooperative or noncooperative.

decides to fight, one alternative to reducing its (uniform) price is to introduce a new brand, sometimes called a **fighting brand**, whose price is low and whose availability is limited to those areas where the small firm is successful. In this way, the large firm can engage in competition without lowering price to all its customers.

A firm that produces many substitute products views price competition in one product as costly because it also affects its revenues from other products. Conversely, a firm that produces complementary products does not view a price war in one product as all that costly because lost profits in one product can be offset by increased profits in others. A firm has less to fear about competitive reaction to its aggressive pricing policy when its rivals produce substitute products, are relatively large, and believe that the firm only wants to occupy a small market niche (Bulow et al. 1985; Fudenberg and Tirole 1984).[27]

Use of Delivered Pricing

A **delivered pricing** system specifies the total delivered price (inclusive of freight) that a buyer must pay as a function of the buyer's location: the price the buyer pays does not depend upon the location of the seller. A delivered pricing system can be created by specifying the total delivered price as the sum of a going market price at some specified location—the so-called **basing point**—plus freight from that location. For example, steel used to be sold with Pittsburgh as the basing point. If an Ohio steel mill shipped steel to Chicago, the price the buyer paid equaled the going price of steel in Pittsburgh plus freight from Pittsburgh to Chicago. The freight charges were calculated from standard published rate schedules.

At first glance, delivered pricing systems seem so bizarre that they inspire suspicion. Indeed, many economists believe that delivered pricing is an odd mechanism adopted only to facilitate collusion. It facilitates collusion because it prevents competing firms from secretly granting discounts disguised as low freight charges. Forcing all firms to charge the same freight and same price makes it easy to detect deviations from a collusive price agreement. The pricing system that many economists predict should emerge with competition is called **FOB pricing** (FOB means *free on board*—the buyer incurs no charge to have the goods loaded onto a transport carrier) in which the total price paid equals the FOB price at the seller's plant plus actual freight. Under such a system, the freight charge to a buyer is different if the firms are located in different places, and firms could cut price by undercharging for freight (which might be difficult for rivals to observe). In such a pricing system, firms at different locations generally quote different prices to a buyer. These effects of FOB pricing can make collusion more difficult by increasing the ease of cheating.

The preceding logic implicitly assumes that firms detect cheating by observing deviations from an agreed-upon price schedule. Another way firms detect cheating is by observing shifts in market share: if firms see that a rival is inexplicably gaining customers,

---

[27] See Bernheim and Whinston (1987) and Whinston (1987) for examples of how multimarket contact and tie-in sales can signal likely competitive responses.

FIGURE 13.5   FOB Pricing Divides the Market

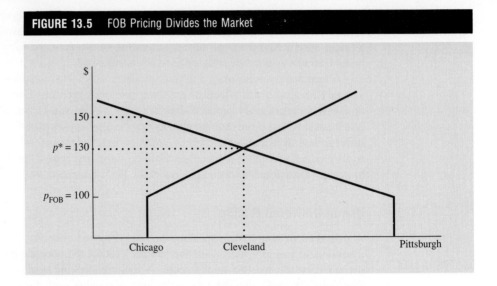

they suspect cheating. A great disadvantage to collusion by delivered pricing is that it fails to allocate the market to sellers. For example, suppose that there are two sellers of steel—one in Chicago and the other in Pittsburgh. Under delivered pricing with Pittsburgh as the basing point, it might be profitable for either a Chicago or Pittsburgh steel mill to sell steel near Chicago. In such a case, no inference of cheating would follow if the Pittsburgh mill were seen selling in the Chicago area. If instead the firms adopted FOB plant pricing plus freight, the market would be clearly divided: consumers closer to Chicago would buy from Chicago, and those closer to Pittsburgh would buy there.

Figure 13.5 illustrates that FOB pricing creates a clean market division precisely because firms charge most buyers different prices. As shown in the figure, suppose each firm agrees to charge the same FOB price at its plant and to charge actual transportation charges. The price lines represent the price that a buyer at any location must pay. They rise as one moves away from the location of each firm to show that transportation costs rise with distance. All customers to the left of Cleveland buy from Chicago, and all customers to the right of Cleveland buy from Pittsburgh.

If the Pittsburgh steel mill were seen selling in the Chicago area, one would infer that it was not adhering to the FOB pricing agreement. In contrast, under delivered pricing, all firms charge the same price, and there is no neat market division. In general, the greater the distance between the firms, and the more important the transportation charges, the better FOB pricing is as a means of market allocation and collusion (Carlton 1983).

There is an important difference between delivered pricing and FOB pricing. In an equilibrium with FOB pricing, all firms must charge the *marginal* buyer the same price ($130 at Cleveland in Figure 13.5). At points other than Cleveland, however, the firms located at Pittsburgh and Chicago charge *different* prices under FOB pricing but not under delivered pricing. Despite this difference between delivered and FOB pricing, it is sometimes possible for the two pricing systems to look alike.

Suppose that many steel consumers are located in both Pittsburgh and Chicago, but that initially all of the many steel mills are in Pittsburgh. If it costs $100 to produce a ton of steel, then in the *competitive* equilibrium, a buyer in Chicago pays $100 plus freight, say $50, from Pittsburgh for a final price of $150. Suppose now that a very small steel mill opens in Chicago. How will the existence of this new steel mill change the equilibrium? At any price below $150, the Chicago steel mill has more business than it can possibly handle (since it is a very small mill). Therefore, there is no reason for the Chicago mill to charge below $150! In this competitive equilibrium, the Chicago mill charges what appears to be a delivered price based on Pittsburgh freight. Yet, it is the competitive equilibrium. The small Chicago mill earns a rent because it has chosen such a desirable location.

Failure to understand that firms at some locations (like Chicago in the example) can charge $150 could lead one to mischaracterize some competitive pricing arrangement as collusive delivered pricing. As more steel mills locate in the Chicago region, they will eventually be unable to sell all their steel in Chicago at $150, and they will start selling outside of Chicago (say, Cleveland). As soon as this occurs, the FOB price can no longer equal $150 in Chicago. If the FOB price is $150 in Chicago and the Chicago mill adds freight to Cleveland, the price to Cleveland exceeds the FOB price at Pittsburgh plus freight (of $30) from Pittsburgh, and no Chicago steel would be sold in Cleveland (see Figure 13.5). Therefore, the new competitive equilibrium must involve an FOB price below $150 in Chicago. Eventually, competitive entry of steel mills in the Chicago region will drive the Chicago price down to a marginal cost of $100. Buyers close to Pittsburgh buy from Pittsburgh, and those close to Chicago buy from Chicago.

Delivered pricing has had an interesting history. In *FTC v. Cement Institute* (333 U.S. 683 [1948]), the FTC alleged a conspiracy among cement producers that was in part facilitated by the use of delivered pricing with basing points. The FTC won the case, but subsequent political pressure from businessmen led to Congressional hearings that seemed to stop the FTC from bringing many more cases.

Recently, spatial pricing policies (that is, variation of price with location) have again come under scrutiny. For example, spatial pricing policies of the lumber industry were attacked in *Boise Cascade*.[28] All plywood used to come from the Pacific Northwest. Beginning in the early 1960s, plywood began being shipped from the South. Initially, the amount of southern plywood was small, but eventually it became significant. The pricing of southern plywood always consisted of the sum of two components, price plus freight, and the freight charge was based on freight charges from the Pacific Northwest. Although it follows from the earlier example of steel why the price of southern plywood was initially quoted in this way, it is harder to explain as the southern plywood industry developed. The lumber firms practicing the policy claimed that it was just a convenient device to facilitate comparisons of price quotes from the South and the Pacific Northwest. They also claimed that the southern FOB price was different from the Pacific Northwest FOB price. The implication was that each FOB price was determined by the forces of supply and demand, and the resulting pricing equilibrium was precisely the competitive FOB

---

[28] *Boise Cascade v. FTC,* 63 E.2d 323 (9th Cir. 1980).

pricing equilibrium predicted by the reasoning of Figure 13.5. For example, suppose that the true competitive price of southern plywood to a buyer in New York is $200 and consists of two parts: $100 of true freight plus $100 of true FOB price. If the freight from the Pacific Northwest is $150, then the quoted price for Southern plywood is $50 FOB plus $150 freight for a total price of $200. The court decided that the pricing scheme did not represent illegal collusive behavior.

In competition, prices reflect costs. Therefore, economists expect that FOB pricing plus actual freight should emerge in competition. In fact, firms in competitive industries often use delivered pricing because it is simple and saves on administrative costs. For example, firms may use uniform delivered pricing as long as freight does not vary much among customers. Typically, furniture stores include delivery in the price of an item, provided that customers live reasonably close to the store. Some firms have zone pricing, in which buyers who live in a firm's region pay lower freight charges than those in more distant regions. It appears that uniform delivered pricing is often followed as long as the variation in freight charges among customers is 10 percent or less (Carlton 1983). It is presumably the convenience of delivered pricing that was at least in part responsible for business opposition to FTC action against firms that practiced delivered pricing.

Cooperative Strategic Behavior and the Role of the Courts

Cooperative strategic behavior requires that firms act together and seems superficially easier to identify and condemn than noncooperative strategic behavior. After all, any agreement or practice that tends to reduce competition is likely to harm society. The problem is that many practices may be chosen not to restrict competition but for efficiency reasons. See Example 13.5. For example, advance notice of price changes may benefit consumers even though it could also facilitate collusion. A policy that condemns practices reached through agreement to limit competition seems correct. A policy that condemns business practices, however chosen (for example, at the insistence of the buyer), that conceivably could affect collusion, is probably too broad and would leave firms in a quandary as to which of their policies were subject to antitrust scrutiny. The result might be to deter firms from adopting efficient practices that their customers desire.

■ SUMMARY

Strategic behavior is an attempt by a firm to influence the market environment in which it competes. This environment includes the beliefs of rivals and customers, the technologies and costs of the firms, and the knowledge of customers. Early models of noncooperative strategic behavior failed to explain why the beliefs of rivals made sense. Later models have stressed that some asymmetry among firms is a key ingredient of successful strategic behavior. The most studied type of noncooperative strategic behavior is predatory pricing. Predatory pricing is a costly policy for a firm to follow. There have been only a few documented cases of successful predatory pricing in which price was below some measure of cost. Other noncooperative strategies, such as price cuts down to (but not below) cost, strategic R&D, or raising rivals' costs, might well be more profitable, and one should expect them to be used more often than predatory pricing. Cooperative strategic behavior requires firms to act together and is actually a direct application of the theory of collusion studied in Chapters 9 and 10. Any practices that firms can use collectively to reduce uncertainty about each other can facilitate collusion.

The proper legal posture toward strategic behavior is complicated. Some strategic behavior helps consumers, for example, by encouraging investments. Other types of strategic behavior harm consumers. Distinguishing the good strategic behavior from the bad can be difficult for any analyst, including courts. The trade-off, unfortunately, is between too little enforcement, which leads to market power, and too much enforcement, which deters healthy competition. Since strategic behavior can create market power for only as long as entry takes, it would make sense not to worry about the effects of strategic behavior in those industries in which entry is relatively rapid. Moreover, in recognition of the difficulty of detecting undesirable strategic behavior, the legal system should normally be used to attack only those instances of strategic behavior where the undesirable effects are unambiguous.

■ Key Terms

basing point
cooperative strategic behavior
credible threat
delivered pricing
extensive form game
fighting brand
FOB pricing
learning by doing

limit pricing
market environment
most-favored-nations contract
noncooperative strategic behavior
predatory pricing
sleeping patents
strategic behavior

■ Discussion Questions

1. Some contracts contain a provision called "meet or release". This provision allows the customer to be released from the contract if the customer can obtain a lower price and the supplier refuses to meet the lower price. Provide an efficiency and anticompetitive reason for the provision.

2. Suppose Firm A and Firm B each produce competing chemicals whose preparation requires a custom-made ingredient that depends on the firm's particular engineering process. How is the possibility of collusion affected if Firm A is Firm B's supplier and Firm B is Firm A's supplier of their specialized ingredients?

3. One method of enforcing a collusive arrangement is for firms to punish a firm that grants discounts to its customers by lowering the industry price temporarily. This, of course, hurts all firms. How is this punishment af-

fected by a retroactive price clause that grants current price discounts to past customers? Will a large or small firm be deterred more by this punishment?

4. Consider a model of price predation. Explain why driving a rival into bankruptcy does not by itself enable the predator to charge monopoly prices. (*Hint:* What happens to the assets of the bankrupt firm?)

5. Suppose that a monopolist produces a product whose only input is a scarce mineral whose only use is to produce this product. The monopolist buys up the scarce mineral in order to prevent entry and earns profits of π_1. Consider another situation in which there is competition in the final product, but a monopolist of the scarce mineral. Will the monopolist of the scarce mineral earn π_1?

■ Problems

1. In several industries, firms engage in *swaps*. For example, a paper firm with a plant in California and a customer in New York will swap one ton of paper with another paper firm with a plant in New York but a customer in California. Often, the customers have many plants located throughout the country. Provide an efficiency explanation for swaps. Provide an anticompetitive explanation. (*Hint:* Consider why assignment of multiplant customers to firms might make monitoring a cartel easier.)

2. Draw a diagram illustrating the extensive form game that corresponds to Table 13.1. Do the same for Table 13.2.

3. If a firm has debt, it must pay interest to the debtholders. Suppose, as Chapter 2 discussed, that there is a blot on a manager's record if the firm he or she operates goes bankrupt. Discuss whether the use of a high ratio of debt to equity among all firms in an industry could be a practice that facilitates collusion. Consider the consequences if firms issue debt in different years and interest rates vary from year to year.

4. Consider the early model of limit pricing. Is it always optimal for a firm to set output at the level that prevents all entry?

5. Return to Example 13.1. Suppose that the Japanese firms were indeed behaving in a predatory way for twenty years in the hope that in year twenty-one and thereafter they could charge a monopoly price. Suppose the annual loss is $1 million for each of the first twenty years, and let m be the annual flow of monopoly profits from year twenty-one onward. If the interest rate is 10 percent, calculate how high m would have to be in order for the predation strategy to be profitable? (*Hint:* The discounted present value of the twenty years of annual loss is $\frac{1}{r}\left[1 - \left(\frac{1}{1+r}\right)^{20}\right]$, and the discounted present value of an annual profit of m beginning in year twenty-one is $\left(\frac{1}{1+r}\right)^{20}\frac{m}{r}$, where r is the interest rate).

Answers to odd-numbered problems are given at the back of the book.

■ References

Alexander, Donald L. n.d. "Price Associations and Competition: The Hardwood Case." Unpublished, Pennsylvania State University.

Areeda, Phillip E., and Donald F. Turner. 1975. "Predatory Pricing and Related Practices Under Section 2 of the Sherman Act." *Harvard Law Review* 88:697–733.

Bain, Joe S. 1956. *Barriers to New Competition*. Cambridge: Harvard University Press.

Bernheim, B. Douglas, and Michael Whinston. 1987. "Multimarket Contract and Collusive Behavior." Harvard Institute of Economic Research, Working Paper no. 1317.

Bulow, Jeremy I., John D. Geanakoplos, and Paul D. Klemperer. 1985. "Multimarket Oligopoly: Strategic Substitutes and Complements." *Journal of Political Economy* 93:488–511.

Burns, Malcolm R. 1986. "Predatory Pricing and the Acquisition Cost of Competitors." *Journal of Political Economy* 94:266–96.

Carlton, Dennis W. 1983. "A Reexamination of Delivered Pricing Systems." *Journal of Law and Economics* 26:51–70.

Dixit, Avinash. 1979. "A Model of Duopoly Suggesting a Theory of Entry Barriers." *Bell Journal of Economics and Management Science* 10:20–32.

Easterbrook, Frank H. 1981. "Predatory Strategies and Counterstrategies." *University of Chicago Law Review* 48:263–337.

Eaton, B. Curtis, and Roger Ware. 1987. "A Theory of Market Structure with Sequential Entry." *The Rand Journal of Economics* 18:1–16.

Farrell, Joseph, and Garth Saloner. 1986. "Installed Base Compatibility: Innovation, Product Preannouncements, and Predation." *American Economic Review* 76: 940–55.

Fudenberg, Drew, and Jean Tirole. 1983. "Capital as a Commitment: Strategic Investment to Deter Mobility." *Journal of Economic Theory* 31:227–50.

———. 1984. "The Fat Cat Effect, the Puppy-Dog Play, and the Lean and Hungry Look." *American Economic Review* 74 (May):361–66.

———. 1986. "A 'Signal-Jamming' Theory of Predation." *Rand Journal of Economics* 17:366–76.

Gaskins, Darius W., Jr. 1971. "Dynamic Limit Pricing: Optimal Pricing Under Threat of Entry." *Journal of Economic Theory* 3:306–22.

Ghemawat, Pankaj, and Barry Nalebuff. 1985. "Exit." *The Rand Journal of Economics* 16:184–94.

Gilbert, Richard J. 1981. "Patents, Sleeping Patents, and Entry Deterrence," in Salop (1981).

———. 1989. "Mobility Barriers and the Value of Incumbency," in Richard Schmalensee and Robert Willig, eds., *Handbook of Industrial Organization*. New York: North Holland.

Gilbert, Richard J., and Marvin Lieberman. 1987. "Investment and Coordination in Oligopolistic Industries." *The Rand Journal of Economics* 18:17–33.

Hurwitz, James D., William E. Kovacic, Thomas A. Sheehan, III, and Robert H. Lande. 1981. "Current Legal Standards of Predation," in Steven C. Salop, ed. *Strategy, Predation, and Antitrust Analyses*. Washington, D.C.: Federal Trade Commission.

Isaac, Mark R., and Vernon L. Smith. 1985. "In Search of Predatory Pricing." *Journal of Political Economy* 93:320–45.

Koller, Roland L. 1971. "The Myth of Predatory Pricing." *Antitrust Law and Economics Review* (Summer) 105–23.

Krattenmaker, Thomas G., and Steven C. Salop. 1986. "Anticompetitive Exclusion: Raising Rivals' Costs to Achieve Power Over Price." *Yale Law Journal* 96: 209–93.

Kreps, David M., Paul Milgrom, John Roberts, and Robert Wilson. 1982. "Rational Cooperation in the Finitely-Repeated Prisoners' Dilemma." *Journal of Economic Theory* 27:245–52.

Kreps, David M., and Robert Wilson. 1982. "Reputation and Imperfect Information." *Journal of Economic Theory* 27:253–79.

Matutes, Carmen, and Pierre Regibeau. 1988. "Mix and Match: Product Compatibility Without Externalities." *Rand Journal of Economics* 19:221–34.

McGee, John S. 1958. "Predatory Price Cutting: The Standard Oil (N.J.) Case." *Journal of Law and Economics* 1:137–69.

Milgrom, Paul, and John Roberts. 1982a. "Limit Pricing and Entry Under Incomplete Information: An Equilibrium Analysis." *Econometrica* 50:443–59.

———. 1982b. "Predation, Reputation and Entry Deterrence." *Journal of Economic Theory* 27:280–312.

Modigliani, Franco. 1958. "New Developments on the Oligopoly Front." *Journal of Political Economy* 66:215–32.

Ordover, Janusz A., and Garth Saloner. 1989. "Predation Monopolization, and Antitrust," in Richard Schmalensee and Robert Willig, eds., *Handbook of Industrial Organization*. New York: North Holland.

Ordover, Janusz A., and Robert D. Willig. 1981. "An Economic Definition of Predation: Pricing and Product Innovation." *Yale Law Journal* 91:8–53.

Porter, Michael E. 1980. *Competitive Strategy: Techniques for Analyzing Industries and Competitors*. New York: The Free Press.

———. 1985. *Competitive Advantage: Creating and Sustaining Superior Performance*. New York: The Free Press.

Salop, Steven C. 1979. "Strategic Entry Deterrence." *American Economic Review* 69:335–38.

———, ed. 1981. "Strategy, Predation, and Antitrust Analysis." Washington, D.C.: Federal Trade Commission.

———. 1986. "Practices That Credibly Facilitate Collusion," in Joseph Stiglitz and G. Frank Mathewson, eds., *New Developments in the Analysis of Market Structure*. Cambridge: The MIT Press.

Salop, Steven C., and David T. Scheffman. 1987. "Cost-Raising Strategies." *Journal of Industrial Economics* 36:19–34.

Schmalensee, Richard. 1982. "Product Differentiation Advantages of Pioneering Brands." *American Economic Review* 72:349–65.

Selten, R. 1978. "The Chain Store Paradox." *Theory and Decision* 9:127–59.

Spence, A. Michael. 1977. "Entry, Capacity, Investment and Oligopolistic Pricing." *Bell Journal of Economics* 8:534–44.

———. 1979. "Investment Strategy and Growth in a New Market." *Bell Journal of Economics and Management Science* 10:1–19.

———. 1981a. "The Learning Curve and Competition." *Bell Journal of Economics* 12:49–70.

———. 1981b. "Competition Entry and Antitrust Policy," in Salop (1981).

Sylos-Labini, Paolo. 1962. *Oligopoly and Technical Progress*. Cambridge: Harvard University Press.

Tenant, Richard B. 1950. *The American Cigarette Industry: A Study in Economic Analysis and Public Policy*. New Haven, Conn.: Yale University Press.

Tirole, Jean. 1988. *The Theory of Industrial Organization*. Cambridge: The MIT Press.

Waldman, Michael. 1987. "Noncooperative Entry Deterrence, Uncertainty, and the Free-Rider Problem." *Review of Economic Studies* 54:301–10.

Whinston, Michael. 1987. "Tying, Foreclosure, and Exclusion." Harvard Institute of Economic Research, Working Paper no. 1343.

Williamson, Oliver E. 1968. "Wage Rates as a Barrier to Entry: The Pennington Case." *Quarterly Journal of Economics* 82:85–17.

———. 1977. "Predatory Pricing: A Strategic and Welfare Analysis." *Yale Law Journal* 87:284–339.

CHAPTER 14

PRICE DISCRIMINATION

All . . . men have their price

SIR ROBERT WALPOLE

Firms in a perfectly competitive market have no discretion in their pricing policies; they must take the market price as given. Most markets, however, are not perfectly competitive, and firms have some discretion over their pricing policies. When a firm does have pricing discretion, it attempts to price its products so as to maximize its profits. If a firm can identify the customers who value its product the most, the firm may profit by charging them a higher price than others do. When a firm charges customers different prices for identical products, the firm is practicing **price discrimination.** On the other hand, if customers are buying different products, or if it costs more to serve a particular group of customers, it is misleading to interpret all price differences as price discrimination.

This chapter first presents several examples to illustrate how common nonuniform prices are. Next, it describes the incentives for engaging in price discrimination and the necessary conditions for it to occur. It then examines some of the most common methods of price discrimination and their effects on society's welfare. The next chapter analyzes more complicated methods of price discrimination, such as two-part tariffs and tie-in sales. The Appendix discusses examples of price discrimination in agriculture.

■ EXAMPLES OF NONUNIFORM PRICING

In competition, oligopoly, or simple monopoly, the price per unit is the same for all customers. When a firm (or group of firms) practices price discrimination, the price can differ across consumers and need not be a constant per unit; that is, there are **nonuniform prices.** Everyday experience confirms that pricing is more complicated than the simple uniform price per unit typically assumed in economic models. We now review five of the most common nonuniform pricing policies. This chapter focuses primarily on the first, and Chapter 15 focuses primarily on the remaining four.

1. Different categories of customers can pay different prices. For example, magazines charge a higher price to people who buy from newsstands than to those who subscribe. Many movie theaters offer discounts to senior citizens. Products are often packaged with discount coupons that entitle the bearer to purchase the product for a lower price next time. In effect, these coupons allow a firm to charge first-time users a higher price than repeat users.

2. A firm can charge a lump-sum admission fee and then a marginal usage fee. This is called a **two-part tariff.** Such a pricing scheme might be used, for example, in a health club, where members pay an annual fee together with usage fees that vary with the intensity of their use of the club's facilities. Another example occurs in amusement parks, where visitors pay an admission fee and then separate fees for certain rides.

3. Prices often depend on quantities purchased. Price discounts for large purchases are quite common. More generally, price often depends on the amount of the product consumed. For example, electricity bills are frequently computed according to a *declining-block* schedule, in which the first units of usage incur one charge, and subsequent units incur lower charges.

4. Firms can use tie-in sales. A **tie-in sale** is the sale of one product under the condition that the purchaser also buy another. A common example of a tie-in sale is the purchase of a durable machine under the condition that the consumer also purchase from the seller all repair services or all repair parts. Other examples are the sale of copy machines under the condition that customers also purchase related supplies (for example, developing chemicals) from the seller and the sale of cameras under the condition that purchasers buy their film from the seller (sometimes buyers have no choice and must buy film from the seller, for example, some Polaroid cameras use only Polaroid film.) Certain tie-in sales are currently a violation of antitrust laws, and therefore were more common before the antitrust laws were passed. However, as Chapter 22 discusses, it is uncertain exactly what constitutes an illegal tie-in sale. A tie-in sale allows a firm to effectively charge higher prices to consumers who use more of the tied product.

5. A firm can offer products of different quality. By offering a high-quality, high-priced product that appeals to consumers who place a high value on the product, and a low-quality, low-priced product that appeals to other consumers, a firm can *separate* the two types of consumers and charge high prices to those most willing to pay them. Therefore, the problem of what range of qualities a monopolist should produce is closely related to the theory of price discrimination.

Although examples of nonuniform pricing are quite common, it would be wrong to conclude that every seller who charges a nonuniform price is practicing price discrimination. There are many other explanations for these pricing practices. For example, a quantity discount may reflect cost savings from dealing with large orders that a manufacturer is passing on to consumers. This chapter and the next, however, focus on explaining how each of these pricing practices can be profitable for a firm with market power.

■ INCENTIVE AND CONDITIONS FOR PRICE DISCRIMINATION

A firm practices price discrimination to increase its profits. However, price discrimination can be practiced only under special conditions. The following section explains why price discrimination increases profits and what conditions are necessary for it to occur, with particular attention to the possibility of resale.

Profit Motive for Price Discrimination

The profit motive for price discrimination is easy to see. Consider a simple monopolist that charges all customers a single price. Recall from Chapter 5 that the monopolist equates marginal revenue with marginal cost. Marginal revenue—the increased revenue that results from selling an additional unit—is the sum of two effects. The first is the increase in revenue from selling one more unit, and the second is the decrease in revenue on all existing output.[1] This decrease in revenue occurs because price must fall slightly to induce the additional sale. The decrease in revenue on all existing units inhibits the monopolist from expanding output. If the monopolist could lower the price on *only* the one additional unit sold, it would clearly do so as long as the price exceeded marginal cost, thus earning its current profit plus an additional amount on the additional unit. The monopolist would then be price discriminating and earning additional profit. All methods of price discrimination can be viewed as attempts to minimize this second effect on marginal revenue from expanding sales. This chapter and the next explain a variety of pricing policies that are designed to minimize the cost to the monopolist of trying to expand output at a lower price to a particular customer without simultaneously offering the same lower price to all consumers.

Conditions for Price Discrimination

Even though firms would like to practice price discrimination, they may not be able to do so. Three conditions are essential for successful price discrimination. Their presence does not always enable price discrimination to occur, but it can never occur without them.

First, a firm (or group of firms) must have some market power; otherwise, it can never succeed in charging any consumer more than the competitive price.[2]

Second, the firm must know or be able to infer the consumers' willingness to pay, and this willingness to pay must vary across consumers or with the number of units any one consumer purchases (an individual's demand curve slopes downward).

Third, a firm must be able to prevent or limit **resale** from customers who pay the lower price to those who pay the higher price. Any attempt to charge one group a higher price than another is doomed to failure if the group charged the lower price can purchase

---

[1] If total revenue equals pQ, then marginal revenue equals $p + Q(dp/dQ)$.

[2] Price discrimination can be practiced by a single firm or a group of firms. To keep the exposition simple, we focus only on a single firm.

the product and resell it at the lower price to the group charged the higher price, because no one in the latter group would ever buy directly from the monopolist. The possibility of resale is of critical importance for all types of price discrimination.

Resale

Any marketing policy that involves charging nonuniform prices can create incentives for retrading and reselling, and thereby destroy or at least reduce the effectiveness of any attempt at price discrimination. For example, if two people pay different prices for the same product, the person facing the lower price has an incentive to resell the product to the person facing the higher price. The person facing low prices thus becomes the purchasing agent for the person facing high prices. This means that any attempt to charge two different prices must fail unless resale can be prevented or is costly. Similarly, if a firm offers quantity discounts for a product, it must ensure that the discount is not so great as to encourage high-volume purchasers to buy the product and then resell it to those with smaller demands.

Several circumstances can prevent or limit resale:

- *Services*. Most services cannot be resold. For example, a dentist may charge Lisa a very high price and Sue a very low price, and it is impossible for Lisa to gain by having Sue purchase the dentist's services for her. For that reason, price discrimination in services is more likely than price discrimination in industries with tradeable products (Kessel 1958).

- *Warranties*. A manufacturer can threaten to void a warranty if a product is resold. For example, a manufacturer could say that the warranty on a product is valid only for the first-time purchaser, which imposes a cost on a buyer who purchases a product from a previous buyer.

- *Adulteration*. A manufacturer can adulterate a product to make it unfit for other uses. For example, suppose that alcohol is used for drinking (alcoholic beverages) and for medicinal purposes (rubbing alcohol). Suppose that a manufacturer of alcohol is a monopolist and wishes to charge a high price to those who drink alcohol, but a low price to those who use alcohol for medicinal purposes. The manufacturer is faced with the problem that the medicinal users could resell to the drinking users. One solution to this problem is to adulterate the medicinal alcohol by adding ingredients that make it unfit for internal consumption yet preserve its medicinal qualities. This effectively prevents the resale of medicinal alcohol for drinking purposes. This solution would not work if medicine consumers were willing to pay more than drinkers, and the manufacturer wanted to prevent the resale of drinking alcohol for medicinal purposes.

- *Tariffs and Transport Costs*. A manufacturer that wants to charge a high price in the United States and a low price in Europe would have to worry about resale from Europe to the United States. However, if there is a large tariff or transportation cost that must be paid by anybody importing the product from Europe to the United States, then the manufacturer does not have to worry as much about resale.

- *Transaction Cost.* Tariffs and transportation costs are special cases of transaction costs that can arise in resale. More generally, if consumers must incur any type of large transaction costs to resell the product, resale is less likely. For example, if some consumers are mailed coupons that entitle them to purchase a product at a lower price than others, it is not likely to be worthwhile for consumers with coupons to purchase the product and then attempt to find consumers without coupons to resell the product to. The time and storage costs of entering into the resale business are simply too high for most consumers.

- *Contractual Remedies.* A firm can contractually forbid resale as part of its terms of sale. For example, many universities and colleges have arranged for students and faculty members to purchase computers at lower than market rates. One condition of these purchases is that each buyer must agree not to resell the computer. In many cases, however, restrictions on resale are not legally binding; therefore, the contractual attempt to prevent resale may not succeed.

- *Vertical Integration.* A firm can solve the problem of resale by vertical integration, which means that the firm produces products internally rather than relying on outside suppliers. Suppose that a manufacturer of aluminum ingot sells it to producers of aluminum wire and producers of aluminum aircraft parts and wants to charge the aircraft producers a much higher price than the wire producers. If the manufacturer did charge two different prices, the wire producers could resell their ingot to the aircraft producers. If the ingot manufacturer vertically integrates into production of aluminum wire, it will have succeeded in eliminating resale and can effectively practice price discrimination. The reason is that the vertically integrated firm can charge final consumers of aluminum wire a low price (that is, effectively charge and pass along a low price for aluminum ingot to its own aluminum wire division) and still charge the aircraft producers a high price for aluminum ingot with no fear of resale. Resale does not arise for two reasons. First, the monopolist controls the actions of its aluminum wire division and would not allow it to resell the aluminum ingot. Second, once the ingot has been made into aluminum wire and sold, it cannot be used by the producers of aluminum aircraft parts. See Example 14.1.

- *Government Intervention.* The government can enact laws that allow firms in a competitive industry to act collectively to prevent resale. For example, government regulations control how much of an orange grower's crop can be sold as fresh fruit and how much as frozen. Appendix 14A briefly describes some government programs in agriculture that foster price discrimination.

The remainder of this chapter assumes that a firm can prevent or control resale of its product and investigates the ways in which a firm can price discriminate. It is useful to emphasize, though, that the very first question that should arise when someone claims that a firm is price discriminating is how resale can be controlled.

EXAMPLE 14.1

VERTICAL INTEGRATION AS A MEANS OF PRICE DISCRIMINATION: ALCOA SHOWS ITS TRUE METAL

The traditional view of why Alcoa (which prior to 1930 was the monopolistic producer of primary aluminum ingot) forward integrated into processing activities (bought firms in these industries) was to demonstrate the technical and commercial feasibility of new aluminum products. Recent research indicates, however, that Alcoa probably vertically integrated in order to price discriminate.

Alcoa Aluminum had considerable monopoly power from 1888 to 1930, which was protected by tariffs abroad and by its control of bauxite lands at home. Further, the disruptions of World War I slowed entry of new firms. Explicit price discrimination was not possible, because aluminum ingots are easy to handle and hence easy to resell. Alcoa overcame this problem by vertically integrating into some industries that purchased aluminum ingots.

Suppose that there are only two downstream industries (or groups of industries) that buy aluminum, and that Industry 1's demand for the product is less price-elastic than Industry 2's demand. Alcoa would like to charge a higher price to Industry 1 than Industry 2. If it does so, however, the industry charged the low price resells its product to the high-price industry.

If Alcoa vertically integrates into the low-price industry (that is, the monopolist buys Industry 2), it need not worry about resale by its own subsidiary. Moreover, since Alcoa supplies its subsidiary with its product internally, the only industry Alcoa explicitly sells ingot to is the high-price industry.

Alcoa only forward integrated into some industries that used primary aluminum. As predicted by this theory, Alcoa integrated into the high-elasticity industries. The five uses of aluminum listed in the following table represented more than 90 percent of Alcoa's output during most of this period. Of these uses, iron and steel production and aircraft manufacturing had the most inelastic demands because of a lack of good substitutes for aluminum in their production process. Alcoa did not integrate into these industries. Alcoa did integrate into the other, relatively elastic industries. Because there were many substitutes for aluminum in the manufacture of cookware (such as tin, glass, steel, iron, and so forth), electric cable (copper), and automobile parts (various metals), their demand for aluminum was relatively elastic.

Major Industries Using Aluminum

Industry	Elasticity of Demand for Aluminum	Integrated by Alcoa?
Cookware	Elastic ($\epsilon \approx -1.6$)	Yes
Electric cable	Elastic (copper substitute)	Yes
Automobile parts	Elastic ($\epsilon \approx -1.5$)	Yes
Iron and steel	Inelastic (no substitutes)	No
Aircraft	Inelastic (no substitutes then)	No

SOURCE: Perry (1980).

■ TYPES OF PRICE DISCRIMINATION

There is a large variety of methods for charging nonuniform prices. This section examines some of the simplest ones and reserves the more complicated ones for the next chapter. We first study *perfect* or *first-degree* price discrimination, in which consumers are left with no consumer surplus. Then we study *third-degree* price discrimination, in which each group of consumers faces its own price per unit. (Chapter 15 examines *second-degree* discrimination, in which the price per unit is not constant and consumers do retain some consumer surplus.)

Perfect Price Discrimination

The point of all methods of price discrimination is to capture from each consumer as much consumer surplus as possible. **Perfect price discrimination,** also called **first-degree price discrimination,** occurs when a monopolist is able to charge so much that consumers have no consumer surplus remaining. Recall that *consumer surplus* is the maximum amount that could be extracted from consumers above and beyond what they are currently paying. Figure 14.1 illustrates the consumer surplus when the per unit price is p.

Suppose that each consumer wants 1 unit of a product and each is willing to pay a different amount for it, as indicated by the demand curve in Figure 14.1. Assume that the firm can identify each consumer and knows the maximum amount that each one is willing to pay. Then, assuming resale can be prevented, the firm could charge each consumer a different price and extract the full consumer surplus from each one. As long as price to the last consumer who buys exceeds marginal cost, the monopolist prefers to sell more of its product to additional consumers, because it makes an incremental profit on the additional sales. Therefore, a profit-maximizing monopolist charges the last consumer who buys marginal cost. The assumption that the monopolist can charge a different price to each consumer entirely avoids the second effect on marginal revenue discussed

FIGURE 14.1   Aggregate Demand Curve and Consumer Surplus

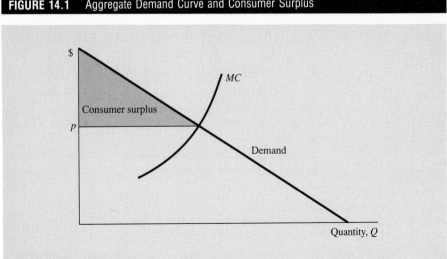

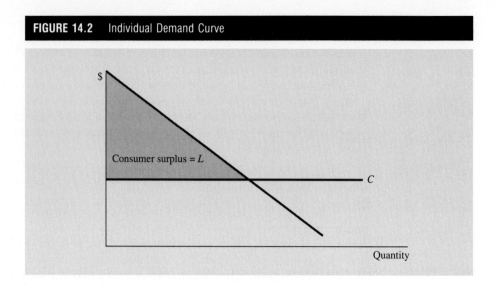

FIGURE 14.2 Individual Demand Curve

earlier—namely, decreased revenues that result from passing along a lower price to everyone who was already purchasing the product—because a low price to one consumer is no longer passed on to another. The effect on marginal revenue of eliminating the second effect is that the demand curve becomes the marginal revenue curve. The monopolist lowers price to only the additional customer and so gains that price as an increase in its revenues from selling one more unit.

An interesting feature of perfect price discrimination is that it yields the same output as would be produced under perfect competition.[3] The reason is that, just as in perfect competition, consumers purchase the product as long as they value it above marginal cost. The main differences between perfect price discrimination and competition are that under perfect price discrimination, consumers each pay different prices and more of their money is transferred to the monopolist. In other words, perfect price discrimination entails no efficiency loss (the price on the last purchase still equals marginal cost) but does affect the distribution of income.

So far, we have assumed that customers differ in their willingness to pay and that each customer demands only 1 unit no matter how low the price. Now consider how perfect price discrimination works when consumers are identical but demand more units as price falls. Suppose that each consumer is identical to all others and has the downward sloping demand curve for the product illustrated in Figure 14.2. Marginal cost is assumed constant at C.

A perfectly discriminating monopolist can charge a different price for each *unit* of the product that is sold and thus, by charging *quantity-dependent* prices, extract all the

---

[3] We ignore income effects—that is, the fact that with price discrimination the monopolist has more money and the consumer less than in competition.

consumer surplus of each consumer. In other words, by charging a high price for the first unit consumed, a lower price for the next unit, and so on until marginal cost, C, is reached, the monopolist can offer the demand curve as the (marginal) price schedule facing consumers.

An alternative and equivalent method of perfect price discrimination in this case would be to charge an optimal two-part tariff. (Recall that a *two-part tariff* consists of a lump-sum fee for the right to purchase plus a per unit charge for each unit consumed.) The monopolist could charge a price of C for each unit consumed and also (regardless of how many units each consumer bought) charge each (identical) consumer L for the right to consume the product, where L is the (common) consumer surplus (see Figure 14.2). This pricing method also yields the competitive output and is equivalent to perfect price discrimination in generating profits (see Example 14.2).

If consumers have downward sloping demand curves but are not identical, the firm still wants to charge each consumer C per unit consumed but wants to charge each one a different lump-sum fee in order to extract all of the consumer surplus. Therefore, the monopolist must have detailed knowledge about each consumer's demand curve in order to design a pricing policy that captures the consumer surplus of each consumer. Especially when consumers are not identical, the information needed to practice perfect price discrimination is often not readily available. In such cases, the monopolist may find it profitable to use the more complicated pricing policies described in the next chapter. However, sometimes it is possible to monitor customers to determine the values they place on products. For example, a firm that rents out copy machines may use a meter in the copy machine to keep track of the number of copies each customer makes and then sets the rent depending upon the number of copies made. This method of pricing maximizes profits if those who make the most copies value their machine the most.

Since perfect price discrimination requires detailed knowledge about individual buyers, it is more likely to occur (or be attempted) when one-on-one bargaining occurs. For example, a car salesperson may try to find out what jobs potential buyers hold, where they live, and where else they have shopped in an effort to estimate the maximum they are likely to spend. Similarly, doctors may be able to successfully price discriminate if they can identify the wealthy people in their area (see Kessel 1958).

Different Prices to Different Groups: Third-Degree Price Discrimination

A firm that does not have enough information to identify each customer and determine what each one is willing to pay is unable to practice first-degree price discrimination and extract all consumer surplus. But suppose a firm can determine whether a particular customer belongs to one group rather than another.[4] If it is possible to prevent (or limit) resale between the two groups, and if the firm knows the different aggregate demand curve of each group, then it is typically profitable to charge one price to one group and another price to the other. This is **third-degree price discrimination,** which occurs when

---

[4] We assume that the customers' demands differ between the two groups.

EXAMPLE 14.2

A Discriminating Labor Union

A powerful labor union may be able to act as a perfectly discriminating monopolist and capture all the consumer surplus. Since it is difficult to charge different prices for each hour of labor, unions use an alternative approach. The union sets both a wage and a minimum number of hours.

As shown in the diagram on the next page, if the labor market were competitive, a wage of w would be charged, and H hours of labor services would be sold. Purchasers of labor services would have consumer surplus equal to areas A and B. If, in contrast, all workers belong to a union, and the union acts like a perfectly discriminating monopolist, it charges a wage equal to the demand curve for each hour of labor services it sells (so that the wage for the last hour it sells is w), and it captures all the consumer surplus.

Alternatively, the union could set a single wage, w^*, and a minimum number of hours, H, and receive the same total amount of compensation. The union offers the firms the following choice: you may buy H hours of labor at w^* (so the total wage bill is Hw^*) or you may buy no hours at all. As shown in the diagram, if the union only set the wage (at w^*) and did not set a minimum number of hours, firms would purchase fewer hours (H^*). The only reason that the firms agree to buy so many hours at this wage is that the alternative is to buy no labor services at all.

As the diagram shows, the firms receive consumer surplus equal to area A for the first H^* hours, and then have negative consumer surplus (equal to area C) for the next H-H^* hours. The union receives profits above the competitive level equal to areas B and C. If w^* is set appropriately so that area A equals area C, the union makes as much profit with this scheme as it would if it perfectly price discriminated.

consumers in different groups face different per unit prices.[5] For example, high transaction costs may prevent resale and enable a firm to charge consumers in California higher prices than those in New York.

Letting subscripts 1 and 2 stand for consumer groups 1 and 2, and letting p stand for price, Q for quantity demanded, and C for (constant) marginal cost, the monopolist's problem is to maximize profits, which are given in Equation 14.1[6]:

---

[5] We have now discussed first-degree and third-degree price discrimination. *Second-degree price discrimination* occurs when customers face a price schedule in which the price per unit depends on the quantity purchased and, as in the case of third-degree discrimination, all consumer surplus is not extracted. Chapter 15 discusses second-degree price discrimination in more detail.

[6] Throughout this chapter and the next, for simplicity, we use examples with no fixed cost and a constant marginal cost.

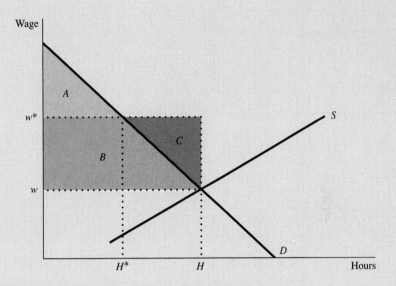

The Longshoremen's union is one well-known union that used this technique. Two-thirds of the union contracts in the transportation industry (excluding railroads and airplanes) had wage-employment guarantees in the early 1970s. In contrast, only 11 percent of union contracts in all industries had such guarantees.

SOURCE: Leontief (1946), U.S. Department of Labor (1975).

$$(p_1 - C)Q_1(p_1) + (p_2 - C)Q_2(p_2) = \text{Profits.} \qquad (14.1)$$

Notice that Q_1 depends on p_1 (not p_2) and Q_2 depends on p_2 (not p_1).

To maximize profits as given in Equation 14.1 requires the monopolist to separately maximize profits from Groups 1 and 2. The description of monopoly in Chapter 5 explains that profits are maximized when marginal revenue equals marginal cost for each group. These two conditions can be expressed as follows:

$$MR_1 = C, \qquad (14.2a)$$
$$MR_2 = C, \qquad (14.2b)$$

where MR_i stands for marginal revenue for Group $i(i = 1,2)$ and C for marginal cost. Equations 14.2a and 14.2b imply that the monopolist equates marginal revenue across

FIGURE 14.3 Price Discrimination

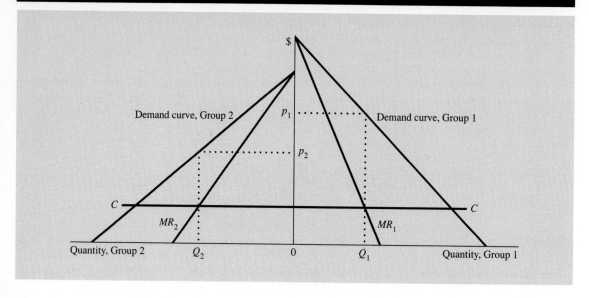

the two markets; that is, in the optimal solution, if the monopolist sells one less unit in Market 1 and one more unit in Market 2 or vice versa, revenues must be unaffected. Otherwise it would pay to reallocate sales between the two markets, and profits could not have been maximized. Equating the common marginal revenue to marginal cost yields maximum profits.[7]

The pricing decision of the discriminating monopolist is illustrated in Figure 14.3. The figure shows two consumer groups, and the demand curve for Group 2 is "flipped" so that their quantity demanded is read in reverse on the left side of the diagram. Setting the marginal revenue of each demand curve equal to marginal cost, C, yields the optimal pricing and output decision (p_1, Q_1) and (p_2, Q_2).

From Chapter 5, we know that Equations 14.2a and 14.2b can be rewritten as follows:

$$\frac{p_1 - C}{p_1} = -\frac{1}{\epsilon_1},$$ (14.3a)

$$\frac{p_2 - C}{p_2} = -\frac{1}{\epsilon_2},$$ (14.3b)

where ϵ is the price elasticity of demand of Group i for $i = 1,2$. These equations make good sense. The percent markup of price over cost $([p_i - C]/p_i)$ is inversely proportional

---

[7] If marginal cost is not constant, the optimal pricing and outputs still satisfy Equations 14.2a and 14.2b, but now C will depend on total output. Unlike the case when C is constant, the optimal pricing and output for one consumer group depend on the optimal pricing and output of the other consumer group.

to Group i's elasticity of demand (willingness to pay): the higher the group's price elasticity of demand, the lower the price and the closer the price is to marginal cost. That is, the group whose demand is more sensitive to price gets charged the lower price.

Equations 14.3a and 14.3b demonstrate the importance of determining which group has the higher elasticity of demand (see Example 14.1). Economic theory is often helpful in solving this problem. For example, suppose that you are in charge of a marketing plan to send out discount coupons to certain groups of users. Recall from the earlier discussion of coupons that there is no need to worry about resale, because it is too costly for consumers to resell inexpensive items. Your problem is to determine which consumer group should receive the coupons. Consumers who increase their purchases the most in response to a special low price, that is, those whose demands are relatively elastic, are the ones who should receive the coupons.

For example, consumers who have a low cost of transportation, who have the space to store items, and who place a low value on time (or who have flexible time schedules) are the most likely to take advantage of special promotions. This suggests that coupons should be sent to families that own a car, that have a nonworking spouse, that do not have young children (so that time can be more flexible), and that live in a house (lower storage costs). Marketing studies done by Blattberg et al. (1978) and Narasimhan (1983) document that, indeed, the consumers who are most likely to take advantage of special promotions own cars, own homes, have one adult family member not working, and have no very young children.

Other Methods of Third-Degree Price Discrimination

Firms can practice third-degree price discrimination in some subtle ways. For example, it often happens that some consumers are better informed than others about prices. One way a firm can charge different prices to consumers is to set a high list price. A **list price** is the price at which an item is marked or listed to sell. The firm charges the list price unless a customer complains that it exceeds the price of the product at other stores. In the event of a complaint, the store matches the lower price. This method of pricing causes uninformed consumers to pay higher prices than knowledgeable ones.[8]

Another example of third-degree price discrimination involves exploiting differences in the value customers place on time (see Example 14.3). High-wage, high-income people typically value their time more than low-wage, low-income people. One clever way to price discriminate between these two groups is to make a special offer that requires consumers to spend time to take advantage of the offer. For example, suppose a store is willing to sell an item over the telephone at the regular price and mail the item to the consumer. The store runs a sale but only gives the low price to consumers who take the time to come in and pick the item up at the store. This is an effective method of price

---

[8] The moral of this story is don't be afraid to complain about high prices. Department stores often have a policy that they will not be underpriced by their rivals. See Chapter 17 for further analysis of how a firm's behavior is affected by the presence of both informed and uninformed consumers.

EXAMPLE 14.3

DISCRIMINATION OVER TIME

The prices initially charged for new products (pocket calculators, personal computers, computer programs, hardcover books, movies) are much higher than those charged in later periods. In some cases, the drop in prices over time is due to decreasing costs of production or increased competition from other firms; in other cases, the decline is due to price discrimination.

Some people insist on being among the first to see the new movie, read the new book, or own the latest electronic gadget. Early purchasers of calculators that could add, subtract, multiply, and divide paid up to several hundred dollars each; yet within a couple of years after they were introduced, the price for simple calculators fell to under $10. Not all firms with market power can profitably price discriminate over time, however. If consumers know that prices will fall in the future, some may postpone their purchase decision. Price discrimination over time will be profitable provided the number who are willing to wait for lower prices is not too large.

SOURCE: Stokey (1979).

discrimination in which consumers who place a high value on time receive the item by mail and pay the regular price, and consumers who place a low value on time pick the item up at the store and pay the low price.

■ WELFARE EFFECTS OF PRICE DISCRIMINATION

The welfare effects of perfect price discrimination are easy to analyze. Output is at the competitive level, but consumers are poorer than they are under competition; therefore, perfect price discrimination does not distort efficiency but does affect the distribution of income.

The welfare effects of third-degree discrimination are more difficult to analyze. As with first-degree discrimination, consumers wind up with less money than under competition. However, unlike the case of first-degree discrimination, it is not possible to make any strong claims about the efficiency of third-degree price discrimination. Equations 14.3a and 14.3b show that third-degree price discrimination involves prices in excess of marginal costs, and therefore it is not as efficient as perfect competition or perfect price discrimination.

Third-degree price discrimination may be better or worse than simple monopoly pricing from an efficiency viewpoint, depending on the shapes of the demand and cost curves. This conclusion holds in general for all forms of imperfect price discrimination. The closer imperfect price discrimination is to perfect price discrimination, the more likely it is that the price discrimination leads to a more efficient outcome than simple monopoly pricing.

Two sources of inefficiency are present in third-degree discrimination. The first is the usual one associated with monopoly: price exceeds marginal cost, which results in an output restriction and hence an output inefficiency. The second is a consumption inefficiency. Because different consumers pay different per unit prices for a product, each consumer's marginal willingness to pay is not the same, which results in an inefficiency because of unexploited opportunities for further trade. For example, suppose Larry is willing to pay $10 to consume the first unit and $9 to consume the second unit for a total of $19 to consume 2 units. If Larry is charged $10 per unit, he consumes only 1 unit. Suppose Andrew is willing to pay $7 to consume the first unit and $4 to consume the second unit for a total of $11 to consume 2 units. If Andrew is charged $5 per unit, he consumes only 1 unit. At the margin, Larry values the product more than Andrew. Larry values an additional unit at $9, and Andrew values the unit that he is consuming at $7. In such a case it is more efficient for Larry to consume 2 units and Andrew none. For example, if Larry paid Andrew $8 for his unit, both Larry and Andrew would be better off. If this trade does not occur (remember resale is assumed impossible), then the price-discriminating monopolist has induced an inefficiency. It follows from this logic that if the price-discriminating monopolist produces the same (or less) output than the simple (nondiscriminating) monopolist, then welfare must decline. The reason is that the price-discriminating monopolist causes a consumption inefficiency that the simple monopolist does not cause.[9]

Third-degree price discrimination can benefit society compared to simple monopoly if it leads to an expansion of output. For example, suppose that there are two groups of consumers, and a simple monopolist finds it optimal to set a price so high that one group is entirely excluded from the market. Then, because a price-discriminating monopolist serves both groups, output expands and consumers are better off.

The welfare effects of simple monopoly pricing and third-degree price discrimination are easy to illustrate. In Figure 14.4, area XYZ represents the familiar deadweight loss from simple monopoly pricing when marginal cost is constant and equals C. The deadweight loss from practicing imperfect price discrimination is the sum of areas $X_1Y_1Z_1$ and $X_2Y_2Z_2$. It is simply not possible, in general, to say whether this sum will be greater or

---

[9] Suppose consumer Group 1 has the demand curve $Q_1 = a_1 - b_1p_1$ and that consumer Group 2 has the demand curve $Q_2 = a_2 - b_2p_2$, where Q_i stands for quantity, p_i for price, and a_i and b_i are numbers, $i = 1,2$. Suppose marginal cost is a constant and equals C. A price-discriminating monopolist chooses the profit-maximizing outputs Q_1^* and Q_2^*, so that

$$Q_1^* = \frac{a_1}{2} - \frac{b_1C}{2} \text{ and } Q_2^* = \frac{a_2}{2} - \frac{b_2C}{2}.$$

A simple monopolist that can set only one price, p, faces the demand curve for total quantity demanded, Q, given by $Q = (Q_1 + Q_2) = (a_1 + a_2) - (b_1 + b_2) p$. If it is optimal to serve both customer groups, the monopolist chooses the profit-maximizing quantity, Q^*, so that

$$Q^* = \frac{a_1 + a_2}{2} - \frac{b_1 + b_2}{2} C.$$

Notice that $Q_1^* + Q_2^* = Q^*$. Hence, it follows that when demand curves are linear and marginal cost constant, welfare always declines with third-degree price discrimination compared to simple monopoly provided the simple monopolist would serve all customer groups. The reason is that the price-discriminating monopolist causes a consumption inefficiency that the simple monopolist does not cause.

FIGURE 14.4 Welfare Effects of Price Discrimination

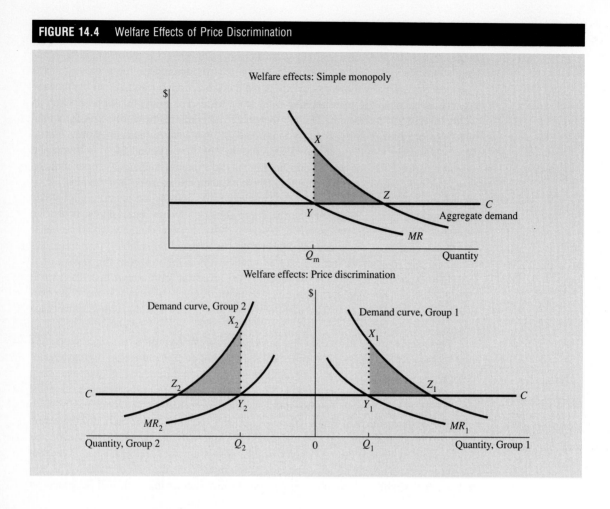

Welfare effects: Simple monopoly

Welfare effects: Price discrimination

less than *XYZ*. In fact, it is not even possible to say in general whether total output is greater with price discrimination than with simple monopoly (whether $Q_1 + Q_2$ will be greater than Q_m in Figure 14.4).[10]

■ SUMMARY

This chapter has investigated the conditions under which price discrimination is feasible and some simple methods of price discrimination. For price discrimination to succeed, a firm must have some market power and must be able to prevent or control resale. In order

---

[10] See Schmalensee (1981), Varian (1985), and Katz (1987). These authors show that under special circumstances it is possible to make unambiguous welfare and output comparisons between simple monopoly and price discrimination, as is done in footnote 9.

to practice the types of price discrimination described, firms must know quite a bit about individual consumers. For perfect, or first-degree, price discrimination, a firm must be able to identify each consumer and know each consumer's demand curve. For third-degree price discrimination, a firm must be able to identify the group that a consumer belongs to and must know the group's demand curve. Sometimes a firm does not have enough information to practice either first-degree or third-degree price discrimination. It must then use more complicated pricing methods to maximize its profits, which are examined in the next chapter.

■ Key Terms

first-degree price discrimination
list price
nonuniform prices
perfect price discrimination

price discrimination
third-degree price discrimination
tie-in sale
two-part tariff

■ Discussion Questions

1. Discuss whether it is sensible public policy to forbid price discrimination. Consider the effects on social welfare and the enforcement difficulties.
2. Suppose a two-part tariff is designed for each customer so as to achieve perfect price discrimination among customers whose downward sloping demand curves differ from each other. Explain why each consumer pays the same (marginal) price per unit but a different lump-sum fee.

3. Suppose that a monopolist has a fixed output, and there are two consumer groups with different demands. Explain why third-degree price discrimination lowers welfare as compared to the effect of simple monopoly on welfare.
4. Suppose that resale cannot be entirely eliminated. Does this mean that price discrimination cannot occur?
5. A magazine purchased at a newsstand is typically more expensive than the same magazine purchased by a subscription. Can you think of a cost justification for this?

■ Problems

1. Return to the case of the monopolist of aluminum ingot who vertically integrates to produce its own aluminum wire. Will any independent aluminum wire producers remain? Could any afford to buy the aluminum ingot at the high price and compete successfully against the low-priced aluminum wire sold by the manufacturer of aluminum ingot?
2. Draw your own diagram like that in Figure 14.4 to show that XYZ can be either above or below the sum of $X_1Y_1Z_1$ and $X_2Y_2Z_2$. (Remember that the aggregate demand is the sum of the demands of the two groups.)

3. It is often difficult to distinguish price discrimination from what are simply different prices for different products. For example, if teachers recommend the magazines they read to students, they are helping to market the magazine. Because they save the magazine some marketing costs, it is profitable for the magazine to encourage teachers to subscribe by offering them a lower price. From the firm's viewpoint, a magazine sold to a teacher is a different product from a magazine sold to someone else. Can you justify a senior-citizen

Answers to odd-numbered problems are given at the back of the book.

discount from movie theatres by appealing to this "different product" argument?

4. Suppose there are two groups of consumers and that it is optimal for a simple monopolist to set $p = \$10$. At that price, no one from the first group chooses to purchase. Now, suppose the monopolist can price discriminate. Will total output expand? Why or why not?

5. Suppose a consumer wants just 1 unit of a good and is willing to pay at most $10. Draw the demand curve and calculate the maximum consumer surplus that can be extracted. Suppose that there is a second consumer who also demands just 1 unit and is willing to pay at most $9. A perfectly discriminating monopolist charges the first consumer $10 and the second consumer $9. Why is there no consumption inefficiency as occurs in third-degree price discrimination?

■ Additional Readings

Several recent papers have extended the analysis of third-degree price discrimination to market structures other than pure monopoly (such as monopolistic competi- tion). See Borenstein (1985), Holmes (1989), Katz (1984), and Lederer and Hurter (1986).

■ References

Berck, Peter, and Jeffrey M. Perloff. 1985. "A Dynamic Analysis of Marketing Orders, Voting, and Welfare." *American Journal of Agricultural Economics* 67: 487–96.

Blattberg, Robert, T. Buesing, P. Peacock, and S. Sen. 1978. "Identifying the Deal-Prone Segment." *Journal of Marketing Research* 15:369–77.

Borenstein, Severin. 1985. "Price Discrimination in Free Entry Markets." *The Rand Journal of Economics*. 16:380-97.

Cave, Jonathan, and Stephen W. Salant. 1987. "Cartels That Vote: Agricultural Marketing Boards and Induced Voting Behavior," in Elizabeth E. Bailey, ed., *Public Regulation: New Perspectives on Institutions and Policies*. Cambridge: The MIT Press.

Gardner, Bruce L. 1984. "Price Discrimination or Price Stabilization: Debating with Models of U.S. Dairy Policy." *American Journal of Agricultural Economics* 66: 763–68.

Garoyan, Leon, and James G. Youde. 1975. *Marketing Orders in California: A Description*. University of California Cooperative Extension Leaflet 2719.

Heien, Dale. 1977. "The Cost of U.S. Dairy Price Support Programs: 1949–1974." *Review of Economics and Statistics* 59:1–8.

Holmes, Thomas J. 1989. "The Effects of Third-Degree Price Discrimination in Oligopoly." *American Economic Review*. 79:244-250.

Ippolito, Richard A., and Robert T. Masson. 1978. "The Social Cost of Government Regulation of Milk." *Journal of Law and Economics* 21:33–66.

Jesse, Edward V., and Aaron C. Johnson, Jr. 1981. *Effectiveness of Federal Marketing Orders for Fruits and Vegetables*. U.S. Department of Agriculture, Economics and Statistics Service, Agricultural Economic Report no. 471.

Katz, Michael L. 1984. "Price Discrimination and Monopolistic Competition." *Econometrica*. 53:1453-72.

———1987. "The Welfare Effects of Third-Degree Price Discrimination in Intermediate Goods Markets." *American Economic Review* 77:154–67.

Kessel, Reuben. 1958. "Price Discrimination in Medicine." *Journal of Law and Economics* 1:20–54.

Kwoka, John E., Jr. 1977. "Pricing Under Federal Milk Market Regulation." *Economic Inquiry* 15:367-84.

LaFrance, Jeffrey T., and Harry de Gorter. 1985. "Regulation in a Dynamic Market: The U.S. Dairy Industry." *American Journal of Agricultural Economics* 67: 821–32.

Lederer, Phillip J., and Arthur P. Hurter, Jr. 1986. "Competition of Firms: Discriminatory Pricing and Location." *Econometrica*. 54:623-40.

Leontief, Wassily. 1946. "The Price Theory of the Guaranteed Annual Wage Contract." *Journal of Political Economy* 54:76–80.

Narasimhan, C. 1983. "A Price Discrimination Theory of Coupons." University of Chicago.

Novakovic, Andrew M., and Robert D. Boynton, 1984. "Do Changes in Farmer-First Handler Exchange Eliminate the Need for Government Intervention?" *American Journal of Agricultural Economics* 66:769–75.

Perry, Martin K. 1980. "Forward Integration by Alcoa: 1888–1930." *The Journal of Industrial Economics* 29: 37–53.

Schmalensee, Richard. 1981. "Output and Welfare Effects of Monopolistic Third Degree Price Discrimination." *American Economic Review* 71:242-47.

Stokey, Nancy L. 1979. "Intertemporal Price Discrimination." 94: *Quarterly Journal of Economics* 355–71.

U.S. Department of Labor, Bureau of Labor Statistics. 1975. *Characteristics of Major Collective Bargaining Agreements, July 1, 1974*. Bulletin 1888. Washington, D.C.: Government Printing Office.

Varian, Hal R. 1985. "Price Discrimination and Social Welfare." *American Economic Review* 75:870–75.

An Example of Price Discrimination: Agricultural Marketing Orders

Federal and state government *marketing orders* foster price discrimination in what would otherwise be competitive agricultural markets. These marketing orders give agricultural firms limited immunity from antitrust prosecution and allows them to collectively price discriminate, advertise, and, in some cases, to restrict output.[1] Since the 1930s, these government created and enforced marketing orders have facilitated collective actions by agricultural firms by forcing all firms to behave in accordance with the wishes of the majority. We first discuss how marketing orders permit farmers to price discriminate and then discuss the efficiency and welfare effects of these programs.

■ MARKETING ORDER RULES

Suppose marketing orders only permitted farmers to price discriminate, but did not require them to do so. If some farmers charged higher prices to some consumers, other competitive firms would undercut their prices, eliminating the differential. Thus, to enable farmers to discriminate effectively, marketing orders not only permit price discrimination, they require it, preventing individual farmers from undermining the price discrimination program.

Classified Pricing Schemes

Many marketing orders require farmers to participate in a *classified pricing* scheme, in which consumers in different markets are charged different prices. Typically, commodities are sold in at least two markets. In most marketing orders, the primary market is the fresh food (or domestic) market, in which the demand elasticity is relatively low and hence price is relatively high. The secondary market is the processed food (or export) market, in which the demand elasticity is relatively high and hence price is relatively low. Since processed foods cannot be converted back into fresh foods, and it is costly to reimport

---

[1] We concentrate on the price discrimination aspects of marketing orders. Apparently Congress first adopted marketing orders to help farmers act collectively to offset the monopsony power of milk processors (Novakovic and Boynton 1984). Modern defenders of marketing orders claim that they are "necessary" to stabilize prices or quantities, a view disputed by many agricultural economists (Jesse and Johnson 1981, Gardner, 1984).

exports, resales between the markets do not occur, so price discrimination is possible. How these market division schemes work varies across marketing orders. The two primary approaches are quantity restrictions and quality restrictions.

Quantity Restrictions. Many marketing orders restrict the share of a farmers' output that can be sold in the primary market. These *quantity share restrictions* increase prices in the primary market, and lower them in the secondary market, where the extra output is sold. Examples include grade A milk, California almonds, Oregon-Washington filberts, Pacific Coast walnuts, California dates, and California raisins (Jesse and Johnson 1981). States that permitted quantity share restrictions in their marketing orders include California, Colorado, Georgia, South Carolina, and Utah (Garoyan and Youde 1975), though many of these programs have been dropped in recent years.

In some cases, a *reserve pool* program is used, where the quantity not sold in the primary market is held in a reserve pool rather than immediately diverted to a secondary market. Later in a marketing year, some of the pool may be sold in the primary market if demand increases. Alternatively, the reserve may be stored for the following marketing year, diverted to secondary markets, or sold for nonfood uses. Cranberries, tart cherries, raisins, hops, and prunes have marketing orders that provide for a reserve pool (Jesse and Johnson 1981).

Some of the marketing orders also enable farmers to price discriminate over time. *Market flow* regulations control when a product may be sold during a marketing season. For example, a lime available today is a different product from one available two months from now. It is quite possible that the prices you pay for these two "products" differ. Market flow regulations separate markets by time rather than by space (domestic versus export sales) or by product type (fresh versus processed). Market flow restrictions are used in most of the citrus orders, California Tokay and desert grapes, Florida celery, South Texas lettuce, and Texas melons (Jesse and Johnson 1981).

Quality Restrictions. Virtually all marketing orders use *quality restrictions* to prevent farmers from selling products that do not meet minimum grade, size, and maturity standards. These restrictions may also result in price discrimination. Although in most marketing orders, the specified standards remain unchanged from one marketing year to another, in a few, the standards are changed frequently. In these latter cases, quality standards are raised to restrict the quantity sold in the primary market during certain periods.

Output Restrictions Programs

In addition to facilitating price discrimination, some marketing orders use explicit *output restrictions*, reducing total output, to create market power for the farmers directly. For example, historical sales levels are used to determine an aggregate quota and quotas for individual producers. A marketing order administrative committee then determines the percent of the quota that may be sold based on its expectations of market conditions. The excess may be placed in a reserve pool. Quota provisions are found in the marketing orders for cranberries, Florida celery, hops, and Far West spearmint oil.

One colorful method formerly used by California peach producers required cooperating farmers to *green drop* fruit: some of the unripe fruit was cut from the trees and allowed to rot. In several years, farmers were given the choice of green dropping or destroying some of their trees in order to control output.

Output restrictions combined with classified pricing schemes allow the collective to act like a discriminating monopolist. When there are no output restrictions, classified pricing schemes, when first introduced, cause farms' profits to rise, which eventually induces entry and additional output. Output expands until the marginal farmers earns zero profits. Thus, in the absence of output restrictions, marketing orders produce a different equilibrium than would a price-discriminating monopolist.

Coverage of Marketing Orders

Most vegetable and noncitrus fruit marketing orders do not cover all production.[2] Since the marketing-order rules only apply to covered producers, the result is that the covered firms act like a dominant firm facing a competitive fringe that consists of uncovered producers who do not restrict or allocate their output. Unless prohibited by law (as in milk markets), unregulated producers only sell in the high-price primary market.

Marketing-order coverage is nearly universal in some markets, however. All the production of tree nuts, dried fruits, hops, tart cherries, olives, and cranberries is covered by Federal Marketing orders. Ninety-five percent of total fresh citrus fruit is marketed through nine separate Federal orders (although including processing use, marketing-order coverage drops to only one-fourth). Federal regulations cover about 80 percent of the grade A milk, and state regulations cover an additional 18 percent, so that virtually all grade A milk is regulated. Grade B milk, however, is unregulated. As a result, about 65 percent of all U.S. milk is federally regulated, and 80 percent is regulated under federal or state laws.[3]

■ EFFICIENCY AND WELFARE EFFECTS OF MARKETING ORDERS

There are both gainers and losers under a price classification scheme, as is shown by a simplified model with fixed supply.[4] The marketing order allocates part of the total output to each of two markets: Class 1 (fresh) and Class 2 (processed), as shown in the figure.

---

[2] According to Jesse and Johnson (1981), only about 10 percent of total noncitrus fruit tonnage is regulated by federal marketing orders. Federal orders only cover fresh potato sales, so that only about 70 percent of the fall potato crop is covered. Federal orders cover less than 50 percent of all other vegetables. Only 13 percent of fresh market vegetables are regulated. Their data are for 1977–1980.

[3] Milk marketing orders typically employ a price-discrimination scheme in which the price for raw grade A milk designated for fluid use is higher than the price paid for the same grade of milk for manufacturing use. In contrast, grade B milk, which is not regulated, passes lower sanitation standards and may only be used for manufactured products.

[4] Ippolito and Masson (1978) and Berck and Perloff (1985) discuss static models. Berck and Perloff (1985) also shows how the analysis changes in a dynamic model, where entry into the industry is slow. Cave and Salant (1987) model the voting behavior in agricultural marketing boards, which determine how marketing orders are run.

Price Discrimination in Agricultural Marketing Orders

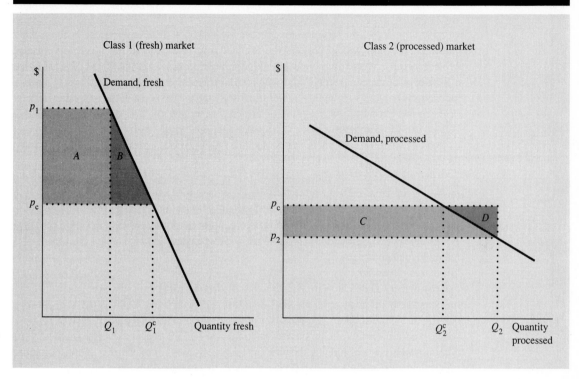

By restricting output in the Class 1 market to Q_1, which is less than the competitive level, Q_1^c, the marketing order drives the price in the Class 1 market, p_1, above the competitive price, p_c. The excess output is sold in the Class 2 market, so Q_2 is greater than the competitive output Q_2^c, and the price in the Class 2 market p_2, is below the competitive price, p_c.

Because the price in the fresh market is above the competitive price, $p_1 > p_c$, consumers of the fresh product lose consumer surplus equal to areas $A + B$. Farmers' profits on the Q_1 units they sell increase by area A ($= [p_1 - p_c]Q_1$), so the net loss (the loss to consumers not offset by a gain to producers) in the fresh market is B.

Consumers of the processed product gain consumer surplus equal to area C due to the lower price, $p_2 < p_c$. Farmers's profits are lower on the Q_2 units of output they sell in the Class 2 market than if a competitive price were charged by areas $C + D$. The net loss in the processed market is D.

Consumers lose areas $A + B$ in the fresh market and gain area C in the processed market, for a net total loss of $A + B - C$. Farmers' profits increase, however. The farmers receive an average, or *blend*, price of $p_b = (p_1 Q_1 + p_2 Q_2)/(Q_1 + Q_2)$. The blend price is higher than the competitive price, or else there would be no point to engaging in such price discrimination. Farmers gain profits of A in the fresh market and lose profits of $C + D$ in the processed market, so their total net gains are areas $A - (C + D)$.

Consumers lose more $(A + B - C)$ than producers gain $(A - C - D)$, for a net total loss of areas $B + D$. Thus, welfare is lower under a classified pricing scheme than under competition.

For simplicity, we assumed that supply was fixed and the only effect of the market allocation program was to redirect the product from the fresh to the processed market. More generally, where supply curves slope upward, marketing orders, by increasing the effective price farmers receive (the weighted average of the fresh and processed prices), increase the amount supplied. Much of the extra supply is directed to the secondary market (to keep the price high in the primary market). Since the price in the secondary market is less than the competitive price (and hence marginal cost), the cost of this extra output exceeds its value to consumers. Thus, social loss can be even greater when supply curves are upward sloping.

The social loss from most classified pricing programs is relatively small because the industries are small. There are, however, large social losses in dairy markets. Based on data from the early 1970s, Ippolito and Masson (1978) estimate that the effect of regulation was to raise the price of Class 1 milk 9.3 percent (at the farm level), to decrease the price of milk for Class 2 product by approximately 5.6 percent, and to increase the blend price facing regulated farmers by 3.7 percent. As a result, Class 1 consumption was 1.9 percent lower than it would have been without regulation, while Class 2 consumption was 9.6 percent higher. They calculate that the classified price regulation was equivalent to a tax on consumers of fresh milk of $333.8 million per year; and Class 2 users received a subsidy of $120.9 million. The producer profits on fresh milk increased by $210.6 million, while producer profits on processed milk fell by $105.2 million a year. Including the administration costs of running the program and the induced inefficiencies in transportation, they calculate that the total social cost was approximately $60 million per year.

Most other researchers, using other approaches, estimate larger costs. Kwoka (1977) estimates that the 1970 classified pricing and pooling schemes had an annual efficiency loss of $179 million. Heien (1977) calculates a total social cost of $175 million. LaFrance and de Gorter (1985) point out that these estimates are based on static analyses that ignore the time that it takes to build up a dairy herd. Using a dynamic model, they estimate that the social cost of the program is three times larger than the static analyses find.

CHAPTER 15

ADVANCED TOPICS IN PRICING

> **A** fool and his money are soon parted. What I want to know is how they got together in the first place.
>
> CYRIL FLETCHER

This chapter continues the examination of methods used to price discriminate, presenting more complicated methods of price discrimination, such as nonlinear pricing, two-part tariffs, tie-in sales, and quality choice. It discusses how these common pricing methods can be used to increase profits, assuming throughout the chapter that firms have market power and can control or prevent resale. The common theme of all the pricing methods in this chapter is that they require a firm to have much less knowledge about consumers than was required to practice the methods of the previous chapter. Because some of these topics become complicated, the details of some of the analyses appear as appendices to this chapter. The appendixes are of above-average difficulty.

■ NONLINEAR PRICING

A common type of price discrimination involves **nonlinear pricing.** A nonlinear pricing schedule is any pricing schedule with the property that the consumer's total expenditure on an item does not rise linearly (proportionately) with the amount purchased. Any pricing scheme in which the total expenditure is not equal to a constant price multiplied by the quantity is a nonlinear pricing scheme. Methods of nonlinear pricing are used to practice **second-degree price** discrimination, which requires a firm to prevent or at least control resale between individuals but does not require it to be omniscient and know the demands of each individual.[1] Rather, these methods assume only that a firm has some idea of the

---

[1] As Chapter 14 shows, nonlinear pricing can also be used to practice first-degree price discrimination when a firm knows each consumer's demand curve. Unlike first-degree price discrimination, second-degree discrimination does not result in a monopolist's being able to extract all surplus from consumers.

underlying distribution of demand in the population—the firm need not be able to say which particular demander has a particular demand curve. This section first presents a simple type of nonlinear pricing schedule—a single two-part tariff—and then discusses the more general problem of nonlinear pricing, illustrating it with an example of a multiple two-part tariff.

Special Case: A Single Two-Part Tariff

Recall from Chapter 14 that a **two-part tariff** consists of a lump-sum fee plus a usage charge per unit.[2] For example, telephone companies commonly charge a monthly subscription fee and then a usage fee that depends upon how many calls are made. Similarly, a person who rents a car often pays a lump sum for the day plus an additional mileage charge. Many firms that rent copy machines charge a minimum rental fee plus a fee that depends upon the usage of the machine. As a final example, suppose that a firm sells cameras whose use requires a special type of film (for example, Polaroid's instant-picture cameras). One can think of the purchase of the camera as the payment of a lump-sum fee and the film purchases as the payment of a usage-sensitive fee.

When a two-part tariff is used, a firm must somehow prevent resale. Otherwise, it would make sense for one customer to pay one fixed fee and purchase all the goods, and then resell them to everyone else, so that only one fixed fee is collected. For example, suppose that a firm requires $100 from each buyer plus a per-unit charge of $1. If Joe and Sam each buy 50 units, they each pay $150, for a total expenditure of $300. However, if Joe buys for both, then the total expenditure is $200. Joe and Sam could therefore each pay $100 and be better off. To prevent this, the firm could try to prohibit Joe from reselling to Sam by making it costly for Joe to ship to Sam by—for example, by making it costly to divide shipped orders. The remainder of this section assumes that firms use one of the methods discussed in the previous chapter to prevent resale. This section analyzes the case in which a firm can use only one two-part tariff; subsequent sections relax this restriction.

When consumers are identical, a two-part tariff can be used to extract all consumer surplus. This point was illustrated in the previous chapter in the section on perfect price discrimination. The more interesting and realistic case occurs when there is more than one type of consumer, but the firm cannot distinguish among consumers. We assume that the firm knows that demands differ within the population but lacks specific knowledge of each individual consumer's demand. For example, the firm may be aware that 50 percent of its customers value its services greatly, while another 50 percent could easily switch to another product. Even though the firm knows the general distribution of demand, it may be unable to determine the group to which a particular customer belongs.

Suppose that there are only two types of consumers, and they have the demand curves of Figure 15.1. A Type 2 customer is willing to buy more at price p than a Type 1 customer and enjoys more consumer surplus than a Type 1 customer. If a firm could identify the type of each customer, then if it chose to charge price p, it could charge a

---

[2] See Oi (1971) and Schmalensee (1981) for a detailed examination of two-part tariffs.

FIGURE 15.1   Two Different Demand Curves

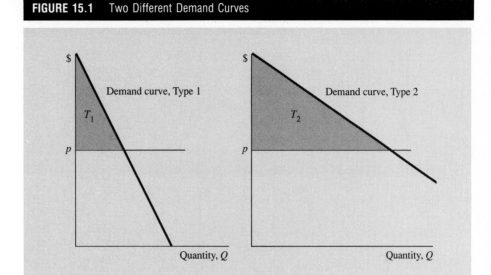

Type 1 customer a fee of T_1, and a Type 2 customer T_2 in addition to the price p per unit. T_2 would be higher than T_1.

Suppose the firm must choose a single two-part tariff. It chooses a lump-sum fee, T, and a per-unit charge, p, so as to maximize profits. As long as p exceeds average variable costs, the firm earns positive net revenues from additional sales and the lump-sum fee. If the firm is unable to distinguish consumer types and charges a single two-part tariff, the lump-sum fee it charges cannot exceed the smaller T_1 if Type 1 consumers are to participate. If the firm tries to charge a lump-sum fee of T_2, Type 1 consumers would simply refuse to purchase the product. The firm now faces an obvious dilemma. If it charges a low price, it sells more of its product, and (as can be seen from Figure 15.1) that enables it to charge a higher lump-sum fee. On the other hand, its ability to charge a high lump-sum fee to extract the consumer surplus of Type 2 consumers is constrained by the low willingness to pay of the Type 1 consumers. In many cases it might pay to ignore Type 1 consumers and only concentrate on Type 2 consumers, letting Type 1 consumers choose not to purchase the product. The diagram illustrates that the less similar Type 1 consumers are to Type 2 consumers, the more difficult it is for the firm to extract consumer surplus from Type 2 consumers with a single two-part tariff (see Appendices 15A and 15B).

The optimal two-part tariff typically generates more profits than a single price, since a single price is a special type of two-part tariff (one with a zero lump-sum fee). The optimal two-part tariff generates less profit than perfect price discrimination (first degree) but may or may not generate less profit than third-degree price discrimination. However, a two-part tariff does not require that the firm be able to identify consumers, while third-degree price discrimination does.

One can think of a two-part tariff as consisting of a fixed charge for one product and a marginal charge for another. For example, the fixed charge could be the price of a

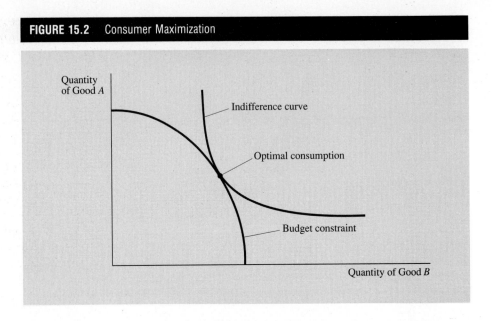

FIGURE 15.2   Consumer Maximization

camera, and the marginal charge that depends on usage could be the price of the film. Appendixes 15A and 15C show that the usage-sensitive price (for example, the price of film) tends to exceed its marginal cost, but the fixed charge may well be below the marginal cost of the item (for example, the camera). In general, the fixed charge increases as the difference between the average purchase and the purchase of the marginal customer decreases, and as the elasticity of demand increases. The usage-sensitive price increases as the elasticity of demand decreases and as the difference between the quantities purchased of the average and marginal customer increases.

The General Case

The two-part tariff just described is one of the simplest examples of a pricing structure in which the average price varies with output—which is a characteristic of any nonlinear pricing scheme. In general, the amount paid can vary with the amount purchased in any prespecified way; that is, the price paid is a function of quantity, and the firm is allowed to choose any function it desires.

The analytics of nonlinear pricing can become quite complicated, and we will not be able to explore them in all their detail.[3] The next two sections discuss the most important general issues. Appendix 15D analyzes the topic in detail and provides an example.

Consumer Maximization.   As always, consumers maximize their utility subject to their budget constraints. If the firm uses a nonlinear outlay schedule, $E(q)$, which is the total expense of purchasing q units, the budget constraint is not a straight line as it is in the

---

[3] See Katz (1983), Spence (1977), Tirole (1988, Ch. 3), and Appendix 15D for more details.

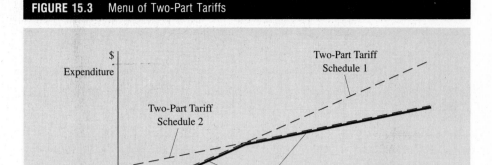

FIGURE 15.3 Menu of Two-Part Tariffs

usual case, in which the price of good is independent of the number of units purchased. Figure 15.2 illustrates how a consumer chooses the optimal combination of goods A and B with a nonlinear budget constraint.

Just as in the usual consumer maximization problem, utility is maximized where the consumer's indifference curve is tangent to the budget constraint. At the point of tangency, the consumer's marginal rate of substitution between the two goods (the slope of the indifference curve) equals the ratio of the goods' marginal prices (the slope of the budget constraint). In the usual case of a single price, prices are constant to all consumers regardless of the number of units purchased, and therefore there is no difference between average price and marginal price. In this more complicated case, the **marginal price** that governs a consumer's actions is the incremental expenditure that a consumer must make to purchase one more unit of the item. For example if the total expenditure when 5 units are purchased is $20, and the total expenditure for 6 units is $23, then the marginal price at 5 units is $3. Technically, if $E(q)$ is the total expense when q units are purchased, the marginal price is the derivative of total expense with respect to q.

Example of Nonlinear Pricing: Two Two-Part Tariffs. Finding the nonlinear pricing policy that maximizes a monopolist's profits is complicated, and some of the details are explored in Appendix 15D. This section presents a simplified example to illustrate the key ideas.

Consider the problem of a firm that offers consumers a choice of two different two-part tariff schedules. Each consumer chooses or *self-selects* that schedule that leads to a higher level of utility. The two schedules are shown in Figure 15.3 as straight, dashed lines. The intercepts on the vertical axis reflect the fixed cost, and the slopes of the curves are the constant marginal costs. From inspection, the consumer can purchase a small

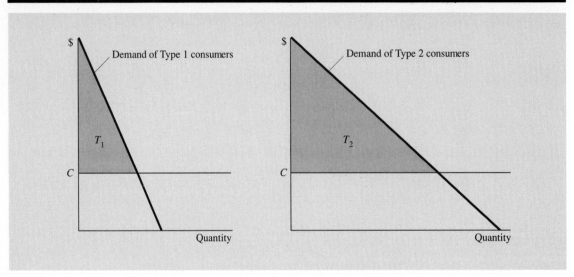

FIGURE 15.4   Optimal Two-Part Tariffs

number of units for less money by choosing Two-part Tariff Schedule 1 and can purchase a large number of units least expensively by choosing Two-part Tariff Schedule 2. Following this reasoning, consumers choose the lower "envelope" of the two curves, which is shown by a solid, kinked line.

The firm chooses its two two-part tariffs in order to maximize its profits. The inability of the firm to identify the willingness to pay of individual customers constrains its pricing policy. The firm only knows the distribution of the different types of consumers in the population; it does not know which type each consumer is. The firm provides a choice of two two-part tariffs in order to separate consumer groups, so that it can lower the price to one group without having to pass along the same low price to the other group. Recall that this was the motivating concern of attempts to price discriminate that were identified in the introductory discussion of Chapter 14.

Suppose there are two groups of individuals, Type 1 and Type 2, and that individuals in each group are identical. *If* the firm knew which consumers belonged to each group (and could prevent resale), the firm could design a two-part tariff for each group. In fact (from the earlier discussion of perfect price discrimination) the optimal policy in such a case is for the firm to charge each consumer a price equal to marginal cost, C, and to extract the surplus of each consumer by charging a lump-sum fee. That means it would charge a Type 1 consumer the amount T_1 and a Type 2 consumer the amount T_2, as illustrated in Figure 15.4.

Suppose the firm simply announced that it had two two-part tariffs: one of (T_1, C) and the other of (T_2, C), where the first number (T_i) in parentheses is the fixed fee, and the second (C) is the marginal price. For the situation represented in Figure 15.4, no consumer would ever choose to consume under the second two-part tariff, because T_2 exceeds T_1; all consumers would choose the first two-part tariff. Consumers always choose

FIGURE 15.5   How a Type 1 Consumer Fares Under the Two Two-Part Tariffs

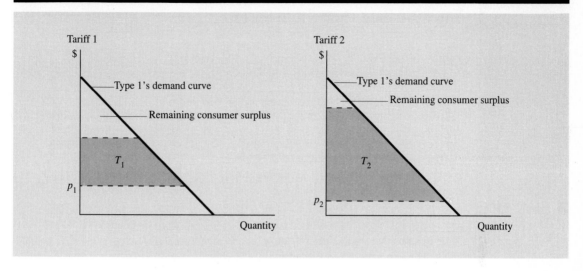

(self-select) the pricing structure that is best for them. This constrains the firm's ability to price discriminate and, as in this example, rules out perfect price discrimination. The difficult problem for the firm is to design a pricing structure that maximizes profits subject to the restriction that neither group prefers the other's two-part tariff. This restriction is sometimes called a **self-selection constraint.** We focus on an optimal solution in which the monopolist serves both types of consumers.

For example, suppose that Type 2 consumers have larger demands than Type 1 consumers at every price. Then it is possible to show (see Appendix 15D) for realistic cases that the fixed fee for the Type 2 consumers, T_2, exceeds T_1, but that the marginal price facing Type 2 consumers, p_2, is below p_1. The reason is that offering a low price to the large demanders allows them to derive a large consumer surplus, which the firm captures through T_2. The high T_2 discourages the small-volume buyers (Type 1), who prefer to pay a higher marginal price on the smaller amounts they purchase. In other words, the high-volume purchasers (Type 2) value low prices much more than the low-volume purchasers (Type 1), and this enables the firm to separate the two groups. This case is illustrated in Figure 15.5 for Type 1 consumers. Notice that a Type 1 consumer prefers (T_1, p_1) to (T_2, p_2) because even though in the second tariff the price is lower $(p_2 < p_1)$, the fixed fee is so much higher $(T_2 > T_1)$ that the remaining consumer surplus is higher under the first tariff. Similarly, Type 2 consumers prefer (T_2, p_2) to (T_1, p_1); their remaining consumer surplus is higher under the tariff (T_2, p_2) because they can take advantage of the low price.

It is possible to show that consumer diversity improves the utility of those (Type 2 consumers) with the greatest willingness to pay for the good. (See Appendix 15D.) The reason is that price discrimination becomes less effective for those with the greatest willingness to pay when there are self-selection constraints.

EXAMPLE 15.1

YOU AUTO SAVE FROM TIE-IN SALES

Instead of purchasing an automobile already assembled—a tie-in sale—you could buy all the parts separately and assemble and paint the car yourself. Doing so would cost you substantially more, however. According to the *Journal of American Insurance*, the cost of buying an assembled 1988 Buick Skylark from a dealer was $12,568. The cost of purchasing the replacement parts for the car (and the paint service) was $40,280.

SOURCE: Boyd, Brendan. 1989. "By The Numbers." *San Francisco Chronicle*, March 3, B5.

■ TIE-IN SALES

A **tie-in sale** occurs when the sale of one good is made contingent upon the sale of other goods. For example, if a supermarket will sell you a pound of coffee only on the condition that you buy sugar from that supermarket, that would be a tie-in sale. The legal restrictions, described in Chapter 22, governing the use of tie-in sales have produced much litigation. One benefit of this litigation is that there are numerous, well-documented examples of firms using tie-in sales. Subsequent sections describe the use of tie-in sales as a method of price discrimination. We use the term *price discrimination* quite broadly in the sense that a tie-in sale enables a monopolist to increase its profit over and above what it would earn without tie-in sales. As with all price discrimination schemes, the reason the tie-in can increase profits is that it enables a firm to charge more to consumers who value the good the most. Although tie-in sales can be used to price discriminate, it is important to recognize that there are many other reasons for tie-in sales that are unrelated to price discrimination. We first explore some of these alternative motives and then turn to a discussion of the motives for price discrimination.

General Justifications for Tie-In Sales

One of the simplest explanations for tie-in sales is based on efficiency. For example, laced shoes are typically sold with laces; everyone who buys laced shoes needs shoe laces. As long as people's tastes for shoe laces do not differ dramatically, it is more efficient (that is, lowers transaction costs) to sell laced shoes with standard shoe laces than to sell the two, shoe laces and shoes, separately. In the extreme, every product can be thought of as composed of multiple products. For example, a radio consists of many individual components. The same is true of an automobile, which could be regarded as a package including an engine, tires, and a car body. Obviously, each of these products could be sold separately, but since consumers desire assembled products, they come tied together. See Example 15.1.

Another efficiency justification for tie-in sales is that they economize on the cost of grading individual units of a product. For example, it may be much easier for a seller to

EXAMPLE 15.2

STUCK HOLDING THE BAG

A large fraction of the world's diamonds is marketed by deBeers Consolidated Mines. A buyer is allowed to specify the average quality of diamond. The buyer is then given a bag containing several diamonds. The buyer has the right to reject or accept the bag in its entirety. A buyer who rejects a bag is not invited back. One rationale for this marketing procedure is that if buyers were allowed to investigate each stone in detail and reject any one stone, then deBeers would be required to spend resources to sort and grade the diamonds more carefully. The cost is avoided by the "take the bag or leave it" selling policy.

SOURCE: Kenney and Klein (1983).

guarantee that a bag containing ten items has a certain average quality than to guarantee that one particular item chosen from the bag has that quality. The law of large numbers states that in a large enough sample, it would be highly unusual for the average to deviate significantly from its expected value. Therefore, if one is selecting, say, potatoes from a bin of a known average weight per potato, it would be quite unusual if a bag containing 100 potatoes weighed on average much less than the average weight of potatoes in the bin. On the other hand, if a single potato is chosen from that bin, that particular potato might easily be either much heavier or lighter than the average. Therefore, if consumers demand that, on average, the quality of their product be at a certain level it is much harder (that is, more costly) to satisfy those preferences when items are sold in small numbers of units. Instead when units are sold together in very large numbers, the law of averages works, and it is much easier for manufacturers to guarantee that the bag satisfies the consumer's desire for a certain average quality. See Example 15.2.

Another common reason for tie-in sales is to evade price controls. Imagine that the government has set price controls on a particular product, for example, steel. Suppose the controlled price is below the market-clearing price (the price at which supply equals demand) by $5.00. One method of circumventing price controls is to sell steel at the controlled price but only on the condition that the consumer also pay $5.25 for a pencil that is actually worth only 25 cents. In this way, the market-clearing price for steel is maintained, and the price controls are still met.

A variant of the preceding example is to use a tie-in sale to circumvent regulation. Some public utilities, like electric utilities, are often subject to rate regulation. If electric utilities were allowed to sell light bulbs and were also allowed to force consumers to buy light bulbs as a condition of receiving electric service, the electric utility could completely circumvent the rate regulation by charging a high price for light bulbs, unless the regulators also regulated the price for light bulbs.

The ability to evade regulation is currently of particular concern in light of the recent divestiture of AT&T. As a result of the divestiture, there are several local regional operating companies in charge of local phone service, which is subject to rate regulation. The local phone companies often ask for the right to enter a business other than local phone service, like the provision of computer time, as uncontrolled firms, free from any sort of regulation. The regulator is concerned that if a local operating company is allowed to enter an unregulated competitive business, the company could tie its regulated product, local phone service, to the purchase of its unregulated product, such as computer services, and by charging a high price for the computer service completely circumvent the rate regulation.

Another motivation for tie-ins is to give a secret price discount. For example, a member of an oligopoly may want to give price discounts secretly, so that rivals cannot discover them (see Chapter 9). One way to do this is to sell a product at the oligopoly price but to tie to that sale another product with a very low price. For example, a firm can give a 10 percent discount on a $100 price by giving as a gift to purchasers of the product another product that is worth $10. Alternatively, the firm could charge customers $10 less than they would have to pay if they purchased the tied product in the competitive market.

Tie-in sales can also be a means to assure quality. For example, Kodak could claim that it tied the development of its film to its film sales because it did not believe that independent developers could develop Kodak film as skillfully as could Kodak.[4] Kodak could have reasoned that if an independent developer made a mistake and produced poor pictures, the consumer would be unable to distinguish whether the film was bad or the developer was bad. The consumer might then be reluctant to purchase film from Kodak in the future.

Another more current example involves NutraSweet. NutraSweet is a nonsugar sweetener that its manufacturer (Searle) claims to be natural and good tasting. Other sugar substitutes, like saccharin, are less expensive than NutraSweet. Beverage manufacturers began using a blend of saccharin and NutraSweet in their diet sodas. Searle felt that the taste of the blend was not as good as NutraSweet alone, and fearing that NutraSweet would be improperly judged, required that users of NutraSweet not use it as a blend.[5] Of course, both Kodak and Searle may have had other motivations for their actions.

A final reason for tie-in sales—the focus of the rest of this chapter—is to increase monopoly profit. That is, if a firm is a monopolist of a product, it may be able to increase its profits by tying another good to the sale of the monopolized good. Tie-in sales can be used to price discriminate in a variety of circumstances, and the way they work is analyzed differently depending on the circumstances. Therefore, after reviewing some general reasons for using tie-in sales as a method of price discrimination, we discuss their use in a variety of different circumstances.

Tie-In Sales as a Method of Price Discrimination

It is useful to distinguish among the various types of tie-in sales that can occur. One type, referred to as a **package tie-in** (also called *bundling*),[6] occurs when goods are sold in

---

[4] Kodak film was once sold only with development included. Purchasers simply mailed the film to Kodak, and it was developed at no additional charge beyond the initial price of the film.

[5] *Newsweek,* January 28, 1985, 57.

[6] See also Adams and Yellen (1976).

fixed proportions. That is, if you buy one jar of coffee, you must buy one bag of sugar. Everyone who buys the product consumes it in the fixed proportions in which it is sold (or else disposes of part of the package). Another type of tie-in sale is a **requirements tie-in** sale. For example, if you purchase Product A from me, you are required to purchase from me all of Product B that you consume. In a famous antitrust case, IBM required that purchasers of its machines that used tabulating cards buy all of their tabulating cards, no matter how many, from IBM.[7] In such a requirements tie, different consumers might well consume different relative amounts of the two products. For example, in the IBM case, a large user of tabulating cards would consume more tabulating cards per machine than a small user. In some cases a requirements tie automatically occurs when the related product is only produced by the firm selling the other product. For example, the only firm that sells film to fit a particular camera may be the camera manufacturer.

As with all methods of nonlinear pricing in which different consumers pay different prices for the same product, a tie-in sale can succeed in price discriminating only if trade between consumers is prevented. For example, in the case of the (fixed proportions) package tie-in, the tie-in will fail if the consumer can break apart the package and resell it on the open market. Similarly, in the case of the requirements tie-in, the consumer must be unable to purchase the tied good elsewhere at the competitive price. One simple way to understand this point is to notice that nonlinear pricing can increase a monopolist's profits by enabling it to charge each group of consumers a different price. Any time resale markets develop, consumers end up paying the same per unit prices for the same goods. That is, if they all have access to the resale market, they will all face the same price. It is for this fundamental reason that resale markets destroy the incentive to use tie-in sales to increase monopoly profits.

The discussion now turns to the various types of tie-in sales and the circumstances under which they increase profits, beginning with an analysis of a package tie-in for the case of products whose demands are independent. Products have **independent demands** if the value a consumer places on one product does not depend on the consumption of the other product. We then turn to an analysis of products whose demands are related.

Package Tie-ins of Independent Products.   There are two relevant situations in which to examine package tie-ins. In one, a firm is a monopolist of both products; in the other, a firm is a monopolist of only one. Let us examine each situation separately.

Package Tie-in with Both Products Monopolized.   Suppose a firm is a monopolist of Product A and of Product B. For example, think of a movie producer that sells movies to theaters. The two movies it owns, A and B, are in great demand. Would the monopolist earn higher profits if it sold A and B separately or as a package? The answer is that it depends on the value that various consumers place on each of the two movies separately

---

[7] *IBM v. U.S.*, 298 U.S. 131 (1936). Customers who bought cards through IBM presumably paid a higher price than they would have if they bought from others.

	Person 1	Person 2
TABLE 15.1 Example of a Profitable Package Tie-in		
Amount willing to pay for A	$ 9000	$10,000
Amount willing to pay for B	$ 3000	$ 2000
Amount willing to pay for A and B together	$12,000	$12,000

versus the value they place on the package (Stigler 1968). Assume that the products are independent, in the sense that a consumer's valuation of A is independent of whether B is consumed.

Consider the example in Table 15.1. Person 1 is willing to pay at most $9000 to purchase A separately and $3000 to purchase B separately. Person 2 is willing to pay at most $10,000 for A separately and $2000 for B. Note that the amount each person is willing to pay for A is completely independent of whether B is also purchased, and vice versa.

Suppose, for simplicity, that the cost of producing the products is zero, and the monopolist wants to maximize the revenues that it receives from selling to these two people. The monopolist has two choices: it can sell A and B separately or as a package. If it sells Product A separately, it maximizes revenue by charging a price of $9000. At that price, both Persons 1 and 2 purchase Product A, and the monopolist receives $18,000. Similarly, in order to maximize the revenue from selling B separately, the monopolist sets a price of $2000 and receives revenue of $4000. Therefore, the total revenues received from selling A and B separately are $22,000.

Now, suppose that the monopolist decides to sell A and B as a package. Person 1 is willing to pay $12,000 for the package, and so is Person 2. If the monopolist sells the package for $12,000, it sells to both consumers and receives $24,000. Revenues are increased by tying the two goods together and selling them as a package instead of selling them separately. By selling the products as a package, the monopolist is effectively able to charge Person 1 a higher price for B ($3000) compared to that charged Person 2 ($2000) and a lower price for A ($9000) compared to that charged Person 2 ($10,000). In other words, when both Persons 1 and 2 buy the same package, they are placing different relative values on the components of the package. This is precisely what methods of price discrimination are designed to do: they enable the monopolist to charge different prices to different people for the same product.

By changing the numbers in Table 15.1, it is possible to show that a tie-in is not always the most profitable strategy. For example, if the willingness to pay is as given in Table 15.2, then it is more profitable for the monopolist to sell the products separately than as a package. In Table 15.2, the maximum profits from selling the products separately are $20,000, while the profits from selling A and B together are only $19,000.

Suppose that both people in Table 15.1 purchase the package of A and B together, break the package apart, and sell A and B separately in a resale market. Because there are two units of Product A, the only market-clearing price that will induce the two

TABLE 15.2 Example of an Unprofitable Package Tie-in		
	Person 1	*Person 2*
Amount willing to pay for A	$9000	$10,000
Amount willing to pay for B	$ 500	$ 2000
Amount willing to pay for A and B together	$9500	$12,000

consumers to hold A, that is the (common) market-clearing price, is $9000. Similarly, the market-clearing price for Product B is $2000. (Students may find the concept of a resale market easier to understand if they assume there are many consumers like Person 1 and an equal number like Person 2.) Now if Person 1 and Person 2 realize that a resale market will develop after they purchase their packages and that the price of A will be $9000 and the price of B will be $2000, they clearly will prefer not to purchase the package. Instead they will wait until the resale market develops and purchase A and B separately for a combined price of $11,000 rather than for the $12,000 in the example. If this occurs, nobody would purchase the package, and the attempt to practice price discrimination through a package tie-in would simply not work. This is another illustration that shows how a resale market destroys the ability of a monopolist to charge effectively different prices for the same product and thereby destroys the ability to price discriminate through tie-in sales.

The example in Table 15.1 depended on a negative relationship between what a person is willing to pay for two items: the person who put a high value on one good placed a low value on the other good. Tie-in sales can be profitable even if there is no such negative relationship (Kenney and Klein 1983, Jennings and Gikas 1985). To illustrate, suppose that a firm sells two items, A and B, and that the value placed on them by a consumer is unknown to the firm. Let the consumer's valuation of A and B, V_A and V_B, be

$$V_A = 10 + E_A,$$
$$V_B = 10 + E_B,$$

where E_A and E_B are two independent random variables that differ across consumers and that, on average, equal zero.[8] The firm is the only one selling either A or B and wishes to choose a price for A and for B, if the two products are sold separately, or a price for the package if they are sold together. Consider the pricing if the firm sells each separately. The firm trades off the increased revenue from a higher price versus the increased likelihood that the price is too high and nothing is purchased. If the firm charges p_A for Product A, the consumer purchases A if p_A is less than V_A or if E_A exceeds $p_A - 10$. A similar calculation applies to the purchase of B. The firm's problem is to choose p_A and p_B to maximize expected revenue. (We continue to assume that production costs are zero.)

Suppose that E_A and E_B each independently equal -3 with probability $\frac{1}{2}$ and 3 with

---

[8] For those who are unfamiliar with random variables, think of picking a number out of a hat containing many numbers whose average is zero.

probability ½. This means that consumers value A at either 7 or 13 (10 − 3 and 10 + 3), and similarly for B. In setting the price for A, the firm could set p_A = $7 and always sell the product for an expected revenue of $7, or choose p_A = $13 and sell Product A only one-half the time for an expected revenue of $6.50. To maximize expected profits, the firm should set p_A = $7. A similar analysis shows that the firm should set p_B = $7. Hence, the firm receives $14 when it sells each product separately.

Suppose the firm ties A and B together and sells them as one package. Using the same numbers as above, consumers have one of the following four pairs (V_A, V_B) of reservation values for A and B: ($7,$7), ($7,$13), ($13,$7) and ($13,$13), each with equal probability. Therefore, the valuation of the package of A and B together is as follows:

$14   with probability ¼

$20   with probability ½

$26   with probability ¼

If the firm sets the package price at $14, its sales are certain, and it earns $14. If the firm sets the package price at $20, it sells the package three-fourths of the time for $20, for an expected revenue of $15. At a price of $26, it sells the package one-fourth of the time for $26, for an expected revenue of $6.50. Therefore, the profit-maximizing strategy is to sell the package for $20. This strategy yields higher expected profits than those ($14) from selling each product separately. The tie-in has increased profits.

Package Tie-ins with One Product Monopolized. Let us change the assumption of the preceding section so that the firm is a monopolist of only Product A. Product B is competitively produced and available for some price, C_B. The question is whether it would pay the monopolist to tie Products A and B together in fixed proportions, again assuming that Product A and Product B are independent, in the sense that consumers' valuation of Product A is unrelated to whether or not they also consume Product B and vice versa.

Before examining this case in more analytic detail, let us use common sense to guess the answer. Suppose that it were profitable for the monopolist to tie a competitive good B to the purchase of Product A. Because A and B are independent products, any competitive product could be tied to Product A to increase the monopolist's profits. In other words, a monopolist of, say, cars, might be expected to tie all sorts of unrelated products to the sale of cars. We rarely, if ever, see a monopolist tie a completely unrelated product to the sale of its own product. Because we do not observe that, it must generally not be profitable for a monopolist to tie an unrelated, competitively available product to the sale of its monopolized product.

Suppose that a monopolist of Product A uses a package tie-in and requires that for every unit of A purchased, one unit of a competitively available Product, B, must also be purchased. To keep the example simple, suppose that the costs of manufacturing A are zero. The monopolist purchases Product B at the competitive price, C_B, inserts it into a package with A, and charges p^* for the package. The profit for every package sold is therefore $p^* - C_B$. In order to show that the package tie-in is not desirable, the following analysis demonstrates that the monopolist would make more money if it sold Product A separately and charged $p^* - C_B$.

Two types of consumers consider purchasing the product. One type likes Product B. If those consumers do not obtain Product B in the package with Product A, they will buy it elsewhere at price C_B. For these consumers, it is as if they are buying Product B at price C_B and paying $p^* - C_B$ for Product A. They are completely indifferent whether they pay $p^* - C_B$ for A and C_B for B separately or whether they buy A and B together in a package for p^*.

The second type of consumer values a unit of B at less than C_B. In other words, if they buy the package, they are forced to consume more of Product B than they would have if they had been allowed to buy B separately at the market price, C_B. For example, a particular consumer may well end up getting Product B when, in fact, this consumer has absolutely no use for Product B and values it at zero. This particular consumer will purchase the package consisting of A and B at p^* only if he or she values Product A at p^* or more.

If Product A were sold separately for $p^* - C_B$, then more from this second type of consumer would purchase Product A separately than purchase the package at p^*. For example, consumers who place no value on B but a value of $p^* - C_B$ on A would buy A separately at $p^* - C_B$, but would refuse to buy the package at p^*. If the monopolist makes a per-unit profit of $p^* - C_B$ when the package is sold, and the same $p^* - C_B$ when Product A is sold separately (at price $p^* - C_B$), the monopolist's profits will be higher when it sells Product A separately, because more units of Product A will be sold. In other words, for any price for a package, p^*, a monopolist can always do better by selling Product A separately for $p^* - C_B$ than by selling the package for p^*. By packaging A and B together, the monopolist is throwing away sales by forcing some consumers to buy a product they do not wish to pay for. This causes some consumers not to buy the package. The key result is that a monopolist never has an incentive to tie in fixed proportions of a good that is competitively produced as long as the goods are independent.

Interrelated Demands.   The analysis so far has been of goods that are independent of each other; that is, the consumption of one good does not affect the value a consumer places on the other good. For many goods, however, this independence assumption is not applicable. For example, the value of a camera depends on the availability of film. The price of film influences the demand for cameras, and vice versa. When two products are not independent, there is an **interrelated demand** for the two. This interrelationship of demand creates incentives for tie-in sales involving package tie-ins and requirements tie-ins in order to price discriminate. Before establishing this point, let us first examine profit maximization with interrelated demands without tie-in sales.

Profit Maximization with Interrelated Demands.   Suppose that there is a monopolist of two products, A and B. If the demands are independent, the demand for Product A depends only on the price of Product A, and the demand for Product B depends only on the price of B. With interrelated demands, the demand for Product A depends on both the price of Product A and the price of Product B; similarly, the demand for Product B depends upon the price of both Products A and B.

Let C denote the (constant marginal) cost of production, p denote price, $D(p)$ the demand curve, and subscripts Products A and B. The monopolist's problem is to maximize profits, π, which are given by the following expression:

$$\pi(p_A, p_B) = (p_A - C_A)D_A(p_A, p_B) + (p_B - C_B)D_B(p_A, p_B).$$

If the profits associated with each product are:

$$\pi_A(p_A, p_B) = (p_A - C_A)D_A(p_A, p_B),$$

and

$$\pi_B(p_A, p_B) = (p_B - C_B)D_B(p_A, p_B),$$

then we can write the firm's profits as

$$\pi(p_A, p_B) = \pi_A(p_A, p_B) + \pi_B(p_A, p_B). \tag{15.1}$$

In choosing the optimal prices to charge, the monopolist not only considers its profits, π_A, from the production and sale of A, but also takes into account how the price of A affects the profits, π_B, from Product B and vice versa. The crucial point about interrelated demands is that a monopolist of interrelated products takes the interrelationship into account. It is possible to illustrate diagrammatically what is happening when demands are interrelated. For example, in Figure 15.6, the demand curve for A shifts out as the price of B falls from \$5 to \$4. By altering price p_B, the monopolist may be able to shift out its demand curve for Product A in such a way that it can extract a large enough profit from the sale of A to more than offset any decline in the monopolist's profit in Market B.[9] (If p_A changes, D_B would shift.) This analysis suggests that a monopolist of two substitute products will set a higher price for each than would separate monopolists.

---

[9] We derive the maximization conditions for choosing p_A and p_B optimally by setting the derivatives of profits, π, in Equation 15.1 with respect to p_A and p_B equal to zero; the maximization conditions are given as follows:

$$\frac{\partial \pi_A}{\partial p_A} + \frac{\partial \pi_B}{\partial p_A} = 0$$

$$\frac{\partial \pi_A}{\partial p_B} + \frac{\partial \pi_B}{\partial p_B} = 0$$

These conditions are different from the conditions that would result if, instead of one monopolist that controls the price of *both* p_A and p_B, there were two monopolists, one setting the price of A and one setting the price of B. Those conditions are

$$\frac{\partial \pi_A}{\partial p_A} = 0, \text{ and } \frac{\partial \pi_B}{\partial p_B} = 0.$$

FIGURE 15.6   Interrelated Demands

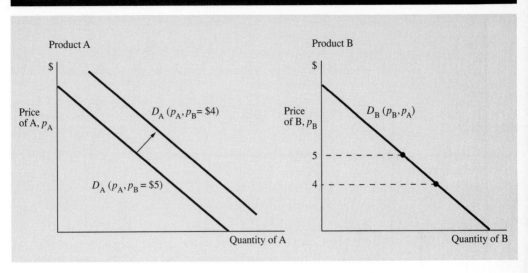

In fact it may pay to set the price of B below its production cost in order to make consumers more willing to purchase Product A. Exactly such a case appeared earlier in this chapter in the discussion of two-part tariffs. Recall that one could interpret the sale of a camera and film as a two-part tariff in which the lump-sum fee is paid for the camera and the usage fee is for the film. The discussion explained how it could be profitable to charge a price below cost for the camera. We now investigate both package tie-ins and requirements tie-ins when demands are interrelated.

Package Tie-ins with Interrelated Demands.   A monopolist of an input might have an incentive for forward vertical integration so that efficient factor proportions will be used in the production of the output. For example, suppose that there is a monopolist of aluminum sheet, but that cars and steel are produced competitively. Cars can be made from various combinations (variable proportions) of aluminum and steel. Figure 15.7 illustrates this example.

Because the choice of the factor proportions of aluminum to steel is based on the ratio of a monopoly aluminum price relative to a competitive steel price, we know that inefficient proportions of aluminum and steel are used. Specifically, too large a proportion of steel to aluminum is being used in the production process for cars. By vertically integrating, the aluminum monopolist can increase its profits and produce cars with more efficient factor proportions.[10]

An alternative to vertical integration is for the aluminum monopolist to specify that 1 unit of its aluminum can be used only with a certain number of units of steel. Suppose

---

[10] This point is developed in detail in Chapter 16.

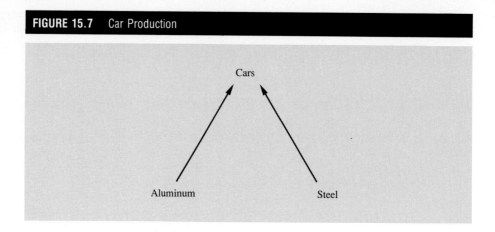

FIGURE 15.7 Car Production

for example, that the monopolist under vertical integration would use 1 ton of aluminum together with 1 ton of steel to make a car. Exactly the same result could be achieved if the aluminum monopolist did not vertically integrate but simply required car manufacturers to use aluminum and steel in one-to-one fixed proportions. The monopolist could impose this restriction by requiring that car manufacturers purchase all their steel through the aluminum monopolist, who could purchase the steel on the competitive market.

The willingness to pay for 1 ton of aluminum depends on the price of steel. Therefore, the case of variable proportions is precisely one in which the valuations of the two inputs are interrelated. This shows that, for the case of interrelated demands, a package tie-in sale could enable a monopolist to achieve the same increase in profits that it could have achieved through vertical integration; thus, a tie-in sale is an alternative to vertical integration. Of course, as with all tie-in sales, if the tie-in is to work, it must be impossible for the consumer, in this case the car manufacturer, to purchase steel secretly on the open market; that is, the consumer must not be able to undo the package tie-in.

Requirements Tie-ins with Interrelated Demands. Perhaps the most common type of tie-in is a requirements tie-in in which consumers buy one good and are then required to make all their purchases of some other related good from the same manufacturer. Several examples of this have arisen in litigation, and Chapter 22 examines several cases. One involves A. B. Dick Company, which sold mimeograph machines.[11] A. B. Dick required that customers who bought mimeograph machines also had to buy all their ink from A. B. Dick, which did not have a monopoly in ink. Another famous tie-in case has already been mentioned: the IBM tabulating card case, in which IBM required purchasers of its machines to buy all their tabulating cards from IBM. It is instructive to explain why these requirements ties were probably profitable.

Suppose that a firm has developed a new machine that automatically sews buttons on shirts. Prior to the development of the machine, buttons were sewn by hand onto shirts,

---

[11] *Henry v. A. B. Dick Co.*, 224 U.S. 1 (1912).

FIGURE 15.8   Demand for Machines

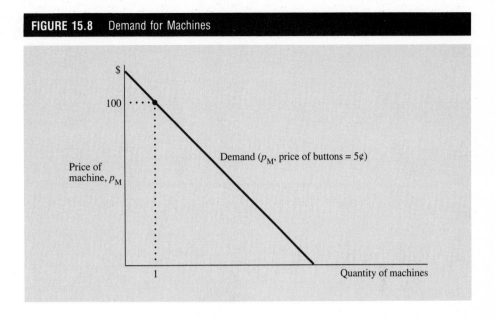

and the labor cost was 1¢ per button. There are many shirt manufacturers. Suppose that the largest one sews on 10,000 buttons per year. That manufacturer is willing to pay $100 per year for the machine because $100 is precisely the savings from reduced labor costs. Another manufacturer that only uses 1000 buttons would be willing to pay only $10 for the machine per year.

To keep the example simple, suppose that a machine lasts for only a year and that the total number of buttons that each manufacturer sews on shirts during a year is unchanged by the advent of the machine. Then if manufacturers can buy buttons competitively at, say, 5¢ per button, we can draw the demand curve for the machine as shown in Figure 15.8. The first shirt manufacturer, who demands 10,000 buttons, is willing to pay $100 for the machine. The one who demands 1000 buttons is willing to pay $10. Thus the demand curve for the machine can be constructed under the assumption that buttons can be purchased competitively at 5¢.

Suppose that the monopolist of the machine decides to allow firms to use the machine for free provided they purchase all their buttons from the monopolist at a price equal to 1¢ (or a shade less than 1¢) above the competitive price, or 6¢. In other words, the monopolist ties the sale of buttons to the sale of the machine and charges a 1¢ premium (or a shade less) on each button. Any firm that has a use for the machine agrees to these conditions because the savings that the machine creates are precisely 1¢ per button. The interesting feature of this tie-in is that the largest users of buttons pay a much higher effective price for the machine. For example, the firm that uses 10,000 buttons effectively pays $100 for the machine; however, the firm that uses only 1000 buttons pays only $10 for it. In other words, a tie-in between buttons and machines enables the monopolist of the machine to charge effectively different prices for the machine to different consumers and, in particular, to charge the most to those who value the machine the most. This tie-

FIGURE 15.9   Shifts in the Demand for Machines and Buttons as a Result of the Tie-In

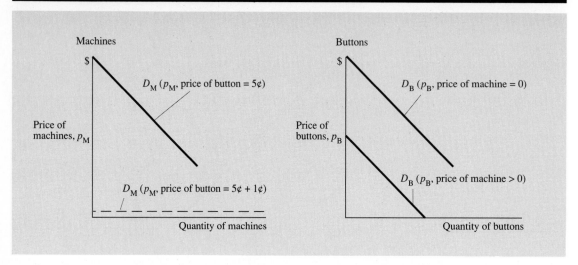

in enables the monopolist to completely extract all consumer surplus from under the demand curve. That is, it allows the monopolist to perfectly price discriminate.

We can relate this example of a tie-in between a machine and buttons to the earlier examination of interrelated demand curves. Figure 15.8 shows that the demand curve for the machine depends on the price of the machine and the price of buttons, 5¢. The tie-in extracts all consumer surplus because of the 1¢ overcharge on the button, so consumers are not willing to pay anything for a machine. As shown in Figure 15.9, the tie-in forces the demand curve for the machine to become a horizontal line at zero because it raises the price of a button by 1¢. In other words, as the price of a button rises from the competitive price of 5¢ to 6¢, the demand curve for the machine collapses to the horizontal axis. The advent of the machine makes the demand curve for buttons shift upward from where it was before the machine existed. If the machine is given to the user for free, the demand curve for buttons rises by precisely one penny above where it was before the machine existed. Therefore, as Figure 15.9 shows, the tie-in does the following: it drops the demand curve for the machine down and raises the demand curve for buttons relative to the positions the demand curves would have if the price of buttons were 5¢ and the machine's price were positive. This turns out to be the most profitable way to exploit the consumers' demands for the machine and buttons.

The preceding example is special in the sense that each firm has a pre-established demand for buttons that is assumed to be unchanged by the tie-in. It is more realistic to assume that each firm has some flexibility over how many buttons it will purchase and that the firms differ in the values they attach to sewing on buttons by machine. In response to a tie-in sale of a machine and buttons in which users are overcharged for buttons, each user might reduce its use of buttons. If this occurs, the tie-in does not allow perfect price discrimination as in the simpler example. However, the tie-in might still make sense, even if all consumer surplus cannot be extracted. The tie-in can be regarded as a two-part tariff in which the machine's price is viewed as a lump-sum payment and the price of buttons is viewed as a per-unit charge. The tie-in sale cannot achieve perfect price discrimination for the same reason, discussed earlier, that a two-part tariff cannot generally achieve perfect price discrimination.[12] The reason is that the firm is unable to separately identify and charge each consumer according to the consumer's willingness to pay.

In the examples in this section, the tie-in serves as a meter of usage. An alternative would be to meter usage explicitly. For example, in the IBM case, IBM could have installed a meter to measure the number of cards each of its customers used. Customers could purchase cards anywhere, but the price they paid IBM for the machine would depend on their card usage. The choice between using a tie-in or an explicit meter depends on the relative costs of the two methods. Meters may be costly, and they may be easy to unhook, trick, or break. Tie-ins, on the other hand, may be hard to police (for example, customers could buy cards elsewhere), and they could distort efficient use. Photocopiers, telephones, and electric utilities often use explicit meters to monitor usage.

■ QUALITY CHOICE

Imagine a monopolist of several goods that differ in quality—for example, a monopolist of cars of high and low quality. Goods of different qualities are typically related on the demand side because consumers can substitute among them. If the qualities of the goods are prespecified, the monopolist's decision about pricing them is the same as the one already examined in the discussion of interrelated demands. However, if the monopolist must also decide on the qualities of the goods to be produced, then it takes the demand interrelationship into account not only when it decides how to price the various quality goods, but also when it decides on the qualities of the goods it will offer for sale (Mussa and Rosen 1978). Thus the monopolist's decisions about levels of quality are influenced by the same forces that have already been examined for nonlinear pricing.

For example, the monopolist may choose to produce only very high quality and very low quality goods. By not providing close substitutes for the high-quality goods, the monopolist may be able to extract more profit from selling them than it could if it also produced medium-quality, low-priced goods that were good substitutes for the high-priced, high-quality goods. The reason is that the firm can charge a high price for the high-quality good and not worry about consumers substituting to the low-priced, low-quality good because it is not a good substitute.

To illustrate how a monopolist can use quality choice to increase its profits, consider the following example. Suppose that there are two different consumers, Type 1 and Type 2, and that each consumes only 1 unit of a product (if it consumes any at all). Type 2 places a much higher value on quality than does Type 1. Let p stand for price, C for cost, U for utility, z for quality, and subscripts for the types of product. The monopolist's

---

[12] If the number of buttons used per shirt is variable, and if, in response to an increase in the price of buttons, shirt manufacturers use fewer buttons, the machine owner may wish to specify as a condition of purchase the minimum number of buttons that can be sewn on per shirt.

problem is to choose a (p_1, z_1) and a (p_2, z_2) in such a way as to maximize its profits. Consumers choose the price-quality combinations most favorable to themselves. That is, there are self-selection constraints that limit the feasible price-quality combinations that the monopolist can choose. This problem is analyzed in Appendix 15E and, in more detail, in Mussa and Rosen (1978).

In summary, when consumers prefer different levels of quality, a monopolist manipulates the qualities of goods produced in the market in order to extract consumer surplus. The monopolist follows the principles already studied regarding price discrimination and chooses the quality spectrum so as to charge a high price to those who value the good the most, and a low price to those who value it the least, without having to pass along the low price to those who value the good the most.

■ OTHER METHODS OF NONLINEAR PRICING

This chapter discusses only some of the many possible pricing schemes that monopolists can adopt as they attempt to maximize profits. A few other pricing schemes are quite common and therefore deserve mention.

- Many sellers specify that their product can be bought only in certain minimum amounts. This can be considered to be a nonlinear pricing schedule in which the price is very high until the minimum purchase level, at which point it falls.

- Sometimes consumers must choose the pricing schedule that will govern their purchases *before* they know how much they will purchase. For example, some telephone companies require consumers to select a pricing schedule at the beginning of the month. Some may elect to pay a large fixed fee and have unlimited calling; others may elect to pay a modest lump-sum fee that entitles them to make calls and pay extra only for those calls in excess of a certain amount. After the month is over, it may turn out that a pricing schedule other than the chosen one would have led to a lower bill. By requiring customers to specify in advance the pricing schedule they will face, monopolists can sometimes discriminate between those who can accurately predict their demands and those who cannot. It contrast, electricity companies generally do not require customers to choose a pricing schedule in advance. Instead, consumers of electricity typically face a declining block schedule where high prices are charged for initial usage and lower prices are charged thereafter. When this schedule is used the bill at the end of the month is independent of the customers' ability to predict their demands.

  Another related example involves the purchase in advance of a fixed amount of a product for a lower price than for smaller, as-needed purchases. For example, many commuter railroads sell individual tickets at much higher prices per ride than monthly passes.

- We have already seen that a tie-in sale affects the use of a complementary product. A monopolist might well require not one good but several to be used in conjunction with its monopolized good. A monopolist could also specify that particular inputs must *not* be used with its monopolized goods.

- Consumers may differ in their desires to obtain the good quickly. A firm could price discriminate by charging more for rapid delivery. For example, a common pricing strategy for new goods is to price high initially and then to lower price over time. Airlines often charge more for tickets ordered one day in advance than for those ordered several weeks in advance. One possible reason for this pricing behavior is that businesspeople, who often travel on short notice, have a less elastic demand than tourists, who do not travel on short notice. (Other reasons related to demand forecasting and inventory control are discussed in Chapter 21.)

- When obtaining a good is uncertain, it may be possible to price discriminate by charging different prices for different probabilities obtaining the good (Harris and Raviv 1981).

- Firms sometimes use auctions to sell a valuable asset.[13] Art, antiques, off-shore oil leases and Treasury bills are some of the many items commonly sold at auctions. The purpose of an auction is typically to obtain the maximum revenue from buyers when the seller does not know which buyers value the goods the most. The objective is to design a pricing mechanism that induces the consumers with the greatest willingness to pay to bid high prices. Several questions arise as to the best way to conduct an auction to obtain the maximum revenue. Should it be an auction in which bids start low and rise until there is no one willing to bid any higher **(English auction)**? Should it be an auction in which the price starts out very high and is slowly lowered until one person agrees to buy at the current price **(Dutch auction)**? Should a minimum bid be specified? The answer to these questions is, under plausible assumptions, surprisingly simple. If buyers maximize expected consumer surplus, then Dutch and English auctions yield the same expected revenues, and it is optimal to specify minimum bids.

- Repeat customers can be charged a different price than first-time purchasers. Providing discount coupons in packages effectively charges repeat buyers lower prices. Special introductory offers are a way of charging new purchasers a lower price.

■ SUMMARY

If a firm with market power lacks knowledge about individual consumers or consumer groups, it cannot perfectly price discriminate, or charge different prices to different consumers. Instead, the firm must offer the same pricing policy to all consumers and let them choose (self-select) how much to pay and consume. However, a firm can earn higher profits than those earned by setting a single price by designing nonlinear pricing policies—like a menu of two-part tariffs—that induce consumers to sort themselves out in such a way that each consumer group pays different prices. The firm's pricing is affected by the self-selection constraints of consumers; that is, the firm must recognize that consumers choose what is best for them.

---

[13] There is a sizeable literature on auctions. See Riley and Samuelson (1981) and McAfee and McMillan (1987).

Aside from using a nonlinear price to price discriminate, a firm can use other policies. One common policy is a tie-in sale. Both package and requirements tie-in sales can increase a firm's profits under appropriate circumstances. One important consideration in analyzing tie-in sales is whether the products are independent or related in demand. A variety of other policies exist that a firm with market power can use to increase its profits over those earned by simple monopolies. These policies include quality choice, auctions, and minimum purchase orders.

■ Key Terms

Dutch auction
English auction
independent demands
interrelated demand
marginal price
nonlinear pricing

package tie-in
requirements tie-in
second-degree price discrimination
self-selection constraint
tie-in sale
two-part tariff

■ Discussion Questions

1. Suppose a firm must use a single two-part tariff. Explain the intuition behind the result that the fixed fee rises and the per-unit charge falls as the population becomes more homogeneous.

2. No study that we are aware of explains the distinction between the pricing in the electric and telephone industries. In the telephone industry, each consumer often has to choose which of many tariffs will govern monthly charges before the month begins. In the electric industry, the rate charged is determined by one rate schedule at the end of the month. Can you think of any reasons for the distinction? (*Hint:* Consider the forecastability of a consumer's demand.)

3. Assume that an incumbent firm makes both peripheral devices and computers. (A peripheral device attaches to a computer. For example, a printer is a peripheral device.) The entrant only makes peripheral devices. Relate the discussion of tie-in sales to the strategic behavior in which the incumbent raises the cost to a rival of attaching the rival's peripheral device to the incumbent's computer.

4. There is an analogy between optimal price discrimination and optimal taxation. Suppose there are two groups with two different demand curves for electricity. The government must raise $100 to finance the provision of an electricity plant. Suppose the variable cost to generate 1 unit of electricity is 1¢. What principles do you think should govern optimal taxation in the presence of different types of consumers if the government can distinguish between the two groups and impose a different per-unit tax on each group? Suppose one group comprises businesses and the other homes. Which group has the more elastic demand? Which should pay a lower price? Suppose the government is able to use a different two-part tariff for each group. How do your answers change?

5. Answer the previous question assuming that the government is unable to distinguish the two groups and uses two two-part tariffs as in Appendix 15D. Is there more deadweight loss than occurs in the previous question when the government uses a two-part tariff for each group?

■ Problems

1. Suppose a firm gives coupons to selected consumers that entitle them to price discounts. Why might the firm limit the number of coupons that a customer can use on a single purchase?

2. Appendix 15D discusses the optimal two two-part tariffs to charge. Why it is optimal to charge the consumer with the highest willingness to pay a marginal price of C?

3. A person who consumes X units of Good 1 and Y units of Good 2 derives utility of $Y + 10X$. Suppose the person has $100, the price of Y is $1, and the nonlinear expenditure for purchasing X units of Good 1 is X^2. How much X should the person consume?

4. Suppose a manufacturer sells a button-fastening machine that saves a firm the labor cost of 1¢ per button sewn on shirts. Suppose firms differ in the total number of buttons they sew on. The manufacturer sells its ma-

chine with a requirements tie-in that requires a purchaser to buy all its buttons from the manufacturer. Suppose the manufacturer can install a meter that measures how many buttons each machine sews. If the manufacturer can charge according to the use measured on the meter, is there any advantage to the tie-in? Would it be sensible to outlaw tie-in sales, but allow the manufacturer to charge according to the metered use?

5. Let the demand for Products 1 and 2 be $q_1 = 10 - 2p_1 + p_2$ and $q_2 = 10 + p_1 - 2p_2$, where q_i = quantity of Good i and p_i = price of Good i. Assume production costs are zero. Calculate the prices that two separate monopolists would charge when each regards the other's price as beyond its control. Calculate the prices that a single monopolist of both goods would charge.

Answers to odd-numbered problems are given at the back of the book.

■ References

Adams, William J., and Janet L. Yellen. 1976. "Commodity Bundling and the Burden of Monopoly." *Quarterly Journal of Economics* 90:475–98.

Harris, Milton, and Arthur Raviv. 1981. "Monopoly Pricing Schemes with Demand Uncertainty." *American Economic Review* 71:347–65.

Jennings, William, Jr., and James Gikas. 1985. "Block Booking: One Method for Dealing with Imperfect Information." Unpublished.

Katz, Michael. 1983. "Nonuniform Pricing, Output, and Welfare under Monopoly." *Review of Economic Studies* 50:37–56.

Kenney, Roy W., and Benjamin Klein. 1983. "The Economics of Block Booking." *Journal of Law and Economics* 26:491–540.

McAfee, R. Preston, and John McMillan. 1987. "Auctions and Bidding." *Journal of Economic Literature* 25:699–738.

Mussa, Michael, and Sherwin Rosen. 1978. "Monopoly and Product Quality." *Journal of Economic Theory* 18:301–17.

Oi, Walter Y. 1971. "A Disneyland Dilemma: Two-Part Tariffs for a Mickey Mouse Monopoly." *Quarterly Journal of Economics* 85:77–96.

Riley, John G., and William F. Samuelson. 1981. "Optimal Auctions." *American Economic Review* 71:381–92.

Schmalensee, Richard. 1981. "Monopolistic Two-Part Pricing Arrangements." *Bell Journal of Economics* 12:445–66.

Spence, A. Michael. 1977. "Nonlinear Prices and Welfare." *Journal of Public Economics* 8:12–18.

Stigler, George J. 1968. "A Note on Block Booking," in Stigler, *The Organization of Industry.* Homewood, Ill.: Irwin.

Tirole, Jean. 1988. *The Theory of Industrial Organization.* Cambridge: The MIT Press.

Varian, Hal R. 1984. *Microeconomic Analysis.* New York: W. W. Norton.

THE OPTIMAL TWO-PART TARIFF

The following problem illustrates the forces that determine the optimal two-part tariff. Let p be the per-unit usage price, T the lump-sum fee, N be the number of demanders, and Q the total amount of the product demanded. The quantity demanded, Q, is a function not only of p (price) but also of the lump-sum fee (T). Imagine that consumers can be indexed by the parameter α. The higher is α, the more consumers are willing to pay for the product. Let $f(\alpha)$ be the density function of the number of consumers of type α, as illustrated in Figure 15A.1. (The number of consumers for each type α is what $f(\alpha)$ reveals.)

The parameter α varies between $\underline{\alpha}$ and $\overline{\alpha}$. For any choice of p and T, there is a critical level, α^*, such that consumers whose α exceeds α^* (who value the product more than the consumers at α^*) purchase the product, while consumers whose α is below α^* choose not to purchase the product. The consumer of type α^* is called the *marginal* consumer. To derive the equation determining the marginal consumer, α^*, let S represent the consumer surplus, in the absence of a fixed fee, which depends on p and the consumer type α^*. Then

$$S(p,\alpha^*) = T. \tag{15A.1}$$

Equation 15A.1 says that the marginal consumer type, α^*, is just indifferent between purchasing the good and not purchasing the good. The surplus obtained from paying price p is exactly equal to the lump-sum fee, T, so that the total surplus from the purchase is zero. Equation 15A.2 determines the number of consumers that purchase the product— the number whose α is greater than α^*.

$$N = \int_{\alpha^*}^{\overline{\alpha}} f(\alpha)d\alpha. \tag{15A.2}$$

If $q(p, \alpha)$ represents the demand curve of individual Type α, then we can write that the total amount demanded as a function of p and T equals the sum of all the demands of consumers whose α exceeds α^*:

$$Q(p, T) = \int_{\alpha^*}^{\overline{\alpha}} q(p, \alpha) f(\alpha)d\alpha. \tag{15A.3}$$

FIGURE 15A.1   Distribution of Consumer Types

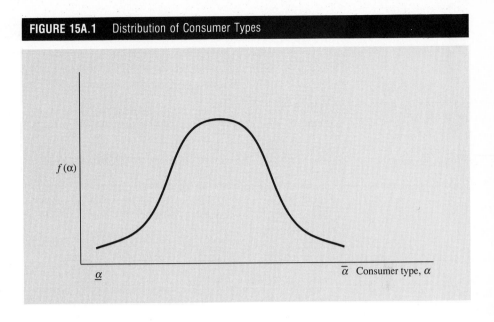

If marginal cost is constant and equals C, then the firm maximizes

$$\text{Profit} = NT + (p - C)Q(p, T) \qquad (15A.4)$$

by choosing p, the price, and T, the lump-sum fee, optimally. Appendix 15B shows that the first-order condition for the determination of price can be written as

$$1 + \frac{p - C}{p}\,E = \frac{q^*}{\bar{q}}, \qquad (15A.5)$$

where $q^* = q(p, \alpha^*),$

$\bar{q} = \dfrac{Q(p, T),}{N}$

and $E = $ price elasticity of demand, holding constant the number of consumers in the marketplace.

Equation 15A.5 is the same as the optimal first-order condition of a simple monopolist, except for the term on the right side, which is the ratio of the purchases of the marginal user (that is, the demand of the α^* consumer) to the purchases of the average user in the marketplace. The ratio $q^*/\bar{q}$ is less than 1 if, as in the usual case, the marginal purchaser buys less of the good than does the average purchaser.

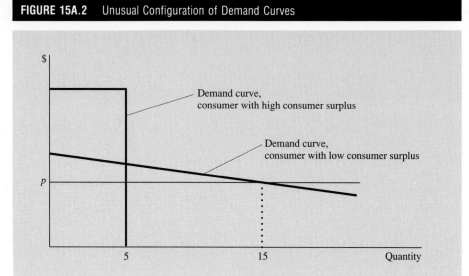

FIGURE 15A.2   Unusual Configuration of Demand Curves

Return to the simple case in which all consumers are identical, so that q^* *equals* $\bar{q}$. Equation 15A.5 becomes

$$\frac{(p - C)}{p} \, \mathrm{E} = 0, \qquad\qquad (15A.6)$$

which implies that price should equal C. That is, when all consumers are identical, it is optimal to charge each consumer marginal cost. All of the profits then come from the lump-sum fee, T. This is exactly the result discussed in Chapter 14 of how perfect price discrimination could be achieved through a two-part tariff in the special case of identical consumers.

It is useful to rewrite Equation 15A.5 as

$$\frac{p - C}{p} = -\frac{1}{\mathrm{E}} \left(1 - \frac{q^*}{\bar{q}} \right). \qquad\qquad (15A.7)$$

In the usual case in which q^* is less than $\bar{q}$, the quantity on the right side of Equation 15A.7 is positive. Thus, in the usual case, price exceeds C. For the usual case the usage sensitive price is closer to C as E increases in absolute value and as consumer diversity, as measured by the difference between 1 and the ratio of the marginal to average purchase, declines. It is possible, however, that in the unusual case it is actually profitable for the usage charge to be below unit cost. This would happen if consumers who get a lot of surplus from the product at a given price buy only small amounts, while the marginal consumers who get very little surplus buy large amounts. This case is illustrated in Figure 15A.2.

In Figure 15A.2, the consumer who purchases 15 units gets very little surplus, and the one who purchases 5 units gets a lot. The intuition in this unusual case is that it is profitable for the firm to lower the price below C in order to raise the lump-sum charge to both types of consumers.

The optimal policy cannot involve a negative value for T, which would mean that people are *paid* a lump-sum fee for the right to consume the good whether or not they consume it. Obviously, if any manufacturer offered to pay people whether or not they consumed the good, everybody would sign up and bankrupt the manufacturer.[1] Hence, in the optimal solution, the lump sum, T, is positive or zero. A two-part tariff generally produces higher profits than a single-price policy because a single price is a special case of a two-part tariff in which the lump-sum fee is zero. Only in the special case, in which the optimal T equals zero, are the two pricing policies equivalent.

---

[1] In fact, this is not precisely true because there are often costs (for example, time) associated with collecting a gift.

DERIVATION OF THE OPTIMAL TWO-PART TARIFF

Using the notation of Appendix 15A, we seek the T and p that maximize profits, which can be written as

$$NT + (p - C)Q(p, T),$$ (15B.1a)

where $N = \int_{\alpha^*}^{\bar\alpha} f(\alpha)d\alpha,$ (15B.1b)

$$T = S(p, \alpha^*),$$ (15B.1c)

and $Q(p, T) = \int_{\alpha^*}^{\bar\alpha} q(p, \alpha)f(\alpha)d\alpha.$ (15B.1d)

Define E as follows

$$E = \int_{\alpha^*}^{\bar\alpha} \frac{q}{Q} \frac{p}{q} \frac{\partial q(p, \alpha)}{\partial p} f(\alpha)d\alpha.$$ (15B.2)

The interpretation of E is that it is the price elasticity of demand of all those *currently* purchasing (those with α's above α^*) at price, p. Notice that it is close to, but is not, the price elasticity of demand. That elasticity would have to account for the fact that as p rises, α^* also rises.

Letting a subscript denote partial differentiation, it follows that

$$-S_p(p, \alpha) = q(p, \alpha),^1$$ (15B.3a)

and from Equation 15B.1c,

$$\alpha_p^* = \frac{-S_p}{S_{\alpha^*}},$$ (15B.3b)

$$\alpha_T^* = \frac{1}{S_{\alpha^*}},$$ (15B.3c)

---

[1] The derivative of the surplus function, $S(p, \alpha)$, equals minus the amount demanded in the absence of income effects. The simple explanation is that if price falls by \$1, the consumer surplus increases by the area of a rectangle with height 1 and width q. A more detailed explanation follows from the theoretical literature on "duality theory." See Varian (1984) for a detailed discussion.

and from Equation 15B.1b,

$$N_{\mathrm{p}} = -\alpha_{\mathrm{p}}^* f(\alpha^*),$$ (15B.3d)

or from Equation 15B.3b,

$$N_{\mathrm{p}} = \frac{S_{\mathrm{p}}}{S_{\alpha^*}} f(\alpha^*),$$

and from Equation 15B.1b,

$$N_{\mathrm{T}} = -\alpha_{\mathrm{T}}^* f(\alpha^*),$$

or from Equation 15B.3c,

$$N_{\mathrm{T}} = \frac{-1}{S_{\alpha^*}} f(\alpha^*),$$

and

$$Q_{\mathrm{p}} = \int_{\alpha^*}^{\bar{\alpha}} \frac{\partial q(p, \alpha)}{\partial p} f(\alpha) d\alpha - \alpha_p^* q(p, \alpha^*) f(\alpha^*),$$

or from Equation 15B.3b,

$$Q_{\mathrm{p}} = \frac{Q}{p} \int_{\alpha^*}^{\bar{\alpha}} \frac{q}{Q} \frac{p}{q} \frac{\partial q(p, \alpha)}{\partial p} f(\alpha) d\alpha + \frac{S_{\mathrm{p}}}{S_{\alpha^*}} q(p, \alpha^*) f(\alpha^*),$$

or

$$Q_{\mathrm{p}} = \frac{Q}{p} \mathrm{E} + \frac{S_{\mathrm{p}}}{S_{\alpha^*}} q(p, \alpha^*) f(\alpha^*).$$

Also,

$$Q_{\mathrm{T}} = -\alpha_{\mathrm{T}}^* q(p, \alpha^*) f(\alpha^*),$$ (15B.4a)

or from Equation 15B.3c

$$Q_{\mathrm{T}} = \frac{-1}{S_{\alpha^*}} q(p, \alpha^*) f(\alpha^*).$$ (15B.4b)

To find the profit-maximizing p and T, take derivatives of Equation 15B.1a with respect to p and T to obtain

$$N_{\mathrm{p}} T + Q(p, T) + (p - C) Q_{\mathrm{p}} = 0,$$ (15B.5a)

and

$$N_T T + N + (p - C)Q_T = 0. \tag{15B.5b}$$

Using (15B.2) to (15B.4), we can rewrite Equation 15B.5 as

$$\frac{S_p}{S_{\alpha*}} f(\alpha^*)T + Q(p, T) + (p - C)\left[\frac{QE}{p} + \frac{S_p}{S_{\alpha*}} q(p, \alpha^*)f(\alpha^*)\right] = 0, \tag{15B.6a}$$

and

$$\frac{-1}{S_{\alpha*}} f(\alpha^*) T + N + (p - C)\left(\frac{-1}{S_{\alpha*}}\right) q(p, \alpha^*)f(\alpha^*) = 0. \tag{15B.6b}$$

To eliminate T from Equation 15B.6, multiply Equation 15B.6b by S_p and add Equation 15B.6a to find

$$Q(p, T) + NS_p + (p - C)\frac{Q}{p} E = 0. \tag{15B.7}$$

Recall that $S_p = -q(p, \alpha^*)$; hence (15B.7) can be written as

$$Q(p, T)\left(1 + \frac{p - C}{p} E\right) = N q(p, \alpha^*), \tag{15B.8}$$

or

$$\left(1 + \frac{p - C}{p} E\right) = \frac{q(p, \alpha^*)}{\bar{q}},$$

where $\bar{q} = \dfrac{Q(p, T)}{N}$.

To eliminate $(p - C)$ from Equation 15B.6, multiply Equation 15B.6a by

$$\frac{1}{S_{\alpha*}} q(p, \alpha^*)f(\alpha^*)$$

and Equation 15B.6b by

$$\frac{Q}{p} E + \frac{S_p}{S_{\alpha*}} q(p, \alpha^*)f(\alpha)$$

and add to obtain

$$T\left[\frac{1}{S_{\alpha*}} q(p, \alpha^*)f(\alpha^*) \frac{S_p}{S_{\alpha*}} f(\alpha^*)\right] - T\left[\frac{Q}{p} E + \frac{S_p}{S_{\alpha*}} q(p, \alpha^*)f(\alpha^*) \frac{f(\alpha^*)}{S_{\alpha*}}\right]$$

$$+ Q(p, T)\frac{1}{S_{\alpha*}} q(p, \alpha^*)f(\alpha^*) + N\left[\frac{Q}{p} E + \frac{S_p}{S_{\alpha*}} q(p, \alpha^*)f(\alpha^*)\right] = 0,$$

or

$$T \frac{-Q}{p} E \frac{f(\alpha^*)}{S_{\alpha^*}} + \frac{f(\alpha^*)}{S_{\alpha^*}} [q(p, \alpha^*) Q(p, T) + NS_p q(p, \alpha^*)] + \frac{NQ(p, T)}{p} E = 0,$$

or recognizing $S_p = -q(p, \alpha^*)$,

$$T \frac{-Q}{p} E \frac{f(\alpha^*)}{S_{\alpha^*}} + \frac{f(\alpha^*)q(p, \alpha^*)}{S_{\alpha^*}} N \left[\frac{Q}{N} - q(p, \alpha^*) \right] + \frac{NQ(p, T)}{p} E = 0.$$

Multiply by p/NQ to obtain

$$T \frac{-E}{N} \frac{f(\alpha^*)}{S_{\alpha^*}} - \beta [q^* - \bar{q}(p, \alpha^*)] + E = 0, \qquad (15B.9)$$

where

$$\beta = f(\alpha^*) \frac{q(p, \alpha^*)}{S_{\alpha^*}} \frac{p}{Q(p, T)} \geq 0,$$

and

$$\bar{q} = \frac{Q(p, T)}{N}.$$

Equations 15B.8 and 15B.9 are the two first-order conditions for p and T. Notice that $E > 0$ and $\dfrac{f(\alpha^*)}{S_{\alpha^*}} < 0$, hence from Equation 15B.9, it follows that

$$\text{sign } T = \text{sign } \{-E - \beta [\bar{q} - q(p, \alpha^*)]\}.[2]$$

---

[2] *Sign T* means the sign (positive or negative) of *T*. If *T* were negative, the monopolist would somehow have to prevent a flood of nonusers (and small users) from receiving the lump-sum payment, *T*. If it could not, the optimal *T* would have to be nonnegative.

TWO-PART TARIFF WHEN TWO PRODUCTS ARE SOLD

Suppose that the two-part tariff is being considered by a manufacturer of a mimeograph machine. The manufacturer wants to charge price T for the machine and price p for the ink that is used. A condition of the sale is that users must buy all their ink from the manufacturer.[1] The unit cost of the ink is C, and the unit cost of the machine is M. The manufacturer's profits are now no longer given by Equation 15A.4, but by

$$\text{Profit} = N(T - M) + (p - C)Q(p, T). \qquad (15C.1)$$

The first-order condition associated with the derivative of profit with respect to p remains as in Equation 15A.5. A derivation like that leading to Equation 15B.9 shows that the first-order condition associated with the derivative of profit with respect to T implies:

$$\text{sign } (T - M) = \text{sign } [-E - \beta(\bar{q} - q^*)], \qquad (15C.2)$$

where $\beta \geq 0$.

Equation 15C.2 determines whether the optimal price for the machine, T, is greater or less than its cost of production, M. Note that the first term in the bracket on the right side of Equation 15C.2 is $-E$, which is a positive number (recall that E is a type of price elasticity that is always negative) that becomes larger as the possibility of substitution away from the product increases. The positive effect from this first term means that T tends to exceed M. However, the second term has precisely the opposite effect, in general. Focusing on the second term, note that, as in Equation 15A.7, the critical distinction is between the average purchase, $\bar{q}$, and the marginal purchase, q^*.

In the normal case, in which q^* is less than $\bar{q}$, the second term in the bracket on the right side of Equation 15C.2 is negative. This tends to make the optimal price, T, *less* than the cost, M.[2] Thus the sign of $T - M$ is ambiguous in the normal case since the

---

[1] This actually occurred when A. B. Dick sold its mimeograph machines, around 1900.

[2] If the optimal T is less than M, the monopolist might consider imposing a minimum purchase requirement on the tied good.

two terms on the right side of Equation (15C.2) are of the opposite signs. Therefore, it should not be viewed as unusual if a monopolist sells a machine for less than its cost. Equation 15C.2 shows that such a policy tends to be more likely, the greater the difference between the marginal and average purchaser and the lower the substitution effect (the smaller is E in absolute value). If consumer diversity is extremely high (as measured by the difference between the average and marginal purchaser) and consumers are not price sensitive to the usage fee, the machine's price will be less than its cost.

If all consumers are alike, it follows from Equation 15C.2 that the price of the machine, T, exceeds the cost of the machine, M. Again, this must be true because when all consumers are identical, the optimal pricing is that p equals C; therefore all profits come through T. Hence, it must be that T exceeds M.

NONLINEAR PRICING WITH AN EXAMPLE

With nonlinear pricing, the consumer faces the following problem:

$$\max U(q, X) \tag{15D.1}$$

$$\text{subject to} \quad E(q) + X = Y,$$

where $E(q)$ is the total expense when q units are consumed of Good 1, X represents all other goods whose per-unit price is normalized to 1, Y is the consumer's income, and U is the consumer's utility function.

Suppose that there are N different consumers. The maximization problem facing a firm that wishes to offer a nonlinear pricing schedule that maximizes its profits can be written as follows:

$$\text{Choose } E(q) \text{ to maximize } \sum_i (E(q_i) - Cq_i) \tag{15D.2}$$

subject to consumer i maximizes as in (15D.1), $i = 1 \ldots N,$

$$C = \text{constant per unit cost, and}$$
$$q_i = \text{amount consumed by consumer } i.$$

The firm chooses $E(q)$ to maximize profit, which equals the sum of the profits made by selling to each consumer, subject to the condition that each consumer maximizes his or her utility. (It immediately follows that each consumer who purchases a good must be better off by doing so than by foregoing consumption of the good entirely.)

The solution to the problem posed in (15D.2) is complicated (Katz 1983, Spence 1977, Tirole 1988, Chapter 3). Rather than present the general solution, we illustrate some of the key ideas that arise in nonlinear pricing through an example.

Consider the problem discussed in the chapter of a firm that faces two types of consumers, Types 1 and 2, and offers two two-part tariffs (T_1, p_1) and (T_2, p_2).[1] Suppose that there is one Type 1 and one Type 2 consumer. If it costs C to produce one unit of

---

[1] The optimal nonlinear price can be more complicated than the two two-part tariffs that are considered. See Tirole (1988, Chapter 3).

the good, and if the Type 1 consumer chooses (T_1, p_1) and the Type 2 consumer chooses (T_2, p_2), then profits equal

$$T_1 + (p_1 - C)q_1(p_1) + T_2 + (p_2 - C)q_2(p_2), \tag{15D.3}$$

where $q_i(p_i)$ = demand curve of Type i. The important additional requirement of the equilibrium in this problem is that Type 1 prefers (T_1, p_1) to (T_2, p_2) and vice versa for Type 2. Let $U_i(T, p)$ be the utility of Type i, which depends on T and p. The self-selection constraints are

$$U_1(T_1, p_1) \geq U_1(T_2, p_2), \text{ and} \tag{15D.4}$$
$$U_2(T_1, p_1) \leq U_2(T_2, p_2).$$

Let $S_i(p)$ be the consumer surplus of consumer type i at price p in the absence of a lump-sum fee. Then utility can be written as $U_i(T, P) = S_i(p) - T$. The pricing problem facing the firm is as follows:

$$\text{Choose } T_1, p_1, T_2, p_2 \text{ to maximize} \tag{15D.5}$$
$$T_1 + (p_1 - C)q_1(p_1) + T_2 + (p_2 - C)q_2(p_2)$$

subject to $\quad S_1(p_1) - T_1 \geq S_1(p_2) - T_2,$
$\qquad\qquad S_2(p_1) - T_1 \leq S_2(p_2) - T_2$
$\qquad\qquad S_1(p_1) - T_1 \geq 0$
$\qquad\qquad S_2(p_2) - T_2 \geq 0.$

The objective function in (15D.5) is the total profits that the firm earns from charging a lump sum, T_1 and T_2, and charging price p_1 when quantity q_1 is consumed and price p_2 when quantity q_2 is consumed. The constraints in (15D.5) are the consumers' self-selection constraints. The first constraint guarantees that the utility of Type 1 with a tariff (T_1, p_1) exceeds the utility from the tariff (T_2, p_2). The second constraint guarantees that the utility of Type 2 at (T_2, p_2) is greater than at (T_1, p_1). These two constraints guarantee that Type 1 chooses (T_1, p_1) as its optimal tariff and Type 2 chooses (T_2, p_2) as its optimal tariff. The last two constraints in (15D.5) simply guarantee that consumers of each type have positive utility. (It is possible that the optimal solution involves satisfying only one consumer type; the other consumer type simply does not consume the good. We focus here on the case in which it is optimal for both types of consumers to purchase the good.)

To illustrate the principles involved in nonlinear pricing, consider the case in which the demand of the Type 2 consumer is larger than that of the Type 1 consumer. In fact, assume that the demand of Type 2 is larger by a factor λ $(\lambda > 1)$ than that of the Type 1 (that is, $q_2(p) = \lambda q_1(p)$). This guarantees that the demand curve of Type 2 lies to the right of the demand curve of Type 1.

Figure 15D.1 shows the indifference curves of consumers in (T, p) space—that is, the combinations of T and p that leave a consumer indifferent. As T falls, p rises along an indifference curve; consumers trade off a higher T for a lower p. They receive higher utility as they move toward indifference curves closer to the origin. Along an indifference

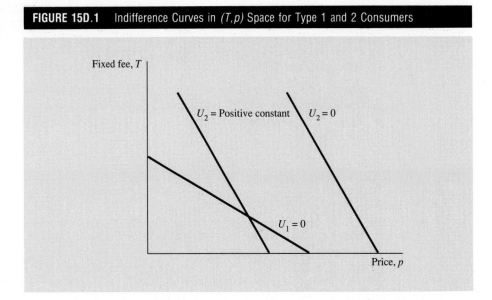

FIGURE 15D.1   Indifference Curves in *(T,p)* Space for Type 1 and 2 Consumers

curve, when p falls, the amount by which T rises depends on the amount that consumers purchase. Those who purchase a large amount of the good are willing to pay a much higher fixed fee as the per-unit price of the good falls. Therefore, as Figure 15D.1 shows, the indifference curve for Type 2 is steeper than the indifference curve for Type 1 when the curves cross.

Along the indifference curve at which Type 2 is just indifferent ($U_2 = 0$) between purchasing the good or not, Type 1 does not purchase the good. This follows because at any price, p, the surplus enjoyed by the Type 2 is higher than it is for Type 1. Therefore along its zero utility curve, Type 2 must pay a fixed fee to totally exhaust its surplus. Type 1 would rather forego consumption of the good than pay such a high fixed fee. Thus the relative position of the zero utility curves for each type are as depicted in Figure 15D.1. The equation of the indifference curve for $U_2 = 0$ is simply $T_2 = S_2(p)$, and that for $U_1 = 0$ is $T_1 - S_1(p)$.

We can now derive the solution to the problem posed in (15D.5). The monopolist's optimal solution involves driving the utility of at least one of the two consumer types down to zero. If both types have positive utilities, the monopolist can raise the fixed fees, continue to sell its product, and still make more money. The monopolist thus continues to raise the fixed fees until one type's utility is driven to zero. Which type will that be? Suppose it were Type 2 whose utility is driven to zero. That means that Type 2 is on its zero utility curve in Figure 15D.1. Where, then, could Type 1 be? Type 1's utility is negative along the $U_2 = 0$ curve; therefore, the only (T, p) combinations that will keep Type 1 in the market are those that lie below the $U_2 = 0$ curve. But if there were a two-part tariff (T, p) that lay below the $U_2 = 0$ curve, Type 2 would prefer that point to the one on the $U_2 = 0$ curve. This proves that in the optimal solution, provided that both Type 1 and Type 2 are purchasing, the solution cannot involve zero utility for Type 2.

FIGURE 15D.2   Possible Equilibrium Configuration

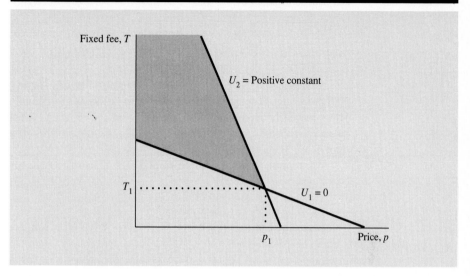

The logic establishes that in the optimal solution involving both consumer types, the utility of Type 1 must be zero.

If (T_1, p_1) lies along the curve $U_1 = 0$, where will (T_2, p_2) be? The answer is that (T_2, p_2) cannot lie below the curve $U_1 = 0$. Otherwise Type 1 would prefer that two-part tariff to its own. The self-selection constraints guarantee that the utility of Type 2 at its two-part tariff cannot be less than the utility at (T_1, p_1). Hence, (T_2, p_2) can only lie within the shaded region of Figure 15D.2. The monopolist wants to extract as much surplus as possible from Type 2 and still satisfy the self-selection constraints. Therefore, (T_2, p_2) lies along the upper part of Type 2's indifference curve that passes through (T_1, p_1). Type 1 would always prefer to remain at (T_1, p_1) rather than at any (T_2, p_2) point that lies above the $U_1 = 0$ curve and along the U_2 curve through (T_1, p_1) and Type 2 is indifferent between (T_1, p_1) and points on its indifference curve through (T_1, p_1).

These insights help solve the problem in (15D.5). We have established two facts. One is that the utility of Type 1 is zero in the optimal solution so that $T_1 = S_1(p)$. Also the utility of Type 2 at (T_1, p_1) must equal its utility at (T_2, p_2). These two facts imply

$$S_1(p_1) - T_1 = 0,$$

and

(15D.6)

$$S_2(p_1) - T_1 = S_2(P_2) - T_2.$$

We can solve for T_1 and T_2 in terms of p_1 and p_2 from Equation 15D.6 and substitute into (15D.5) to reexpress the problem facing the firm as follows:

Choose p_1 and p_2 to maximize

$$S_1(p_1) + (p_1 - C)q_1(p_1) + S_2(p_2) - S_2(p_1) + S_1(p_1) + (p_2 - C)q_2(p_2). \quad (15D.7)$$

By assumption, for any p, $\lambda q_1(p) = q_2(p)$, and therefore $\lambda S_1(p) = S_2(p)$, and so we can rewrite (15D.7) as

$$S_1(p_1) + (p_1 - C)q_1(p_1) + \lambda S_1(p_2) - \lambda S_1(p_1) \qquad (15D.8)$$
$$+ S_1(p_1) + \lambda(p_2 - C)q_1(p_2).$$

Notice that $(p_1 - C)q_1(p_1)$ is just the profits that a simple monopolist earns at price p_1. Let us refer to the expression $(p - C)q_1(p)$ as $SP(p)$ (simple profits). The function $SP(p)$ reaches a maximum, as shown in Figure 15D.3, at p^*, which is the price a simple monopolist would charge. To the left of p^*, the slope of $SP(p)$ is positive, and to the right of p^*, the slope of $SP(p)$ is negative.

We are now ready to choose p_1 and p_2 to maximize Equation 15D.8. The optimal conditions are

$$\frac{d}{dp}[SP(p_1) + (2 - \lambda)S_1(p_1)] = 0, \qquad (15D.9a)$$

and

$$\frac{d}{dp}[SP(p_2) + \lambda S_1(p_2)] = 0. \qquad (15B.9b)$$

Since $\dfrac{dS_1}{dp}(p_1) = -q_1(p_1)$ and $\dfrac{dS_2}{dp}(p_2) = -q_2(p_2)$,[2] we can write (15D.9) as follows:

$$\frac{d}{dp}[SP(p_1)] = (2 - \lambda)q_1(p_1), \qquad (15D.10a)$$

and

$$\frac{d}{dp}[SP(p_2)] = \lambda q_1(p_2), \qquad (15D.10b)$$

where $\lambda > 1$.

If $\lambda > 2$, Equation 15D.10a tells us that p_1 should be chosen where the slope of $SP(p)$ is negative; that is, p_1 will exceed p^*. Equation 15D.10b tells us that p_2 should be chosen where the slope of $SP(p)$ is positive; hence p_2 will be less than p^*. In other words, when the demand of the Type 2 customer is large ($\lambda > 2$) relative to that of the Type 1 customer, the Type 1 customer is charged a very high price—indeed, a price above the simple profit-maximizing price—so that Type 2 can be charged a low price and a high lump sum. Although profits are foregone from Type 1 by charging it a price

---

[2] As price falls by \$1, the additional surplus precisely equals the quantity consumed (ignoring income effects).

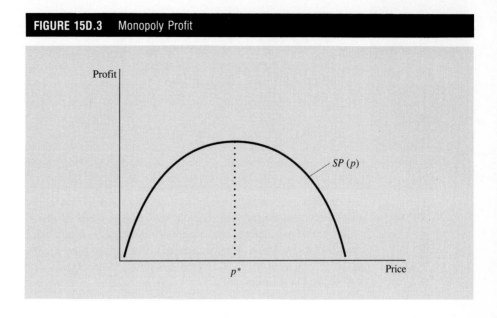

FIGURE 15D.3   Monopoly Profit

above p^*, profits are more than made up from Type 2. Type 1's price is high to prevent making the (T_1, p_1) tariff attractive to Type 2, thereby allowing Type 2 to be charged a high T_2. By using two two-part tariffs, it is possible to separate Types 1 and 2 and limit the problem of having to pass along the low p_2 to Type 1 and the low T_1 to Type 2.

When $\lambda < 2$ (recall that λ always exceeds 1 because, by assumption, the Type 2 customer buys more than the Type 1 customer), Equation 15D.10a shows that at p_1 the slope of $SP(p)$ is positive. This means that $p_1 < p^*$. From Figure 15D.2, we know that $p_2 \leq p_1$. Hence, $p_2 < p_1 < p^*$.

There is one additional insight regarding the optimal solution. The most efficient method of price discrimination against Type 2—and one that does not interfere with self-selection by Type 1—is to set price at marginal cost and charge a high lump-sum fee. Hence $p_2 = C$ in the profit-maximizing solution.

In summary, the optimal tariff depends upon how large λ is. The per unit price to Type 1 always exceeds that to Type 2, and the fixed fee to Type 1 is always less than that to Type 2. The per unit price to Type 2 equals marginal cost. The presence of Type 1 constrains the T_2 and p_2 that Type 2 can be charged. The larger the relative demand of Type 2 (higher λ), the more profitable it is to forego profits on Type 1 (that is, charge p_1 in excess of p^*) in order to charge a high lump-sum fee and low per unit price to Type 2. Type 2 is better off when Type 1 is present in the market than when it is not. From the solution to (15D.5), we know that $U_2(T_2, p_2) > 0$, but if Type 2 was the only consumer the optimal two-part tariff would extract all consumer surplus from it, and U_2 would be zero. Consumer diversity helps those with the greater willingness to buy the good. In contrast, Type 1's utility is completely unaffected by the presence of Type 2. The moral is that consumer diversity makes it harder to capture the surplus of inframarginal consumers.

QUALITY CHOICE OF A MONOPOLIST

The problem of optimal range of qualities is similar to that involving the optimal choice of two two-part tariffs; thus the solution involves many of the same insights developed in that problem. Suppose that there are two consumers, Type 1 and Type 2. Each consumer desires at most 1 unit. We focus on the case in which each consumer consumes 1 unit in the optimal solution. Type 2 values quality more than Type 1. The monopolist's problem can be written as follows:

$$\text{Choose } (p_1, z_1) \text{ and } (p_2, z_2) \text{ to maximize profit,} \qquad (15\text{E}.1)$$

where

$$\text{Profit} = [p_1 - C_1] + [p_2 - C_2]$$

subject to

$$U_1(p_1, z_1) \geq U_1(p_2, z_2),$$
$$U_2(p_2, z_2) \geq U_2(p_1, z_1),$$
$$U_1(p_1, z_1) \geq 0,$$
$$U_2(p_2, z_2) \geq 0.$$

where p_i = price of good i, z_i = quality of good i, and C_i = constant marginal cost of good i. The profit function is straightforward because by assumption only 1 unit of the good is consumed by each consumer. The constraints in Equation 15E.1 are the self-selection constraints that guarantee that the Type 1 consumer prefers consuming the combination (p_1, z_1) to the combination (p_2, z_2) and similarly that the Type 2 consumer prefers (p_2, z_2) to (p_1, z_1). The last two constraints in (15E.1) simply guarantee that each consumer is better off consuming the goods than not doing so.

Consider the shapes of the indifference curves of consumers in price-quality space illustrated in the figure on p. 501. Along any indifference curve, as price increases, quality must also increase if a consumer is to remain at the same level of utility. Therefore, indifference curves slope up. Holding quality constant, the utility levels of consumers increase with lower prices. Since the Type 2 consumer values quality more than the Type 1 consumer, the slope of the indifference curve for Type 2 is steeper than that for Type 1 when the curves cross. The reason is that for any given increase in quality, price must rise by a greater amount for Type 2 than for Type 1 in order to leave the consumer at the same level of indifference. That follows because Type 2 values quality more than Type 1. As in the solution to the problem in (15D.5), the solution here involves the utility

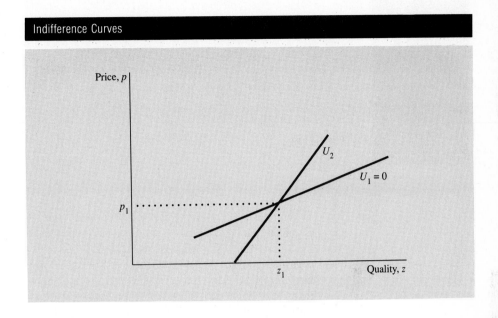

Indifference Curves

of either Type 1 or Type 2 being set to zero. By the same logic used to analyze the problem in (15D.5), it follows that the utility of Type 1 is driven to zero in the optimal solution. It also follows that the optimal (p_2, z_2) must lie along the indifference curve of Type 2 that goes through the optimal point (p_1, z_1). That is true because the self-selection constraints require that Type 2 achieve a utility level no lower than the level it could achieve if it consumed at (p_1, z_1). Using exactly the same logic as before, it also follows that the equilibrium (p_2, z_2) can lie only above the $U_1 = 0$ line. If (p_2, z_2) lay below the $U_1 = 0$ line along the U_2 indifference curve through (p_1, z_1), then Type 1 would prefer (p_2, z_2) to (p_1, z_1). Hence, one of the self-selection constraints would be violated.

Figure 15E.1 shows that one consequence of a lower z_1 is that it enables a monopolist to drive the utility of Type 2 down further, because as one moves to the left in the figure, utility falls. Because the monopolist derives the most surplus from Type 2 (who values the good the most), it may well be profitable for the monopolist to have more flexibility in extracting surplus from Type 2 than it could achieve by choosing z_1 at a high level. In other words, by choosing (p_1, z_1) down to the left in Figure 15E.1, the monopolist provides Type 2 with a very poor alternative to (p_2, z_2) and can therefore charge a high price, p_2, for a high-quality product. Intuition thus suggests that when a monopolist can choose product quality, it tends to spread out the quality spectrum so as not to provide good substitutes to consumers who value high quality. In this way, the monopolist extracts more money (or, equivalently, lowers Type 2's utility more) than it could if its lower quality product had enough quality to be a close substitute to its higher quality product.

CHAPTER 16

VERTICAL INTEGRATION AND VERTICAL RESTRICTIONS

> **O**utside the firm, price movements direct production, which is co-ordinated through a series of exchange transactions on the market. Within a firm, these market transactions are eliminated and in place of the complicated market structure with exchange transactions is substituted the entrepreneur-co-ordinator, who directs production. It is clear that these are alternative methods of co-ordinating production.
>
> RONALD COASE (1952, 333)

A firm that participates in more than one successive stage of the production or distribution of goods or services is **vertically integrated.** Nonvertically integrated firms buy the inputs or services they need for their production or distribution processes from other firms. A nonintegrated firm may write long-term, binding contracts with the firms with which it deals, in which it specifies price and other terms. Such contractual restraints are called **vertical restrictions.** For example, manufacturers commonly restrict their distributors by determining their sales territories, setting inventory requirements, and, where legal, setting the minimum retail price they can charge.

Some firms choose to vertically integrate and perform all production and distribution activities themselves. Others partially vertically integrate. For example, they may do all the producing themselves but rely on others to market the products. Some firms are not vertically integrated, but buy from a small number of suppliers or sell through a small number of distributors.[1] These firms often write complex contracts that restrict the actions of those with whom they deal. These vertical restraints can approximate the outcome from vertically merging. Other firms buy in the open market

---

[1] Any firm that engages in successive steps in its production process is at least partially integrated. For example, a restaurant that bakes its own pies instead of buying them ready-made is partially integrated. Thus, most firms are at least partially integrated.

from any number of anonymous firms. For example, they may buy wheat from a wheat broker without knowing who grew it or using any formal long-term contracts. Such firms place no restrictions on their suppliers.

A firm's decision to vertically integrate, write complex contracts with vertical restrictions, or rely on markets is a basic strategic decision. It affects the subsequent pricing and promotional behavior of that firm and other related firms. Chapter 2 notes that a firm may choose to vertically integrate because it is cost-effective to do so. This chapter expands upon that analysis and examines vertical restrictions. Vertical restrictions between manufacturers and distributors are of particular interest and have been the subject of lengthy antitrust litigation. This chapter explores the procompetitive as well as the anticompetitive reasons for such restrictions.

The analysis begins by examining why some firms vertically integrate, whereas others do not. That analysis provides a story of the life-cycle of firms, in which they integrate at certain times and not at others. We then examine how some firms use vertical restrictions to achieve many of the advantages of vertical integration. Next there is a brief discussion of the relevant antitrust laws. Finally, we present some empirical evidence on franchising, an increasingly important vertical relationship, and the motives for vertical integration and vertical restrictions. We analyze four key issues:

1. Why do firms vertically integrate? Why not rely on the market (other firms) to supply inputs and distribute products?

2. What should public policy be towards vertical integration? We know that horizontal mergers sometimes have anticompetitive effects; is the same true for vertical mergers?

3. Why do some manufacturers establish vertical restraints that give their distributors some of their monopoly power?

4. What should public policy be toward vertical restraints? Do these restrictions necessarily hurt retailers and consumers?

■ THE REASONS FOR AND AGAINST VERTICAL INTEGRATION

If you want something done right, do it yourself.

He is a slave of the greatest slave, who serves nothing but himself.

Most of the reasons why firms choose to vertically integrate have to do with reducing costs or eliminating a market externality. In general, a firm needs a good reason to vertically integrate, for it involves substantial costs.

There are three chief costs of vertical integration. First, the cost of supplying its own factors of production or distributing its own product may be higher for a firm that vertically integrates than one that depends on competitive markets, which serve these needs efficiently. Second, as a firm gets larger, the difficulty and cost of managing it increase. The advantage of dealing with a competitive market is that someone else supervises production. Third, there are often substantial legal fees to merging with another firm. These may include defending the merger before a government agency such as the Federal Trade Commission or the Justice Department.

Because of these costs, firms vertically integrate only if the benefits outweigh the costs. There are at least six major advantages to integrating[2]:

1. A firm may lower its transaction costs by vertically integrating. For example, the transaction costs of buying from or selling to other companies are avoided.

2. A firm may be able to avoid government restrictions, regulations, and taxes by vertically integrating. Examples of government interventions include price controls, regulations that restrict profit rates (see Chapter 23), and taxes on revenues or profits.

3. A firm may vertically integrate to increase or create its market power. For example, a sole supplier of a vital input may *vertically integrate forward*, buying the manufacturing firms, to monopolize the final product market, and thereby increase its monopoly profits. Further, by vertically integrating, a firm may create or increase its monopoly profits by being able to price discriminate, eliminate competition, or foreclose entry.

4. A victim of another firm's market power may vertically integrate to eliminate that power. For example, around the turn of the century, dairy farmers contended that they faced a single processor that bought their milk at a low, monopsonistic price. To raise the price of milk, dairy farmers vertically integrated forward to form their own processors.

5. A firm may vertically integrate to assure itself a steady supply of a key input. To do so, the firm may *vertically integrate backwards*, buying or building the capacity to produce that input. Delivery problems may thus be reduced, because it is often easier to exchange information within a firm than between firms.

6. A firm may vertically integrate to correct market failures due to externalities by internalizing those externalities. For example, McDonald's, by owning or controlling all its restaurants, can ensure a uniform quality, which results in a positive reputation (externality). Consumers, as they travel around the country know that they can expect a certain minimum quality at any of this chain's restaurants.

The following sections consider each of these issues in more depth.

Integration to Lower Transaction Costs

It is well known what a middle man is: he is a man who bamboozles one party and plunders the other. —BENJAMIN DISRAELI

Chapter 2 contained an extensive discussion of the forces that lead a firm to perform productive activities itself rather than rely upon other firms. One of the most important reasons had to do with *transaction costs,* such as the costs of writing and enforcing contracts (Williamson 1975, Klein, Crawford, and Alchian 1978). When such costs are

---

[2] See Perry (1989) for an excellent survey that discusses these and other explanations.

high, one firm may take advantage of another through **opportunistic behavior.** These opportunities for exploitation are greater when one firm is wholly dependent on another. For example, to respond to a sudden increase in demand, an automobile manufacturer needs more supplies. If there is only one supplier of a critical part, that supplier can raise its prices, and the auto manufacturer has nowhere to turn in the short run. Even when such complications and dependencies can be foreseen, it may be difficult to structure a contract that completely removes the incentives for either firm to behave opportunistically towards the other. For example, the Intel Corporation designs and sells many embedded control-function semiconductor chips, which are customized to do one job quickly and well. But buyers who start using these chips in their products have only one source, because Intel is not expected to allow other companies to produce the new chips. As one observer noted, "If they can get customers to make the transition, they now have captives."[3]

Chapter 2 explains that one response to these high transaction costs is for a firm to vertically integrate and perform the activity itself. Such vertical integration transforms the monitoring problem from monitoring between firms to monitoring employees within the firm. Within a firm, a boss can coordinate the decisions of different divisions and can monitor workers in ways that are not possible when firms are completely independent. On the other hand, an employee on a fixed salary may work less hard than an owner of a subcontracting firm.

The theory in Chapter 2 holds that the desirability of vertical integration is higher, the higher the transaction costs of using the market place. There are four types of transactions in which transaction costs are likely to be substantial enough to make vertical integration desirable: they involve *specialized assets, uncertainty* that makes monitoring difficult, *information,* or *extensive coordination.*

Specialized Assets. A **specialized asset** is one tailor-made for one or a few specific buyers. To illustrate why the use of specialized assets provides a reason to integrate, consider a supplier that has custom-designed its facility to suit a particular buyer's needs. That supplier will be at the mercy of the buyer should any disputes arise subsequent to the construction of the supplier's plant. In this case, we expect to see vertical integration because of asset specificity, which takes three main forms involving (Williamson 1985, 95–96): specific physical capital, specific human capital, and site-specific capital.

Specific physical capital includes buildings and machines that can be used for only one or a few buyers. As an example, suppose specific dies are needed on a machine press to produce a particular part for one buyer. If the supplier that owns the machine press also owns the dies, there is a chance for opportunistic behavior: the supplier can raise the price, and the buyer may find it prohibitively expensive to switch suppliers in the short run. If the buyer owns the dies and has other firms bid to provide the machine-press services, no opportunistic problems arise. In this case, vertical integration is not necessary. Only **quasi-vertical integration** (or quasi-integration), where the firm owns the specific

---

[3] Slater, Michael, editor of *Microprocessor Report,* quoted in Clark, Don. 1988. "Intel Corp. Planning New Chip Campaign." *San Francisco Chronicle,* April 2, B1 and B20.

physical asset (the dies), is required to avoid opportunistic behavior. If the machine press itself is unique, however, this method cannot be used, and vertical integration may be necessary.

A firm may need specially trained workers *(specific human capital)*, such as accountants, economists, or engineers, to produce a particular product. If it uses outside contractors as opposed to its own employees, opportunistic behavior is possible. For example, a contractor who knows that a firm is facing a deadline may demand more money or lower the quality of its output to meet its own deadline. Vertical integration in the form of an employment relationship can avoid such problems.

If successive stages of a production process must be located adjacent to each other (that is, they involve *site-specific capital*), vertical integration is likely. The reason is that if a manufacturing firm stops demanding the input of a supplying firm, that supplying firm must relocate, which can be extremely costly. Opportunistic behavior can be avoided by integrating. The empirical section at the end of this chapter discusses three studies of the importance of specific physical assets and site-specific capital in the automobile and airplane manufacturing industries and in manufacturing as a whole.

Uncertainty and Monitoring.   As an example of the second transaction-cost reason for vertical integration, uncertainty, suppose that it is hard for a buyer to monitor the quality of the product a supplier provides. For example, imagine a durable machine whose useful life cannot be determined for many years. In such a case, the best way to monitor quality may be to observe the method by which the machine is constructed. Because quality controls on construction may be hard for an outside firm to monitor, vertical integration often occurs in such situations.

Transactions Involving Information.   The third transaction-cost reason for vertical integration concerns transactions involving information. It may be difficult to structure a contract that gives the supplying firm the appropriate incentives to develop the information. For example, if one firm pays another firm a fixed fee to obtain information on newly developing markets, the hired firm does not have an incentive to work hard at the margin to uncover all the information, and the buyer has no way of determining if the supplier did a good job. As Chapter 2 shows, disputes on payments may well arise and be difficult to resolve. Such problems can be avoided by vertical integration.

Extensive Coordination.   The fourth transaction-cost reason to vertically integrate is to facilitate extensive coordination. Network industries, such as railroads, provide an example. A railroad depends heavily on developing feeder traffic for its through routes. Although it might be possible to devise a price system for each link in the network, such a system would be inherently very complicated. As a result, there is an incentive for railroads to merge to deal with these coordination problems (Carlton and Klamer 1983). The same incentive arises in the airline industry.

Notice that *technological conditions alone do not explain the vertical integration of a firm*. For example, a common case of vertical integration is a steel mill that produces its own pig iron. The molten pig iron is run directly into the steel furnace. Although it is inefficient to allow the pig iron to cool down and then ship it to a steel furnace where it must be heated again, it is not necessary that one firm produce both pig iron and steel:

EXAMPLE 16.1

BIOTECH FIRMS

Over time, the decision whether to vertically integrate can change. For example, a pharmaceutical company that decides to quickly enter the new biotechnology field of genetic engineering has several options. It can start its own research program, merge with an existing (typically small, start-up) firm, or engage in a joint venture with another firm. Starting its own new research program takes a long time. In the interim, it may pursue one of the other two options.

In 1978, only six established firms had in-house biotechnology research and development (R&D) programs, although many established firms have started internal R&D programs since then. Even by 1981, most established firms relied on new biotech R&D firms and other external sources for R&D. All of 39 large U.S. pharmaceutical companies had in-house biotech R&D programs and agreements with new biotech R&D firms, nonprofit organizations, and universities, or with other established companies. Only one did not have an agreement with a new biotech R&D firm, and most had multiple agreements.

Similarly, a new biotech R&D firm must decide whether to manufacture in-house or rely on pharmaceutical companies to manufacture and sell its new discoveries. One recent survey found that 78 percent of new biotech firms did their manufacturing in-house, and some are even considering integrating forward into distribution.

A statistical analysis of R&D projects of the world's 50 largest pharmaceutical companies in 1982 indicates that opportunistic behavior and experience are important in determining whether pharmaceutical firms engage in internal research or in joint ventures. Because a research project often provides a starting point for later research, each firm in an agreement is vulnerable to opportunistic behavior by the other firm. For example, if there are few R&D firms, a pharmaceutical firm may find it difficult to obtain a new partner for a follow-up project if the first partner proves unsuitable. As a result, an opportunistic R&D firm may demand a larger share of the joint profits to keep it from pulling out of the follow-up project. The statistical study finds that a decrease in the average number of R&D firms in a product area from 6 to 5 firms increases the probability that an established pharmaceutical firm engages in internal R&D by 7 percent, presumably to protect itself against opportunistic behavior.

The statistical analysis also concludes that extra experience makes it substantially easier for firms to engage in in-house R&D. Thus, as the number of other R&D companies decreases and as a pharmaceutical company's experience increases, it is much more likely to engage in in-house research. It is no surprise then, that pharmaceutical companies are increasingly conducting their own research.

SOURCE: Pisano (1988).

two firms can locate side by side. However, because pig iron production and steel production are so interrelated, there is a potential for opportunistic behavior if two separate firms are involved. Therefore, vertical integration often arises when production processes at different stages are closely interrelated. See Example 16.1.

EXAMPLE 16.2

OWN YOUR OWN STEEL MILL

A legal case, *Perlman v. Feldmann* (219 F.2d 173, Cert. denied), illustrates the incentive for vertical integration in the presence of rationing. Feldmann controlled a majority of the stock of Newport Steel Corporation, which produced steel products. In 1950 steel supplies were becoming tight, apparently due to fear of Korean War price controls. Feldmann arranged for the sale of a controlling interest of Newport's stock to the Wilport Corporation, which was a user of steel. Wilport, by obtaining controlling interest, would be able to control the allocation of steel (to itself) in times of shortages.

The plaintiff in this case was a shareholder who complained that the high price Feldmann received for his shares ($20 versus $12 for noncontrolling shares) represented a value that other shareholders were entitled to, since it represented the value of steel at uncontrolled market prices. The Court ruled that Feldmann was not entitled to receive the entire value of the right to control allocation, but was only entitled to his pro-rata share of that value. Even though Feldmann was only entitled to his pro-rata share, his activities reflect the incentive created by price controls to vertically integrate.

Integration to Avoid Government Intervention

The only thing that saves us from the bureaucracy is its inefficiency.
EUGENE MCCARTHY

Government intervention can affect incentives to vertically integrate in a variety of ways. For example, the government has placed *price controls* on steel products several times since World War II, which set a maximum price that may be charged for steel. Under binding price controls, a firm that buys steel is unable to purchase all the steel that it wants at the controlled price because producers choose to ration steel rather than supply as much as is demanded at the controlled price. A firm that badly needs more steel for its production process may find that it pays to purchase the company that supplies it with steel. Because transactions within a company are unaffected by price controls, a buyer who really wants steel can get it by purchasing a steel company and producing all the steel it needs. Purchasing a steel company is thus a simple way to avoid price controls (see Example 16.2). Indeed, if there are no transaction costs to buying steel companies, and if owners of steel mills are entitled to steel in proportion to their ownership, then price controls on steel are completely ineffective because all users vertically integrate by acquiring ownership interests in steel mills.

Similarly, *taxes* encourage vertical integration. Depending on where firms are located, they may be subject to different taxes. For example, tax rates differ by state as well as by country. A vertically integrated firm may be able to shift profits from one location to another simply by changing the *transfer price* at which it sells its internally produced materials from one division to another (see Example 16.3). By shifting profits from a high tax jurisdiction to a low tax jurisdiction, a firm can increase its profits. The Internal

EXAMPLE 16.3	# OIL DEPLETION ALLOWANCE

In what some Texans view as the Good Old Days, the federal government allowed owners of oil wells to take a tax savings for selling their oil. Specifically, a firm could reduce its corporate income tax by an oil *depletion allowance* equal to roughly 27.5 percent of the value of the crude oil sold. The Revenue Act of 1924 limited the depletion allowance to no more than 50 percent of a property's taxable income before depletion but after deduction of expenses directly associated with the producing property. As amazing as it seems, firms were actually recompensated for using up their own reserves.

The oil depletion allowance gave oil companies a strong incentive to vertically integrate. If a company owned the wells, processed the crude oil, and sold gasoline and other products to final consumers, it could control the price it charged its own units for the oil. By charging a very high internal transfer price for the oil, the firm could increase its allowance, which depended on the *value* of the crude oil sold.

Needless to say, oil companies took advantage of this tax loophole with enthusiasm by vertically integrating. With the end of this opportunity in 1974, there was large-scale divestiture of firms' downstream retailers.

SOURCE: Bolch and Damon (1978).

Revenue Service is, of course, aware of such shifting and insists that firms use internal transfer prices that reflect prices in the marketplace.

Government *regulation* can create an incentive for a firm to vertically (or horizontally) integrate when the profits of only one division of a firm are regulated. For example, the profits that local telephone companies earn on local services are regulated, but their profits on other services, such as selling telephones in competition with other suppliers, are not regulated. If a telephone company can shift profits from its regulated division to its unregulated division, it can effectively avoid the regulation of its local telephone service.

Suppose, for example, that such a firm is able, through accounting conventions, to transfer costs from its unregulated division to its regulated division, which lowers its reported profits in the regulated line of business and raises them in the unregulated line. At the next rate hearing, the telephone company may argue that it is entitled to increase its rates to raise its profits in its regulated business. By shifting profits from the regulated to the unregulated division, the telephone company can thus increase its overall profits. It may be the fear that profits will be transferred from a regulated business to an unregulated business, and the difficulty of detecting such transfers, that has motivated the government to control the entry of local telephone companies into unregulated businesses (see Example 16.4).[4]

---

[4] Even if some avoidance of regulation does occur, there may be offsetting efficiencies to society from allowing the telephone company to enter new businesses. See Chapter 23 on regulation.

EXAMPLE 16.4

THE BREAKUP OF AT&T

In 1984, AT&T and the Department of Justice settled the antitrust case against AT&T. AT&T agreed to break itself up into several firms. One firm, AT&T, provides long-distance service, and the other firms provide local telephone service. Lawyers at the Department of Justice apparently felt that a vertically integrated telephone company, one that provided local and long-distance service, was not required for productive efficiency, or that there were other offsetting gains from the divestiture.

According to the Department of Justice, the vertical structure of the company provided an opportunity for unfair competition against other providers of long-distance service. For example, by charging high local rates or by providing poor local service to other providers of long-distance service (which require local service), AT&T could harm interexchange competitors. Another concern of the Department of Justice was the difficulty of monitoring cost-shifting among AT&T's regulated (telephone) and other relatively unregulated businesses (such as the manufacture of telephones and other equipment). The resulting breakup of the telephone company presumably mitigated these concerns of the Department of Justice.

SOURCE: Lavey and Carlton (1983).

Integration to Increase Monopoly Profits

God helps them that helps themselves.

A firm may be able to increase its monopoly profits in two ways by vertically integrating. First, a firm that is a monopolistic supplier of a key input in a production process used by a competitive industry may be able to vertically integrate forward, monopolize the production industry, and increase its profits. Second, a vertically integrated monopolistic supplier may be able to price discriminate.

Vertical Integration to Monopolize Another Industry.   In some cases, a monopolistic supplier of an input can increase its profits by vertically integrating to monopolize the producing industry. When does it pay to forward integrate to extend monopoly power? The answer depends on the production process, as the following model illustrates.

In the industry illustrated in Figure 16.1, consumers purchase Q units of a competitively produced good at price p. The competitive industry produces that good using a production function, F,

$$Q = F(M,L). \tag{16.1}$$

FIGURE 16.1   Vertical Organization of an Industry

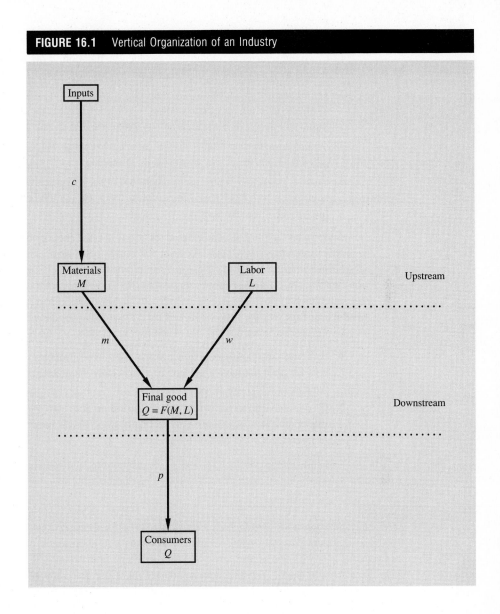

that depends on inputs of a particular material, M, and labor, L. These inputs are sold to competitive firms at prices m and w (for wage), respectively. The firms that supply the inputs in the production process are referred to as the **upstream** firms, and the firms that produce the good are called **downstream** firms. In the past, firms often located along a river and the upstream firms used the flow of the river to take their products downstream on boats or barges to the processors, who in turn sent it downstream to consumers.

We make four assumptions about the industry in Figure 16.1:

1. *Constant returns to scale:* The production function, *F(M,L)*, exhibits constant returns to scale. That is, if both inputs are doubled, output exactly doubles.

2. *The inputs are produced at constant marginal cost:* The producing firms can buy as much labor, *L*, as they want at a wage of *w* (the supply curve of labor is horizontal at *w*). The material, *M*, is produced at a constant marginal cost of *c*.

3. *No entry upstream:* The upstream firm that supplies materials does not fear that entry by other firms will eliminate its monopoly.

4. *Costs of vertically integrating:* There are costs to vertically integrating, such as negotiation and legal fees. Thus, unless there are sizable benefits from vertically integrating, the firm does not integrate.

Under what additional conditions does it pay for the monopolistic supplier of *M* to vertically integrate forward and take over the downstream firm? The answer depends on whether the industry has a fixed-proportions production or a variable-proportions production function. In a **fixed-proportions production function** the inputs are always used in the same proportions, regardless of relative factor prices. In a **variable-proportions production function** the ratio of factors used is sensitive to relative factor prices.

Given the four assumptions, there are two key results:

1. If the downstream production process uses fixed proportions, the upstream monopolist does not have an incentive to vertically integrate. It makes the same profit whether it integrates or not.

2. If, alternatively, the downstream production process uses variable proportions, the monopolist has an incentive to vertically integrate. It integrates if its increase in profits exceeds the cost of integration.

The following sections examine fixed proportions and variable proportions in turn and then present a numerical example to illustrate how the two cases differ.

Fixed-Proportions Production Function. In a fixed-proportions production process it is impossible to substitute one input for another. A nonrealistic example illustrates the basic idea. Suppose there are two input markets: one makes left shoes, and the other makes right shoes. The production industry takes one left shoe and one right shoe and produces a pair of shoes. If the cost of left shoes rises to three times the price of right shoes, the production firm still uses the same proportions of left and right shoes, because it cannot substitute right shoes for left shoes.

Graphically, such a production process has an *isoquant* (a curve that shows the various combinations of the inputs that produce a given output level) in the shape of an L, as shown in Figure 16.2. The isoquant shows the various combinations of left and right shoes that can be used to make one pair. The firm can make one pair of shoes using one left and one right shoe. If it has two left shoes and a right shoe or one left shoe and two right shoes, it can make only one pair.

Also shown in the figure is an *isocost* line (which shows the various combinations

FIGURE 16.2   Fixed-Proportions Isoquant and Isocost Curves

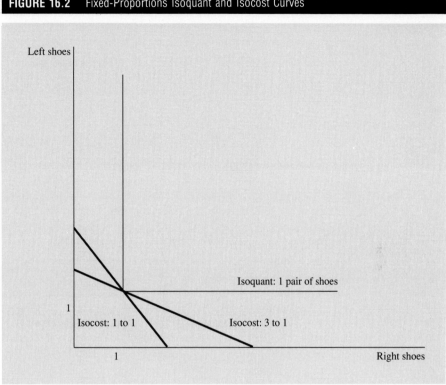

of the inputs that cost a given amount), where the prices for left and right shoes are equal (1 to 1) and another isocost line where left shoes cost three times as much as right shoes (3 to 1). Regardless of the relative price of the two inputs, the cost-minimizing combination of inputs is to use one left shoe and one right shoe to make a pair of shoes. This cost-minimizing solution is shown in the figure, since both isocost curves hit the isoquant at that point.

Now we can compare the profits that the materials monopolist makes if it vertically integrates and if it does not. For simplicity, suppose that it takes 1 unit of M and 1 unit of L to make 1 unit of Q.[5]

If the monopolist integrates forward, it is the only producer of the final product (because M is an essential input in the production process). For example, many goods, such as IBM mainframe computers, Xerox machines, and Tupperware, are only (or

---

[5] By choosing units appropriately, we can always ensure that it takes 1 unit of each input to make 1 unit of output. Mathematically, this fixed-proportion production function is $Q = \min (M,L)$. That is, Q equals the minimum of the quantity of the two inputs, M and L. For example, if we have 3 units of L and 2 units of M, we can make 2 units of Q.

FIGURE 16.3   Fixed-Proportions Production Function

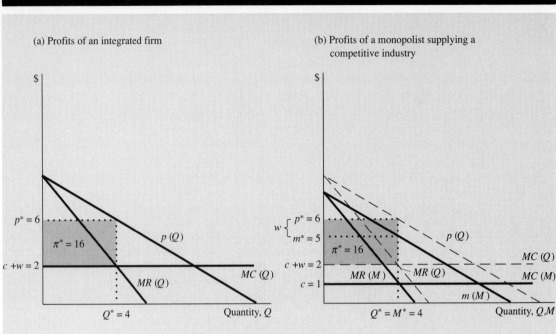

(a) Profits of an integrated firm

(b) Profits of a monopolist supplying a competitive industry

primarily) sold by the manufacturers' own retailers or sales staff and are examples of a manufacturer integrating into distribution.

The integrated monopolist's cost of producing a unit of Q is $c + w$. That is, it takes 1 unit of M, which costs the firm c to make, and 1 unit of L, which can be hired at a cost of w. Figure 16.3a shows this per-unit, or marginal, cost, $MC(Q) = c + w$. Also in the figure is the inverse demand curve for the final product, $p(Q)$, which shows the price consumers are willing to pay to buy Q units of the product, and the corresponding marginal revenue curve, $MR(Q)$.

The integrated monopolist maximizes its profits by producing Q^* units of output so that its marginal cost equals its marginal revenue: $MC(Q^*) = c + w = MR(Q^*)$. It uses $M^* = L^* (= Q^*)$ units of inputs. It charges p^* and has profits of

$$\pi^* = [p^* - (c + w)]Q^*. \tag{16.2}$$

We can contrast the vertically integrated industry to one in which the materials monopolist supplies a competitive industry. The nonintegrated material monopolist's marginal cost of producing M, $MC(M)$, is c and is shown as a solid line in Figure 16.3b. It faces an inverse demand, $m(M)$, for its product from the competitive industry, shown in the figure as a solid line. This line shows the highest price, m, that the competitive industry will pay for M units of materials. The corresponding marginal revenue curve is $MR(M)$.

The output market curves of Figure 16.3a are also shown in Figure 16.3b as dotted lines for comparison. Both sets of curves can be shown in the same diagram because both sets of curves are scaled the same (it takes 1 unit of M to produce 1 unit of Q).

The demand curve facing the upstream monopolist can be derived from the demand curve facing the competitive downstream industry. The monopolist views its demand curve as the highest price it can charge the downstream firms for a given quantity of M. The price a competitive upstream firm receives for a unit of its output is p. To produce that unit of output, it must spend w for a unit of labor. Thus, the most it will pay for a unit of M is $m = p - w$. As a result, the demand curve facing the input monopolist equals the demand curve facing the competitive industry minus w. As shown in the figure, the monopolist's demand curve, $m(M)$, is just the industry's demand curve, $p(Q)$, shifted down by w.[6]

The materials monopolist sets its output as M^* so as to equate its marginal revenue, $MR(M)$, with its marginal cost, $MC(M) = c$. The material monopolist maximizes $[p(m) - (c - w)]M$, which is identical to what the vertically integrated firm maximizes, Equation 16.2, because $M = Q$. It charges m^*. As the diagram shows, $M^* = Q^*$ from the vertically integrated industry. That is, the industry output and the amount of materials used are the same whether the industry is vertically integrated or not. The materials monopolist's profits,

$$\pi^* = (m^* - c)M^* = [(p^* - w) - c]M^*,$$

are the same as before. The monopolist now only receives m^* (which is $p^* - w$) instead of p^* per unit sold, but its costs are only c instead of $c + w$ per unit produced.

Thus, since the upstream firm earns the same profits whether it integrates or not, and there is a cost to integration, it chooses not to integrate. What is the intuition behind this result? The key point is that when the nonintegrated monopolist raises its price for a unit of M by $1. the price to consumers also goes up by $1. That is, the materials monopolist can perfectly control the final price consumers pay without vertically integrating. Not only can it raise the price, but it captures all the resulting profits. None go to the competitive industry, which merely passes on higher factor costs to consumers. The reason that the nonintegrated monopolist can control the downstream price perfectly is that the downstream firms cannot substitute away from the input produced by the monopolist.

---

[6] We can derive the materials monopolist's derived demand curve mathematically. Since the downstream industry is competitive, the price it sets for its product equals the marginal cost of producing it,

$$p(Q) = m + w,$$

where its marginal cost, $MC(Q) = m + w$, because it must pay m for 1 unit of materials to the upstream monopolist and w for 1 unit of labor. Because the monopolist must lower its price to sell more units, m is a function of M. Thus, we can rewrite the equation as

$$p(M) = m(M) + w.$$

We have written $p(M)$ instead of $p(Q)$, since $M = Q$. Finally, we can rearrange terms in this last equation to obtain

$$m(M) = p(M) - w.$$

That is, the derived demand curve facing the upstream monopolist equals the demand curve facing the competitive industry minus the cost of a unit of labor.

FIGURE 16.4   Variable-Proportions Isoquant and Isocost Curves

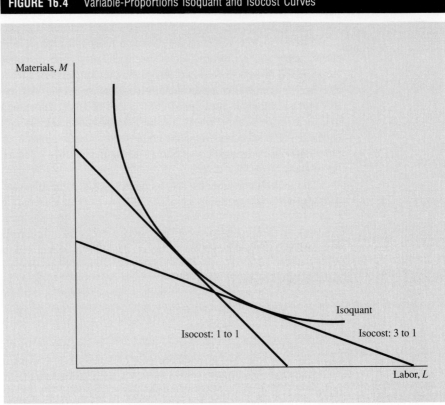

Variable-Proportions Production Function.   The preceding intuition suggests that the results are different if the competitive downstream industry faces a variable-proportions production function, with which the downstream industry substitutes away from the input monopolist's product if the price rises.

Figure 16.4 shows the isoquant of a variable-proportions production function. Unlike the fixed-proportions production function, it is a smooth curve, showing that the products are (imperfect) substitutes. As a result, as the relative costs of the inputs change, as shown by a shift in the slope of the isocost curve, the firm substitutes more of the now less expensive input for the more expensive input.

With a variable-proportions production function, if the upstream monopolist increases its price to the competitive downstream industry, firms in that industry substitute more labor for the monopolist's product. If the monopolist raises its price by a dollar, the price of the final good no longer increases by a dollar, and the amount of M used falls by more than Q does.

Consider a more extreme case where the two inputs are perfect substitutes in the production process. Here, the isoquant is a straight line. For example, if the two inputs are palm oil and coconut oil, and the downstream food processing firms do not care which oil they use, then the products are perfect substitutes (and the isoquant is a straight line with a slope of negative 1). If a monopolist in palm oil increases its price above that of coconut oil, all the downstream firms switch to coconut oil. In this case, the upstream monopolist cannot raise the price consumers pay.

In short, with a variable-proportions production process, the upstream monopolist does not have complete control over the downstream industry: Every time it raises its price, the downstream industry substitutes away from its product. More importantly, this substitution, in general, leads to inefficient production, because efficiency requires the slope of the isoquant to equal the ratios of the input's marginal costs. Downstream firms are using too much L and too little M. This inefficiency means that there are less profits for the monopolist to seize.

If the upstream firm integrates forward so that it monopolizes the downstream industry, it has complete control and can use the inputs in the most efficient combination. Thus, its profits increase. If profits increase by more than the cost of vertical integration, the firm will vertically integrate.

An Example: Fixed vs. Variable Proportions.   Thus, with a fixed-proportions production process, vertical integration cannot increase profits, whereas with variable proportions profits can rise. This difference between fixed proportions and variable proportions can be illustrated using an example with the following properties:

- *Demand:* The final goods market has a linear inverse demand curve of

$$p = 10 - Q. \qquad (16.3)$$

- *Input costs:* The marginal cost of the two inputs, M and L, are $c = w = 1$.
- *Production process:* By construction, 1 unit of M and 1 unit of L produce 1 unit of Q, and the production process exhibits constant returns to scale.

We consider both a fixed-proportions and a variable-proportions production function. Both production processes have constant returns to scale and the property that 1 unit of M and 1 unit of L produce 1 unit of Q.

We start by considering the outcome if all markets are competitive. Competitive markets are socially optimal because welfare, defined as consumer surplus plus profits, is maximized. We then compare monopoly of M with fixed proportions and variable proportions to competition and to each other. The fixed- and variable-proportions production functions are chosen so that the integrated monopoly outputs are the same for both. Table 16.1 shows the properties of the three cases, and Appendix 16A derives the values in Table 16.1.

The first column of Table 16.1 shows what happens if all the markets are competitive. The factor markets are competitive, so the price of M, m, equals its social cost, c. Since 1 unit of M and 1 unit of L produce a unit of Q, the marginal cost and hence the price of Q is 2 ($= cM + wL = 1 \times 1 + 1 \times 1$). At that price, 8 units of Q are produced using 8 units each of M and L. Under competition, there is no deadweight loss nor any losses from inefficient production, and consumer surplus and welfare are maximized (at 32). The rest of this example concerns a single, monopolistic firm that produces M.

		Monopoly of M			
TABLE 16.1 Effects of Vertical Integration					
		Fixed Proportions		Variable Proportions	
	All Markets Competitive	Not Integrated	Integrated	Not Integrated	Integrated
Price, p	2	6	6	5.63	6
Quantity, Q	8	4	4	4.37	4
Consumer surplus	32	8	8	9.55	8
Profits to owner of M	0	16	16	10.75	16
Deadweight loss from monopoly pricing	0	8	8	6.59	8
Loss from inefficient production	0	0	0	5.11	0
M	8	4	4	1.55	4
L	8	4	4	12.30	4
m	1	5	1	7.93	1

Inverse demand function: $p = 10 - Q$

Factor costs: $w = c = 1$

Fixed-proportions production function: $Q = \min(L, M)$

Variable-proportions production function: $Q = L^{.5} M^{.5}$

If the production process uses fixed proportions, so that the input proportions used are insensitive to change in the relative factor prices (m/w), profits to the upstream monopolist are the same whether or not it vertically integrates. As shown in the second and third columns of Table 16.1, final good price and quantity, consumer surplus, and deadweight loss are the same in either case.[7] The price, $p = 6$, is the one that maximizes monopoly profits. The only difference in the two columns is that when the firm is vertically integrated, as in Figure 16.3, the monopolist charges itself $m = c = 1$, whereas in the absence of vertical integration, the monopolist charges the final goods industry $m = 5$.

Whether or not the firm integrates, production is efficient, because the cost-minimizing choices of M and L are used ($M = L = Q = 4$). There is, however, a deadweight loss from monopoly pricing of 8, which stems from setting the monopoly price, 6, above the true social marginal cost (competitive price), 2. As a result, total welfare falls by the deadweight loss of 8 from 32 in the competitive case to 24 (consumer surplus = 8, plus profits to the owner of M = 16). Consumer surplus falls from 32 in the competitive case to 8, so consumers are much worse off due to monopoly pricing.

---

[7] Because the demand curve is linear, the consumer surplus is the triangle under the demand curve and above the price: $(10 - p)Q/2$. The deadweight loss is also a triangle: $(p - 2)(8 - Q)/2$. One side is the difference between the price and the social marginal cost, 2, and another side is the difference between the quantity and the quantity that would have been produced if price equaled the social marginal cost, 8.

With a variable-proportions production function, most of these variables differ in the integrated and nonintegrated market organizations. In Table 16.1, a Cobb-Douglas production function is used:

$$Q = L^{.5}M^{.5}. \tag{16.4}$$

Here, L and M are (imperfect) substitutes. Corresponding isoquants look like the one in Figure 16.4. This production process was chosen so that if the firm is integrated, price, quantity, profits, consumer surplus, and so forth are the same as with a fixed-proportions integrated monopolist.

If the monopolist vertically integrates, it charges itself $m = c = 1$, and produces efficiently ($M = L = Q = 4$), so that costs are minimized. The results are different, however, if the monopolist does not vertically integrate. Without integration, if the monopolist increases its price, m, the downstream firms substitute away from M and towards L, as shown in Figure 16.4. As a result, the marginal cost does not rise as much as m does. The final goods producers face a marginal cost of

$$MC = 2(wm)^{.5} = 2m^{.5}, \tag{16.5}$$

since $w = 1$. Thus, if m doubles, the marginal cost only increases by 41 percent.

Because of the substitution by downstream firms, M and L are no longer used in equal proportions. Rather, at the profit-maximizing choice of m, 7.93, nearly 8 times as much L as M is used. The marginal cost, and hence price, of the downstream competitive firms is 5.63, so consumers are better off than in the integrated case: their consumer surplus is 19 percent higher.

There is now a second social loss, beyond that from monopoly pricing, due to inefficient production. The least expensive way to produce the quantity sold, $Q = 4.37$, is to use 4.37 units of M and L at a social cost of 8.74. Instead, $M = 1.55$ and $L = 12.30$, with a social cost of 13.85. Thus, the social loss from inefficient production is $5.11 = 13.85 - 8.74$.[8] This social loss represents 16 percent of the consumer surplus in the competitive case, and 54 percent of the consumer surplus in this case. Because the integrated firm can avoid this social loss and charges a higher price, its profits are larger: 16 versus 10.75. Thus, the upstream monopolist has a substantial incentive to vertically integrate when the final goods market uses a variable-proportions production function. It integrates if this increase in profits exceeds the cost of integrating.[9]

Consumer surplus is higher (9.55 versus 8) without integration than with it, because the nonintegrated price, 5.63, is less than the integrated price, 6, although it is still above the competitive level, 2. Society's welfare is lower than in the integrated case ($20.3 = 9.55 + 10.75$ versus $24 = 8 + 16$). This drop in welfare of 3.7 reflects the

---

[8] The sum of consumer surplus, profits to the owner of M, deadweight loss, and loss from inefficient production is the same in all five cases. The reason is that they collectively equal the area above the social marginal cost ($= 2$) and below the demand curve. That is, they equal the consumer surplus in the competitive case.

[9] Table 16.1 does not include a cost of integrating. The profits in the integrated case should be lowered by any such cost.

loss from inefficient production of 5.11 that outweighs the reduction in deadweight loss due to monopoly pricing of 1.41 (8 − 6.59).

Thus, welfare is highest if all markets are competitive. In this example, assuming no cost of integrating, welfare is the same with fixed or variable proportions if a materials monopolist vertically integrates. If integration does not take place (perhaps because of a legal prohibition), welfare is lower with variable proportions than with fixed proportions because there is a loss due to inefficient production in addition to the loss from monopoly pricing.

The results of this example do not always hold, however. It is possible for both consumer surplus and welfare to rise when a monopolist vertically integrates to extend its monopoly power. It may happen that the loss due to the increase in monopoly power is more than offset by an increase in production efficiency (Mallela and Nahata 1980).[10]

Price Discrimination.   A monopolistic supplier may vertically integrate so that it can successfully price discriminate. Chapter 14 explains that an essential element for successful price discrimination is the ability to prevent resale of the product by those who pay a low price to those who pay a high price. If resale cannot be prevented, it is impossible to price discriminate. Vertical integration can be used to prevent resale.

For example, aluminum is used in many products (see Example 14.1). For simplicity, initially, suppose that there are only two uses for aluminum: in wire and aircraft. There are good alternatives for aluminum wire in electric cables, such as copper, but there are no good alternatives in airplanes. As a result, the elasticity of demand for aluminum by wire manufacturers is much higher than it is for airplane manufacturers. Thus, it is profitable to charge airplane manufacturers a higher price than aluminum wire producers.

If the aluminum monopolist charges a higher price to airplane manufacturers without integrating, the aluminum wire producers can purchase aluminum at a relatively low price and resell to the airplane manufacturers at a lower price than the monopolist charges. To prevent this resale, the aluminum monopolist can vertically integrate forward and become the only producer of aluminum wire. It can then charge a very high price for aluminum to the aircraft manufacturers, without worrying about resales from wire manufacturers. By transforming the product from aluminum ingot to aluminum wire, the vertically integrated firm prevents resales.

Integration to Eliminate Market Power

Just as a firm can increase monopoly profits by vertically integrating, another firm can reduce or eliminate monopoly power by vertically integrating. Suppose, for example, that only one firm sells an input that is essential for your production process. If that firm is charging you a high, monopoly price, you should determine whether it is cost-effective for you to vertically integrate backwards and produce that product yourself. You might, for example, either build a new production plant to produce that input or try to buy the existing firm.

---

[10] Earlier works on this issue include Vernon and Graham (1971) and Warren-Bouton (1974).

Let us return to the example given above, where the upstream firm is a monopolist supplying a competitive industry. Does a downstream firm have an incentive to vertically integrate backward and produce the input for itself? Although the answer appears to be yes, the full answer is complicated.

If the downstream firm can produce the product that the monopolist is supplying at the same cost, then the firm has an incentive to vertically integrate and avoid paying a price above the competitive price for the product. If, however, the downstream firm has such productive capability, it is likely that other firms have it as well. It is therefore unlikely that the upstream firm can remain a monopolist for very long. If other firms can produce this product at the same cost, it will eventually be supplied competitively. Thus, the downstream firm does not have to vertically integrate.

Suppose, however, that the upstream firm is a monopolist and no other firm, including the downstream firms, can produce at the same cost. For example, the upstream firm might own a patent that enables it to produce at lower cost than anyone else. In such a case, is there an incentive for a downstream firm to purchase the upstream firm? The answer is not obvious because the upstream firm will sell to the downstream firm only if the price offered is high enough. The monopolist is willing to sell its firm for a price that reflects its monopoly profits. Whether the downstream firm pays the monopolist slowly over time in the form of a high price per unit or instead pays it all at once in a lump-sum payment, it must pay the monopoly price. As in the previous section on increasing monopoly profits, which alternative is superior for the downstream firm depends on the production technology.

Fixed-Proportions Production Function.   Suppose that downstream firms use fixed-proportions production processes. If a downstream firm acquires the monopolist, it is able to save the difference between the monopoly price for M, m, and the per-unit cost of producing it, c, times the number of units it uses. For example, suppose that the downstream firm buys 10 units of M at the monopoly price of \$10, and the per-unit cost of production is \$2. Then the firm is willing to pay \$80.[11] The total amount of money that the downstream firm must spend to acquire the monopolist precisely equals the amount of money that it has to pay in monopoly overcharges if the firms remain separate. Therefore, when the production process uses fixed proportions, the downstream firm's profits are *unaffected* by whether or not it purchases the upstream firm.

Variable-Proportions Production Function.   Now, suppose that downstream firms have variable-proportions production functions, so they can substitute one factor for another to some extent. If the upstream firm charges a monopolistic price, the downstream firms substitute away from that product. The cost-minimizing (efficient) choice of factors is used only if both inputs are sold at their marginal costs. That is, efficiency requires that the slope of the isoquant at the chosen production point equals the ratio of the marginal

---

[11] This example assumes that there is only one time period. If there are many periods, an appropriately discounted value for the future stream of monopoly profits should be used.

costs of the two inputs. Downstream firms choose the production point so that the slope of the isoquant at the chosen production point equals the ratio of the input prices. Thus, if the upstream monopolist charges more than its marginal cost $(m > c)$, the downstream firms produce inefficiently, using too much L and too little M to produce a given level of Q.

Suppose that a downstream firm acquires the upstream monopolist. As discussed above, the new integrated firm produces efficiently, since it uses c rather than m in deciding the optimal input mix. The downstream firm can afford to pay the monopolist an amount equal to its monopoly profits (before vertical integration) and still make money, because of its increased efficiency. Of course, the upstream firm can vertically integrate forward, taking over a downstream firm and increasing its profits. Thus, the upstream monopolist is not willing to sell for an amount equal to its preintegration profits, but insists on a purchase price equal to the postintegration profits.

The key point is that *when there are variable proportions in production, the input should not be sold at the monopoly price*. Any firm that faces a monopoly price is forced to use inefficient methods of production, which provides an incentive for vertical integration.

Integration to Assure Supply

One of the most common reasons given for vertical integration is to assure supply of important inputs, as was mentioned in the discussion of how price controls distort market operations. Here we assume that there are no such controls.

Why is there concern about obtaining assured supplies when the standard models of monopoly or competition never predict shortages? It appears that obtaining timely delivery of an item *is* of concern to business people, so these standard models of competition must be inadequate to describe many real-world businesses. Assurance of supply is important in markets where price is not the sole device used to allocate goods (see Chapter 21). Nonprice allocation occurs in a wide range of common situations. For example, a bakery frequently runs out of bread by the end of the day and yet does not raise its price. Instead, late-arriving customers cannot buy the bread. Similarly, grocery stores frequently run out of produce without raising prices. In many producer-good industries, good customers often get the product during "tight" times, and other customers must wait. It is the marketing department, not customer responses to short-run price movements, that allocates goods. Such rationing has occurred in many industries, such as paper, chemicals, and metals.

When rationing is a possibility, there is an incentive to vertically integrate in order to raise the probability of obtaining the product. A firm has an incentive to produce its own supplies to meet its predictable level of demand and relies on other firms for supplies to meet its less stable demand. Outside suppliers respond to this risky environment by raising prices. This arrangement, in which outside suppliers bear the risky demand, may not be the most efficient system for reliably providing the product but may provide a strong incentive for a firm to vertically integrate (Carlton 1979).

Integration to Eliminate Externalities

A firm may integrate to internalize externalities (see Chapter 6). If all Radio Shack stores carry the same products, maintain certain standards of service, and provide advice on the use of their products, a regular customer who moves from one city to another goes to the Radio Shack in the new city. That is, there is a positive reputation externality. A consumer who likes one of the outlets knows that the others are similar. Obviously, then, it is in the chain's best interest to maintain uniform standards. A bad store can harm the business of all distributors, and lower the profits of the firm, Tandy, that supplies the products sold by these distributors. Thus, Tandy has an incentive to integrate forward into distribution (own Radio Shack stores) to control this externality.

■ THE LIFE CYCLE OF A FIRM

Firms vertically integrate if the benefits outweigh the costs. Stigler (1951) and Williamson (1975), building on Adam Smith's theorem that "the division of labor is limited by the extent of the market," have used the ideas discussed in the preceding section to develop a theory of the life cycle of firms. They explain why firms rely on markets during certain periods, whereas during other periods, they vertically integrate.

If the demand for a product is small, so that the collective output of all the firms in the industry is small, each firm must undertake all the activities associated with producing the final output itself. For example, a firm must collect information on where it can buy certain inputs at the lowest price, produce the output, and sell it. Some of these functions, however, are subject to increasing returns to scale. It may be that all the industry's output can be produced by one firm at lower cost than if many firms produce it. Similarly, each firm duplicates the cost of gathering information about factor prices, even though it is less expensive for one person to collect the information and make it available to all firms.

What keeps a firm from taking advantage of these economies of scale? The answer is that when the industry is small it does not pay for a firm to specialize in an activity that yields increasing returns to scale. A specialized firm may have large setup (fixed) costs. If the specialized firm produces large quantities of output, the average setup or fixed cost per unit is small. In a small industry, however, the setup costs per unit are large, so that the specialized firm's price is higher than the cost of each firm that produces everything for itself. Similarly, a specialized firm's transaction costs of contracting to supply a small amount or a large amount of the specialized service may be about the same. Thus the smaller the number of units sold to firms, the higher the average cost (including the per-unit transaction cost).

As the industry expands it becomes profitable for a firm to specialize, since the per-unit transaction costs fall.[12] That is, as the industry grows, firms *vertically disintegrate*.

---

[12] A specialized firm cannot charge a price for its product that is higher than the average cost of the product if one of the nonspecialized firms produces it itself.

When the industry is small, each firm produced all successive steps of the production process, so that all firms were *vertically integrated*. In the larger industry, each firm does not handle each stage of production itself, but buys services or products from specialized firms.

For example, in the 1860s, Birmingham was the leading production center of the small-arms industry.[13] Virtually all of the 5800 people working in this industry were located in a small district near St. Mary's Church. They were localized because large numbers of firms specialized in particular processes, so parts had to be frequently transported from one workshop to another. The master gun manufacturer owned a warehouse rather than a factory or workshop. These entrepreneurs purchased semifinished parts from "material-makers" such as barrel-makers, lock-makers, sight-stampers, trigger-makers, ramrod-forgers, gun-furniture makers, and bayonet-forgers. The gun-maker then sent the parts to a succession of "setters-up", or specialized craftsmen, who assembled them into guns. For example, jiggers worked on the breech end, stockers dealt with the barrel and lock and shaped the stock; barrel-strippers prepared the gun for rifling and proofing; hardeners, polishers, borers and riflers, engravers, browners, and finally the lock-freers adjusted the working parts.

As an industry matures further, new products often develop and reduce much of the demand for the original product, so that the industry shrinks in size. As a result, firms again vertically integrate.

In 1919, 13 percent of manufacturing companies studied had two or more establishments making successive products, where the product of one was the raw material of the next (Stigler 1951, 135). In 1937, successive functions were found in 10 percent. Similarly, in 1919, 34.4 percent of all complex central offices had successive establishments (companies with establishments in two or more vertically related industries); in 1937, only 27.5 percent did. Apparently, there has been no overall trend in vertical integration since 1929 (Adelman 1955, Laffer 1969, Livesay and Porter 1969).

■ VERTICAL RESTRICTIONS

I don't trust him. We're friends. —BERTOLT BRECHT

It is often preferable (cheaper) for a firm to rely on other firms for a good or service than to provide it itself. Product distribution is a good example. Manufacturers often rely upon independent firms to distribute their products rather than doing it themselves, because the costs of monitoring internal employees in a distribution setting often exceeds the costs of using independent firms. For example, the distribution centers may be far apart, making it costly for employees to travel to them and spend time becoming familiar enough with local market conditions to be able to judge the efficiency of a particular retail outlet. Every manufacturer, regardless of whether it is a monopolist or a competitive firm, wants its product distributed at the lowest possible costs. The manufacturer also wants the distributors to price and sell in a manner that is best for the manufacturer.

---

[13] This discussion is based on Allen, G. C. 1929. *The Industrial Development of Birmingham and the Black Country, 1860–1927*. London, pp 56–57, 116–17, cited by Stigler (1951).

Economists describe the relationship between a manufacturer and a distributor as a **principal-agent** relationship. The *principal*, the manufacturer, has its *agent*, the distributor, sell its product. The manufacturer, typically, cannot perfectly observe the sales effort of the distributor and realizes that its agent may try to take advantage. For example, the distributor may advertise less than it is supposed to, in order to save money and *free ride* on the manufacturer's reputation. **Free riding** occurs when one firm benefits from the actions of another without paying for it. Where free riding is possible, the distributor has an inadequate incentive to advertise; it prefers to rely on the efforts of others and does not do its share.[14] These principal-agent problems are often addressed through vertical restrictions that the manufacturer places on the distributor beyond requiring it to pay the wholesale price for the product. These vertical restrictions are determined through contractual negotiations between the manufacturer and the distributor, and try to approximate the outcome that would occur if the firms vertically integrated. They include requirements that the distributor sell a minimum number of units, that distributors not locate near each other, that distributors not sell competing products, and that distributors charge no lower than a particular price. Although principal-agent problems do not arise exclusively in the distribution context, the most interesting vertical restrictions have been developed for such situations.

Economists and the courts initially were uneasy about vertical restrictions because several vertical restrictions, such as forbidding the distributor to lower its price or sell competing products, appear at first glance to restrain competition and should not occur in a perfectly competitive market. But this observation may only tell us that the economic models of perfect competition, in which distribution is taken to be a costless activity, are not applicable here. Simple models of competition ignore the cost of sales efforts. Where it takes resources to distribute a product, a manufacturer must pay somebody to do it and wants to control how the distribution takes place. Thus, models of perfect competition that ignore the cost of distribution do not provide good intuition for markets that rely on substantial sales effort.

The following sections identify a number of problems that arise when vertical integration is impossible and describe the vertical restrictions that are used to deal with these problems. We then discuss the pro- and anticompetitive implications of these vertical restrictions.

Vertical Restrictions Used to Solve Problems in Distribution

Four problems commonly arise when distribution is costly and a manufacturer retains a distributor to retail its products:

1. There is a double monopoly markup by successive monopolists in manufacturing and distribution.
2. Some distributors may free ride (not do their share in promoting the good) on other distributors.

---

[14] Free riding is an externality analogous to those discussed in Chapter 6.

3. Some manufacturers may free ride on other manufacturers.

4. There may be a lack of coordination among distributors that leads to externalities.

Each problem is discussed in order along with the vertical restrictions designed to deal with each.

Double Monopoly Markup.   If the manufacturer and the distributor are both monopolists, each adds a monopoly markup (the difference between its price and its marginal cost is positive), so consumers face two markups instead of one. This double markup provides an incentive for firms to either vertically integrate or use vertical restrictions to promote efficiency and thereby increase joint profits. We first illustrate the losses due to the double monopoly markup and then show how vertical restrictions can be used to prevent these losses where vertical integration is not practical.

An Example of the Loss from a Double Monopoly Markup.   To illustrate the effect of a double markup, we contrast a market in which a manufacturer is vertically integrated into distribution to one with two successive monopolists. Both consumers and firms lose from the double markup.

Suppose the vertically integrated, monopolistic manufacturer-distributor faces a downward sloping demand curve, D_1, for its product, as shown in Figure 16.5a. The firm produces Q^* units so as to equate its marginal cost of production, c, and its marginal revenue, MR_1.[15] Its profits π^*, the shaded area in the figure, equal the monopoly markup per unit (the difference between the sales price, p^*, and the cost per unit) times the number of units, Q^*.

Now suppose that the monopolistic, upstream manufacturer uses a monopolistic, downstream firm to distribute its product. Since each firm adds a monopoly markup to its per-unit costs, there is a double monopoly markup. Here, the distributor faces the same downward sloping demand curve, D_1, and marginal revenue curve, MR_1, as in Figure 16.5a. The manufacturer charges the distributor a wholesale price, p_2, per unit. The distributor treats this wholesale price as its marginal cost. It maximizes its profits by selling Q_1 units, such that its marginal cost, p_2, equals its marginal revenue, $MR_1(Q_1)$, which is a function of Q_1, as shown in Figure 16.5b. Because distribution cost are assumed to equal 0, $p_2 = p^*$.

The number of units of the manufactured good the distributor demands depends on the manufacturer's wholesale price, p_2 and is determined by the intersection of the MR_1 curve with the horizontal line at p_2. This demand curve facing the manufacturer, D_2, equals the distributor's marginal revenue curve, MR_1 (by the same reasoning that was used in the previous section on vertically integrating to extend monopoly power). The manufacturer maximizes its profits by choosing its output level, Q_2, so that its marginal cost, c, equals its marginal revenue, MR_2 (the curve marginal to D_2).

Figure 16.5b shows the resulting double markup. The manufacturer charges p_2, which is above its marginal cost of c; the distributor charges p_1, which is above its marginal cost of p_2. Because Figure 16.5 uses linear demand curves, $p^* = p_2 < p_1$. Consumers facing the double markup buy less output, Q_2, than when there is an integrated firm, Q^*.

---

[15] For graphic simplicity, we ignore the costs of distribution for now.

FIGURE 16.5   Monopolies in Both Manufacturing and Distributing

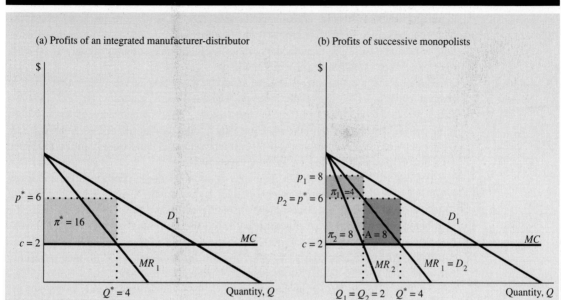

(a) Profits of an integrated manufacturer-distributor

(b) Profits of successive monopolists

As a result, they are worse off. Using the same demand curve, $p = 10 - Q$, as in the preceding example, and setting marginal cost, c, equal to 2, $p^* = p_2 = 6$ and $p_1 = 8$.[16] Thus consumers pay a third more due to the successive monopoly markup than if the firms were integrated. They buy half as many units: down from $Q^* = 4$ to $Q_1 = Q_2 = 2$.

The firms' collective profits are also lower. The profits of the integrated firm are $\pi^* = 16$. With the successive monopolists, the retailer's profits, π_1, are 4 and the manufacturer's profits, π_2, are 8. As Figure 16.5b shows, π^* equals π_2 plus area A, the profits lost due to reduced sales from the higher price. Total profits drop by Area A $- \pi_1 = 8 - 4 = 4$. That is, the total profits of the successive monopolists are 25 percent lower than those for the integrated firm.

Thus, both consumers and firms are worse off with successive monopolists than when there is a single, integrated monopolist. These losses provide a strong incentive to integrate. It is not always practical to do so. For example, the manufacturer might be Japanese and the distributor, French. It may be too costly for the Japanese firm to vertically integrate into distribution. One alternative is to use vertical restrictions.

---

[16] In this example, $p_1 = D_1(Q_1) = 10 - Q_1, MR_1 = p_2 = D_2(Q_2) = 10 - 2Q_2$, and $MR_2 = 10 - 4Q_2$. Equating marginal cost and marginal revenue for the upstream firm, $c = 2 = 10 - 4Q_2 = MR_2$, implies that $Q_2 = 2$, so $p_2 = 10 - (2 \times 2) = 6$. As a result, $p_2 = 6 = 10 - 2Q_2 = MR_1$, and $p_1 = 10 - 2 = 8$.

Vertical Restrictions.   The problem with the successive monopolists is that the distributor has an incentive to restrict output and raise price. The manufacturer does not want its distributor to further restrict output—or, equivalently, to increase its price, p_1, above the wholesale price, p_2—because profits from the distributor's markup go to the distributor, not the manufacturer. The manufacturer wants as efficient a distribution system as possible (that is, with the smallest distributor's markup).

Ideally, the manufacturer wants to induce competition at the distribution level in order to drive p_1 to the wholesale price, p_2. There are many instances, however, when it is not possible to have competition in distribution, so the manufacturer is stuck with a monopolistic distributor. Before discussing why competition at the distribution level may be impossible, we examine three vertical restrictions that manufacturers can use to induce a monopoly distributor to behave more competitively.

Where it is legal, the manufacturer may be able to impose contractually a *maximum retail price*, $\bar{p}$, that the distributor can charge. By so doing, a manufacturer prevents a distributor from raising its price much above the wholesale price, p_2. As a result, the distributor sells more units. If $\bar{p}$ is set equal to p_2, the distributor behaves like a competitive firm, sells Q^* units, and the outcome is the same as with an integrated firm. If the distributor does not accept this restriction, and $\bar{p}$ is set between p_2 and p_1, then a quantity between Q_1 and Q^* is sold. Such contract clauses were common in the United States before 1976, when a change in the law made it illegal for manufacturers to control the retail prices of independent distributors.

A manufacturer may also impose a sales **quota** on a distributor and require that the distributor sell at least $\bar{Q}$ units. With this restriction, generally referred to as **quantity forcing,** a manufacturer does not have to restrict a distributor's price. Sales quotas induce distributors to expand their output by lowering their prices. Many automobile dealerships and computer retailers have sales quotas.

Another tactic is for a manufacturer to adopt a more complicated pricing scheme than merely charging a distributor p_2 per unit of output. A manufacturer can use a two-part pricing scheme, as described in Chapter 15. It charges the distributor one price for the product and a second price for the right to sell the product. That is, the manufacturer sells the **franchise** rights, or rights to sell the product, to the distributor, for a *franchise fee*.

Why would a manufacturer want to use two prices? Suppose that instead of charging the distributor a price per unit of p_2, which is greater than its marginal cost, c, the manufacturer charges its marginal cost. Here, the distributor equates marginal revenue to its marginal cost, c, and sells Q^* units, which is the same outcome as with a vertically integrated firm. Thus, by setting $p_2 = c$, the manufacturer prevents the second monopoly distortion.

If the manufacturer charges c per unit, however, it earns zero profits, and the distributor earns all the monopoly returns. The manufacturer may, however, make positive profits from its franchise fee. Indeed, so long as there are many *potential* distributors, this approach allows the manufacturer to earn the same profits as it would if it were vertically integrated into distribution. The manufacturer can offer for sale the *right* to be the sole distributor of its product with a contractual guarantee that the wholesale price to the distributor is c per unit. The largest franchise fee a distributor is willing to pay is the value of the monopoly profits, π^*, as shown in Figure 16.5a. If a large number of firms want the monopoly franchise rights, competitive bidding ensures that the franchise fee equals the present value of the monopoly profits. Thus, the manufacturer can achieve the equivalence of vertical integration by charging a franchise fee initially and then charging the marginal cost for its product.

In summary, if there is only one distributor, the problem of double monopoly markups may occur. If vertical integration is not feasible, vertical restraints such as maximum retail prices, quotas, or franchise fees may reduce or eliminate the problem. With more than one distributor, other problems may occur.

Free Riding Among Distributors.   In a typical distribution arrangement, several independent firms distribute one manufacturer's product. Each distributor benefits from the promotional activities of other distributors without having to pay for them. The following sections identify several situations where free riding by distributors is likely to occur and then discuss some vertical restraints that may minimize free riding.

The Problem of Free Riding Among Distributors.   Where distributors must expend substantial sales effort (advertising, showrooms, training a sales staff, training purchasing agents, maintaining quality) in order to sell a product, free riding is likely, since some of that effort helps other distributors. A distributor that cannot reap the full benefits of its sales efforts has an incentive to reduce those efforts and thereby sell less of the manufacturer's product. Free riding, therefore is a problem that arises because distributors are not compensated *separately* for sales efforts; instead, they are compensated for sales efforts on behalf of a particular product only when they sell that product.

Suppose that one distributor heavily *advertises* a manufacturer's product that is also carried by another distributor. The first distributor creates a demand for the product that benefits both distributors, but the second distributor incurs no cost at all. Unless something is done, the first distributor has little incentive to advertise, because it does not capture the full benefits of its advertising.

There are many other examples of free riding other than advertising. Selling many durable goods (for example, automobiles, stereo equipment, and other appliances) requires a large showroom to display products, so that consumers can select the best model to satisfy their particular needs. Showrooms, of course, cost money, as does the inventory on display. If only one distributor has a well-stocked showroom, all customers go to that showroom to decide which product to buy, but they may very well buy from other distributors with less fancy showrooms and smaller inventories. These distributors can charge a lower price than the first distributor because their costs are lower. Thus no dealer has an incentive to maintain a pleasant, well-stocked showroom.

There was a clear example of this behavior near the Berkeley campus of the University of California. A discounter opened a store next door to a retailer that sells stereo equipment in a fancy, well-stocked showroom with carpets and attractive lighting. The discounter had only piles of stereo equipment in their original boxes on linoleum floors with minimal lighting. The discounter had a crude, handwritten sign in its window that said "Go next door, see which equipment you want, then come here for a lower price."

Another example of free riding occurs when a distributor's *sales staff* must be well-trained in order to sell a product. Computer salespeople are a good example. If one distributor has highly trained sales people, customers go to that store and learn a great deal about the product. Some of them subsequently may buy from a distributor (often a mail-order house) without a trained staff at a lower price. The discount distributors can sell at lower prices because they do not incur training costs. Again, the first distributor has a reduced incentive to maintain a well-qualified staff.

Another example of free riding concerns **certification.** Here, there are no explicit services; what is provided is the distributor's reputation that the product it carries is of high quality. For example, certain department stores are known as trendsetters in fashion. They carry only items that they deem to be trendy and of high quality. Presumably they have built this reputation by hiring qualified staff who are able to spot trends in fashion as well as high-quality clothes.

Other stores that carry the same merchandise as that stocked by the "certifying" fashion store reap a benefit: their goods have been certified by the fashionable store as being of high quality and trendy. The other stores are free riding on the reputation of the certifying store and do not invest in building up their own reputations. This free riding creates a dilemma for the manufacturer (Marvel and McCafferty 1984). If the manufacturer only sells to the highest quality stores, it may not get large enough distribution of its product. If it sells to every low quality store, high-quality distributors may be unable to capture fully the returns on their reputations.

A final example of free riding occurs when the *reputation of the product,* which the dealer can affect, influences the overall demand for the product. For example, imagine a chain of independently owned food shops all selling under the same brand name (McDonald's, Burger King, or Wendy's). The brand name carries a certain reputation that attracts buyers. If one shop decides to chisel on quality and produce a lower quality than the other shops, the brand's reputation declines and all distributors suffer. The chiseling firm loses reputation, but if customers primarily rely on brand reputation (and not an individual store's reputation), the decline in demand facing the chiseling store may be more than offset by the decline in that store's cost. If so, it is profitable for the firm to lower quality and free ride on the brand's reputation. When a large proportion of a store's sales are to nonrepeat customers, such as tourists, a store's reputation matters less than brand reputation (since few buyers are familiar with the store's reputation), and chiseling is more of a problem.

Vertical Restrictions.   Manufacturers want to encourage sales efforts by distributors because it increases the demand for the product, thereby increasing the manufacturer's profits. Because free riding reduces the incentive of distributors to promote a manufacturer's product, manufacturers have designed a variety of vertical restrictions to deal with the free-riding problem. Several of these restrictions create a *property right* (see Chapter 6) in the sales efforts that distributors expend on behalf of a manufacturer. That is, these restraints are designed so that distributors reap the benefits of their sales effort.

 One of the most common vertical restraints is an **exclusive territory,** in which a single distributor is the only one that can sell: the distributor obtains monopoly rights to customers in its territory. Because it is often hard to monitor the location of customers and in any event may be difficult to prevent a customer in one territory from buying from a distributor in another, exclusive territories usually involve a promise by the manufacturer that other distributors will not be allowed to locate within certain geographic proximity

EXAMPLE 16.5

EXCLUSIVITY IN BEER

Beer distributors often have exclusive territories. So long as the establishment of these exclusive territories does not lessen competition, they are legal. The courts are often uncertain, however, whether a particular restriction lessens competition. For that reason, the National Beer Wholesalers Association and the U.S. Brewers Association have lobbied for the Malt Beverage Interbrand Competition Act, which would grant antitrust immunity for exclusive territories. Some proponents argue that the bill would help solve free-riding problems, pointing to a similar bill enacted for the soft drink industry in 1981. Some opponents claim the bill would only reduce competition and raise prices. The opponents support their case by pointing to a study by the New York City Department of Consumer Affairs showing that beer prices rose 30 percent in 1983, the year that Miller Brewing and Anheuser-Busch set up exclusive agreements. (See also Example 23.9 on a proposed California law.)

SOURCE: *Fortune.* 1985. December 9, p 135.

to the existing distributor. For example, a distributor of Cadillacs may have a clause in its contract with General Motors (GM) that prevents GM from opening any other Cadillac dealership within a radius of several miles of it. By granting a geographic monopoly to the distributor, the manufacturer insulates it from competition. This insulation from competition may be essential if the distributor is to reap the benefits of its sales efforts (see Example 16.5). Of course, creating market power for the distributor creates the problem of a double monopoly markup. Thus, the manufacturer may have to impose other vertical restrictions as well.

A second type of vertical restraint manufacturers use to stimulate sales efforts is to *limit the number of distributors*. The effect of this limitation is similar to that of exclusive territories. That is, price competition is limited, and more of the gain from sales efforts accrues to the distributor that makes the efforts. Again, the manufacturer must contend with the problem of a double monopoly markup due to the market power it confers on individual distributors.[17]

Resale price maintenance is another method of controlling free riding.[18] Under a resale price maintenance agreement, the manufacturer sets a *minimum* price that may be

---

[17] In addition to limiting distributors, the manufacturer may choose to reward dealers who sell a large amount because of extensive sales effort by sending them larger or more timely shipments.

[18] See Overstreet (1983) and Yamey (1966) for detailed discussions of several instances of retail price maintenance. See Telser (1960) for a discussion of why manufacturers want resale price maintenance agreements, which used to be allowed in the United States under what were called *fair trade laws*. See Mathewson and Winter (1984), Marvel and McCafferty (1984), and Perry and Porter (1986) for further discussions of vertical restraints to deal with free riding.

charged by retailers, which creates an incentive to compete for customers in other dimensions, such as sales effort. For example, if the wholesale price the distributor pays is $10, and the minimum resale price is $20, each dealer has an incentive to spend up to $10 to attract customers. Thus, up to $10 per unit is invested in advertising, trained sales staff, or fancy showrooms. Minimum price restrictions channel competition among distributors toward sales effort and away from price cutting. They lead to more sales effort than occurs without them.

Many countries have banned resale price maintenance. It was abandoned by Canada in 1951, Sweden in 1954, Denmark in 1955, the United Kingdom in 1965 (though exemptions may be requested), and the United States in 1976.

Where legal, resale price maintenance is often widely used.[19] One study estimates that, before resale price maintenance was banned in the United Kingdom in 1956, 44 percent of consumer expenditures on goods were on price maintained items. Other studies indicate that the rate was 25 percent to 40 percent by 1960. A Canadian study estimates that 20 percent of goods sold in grocery stores and 50 percent of goods sold in drug stores were price maintained. In Sweden, 30 percent of consumer goods were covered by resale price maintenance. Another study indicates that, before the ban, coverage in the United States varied from 4 percent to 10 percent of retail sales.

A fourth approach to dealing with free riding is for the manufacturer to *advertise on behalf of its distributors*. If the manufacturer takes over the sales effort and handles the advertising, it does not have to worry about free riding among distributors, who can only free ride on the sales efforts of other distributors. A manufacturer that advertises and stimulates demand for its product can charge each distributor for that service through higher wholesale prices or a higher franchise fee. The problem with the manufacturer taking over the marketing and advertising function is that the appropriate advertising and marketing may differ by locale, and a local distributor is in a better position than the manufacturer to determine the best strategy for its area. After all, if local distributors have no comparative advantage in marketing, the manufacturer probably should vertically integrate.

One solution to this problem is cooperative advertising, in which the manufacturer agrees to pay some of the distributors' advertising costs. The cooperative arrangement can place the responsibility for choosing the advertising in the hands of the knowledgeable party, the local distributor, and the advertising subsidy from the manufacturer to the dealer prevents the free riding problem from eroding the distributor's incentive to advertise. In such cooperative arrangements the manufacturer in effect monitors and pays for the sales efforts of the distributor.

A fifth solution to the free-rider problem is for the manufacturer to monitor each dealer's sales effort and compensate each accordingly. This monitoring is costly.

Free Riding by Manufacturers.   It is also possible that competing manufacturers can free ride the efforts of each other. Suppose that two competing manufacturers both use

---

[19] See the survey of studies in Overstreet (1983, 113; 152–56). The following numbers on the percentage of goods covered by resale price maintenance agreements are based on his summary. There is an extensive discussion of various countries' laws in Yamey (1966).

EXAMPLE 16.6

REQUIRING EXCLUSIVITY

Coors Beer used to have exclusivity requirements with some retailers who sold its beer for on-premise consumption, such as restaurants and taverns. Coors required the retailers to sell only Coors draught beer and no other light-colored draught beer, which is beer that is dispensed from a tap or faucet. Retailers were allowed to sell dark draught beers and any brand of beer in a bottle or can. The Federal Trade Commission challenged this practice and obtained a court order stopping Coors from requiring exclusivity.

Shishido-Topel argues that this practice was designed to prevent retailers from switching brands on customers. Coors spends money to advertise its product and thereby increases the customer demand in taverns that serve Coors. A customer who consumes Coors beer in a can or in a bottle can tell if it is Coors. A customer who consumes draught beer can only determine if it is Coors by its taste and color. Coors' restriction applied only to other light-colored draught beers because most customers would realize that a dark beer was not Coors. If the customer does not get Coors, then Coors' advertising is benefiting some other beer company. By allowing only Coors beer to be served, Coors guaranteed that it reaped the full rewards of its advertising.

Presumably, Coors could spot check its retailers to prevent such switching activity, but the costs of Coors might be higher than enforcing its previous restrictions. It is possible, of course, that Coors had other motives for this requirement as well.

SOURCE: Shishido-Topel (1984).

the same distributor to sell their product and that one manufacturer conducts a massive advertising campaign to entice consumers to go to the distributor to buy its product. This manufacturer has no way to prevent the second manufacturer from benefiting from the increased customer flow. In fact, since the free riding manufacturer does not advertise, it has lower costs than the first manufacturer and can sell at a lower price. The distributor then can (correctly) tell a customer who was enticed into the store by the advertising of the first manufacturer, that the second manufacturer's product is a much better deal because it has a lower price. See Example 16.6.

Another example of free riding among manufacturers occurs when one manufacturer trains its distributors to repair or sell its product. To the extent that such training is costly and can be applied to other products, a second manufacturer can free ride on these training expenditures by using the same distribution outlets as the first manufacturer. Again, the free rider has lower costs and can out-compete the manufacturer that pays for the training.

A final example of free riding among manufacturers occurs when one manufacturer provides a list of potential customers to a distributor. If the distributor also sells the competing products of a second manufacturer, the second manufacturer benefits from the first manufacturer's customer list. These examples of free riding among manufacturers are similar in their effects to free riding among distributors. If the free riding is unchecked, manufacturers have reduced incentives to advertise, provide training for distributors, or develop customer lists. The solution to these free-rider problems is to create a system that allows manufacturers to obtain the full reward for their sales efforts. One common solution, **exclusive dealing,** is for manufacturers to forbid their distributors to sell the products of competing manufacturers (Marvel 1982). Recently, several ice cream manufacturers have alleged that a rival has required its distributors to carry only its products.

Externalities Due to a Lack of Coordination Among Distributors. A manufacturer that relies upon independent distributors that compete with each other usually wants to coordinate or restrict the ways in which they compete. For example, distributors often compete with each other on location (see Chapter 11 on monopolistic competition). The optimal location from a manufacturer's viewpoint may differ from the one that emerges under monopolistic competition by independent retailers.

A manufacturer may want to insure that its goods are available wherever consumers are apt to buy. For example, by selling at unprofitable locations, the manufacturer may prevent buyers from trying other products and thereby develop brand loyalty. This strategy can raise profits elsewhere, and hence total profits. Since an independent dealer sells only where its profits are nonzero, a conflict arises between the locational desires of the manufacturer and its distributors.

Competition between distributors depends on how each distributor thinks the others will react to its behavior. This competitive interaction among dealers can lead to a price and service quality that is different from what the manufacturer prefers. As shown in Chapters 10 and 11, price and quality vary depending on rivals' behavior toward each other, so it is unlikely that any particular oligopolistic outcome is consistent with the manufacturer's desires. Again a conflict arises between the manufacturer's desires and the outcome of competition among distributors.

As a final example, suppose that consumers search to find the lowest price (see Chapter 17). Searching uses resources, so it is only undertaken if consumers believe there are price differences across locations. If a manufacturer can require its distributors to set identical prices, then the incentive to search (and thereby the costs of searching) is eliminated. The problem of competing distributors can be restated in the framework of Chapter 15. Suppose that different distributors sell different products that are substitutes for one another. As Chapter 15 shows, if consumers substitute between Products A and B, it is more profitable to have a single monopolist coordinate their prices than to have two separate firms setting prices. The point here is the same, although now it is not just price that matters. By controlling competition among all dealers, a manufacturer can profitably coordinate their pricing, sales efforts, and locations and achieve higher profits than those that result from uncoordinated decision making among competing distributors. Table 16.2 summarizes the main problems arising in distribution and the possible solutions for a manufacturer.

The Effects of Vertical Restrictions

The preceding sections have discussed a variety of vertical restrictions that manufacturers can and do impose on distributors to control the problems of double monopoly markup,

TABLE 16.2 Problems That Arise in Distribution and Manufacturers' Responses	
Problems in Distribution	*Manufacturers' Responses*
Double monopoly markup	Encourage competition at distribution Sell at marginal cost and charge a franchise fee Establish sales quotas or maximum prices
Free riding among distributors	Establish exclusive territories or restrict the number of dealers Establish minimum price (resale price maintenance) Have the manufacturer take over the marketing effort Have the manufacturer subsidize dealer sales effort Have the manufacturer monitor and pay for sales effort
Free riding among manufacturers	Impose exclusive dealing on dealers
Lack of coordination among dealers leading to externalities	Use a combination of the policies above

free riding, and competitive interaction. In general, distribution arrangements include various combinations of these policies. These restrictions typically limit the amount of competition that can occur in a market and, at the same time, encourage additional efforts to sell the product.

A restriction in competition is something that an economist abhors, as it may increase market power. On the other hand, an increase in sales efforts is something that an economist applauds. So, should an economist conclude that vertical restraints are desirable or undesirable? There is no clear-cut answer to this question, but one can make several observations about the trade-off between restrictions and additional sales effort. The following sections describe markets where vertical restrictions benefit both firms and consumers, where the effects are ambiguous, and where vertical restrictions harm consumers. Finally, we note the implications of banning vertical restrictions.

Desirable Effects of Vertical Restrictions.   Vertical restrictions that benefit both firms and consumers are unambiguously desirable. It is often in a manufacturer's selfish interest to use vertical restrictions that help consumers. Any manufacturer, even one with substantial monopoly power, wants its product distributed at the lowest cost. Distribution is viewed by the manufacturer as an input necessary to make a sale, just as a raw material is an input in the manufacturing process. A monopolistic manufacturer tries to distribute the product as efficiently as possible, just as it tries to produce the good in the most efficient manner. Thus, although in some cases vertical restrictions can be used for anticompetitive purposes, a number of economists believe that many if not most vertical restrictions benefit consumers by lowering prices or increasing services.[20]

Vertical restrictions may lower prices, either because they increase the output of existing firms or encourage new firms to enter markets. Vertical restrictions that allow a firm to more effectively promote its product and that lead to more output sold at a lower

---

[20] For examples of instances when vertical restrictions are procompetitive, see several of the case studies in Lafferty, Lande, and Kirkwood (1984).

price help both firms and consumers. For example, competition between different brands is heightened if competing firms can effectively promote their products. That is, although competition among dealers of the same brand is restricted, competition across brands is encouraged, because the vertical restrictions stimulate sales efforts for each brand. Vertical restrictions also may make entry easier, which leads to lower prices. Without vertical restrictions, new products that rely heavily on sales efforts have difficulty breaking into a market.

In many cases, consumers view the *relevant product* as both the good and the service provided with it. Consumers who cannot get full use from a good without instruction from the seller suffer if the good is sold without service. For example, a neophyte photographer is well advised to buy a camera from a local store that provides instructions on how to use it. Although the camera can be purchased at a lower price from a mail-order distributor, the extra service from the local store may be worth the difference in price. In such cases, the good-with-service is really an entirely different product than the good without service. Vertical restrictions allow the good to be sold with service (sales effort). Without the restrictions, the price is lower, but fewer services are provided.

Ambiguous Effects of Vertical Restrictions.   Whether a vertical restriction is desirable depends on the same factors that influence the social desirability of product choice. Imagine two groups of buyers: those who know how to use a good (experienced users) and those who do not (beginners). With no training provided, experienced users buy the good at $10 and beginners go without it. With vertical restrictions that allow beginners to receive instruction, both groups buy the good for $11. The experienced users are worse off with the vertical restrictions, since they spend more per unit but do not benefit from the availability of training. The beginners, however, are better off because if they purchased the good, it must be worth at least $11 to all of them, and some may receive consumer surplus. Although it is impossible to say that a vertical restriction that leads to more services benefits all groups of consumers, in some cases most or all consumers benefit from a vertical restriction. For example, most farmers receive detailed instructions on how to use fertilizers and pesticides from sales agents.

Training is not the only useful sales effort. For example, showrooms are very useful to automobile, camera, computer, and stereo buyers. Without showrooms, potential customers could not easily examine the various products before purchase. Many, if not most, consumers would prefer to pay a slightly higher price and have a chance to test drive a car before purchasing it.

Vertical restrictions, just like vertical integration, can be used to price discriminate. Suppose consumers in California have an inelastic demand for some product, and consumers in Illinois have an elastic demand. The manufacturer wants to charge a high wholesale price to the distributor in California and a low one to the distributor in Illinois. If the manufacturer tries to do so, however, the independent Illinois distributor can profitably resell the product it buys from the manufacturer in California. By granting exclusive territories to the independent distributors in exchange for no resale agreements, the manufacturer can charge a low wholesale price in Illinois and a high one in California. As explained in Chapters 14 and 15, however, imperfect price discrimination has ambiguous welfare effects and can increase or decrease welfare compared to simple monopoly pricing. Vertical restrictions that allow a manufacturer to control the externalities among the distributors can also have ambiguous welfare effects (Rey and Stiglitz 1986, Rey and Tirole 1986).

Undesirable Vertical Restrictions.   In some cases, vertical restrictions (and vertical integration) can be used for anticompetitive purposes. For example, they may be used to cartelize an industry or prevent entry.

Vertical restrictions can lead to either distributors' or manufacturers' cartels. A group of dealers can impose vertical restraints that lead to monopolization. For example, suppose a group of dealers are the only ones who can distribute some product. They may force the manufacturer to grant exclusive territories, leading to local monopolies and restricted competition among dealers. As discussed in Chapter 9, allocating territories is an effective way to cartelize, and leads to higher consumer prices. This outcome is likely only if entry into distribution is difficult, so that a manufacturer has no choice but to act as the *cat's paw* for a dealer cartel.

Similarly, vertical restrictions can help to perpetuate a cartel of manufacturers. Suppose a group of manufacturers wants to collude. It may be difficult for them to observe the price that each is charging its dealers. If they all agree to charge the same price at retail, however, and enforce this agreement with vertical restrictions (such as resale price maintenance) on dealers, it is easier for them to detect if any manufacturer cheats on the agreement by lowering price, since it is easier to observe retail prices than wholesale prices.

Vertical restrictions may be used to increase the difficulty of entering an industry. For example, Chapter 13 shows how an incumbent can make it difficult or impossible for a rival to enter by tying up scarce distribution channels. Exclusive dealing is one way for manufacturers to tie up distribution. Under such agreements, both parties to the contract agree to rely only on each other, not on other firms. Such strategic behavior can successfully raise the cost of entry only if the channels of distribution are limited.

Banning Vertical Restrictions

Even where vertical restrictions are undesirable, in some cases little is accomplished by banning them. If vertical restrictions are outlawed, a manufacturer has an incentive to vertically integrate and handle its own distribution, so that it can impose the desirable restrictions. It would be a bit odd to enact a law preventing contracts between independent firms when a firm could easily avoid such prohibitions by vertically integrating and distributing the product itself. Only where the cost of vertically integrating is much higher than the cost of imposing vertical restrictions does a ban on vertical restrictions effectively end such practices.

Thus, although manufacturers impose vertical restrictions to increase their profits by generating more sales efforts, consumers may either gain or lose. Courts have recognized the value of increasing competition by encouraging promotional efforts. The courts have tried to bar certain vertical restrictions such as those that enhance or create a dealer or manufacturer cartel or raise costs of entry. Unfortunately, forbidding undesirable vertical restrictions does not prevent the associated harms unless vertical integration is prohibitively expensive.

■ LEGAL STATUS UNDER ANTITRUST LAWS

Restrict: *To limit; to confine. A word scarce English.* —DR. SAMUEL JOHNSON

Vertical integration that occurs through internal expansion is generally beyond the reach of the antitrust laws, as is discussed in more detail in Chapter 22.[21] Vertical integration achieved through merger can be challenged under the antitrust laws if the effect is to lessen competition.

Under the antitrust laws, most nonprice vertical restrictions are judged under a **rule of reason.** That is, vertical restrictions are not **per se illegal** (always illegal); each case must be considered separately on its merits. The courts attempt to weigh the procompetitive features of the restriction against the anticompetitive ones in deciding whether to prohibit the restriction.

The courts sometimes phrase the evaluation of a vertical restriction in terms of the promotion of interbrand competition (competition between brands) versus the restriction of intrabrand competition (competition in the selling of one brand), but this distinction can be a misleading characterization. First, sales efforts can stimulate sales even if there are no competing brands. Second, as long as vertical restrictions do not create or enhance market power, they do not limit intrabrand competition, as discussed in the previous section. A manufacturer can already affect the retail price by setting the wholesale price. A manufacturer may rely on vertical restrictions because it cannot otherwise control promotional efforts. Vertical restrictions do not necessarily give a manufacturer greater control over retail price, but they do give it greater control over sales efforts, which may benefit consumers.

Political pressures to forbid certain types of vertical restrictions are strong. In some states, for example, auto dealers have successfully lobbied for laws that limit the control that auto manufacturers have over them. In some states existing franchisees can influence the location of new franchisees that the franchisor wants to place near them.

Although most nonprice vertical restrictions are subject to a rule of reason, vertical restrictions on price are now per se illegal. That is, the courts consider the facts of the case to determine whether a particular nonprice vertical restriction is harmful, but they view any vertical restriction on price as illegal and do not consider any mitigating circumstances or offsetting benefits. Thus, resale price maintenance is now against the law. Until federal repeal on January 1, 1976, under the Miller-Tidings Act of 1937 and the related McGuire Act of 1952, however, states could give manufacturers the right to set prices for their products at retail levels. In the early 1950s, resale price maintenance laws or fair trade laws were enforced in all states except Alaska, Missouri, Texas, and Vermont.

---

[21] *U.S. v. Alcoa*, 148 F.2d 416 (2d Cir. 1945) is an exception. The court found that Alcoa's internal expansion into bauxite and electric power amounted to an exclusionary practice.

By the time of repeal, only 36 states had fair-trade laws, and the laws were not actively enforced in many. As a result, Consumers Union estimated that the proportion of retail sales subject to fair trade fell by half between 1959 and 1974 (Shepard 1978).

In *Monsanto v. Spray-Rite* (465 U.S. 752 [1984]), Spray-Rite, a distributor, complained about the control that Monsanto exerted over its prices. Because of an explicit congressional prohibition, the U.S. Department of Justice, which filed a brief in the case, was not allowed to argue in favor of resale price maintenance. Opponents of resale price maintenance (for example, discount stores) persuaded Congress to enjoin the Department of Justice from supporting resale price maintenance. In its decision in the case, the U.S. Supreme Court refused to rule that resale price maintenance could (even sometimes) be legal. Therefore, resale price maintenance remains a per se violation of the antitrust laws. For example, in 1989, although denying any wrongdoing, Panasonic Co. agreed to refund as much as $16 million to consumers to settle charges that consumers paid 5 to 10 percent too much because of price fixing. Panasonic was alleged to have threatened to discontinue supplying retailers that sold for less than the suggested retail price.[22]

As discussed above, all vertical restrictions have the potential for both procompetitive and anticompetitive effects. Thus, there is no economic reason to distinguish resale price maintenance from other types of vertical restrictions.

■ FRANCHISING

One special type of vertical relationship that has become increasingly important in the United States and elsewhere is that between a **franchisor** and a **franchisee** (Caves and Murphy 1976; Rubin 1978). The franchisor, a firm such as McDonald's, sells a proven method of doing business to the individual franchisee (the owner of a McDonald's outlet). When the franchisor provides a total system of doing business, it is referred to as a *business-format* franchise.

In the last 10 years, the number of franchisors has roughly doubled to about 2000, and the number of individual franchisees has grown from about 220,000 units to over 300,000. In 1985, business-format franchise sales accounted for over $141 billion.[23] Franchises include fast-food outlets, service stations, auto dealers, and soft-drink bottlers. The six fastest growing business-format franchises appear in Table 16.3.

Franchisees have a much lower failure rate than independent nonfranchisee businesses: 20 percent versus 80 percent.[24] The franchisor provides the franchisee with training and other assistance, which often includes advice on purchasing, pricing, choice of location, accounting procedures, and advertising. The franchisee agrees to run the business in the manner stipulated by the franchisor, who continues to monitor the franchisee's performance to make sure it abides by the franchisor's methods. The franchisor's vertical restrictions greatly limit the way a franchise is run (though federal antitrust and state laws often limit

---

[22] "Panasonic Plans Mass Refund in Price-Fix Case." 1989. *San Francisco Chronicle*, January 19, A1, A14.

[23] *The 1986 Franchise Annual*. 1986. Lewiston, N.Y.: Info Press, H55.

[24] Ibid., H38.

TABLE 16.3 Fastest Growing Franchises			
Franchisor	*Company-owned/ Franchisee*	*Franchise Fee*	*Royalty Fee on Sales*
Domino's	804/1970	$6500	5.5%
McDonald's	2165/6150	$12,500	11.5%
Burger King	778/3555	$40,000	3.5%
Jazzercise	0/3073	$500	30.0%
Fantastic Sam's	3/860	$25,000	$131 per week
Wendy's	1135/2106	$30,000	4.0%

NOTE: Sample includes only business-format franchises for which data on the last two fiscal years were available.
*Advertising and initial start-up costs also differ across franchises.
SOURCE: *Venture*. November 1986, 52–53.

aspects of franchisor control, as discussed in Chapter 22). Franchisee agreements can typically be terminated by the franchisor. As compensation to the franchisor, the franchisee usually pays a franchise fee plus a percentage, or royalty, on sales, which is usually in the range of 0–10 percent, with 5 percent a typical value.

The franchisor-franchisee relationship requires each party to rely on the efforts of the other—efforts that may be difficult to observe. Because a franchisor has difficulty monitoring how well a franchise is run, it provides incentives to the franchisee by making it the *residual claimant*, the one who receives any extra profits that arise from the franchisee's hard work. That is, if a franchisor receives a fixed amount each year, then all extra profits generated through the franchisee's efforts go to the franchisee. Thus, the franchisee has an incentive to work harder than a salaried employee of the franchisor would.

Where it is not difficult to monitor the behavior of the franchisee, the franchisor may own the outlet itself. Many franchisors own and operate a substantial fraction of their outlets. In the United States, about 26 percent of franchisor sales come from company-owned outlets.[25] Company owned outlets tend to be larger than independent franchises and tend to be located closer to a regional headquarters of the franchisor than independent franchises. There appears to be a long-run tendency for the proportion of company owned outlets to decline as the franchisor continues to expand (Martin 1988, Brickley and Dark 1987).

After entering into the agreement, the franchisee expects the franchisor to continue to offer services and to make sure that the other franchisees maintain the reputation of the brand. If the franchisor sells franchises to inept people, the brand name declines in value and so does the business of each franchisee—even those run efficiently. By linking the franchisor's fee to a percentage of sales, the franchisor has an incentive to continue to assist and monitor franchisees and to make sure that they succeed. If total sales fall, the franchisor's fee falls.

A more difficult question is why the franchisor's fee depends on sales and not profits.

---

[25] International Trade Administration, U.S. Department of Commerce. 1987. *Franchising in the Economy: 1985–1987*. Washington, D.C.: U.S. Government Printing Office.

After all, it is profits, not sales, that franchisees and franchisors want to maximize. One answer is that it is easier to measure sales rather than profits (which, for example, requires a determination of depreciation). Another answer, which is hard to verify, is that a fee based on sales, and not profits, better induces the franchisor to monitor other franchisees.

■ EMPIRICAL EVIDENCE ON VERTICAL INTEGRATION AND VERTICAL RESTRICTIONS

Several explanations of why firms vertically integrate or impose vertical restrictions have been discussed in this chapter. Real world evidence illustrates how significant the explanatory power of the various theories are in predicting where vertical integration and vertical restrictions occur. We first examine the evidence on vertical integration and then that on vertical restrictions.

Evidence on Vertical Integration

Most of the existing studies of the reasons for vertical integration focus on the transaction costs or market power theories discussed in this chapter. Williamson's (1975, 1985) transaction costs or specific assets theory holds that when either firm in a vertical relationship must invest in a specific asset (one with no alternative use), vertical integration may be used to avoid opportunistic behavior. Opportunistic behavior typically involves reneging on implicit or explicit contracts or promises, with the intent of extracting a larger share of the rents generated by the transaction. The firm does whatever is least expensive—vertically integrate or rely on markets—taking into account possible opportunistic behavior by other parties. The market power theory holds that firms vertically integrate to increase profits or eliminate market power. This section presents three empirical studies that examine why firms produce some products internally but obtain others through market procurement.

Monteverde and Teece (1982) examine quasi-integration by automobile manufacturers. They explain why, in some cases, a manufacturer owns a machine necessary to produce a part, rather than buying the part from another firm that owns the machine. For example, suppose that the machine to make a specialized part that can only be used by that manufacturer must be custom built. If another firm owns that machine, it is at the mercy of the manufacturer, which could suddenly announce it is no longer willing to buy the parts, making the machine virtually worthless. This opportunistic behavior can be avoided if the manufacturer vertically integrates backwards and owns the other firm. A less extreme solution is quasi-vertical integration, in which the manufacturer owns only the machine, not the other firm. The other firm runs the machine for the manufacturer and charges an hourly rate.

Monteverde and Teece examine a sample of manufactured components from two divisions of a major U.S. automobile supplier, all of which require special machinery and cannot be purchased on the open market. Monteverde and Teece test whether the possibility of opportunistic behavior leads to quasi-integration. Opportunistic behavior is likely if the value of the specialized asset to the downstream firm is much higher than for its next most valuable use. To illustrate this point, suppose that the machine to make a specialized part can be easily converted to produce parts for other firms. In that case, the opportunities for exploitation of this firm by the manufacturer are much less than if there is no other use for the machine. Monteverde and Teece believe that opportunistic behavior is more likely, the higher the tooling cost (the cost of producing the special machines to produce the part) and the more specialized the part (the higher the cost of converting the machine to its next best use). Their empirical evidence for automotive suppliers supports this hypothesis.

Masten (1984) studies vertical integration in the aerospace industry. Firms can either make various components used in the industry themselves or buy from others. As in the previous study, integration is more likely when specialized assets are used. Masten employs two measures of asset specificity. The first, design specificity, reflects whether the item is used exclusively by this company (highly specialized), is easily adaptable for use by other aerospace firms (somewhat specialized), or is used in other industries (relatively standard). For example, transistors and resistors are standard items, and hybrid circuits designed for specific firms are highly specialized. The second, site specificity, reflects whether having the product produced nearby reduces costs. Masten also measures the complexity of the product: the more complex the product, the more things that can go wrong and the greater the possibility of opportunistic behavior.

His statistical analysis shows that products that are highly complex and highly design-specific are more likely to be produced internally, but that site specificity, at least in this industry, is not an important factor. If the product is both design-specific and complex, there is a 92 percent probability that it is produced internally. If it is design specialized but not complex, there is a 31 percent probability of internal production. The probability drops to 2 percent or less if it is not design specialized, regardless of whether or not it is complex. Thus, design specialization appears to be the most important factor.

Spiller (1985) tests whether the specific-asset or market-power theories explain the occurrence of vertical mergers, in which the acquiring firm vertically integrates by buying either a supplier or a customer. Firms often vertically merge to avoid opportunistic behavior when a specific asset is involved. Spiller argues that there is less of a need to integrate, the more similar are the market conditions faced by both firms. For example, if both the seller and the buyer know when either firm's costs change, the supplier is less likely to claim falsely that it must raise its prices due to a cost increase. Determining whether the other firm's costs changed is easier if the market conditions facing both firms are highly correlated.

The market-power explanation is that a firm may vertically merge to obtain or eliminate market power in the input market. All else the same, the gains from merging should depend on whether the input market is concentrated.

Spiller tests these two explanations by analyzing the size of the total gains to the two firms and the distribution of the gains from a merger between the acquiring and target firms. This information is derived from the unexpected changes in the firms' stock market values at the time of the merger announcements. The specific-asset rationale suggests that the total gains to the two firms increase with the degree of asset specificity by the two firms.

Spiller uses site specificity (the proximity of the two firms) as a measure of asset specificity, and the concentration ratio of the industry as a proxy for a firm's market power. Spiller finds, as predicted by the asset-specificity argument, that the total gains from merging are less, the greater the distance between the plants involved. The evidence does not support the market-power explanation. Through these and other tests, Spiller infers that the observed mergers are more likely due to asset specificity than to efforts to extend or eliminate market power.

Evidence on Vertical Restrictions

Most of the empirical studies of vertical restrictions have concentrated on the effects of resale price maintenance.[26] This section examines two studies based on a comparison of the periods before and after the law changed. Most of the studies presented to Congress in 1975, when it was debating making resale price maintenance illegal, found that maintained prices were from 16 to 19 percent higher than those in states that did not enforce fair trade laws. A Library of Congress study estimated that consumers paid between $1.66 billion and $6.23 billion more on retail transactions covered by fair-trade laws than in free-trade states. Thus, families in fair-trade states may have paid $150 more per year for maintained prices (Shephard 1978).

If these studies are correct, the federal ban in 1976 should have lowered prices, diminished nonprice competition, and led to a consolidation among retailers. A study by Shepard (1978) of the eighteen-month period following repeal (January 1976 to June 1977) finds some evidence of these effects and suggests that consumers paid up to $6.5 billion more in fair-trade states. The prices of discount firms are estimated to have fallen 11.6 percent relative to the prices they were forced to charge in December 1975, and specialty store (nondiscounter) prices fell by only 1.8 percent. Price differentials between discounters and nondiscounters in furniture, apparel, and tools became very large, from 20 to 30 percent. Nonprice competition probably fell as a result. A survey of retailers in California, a fair-trade state, found that nondiscount specialty stores discounted some product lines sold at nearby discount outlets. Moreover, 15 percent of surveyed retailers claimed they or their rivals had reduced their advertising budgets following repeal. This claim is supported by average advertising linage purchased by retailers in major newspapers in the 108 largest U.S. cities. In 1975, prior to repeal, mean advertising in the 82 fair-trade cities was 16.2 percent higher than in free-trade cities. In 1976, after repeal, advertising in these cities was only 12.7 percent higher.

Ornstein and Hanssens (1987) consider whether resale price maintenance of liquor increased or decreased welfare. Presumably, if resale price maintenance increases efficiency in distribution, it increases output and thereby raises consumer surplus.[27] They compare states with resale price maintenance to others for the period 1974–78. They find that the presence of resale price maintenance lowers per capita consumption by 8 percent,

---

[26] Ekelund *et al.* (1987), analyzes the effect of exclusive territories on the price of beer. They conclude that, when account is taken of state advertising restrictions on price, there is no evidence that exclusive territories raise price.

[27] More liquor sold at a lower price increases consumer surplus from direct consumption. More consumption, of course, could cause substantial harm, such as from drunk driving. These indirect harms are not included in the welfare calculations reported below.

holding other factors constant. They also compare the effects in California counties for eight years prior to the repeal and in 1984. The repeal of the law had a significant negative impact on liquor store license values of between 23 and 25 percent. This large loss is consistent with the belief that resale price maintenance was used to establish prices above the competitive level. It is also consistent with the view that resale price maintenance was used to create some profits in the distribution sector in order to encourage sales effort.

Using a cross-state analysis, they estimated the welfare loss from resale price maintenance, ignoring the negative externalities from drink. Based on estimates of the price elasticity of demand for liquor that range from -0.5 to -1.5, their estimates of the direct welfare loss range from $2.5 to $7.5 million. The wealth transfer from consumers to firms was more substantial: $226.6 million in 1978, or 4.5 percent of estimated retail sales in the affected states. Thus, the deadweight loss from resale price maintenance appears to be a small percent (1.1 to 3.3 percent) of the redistribution of income. Given the problems in estimating welfare losses, Ornstein and Hanssens say these figures should be viewed as suggestive only.

■ SUMMARY

Vertical integration results for the same reasons that firms are created in the first place. Although firms may vertically integrate to increase monopoly profits, they also have many efficiency-related motives. When firms decide not to vertically integrate, they may impose vertical restrictions on the firms with which they deal. It is often in the best interest of a manufacturer to use vertical restrictions to give limited monopoly power to distributors. By doing so, the manufacturer induces the distributor to put forth more sales effort. These vertical restrictions can stimulate product sales and promote competition. In certain circumstances, vertical integration and vertical restriction may also be used for purely anticompetitive reasons. Although there may be exceptions, in general it is extremely difficult to show that either vertical integration, or vertical restrictions decrease welfare; therefore policy interventions should be limited.

■ Key Terms

certification
downstream
exclusive dealing
exclusive territory
fixed-proportions production function
franchise, franchisee, franchisor
free riding
opportunistic behavior

per se illegal
principal-agent
quantity forcing
quasi-vertical integration
   (quasi-integration)
quota
resale price maintenance
rule of reason

specialized asset
upstream
variable-proportions production function
vertical restrictions
vertically integrated

■ Discussion Questions

1. Suppose that there are many car manufacturers. One is a monopsonistic buyer of aluminum from suppliers located near its plant. Under what circumstances is it efficient for vertical integration to occur?

2. Explain why a manufacturer of fashion clothes might want to prevent its clothing from being sold in discount stores.

3. Should the controls that a franchisor places on a franchisee be subject to government regulation if the franchisor competes with other franchisors?
4. Does it make sense to allow vertical integration through internal expansion but not through a merger?
5. Argue for or against the following statement: "Firms are not just vertically integrated or not vertically integrated. There is a continuum of relations between these two extremes."
6. When should a firm vertically integrate (take over a supplier or purchaser) and when should it only pursue quasi-vertical integration (obtain control of an asset such as a machine, but not own the other firm)?

■ Problems

1. Show that it is more efficient (larger joint profits) for a franchisor to collect a royalty from a franchisee that is a percent of profits rather than sales. Why do most franchisors collect royalties as a percent of sales?
2. Suppose a monopolistic upstream firm sells to a number of downstream firms, and one of these is a monopolist in its retail market. If vertical integration is impractical, what might the government do to reduce the distortions from the double monopoly markup?
3. If a pure profits tax (a percentage of the economic profits) is collected at the retail level, does a downstream monopolist's incentive to vertically integrate change? Does the incentive change if the tax is collected at both upstream and downstream levels? Does a sales tax (at the retail level) affect the incentive to vertically integrate?
4. A monopolistic producer uses a dealer network, in which it limits the number of dealers and restricts them to exclusive territories, to sell its product in the United States. The producer also sells its product in another country. Some importers buy the product in the other country and sell it in the United States. Such imported products are said to be sold on the *gray market*. Explain why the manufacturer might not act to prevent such gray market sales.
5. A woman wants to present a friend with a gift and, as an inside joke, wants to present it inside an empty red and white striped barrel of Kentucky Fried Chicken. She tries to buy the empty carton from a fast food chain that sells Kentucky Fried Chicken and is told that it costs $10! The barrel full of chicken costs $10.99. The reason is that the corporate headquarters keeps its inventory on the amount of chicken sold by the number of cardboard containers sold.[28] To make sure of an accurate count, the parent firm may have required the franchisees to purchase cartons only from it. Should society bar the franchisor from requiring such purchases by franchisees? Why does the franchisor want to use this method? How can it try to get around this restriction?
6. One possible measure of the degree of vertical integration is the ratio of value added (sales minus material and energy costs) to sales. Contrast this measure for an oil producing firm that owns an oil well to a car producing firm.

Answers to odd-numbered problems are given at the back of the book.

[28] DeLeon, Clark. 1980. "The Colonel: That will work, won't it?" *Philadelphia Inquirer*, December 30, 2-B.

■ Recommended Readings

For an excellent, relatively nontechnical survey of the entire literature on vertical relations, see Perry (1989). The classic articles on vertical integration are Coase (1937) and Stigler (1951). The two books by the leading proponent of the transaction costs approach, Williamson (1975, 1985), are relatively nontechnical and are fascinating reading. Blair and Kaserman (1983) is a clear, but more technical analysis. Telser (1960) is probably the first article to present the modern rationale for vertical relations and is nontechnical. A clear, recent statement on that topic is White (1985).

■ References

Adelman, Morris A. 1955. "Concept and Statistical Measurement of Vertical Integration," in George J. Stigler, ed., *Business Concentration and Price Policy*. Princeton, N.J.: Princeton University Press.

Blair, Roger D., and David L. Kaserman. 1983. *Law and Economics of Vertical Integration and Control*. New York: Academic Press.

Bolch, Ben, and William W. Damon. 1978. "The Depletion Allowance and Vertical Integration in the Petroleum Industry." *Southern Economic Journal* 45:241–49.

Brickley, J., and F. Dark. 1987. "The Choice of Organizational Form: The Case of Franchising." *Journal of Financial Economics* 18:401–20.

Carlton, Dennis W. 1979. "Vertical Integration in Competitive Markets Under Uncertainty." *Journal of Industrial Economics* 27:189–209.

Carlton, Dennis W., and M. Klamer. 1983. "The Need for Coordination Among Firms with Special Reference to Network Industries." *University of Chicago Law Review* (Spring).

Caves, Richard E., and William F. Murphy. 1976. "Franchising: Firms, Markets, and Intangible Assets." *Southern Economic Journal* 42:572–86.

Coase, Ronald H. 1937. "The Nature of the Firm." *Economica* 4:386–405. Reprinted in George J. Stigler and Kenneth Boulding, eds., *Readings in Price Theory*. Homewood, Ill.: Richard D. Irwin, 1952.

Ekelund, Robert B., Jr., John D. Jackson, David S. Saurman, William F. Shugart III, and Robert D. Tollison. 1987. "Exclusive Territories and Advertising Restrictions in the Malt Beverage Industry." Manuscript.

Klein, Benjamin, Robert G. Crawford, and Armen A. Alchian. 1978. "Vertical Integration, Appropriable Rents, and the Competitive Contracting Process." *Journal of Law and Economics* 21:297–326.

Laffer, Arthur B. 1969. "Vertical Integration by Corporations, 1929–1965." *Review of Economics and Statistics* 51:91–3.

Lafferty, Ronald N., Robert H. Lande, and John B. Kirkwood, eds. 1984. *Impact Evaluations of Federal Trade Commission Vertical Restraint Cases*. Washington, D.C.: Bureau of Competition, Bureau of Economics, Federal Trade Commission (August).

Lavey, Warren, and Dennis W. Carlton. 1983. "Economic Goals and Remedies of the AT&T Modified Judgment." *Georgetown Law Review* 17:1497–1518.

Livesay, Harold C. and Patrick C. Porter. 1969. "Vertical Integration in American Manufacturing, 1899-1948." *Journal of Economic History* 29:494–500.

Mallela, Parthasaradhi, and Babu Nahata. 1980. "Theory of Vertical Control with Variable Proportions." *Journal of Political Economy* 88:1009—25.

Martin, R. 1988. "Franchising and Risk Management." Mimeo.

Marvel, Howard P. 1982. "Exclusive Dealing." *Journal of Law and Economics* 25:1–25.

Marvel, Howard P., and Stephen McCafferty. 1984. "Resale Price Maintenance and Quality Certification." *Rand Journal of Economics* 15:246–359.

Masten, Scott E. 1984. "The Organization of Production: Evidence from the Aerospace Industry." *Journal of Law and Economics* 27:403–17.

Mathewson, G. Frank, and Ralph A. Winter. 1984. "An Economic Theory of Vertical Restraints." *Rand Journal of Economics* 15:27–38.

Monteverde, Kirk, and David J. Teece. 1982. "Appropriable Rents and Quasi-Vertical Integration." *Journal of Law and Economics* 25:403–18.

Ornstein, Stanley I., and Dominique M. Hanssens. 1987. "Resale Price Maintenance: Output Increasing or Restricting? The Case of Distilled Spirits in the United States." *Journal of Industrial Economics* 36:1–18.

Overstreet, Thomas R., Jr. 1983. *Resale Price Maintenance: Economic Theories and Empirical Evidence*. Washington, D.C.: Federal Trade Commission, Bureau of Economics Staff Report (November).

Perry, Martin K. 1989. "Vertical Integration: Determinants and Effects," in Richard Schmalensee and Robert Willig, eds., *Handbook of Industrial Organization*. New York: North Holland.

Perry, Martin K., and Robert H. Porter. 1986. "Resale Price Maintenance and Exclusive Territories in the Presence of Retail Service Externalities." Bell Communications Research, Inc., Economics Discussion Paper #20 (May).

Pisano, Gary P. 1988. *Innovation Through Markets, Hierarchies, and Joint Ventures: Technology, Strategy, and Collaborative Arrangements in the Biotechnology Industry*. Ph.D. diss., University of California, Berkeley.

Rey, Patrick, and Joseph E. Stiglitz. 1986. "The Role of Exclusive Territories." Manuscript.

Rey, Patrick, and Jean Tirole. 1986. "The Logic of Vertical Restraints." *American Economic Review* 76:921–39.

Rubin, Paul H. 1978. "The Theory of the Firm and the Structure of the Franchise Contract." *Journal of Law and Economics* 21:223–33.

Shepard, Lawrence. 1978. "The Economic Effects of Repealing Fair-Trade Laws." *The Journal of Consumer Affairs* 12:220–36.

Shishido-Topel, L. 1984. "An Economic Analysis of Exclusive Dealing." Ph.D. diss., University of California, Los Angeles.

Spiller, Pablo T. 1985. "On Vertical Merger." *Journal of Law, Economics, and Organization* 1:285–312.

Stigler, George J. 1951. "The Division of Labor Is Limited by the Extent of the Market." *Journal of Political Economy* 59:185–93.

Telser, Lester G. 1960. "Why Should Manufacturers Want Fair Trade? *Journal of Law and Economics* 3:86–105.

Vernon, John M., and Daniel A. Graham. 1971. "Profitability of Monopolization by Vertical Integration." *Journal of Political Economy* 79:924–25.

Warren-Boulton, Frederick R. 1974. "Vertical Control with Variable Proportions." *Journal of Political Economy* 82:783–802.

White, Lawrence J. 1985. "Resale Price Maintenance and the Problem of Marginal and Inframarginal Customers." *Contemporary Policy Issues* 3:17-22.

Williamson, Oliver E. 1975. *Markets and Hierarchies: Analysis and Antitrust Implications*. New York: The Free Press.

———. 1985. *The Economic Institutions of Capitalism*. New York: The Free Press.

Yamey, B.S., ed. 1966. *Resale Price Maintenance*. Chicago: Aldine.

VERTICAL INTEGRATION UNDER FIXED AND VARIABLE PROPORTIONS

The example in Table 16.1 illustrates the effects of vertical integration for both fixed- and variable-proportions production functions. The example assumes the market demand curve is linear,

$$p = a - bQ, \tag{16A.1}$$

where p is the price of the downstream good, Q. As a result, the marginal revenue curve is

$$MR = a - 2bQ. \tag{16A.2}$$

In the fixed-proportions case, the downstream production function is

$$Q = \min(M,L), \tag{16A.3}$$

where M is the input produced by the upstream monopolist, and L, labor, is the other input. This production function exhibits constant returns to scale.

In the variable-proportions case, the downstream production function is

$$Q = \alpha M^{.5} L^{.5}, \tag{16A.4}$$

which is called a *Cobb-Douglas production function*. Because the powers to which M and L are raised add to 1 (.5 + .5 = 1), this production function exhibits constant returns to scale. Because both production functions exhibit constant returns to scale, in the absence of integration, when the downstream firms are price takers, the number of downstream firms is arbitrary. To facilitate comparison of the two cases, the parameter α is chosen so that the marginal costs are the same under both production functions when the firms are vertically integrated.

■ THE FIXED-PROPORTIONS PRODUCTION FUNCTION

With a fixed-proportions production function, the same amount of final output is produced whether the firms are integrated or not integrated. As a result, the price and combined profits are the same. Thus, if there is any cost to integrating, the firms do not integrate.

Vertically Integrated

When an upstream monopolist vertically integrates forward, it chooses its output, Q, so that its marginal cost for producing the final good equals the marginal revenue given by Equation 16A.2. With the fixed-proportions production function, 1 unit of M and 1 unit of L are used to produce 1 unit of Q. As a result, the integrated firm's marginal cost is $c + w$, where c is the cost of producing a unit of M, and w is the wage of L. Equating $c + w$ with the right side of Equation 16A.2, the integrated monopoly output is

$$Q_i = \frac{a - c - w}{2b}. \tag{16A.5}$$

Not Vertically Integrated

If the firms are not vertically integrated, the downstream firms sell at a price, p, equal to their marginal cost. Their marginal cost is $m + w$, where m is the price the upstream monopolist in M charges. Rewriting $p = m + w$, we can derive the demand curve that the upstream monopolist faces,

$$m = p - w = a - bQ - w = a - bM - w, \tag{16A.6}$$

using Equation 16A.1 and noting that $Q = M$, given the fixed-proportions production function.

The upstream monopolist maximizes its profits,

$$\pi = (m - c)M = (a - bM - w - c)M, \tag{16A.7}$$

where $(m - c)$ is its monopoly markup per unit of M sold. It chooses M to maximize Equation 16A.7. The first-order condition is

$$a - w - c - 2bM = 0. \tag{16A.8}$$

Since M equals Q_n, the nonintegrated output, this expression can be rewritten as

$$Q_n = \frac{a - c - w}{2b}, \tag{16A.9}$$

which is the same output as the integrated firms produce, Equation 16A.5.

If $a = 10$ and $b = c = w = 1$, then $Q_n = Q_i = 4$. The corresponding price, p, is 6. In the nonintegrated case, using 16A.6, m equals 5, so $m + w = 6 = p$.

■ THE VARIABLE-PROPORTIONS PRODUCTION FUNCTION

When a variable-proportions production function is used downstream, output, price, and profits differ depending on whether the industry is integrated or not. To show this, we start by determining the cost function for the downstream firms.

Cost Function

Downstream firms combine M and L to produce a given level of output at the lowest possible cost. Thus, the cost function, conditional on factor prices and a given level of output, is

$$c(m,w,Q) = \min_{L,M} mM + wL \tag{16A.10}$$

subject to Equation 16A.4, which, by substituting for L using (16A.4), can be written as

$$c(m,w,Q) = \min_{M} mM + \frac{wQ^2}{m\alpha^2}. \tag{16A.10'}$$

Solving the first-order condition for Equation 16A.10', we obtain the demand for M conditional on the factor costs and output:

$$M(m,w,Q) = \left(\frac{w}{m}\right)^{.5} \frac{Q}{\alpha}. \tag{16A.11}$$

The expression for $L(m,w,Q)$ is the same, except that w and m are reversed. The total cost, $C(m,w,Q) = mM(m,w,Q) + wL(m,w,Q)$, which we can write as

$$C(m,w,Q) = \frac{2Q}{\alpha}(wm)^{.5}. \tag{16A.12}$$

Vertically Integrated

The vertically integrated firm maximizes its monopoly profits by equating the marginal revenue, Equation 16A.2 with its marginal cost. Its marginal cost is obtained by setting $m = c$ in (16A.12) and differentiating with respect to Q: $MC = 2(wc)^{.5}/\alpha$. Thus, the output of the integrated firm is

$$Q_i = \frac{a - 2(wc)^{.5}/\alpha}{2b}. \tag{16A.13}$$

Using the same parameters as before and setting $\alpha = 1$, $Q_i = 4$. That is, when we choose $\alpha = 1$, we get the same output in the integrated case as with the fixed-proportions production function.

Not Vertically Integrated

Where the firms are not integrated, the demand facing the upstream monopolist is derived by setting p, from Equation 16A.1, equal to marginal cost, obtained by differentiating Equation 16A.12, and substituting for Q, using Equation 16A.11:

$$M = \frac{a(w/m)^{.5} - 2w/\alpha}{b\alpha}. \qquad (16A.14)$$

The upstream monopolist maximizes its profits, $(m - c)M$, using Equation 16A.14 for M. Its first-order condition (maximizing profits through its choice of m) is

$$aw^{.5} - \frac{2}{\alpha} wm^{.5} - \frac{1}{2}(m - c)a\frac{w}{m} = 0. \qquad (16A.15)$$

Using the same parameters as before, Equation 16A.15 implies that $m = 7.9265$. The marginal cost is $2m^{.5} = 5.6308 = p$. Using the demand curve in Equation 16A.1, $Q_n = 10 - 5.6308 = 4.2692$. Thus, with this constant-returns-to-scale, variable-proportions production function, $Q_i < Q_n$.

CHAPTER 17

INFORMATION

There is no absolute knowledge. . . . All information is imperfect.
We have to treat it with humility.

J. BRONOWSKI

Although most of the economic models discussed in previous chapters assume that consumers have perfect information, consumers often do not know which store sells a good at the lowest price or how quality varies across brands. Providing consumers with information about product prices, attributes, or quality alters their purchasing behavior and thereby affects market structure. The results of recent research on markets in which consumers have limited information are startling and contradict the strongest conclusions from the standard economic models based on perfect consumer information. In markets in which consumers have limited information, high-quality products may not be supplied, some of the desirable effects of perfect competition vanish, and firms may have an incentive to reduce consumers' information.

This chapter examines the problems that arise from limited consumer information. It begins by showing that if consumers have limited information about a product's quality, one of two serious problems occurs: either the market does not exist, or if it does exist, the quality produced is different (usually lower) than in a world of perfect information.[1] For example, often only the lowest-quality products are produced. Providing information through experts, standards, and certification is socially desirable if the benefits to consumers outweigh the costs of collecting and disseminating the information. Warranties or guarantees may also eliminate problems due to limited information.

Next, we show that imperfect consumer information about prices may eliminate a

---

[1] Many economists call the limited information equilibrium *nonoptimal, inefficient,* or say that it is a *market failure.* Because it is common (though perhaps confusing) terminology we will refer to departures from perfect competition as inefficient. This terminology implies that a problem exists and can and should be fixed. It is, however, costly to provide perfect information, and the costs of providing perfect information may exceed the benefits. Thus, even though such departures from a perfect world are commonly referred to as nonoptimal, it may not be optimal or even possible to correct this inefficiency or market failure.

market, enable even small firms to set their prices above marginal cost, or lead to a variety of prices being charged for a homogeneous good. That is, with imperfect consumer information, perfect competition is impossible. In this sense, the *law of supply and demand* and the *law of a single price* do not hold in markets with limited information.

Then, we show that firms may purposely raise consumers' costs of search so as to obtain market power. For example, a firm may charge different prices for the same good at various locations or under different brand names so as to make it more difficult for consumers to find the low-priced brand. Finally, we present some theories that show that improving consumer information can sometimes lower average price. Some empirical evidence is presented to support these theories.

■ WHY INFORMATION IS LIMITED

Research by psychologists, economists, marketing experts, and others shows that consumers have imperfect knowledge of prices and qualities in the marketplaces where they shop. There are five chief reasons for this limited knowledge (Federal Trade Commission 1978).

First, information varies in reliability. Not all "information" is accurate, and hence a rational consumer should not rely equally on information from all sources. Information that was once correct may become dated and therefore inaccurate.

Second, there is a cost to collecting information. It does not pay for consumers to collect information beyond the point where the marginal benefit equals the marginal cost of collecting it. For example, going to several stores to determine which has the lowest price on a candy bar almost certainly does not make sense. See Example 17.1.

Third, consumers can remember and readily recall only a limited amount of information. (Example 17.2, p. 557). They are, of course, more likely to retain and recall relatively important information. Information is easier to retain if it is easily "encoded" by the brain, and such encoding is easier if it fits into an existing pattern. Unfortunately, the prices charged by different stores for the hundreds of products a consumer typically buys are not easily arranged into meaningful patterns. Moreover the typical distribution of prices for a given item is large. One survey of prices in the Boston area found that for 18 of 39 randomly chosen products, the highest price was over twice the lowest, and for 4 products, the higher price was five or more times greater than the lowest (Pratt, Wise, and Zeckhauser 1979).

Fourth, it is often efficient for consumers to use simplified rules to process information. That is, they rationally use only some of the information they have collected because it is costly to process it. A customer may check a restaurant bill to see if any nonordered items were included but may not check the addition. A sensible consumer processes information up to the point where the marginal benefit equals the marginal cost of processing more information. Such behavior is referred to as **bounded rationality.**[2]

Fifth, consumers do not have sufficient education or intelligence to process available information on all products correctly. For example, some quite intelligent people do not know how to determine the quality of various computers or industrial organization text-

---

[2] See Simon (1957; 1959), Cyert and March (1963), and Williamson (1964).

EXAMPLE 17.1

SOURCES OF CONSUMER INFORMATION

A national study of 2430 U.S. consumers selected randomly from the telephone directories in 1979–80 shows how consumers obtain their information about grocery stores. Two-thirds (68.8 percent) claim they read food store advertisements. The proportion of shoppers reading newspaper ads increases with family size. Presumably, the larger a family, the higher the return to finding the lowest food prices. Over half (54.1 percent) of the shoppers who read newspaper ads say that the advertisements influence where they shop. Consumers who read ads read an average of 2.5 per week.

Almost half (47.6 percent in 1979–80 compared to 40.7 percent in 1977) view food-store commercials, seeing an average of 1.8 ads per week. However, only 18.3 percent of these television viewers say the commercials influence where they shop.

Almost three-quarters of the consumers compare prices between different supermarkets (74.4 percent), compared to only about two-thirds who compared in 1977. The main method for comparative pricing is reading newspaper ads; the second most likely method is store visits.

The typical consumer shops in 2.2 different supermarkets during a one month period. The average number of shopping trips is 1.4 per week (although only 26.7 percent of consumers shop more than once a week). Shopping in more than one store is more likely, the larger the family size and the more spent per week.

Shoppers tend to remain loyal to certain stores. Annually, only 18.2 percent of the respondents changed the supermarket where they did most of their shopping. The greatest switching behavior is among the younger age groups and larger families. The main reason (given by 36.8 percent in 1979–80 compared to 25.6 percent in 1977) for changing supermarkets is lower prices.

Thus, consumers gather information in a variety of ways. Consumers with large families, who benefit the most from the information, collect more of it and are more likely to use it.

SOURCE: Burgoyne, Inc. 1977 and 1979–80. *The National Study of Supermarket Shoppers.*

books, the healthfulness of foods, or the probability that a given plant will survive in their yard. Others lack the math skills to compare the cost of buying a car by paying all the money at once to its cost if they pay for it in relatively small amounts each month for years. See Example 17.3, p. 558.

■ LIMITED INFORMATION ABOUT QUALITY

> *Lord Bowen's definition of hard work: Answering yes or no on imperfect information.*

In many markets, consumers do not know how quality varies across brands. Markets where consumers are often unsure about quality include those for professional services

EXAMPLE 17.2

Do Consumers Know How Much They Pay?

Do consumers know the exact prices they pay in grocery stores? The answer is no. In a survey of 560 shoppers in four Providence and Boston area supermarkets in July 1974, consumers were asked to state the price of 44 popular brand-name and nationally advertised items. Only 24 percent of the shoppers tested knew the correct price (within 5 percent) of a specific product; the comparable figure for a similar study in 1963 was 32 percent.

The same is true in Great Britain. A random sample of housewives in Nottingham, England were asked to recall the prices they paid for seven common grocery items within the previous week. Any departure from the actual price was classified as incorrect. Across all social groups and all types of retail outlets, 57.0 percent of prices were accurate, 25.4 percent were wrong, and 17.6 percent were not known by the consumer. Thus, one-quarter of the housewives believed they knew the price but were wrong; and 4 out of 10 either did not know the price or gave the wrong one. The percent correct varied across commodities from 34.8 percent for breakfast cereal to 79.3 percent for tea.

Of those prices that were incorrect, 43.2 percent differed from the correct price by not more than 5 percent, roughly equally split between the positive and negative bias. If the researchers had classified a price as correct if the deviation did not exceed 5 percent, the percentage correct would have been 65.3 percent; with a 10 percent criterion, the number would be 73.1 percent.

Accuracy declined as wealth or the number of items bought increased. The social group with the lowest percent correct was the well-to-do, and the second lowest was the professional middle class. Thus, consumers who spend a relatively small percent of their income on food are relatively less likely to know accurately the prices they paid.

SOURCES: *The Progressive Grocer,* November 1974: 39, and Gabor and Granger (1961).

(doctors, lawyers, plumbers, and electricians), processed foods, used goods, and complex mechanical or electronic products. In these markets, there is *asymmetric information:* sellers know the quality of the good, but buyers do not. Asymmetric information about quality can have either of two undesirable results: the equilibrium may not exist, or, if the equilibrium exists, resources are used inefficiently compared to markets with perfect information.

The Market for "Lemons"

Probably the best-known study of the way limited information can disrupt a market is Akerlof's (1970) classic analysis of the market for lemons. Akerlof shows that where sellers have perfect information and consumers have extremely limited information, a market may not exist, or only the lowest-quality product may be sold.

Consider first the market for cars. Neither the seller nor the buyer of a new car knows

EXAMPLE 17.3

Understanding Consumer Information

Consumers often cannot understand potentially valuable information due to lack of training or intelligence. The following four examples indicate that many consumers have difficulty understanding potentially useful information.

Unit Pricing: A shopper can use unit pricing information in grocery stores to determine which brands or sizes are relatively inexpensive per unit. In 300 postshopping interviews in 1975, 39 percent of shoppers claimed to use unit pricing frequently and another 32 percent occasionally. Only about 19 percent said they seldom or never used shelf tags for price comparisons, and only 10 percent admitted they had never noticed the tags. Thus, over 7 out of 10 customers said they occasionally used unit pricing, whereas only 22 percent rated unit pricing as "not helpful."

One reason consumers may not use unit pricing is that they cannot process the information. One experiment found that understanding the unit price information varied with education.

Education level	Percent Who Understood Unit Pricing
Grade school	47.7
Some high school	71.1
High school graduate	75.0
Some college	80.9
College graduate	82.7

Insurance Cost: Surveys show that the model life insurance cost-disclosure format adopted by the National Association of Insurance Commissioners is incomprehensible to the average consumer. Only 38 percent of life insurance purchasers knew that a policy's index number could be used to compare the costs of life insurance policies. Only 21 percent knew that the lower the policy's index number, the lower its cost, and 61 percent said they did not know how to use an index number.

if it is a good car or a bad one (a "lemon") that will break down repeatedly. An owner learns the quality of a car after owning it for a while.

Now consider the used-car market, in which there is asymmetry of information between buyers and sellers. The sellers, who are the current owners, know the quality of the cars, but the buyers do not. At best, a potential buyer knows the probability of getting a good car. As a result, both good and bad used cars must sell for the same price, since buyers cannot tell them apart.

Bad Products Drive Out Good Products.   Bad cars are overvalued and good cars are undervalued in this market. For example, suppose consumers believe that half the used cars in the market are lemons worth $100 and the other half are good cars worth $200. Suppose also that consumers are risk-neutral: they are indifferent between having a dollar and having something that has a 50 percent probability of being worth nothing and a 50

Brightness of Light Bulbs: Since 1970, the Federal Trade Commission has required the disclosure of brightness information for light bulbs. Five years after the rule was promulgated, most consumers did not understand the concept of "lumens," which measure brightness. In a survey of 168 people, only 1 mentioned lumens as a pertinent factor in selecting light bulbs.

Nutrition: The Food and Drug Administration requires that nonstandard food items must be labeled, yet many consumers (including the authors of this text) find it hard to understand the meaning of certain terms. For example, if a product is not the real thing or is nutritionally inferior to the real thing, it must be called *imitation*. If the product is not real but is nutritionally equivalent, it may be called a *substitute*. The terms *salt free*, *no salt*, *no salt added*, *unsalted*, and *without salt* may be misleading to many consumers. These phrases mean that no salt has been added during processing, but the original product may be very high in salt or sodium.

Moreover, many consumers assume that food labels must provide all relevant information. Yet food that is repackaged by a store need not be labeled if the information is posted nearby. Substances that migrate from equipment or the package to a food item are not included on the label. For example, cold cereals need not list preservatives on their labels even if they are packed in boxes coated with preservatives that leach into the cereals.

SOURCES: *The Progressive Grocer*, October 1975: 48; McCullogh, D. and D. I. Padberg. 1971. "Unit Pricing in Supermarkets." *Search: Agriculture*. 1:18, Table 22; Federal Trade Commission (1979 93–94); Margen, Sheldon, and Dale Ogar. 1986. "To Your Health: The Writing on Food Labels Often Confuses." *San Francisco Chronicle*. 1986. October 22, FF4; Margen, Sheldon, and Dale Ogar. 1986. "To Your Health: Labels on Our Food Don't Tell the Whole Story." *San Francisco Chronicle. 1986. October 29, FF 3.*

percent probability of being worth $2. Then the value to a typical consumer of a randomly selected car is $150 (= 0.5 [100] + 0.5 [200]). A buyer who thinks that a car might turn out to be good is willing to pay more than the value of a bad car ($150 > $100), but the buyer also thinks that it might turn out to be bad and thus is not willing to pay the full value of a good car ($150 < $200).

A kind of "Gresham's law" for used cars operates: bad cars drive out good cars.[3] Although an owner of a bad car is delighted to sell it for more than it is worth, an owner

---

[3] Gresham's law, formulated by Sir Thomas Gresham, (1519–79), holds that "bad money drives out good." That is, if two monetary measures circulate at values different from their true value, then only the lower value measure survives. For example, if both gold and silver coins are used, and their face values are lower than their metal's value, the more undervalued coins will be melted down first. Akerlof points out that the analogy is not perfect, because both buyers and sellers of the coins know the relevant facts.

of a good car is unwilling to sell it for less than its value and hence keeps it. Thus, in a market with only two types of cars, only the bad cars are sold. Because only bad cars are sold, buyers know they are getting lemons and will only pay the value of a lemon. There is no market for good-quality used cars.

This example can be extended to many qualities of cars, but the result is the same. The lowest-quality cars eventually drive all other cars out of the market by the same sort of reasoning.[4]

These sorts of problems also arise in markets for insurance and for home repair. Healthy senior citizens often have problems buying medical insurance. Why don't insurance companies merely adjust the price of a policy to match the risk? The reason appears to be the same sort of **adverse selection** as in the used-car example: as the price of a policy rises, only the worst risks are interested in buying the policy. If the individual can better determine his or her own health than can the insurance company, the insurance company sells a disproportionate number of policies to the least healthy members of society. As the price level rises (for example, with age), only those who believe they have increasingly high risks buy insurance. Akerlof reports that although 63 percent of a sample of people aged 45 to 54 had hospital insurance, only 31 percent over 65 had such insurance.

Similarly, suppose that some good carpenters use high-quality materials and bad carpenters use low-quality materials. If homeowners cannot tell the honesty of a carpenter for many years (for example, bad materials break down in 5 years and good materials last 10 years) and must pay both types the same amount, the bad carpenters drive out the good ones whose costs are higher.

Asymmetric Information Lowers Quality.   Although not all markets with asymmetric information degenerate so that only the lowest-quality item is sold, there is always inefficiency in these markets relative to a world with perfect information: quality levels are too low (Leland 1979a, 1979b). The inefficiencies stem from a discrepancy between private and social returns. Unfortunately, these inefficiencies relative to a perfect world usually cannot be remedied by government intervention, since providing perfect information is often prohibitively expensive.

In an equilibrium with imperfect information, the marginal firm faces a market price just equal to its opportunity cost, such as the value of the used car to the firm. That is, the marginal seller is indifferent between selling and not selling. Since the opportunity cost of higher-quality units is above the market price, the marginal seller's product is the highest quality actually observed in the market.

In such a market, the social value of a unit of the highest quality exceeds the social value of a unit of the average quality level. That is, if consumers can tell the difference in quality, they are willing to pay more for a better-quality product. Unfortunately, the private value (the amount that a buyer is willing to pay) of the highest quality is equal to the average value in equilibrium because buyers cannot distinguish good products from bad ones.

---

[4] Kim (1985), however, shows that if people are free to choose whether they are buyers or sellers, the results may differ. The pure Akerlof model applies better to insurance and similar markets where people cannot easily switch between being buyers and sellers.

Thus, the market failure can be explained in terms of an *externality*.[5] When a relatively high-quality seller offers a good or service to the market, the average quality rises, and buyers are willing to pay more for all products. The high-quality seller must, therefore, split the benefits of its high-quality product with sellers of lower-quality products by raising the average price to all. Because marginal sellers are not recognized as providing the best available quality, they do not receive the value of their full contribution to social welfare. This wedge between social and private benefits results in quality that is too low and economic inefficiency.

In the used-car example, sellers could not vary the quality of their products; however, firms in most markets can vary the quality of their products. If firms cannot fully capture the value of producing higher-quality goods (an externality), they have an incentive to produce goods of relatively low quality.

Solving the Problem: Equal Information

I only ask for information. —CHARLES DICKENS

The problem of bad products driving out good ones results from the asymmetry of information. Where information is symmetric, markets are more likely to exist. There are two types of symmetric information: either both sides costlessly know the quality of a product, or neither knows.

If both buyers and sellers know the quality of used cars, prices reflect the true values of cars. Good-quality cars sell for more than bad-quality cars. There are no inefficiencies. We studied competitive markets with perfect information in Chapter 4.

If sellers know no more than buyers (as with new cars), then good and bad cars are sold at a price that reflects an average of the two qualities. That is, the price does not reflect the true value of a given car, but it does equal the expected value. Thus, where there is symmetric but imperfect information, markets do not vanish. Whether it pays for consumers (or sellers) to obtain information, however, depends on the costs of obtaining it as well as its benefits. Where costs of obtaining information are relatively low, consumers obtain the information and markets function smoothly; if costs are high, the information is not gathered and inefficiency results.[6] See Examples 17.4 and 17.5.

---

[5] See Chapter 6 for a discussion of externalities. An externality arises when the benefits from a firm's actions are not completely captured by the firm.

[6] In some markets, price may convey the information necessary for consumers to infer relative qualities of different products; in others, price is not a good indicator. See Grossman and Stiglitz (1980) and Cooper and Ross (1984). Ginter, Young, and Dickson (1987) survey studies of the relationship between price and quality in many different types of markets (clothing cameras, shoes, food, small appliances, and others) and find that the correlation between price and quality is almost always low. In all studies, the average correlation was less than 0.29. On the other hand, price does correlate well with some major purchases of durable goods (Gerstner 1985; Tellis and Wernerfelt 1987; and Curry and Reisz 1988). Smallwood and Conlisk (1979) and Chan and Leland (1982) contend that high prices should be correlated with high quality when there are informed consumers. Bagwell and Riordan (1988) show that when quality is fixed, a high price can signal high quality if a higher-quality good costs more to produce. Klein and Leffler (1981) argue that high prices signal high quality as a payoff for the repeated choice of the high-quality good by consumers. These theoretical issues are discussed in more detail below and in the next chapter.

Consumers obtain information in at least five ways. First, by providing credible **guarantees** or **warranties,** sellers of high-quality goods credibly convey the information to consumers that their products are of high quality. By providing consumers with equal information, such firms are able to charge higher prices that reflect the higher quality of their goods.

Guarantees only convey this information if they are credible. For example, a guarantee on a used car provided by an established dealer is more credible than one from an individual. After all, a buyer only believes a guarantee is valuable if the buyer believes the seller can be found and made to honor the guarantee in the future. Thus, guarantees or warranties are only offered where the seller can establish credibility.[7]

Typically, guarantees are only provided if the life of a product does not depend heavily on how consumers use it. Otherwise, buyers have an incentive to use the product relatively carelessly and rely on the seller to fix problems under the warranty. This incentive for a consumer to behave carelessly when the product is covered by a guarantee that the seller will fix all problems (even those caused by the consumer) is called a **moral hazard.**

Second, a store or manufacturer may rely on its reputation to signal that its goods are of high quality. A store that expects repeated purchases by a consumer if it provides high-quality products has a strong incentive not to provide defective products.

Third, liability laws may also serve the same function as explicit warranties. If consumers know that liability laws or contract laws force the manufacturer to make good on defective products, then the manufacturer need not provide an additional warranty. The problem with relying on legal recourse, however, is that the transaction costs are very high. Thus, manufacturers may find that explicit warranties are still necessary.

Fourth, a disinterested party, an expert, may be able to provide consumers with reliable information. For example, if a potential purchaser of a used car can take it to a mechanic and get it appraised, then any information asymmetry may be eliminated.

Fifth, the government, consumer groups, industry groups or others may provide information in the form of **standards** and **certification.** Standards are established for a particular good by defining a metric, or scale, for evaluating that product. For example, the R-value of insulation tells how effectively it works. Certification means that a particular product has been found to meet a standard.

Industry groups may set their own standards and get an outside group or firm, such as Underwriters' Laboratories (UL) or Factory Mutual Engineering Corporation (FMEC), to certify that their products meet these standards. Often standards are set to guarantee conformity across brands. For example, a VHS video-recorder owner is assured that a VHS tape manufactured by another firm works in that machine.

Government agencies may require manufacturers to disclose information about their products, such as the energy consumption of an electric appliance or the potentially harmful side-effects of certain drugs. Governments may set and enforce minimum quality standards by requiring that professionals be licensed or that drugs be effective. Governments also

---

[7] A Federal Trade Commission study found that only 4.8 percent to 14.8 percent of consumers carefully study guarantees and warranties before purchasing; thus, in many markets, they may be provided for other reasons than to signal quality before purchase (Crocker 1986).

may set fines to guarantee that firms meet standards or liability rules requiring firms to recompense consumers if products malfunction.

Consumer groups may publish comparisons of different brands, as in Consumers Union's *Consumer Reports*. Some consumer groups set their own standards, such as the National Society for the Prevention of Blindness, a prime mover in setting standards that promote eye safety (Hemenway 1975, 62). For an outside organization to provide believable information, it must convince consumers that it is trustworthy and is not deceiving them. For example, Consumers Union attempts to establish its trustworthiness by refusing advertising or other payments from firms.

Objective information supplied by outside organizations is rare because information is a **public good:** a good that, if it is supplied to anyone, can be supplied to others at no extra cost. Information is socially valuable if it is worth more (say to consumers) than it costs to provide it. Although socially valuable information may exist, it is possible that no firm can profitably provide it because it cannot capture all the benefits. Consumers Union does not capture the full value of its information through subscriptions because subscribers to *Consumer Reports* lend their copies to friends, libraries stock the journal, and newspapers report on its findings. As result, Consumers Union does not engage in as much research as it otherwise would.

Standards and Certification May Help or Hurt

Unfortunately, standards and certification may either help or hurt. They are harmful if their information is degraded or misleading, or if they are used for anticompetitive purposes. Where consumers are inexpensively informed of the relative quality of all goods in a market, the information is unambiguously useful. Often, however, information is degraded. For example, although quality may vary along a continuous scale, only a high- versus low-quality rating may be used. In this case, products are likely to be made so that they have either the lowest possible quality (and hence cost of manufacture) or just barely a high enough quality level to obtain the high-quality rating.

Such high-low rating schemes are often combined with the exclusion of low-quality goods or services. For example, many state and local governments license professionals, and only those meeting some minimum standards are granted licenses and allowed to practice. In most states dozens, if not hundreds, of professions and crafts are licensed, such as electricians, plumbers, dentists, psychologists, contractors, and beauticians. Licensing has two offsetting effects (Leland 1979a, 1979b). First, the restrictions raise the average quality in the industry by eliminating low-quality goods or services. Second, these restrictions raise the prices consumers pay. The number of people providing services is reduced because the restrictions screen out some potential suppliers. Moreover, consumers are unable to obtain the lower-quality and less expensive goods or services. As a result, welfare may go up or down depending on whether the increased-quality or the higher-price effect dominates. Only by setting the standard properly and changing it as necessary over time can welfare be raised. Whether such restrictions can be set properly and cost-effectively by government agencies is debatable.

A better solution than trying to set the best possible standard is to provide consumers with objective information on the relative quality of each brand or professional, and let them judge whether the price savings justifies purchasing a low-quality good or service. Restrictions may be superior to providing such information only if consumers are unable to understand more subtle grading systems or it is too costly for consumers to train themselves to use this information.

A further problem with licensing or mandatory standards and certification is that they can be used for anticompetitive purposes, such as erecting entry barriers to new firms and products. For example, many model plumbing and building codes required that pipes be made of copper or a few other types of materials and have certain dimensions (Federal Trade Commission 1978, 162–63). As a result, manufacturers of plastic pipe faced problems in introducing their products.[8] These mandatory standards in building codes impeded the diffusion of innovations (Oster and Quigley 1977), as discussed in Example 23.3.

Many professions license themselves under government auspices. Thus, doctors, lawyers, electricians, and others may set their own licensing standards. These groups may define standards that prevent entry of professionals from other states or those who have just finished their education, so as to keep the wages of currently licensed professionals high. Here, licensing is very likely to be socially harmful, since it excludes qualified professionals and raises consumers' costs. Unfortunately for economists, their profession is not licensed so they cannot act in this anticompetitive manner to limit supply and raise their wages.

Consumer Misperceptions

If consumers have misperceptions about product quality, such as not knowing the probability that a product will fail, a competitive market may provide less information than they would in a world with perfect information, forcing consumers to bear more risk. Spence (1977) shows that several departures from the world of complete information may occur.

He first considers the case where consumers are risk-neutral: they are willing to take a fair bet. The risk-neutrality assumption is reasonable when the loss to the consumer from a product failure is small. In this case, if consumers initially underestimate the quality (for example, safety) of a product, it is undersupplied by a competitive market. If a product-liability rule is in effect (where liability equals the loss to consumers in dollars if a product fails), then a competitive market provides a socially optimal quantity. Again, in the absence of a liability rule, firms could use guarantees to correct consumers' misperceptions about the quality of such products.

Spence next considers markets in which consumers are risk-averse: they are not willing to take a fair bet. Here, if consumers underestimate the probability of failure, the market provides below-optimal levels of insurance or guarantees.[9] Spence shows that a

---

[8] One reason for the building-code restriction on plastic pipes is that they can be installed more quickly and by less skilled labor than copper pipes. As a result, plumbing unions supported the restrictive codes in order to increase the demand for their skilled labor.

[9] Under somewhat different assumptions, Heal (1977) shows that profit-maximizing firms overguarantee their products if they are less risk-averse than consumers and have accurate information.

competitive market may either supply too high or too low a quality level from a social standpoint.

He also shows that if the government can perfectly determine quality, it can eliminate the market inefficiency by imposing appropriate fines on firms in the event of a product breakdown (or by providing consumers with the information).[10] Further, Spence demonstrates that if firms can provide information through both price and guarantees, a market functions optimally so long as there is no moral hazard, consumers' actions do not affect the probability of failure, and consumers suffer only monetary losses in the event of a product failure (that is, they are not irreparably injured).

■ LIMITED INFORMATION ABOUT PRICE

Firms obtain market power from consumers' lack of knowledge about prices and quality. Limited information can lead to a monopolistic price in what would otherwise be a competitive market. For example, suppose that many stores in an area sell the same good. If one store raises its price above the level of others, *and all consumers know it,* that store loses all its business. Because the store faces a demand curve that is horizontal at the going market price, it has no market power.

In contrast, suppose that *some or all customers do not know* that other stores charge lower prices. Then the store can raise its price without losing all its sales. That is, the store faces a downward sloping demand curve and has some market power. This concept is employed in a formal model developed by Diamond (1971).[11] We call a simplified version of his model the *tourist-trap model.*

The Tourist-Trap Model

A typical tourist, Lisa, arrives in a small town filled with souvenir stands. Each stand sells a mug with the town hall painted on it. Lisa, by chance, wanders by one of these stands and sees the mug. For reasons better left to a sociologist or a psychologist, she decides she should buy a mug for her father (and, if it is inexpensive enough, one for her mother as well). She has but a short time before her bus leaves, and she does not expect to return to this town again. Thus, she does not have time to check the prices at each souvenir stand, and she cannot use information obtained through even a limited search in the future. If there are many such tourists, what prices do the stands charge for these mugs?

---

[10] The government, of course, is not omniscient and cannot be relied upon to set standards, fines, or other regulations appropriately in all cases. For example, for a product with many quality dimensions, people of goodwill differ on how to set a standard or provide information in a way that is meaningful to consumers. Further, the cost of collecting the information to set the standard may be prohibitively high.

[11] Probably the first paper to clearly make this point was Scitovsky (1950). Diamond (1971) was the first to present a formal mathematical analysis. Salop (1976) and Stiglitz (1979) provide excellent, relatively non-technical surveys of this literature.

To answer this question, we make four assumptions for specificity:

1. All firms (souvenir stands) have the same costs and sell the identical product.
2. All consumers have identical demand functions.
3. A guide book provides each consumer with the general distribution of prices (how many stores charge each price) but does not give the particular price each store charges.
4. The tourist's cost of going to a stand to check the price or buy is c, which reflects the tourist's time and expenses (taxi rides).

Thus, if Lisa goes to two souvenir stands, the search costs are $2c$. If she buys a mug at the second stand at price p, the total cost of that mug is $p + 2c$. The least she can pay is $p + c$, since she must visit at least one stand to buy a mug.

Fixed Number of Firms. Initially, assume that there are a fixed number of souvenir stands, n. How much does each one charge for the mug? We start by considering whether each stand charges the full-information, competitive price, p^c, which equals marginal cost.

Breaking the Full-Information, Competitive Equilibrium. There cannot be a full-information, competitive equilibrium (price equal marginal cost) when consumers have limited information. Suppose all firms initially set the competitive price, p^c. Each firm has an incentive to charge a price higher than p^c; that is, each firm has an incentive to **break the equilibrium.** Thus, competitive pricing cannot persist, and competitive pricing is not an equilibrium.

If all other stands charge p^c, it pays for a deviant firm to set a higher price. Suppose the deviant firm charges a price $p^* = p^c + \epsilon$, where ϵ is a small, positive number. If every consumer knows the price at every store before visiting stores, no one goes to the deviant firm, and the competitive equilibrium holds. If consumers do not know the price in each store, however, a store can charge a relatively high price and still get customers. It costs a consumer time and effort to check prices at various souvenir stands. Because foregone time spent checking the price at one more souvenir stand might be spent seeing sights or having a cool drink, our tourist values this time at c.

Lisa walks into the deviant store and sees that the mug sells for p^*. Her guide book tells her that all the other souvenir stands charge p^c. "What amazingly bad luck," she thinks to herself (or something to that effect), "I've hit the only expensive stand in town." She is annoyed and considers going elsewhere. She knows with certainty that any other store charges less. Nonetheless, she does not go to another store if the cost of search, c, is greater than the price overcharge in this store, ϵ. That is, she does not search (go) elsewhere if the price in this store, p^*, is less than the price at another store *including* the additional cost of getting to that store or if $p^* < p^c + c$.

Thus, it pays for the deviant store to raise its price by an amount just less than the cost of additional search. If it pays for this store to raise its price, though, then it pays for all other stores to raise their prices to p^*. The proposed equilibrium where all stores charge the competitive price, p^c, can be broken. That is, it is in each store's best interest to raise its price from the proposed equilibrium price.

Now suppose every store charges p^*. Can this proposed equilibrium be broken? Yes, it pays stores to raise their prices still further, by the same argument. A deviant store considers raising its price to $p^{**} = p^* + \epsilon = p^c + 2\epsilon$. Again, it is not worthwhile for a tourist unlucky enough to enter that store to search further. Moreover, if it pays one store to raise its price to p^{**}, then it pays for all to do so. This argument can be repeated, but does that mean that stores raise their prices without limit? No, they do not raise their prices above the monopolistic or profit-maximizing level, p^m.

When Lisa learns the price at the souvenir stand, she decides how many mugs to buy. If the price is set too high, the stand loses sales and hence profits (marginal revenues exceed marginal costs). Only when the price is set so that marginal revenue equals marginal cost are profits maximized. Although the store can charge a higher price without losing all its sales, it has no incentive to do so. Thus, the only possible single-price equilibrium is at p^m.

Reducing Search Costs.   Can reducing search costs lower the equilibrium price? The startling answer is that the equilibrium price does not change so long as search costs are positive and there is a single-price equilibrium. Suppose, now, that the government or a private firm sells firm-specific price information. For a price of $c/2$, the consumer can obtain the price at any given store.

Now repeat the previous analysis. Suppose all stores initially charge the competitive price, p^c, and a deviant considers raising its price. So long as it raises its price by no more than $c/2$, an unlucky consumer who goes to the deviant store does not search further. That is, at each step in the argument, the deviant store raises its price by a smaller amount, the lower are search costs; but it raises its price nonetheless. Although the price deviation is smaller than before, any proposed single-price equilibrium at a price less than p^m can still be broken. Again, the only possible single-price equilibrium is at p^m.

Thus, *lowering search costs has no effect on the single-price equilibrium until search costs fall to zero*. If search costs fall to zero, consumers have full information, so the only possible equilibrium is at p^c, which equals marginal cost.

Breaking the Single-Price Equilibrium.   Where search costs are positive, can the proposed equilibrium where all firms charge p^m be broken? The answer depends on the shape of consumer demand curves, the number of firms in the industry, and on the search costs. The following discussion first shows that, for demand curves of certain shapes, consumers buy nothing if firms charge p^m. Then it shows that for any demand curve, it may pay for a firm to deviate from a high-price equilibrium.

If the equilibrium price is p^m, a tourist may not visit even one store (Stiglitz 1979, 340). In other words, a market does not exist. Suppose each tourist buys exactly one mug so long as the price is no more than p^u. That is, the demand curve is a vertical line at a quantity of 1 up to a price of p^u. Given this demand curve, $p^m = p^u$. After all, once Lisa enters the shop, she is willing to pay up to p^u for one mug and buys no more mugs at a lower price.

To go to even one store, a consumer must incur a search cost, c. As a result, the full cost of a mug, the price plus the search cost, is $p^m + c$. Thus, the full cost of shopping for the mug, $p^m + c = p^u + c$, exceeds the maximum value the consumer places on the mug, p^u, so the consumer does not shop at all.

In attempting to take advantage of the tourists, the souvenir stands have set their prices so high that consumers do not find it worthwhile to shop. Thus, if consumers have this type of demand curve, p^m is not an equilibrium. Should the stores lower their prices from p^m?

If all other stores are charging p^m, it may pay for a store to deviate by lowering its price.[12] As previously shown, if consumers have an inelastic demand up to some maximum price, p^u, stores have no customers if they all charge p^m, so that a store might do better by lowering its price to attract customers. Even when demand curves slope down so that a single price equilibrium may exist and stores earn positive profits if all charge p^m, it may still pay a store to lower its price.

It can only pay a deviant store to lower its price if the decrease is substantial enough to induce consumers to search for this low-price store.[13] If search costs are c, and if the store lowers its price by less than c, then consumers have no incentive to search for this low-price store. Thus the store makes less on each sale, so that its profits must fall. It may, however, pay for a store to deviate by dropping its price by more than c. If there are few stores, consumers may search for this low-price store. Although the store makes less per sale than the high-price stores, its profits may be higher due to greater volume.

The deviant does not attract the extra business, however, if it cannot easily induce search by slightly lowering its price. If there are a large number of stores, then consumers do not search for the low-price store because their chances of finding it are low. As a result, when a large number of stores makes searching for a low-price store impractical, the proposed single-price equilibrium at p^m cannot be broken.[14] Thus, in general, where search costs are positive and there are a large number of firms, the only possible equilibrium is a single-price equilibrium at the monopoly price, p^m.

If, however, there are few stores, price-cutting is profitable, and the high-price equilibrium can be broken. Thus, where there are relatively few firms so that the monopoly price equilibrium can be broken, there is no single-price equilibrium. The only possible equilibrium is for various firms to charge different prices. Multiple-price equilibria are discussed after the following discussion of the effects of entry.

Free Entry. With a small number of stores each charging the monopoly price, each one may earn large profits. If there are no barriers to entry, these profits attract new stores. Even though they incur entry costs, new stores enter the industry, so the number of tourists going to any one souvenir stand falls, and profits fall. Entry continues until profits are driven to zero. Depending on the shape of the demand curve, each store may continue

---

[12] It cannot pay for a store to deviate by charging more. With the inelastic demand curves just discussed, $p^m = p^u$, and raising price does not attract any more customers; thus stores continue to make no sales. With normally shaped demand curves, p^m is the profit-maximizing price for a store. If it raises its price further, the reduction in the number of units sold more than offsets the greater revenue from each sale, so the deviant loses profits.

[13] We continue to use the assumption of the model that consumers know the distribution of prices but not which particular store has the lowest price.

[14] It may be possible, however, for firms to advertise that they have low prices and thereby overcome the high search-cost problem, as discussed in the next chapter.

to charge the same price even after entry occurs.[15] A *monopolistically competitive* equilibrium results: price is above marginal cost, but each firm's profits are zero.[16]

In contrast to a market where consumers have full information, the additional entry does not necessarily lower price if consumers have limited information. Additional entrants must sink some costs (buy a souvenir stand), so society is worse off with free entry here: consumers do not gain from entry, all monopoly profits are dissipated in excess entry (firms earn zero profits), and social expenditures on sunk costs rise.

Indeed, reducing the number of firms, under certain circumstances, may increase *effective* competition. For example, if several stores merge to form a chain of souvenir stands and collectively lower prices, they may be able to induce individuals to search for one of the stands in this low-price chain (Stiglitz 1979, 340). Thus, by reducing the number of independent stores (but not necessarily the number of souvenir stands), effective competition may be increased and prices lowered.

This reasoning suggests a result that is the exact opposite of that for a market where consumers have full information. With imperfect consumer information, competition may be socially wasteful because of entry costs, so that monopoly may be superior to competition.[17]

The Tourists-and-Natives Model

A fool must now and then be right, by chance. — WILLIAM COWPER

Our analysis of the tourist-trap model raises two questions about markets in which consumers have limited information about price. First, is a multiple-price equilibrium possible? That is, is there an equilibrium where stores charge different prices for the identical good so that there is a **price dispersion?** Second, if some consumers are fully informed, even though others have limited information, can there be a full-information equilibrium where price equals marginal cost?

Both questions can be examined by modifying the tourist-trap model so that there are two types of consumers. A persistent price dispersion requires that at least some consumers must be unable or unwilling to learn which stores charge the low price.[18] The

---

[15] For example, if the elasticity of demand facing each firm is unchanged as demand shifts down, price is unchanged.

[16] If consumers' demand curves are downward sloping, the equilibrium resembles that of the standard monopolistically competitive industry illustrated in Figure 11.1. Price is above marginal cost (at the quantity where marginal revenue equals marginal cost), and the demand curve is tangent to the average cost curve (so that profits are zero). Thus equilibrium requires that there be a fixed cost if marginal cost is constant.

[17] Some of the surprising results of the tourist-trap model change when there are repeated transactions. We discuss the roles of repeated transactions and reputations in more detail in the next chapter.

[18] Stigler (1961) shows that if there is a price dispersion, consumers search for low prices, and that if the search is costly, they do not conduct sufficient searches to learn the entire price distribution. A number of papers present models where firms have different costs, and random changes affect the market so that the store with the lowest price keeps changing, and hence consumers cannot easily learn the identity of the low-cost store in a given period. The explanation that follows assumes the firms have identical cost functions and there are no random changes. See also Reinganum (1979).

EXAMPLE 17.6

PRICE DISPERSION

A survey in England recorded twice a month the prices charged for nine branded goods by retailers in the same shopping area over a period of seven months. The following table gives the largest price differences as percentages of the lowest price.

Good	Number of Stores	Largest Percentage Price Difference
McDougall's SR Flour	4	40.0
Fairy Liquid	5	33.3
Bird's Eye Frozen Peas	3	30.0
Ambrosia Creamed Rice	4	27.3
Heinz Chicken Soup	4	26.6
Nescafe	4	19.3
Heinz Baked Beans	4	17.3
Typhoo Tea	4	16.7
Pal Dogfood	5	13.3

A similar study in the United States also found large spreads. For example, out of 17 items studied, the highest price exceeded the lowest by 100 percent or more in 42 percent of the items, and the highest price exceeded the lowest by 50 percent to 99 percent in 23 percent of the items. In only 23 percent of the items was the spread less than 30 percent. The U.S. study found that consumers' perception of the degree of price dispersion was most accurate for items with relatively small actual price dispersion, such as food items and heating oil. Consumers tended to underestimate the spread of prices for high dispersion items such as consumer durables.

SOURCES: Gabor (1980); Maynes and Assum (1982).

discussion shows that where some consumers are fully informed and others have limited information, either a multiple-price equilibrium (Example 17.6) occurs, or there is a single-price equilibrium at marginal cost.

Consider a market in which all firms have identical costs, but consumers' search costs differ. One group of consumers, the natives, who are the *informed* consumers, have zero search costs: they know the entire distribution of prices in the market. The other group, the tourists, who are the *uninformed* consumers, have search costs of c, as before. For example, natives in a town might know the prices charged by each restaurant, but a tourist has to spend the time (search costs) to visit each one to learn its price.

Even if some consumers are ignorant of the distribution of prices charged by different stores, others who are knowledgeable only buy at low-price stores, so that prices sometimes are driven to the (low) competitive-equilibrium price. Obviously, for price to be driven to marginal cost, there must be a substantial number of knowledgeable consumers. In a rigorous version of this model, Salop and Stiglitz (1977) show that with many informed and many uninformed consumers, a single, competitive-price equilibrium may exist, but

FIGURE 17.1   Single-price Market

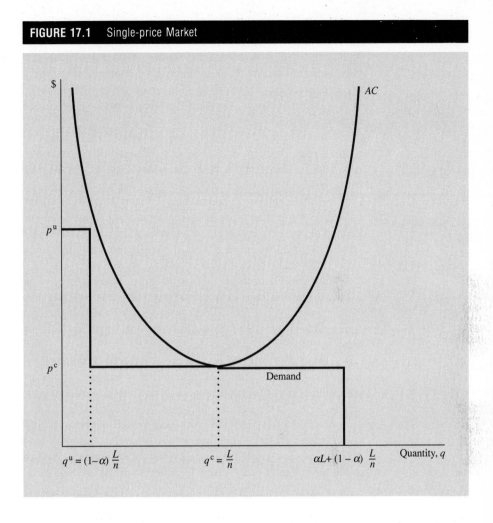

p^u

p^c

AC

Demand

$q^u = (1-\alpha)\dfrac{L}{n}$ $q^c = \dfrac{L}{n}$ $\alpha L + (1-\alpha)\dfrac{L}{n}$ Quantity, q

$

it is also possible that there is a single-price equilibrium at a higher price, or a multiple-price equilibrium.

To illustrate their result, suppose that of the L consumers in this market, αL are informed and $(1 - \alpha)L$ are uninformed. Each consumer buys 1 unit of the good so long as the price is no higher than p^u. There are n firms. Consider a proposed equilibrium where all stores set price equal to marginal cost, so that their price and quantity are p^c and q^c. If all firms set the same price, each is assumed to obtain an equal share of the consumers, so $q^c = L/n$.

Suppose a deviant firm raises its price to $p^* = p^c + \epsilon$. By the same reasoning as in the tourist-trap model, this firm obtains no informed customers, but still obtains its share of uninformed customers, so long as $\epsilon < c$. Thus, the firm's sales fall to $(1 - \alpha)q^c$.

Many Informed Consumers.   If there are many informed consumers, it does not pay for a firm to deviate by raising its price above p^c. As shown in Figure 17.1, the demand curve facing the deviant firm consists of four parts. If the firm's price is above p^u, its sales are zero.[19] If its price is below p^u but above p^c, its sales equal $q^u = (1 - \alpha)q^c$, because it loses all its informed customers. If its price equals p^c, its sales are q^c. If its price is slightly below p^c all the informed consumers shop there as well as its share of the uninformed consumers, so its sales are $\alpha L + (1 - \alpha)q^c$. The deviant is uninterested in charging less than p^c, because that price is below its average cost, so that it makes negative profits.

With the demand curves as shown in Figure 17.1, it does not pay for the deviant to raise its price, because it loses money. Although it makes more per sale ($p^u > p^c$), it makes so few sales that its costs exceed its revenues. Profits must be negative because the demand curve is to the left of the firm's average cost at p^u.

Thus, the proposed equilibrium at p^c cannot be broken. There are so many informed consumers that a store charging more than p^c loses so much business that it loses money. Thus, if there are enough informed consumers, the price is the same as the full-information, competitive-equilibrium price, even if some consumers are uninformed.

Few Informed Consumers. In contrast, if there are relatively few informed consumers, a deviant firm can raise its price and lose relatively few customers. As shown in Figure 17.2, it pays for the firm to deviate because it makes higher profits: at p^u the deviant firm's demand curve is to the right of its average cost curve. The firm makes zero profits at p^c, so it has an incentive to raise its price.

Thus, if α is relatively large, it does not pay for a firm to deviate from the competitive equilibrium (p^c, q^c). That is, if there are many informed consumers, all firms charge the competitive price. In contrast, if there are relatively few informed consumers (α is relatively small), it pays to deviate, and the proposed equilibrium is broken.

This reasoning shows that no single-price equilibrium exists at p^c if there are relatively few informed consumers. A firm profits by raising its price if the demand at p^u is above average cost. Let $q^a(p^u)$ be the quantity such that the average cost equals p^u, $AC(q^a) = p^u$, as shown in Figure 17.2. It pays for a firm to deviate so long as $(1 - \alpha) q^c > q^a(p^u)$ or

$$\alpha < 1 - \frac{q^a(p^u)}{q^c}, \tag{17.1}$$

and a single-price equilibrium at p^c is impossible. As Equation 17.1 shows, the number of informed consumers needed to produce a single-price equilibrium depends on the shape of the average cost curve and the maximum price consumers are willing to pay, p^u.

Can there be an equilibrium where all firms charge p^u? No, a clever firm can lower its price to any amount less than p^u and obtain all the informed consumers. It makes large profits if its price is only slightly below p^u because it has more sales at approximately

---

[19] We assume that the deviant raises its price to p^u. As explained in the tourist-trap model, the deviant charges ϵ more than the price other firms are charging, or p^u (the maximum price a consumer is willing to pay), whichever is less. If the deviant firm charges p^u, it must be true that $p^c + c \geqq p^u$. That is, we are assuming that search costs, c, are large.

FIGURE 17.2   Two-price Market

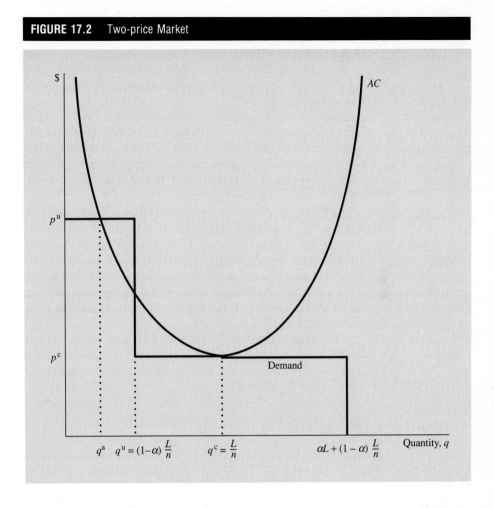

the same price. Another firm, seeing that the first firm has captured all the informed consumers, can set its price slightly below that of the first firm and gain all the informed consumers' business. In this fashion, competition (similar to the Bertrand competition described in Chapter 10) drives the price for the informed consumers to the full-information, competitive level, p^c.

If there is a two-price equilibrium where one or more firms charge p^c and the remaining firms charge p^u, all the informed customers shop at the low-price stores, and the uninformed consumers shop randomly. As a result, some uninformed consumers buy at the high-price stores, and others buy at the low-price stores.

Is it possible that there can be more than two prices? Suppose there is a three-price equilibrium with some stores charging $p^1 = p^u$; others charging p^2, $p^u > p^2 > p^c$; and the rest charging $p^3 = p^c$. The stores charging p^2 make no sales to informed customers. They have, on average, the same number of uninformed customers as stores charging p^u, but they make less money than those stores. As a result, if a store charging p^2 raises its price, it loses no customers and receives higher profits, so that this proposed three-price equilibrium can be broken. Thus, it does not make sense for a store to charge less than p^u and more than p^c.

By such reasoning, we can reject three-price, four-price, and other multiple-price equilibria with large numbers of prices. The only possible multiprice equilibrium is a two-price equilibrium.[20]

In the two-price equilibrium, the low-price stores charge p^c and have sales of q^c. The high-price stores charge p^u and sell q^u units. The low-price stores get all the informed consumers (natives) and some of the uninformed consumers (lucky tourists), so their share of the market (sales per store divided by total sales) is greater than the proportion of informed consumers.[21] Appendix 17A calculates the number of firms in the equilibrium and the shares of each type of firm.

In the two-price equilibrium, all firms must make the same profits, or a firm has an incentive to change its pricing policy. The low-price stores make zero profits (because $p^c = AC(q^c)$ as shown in Figure 17.2). Thus, in equilibrium, the high-price stores must also make zero profits. Suppose instead that they make positive profits. Then either new firms enter the market as high-price stores, or low-price stores start charging high prices. As the number of high-price stores increases, each one sells less (as the uninformed consumers are spread over more stores). The number of high-price stores increases until profits are driven to zero.

To summarize, where only a relatively small number of customers are informed, there is a two-price, monopolistically competitive equilibrium. The low-price stores charge a price equal to marginal cost (the full-information, competitive price), and the high-price stores charge the monopolistic price. Both types of stores make zero profits in equilibrium because of entry. All the informed consumers and some of the uninformed consumers shop at the low-price stores, so these stores have a disproportionately large share of the market.

■ THE NOISY MONOPOLIST: PRICE DISCRIMINATION

People who make no noise are dangerous.—JEAN DE LA FONTAINE

As the preceding discussion shows, limited consumer information can lead to higher prices. Thus, it may be in a firm's best interests to create *noise* in the market by charging different prices for nearly identical products or for the same product at different stores.

---

[20] With other, less restrictive assumptions, there may be many different prices in a market. For example, if consumers know about some but not all firms, firms may charge a full range of prices (Butters 1977). Rothschild (1974) provides a good survey of search theories, which explain price distributions. Where there are many prices charged, as the number of firms increases, obtaining information may be more difficult. As a result, some firms may charge higher prices as new firms enter. A study of the prices of primary-care physicians' services in 92 metropolitan areas concludes that factors that increase search costs, such as number of providers, increase average prices (Pauly and Satterthwaite 1981).

[21] Thus, consumers who go to large stores and buy brands with large shares of the market may be acting rationally (Smallwood and Conlisk 1979). If uninformed consumers observe market shares, they become informed. It is possible, however, that if consumers use share as a signal, then the first entrant in a market may maintain its high share solely as a result of its historical monopoly rather than its superior product.

That is, by creating price dispersion, they may be able to reduce consumers' information.

For example, some durable goods manufacturers sell nearly identical products under two or more brand names. A product may be available under the manufacturer's own brand name at a relatively high price and be available under another brand name at a lower price.

A model by Salop (1977) shows when it pays for a firm to price discriminate in this way.[22] Salop points out that a firm has conflicting objectives. On the one hand, because search by consumers is costly and may lead them to drop out of the market by raising the total cost of a product, the firm wants to reduce price dispersion to eliminate unnecessary search costs. That is, because search costs raise the price to consumers but do not directly benefit the firm, they should be eliminated, all else the same.

On the other hand, when consumers have different costs of collecting information, price dispersion may benefit the firm by allowing it to price discriminate. That is, informed consumers (people who search a lot) are able to find the low-price items, but many of the uninformed consumers (people who do little search) pay the higher price. In short, this model is similar to the tourists-and-natives model.

Thus, dispersion is a costly device for sorting consumers into groups for the purpose of price discrimination. If search does not cost enough to drive consumers from the market and if demand elasticities vary in a certain direction (as in the following example), then creating dispersion is more profitable than charging a single price.

For example, suppose that a monopolist has n retail stores and there are two types of consumers. Of the L consumers, αL are natives who have no search costs and buy 1 unit of the monopolist's product if the price is no higher than p^n. The $(1 - \alpha)L$ consumers who are tourists have extremely high search costs and buy 1 unit of the product if the price is no higher than p^t, where $p^t > p^n$. That is, natives are willing to pay less per meal at local restaurants than are tourists, and natives have perfect information about prices. Tourists typically choose restaurants randomly because they do not know where the low-price (or high-quality) restaurants are located.

Imagine further that one company owns all the restaurants and that they all serve the same type of food. Does it pay for the company to vary its prices across locations? No restaurant can charge more than p^t, because at a higher price, the restaurant draws no customers. Similarly, no restaurant should charge less than p^n because, by assumption, natives have an inelastic demand for a meal up to a price p^n. Lowering the price from p^n does not increase the number of meals the company can sell, so its profit-maximizing price is at least p^n. If it pays for the monopolist to charge different prices at various locations, it sets a low price, p^n, at only one restaurant, because natives always search for the minimum price, and tourists never go to more than one outlet. All the other restaurants charge a higher price, because tourists discover restaurants by chance.

Suppose for simplicity that the monopolist can produce meals at zero cost. If the monopolist charges more than p^n, no native dines at local restaurants. In that case, profits on meals sold to tourists are maximized by setting price at p^t. Profits on the tourists' meals are given by

$$(1 - \alpha)Lp^t, \tag{17.2}$$

---

[22] The following presentation is partly based on Calvo (n.d.).

where $(1 - \alpha)L$ is the number of meals sold at price p^t.[23]

If the monopolist charges p^n at one location and p^t at all other locations, then it sells meals to all L potential consumers. All the natives eat at the low-price restaurant, so the profits on meals sold to natives are $\alpha L p^n$. Most ($[n - 1]/n$) tourists eat at the high-price restaurants, but $1/n$ of the tourists are lucky and find the low-price restaurant. Thus, the monopolist's expected profits are

$$\alpha L p^n + \frac{1}{n}(1 - \alpha)L p^n + \frac{(n - 1)}{n}(1 - \alpha)L p^t, \qquad (17.3)$$

where the first term is the profits from the (αL) natives, the second term is the expected profits from the ($[1 - \alpha]L/n$) lucky tourists who find the low-price restaurant, and the last term is the expected profits from the ($[1 - \alpha]L[n - 1]/n$) unlucky tourists who pay the high price.

If the monopolist receives higher profits when it charges two prices (Expression 17.3) than when it charges a single price of p^t (Expression 17.2), it pays for the monopolist to be "noisy" and price discriminate. The difference in profits between discriminating and setting a single price (Expression 17.3 − Expression 17.2) is

$$\alpha L p^n - \frac{1 - \alpha}{n}L(p^t - p^n). \qquad (17.4)$$

It pays for the monopolist to price discriminate if the difference in profits between price discriminating and setting a single price (Expression 17.4) is positive. Since the first term in (17.4) is positive, and the second term is negative, price discrimination is more likely as the second term becomes small in absolute value relative to the first term. By inspection, as the share of tourists, $(1 - \alpha)$, falls or as the number of firms, n, increases, the second term gets closer to zero, and price discrimination becomes relatively more attractive.

As the number of tourists becomes small, it pays the monopolist to sell to natives as well as tourists. Thus, it becomes more likely that the monopolist gains by price discrimination as $(1 - \alpha)$ shrinks.[24] Similarly, as the number of restaurants, n, rises, price discrimination is more likely to pay.[25] Suppose, for example, that the monopolist can operate extra restaurants at little or no additional cost. It can then choose the number of restaurants, n, large enough that the second term in (17.4) is essentially zero, and

---

[23] If the monopolist is going to charge a single price at all locations, it may pay to charge p^n instead of p^t to induce natives to also patronize the restaurants. It pays to set a single price of p^n if $(1 - \alpha)L p^t < L p^n$, or $(1 - \alpha) < p^n/p^t$. That is, as the relative share of natives, α, increases, or the maximum price natives are willing to pay approaches that of tourists, it pays to set a low price. Similarly, as the share of tourists increases, or as the amount they are willing to pay relative to natives increases, it pays to set a high price. We do not further consider charging a single price of p^n, because price discriminating by charging p^n at one restaurant and p^t at all others produces higher profits than charging p^n at all restaurants.

[24] Differentiating (17.4) with respect to α gives $L[p^n + (p^t - p^n)/n] > 0$.

[25] Differentiating (17.4) with respect to n gives $(1 - \alpha)L(p^t - p^n)/n^2 > 0$.

hence it pays to be noisy. That is, if the monopolist can make it so hard to find the low-price restaurant that relatively few tourists find it, it pays to price discriminate.

Thus, where there are both informed and uninformed consumers in a market, it often pays for a monopolist to create *noise;* that is, it has an incentive to charge different prices for a homogeneous good at various locations to make it more difficult for uninformed consumers to find the low-price store. The monopolist is able to price discriminate because search costs prevent consumers from buying at the low-price restaurants.

■ PROVIDING CONSUMER INFORMATION LOWERS PRICE

> *It is a great nuisance that knowledge can only be acquired by hard work. It would be fine if we could swallow the powder of profitable information made palatable by the jam of fiction.* —W. SOMERSET MAUGHAM

It seems intuitively obvious that providing consumers with comparative price information should lower the average price observed in the market. Yet, as the tourist-trap model shows, lowering the cost of search has no effect so long as the cost is positive. That result may not be as perplexing as it first appears because merely decreasing the cost of search does not provide consumers with extra information. In fact, that result indicates that in equilibrium, no further searches occur when the costs of search are lowered, so consumer information does not increase.

An information program that actually provides consumers with comparative price information may, then, have an effect where merely lowering the cost of search does not. The following discussion first presents a theoretical argument that supplying more consumer information results in a lowered equilibrium price and then presents some empirical evidence that supports this conclusion.

How Information Lowers Prices

At least two types of models show that improving information can lower prices. First, as the tourists-and-natives model with many firms shows, as more consumers become informed, the market share of low-price firms increases. A second model developed below shows that where information is provided that allows consumers to better estimate true prices, the average price may fall. This latter model explains the existence of a single-price equilibrium, where the price lies between the monopolistic and the full-information, competitive price (marginal cost).

Suppose a consumer wishes to shop at the lowest-price store but does not know which store has the lowest prices. Typically, consumers collect information from various sources (shopping at various stores, reading advertisements, watching commercials, asking friends) to determine which stores are relatively inexpensive (see Example 17.1).

Consumers form estimates based on available information of the prices at each store and then choose the store they estimate has the lowest price (Perloff and Salop 1986). Consumers do not know the prices exactly, so a store may raise its price without losing all its customers. That is, the demand curve facing each store changes from being perfectly elastic under full information to being less elastic under limited consumer information.

TABLE 17.1   Consumer Price Estimates

	Price Estimates of Consumers			
	(1/3)L	*(1/3)L*	*(1/3)L*	*Share of Sales*
Store 1	$9.00	$10.00	$11.00	*(2/3)L*
Store 2	$9.50	$10.50	$11.50	*(1/3)L*

Firms' demand curves are not perfectly elastic so long as consumers use their estimates of relative prices to choose the stores at which they shop. If they treat their price estimates as their best information and go to the store that they believe has the lowest price, they may make a mistake; thus, a store that raises its price slightly may not lose all its customers because some of them believe (incorrectly) that other stores charge even higher prices. If consumers gain more information, or the number of stores increases, prices may fall.

Improved Consumer Information.   The following example illustrates the effect of an increase in consumers' information. Suppose there are only two stores: Store 1 and Store 2. Store 1 charges $10 for a given good. Consumers, however, have imperfect information, so their estimates of this price are not always correct. Consumers form unbiased estimates, so, on average, they estimate the correct price, but any one consumer may have an inaccurate estimate. Initially, suppose that one-third of all consumers believe that Store 1 charges $9, one-third believe it charges $10, and the remainder believe that it charges $11.

Now suppose Store 2 actually charges $10.50. One-third of all consumers believe it charges $9.50, one-third believe it charges $10.50, and the remainder believe its price is $11.50. If consumers form their estimates independently for the two stores, some consumers shop at Store 2 even though its price is higher. That is, some consumers estimate that Store 1 charges $11, and they estimate that Store 2 charges $9.50 or $10.50. If there are L consumers, each of whom buys exactly 1 unit of the good, then Store 1 sells $(\frac{2}{3})L$ units and Store 2 sells $(\frac{1}{3})L$ units if consumers shop at the first store they visit. This example is summarized in Table 17.1.

Now assume that the consumers obtain better information, so their estimates of the two stores' prices become more accurate, as shown in Table 17.2. If Store 2 charges 50¢ more than Store 1, as before, it loses half its customers. In the first example, one-ninth of the customers correctly estimate the price at Store 2 and overestimate the price at Store 1, so they shop at Store 2. Another ninth of the customers in the first example shop at Store 2 because they underestimate the price at Store 2 and correctly estimate the price at Store 1. In the second example, where consumers have better information, both of these types of customers shop at Store 1. In both examples, some of those consumers who underestimate the price at Store 2 and overestimate the price at Store 1, buy at Store 2.

With better information, Store 2 loses more sales if it raises its price above that of

TABLE 17.2	More Accurate Consumer Price Estimates			
	Price Estimates of Consumers			
	(1/3)L	*(1/3)L*	*(1/3)L*	*Share of Sales*
Store 1	$9.70	$10.00	$10.30	*(8/9)L*
Store 2	$10.20	$10.50	$10.80	*(1/9)L*

Store 1. So long as there is some limit to consumers' information, however, Store 2 can charge more than Store 1 and retain some customers. The amount more that it can charge varies inversely with the amount of information consumers have: the better their information, the higher the elasticity of demand facing the firm. With perfect information, each store's elasticity of demand is infinite, and a store must charge a price as low as other stores or lose all its customers.

More Firms.   If firms can enter the industry without limit, then (even given imperfect information) prices are driven to the full-information, competitive price (marginal cost) under certain plausible assumptions. Suppose each consumer forms an unbiased estimate of each store's price as previously described. Then as the number of stores increases, the number of estimates increases. Suppose every existing firm is duplicated 10 times, so that the new firms charge the same prices as the original ones, and the true price distribution remains unchanged. As the number of stores increases, however, the probability that a customer thinks that another store charges roughly the same price as the one previously estimated to have the low price rises. That is, the elasticity of demand facing each store falls, and hence its price falls.

To summarize, increasing consumer information (in the sense that consumers can more accurately estimate stores' true prices) initially increases the share of low-price stores. The elasticity of demand facing stores rises, so they have an incentive to lower their prices. As a result, the average price and the spread in prices is likely to fall. Similarly, increasing the number of stores increases the elasticity of demand facing each one, so the average prices and the spread in prices is likely to fall.

An Example: Grocery Store Information Programs

Does providing consumers with information increase the market shares of relatively low-price stores, lower the average market price, and reduce the variance in prices across stores? A 1974 experiment by the Food Price Review Board of Canada was designed to answer these questions for grocery stores.[26] There were three phases in the experiment. During Phase 1 (a 17-week period), supermarket price information was collected in both

---

[26] Devine and Marion (1979) and Devine (1978). Lesser and Bryant (1980) critique Devine and Marion (1979), who respond in Devine and Marion (1980).

the control city, Winnipeg, and in the experimental city, Ottawa-Hull. Only during Phase 2 (a 5-week period) was the information on grocery store prices in Ottawa-Hull published in newspapers and mailed to some consumers whose behavior was monitored in detail. At no time was the information publicized in the control city, Winnipeg. In the final phase (6 weeks), price information was again collected in both cities but not disseminated.

Average food prices declined in Ottawa-Hull by 1.5 percent during the first week of Phase 2, by 3.0 percent the following week, and then remained steady for the next three weeks. During the first week following the end of Phase 2, prices dropped an additional 2.5 percent. Thus, the total decline over this 6-week period was 7.1 percent. Prices in the control market declined by 0.6 percent during Phase 2. Thus, prices in the experimental city fell relative to prices in the control city by 6.5 percent during the 6-week period that included the first week of Phase 3 (see Figure 17.3).

During the experimental period, prices at the higher-price stores (and chains) fell more than those at initially low-price stores. The difference in price index levels between high- and low-price stores dropped from a maximum of 15 percent during the preinformation period to a low of 5.4 percent at one point in Phase 2. The differential for chains fell from a maximum of 7.3 percent to a low of 3.1 percent. The average range of prices during the 12-week period prior to the information program was 9.71 percent compared to 7.83 percent during Phase 2.

The high-price stores had more volatile prices as measured by the index of in-store price variation. High-price stores were more common in the underprivileged areas than in the more affluent areas. Stores with the highest prices generally dropped prices to meet those of their lower-price competitors.

A consumer survey found that 43 percent of the consumers in the test market indicated that they had changed stores as a direct result of the comparative price program. As a result of this shift, the top four corporate chains increased their share of the market from 74 percent to 81 percent. Lower-priced chains increased their share relative to others.

Average retail food prices in the test market began to rise within two weeks after the termination of the information program and increased 8.8 percent by the end of the research period. One interpretation of these results is that during the information period, a once-and-for-all drop in average prices occurred. With the end of the information program, prices increased to their preinformation levels.[27] It appears that stores realized the experiment would be short-lived and were particularly aggressive in trying to convince consumers that they had relatively low prices while the program was in effect. Apparently, to maintain low prices, information must be continuously supplied.

A back-of-the-envelope calculation of the welfare gain (consumer surplus minus profits) indicates that it could significantly exceed the costs of collecting the information. Nonetheless, gains per family may be small. Interviewed consumers were willing to pay $1.36 per month for this information, which implies a consumer surplus gain of approximately $2 million per year for the city.

---

[27] The test market basket of goods was 2 percent higher than that in the control market at the beginning of the information program. During the final week of the monitoring program, prices were 1.3 percent lower in the test market. It is possible that prices in the experimental city had not completely caught up with prices in the control city by the end of the Phase 3 monitoring period.

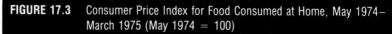

FIGURE 17.3   Consumer Price Index for Food Consumed at Home, May 1974–
March 1975 (May 1974 = 100)

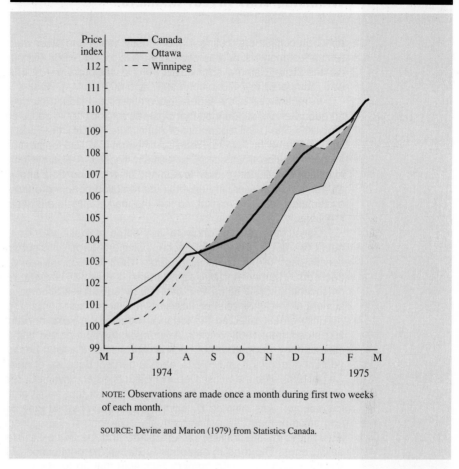

NOTE: Observations are made once a month during first two weeks
of each month.

SOURCE: Devine and Marion (1979) from Statistics Canada.

The basic results of this experiment were largely confirmed in another experiment conducted in the province of Saskatchewan in October 1975 to determine the long-run effects of an information program (Devine 1978). During the experiment, prices were monitored in six Saskatchewan cities and in Calgary and Winnipeg, located in neighboring provinces. The relative prices were published weekly for six consecutive months in two test markets in Saskatchewan: Regina and Saskatoon.

The price index levels in the test markets fell more than the price declines recorded in the control cities of Winnipeg and Calgary outside the province. In particular, Regina led the national decline in the Statistics Canada Consumer Price Index for Food Consumed at Home during the latter part of the publication period. Although average prices in Saskatoon declined more rapidly than in the paired control market (Winnipeg) during most of the information period, this result was reversed during the last six weeks of the program.

EXAMPLE 17.8

A COST-BENEFIT ANALYSIS OF PROVIDING MORE ACCURATE INFORMATION

Providing information only makes sense if the benefits from the information outweigh the costs of providing it. A cost-benefit study was conducted concerning accurate interpretation of weights reported on chicken labels in grocery stores.

Some foods, such as meats and poultry, accumulate moisture during processing and lose moisture during packing and storage. The accumulation or loss depends on the biological characteristics of the product and handling conditions such as temperature and storage time. As a result, the actual weight of the meat purchased is often different from the weight stated on the label.

To be sure they are in compliance with labeling requirements, some firms label packages with weights less than the actual weights, a technique referred to as *overpacking* by the industry. Because different states use different standards—some use wet weights and others use dry weights—the difference between labeled and actual weight is probably substantial across the country. The U.S. Department of Agriculture examined the drained and labeled weights of packages of whole, cut-up chickens from various states. In roughly half the sample the drained weight was higher; in the other half the labeled weight was higher.

Presumably, consumers would be willing to pay more per pound if they knew that a package contained more product than was indicated on the label. One estimate of the gain from the information about accurate weights in 1978 was $2.1 million, which is only 0.01 percent of the total expenditures on chicken. The estimated cost of providing drained-weight information is at least $59 million annually. Thus, in this case, the costs of providing the information would easily outweigh the benefits.

SOURCE: Sexton (1981).

Thus, a number of studies have shown that providing consumers with information can lower average price. When the information programs are ended, however, the average price tends to rise to its original level. Providing information to consumers, however, does not always increase welfare: see Examples 17.7 and 17.8.

■ SUMMARY

There are five major results from models in which consumers have limited information about quality or prices. First, if consumers have limited information about the quality of a product, either there is no market or, where the market exists, quality levels are usually lower than the levels produced if consumers have full information. Expert information, reputation, standards, and certification may provide consumers with information about quality and hence rectify these problems; however, standard setters can behave anticompetitively.

Second, where consumers have limited information about prices, markets may not exist or, if they do exist, even small firms may set prices above marginal costs. Thus, perfect competition may be impossible. Even with a homogeneous good, stores may charge different prices. In this sense, the law of supply and demand and the law of a single price do not hold. Indeed, with this type of limited information, monopoly may be socially preferable to competition.

Third, where some consumers know the prices at all stores and others must incur search costs to determine the price at any given store, two types of equilibria are possible. If there are enough informed consumers, the equilibrium price equals marginal cost. If there are relatively few informed consumers, a two-price equilibrium is likely, where some stores charge a high price and others charge marginal cost. Fourth, in such a market, a monopolist may charge different prices at its different stores in order to price discriminate between informed and uninformed consumers.

Fifth, lowering the cost of gathering information may not lower average prices. For example, in a single-price equilibrium, reducing search costs for all consumers may have no effect. In contrast, providing consumers with the location of the lowest-price store may lower average price.

Thus, markets with limited information differ from those with perfect information. Providing information or lowering the cost of obtaining information may not always increase welfare when the costs of providing the information or lowering the search costs are taken into account. The next chapter examines the incentives of individual firms to inform or misinform consumers by using advertising and the effects of such advertising.

■ Key Terms

adverse selection
bounded rationality
break the equilibrium
certification

guarantees
moral hazard
public good

price dispersion
standards
warranties

■ Discussion Questions

1. Under what conditions does providing consumers with extra information increase social welfare?
2. Many states and local governments license many professions. To practice those professions, one must pass a test showing a high ability level. In a few locations, the government merely tests professionals and makes that information available to consumers; low-ability workers are not excluded from the market. This latter approach is called certification. Under which circumstances is licensing preferable and under which circumstances is certification preferable?
3. In which markets do you think the government could successfully intervene to overcome problems due to inadequate consumer information? That is, in which markets do you expect the benefits to exceed the costs of intervention? How do you think the government could obtain the necessary information to provide to consumers? Can you give a real-world example of successful government intervention?
4. Is a large difference between the highest and the lowest price in a market a sign of a market failure? If so, what should or could be done about it?
5. Organizations like Consumers Union provide a valuable service. How can society encourage such organizations to provide the optimal amount of information to consumers? How should the optimal level be determined?

■ Problems

1. Describe how a manufacturer could act like a noisy monopolist by using discount coupons provided to some consumers in newspapers or magazines. Under what conditions should a manufacturer use this technique?

2. Suppose that there are two types of firms. All firms have U-shaped average cost curves, where n firms have average costs of $AC(q)$ and m firms have average cost curves of $AC(q) + k$. There are two types of consumers: the natives have zero search costs, and the tourists have very high search costs. Describe the resulting equilibrium.

3. Suppose two economists write a textbook. Their publisher offers them royalties on sales of the book equal to α percent of the sales revenue. The economists are concerned. They believe that such a royalty system causes the publisher to sell less than the joint profit-maximizing number of copies of the book. Demonstrate this reasoning. They believe that a royalty in the form

of a lump-sum payment, L, or β percent of profits does not cause the publisher to publish too few books. Why do they agree to the α percent royalty? *Hint:* One explanation concerns asymmetric information on the part of the publisher.

4. Determine the equilibrium prices, quantities, and number of high- and low-price stores in the tourist-and-native model if consumers have downward sloping, linear demand curves: $q = a - bp$, where a and b are positive constants.

5. By reinterpreting the first model discussed in Appendix 11C (a representative consumer-spatial model), develop a model of how extra information may affect price. *Hint:* Suppose a consumer's estimate of the price charged by store i is its price plus an error term, $\beta\epsilon$, where the mean of $\epsilon = 0$ and β is a constant. Better information could be interpreted as a smaller β.

Answers to odd-numbered problems are given at the back of the book.

■ Recommended Readings

In addition to the articles cited in the chapter, the following provide important background reading. Two nontechnical papers that give a good overview of many of the main issues are Salop (1978) and Beales, Craswell, and Salop (1981).

The rest of these articles are more technical. Uncertainty, information, and welfare are examined in Colantoni, Davis, and Swaminuthan (1965); Allen (1981); Kahne-

mann, Slovic, and Tversky (1982). Important work on the value of information includes Lave (1963), Gould (1974), and Antonovitz and Roe (1986). Work on search and strategic behavior by firms includes Wilde and Schwartz (1979) and Varian (1980). The role of information in oligopolistic or monopolistic competition is discussed in Shapiro (1982), Wolinsky (1986), and Ross (1988).

■ References

Akerlof, George A. 1970. "The Market for 'Lemons': Quality Uncertainty and the Market Mechanism." *Quarterly Journal of Economics* 84:488–500.

Allen, Beth. 1981. "Generic Existence of Completely Revealing Equilibria for Economies with Uncertainty When Prices Convey Information." *Econometrica* 49:1173–99.

Antonovitz, Frances, and Terry Roe. 1986. "A Theoretical and Empirical Approach to the Value of Information in

Risky Markets." *Review of Economics and Statistics* 68:105–14.

Bagwell, Kyle, and Michael Riordan. 1988. "High and Declining Prices Signal Product Quality." Northwestern University working paper (October).

Beales, Howard, Richard Craswell, and Steven Salop. 1981. "Efficient Regulation of Consumer Information." *Journal of Law and Economics* 24:491–539.

Boynton, Robert D., Joseph N. Uhl, Brian F. Blake, and

Vicki A. McCracken. 1981. "An Analysis of the Impacts of Comparative Foodstore Price Reporting on Price Structures and Consumer Behavior." Purdue University Agricultural Experiment Station Research Bulletin 968 (August).

Butters, Gerard R. 1977. "Equilibrium Distribution of Sales and Advertising Prices." *The Review of Economic Studies* 44:465–91.

Calvo, Guillermo. n.d. "The Noisy Monopolist: Salop Simplified." Mimeo.

Chan, Yuk-Shee, and Hayne E. Leland. 1982. "Prices and Qualities in Markets with Costly Information." *The Review of Economic Studies* 49:499–516.

Colantoni, C.S., O.A. Davis, and M. Swaminuthan. 1965. "Imperfect Consumers and Welfare Comparisons of Policies Concerning Information and Regulation." *The Bell Journal of Economics* 7:602–15.

Cooper, Russell, and Thomas W. Ross. 1984. "Prices, Product Qualities, and Asymmetric Information: The Competitive Case." *The Review of Economic Studies* 51:197–207.

Crocker, Keith J. 1986. "A Reexamination of the 'Lemons' Market When Warranties are Not Prepurchase Quality Signals." *Information Economics and Policy* 2:147–62.

Curry, D., and P. Reisz. 1988. "Prices and Price/Quality Relationships: A Longitudinal Analysis." *Journal of Marketing* 52:36–51.

Cyert, R.M., and J.G. March. 1963. *A Behavioral Theory of the Firm*. Englewood Cliffs, N.J.: Prentice-Hall.

Devine, D. Grant. 1978. "A Review of the Experimental Effects of Increased Price Information on the Performance of Canadian Retail Food Stores in the 1970s." *Canadian Journal of Agricultural Economics* 26:24–29.

Devine, D. Grant, and Bruce W. Marion. 1979. "The Influence of Consumer Price Information on Retail Pricing and Consumer Behavior." *American Journal of Agricultural Economics* 61:228–37.

———. 1980. "The Influence of Consumer Price Information on Retail Pricing and Consumer Behavior: Reply." *American Journal of Agricultural Economics* 62:267–69.

Diamond, Peter. 1971. "A Model of Price Adjustment." *Journal of Economic Theory* 3:156–68.

Federal Trade Commission, Bureau of Consumer Protection. 1978. *Standards and Certification, Proposed Rule and Staff Report*. Washington, D.C.: U.S. Government Printing Office.

Federal Trade Commission. 1979. *Consumer Information Remedies, Policy Review Session*. Washington, D.C.: U.S. Government Printing Office.

Gabor, André. 1980. "Price and Consumer Protection," in D. Morris, ed., *Economics of Consumer Protection*. London: Heinemann Educational Books.

Gabor, André, and C. W. J. Granger. 1961. "On the Price Consciousness of Consumers." *Applied Statistics* 10:170–88.

Gerstner, E. 1985. "Do Higher Prices Signal Higher Qualities?" *Journal of Marketing Research* 22:209–15.

Ginter, James L., Murray A. Young, and Peter R. Dickson. 1987. "A Market Efficiency Study of Used Car Reliability and Prices." *The Journal of Consumer Affairs* 21:258–76.

Gould, John P. 1974. "Risk, Stochastic Preference, and the Value of Information." *Journal of Economic Theory* 8:64–85.

Grossman, Stanford J., and Joseph E. Stiglitz. 1980. "On the Impossibility of Informationally Efficient Markets." *American Economic Review* 70:393–408.

Heal, Geoffrey. 1977. "Guarantees and Risk-Sharing." *The Review of Economic Studies* 44:549–60.

Hemenway, David. 1975. *Industrywide Voluntary Product Standards*. Cambridge, Mass.: Ballinger.

Kahnemann, Daniel, Paul Slovic, and Amos Tversky, eds. 1982. *Judgement Under Uncertainty: Heuristics and Biases*. Cambridge: Cambridge University Press.

Kim, Jae-Cheol. 1985. "The Market for 'Lemons' Reconsidered: A Model of the Used Car Market with Asymmetric Information." *American Economic Review* 75:836–43.

Klein, Benjamin, and Keith Leffler. 1981. "The Role of Market Forces in Assuring Contractual Performance." *Journal of Political Economy* 89:615–41.

Lacko, James M. 1986. *Product Quality and Information in the Used Car Market*. Federal Trade Commission, Bureau of Economics Staff Report. Washington, D.C.: U.S. Government Printing Office.

Lave, Lester B. 1963. "The Value of Better Weather Information to the Raisin Industry." *Econometrica* 31:151–64.

Leland, Hayne E. 1979a. "Quacks, Lemons, and Licensing: A Theory of Minimum Quality Standards." *Journal of Political Economy* 87:1328–46.

———. 1979b. "Minimum Quality Standards in Markets with Asymmetric Information," in Simon Rottenberg, ed., *Occupational Licensure*. Washington, D.C.: American Enterprise Institute.

Lesser, William H., and W. Keith Bryant. 1980. "The Influence of Consumer Price Information on Retail Pricing and Consumer Behavior: Comment." *American Journal of Agricultural Economics* 62:265–66.

Lynch, Michael, Ross Miller, Charles R. Plott, and Russell Porter. 1986. *Experimental Studies of Markets with Buyers Ignorant of Quality Before Purchase: When Do 'Lemons' Drive Out High-Quality Products?* Bureau of Economics, Federal Trade Commission. Washington, D.C.: U.S. Government Printing Office.

Maynes, Scott E., and Terje Assum. 1982. "Informationally Imperfect Consumer Markets: Empirical Findings and Policy Implications." *The Journal of Consumer Affairs* 16:62–87.

McCracken, Vicki A., Robert D. Boynton, and Brian F. Blake. 1982. "The Impact of Comparative Food Price Information on Consumers and Grocery Retailers: Some Preliminary Findings of a Field Experiment." *The Journal of Consumer Affairs* 16:224–39.

Oster, Sharon M., and John M. Quigley. 1977. "Regulatory Barriers to the Diffusion of Innovation: Some Evidence from Building Codes." *The Bell Journal of Economics* 8:361–77.

Pauly, Mark V., and Mark A. Satterthwaite. 1981. "The Pricing of Primary Care Physicians' Services: A Test of the Role of Consumer Information." *The Bell Journal of Economics* 12:488–506.

Perloff, Jeffrey M., and Steven C. Salop. 1986. "Firm-Specific Information, Product Differentiation, and Industry Equilibrium." *Oxford Economic Papers* 38:184–202.

Pratt, John W., David A. Wise, and Richard Zeckhauser. 1979. "Price Differences in Almost Competitive Markets." *Quarterly Journal of Economics* 93:189–211.

Reinganum, Jennifer F. 1979. "A Simple Model of Equilibrium Price Dispersion." *Journal of Political Economy* 87:851–58.

Ross, Thomas W. 1988. "Brand Information and Price." *The Journal of Industrial Economics* 36:301–14.

Rothschild, Michael. 1974. "Models of Market Organization with Imperfect Information: A Survey." *Journal of Political Economy* 82:1283–1308.

Salop, Steven C. 1976. "Information and Monopolistic Competition." *American Economic Review* 66:240–45.

———. 1977. "The Noisy Monopolist: Imperfect Information, Price Dispersion, and Price Discrimination." *The Review of Economic Studies* 44:393–406.

———. 1978. "Parables of Information Transmission in Markets," in Andrew A. Mitchell, ed., *The Effect of Information on Consumer and Market Behavior*. Chicago: American Marketing Association, 3–12.

Salop, Steven C., and Joseph Stiglitz. 1977. "Bargains and Ripoffs: A Model of Monopolistically Competitive Price Dispersion." *The Review of Economic Studies* 44:493–510.

Scitovsky, Tibor. 1950. "Ignorance as a Source of Oligopoly Power." *American Economic Review* 40:48–53.

Sexton, Richard. 1981. "Welfare Loss from Inaccurate Information: An Economic Model with Application to Food Labels." *Journal of Consumer Affairs* 15:214–31.

Shapiro, Carl. 1982. "Consumer Information, Product Quality, and Seller Reputation." *The Bell Journal of Economics* 13:20–35.

Simon, Herbert A. 1957. *Models of Man*. New York: John Wiley and Sons.

———. 1959. "Theories of Decision-Making in Economics and Behavioral Science." *American Economic Review* 49:253–83.

Smallwood, Dennis E., and John Conlisk. 1979. "Product Quality in Markets Where Consumers are Imperfectly Informed." *Quarterly Journal of Economics* 93:1–23.

Spence, A. Michael. 1977. "Consumer Misperceptions, Product Failure, and Producer Liability." *The Review of Economic Studies* 44:561–72.

Stigler, George. 1961. "The Economics of Information." *Journal of Political Economy* 69:213–25.

Stiglitz, Joseph. 1979. "Equilibrium in Product Markets with Imperfect Information." *American Economic Review* 69:339–45.

Tellis, Gerard J., and Birger Wernerfelt. 1987. "Competitive Price and Quality Under Asymmetric Information." *Marketing Science* 6:240–53.

Varian, Hal. 1980. "A Model of Sales." *American Economic Review* 70:651–59.

Wilde, Louis L., and Alan Schwartz. 1979. "Equilibrium Comparison Shopping." *The Review of Economic Studies* 46:543–53.

Willamson, Oliver E. 1964. *The Economics of Discretionary Behavior*. Englewood Cliffs, N.J.: Prentice-Hall.

Wilson, Charles. "The Nature of Equilibrium in the Markets with Adverse Selection." *The Bell Journal of Economics* 11:108–13.

Wolinsky, Asher. 1986. "True Monopolistic Competition as a Result of Imperfect Information." *Quarterly Journal of Economics* 101:493–511.

MARKET SHARES IN THE TOURIST-AND-NATIVE MODEL

In the two-price equilibrium in the tourist-and-native model, the low-price stores charge p^c, sell q^c, and have β share of the market, while the high-price stores charge p^u, sell q^u, and make up $1 - \beta$ share of the market. The high-price stores only sell to their share of the $(1 - \alpha)L$ uninformed consumers, $(1 - \alpha)L(1 - \beta)$, so each high-price firm sells

$$q^u = \frac{(1 - \alpha)\, L\, (1 - \beta)}{n(1 - \beta)} = \frac{(1 - \alpha)L}{n}. \qquad (17A.1)$$

The high-price stores' share of the market is

$$1 - \beta = \frac{q^u}{L} = \frac{1 - \alpha}{n}. \qquad (17A.2)$$

Each low-price store sells to its share of the αL informed consumers and to its share of the $\beta(1 - \alpha)L$ uninformed consumers who are lucky enough to find a low-price store:

$$q^c = \frac{\alpha L + (1 - \alpha)L\beta}{n\beta}. \qquad (17A.3)$$

The market share of low-price stores is

$$\beta = \frac{q^c}{L} = \frac{\alpha + (1 - \alpha)\beta}{n\beta}. \qquad (17A.4)$$

In equilibrium the low-price stores get all the informed consumers and some of the uninformed consumers (the lucky tourists), so their share of the market is greater than the proportion of informed consumers: $\beta > \alpha$.

Let q^a be the quantity at which average cost equals p^u. That is, $q^a = q^u$, so that

$$q^a = \frac{(1 - \alpha)L}{n}. \qquad (17A.5)$$

Similarly, q^A is the quantity at which average cost equals p^c, so $q^A = q^c$, and

$$q^A = \frac{\alpha L + (1 - \alpha)L\beta}{n\beta}. \tag{17A.6}$$

Equations 17A.5 and 17A.6 are equations in two unknowns, β and n. Rearranging (17A.5) yields

$$n = \frac{(1 - \alpha)L}{q^a}. \tag{17A.7}$$

Substituting from Equation 17A.7 into (17A.6) and rearranging terms,

$$\beta = \frac{\alpha q^a}{(1 - \alpha)(q^A - q^a)}. \tag{17A.8}$$

The two-price equilibrium is characterized by n and β (determined by Equations 17A.7 and 17A.8). The βn low-price stores sell $q^A = q^c$ (Equation 17A.6) units at p^c, and $(1 - \beta)n$ high-price stores sell $q^a = q^u$ (Equation 17A.5) at p^u.

CHAPTER 18 | ADVERTISING AND DISCLOSURE

> **A**dvertisements contain the only truth to be relied on in a newspaper.
>
> THOMAS JEFFERSON
>
> **A**dvertising is a racket . . . its constructive contribution to humanity is exactly minus zero.
>
> F. SCOTT FITZGERALD

Firms use advertising for many purposes; it can be used to inform consumers that a firm has a new product or the lowest prices, or it can differentiate one product from another. A firm wants consumers to know its product's strengths but not its weaknesses. Firms grudgingly disclose some facts to consumers, enthusiastically advertise other claims, and hide yet other product attributes. This chapter examines the motives for advertising and for truthful or untruthful disclosure.

The 100 largest domestic advertisers in the United States spend more than $27 billion a year.[1] As shown in Table 18.1, the firm with the highest advertising budget in the United States, Procter & Gamble, spent $1.435 billion in 1986 to advertise soaps, cleaners, and other products. Number 2, Philip Morris, a cigarette firm, spent $1.364 billion. The U.S. Government spent $306 million, and was the 39th largest advertiser.

Advertising as a percentage of sales varies widely. For example, General Motors, the fifth largest advertiser, spent only 0.9 percent of its sales revenues on advertising, whereas Warner-Lambert Co., which produces pharmaceuticals and is the 12th largest advertiser, spent 32.3 percent.

Advertisers pay for television and radio broadcasts. It is hard to imagine life without Saturday morning cartoons supported by toy and cereal ads. Firms may also influence

---

[1] *Advertising Age*. 1987. September 24, 162.

TABLE 18.1	Fifty Leading National Advertisers		
	Rank	*U.S. Advertising in 1986 ($thousands)*	*Advertising as percent of U.S. Sales*
Airlines			
Allegis Corp.	48	171,746	N/A
Automotive			
Chrysler Corp.	20	426,000	2.1
Ford Motor Co.	6	648,500	1.3
General Motors Corp.	5	839,000	0.9
Honda Motor Co., Ltd.	41	205,082	N/A
Nissan Motor Co., Ltd.	47	180,136	N/A
Toyota Motor Corp.	40	208,877	N/A
Chemicals & Petroleum			
American Cyanamid Co.	35	248,460	2.9
Mobil Corp.	50	167,777	0.9
Electronics & Office Equipment			
Eastman Kodak Co.	34	255,586	2.9
General Electric Co.	25	354,250	N/A
International Business Machines	31	295,498	1.2
Tandy Corp.	33	262,161	N/A
Entertainment and Media			
CBS, Inc.	46	184,837	4.5
Time, Inc.	44	190,587	N/A
Walt Disney Co.	38	219,138	N/A
Financial			
American Express Co.	45	190,002	1.6
Food			
BCI Holding	13	535,852	9.2
Campbell Soup Co.	42	204,233	5.7
General Mills	11	551,561	N/A
H. J. Heinz Co.	39	217,413	7.8
Kellogg Co.	23	374,142	16.5
Kraft, Inc.	19	437,952	7.0
Nestle SA	30	305,451	N/A
Pillsbury Co.	16	494,877	9.0
Quaker Oats Co.	28	309,239	N/A
Ralston Purina Co.	17	478,031	N/A
RJR Nabisco	4	935,036	5.9
Sara Lee Corp.	32	271,623	3.5

newspapers' reporting by threatening to remove advertising. In spite of this pervasive role of advertising in our daily lives, standard models of competition ignore promotional efforts. This chapter incorporates those efforts into models of competitive and noncompetitive behavior.

TABLE 18.1	Fifty Leading National Advertisers *continued*		
	Rank	*U.S. Advertising in 1986 ($thousands)*	*Advertising as percent of U.S. Sales*
Government			
U.S. Government	29	306,094	N/A
Gum & Candy			
Mars Inc.	27	312,607	N/A
Pharmaceuticals			
American Home Products Corp.	22	395,718	10.7
Bristol Myers Co.	26	330,997	9.5
Johnson & Johnson	21	410,672	10.3
Pfizer, Inc.	49	171,139	6.9
Schering-Plough Corp.	43	203,359	14.4
Sterling Drug	37	220,727	17.6
Warner-Lambert Co.	12	548,726	32.3
Retail			
J. C. Penney Co.	15	496,241	3.5
K-Mart Corp.	9	590,350	N/A
Sears, Roebuck & Co.	3	1,004,708	N/A
Restaurants			
McDonald's Corp.	8	1,004,708	N/A
Soap & Cleaners			
Colgate-Palmolive Co.	36	237,867	10.4
Procter & Gamble Co.	1	1,435,454	N/A
Unilever N.V.	14	517,746	10.7
Soft Drinks			
Coca-Cola Co.	24	370,379	8.0
PepsiCo, Inc.	10	581,309	7.2
Telephone			
American Telephone & Telegraph	18	439,919	N/A
Tobacco			
Philip Morris	2	1,364,472	7.8
Wine, Beer, & Liquor			
Anheuser-Busch	7	634,522	N/A

SOURCE: *Advertising Age*. 1987. September 24, 162.

We start by discussing how product types affect the informational content of advertising, contrasting advertisements that inform to those that attempt to persuade without using many facts. Next, we examine the profit-maximizing advertising level and then consider whether the profit-maximizing level of advertising is socially optimal. The effects of advertising on prices, entry barriers, and consumer welfare are described.

We then consider when firms advertise truthfully and when they lie, and discuss the optimal level of enforcement of truth-in-advertising laws. Finally, we analyze a firm's decision to disclose or hide information. Although a firm may have strong incentives to tell consumers about the high quality of its products or its low prices, it may hesitate to disclose facts about weaknesses in its products, such as side-effects and bad repair records. Indeed, as Chapter 17 shows, a firm may gain market power by reducing consumers' information. In many cases, however, it is in the firm's best interest to disclose information. Although truth-in-advertising laws encourage truthful disclosures, we show that mandatory disclosure laws may have a perverse effect.

■ INFORMATION AND ADVERTISING

Advertising may convey hard facts, vague claims, or try to create a favorable impression of a product. Some advertisements list a store's prices. If consumers learn that a firm has the lowest prices in town, the demand for its products increases. In contrast, other advertisements merely show a product being used in a pleasant setting. An attractive person consuming a soft drink near a waterfall may convey to consumers the impression that this product is refreshing. By convincing consumers that its product has certain desirable traits, a firm can differentiate it from other products. As its product becomes differentiated, a firm may face a higher and less elastic demand curve, so that it can charge a higher price and earn greater profits (see Chapter 11). For example, a heavily promoted brand of bleach sells at a higher price than many other bleaches whose chemical compositions are virtually identical.

Promotions

Advertising can be subtle and indirect or hit you over the head with its bluntness. Advertising is only one of many ways to promote a product; firms also use price discounts and sales staffs. When it is hard to describe a product, a firm may include a discount coupon in its advertisement to encourage consumers to try the product. Salespeople act like living advertisements. In addition to advertising in newspapers, on radio, and on television, firms may advertise indirectly by establishing a brand name or otherwise establishing a positive reputation.

For example, some agricultural firms now sell their fruits and vegetables under brand names (Example 18.1). Unlike sellers of unbranded produce, these farmers are trying to develop a reputation for producing a particular (presumably high) quality of produce. Such branding can help overcome the "lemons" problem discussed in Chapter 17. Although this chapter concentrates on advertising, most of the discussion applies equally well to other types of promotions.

"Search" versus "Experience" Goods

The informational content of advertising depends on whether consumers can determine the quality of a product prior to purchase (Nelson 1970, 1974). If the consumer can

EXAMPLE 18.1	# BRANDING AS ADVERTISING

Most fruits and vegetables are sold without a brand name. Consumers assume that a tomato is a tomato and that there is little variability across firms. That is, these markets competitively provide perfectly homogeneous products. Recently, however, several firms (Natural Pak Produce Inc., Campbell Soup Co. and Dart & Kraft Inc.) have started selling branded tomatoes.

Thanks to new breeding techniques based on recent advances in DNA research and better storage methods, these companies believe they can provide produce that tastes better and remains fresh longer. A company has no incentive to provide a better product (at presumably higher cost) if the credit for higher quality goes to the market as a whole rather than to the firm in particular (see Chapter 17).

Consumers are willing to pay more for products they believe are superior. Sunkist oranges, Dole pineapples, and Chiquita bananas have gross profit margins 10 percent to 60 percent higher than generic produce. When introduced, one branded tomato sold at about $1 per pound or 30¢ more than unbranded tomatoes.

There are risks associated with building a brand. Unless firms can provide better produce consistently, consumers may eventually hold a brand's name against it. After all, why pay more for a product that's no better than the unbranded produce? Further, even if consumers view the product as superior and pay a premium for it, the premium may not be high enough to cover the extra costs of producing higher quality and establishing a brand name. Castle & Cooke, Budd Co., and other smaller firms did not recoup their investment on branded cauliflower, grapes, and broccoli.

SOURCE: Eklund, Christopher S. 1985. "Will a Tomato by Any Other Name Taste Better?" *Business Week*, September 30, 105.

establish a product's quality prior to purchase by inspection, the product has **search qualities.** Examples are furniture, clothing (determining style), and other products whose chief attributes can be determined by visual or tactile inspection. If the consumer must consume the product to determine its quality, it is said to have **experience qualities.** Examples are processed foods, software programs, and psychotherapy.[2]

Advertising provides direct information about the characteristics of products with search qualities; advertisements for search products are likely to include photographs. In some cases a consumer cannot directly observe a physical attribute, but it can be concisely described. For example, food and drink advertisements may claim that their products are low in calories. In contrast, for experience goods, the most important information may be conveyed simply by the presence of the advertising; some advertisements do little more

---

[2] Some economists identify a third category, in which the quality of some goods cannot be determined even after consumption. Darby and Karni (1973) call these *credence* goods. Examples include many repair services and medical care, where the consumer must rely on the provider's assurances that the work was done properly.

than mention the name of the firm to enhance its reputation. Such advertisers hope that consumers infer the quality or reputability of a firm by the expense of its advertising: fly-by-night firms may be less likely to advertise in expensive publications or on national television.

Some firms claim that all their products are excellent. Their advertisements contend that if you have experienced and liked one of their products, you will like all of them (Duncan Hines, Green Giant). Such advertisements may do little more than show the company's name; they do not describe the properties of each of its products. Alternatively, a firm may try to convince consumers that its product is different and superior to other, similar brands—that is, it attempts to differentiate its product (for example, Bayer vs. generic aspirin, Coke vs. Pepsi, Tide vs. All laundry detergents).

Informational versus Persuasive Advertising

Some economists distinguish between **informational advertising,** which describes product characteristics, and **persuasive advertising,** which is designed to shift consumers' tastes. For example, informational advertising may cite the price of a product, compare the advertising store's price to its rivals' prices, describe the features of the product, or list its uses. Persuasive advertising may explicitly or implicitly make claims such as "smoke these cigarettes to look more mature and sexier."

It seems reasonable that producers of search goods are more likely to use informational advertising and experience goods producers are more likely to use persuasive advertising, but this division is not perfect. The advertising/sales ratio for products classified as experience goods is three times greater than that for products classified as search goods, and the difference is statistically significant (Nelson 1974, 738–40). A possible inference is that images (such as often used in persuasive advertising) are forgotten more quickly than facts (such as used in informative advertising). Thus, consumers may learn and remember that a particular good has fewer calories (is "less filling") in one or a few exposures to an advertisement, but need to be bombarded with repeated exposures to be convinced that a product "tastes great."

Such empirical evidence must be viewed with caution, however, since it is difficult to classify products as either experience or search goods or as using either informational or persuasive advertising. If your younger brother's utility depends on the need to be "cool," and he sees a cool person such as a well-known actor or singer using a particular brand of sunglasses, he may interpret the advertisement as being informative.[3] It tells him and his friends that this particular brand of sunglasses is cool. Others, such as you, may view such testimonial advertising as persuasive, having little information content.

---

[3] Honus Wagner became the father of endorsement advertising in 1905 when he let his autograph be imprinted on a Louisville Slugger bat. Boyd, L. M. 1988. "The Grab Bag." *San Francisco Examiner*, September 4, "Sunday Punch" section, 7.

Profit-Maximizing Advertising

The codfish lays ten thousand eggs,
The homely hen lays one.
The codfish never cackles
To tell you what she's done.
And so we scorn the codfish,
While the humble hen we prize,
Which only goes to show you
That it pays to advertise. — Anon.

All advertising is designed to increase the demand for a firm's product whether facts are used or merely smoke and mirrors. In Figure 18.1, an increase in informative or persuasive advertising expenditures by E dollars, which increases a firm's advertising from α to α', causes an outward shift of the demand curve facing a firm.[4]

The outward shift in the demand curve increases profits (not adjusted for advertising expenditures) for two reasons. First, profits increase by areas B and C because the firm increases its sales from Q to Q'. This extra profit is $(p' - AC)(Q' - Q)$, where AC is the average (and marginal) production cost, so $(p' - AC)$ is the profit per unit. Second, the firm makes more profits on the Q units it used to sell, area A. Since price rises from p to p', its profits on the first Q units increase by $(p' - p)Q$. Thus, profits (ignoring advertising costs) increase by the sum of areas A, B, and C due to the extra advertising.

So long as the extra expenditure on advertising, E, is less than or equal to the increase in profits, $A + B + C$, the extra advertising pays. If profits rise by more than the advertising expenditures, then advertising expenditures should be increased even more. A profit-maximizing firm sets its advertising expenditures so that the last dollar spent on advertising increases its profits, excluding advertising costs, by exactly one dollar (Appendix 18A). That is, the firm maximizes its profits by setting the marginal cost of advertising equal to the marginal benefit, as illustrated in Example 18.2, p. 601.

The lower the cost, the more advertising in a society. In ancient Egypt, some entrepreneurs used criers to announce ship and cargo arrivals. By 1630, printing lowered the cost of advertising sufficiently that wide-scale public advertising became common. More recently, radio and television again lowered the cost of advertising. Today the largest advertisers spend over a billion dollars a year on advertising so that we are constantly exposed to it.

The model of perfect competition (Chapter 4) ignores selling cost and assumes that firms can sell all they want at the market price. In fact, most firms do incur selling costs. Usually, firms with market power incur promotional expense to cause their demand curves to shift out or become more inelastic, so they can sell more at higher prices. However,

---

[4] The following analysis ignores the effects of the firm's advertising and quantity decisions on other firms. Empirical evidence suggests, however, that the amount of advertising is influenced by market structure (Weiss, Pascoe, and Martin 1983). Lambin (1976) finds that advertising by rivals roughly lowers a firm's market share by as much as its own advertising increases it.

FIGURE 18.1 Advertising

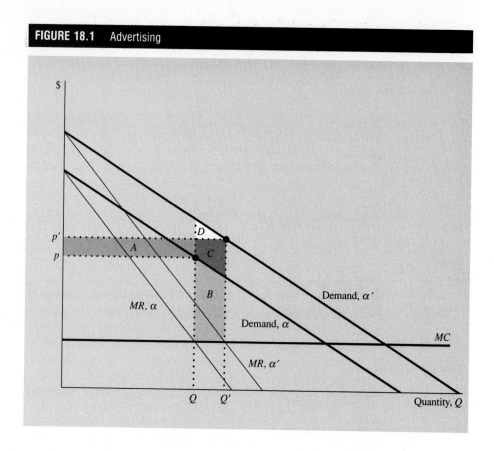

it is possible for firms to advertise and still face very elastic demand curves. For example, such a firm may act as a price-taker, but needs to inform customers where it is located. That is, advertising need not be inconsistent with price-taking behavior.

■ EFFECTS OF ADVERTISING ON WELFARE

> *Advertising may be described as the science of arresting human intelligence long enough to get money from it.* — STEPHEN LEACOCK

Many social commentators attack advertising. Yet the Federal Trade Commission (FTC), which is supposed to protect consumers, fights groups that want to forbid advertising, arguing that some advertising benefits consumers. This section examines research on the effects of advertising on welfare. Substantial empirical evidence indicates that advertising about relative prices can increase competition and raise welfare. In some cases, nonprice advertising can overcome the lemons problem discussed in Chapter 17. Theoretical models, however, differ as to whether other types of advertising promote welfare.

EXAMPLE 18.2

MILK ADVERTISING

State and federal milk-marketing programs fund over $200 million annually for generic milk advertising and promotion. There is a mandatory assessment of 15¢ per hundredweight on all milk marketed for commercial use in the contiguous 48 states. Of the 15¢, at least one-third goes to national advertising and promotion programs, and the rest goes to qualified local promotion programs.

Liu and Forker assume that consumers forget at a constant rate, so that there is an incentive to continue advertising. They estimate, for New York City, that a 1 percent permanent increase in advertising causes the demand for milk to rise and reach a new higher level in about six months. The long-run demand elasticity with respect to advertising is 0.0028. With current levels of advertising, 18.27 pounds are consumed per month per capita. If advertising were only 10 percent of historical levels, all else the same, consumption would fall 1.5 percent to 17.99 pounds per month per capita.

They calculate that at the historical levels of advertising, dairy farmers receive back $1.50 in additional sales revenue for each promotional dollar. Nonetheless, they calculate that the optimal level of advertising (where marginal benefit equals marginal cost) is about 55 percent of the historical level. The following table shows the ratio of estimated marginal benefit to marginal cost.

Advertising as a Percentage of Historical Levels	Marginal Benefit / Marginal Cost
10	4.16
20	2.44
30	1.74
40	1.35
50	1.11
60	0.94
70	0.81
80	0.72
90	0.64

Had advertising levels been reduced to the optimal level, each extra dollar of advertising would generate an additional $2 of sales.

SOURCE: Liu and Forker (1988).

Price Advertising Increases Welfare

Advertising that provides relative price information tends to lower the market price. Truthful advertising lets consumers know where to buy at the lowest price. Since it is costly to advertise, however, firms do not engage in it unless the costs are at least covered by the additional revenues from an increase in demand.

EXAMPLE 18.3

I SEE THE SOCIAL GAIN TO ADVERTISING: EYEGLASSES

In the past, price advertising for eyeglasses was forbidden in some states, but permitted in others. A cross-state comparison of prices for eyeglasses in 1963 shows that they were substantially higher in states that banned advertising than in those that had no restrictions. Adjusting for differences across states in income, age, sex, and family structure, the cost of eyeglasses was $7.37 higher in states with complete advertising restrictions. Since the average price was $26.34 in states with no restrictions, the restrictions increased the average cost by 28 percent.

There was only a $1.32 difference (which was not a statistically significant difference) among states that had restrictions on price advertising but not other forms of advertising and those that had no restrictions. Thus, only complete bans on advertising substantially increase price.

A 1980 Federal Trade Commission study also reports that prices were lower in cities that allowed advertising than in those that did not. Moreover, they found that the quality of the glasses was the same in both sets of cities. In cities without advertising bans, even optometrists who did not advertise charged an average of $20 less for an exam and glasses than did their counterparts in cities that banned advertising.

In 1978 the Federal Trade Commission (FTC) proposed a trade regulation prohibiting states and trade organizations from restricting price advertising for eyeglasses and related services. The basis for this rule was the economics literature showing that such restrictions increase average price and the dispersion of prices in the market.

SOURCES: Benham (1972), Bond et al. (1980), and Ippolito (1986).

If relatively low-price stores advertise their prices and attract more customers, these stores gain in size and the average price in the market falls (Smallwood and Conlisk 1979). In the tourist-and-native model (Chapter 17), if tourists can gather information only by visiting local stores, the cost of information gathering may be sufficiently high to create a two-price equilibrium, where some stores charge natives low prices and others charge tourists high prices. If, however, relatively low-price stores can advertise in the local paper, the cost to tourists of gathering information falls, so that more consumers become informed, and the market share of low-price stores increases. If enough consumers become informed, all stores may charge the low price. Thus, without advertising, no store may find it profitable to charge low prices; but with advertising, all stores may charge low prices.[5]

Many empirical studies show that advertising about price lowers the average price consumers pay for products such as drugs (Cady 1976), eyeglasses (Benham 1972, Example 18.3), liquor (Luksetich and Lofgren 1976), toys (Steiner 1973), and retail

---

[5] Butters (1977) shows that the less expensive is advertising or consumer search, the lower is the average price in a market. He also demonstrates that a free market generates the optimal amount of advertising and the maximum possible welfare. Butters shows that there can be a multiple-price equilibrium when it is costly to inform consumers about price and firms can advertise.

gasoline (Maurizi 1972). Other studies show that although advertising can lower the price of legal and optometric services, advertising may also cause quality to fall in such markets (Arnould 1972, Muris and McChesney 1979, Kwoka 1984).

Benham (1972) finds that the price of eyeglasses in states prohibiting price advertising, but not other advertising about eyeglasses, was only slightly higher than in states that allowed price advertising. It was, however, significantly below that in states banning all advertising. Thus, even nonprice advertising may lower prices (Bagwell and Ramey 1988).

Because advertising can lower price in a market, professional groups want it banned. Until Supreme Court decisions stopped them, doctors, dentists, and lawyers prevented advertising on the grounds that it was unprofessional. Today, 16 percent of Florida's lawyers place display ads in the Yellow Pages, and some law firms issue press releases after victories, mail brochures to prospective clients, and hire public relations firms to help penetrate the market.[6]

Advertising to Solve the Lemons Problem

In some markets, firms cannot profitably sell high-quality products because consumers are unable to distinguish between high-quality and low-quality products, as in the lemons model (Chapter 17). If firms can use guarantees or warranties to signal high quality, the lemons problem can be avoided. Similarly, advertising may solve the lemons problem if it signals quality.[7]

Suppose, for example, a firm wants to start selling a high-quality experience good. It believes that if consumers try its product, they will like and purchase it repeatedly. That is, the firm's incentive to provide high-quality goods is to induce repeat sales (Klein and Leffler 1981; Shapiro 1983; Rogerson 1986). The firm hopes to make large profits by signaling its high-quality and getting consumers to try its product.

To keep this example simple, let us make two additional assumptions. First, assume that consumers can only find out about a product's quality by trying the good; otherwise, the firm could produce a few items, give them away to some consumers, and rely on word-of-mouth to sell its product. Second, we assume that the firm's marginal and average variable costs of production are the same as those of firms that produce low-quality goods (this assumption is dropped later in this chapter). As a result, if the high-quality firm sells more units than low-quality firms at the same price, it makes higher profits on these sales.

The high-quality firm has a greater incentive to advertise than does the low-quality firm. The high-quality firm's advertising leads to repeated sales, whereas the low-quality firm's advertising leads to sales only in the current period. Since both types of firms have the same costs of production and advertising and since the rewards to advertising are greater for the high-quality firm, it engages in more advertising.[8]

---

[6] Naisbitt, John. 1985. "Trendnotes." *San Francisco Chronicle*, March 5, 51.

[7] Nelson (1974), Schmalensee (1978), Klein and Leffler (1981), Shapiro (1983), Wolinsky (1983), Kihlstrom and Riordan (1984), Milgrom and Roberts (1986), and Rogerson (1986). For a different view see Allen (1984).

[8] Rogerson (1986) discusses the complications in this type of model.

When Advertising Is Excessive

Advertising is the rattling of a stick inside a swill bucket. — GEORGE ORWELL

Newspaper articles, movies, and social philosophers often argue that there is too much advertising because it induces consumers to buy goods they do not "need." Recently, these arguments have been formalized to show that where products are differentiated, firms engage in more than the socially optimal amount of both persuasive and informative advertising. We explain why this conclusion may not always be correct.

Advertising for a Single Product.   Until recently, most economists concluded that very little could be said about the welfare effects of persuasive advertising.[9] They reasoned that if advertising changes consumers' tastes (as reflected by consumers' utility functions), then there is no fixed basis for comparing welfare before and after advertising.

Suppose an advertisement convinces many consumers that using a cologne makes them more attractive and thus results in more sales at a higher price. Are consumers better off? The price is higher than before, but some consumers are receiving more pleasure from using the cologne than before. Most social commentators who are not economists say that the consumers just "think they are better off," and hence their greater pleasure after advertising is spurious and should be discounted. Economists typically argue, however, that consumers are the best judges of their own tastes. Unfortunately, it is difficult to compare consumers' pleasure before and after advertising if the scale on which the pleasure is measured has changed.

In a clever but controversial article, Dixit and Norman (1978) argue that strong welfare conclusions can be drawn. They use the two natural extremes of consumers' preadvertising and postadvertising tastes (utilities) as the basis for their conclusions. For example, if one believes that advertising is pure deception, one could use preadvertising tastes in evaluating welfare. If instead, one believes that postadvertising tastes represent the consumers' true interest, one should use those tastes. If on the basis of both sets of tastes one gets the same welfare results, then Dixit and Norman argue that the results hold regardless of one's underlying assumptions about the appropriate set of tastes.

We start by examining the welfare effects of advertising on a monopolist and its customers. The monopolist has a constant marginal cost of production. Advertising is supplied at constant cost, so that advertising agencies do not receive unusual profits, and hence the advertising cost is the same for the firm and for society. As a result, the welfare analysis can ignore the advertising agencies; they receive zero profits regardless of the amount of advertising.

Let α be the initial level of advertising that is increased to a new level α'. We refer to α as the *preadvertising* level and α' as the postadvertising level. In Figure 18.1, the additional advertising expenditure, $E = \alpha' - \alpha$, causes the demand curve to shift outward: at any given price, consumers demand more output, postadvertising. The price, p', and the quantity, Q', are higher in the postadvertising monopolistic equilibrium than in the original equilibrium (with price p and output Q).[10]

As an initial standard, we use the preadvertising preferences of consumers, as reflected

---

[9] For an earlier debate on the welfare effects of advertising, see Kaldor (1949–50) and Telser (1966).

[10] If output falls, then welfare definitely falls, and no further analysis is necessary.

by the preadvertising demand curve with α advertising. In the postadvertising equilibrium, consumers appreciate this product more than before, so consumers buy $Q' - Q$ more units. The additional consumer surplus from these extra units is the area under the preadvertising demand curve, because we are evaluating welfare at the preadvertising level, between Q and Q'. The cost of producing these units is the area under the marginal (and average) cost curve between Q and Q'. Thus, the net social gain from these extra units is the difference between the extra consumer surplus and the cost of producing them, area B, less the cost of the additional advertising, E.

Using the postadvertising preferences as our standard, consumer surplus increases by the area under the postadvertising demand curve between Q and Q'. Thus, the change in welfare is the increase in consumer surplus above the marginal cost curve, $B + C + D$, minus the additional cost of advertising, E. That is, using the postadvertising preferences, welfare changes by $B + C + D - E$, instead of just area $B - E$, using the preadvertising preferences. For small amounts of advertising, C and D are generally very small relative to B, so that there is little difference in the change in welfare between the two standards.

In either case, the gain to advertising is the area under the *relevant* demand curve (either the pre- or postadvertising demand curve) between Q and Q' and above the marginal cost curve, less the additional advertising expenditures, E. That is, we are measuring the social value of a change in output from Q to Q' using the relevant standard.

Again, the outward shift of the consumers' demand curve due to advertising increases the monopolist's profits for two reasons. First, the monopolist sells $Q' - Q$ more units of output. Second, the monopolist sells each unit of output at a price that is $p' - p$ dollars more per unit than before. Thus, the monopolist's profits increase by the sum of areas A, B, and C, less the cost of advertising, E. The increase in price due to the advertising makes firms better off by raising profits, $A + B + C - E$, but makes consumers worse off by raising the cost of the original output, $A = (p' - p)Q$. The change in welfare, using either standard, approximately equals the increase in profits to the monopolist less the extra expenditures, A, by consumers.

Using the preadvertising preferences, the change in welfare is approximately the difference between the extra profits of the monopolist, $A + B + C - E$, and the higher cost to consumers for the original output, A, or $B + C - E$. For small changes in advertising expenditures, C is small relative to B, so that $B + C - E$ approximately equals $B - E$, the change in welfare. Area A represents a transfer of wealth from consumers to the monopolist and hence does not affect total welfare: the monopolist's gain offsets the consumers' loss.

Welfare cannot rise unless the monopolist finds advertising profitable. The change in welfare, $B - E$, is less than the increase in profits, $A + B + C - E$. Thus, *unless an increase in advertising increases profits, welfare cannot rise.* Alternatively stated, profitability is a *necessary* condition for additional advertising to increase welfare; it is not a *sufficient* condition, because profits could go up ($A + B + C - E > 0$), and yet welfare could fall ($B - E < 0$).

Using postadvertising preferences, the change in welfare is $B + C + D - E$. For a small increase in advertising, C and D are small relative to A and B. Again, welfare cannot increase unless profits, $A + B + C - E$ are positive. Thus, using either set of preferences, profitability is a necessary condition for welfare to rise.

In equilibrium, the monopolist increases advertising until the extra expenditure on advertising, E, exactly equals the marginal increase in profits net of advertising, $A + B + C$. That is, in equilibrium, the change in the monopolist's marginal profits, including advertising expenditures from one more dollar of advertising, is zero. Because the change in welfare is marginal profits (which is zero in equilibrium) minus the extra consumer expenditures due to advertising (which are positive), the marginal change in welfare is negative for the last advertising dollar. Regardless of the welfare standard—preadvertising or postadvertising preferences—a marginal increase in advertising causes welfare to fall by approximately area A, the extra consumer expenditures. That is, advertising is excessive: *in equilibrium, a small decrease in advertising increases welfare.*

Dixit and Norman (1978) show that these results hold in oligopolistic and monopolistically competitive markets as well. They conclude that in all these markets,

- A small increase in advertising raises welfare only if the firm finds it profitable. There cannot be too little advertising, because if society benefits from the advertising, the firm provides it.
- Reducing advertising from the profit-maximizing level raises welfare. This result holds even using the postadvertising preferences of consumers.

That is, it is possible that a low level of profitable advertising maximizes welfare, but that firms advertise at a higher level. Even at that excessive level, however, welfare may be higher than with no advertising.

Two serious criticisms of Dixit and Norman's (1978) conclusions have emerged.[11] First, as Fisher and McGowan (1979) explain, in general, one should not compare welfare on the basis of just preadvertising or just postadvertising preferences. Suppose an improvement in the product's quality, instead of advertising, shifted demand. Dixit and Norman's analysis would imply that there is an overinvestment in product quality. The reason for this counterintuitive result is that Dixit and Norman compare welfare before and after advertising using either the preadvertising or postadvertising preferences for both equilibrium outcomes. If the preadvertising equilibrium based on the preadvertising preferences is compared to the postadvertising equilibrium based on the postadvertising preferences, the welfare effects of advertising are ambiguous. If advertising changes preferences, the utility levels of consumers pre- and postadvertising cannot be directly compared. Here it is inappropriate to use just one or the other set of preferences to evaluate the welfare effects.

Second, Shapiro (1980) explains that if advertising serves to inform consumers that a product exists rather than to shift tastes, there is too little advertising. In Shapiro's example, some consumers are unaware of the product before it is advertised. After exposure to advertising, they become aware of the product and purchase it, but no consumer's tastes have changed. Unless the monopolist can price discriminate, it advertises too little,

---

[11] Dixit and Norman (1979, 1980) respond to these criticisms.

because it bears the full cost of advertising but does not receive the full benefits (it does not capture all the additional consumer surplus).[12]

Advertising About Differentiated Goods.   Grossman and Shapiro (1984) show that in markets with differentiated products there is excessive informative advertising. In their model, firms sell differentiated products, and consumers can only learn about the existence of a particular brand through an advertisement.[13] To reach more consumers, a firm must place ads in more magazines, send out more flyers, and so forth. Once a consumer becomes aware of the firm's product, additional advertising reaching that consumer is wasteful.

When products are differentiated, advertising that leads to a better matching of consumers and brands increases welfare. This positive effect depends crucially on the degree of differentiation. If the products are identical, advertising shifts consumers from one firm to another and can be socially wasteful.

Grossman and Shapiro show that the market equilibrium has too many firms (excessive diversity of products) and that each firm advertises less than the socially optimal level per firm. Given the actual number of firms in the industry, however, there is too much advertising. They conclude that the beneficial effect of improved matching of consumers and products is outweighed by the wasteful effect of merely shuffling consumers between firms. As a result, the private return to advertising exceeds the social return, and there is excessive advertising.

If firms target their advertising to only the relevant group of consumers, there is less waste from redundant advertising. If some consumers read *Popular Mechanics,* whereas others read only *Cosmopolitan,* a firm selling power saws can advertise to the first group without wasting money on the uninterested second group. See Example 18.4. When targeting can produce greater efficiency in advertising, the industry becomes more competitive and prices fall.

Even when products are differentiated, however, one can easily imagine situations where firms provide too little informative advertising. For example, many farmers obtain most of their information about how to use new pesticides, equipment, and other products from sales agents. Here, the information not only helps farmers decide which products to use, but also tells them how to use the products. A firm provides too little of this informative advertising if it does not capture the full benefit of the advertising. For example, if the proper use of pesticides by farmers results in fewer sales, the pesticide company provides too little information. Thus, in differentiated goods markets, whether there is too little or too much informative advertising depends on the particular circumstances.

---

[12] See Shapiro (1980) for a graphic analysis. A similar point is made by Diamond and Rothschild (1978). Shapiro (1980) and Dixit and Norman (1980) also debate the welfare effects when advertising affects consumers differently.

[13] Grossman and Shapiro use Salop's (1979) circle model of differentiated products (discussed in Chapter 11) and the information transmission function of advertising from Butters (1977).

EXAMPLE 18.4

DIFFERENT STROKES FOR DIFFERENT FOLKS

Firms must use different advertising techniques to reach different groups of consumers. Over two-thirds (68.8 percent) of all consumers read food store ads in newspapers. As is to be expected, the larger the family (and hence the greater the payoff of lower prices), the more likely were the ads to be read. Although only 59.5 percent of people living alone read the ads, 70.6 percent of three-person families and 73.4 percent of families of five or more people read the ads.

Less than half of the people surveyed saw television ads for food stores. Lower income groups were more likely than higher income groups to see these ads. Only 18.3 percent of those who saw television ads said they were influenced by them as to where to shop, compared to 54.1 percent who said they were influenced by newspaper ads. One possible explanation is that the newspaper ads contain more price and availability information than television ads, which stress "quality" or other abstract reputation concepts, and that food stores prefer to convey "hard" information.

SOURCE: Burgoyne, Inc. *The National Study of Supermarket Shoppers 1979–80: Census Profile* and *Demographic Profile*, n.d.

Advertising as a Barrier to Entry.   The Dixit and Norman (1978) and Grossman and Shapiro (1984) studies do not argue that all advertising is harmful; they only contend that there is too much of some types in certain circumstances. Many people, however, argue that persuasive advertising is anticompetitive and should be banned.

Persuasive advertising is said to be anticompetitive for two reasons (Bain 1956, Comanor and Wilson 1974). First, advertising may cause some consumers to conclude mistakenly that physically identical brands differ, which is called **spurious product differentiation.** For example, some people pay a premium for branded bleaches that are chemically identical to many generic brands. Because buying behavior depends on consumers' perceptions of products rather than on the products' physical characteristics, advertising leads to higher prices for some brands than for others. It is not clear whether consumers are fooled in these cases by claims that a particular brand is superior in some unspecified way. They may be concerned that some generic brands are weak or contaminated and thus find it worth paying the premium for a branded good to avoid this (possibly false) worry.

Second, some economists argue that advertising by firms already in the industry may make entry by new firms more difficult. A potential entrant must advertise extensively to overcome the goodwill created by an incumbent firm's advertising, but the incumbent did not have to incur this introductory advertising expense when it first entered the market. Such a barrier to entry increases the market power of incumbent firms, and they charge higher prices as a result.

If the incumbent has no long-run advantage over a potential entrant in advertising, then advertising does not restrict entry even if the incumbent has built up goodwill through its past advertising (Schmalensee 1974) If a potential entrant can advertise as effectively as an incumbent, eventually it will be on an equal footing with the incumbent. The potential entrant, forseeing that day, is not deterred from entering, and there is no barrier to entry as defined in Chapter 7 (see also von Weizsäcker 1980). Moreover, in many cases the entrant incurs lower advertising costs than the incumbent, especially if the incumbent has already persuaded consumers that the product is desirable. On the other hand, if (as in Chapter 13) the second entrant faces higher marketing costs than the first, there is a barrier to entry. Although one can create theoretical arguments on both sides of this issue, the debate can only be resolved with empirical evidence. There is evidence that the presence of advertising and product differentiation can sometimes create entry barriers (see Chapter 7).[14] There are almost as many studies showing that advertising is not anticompetitive as those showing that it is, however.

Many studies examine whether concentration ratios are related to advertising.[15] Studies finding that advertising increases concentration (Mann, Henning, and Meehan 1967; Ornstein et al. 1973; Strickland and Weiss 1976) are no more common than those finding that it either has no effect or lowers concentration (Telser 1964, 1969, Ekelund and Maurice 1969, Ekelund and Gramm 1970, Vernon 1971, Edwards 1973). Whether these studies actually test that advertising causes barriers to entry is open to question (Schmalensee 1976). For example, Weiss, Pascoe, and Martin (1983) infer that market structure, as measured in part by concentration ratios, determines advertising/sales ratios. The connection between concentration ratios and market power is tenuous at best, and the direction of causality between concentration ratios and advertising is not clear. Indeed it is likely that both are determined simultaneously, rather than one determining the other.[16]

Another approach (Comanor and Wilson 1974, Miller 1969, Weiss 1969) examines the relationship between various accounting measures of profit and advertising. Again, the causality of any such relationship is open to question (Butters 1977). Moreover, if advertising is long-lived in the sense that advertising today affects purchasing decisions in the future, then short-run profitability differences associated with advertising may be misleading.[17] Firms may incur costs today, lowering current profits, that raise profits in the future. Ayanian (1983) estimates that the average stock of advertising (the cumulative effect of many advertisements) typically lasts seven years. After adjusting profits for the stock of advertising, he concludes that advertising does not cause entry barriers that result in unusual profits.

---

[14] Comanor and Wilson (1979, 470) conclude from a survey of the available studies that "The weight of available evidence is consistent with the hypothesis that heavy advertising can have substantial anticompetitive consequences. However, because the distribution of advertising intensities is highly skewed, there is no indication that these effects are pervasive throughout the economy, or even within the manufacturing sector."

[15] Telser (1964) was probably the first to do so. Many of these studies are reviewed in Ornstein (1977) and Comanor and Wilson (1979).

[16] Lambin (1976) and Schmalensee (1973) attempt to measure separately the effects of advertising by firms on their own demand curves and on the industry's demand curve. Unfortunately, their data do not allow them to precisely measure these effects.

[17] Lambin (1976, 97) reports that the elasticity of sales with respect to advertising expenditures is usually greater in the long run. The short-run elasticity for electric shavers is 0.229 (a 1 percent increase in advertising expenditures leads to a 0.229 percent increase in sales), but the long-run elasticity is over twice that, 0.597. Similarly, the short-run and long-run elasticities for cigarettes are 0.154 and 0.752; for detergents, 0.055 and 0.659; and for soft drinks, 0.057 and 0.415.

As previously discussed, a number of studies show that informative advertising about prices can lower the average price in a market. Persuasive advertising, by enabling new firms to differentiate their products, may sometimes facilitate entry. Thus, even if it could be shown that persuasive advertising can create barriers to entry, restricting advertising would also reduce its desirable effects.

■ FALSE ADVERTISING

Advertising is legalized lying. — H. G. WELLS

False advertising is illegal. Where enforcement is lax, however, firms can advertise for years in a false, deceptive, or misleading manner with few if any penalties. This section considers the circumstances in which firms are most likely to engage in false advertising and whether truth-in-advertising or antifraud laws are desirable. The results are surprising: under some circumstances, antifraud laws can lead to more false advertising.

Limits to Lying

The truth is the safest lie.

Why don't all firms lie in their advertising? One answer is that most consumers are hard to fool (Nelson 1974, Schmalensee 1978). Nelson (1974, 749) proposes a consumer decision rule that usually prevents a consumer from being deceived: "[B]elieve an advertisement . . . qualities when it tells about the functions of a brand; do not believe the advertisement when it tells how well a brand performs that function." The functions of a brand are easily tested before purchase (search qualities), whereas the performance can only be confirmed after purchase (experience qualities). A firm's claim that it sells king-size beds is much easier to confirm than the claim that the bed will last for 50 years. Thus, the first claim is more plausible than the second.

False advertising is more likely for experience goods than for search goods. For example, in a six-month period, all 58 Federal Trade Commission cases of deceptive advertising about product attributes concerned experience qualities rather than search qualities (Nelson 1974, 750). A false claim about a search good leads to no additional purchases if the claims can be inexpensively confirmed prior to purchase. Making such a false claim only damages a firm's reputation. As a result, firms have no incentive to make such false claims. In contrast, they may have an incentive to lie about experience goods, since the lie may cause consumers to make a trial purchase.

Nonetheless, the amount of false advertising about experience goods may be minimized by high-quality firms' incentives to advertise the truth.[18] A consumer who tries and enjoys a high-quality item is likely to make repeated purchases, whereas a consumer disappointed by a low-quality product does not buy it again. Thus, the benefit to having

---

[18] The conditions under which advertising can serve as a signal of quality are discussed in Nelson (1974), Schmalensee (1978), Klein and Leffler (1981), Shapiro (1983), Wolinsky (1983), Allen (1984), Kihlstrom and Riordan (1984), Milgrom and Roberts (1986), and Rogerson (1986, 1988).

a consumer try its product is greater for a high-quality firm than for a low-quality firm if both have the same costs. As a result, high-quality firms tend to advertise more than low-quality firms do, so that even the *amount* of persuasive advertising may be a signal of quality.

This argument appears sound as far as it goes: high-quality firms have a greater incentive to advertise extensively than low-quality firms do, assuming that both have the same costs, as argued earlier. In many, if not most, markets, however, low-quality or fraudulent firms have relatively low costs. A fly-by-night firm could sell a worthless product that is almost costless to produce, so that its costs are substantially below those of a high-quality firm. The fly-by-night firm makes larger profits on its initial sales because it makes higher profits per unit; however, it expects no repeat business and has no intention of being around for very long. In such markets, therefore, it is unclear whether a high-quality firm with a relatively high cost of production advertises more or less (Schmalensee 1978; Kihlstrom and Riordan 1984; Milgrom and Roberts 1986).

We would expect high-quality products to be advertised more if the variable costs of the high-quality firm are no higher than those of low-quality firms and if consumers cannot learn about a product's quality except through consumption (Shapiro 1983, Rogerson 1986).[19] If the high-quality firm has relatively high costs, a large amount of advertising may not signal high quality.[20] Thus, either high-quality or low-quality firms may advertise more, so extensive advertising is not necessarily associated with high quality. For example, Kotowitz and Mathewson (1986) do not find evidence in either automobiles or whole-life insurance that greater advertising indicates either better buys or signals more experience quality.

Antifraud Laws

> *An advertisement for a carburetor to save gasoline ended with, ". . . If not satisfactory, money will be returned." When some customers complained, they were told, "So far, all money we have received has been satisfactory."* [21]

A company that sells an unsafe or otherwise substandard product typically can produce at lower cost than can firms producing a safe or standard product. Such firms may engage in deceptive advertising that implies that their products are safe and useful in order to induce consumers to buy. Although there are no repeat sales from satisfied customers, a company may make money if its costs are low enough. One approach to dealing with deceptive ads is to prosecute such firms under antifraud laws.

Paradoxically, more deception may occur when an antifraud law is moderately enforced than when it is not enforced at all (Nelson 1974, 749–51). Suppose, for example, that the law prohibits the mislabeling of the fabric content of clothing. If the law is almost

---

[19] If potential consumers can learn about quality through word-of-mouth from others who have tried the product, a high-quality firm need only sell a small amount of output at low introductory rates to convince consumers that it has an outstanding product, and hence it has no incentive to advertise extensively.

[20] Even in this case, however, extensive advertising signals quality under some circumstances (Milgrom and Roberts 1986).

[21] Boyd, L. M. 1988. "Grab Bag." *San Francisco Chronicle*, April 2, C12.

EXAMPLE 18.5

TAKING CANDY FROM BABIES

Consumers are often unable to determine easily whether foods are impure or mislabeled. From 1978 through 1982, Beech-Nut Nutrition Corp., the second largest U.S. manufacturer of baby-food products, distributed phony apple juice for babies. Indeed, the product, labeled as containing pure apple juice, consisted of "a chemical cocktail" that contained little if any apple juice, according to a Beech-Nut chemist. An employee blew the whistle, and the federal government brought suit. The government believes that the company saved about $750,000 by buying the adulterated concentrate. Once Beech-Nut realized that the concentrate was not pure apple juice, it avoided a loss of about $3 million by selling the bogus juice instead of destroying it, according to the government.

Beech-Nut pleaded guilty to 215 federal counts of shipping mislabeled products with the intent to defraud and mislead the public. The firm agreed to pay a $2 million fine, which government officials said was at least six times as great as any paid under the Food, Drug and Cosmetic Act of 1938. Beech-Nut agreed to pay $140,000 in investigative costs to the Food and Drug Administration. Beech-Nut also settled a class-action suit for $7.5 million, which provided $2.5 million in Beech-Nut and affiliated products to certain retailers and a $5 million cash fund for consumers who purchased the misrepresented juice. One estimate is that Beech-Nut has paid about $10 million in fines and civil suit settlements. In addition, it paid its ex-employees' legal bills, which may have been in the millions of dollars. Presumably, Beech-Nut also suffered significant losses to its reputation.

SOURCES: Buder, Leonard. 1988. "Two Former Executives of Beech-Nut Guilty in Phony Juice Case." *New York Times*, February 18, 1, 27. Gordon, Al. 1988. "Beech-Nut Baby Food: How Firm Was Caught Selling Fake Juice." *San Francisco Chronicle*, June 14, A8. Consumers Union. 1989. "Beech-Nut Convictions Overturned." *Consumer Reports*, June, 354.

always enforced, consumers believe that a clothing label is usually correct, thereby giving a manufacturer an incentive to mislabel. That is, if consumers believe that labels are accurate, false labels fool them. See Example 18.5. In contrast, in the absence of any enforcement, consumers generally do not trust clothing labels unless it is in the self-interest of the manufacturer to provide the correct information.[22] Here, deceptive labels do little harm, since no one believes them. As a result, firms have little incentive to make deceptive claims.

Does it follow that we should not have antifraud laws or not enforce the laws? Such a conclusion is too strong. These laws induce firms to make more information available

---

[22] For example, Eaton and Grossman (1986) show that a firm may have an incentive to accurately disclose information if its product is very different from those of its rivals.

to consumers. If a firm knows that consumers do not believe its claims in the absence of an antifraud law, it does not bother making any. Thus there is a trade-off between having more claims (and perhaps more information) and having more deception.

The government must determine the optimal level of enforcement. Preventing all false claims, even if feasible, would be prohibitively expensive. Eliminating the laws or making it known that they are not enforced would greatly reduce the incentives of firms to provide consumers with information. Thus, the optimal level of enforcement lies in the middle range between no enforcement and testing all claims.

Disclosure Laws

Do you promise to tell the truth, the whole truth, and nothing but the truth?

Disclosure laws require firms to reveal truthfully to consumers certain information about their products. Antifraud laws only require that any information voluntarily disclosed by firms be truthful. A firm advertises primarily to inform consumers about desirable properties of its products, but it may also disclose undesirable properties, such as side effects of drugs, for various reasons. Appropriate warnings may protect a firm against liability suits, or the firm may decide that full disclosure is profit-maximizing. In some markets, the government requires firms to make disclosures about all *material* facts: all the good and bad factors that should influence the decision to buy the product.

As discussed in the previous chapter, a market for lemons may develop if high-quality sellers cannot practically differentiate their products from those of low-quality sellers, so that consumers remain uninformed. Here, however, we consider markets in which high-quality sellers have both an incentive and the ability to distinguish their products.[23]

Recall from the previous chapter that when statements about a product's quality can be established after the sale at low cost, firms not only tell the truth, they provide warranties or guarantees to establish that they are telling the truth. For example, if a firm states that its box of oranges contains six oranges, a consumer can verify this claim upon opening the box at virtually no cost.

Where statements about a product's quality are costly to convey to consumers or costly to verify after the sale, standard guarantees cannot be offered. For example, the quality of an automobile's construction is difficult to describe or to verify even after purchase. We do not expect to see a guarantee that all the parts of an automobile are of high quality and were properly assembled. It is relatively easy, however, to determine whether or not the car breaks down. If high-quality cars have a lower probability of failure than low-quality cars, guarantees covering breakdowns can be used instead of direct guarantees of construction. We now consider the need for and effects of disclosure laws under various assumptions about the buyers and sellers.

Sellers Are Known to Have Information.   Suppose a firm knows all about its new product with which consumers have no experience. Moreover, the consumers have no need to deal with the producer further in the future. Here, one expects that the firm has

---

[23] This discussion is based on Grossman and Hart (1980), Milgrom (1981), and especially Grossman (1981).

a substantial incentive to mislead. Surprisingly, however, it may not be able to mislead rational consumers about the quality of the product; indeed, it may have to make full disclosures in the absence of a disclosure law. Suppose antifraud laws, which make it illegal to lie about a product, are fully and completely enforced in the relevant market and that the penalties for lying are substantial. Thus the firm has the option of telling the truth about the product or saying nothing.

The surprising result that the firm reveals information about the product stems from consumers' cynicism. The box of oranges example can be used to illustrate this effect. The firm has the choice of saying nothing, putting the true number of oranges on the box label, or making a true but imprecise statement, such as, "There are at least three oranges in the box." Suppose that prior to purchase a consumer cannot tell from looking at it how many oranges are in the box. How would a rational consumer react to each of the three types of labels?

First, if the label says there are three oranges, a consumer may believe there are exactly three oranges. This consumer believes the antifraud laws prevent the firm from lying.

Second, if the label says "There are at least three oranges in the box," a consumer may assume there are *exactly* three oranges. After all, if there were four oranges, surely the label would say so, since it is in the firm's best interests.

Third, if the label says nothing, a consumer may assume there are *no* oranges. If there were an orange in the box, the label could say, after all, that there is "at least one orange in the box." If consumers have no other reason except the label to believe that there are oranges in the box, they realize that it is in the firm's best interest to state the correct number of oranges in the box.

In short, *the rational consumer expects the worst:* the quantity expected is the lowest possible one consistent with the firm's disclosure. The consumer knows that the price is higher the more oranges there are in the box and hence knows that the firm has an incentive to list the largest number consistent with the truth. In other words, the consumer expects the seller to make the most optimistic, truthful statement possible. Thus, at least where the law prohibits false statements and is strictly enforced, the firm has an incentive to make full disclosures.[24] The implication of this argument is that where information or warranties are costless and consumers can understand the information, the government need not require disclosures if it enforces a law prohibiting false statements: firms voluntarily make full disclosures about quality.

Why not require disclosure even if it is unnecessary? The reason is that disclosure laws raise disclosure costs. Disclosure laws are typically very broad and, for example, require an issuer of a new stock or the seller of a house to disclose all facts that are material to a purchaser. If a bad event occurs that was not perfectly predictable, a buyer can bring suit, claiming that a material fact was not disclosed regarding that bad event. After the event, a buyer may search the seller's records for evidence that the seller knew the event was possible but did not disclose it. Because such suits and searches are costly,

---

[24] Where only some consumers become informed, the result changes, as discussed in the noisy monopolist model in Chapter 17.

the seller, anticipating these costs, discloses more information than in the absence of such laws. Thus, such laws could convert a situation with costless disclosure of truly material facts into a situation where both the buyer and seller must bear costs. Here, welfare could be higher in the absence of disclosure laws.

These arguments, however, are based on the assumption that the seller already has the relevant information. The next question to consider, then, is whether these arguments hold if the seller has the option to remain ignorant.

Sellers Decide Whether to Obtain and Disclose Information. Do firms voluntarily run tests of quality and disclose the results? To answer this question, we again assume that there is a single seller who is prevented from lying by antifraud laws. Again, there is a surprising result: only if disclosure is mandatory does a seller fail to test and disclose (Matthews and Postlewaite 1985).

By the preceding reasoning, if consumers know that a firm knows the quality of its product, the consumers assume the worst if it makes no disclosure. Now, however, suppose that the firm does not initially have quality information, but it can test costlessly. Whether it should test and disclose the test results depends on whether consumers assume it already has the relevant information and whether there is a disclosure law.

If consumers can *verify* that the firm has not tested for quality, the firm can refuse to test, and therefore make no disclosures, without consumers necessarily believing the worst about the product. If there is no disclosure rule and if the firm cannot credibly prove it has not tested its product, the same reasoning applies as in the case where consumers know the firm has the information. Consumers assume that the firm has tested and hence assume the worst about the product if it makes no disclosures. Thus, the firm has nothing to lose by testing and disclosing the results, and does so. Again, only antifraud rules are required.

Surprisingly, when consumers are uncertain whether the seller has tested the product, disclosure rules are harmful. They require firms to report all the relevant facts they know. Because consumers know that firms must fully disclose any test results, if a firm makes no disclosure, consumers conclude that it did not test. As a result, consumers do not necessarily draw negative inferences from the lack of disclosure. Therefore, a firm may not test, and hence make no disclosures, especially when it believes the test results will be below consumer expectations. When there is a disclosure law, a firm is not forced to test to dispel cynicism about its product quality. No disclosure only means no tests were conducted, not that quality is necessarily low. Thus, a firm discloses when there is no disclosure rule and may not disclose when there is a rule.

Matthew and Postelwaite's result depends crucially on costless testing. If testing or disclosing is known to be costly, claiming that the firm did not test may be credible (Jovanovic 1983). Where testing is costly, a monopolist performs fewer than the socially optimal number of tests (Nelson 1959, Arrow 1962, Kwerel 1980) because it cannot capture the full benefit from testing but must bear the full cost.

Thus, this literature draws four major conclusions about disclosure when a monopolist must test to determine the quality of its own product and antifraud laws are fully enforced. First, where consumers cannot verify whether a firm has tested, if test costs are low, the firm is relatively likely to test and disclose in the absence of a mandatory disclosure law.

Second, where consumers can verify whether or not a firm tests, it does not test and disclose if it fears bad results. Third, since a mandatory disclosure law allows consumers to determine whether or not a firm has tested, a firm may not test under such a law. Fourth, if testing is costly, a firm conducts less than the optimal amount of testing, so disclosure laws may be desirable.

Empirical Evidence. Disclosure laws are common in financial markets, housing markets, and other markets where the quality of products is complex and sellers have substantially more information than buyers. These markets do not satisfy all of the assumptions of the previous sections: there are many firms, consumers differ in knowledge and reasoning ability, quality means different things to different consumers, firms can change quality, and antifraud laws are not always enforced. Thus, disclosure laws may be useful in these markets. We now review empirical studies in two areas where disclosure laws are important.

Federal securities legislation was designed to prevent the overpricing of new stock issues resulting from buyers' ignorance about undesirable attributes of these new stocks (Benston 1973, Hilke 1984). Stigler (1964) and Jarrell (1981) compare the rates of return and the associated risks of investing in new issues before and after the 1933 Securities Act that imposed stringent disclosure requirements. They find, at most, small differences in relative performance across periods, although one researcher finds that fewer risky new stocks were available after the disclosure requirements.[25]

Another type of study examines the purchase of consumer durables. McNeil et al. (1978) find that the poor pay more for used cars, are less likely to receive redress for defects discovered after purchase, and are less satisfied and more likely to believe something was misrepresented. That is, consumers may differ in their abilities to determine quality before purchasing, in their bargaining power, and in the gains they provide to firms when they are satisfied. This study finds that the adoption of disclosure regulations in Wisconsin, however, did not help. In short, there is little evidence to show that disclosure laws have been useful in either financial or used car markets.

■ SUMMARY

Firms have an incentive to inform consumers about the strengths of their products and to try to shift their tastes. In addition to advertising in newspapers, on radio, and on television, firms may advertise indirectly by establishing brand names or otherwise establishing positive reputations.

A firm determines the profit-maximizing amount of advertising by setting the marginal cost of advertising equal to the marginal benefit stemming from increased sales. Existing empirical studies find that firms generally spend more on advertising for experience goods (goods that the consumer must try in order to determine if they are desirable) than on search goods (goods that consumers can instantly appraise).

---

[25] Hilke (1984), commenting on these studies, questions whether the mandatory disclosure requirements of the 1933 Security Act significantly increased disclosure requirements.

The welfare effects of advertising are complex and depend on the type of product and type of advertising. Advertising about prices of homogeneous products typically lowers the average price consumers pay, as shown in studies of eyeglasses and other products. These studies only show, however, that some advertising is desirable; they do not show that firms engage in the socially optimal amount of advertising. When persuasive advertising changes consumers' utility, one cannot determine if there is too much or too little advertising.

Advertising that leads to the spurious differentiation of goods and results in higher prices for consumers is harmful. Advertising may also be a barrier to entry, but the evidence supporting this view is mixed. Thus, the effects of advertising on consumer welfare are generally ambiguous. In some markets, advertising can make entry easier for a firm without a reputation, but it can also lead to the creation of market power.

Skepticism by consumers discourages false advertising. Paradoxically, antifraud laws can increase the amount of both truthful and false advertising. Society must, therefore, trade off the cost of enforcing antifraud laws and the harm of false advertising against the benefit from an increase in truthful advertising in order to determine how strictly to enforce these laws.

When antifraud laws are fully enforced, firms generally have an incentive to disclose relevant information to consumers. Surprisingly, under some circumstances, mandatory disclosure laws can reduce the extent of such disclosures. The empirical studies of mandatory disclosure laws fail to reveal a beneficial effect in securities or used car markets.

Based on the theory and empirical work to date, three tentative policy conclusions can be drawn. First, advertising about price levels is desirable, as it often leads to lower prices. Second, partial enforcement of antifraud laws may lead to increased deception. Third, care must be shown in requiring mandatory disclosures, as such laws sometimes may be counterproductive.

■ Key Terms

experience qualities
informational advertising
persuasive advertising

search qualities
spurious product differentiation

■ Discussion Questions

1. Which industries do you think advertise excessively? Which do too little advertising? Why?
2. What are the advantages and disadvantages of truth-in-advertising or antifraud laws? Can these laws serve as a substitute for disclosure laws?
3. Is there too little or too much advertising of prices? Why?

4. On balance, are more mandatory disclosure laws desirable? Why?
5. If it is not practical to enforce the laws fully, how should antifraud and mandatory disclosure laws be changed?

■ Problems

1. Use a graph to illustrate Shapiro's (1980) critique of the Dixit and Norman (1978) argument that if a monopolist's advertising only informs consumers that a product exists rather than shifting tastes, there is too little advertising. Assume demand is linear and marginal costs are constant.

2. What is the profit-maximizing rule for advertising if advertising depreciates (that is, consumers forget about it over time if not reminded)?

3. What happens if a firm advertises, but only some people see the ads? *Hint:* Consider the tourist-and-native model in Chapter 17.

4. A manufacturer uses vertical restraints in its contract with its dealer network (see Chapter 16) to encourage them to advertise locally. Under what conditions are such vertical restraints socially desirable?

5. Using the model in Appendix 18A, suppose the inverse demand curve facing a monopolist is $p = a + \alpha - bQ$, where α is the amount of advertising, and the cost function is cQ. Determine the optimal level of advertising and output.

Answers to odd-numbered problems are given at the back of the book.

■ Recommended Readings

The following are relatively nontechnical (or have nontechnical sections). To get a good overview of the literature on advertising, see Schmalensee (1973) and Comanor and Wilson (1974, 1979). A more recent survey is Ekelund and Saurman (1988). Grossman (1981) clearly explains the basic arguments concerning deception.

■ References

Allen, Franklin. 1984. "Reputation and Product Quality." *Rand Journal of Economics* 15:311–27.

Arnould, Richard J. 1972. "Pricing Professional Services: A Case Study of the Legal Services Industry." *Southern Economic Journal* 38:495–507.

Arrow, Kenneth. 1962. "Economic Welfare and the Allocation of Resources for Invention," in Universities-National Bureau of Economic Research Conference Series, *The Rate and Direction of Economic Activity: Economic and Social Factors*. Princeton: Princeton University Press.

Ayanian, Robert. 1983. "The Advertising Capital Controversy." *Journal of Business* 56:349–64.

Bagwell, Kyle, and Garey Ramey. 1988. "Advertising, Coordination, and Signaling." Northwestern University, Center for Mathematical Studies in Economics and Management Science, Discussion Paper No. 7897.

Bagwell, Kyle, and Michael Riordan. 1988. "High and Declining Prices Signal Product Quality." Northwestern University working paper (October).

Bain, Joe S. 1956. *Barriers to New Competition: Their Character and Consequences in Manufacturing Industries*. Cambridge: Harvard University Press.

Benham, Lee. 1972. "The Effect of Advertising on the Price of Eyeglasses." *Journal of Law and Economics* 15:337–52.

Benston, George J. 1973. "Required Disclosure and the Stock Market: An Evaluation of the Securities Exchange Act of 1934." *American Economic Review* 63:1323–55.

Bond, Ronald S., John E. Kwoka, Jr., John J. Phelan, and Ira Taylor Whitten. 1980. "Staff Report on Effects of Restrictions on Advertising and Commercial Practice in the Professions: The Case of Optometry." Bureau of Economics, Federal Trade Commission. Washington, D.C.: U.S. Government Printing Office.

Butters, Gerard R. 1977. "Equilibrium Distributions of Sales and Advertising Prices. *The Review of Economic Studies* 44:465–91.

Cady, John F. 1976. "An Estimate of the Price Effects of Restrictions on Drug Price Advertising." *Economic Inquiry* 14:493–510.

Comanor, William S., and Thomas A. Wilson. 1974. *Advertising and Market Power*. Cambridge: Harvard University Press.

———. 1979. "Advertising and Competition: A Survey." *Journal of Economic Literature* 17:453–76.

Darby, Michael R., and Edi Karni. 1973. "Free Competition and the Optimal Amount of Fraud." *Journal of Law and Economics* 16:67–88.

Diamond, Peter A., and Michael Rothschild. 1978. *Uncertainty in Economics*. New York: Academic Press.

Dixit, Avinash, and Victor Norman. 1978. "Advertising and Welfare." *The Bell Journal of Economics* 9:1–17.

———. 1979. "Advertising and Welfare: Reply." *The Bell Journal of Economics* 10:728-29.

———. 1980. "Advertising and Welfare: Another Reply." *The Bell Journal of Economics* 11:753–54.

Dorfman, Robert, and Peter O. Steiner. 1954. "Optimal Advertising and Optimal Quality." *American Economic Review* 44:826–36.

Eaton, Jonathan, and Gene M. Grossman. 1986. "The Provision of Information as Marketing Strategy." *Oxford Economic Papers* 38:166–83.

Edwards, Franklin R. 1973. "Advertising and Competition in Banking." *Antitrust Bulletin* 18:23–32.

Ekelund, Robert B., Jr., and Charles Maurice. 1969. "An Empirical Investigation of Advertising and Concentration: Comment." *Journal of Industrial Economics* 18:76–80.

Ekelund, Robert B., Jr., and William P. Gramm. 1970. "Advertising and Concentration: Some New Evidence." *Antitrust Bulletin* 5:243–49.

Ekelund, Robert B., Jr., and David S. Saurman. 1988. *Advertising and the Market Process*. San Francisco: Pacific Research Institute for Public Policy.

Fisher, Franklin M., and John J. McGowan. 1979. "Advertising and Welfare: Comment." *The Bell Journal of Economics* 10:726–27.

Grossman, Gene M., and Carl Shapiro. 1984. "Informative Advertising with Differentiated Products." *The Review of Economic Studies* 51:63–81.

Grossman, Sanford J. 1981. "The Informational Role of Warranties and Private Disclosure About Product Quality." *Journal of Law and Economics* 24:461–83.

Grossman, Sanford J., and Oliver Hart. 1980. "Disclosure Laws and Takeover Bids." *Journal of Finance*. 35: 323–334.

Hilke, John C. 1984. "Early Mandatory Disclosure Regulations." Bureau of Economics, Federal Trade Commission Working Paper No. 111. Washington, D.C.: U.S. Government Printing Office.

Ippolito, Pauline M. 1986. "Consumer Protection Economics: A Selective Survey," in Pauline M. Ippolito and David T. Scheffman, eds., *Empirical Approaches to Consumer Protection Economics*. Federal Trade Commission. Washington, D.C.: U.S. Government Printing Office.

Jarrell, Gregg A. 1981. "The Economic Effects of Federal Regulation of the Market for New Security Issues." *Journal of Law and Economics* 24:613–75.

Jovanovic, Boyan. 1983. "Truthful Disclosure of Information." *The Bell Journal of Economics* 13:36–44.

Kaldor, Nicholas. 1949–50. "The Economic Aspects of Advertising." *The Review of Economic Studies* 18: 1-27.

Kihlstrom, Richard, and Michael Riordin. 1984. "Advertising as a Signal." *Journal of Political Economy* 92:427–50.

Klein, Benjamin, and Keith Leffler. 1981. "The Role of Market Forces in Assuring Contractual Performance." *Journal of Political Economy* 89:615–41.

Kotowitz, Yehuda, and G. Frank Mathewson. 1986. "Advertising and Consumer Learning," in Pauline M. Ippolito and David T. Scheffman, eds., *Empirical Approaches to Consumer Protection Economics*. Federal Trade Commission. Washington, D.C.: U.S. Government Printing Office, 109–34.

Kwerel, Evan R. 1980. "Economic Welfare and the Production of Information by a Monopolist: The Case of Drug Testing." *The Bell Journal of Economics* 11: 505–18.

Kwoka, John E., Jr. 1984. "Advertising and the Price and Quality of Optometric Services." *American Economic Review* 74:211–16.

Lambin, Jean Jacques. 1976. *Advertising, Competition and Market Conduct in Oligopoly over Time*. Amsterdam: North-Holland.

Liu, Donald J., and Olan D. Forker. 1988. "Generic Fluid Milk Advertising, Demand Expansion, and Supply Response: The Case of New York City." *American Journal of Agricultural Economics* 70:229–36.

Luksetich, William, and Harold Lofgren. 1976. "Price, Advertising, and Liquor Prices." *Industrial Organization Review* 4:13–25.

Mann, H. Michael, John A. Henning, and James W. Meehan, Jr. 1967. "Advertising and Concentration: An Empirical Investigation." *Journal of Industrial Economics* 16:34–45.

Matthews, Steven, and Andrew Postlewaite. 1985. "Quality Testing and Disclosure." *The Rand Journal of Economics* 16:328–40.

Maurizi, Alex R. 1972. "The Effect of Laws Against Price Advertising: The Case of Retail Gasoline." *Western Economic Journal* 10:321–29.

McNeil, Kenneth, John R. Nevin, David M. Trubek, Richard E. Miller, and Lauren Edelman. 1978. "Market Discrimination Against the Poor and the Impact of Consumer Disclosure Laws: The Used Car Industry." Institute for Research on Poverty Discussion Paper No. 486-78, University of Wisconsin-Madison.

Milgrom, Paul. 1981. "Good News and Bad News: Representation Theorems and Applications." *The Bell Journal of Economics* 12:380–91.

Milgrom, Paul, and J. Roberts. 1986. "Price and Advertising Signals of Product Quality." *Journal of Political Economy* 94:796–821.

Miller, Richard A. 1969. "Market Structure and Industrial Performance: Relation of Profit Rate to Concentration, Advertising Intensity, and Diversity." *Journal of Industrial Economics* 17:104–18.

Muris, Timothy J., and Fred S. McChesney. 1979. "Advertising and the Price and Quality of Legal Services: The Case for Legal Clinics." *American Bar Foundation Research Journal* 1979:179–207.

Nelson, Richard. 1959. "The Simple Economics of Basic Research." *Journal of Political Economy* 67:297–306.

Nelson, Phillip. 1970. "Information and Consumer Behavior." *Journal of Political Economy* 78:311–29.

———. 1974. "Advertising as Information." *Journal of Political Economy* 81:729–54.

Ornstein, Stanley I., J. Fred Westen, Michael Intriligator, and Ronald Shrieves. 1973. "Determinants of Market Structure." *Southern Economic Journal* 39:612–25.

Ornstein, Stanley I. 1977. *Industrial Concentration and Advertising Intensity.* Washington, D.C.: American Enterprise Institute for Public Policy Research.

Rogerson, William P. 1986. "Advertising as a Signal When Price Guarantees Quality." Center for Mathematical Studies in Economics and Management Science Discussion Paper No. 704, Northwestern University.

———. 1988. "Price Advertising and the Deterioration of Product Quality." *The Review of Economic Studies* 55:215–29.

Salop, Steven C. 1979. "Monopolistic Competition with Outside Goods." *The Bell Journal of Economics* 10:141–56.

Satterthwaite, Mark A. 1979. "Consumer Information, Equilibrium Industry Price, and the Number of Sellers." *The Bell Journal of Economics* 10:483–02.

Schmalensee, Richard. 1973. *The Economics of Advertising.* New York: Humanities Press.

———. 1974. "Brand Loyalty and Barriers to Entry." *Southern Economic Journal* 40:579–88.

———. 1976. "Advertising and Profitability: Further Implications of the Null Hypothesis." *Journal of Industrial Economics* 25:45–54.

———. 1978. "A Model of Advertising and Product Quality." *Journal of Political Economy* 86:485–03.

Shapiro, Carl. 1980. "Advertising and Welfare: Comment." *The Bell Journal of Economics* 11:749–52.

———. 1983. "Premiums for High-Quality Products as Returns to Reputation." *Quarterly Journal of Economics* 98:659–79.

Smallwood, Dennis E., and John Conlisk. 1979. "Product Quality in Markets Where Consumers are Imperfectly Informed." *Quarterly Journal of Economics* 93:1–23.

Steiner, Robert L. 1973. "Does Advertising Lower Consumer Prices?" *Journal of Marketing.* 37:19–26.

Stigler, George J. 1964. "Public Regulation of the Securities Markets." *Journal of Business.* 37:117–42.

Strickland, Allyn D., and Leonard W. Weiss. 1976. "Advertising, Concentration, and Price-Cost Margins." *Journal of Political Economy* 84:1109–21.

Telser, Lester G. 1964. "Advertising and Competition." *Journal of Political Economy* 73:537–62.

———. 1966. "Supply and Demand for Advertising Messages." *American Economic Review* 56:457–66.

———. 1969. "Another Look at Advertising and Concentration." *Journal of Industrial Economics* 18:85–94.

Vernon, John M. 1971. "Concentration, Promotion, and Market Share Stability in the Pharmaceutical Industry." *Journal of Industrial Economics* 19:246–66.

von Weizsäcker, C. C. 1980. "A Welfare Analysis of Barriers to Entry." *The Bell Journal of Economics* 11:399–420.

Weiss, Leonard W. 1969. "Advertising Profits and Corporate Taxes." *Review of Economics and Statistics* 51:421–30.

Weiss, Leonard W., George Pascoe, and Stephen Martin. 1983. "The Size of Selling Costs." *Review of Economics and Statistics* 65:668–72.

Wolinsky, Asher. 1983. "Prices as Signals of Product Quality." *The Review of Economic Studies* 50:647–58.

PROFIT-MAXIMIZING ADVERTISING

Suppose the price a firm may charge, p, is a function of its output, Q, and advertising, α.[1] That is, its inverse demand curve is

$$p = p(Q,\alpha). \tag{18A.1}$$

Its revenues, then, are

$$R = p(Q,\alpha)Q \equiv R(Q,\alpha). \tag{18A.2}$$

The firm's costs are the sum of its production costs, $C(Q)$, and its advertising costs, α, where \$1 of advertising costs \$1.

In a one-period model that ignores the effect of advertising on future purchasing behavior, the firm maximizes its profits through its choice of price and advertising levels:

$$\max_{Q,\alpha} \pi = R(Q,\alpha) - C(Q) - \alpha. \tag{18A.3}$$

The two first-order conditions are

$$\pi_Q = R_Q - C' = 0, \tag{18A.4}$$

$$\pi_\alpha = R_\alpha - 1 = 0, \tag{18A.5}$$

where $R_Q \equiv \partial R/\partial Q$ and $R_\alpha \equiv \partial R/\partial \alpha$. The optimal Q and α must simultaneously satisfy Equations 18A.4 and 18A.5. Equation 18A.4 says that output should be chosen so that marginal revenue from an extra unit of output, R_Q, equals the marginal cost of producing an extra unit, C'. Equation 18A.5 says that the firm should advertise until the marginal revenue resulting from an increase in advertising, R_α, equals the marginal advertising cost, 1.

---

[1] In the following analysis, the firm chooses output and advertising levels. Many analyses instead have the firm choose price and advertising levels. See, for example, Dorfman and Steiner (1954).

CHAPTER 19

DECISION MAKING OVER TIME: DURABILITY

Time is nature's way of keeping everything from happening at once.

T his chapter is the first of two that analyze firms' decision making over time. Here, we examine markets for goods that last for several time periods—**durable goods.** Examples of durable goods include light bulbs, automobiles, washing machines, and X-ray machines. In the United States, durable goods expenditures are 14 percent of all personal consumption expenditure and 29 percent of expenditures on all goods.[1]

Manufacturers of durable goods must decide how long their products should last. By spending more money initially, a manufacturer can make the product last longer. This chapter answers two questions about durability. First, does market structure affect the durability of products? For example, does a monopolist produce as durable a product as a competitive firm? Second, does it matter whether a monopolist rents or sells its goods?

■ HOW LONG SHOULD A DURABLE GOOD LAST?

In the long run, we are all dead.— JOHN MAYNARD KEYNES

When buying a durable good, consumers consider how long it lasts and its resale value in future years. For example, manufacturers of expensive cars often argue that consumers are better off buying better cars than less expensive ones because the better cars last longer

---

[1] Charles Schaninger and W. Christain Buss, of the State University of New York at Albany, tracked the spending habits of 310 couples, and found that during the first three years, couples who would remain happily married spent 30 percent more on appliances, 33 percent more on homes, and 41 percent more on other durable goods. Couples who later divorced spent more on stereos and televisions. Concludes Buss: "Happily married couples tend to spend more on products that are less easily divisible and would lose value if the marriage broke up." (*San Francisco Chronicle*, November 6, 1986, 27).

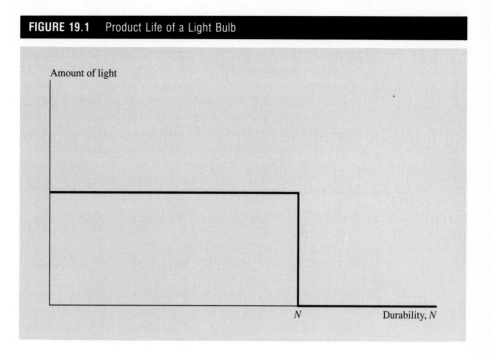

FIGURE 19.1   Product Life of a Light Bulb

and can be resold for a higher percent of their initial purchase price in any future year.

A firm must trade off higher initial manufacturing costs against a longer-lived product that it can sell at a higher price. The firm's optimal policy is to increase initial expenditures up to the point where the marginal cost of greater durability equals the marginal benefit from a higher sales price. The firm's decision may be influenced by a number of factors, including its market power and the presence or absence of a resale market. We start by examining a competitive firm's decision and then a monopolistic firm's decision.

Competitive Firm's Choice of Durability

> *I'm not afraid to die. I just don't want to be there when it happens.*
> —WOODY ALLEN

Consider a competitive light bulb manufacturer's tradeoff. The firm manufactures a light bulb that lasts N periods under normal use. A light bulb that is N periods old is just as useful—provides as much light—as a brand new one. At the end of N periods, the light bulb dies and must be replaced; it does not pay to fix it. Figure 19.1 illustrates the product life of a light bulb.[2]

---

[2] A light bulb differs from many other products, since an older light bulb is as useful as a new one until it suddenly dies. The main results of this section, however, do not depend on this special property of light bulbs.

When one says that a light bulb is useful, one refers to the **service**—the light of a specified intensity—that the light bulb provides. The light bulb is a machine or **capital asset** (something that lasts for many periods) that provides a service in each period.[3]

The manufacturer must decide how durable to make the light bulb; that is, the manufacturer must choose N. The constant marginal cost of manufacturing a light bulb that lasts N years is $C(N)$. The more durable (long-lived) is the light bulb, the higher the cost of manufacture. Thus the firm faces a trade-off between greater durability and lower initial cost. The competitive firm must pick the optimal trade-off because if it cannot produce efficiently, other firms will drive it out of business.

What is the cost of providing one light bulb's worth of service forever? In the first period, the bulb costs $C(N)$. No replacement is needed until N periods later, at which time $C(N)$ dollars must again be spent to replace the bulb. Thereafter, every N periods, the bulb must be replaced at a cost of $C(N)$ dollars.

Costs in the future, however, are less important than costs today because future dollars are worth less. For example, if the interest rate is 10 percent, a dollar today is worth $1.10 next period. Alternatively stated a dollar next period is worth only $0.91 ($\approx 1/1.1$) today. To calculate the present value of a stream of costs, then, we *discount* expenditures in the future. Thus, if one is committed to pay $1 this year and $1 next year, the *present value* of this commitment, assuming a 10 percent interest rate, is $1 + $0.91 or $1.91. Therefore, the present value of the cost of providing one light bulb's worth of service forever is the cost of producing it today, plus the discounted cost of producing another after N periods, plus the discounted cost of producing another in $2N$ periods, and so on.

Suppose, then, that a firm can produce one type of bulb that lasts 5 years at relatively low cost and another that lasts 10 years at higher cost. Which type of bulb has the lowest present-value cost? The answer depends on both the manufacturing costs and the interest rate. Table 19.1 provides an example.

Suppose the bulb that lasts 5 years costs $1 to manufacture and the manufacturing costs remain constant over time. Thus, to provide perpetual light, a bulb must be manufactured every 5 years. The first bulb costs $1. The second bulb, manufactured 5 years later, costs $1 then, but the present value of that cost at a 10 percent interest rate is only 61¢. Similarly, the present value of manufacturing another bulb 10 years from now is only 37¢. Adding up all these costs in present-value terms shows that the present-value cost of providing one light bulb's worth of light forever is $2.54. Table 19.1 also shows that if a bulb that lasts 10 years costs $1.61 to manufacture initially, the present value of providing one bulb's worth of service forever is the same as for the 5-year bulb, $2.54. Although the 10-year bulb costs more to manufacture, it needs to be replaced only half as frequently as the 5-year bulb.

Thus, both bulbs have the same present value of costs in the table. If the initial cost of the 10-year bulb is slightly higher, say $1.75 instead of $1.61, then it is cost-effective to manufacture the 5-year bulb. Similarly, if the interest rate is 15 percent instead of 10

---

[3] The light bulb, a machine, is a *stock,* which has no time dimension, and the service is a *flow,* which has a time dimension: the amount of light *per period.* Another common term for a machine is a *capital asset.*

TABLE 19.1 Cost of Producing Bulbs of Different Durations

	Duration of a Bulb	
Years	5 years	10 years
0	1.000000	1.606530
5	0.606531	0
10	0.367879	0.591009
15	0.223130	0
20	0.135335	0.217420
25	0.082085	0
30	0.049787	0.079984
35	0.030197	0
40	0.018316	0.029425
45	0.011109	0
50	0.006738	0.010825
55	0.004087	0
60	0.002479	0.003982
65	0.001503	0
70	0.000912	0.001465
75	0.000553	0
80	0.000335	0.000539
85	0.000203	0
90	0.000123	0.000198
95	0.000075	0
100	0.000045	0.000073
105	0.000028	0
110	0.000017	0.000027
115	0.000010	0
120	0.000006	0.000010
125	0.000004	0
130	0.000002	0.000004
135	0.000001	0
140	0.000001	0.000001
145	0.000001	0
Present-value cost at interest rate = 10%	2.541494	2.541494

percent, the 5-year bulb is a better value than the 10-year bulb. Because costs in the future matter less, the advantage of having to replace a bulb less frequently is less valuable. In the extreme case, if the interest rate approaches infinity, so that consumers do not care about the future at all, then only the initial cost of manufacturing matters, and the firm produces the shortest duration (lowest initial cost) bulb possible.

Figure 19.2 illustrates the effect of interest rates. The figure plots the present value of costs as a function of N, the durability of the bulb, for a particular cost function.[4] One line assumes an interest rate of 10 percent, and the other assumes a rate of 20 percent.

---

[4] The cost function is $C(N) = N^\alpha$, where $\alpha = .487$ in Figure 19.2. Appendix 19A analyzes this problem mathematically.

FIGURE 19.2   Present Value of Costs

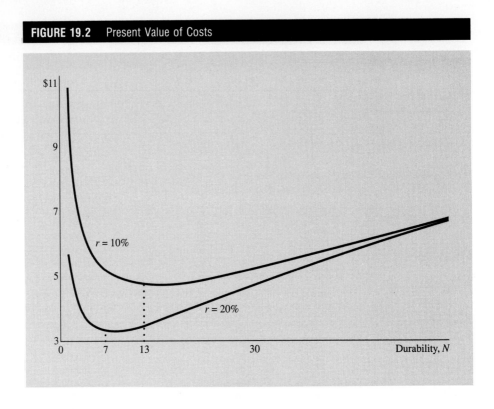

If the interest rate is 10 percent, the minimum present value of cost occurs where $N = 13$ years. If the interest rate is 20 percent, the minimum cost occurs at $N = 7$ years. Thus, the higher the interest rate, the less durable the bulb should be because the future savings from delaying replacement of the bulb diminish, whereas the cost of making the good more durable is borne currently and not discounted. Thus, a competitive firm picks the durability, N, that minimizes the present discounted costs of providing 1 unit of light bulb service forever. Does a monopolist make a different decision?

The Monopolist's Choice of Durability

The meaning of life is that it stops.— FRANZ KAFKA

Suppose only one company produces light bulbs. Its choice of durability may depend on whether it rents or sells the product. We start by analyzing this problem if the monopolist rents; that is, it sells light services rather than light bulbs. The sales problem is analyzed later.

Renting.   Let $Q(R)$ be the number of units of light services that consumers demand in each period when the rental price is R. That is, the demand curve, $Q(R)$, does not change over time. If the monopolist rents the bulbs in each period at price R, it receives a continuous flow of revenue equal to $RQ(R)$ in each period. In contrast, the monopolist's costs of producing $Q(R)$ units per period are not incurred continuously. To provide $Q(R)$ units per period, the monopolist must initially produce $Q(R)$ bulbs, then produce another $Q(R)$ bulbs N periods later, and so on.

The monopolist chooses a rental price, R, and a durability, N, that maximize profits, where profits equal the discounted present value of rentals minus production costs. The choice of durability, however, does not concern consumers. Consumers only care about the rental cost of the light service. How long the bulb lasts is irrelevant to consumers if the monopolist instantly replaces burnt-out bulbs with new ones. As a result, the monopolist should choose the N that minimizes the discounted present value of the cost of producing $Q(R)$ units of service forever. Because there are constant returns to scale, the N that minimizes total cost minimizes the cost of producing one unit.

Thus, both a competitive firm and a monopolist choose the same N: the one that minimizes the cost of producing a unit of light service. This result should not be surprising because both a monopolist and a competitive firm always produce so as to minimize costs. If the choice of durability affects only costs, both competitive and monopolistic firms choose the same durability. Thus, if there are no scale economies and durability does not affect demand, *the optimal durability is identical for a monopolist and a competitor.*[5]

Once the optimal N is chosen, the monopolist must choose how many bulbs, Q, to rent. The monopolist sets marginal revenue equal to marginal cost so as to maximize profits. A competitive firm chooses its output level so that its marginal cost equals price. Thus, although both the competitive industry and the monopolist choose the same durability, the monopolist produces fewer units at a higher price.

Selling.   Whether the monopolist rents or sells does not affect this analysis if the monopolist can convince consumers that it will stick to a particular pricing policy in the future. Table 19.2 shows the pattern of revenues and costs for the monopolist over time. The top line shows the rental revenues. The firm receives rents of R in each period for each bulb. The bottom line shows the monopolist's expenditures over time to produce the bulb; the firm has chosen R and N to maximize profits.

Now suppose the monopolist, instead of collecting rent R in each period, allows the rents to accumulate and only collects the rent every N periods. The monopolist collect rents of $R\gamma$, where $R\gamma$ is the present value of the rental for N periods collected all at once

---

[5] Schmalensee (1979) and Liebowitz (1982) survey the durability literature. Swan (1970) was the first to show that a monopolist chooses the same durability as competitive firms under constant returns to scale (cost is increasing in durability but constant with respect to the level of output). Sieper and Swan (1973) relax the constant-returns-to-scale assumption by introducing a fixed-capacity cost. They show that durability is independent of market structure in the long-run equilibrium (though not necessarily in the short run). Kamien and Schwartz (1974) show that with rising average-cost curves, a monopolist chooses a lower durability than competitive firms. Swan (1977) notes, however, that if the monopolist has access to the same technology as the competitive industry (many plants), then the independence result continues to hold. More recently, Abel (1983) finds that the independence result holds under weaker conditions than constant returns to scale, but that without constant returns to scale, the independence result need not hold. We show later that when the product is sold instead of rented, the monopolist may opt for a shorter-lived product.

TABLE 19.2		Time Pattern of Revenues and Costs								
Period	1	2	3	4	. . .	N	N + 1	N + 2	N + 3	. . .
Rental revenue	R	R	R	R	. . .	R	R	R	R	. . .
Sales revenue	Rγ	0	0	0	. . .	0	Rγ	0	0	. . .
Costs	C(N)	0	0	0	. . .	0	C(N)	0	0	. . .

rather than every period for N periods.[6] For example, if the rent, R, is \$1 per period, the duration, N, is 3 periods, and the interest rate is 10 percent, then the present value of the rent for 3 periods is $R\gamma$ = \$1 + \$0.9048 + \$0.8187 ≈ \$2.72. Only \$2.72 is collected rather than \$3 because rent in the future is worth less than rent today.

Both the monopolist and consumers are indifferent between a rent of \$1 per period and a payment collected every three periods of \$2.72 if transaction costs are negligible, *and consumers are convinced that prices will not change in the future*. The monopolist is indifferent between receiving the payment of \$2.72 every three periods or a rent of \$1 each period. The monopolist has no incentive to charge a sale price different from \$2.72 if that is the profit-maximizing rental. A lower or higher price would reduce profits.

As a result, if the bulb is sold rather than rented, the monopolist sells it for $R\gamma$, which is equal to the present value of the rental stream: the present value of the profits from selling and from renting are the same. Because the costs are the same in both cases, and (by construction) the present value of revenues collected over N periods is the same, the results of the rental analysis also hold for the sales case, and the monopolist chooses that durability that minimizes costs, just as in the competitive case.

Costly Installation and Maintenance

We have just shown that, under certain conditions, durability is the same under competition as it is for a monopolist that rents, and for a monopolist that sells. When installation is costly or better maintenance can extend a product's life, however, durability differs across these market structures.

Costly Installation. Suppose that it is costly to replace a light bulb; for example, suppose that a maintenance person must change the bulb. If the costs are the same for each consumer, both the monopolist and competitive firm choose the same durability that minimizes the full cost of changing the bulb, including the installation.

In contrast, suppose the costs of changing light bulbs vary across consumers, so that the total costs of buying and installing a light bulb differ across consumers. Those consumers with relatively high replacement costs prefer relatively expensive, long-lived bulbs. In contrast, those with relatively low costs prefer relatively inexpensive, short-lived bulbs. In this case, durability is an attribute of the product that the monopolist can use to segregate

---

[6] The discount factor $\gamma = (1 - e^{-rN})/(1 - e^{-r})$, where r is the interest rate.

FIGURE 19.3   Production of Machine Services

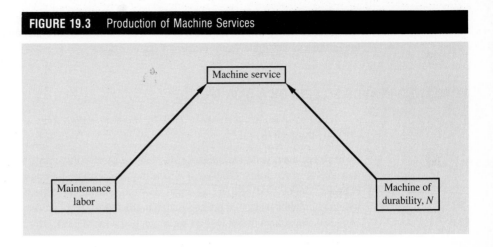

consumer groups. In this case, the problem becomes one of quality choice. The analysis in Chapter 15 shows that the monopolist typically produces a different range of durabilities than does a competitive industry.

Maintenance.   Let us now complicate the problem further. Suppose that the durability of the product is determined by consumer behavior as well as by the manufacturer. ("If I had known that I was going to live this long, I would have taken better care of myself.") For example, a consumer may be able to use labor to maintain a machine, such as a typewriter or a car, in order to make it last longer. The consumer purchases labor in a competitive market and combines the labor with the machine to produce machine services, as shown in Figure 19.3.

The production of machine services involves variable proportions: the services are produced by a machine of a particular durability combined with labor. If the price of a machine is relatively high, consumers maintain it longer in order to economize on the number of times the expensive machine must be purchased. For example, when the price of new cars increases, consumers keep their old cars longer.

This problem is analogous to the case of vertical integration with variable proportions discussed in Chapter 16. A monopolist of a machine does not want its consumers substituting away from the machine and toward labor. Firms may try to prevent this substitution by contracts that place vertical restraints on consumers; for example, a firm may *tie* maintenance to the purchase of the machine[7]. Maintenance is also tied to the machine if a firm refuses to sell the machine and instead only rents it with maintenance included.

In a famous antitrust case in 1947, United Shoe was charged with attempting to monopolize the market for machines that manufacture shoes. One of United Shoe's tactics that was attacked was its refusal to sell machines outright. Prior to the antitrust verdict,

---

[7] Epple and Raviv (1979) show these results also hold when durability is stochastic (varies randomly around an average).

United Shoe only leased its machines with maintenance included. One possible explanation for this *lease only* policy is that it prevents consumers from maintaining their machines longer than is desirable from the firm's point of view.

■ RENTING VERSUS SELLING BY A MONOPOLIST

> *It is better to buy a quart of milk by the penny than keep a cow.*
> —JAMES HOWELL

Even where there is no maintenance involved, a monopolist may prefer to rent rather than to sell. The preceding example, in which the monopolist and consumers were indifferent between renting and selling, assumed that the consumers believed that the monopolist would maintain a particular pricing policy in the future. If, however, the monopolist cannot convince consumers that it will do so, it can make more money by renting than by selling. Indeed, where the monopolist must sell the durable good, it may lose much (or even all) of its market power. To illustrate this result, the following sections first examine the effect of consumers' ability to resell the product, then consumers' behavior, and finally the monopolist's behavior.

Resale Market

Until now, we have assumed that consumers keep a machine until it dies. This section examines the effect of consumers' reselling the machine on a durable goods monopolist, assuming that consumers believe that the monopolist will continue to charge its announced price.

Suppose a monopolist that produces a nondurable good, which is completely consumed in one period, sells Q^* units at \$10 to those who value the product the most. If those Q^* consumers are subsequently allowed to resell the product, there are no further transactions because, by assumption, those Q^* consumers who valued the product most already own it, and no one else is interested in bidding the product away. The market price remains at \$10.

So long as the consumers who value the machine the most do not change over time, the same result holds for durable goods. Suppose a monopolist sells durable machines with a lifetime of N and that it is profit maximizing to sell Q^* units every N periods; that is, customers are consuming Q^* units of machine service (for example, light) each period. The initial consumers who purchase the machines are those who value it the most, and by assumption they continue to be the ones who value it the most, so there are no resales. The opportunity for resales leaves the optimal (sales) solution unaffected.

Suppose now that the overall demand curve for the machine services each period does not vary over time, but the consumers who value the machine the most do change. In this case, there are resales from owners who now place less value on the machines to consumers who now value the machines highly but do not own them. Since Q^* machines are available each period, which is the optimal number from the monopolist's point of view, the value consumers place on consuming the product per period (the implicit rental price) is unchanged as long as the total demand curve for services is unchanged. The initial sales of the machine reflect the discounted present value of these consumer values. As in Table 19.2, resale does not affect R (the implicit rental price), so the solution is the same as in the case where the identity of those who value the good the most is unchanged.

These results can be illustrated using the previous example: suppose consumers are willing to pay $1 per period per light bulb; the interest rate is 10 percent ; the identity of consumers wanting light bulbs does not change from period to period; and the monopolist's optimal solution is to produce 50 light bulbs, each of which lasts 3 periods. As already calculated, the present value of a bulb given a rental of $1 for 3 periods is $2.72.

Now suppose that consumers' desires change over time so that resales occur each period but that overall demand for services each period is unchanged. If an initial owner in the first period sells the bulb a year later to another consumer, then the discounted value in the initial period from the resale in the beginning of the second period is $1.72.[8] That is, after reselling the bulb, the initial owner has spent $2.72 − $1.72 = $1 for the use of the bulb for one year, which equals the rental rate for one year. It is, of course, of no interest to the monopolist if this resale occurs because the total demand it faces has not changed: the same number of bulbs are demanded in each period as when consumer' desires were unchanging. With a resale market, the optimal solution to the monopolist's problem is the same whether consumers' preferences change or do not change because the full monopoly profits are obtained in the initial sales of the machines.[9] The presence of a resale market does constrain the price that can be charged by the monopolist in the periods subsequent to the initial sale. See Example 19.1.

Without a resale market, when the consumers who value the good the most change over time, the monopolist cannot obtain as high profits as it would if the same consumers always valued the good the most. For example, suppose you only have use for a durable good a short time (you want the use of a refrigerator for only this school year). If you cannot resell it, you are not willing to pay as much for it as you would if you planned to keep it for its entire product life. Resales help the monopolist and consumers by effectively lowering the cost of providing each unit of service to consumers

Suppose there is an aluminum monopoly and an owner of an aluminum pot cannot sell it as a pot but can sell it to a recycling firm, which melts it back into aluminum for refabrication. This recovery industry creates a source of aluminum, called a *secondary market,* that competes with the original monopolist. The market outcome is similar regardless of whether the pot is sold as a pot or is recycled. In contrast, suppose that the owner of the pot throws it out and a scrap dealer retrieves it and recycles the aluminum. Here, consumers are not willing to pay as much for the aluminum as they would if they could resell it. The secondary market still constrains the monopolist, but consumers' incentives differ from when they received the value of the recycled pot.

---

[8] The original owner receives $1.9048 in the second period, so the discounted value of this resale in the initial period is $1.72.

[9] One qualification to this result is that the optimal rental solution (that prevents resale) does not require the monopolist to reduce output over time. A sales policy cannot always duplicate a rental policy when cutbacks in output are required over time.

EXAMPLE 19.1

THE IMPORTANCE OF USED GOODS

In 1985, Deere & Co. proposed to acquire the farm machinery division of Versatile Co., a Canadian company. Deere & Co. is one of the world's largest manufacturers of a variety of tractors. Versatile was one of the largest producers of four-wheel-drive (4WD) tractors, which have power to all four wheels. Unlike two-wheel-drive tractors, four-wheel-drive tractors have four (not two) enormous wheels.

Versatile and Deere were the top two North American producers of 4WD tractors in 1985, were of roughly equal size, and between them had a substantial share of the sales of new tractors. There were only two other major producers of 4WD tractors. Just a few years earlier there had been double the number of firms, but the precipitous collapse of the farm economy had reduced the demand for 4WD tractors to about 30 percent of its 1981 levels as shown in the table below:

Sales of 4WD Tractors in North America, 1976–85	
Year	*Number Sold*
1976	13,752
1977	10,303
1978	11,500
1979	14,710
1980	14,568
1981	14,021
1982	9,964
1983	7,647
1984	6,494
1985	5,093

Tractors are a durable good, and 4WD tractors are especially durable, lasting anywhere from 15 to 30 years. There is a well-organized market for used tractors, and many farmers can substitute between new and used equipment. As a result, there is a close relationship in the price movements of new and used goods.

If new and used goods are substitutes, then market shares based on new sales have only limited meaning. Even if a firm suddenly becomes a monopolist of new sales, but new sales account for only a small fraction of total tractors in use, the monopolist could not raise the price of new tractors significantly.

The rental rate of tractors is determined by the intersection of the supply curve of tractor services with the demand curve. The price equals the discounted present value of future rentals. In any year, the supply of tractor services equals the services available from the new stock plus those available from the old stock. The supply of services from the old stock equals the (depreciated) service left in tractors sold in previous years.

The supply curve in year t can be written as a function of the year and the rental rate, R:

$$S(R, t) = S_o(R, t) + S_n(R, t),$$

where $S_n(R, t)$ = new supply at rental rate R, in year t
                 $S_o(R, t)$ = old supply at rental rate R in year t.

If we ignore maintenance, the rental rate, R, does not affect the supply from previous years, so we need not write supply as a function of the rental rate. An econometric analysis indicates that the annual depreciation rate was about 8 percent per year. Since 92 percent of the previous year's supply is available in a given year, the supply in 1985 is

$$S_o(1985) = .92\, S_n(1984) + .92 \times .92\, S_n(1983) + \ldots$$

Using this formula and the data from the table, the ratio of new tractors to existing stock in 1985 is low: less than 10 percent. Since older tractors dominate the stock of tractors in use and are likely to do so for years to come, even a monopolist of new tractors could not profitably and significantly reduce total industry supply (and hence significantly raise prices) for several years.

The U.S. Department of Justice, in deciding whether to permit mergers, is primarily concerned about the effect of a merger on prices. Thus, if a merger created a firm with a large share but no ability to raise prices, the merger is likely to be permitted. The Department of Justice felt that the acquisition posed anticompetitive problems. The Department of Justice understood the constraining effect of used equipment, but felt that is was not significant enough to prevent price from rising over the foreseeable future. The Department of Justice said it would allow the acquisition if there was no other potential buyer in deference to the Canadian government's plea that otherwise Versatile would exit the industry. The transaction was never completed.

This case raises a host of complicated issues dealing with durable goods. The analysis suggests that any durable good with a low depreciation rate and a large outstanding stock might be hard to monopolize, at least initially (Carlton and Gertner 1989). For example, in the automobile industry, the depreciation rate (23 percent) is about three times higher than that for tractors. Thus, all else the same, a monopolist in automobiles could raise prices sooner than one in tractors because used goods constrain for a shorter time in the automobile industry. This reasoning shows that if a firm intends to monopolize an industry, it should understand the constraining effect of used equipment. Moreover, it can be shown that in a durable good industry, competition among oligopolists is likely to be more intense than in a nondurable good industry (Carlton and Gertner 1989). The intuition behind this result is that a firm that makes an extra sale today is taking current and future sales from rivals, increasing the incentive to make sales today relative to that for a nondurable good.

NOTE: Carlton worked as a consultant to Deere & Co.
SOURCES: Farm and Industrial Equipment Institute. *State of the Industry 1985 Update* and *The State of the Industry 1978–1980;* Canadian Farm and Industrial Equipment Institute. *Industry Outlook 1986;* U.S. Department of Agriculture, Economic Research Service. *Outlook and Situation Report* August 1985.

EXAMPLE 19.2

THE ALCOA CASE: SECONDHAND ECONOMICS

In 1945, Judge Learned Hand, writing for a panel of three judges, found the Aluminum Company of America (Alcoa) guilty of monopolizing the domestic aluminum market. The case turned, in large part, on the court's finding that the relevant market consisted only of domestic aluminum production and net imports of primary ingot. The court held that secondary aluminum, which is obtained by remelting aluminum scrap, was *not* part of the market. Judge Hand's reasoning was that although secondary aluminum is a close substitute for primary aluminum, Alcoa controlled the secondary production through its domination of primary production. Essentially, he contended that the existence of secondary aluminum producers did not substantially curtail Alcoa's monopoly profits from the sale of primary aluminum.

Several economists have examined whether Judge Hand was correct. Gaskins (1974) estimates the demand for aluminum and supply of secondary aluminum and uses other data to simulate the long-run effects of having a secondary market. He compares simulations with and without a secondary market. His analysis has two key results. First, the presence of a secondary market causes a durable goods monopolist to set a higher price initially. Second, because the demand for aluminum was growing over time, the constraining effect of the secondary market was small.

For one set of parameters he studies, the initial price is 6 percent above the monopoly price without a secondary market and nearly 3.5 times larger than the competitive price (long-run marginal cost). The long-run monopoly equilibrium price with a secondary market is 14 percent less than the monopoly price without a secondary market, but 2.8 times higher than the competitive price. According to the simulations, the monopoly price with a secondary market falls slowly over time, so that it takes 100 years for the price to fall within 5 percent of its long-run equilibrium value.

Swan (1980), using different models, conducts other simulations that reach the same conclusion: Alcoa's predicted price was only slightly below the monopoly price without a secondary market and well above the competitive price (based on Alcoa's own cost figures).

The importance of a secondary market was debated in a famous antitrust case involving Alcoa. Alcoa was the sole supplier of aluminum ingot; however, aluminum products can be recycled to obtain aluminum ingots. The legal question became whether Alcoa had market power since it did not control the secondary scrap market directly. The recycling market constrained the price Alcoa could charge in subsequent periods for its aluminum. When demand is growing over time, the constraint of the secondary market on the monopolist's pricing is an empirical issue (see Example 19.2 and Martin 1982). If demand is growing extremely rapidly so that the supply of the resold material does not account for a large fraction of demand, then there is little constraint on the monopolist. Most recent analyses of the Alcoa case (Example 19.2) find that Alcoa was little constrained by the secondary market due to growing demand.

Gaskins explains why the first-period price is higher than the short-run monopoly price. His argument has three steps. (1) Initially, there is no stock of aluminum, so there is no secondary market. Later, for a given stock of aluminum in the world, the higher the price for aluminum, the more it pays to convert scrap aluminum to pure aluminum, so the supply of secondary aluminum is increasing in price. (2) When maximizing the present discounted profits, a firm must trade off short-run versus long-run profits. Thus, the firm must be concerned that higher production in the short run will lead to a larger stock of aluminum later and hence more competition from the secondary market. (3) Therefore, in the initial period, the primary-producer monopolist sells even less than the short-run profit-maximizing level of output and charges a higher than monopoly price.

Gaskins concludes that Judge Hand's contention that monopoly control of primary production is nearly equivalent to a pure monopoly in its welfare implications was approximately correct in this case; that is, leaving out the secondary market did not substantially bias the results. Including the secondary market still would have left Alcoa with a large market share and would have led to the same conclusion. Because in other cases the secondary market can constrain pricing in the primary market, it is, in general, a mistake to ignore it (Fisher 1974).

Suslow (1986b) argues that, since new and used aluminum are not perfect substitutes, Alcoa's market power was not as constrained by the fringe as it would have been were they perfect substitutes. Similarly she notes that there are lengthy recycling lags, so Alcoa faced limited recycling in its early years. She estimates that before 1940, Alcoa's markup of price over its short-run marginal cost was 59 percent. That is, she concludes that the "Alcoa problem" was not very important to Alcoa.

TECHNICAL NOTE: In the simulations of Gaskins and Swan, Alcoa is assumed to be able to set its pricing in the initial period and to stick to that pricing. Thus, these results differ from the more appropriate model that assumes Alcoa changes its policy over time. See the discussion in the chapter on consumer expectations and Suslow (1986a).

Consumers' Expectations Constrain the Monopolist

We should all be concerned about the future because we will have to spend the rest of our lives there. —CHARLES FRANCIS KETTERING

When resales are possible, the price consumers are willing to pay for a durable good depends on both the value of the services of the durable good during the period the consumer owns it and the resale value at the end of that period. That is, consumers' expectations about the future resale price affect the initial price. For example, if you buy a house, the amount you are willing to pay depends in part on how much you think you will receive when you sell it years later. This section analyzes the effects of consumers' price expectations on a monopolist.

Products that are likely to be fads, and hence worthless in the future, tend to sell for less today than products that will remain valuable. In general, consumers' price expectations depend on what they believe about the demand curve and the output of a monopolist in subsequent periods, because demand and output levels determine the resale price.

The constraining effect of consumers' expectations leads to a surprising result, sometimes called the **Coase conjecture** (Coase 1972): a durable goods monopolist that sells its product has less market power—indeed, in the extreme case, no market power—when compared to a monopolist that rents the durable good.[10] The intuition behind this result is that a monopolist that sells has an incentive to cut price in the future, whereas such behavior does not occur if the monopolist only rents. The following sections illustrate this result through a series of examples.

Examples Where Consumers Do Not Expect Price Cuts. First, consider a nondurable good that lasts for only one period and for which there are no costs of production. The demand curve for the services of the good is

$$Q(R) = 20 - R, \tag{19.1}$$

where R is the rental price and $Q(R)$ is the amount demanded at rental rate R. In this one-period market, the optimal policy for the monopolist is to charge \$10 and sell 10 units.[11] The monopolist's profits (revenues) are \$100. In this case, of course, it makes no difference whether the monopolist rents or sells because there are no future periods: renting is identical to selling.

Now consider a world that lasts for two periods, and a durable good that lasts for two periods. The demand curve for services given in Equation 19.1 holds in both periods. The monopolist can sell Q_1 units in Period 1 and an additional Q_2 units in Period 2. If the monopolist only rents the good and the demand curve remains constant, the optimal policy is for the monopolist to rent 10 units of the good in Period 1 for \$10 and 10 units in Period 2 for \$10, producing all 10 units in Period 1 and no units in Period 2. With this policy, the monopolist earns \$200 total (assuming the interest rate is zero for simplicity).

Now consider the sales policy. Suppose the monopolist sells 10 units at the beginning of Period 1 for \$20. Consumers are willing to buy 10 units at that price because, according to Equation 19.1, consumers are willing to pay \$10 per period per unit in Periods 1 and 2. The monopolist earns \$200 in Period 1 and no revenue in Period 2. This argument is the same as the one made previously with respect to Table 19.2. Thus, the optimal sales policy is equivalent to the optimal rental policy and gives the monopolist \$200 in profits.

---

[10] See Stokey (1981), Bulow (1982), and Gul, Sonnenschein, and Wilson (1986) for proofs of the Coase conjecture under various conditions. Bagnoli, Salant, and Swierzbinski (1988) show that the Coase conjecture proof of Gul, Sonnenschein, and Wilson (1986) depends on a continuum of consumers.

[11] The monopolist's profits are equal to revenues $= 20R - R^2$. The first-order condition for profit-maximization is $20 - 2R = 0$, or $R = 10$.

Consumers Expect Future Price Cuts.   For the optimal rental policy and the optimal sales policy to be equivalent, the monopolist must sell 10 units in Period 1 and nothing in Period 2. Is such a policy believable? We now show that the monopolist has an incentive to produce in the second period, so that the price in Period 2 is less than in Period 1, and rational consumers anticipate this fall in price.

Consider the demand curve the monopolist faces in Period 2. Because only one period remains at the beginning of Period 2, a consumer willing to rent the good for R in Period 2 is willing to pay R to purchase the good. That is, in the last period there is no difference between the sales price and the rental price for a durable product. Therefore the demand curve the monopolist faces in Period 2 equals the demand given in Equation 19.1 minus the 10 units that are already in the marketplace. This residual demand curve in Period 2 is shown in Equation 19.2, where R_2 is the rental rate that is equivalent to the selling price of the good in Period 2, and $Q_2(R_2)$ is the number of additional units beyond those already sold in Period 1 that the monopolist sells in Period 2 for R_2:

$$Q_2(R_2) = (20 - R_2) - 10 = 10 - R_2. \tag{19.2}$$

Given this residual demand curve in Period 2, will the monopolist decide to produce zero units in Period 2? The answer is clearly no. The monopolist faced with the demand curve of Equation 19.2 sets $R_2 = \$5$, sells $Q_2 = 5$, and receives revenues of $25 in Period 2. Thus the monopolist has an incentive to produce a positive amount in Period 2. The sales policy in which the monopolist produces 10 units in Period 1 and 0 units in Period 2 is not credible to consumers, who recognize that the monopolist has an incentive to produce a positive amount in Period 2.

Won't these sales in Period 2 be good for the monopolist? Surprisingly, the answer is no. If the monopolist can sell 10 units in Period 1 for $200 and then sell 5 more units in Period 2 for an additional $25, it appears that the monopolist earns a total of $225. Unfortunately for the monopolist, this calculation is wrong.

A monopolist that only rents is unconstrained in setting the rental fees that are profit-maximizing. In that calculation above, the highest total profit it can earn is $200; hence earning more is impossible, because $200 *is* the profit-maximizing solution. The problem with the reasoning in the sales calculation is that no one is willing to pay $20 per unit in Period 1 if the monopolist is going to sell the same unit in Period 2 for only $5.[12] In other words, consumers in Period 1 are only willing to pay $R_1 + R_2$ for a machine, where R_1 is the implicit rental value they place on the machine in Period 1 ($10) and R_2 is the rental value in Period 2 ($5). No consumer values the good at $10 in Period 2 if it can be purchased for only $5. If the monopolist produces additional units in Period 2, so that R_2 equals $5 instead of $10, consumers are only willing to pay $15 (rather than $20) to purchase the good in Period 1. Thus, the total amount the monopolist

---

[12] The consumers are assumed to be rational and have perfect foresight about the monopolist's behavior in Period 2. If consumers are myopic and do not expect the monopolist to produce in the second period, then consumers' expectations not only do not constrain the monopolist, but benefit the monopolist, who can earn profits of $225.

earns from sales is actually $\$15 \times 10 + \$5 \times 5 = \$175$, which is less than the $200 in the rental case.

This example illustrates an important point: When the monopolist sells the good rather than rents it, it has an incentive to produce and sell a positive number of additional units in Period 2. These additional sales drive the price down in Period 2 below what it would have been had no additional units been produced. This lower price, in turn, causes consumers to lower the amount they are willing to pay for the good in Period 1. Moreover, consumers recognize the monopolist's incentive to produce in Period 2 and *expect* such additional production to occur. Their expectations influence their behavior in Period 1.

In the rental solution, the monopolist faces no constraints from consumers' price expectations. It can produce more in later periods without affecting the rental rate in the first period, because consumers do not care about future production. It is not, however, optimal for the monopolist to produce and rent additional units in Period 2: if it tries to rent more units in Period 2, the rental rate is driven down below the profit-maximizing level.

Thus, a monopolist that must sell the good is actually constrained in a way that does not occur in the rental case. When selling, the monopolist cannot credibly commit to producing zero units in Period 2, in contrast to the rental case. It cannot credibly commit in the sales case because consumers know that it is *not* optimal for the monopolist to produce nothing in the second period.

Since the rental solution was an unconstrained profit maximization, a monopolist earns as high or higher profits from renting as it does from selling. The monopoly is harmed in the selling case by being unable to credibly restrain itself from producing in the future. In other words, the monopoly is cursed by having an incentive to profitably produce additional units in Period 2. United Shoe Company, IBM, and Xerox all initially only rented their durable products; however, they are now required to sell them (Bulow 1982, 318).

There are several methods whereby a monopolist can overcome the problem caused by consumers' expectations. Before discussing them, however, let us return to the problem of the monopolist who must sell a durable good in a two-period world and determine its *second-best* policy (its "optimal" policy given that it must sell rather than rent).

The Monopolist's Optimal Sales Policy.   To determine the monopolist's second-best sales policy, we work backwards starting in Period 2 (see also Appendix 19B). Suppose the monopolist sells Q_1 in Period 1. Then the residual demand curve facing the monopolist in Period 2 is

$$Q_2(R_2) = 20 - R_2 - Q_1, \tag{19.3}$$

which is a generalization of Equation 19.2, where we replace the number 10 with Q_1. The monopolist solves for the optimal rental rate, R_2, that maximizes profits, where demand depends on the quantity sold in Period 1.

The residual demand curve in Figure 19.4 hits both the R_2 and Q_2 axes at $20 - Q_1$. The marginal revenue curve, *MR*, corresponding to this residual demand curve hits the Q_2 axis at half the distance from the origin, $10 - (Q_1/2)$, as does the demand curve, since the demand curve is linear. Because costs (and hence marginal costs) are zero,

FIGURE 19.4   Profits in the Second Period

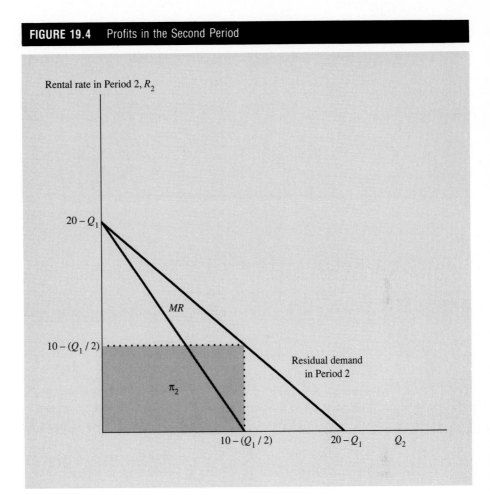

profits are maximized where $MR = 0$. As the figure shows, that occurs where $R_2 = Q_2 = 10 - (Q_1/2)$. Total profits in Period 2, π_2, are shown as the shaded box in the figure. Thus, output, rents, and profits in the second period all depend on output in the first period, Q_1.

The monopolist wants to maximize the present value of profits in the two periods combined, which are equal to profits in Period 1 plus profits in Period 2 (assuming the interest rate is 0, so that profits in Period 2 are not discounted). That is, the present value of profits (PVP) is

$$PVP = \pi_1 + \pi_2 = (R_1 + R_2)Q_1 + R_2Q_2. \tag{19.6}$$

The sales price in Period 1 equals the rental rate in that period plus the rental rate in Period 2. The sales price in Period 2 equals the rental rate in that period. The rental rate in Period 2 depends on the total amount consumed in Period 2, $Q_1 + Q_2$.

TABLE 19.3 Profits in a Two-Period Model

Sales Period 1, Q_1	Rental Rate Period 1, R_1	Sales Period 2, Q_2	Rental Rate Period 2, R_2	Profits Period 1, π_1	Profits Period 2, π_2	Present Value of Profits, $PVP = \pi_1 + \pi_2$
1	19	9.5	9.5	28.5	90.25	118.75
2	18	9	9	54	81	135
3	17	8.5	8.5	76.5	72.25	148.75
4	16	8	8	96	64	160
5	15	7.5	7.5	112.5	56.25	168.75
6	14	7	7	126	49	175
7	13	6.5	6.5	136.5	42.25	178.75
8	**12**	**6**	**6**	**144**	**36**	**180**
9	11	5.5	5.5	148.5	30.25	178.75
10	10	5	5	150	25	175
11	9	4.5	4.5	148.5	20.25	168.75

$\pi_1 = (R_1 + R_2)Q_1$

$\pi_2 = R_2 Q_2$

$Q_2 = 10 - Q_1/2$

Having shown that the monopolist's choice of R_2 and Q_2 depends on Q_1, we now examine how profits depend on Q_1. (Equation 19.1 shows R_1 depends on Q_1 so that, with Equation 19.6, PVP can be expressed in terms of only Q_1.) These calculations are shown in Table 19.3. Where $Q_1 = 8$ (bold line), the present value of profits is maximized at $180. See Appendix 19B.

Notice that a PVP of $180 is higher than the $175 (discussed previously) that is obtained when $Q_1 = 10$. Setting $Q_1 = 10$ leads to higher profits in the first period than when $Q_1 = 8$, but profits in the second period are enough lower that PVP is lower when $Q_1 = 10$. Even at a PVP of $180, the monopolist is worse off than if it only rented, where the PVP is $200.

Figure 19.5 presents the same information as Table 19.3. The upper diagram, Figure 19.5a, shows the marginal profits in each of the two periods and the marginal total present value of profits *(MPVP)* as a function of output in the first period. Marginal profits in Period 1, MP_1, are decreasing in Q_1, but are positive where $Q_1 < 10$ and negative where $Q_1 > 10$. That is, profits in Period 1 reach their maximum at 10, as shown in Figure 19.5b.

Marginal profits in Period 2, MP_2, rise as Q_1 increases. This curve hits 0 at 20. That is, profits in Period 2 are minimized at 20 (see Figure 19.5b).

The present value of total profits, $PVP = \pi_1 + \pi_2$, reaches its maximum, as shown in Figure 19.5b and Table 19.3, at 8. The marginal present value of total profit (Figure 19.5a), falls as Q_1 increases and hits 0 at 8. The monopolist increases Q_1 until the marginal present value of total profits equals 0, because that is the point where total profits are maximized.

FIGURE 19.5   Marginal and Total Profits in a Two-period Model

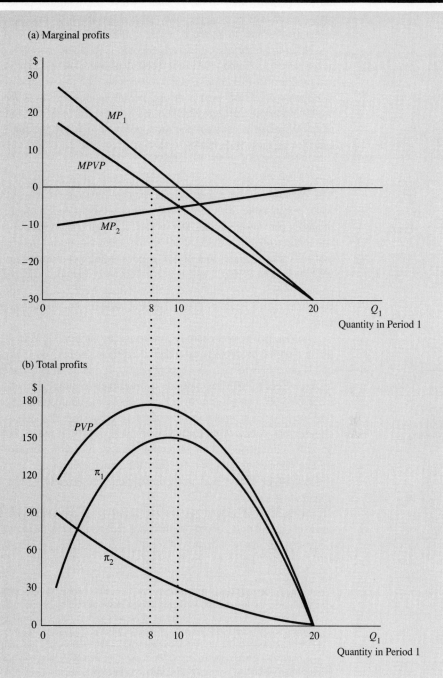

The marginal present value of total profits must equal the sum of marginal profits in the two periods, $MP_1 + MP_2$. Thus, where the marginal present value of total profits equals zero, $MP_1 = -MP_2$. The marginal profits in Period 1, MP_1, equal the negative of marginal profits in Period 2, $-MP_2$, at 8 also.

What these curves tell us is that as the monopolist increases Q_1, marginal profits fall in the first period and rise in the second period. The monopolist increases Q_1 until the marginal profits in Period 1 equal the negative of the marginal profits in Period 2. The monopolist trades off profits in one period against profits in the other. If the marginal profits in Period 1 are greater than the negative of marginal profits in Period 2 (as they are at $Q_1 = 6$), it pays for the monopolist to increase Q_1, since the loss in Period 1 is less than the gain in Period 2.

The Paradox.   The preceding analysis demonstrates that a monopolist's profits are lower when it sells rather than rents. The reason selling is less profitable is that the monopolist produces too much in the later periods. In our example, the monopolist is better off committing not to produce at all in the second period. Unfortunately for a monopolist that sells the machine, that policy is not credible: consumers realize that the monopolist will produce in Period 2 and hence the price in Period 2 will be below that in Period 1, so they will pay less in Period 1 than if they expected no production in Period 2. This consumer expectations problem does not arise in our example when the monopolist only rents.

In our two-period example, the price in Period 2 is below that in Period 1. When the two-period example is extended to cover many periods (Appendix 19B), the monopolist's price falls in each subsequent period. It can be shown that the price eventually falls to zero. Because the time periods can be made arbitrarily small, a monopolist that sells a durable good can never receive a price above the competitive price (zero in our example). One way to think about this puzzling result is that if the monopolist cannot credibly commit to a policy of no further production, it is as if the monopolist is a different firm in each future period. With an infinite number of future periods, it is as if there were an infinite number of competitors. Thus the monopolist of the future is competing with the monopolist of today, and this competition immediately drives the price down to the competitive level.[13]

This result is indeed bizarre and arises from the extreme assumption that has been made about the cost conditions. It is not the assumption that costs are zero that turns out to be critical: the results hold for any (constant) positive level of marginal costs. The

---

[13] We ignored depreciation of the durable good in our discussion. Bond and Samuelson (1984) and Suslow (1986a) examine the durable goods monopolist problem with depreciation. Kahn (1986) and Karp (1987) show that if the monopolist sells an infinitely durable product with an increasing marginal cost of production, the sales policy results in a lower level of stock (that is, cumulative sales) than the socially optimal level, but that the monopolistic stock asymptotically approaches the socially optimal long-run solution. If the good is not infinitely durable, the asymptotic stock under the monopoly sales policy is less than the socially optimal long-run solution.

critical assumption is that the output level can be increased costlessly as fast as the monopolist desires. If consumers know that the monopolist cannot expand output costlessly, they believe that its output in the future is constrained and therefore so is its markup above the competitive price. This insight leads to a variety of policies that a monopolist can undertake to get around the expectations problem.

How the Monopolist May Solve Its Expectations Problem

We have just shown that a durable goods monopolist that sells its product loses monopoly power when consumers form their own expectations as to the monopolist's future behavior.[14] A monopoly can only overcome this problem by credibly committing itself not to take advantage of certain profitable opportunities in the future. There are at least five ways the monopoly may avoid the expectations problem (Bulow 1982, 329–31).

First, the monopoly can refuse to sell the product and only *rent* or lease it. Renting or leasing avoids the expectation problem.

Second, because the problem of expectations only arises for durable goods, the monopoly can produce *less durable* goods. The monopolist can use **planned obsolescence,** making the durable good short-lived, as a way of limiting its ability to lower its price in the future. Having new models each year, as with automobiles or high-fashion dresses, may be examples of planned obsolescence; however, the costs of redesigning products frequently limit the monopoly's ability to use this technique.

Third, the monopoly can construct its production process in such a way that it is prohibitively costly to expand output in the future. Consumers know that this *capacity constraint* limits its production in the future. An extreme example is an artist who destroys the plate used to produce a print after a fixed number are produced in the first period.

Fourth, the monopoly can *guarantee* to buy back products from any consumers at the price they paid for it. This *buy-back* provision protects the consumer in case the monopolist expands output and thereby lowers price in the future. This policy is not feasible where consumer abuse may lower the value of a product, as with automobiles, or if the products cannot be easily transferred, as with railroad tracks.

Fifth, if the firm cannot explicitly contract to control its future production, it may attempt to acquire a *reputation* for never lowering price. For example, deBeers, the South African diamond monopolist, claims it has a policy of never reducing the nominal price of its diamonds (although it apparently has on occasion). As another example, IBM recently announced prices at future dates for its PS2 line of computers.

Thus, there are a number of ways in which a durable goods manufacturer may precommit itself to assure consumers that goods purchased today will not drop in value tomorrow. A durable good monopolist can maintain its market value by renting or by selling "with strings attached." What is striking in this case is that the strings bind the monopolist, not the consumers, and that the monopolist likes it that way.

---

[14] For a discussion of durable goods and oligopoly, see Ausubel and Deneckere (1987), Gul (1987), and Carlton and Gertner (1989).

■ SUMMARY

The future isn't what it used to be.

Market structure usually does not affect the durability of a good when durability, by itself, is not important to consumers and when firms are not constrained by consumer expectations. In rental markets, both competitive and monopolistic firms choose the durability that minimizes the cost of providing the services.

Generally, a monopolist is better off if it can rent its product than if it must sell it. When the monopolist must sell the product with no strings attached, consumers can invest more in maintenance, so they need less in the future. Moreover, rational consumers expect that a monopolist will produce more units in the future, thereby lowering both future prices and resale values, and as a result, the initial purchase price. Under certain conditions, a monopolist that sells a durable good may make no monopoly profits at all. It is therefore in the monopolist's best interest to *credibly* commit itself to not expand future output and not lower prices in the future. If it can do so, it can make monopoly profits from selling as well as from renting.

■ Key Terms

capital asset
Coase conjecture
durable goods

planned obsolescence
service

■ Discussion Questions

1. Should textbook publishers encourage authors to revise their textbooks frequently? *Hint:* Consider what frequent revisions do to the price a student is willing to pay and to the publisher's costs.
2. Contrast how the resale markets affect the prices consumers pay in Examples 19.1 and 19.2.
3. Comment on the following assertion: "The Department of Justice should not concern itself with anticompetitive mergers in durable goods industries. Coase shows that the competitive price prevails in such industries."

4. What could a government do to reduce the price of diamonds to its citizens who buy from a durable goods monopolist?
5. Can a durable goods manufacturer use a most-favored-nations clause in its sales contracts to solve its expectations paradox? Such a clause, for example, could require the monopolist to lower the price to an earlier purchaser if it sells the good to a later purchaser at a lower price.

■ Problems

1. Use Example 19.1 to calculate the elasticity of demand facing a monopolist producer of four-wheel drive tractors, assuming it rents in the future but has sold units in the past, of which 20 units remain. Show how the elasticity is affected by the ratio of new to used equipment.
2. Explain how the analysis in Problem 1 is affected if farmers can maintain tractors forever.

Answers to odd-numbered problems are given at the back of the book.

3. Explain how the analysis in Problem 1 is affected if farmers never sell or buy used tractors (that is, transaction costs are too high for a used tractor market to develop).

4. Explain how the analysis in Problem 1 is affected if an investment tax credit (which lowers a firm's taxes in proportion to the amount spent on new capital) encourages overconsumption of tractors.

5. Explain how the analysis in Problem 1 is affected if four-wheel drive tractors are close substitutes for other types of tractors.

6. Suppose the cost of producing a machine that lasts N periods is $C(N) = N^{.5}$. If the interest rate is 5 percent, what duration should the firm plan for its machine? How should it modify its behavior if consumers can maintain the machine for one extra year at an expense of $1? Does your answer depend upon whether the manufacturer rents or sells the machine?

■ References

Abel, Andrew B. 1983. "Market Structure and the Durability of Goods." *The Review of Economic Studies* 50:625–37.

Ausubel, Lawrence, and Raymond J. Deneckere. 1987. "One Is Almost Enough for Monopoly." *Rand Journal of Economics* 18:255–74.

Bagnoli, Mark, Stephen W. Salant, and Joseph E. Swierzbinski. 1988. "Pacman Refutes the Coase Conjecture: Durable-Goods Monopoly with Discrete Demand." Department of Economics, University of Michigan working paper.

Bond, Eric W., and Larry Samuelson. 1984. "Durable-Good Monopolies with Rational Expectations and Replacement Sales." *Rand Journal of Economics* 15:336–345.

Bulow, Jeremy I. 1982. "Durable-Goods Monopolists." *Journal of Political Economy* 90:314–32.

Carlton, Dennis W., and Robert Gertner. 1989. "Market Power and Mergers in Durable Good Industries." *Journal of Law and Economics* 32.

Coase, Ronald H. 1972. "Durability and Monopoly." *Journal of Law and Economics* 15:143–49.

Epple, Dennis, and Artur Raviv. 1979. "Product Reliability and Market Structure." *Southern Economic Journal* 46:280–87.

Fisher, Franklin M. 1974. "Alcoa Revisited: Comment." *Journal of Economic Theory* 9:357–59.

Gaskins, Darius W., Jr. 1974. "Alcoa Revisited: The Welfare Implications of a Secondhand Market." *Journal of Economic Theory* 7:254–71.

Gul, Faruk. 1987. "Foundations of Dynamic Oligopoly." *Rand Journal of Economics* 18:248–54.

Gul, Faruk, Hugo Sonnenschein, and Robert Wilson. 1986. "Foundations of Dynamic Monopoly and the Coase Conjecture." *Journal of Economic Theory.* 39:155–90.

Kahn, Charles. 1986. "The Durable-Goods Monopolist and Consistency with Increasing Costs." *Econometrica* 54:275–94.

Kamien, Morton I., and Nancy L. Schwartz. 1974. "Product Durability Under Monopoly and Competition." *Econometrica* 42:289–301.

Karp, Larry S. 1987. "Consistent Policy Rules and the Benefits of Market Power." Giannini Foundation Working Paper, University of California, Berkeley.

Liebowitz, S. J. 1982. "Durability, Market Structure, and New-Used Goods Models." *American Economic Review* 72:816–24.

Martin, Robert H. 1982. "Monopoly Power and the Recycling of Raw Materials." *Journal of Industrial Economics* 30:405–19.

Schmalensee, Richard. 1979. "Market Structure, Durability, and Quality: A Selective Survey." *Economic Inquiry* 17:177–96.

Sieper, E., and Peter L. Swan. 1973. "Monopoly and Competition in the Market for Durable Goods." *The Review of Economic Studies* 40:333–51.

Stokey, Nancy. 1981. "Rational Expectations and Durable-Goods Pricing." *The Bell Journal of Economics* 12:112–28.

Suslow, Valerie Y. 1986a. "Commitment and Monopoly Pricing in Durable-Goods Models." *International Journal of Industrial Organization* 4:451–60.

———. 1986b. "Estimating Monopoly Behavior with Competitive Recycling: an Application to Alcoa." *Rand Journal of Economics* 17:389–403.

Swan, Peter L. 1970. "Durability of Consumption Goods." *American Economic Review* 60:884–94.

———. 1977. "Product Durability Under Monopoly and Competition: Comment." *Econometrica* 45:229–35.

———. 1980. "Alcoa: The Influence of Recycling on Monopoly Power." *Journal of Political Economy* 88:76–99.

How durable should a product be? In the light bulb example, the number of periods that the bulb should last, N, depends on the cost of producing a bulb of a given durability, $C(N)$, and the interest rate, r.

The total present value of the cost of producing 1 unit of light bulb service forever is:

$$C(N) (1 + e^{-rN} + e^{-2rN} + \ldots) = \frac{C(N)}{1 - e^{-rN}}. \qquad (19A.1)$$

The left side of Equation 19A.1 can be rewritten as

$$C(N) + C(N) (e^{-rN} + e^{-2rN} + \ldots).$$

The first term is the current cost of producing a bulb of duration N, and the second term represents the costs in the future. Thus, the first term reflects the costs of higher quality, and the second term reflects the benefits: lower replacement costs in the future. Since only the second term depends on the interest rate, r, a change in the interest rate only affects the benefits. Intuitively, the lower the interest rate, the more we value the future, so the higher the value of durability.

Formally, we can minimize Equation 19A.1 by differentiating the equation with respect to N, setting that derivative equal to zero, and rearranging terms to obtain:

$$\frac{C'(N)}{1 - e^{-rN}} - \frac{C(N)re^{-rN}}{(1 - e^{-rN})^2} = 0. \qquad (19A.2)$$

The first term in Equation 19A.2 represents the present value of the increased cost from initially producing a more durable bulb. The second term represents the savings that come from reducing the number of times that a light bulb must be replaced as it becomes more durable.

Equation 19A.2 can be simplified:

$$\frac{C'(N)}{C(N)} = \frac{r}{e^{rN} - 1} \qquad (19A.3a)$$

In the example of Figure 19.2, the cost function was $C(N) = N^\alpha$. With that cost function, Equation 19A.3 becomes, after simplifying,

$$\frac{\alpha}{N} = \frac{r}{e^{rN} - 1}, \qquad (19A.3b)$$

or $\alpha = rN/e^{rN} - 1$. For $\alpha = .4870197$ (the α used in Figure 19.2), the N that minimizes that expression is 13 when $r = 10$ percent.

The monopolist rents $Q(R)$ units if the rental rate is R per period. The present discounted value of renting is

$$\int_0^\infty RQ(R) \, e^{-rt} \, dt = \frac{C(N)}{1 - e^{-rN}} \, Q(R), \qquad (19A.4)$$

where the first term represents the discounted present value of receiving a revenue stream of $RQ(R)$ in each period, and the second term is the cost of producing $Q(R)$ units of service forever, based on Equation 19A.1.

The monopolist maximizes Equation 19A.4 with respect to R and N. The first-order condition with respect to N is the same in Equation 19A.2, where the entire left side has been multiplied by $Q(R)$. Since $Q(R)$ is positive, the first-order condition is identical to (19A.2). Thus both a competitive firm and a monopolist choose the same N: the one that minimizes costs. One way to understand this result is to note that N only enters the monopolist's profits in Equation 19A.4 in the second term, so choosing N to maximize profits is the same as choosing N to minimize per unit costs.

MULTIPERIOD DURABLE GOODS MONOPOLIST

A monopolist that sells, rather than rents, a durable good in many periods earns less than one that only rents, as discussed in the chapter. Here, we determine the output and prices in each period. We start by considering a two-period world.

■ TWO-PERIODS

A monopolist is considering selling a durable good that lasts two periods. For simplicity, we assume that:

- There is no cost of production (so marginal cost $= 0$).
- The interest rate $= 0$.
- The duration of the good is given and equals two periods.
- Resales are allowed.
- Total demand is unchanged over the two periods and equals:

$$Q_i = 20 - R_i, \tag{19B.1}$$

where Q_i is the output sold in Period i and R_i is the rental rate in that period.

In order to determine the monopolist's optimal policy, we must work backwards starting in Period 2. Suppose that the monopolist sells Q_1 in Period 1. Then the residual demand curve facing the monopolist in Period 2 is:

$$Q_2(R_2) = 20 - R_2 - Q_1. \tag{19B.2}$$

The monopolist solves for the rental rate in Period 2, R_2, that maximizes profits, where demand depends on the quantity sold in Period 1.

Since there is, by assumption, no cost of production, the monopolist's profits in Period 2 are equal to the revenues:

$$\pi_2(R_2,Q_1) = R_2 Q_2(R_2) = R_2 (20 - R_2 - Q_1). \tag{19B.3}$$

Notice that profits in the second period are a function of the rental rate in Period 2 and output in Period 1: $\pi_2(R_2, Q_1)$.

Differentiating Equation 19B.3 with respect to R_2, setting the resulting partial derivative equal to zero, and rearranging terms gives the profit-maximizing rental rate in the second period:

$$R_2 = \frac{20 - Q_1}{2}. \qquad (19B.4)$$

This same result is shown in Figure 19.4. By substituting Equation 19B.4 into (19B.2), we find that the profit-maximizing output in the second period is

$$Q_2 = \frac{20 - Q_1}{2}. \qquad (19B.5)$$

By substituting for R_2 and Q_2 in Equation 19B.3 using (19B.4) and (19B.5), we find that profits in Period 2 are

$$\pi_2 = \frac{(20 - Q_1)^2}{4}. \qquad (19B.6)$$

Thus, output, rents, and profits in the second period all depend on output in the first period, Q_1.

The monopolist wants to maximize the present value of profits in the two periods. The present value of profits, *PVP*, equals profits in Period 1 plus discounted profits in Period 2 (we assume that the interest rate equals 0, so profits in Period 2 are not discounted),

$$PVP = \pi_1 + \pi_2 = (R_1 + R_2)Q_1 + R_2Q_2, \qquad (19B.7)$$

because the sales price in Period 1 equals the rental rate in Period 1 plus the rental rate in Period 2. By substituting for π_2 from Equation 19B.6 into Equation 19B.7 and noting that demand in the first period is $Q_1 = 20 - R_1$ or $R_1 = 20 - Q_1$, we obtain

$$PVP = \left[(20 - Q_1) + \frac{(20 - Q_1)}{2} \right] Q_1 + \frac{(20 - Q_1)^2}{4}. \qquad (19B.8)$$

Equation 19B.8 expresses the present value of profits as a function of just Q_1. Once Q_1 is determined, Q_2 is determined, and in turn, the rental and sales rates for both periods are determined.

To maximize the present value of profits, we must differentiate Equation 19B.8 with respect to Q_1 and set that derivative equal to zero, which shows that the Q_1 that maximizes the *PVP* is 8. Substituting $Q_1 = 8$ into the other equations shows that $R_2 = 6$, $Q_2 = 6$, $R_1 = 12$, $\pi_2 = 36$, $\pi_1 = 144$, and $PVP = 180$ (which is less than the present value of the optimal rental profits of 200).

■ INFINITE NUMBER OF PERIODS

Suppose, now, that the monopolist sells in each of T periods, where T is arbitrarily large. It is possible to show that the rental rate in period i is

$$R_i = \beta_i R_{i-1}, \qquad \beta_i < 1, \tag{19B.9}$$

where β_i is a constant for Period i. From Equation 19B.9, it follows that the rental rate in Period i can also be expressed as a function of the rental rate in the initial period, R_0:

$$R_i = (\beta_i \, \beta_{i-1} \, \beta_{i-2} \ldots \beta_1) \, R_0. \tag{19B.10}$$

It is possible to show that the product of the β's must approach zero as i grows large (Stokey 1981). The length of a time period is arbitrary; thus, if the time periods are very short, so that there are many periods within any given time interval, the rental rate immediately falls to zero by this reasoning. A striking implication of this result is that a monopolist of a durable good receives a price of zero, which is the competitive price, because we have assumed that the cost of production is zero.

CHAPTER 20

PATENTS AND TECHNOLOGICAL CHANGE

> **T**he Congress shall have power . . . to promote the progress of science and useful arts, by securing for limited times to authors and inventors the exclusive right to their respective writings and discoveries.
>
> U.S. CONSTITUTION, ARTICLE I, SECTION 8.

Patents, which give the inventor of a new product an exclusive right to sell it, have both desirable and undesirable effects. The chief benefit is that the possibility of obtaining monopoly profits encourages more inventive activity. Without patents or other similar incentives there may not be enough inventive activity. The chief disadvantage is that new products may be sold at excessively high (monopoly) prices.[1]

Were it not for these exclusive rights, it might not pay for a drug company to invest large sums to discover a drug that cures cancer or prevents heart attacks. But once the drug is discovered, setting the price tens of thousands of times higher than the manufacturing cost puts the drug beyond the reach of many consumers who would gladly pay a competitive price or even all their wealth for it.

This chapter begins by discussing the various methods of granting inventors and other creators exclusive rights to encourage their work. The remainder of the chapter concentrates on answering five questions relating to patents and imperfect competition:

1. If there were no patents or other government incentives, would there be too little research and development (R&D)?

2. If there would be too little research, should the patent system be used to encourage research rather than other incentives, such as prizes, research contracts, and joint ventures?

---

[1] A patented product may face competition from other products. Just because a product is protected by a patent does not guarantee that it is sold for more than the competitive price.

3. Given that we keep the patent system, how long should patent protection last to obtain the best possible trade-off between incentives to invest and the harms from monopoly?

4. Are monopoly profits higher if a patent-holder produces the invention or licenses it to others for production?

5. How does the structure of product and research markets affect the incentives to conduct research and the timing of innovations?

■ PATENTS, COPYRIGHTS, AND TRADEMARKS

Patents, copyrights, and trademarks give a creator exclusive property rights. The three types of protection differ in what they cover and how long they last.

Patents

Patents provide an inventor with exclusive rights to a new and useful *product, process, substance,* or *design.* New products include machines (mechanisms with moving parts) or manufactured articles, such as tools, without moving parts. New processes, or methods, include chemical processes for treating metal or manufacturing drugs, mechanical processes for manufacturing goods, or electrical processes. New substances include chemical compounds and mixtures; the concept covers the composition of matter. New forms of plants can also be covered.[2] New designs include the shapes of products where the shapes serve a functional purpose. In addition, *improvements* on products, processes, and substances may be patented.

In the United States, patents provide 17 years of protection for these inventions. Patent protection is provided for new designs for a term of 14 years. Unlike many European countries, the United States imposes no tax to maintain a patent for its full life, nor does it require that the patent-holder permit others to use the discovery during this period. To obtain a patent, the inventor must prove that the invention is useful (especially for new chemicals), **novel** and **nonobvious** (you cannot patent a slight modification of something known to everyone in the business), and provide a working model. Approximately three-quarters of patent applications eventually are granted.

Copyrights

Copyrights give a creator the exclusive production, publication, or sales rights to artistic, dramatic, literary or musical works. Examples include articles, books, drawings, maps,

---

[2] In April 1988, Harvard University received the first animal patent on a genetically altered mouse. There is extensive work underway to create hogs that produce pork with 70 percent less cholesterol and cows that produce more milk. Farm groups lobbied the Congress claiming that royalty charges for the offspring of such animals would put many small farmers out of business. A bill passed the House exempting farmers from charges of infringement if they breed or sell patented animals' offspring. Such a law might make animal patents worthless. The bill did not pass the Senate, but may be reintroduced in later sessions. (Andrews, Edmund. 1988. "Farmer Exemption Bill Dies." *San Francisco Chronicle,* October 22, A5.)

musical compositions, or photographs. Copyright law covers original "works of authorship" as long as they are "fixed" in a "tangible medium," such as a book.[3]

In the United States, copyrights to businesses last 75 years, and copyrights to individuals last for life plus 50 years. Many countries provide protection for different lengths of time. For example, in Japan copyright protection lasts 50 years after the death of the artist, but actual recordings are only protected for 20 years. Copyrights have exceptions, like the *Fair Use doctrine,* which allows individuals to make copies for their own use of a short passage from a book.[4] *International copyrights* are reciprocal arrangements extending copyright protection to citizens of other participating countries.

Trademarks

Trademarks are words, symbols, or other marks used to distinguish a good or service provided by one firm from those provided by other firms. A trademark may be registered with the Patent Office in the United States. Examples include Kodak film, Exxon gasoline, Apple computers, Chlorox bleach, Bib the Michelin Man who symbolizes tires for the Michelin Company; and a stylized penguin that symbolizes paperback books published by Penguin Books. Unlike copyrights and patents, trademarks do not last for a fixed term, but are subject to variable limits. If a word comes to signify all products in an industry, it no longer distinguishes a particular brand and the trademark protection ends.

To keep from losing its trademark, General Foods stresses "Sanka-*brand* decaffeinated coffee," so that Sanka will not come to describe all decaffeinated coffee. Xerox recently took out an ad (*ABA Journal,* May 1, 1988) that says in part: "Once a trademark not always a trademark. . . . We need your help. . . . Whenever you use our name, please use it as a proper adjective in conjunction with our products and services: e.g., Xerox copiers or Xerox financial services. And never as a verb: 'to Xerox' in place of 'to copy,' or as a noun: 'Xeroxes' in place of 'copies.' With your help and a precaution or two on our part, it's 'Once the Xerox trademark, always the Xerox trademark.'" Examples of trademarks that have become generic names are aspirin, cellophane, cornflakes, dry ice, escalator, high-octane, kerosene, linoleum, mimeograph, nylon, raisin bran, shredded wheat, thermos, trampoline, and yo-yo (Landes and Posner 1987).

---

[3] Computer software on floppy disks and music on records are other examples of works preserved on tangible media.

[4] There may be another strange copyright exemption. In a recent case, *BV Engineering v. University of California, Los Angeles,* 858 F.2d 1394 (9th Cir.), a federal appeals court concluded that state institutions can "violate the federal copyright laws with virtual impunity" due to the immunity clause in the 11th Amendment to the Constitution, which prohibits suits against states for damages, and parts of the Copyright Act, which has sections that exempt states. Apparently a copyright holder can get an injunction against officials of state institutions to stop violating copyrights, but no damages can be collected. The court suggests, however, that by rewriting the law more explicitly, Congress can eliminate this loophole. (Salant, Nathan. 1989. "No Damages from States." *ABA JOURNAL,* March, 32.

Distinctions between Patents, Copyrights, and Trademarks

The remainder of this chapter concentrates on patents. Copyrights can be analyzed similarly to patents, as protections designed to encourage creation. Trademarks, too, can be analyzed as providing protection by encouraging firms to develop reputations that convey information to consumers, allowing them to identify which products they like and dislike (Landes and Posner 1987).

One important distinction between patents and copyrights is that copyrights protect the particular expression of an idea, whereas patents protect any tangible embodiment of the idea itself. Two versions of the same story told in two different ways (*Romeo and Juliet* and *West Side Story*) can be copyrighted. A patent, however, prevents others from using an application of an idea in their products.

Therefore, patents allow greater exclusivity. Patents, though, are much harder to obtain than copyrights. As the following discussion shows, society must choose a trade-off between more stimulus to invention and more monopoly power. Because the greater the monopoly power, the sooner one can make large profits, it is not surprising that society sets patent terms shorter than those for copyrights.

■ INCENTIVES FOR INVENTIONS ARE NEEDED

> *Progress might have been all right once, but it has gone on too long.*
> —OGDEN NASH

> *If you took away everything in the world that had to be invented, there'd be nothing left except a lot of people getting rained on.* —TOM STOPPARD

Most economists and policy makers believe that without patents or other government incentives, there would be too little research. The chief reason is that inventions are fundamentally new information, and information leads to externalities (see Chapter 6).[5] If you eat a hot dog, I can't eat that same hot dog. However, if you possess some information, I can possess and benefit from that same piece of information. Thus, your knowledge of the information doesn't prevent me from using it. If some consumers of the information can obtain it costlessly (for example, you can read a book in a library), the producer of the information has less incentive to produce it than if everyone had to pay for it. Why would one be willing to incur the entire expense of developing new information, processes, or products if people could benefit from them for free? Although some people like to invent for its own sake, many current inventors and firms undertake research for the pecuniary rewards. Thus, if they could not benefit from their new developments, this latter group would not engage in research.

Eliminating most such research would harm society because it has social value. New manufacturing methods lower the costs of producing existing products and allow society to produce more output with the same amount of input. New products increase productivity (for example, improved seeds with higher output or better quality) or give pleasure (video

---

[5] See, for example, Arrow (1962). Where secrecy about a discovery can be maintained, this problem may be eliminated (Taylor and Silberston 1973, Ch. 9; Kitch 1975; and Cheung 1982).

cassette recorders). Indeed, society becomes dependent upon many new inventions. For example, 46 percent of Americans say they do not know how they could get along without Scotch tape.[6] Although 11 percent of Americans say the wheel is the greatest invention of all times, 10 percent say the automobile is.[7] How would our world survive without perforated toilet paper, invented in the 1880s by English manufacturer Walter James Alcock; the zipper, designed for boots and shoes by Chicago engineer Whitcomb L. Judson, who filed for a patent in 1893; or the Barbie doll, developed by Ruth Handler in 1959.[8] Of course, not everyone believes all new products are desirable: 67 percent of Iowans think music videos are among the "least useful changes" in modern life.[9] Further, 0 percent of American car owners keep gloves in their glove compartments.[10]

To create new products, many firms invest large amounts of money. For example, IBM Corp. spent $4 billion in 1987. Research and development expenditures as a percent of sales, however, vary substantially across firms: in 1987 Chevron (oil) invested 1.0 percent of its sales in R&D, Hewlett-Packard (equipment, computers) invested 11.1 percent, Software Publishing, 19.9 percent; Advanced Micro Devices, 24.9 percent; Genentech (biotechnology), 30.9 percent; and Alza (biotechnology), 36.9 percent.[11]

Imitation Discourages Research

Men often applaud an imitation and hiss the real thing. — AESOP

Without a patent, any one could use new information, and *imitations* of new inventions could be sold legally. Suppose you discovered a cure for cancer. You could sell your new drug for large sums of money if a patent gave you exclusive rights. Without a patent, other companies could duplicate your drug, and competition would drive the price to the competitive level. You would incur all the research costs and no private benefit (profits). For example, Ford's innovation of an assembly line was quickly duplicated by others. Every firm wants to copy others' inventions, and no firm wants to go to the expense of inventing anything itself. Thus, without patents consumers could buy new inventions at competitive prices, but there would be few new inventions. Indeed, society tries to reduce the number of certain types of new inventions by not offering patent protection. For example, in the United States, you cannot patent a gambling device such as a slot machine.

Even with patents, the return to the inventor of a new invention may be less than its value to society. For example, although Xerox earns substantial returns from its plain

---

[6] Roper Organization, as cited in Lapham, Pollan, and Etheridge (1987).

[7] R. H. Bruskin, as cited in Lapham, Pollan, and Etheridge (1987).

[8] Wallace, Irving, David Wallechinsky, and Amy Wallace. 1988. "The Column of Lists: Anonymous Inventions." *San Francisco Chronicle,* August 10, B3.

[9] Des Moines Register and Tribune Company, as cited in Lapham, Pollan, and Etheridge (1987).

[10] Runzheimer International, as cited in Lapham, Pollan, Etheridge (1987).

[11] Clark, Don. 1988. "High Tech Bucks R&D Trend." *San Francisco Chronicle,* June 14, C1, C16. These comparisons may be somewhat misleading. For example, oil companies appear to do little R&D because their value added as a fraction of sales is low. Oil companies appear more R&D-intensive if we compare R&D to value added or scientists to total employment.

TABLE 20.1 Estimated Percentage Increase in Imitation Cost Due to Patents For 33 New Products in the Chemical, Drug, Electronics, and Machinery Industries

Percent Increase in Imitation Cost	Number of Products	Percent of Cases Studied
Under 10%	13	39%
10-19%	10	30%
20–49%	4	12%
50–99%	0	0%
100–199%	3	9%
200% and more	3	9%
Total	33	100%

SOURCE: Mansfield (1984).

paper copier, other companies, upon seeing Xerox's success, were able to invent similar but not identical products. They were able to capture some of Xerox's plain paper copier business in spite of existing patents. During a 10-month period in 1974, 16 companies, including IBM, Kodak, 3M, Addressograph-Multigraph, Bell & Howell, GAF, Litton, and Pitney-Bowes, obtained 390 patents in the field of xerography (Scherer 1981, 292). In many cases, then, competitors can "invent around" a patent, lowering the patent's value to its inventor.[12]

A recent survey of high-level R&D managers in 129 lines of business finds that even for major new or improved products, many firms are capable of duplicating an innovation (Levin et al. 1987). In 2 percent of the cases, no firm is capable of duplication; however, in 25 percent of the cases, 1 or 2 firms are capable of duplicating; in 73 percent of the cases 3 to 5 firms are capable; in 25 percent, 6 to 10 firms; and in 4 percent, more than 10 firms. For a typical new product, the corresponding numbers are 1 percent, 5 percent, 33 percent, 63 percent, and 26 percent. That is, for a typical new product, in 89 percent of the cases, 6 or more firms can produce an imitation.

Work on copying innovations can start quickly. Information about R&D programs in manufacturing industries are in the hands of at least some rivals within a year to a year and one-half after the development decision is made (Mansfield 1985). Information spreads due to movements of employees between firms, formal and informal communications among engineers and scientists at various firms (especially at professional meetings), reports of input suppliers and customers, and reverse engineering of new products.

Even if the patent restrictions can be circumvented, patents increase the cost of imitation, as shown in Table 20.1. At the very least, they typically delay the time when imitators enter the market. Mansfield (1968) reports that in the United States, the time between the first use of a major innovation and the time when 60 percent of all related products have imitated the innovation can be as short as a month (ball-point pens: see Example 8.3) or a year (packaging beer in tin cans), or as long as several decades (by-

---

[12] To prevent entry by rivals, defensive *sleeping patents* may be obtained by the original inventor. These similar patents are not used but prevent others from patenting these similar products. See Gilbert and Newbery (1982) and the following discussion.

TABLE 20.2   Cost of Duplicating an Innovation as a Percentage of the Innovator's R&D Cost: Frequency Distribution of Median Responses

Type of innovation	Less Than 25%	26%-50%	51%-75%	76%-100%	More than 100%	Timely duplication not possible
Major new process						
Patented	1	5	19	66	26	10
Unpatented	5	10	55	49	6	2
Typical new process						
Patented	2	15	61	41	6	2
Unpatented	8	43	58	14	4	0
Major new product						
Patented	1	4	17	63	30	12
Unpatented	5	13	58	40	7	4
Typical new product						
Patented	2	18	64	32	9	2
Unpatented	9	58	40	15	5	0

NOTE: Each row adds to 127, reflecting the 127 lines of business surveyed.
SOURCE: Levin, Klevorick, Nelson, and Winter (1987, Table 8, 809).

product coke oven for steel mills and continuous annealing of tin-plated steel). Of 48 firms interviewed, the median estimate of the increase in the cost of imitation due to patents is 11 percent overall, 30 percent in ethical drugs (pharmaceutics without advertising directed at consumers), 10 percent in chemicals, and 7 percent in electronics and machinery (Mansfield et al. 1982).

The Levin, Klevorick, Nelson, and Winter (1987) survey finds similar results. They find, as shown in Table 20.2, that the cost of duplicating an innovation as a percentage of the innovator's cost was higher for patented than unpatented major or typical processes or products. They also find that on average it takes longer to duplicate a major new product if it is patented than if it is not.

As a result, even though obtaining a patent requires revealing information to potential imitators, many firms obtain patents. In 1987, General Electric Co. and its subsidiary RCA Corp. received 1283 patents (more than any other company in the world); Canon, 847; Hitachi Ltd, 845; and Toshiba Corp, 823.[13]

Patents Encourage Research

By imposing costs on potential imitators, patents can give market power to patent holders. The resulting monopoly profits can be a strong inducement to be the first to invent a new product.

A rational inventor engages in costly research up to the point where the expected marginal return from more research equals its marginal cost. If the inventor's return is less than society's, the inventor tends to underinvest in research. Patents may permit inventors to capture a large share of the benefits (internalize the externality) associated

---

[13] "Patent Report." 1988. *San Francisco Chronicle,* April 2, B20.

EXAMPLE 20.1

Do Patents Lead to More R&D?

Economic theory predicts that without patents or other incentives to engage in research and development there could be too little research, especially when imitation is rapid. A survey of 27 British companies in research-oriented industries suggests that the reduction in R&D if patents did not exist would be minor in some industries, but substantial in others.

The survey found that the percent of R&D expenditure that executives of the firms estimated was due to patents were:

Chemicals	
Pharmaceuticals	64%
Other finished and specialty	25
Basic	5
Mechanical Engineering	
Plant, machinery & equipment	7
Components and materials	2
Electrical Engineering	Negligible

Although these figures are subjective, they suggest that the importance of patents varies substantially across industries.

SOURCE: Taylor and Silberston (1973).

with the production of knowledge by insulating them from competition. By granting these exclusive rights through patents, society encourages more inventions in some industries, as shown in Example 20.1.

Patents may also encourage too much innovation (Hirshleifer 1971, Mansfield et al. 1977). For example, suppose an improved method of weather prediction is developed that allows accurate prediction of crop yields after all planting decisions have been made. The inventor can make a fortune speculating on future farm prices. Despite the profits from speculation, there may be little efficiency gain to society from the new forecasting technique.

Patents Encourage Disclosure

Some countries' patent laws encourage disclosure of new discoveries sooner than other countries' laws. To obtain a patent, an inventor must demonstrate that the invention is novel and nonobvious. By providing patent protection to inventors, society obtains two valuable results: greater incentives for additional research and development and an acceleration of innovation through disclosure of inventions.[14] Section 112 of the patent law states, "the specification shall contain a written description . . . in such full, clear, concise and exact terms as to enable any person skilled in the art . . . to make and use the same." Such disclosure can increase the pace of invention as one inventor builds on the work of another.

For example, the government has a "microbe zoo" in Rockville, Maryland, where $70 (or $40 for nonprofit organizations) buys virtually anyone with a college degree in science a vial of the same genetically altered cells that Genentech developed at a cost of $200 million to produce TPA, a clot-dissolving drug designed to prevent heart attacks.[15] The TPA-producing cells are just one of more than 8000 patented life forms at the American Type Culture Collection. For $560 a firm may make a deposit consisting of six vials of living materials. The fee covers 30 years of storage. By depositing here, a company partially meets the patent requirement to supply enough information to allow a skilled specialist to reproduce its invention. It has been estimated, however, that only 1 percent of recombinant DNA patents need a deposit today; the general scientific community has a good understanding of the technology, so that a written description is sufficient. For a $100 fee, a depositor obtains a list of all the people requesting a sample of its patented organism, which may be useful to check for patent infringement.

Some firms do not patent discoveries so that their competitors will not learn about them. Thus, to the degree that firms use the patent system, there is greater disclosure.

Competing firms often make similar discoveries at virtually the same time. In most countries except the United States and Canada, there is a *first-to-file* rule: the first applicant receives the patent. In the United States and Canada, a *first-to-invent* rule is used: the patent is issued to the first inventor, provided the date can be documented. In Japan, a Japanese firm, Sankyo, was granted a patent for a new anticholesterol drug, whereas an American firm, Merck, was granted the patent in the United States because of the difference in these rules. Sankyo's application predated Merck's in both countries, but Merck could document prior invention. There is a deterrent to disclosure under the first-to-invent rule because a firm is not in as much of a hurry to apply for a patent. So long as it can document when it achieved its discovery, a firm may wait until another firm applies for a patent to make its claim and disclose its discovery.

The novelty requirement greatly affects possible profits and the incentive to disclose. The more extreme the requirement that an innovation differ from previous ones, the harder it is to obtain a new patent, and the longer the owner of a current patent can earn monopolistic profits. As a result, the more stringent the novelty requirement, the greater the reward to a patent and hence the greater the incentive to engage in research. On the other hand, the less frequently patents are issued, the less disclosure there is, which tends to slow research by others. Thus, the stringency of a novelty rule affects the trade-off between rewards and incentives.[16]

---

[14] This section is based on Scotchmer and Green (1988).

[15] Russell, Sabin. 1988. "'Microbe Zoo' Stores Life Forms." *San Francisco Chronicle*, May 23, C1, C5.

[16] Scotchmer and Green (1988) show that a weaker novelty rule is better than a stronger rule in some markets, but they do not claim that their result holds in all markets. They argue, however, that first-to-file is better than first-to-invent in virtually all cases.

■ PATENTS, PRIZES, RESEARCH CONTRACTS, AND JOINT VENTURES

Most of the economic research on how to encourage inventive activity has centered on choosing the optimal patent system. But why should society only use patents? Why not use other incentives such as prizes and research contracts?[17] For example, the government could offer a cash **prize** to the first person who discovers a cure for AIDS, or it could give **research contracts** to firms or individual researchers to work on an AIDS cure. Alternatively, the government could relax antitrust prohibitions to allow firms to coordinate research activities through research **joint ventures**.

The following example illustrates how patents, prizes, research contracts, and joint ventures affect research effort; Appendix 20A has a corresponding mathematical analysis. Suppose there is an industry for research with the following properties:

- There are an unlimited number of identical firms that can each undertake one research project. The number of firms currently in the industry, and hence the number of projects undertaken, n, is shown in the first column of Table 20.3.

- Each research firm can conduct one research study at a constant marginal (and average) cost: $c = 1$. Thus, the total cost of research for n firms is $C(n) = nc = n$. Table 20.3 shows the per-firm (marginal) cost, c, in Column 2, and the industry (social) cost, $C(n)$ in Column 7.

- The more firms actively searching for a particular invention, the higher the probability that at least one of them will discover it. Thus, $\rho(n)$, the probability of success, is an increasing function of the number of firms, n, as shown in the fifth column of Table 20.3.

- If successful, the research will allow production of a new product at a constant marginal cost. If the present value of the potential benefit to society (the present value of the consumer surplus at the competitive price) from a successful invention is $B = \$25$, then the expected social benefit of having n firms race to make the discovery is $B\rho(n)$: the benefits times the probability of success, shown in Column 6 of Table 20.3.

- Research takes place in period $t = 0$. If the discovery is made in that period, society benefits in subsequent periods ($t = 1, 2, \ldots$). For simplicity, we assume that research does not take place in subsequent periods if the discovery is not made in the initial period.

The analysis begins by determining the optimal number of firms racing to be the first to make the discovery. Next, we suppose that the government has as much information as firms about all possible research projects and ask how many firms would race under five possible government incentive programs: no government incentives, government research programs, government prizes, legal joint ventures (research projects funded by two or more firms), and patents. Finally, we examine how the analysis changes if the government has less information than research firms have.

---

[17] The following comparison of prizes, research contracts, and patents is based in large part on Wright (1983).

TABLE 20.3	Costs and Benefits of Research Programs						
Number of Projects n	Marginal Cost c	Expected Marginal Social Benefit	Expected Payoff with a Prize = B	Probability of Success ρ(n)	Expected Social Benefit Bρ(n)	Social Cost C(n)	Net Social Benefit Bρ(n) − C(n)
1	1.00	4.14	4.60	0.18	4.60	1.00	3.60
2	1.00	3.38	4.17	0.33	8.35	2.00	6.35
3	1.00	2.76	3.80	0.46	11.41	3.00	8.41
4	1.00	2.25	3.48	0.56	13.91	4.00	9.91
5	1.00	1.84	3.19	0.64	15.94	5.00	10.94
6	1.00	1.50	2.93	0.70	17.61	6.00	11.61
7	1.00	1.23	2.71	0.76	18.97	7.00	11.97
8	**1.00**	**1.00**	**2.51**	**0.80**	**20.08**	**8.00**	**12.08**
9	1.00	0.82	2.33	0.84	20.98	9.00	11.98
10	1.00	0.67	2.17	0.87	21.72	10.00	11.72
11	1.00	0.54	2.03	0.89	22.32	11.00	11.32
12	1.00	0.44	1.90	0.91	22.81	12.00	10.81
13	1.00	0.36	1.79	0.93	23.22	13.00	10.22
14	1.00	0.30	1.68	0.94	23.54	14.00	9.54
15	1.00	0.24	1.59	0.95	23.81	15.00	8.81
16	1.00	0.20	1.50	0.96	24.03	16.00	8.03
17	1.00	0.16	1.42	0.97	24.21	17.00	7.21
18	1.00	0.13	1.35	0.97	24.35	18.00	6.35
19	1.00	0.11	1.29	0.98	24.47	19.00	5.47
20	1.00	0.09	1.23	0.98	24.57	20.00	4.57
21	1.00	0.07	1.17	0.99	24.65	21.00	3.65
22	1.00	0.06	1.12	0.99	24.71	22.00	2.71
23	1.00	0.05	1.08	0.99	24.77	23.00	1.77
24	1.00	0.04	1.03	0.99	24.81	24.00	0.81
24.84	1.00	0.03	1.00	0.99	24.84	24.84	0.00
25	1.00	0.03	0.99	0.99	24.84	25.00	−0.16

$c = 1$, per-firm cost of a research project.
$B = 25$, present value of the discovery.
$\alpha = 0.2031$.

$\rho(n) = (1 - e^{-\alpha n})$, probability
    of success with n projects.
Optimal prize = \$9.96.

Determining the Optimal Number of Firms

Society should choose the number of firms racing to make discoveries that maximizes expected *net social benefit,* which is the expected social benefit, $B\rho(n)$, minus the social cost, $C(n) = nc = n$. In our example, net social benefit is maximized at 8 firms, as shown in Table 20.3 (bold row) and Figure 20.1a.

Figure 20.1a shows that the social costs of a research program, $C(n) = n$, increases with the number of research programs. The expected social benefits, $B\rho(n)$, increase with n as well. Where there are few firms, adding one more firm substantially increases the probability of success. However, as more firms join the race, the probability of success approaches 1 (certainty), so that adding more firms to the race has little effect on expected

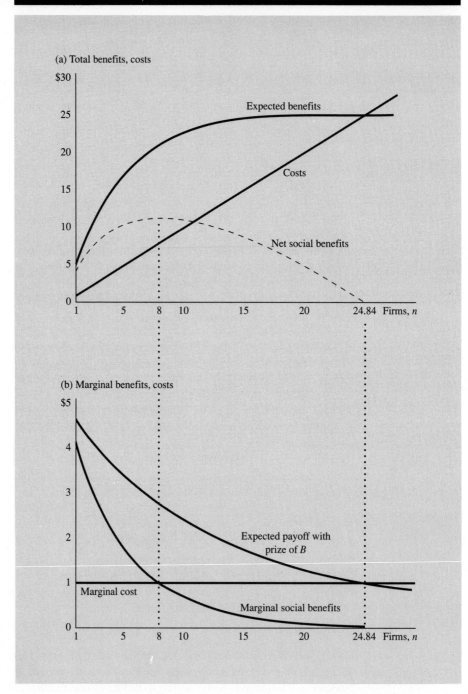

FIGURE 20.1 Costs, Expected Benefits, and Net Social Benefits from R&D

benefits. Thus, expected benefits first rise rapidly and then level off. A dashed line representing the expected net social benefit is shown in Figure 20.1a; it is identical to the gap between the expected benefits and costs. The gap between benefits and costs and the height of the net social benefits curve is maximized at 8 firms.

Another way to describe that result is to say that the marginal (social) cost equals the marginal social benefit at 8 firms (see Figure 20.1). The marginal social cost of one more research program is $c = 1$, which is the height of the marginal cost curve in Figure 20.1b and the slope of the cost curve in Figure 20.1a. The marginal benefit curve in Figure 20.1b equals the slope of the expected benefit curve in Figure 20.1a. The dotted line in Figure 20.1a at $n = 8$ shows where the gap between expected benefits and costs is greatest—where the slope of the benefit and cost curves are equal (in the example both slopes equal 1).

Suppose one more firm undertakes a research project. The expected benefit increases from 20.08 to 20.98 (see Table 20.3), but the marginal cost of that extra research project is 1, so net benefits fall by 0.1 ($= 1 - 0.9$), from 12.08 to 11.98.[18]

No Government Incentives

Is it progress if a cannibal uses knife and fork?—STANISLAW LEM

In the absence of patents and other incentives to invent, few, if any, inventions may be produced. Once a discovery is made, everyone can copy it, so a new product is sold at a competitive price, and the inventor makes no economic profits. If inventors bear the full private and social cost of research ($c = 1$) but receive no private financial benefits from their inventions, the profit-maximizing solution for inventors is to engage in no research.

Government-Financed Research

Twenty-two percent of new U.S. government R&D spending went to Star Wars in 1986.[19]

A government can encourage more research by subsidizing research costs. The U.S. government has, for example, given 20 percent tax credits for R&D expenditures. More directly, the government can pay firms to conduct research.

In the preceding example (Table 20.3) the government can ensure that the optimal number of research projects are undertaken by offering eight research contracts to the lowest bidders and retaining the rights to successful products. Competitive bidding drives the price to $c = 1$. Assuming that the firms engage in energetic research even though payments are independent of success, this approach leads to the optimal solution. Of course, the government can only pick the optimal number of firms if it knows the true

---

[18] In Table 20.3, the marginal benefit at $n = 8$ only approximately equals the difference between benefits at $n = 7$ and $n = 8$. The marginal benefits at 8 are defined as the derivative of $B\rho(n)$ with respect to n, which only approximately equals $B\rho(n + 1) - B\rho(n)$.

[19] Carroon and Black in *Space*, as cited in Lapham, Pollan, and Etheridge (1987).

EXAMPLE 20.2

JOINT PUBLIC-PRIVATE R&D

Many research projects at land-grant universities in the United States and other public institutions are jointly funded by the public and private sectors. One fear is that the private funding distorts research away from maximizing the public good to maximizing private returns.

A case study of Canadian malting barley, which is used in the production of beer, illustrates how sources of funding affect research. Public research costs are shared by Agriculture Canada, universities and associated research institutions, and the Canadian Grain Commission; private costs are borne by the Brewing and Malting Barley Research Institute. The private contribution was 28.3 percent of the total in 1951, but fell to 6.7 percent by 1981.

Research can improve the yield or quality of barley. Ulrich, Furtan, and Schmitz (1986) calculate the public (social) return and the private (industry) return. Their calculations show that the social rate of return would be at least 40 percent higher if only yield research were funded. The (relatively small) grants and liaison work from the private sector, however, are likely to keep public research institutes concentrating on a research path that produces both yield and quality improvements. The private sector's best strategy is to provide just enough funding to encourage the "right kind" of public funded research. They calculate that every $1 spent by the private sector costs the public sector $25.74 from distorted research that reduces social welfare.

Thus, the interaction between the public and private sectors can cause two problems. The problem that economists have traditionally worried about is that public investment in research displaces private investment. The private sector's share of R&D expenditures on barley has fallen substantially over time. A second problem is that relatively small private contributions may distort public research programs. At least with barley, the social loss from this distortion is large.

research costs and expected benefits. With adequate information, this approach is efficient if the research is funded efficiently (for example, the government raises the money through nondistorting taxes, such as lump-sum taxes).

Government-financed research is common in many countries. For example, expenditures by Commonwealth Departments and Authorities on research and development account for roughly half of total Australian expenditures (Tisdell 1974). Similarly, just less than half of all U.S. expenditures on R&D are paid for by the federal government.[20] Moreover, one-third of all U.S. R&D performed by industrial firms is paid for by the government.

A study of 25 major firms in chemical, oil, electrical equipment, and primary metals industries in the United States concludes that without government support these firms

---

[20] U.S. National Science Foundation. 1983. *Defense and Economy Major Factors in 7% Real Growth in National R&D Expenditures in 1984*. NSF 83-316. Washington, D.C.: U.S. Government Printing Office.

PRIZES

On a few occasions, prizes have been used to spur research. Two important examples are the development of the chronometer and the introduction of canning.

In 1713, prizes were offered in England to encourage the discovery of the measurement of longitude at sea. One of the important discoveries was that of Mayer who was able to accurately predict the moon's position, which allowed a calculation of a ship's longitude. For this discovery, Mayer's widow received £3000. Awards of £10,000, £15,000, and £20,000 were offered for a chronometer that measured longitude to within 60, 40, and 30 minutes respectively. In 1762, 49 years later, John Harrison claimed the £20,000 reward. Payment was completed in 1773. By 1815, £101,000 in prizes had been awarded.

In 1795, Napoleon's Society for the Encouragement of Industry offered a prize of 12,000 francs for a method of food preservation that could be employed by the military. Fifteen years later, in 1810, Nicolas Appert received the prize for his method of food canning that used heat treatment of food in sealed champagne bottles.

SOURCES: Wright (1983, 704) and Stigler (1986).

would have funded only between 3 percent and 20 percent of the energy R&D that they performed with government support (Mansfield 1984). A recent study of the entire private sector finds that federal R&D expenditures do not statistically significantly raise or lower private-sector expenditures (Lichtenberg 1987). Thus, the government can increase the total amount of research by offering government contracts because its funding does not reduce private research efforts by an equal amount (see, however, Example 20.2). A reduction in private research is even less likely if the government funds research that private industry would otherwise ignore.

Government Prizes

Prizes bring bad luck. Academic prizes, prizes for virtue, decorations, all these inventions of the devil encourage hypocrisy, and freeze the spontaneous upsurge of a free heart. —CHARLES BAUDELAIRE

The government, with little risk, can induce firms to engage in research by offering prizes for successful research because if no one makes the discovery, the government has no cost. Even if anyone can copy the discovery once the prize is awarded, a large enough prize can induce firms and inventors to undertake research (see Example 20.3). If the government sets the prize properly, the optimal number of firms race to win it; setting a higher prize, however, stimulates excessive research.

Optimal Prize. A firm undertakes a research project in an attempt to win a prize if its expected winnings are at least as great as its costs.[21] The number of firms racing to win the prize is determined by the size of the prize. To induce the optimal number of firms, n^*, to compete for a prize, the government must set the prize so that if n^* firms race to be first, each firm's expected earnings equal its research costs.

The probability that at least one firm makes the discovery is $\rho(n)$.[22] If each of the n firms believes it has an equal chance of winning, then its expected gain is $\rho(n)/n$ times the prize. From the preceding analysis, we know that at the optimal number of firms, n^* = 8, the cost of a research project, c = 1, exactly equals the expected marginal social benefit of having n^* firms race to make the discovery. The optimal prize, then, is determined by dividing the expected marginal social benefit at n^* = 8, which is 1, by a firm's probability of winning, $\rho(8)/8$. That is, using the numbers shown in Table 20.3, the optimal prize is $9.96 = \$1/(.80304/8)$.[23]

With this prize, each firm's expected winnings are the same as the expected marginal social benefits shown in Table 20.3. With n = 8, each firm's expected winnings are $1.00, which equals its costs. A ninth firm considering joining the race calculates that its expected winnings are $0.93, or less than its cost of $1.00, and decides that it is not worth joining the race. As a result, only the optimal number of firms, 8, compete for the prize. Net social benefit is maximized at $12.08. So long as the government has the necessary information to set the prize optimally, and so long as the prize is financed without distortions, prizes can efficiently induce innovation.

Too High a Prize and the Common-Pool Problem. It might appear reasonable to set the prize equal to the social value of the discovery, B = $25, rather than $9.96. That prize is so high, however, that too much research is undertaken. As Edward Abbey is reputed to have said, "Growth for the sake of growth is the ideology of the cancer cell."

The *Expected Payoff with a Prize = B* column in Table 20.3 shows a firm's expected benefit from engaging in research if the prize is $25. If 24 firms engage in research, the probability, $\rho(24)$, that at least one will be successful is 99.24 percent, so the probability that a particular firm wins the prize is $0.9924/24$ = 4.13 percent. As a result, each firm's expected prize is $25 times 4.13 percent, or $1.03, as shown in Table 20.3. With 25 firms competing, each firm's expected earnings are $0.99 (less than the cost of a research project). Thus, if there can only be a whole number of firms racing for the prize, 24 firms compete.

That much research is excessive because the competition dissipates almost all of the rents from research. Table 20.3 shows that the net social benefit when n = 24 is $0.81: the social cost of the research nearly equals the expected benefits. This problem is analogous to the fishing, or *common-pool*, problem in Chapter 6. Each firm considers its private

---

[21] For simplicity, this example assumes that firms are risk-neutral and are willing to take a fair bet. That is, they participate in a gamble if their expected winnings equal their expected costs.

[22] If there is a tie, the prize is either split equally or awarded randomly to one of the successful firms.

[23] The prize equals $B\rho'(n^*)/[\rho(n^*)/n^*]$, where $B\rho'(n^*)$ is the expected marginal social benefit from having n^* compete, and $\rho(n^*)/n^*$ is the probability that one of the n^* firms will be the first to make the discovery (see Appendix 20A).

return rather than the social return when deciding whether to undertake research. If there can be a fractional number of research projects, 24.84 projects are undertaken, and net social benefits are completely dissipated. Figure 20.1b shows the expected returns from each research project, which are equal to the marginal cost, $1.00, when there are 24.84 projects. In contrast, the expected marginal benefit to society from having the last project is only about 3¢, as shown in Table 20.2.

To summarize, when the prize is set at $9.96, only 8 firms compete, and the probability that at least one will make the discovery is only 80 percent. When the prize is set at $25, 24 firms compete and the probability rises to 99 percent. Increasing the probability by these extra 19 percentage points, however, requires that the social cost of the research rise from $8 to $24, or 300 percent. Thus, raising the probability by 19 percent does not pay. With a prize of $9.96, net social benefit is maximized at $12.08, whereas with a prize of $25, net social benefits are essentially eliminated.

Relaxing Antitrust Laws: Joint Ventures

The reason why there is too little research without additional incentives such as prizes and government research contracts is that there is an externality if an inventor cannot capture the full value of a new discovery. In the absence of patent laws, each firm interested in producing a new product prefers to copy the discovery of another firm that paid to develop the new product. As a result, each firm may wait for others to bear the cost, and little research is undertaken.

If all the firms in an industry, however, agree to share the cost of development in a research joint venture, this externality problem can be avoided. Firms may fear, however, that such joint research activity may lead to antitrust prosecutions. When the firms meet to agree on funding the research and sharing existing knowledge, the government may suspect that they also conspire to set the price for the new product at the monopoly level. Many policy makers and economists (Ordover and Willig 1985, Grossman and Shapiro 1986) argue that antitrust laws and polices should be changed to encourage joint research activities (but not joint price setting).

It is unclear, in the preceding example, whether a joint venture finances the optimal number of research projects. On the one hand, a joint venture may be able to avoid needless duplication of research projects, and hence its costs of research may be lower than when there is competition. On the other hand, if the joint venture cannot capture the full expected social value, $B\rho(n)$, the joint venture undertakes too little research, because it bears the full social cost.[24] Except for a discriminating monopolist, joint ventures typically capture less than the full social value of a new product, which includes consumer surplus. Moreover, in an industry where research can be easily copied by firms outside the joint venture, the joint venture may capture little of the social value of a discovery. Joint ventures are unlikely to generate substantial research in such markets.

---

[24] If the firms currently in the industry can obtain patent protection for a discovery they jointly finance, they can make it more difficult for other firms to enter the industry. This barrier to entry stems from the patent and not from the joint venture. Without such patent protection, however, firms are less likely to undertake joint ventures, because new entrants can profit from their discoveries.

EXAMPLE 20.4	# A PATENT MONOPOLY

The Bell System monopoly was based on patents. The original Bell patents were filed in 1876 and 1877 and were offered to Western Union for $100,000. Although the telegraph company turned down this offer, it later acquired other telephone patents of Amos Dolbear, Thomas A. Edison, and Elisha Gray. A 4–3 Supreme Court decision awarded the basic patent right of the telephone to the Bell interests in 1876. Western Union, in later negotiations, acknowledged the validity of the Bell patent, licensed Bell its own Gray patents, withdrew from the telephone industry and promised not to reenter, and agreed to pay 20 percent of the costs of Bell's new patents developed or acquired by the Bell interests. In return, Bell agreed to stay out of the telegraph industry and to reimburse Western Union for royalties on Bell patents.

Upon securing its patents, Bell filed over 600 patent suits against competing companies and individuals, including 200 alone against the American Cushman Telephone Company. As a result, most of these firms left the business. It was not until 1894, when the original telephone patent expired that independent companies started entering the industry.

Meanwhile, Bell developed more patents so that by the 1930s, it had acquired or developed some 9000 patents, had filed 1200 patents, and had licensed 6000 others. These patents gave Bell a virtual monopoly in the technology of long distance transmission for years.

SOURCE: Irwin (1971).

Joint ventures in technological fields, where R&D costs are high, are becoming increasingly common in the United States (see Example 16.1 on biotech joint ventures). Under the National Cooperative Research Act, 111 cooperative endeavors were registered between January 1985 and June 1988 (Jorde and Teece 1988). Joint ventures are much more common in Japan and Europe.

Patents

Patents, which grant exclusive rights to successful inventors, also induce research. Unlike prizes or government research contracts, however, patents lead to distortions due to monopoly pricing. Thus, they are less efficient than optimal prizes or research contracts if the government has sufficient information to induce the optimal amount of research. There are reasons to use patents, however, because the government typically has limited information. In any case, patents are an extremely common method of inducing research throughout the world. For example, the Soviet Union, which one might expect to rely on government-directed research, issues one and one-half times as many patents as the United States.[25] An important U.S. example of an industry affected by patents is discussed in Example 20.4.

---

[25] Boyd, L. M. 1988. "The Grab Bag." *San Francisco Examiner*, July 24, "This World" section, 7.

Value of a Patent.   Suppose that the first successful firm receives a patent granting exclusive rights to sell the product. Does this reward of monopoly profits induce the optimal number of firms to conduct research? To determine how many firms engage in a **patent race** to be the first to make the discovery and be granted the patent, one needs to find out how much the patent is worth.

Continuing to use the same example, we add four (consistent) assumptions to calculate the value of the patent:

1. The demand in each period for the new product is linear:

$$p = 6 - 5Q, \qquad\qquad (20.1)$$

where p is the price and Q is the number of units sold.

2. The marginal (and average) cost of production is 1.
3. If two firms make a discovery simultaneously, they split the patent rights.[26]
4. The interest rate is 10 percent.

A firm that obtains exclusive rights under a patent acts like a monopolist and maximizes its profits by setting marginal revenue equal to marginal cost. In the example, the monopolist charges price p_m = $3.50, sells q_m = 0.5 units and makes annual profits of π_m = $1.25. With monopoly pricing, the annual consumer surplus is $0.625, which is one-fourth the consumer surplus of a competitive industry. These calculations show how much monopoly rights to sell the new good are worth per year. How much the patent is worth over time depends on how long it lasts. We consider two cases: a patent that lasts forever and one that lasts for only a few years.

Permanent Patent.   If a patent lasts forever, the patent holder earns monopoly profits forever. These large potential rewards may induce many firms to race to win the patent, resulting in excessive research effort.[27] As Tom Stoppard said, "Eternity is a terrible thought. I mean, where's it going to end?"

If the patent lasts forever, and the interest rate r = 10 percent, the present value of the patent is π_m/r = $12.50. That is, the present value of a stream of monopoly profits of $1.25 every year forever is $12.50. If you put $12.50 in a bank account that paid 10 percent interest, you would receive $1.25 in interest each year. The present value of a

---

[26] With modern, complex discoveries, expensive court fights over patent rights are frequent. Recent disputes include Hoffmann-La Roche vs. Burroughs Wellcome over alpha interferon (cancer treatment); Amgen vs. Genetics Institute, Chgai, and Integrated Genetics over EPO (anemia treatment); Scripps & Revlon vs. Genentech over Factor VIII (blood-clotter); Genentech vs. Eli Lilly over human growth hormone (dwarfism treatment); and Genentech vs. Wellcome Foundation over TPA (heart-attack treatment). Lehrman, Sally. 1988. "The Patent Game Muscles Up." *San Francisco Examiner,"* September 18, D1.

[27] There is a large literature on patent races. Early articles include Usher (1964) and Barzel (1968). A later literature—Loury (1979), Dasgupta and Stiglitz (1980), Lee and Wilde (1980), Reinganum (1982)—which is surveyed in Reinganum (1984), investigates *poisson* patent races, in which the probability that a firm makes a discovery first depends only on its current R&D expenditures and not on its experience to date. An even more recent literature, where experience matters, is discussed later in this chapter.

TABLE 20.4 Optimal Patent Length

Length of Patent, t	Fractional Firms Possible			Fractional Firms Impossible	
	Number of Projects, n	Net Social Benefit		Number of Projects, n	Net Social Benefit
5.35	0.50	$1.66		0.	$0.00
5.71	1.00	3.10		1.00	3.20
6.53	2.00	5.35		2.00	5.35
7.47	3.00	6.91		3.00	6.91
8.56	4.00	7.91		4.00	7.91
9.00	4.35	8.14		4.00	7.84
9.87	5.00	8.44		5.00	8.44
10.00	5.09	8.47		5.00	8.42
11.00	5.74	8.60		5.00	8.29
11.4405	**6.00**	**8.608906**		**6.00**	**8.60891**
11.4475	**6.004**	**8.608908**		**6.00**	**8.60793**
12.00	6.31	8.59		6.00	8.53
13.00	6.82	8.51		6.00	8.41
13.40	7.00	8.47		7.00	8.47
14.00	7.26	8.39		7.00	8.39
15.94	**8.00**	**8.08**		**8.00**	**8.08**
19.51	9.00	7.48		9.00	7.48
25.36	10.00	6.72		10.00	6.72

permanent patent, in our example, is 50 percent ($= \$12.50/\$25$) of the net social value of the invention if the product were sold at competitive prices.

Each firm has an equal chance of obtaining the patent, so the expected return to a firm undertaking research is $12.50 times the probability that it makes the discovery first, $\rho(n)/n$. A firm joins the patent race so long as its research costs, $c = 1$, are less than its expected benefits from winning the race.

In the example, 11.22 research projects are undertaken given permanent patent rights (see Appendix 20.A) if fractional projects are possible, or 11 if fractional projects are impossible. Thus, in the example, a permanent patent leads to excessive research: 40 percent more research projects than the optimal number, 8.[28]

Finite Patent Length. By having patents last shorter periods of time, t, the government can reduce the incentive for excessive research. Having exclusive rights for only t years reduces the present value of the flow of monopoly profits; thus the expected private benefit to each firm is lower, so fewer firms engage in research.

Unlike a prize or a research contract, a patent causes a pricing distortion after a discovery. That is, the price set at the monopoly level is too high. The government is faced with a trade-off: the longer the patent, the greater the inducement for research but

---

[28] This result stems, in part, from the particular probability function used in the example: $\rho(n) = 1 - e^{-\alpha n}$, where $\alpha = .2031$. If we choose $\alpha = 0.1342$, the optimal number of projects is 9, but a permanent patent leads to 8.51 projects, which is fewer than the optimal number.

FIGURE 20.2   Net Social Benefit Varies with Patent Length

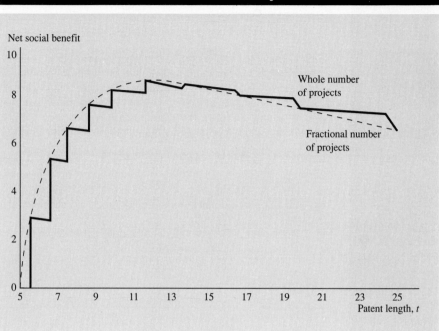

the larger the cost due to more research projects and the monopoly loss. Given that the government uses patents, then, it should choose the length, t, to maximize expected net social benefit, taking into account monopoly pricing. Table 20.4 and Figure 20.2 show the net social benefits corresponding to various patent lengths, t.[29] Both show the number of projects and associated net social benefits if fractional numbers of projects are possible and if only whole numbers of projects are possible.

As shown in Table 20.4, if fractional numbers of projects are possible, net social benefit is maximized when $t = 11.4475$, there are $n = 6.004$ projects, and net social benefit $= \$8.608908$. If there can only be whole numbers of projects, the best solution is $t = 11.4405$, $n = 6$, and net social benefit $= \$8.608906$. If t is set at 15.94, there are 8 projects, and net social benefit is $8.08.

Because of the distortions associated with patents, society only wants approximately 6 projects rather than the 8 desired with prizes or research contracts. To get 8 projects rather than 6 using patents, the length of time for the grant of exclusive rights must be increased 39 percent from 11.44 to 15.94. An increase in the number of projects from 6 to 8 only increases the probability of success from 70 percent to 80 percent (Table 20.3),

---

[29] We assume that the patent holder does not price discriminate. See, however, Hausman and MacKie-Mason (1988), who discuss the social desirability of price discrimination by patent holders and the effect of such discrimination on the optimal length of a patent.

EXAMPLE 20.5

EUROPEAN PATENTS

In many countries, patent-holders must pay an annual renewal fee to maintain their monopoly rights under the patent. A firm only renews a patent if the expected returns to one more year of exclusive rights exceed the cost of renewing. By examining the data from France and Germany, Pakes (1986) estimates the distribution of the value of holding patents and how this distribution changes over the lifetime of a patent. This information tells us the value to patent-holders of the proprietary rights created by the patent.

There is no renewal fee in France until a patent is 2 years old, 3 years old in Germany, or 5 years old in the U.K. A patent can only be renewed until it is 16 years old in the U.K., 18 in Germany, and 20 in France. Renewal fees are relatively low in all three countries in the early years, but increase significantly faster in Germany in later years.

The estimated average returns on a patent, based on renewal data, for France and Germany for the first five years are:

Year	France	Germany
1	$ 380	$1609
2	1415	3401
3	1432	3225
4	1339	2899
5	1193	2641

which does not fully offset the additional costs. The net social benefit falls 6.2 percent, from $8.61 to $8.08 (Table 20.4).

Patents last 17 years in the United States. Setting a fixed length for a patent for all types of products probably means that monopoly power is granted for too long a period for some types of products and too short a time for others.[30] To partially compensate for this problem, the Drug Price Competition and Patent Term Restoration Act of 1984 extends patent lives of pharmaceuticals to offset the delays in introducing new drugs as a result of regulatory requirements. However, where the pace of invention is rapid, the length of a patent may be irrelevant because new products eliminate the demand for older ones, even though the latter still have patent protection. In many European countries, patent lengths vary because patent-holders must pay annual fees to maintain their monopoly rights under patents (Example 20.5).

---

[30] Nordhaus (1969), however, argues that 17 years is close to optimal for many industries. Compare DeBrock (1985) and Dasgupta and Stiglitz (1980).

In France, the mean initial return to a patent is $380. In that year, one-fifth of the French patent-holders discover a use for the patent, allowing them to increase subsequent returns. Over 6 percent find that their patented ideas cannot be profitably exploited, so they do not pay the renewal fee in the second year. The rest renew, maintaining the option of patent protection while continuing to look for profitable uses. The average return on remaining patents rises to $1415. The next year, another 9 percent fail to renew, and the average return increases to $1432. Learning about profitable uses of the patent decreases over time, so that by the fifth year, virtually no more learning takes place, and obsolescence starts dominating learning. The average return on remaining patents falls to $1193.

In contrast, the average initial value of German patents, $1608, is much higher than French patents. One reason may be that 93 percent of French applicants are granted patents, whereas only 35 percent of German applicants are granted patents. As a result, fewer Germans bother to apply for patents of questionable value. A second factor is that the French data contain all applicants, but the German data include only successful ones. The average value of German patents is $3401 in the second year, $3225 in the third, $2899 in the fourth, and $2641 in the fifth.

These results show that most patents have very low initial value. Indeed, most patent-holders do not find a use for their patents within the first few years, and hence do not renew the patent. Of those who do find a use for a patent, they find it within the first couple of years, before the discovery becomes obsolete. The average annual return from holding a patent was 15.56 percent of the R&D expenditures in France and 13.83 percent in Germany, in 1963.

Government Uncertainty

The example in Tables 20.3 and 20.4 demonstrates that if the government has as much information as research firms, it can set prizes or research contracts so as to induce the optimal level of research, maximizing net social benefit. When the government has full information, patents and joint ventures are less desirable than prizes or research contracts because they distort pricing. With prizes or research grants, after the discovery is made, the new product is sold at competitive prices, and consumer surplus is maximized.[31] For the life of a patent, a new product is sold at a monopolistic price, which leads to too few sales. However, if inventors have more information before they start inventing than do government officials, as seems likely, then patents and joint ventures may be superior.

Suppose the government sets a prize, research contract, or patent length before the value of an invention is known. If the researcher believes correctly that the invention is

---

[31] If government-financed research is patented, however, this advantage is lost. Such patenting occurs in Australia (Tisdell 1974).

worth more than the value the government has set, then the patent may induce more research than the prize or government contract. Of course, if the length of the patent is very short, then prizes or research contracts, even if set too low, may be superior.[32]

In general, it is difficult for anyone, even the potential inventor, to predict the value of an invention beforehand. Indeed, even after it is invented, its value may be quite uncertain because demand is hard to predict or because of legal uncertainties about the ownership of the patent. For example, the inventor of the shoe-lace made $2.5 million on his patent, whereas the inventor of the safety pin earned only $400.[33] Indeed it is estimated that less than 1 out of every 50 patent-holders makes money from it.[34]

Patent-Holders May Manufacture or License

A patent gives the inventor the monopoly on an idea for a fixed period of time. The patent-holder may produce the product or **license** (permit) others to produce it in exchange for a payment called a **royalty**. We will now show that a profit-maximizing inventor is indifferent between being the only seller of the product and licensing others to produce and sell it, so long as the product market was competitive prior to the invention.[35]

Suppose a market was originally competitive and all firms produced at constant (marginal and average) cost c.[36] The competitive price of the good was c, and Q units were sold. Now suppose someone develops a new process that allows the same good to be produced at a lower cost, $\underline{c}$, as shown in Figure 20.3a.

If the firm that owns the new patent decides to sell the product itself, it is essentially a low-cost dominant firm that faces a competitive fringe (see Chapter 8). The lowest price it considers charging is $\underline{c}$: any lower price leads to losses. The highest price it can charge is c: any higher price allows the fringe to undercut its price. Suppose that it is optimal for the dominant firm to charge just slightly less than c to prevent the fringe from making any sales. The profits from the invention are the difference between the old cost and the new cost times the number of units sold. This amount is labeled *Royalties* in Figure 20.3a.

Now suppose the firm considers licensing other firms to use the new technology. The firm charges a royalty per unit of output sold by the other firms *(royalty rate)*. For example, in 1988, IBM announced that it would charge 1 percent on sales of computers based on its PS/2 line that used an IBM patent, and up to 5 percent on products employing more than one patent.[37] Licensing arrangements are often very complex, especially if firms

---

[32] In a sophisticated analysis, Brian Wright (1983) identifies the conditions under which patents, prizes, or research contracts are likely to be best in a world of uncertainty. Patents are likely to be best when the probability of success is low and the elasticity of supply of research is relatively high.

[33] Boyd, L. M. 1988. "The Grab Bag." *San Francisco Examiner*, March 27, "This World" section, 7.

[34] Ibid. 1987. September 6, "Sunday Punch" section, 7.

[35] This section focuses on only a small aspect of licensing. Gallini (1984), Gallini and Winter (1985), and Katz and Shapiro (1985, 1986) discuss these and other important issues. For example, Gallini (1984) and Gallini and Winter (1985) note that, under certain circumstances, licensing may reduce inefficient R&D expenditures.

[36] This graphic presentation follows Arrow (1962), McGee (1966), Nordhaus (1969), and Dasgupta and Stiglitz (1980). This presentation is very similar to the low-cost dominant firm analysis in Chapter 8.

FIGURE 20.3   License Royalties

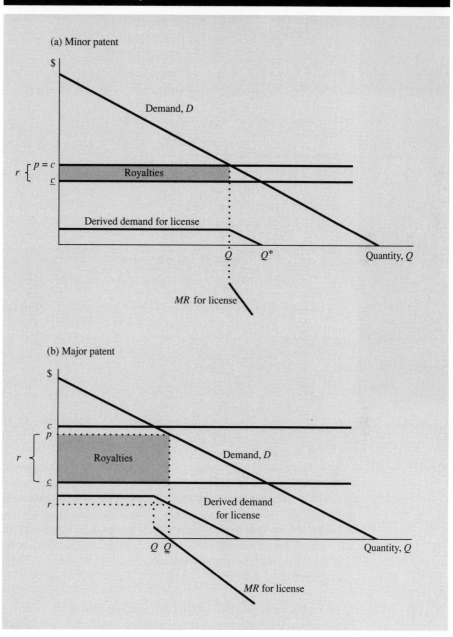

EXAMPLE 20.6

INTERNATIONAL LICENSES

Today, international technology trade in patents and know-how is widespread. The primary methods for transferring new and improved products and production methods between countries include the use of subsidiaries or joint ventures with local partners, licensing or sales of patents and other intellectual property, and the sale of machinery and equipment or the supply of *turn-key* plants (plants that include all the equipment and instructions necessary to start producing at once).

The major sources of supply of new technology are the United States, the United Kingdom, France, Germany, and Japan, who supply 85 percent of the transactions. The United States supplies between 50 and 75 percent of technology for most importing countries. Most countries—except the United States, the United Kingdom, Sweden, and Switzerland—are net importers of technology. In 1983, the United States had net receipts from the sale of technology of $7.3 billion, the United Kingdom, $201 million, and Sweden, $45 million. Countries with negative net balances include Spain with $489 million; Germany, $457 million; Italy, $452 million; Belgium/Luxembourg, $190 million; and Japan, $162 million.

International payments for patents, licenses, and know-how were worth at least $11 billion in 1982 and $12 billion in 1983. In constant terms, the payments have increased by 2 percent per year between 1975 and 1983. The sales of licensed products manufactured overseas equal approximately 5 to 10 percent of sales from foreign direct investment.

SOURCE: Vickery (1986).

cross-license each others' patents; more than 100 companies now license from or partially cross-license with IBM.[38]

What royalty rate maximizes the firm's profits? To answer this question, we must determine the derived demand for a patent license: the maximum price a producer is willing to pay for a license. Figure 20.3a shows an example for a run-of-the-mill or minor invention that only slightly reduces the cost of production. The derived demand for licenses is the difference between the residual demand curve facing the patent-holder and the cost of producing under the new process, $\underline{c}$. That is, the maximum royalty a competitive firm will pay for a license is the difference between the competitive price and the cost under the patented process. Thus, for the first Q units (the amount sold by a competitive industry), the competitive price is c, so the maximum royalty is $c - \underline{c}$, which is labeled the *derived demand for license* in Figure 20.3a. If more units are sold, the value of the license drops,

---

[37] Reuters. 1988. "IBM to Seek Better Terms on Patent Licenses." *San Francisco Chronicle*, April 9, B2.

[38] Cringely, Robert X. 1988. "Notes from the Field." *InfoWorld*, November 28, 94.

so the derived demand falls. Indeed, at Q^*, the value of a license is zero, since the competitive price equals the cost of production under the new process.

The profit-maximizing royalty occurs where the marginal revenue *(MR)* from selling one more license equals the marginal cost of a license. The marginal cost of a license is zero. Thus, the profit-maximizing royalty is determined by the intersection of the marginal revenue curve for a license with the quantity axis. In the case shown, that occurs at quantity Q and a royalty rate $r = c - \underline{c} = p - \underline{c}$. That is, the profit-maximizing royalty is the *total* per unit savings from using the new process. This amount equals the earnings if the firm did not license the product, but sold it itself.

Figure 20.3b uses the same types of curves to examine the case of a major new process that produces a dramatic fall in costs. Here, the marginal revenue for the derived demand for licenses equals zero at $\underline{Q}$. The profit-maximizing price, p, lies between c and $\underline{c}$. As a result, the royalty rate ($r = p - \underline{c}$) is less than the cost reduction ($c - \underline{c}$), but $\underline{Q} > Q$ licenses are sold.

There are two results of this analysis. First, if the inventor can produce as efficiently as others, the inventor is indifferent between selling the product and licensing it because the competitive fringe restricts the monopolist equally in both cases. Licensing is likely when licensees have lower manufacturing costs than the inventor. As Example 20.6 shows, licensing provides an important mechanism through which new discoveries can be implemented throughout the world.

Second, the inventor captures all the gains of minor discoveries, but not of major discoveries. With minor discoveries, consumers continue to buy the same quantity at the same price, so they are unaffected by the discovery. With major discoveries, price falls and quantity rises so that consumer surplus rises. So with major discoveries, the inventor's gain is less than the total social gain.

■ MARKET STRUCTURE

The incentives to conduct research, the timing of innovations, and the nature of patent races are all determined by the market structures in the product and research industries. Joseph Schumpeter (1950) initiated modern research about the effects of market structure on innovation by stressing the role of economic agents in technological progress. In the Schumpeterian view, there is a positive relationship between innovation and market power, and large firms are more innovative than small firms (see Example 20.7).[39]

The Schumpeterian argument is that innovation is more important than price competition because it is a more effective means of gaining an advantage over competitors. Two connections exist between market structure and innovation. First, patents allow one to gain market power by innovating. Second, a firm with market power may be able to prevent entry and imitation through defensive patents, or maintain its power through the introduction of new products. If it is difficult to raise money for R&D, a monopoly may be better able than new firms to finance research for these new products because of its monopoly profits.

---

[39] See Schumpeter (1950), Galbraith (1952), Nelson and Winter (1982), and Kamien and Schwartz (1982).

EXAMPLE 20.7

SIZE AND INNOVATION

Recently, a number of policy makers have argued that we should relax the antitrust laws to allow firms to grow larger and innovate more. Their argument assumes that larger firms make more innovations and that the return to these innovations exceeds the loss from greater market power. It is worth checking, then, whether large firms disproportionately innovate.

Joseph A. Schumpeter (1950) started this debate by contending that large corporations with monopoly power were likely to advance industrial technology because of superior access to capital, ability to pool risks, and economies of scale in the maintenance of R&D laboratories. Critics argue that large bureaucracies stultify R&D.

According to Scherer (1984, Ch. 11), Gelman Research Associates' large data base of major innovations indicates that small firms are relatively more likely to make major innovations. Companies with fewer than 1000 employees are responsible for 47.3 percent of important innovations, a share greater than their 41.2 percent of total employment. Companies with over 10,000 employees are responsible for 34.5 percent of the innovation, but 36 percent of total employment. Thus, large firms innovate in proportion to size, small firms innovate out of proportion, and medium-sized firms do relatively little innovating.

Also according to Scherer (1984, Ch. 11), in another sample of major innovations reported in *Industrial Research & Development,* 72 percent of the major innovations came from U.S. profit-seeking firms, 12.9 percent from government laboratories, 10.7 percent from foreign corporations, 2.4 percent from academic institutions, and 2.3 percent from other nonprofit organizations. Large firms in the Federal Trade Commission's (FTC) line-of-business survey account for 73 percent of both company-financed

---

The two key questions considered in the remainder of this section are (1) Does a competitive or a monopolistic firm have a greater incentive to invent? (2) Which type of firm innovates faster?

The analysis first demonstrates that if firms do not have to worry about others inventing the product first, a competitive firm has a greater incentive to invent than a monopolistic firm. Then it finds that a competitive firm sometimes innovates too quickly, and certainly more quickly than a monopolistic firm. Finally, it shows that a monopolistic firm that must worry about a potential rival entering its market by inventing has an incentive to innovate to prevent entry. This threat of competition gives the monopolistic firm a greater incentive to invent than a competitive firm. Thus, which type of firm has a greater incentive to invent depends on whether a patent race is possible.

Market Structure Without a Patent Race

Suppose that one firm, which is uniquely suited to innovate, believes that if it does not invent a new process, no other firm will. In this case, a competitive firm is likely to have

and federal contract industrial R&D expenditures, 55–60 percent of manufacturing sales, and 55 percent of the major innovations. Again, there is no strong evidence that size leads to more innovation, at least in the United States. The large firms in the FTC data account for only 61 percent of all patented inventions, a lesser percent than their 73 percent share of the R&D expenditures.

Cohen, Levin, and Mowery (1987) find, using a statistical analysis of the FTC's line-of-business data, that business-unit size has no effect on the R&D intensity (R&D as a percent of sales) of firms conducting R&D but does affect the probability of engaging in R&D. Moreover, business-unit and firm size collectively explain less than 1 percent of the variance in R&D intensity, in contrast to industry effects, which explain nearly half the variance.

Bound, Cummins, Griliches, Hall, and Jaffe (1984) find, using sophisticated statistical techniques to control for the underreporting of R&D, that R&D expenditures increased with sales and gross plant size in 1976. At the sample mean, a 1 percent increase in sales causes a 0.7 percent increase in R&D. The impact of size is nonlinear, however, so that very small and very large firms are more R&D intensive than average-sized firms. Small firms that do research tend to patent more per R&D dollar than larger firms, and firms with large R&D programs tend to have a constant ratio of patenting to R&D. Jensen (1987) finds that there are no advantages or disadvantages to locating a given R&D program in a larger firm in the pharmaceutical industry. Thus, these studies do not confirm the Schumpeter hypothesis for the United States. See, however, Example 20.10.

a greater incentive to invent a cost-saving process than does a monopolistic firm. The basic intuition is that the competitive firm earns profits from its new process over more units than does a monopolistic firm (Arrow 1962).

Let us stick to the minor cost-reducing inventions discussed in the preceding section. We assume that a royalty fee is collected from each firm that produces the product in the final goods market, and consider two contrasting market structures. In one, the inventing firm is part of a competitive industry; in the other, the inventing firm monopolizes the product market, and barriers to entry prevent future competition.

If the product market is competitive, and the competitive price before invention is c, after invention, the price is $\underline{c} + r$, where r is the per-unit royalty rate, as shown in Figure 20.4. For a minor innovation, the new price, $\underline{c} + r$, equals c, as discussed above. Thus the competitive price and quantity, Q, are the same before and after the invention. In contrast, a monopolist sets marginal revenue equal to marginal cost. Figure 20.4 shows the original price, p_m, corresponding to the original cost c, and the new price $\underline{p}_m$ corresponding to cost $\underline{c}$. The corresponding quantities are Q_m and $\underline{Q}_m$.

The monopolist earns more on the original Q_m units and makes a profit on the extra

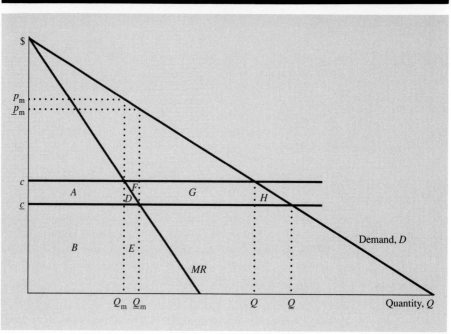

FIGURE 20.4   Gains to Discoveries Vary with Market Structure

$Q_m - Q_m$ units, so its profits must rise. Its original costs were cQ_m = areas $A + B$. After the discovery, its costs are $\underline{c}\,\underline{Q}_m$ = areas $B + E$. Thus, the change in its costs is $(A + B) - (B + E) = A - E$. Its revenues increase by the area under the marginal revenue curve between Q_m and $\underline{Q}_m$, or areas $D + E$. Thus, its profits rise by $(D + E) + (A - E) = D + A$.

This diagram shows that a monopolist gains less from the invention than an inventor in a competitive industry. The optimal royalty level for the inventor in the competitive market is $r = c - \underline{c}$. Thus, in a competitive market, the inventor earns $rQ = (c - \underline{c})Q$ = areas $A + D + F + G$ in Figure 20.4. In other words, the gain to the inventor in the competitive industry is $F + G$ more than the gain to the monopolist. Indeed, on just the first Q_m units, the competitive inventor earns $A + D + F$, whereas the monopolist only earns $A + D$. The royalties on the $Q - Q_m$ extra units sold in a competitive industry are "gravy." Thus, in this example, a product-market monopolist has less of an incentive to conduct research than a competitive industry.

Even the return to the competitive industry, however, is less than the full social benefit, $A + D + F + G + H$, the area bounded by the lines at c, $\underline{c}$, and the demand curve. Thus, society has a greater incentive for research than a competitive industry, which in turn has a greater incentive than a product-market monopolist.

It is important to stress that these results hold *only* where a firm does not fear a patent race. Where other firms may beat your firm to a new invention, your firm has a greater incentive to invent first.

Optimal Timing of Innovations

Things have never been more like the way they are today in history.
—DWIGHT DAVID EISENHOWER

Because only the first firm to produce an innovation can collect royalties on it, competing firms have a strong incentive to be the first to invent. This incentive may be so strong that competitive firms innovate before a monopolist would. A monopolistic firm does not have to worry about being in a patent race, so it innovates at whatever rate it considers optimal.

Two decades ago, several firms had the knowledge and ability to construct a supersonic transport (SST). Nonetheless, actual production took an enormous investment. In the race between Americans, the British-French *Concord* team, and the Russians, the SST may have been produced too soon. Indeed, it is not clear that the SST will ever be profitable.

To illustrate that competing firms may innovate before monopolistic firms, consider a new example.[40]

- The knowledge to make a minor innovation is costlessly available, but it takes an investment of $2000 to put it into operation. Once developed, the innovation can be used forever at no additional cost.

- This minor innovation saves $1 per unit of output in a particular production process. As previously discussed, the inventor sets the royalty rate for use of the innovation at $1.

- In Year 1, 60 units are demanded at the market price. With price held constant, demand grows, and output increases by 10 units each year. This growth in demand makes the innovation progressively more profitable. By Year 15, demand has grown to 200 units (see Table 20.5).

- The interest rate is 10 percent.

There are four alternative earning streams. First, the inventing firm could put the innovation into effect immediately (the second column of Table 20.5). Because 60 units are sold in that year and the royalty rate is $1 per unit, the firm earns $60 that year, and in each successive year it earns $10 more. The present discounted value of these earnings, at 10 percent interest, is $1600, which is less than the initial investment of $2000.

The second strategy (Column 3) is to invest the $2000 elsewhere and earn 10 percent interest, or $200, forever. The present discounted value of this strategy is $2000.

The third strategy (Column 4) is to put the $2000 in the bank earning 10 percent interest until the fifth year, when the innovation is activated. The firm earns $200 in Years 1–4, $100 in Year 5, $110 in Year 6, and so forth. The present discounted value of these earnings is $2000.

The final strategy has the largest present value: the firm leaves the $2000 in the bank until Year 15, when it puts the innovation into service. The present discounted value of this stream of earnings is $2263.33. Making the switch from the bank to innovating at

---

[40] The following example is based on Barzel (1968). See Kamien and Schwartz (1982, ch. 4) for a rigorous version of a similar model.

TABLE 20.5   Earning Streams from Four Alternative Investment Policies of Investing $2000

Year	Innovate Immediately	Invest Elsewhere	Innovate in Year 5	Innovate in Year 15
1	$ 60	$ 200	$ 200	$ 200
2	70	200	200	200
3	80	200	200	200
4	90	200	200	200
5	100	200	100	200
6	110	200	110	200
7	120	200	120	200
8	130	200	130	200
9	140	200	140	200
10	150	200	150	200
11	160	200	160	200
12	170	200	170	200
13	180	200	180	200
14	190	200	190	200
15	200	200	200	200
16	210	200	210	210
17	220	200	220	220
18	230	200	230	230
19	240	200	240	240
20	250	200	250	250
·	·	·	·	·
·	·	·	·	·
·	·	·	·	·
Present Value	$1600	$2000	$2000	$2263.33

either an earlier or later year produces a lower present discounted value of earnings. The present value of earnings from the fourth option is the highest. As Table 20.5 shows, that strategy has as high or higher earnings than any of the other strategies in each year.

The optimal time to innovate is when the present value of the savings per unit of time due to the innovation equals the present value of the alternative earnings of the original investment. That is, innovation should occur when the marginal revenues (from royalties) become large enough to cover the marginal cost of the foregone interest ($200). A monopolistic firm facing this schedule uses that strategy.

Competitive firms may not behave like the monopolist, however, because they race to be first. Suppose you run a firm that could produce the innovation. You know that if you are the first to produce it, you can collect royalties forever. Moreover, you know that if you are the first to innovate and your innovation occurs in Year 15, your profits from the royalties will be maximized. You may not be able to wait until Year 15, however. You know that it is profitable to innovate from any year after the fifth. You also know that if you wait, someone else may innovate first. If, in an attempt to be first, you innovate in Year 5, you are indifferent between making the investment and leaving your money in the bank.

EXAMPLE 20.8

ADOPTION OF A NEW TECHNOLOGY: OPTICAL SCANNERS

Market structure not only affects the amount of R&D in an industry, it also affects the speed of adoption of new technology. Optical scanners at checkout counters of grocery stores provide a recent example.

Scanners were available in 1972, the standardized Uniform Product Code was adopted in 1973, and the first installation of a scanner was in 1974. By August 1981, 4216 groceries—about one in eight stores—used them.

According to a statistical analysis, a firm was more likely to adopt scanners, holding other factors constant, if it had a large share of the market. A 1 percent higher market share increased the likelihood of initially adopting scanners by almost 16 percent during the first four years, and by 7 percent thereafter.

In the early period, firms were 6.7 percent less likely to adopt for each 1 percent higher the four-firm concentration ratio was. This effect is half as strong in the later period. Thus, holding market concentration constant, large firms were likely to adopt sooner, but adoption was slower in highly concentrated markets.

SOURCE: Levin, Levin, and Meisel (1987).

Thus, given the schedules in Table 20.5, a competitive industry innovates before a monopoly. A firm with a monopoly on information introduces the innovation at the time that is optimal for it. With a permanent patent, a competitive industry may overinvest in research, as previously shown, *and* the research may occur *too soon*.

In general the year a firm chooses to innovate depends on a variety of factors, such as the cost and demand functions and the number of rival firms. It is possible to construct examples in which competitive firms innovate before or after monopolistic firms. One reason for this uncertainty is that monopolistic firms charge more for the new product than competitive firms, so they face different benefit schedules in general from the innovation. It is clear, however, that the innovation time of a competing firm is after the zero profit introduction time (Kamien and Schwartz 1982).

So far, we have shown that competitive firms may conduct research more quickly than a monopolist that is not involved in a patent race. The analysis of rates of adoption of new technologies is similar; see Example 20.8. We now turn our attention to the case where a monopolist faces a patent race.

Monopolists in Patent Races

> *It were good therefore that men in their innovations would follow the example of time itself, which indeed innovateth greatly, but quietly and by degrees scarce to be perceived.* —FRANCIS BACON

Suppose a monopolist fears that a potential rival will invent a new, similar product and enter the monopolist's market. Both firms have an incentive to invent the new product. If the monopolist gets there first, it maintains its monopoly power. If the potential rival

EXAMPLE 20.9

COMPULSORY LICENSES AND SLEEPING PATENTS

Newspaper articles and lawsuits often allege that firms acquire patents and do not use them to prevent potential competitors from obtaining them. One way to prevent such abuses is to force the patentee to let others use the invention.

Many countries' patent laws require compulsory licensing of an invention at "reasonable" terms if the patentee does not utilize the invention within a specified time or otherwise abuses the rights of the patent grant. As Example 20.5 shows, many patents are not used.

These compulsory licensing laws are seldom used, however. The table on p. 687 shows the number of compulsory licenses filed and granted in selected countries that have compulsory licensing provisions in their patent laws. Thus, it appears either that firms do not sit on patents to deny their use by competitors or that compulsory licensing is not a good solution. Suppose one firm goes to the trouble and cost of proving another firm's patent is not being used in order to obtain the compulsory license. Once that is done, other firms can obtain the compulsory license at lower cost because they do not have to prove the patent is not being used. That is, the first firm bears more of the costs than subsequent firms, so there is an externality problem. Each potential licensing firm would like another to go to the expense of obtaining the first license. As a result, firms are slow to obtain licenses.

SOURCE: Gilbert (1981, 249–50), based on data from UNCTAD. 1975. *The Role of the Patent System in the Transfer of Technology to Developing Countries.* New York: United Nations.

is first to invent, it competes with the incumbent and duopoly results. Thus, the rewards are asymmetric: the monopolist stands to lose more from failing to be first than the rival. The rival loses only its R&D expenditures, whereas the monopolist loses its R&D expenditures and some of its monopoly profits.

Not losing is the monopolist's primary aim; it does not care particularly if it makes or implements the new discovery—it only cares that its rival does not. Indeed, the monopolist may let its patent "sleep." That is, it may patent related products so as to prevent anyone else from doing so and then not use the new patents. Sleeping patents are discussed in Chapter 13 and in Example 20.9.

Suppose someone invents a product that is superior to the one the monopolist is currently selling. The monopolist is willing to bid more for the patent than a potential rival. The monopolist can use the new invention to maintain its monopoly power, whereas

Country	Period Covered	Number Filed [a]	Number Refused	Number Abandoned	Number Granted
Developed Market Economies					
Australia	1958–63	None	—	—	None
Canada	1935–70	192	14	72	79
Denmark	[b]	7	—	1	3
Ireland	[b]	1	—	—	None
Japan	1958–63	None	—	—	None
Netherlands	1958–63	None	—	—	None
New Zealand	1955–63	None	—	—	None
Norway	1910–63	27	2	11	11
Switzerland	1952–63	None	—	—	None
United Kingdom	1959–68	57	—	—	6
Developing Countries					
Cuba	1958–63	None	—	—	None
India	[b]	4	—	—	1
Israel	[b]	3	—	—	None
Morocco	1958–63	None	—	—	None
Philippines	[b]	8	—	—	None
Republic of Korea	[b]	1	—	—	1
Socialist Country					
Poland	[b]	7	—	—	None

[a] Including applications pending at the end of the period covered.
[b] Precise period not specified, but reference to "over a recent 5-year period."

the rival only can use it to become a duopolist (see Chapter 13). Thus, the monopolist is willing to bid more than the potential rival, up to the difference between monopoly and duopoly profits. An incumbent firm also may have an advantage making new discoveries because of experience (see Example 20.10).

Unfortunately for the monopolist, it is not always able to bid for new inventions. The monopolist gets the patent if it invents first, otherwise a potential rival obtains it. If the potential rival could sell the patent to the monopolist, it would earn more than if it competes as a duoplast, but antitrust laws are intended to prohibit such practices.

How then can a monopolist maintain its monopoly power? Or, restated, how can the monopolist guarantee it is the first to invent (Gilbert and Newbery 1982, Kamien and Schwartz 1982, Fudenberg et al. 1983, and Harris and Vickers 1985)? One way is to obtain such a head start in a patent race that all potential rivals drop out of the race. A

EXAMPLE 20.10

LEARNING BY DOING, INNOVATION, AND MARKET STRUCTURE

An empirical study, Lieberman (1987), shows that *learning by doing* has an important effect in the chemical industry. The earlier the innovation, the sooner a firm's employees can learn by doing, which leads to more innovation and lower costs. A 1 percent increase in the growth rate of cumulative output (a proxy for experience) increases the expected number of patents in a given year by 8 percent, holding other factors constant. Moreover, prices fall with experience: a doubling of cumulative output leads to price reductions of 23 percent.

Lieberman finds that R&D expenditures in chemicals have little impact on the rates of patenting, but that firm size and market structure are important. Larger firms have higher patent rates: a 1 percent increase in firm size leads to a 0.3 percent increase in the patent rate. (Thus, in contrast to the studies reported in Example 20.7, the Schumpetarian hypothesis is supported in the chemical industry.) The larger a firm's market share, the more likely it is to file patents. The greater the industry concentration, however, the lower is a firm's propensity to patent.

This concentration result is consistent with two possible explanations. Firms in concentrated industries may prefer to maintain secrecy by not patenting discoveries instead of erecting new barriers to entry through patenting. Alternatively, a firm in an industry with barriers to entry does not have to worry about potential rivals beating it to a discovery, so it has lower incentives to invent than firms in more competitive industries.

The effects of patents on prices are complex. Patenting by producer firms slows the rate of price reduction. Cost-saving techniques used by all firms lower prices. If, however, one firm makes a discovery first and is able to patent it, that firm can capture the value of the invention and keep prices from falling by collecting royalties from other firms.

Patents by nonproducers and by foreign firms lead to price reductions, whereas those by domestic producers do not. The average patent by a U.S. nonproducing firm results in a 0.9 percent fall in output prices. An average foreign patent leads to a 0.15 percent price reduction. These results indicate that domestic producers are more likely to capture the full value of a discovery than other firms. One possible explanation is that producers discover many minor cost-saving processes, whereas nonproducing domestic firms and foreign firms discover many major cost-saving processes.

firm with a relatively small head start can discourage its rivals from entering a patent race. A trailing firm with no chance of catching up should drop out of the race immediately. In this case, the monopolist can maintain its market power, but it may be forced to innovate faster than it prefers. Alternatively, if the trailing firm has a good chance of gaining the lead ("leapfrog" ahead), then it should stay in the race, and there is a competitive patent race.

A recent survey of high-level R&D managers in U.S. firms, however, suggests that in many cases patents are not an important means of protecting a competitive advantage,

TABLE 20.6   Effectiveness of Alternative Means of Protecting the Competitive Advantages of New or Improved Processes and Products

| | Averages* | |
Method of Appropriation	Processes	Products
Patents to prevent duplication	3.52	4.33
Patents to secure royalty income	3.31	3.75
Secrecy	4.31	3.57
Lead time	5.11	5.41
Moving quickly down the learning curve	5.02	5.09
Sales or service efforts	4.55	5.59

*Based on a survey of 650 high-level R&D managers of a cross-section of U.S. firms. Each manager answered on a 1–7 scale, where 1 = not at all effective and 7 = very effective.
SOURCE: Levin et al. (1987, Table 1, 794).

as shown in Table 20.6 (Levin et al. 1987). Patents were rated the least effective mechanisms of appropriating the returns from a competitive advantage for new processes. Secrecy, lead time, moving quickly down the learning curve (gaining experience that leads to lower production costs), and sales or service efforts were all rated higher. Patents ranked above secrecy, but below lead time, moving quickly down the learning curve, and sales or service efforts for new products. These averages across all industries, however, do not give the full picture. Patents were ranked effective for protecting new products in inorganic chemicals, organic chemicals, drugs, and plastic materials. Thus, patent races are relatively less likely for new processes and relatively more likely for new products in certain industries with high levels of R&D.

■ SUMMARY

This chapter examines five questions concerning patents and technological progress and reaches the following conclusions. First, without patents or other government incentives to conduct research, there is typically too little R&D and hence too little technological progress. Too little effort is put into R&D because information externalities prevent inventors from capturing the values of their discoveries in the absence of property rights. Patents, prizes, government research contracts, and joint ventures can overcome this problem.

Second, although patents encourage inventive activity, they cause monopoly pricing distortions. By adjusting the length of a patent, governments can trade off more inventive activity versus more efficient pricing. Shortening the length of a patent reduces the harms from monopoly pricing but also reduces the incentive to invent. In most cases, the best trade-off is obtained with a finite-length patent. Many, if not most governments rely primarily on grants of monopoly power for a fixed maximum number of years in the form of patents to encourage research. In some cases, welfare may increase with changes in the lengths of patents, greater use of prizes or research contracts, and possibly from compulsory licensing of unused patents.

Third, government prizes and research contracts stimulate R&D and do not have the same drawback as patents and joint ventures of monopoly pricing. Patents, however, may come closer in stimulating the optimal amount of R&D if the government lacks the information or ability to set prizes or research contracts properly. The government may be unable to set them properly if it has less information than researchers about the value of potential new discoveries or the likelihood of making a discovery.

Fourth, a patent-holder achieves the same profits by being the sole producer of the product as it does by licensing it and receiving royalties if production costs are the same across manufacturers. The patent-holder can capture virtually all the benefits from many minor cost-saving inventions, but not from major ones.

Fifth, market structures affect rates of research. Competitive firms, racing to obtain patents, may innovate too rapidly. If a monopolist does not fear competition, it innovates more slowly than would a competitive firm. When a monopolist faces potential entrants, it tries to innovate more rapidly than it otherwise would to maintain its monopoly profits. A monopolist can prevent a patent race, however, if it can obtain a sufficient lead in research. A monopolist wants to preempt other firms from engaging in a patent race, because patents are worth more to it than to competitive firms. If the monopolist makes the discovery first, it maintains its monopoly power, whereas if the competitive firm makes the discovery first, it must compete with the former monopolist. Because of these offsetting effects, whether greater monopoly power would stimulate innovation in a particular industry remains an unresolved empirical question.

■ KEY TERMS

copyrights	patents	research contracts
joint ventures	patent race	royalty
license	prize	trademarks
novel (nonobvious)		

■ Discussion Questions

1. Under what conditions is there too little research and under what conditions is there too much?
2. Argue for or against the following proposition: "The lengths of patents should be set differently in different industries and for different types of inventions."
3. Argue for or against the following proposition: "Artists get pleasure out of creating; therefore, copyrights should be shorter than patents."
4. Should copyrights or patents be offered for paintings? Can you think of a better incentive for painters? For

example, should they receive a fraction of the profits from the resale of their paintings at later dates?

5. Argue for or against the following proposition: "If a patent is not put into use within one year, the patent-holder should automatically lose exclusive rights, and anyone should be able to use the invention."
6. Under what conditions does one expect large or monopolistic firms to invent more than small, competitive firms? Under what conditions does one expect the opposite?

■ Problems

1. What is the effect of a sales (revenue) tax on the incentive to invent under a patent system?
2. What is the effect of a profits tax on the incentives to invent?
3. Graphically illustrate (using the benefit and cost curves in Figure 20.1) the effect of a longer patent life on the incentive to invent.
4. If the government could only observe prices, quantities, and royalty rates (but did not know the demand curves or the marginal cost curves), could it determine if a royalty was for a minor or major patent?
5. Using an argument similar to that for monopolistic competition (Chapter 11), show that firms operate on the downward sloping section of their average cost curves for inventive activities.

Answers to odd-numbered problems are given at the back of the book.

■ Recommended Readings

Arrow (1962) and Barzel (1968) are two important early papers that are relatively nonmathematical. For a good survey of the history of research on innovation and theory, see Kamien and Schwartz (1982). Some parts of that book are technical, but others are nontechnical. A good collection of recent empirical research on patents is contained in Griliches (1984). See Novos and Waldman (1984) on copyrights and Landes and Posner (1987) on trademarks. See Wright (1983) for a discussion of patents and alternatives.

■ References

Arrow, Kenneth J. 1962. "Economic Welfare and the Allocation of Resources for Invention," in National Bureau of Economic Research, *The Rate and Direction of Inventive Activity*. Princeton, N.J.: Princeton University Press.

Barzel, Yoram. 1968. "Optimal Timing of Innovations." *Review of Economics and Statistics* 50:348–55.

Bound, John, Clint Cummins, Zvi Griliches, Bronwyn H. Hall, and Adam Jaffe. 1984. "Who Does R&D and Who Patents?" in Zvi Griliches, ed., *R&D, Patents, and Productivity*. Chicago: University of Chicago Press, 21–54.

Cheung, Steven N. S. 1982. "Property Rights in Trade Secrets." *Economic Inquiry* 20:40–52.

Cohen, Wesley M., Richard C. Levin, and David C. Mowery. 1987. "Firm Size and R&D Intensity: A Re-Examination." *The Journal of Industrial Economics* 35:543–65.

Dasgupta, Partha, and Joseph E. Stiglitz. 1980. "Uncertainty, Industrial Structure, and the Speed of R&D." *The Bell Journal of Economics* 11:1–28.

DeBrock, Lawrence M. 1985. "Market Structure, Innovation and Optimal Patent Life." *Journal of Law and Economics* 4:223–44.

Fudenberg, Drew, Richard Gilbert, Joseph E. Stiglitz, and Jean Tirole. 1983. "Preemption, Leapfrogging, and Competition in Patent Races." *European Economic Review* 22:3–31.

Galbraith, John K. *American Capitalism*. 1952. Boston: Houghton Mifflin.

Gallini, Nancy T. 1984. "Deterrence Through Market Sharing: A Strategic Incentive for Licensing." *American Economic Review* 74:931–41.

Gallini, Nancy T., and Ralph A. Winter. 1985. "Licensing in the Theory of Innovation." *Rand Journal of Economics* 16:237–52.

Gilbert, Richard J. 1981. "Patents, Sleeping Patents, and Entry Deterrence," in Steven C. Salop, ed., *Strategy, Predation, and Antitrust Analysis*. Washington, D.C.: Federal Trade Commission, 205–69.

Gilbert, Richard J., and David M. G. Newbery. 1982. "Preemptive Patenting and the Persistence of Monopoly." *American Economic Review* 72:514–26.

Griliches, Zvi, ed. 1984. *R & D, Patents, and Productivity*. Chicago: University of Chicago Press.

Grossman, Gene, and Carl Shapiro. 1986. "Research Joint Ventures: An Antitrust Analysis." *Journal of Law, Economics, and Organization* 2:315–37.

Harris, Christopher, and John Vickers. 1985. "Patent Races and the Persistence of Monopoly," in P. A. Geroski, L. Phlips, and A. Ulph, eds., *Oligoply, Competition, and Welfare*. New York: Basil Blackwell.

Hausman, Jerry A., and Jeffrey K. MacKie-Mason. 1988. "Price Discrimination and Patent Policy." *The Rand Journal of Economics* 19:253–65.

Hirshleifer, Jack. 1971. "The Private and Social Value of Information and the Reward to Inventive Activity." *American Economic Review* 61:561–74.

Irwin, Marley R. 1971. "The Communication Industry," in Walter Adams, ed., *The Structure of American Industry*. New York: Macmillan.

Jensen, Elizabeth J. 1987. "Research Expenditures and the Discovery of New Drugs." *The Journal of Industrial Economics* 36:83–95

Jorde, Thomas M., and David J. Teece. 1988. *Innovation, Cooperation, and Antitrust*. Berkeley: University of California, Berkeley, School of Business Administration.

Kamien, Morton I., and Nancy L. Schwartz. 1982. *Market Structure and Innovation*. Cambridge: Cambridge University Press.

Katz, Michael L., and Carl Shapiro. 1985. "On the Licensing of Innovations." *Rand Journal of Economics* 16:504–20.

————. 1986. "How to License Intangible Property." *Quarterly Journal of Economics* 101:567–90.

Kitch, Edmund W. 1975. "The Nature and Function of the Patent System." *Journal of Law and Economics* 13:1–37.

Landes, William M., and Richard A Posner. 1987. "Trademark Law: An Economic Perspective." *Journal of Law and Economics* 30:265–309.

Lapham, Lewis H., Michael Pollan, and Eric Etheridge. 1987. *Harper's Index Book*. New York: Henry Holt and Company.

Lee, Tom, and Louis Wilde. 1980. "Market Structure and Innovation: A Reformulation." *Quarterly Journal of Economics* 94:429–36.

Levin, Richard C., Alvin K. Klevorick, Richard R. Nelson, and Sidney G. Winter. 1987. "Appropriating the Returns from Industrial Research and Development." *Brookings Papers on Economic Activity* 3: (Special Issue on Microeconomics) 783–820.

Levin, Sharon G., Stanford L. Levin, and John B. Meisel. 1987. "A Dynamic Analysis of the Adoption of a New Technology: The Case of Optical Scanners." *Review of Economics and Statistics* 69:12–17.

Lichtenberg, Frank R. 1987. "The Effect of Government Funding on Private Industrial Research and Development: A Re-Assesment." *The Journal of Industrial Economics* 36:97–104.

Lieberman, Marvin B. 1987. "Patents, Learning by Doing, and Market Structure in the Chemical Processing Industries." *International Journal of Industrial Organization* 5:257–76.

Loury, Glenn C. 1979. "Market Structure and Innovation." *Quarterly Journal of Economics* 93:395–410.

Mansfield, Edwin. 1968. *Industrial Research and Technological Innovation: An Econometric Analysis*. New York: W. W. Norton & Co.

Mansfield, Edwin, et al. 1977. "Social and Private Rates of Return from Industrial Innovations." *Quarterly Journal of Economics* 91:221–40.

Mansfield, Edwin, Anthony Romeo, Mark Schwartz, David Teece, Samuel Wagner, and Peter Brach. 1982. *Technology Transfer, Productivity, and Economic Policy*. New York: W. W. Norton & Co.

Mansfield, Edwin. 1984. "R&D and Innovation: Some Empirical Findings," in Zvi Griliches, ed. *R&D, Patents and Productivity*. Chicago: University of Chicago Press.

————. 1985. "How Rapidly Does New Industrial Technology Leak Out?" *Journal of Industrial Economics* 34:217–23.

McGee, John S. 1966. "Patent Exploitation: Some Economic and Legal Problems." *Journal of Law and Economics* 9:135–62.

Nelson, Richard R., and Sidney G. Winter. 1982. "The Schumpeterian Tradeoff Revisited." *American Economic Review*. 73:114–32.

Nordhaus, William D. 1969. *Inventions, Growth, and Welfare: A Theoretical Treatment of Technological Change*. Cambridge, Mass.: Massachusetts Institute of Technology Press.

Novos, Ian E., and Michael Waldman. 1984. "The Effects of Increased Copyright Protection: An Analytical Approach." *Journal of Political Economy* 92:236–46.

Ordover, Janusz A., and Robert D. Willig. 1985. "Antitrust for High-Technology Industries: Assessing Research Joint Ventures and Mergers." *Journal of Law and Economics* 28:311–33.

Pakes, Ariel. 1986. "Patents as Options: Some Estimates

of the Value of Holding European Patent Stocks. *Econometrica* 54:775–84.

Reinganum, Jennifer F. 1982. "Dynamic Games of R&D: Patent Protection and Competitive Behavior." *Econometrica* 50:671–88.

———. 1984. "Practical Implications of Game Theoretic Models of R&D." *American Economic Review* 74:61–66.

Scherer, F. M. 1981. "Comments on 'Patents, Sleeping Patents, and Entry Deterrence,'" in Steven C. Salop, ed., *Strategy, Predation, and Antitrust Analysis*. Washington, D.C.: Federal Trade Commission.

———. 1984. *Innovation and Growth: Schumpeterian Perspectives*. Cambridge, Mass.: The MIT Press.

Schumpeter, Joseph. 1950. *Capitalism, Socialism, and Democracy*. 3rd ed. New York: Harper and Row.

Scotchmer, Suzanne, and Jerry Green. 1988. "Novelty and Disclosure in Patent Law." Graduate School of Public Policy, University of California, Berkeley, Working paper no. 148.

Stigler, Stephen M. 1986. *The History of Statistics*. Cambridge, Mass.: Harvard University Press.

Taylor, Charles T., and Z. Aubrey Silberston. 1973. *The Economic Impact of the Patent System*. Cambridge: Cambridge University Press.

Tisdell, Clem. 1974. "Patenting and Licensing of Government Inventions—General Issues Raised by Australian Policy." *Australian Economic Papers* 13:188–208.

Ulrich, Alvin; Hartley Furtan; and Andrew Schmitz. 1986. "Public and Private Returns from Joint Venture Research: An Example from Agriculture." *Quarterly Journal of Economics* 101:103–29.

Usher, Dan. 1964. "The Welfare Economics of Invention." *Economica* 31:279–87.

Vickery, Graham. 1986. "International Flows of Technology—Recent Trends and Developments." *STI Review* (Autumn):47–84.

Wright, Brian D. 1983. "The Economics of Invention Incentives: Patents, Prizes, and Research Contracts." *American Economic Review* 73:691–707.

PATENTS, PRIZES, AND RESEARCH CONTRACTS

This appendix compares prizes, research contracts, and patents and is based, in large part, on Wright (1983). Suppose that each firm in a competitive research industry can undertake one research project at a constant cost, c. The total cost, then, for n firms is $C(n) = nc$. The firms are racing to make a discovery. The probability that at least one firm will succeed is $\rho(n)$. The larger the number of firms, the higher the probability, $\rho'(n) > 0$; but the increase in probability occurs at a decreasing rate, $\rho''(n) < 0$. If the value to society of the discovery is B, the expected value of the discovery, prior to the research, is $B\rho(n)$.[1]

Research takes place in period $t = 0$. If a discovery is made, society benefits from it for the rest of time. For simplicity, we do not consider research in later periods if the discovery is not made in $t = 0$.

Society wants to choose the number of competing research projects (firms), n, to maximize net social benefit, which equals expected benefit minus industry costs:

$$\max_{n} S(n) = B\rho(n) - C(n) = B\rho(n) - nc. \qquad (20A.1)$$

S is maximized at n^*, where

$$S'(n^*) = B\rho'(n^*) - C'(n^*) = B\rho'(n^*) - c = 0. \qquad (20A.2)$$

That is, marginal benefit, $B\rho'(n^*)$, equals marginal cost, c.

If, by assumption, $\rho(n) = 1 - e^{-\alpha n}$ (as in Table 20.2 and Figure 20.1), we can rewrite Equation 20A.2 as follows:

$$S'(n^*) = \alpha B e^{-\alpha n^*} - c = 0. \qquad (20A.2')$$

---

[1] B is the present value of consumer surplus at the competitive price. That is, B equals the consumer surplus in a single period divided by r, the social discount rate.

We can solve Equation 20A.2' for n^*:

$$n^* = -\frac{1}{\alpha} \ln\left(\frac{c}{\alpha B}\right).$$

(20A.3)

In Table 20.2, $c = 1$, $B = 25$, and $\alpha = .2031$, so $n^* = 8$.

Government Prizes

Suppose a firm were offered a prize equal to the value of the discovery, B, for being the first to discover it. The probability that the discovery is made is $\rho(n)$. In the case of ties, either the prize is shared or awarded randomly to one of the successful firms, so the probability that any one of the n firms wins the prize is $\rho(n)/n$. In this case, a profit-maximizing firm undertakes a research project only if the expected benefit is greater than or equal to the expected cost:

$$\frac{B\rho(n)}{n} \geq c.$$

(20A.4)

In the example in Table 20.2, the equality holds in Equation 20A.4 when $n = 24.84$.

A prize equal to $Bn^*\rho'(n^*)/\rho(n^*)$ leads to the optimal number of research projects. Each firm's expected payoff equals $B\rho'(n^*)$, and from Equation 20A.2, that payoff leads to the optimal number of firms $= n^* = 8$. Since $\rho''(n) < 0$, the average probability of making the discovery is greater than the marginal probability: $\rho(n)/n > \rho'(n)$. Thus, $Bn\rho'(n)/\rho(n) < B$, so this alternative prize is smaller than B; thus it leads to fewer research projects.

Government Research Contracts

The government can achieve the optimal number of projects, $n^* = 8$, by offering to pay for them directly and regardless of success. It can call for competitive bidding for 8 contracts. Competition drives the price to $c = 1$.

Patents

Suppose that the first successful firm receives a patent giving it exclusive rights to sell the product. In case of ties, patent rights are shared or awarded randomly to one of the successful firms. To determine how many firms engage in research, we need to find out how much the patent is worth.

In the example, demand is linear and the costs of producing are constant. The demand for the product is

$$p = a - bQ,$$

(20A.5)

where $a = 6$ and $b = 5$. The marginal cost of producing the product is $k = 1$. Thus, if the product is sold at a competitive price ($= k$), then $q = 1$. The corresponding consumer surplus (benefit of the discovery) in any period is the area under the demand curve above $k = 1$: $CS = (a - k)^2/(2b) = \$2.50$. The present value of consumer surplus, given competitive pricing, is CS/r, where r is the interest rate. If $r = 10$ percent, then the present value of consumer surplus $= \$25 = B$, the social benefit from the discovery.

A monopolist maximizes profits by setting marginal revenue equal to marginal cost. Here, the revenues $= aq - bq^2$, so marginal revenue $= a - 2bq$, and marginal cost $= k = 1$. Thus, a monopolist charges a price of $p_m = (a + k)/2 = \$3.50$, sells $q_m = (a - k)/(2b) = 0.5$ units, and makes profits of $\pi_m = \$1.25$. The consumer surplus, given monopoly pricing, is $CS_m = \$0.625$ per period, or one-fourth the consumer surplus of a competitive industry.

If the patent lasts forever, given that the discovery is made, present value of the monopoly profits is $\pi_m/r = \$12.50$. If each firm has an equal chance of obtaining the patent, then the expected return to a firm undertaking research is $\$12.50\rho(n)/n$. Firms undertake projects if $c = 1 \leq 12.50\rho(n)/n$. With a permanent patent, a firm's net expected return, $12.50\rho n/n - 1$, equals zero when there are 11.22 firms racing to make the discovery. If a fractional number of firms is impossible, it does not pay for a firm to compete if there are more than 11 firms. A permanent patent leads to excessive research ($11.22 > 8$).

How long should the patent last to induce $n^* = 8$ firms to enter the patent race? The present value of a patent, $PVP(t)$, that lasts t years is

$$PVP(t) = \pi_m \int_0^t e^{-rs}ds = \frac{\pi_m}{r}(1 - e^{-rt}). \qquad (20A.6)$$

The expected return to any given firm in the patent race is $PVP(t)\rho(n)/n$. A firm enters the race if the expected return is greater than or equal to the marginal cost, or $PVP(t)\rho(n)/n \geq c$. In the example, the length of a patent, t^*, such that $n = 8$ firms is determined by solving the following: $PVP(t^*)\rho(8)/8 = 1$. Thus, $t^* = -10 \ln(1 - 8/[12.50\rho(8)]) = 15.94$.

Unlike prizes, however, patents cause a distortion after the discovery: the price, set at the monopoly level, is too high. Thus, the government is faced with a trade-off. The longer the duration of the patent, the greater the chance of success, but the larger the cost due to more research projects and the monopoly loss.

Given that the government uses patents, then it should choose their length, t, to maximize expected net social benefit taking into account monopoly pricing. Expected net social benefit for a patent of length t is

$$NSB(t) = \left[(CS_m + \pi_m) \int_0^t e^{-rs}ds + \frac{CS}{r}e^{-rt} \right] \rho(n_m) - n_m c, \qquad (20A.7)$$

where the first term on the right side is the present value of the sum of consumer surplus and profits for the t years that the patent grants exclusive rights, the second term is the present value of the consumer surplus for the rest of time after the patent expires, $\rho(n_m)$ is the probability of success if n_m firms race, and the last term is the total cost of research for n_m firms. Firms enter until marginal cost equals their expected marginal return:

$$c = 1 = \frac{\pi_m \, \rho(n)}{r \, n_m} \, (1 - e^{-rt}). \qquad (20A.8)$$

For a given t, there is a value for n_m that solves this expression. This formula is used for the calculations in Table 20.3.

To find the optimal solution, the government should maximize Equation 20A.7 with respect to t, subject to Equation 20A.8. The resulting $t = 11.4475$ leads to a $n_m = 6.004$, which is smaller than $n^* = 8$. See Table 20.3.

CHAPTER 21

HOW MARKETS CLEAR: THEORY AND FACTS

Fortune is like the market, where many times, if you can stay a little, the price will fall.

FRANCIS BACON

Most of the discussion in this text has assumed that **market clearing**—the equilibration of the quantities supplied and demanded—occurs exclusively through the price mechanism.[1] Price alone determines how much consumers buy and firms sell. In many, if not most, markets, more than just price adjustments are used to allocate goods to consumers. This chapter examines the evidence on how goods are allocated to customers and presents some recent theories that explain some of the evidence.[2] Much of industrial organization seems fixated on explaining how market behavior differs as industry concentration changes. Although this is certainly an interesting question, industry concentration is only one of many ways in which markets can differ. For example, heterogeneity of products, variability in demand and supply, the ability to hold inventories, and the ability to plan are also important characteristics, and differences in them lead to different market behavior. Yet the effects of these other characteristics have received much less attention from industrial organization economists than the effects of differences in industry concentration. This chapter discusses some of these other characteristics and their effects.

The chapter begins with a brief review of some simple theories that have already been discussed about the ways in which markets clear. These theories focus on price as the mechanism for achieving resource allocation and investigate how the price-clearing function is altered depending upon whether the market is a competitive one, an oligopoly, or a monopoly. We then provide evidence on what is known about price behavior. The evidence varies sufficiently from the predictions of the simple theories that it raises serious

---

[1] One exception was the discussion of search in Chapter 17.

[2] This chapter is a revised version of Carlton (1989a).

questions about their usefulness for explaining price behavior in many markets. Next, a variety of alternative theories are examined that help explain some of the observed puzzles in the data on price. In particular, we present a general theory of market behavior without relying on price as the exclusive market-clearing mechanism. Finally, features of market structure other than the degree of market concentration are used to show how market structure matters in explaining the response of various industries to shocks in either supply or demand. Since the failure of markets to clear through price movements is a key assumption in several macroeconomic theories, the issues discussed in this chapter have been receiving widespread attention from macroeconomists.

■ HOW MARKETS CLEAR: THREE SIMPLE THEORIES

This section briefly reviews the three most important simple models of the ways in which markets operate. These simple models form the background against which the next section analyzes the evidence on prices. Although these models are admittedly simple, understanding where they fail is important for developing better models.

Competition

Probably the simplest and most frequently used model for evaluating industry behavior is the standard competitive model in which price adjusts so as to equate supply to demand. This model assumes a well-functioning market in which transactions take place at no cost and with no uncertainties affecting suppliers or demanders.

In this model the price mechanism alone clears the market. Given the standard assumptions of a perfectly competitive model, price responds to shifts in either supply or demand. For example, we can write, in equilibrium, that

$$D(p) = S(p),$$

where D is the demand curve, S is the supply curve, and p is the price. In response to shifts in either the demand or supply curve, price changes so as to equilibrate supply and demand.[3] The amount of the price change depends not only on the size of the shifts in either supply or demand, but also on the shapes of the supply and demand curves—in particular, their price elasticities.

The insights from the competitive model usually stop there. Once analysts know the elasticities of supply and demand, they can predict price changes. Typically not much attention is paid to the economic explanations of the likely magnitude of the elasticities.

The competitive model is elegant in its simplicity and in its predictions. When either demand or supply changes, price adjusts to clear the market. The amount by which price must adjust depends on the supply and demand elasticities. There are no unsatisfied

---

[3] It is unclear how price adjusts to a new equilibrium. For example, which firm first changes its price and why? See Arrow (1959).

FIGURE 21.1 Kinked Demand Curve

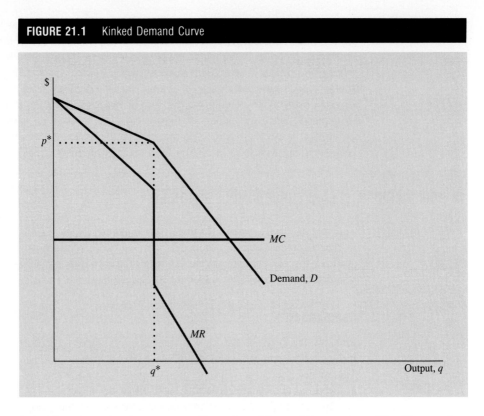

demanders at any instant nor any sellers who wish to sell but cannot. All sellers receive and all buyers pay the same price, and price changes are perfectly correlated across different buyers.

Oligopoly Models

As has been shown, the competitive model is inappropriate if there are only a few firms in the marketplace and if they recognize their mutual interdependence. No single model of oligopoly behavior is universally accepted today. However, most models of oligopoly assume that there are no unsatisfied demanders or sellers at whatever price is set, that price changes are passed along to all buyers simultaneously, and that it is not costly to transact in the market.

One common theme of most models of oligopoly is that the behavior of price is much different than it is in a competitive market. This insight is useless, though, unless it is possible to describe the types of differences one expects. One early attempt was to use the model of the kinked demand curve (Appendix 10B) to explain oligopoly pricing.[4] As Figure 21.1 shows, under this theory of oligopoly pricing every firm faces a demand curve that is much more elastic above a price, p^*, than it is below that price. If firms do

---

[4] Other recent models yielding kinked demand curves include Salop (1979) and Schmalensee (1982).

face such demand curves, they have a tendency to price at p^* for a range of different marginal costs. The marginal cost *(MC)* curve goes through the vertical segment in the marginal revenue *(MR)* curve. The kinked demand theory of oligopoly behavior therefore predicts that prices tend to remain unchanged for small changes in costs.

Unfortunately, the theory is silent on how price is initially set. The kinked demand curve theory is certainly not one that explains price levels. At best, it explains why price does not change in response to moderate shifts in cost. In response to large shifts in cost, the theory predicts that price should change, although it provides no guidelines as to how the new price level is set. (See Appendix 10B.)

The view of price as unresponsive to some cost fluctuations is preserved in most discussions of oligopoly theory whether or not they are based on the kinked demand curve. The reasoning is that in oligopolies prices fluctuate less in response to cost changes (especially small ones) than they would otherwise in order not to disturb existing oligopolistic discipline. Any time a price change occurs in an oligopoly, there is the risk of a price war. Hence, firms are reluctant to change price.

Monopoly

In the theory of monopoly, a firm equates marginal revenue to marginal cost. Again, the basic theory of monopoly does not typically analyze how the shapes of either the demand curve or marginal cost curve are influenced by the economic motivations facing consumers or the firm. The implication of the theory of monopoly is that price exceeds marginal cost. Again, as in the models of competition and oligopoly, there are no unsatisfied demanders at the market price, and the cost of allocating goods (that is, the cost of using a market price to allocate goods) is assumed to be zero. One assumes the demand curve is known and that price changes across different buyers are perfectly correlated.

The theory of monopoly explains how a monopolist reacts to shifts in either supply or demand. For example, if marginal cost changes, the new price is determined by the intersection of the new marginal cost curve with the marginal revenue curve.

It is commonly stated that a monopolist's price varies less than the competitive price in response to changes in costs. This statement seems to be based on the assumption that demand curves are linear, so that any change in marginal costs translates into a change in the monopoly price that is *less* than the change in marginal costs. In the competitive case, since price equals marginal cost, the changes in price and marginal cost are equal. For example, if the demand curve equals

$$Q = 9 - p,$$

and marginal cost equals \$1, the monopoly price is \$5. If marginal cost rises from \$1 to \$3, the monopoly price goes up from \$5 to \$6. That is, price rises by one-half of the cost increase. In contrast, if this industry were competitive, price would increase by the same amount as marginal cost.

It is also possible to construct examples in which the monopolist's price varies more than the competitive price in response to cost changes. For example, suppose a monopolist faces a demand curve with a constant elasticity of demand and has a constant marginal cost. Then the monopolist's price equals a constant markup above marginal cost. Since the markup exceeds 1, it follows that the price increases by more than the increase in marginal cost. For example, if the elasticity were -2, the monopolist would charge a price of $2 if marginal cost were $1. If marginal cost were to rise by $2 to become $3, the optimal price would rise by $4 and become $6. The increase in price would exceed the increase in cost. In the competitive case, the price increase would exactly equal the increase in cost.

These examples regarding price variability show that the relation of price changes to cost changes varies with the shape of the demand curve. Therefore, it is not possible to make any general statements about the variability of price in relation to the variability of cost based upon whether a market is competitive or monopolized. Moreover, since oligopolies range from almost competitive industries to almost monopolized industries, the three simple theories do not allow any differential predictions of price flexibility for large cost changes that depend solely on the degree of competitiveness of the market. (For small cost changes, some theories of oligopoly suggest that prices may remain unchanged.)

■ EMPIRICAL EVIDENCE ON THE ROLE OF PRICE IN ALLOCATING GOODS

Several types of evidence are available on the role that price plays in clearing markets. One type is casual observation which, although not terribly scientific, is better than no observation at all. Another type comes from surveys of prices paid, as best they can be measured, for different commodities across time.

Casual Observation

Even someone who has never studied the actual empirical distributions of prices across markets has probably been a consumer and transacted in many markets. Consumers know that it is not unusual to go to the supermarket to buy a product and find that the supermarket is out of stock. Consumers know that if there are three cars ahead of them at the gas station, the price of gasoline at the pump will not rise; rather they will have to wait to get their car filled up. In fact, for many items commonly purchased, prices stay fixed for a while once they are set.

Newspaper articles often describe how some companies have difficulty assuring themselves of supply during periods of high demand. Histories of business, such as Chandler's (1977), explain in detail that many firms vertically integrate, not necessarily to get a lower price for a product, but simply to get the product on a reliable basis. Waiting for a good and being unable to purchase a good when one wants it are typical rather than atypical experiences in many markets. In periods of tight supply, preferred customers get delivery, while new customers are often unable to assure themselves of a supply at the same price as steady customers. In fact, short-term customers may be unable to get the product at all.

Such observations suggest that in many markets, price may not be the sole mechanism used to clear the market. None of the simple theories of the previous section are able to explain the existence of unsatisfied demanders, yet they appear to be an observed feature of many markets.

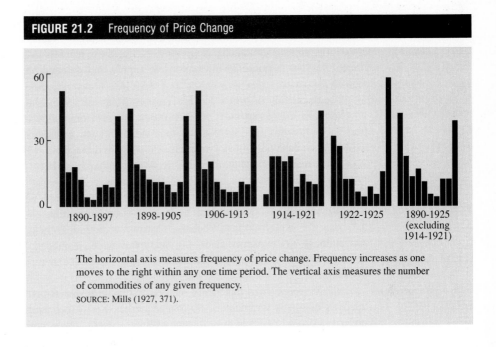

FIGURE 21.2   Frequency of Price Change

The horizontal axis measures frequency of price change. Frequency increases as one moves to the right within any one time period. The vertical axis measures the number of commodities of any given frequency.
SOURCE: Mills (1927, 371).

Studies of Price Statistics

One obvious way to learn how price clears markets in response to changes in supply or demand is to study actual price behavior. There have been many such studies, and their findings are sometimes quite startling. The following sections review the early studies and then some more recent ones. They also discuss what is known about the behavior of price-cost margins during business expansions and contractions and finally consider some studies of foreign prices.

Early Studies.   Frederick Mills (1927) conducted one of the earliest studies regarding the flexibility and behavior of prices. Mills examined numerous price statistics gathered by the U.S. Bureau of Labor Statistics (BLS) for frequency of change and amplitude of change. His work represents an outstanding contribution to our knowledge of price behavior.

Figure 21.2 presents some of Mills' findings regarding the frequency of price change over various time periods. The diagrams show that the distribution across markets of the frequency of price changes is U-shaped; that is, there are many products whose prices change frequently, and many whose prices change infrequently. We are unaware of any attempt by economists to explain empirically the shape of these functions. Of course, it is possible that supply and demand are in equilibrium in all industries and that what Mills is showing reflects simply the distribution of shocks to various supply and demand curves. So, for example, there are many markets in which shocks and the resulting price changes are frequent and also many markets in which shocks and the resulting price changes are few. Another possibility is that in some markets prices change frequently and are the exclusive device used for market clearing, while in other markets prices do not vary frequently, and something else is working to clear those markets. Markets in which prices do not vary in response to fluctuations in supply and demand are said to show **price rigidity**.

The next study of prices was by Gardiner Means in 1935. Unlike Mills, Means had an enormous effect not only on economists but also on policy makers. His influence persists to this day. Means claimed that the traditional economists' models could not explain price behavior in many markets. He suggested that the Great Depression occurred because in many markets the laws of supply and demand had been "repealed," and prices no longer fluctuated to clear the markets. Means' arguments attracted widespread attention. Here was a man claiming that the Great Depression, which was inexplicable to most economists, was caused by a breakdown in market clearing, which formed the basis for all economists' beliefs.[5] Means' hypotheses challenged the profession, and although (as explained later) his inferences were misguided, they were motivated by the inability of the simple theories to explain price behavior very well on certain markets.

Means' theory was that many markets had **administered prices,** which meant that the laws of supply and demand no longer predicted price behavior; instead, prices were under the control of firms that, for unexplained reasons, chose not to vary them to clear markets. Means claimed that price changes in administered markets were much less frequent and that when they did occur, they were much larger in amplitude than those in competitive markets. According to Means, because administered markets had long stretches of unchanging or rigid prices, prices were failing to clear these markets, and this failure caused the disequilibrium of which the Great Depression is an example.

Means seems to have resisted equating administered prices to prices in markets with high concentration, and there was confusion as to what exactly an administered price was. A voluminous and contentious literature developed that attempted to give structure to Means' arguments and test them.[6] The result of that literature has been to confirm that something unusual is going on in the behavior of some prices.[7]

Mills' (1927) earlier work, which attracted much less attention than that of Gardiner Means, does not indicate a significant increase in price rigidity from the 1890s to the mid-1920s (see Figure 21.2). We are unaware of any study that shows greater rigidity of prices right after 1929. Means may well have been right to point out that economists had

---

[5] Macroeconomists, notably Keynes, soon developed theories to explain the Great Depression. These theories were based upon an assumption that wages (not prices) did not fluctuate to clear markets. Wage rigidity may be less important than price rigidity, and the reliance by macroeconomists on wage rigidity is probably misplaced. Evidence of how real wages (wages corrected for inflation) behave over the business cycle can help one determine whether wages are stickier than prices. If a variable rises during booms and falls during bad times, then the variable is said to be procyclical. The reverse behavior is called countercyclical. If prices are stickier than wages, real wages should be procyclical, while if wages are stickier than prices, real wages should be countercyclical. There is evidence (Zarnowitz 1985) that real wages are procyclical.

[6] The interested reader is referred to Beals (1975), Lustgarten (1975), Qualls (1979), Scherer (1980, Ch. 13), Weiss (1977), and Weston and Lustgarten (1974), and the references cited therein.

[7] See, for example, Weiss (1977), but see Stigler and Kindahl (1973) for a different point of view.

inadequate theories for predicting the flexibility of prices, but the phenomenon he was talking about was not confined to the period of the Great Depression. Indeed, the following pages show that the phenomenon of rigid prices characterizes the U.S. economy today.

Later Studies.   The major criticism of Means' work is that it relies on price statistics gathered by the U.S. Bureau of Labor Statistics (BLS). A study done by McAllister (1961) for a Congressional Committee on Price Statistics shows that the BLS data typically do not reflect price discounts. Moreover, an examination of the way in which the BLS gathered price statistics shows that the number of firms reporting prices to the BLS varies from market to market. The more firms reporting price, the more likely is the observation of some flexibility in an average price. This is especially true when products are heterogeneous. The McAllister study shows that the flexibility of average prices, as determined from BLS data, is closely linked to the number of firms reporting to BLS surveys.

Recognizing the inadequacies of BLS price statistics, Stigler and Kindahl (1970) collected data on individual transaction prices based on actual transactions between buyers and sellers. Although the Stigler-Kindahl data undoubtedly contain reporting errors, they are probably the best source of information on pricing behavior available to economists today. Stigler and Kindahl construct indices of prices (averages of individual prices) for individual commodities and find that their price indices move much more smoothly than those of the BLS: price indices based on actual transaction prices are much more flexible than those based on BLS data. Although Stigler and Kindahl do not explicitly claim that their findings are completely in accord with any of the simple theories of market clearing, they do suggest that their work goes a long way toward explaining the unusual findings of price investigations based on BLS data. Their explanation is that the BLS data are misleading.

Stigler and Kindahl recognize that there are some puzzling features even in their own data set. For example, they note that the typical pattern of buyer-seller behavior is for buyers and sellers to remain in contact with each other for long periods of time, even for transactions involving apparently homogeneous goods. This suggests that buyers and sellers build up valuable ways of doing business with each other and that the relationship is worth preserving. As shown later, this insight can be used to explain a great deal of what appears to be unusual pricing behavior. Another puzzling feature is that the Stigler-Kindahl data produce price indices that in addition to being more flexible than the BLS indices have different general trends from the BLS indices during some time periods. The BLS data are primarily based on price quotations for immediate delivery. The Stigler-Kindahl data are based on prices from long-term relationships between buyers and sellers. Therefore, it is likely that the BLS index will reflect fewer long-term contracts than the Stigler-Kindahl index does (see Stigler and Kindahl 1970, 6). A comparison of the Stigler-Kindahl and BLS price indices suggests that over the course of the business cycle there are systematic differences between how spot prices (prices for immediate delivery) behave and how long-term contract prices behave: during booms, spot prices rise relative to long-term contract prices. There have been only a few attempts to explain why such differences exist.[8]

---

[8] See Stigler and Kindahl (1970), Carlton (1979), and Hubbard and Weiner (1986).

Another interesting feature noted by Stigler and Kindahl is that most of the transactions, although they last a long time and although they may be pursuant to a contract, seem to specify neither a price nor in many cases a quantity. It is simply wrong to think of most contracts as rigidly setting both the price and the quantity terms in a market place.[9]

Weiss (1977) weighs the evidence of Stigler and Kindahl against the evidence put forward by Means (1935, 1972). Although recognizing the difficulty of giving theoretical content to Means' hypothesis, Weiss concludes that the evidence on pricing does appear unusual in the sense that the simple theories do not do a good job of explaining pricing behavior.

Carlton (1986) also analyzes the Stigler-Kindahl price data. Unlike Stigler and Kindahl, Carlton does not construct indices of prices to examine how a price index behaves over time, because indices can mask interesting behavior. For example, it is possible for an index of prices to be perfectly flexible even if most contracts are characterized by rigid prices. This could occur if new buyers pay different prices than old buyers. Yet, it is surely important to know whether price is being used to allocate goods to some buyers and not to others, and whether some other mechanism, such as a seller's knowledge of each buyer's requirements, is being used to allocate goods.[10] Instead of examining indices, Carlton examines how prices to individual buyers change relative to each other during the course of a 10-year period. He also analyzes how often a price changes once it has been set to an individual buyer.

Table 21.1 presents a summary of some of Carlton's findings. It shows that the degree of price rigidity—the average length of time during which prices are unchanged—differs greatly across industries from roughly 6 months in household appliances to over 18 months in chemicals.[11] There are several instances of transactions in the Stigler-Kindahl data in which the price paid by a buyer does not change for periods of well over five years. Although the evidence in Table 21.1 could conform to the simple theories under some extreme assumptions, we think it is better viewed as casting doubt on them. For example, one could argue that in industries with very rigid prices, the supply and demand conditions are virtually stable over time, while in the other industries with flexible prices the supply and demand conditions change frequently. The duration of the rigidity in some prices to individual buyers is so long that this explanation is not credible.

---

[9] Williamson (1975) makes this same point.

[10] Rigid prices are troubling to an economist because they suggest that prices may not be clearing markets. However, it is not *rigidity* itself that should bother economists, but rather the inference from the rigid prices that prices are not clearing markets. For example, even if prices were perfectly indexed to inflation and hence were always changing, it would still be troubling if there were unsatisfied buyers indicating that price was not clearing markets. The simple models predict inefficient resource allocation when the *marginal* price (the price of an additional unit) fails to clear markets. A contract that specifies a fixed quantity at a fixed price is *not* a rigid price that can induce inefficiency because the price of an additional unit is the price of buying that unit in the marketplace. When the quantity term is left open, as appears to be the case for the Stigler-Kindahl data, the contract price is the marginal price.

[11] Cecchetti (1985) analyzes newstand prices of magazines and finds that they changed infrequently, every seven years, on average, in the 1950s and every three years, on average, in the 1970s.

TABLE 21.1   Price Rigidity by Industry

Industry	Average Duration of Price Rigidity (months)
Steel	17.9
Nonferrous metals	7.5
Petroleum	8.3
Rubber tires	11.5
Paper	11.8
Chemicals	19.2
Cement	17.2
Glass	13.3
Truck motors	8.3
Plywood	7.5
Household appliances	5.9

SOURCE: Carlton (1986, Table 1).

The Stigler-Kindahl data allow one to examine the correlation (co-movement) of price changes across different buyers of an identical commodity. In all of the simple theoretical models of market clearing, price changes across different buyers of the same commodity should be highly correlated. Although this is true for some markets, there are several markets in which price changes seem to be poorly correlated across buyers. Carlton's interpretation of these results is that the simple models that rely exclusively on price to clear markets fail to explain how many markets operate. It remains to be explained why price changes in some markets are highly correlated across buyers, while price changes in other markets are not.

One of Carlton's findings is a strong positive relationship between industry concentration and price rigidity. The more highly concentrated an industry, the greater the likelihood that its prices remain unchanged for long periods of time. Recall that the simple models make no predictions relating price rigidity to the amount of concentration in a market.[12]

In summary, detailed examination of the Stigler-Kindahl data uncovers a number of anomalies in price behavior. These anomalies do not support any of the simple models of market clearing. We think it wrong to assert that these findings necessarily prove that markets are operating inefficiently. Instead, these findings prove that the simple models of price clearing are inapplicable to certain markets.

---

[12] Although the theory of oligopoly can justify price rigidity in the face of small cost changes, notice that as the industry becomes more concentrated and an oligopoly becomes more powerful, the oligopoly should behave more like a monopolist for whom, according to the simple theory of monopoly, prices should not be rigid.

Other Recent Studies. There have been numerous empirical investigations of the relationships among price, cost, business cycles, and concentration.[13] Here we describe several recent studies that improve on earlier studies by using more comprehensive data.

Domowitz, Hubbard, and Peterson (1986a, 1986b, 1987) examine the behavior of manufacturing prices in the United States over the period 1958–81, using data on over four hundred industries. They reached three interesting conclusions. First, price-cost margins (which theoretically equal the ratio of price minus marginal cost to price) in concentrated industries are *procyclical*: they rise in booms and fall in recessions.[14] Second, price-cost margins in relatively unconcentrated industries "tend" to be *countercyclical*: the fall in booms and rise in recessions. Third, extensive unionization, which is more common in concentrated industries, keeps wages in those industries relatively stable over the business cycle.

Domowitz et al. explain their finding of procyclical margins in concentrated industries by showing that costs, in particular real wages, are more rigid in those industries. That is, during a boom, a firm in a concentrated industry experiences a price increase that is accompanied by only a modest cost increase, so that the gap between price and (marginal) cost rises. Unions provide one explanation for the greater rigidity of wages in concentrated industries because unionization and concentration are positively correlated.

This finding of procyclical margins in concentrated industries has important implications about how concentrated markets work. A firm raises its price-cost margin only if its demand curve becomes less elastic. There is no apparent reason why industry demand elasticities should decrease in booms. Therefore, some other explanation is needed to explain procyclical margins in concentrated industries. Possible explanations could rely on either oligopolistic interdependence (for example, incentives to cheat on the oligopoly price in booms versus recessions) or on the long-term relationship of the buyer and seller.

Some research reaches conclusions opposite to those of Domowitz et al. For example, Scherer (1980, ch. 9), in reviewing the literature, concludes that margins in concentrated industries are likely to be countercyclical. His view is based on studies that find slow adjustment of prices to cost changes in concentrated industries.

Another contradiction to the procyclical nature of margins comes from the work of Bils (1987), who finds that marginal cost is procyclical and that, in general, margins are countercyclical. He finds no effect of concentration on this relationship; however, his investigation of the concentration effect relies on fewer observations than does the work of Domowitz et al. Bils takes special care to measure marginal as opposed to average variable cost. In contrast, Domowitz et al. are forced to use average variable cost in their measure of margins. If marginal cost is rising, then the true price-cost margin could be unchanging or even falling over the business cycle, even though Domowitz et al. measure an increasing margin. While the different definition of costs may not completely explain the discrepancy between Bils and Domowitz et al., it surely reconciles at least part of the discrepancy.

A final piece of contradictory evidence to procyclical margins comes from Mills (1936). Mills studies the behavior of margins during the period before and after the Great Depression and finds them to be strongly countercyclical. Although Mills does not in-

---

[13] See Chapter 12 and Scherer (1980, chapters 9 and 13) for a survey of some of these studies.

[14] Qualls (1979) also finds this procyclical effect.

vestigate the relationship of margins to concentration, his strong finding across all industries does contrast with the finding of Domowitz et al. of a "tendency" for countercyclical behavior of margins and then only in unconcentrated industries.

International Studies.   Several studies analyze the different price flexibilities in various countries. One of the best studies is by Encaoua and Geroski (1984).[15] They use a detailed data base to estimate the relationship between price, cost, and concentration across several countries (Canada, Japan, Sweden, United Kingdom, United States) and commodities. They find, in general, that the higher the degree of concentration in a market, the slower is the adjustment of price to cost changes.[16] They show that the more an industry is characterized by new entry and competition (measured by imports), the more likely it is that prices rapidly adjust to cost changes. They also find that price flexibility varies across countries; Japan, for example, has more flexible prices than the United States. Understanding the reasons for the differential flexibility of prices across countries remains an important task.

■ EXPLAINING THE EVIDENCE

The evidence on price behavior reveals that some markets are well described by the simple models of market clearing, but others are not. Markets differ greatly in price flexibility, with the degree of concentration being an important determinant of flexibility. In some markets, price changes to one buyer are uncorrelated with those to another buyer, suggesting that other factors, such as a seller's knowledge of a buyer, are involved. In many markets, long-term relationships between buyers and sellers are important.

There are several approaches to reconciling economic theory and the observed evidence.[17] One approach is to extend and improve the simple theories. That approach can be quite fruitful, and we describe some of the most useful extensions. However, extensions to the simple theories help resolve only some of the inconsistencies between the theory and the evidence, and the remainder of this section explores alternative theories that are useful in explaining the evidence.[18]

Extensions to the Simple Theory: The Introduction of Time

The expositions of the simple theories stress price as the market-clearing mechanism and ignore the possibility of delaying consumption or production to a later time. However, nothing in the theory prevents it from taking account of such substitution over time, which is known as **intertemporal substitution.** For example, it is a straightforward extension

---

[15] See also Gordon (1983).

[16] The empirical findings of Domberger (1979) for the United Kingdom are precisely opposite. Domberger's explanation of his results is that market information should be easier for firms to gather as concentration increases, and thus prices should respond more rapidly to market changes. See also Eckard (1982).

[17] See Tucker (1938) for an early attempt.

[18] We do not explore the importance of risk aversion in explaining price rigidity. Empirical work (Carlton 1986) indicates that it is not important. See Polinsky (1985) for a detailed study of risk aversion and pricing. We also do not explicitly examine pricing under conditions of natural monopoly (see Hall 1984).

of the simple competitive model to date goods and treat a good at one date as different from the same good at a different date.[19] Once dynamic elements are introduced in this way, it is clear that a potential customer faces many substitutes to consuming a product today, not only from other products but also from the same product consumed in the future. Similarly, a supplying firm can substitute production today for production tomorrow by holding inventories.

The introduction of time into any of the simple models of competition, oligopoly, or monopoly makes them more realistic by emphasizing the importance of intertemporal substitution on both the demand side and the supply side. The following sections describe how each of the three simple theories is altered by the introduction of time.

Competition.   By the device of dating commodities, time can be introduced into the analysis of competition. Each commodity at each separate date is regarded as a distinct commodity. The insight is that intertemporal substitution on both the demand and supply side becomes an important factor in understanding how prices are determined.

The demand curve for a product at a particular time depends on consumers' perceptions about what the price of the product will be in the future. If consumers are not impatient about consuming the product, then the price today cannot deviate very far above the price expected to prevail in the future without inducing consumers to cease purchasing today and wait to do so in the future. That is, the elasticity of demand for purchases today (all else equal) will be very high. Similarly, on the supply side, intertemporal substitution affects the willingness of firms to supply the product today at a given price. Firms recognize that an alternative to producing and selling today is to produce and sell tomorrow, or perhaps to produce today, hold goods in inventory, and sell them tomorrow. The ability of a firm to decide on the optimal time path of production and the optimal employment of factors of production, one of which is inventory, affects the shape of the short-run marginal cost curve (all else equal).

A competitive equilibrium involves a separate price for each date at which the commodity may be consumed. Anything that changes production cost today or in the future or demand today or in the future affects the entire vector of prices over time. Thus a shock to demand today affects the price of a good not only today but also in the future, which raises the possibility that shocks to supply or demand today may be absorbed primarily by something other than prices today. In fact, it is quite conceivable that in response to only slight changes in the vector of prices in the future, consumers will significantly rearrange their consumption of a good over time. In such a case, an increase in demand today may have a small effect on prices today and in the future, but may shift a significant amount of consumption from today to the future.

The important insight from this view of competition is that even though prices are equating supply and demand, the necessary equilibrating price changes can be quite small: quantity shifts among different goods (in particular, the good consumed at different periods of time) may bear the brunt of the adjustment and not price.

If there are large shifts in the timing of consumption as demand or supply conditions change, the data should reveal large swings in delivery lags (the lag between the placement

---

[19] See Debreu (1959, Ch. 7).

		Standard	Median
	Standard	Deviation	Delivery
	Deviation	of log of	Lag
Industry	of log of Price	Delivery Lag	(months)
Textile mill products	.06	.17	1.26
Paper and allied products	.05	.08	.46
Steel	.03	.25	1.95
Fabricated metals	.03	.18	3.06
Nonelectrical machinery	.04	.25	3.63
Electrical machinery	.05	.10	3.86

TABLE 21.2   Price and Delivery Lag Fluctuations

SOURCE: Carlton (1983b, Table 1).

and shipment of an order). Many markets are characterized by large fluctuations in delivery dates and small fluctuations in price. For example, Table 21.2 presents measures of the variability of price and delivery lags for several major manufacturing industries. (The measure of variability, the standard deviation of the logarithm, describes the variability in percent changes.) As the table shows, the measure of variability of delivery lags is 1.6 to 8.3 times larger than the measure of variability in price for many industries. This evidence is consistent with the theory just outlined of competitive market clearing. The insight of the theory is that the price fluctuations that clear markets may be lower than those predicted by a simple model that ignores the importance of intertemporal substitution.

The importance of delivery lags in market clearing has not been extensively studied. Zarnowitz (1962, 1973) appears to have been the first to stress the importance of delivery lags as market-clearing phenomena.[20] Carlton (1985) estimates the importance of delivery lags as determinants of demand, as shown in Table 21.3. In conjunction with Table 21.2, these results imply that for many markets the fluctuations in delivery lags are almost as important to the equilibration of demand and supply as fluctuations in price. For example, Tables 21.2 and 21.3 imply that an increase of one standard deviation in the log of the price of steel causes demand to fall by about 0.43 percent while an increase of one standard deviation in the log of delivery lags causes demand to fall by about 0.20 percent.[21]

Several studies estimate the time paths by which firms adjust factors of production in an attempt to meet fluctuations in demand.[22] These studies explicitly recognize that firms can vary price, inventories, labor, and other factors of production to achieve their desired sales. Such studies of intertemporal substitution in production provide a better understanding of the behavior of price over time. For example, if it is costless to store inventories, prices cannot be expected to increase. If prices were expected to increase, there would be an incentive to sell less today and hold more inventory for the future,

---

[20] See also Maccini (1973) and Carlton (1983b).

[21] $0.43 = 0.03 \times 14.36$ and $0.20 = 0.25 \times 0.78$.

[22] See, for example, Nadiri and Rosen (1973), Haltwanger and Maccini (1983), and Topel (1982).

TABLE 21.3 Elasticities of Demand		
Industry	*Price*	*Delivery Lag*
Paper and allied products	− 1.37	− .40
	(7.9)	(3.7)
Steel	− 14.36	− .78
	(2.8)	(3.0)
Fabricated metals	− 1.75	− .30
	(1.8)	(3.6)
Nonelectrical machinery	− 3.5	− .35
	(5.4)	(3.5)
Electrical machinery	− 1.60	− .64
	(2.2)	(3.3)

Absolute values of *t*-ratios in parentheses. (A *t*-ratio in excess of about 2.0 in absolute value indicates that the estimated coefficient is statistically different from zero using commonly applied statistical criteria.)
SOURCE: Carlton (1985).

driving current price up. If prices were expected to fall, then firms would sell their current inventory today, tending to drive price down. Therefore, the possibility of inventory holding tends to stabilize price.

Intertemporal substitution affects the firm's supply curve, so too does the firm's choice of production technology. Mills and Schumann (1985) investigate which firms adopt a production technology that is flexible in the sense that the firm can, at low cost, vary its production over a wide range of outputs. For example, a firm with a flexible production technology may find it efficient to produce any output between 10 and 100, while another firm with an inflexible production technology may find it cost efficient to produce outputs only in the range 45 to 55. An understanding of the choice of flexibility of production enables an analyst to better predict the likely supply responses available in the short run to help meet changes in demand (Stigler 1939). Mills and Schumann find that small firms have more flexible production technologies than large firms. This suggests that industries in which entry and survival are difficult for small firms are less able to expand production during booms than industries with no such entry and survival difficulties. In such industries, large price fluctuations are the likely response to large changes in demand.

In summary, the introduction of time[23] into the simple competitive model helps a great deal in explaining how markets may respond to shocks without large changes in

---

[23] An analysis that recognizes the quality of goods is conceptually the same as one involving time. If goods are described by a vector of characteristics, q, then in response to a perturbation in either supply or demand, not only does the price of the good change but also its quality, q (Rosen 1974). Thus, in a perfectly competitive model, adjustments to demand or supply shocks can occur through changes in q as well as through changes in price. Although it appears that delivery lags are one of the most important quality components of a good that seem to fluctuate, there may well be others, depending upon the particular commodity. For example, in response to an increase in the demand for bus transportation during rush hour, each bus may be much more crowded than during nonrush hours. That is, a less desirable product has been substituted, and prices have remained unchanged.

current prices. Instead of large price changes, large shifts over time in the quantities consumed or produced may occur as firms or consumers take advantage of intertemporal substitution.

Oligopoly.   The introduction of time affects oligopoly models for many of the same reasons just discussed for the competitive model. That is, the ability of consumers to substitute across time periods and the ability of firms to produce across different time periods affect how the market responds to changes in supply or demand. Recent work, discussed in Chapters 9 and 10, has shown that the introduction of time adds a new element to the analysis of oligopolies that is lacking in the analyses of static oligopoly or dynamic competition. The key insight is that firms in an oligopoly are playing a game with each other over time; they are attempting to send each other signals about the likelihood of successful collusion.

In Chapters 9 and 10 we discussed the pricing implications of several different models of oligopoly over time. In Rotemberg and Saloner (1986), price wars break out in booms, while in Stigler (1964) and Porter (1983) and Green and Porter (1984), price wars break out in downturns in business activity or when economic uncertainty increases, as in inflationary times (Vining and Elwertowski 1976).[24] The empirical evidence discussed in Chapter 9 does not seem to support the Rotemberg and Saloner model.[25]

Monopoly.   The introduction of dynamic elements into the study of monopoly raises the same issues about intertemporal substitution in demand and supply discussed for competition. (Chapter 19 has already discussed the special dynamic issues that arise for a durable-goods monopolist.) For example, a monopolist that can hold inventory takes into account the relation among the marginal revenue curves at different points in time in setting its price. By taking account of these interactions one can show that the monopolist is led to choose a more stable price policy than the simple models of monopoly would suggest (Amihud and Mendelson 1983, Blinder 1982, Phlips 1983, and Reagan 1982).

The introduction of time raises one additional element in the case of monopoly (or perhaps among firms in an oligopoly) that does not arise in the case of competition. A monopolist is concerned not only with the influence of today's price on current demand, but also with its influence on future demand. For example, an increase in the price of steel scrap may lead some steel producers to alter their plans for building new steel furnaces, and this in turn affects the future demand for steel scrap. To the extent that consumers adjust their future behavior in response to price changes today, a monopolist takes that adjustment into account in setting price. In contrast, a competitive firm has no control over its price today or in the future and therefore cannot respond to incentives to influence future demand.

For example, if costs rise unexpectedly in the short run but the monopolist knows that the increase is only temporary, the monopolist may not raise its price and pass these

---

[24] See Carlton (1983a) for a further discussion of the effects of inflation on price behavior.

[25] Rotemberg and Saloner (1985) have also explored how their model can help explain inventory holdings over the business cycle.

costs on to consumers for fear that they will misinterpret the current price increases as permanent and react to them in the long-run by substituting away from the product. Therefore, a monopolist may have an incentive to absorb temporary cost increases so that the current price is a good indicator to consumers of the future price.

Fixed Costs of Changing Price

If a fixed cost must be incurred every time a price is changed, a firm will not continuously vary prices as predicted by a simple market-clearing model under either competition or monopoly. Instead, an established price will remain fixed until a new price can exceed the old one by an amount sufficient to justify incurring the fixed costs (Barro 1972).

This theory clearly accounts for price rigidities, but to be believable, it must explain the source of the fixed costs of changing a price. For example, it may cost money to publish a new catalog, print a new menu, or re-mark items already on the shelf.

Aside from the costs of having to relabel items, send out new catalogs, or print new menus, there is another reason why firms might be reluctant to change prices and might act as if they faced fixed costs for doing so. Some customers settle on a firm to buy from only after a search in which they have compared the price of that firm to the prices of other firms. As long as they believe nothing has changed, customers remain with the initially chosen firm. If they interpret a change in price by the firm as a signal that market conditions have changed, they may decide to search again to see if the chosen firm still has attractive prices.

If the fixed costs of changing prices are high, then small price changes will tend not to occur. Carlton (1986) tabulates the smallest observed price changes across a wide variety of products sold at the intermediate level of manufacturing. Table 21.4 presents the smallest price changes observed and shows that for the large majority of commodities examined, the smallest price changes are quite small. This evidence indicates that small price changes occur in many transactions and suggests that, at least for these transactions, the fixed costs of changing prices are small.[26]

Implications of an Unchanging Price

Several studies (Carlton 1986, Cecchetti 1985) show that for many products, the price, once set, does not change for some time thereafter. Models where price is temporarily fixed have different implications from the standard ones. The new features of models with temporarily fixed prices are that prices no longer instantaneously adjust to allocate goods to consumers, who therefore run some risk of not being able to satisfy their demands. The standard theories never consider the possibility that a product may be unavailable. Yet unavailability of a product is a fact of life in many markets and is one that our economic theories should deal with.

---

[26] We use the word *suggest* because it is possible that we observe small price changes only when the new supply and demand conditions are expected to persist for a long time. The evidence could then be consistent with significant fixed costs of changing prices that cause prices to remain rigid for temporary shifts in supply and demand, but not for permanent ones. Although this explanation is possible, we have seen no evidence to support it.

TABLE 21.4   Fraction of Price Changes Accounted for by Small Price Changes

Product	Contract Type	Size of Price Change			
		<0.25%	<0.50%	<1%	<2%
Steel	Annual	.04	.08	.11	.27
	Quarterly	.05	.11	.17	.24
	Monthly	.09	.20	.36	.52
Nonferrous metals	Annual	.02	.05	.09	.27
	Quarterly	.02	.05	.12	.25
	Monthly	.08	.15	.28	.49
Petroleum	Annual	0	0	.08	.24
	Quarterly	0	0	.02	.17
	Monthly	.01	.05	.19	.47
Rubber tires	Annual	.12	.21	.30	.44
	Quarterly	.07	.11	.18	.34
	Monthly	.13	.23	.38	.63
Paper	Annual	.04	.09	.08	.27
	Quarterly	0	.19	.24	.33
	Monthly	.13	.23	.43	.62
Chemicals	Annual	.04	.08	.13	.24
	Quarterly	0	.05	.11	.24
	Monthly	.05	.14	.30	.42
Cement	Annual	.14	.22	.32	.46
	Quarterly	0	0	.01	.19
	Monthly	.71	.75	.85	.94
Glass	Annual	0	0	.07	.19
	Quarterly	0	0	.20	.40
	Monthly	.03	.20	.45	.67
Truck motors	Annual	.03	.03	.12	.20
	Quarterly	0	0	0	.08
	Monthly	.12	.27	.50	.75
Plywood	Annual	—	—	—	—
	Quarterly	.01	.02	.06	.19
	Monthly	.19	.38	.54	.72
Household appliances	Annual	0	0	0	.25
	Quarterly	—	—	—	—
	Monthly	.22	.44	.70	.95

SOURCE: Carlton (1986, Table 3).

Mills (1962) examines the behavior of a monopolist that must set price and production before observing demand. The optimal policy for the monopolist is to have enough output available so that the expected price equals marginal cost. The expected price equals the price charged times the probability that a customer arrives and purchases the output. The optimal inventory-holding policy of the firm depends on the markup of price above cost. The closer price to cost, the smaller the optimal inventory; conversely, the higher the markup, the larger the optimal inventory. The incentive to hold inventory declines as the markup falls because the profit from making a sale falls, while the cost of holding unsold goods remains unchanged. What is interesting about this relationship is that the probability of *stock-outs* (shortages) increases as the market price falls to marginal production cost.

Models analyzing the availability of goods in competitive markets are developed in Carlton (1977, 1978, 1984b, 1989b), DeVany and Saving (1977), and Gould (1978). In these models, consumers judge a firm not only by its pricing policy but also by its inventory policy. Consumers care not only about the price but also about the probability that a good is available. Inventory policy affects the probability that a firm has the good available. Some consumers prefer to shop at high-price stores that run out of goods infrequently, while others prefer to shop at stores that charge low prices but may run out of goods frequently.

Since a firm must maintain a relatively large inventory to satisfy customers whose demands fluctuate a great deal, the variability of consumers' demand for a product affects a firm's costs. Thus, the cost function of the firm depends upon the demand characteristics of consumers. The simple separation between supply curves and demand curves is lost in these models.

If variability of demand influences a firm's costs, the firm will want to charge different consumers different prices based on their respective variability of demand. These price differences do not represent price discrimination; they reflect cost differences. Prices to consumers differ according to each consumer's variability of demand, even if each purchases the same quantity of a physically identical product in the long run. Moreover, if the variability of one customer's demand changes, then the price to that consumer would change while the prices to other consumers remain unchanged. The result would be a low correlation of price changes across consumers—a finding that characterizes many markets.

Asymmetric Information and Moral Hazard

In many economic transactions, buyers and sellers have different information. For example, a person who buys a house generally knows less about it than the seller, who has lived there for a long time. Some buyers of IBM stock may know less about IBM than other investors who are employed by IBM. Does the introduction of this kind of asymmetric information affect how markets reach equilibrium? Akerlof (1970) shows that it does. He shows that with asymmetric information, equilibrium no longer requires supply to equal demand. Moreover, not only does asymmetric information affect how prices are set, it can also cause markets to vanish completely.

Akerlof uses a simple example to illustrate his point. Consider a market in which buyers purchase used cars that differ in quality. Buyers know nothing about the quality of particular used cars; they only know the quality of the average car sold. Sellers, on the other hand, know exactly the quality of their used cars. At any price, p, an owner is willing to sell a car only if its value is *less than or equal to p*. If only cars whose quality is valued at p or *less* are placed on the market, then the *average* quality of cars offered at price p will be valued at less than p. But if the average quality of a car offered at p is not valued at p, the price will fall. A simple repetition of the argument shows that no matter how low the price falls, the average quality offered in the marketplace is always valued at less than the stated price. This causes the market to vanish entirely: the price mechanism does not clear the market, and there is no market left to clear. This collapse of a market can occur even though there may be buyers and sellers who, in a world of perfect information, would find it mutually beneficial to transact with each other. (Akerlof's model is described in more detail in Chapter 17.)

Akerlof's model can be extended to show how equilibrium may be characterized by either excess demand or supply (Stiglitz 1976, 1984). For example, suppose a firm wishes to hire a worker of a particular skill level. The firm obviously wants to pay as little as possible for such a worker. However, if the firm advertises a low wage, the people who apply for the job are likely to be low-quality workers. The higher the wage rate offered, the higher the average quality of the applicant.[27] Therefore, when a firm has difficulty measuring worker quality in advance, it is sensible for it to set a wage high enough to attract more than one applicant. Equilibrium, therefore, involves setting a high wage and having an excess supply of labor apply to the firm.

Akerlof's model has been extended to a variety of other markets. For example, Keeton (1980) and Stiglitz and Weiss (1981) examine the market for loans. They observe that when a bank makes a loan, it cannot perfectly monitor the riskiness of the borrower's investments. One response of a borrower to a higher interest rate might be to take on riskier projects. A bank may sometimes be unwilling to raise the interest rate in the face of excess demand for loans for fear that the increased interest rate will drive borrowers to pursue riskier projects, to the bank's disadvantage. Therefore, the bank might refuse to make additional loans rather than raise the interest rate. In this example asymmetric information leads to an equilibrium in which supply does not equal demand and there is a rigidity in a price variable, the interest rate. In short, asymmetric information creates incentives for **adverse selection**, in which the worst risks respond to the uninformed's offer (only bad workers show up for a low-paying job), and for **moral hazard**, in which individual's alter their actions in response to the uninformed's offer (borrowers choose riskier investments in response to higher interest rates), and can, as a result, lead either to the disappearance of markets or to a market equilibrium in which supply does not equal demand and there are rigidities in the relevant price variables.

Toward a General Theory of Allocation

This section sketches a theory that explains some of the puzzling evidence on price behavior that has already been reviewed. The theory relies on the simple insight that if it is costly to use a price system, then alternative allocation mechanisms may develop.[28]

The Cost of Creating a Market That Clears by Price Alone.   The key feature that the simple theories of market clearing ignore is that it is costly to create a market in which price allocates goods to buyers. The standard theory often pretends that a fictional auc-

---

[27] The average quality rises with the wage because higher quality workers (in addition to the lower quality workers who applied at the lower wage) apply for a job as the wage rises.

[28] The theories in this section are developed in detail by Carlton (1989b). See also Okun (1981) and Williamson (1975).

TABLE 21.5 Death Rates of Futures Markets	
Age (years)	Probability of Dying at the Given Age or Less
1	.16
2	.25
3	.31
4	.37
5	.40
10	.50

SOURCE: Carlton (1984a, Table 5).

tioneer adjusts prices to clear markets. But in most markets, there is no such person. The markets that probably come closest to the textbook model of competitive markets are financial markets, such as futures markets. In a futures market, transactions for the right to buy or sell in the future occur. For example, Daniel agrees to buy and Lisa agrees to sell 1 bushel of wheat on April 1 of next year at an agreed-upon price. It is costly to run a futures market. Aside from the actual physical space required, there is the time cost for all those who participate in the market. For example, at the Chicago Board of Trade, there are floor traders, employees of the brokerage firms, as well as the members of the associated clearinghouses. The users of futures markets must somehow pay all the people who work either directly or indirectly in making the transactions for customers.[29] These payments can take several forms, such as direct commissions or bid-ask spreads.[30]

An important cost of making markets is the time cost of the actual customers (Becker 1965). A market in which customers had to spend large amounts of their own time in order to transact could be inefficient. The purpose of a market is not merely to create transactions, but to create transactions at the lowest cost.

Because the creation of markets is itself a productive activity that consumes resources, it makes sense to regard the making of markets as an industry. There has not been much research on the "making of markets," but just as there is competition to produce a better mousetrap, so too there is competition to produce better and more efficient markets. The New York Stock Exchange competes with the American Stock Exchange; the Chicago Mercantile Exchange competes with the Chicago Board of Trade, and so on.[31]

Lest one think that it is easy to create a successful futures market, one need only consult the historical record. Table 21.5 presents the average failure rates of new, successfully introduced futures markets (those listed in the *Wall Street Journal*) in the United States. The table indicates that about 40 percent of all futures markets fail by their fifth year. The making of successful markets is a risky activity, and as the exchanges themselves well know, it is hard to predict which markets will succeed and which will fail.

---

[29] Markets benefit nonusers too by providing price information. This creates a free-rider problem.

[30] If the *bid* price—the price the trader buys at—is below the *ask* price—the price the trader sells at—the trader can make a profit on each transaction.

[31] See Carlton (1984a) for a study of the competition in the introduction of new futures markets.

Futures markets are markets that clear by price alone, and such markets exist for only a handful of commodities. Because there are definitely social benefits to the creation of such markets, and because at least some of these benefits can probably be privately appropriated, the paucity of such markets emphasizes that it must be costly to create them.

Heterogeneity of the Product.   The heterogeneity of the product is perhaps the most critical characteristic in determining whether an organized market (for example, one with an auctioneer) can be created that clears by price alone. If buyers prefer to buy at different firms or at different times or have different preferences for quality, it becomes more difficult to create an organized market that clears by price alone. Attempts to do so in the face of widespread product heterogeneity lead to markets with only a few traders in any given product, and the traders will not be able to pay for the cost of running the market (Telser and Higgenbotham 1977).

Suppose that each buyer can purchase a standardized product or one specifically designed for the buyer. The advantage of a specially designed product depends on how idiosyncratic the buyer's needs are. The disadvantage is that the buyer is forced to transact in a less liquid (higher transaction cost) market. (There are few firms that can supply the buyer, and hence the transaction costs, studied in Chapter 2, rise.) The greater the benefits from custom-designing a product to one's own specifications, the less likely it is that a market can be created that clears by price alone. Indeed, in the extreme case, in which every buyer demands a slightly different product, it is impossible for traders to trade with each other without enumerating each product's characteristics, and the incentive to create an organized market is small.

Marketing Clearing in the Absence of Organized Markets.   When an organized market does not exist, firms cannot costlessly discover the market clearing price, and they must rely on other methods to determine how to allocate their products to buyers. A wide variety of mechanisms other than the auction-price mechanism can be used to clear a market. One alternative suggested by Stigler (1961) is customer search. In Stigler's model, there is no organized market in which price equates supply to demand. Instead, buyers must search across different sellers in order to discover prices (see Chapter 17). Buyers' search costs become the resource cost of operating the market.

Firms posting prices and consumers searching across firms is only one of many ways in which markets can function. An alternative is for firms to hire salespeople whose task it is to become knowledgeable about the demands of individual customers. Even if it is difficult for the firm to set the market-clearing price, it may be possible to identify those customers who should obtain the goods so that goods are efficiently allocated.[32] The firm could use price to identify those buyers who want the goods the most and then could use its knowledge of each buyer's needs to decide which of those buyers should receive the goods. So, for example, it would not be uncommon during times of tight supply for

---

[32] For example, imagine that a firm with a capacity of 100 units has only two buyers who are known to be identical. If the firm is supply-constrained (that is, each buyer's demands are high at the stated price), then the efficient allocation is obvious (50–50), but the market-clearing price is not. (See Carlton 1989b for more details.)

steady customers to get delivery while new customers stand waiting. It would also not be unusual for buyers and sellers to enter into long-term relationships so that they could better understand each other's needs.

If price is not the sole mechanism used to allocate goods, prices may remain rigid even though goods are being efficiently allocated. Although rigid prices can imply inefficiency under any of the simple models in which price is the exclusive mechanism for efficient resource allocation, they do not necessarily imply inefficiency in a world in which price is but one of many methods firms use to allocate goods.

A theory that combines price with nonprice methods of allocation has the following implications[33]:

- The longer the buyer and seller have dealt with each other (the better they know each other), the less need there is to rely on price to allocate goods efficiently. A seller's knowledge of a buyer's need can be a substitute for an impersonal (auction) market that clears by price alone.

- The length of time over which a buyer and seller do business becomes a characteristic of the transaction and can make one buyer different from another from the seller's viewpoint. Therefore, observing differences in price movements to different buyers who buy identical physical commodities may reveal nothing about allocative efficiency; prices for different "products" should be expected to move differently from one another. The evidence from Stigler and Kindahl (1970) that indices of spot prices and long-term contract prices do not always move together is consistent with this implication, as is the evidence that the correlation of price movements across buyers of the same product is often low.

- The pattern of a buyer's demand over the business cycle or, alternatively, the co-movement of one buyer's demands with those of other buyers, is crucial information for the seller because it permits the seller to plan capacity to customer needs. Even though two buyers purchase identical commodities, they may be charged different prices and have their prices change differently simply because they have different buying patterns over time. The evidence on different price movements for different buyers of the same product is consistent with this observation.

- Rapid turnover of customers prevents the use of long-term relationships in which a seller's knowledge of customers is used to allocate goods. Industries with significant new entry or with customers that have little firm or brand loyalty, should rely on price as the primary mechanism to allocate goods.

- The establishment of a new futures market disrupts the traditional pricing policies of existing firms in an industry. These firms should be expected to complain about the introduction of the new futures market. If the allocation of goods is a productive activity that requires resources, then a futures market acts as a competitor to the marketing departments of firms in the industry. Futures markets create marketing information. Without futures markets, other agents, such as salespeople, must create

---

[33] Additional implications regarding behavior during periods of price controls, speed of price adjustment, behavior of price indices, and the role of marketing departments are discussed and tested in Carlton (1986, 1989b).

this marketing information and be compensated for doing so. If a futures market is established, there is increased competition in marketing, and the value of marketing skills declines. Therefore, it is natural for firms that were successfully performing the marketing function before the introduction of the futures market to complain about the increased competition.

There is some evidence of hostility towards the creation of new futures markets from members of the affected industries. For example, the aluminum futures market was established in the late 1970s. Aluminum producers opposed its establishment (*American Metal Market*, Jan. 6, 1978, p 9). One possible motivation for the opposition of the aluminum companies is that the resources they had invested in marketing were now competing with the resources of a futures market to market the product, and the competition would reduce the anticipated returns on their marketing investment.

■ MARKET STRUCTURE IS MORE THAN CONCENTRATION

Industrial organization economists often examine how market behavior differs as concentration in a market changes.[34] However, there are many other features of market structure that matter a great deal in explaining how markets behave and, in particular, how they respond to shocks in either supply or demand. For example, the previous sections show that market operation is significantly influenced by the ability of consumers and suppliers to substitute over time, and by the market's reliance on price to allocate goods. This section presents two illustrations of market characteristics that influence an industry's responses to shifts in either supply or demand.[35] The two illustrations involve whether an industry holds inventories and whether an industry has a fixed price in the face of random demand. Although we treat these characteristics as given and proceed to analyze the subsequent industry behavior, the reader should recognize that these characteristics themselves depend on underlying economic conditions.

Produce-to-Order versus Produce-to-Stock

Industries can be organized in two basic ways: they can wait for orders to come in and then produce (**produce-to-order**), or they can produce first, hold inventories, and then hope to sell the products (**produce-to-stock**).[36] Although there is not much research on this topic, our economy has probably increased its reliance on industries that produce to order versus those that produce to stock, especially with the relative growth of the service sector in recent times.

---

[34] This experiment only makes sense if concentration in a market is an exogenous variable. Research has suggested that concentration is an endogenous variable and is influenced by the relative efficiency of firms (Demsetz 1973, Peltzman 1977). See Schmalensee (1985) for a different viewpoint.

[35] Other illustrations include the incentives the industry has to plan (Carlton 1982), the degree of vertical integration, (Carlton 1983a, Wachter and Williamson 1978), the importance of new products (Shleifer 1986), and the effect of search (Lucas 1981, Diamond 1982).

[36] See Zarnowitz (1973) and Belesley (1975).

An industry that produces to stock can satisfy customers more quickly and can take greater advantage of economies of scale than an industry that produces to order. On the other hand, an industry that produces to order eliminates the cost of inventory holdings of the final good (though not necessarily of inputs), can custom-design products to closely match buyers' specifications, and can, perhaps, use flexible technologies to compensate for its lack of inventory holdings of the final output. The need to cut or raise prices significantly in order to clear markets is greater in produce-to-stock industries than in produce-to-order ones. Moreover, the transmission of shocks to other sectors of the economy or into the future depends on whether an industry produces to stock (that is, holds inventories). For example, if either firms or final consumers are holding inventories, a temporary increase in demand is at least partially accommodated by a decrease in inventory that, next period, will lead to an increase in production as the inventory is replenished. If inventory is not being held, the increase in demand may drive up only current prices, with little, if any, increase in production in the current or subsequent periods.

Transmission of Shocks in Industries with Fixed Prices

Suppose that once prices in a particular industry are set, they don't change for some period of time. (This assumption is consistent with the earlier evidence.) The production of the goods must occur before demand is observed, and therefore there is some risk that firms will run out of the good. Carlton (1977) shows that the ratio of inventory to average demand depends on the ratio of price to cost. The reason is that the opportunity cost of a lost sale rises with price, so that the incentive to hold inventories increases with price. If price exceeds cost by a large amount, the amount of goods produced exceeds the amount demanded, on average. In the contrasting case, price is close to cost, so that inventory on hand is small relative to the average level of demand—and the firm will frequently run out of stock.

Carlton (1977) also shows that in response to an increase in the riskiness of demand, firms increase their inventory holdings when price significantly exceeds marginal cost and decrease them when price is close to marginal cost. Firms that operate with little extra inventory are not able to cushion demand shocks. Therefore, when prices are temporarily unchanging and demand becomes riskier, an economy is more vulnerable to disruption (stock-outs) from shocks the closer prices are to marginal costs.

Economists have recently investigated the aggregate macroeconomic implications of models involving fixed costs of price changes (Akerlof and Yellen 1985), Mankiw 1985, and Blanchard and Kiyotaki 1987).[37] This work shows that the need to adjust prices may be less important for a firm than for the economy as a whole. The reason is that firms are assumed to have market power, so that there is a gap between price and marginal cost. So, for example, the firm's decision to change price in response to a demand change depends on whether the resulting increased profit, which depends on the gap between the new marginal revenue and marginal cost, offsets the fixed cost of the price change.

---

[37] See also Dreze (1975), Fischer (1977), Hall (1978), Malinvaud (1979), Rotemberg (1982), and Phelps and Taylor (1977).

Society's increased welfare from the price change depends on the gap between price (not marginal revenue) and marginal cost and the fixed cost of the price change. If the firm was initially maximizing profits, so that marginal revenue equals marginal cost, then for small changes in demand the firm has no incentive to lower price even if society would benefit. Therefore, a firm's incentive to incur a cost to change price and society's incentive to do so may diverge.[38]

■ SUMMARY

This chapter surveys what economists know about the way markets clear. The evidence about price behavior is sufficiently inconsistent with the simple theories of market clearing that economists are now exploring more sophisticated theories. Prices for some products are much more rigid than any of the standard theories predict. The availability of a good is an important concern in many markets, yet that concern never arises in the standard theories. New theories have been developed to account for some of the more puzzling features of market clearing. These theories recognize that intertemporal substitution matters, that marketing is a costly activity, that an impersonal price mechanism is not the only device used to allocate goods, and that price adjustments in conjunction with nonprice methods are often used for allocation.

■ Key Terms

administered prices
adverse selection
intertemporal substitution
market clearing

moral hazard
price rigidity
produce-to-order
produce-to-stock

■ Discussion Questions

1. The Smiths plan to celebrate their anniversary in three months by going out to dinner. They decide to line up a babysitter now to take care of their young children. The Smiths will place an ad in the local weekly newspaper. Is it a good strategy for them to offer to pay 25¢ an hour and see if anyone responds and, if not, then raise the offer to the more standard $5 per hour? Explain.
2. Price rigidity implies an inefficiency. Explain.

3. As the supply curve shifts, price responds in the competitive model. Show how the price response changes as the price elasticity of demand increases.
4. If a monopolist suffers a decline in demand because of a recession, is it possible to say what is likely to happen to price?
5. Inventories help firms meet unexpected surges in demand. If firms could predict surges in demand, they would need less inventory. Would improved communications between firms lead to less inventory?

---

[38] A closely related point is that in the presence of distortions between price and marginal cost, the value of an output expansion can be greater to society than to a firm (see Harberger 1971). Hart (1982) and Hall (1988) apply this principle in a macroeconomic setting.

■ Problems

1. Suppose a bakery must bake bread before it observes the demand for bread. There will be either 100 or 50 customers; each outcome is equally likely. Let each customer have a demand for one loaf of bread, provided the price is $5 or less, and let the constant unit cost of production be $1. What are the optimal price and number of loaves if the bakery is a monopoly? Suppose the most consumers would pay for a loaf of bread is $1.50. How do your answers change?

2. Suppose an industry produces to order. What economic conditions would have to change for it to become a produce-to-stock industry?

3. Suppose that a firm has an upward sloping marginal cost curve. Illustrate how the price-cost margin behaves as price increases. (Use marginal cost to measure cost.) What happens to your answer if average variable cost is used instead of marginal cost in the definition of the price-cost margin?

4. Is the establishment of an organized auction market more likely to benefit small firms or large firms?

5. Suppose two customers pay different prices for the identical physical product. When would it be appropriate for an analyst to conclude that there is no price discrimination?

_____

Answers to the odd-numbered problems are given at the back of the book.

■ References

Akerlof, George A. 1970. "The Market for 'Lemons': Quality, Uncertainty, and the Market Mechanism." *Quarterly Journal of Economics* 84:488–500.

Akerlof, George A., and Janet L. Yellen. 1985. "A Near-Rational Model of the Business Cycle, With Wage and Price Inertia." *Quarterly Journal of Economics* 100(Supp.):823–38.

Amihud, Yakov, and Haim Mendelson. 1983. "Price Smoothing and Inventory." *Review of Economic Studies* 50:87–98.

Arrow, Kenneth J. 1959. "Toward a theory of Price Adjustment," in Moses, Abromovitz et al., *The Allocation of Economic Resources*, Stanford, Calif.: Stanford University Press.

Barro, Robert J. 1972. "A Theory of Monopolistic Price Adjustment." *Review of Economic Studies* 39:17–26.

Beals, R. 1975. "Concentrated Industries, Administered Prices, and Inflation: A Survey of Empirical Research." *Council on Wage and Price Stability*. Washington D.C.

Becker, Gary. 1965. "A Theory of Allocation of Time." *Economic Journal* 75:493–517.

Belesley, David A. 1975. *Industry Production Behavior*. Amsterdam: North Holland.

Bils, Mark. 1987. "The Cyclical Behavior of Marginal Cost and Price." *American Economic Review* 77:838–55.

Blanchard, Oliver, and N. Kiyotaki. 1987. "Monopolistic Competition and the Effects of Aggregate Demand." *American Economic Review* 77:647–66.

Blinder, Alan S. 1982. "Inventories and Sticky Prices: More on the Microfoundations of Macroeconomics." *American Economic Review* 72:334–48.

Carlton, Dennis W. 1977. "Uncertainty, Production Lags, and Pricing." *American Economic Review* 67:244–49.

_____. 1978. "Market Behavior with Demand Uncertainty and Price Inflexibility." *American Economic Review* 68:571–87.

_____. 1979. "Contracts, Price Rigidity, and Market Equilibrium." *Journal of Political Economy* 87:1034–62.

_____. 1982. "Planning and Market Structure," in John J. McCall, ed., *The Economics of Information and Uncertainty*. Chicago: University of Chicago Press, 47–72.

_____. 1983a. "The Disruptive Effect of Inflation on the Organization of Markets," in Robert Hall, ed., *Inflation*. Chicago: University of Chicago Press, 139–52.

_____. 1983b. "Equilibrium Fluctuations When Price and Delivery Lag Clear the Market." *Bell Journal of Economics* 14:562–72.

_____. 1984a. "Futures Markets: Their Purpose, Their History, Their Growth, Their Successes and Failures." *Journal of Futures Markets* 4:237–71.

————. 1984b. *Market Behavior Under Uncertainty*. New York: Garland Press.

————. 1985. "Delivery Lags as a Determinant of Demand." Unpublished.

————. 1986. "The Rigidity of Prices." *American Economic Review* 76:637–58.

————. 1989a. "The Theory and Facts of How Markets Clear: Is Industrial Organization Useful for Understanding Macroeconomics?" in Richard Schmalensee and Robert Willig, eds., *The Handbook of Industrial Organization*. Amsterdam: North Holland Press.

————. 1989b. "The Theory of Allocation and Its Implications for Marketing and Industrial Structure." Unpublished.

Cecchetti, Stephen G. 1985. "Staggered Contracts and the Frequency of Price Adjustment." *Quarterly Journal of Economics* 100:935–59.

Chandler, Alfred D., Jr. 1977. *The Visible Hand: The Managerial Revolution in American Business*. Cambridge, Mass.: Harvard University Press.

Debreu, Gerard. 1959. *Theory of Value: An Axiomatic Analysis of Economic Equilibrium*. New York: John Wiley and Sons.

Demsetz, Harold. 1973. "Industry Structure, Market Rivalry, and Public Policy." *Journal of Law and Economics* 16:1–9.

DeVany, Arthur S., and Thomas R. Saving. 1977. "Product Quality, Uncertainty, and Regulation: The Trucking Industry." *American Economic Review* 67:583–94.

Diamond, Peter. 1982. "Aggregate Demand Management in Search Equilibrium." *Journal of Political Economy* 90:881–94.

Domberger, Simon. 1979. "Price Adjustment and Market Structure." *The Economic Journal* 89:96–108.

Domowitz, Ian, Glenn R. Hubbard, and Bruce C. Petersen. 1986a. "The Intertemporal Stability of the Concentration-Margins Relationship." *Journal of Industrial Economics* 35:13–34.

————. 1986b. "Business Cycles and the Relationship Between Concentration and Price-Cost Margins." *Rand Journal of Economics* 17:1–17.

————. 1987. "Oligopoly Supergames: Some Empirical Evidence on Prices and Margins." *Journal of Industrial Economics* 35:379–98.

Dreze, Jacques H. 1975. "Existence of an Exchange Equilibrium Under Price Rigidities." *International Economic Review* 16:301–20.

Eckard, E. Woodrow, Jr. 1982. "Firm Market Share, Price Flexibility and Imperfect Information." *Economic Inquiry* 20:388–92.

Encaoua, David, and Paul Geroski. 1984. "Price Dynamics and Competition in Five Countries." University of Southampton, Working Paper no. 8414.

Fischer, Stanley. 1977. "Long-Term Contracts, Rational Expectations, and the Optimal Money Supply Rule." *Journal of Political Economy* 85:191–205.

Gordon, Robert. 1983. "A Century of Evidence on Wage and Price Stickiness in the United States, The United Kingdom, and Japan," in James Tobin, ed., *Macroeconomics, Prices, and Quantities: Essays in Memory of Arthur M. Okun*. Washington, D.C.: The Brookings Institution, 85–134.

Gould, John P. 1978. "Inventories and Stochastic Demand: Equilibrium Models of the Firm and Industry." *Journal of Business* 51:1–42.

Green, Edward J., and Robert H. Porter. 1984. "Noncooperative Collusion Under Imperfect Price Information." *Econometrica* 52:87–100.

Grossman, Sanford J., and Joseph E. Stiglitz. 1980. "On the Impossibility of Informationally Efficient Markets." *American Economic Review* 70:393–408.

Hall, Robert E. 1978. "The Macroeconomic Impact of Changes in Income Taxes in the Short and Medium Runs." *Journal of Political Economy* 86:571–85.

————. 1984. "The Inefficiency of Marginal Cost Pricing and the Apparent Rigidity of Prices." National Bureau of Economic Research, Working Paper no. 1347.

————. 1988. "A Non-Competitive Equilibrium Model of Fluctuations." National Bureau of Economic Research, Working Paper no. 2576.

Haltwanger, John, and Louis J. Maccini. 1983. "A Model of Inventory and Layoff Behavior Under Uncertainty." Unpublished.

Harberger, Arnold C. 1971. "Three Basic Postulates for Applied Welfare Economics: An Interpretive Essay." *Journal of Economic Literature* 9:109–38.

Hart, Oliver. 1982. "A Model of Imperfect Competition with Keynesian Features." *Quarterly Journal of Economics* 97:109–38.

Hubbard, Glenn, and Robert Weiner. 1986. "Contracting and Price Flexibility in Product Markets." Unpublished.

Keeton, William R. 1980. *Equilibrium Credit Rationing*. New York: Garland Press.

Lucas, Robert E., Jr. 1981. *Studies in Business-Cycle Theory*. Cambridge: The MIT Press.

Lustgarten, Steven H. 1975. "Administered Inflation: A Reappraisal." *Economic Inquiry* 13:191–206.

McAllister, Henry. 1961. "Government Price Statistics." Hearings before the Subcommittee on Economic Statistics of the Joint Economic Committee, 87th Cong., 1st Session. Washington, D.C.: U.S. Government Printing Office.

Maccini, Louis J. 1973. "On Optimal Delivery Lags." *Journal of Economic Theory* 6:107–25.

Malinvaud, E. 1979. *The Theory of Unemployment Reconsidered*. New York: Halsted Press.

Mankiw, N. Gregory. 1985. "Small Menu Costs and Large Business Cycles: A Macroeconomic Model." *Quarterly Journal of Economics* 100:529–38.

Means, Gardiner C. 1935. "Industrial Prices and Their Relative Inflexibility." Senate Document 13, 74th Congress, 1st session. Washington, D.C.: U.S. Government Printing Office.

———. 1972. "The Administered Price Thesis Reconfirmed." *American Economic Review* 63:292–306.

Mills, David E., and Laurence Schumann. 1985. "Industry Structure with Fluctuating Demand." *American Economic Review* 75:758–67.

Mills, Edwin. 1962. *Prices, Output and Inventory Policy*. New York: John Wiley and Sons.

Mills, Frederick C. 1927. *The Behavior of Prices*, New York: National Bureau of Economic Research.

———. 1936. *Prices in Recession and Recovery*. New York: National Bureau of Economic Research.

Nadiri, M. Ishaq, and Sherwin Rosen. 1973. *A Disequilibrium Model of the Demand for Factors of Production*. New York: National Bureau of Economic Research and Columbia University Press.

Okun, Arthur. 1981. *Prices and Quantities: A Macroeconomic Analysis*. Washington, D.C.: The Brookings Institution.

Peltzman, Sam. 1977. "The Gains and Losses from Industrial Concentration." *Journal of Law and Economics* 20:229–63.

Phelps, Edmund S., and John B. Taylor. 1977. "Stabilizing Powers of Monetary Policy Under Rational Expectations." *Journal of Political Economy* 85:163–90.

Phlips, Louis. 1983. *The Economics of Price Discrimination: Four Essays in Applied Price Theory*. New York: Cambridge University Press.

Polinsky, A. Mitchell. 1985. "Fixed-Price versus Spot-Price Contracts: A Study in Risk Allocation." Stanford Law School, Working paper no. 20.

Porter, Robert H. 1983. "Optimal Cartel Trigger-Price Strategies." *Journal of Economic Theory* 29:313–38.

Qualls, P. David. 1979. "Market Structure and the Cyclical Flexibility of Price-Cost Margins." *Journal of Business* 52:305–25.

Reagan, Patricia B. 1982. "Inventory and Price Behavior." *Review of Economic Studies* 49:137–42.

Rosen, Sherwin. 1974. "Hedonic Prices and Implicit Markets: Product Differentiation in Pure Competition." *Journal of Political Economy* 82:34–55.

Rotemberg, Julio J. 1982. "Sticky Prices in the United States." *Journal of Political Economy* 90:1187–1211.

Rotemberg, Julio J., and Garth Saloner. 1985. "Strategic Inventories and the Excess Volatility of Production." Sloan School of Management, MIT, Working Paper no. 1650-85.

———. 1986. "A Supergame-Theoretic Model of Price Wars During Booms." *American Economic Review* 76:390–407.

Salop, Steven C. 1979. "Monopolistic Competition with Outside Goods." *Bell Journal of Economics* 10:141–56.

Scherer, Frederic M. 1980. *Industrial Market Structure and Economic Performance*. Chicago: Rand McNally.

Schmalensee, Richard. 1982. "Product Differentiation Advantages of Pioneering Brands." *American Economic Review* 72:349–65.

———. 1985. "Do Markets Differ Much?" *American Economic Review* 75:341–51.

Shleifer, Andrei. 1986. "Implementation Cycles." *Journal of Political Economy* 94:1163–90.

Stigler, George J. 1939. "Production and Distribution in the Short Run." *Journal of Political Economy* 47:305–27.

———. 1961. "The Economics of Information." *Journal of Political Economy* 69:213–25.

———. 1964. "A Theory of Oligopoly." *Journal of Political Economy* 72:44–61.

Stigler, George J., and James K. Kindahl. 1970. *Behavior of Industrial Prices*. New York: National Bureau of Economic Research.

———. 1973. "Industrial Prices, as Administered by Dr. Means." *American Economic Review* 63:717–21.

Stiglitz, Joseph E. 1976. "Prices and Queues as Screening Devices in Competitive Markets." IMSS Technical Report no. 212. Stanford University.

———. 1984. "Price Rigidities and Market Structure." *American Economic Review* 74:350–55.

Stiglitz, Joseph E., and Andrew Weiss. 1981. "Credit Rationing in Markets with Imperfect Information." *American Economic Review* 71:393–410.

Telser, Lester G., and Harlow N. Higgenbotham. 1977. "Organized Futures Markets: Costs and Benefits." *Journal of Political Economy* 85:969–1000.

Topel, Robert H. 1982. "Inventories, Layoffs, and the Short-Run Demand for Labor." *American Economic Review* 72:769–87.

Tucker, Rufus. 1938. "The Reasons for Price Rigidity." *American Economic Review* 28:41–54.

Vining, Daniel R., Jr., and Thomas C. Elwertowski. 1976. "The Relationship Between Relative Prices and the General Price Level." *American Economic Review* 66:699–708.

Wachter, Michael L., and Oliver E. Williamson. 1978. "Obligational Markets and the Mechanics of Inflation." *Bell Journal of Economics* 9:549–71.

Weiss, Leonard W. 1977. "Stigler, Kindahl, and Means on Administered Prices." *American Economic Review* 67:610–19.

Weston, Fred, and Stephen Lustgarten. 1974. "Concen-tration and Wage-Price Changes," in Harvey J. Gold-schmidt, ed., *Industrial Concentration: The New Learning*. Boston: Little, Brown, 307–38.

Williamson, Oliver, E. 1975. *Markets and Hierarchies—Analysis and Antitrust Implications: A Study in the Economics of Internal Organization*. New York: The Free Press.

Zarnowitz, Victor. 1962. "Unfilled Orders, Price Changes, and Business Fluctuations." *Review of Economics and Statistics* 44:367–94.

———. 1973. *Orders, Production, and Investment: A Cyclical and Structural Analysis*. New York: National Bureau of Economic Research.

———. 1985. "Recent Work on Business Cycles in His-torical Perspective: A Review of Theories and Evi-dence." *Journal of Economic Literature* 23:523–80.

GOVERNMENT POLICIES AND THEIR EFFECTS

CHAPTER 22

ANTITRUST LAWS AND POLICY

The first thing we do, let's kill all the lawyers.

WILLIAM SHAKESPEARE

T he **antitrust laws** are the major policy vehicle that the United States government uses to influence the ways in which firms compete with each other. The antitrust laws do not make monopoly illegal. They do control how firms can attain and maintain their market positions. This chapter describes the antitrust laws and how they affect efficiency. It is not intended as a complete course in the antitrust law; it is designed to provide an overview of the most important developments and issues in federal antitrust policy.[1]

The chapter first presents the major antitrust statutes and their major objectives. As with most laws, a literal reading of the statutes does not convey how the laws have been applied. After discussing the laws, we discuss the concept of market power, which is a central focus of the antitrust laws. This concept is used to interpret the decisions of the courts. We then examine the two major areas to which the antitrust laws apply. The first deals with agreements among competitors, such as price-fixing agreements and agreements to merge. The second deals with the actions of a single firm that allegedly harm rivals. These actions involve strategic behavior like predatory pricing, vertical relationships among firms, and tie-in sales. We next review the antitrust doctrines on price discrimination and on regulated industries and conclude with an overall economic assessment of the effect of the major antitrust doctrines on firm organization.

---

[1] The interested reader is referred to Posner and Easterbrook (1980), Posner (1976), Bork (1978), Areeda and Turner (1978, 1980), and Areeda (1986) for more detailed examination of antitrust issues. See Scherer (1980, Chs. 19–21) for a slightly different economic perspective. The presentation and analysis of the cases in this chapter rely heavily on Posner and Easterbrook (1980). This chapter deals only with federal antitrust law and not with state antitrust law.

■ THE ANTITRUST LAWS AND THEIR PURPOSES

The antitrust laws are surprisingly simple to state, but have proved difficult to apply. Indeed, the Supreme Court has changed its mind several times on the proper interpretation of the laws. This section describes the laws, their enforcement, and their purposes, explaining who can sue under the antitrust laws and how damages are paid.

Antitrust Statutes

The three major statutes governing antitrust policy are the Sherman Act, passed in 1890; the Clayton Act, passed in 1914; and the Federal Trade Commission Act, also passed in 1914. There have been various amendments, additions and deletions over the years. Even prior to the passage of the Sherman Act, however, there were legal principles that governed competition among firms. Under the common law, price-fixing among firms, though not illegal, was unenforceable: a court would not enforce a contract in which one firm agreed with a competitor to fix prices. Similarly, agreements not to compete that accompanied the sale of a business or an employment relationship were also unenforceable if they were judged "unreasonable." Agreements among workers to either fix wages or strike were often held to violate the law. Practices by which firms attempted to exclude competitors (for example, predatory pricing) were not considered to violate the law unless accompanied by additional illegal actions such as fraud (Posner and Easterbrook 1980, 18).

The antitrust statutes were passed at a time of great upheaval in American industry. As Chapters 2 and 7 describe, the time period around 1890 witnessed the rise of the modern American corporation, the rise of large-scale firms of national reputation, and the creation of very large firms through mergers. In fact, the merger wave in the 1890s and early 1900s, as Chapter 7 explains, was the largest in our history, after adjusting for the size of the economy.

The **Sherman Act** was, in part, a response to the changes in the U.S. economy and was the first federal antitrust legislation. Section 1 of the Sherman Act states that "every contract, combination in the form of trust or otherwise, or conspiracy, in restraint of trade or commerce among the several States, or with foreign nations, is declared to be illegal. . . ." Thus, Section 1 forbids explicit cartels.

Section 2 states that "every person who shall monopolize or attempt to monopolize, or combine or conspire with any other person or persons, to monopolize any part of the trade or commerce among the several States, or with foreign nations, shall be deemed guilty of a felony. . . ."

One might read Section 2 as saying that it is illegal to be a monopolist. That is *not* what courts have interpreted it to mean. As explained later, it is not a crime to be a monopolist as long as the monopolist has committed no "bad acts."

The courts' interpretation of the Sherman Act left doubt as to whether the act prohibited certain industry behavior. This led legislators to pass the additional antitrust legislation: the Clayton Act and the Federal Trade Commission Act, both passed in 1914. The **Clayton Act** is directed primarily against four specific practices. Section 2 of the Clayton Act (amended in 1936 by the Robinson-Patman Act) prevents price discrimination that lessens competition. Section 3 prohibits the use of tie-ins and exclusive dealing when the result is to lessen competition. Section 7 (amended in 1950 by the Celler-Kefauver Act) prohibits mergers that reduce competition. Section 8 deals with the creation of interlocking directorates among competing firms (that is, the control of competing firms by interrelated Boards of Directors). The Clayton Act also allows an injured party to recover **treble damages** (three times actual damages) plus attorneys' fees.

The **Federal Trade Commission Act** of 1914 created a new government agency, the Federal Trade Commission (FTC), whose duties include the enforcement of the antitrust laws and the adjudication of disputes under the antitrust laws, as articulated in the Federal Trade Commission Act. The main antitrust provision of the FTC Act is Section 5, which prohibits "unfair" methods of competition. The FTC's other main responsibilities include consumer protection and the prevention of deceptive advertising.

It is quite common for an antitrust complaint to list violations of several of the antitrust statutes simultaneously. So for example, an antitrust complaint regarding tie-in sales could list violations of both the Sherman Act and the Clayton Act.

Enforcement

Both the FTC and the Department of Justice are responsible for administering the antitrust laws. A suit brought by the Justice Department is adjudicated in federal courts, while an action brought by the FTC is heard and decided by an administrative law judge at the FTC and then reviewed by the Federal Trade Commissioners.[2] After the FTC has completed its proceedings, defendants can appeal adverse decisions to the federal courts.

An action brought by the FTC can result in a *cease and desist* order, which prohibits specific acts. A suit brought by the Department of Justice can result in a similar type of order, an *injunction*. The Department of Justice can also bring a suit (called a criminal suit) that can result in criminal fines or jail sentences. Aside from its enforcement responsibilities, the Department of Justice can sue to recover the cost of the suit plus the damages that arise when the U.S. government is a victim of an antitrust offense. A private individual or firm can bring an antitrust suit and, if victorious, receive treble damages (three times damages) plus the cost of the suit including attorneys' fees. Such private litigation comprises a significant share of antitrust litigation (White 1989).

Goals of the Antitrust Laws

To most economists, the antitrust laws should have a very simple goal: to promote efficiency. That is, they should prevent practices or amalgamations of firms that would harm society through the exercise of market power.

One can reject the efficiency basis for the antitrust laws and instead regard them as an attempt to help certain groups and harm others. For example, some may argue that the antitrust laws are designed to help small firms that compete with large firms, whether

---

[2] The FTC can also bring an action in federal court to obtain a preliminary injunction preventing consummation of a merger.

or not this promotes efficiency. In fact, the antitrust laws against price discrimination were passed in response to political lobbying by many small firms that were complaining of larger firms' ability to secure lower prices in their purchases of supplies (Ross 1984).

Another example of the way firms can use the antitrust laws to help themselves concerns exemptions from the antitrust laws. One effective method of competing is to disadvantage actual or potential rivals. Because the antitrust laws constrain what firms can do, those that succeed in obtaining a unique exemption from the antitrust laws obtain a benefit that their rivals lack.

A group of firms that obtain a general exemption from the antitrust laws can reduce competition and thereby benefit. Many groups have succeeded in obtaining exemptions from the antitrust laws. Workers who unionize in order to raise their wages are specifically exempted from the antitrust laws, as are certain agricultural groups and export associations. Moreover, as Chapter 23 shows, legislators have made numerous attempts to protect certain groups from competition that would be legal under the antitrust laws. It is perfectly legal for firms to attempt to influence legislation in order to protect themselves from competition and insulate themselves from antitrust liability.[3]

The view that the guiding principle of the antitrust laws should be efficiency rather than the taking of resources from one group and granting them to another has gained increasing acceptance among legal and academic scholars. One appeal of such a simple proposition is that it provides a much clearer guide as to what antitrust policy should be, as compared to the alternative, which is to help the group that has the most political power at the expense of everyone else.

Even if one accepts the proposition that the goal of the antitrust laws is to promote efficiency, it can sometimes be difficult to figure out exactly what practices or actions result in inefficient behavior, even using the most sophisticated economic analysis. For example, suppose that two firms merge and the resulting reduction in competition causes price to rise. That sounds bad. However, suppose also that as a result of the merger, the merged firm develops a new and better product or provides the same product but offers better services or develops a lower cost method of production. That sounds good. Should the antitrust laws ban all mergers if they significantly eliminate competition or should they also pay attention to the potential efficiency gains and balance the two?

To see how the trade-off between an increased price and improved efficiencies can be calculated, suppose that as a result of a merger a firm is able to elevate price from $1 to $1.01 because of the elimination of competition. Suppose that the merger also enables the firm to improve efficiency and lower its constant marginal cost from $1 to $0.92. The deadweight loss caused by the price elevation is illustrated as *BEF* in Figure 22.1.

---

[3] This lobbying is protected by what is called the Noerr-Pennington doctrine. *Eastern Railroad Presidents Conference v. Noerr Motor Freight, Inc.*, 365 U.S. 127 (1961), and *United Mine Workers of America v. Pennington*, 381 U.S. 637 (1965).

We cite cases primarily from the U.S. Reporter, Federal Reporter (F2d), and the Supreme Court Reporter (S.Ct.), which are standard legal references. For example, the preceding citation means vol. 381 of the U.S. Reporter, page 637. The case was decided by the Supreme Court in 1965. A case is first decided in a District Court. It can then be appealed to the Court of Appeals in the relevant region (called a Circuit Court) and after that to the Supreme Court.

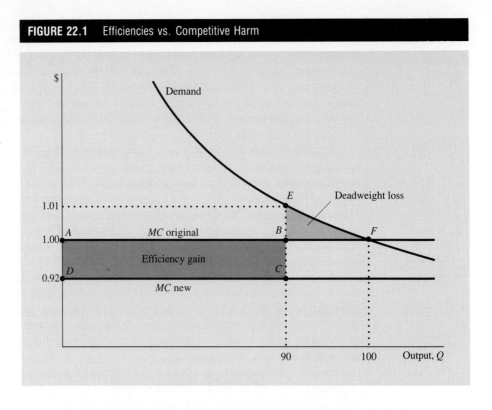

FIGURE 22.1 Efficiencies vs. Competitive Harm

The gain to society from the improved efficiencies of the lower production cost is illustrated as the box *ABCD*. If the triangular area representing the deadweight loss from the price increase is less than the rectangular area of efficiency gain, the merger is, on balance, good for society. The relative size of these two areas depends on the particular example. The larger the quantity sold in the marketplace, the more important the efficiency gains, and the larger the area of the rectangle compared to the triangle. In general, even small reductions in costs per unit can result in efficiency gains that swamp deadweight loss in importance.[4] For example, suppose that the initial quantity is 100 units, and the postmerger quantity is 90. Since the efficiency savings are $0.08 per unit, the efficiency gains equal $7.20, but the deadweight loss from the price increase approximately equals only $0.05. The efficiency gains outweigh the deadweight loss.[5]

These types of calculations can obviously be quite complicated to do, and it is a matter of debate whether courts should be charged with making such calculations in deciding the legality of a merger (Williamson 1968–69). The most recent policy guide

---

[4] The reason is that efficiency gains depend on the total quantity produced, while deadweight loss depends on the restriction in output resulting from the merger. The output restriction is usually a small percent of the total quantity produced.

[5] These calculations are based on a demand curve with a constant elasticity of −11.3.

of the Department of Justice, the 1984 Merger Guidelines, explicitly recognize the importance of efficiency gains in evaluating mergers. However, it is unclear whether the Department of Justice would allow a merger to go forward unchallenged if there were an anticompetitive effect (a price increase) even if there were offsetting efficiency gains.

In judging the behavior of firms, a logical question is, what standard should the courts use to see if an industry is behaving properly? It would be a grievous error to use the perfectly competitive model of Chapter 4 as a standard of industry behavior because few if any industries satisfy the conditions of that model. Therefore, it is pointless to use it as the standard to which all firms must adhere if they are to avoid antitrust liability. Requiring courts to apply sophisticated economic analyses to evaluate behavior may be unrealistic. Moreover, the courts must often face economic problems that economists have not yet thought about. Courts don't have the luxury of taking as much time as necessary to solve a problem. Still, it is hard to argue that economic knowledge should be ignored. There has been an increasing use of economics in antitrust proceedings. One effect has been that economics can now be the centerpiece of a case; another effect has been that litigation is more complicated.

Who Can Sue?

The question of who has **legal standing,** which is the right to bring a suit under our antitrust laws, is a complicated one. Individuals and firms, in addition to the Department of Justice and FTC, can bring antitrust suits. The question often arises as to whether a plaintiff has suffered an injury that the antitrust laws were designed to prevent.

Consider the case of a competitor who brings an antitrust suit claiming that a proposed merger of rivals will be anticompetitive. If the merger is indeed anticompetitive as a result of increasing market concentration, then presumably, prices should rise. If prices rise, each competitor in the market benefits from the decrease in competition; therefore no competitor is harmed by the merger. If instead of creating market power, the merger creates a more efficient firm, then a competitor is likely to be harmed by the increase in competition. However, this increase in competition presumably will lead to lower prices and benefit consumers. In this case, the harm that a competitor suffers from a merger is not the type of harm that the antitrust laws were designed to prevent, because consumers are benefiting from the low prices.[6]

Suppose, however, that a competitor claims that as a result of the merger, the merged firm will be more likely to engage in certain predatory activities designed to drive it out of business; that is, the merged firm may be better able to violate the law, drive competitors out of business, and then harm consumers by raising prices. The description in Chapter 13 of the difficulty of proving predatory behavior, even when the facts are readily available, suggests that it is difficult to forecast the likelihood of predatory behavior in the future. Moreover, even if there is a likelihood of predatory behavior in the future, it can be dealt

---

[6] *Brunswick Corp. v. Pueblo Bowl-O-Mat, Inc.*, 429 U.S. 477 (1977) and *Cargill Inc. v. Monfort of Colorado*, 197 S. Ct. 484 (1986).

with in the future when it occurs. It is not clear that mergers should be blocked on so flimsy a ground as the possibility of predatory behavior, especially given the difficulty of concluding that future predation is likely.

Suppose that a group of manufacturing firms engages in a conspiracy to raise prices and that they sell their products to a retail department store, which then sells it to final consumers. The retail department store is not engaged in any conspiracy and simply charges the normal retail profit. Who should be allowed to sue the manufacturers who are engaged in the conspiracy? The department stores, which are direct purchasers from the conspiring parties, certainly have the right to sue. The question is whether the final consumers (indirect purchasers) have a right to sue: it would be double counting if both final consumers and the direct purchasers, namely the retail stores, were allowed to recover damages for the same price overcharge. In the *Illinois Brick* case, the Court limited the right of indirect purchasers to sue.[7] One possible justification for this decision is the difficulty of determining all of the potential indirect and direct parties who would be entitled to sue and obtain duplicative damages for the same price overcharge from the plaintiffs (Landes and Posner 1979).

Suppose that individual consumers are the direct purchasers of a product from firms who have engaged in a conspiracy. Would an individual purchaser have the incentive to sue if all that could be recovered was the price overcharge on the product, trebled, plus attorneys' fees? Usually no. In an effort to create greater incentives to bring suits, courts allow attorneys to file class-action suits on behalf of all consumers. Attorneys are entitled to legal fees, and this provides an incentive for them to bring such suits. Of course, attorneys might well have an incentive to bring too many such cases if they are over-compensated. Several class-action antitrust suits have led to enormous settlements totaling hundreds of millions of dollars.

Economic Theory of Damages

Economic theory has a great deal to say about the optimal amount of damages that a guilty defendant should pay. Although economic theory has had an enormous impact on the determination of antitrust liability, it has had much less effect on damage determination.

The economic theory of damages starts from the proposition that the purpose of damages is to deter inefficient activity but not to be so burdensome as to deter efficient activity. For example, suppose that the death penalty were imposed any time a firm was convicted of illegally conspiring with another firm. As will be shown, it is not so easy to determine when an agreement among firms is an illegal one. If the penalty were death (or extremely harsh), many firms might be dissuaded from activity that could be perfectly lawful, such as the creation of a trade association that sets product safety standards. Therefore, there is a necessary balance between making penalties too harsh or too lenient. The optimal penalty is one that balances the beneficial and the nonbeneficial aspects of deterrence.

---

[7] *Illinois Brick Company v. Illinois*, 431 U.S. 720 (1977). The word *court* spelled with a capital C refers to the Supreme Court of the United States.

An optimal penalty tries to eliminate the incentive to engage in illegal activity. For example, suppose that a group of firms, if they conspire, could raise their profits by $100. If this conspiracy could be detected with certainty and at no cost by enforcement officials, then a penalty of $100 would suffice to deter the activity. Of course, deterrence is not perfect, and it takes resources to discover illegal activity. It might well make sense, therefore, to charge a penalty higher than $100 in order to adjust for the less-than-certain probability of detection. For example, suppose that price-fixing conspiracies are detected in only one-third of all cases. Then, as a first approximation, charging a penalty of $300 should be enough to deter the illegal activity.[8]

Suppose that a group of firms is convicted of violating the antitrust laws. How should the penalties be apportioned among the firms? Should one defendant pay all of the damages, or should there be some pro rata sharing rule? In particular, suppose that of the two defendants to a lawsuit, one defendant settles with the plaintiff (for example, pays the plaintiff $100 to be dismissed from the lawsuit) before the case goes to trial. At the trial, the damage award to the plaintiff is several times the amount of the settlement. Should the remaining defendant be forced to pay the entire amount? The Court has ruled that an antitrust defendant is not entitled to **contribution** (payments) from other culpable parties.[9] The decision has been criticized on the grounds that it appears unfair. However, the incentive to settle will be greatest if, once the settlement is achieved, no further liability can be assumed, and therefore a large damage award can be avoided. This greatly increases the incentive to settle, with a resulting savings in litigation costs (Easterbrook, Landes, and Posner 1980).

■ MARKET POWER AND THE DEFINITION OF MARKETS

The antitrust laws deal extensively with situations involving market power and try to control the creation and maintenance of market power. This section defines market power, discusses how to measure it, and points out that it is sometimes hard to measure market power accurately. One rough way to measure market power is to first define a market and then calculate the market share of the firm under analysis. A high market share is interpreted as an indicator of market power. The section describes the principles that should be used to define a market and provides a background against which the cases can be interpreted.

Market Power

The precise economic definition of market power is easy to state. Market power arises whenever a firm (or group of firms acting together) is able to profitably charge a price above that which would prevail under competition, which is usually taken to be marginal cost. This ability to set price above marginal cost implicitly uses the model in Chapter 4

---

[8] For more on optimal damages in antitrust cases, see Landes (1983) and White (1989). Landes explains that the optimal penalty equals the harm the firms impose on others.

[9] *Texas Industries, Inc. v. Radcliff Materials, Inc.,* 451 U.S. 630 (1981).

of perfect competition as a benchmark against which to measure the behavior of firms. If this definition is applied literally, probably every firm in the United States has at least a tiny bit of market power. The model of perfect competition is an extreme one that describes few, if any, actual industries. Therefore, presumably, when courts find that a firm has market power, they must mean a substantial amount of market power, even though they have failed to articulate what exactly they mean by *substantial*. For example, does it mean a 5 percent deviation of price from marginal cost? A 10 percent deviation?

It is difficult to measure marginal cost and therefore difficult to measure the deviation between price and marginal cost, even if some standard could be agreed upon as to what is a substantial enough deviation to constitute significant market power. An alternative approach is to estimate the price elasticity of the demand facing an individual firm (or group of firms). This elasticity of demand facing a firm summarizes the ability of a firm (or group of firms acting together) to exercise market power since the price-cost margin depends on the inverse of the elasticity of demand.[10] If the elasticity is large, the firm has little market power. It should be noted that most empirical attempts to estimate demand curves for individual firms selling branded products rarely find the absolute value of price elasticities to be higher than 5–10 (Telser 1972, 274–306). Elasticities of 5 to 10 imply that prices in these industries exceed marginal costs by roughly 10 to 25 percent in what many economists would deem to be competitive industries.[11]

Whether a firm currently has market power is a much different question from whether, as a result of a merger, it could acquire and exercise *additional* market power. The first question is whether price is already elevated significantly above competitive levels. This can be answered directly by looking at price and marginal cost, or indirectly by looking at the elasticity of demand facing the firm. The second question is not whether the price is currently above the competitive level, but rather, whether price, at whatever level it currently happens to be, will rise significantly as a result of the merger activity. This question can be answered directly by predicting how price will change or indirectly by predicting how the elasticity of demand facing the firm will change as a result of the merger.

For example, suppose a firm makes some differentiated product, Product A. The firm's demand curve for Product A can be estimated as a function of the price of Product A and the price of substitute products, for example, Product B. If the direct elasticity of Product A at current prices is very large, then the firm producing Product A has no market power. In a merger case, the analyst can attempt to predict how the elasticity of each product will change as a result of the merger. For example, suppose the firms producing Products A and B want to merge. The merger between the firms will allow the merged firm to set prices jointly, and the analyst can calculate the resulting prices based on the demand curve facing the merged firm. The merger increases market power if the post-merger prices are higher than the premerger ones (Baker and Bresnahan 1985).

---

[10] Recall from Chapter 5 that $\dfrac{p - C}{p} = \dfrac{-1}{\epsilon}$ where p is price, C is marginal cost and ϵ is the price elasticity of demand (which is a negative number). In a static model, the elasticity completely summarizes a firm's market power and determines its pricing. In a dynamic model, one must analyze the responses of consumers and firms over time in order to understand pricing.

[11] With the formula in footnote 10, if $\epsilon = -5$, then $p = 1.25\ C$, and if $\epsilon = -10$, then $p = 1.11\ C$.

Market Definition

Sometimes accurate econometric (statistical) estimation of price elasticity may not be possible because of, for example, inadequate data. In an attempt to reach some workable solution to the problem of determining market power, analysts and the courts often define a market and construct a measure of market share. If the market share of the firm (or firms) under analysis is high, the suggestion is that market power exists. In a merger case, one looks at whether there will be a significant increase in concentration as a result of the merger. There is no agreement, however, as to exactly what share (or change in share) is "high," but many economists would regard a share in the range of 30–50 percent as too low to indicate significant market power in an industry with a competitive fringe comprising the remainder of the market. Market shares alone are not completely determinative of whether a firm has market power, and additional analysis of the economic conditions is necessary before one can reach a conclusion about market power. For example, if entry is easy, then the industry pricing will be severely constrained, regardless of whether one firm currently has a large market share. Similarly, many of the factors discussed in the chapter on oligopoly that show how oligopoly discipline is likely to break down would also be relevant. Still, market shares can be a useful initial step in analyzing the competitiveness of an industry.

The use of market shares is a reasonable, though crude, way of judging whether market power either exists or is likely to exist in the future. Of course, in order for the market share to be sensible, the market must be properly defined. Alfred Marshall (1920, 324) defined a market as an area in which "prices of the same goods tend to equality with due allowance for transportation costs." Since Marshall's time, economists and lawyers have been refining the definition of a market. There are two dimensions of **market definition:** which products to group together and which geographic areas to group together.

Consider the product dimension of market definition. A proper definition of a market should include all those products that are good substitutes on the demand and supply sides.[12] Product B is a demand substitute for Product A if an increase in the price of A causes consumers to use more Product B instead. Product B is a supply substitute for Product A if in response to an increase in the price of Product A, firms that are producing Product B switch some of their production facilities to the production of Product A.[13] In

---

[12] The relevant economic market is not necessarily the same as the *market* that a salesperson might refer to. Substantial confusion has sometimes resulted when market definition is based on memos written by marketing personnel. For that reason, some companies may instruct marketing personnel to avoid the use of the word *market* in memos.

[13] The relationship between the demand elasticity facing a firm and supply and demand substitutes can be illustrated in terms of the model for a dominant firm facing a competitive fringe. Let ϵ_{DF} = demand elasticity facing the dominant firm, ϵ = market demand elasticity, M = market share of the dominant firm and η = supply elasticity of the fringe. Then, from Chapter 8, we know that $\epsilon_{DM} = \dfrac{1}{M}\epsilon - \dfrac{1-M}{M}\eta$. As ϵ increases (more demand substitutes) and as η increases (more supply substitutes) and as M falls, ϵ_{DM} rises and the dominant firm has less market power. See Landes and Posner (1981).

both cases, the presence of Product B significantly constrains the pricing of Product A, provided that an increase in the price of A would result in a significant decline in the quantity of A consumed as consumers switch from A to B or a signficiant increase in the supply of A as firms switch production from B to A.

The degree of substitution between products depends upon the current prices of the two products. At a high price for Product A, Products A and B may be highly substitutable, but not at a low price for Product A. Even a monopolist may raise its price sufficiently above competitive levels so that eventually it faces some competition from other products. The mere fact that at the monopoly price a monopolized product faces demand substitutes does *not* mean that the firm producing the product has no market power. (It may mean that the firm could not acquire additional market power to raise price more.) It is only if the substitution possibilities are so large as to generate a highly elastic demand that the monopolist has no significant market power. This discussion illustrates the difficulty in deciding which products to include in the market definition and why market shares may be only a crude indicator of market power.

The *Cellophane* case illustrates these difficulties in defining a market.[14] The Court was investigating whether DuPont had market power in the pricing of cellophane. The Court reasoned that DuPont lacked market power because at the current market prices, a user of cellophane had many substitutes, like paper bags, and DuPont's share of the market including these substitutes was not large. However, there was also evidence that price substantially exceeded marginal cost. Based on the foregoing discussion, it was an error to include other wrapping materials in the market definition because they did not prevent the exercise of market power and constrain the price of cellophane to competitive levels. (If, instead of investigating whether DuPont had market power, the Court had investigated whether a proposed merger would raise the cellophane price, then its market definition may have been appropriate.)

Numerous methods are used to identify the good substitutes for a particular product. One obvious way is to interview producers in the industry, who presumably know both their customers and their potential competitors from other industries. In the *Brown Shoe* case, the Supreme Court articulated a laundry list of criteria that can be used to define markets.[15] It said: "The boundaries of such a submarket may be determined by examining such practical indicia as industry or public recognition of the submarket as a separate economic entity, the product's peculiar characteristics and uses, unique production facilities, distinct customers, distinct prices, sensitivity to price changes, and specialized vendors." The application of this laundry list of criteria has not led to precision in defining a market for antitrust purposes.[16]

---

[14] *United States v. E.I. du Pont de Nemours & Co.,* 351 U.S. 377 (1956).

[15] *Brown Shoe Company v. United States,* 370 U.S. 294 (1962).

[16] The courts, in addition to defining economic markets, have occasionally attempted to define economic *submarkets* that are contained within an economic market. Presumably competition between two products in the same economic market is more intense if the two products also belong to the same submarket. The distribution between *market* and *submarket* is not very useful, and we will not refer to it or even attempt to give an economic definition of the term *submarket*.

If Products A and B are in the same economic market, then their prices should tend to move closely together. Therefore, a *first* step in defining economic markets is to examine the price correlations among different products that are under consideration for inclusion in the same product market. If the prices of two goods in the same economic market do not move together, then one would expect to see dramatic quantity shifts from one good to the other in response to relative price shifts.[17]

Although no standard levels of correlation have been established to determine if two products are in the same market, the available data may often be used to develop such standards. For example, suppose that everybody agrees that two different types of plastic materials are in the same economic market. One could compute the correlation between their prices and use it as a benchmark to determine whether some third plastic material belongs in the same economic market with the other two products.

As already discussed, it is the direct price elasticity, *not* the **cross-elasticity of demand,** that matters in the determination of market power. The cross-elasticity is the percentage change in quantity demanded in response to a 1 percent change in another product's price. There is a lot of discussion in court decisions as to the importance of cross-elasticity of demand in defining markets. Courts often use the term loosely to indicate that products are substitutes. Analytically, the relationship between cross-elasticity and direct elasticity is as follows: When the cross-elasticity of demand tends to be high, then the direct elasticity of demand tends to be high. This follows from a well-known result in economic theory: The sum of the direct elasticity plus all cross-elasticities of demand equals 0.[18] Therefore, if a cross-elasticity is high, the direct elasticity is likely to be high.

The *cross-elasticity of demand* is not a completely accurate expression. One must define whether it is the cross-elasticity of Product A with respect to the price of Product B or vice versa. These two different cross-elasticities are usually not distinguished in court decisions, but they are not generally equal. The relevant cross-elasticity of demand when the question is whether the market for Product A should include Product B is the cross-elasticity of demand for Product A with respect to the price of Product B.[19]

In considering the geographic aspect of the market definition, the defining theoretical question is: which geographic areas significantly constrain the pricing of the product in the location under analysis. The process of determining those areas proceeds along exactly

---

[17] Price correlations are a useful first step in defining markets. However, high correlations need not always indicate that two products are in the same market. For example, dissimilar products made from similar inputs may have high price correlations. Similarly, low correlations need not always indicate that products are not in the same market provided large quantity shifts accompany the relative price shifts.

[18] See, for example, Henderson and Quandt (1980, 31–33).

[19] Let the cross-elasticity of demand of product i with respect to the price of product j be defined as $\epsilon_{ij} = \dfrac{\partial Q_i}{\partial p_j} \dfrac{p_j}{Q_i}$ where Q_i is the (income-compensated) demand for product i, and p_j is the price of product j. Then economic theory requires that $0 = \epsilon_{ii} + \sum_j \epsilon_{ij}$. The cross-elasticity of demand is positive for substitutes, and the direct price elasticity is negative. Notice that the direct elasticity can be large even if no individual cross-elasticity is large. It is also true that $\dfrac{\partial Q_i}{\partial p_j} = \dfrac{\partial Q_j}{\partial p_i}$. This last relationship does not imply that $\epsilon_{ij} = \epsilon_{ji}$. See Henderson and Quandt (1980, 30).

the same lines as discussed for the product market definition and involves similar reasoning. For example, consider the consumption of apples in Chicago. Although some apples may be grown inside the city, most are shipped to Chicago from outside the city limits. The geographic areas that ship to Chicago (or could profitably do so if price rose slightly) are in the same economic market as Chicago because they contain apple producers whose output significantly influences the price of apples in Chicago. Notice that these same apple producers could also significantly affect the price of apples in Milwaukee. Thus Milwaukee and Chicago would be in the same economic market, and the price of apples in Chicago would generally be closely related to the price of apples in Milwaukee.[20] Example 22.1 discusses how the government applies the principles of market definition in its antitrust enforcement policy toward mergers.

■ COOPERATION AMONG COMPETITORS

This section explores the restrictions that the antitrust laws place on cooperation among competitors. We first examine explicit agreements to set price or output and then explicit agreements that lead to new products being produced, as well as information-sharing among rivals. We then analyze oligopoly behavior in which firms behave similarly, though not as a result of explicit agreements. Finally, we examine mergers among competitors.

Price-Fixing and Output Agreements

Soon after the passage of the Sherman Act, the courts had to deal with the treatment of firms that cooperatively set prices and allocated customers. In *Trans-Missouri Freight Association,* a group of competing railroads entered into agreements about what rates to charge.[21] The railroads claimed that the rate agreements resulted in reasonable rates that prevented ruinous competition. The Court rejected these arguments and instead ruled that "The claim that the Company has the right to charge reasonable rates and that therefore it has the right to enter into a combination with competing roads to maintain such rates cannot be admitted. . . . Competition will itself bring charges down to what may be reasonable. . . ."

After the decision limiting their ability to fix rates, railroads continued to push for the ability to set their rates and avoid competition. They were ultimately allowed to do so by legislation. Recently, the Staggers Act of 1980 eliminated many of the restrictions on competition. Apparently as a result, there has been a consolidation through mergers among railroads recently.

Almost concurrent with *Trans-Missouri* was another case involving price-fixing, the *Addyston Pipe* case.[22] A group of manufacturers of cast-iron pipe met to set price terms

---

[20] See Landes and Posner (1981), Scheffman and Spiller (1987), and Stigler and Sherwin (1985) for further analysis of market definition.

[21] *United States v. Trans-Missouri Freight Association,* 166 U.S. 290 (1897).

[22] *United States v. Addyston Pipe & Steel Co.,* 175 U.S. 211 (6th Cir. 1899).

EXAMPLE 22.1

MARKET DEFINITION: 1984 MERGER GUIDELINES

The definition of a market is an activity that economists engage in primarily because they are analyzing antitrust cases. Were it not for that, it is doubtful whether as large a body of economic research would have developed to define markets.[1] Probably the most careful statement of government policy on the definition of markets is the *Merger Guidelines* that the Department of Justice issued in 1984. (The FTC has similar, but less detailed, guidelines.)

These *Guidelines* set forth the principles that the government uses to define relevant economic markets in its enforcement of the antitrust laws regarding merger activity. For the most part, the *Guidelines* are consistent with the economic principles that have been articulated in this chapter and represent an improvement over previous government policy. The *Guidelines* indicate that an HHI[2] (see Chapter 12) should be calculated for a properly defined economic market.[3] The government will not generally challenge a merger between two firms if the postmerger HHI in the industry is below 1000. If the postmerger HHI is between 1000 and 1800, the merger will generally be challenged if the change in the HHI resulting from the merger is 100 points or more. If the industry's postmerger HHI is over 1800, then a merger will generally be challenged if the change in the HHI resulting from the merger is 50 points or more.

For example, suppose an industry consists of four firms, each with a 25 percent market share, and two of the firms want to merge. The *Guidelines* would calculate the premerger HHI as $(25 \times 25) + (25 \times 25) + (25 \times 25) + (25 \times 25) = 2500$, and the postmerger HHI as $(50 \times 50) + (25 \times 25) + (25 \times 25) = 3750$. Since the postmerger HHI exceeds 1800, and the change in the HHI exceeds 50, the merger would generally be challenged.

The application of the *Merger Guidelines* implicitly assumes that after a merger the firms involved will be able to maintain their premerger market shares, and the merged firm will enjoy a market share equal to the sum of the premerger shares of the firms that are merging. When this is not a reasonable assumption, the analysis should be modified in order to properly reflect the merged firm's market share.

[1] The research on the performance of concentrated markets (see Chapter 12) also requires a proper definition of the market.
[2] Recall that the Herfindahl-Hirshman Index equals the sum of the squared market shares of the firms in the industry.
[3] The *Guidelines* define a market as the smallest group of products and the smallest area such that a hypothetical monopolist of all those products in the area could raise price by a certain amount (for example, 5 or 10 percent) above prevailing or likely future levels. There are some problems with this definition. For example, two large firms could by themselves constitute a market, even though fringe firms existed that produced the identical product. Moreover, there is sometimes a tendency in applying the *Guidelines* to exclude firms or products whose supply elasticity is low. As footnote 13 shows, such firms and products can indeed constrain price and affect the elasticity facing a firm that attempts to exercise market power. See Stigler and Sherwin (1985) for additional discussion of the deficiencies of the *Guidelines*.

in certain geographic areas. Their defense was that the prices they set were fair and reasonable and restrained the deleterious effects of ruinous competition. The Court re-affirmed its rejection of this type of argument. Several months after the adverse decision, all of the defendants merged into a single firm. The government did not challenge the merger. Therefore, the firms were able to achieve through merger what they were unable to achieve through horizontal agreements.

These two early important price-fixing cases both involved industries with high fixed costs that made claims of ruinous competition. Recall that in such industries, it is possible (see Chapter 4) for no equilibrium to exist without additional restrictions on competition.[23]

The Court reinforced its views against price-fixing in the *Trenton Potteries* case.[24] In that case, the firms that manufactured and distributed 82 percent of the bathroom fixtures produced in the United States attempted to set list prices and urged adherence to these prices. Without investigating whether the agreement could successfully affect prices, the Court ruled: "The aim and result of every price-fixing agreement, if effective, is the elimination of one form of competition. The power to fix prices, whether reasonably exercised or not, involves power to control the market and to fix arbitrary and unreasonable prices. The reasonable price fixed today, may, through economic and business changes, become the unreasonable price of tomorrow. . . . We should hesitate to adopt a construc-tion making the difference between legal and illegal conduct . . . depend upon so uncertain a test as to whether prices are reasonable." The Court left no doubt that the reasonableness of price was no justification for price-fixing.

During the 1930s, there was a widespread belief that the forces of competition were, in large part, the cause of the Great Depression. As a result, many policymakers advocated the formation of explicit cartels. In 1933, in an apparent response to the current thinking of the time, the Court reached a decision that appeared to contradict its previous rulings on price-fixing. In *Appalachian Coals,* a group of coal mines agreed to sell their coal through an exclusive common selling agency, which is a device that a cartel can use to collude.[25] The defendants explained that the purpose of the selling agency was to assist them in selling their coal during very difficult financial circumstances. The Supreme Court ruled that the exclusive selling agency was not a violation of the antitrust laws.

The anomalous decision in *Appalachian Coals* was soon overruled by the Supreme Court. In the *Socony-Vacuum* case, the Court reaffirmed its previous views regarding price agreements among competitors.[26] In that case, a group of oil producers formed an or-ganization whose purpose was to raise prices in order to rescue the industry from its serious financial plight. The Court ruled, "The elimination of so-called competitive evils is no legal justification" for such programs.

Aside from explicit price-fixing among competitors, the Court has also condemned attempts by competitors to use collective boycotts to restrict competition. In the *Eastern*

---

[23] See Bittlingmayer (1982) for an analysis of the *Addyston Pipe* case from this point of view.

[24] *United States v. Trenton Potteries Co.,* 273 U.S. 392 (1927).

[25] *Appalachian Coals, Inc. v. United States,* 288 U.S. 344 (1933).

[26] *United States v. Socony-Vacuum Oil Co.,* 310 U.S. 150 (1940). This case is also referred to as *Madison Oil* because it was tried in Madison, Wisconsin.

| EXAMPLE 22.2 | **ANTITRUST LAWS IN OTHER COUNTRIES** |

Many countries take a much different view towards agreements among competitors than that taken in the United States. For example, Germany, Japan, and the United Kingdom allow the formation of cartels that the government believes will promote efficiency. Although competition is generally viewed as desirable, these countries also believe that in certain circumstances competition may not lead to efficiency. For example, West Germany and Japan both allow for cartelization so that firms can reduce capacity during periods of excess capacity. Audretsch (1987) shows that in West Germany, prices rise during the cartelization period and fall after the cartel dissolves. In the United Kingdom the trend recently has been to rely more on competition. This policy shift has led to an increase in mergers as the antitrust scrutiny of agreements among competitors has increased. This observation is similar to Bittlingmayer's (1985) that application of the Sherman Act to agreements among competitors accelerated the merger movement in the United States in the late 1890s and early 1900s.

SOURCES: Audretsch (1987), Swann et al. (1974).

States case, the Court condemned the actions of a group of retail lumber dealers who blacklisted and presumably refused to deal with any wholesale lumber dealers who tried to sell at retail.[27]

The Court's views on price-fixing and output agreements are that an agreement whose sole purpose is to eliminate competition and raise prices above competitive levels—that is, a "naked" agreement to eliminate competition—is illegal. No inquiry as to the reasonableness of the price set is necessary to reach the conclusion that the agreement violates the law. When no additional inquiry is necessary to analyze the facts of a situation in order to determine the legality of the conduct, the conduct is said to be **per se** illegal. Therefore, it is often said that price-fixing and output agreements are per se violations of the antitrust laws. Example 22.2 discusses the approach that other countries have taken toward such agreements among competitors.

cIt is peculiar to many economists that an agreement among two competitors in a very competitive industry where the two together cannot affect the market price is a per se violation of the antitrust laws. This violation is even more peculiar when one realizes that a merger of the two firms is legal under the antitrust laws. This asymmetry in the treatment of agreements between independent firms and mergers of independent firms seems to have little basis in economic logic.[28]

---

[27] *Eastern States Retail Lumber Dealers Ass'n v. United States,* 234 U.S. 600 (1914).

[28] If agreements among competitors can never generate efficiencies, then there is a benefit from an enforcement viewpoint in banning both effective and ineffective agreements to fix price among competitors. However, just like a merger, agreements among competitors can generate efficiencies, so it is peculiar to distinguish between the two.

Not All Agreements among Competitors Are Illegal

Although it is true that an agreement whose sole purpose is to fix prices or restrict output is a per se violation of the antitrust laws, it is not true that every agreement that results in prices being fixed is illegal per se. The Supreme Court has indicated that if the agreement is ancillary to achieving another procompetitive purpose, then the price-fixing may well be deemed lawful. In such situations, it is necessary to investigate whether the price-fixing agreement is necessary to achieve the procompetitive purposes for which the agreement was entered into.

The Court long ago recognized that competitors must often cooperate and that this cooperation may affect price. Rather than applying a per se rule of illegality to such agreements, the courts apply a **rule of reason** analysis, in which the reasonableness of the restraint is analyzed. One famous, early case in which the rule of reason is eloquently articulated is the *Chicago Board of Trade* case.[29] In that case, members of the Board of Trade (who compete with each other to buy and sell contracts involving grains) agreed among themselves that after the Board had closed, no member of the Board of Trade could transact in a certain type of grain at a price other than the closing price that day. The Board of Trade was open during the early part of each day, and during that time, members transacted at prices that were determined by their willingness to buy or sell. The last price of the day was the closing price. The rule that no members could trade after the Board had closed except at the closing price made it more difficult for members to transact after closing, because supply and demand were likely to have moved the equilibrium price away from the closing price. The effect of this rule, therefore, was to create an incentive for members who wanted to trade to trade during the time when the Board was open.

An organized exchange provides a valuable service. It amalgamates the information flows of buyers and sellers in such a way as to create a market price. An exchange is compensated for its activities by charging in some way for each trade that occurs. If someone could costlessly observe the prices at the Board of Trade without having to pay any fees to it, they could free ride on the informational activities at the Board of Trade. By waiting to trade until after hours, one could use the information generated during the trading session by the Board of Trade yet avoid paying any fee. Therefore, two effects of the rule under discussion are that (1) it created an incentive to conduct more trades during the day on the exchange (hence the market becomes a larger one that can process more information), and (2) it reduced the free-riding problem by discouraging trading after hours. The Court ruled that this agreement was not a per se violation of the antitrust laws. The opinion, written by Justice Brandeis, said that

> The case . . . rested upon the bald proposition, that a rule or agreement by which men occupying positions of strength in any branch of trade, fixed prices at which they would buy or sell during an important part of the business day, is an illegal restraint of trade under the antitrust law. But the legality of an agreement or regulation cannot be determined by so simple a test, as whether it restrains competition. Every agreement concerning trade, every regulation of trade, restrains. To bind, restrain, is of their very essence. The

---

[29] *Board of Trade of City of Chicago v. United States*, 246 U.S. 231 (1918).

true test of legality is whether the restraint imposed is such as merely regulates and perhaps thereby promotes competition or whether it is such as may suppress or even destroy competition. To determine that question, the Court must ordinarily consider the facts peculiar to the business to which the restraint is applied;

This famous decision clearly recognized the principle that sometimes a cooperative agreement among rivals about pricing can promote competition.

In *Broadcast Music, Inc., v. Columbia Broadcasting System,* the Supreme Court investigated the way in which music is licensed.[30] Copyright owners of musical scores have property rights to their material. No one is allowed to use that material without permission and the payment of the agreed-upon fees. For example, any time a copyrighted song is played on the radio or on television, the copyright owner of that musical score must be compensated. It obviously would be very costly for television and radio stations to locate and pay the copyright owner of each of the musical scores that it uses. Similarly, it would be very difficult for copyright owners to constantly monitor radio and television to determine if their musical scores were being performed.

To get around these horrendous transaction problems, two organizations have been formed. One is the American Society of Composers, Authors, and Publishers, (ASCAP) and the other is Broadcast Music, Inc. (BMI). Copyright owners belong to one or both of these organizations and rely upon them to collect revenues on their behalf. These organizations monitor musical productions and issue blanket licenses that enable the licensee to use any song listed in the blanket license. Fees for blanket licenses are ordinarily flat dollar amounts or percentages of total revenues. Therefore, ASCAP and BMI do in some sense fix prices, and they are, of course, organizations of competitors, handling the many songwriters.

The Supreme Court realized that ASCAP and BMI were providing an important service that lowered transaction costs and that the only way they could provide it was to set the price. In this sense, then, both BMI and ASCAP were performing procompetitive functions, and by lowering transaction costs they were expanding the amount of consumption that could occur. The Supreme Court therefore recognized that the per se rule was not appropriate here; instead, it decided that a rule of reason was necessary to analyze the reasonableness of the restraint. The Court ruled,

A bulk license of some type is a necessary consequence of the integration necessary to achieve these efficiencies and the necessary consequence of an aggregate license is that its price must be established. . . . The blanket license, as we see it, is not a "naked restraint of trade" with no purpose except the stifling of competition, but rather accompanies the integration of sales, monitoring, and enforcement against unauthorized copyright use.

This case, then, emphasizes that cooperative agreements need not always violate the antitrust laws.

In the *NCAA* case, the Supreme Court investigated a restriction placed on the televised broadcasting of college football events by an association of colleges, the National Collegiate

---

[30] *Broadcast Music, Inc., v. Columbia Broadcasting System, Inc.* 441 U.S. 1 (1979).

Athletic Association (NCAA).[31] The Court recognized the need for the competitors, the individual colleges, to cooperate among themselves in order to produce the product, football games. Therefore, the Court ruled that any restrictions entered into had to be investigated under a rule of reason, rather than a per se rule. In that case, the Court ruled that the restrictions on television broadcasting of college football games were an unnecessary restraint of trade. The Court felt that the restrictions on television broadcasting were not necessary in order for the NCAA to succeed in its task of staging football games.

The courts have often treated collective action like a group's refusal to deal as a per se violation. Recently, two cases have indicated a change in view. In *Northwest Wholesale Stationers, Inc., v. Pacific Stationery and Printing Company,* the Court refused to apply the per se rule to a case involving an agreement among competitors.[32] This case involved the expulsion of one member from a cooperative buying agency (a group of firms that buy products as one purchaser). The Court determined that the cooperative buying agency, through an agreement among competitors, did not necessarily engage in a per se violation by expelling the plaintiff and refusing to deal with him. The Court ruled that in the absence of proof that the cooperative had market power or unique access to a critical resource necessary for effective competition, it was not appropriate to treat the conduct as a per se violation, and instead it had to be subjected to a rule of reason.

In the *Indiana Federation of Dentists* case, the Court again declined to apply a per se analysis to agreements among competing dentists.[33] The dentists did not want to submit X-rays to dental insurers in connection with verification of claims for insurance. The Federation forbade its members to submit the X-rays. The Court ruled that the horizontal agreement was not necessarily a per se violation of the antitrust laws and, again, that a rule-of-reason analysis was necessary. The Court ultimately struck down the agreement. However, these recent decisions regarding agreements among competitors seem to indicate a recognition that cooperation may often be essential in achieving efficiency and that agreements among competitors (other than agreements whose sole purpose is to fix price or restrict output) should be judged under a rule of reason.[34]

Information Exchanges among Competitors

A common and natural form of association among competitors is a trade association, which is an organization composed of firms in similar businesses. Trade associations often collect information on the industry that is valuable to its members. Of course, trade associations can also serve as a vehicle by which prices are fixed. However, it is important to recognize the legitimate information-generating services that trade associations can provide, such as revealing cost information to their members, or even revealing transaction prices to market participants, provided there is not collusion.

---

[31] *NCAA v. University of Oklahoma,* 468 U.S. 85 (1984).

[32] *Northwest Wholesale Stationers, Inc., v. Pacific Stationery and Printing Company,* 105 S. Ct. 2613 (1985).

[33] *Federal Trade Commission v. Indiana Federation of Dentists,* 106 S. Ct. 2009 (1986).

[34] See Carlton and Klamer (1983) and Halverson (1988) for further discussion.

In the *Hardwood* case, the Court investigated the activities of the American Hardwood Manufacturers' Association, which consisted of about 400 members.[35] The association was engaged in gathering and reporting information about the sales, production, and inventory and pricing activities of each member and making such information available to the members. Moreover, at meetings it was quite frequent for business conditions to be discussed along with the suitability of increases or decreases in industry production in light of market conditions. A cartel with 400 members would be a difficult one to police and is therefore not likely to be successful in raising price for long. Therefore, it is likely that the information that was distributed probably improved the knowledge of market conditions without increasing price. Despite this, the Court ruled that these activities were illegal (see Example 13.6).

Justice Brandeis disagreed with his colleagues on the Supreme Court about the *Hardwood* case and wrote an eloquent dissenting opinion. He explained that had there been a centralized market, much of the information collected by the trade association would have been automatically available. The provision of information, therefore, was viewed by Brandeis as a beneficial effect of the trade association:

> Surely it is not against the public interest to distribute knowledge of trade facts, however detailed. The cooperation which is incident in this plan does not suppress competition. On the contrary, it tends to promote all in competition, which is desirable. By substituting knowledge for ignorance . . . it tends also to substitute research and reasoning for gambling and piracy. . . . In making such knowledge available to the smallest concern, it creates among producers equality of opportunity. In making it available, also, to purchasers in the general public, it does all that can actually be done to protect the community from extortion. If, as is alleged, the plan tends to substitute stability of prices for violent fluctuations, its influence in this respect is not against the public interest.

Brandeis understood the value of information and the role of a centralized market in providing such information.

A few years later, in a similar case, the Court again examined a trade association, this time the Maple Flooring Manufacturers' Association.[36] This association consisted of twenty-two defendants, who accounted for roughly 70 percent of the total production of hardwood-type floors. The association provided information on costs, freight, quantities sold, and prices received by individual members, and held meetings at which various industry members exchanged views about the state of the industry. The Court ruled that this activity was not a violation of the antitrust laws and cited the procompetitive benefits that result from a free flow of information and having industry participants apprised of market conditions. Using the economic theories about number of participants developed in our discussion of cartels, it appears that the trade association was much more likely to act successfully as a collusive device in the *Maple Flooring* case than it was in the *Hardwood* case. Despite this, the Maple Flooring Association was exonerated, but not the Hardwood Association.

---

[35] *American Column & Lumber Company v. The United States,* 257 U.S. 377 (1921).

[36] *Maple Flooring Manufacturers' Association v. United States,* 268 U.S. 563 (1925).

In the *Container* case, the Court investigated exchanges of price information among producers of corrugated containers.[37] One competitor would request information from another on the most recent price that it had offered. The industry was concentrated, with the defendants accounting for about 90 percent of the shipments of corrugated containers from plants in the southeastern United States. After examining the economic factors of the industry, the Court concluded that "price information exchanged in some markets may have no effect on a truly competitive price, but the corrugated container industry is dominated by relatively few sellers. The product is fungible and the competition for sales is price. . . . The inferences are irresistible that the exchange of price information has had an anticompetitive affect in the industry." In other words, the Court examined the economic factors in the industry and concluded that the exchange of price information was anticompetitive.

The discussion of oligopoly theory in Chapters 9, 10, and 13 shows that exchanges of information can assist in collusion. For this reason, courts have paid careful attention to the activities of trade associations. At the same time, the courts recognize that information is a scarce commodity and that its dissemination can often be valuable. Balancing these two offsetting effects is typically difficult.

Oligopoly Behavior

The enforcement of the antitrust laws has often focused on explicit agreements among competitors. The prosecution effort centers on showing evidence of an agreement, rather than on showing the effect of an agreement. The search for the incriminating document rather than the effect upon price is the focus of many investigations. It is inevitable that business managers, with the thousands of documents that they write, occasionally write down something that, taken out of context, could give rise to a charge that there is an actual agreement. For example, competing companies may naturally communicate with each other about matters other than market conditions, such as safety precautions, or firms in the same industry may purchase goods from each other, as might occur if one firm had a temporary plant failure. These natural occasions for interaction among firms could lead to charges of conspiracy, when in fact the interactions consist of innocent economic transactions. The difficulty with looking for evidence of an agreement is especially acute in the application of the antitrust laws to oligopoly behavior. We have noted that in an oligopoly price need not be at the competitive level. The question the courts had to address early on was whether such oligopoly behavior can be regarded as the result of an agreement among competitors that violates the antitrust laws.

The Court addressed the question of when one could infer that a conspiracy or agreement had been made among competing firms in the *Interstate Circuit* case.[38] The managers of two competing firms that owned chains of movie houses sent out letters to distributors of movies telling them not to distribute their films to movie theaters that charged admission fees of less than 40¢ for first-run movies or less than 25¢ for second-

---

[37] *United States v. Container Corp. of America*, 393 U.S. 333 (1969).

[38] *Interstate Circuit, Inc., v. United States*, 306 U.S. 208 (1939).

run movies. The Court said, "In order to establish agreement, it is compelled to rely on inferences drawn from the course of conduct of the alleged conspirators." The Court ruled that the similarity in behavior was enough to constitute evidence of an agreement.

In the *American Tobacco Case* the Court examined in detail the behavior of the cigarette industry in the 1930s.[39] List prices of the three major companies (the "big three"), Reynolds, American, and Liggett & Myers, were identical most of the time. During the height of the Depression, the cigarette companies all raised their prices, despite the fact that their costs had fallen. Profits increased. As the Court said, "This was one of the three biggest years in their history." After prices rose, new competitors entered the cigarette industry and were able to sell their 10-cent brands in successful competition with the 15-cent brands of the three majors. The market shares of the big three started to erode, and they had lost roughly 22 percent of total cigarette sales by 1932. The big three responded by cutting prices, and sales of the 10-cent brands fell considerably: the market share of the 10-cent brands was reduced to around 6.5 percent by 1933. The three major cigarette companies used their influence to make sure that no retail store sold the brands of the big three for more than 3 cents above the price of the 10-cent brands. See Example 13.3.

The Court found that the similarity of conduct among the three majors provided a basis to infer that an unlawful conspiracy had occurred: "Where the circumstances are such as to warrant a jury in finding that the conspirators had a unity of purpose for a common design and understanding, or meeting of minds in an unlawful arrangement, the conclusion that a conspiracy is established is justified."

Interestingly, several histories of the cigarette industry have shown that the similarity of list prices has characterized that industry since its formation, and that it is not at all unusual for the list prices of major brands of cigarettes to be absolutely identical (Tennant 1950, Nicholls 1951). The Court appeared to be reacting to what it perceived as peculiar conduct in the Depression; namely, when all the other firms were losing heavily, the cigarette companies were doing very well.

After the *American Tobacco* case, it was unclear exactly what type of oligopoly behavior would be subject to the antitrust laws. Was merely parallel behavior, in which firms who recognize each other's interdependence act similarly, a violation of the antitrust laws? In a series of cases involving delivered pricing, the Court went to great lengths in attacking oligopoly behavior. (See the discussion in Chapter 13 of the cases involving delivered pricing.) However, in 1954 the Court indicated a change in direction. In the *Theatre Enterprises* case, the Court addressed the question of parallel behavior involving movie theatres.[40] In that case, a newly refurbished theater sought to obtain the rights to run first-run feature movies from several distributors. The distributors refused because they already had theatres lined up for their first-run features. The Court ruled that "business behavior is admissible circumstantial evidence from which the fact finder may infer agreement . . . but this Court has never held that proof of parallel business behavior conclusively establishes agreement or, phrased differently, that such behavior itself con-

---

[39] *American Tobacco Company v. United States*, 328 U.S. 781 (1946).

[40] *Theatre Enterprises Inc. v. Paramount Film Distributing Corp.*, 346 U.S. 537 (1954).

stitutes a Sherman Act offense." In other words, the common action of the distributors in refusing the movie theatre the right to run first-run movies did not constitute a violation of the antitrust laws. This case is often interpreted to mean that parallel behavior, the kind that naturally results from a few firms' competition with each other in an oligopoly, cannot by itself lead to an antitrust violation; there must be some additional offense for the behavior to constitute an illegal action.

The view that parallel behavior alone is not sufficient for an antitrust violation has been reaffirmed in several recent cases that the Federal Trade Commission has unsuccessfully brought, in which it has alleged that either markets are so-called shared monopolies[41] (firms don't compete for the same customers and instead have local monopolies) or are not competitive because of certain business practices adopted independently by each firm. For example, in the *DuPont* case, the FTC charged that the noncollusive adoption of certain common business practices, such as notification to buyers of price increases, the use of a most-favored nations clause (see Chapter 13), the use of uniform delivered pricing, and public announcements in the press all constituted business practices that facilitated noncompetitive pricing.[42] The Court of Appeals for the Second Circuit rejected such arguments as indicating violations of the antitrust laws. "The mere existence of an oligopolistic market structure in which a small group of manufacturers engage in consciously parallel pricing of an identical product does not violate the antitrust laws."

Mergers

The antitrust laws attempt to prevent the creation of additional market power through mergers of competitors. The issue in a merger case is not whether the industry is currently competitive, but whether it will be less competitive as a result of a merger. Because mergers can generate efficiencies, a merger policy that overdeters merger activity imposes a significant cost on society. Conversely, too lenient a policy leads to the creation of additional market power. We first discuss mergers among competitors and then among potential competitors.

Mergers Among Competitors. In an early decision, *Northern Securities Company,* the Supreme Court investigated the creation of a holding company that would control two large, competing railroads: The Great Northern Railroad Company and the Northern Pacific Railway Company.[43] The creation of this holding company, which would exercise control over these two previously competing railroads, was deemed to violate the antitrust laws. The *Northern Securities* decision in 1904 coincided with the end of the widespread merger movement in the early 1900s (see Chapter 7).

---

[41] See *FTC v. Kellogg et al.*, Docket No. 8883, 99 FTC Reporter 8, 1982. The FTC eventually dismissed the case. See Schmalensee (1978) for an analysis of this case.

[42] *E.I. du Pont de Nemours & Co. v. FTC*, 729 F.2d 128 (2d Cir. 1984). This case is also sometimes called the *Ethyl* case. Ethyl was a participant in the case. See Example 13.5.

[43] *Northern Securities Company v. United States*, 193 U.S. 197 (1904).

Soon after the *Northern Securities* decision, the Court reached another decision involving market power acquired through merger. In the *Standard Oil* case, the Court investigated the creation of the Standard Oil Company and the practices it followed in acquiring businesses related to petroleum products.[44] John D. Rockefeller, together with others, was the defendant in the lawsuit. The charge was that the defendants "purchased and obtained interest . . . and entered into agreements with . . . various persons . . . engaged in purchasing, shipping, refining, and selling petroleum and its products . . . for the purpose of fixing the price of crude and refined oil and the produce thereof, limiting production thereof, and controlling the transportation therein, and thereby restraining trade . . . and monopolizing interstate commerce." It was also charged that refineries that refused to enter into the agreement were driven out of business through a variety of predatory tactics such as low prices. Other charges included unfair practices against competing pipelines, contracts with competitors, espionage, and division of the United States into districts and limiting the amount of competition in each district. The Court ruled that the actions indicated "a conviction of a purpose and intent" to monopolize, and it ordered the dissolution of the combination. This case is famous for refusing to apply a per se ban to mergers among competitors and introducing the concept of the rule of reason, in which one had to investigate whether the resulting effect of the merger was an unreasonable restraint of trade.

In the *United States Steel* case, the Court seriously retrenched from vigorously applying the antitrust laws to enjoin merger activity.[45] The case involved the creation of the United States Steel Company, which was formed by a merger of approximately 180 independent concerns. Measured by the amount of production, U.S. Steel produced 80 to 90 percent of the entire steel output of the country. The Court refused to find the creation of United States Steel illegal, and seemed to indicate that because U.S. Steel, unlike Standard Oil, did not engage in improper behavior, the combination was lawful (see Example 8.4).

Dissatisfaction with the Supreme Court's treatment of mergers (especially in light of a failure to block another acquisition)[46] led Congress to pass the **Celler-Kefauver Act** in 1950, which strengthened Section 7 (on merger activity) of the Clayton Act.

In *Brown Shoe,* the Supreme Court applied the new standards of the amended Section 7 of the Clayton Act to a proposed merger between G. R. Kinney Company and Brown Shoe Company.[47] Kinney and Brown were both manufacturers and sellers at retail of shoes. The government attacked both the horizontal and vertical elements of the transaction. One horizontal element that was attacked was the concentration that would result in shoe retailing. In 32 cities the share of women's shoes sold by the two companies combined exceeded 20 percent. In 31 cities the combined share of children's shoes exceeded 20

---

[44] *Standard Oil Company of New Jersey v. United States,* 221 U.S. 1 (1911). For an analysis of this case, see McGee (1958).

[45] *United States v. United States Steel Corporation,* 251 U.S. 417 (1920).

[46] *United States v. Columbia Steel Company,* 334 U.S. 495 (1948).

[47] *Brown Shoe Company v. United States,* 370 U.S. 294 (1962). For a detailed analysis of *Brown Shoe,* see Peterman (1975).

percent and in 6 cities, their combined share exceeded 40 percent. The language of the Court's decision indicated that a combined share of 5 percent in a city was excessive, taking into account the trend toward increasing concentration in this industry. The Court ruled that this horizontal conglomeration was the type of merger activity that Congress intended to stop by the 1950 amendment to Section 7 of the Clayton Act. The Court emphasized that enforcement of the amended Clayton Act with respect to mergers should be for the "protection of competition, not competitors, and its desire to restrain mergers only to the extent that such combinations may tend to lessen competition." The Court also issued its famous laundry list of criteria, discussed in the section on market definition, to use in defining a market.

The Court continued its hard line on mergers among competitors in the *Philadelphia Bank* case.[48] In that case, it prohibited a merger between the Philadelphia National Bank and the Girard Trust Corner Exchange Bank. At the time, these were the second and third largest of the commercial banks in the Philadelphia metropolitan area. The merged entity would have had roughly 36 percent of a four-county area's total assets and deposits. The Court stated, "A fundamental purpose of amending Section 7 was to arrest the trend toward concentration, the tendency to monopoly, before the consumer's alternatives disappeared through merger. . . ." The Court also addressed whether it was appropriate for it to consider the benefits that would arise from the merger for efficiency reasons. Its response was as follows: "We are clear, however, that a merger, the effect of which may be substantially to lessen competition, is not safe because, on some ultimate reckoning of social and economic debits and credits, it may be deemed beneficial. . . . A value choice of such magnitude is beyond the ordinary limits of judicial confidence. . . ." Congress "proscribed anti-competitive mergers, the benign and malignant alike, fully aware, we must assume, that some price might have to be paid." Thus, the Court clearly rejected a consideration of the efficiency benefits of a merger.

The Supreme Court took its most aggressive stance ever in enforcing Section 7 of the Clayton Act in the *Von's* case.[49] In that case, Von's Grocery Company sought to acquire a competitor, Shopping Bag Food Stores. Both Von's and Shopping Bag were retail grocery companies in Los Angeles. Together, their sales accounted for 7.5 percent of all sales in the Los Angeles market. Again relying on the trend toward increasing concentration in this market, the Supreme Court prevented this acquisition from occurring. At about the same time of the *Von's* decision, the Department of Justice issued guidelines for enforcement policy in merger cases. See Example 22.3.

It is clear that the courts are reluctant to allow any proposed efficiency savings or benefits flowing from a merger to be used as a defense to justify a merger that will result in an increase in concentration in a market. The application by the Department of Justice and the FTC of the current merger guidelines, which recognize the value of efficiencies, suggests that efficiencies alone generally do not provide sufficient justification for a merger in which prices are expected to rise. (Efficiencies can provide a justification for a merger that results in increased concentration if the efficiencies would lead to lower prices.)

---

[48] *United States v. Philadelphia National Bank,* 374 U.S. 321 (1963).

[49] *United States v. Von's Grocery Company,* 384 U.S. 270 (1966).

EXAMPLE 22.3

1968 MERGER GUIDELINES

In 1968, at about the same time as the *Von's* decision, the Department of Justice issued merger guidelines to inform firms as to which types of horizontal mergers (mergers among competitors) it would contest. It defined a highly concentrated market as one in which the four largest firms had a 75 percent market share. In these markets, the Department indicated that it would ordinarily challenge a merger in the following situations:

Acquiring Firm	Acquired Firm
4 percent	4 percent or more
10 percent	2 percent or more
15 percent or more	1 percent or more

In markets in which the four-firm concentration ratio was below 75 percent, the Department indicated it would challenge mergers under the following conditions:

Acquiring Firm	Acquired Firm
5 percent	5 percent or more
10 percent	4 percent or more
15 percent	3 percent or more
20 percent	2 percent or more
25 percent or more	1 percent or more

It is interesting to contrast the stringency of these 1968 guidelines with the merger guidelines currently in effect (discussed in Example 22.1). In a market that is not highly concentrated, the 1968 guidelines imply that a merger that resulted in a change in the HHI of 50 (for example, a 5 percent firm acquiring a 5 percent firm) would violate the Justice Department standards. Under the current merger guidelines, such a change in a HHI would never trigger an enforcement action unless the market were highly concentrated. The new guidelines represent a considerable relaxation of the criteria articulated in the 1968 guideline policy.

One defense that courts have allowed in merger cases is the *failing-firm defense*, in which the firms explain that if the proposed merger is not allowed, one of the firms will go out of business. If the proposed transaction is the least anticompetitive one that can prevent the assets from leaving the industry, the Department of Justice or FTC will not challenge the merger. However, if the failing firm were to go bankrupt but the creditors continue to operate the firm, then the bankruptcy would not affect competition, and there is no reason to allow a failing-firm defense.

The failing-firm defense can be regarded as a recognition that current market shares may not reflect the future importance of the competitor that will vanish as a result of the merger. If a firm will go out of business unless it can merge with others, then the fact that it currently has a high market share is irrelevant in considering whether the merger should go through or not. Merger policy should be forward-looking, and it is really the future competitive significance of the merging firms that is important in understanding whether a merger is anticompetitive or not.[50] This principle is recognized by the Supreme Court in several court cases in which it argues that current market shares may be inaccurate indicators of the future competitive significance of a firm.[51]

The Court's and government's approach and criteria for analyzing mergers have obviously evolved considerably since the Celler-Kefauver Act in 1950. As the Court has worked out some of the inconsistencies in its opinions in defining markets, and as economists and lawyers have become more sophisticated about defining markets and understanding the effects of market concentration, government policy toward mergers has become more systematic. A merger like that attacked in *Von's* would probably not be attacked today. Moreover, as Example 22.4 explains, both the FTC and Department of Justice allow firms to remedy an anticompetitive merger by restructuring the proposed transaction.

Mergers Among Potential Competitors.   Suppose two firms do not currently compete in the same market and wish to merge. Can the merger be blocked if someone thinks it likely that the two firms would have competed in the future? Logically, there is nothing wrong with blocking a merger if it will improve future competition. Practically, it is very difficult to figure out exactly who is a potential competitor. The decisions of the Court have evolved over time so that a merger between potential competitors is now much less likely to be considered anticompetitive than previously.

An early case involving a merger between potential competitors was the *El Paso Natural Gas* case.[52] In that case, El Paso Natural Gas sought to acquire the assets of Pacific Northwest Pipeline Corporation. Both companies operated large natural gas pipelines. Only one of them, El Paso, delivered natural gas into California, a market in which the government contended competition would be lessened if the acquisition occurred. Even though Pacific Northwest had never sold gas in California, it had on several occasions attempted to obtain the necessary regulatory approval to deliver gas into California. In fact, Pacific Northwest had conducted lengthy negotiations with a large customer in Southern California. The result of these negotiations was to heighten competition, even though El Paso eventually won away the customer. The Court ruled that even though Pacific Northwest was not a successful seller in California, it was indeed a competitor: "Unsuccessful bidders are no less competitive than the successful ones." The acquisition

---

[50] Suppose there are three firms in an industry with market shares of 30 percent, 30 percent, and 40 percent. Suppose the one with 40 percent is failing. If it fails, the remaining firms will have 50 percent and 50 percent. If, instead, the failing firm is acquired by one of the remaining firms, the shares will be split 70–30. It appears that concentration (as measured by the HHI) is worsened by the transaction. This example illustrates an important principle. The comparison of HHIs is *irrelevant* if the output level is different in the two situations being compared. If as a result of the acquisition, more assets remain in the industry, and output is permanently higher, then consumers are better off even if market concentration increases from what it would have been if no acquisition occurred, the failing firm failed, and its assets exited the industry.

[51] *United States v. General Dynamics Corporation,* 415 U.S. 486 (1974).

[52] *United States v. El Paso Natural Gas Company,* 376 U.S. 651 (1964).

EXAMPLE 22.4	# How Firms Merge

When two firms propose to merge, the merger comes under the scrutiny of either the FTC or the Department of Justice, one of which analyzes the economic conditions surrounding the merger and decides whether to challenge the merger. If the FTC or Department of Justice decides that the proposed transaction would violate the antitrust laws, it can ask a court to grant a preliminary injunction forbidding the transaction. If the court decides to grant such an injunction, the merger is often called off because the only way to fight such an injunction is to litigate the case, which is often a costly and lengthy procedure. Moreover, a court can require that during the course of the litigation, the two companies be held as separate and not combined. Alternatively, the Department of Justice or FTC can allow a merger to go through and then bring an action requiring a remedy such as a division of the merged company into two companies. Obviously, once the two companies are combined, it can be difficult to unscramble them again.

Many companies, in order to avoid a challenge by either the FTC or the Department of Justice, may attempt to remedy any perceived anticompetitive effects of a proposed acquisition. So, for example, if two firms wish to merge, they can try to explain to the Department of Justice why their merger will not be anticompetitive. But if they are unsuccessful, and the Department of Justice raises some anticompetitive concerns for one of the many products that the firms produce, it is possible for the transaction to be modified. For example, the anticompetitive concerns surrounding the merger may be eliminated by having one of the merging firms spin off one of its product lines to a third firm so as not to concentrate the market that the Justice Department is concerned about. This "fix-it-first" policy has been practiced extensively during the 1980s.

was barred. This case can be interpreted as one involving actual competitors, even though one had not yet been successful in entering. Alternatively it can be regarded as a case involving potential competitors. Since Pacific Northwest had actually bid for business, it seems more reasonable to regard it as a case between actual rather than potential competitors.

Another important case involving potential competition was the *Procter & Gamble* case.[53] In this case, Procter & Gamble Company acquired Clorox Chemical Company. Clorox was the leading manufacturer of household liquid bleach, having about 50 percent of U.S. sales. Procter & Gamble did not manufacture or sell bleach, but was a major manufacturer and seller of many other household products sold through grocery, drug, and department stores. The Court decided that the acquisition should be blocked because P & G was a likely entrant into the liquid-bleach market.

---

[53] *Federal Trade Commission v. Procter & Gamble Company*, 386 U.S. 568 (1967).

The FTC also feared that "the substitution of Procter, with its huge assets and advertising advantages, for the already dominant Clorox would dissuade new entrants and discourage active competition from the firms already in the industry due to fear of retaliation by Procter." The Court was concerned that the acquisition would raise barriers to entry into the industry. The Court rejected Procter & Gamble's efficiency arguments and stated, "Possible economies cannot be used as a defense to illegality." As a result of the decision, Clorox was divested in 1969 (12 years after the original merger).

The Court returned to the potential competition theory in an analysis of a proposed joint venture between Pennwalt Chemicals Corporation and Olin Mathieson Chemical Corporation.[54] In this case, two large producers of sodium chlorate engaged in a joint venture to develop a new sodium chlorate plant in the southeastern United States. This was an area of the country where neither of these companies sold their products and neither was an important market force. The district court allowed the joint venture to proceed because it concluded that it was unlikely that both firms would independently enter the market there in the southeastern United States. The Supreme Court sent the case back to the district court, claiming that the relevant consideration was not whether both companies would have entered the market, but whether one company would have entered the market with the other company still remaining on the sidelines as a potential competitor. The district court determined that neither company would have entered alone and therefore allowed the joint venture.

The potential competition doctrine was again used by the Supreme Court in *United States v. Falstaff Brewing Corporation*.[55] Falstaff, one of the nation's largest brewers, sought to acquire Narragansett, which was the largest brewer in the New England area—an area in which Falstaff did not compete. The government argued that the merger should be enjoined because Falstaff was a likely entrant into the New England area. The district court had found that Falstaff had no intentions of otherwise entering the New England area, but the Supreme Court ruled that this alone did not eliminate the possibility that Falstaff affected competition in New England, because Falstaff might have been perceived as a potential entrant into the New England area and therefore might have restrained prices. The district court subsequently found that Falstaff was not perceived as a potential entrant. Although it is logically correct that a perceived potential competitor could influence the market, a perceived potential competition doctrine seems to depend upon the state of mind of the competitors and not on any easily verifiable facts. Therefore, even though it is logically consistent, it turns out to be extremely complex to litigate such a case, which is based on the opinions of competitors who may be interested in preventing a merger that would result in an efficient competitor and rival being created.

The Supreme Court significantly constrained the application of the potential competition theory in the *Marine Bancorporation* case.[56] In this case, the government challenged a proposed merger between two commercial banks, which were not direct competitors, even though both were located in the same state: one was in Seattle, and the

---

[54] *United States v. Penn-Olin Chemical Co.*, 378 U.S. 158 (1964).

[55] *United States v. Falstaff Brewing Corporation*, 410 U.S. 526 (1973).

[56] *United States v. Marine Bancorporation Inc.*, 418 U.S. 602 (1974).

other was in Spokane. The government challenged the merger on the grounds that the acquiring bank would have found an alternative and more competitive means for entering the Spokane area. The Court ruled that "the potential competition theory requires two ingredients: first, that there are feasible means for entering the market other than acquisition; and secondly, that these means offer a substantial likelihood of procompetitive effects." The Court was unconvinced that an alternative method of entry would achieve the same procompetitive effects as this acquisition. Notice the Court's emphasis on alternative feasible means of entry. If there are no entry barriers, there can be no anticompetitive effect because entry will constrain price. It appears, then, that the Court's decision requires a showing that first, there is some unique advantage to entry that the potential competitor has; and second, that this means of entry would allow the potential competitor to come in and prosper. Since the *Marine Bancorporation* decision, the potential competition doctrine has not fared well (Posner and Easterbrook 1980, 531). Of course, if markets are broadly defined, there is little need for a potential competition doctrine since the potential competitors are considered part of the market.

■ EXCLUSIONARY ACTIONS AND STRATEGIC BEHAVIOR OF A SINGLE FIRM

So far, this chapter has described how agreements between competing firms, such as a price-fixing conspiracy or a merger, can lead to the creation of market power that the antitrust laws attempt to prevent. This section examines those actions by a single firm that have been claimed to help maintain its monopoly or facilitate its acquisition of a monopoly. These actions, which are called **exclusionary actions,**[57] exclude or harm rivals and thereby either help to maintain or create a monopoly to the disadvantage of consumers. These actions, or bad acts, include predatory pricing, denial of key products to rivals, vertical relationships among firms, and tie-in sales. Antitrust cases aimed at these practices typically involve a violation of Section 2 of the Sherman Act. Hence, these cases are often called *Section 2 cases*.

The category of bad acts that Section 2 has been used to attack is so general that sometimes it is hard to distinguish a bad act from ordinary desirable competitive behavior. We first discuss the type of rivalrous behavior that has been attacked under Section 2 and then discuss vertical relationships and tie-in sales. The section concludes with a discussion of the complexities of litigation under Section 2 of the Sherman Act.

Rivalrous Behavior

No competitor wants its rivals to succeed. In general, competition benefits consumers. But some forms of competitive behavior can harm competition, as shown in Chapter 13. This section reviews some of the main types of rivalrous behavior that the Court has found to violate the antitrust laws. We begin with a general discussion of some famous

---

[57] This terminology is taken from Posner and Easterbrook (1980).

cases in which the Court has deemed certain behavior undesirable and then discuss specific examples of undesirable behavior, such as predatory pricing and denial of key products to rivals.

Undesirable Competitive Behavior. One of the most famous Section 2 cases is the *Alcoa* case.[58] Alcoa was engaged in the production and sale of aluminum ingot and also fabricated the aluminum ingot into many finished and semifinished goods. Alcoa owned or licensed many of the original patents, and until 1909 no one could compete effectively. After 1909 the United States alleged that Alcoa maintained its market power through a series of exclusionary tactics, among them (1) the signing of power contracts that forbade the power companies to sell power to anyone else who made aluminum; (2) outright price-fixing agreements with foreign producers of aluminum to prevent imports into the United States; (3) a price squeeze, in which the price of aluminum ingot was raised to independent aluminum-sheet fabricators, who were then unable to make a profit fabricating the sheet and selling it in competition with Alcoa at the prices Alcoa was setting for aluminum sheet; and (4) a strategy of expanding capacity with the intention of eliminating competition. Alcoa remained the sole domestic producer of aluminum until 1945.

One of Alcoa's defenses was that the profit it earned was not very high. The Court ruled that whether profits are high or low is irrelevant: "[Congress] did not condone good trusts and condemn bad ones; it forbade all." The Court stated that the mere acquisition of a monopoly by itself was not necessarily illegal. "It does not follow that because Alcoa had such a monopoly, that it 'monopolized' the ingot market; it may not have achieved the monopoly; monopoly may have been thrust upon it. . . . A single producer may be the survivor out of a group of active competitors, merely by virtue of his superior skill, foresight, and industry. . . . The successful competitor, having been urged to compete, must not be turned upon when he wins."

Despite this language, which appeared to recognize that efficient firms that grow should not be penalized, the Court also looked with disfavor on Alcoa's policy of anticipating demand and building capacity for it in advance. "It was not inevitable that it should always anticipate increases in demand for ingot and be prepared to supply them. . . . It insists that it never excluded competitors; but we can think of no more effective exclusion than progressively to embrace each new opportunity as it opened." The Court's reasoning is perplexing. It is difficult for an economist to distinguish evil capacity expansion from desirable capacity expansion that occurs as a result of foresight.

The Court also ruled that "The monopolist must have both the power to monopolize, and the intent to monopolize." By stressing intent, the frame of mind of the violator becomes relevant in an antitrust suit. Endless litigation can result when someone's frame of mind, rather than the actual effects of the economic actions, are the subject of the litigation. The Court also ruled that Alcoa's price-squeeze policy was unlawful.

A fascinating issue in the *Alcoa* case was the definition of the market. Aluminum ingot, once it is made into fabricated aluminum, can be recycled as scrap aluminum. Scrap aluminum competes with primary ingot for many uses. The question arose as to

---

[58] *United States v. Aluminum Company of America,* 148 F. 2d 416 (1945).

whether the secondary market should properly be considered as part of the market in which virgin aluminum ingot competes. The Court ruled that secondary aluminum should not be part of the market definition and concluded that a market share for virgin ingot of 90 percent would definitely indicate monopoly power; 67 percent might indicate monopoly power; but 33 percent would not. As was explained in Chapter 19 (see Example 19.2), secondary and primary products definitely compete with each other, but such competition need not erode the initial market power in the primary product. Once the primary product is sold, there may be no further monopoly profits to be made, and the secondary market does constrain the *subsequent* pricing of primary aluminum, even though it does not constrain the initial price.[59]

The Court remanded the case to the district court for reconsideration.[60] The main antitrust divestiture order facing Alcoa, resulting from the antitrust litigation, was one regarding its Canadian properties. During the time period of the district court's reconsideration, the United States government sold off aluminum facilities built for it during World War II and thereby set up Reynolds and Kaiser as two competitors to Alcoa. The monopoly on aluminum that Alcoa had enjoyed in the United States disappeared. By 1958, Alcoa's share of primary aluminum ingot capacity had fallen to 35 percent.

The *Alcoa* decision had far-reaching implications for the way a dominant firm should behave. It was unclear if there was anything a dominant firm could do to avoid being charged with consciously seeking to maintain control of the market; furthermore, it was unclear how one would determine whether its monopoly condition was "thrust upon it," maintained by clever but legal business practices, or maintained by practices that the Court would find illegal.

Another major case involving Section 2 was the *United Shoe* case.[61] In that case, the government charged that United Shoe maintained its market share of 75–85 percent of American shoe machinery primarily through the practice of refusing to sell its equipment, agreeing only to lease it. The government maintained that United, by only leasing its equipment, created barriers to entry. The reason was that because United repaired its own equipment, there were no independent repair organizations that a competitor could rely on; therefore, if a competitor sought to enter the field, it would have to enter with repair service. The Court also ruled that the leasing system, under which United leased the machines for 10 years, would "deter a shoe manufacturer from disposing of a United machine and acquiring a competitor's machine." The Court ruled that the leases were "so drawn and so applied as to strengthen United's power to exclude competitors." Although the Court recognized the superiority of many of United's products and services, it felt that the leasing system contributed to its market power. The Court required United to

---

[59] Another issue in the definition of the market involved whether imports should be included in the market or not. The Court correctly decided to include them.

[60] The *Alcoa* case was decided by a court of appeals rather than the Supreme Court; the Supreme Court was unable to hear the case because of a conflict of interests involving several of the Justices. The Court of Appeals for the Second Circuit was designated as the court of last resort for the *Alcoa* case, and Judge Learned Hand wrote the decision.

[61] *United States v. United Shoe Machinery Corporation*, 110 F. Supp. 295 (1953). This citation refers to the Federal Supplement, a standard legal reference in which the opinions of the district courts appear.

offer for sale any machines that it leased. The *United Shoe* case illustrates an important concept that has already been presented in Chapter 19: a monopolist would prefer to lease rather than sell its machines.

The Court's views on the 10-year period of the lease are troublesome. If leases come up for renewal over time, and if there can be competition to obtain the customer whose lease has expired, then it is unclear why competition is injured by the leases. Only if the slow turnover of customers prevents a rival from attaining some critical mass necessary for its survival as an efficient competitor would there seem to be an antitrust concern.[62] Even in that case, one would also want to consider any benefits that arise as a result of the long-term nature of the contract.

In *Griffith,* the Court considered the buying practices of chains of motion picture theaters.[63] These motion picture theaters paid for the movies through rentals that were based on the total attendance of the entire chain, rather than at any particular theater. That meant that if a chain had a theater in a town in which it was competing with a single, independent theater, the chain could obtain the same movie at a lower price than the single theater. The Court ruled that this placing of single competitors at a disadvantage was a violation of Section 2 of the Sherman Act. The Court also ruled that "It is . . . not always necessary to find a specific intent to restrain trade or to build a monopoly in order to find that the antitrust laws have been violated. It is sufficient that a restraint of trade or monopoly results as a consequence of a defendant's conduct of business arrangements." This view, that it is the effect of the action rather than the intent of the person conducting the action, was an important development that made for more manageable litigation proceedings.

In the *Berkey* case the Court of Appeals for the Second Circuit examined the duty that a monopolist has towards its rivals.[64] Kodak was a dominant firm in the markets for cameras and for film. In 1972, it introduced the 110 pocket Instamatic camera. It simultaneously introduced a film format to fit that camera. Berkey was a manufacturer of cameras and a processor of film. One of Berkey's claims was that because Kodak refused to predisclose the format of its 110 film, Berkey was unable to manufacture cameras to fit the 110 format film until well after its introduction. Berkey claimed that Kodak's dominance in both film and cameras required it to predisclose to its competitors any changes in film format that would affect competition in the camera market. The court ruled that predisclosure was not a duty imposed on a dominant firm by the antitrust laws. The court recognized that the antitrust laws, especially Section 2, do not prevent monopolies. The Court of Appeals reiterated that the standard for a Section 2 offense is the possession of market power and the willful acquisition or maintenance of that power, as distinguished from growth or development as a consequence of a superior product, business acquirement, or historic accident.[65] See Example 13.4.

---

[62] Aghion and Bolton (1987) have analyzed models in which long-term contracts can create anticompetitive harm.

[63] *United States v. Griffith,* 334 U.S. 100 (1948).

[64] *Berkey Photo, Inc. v. Eastman Kodak Company,* 603 F. 2d 263 (S2d Cir. 1979) cert. denied, 444 U.S. 1093 (1980).

[65] See also *United States v. Grinnell Corp.,* 384 U.S. 563 (1966).

Predation.   As discussed in Chapter 13, one of the classic bad acts is predatory pricing; however, there is a danger of confusing predatory pricing with aggressive competition. The *Utah Pie* case involved a claim of predatory pricing.[66] Utah Pie Company sold frozen dessert pies in Utah. Continental Baking Company, Carnation Company, and Pet Milk Company sold pies in competition with Utah Pie. The Salt Lake City market was the scene of dramatic price competition, and there was evidence to show that prices of the defendants' products were lower in Salt Lake City than they were elsewhere. There was also evidence to suggest that the prices of the defendants' products, at least some of them, was less than their direct cost plus an allocation for overhead. There was evidence that one of the defendants had employed an industrial spy to infiltrate the Utah Pie plant to obtain information. The Court ruled that the price discrimination eroded competition and, therefore, was predatory in violation of the law.

The language of *Utah Pie* suggests that price discrimination can violate Section 2, even if prices exceed average cost. As shown in the discussion of predatory pricing in Chapter 13, fully allocated cost is a mistaken standard to use in determining if prices are predatory.

In the *Telex* case, the Court of Appeals for the Tenth Circuit investigated IBM's pricing behavior with regard to peripheral devices (like disk drives) that plugged into an IBM central processing unit.[67] Telex claimed that IBM had violated the antitrust laws by its decision to slash prices on its peripheral devices in order to compete with Telex. The Court found that because the price was not below IBM's production costs, there were no grounds to the complaint.

In the *Matsushita* case, the Supreme Court again investigated a charge of predatory pricing.[68] This case involved a claim that certain Japanese manufacturers were engaged in predatory pricing over a 20-year period. The Court recognized the irrationality of such a scheme (it would obviously be unprofitable to lose money for 20 years) and dismissed the case (see Example 13.1).

Essential Facilities.   Another type of strategic behavior that has been attacked under the antitrust laws has to do with denial of a competitor's access to **essential facilities,** which are defined as facilities essential to a competitor's survival. Under the essential facilities doctrine, the owner of the essential facility must make the facility available to competitors. For example, a trucking firm that owns the sole bridge leading to an island owns a facility that is essential to rival trucking firms that deliver to the island. The Court has often not concerned itself with the price at which the facility must be made available, though presumably it would have to be at a price reasonable enough to allow the competitor to compete.

In the *Terminal Railroad* case, the Court investigated a situation in which all the railroad bridges in St. Louis were owned by a group of railroads.[69] The concern was that this control could allow the owning railroad companies to harm rival railroads. The Court

---

[66] *Utah Pie Company v. Continental Baking Company,* 386 U.S. 685 (1967). See Elzinga and Hogarty (1978) for an economic analysis of this case.

[67] *Telex Corp. v. International Business Machines Corp.,* 510 F.2d 894 (1975).

[68] *Matsushita Electric Industrial Co. v. Zenith Radio Corporation,* 106 S. Ct. 1348 (1986).

[69] *United States v. Terminal Railroad Association of St. Louis,* 224 U.S. 383 (1912).

ruled that the owning group had to provide access to rival railroads on reasonable terms.

The doctrine of essential facility applies only in cases where one competitor must rely on another for a scarce input. The doctrine is best understood using the theories of cost-raising strategies and the natural advantage of an incumbent discussed in Chapter 13.

Vertical Arrangements Between Firms

So far, the section has described how one competitor can commit bad acts against another. The antitrust laws have also characterized certain types of vertical relationships among noncompeting firms, typically a manufacturer and distributor, as bad acts that harm competitors. We now analyze vertical integration, resale price maintenance, exclusive territories, and exclusive dealing, concluding with an economic assessment of antitrust policy aimed at vertical relationships between firms. The area of the law dealing with vertical relationships has changed rapidly, and several economic anomalies are still associated with it.

Vertical Integration.   The Court's early views on vertical issues, in general, and vertical integration, in particular, were confused. These views suggest that the Court was concerned with a *foreclosure of competition*. This means that if a firm that manufactures shirts vertically integrated backward into producing buttons, the firm would have foreclosed competition in the button market because other button manufacturers could now no longer sell to that firm.

In the *Yellow Cab* case, the Court suggested that vertical integration through merger might be per se illegal.[70] However, soon thereafter it reached the much more sensible conclusion in *Columbia Steel* that "it is clear to us that vertical integration, as such without more, cannot be held violative of the Sherman Act."[71]

The next major case involving vertical integration was the *DuPont* case.[72] DuPont was a major supplier to General Motors of automotive finishes and fabrics. Since 1920 (or earlier), DuPont had owned a 23 percent stock interest in General Motors. The United States government brought suit, claiming that the vertical relationship violated the antitrust laws. It was unclear how consumers would be adversely affected by this vertical integration. Nevertheless, the Court ruled that DuPont's ownership violated the antitrust laws.

It appears that since the *DuPont* case, enforcement policy toward vertical mergers has been in line with the reasonable economic logic of *Columbia Steel*. The current vertical guidelines of the Department of Justice emphasize that vertical integration alone is not objectionable; instead they focus on whether the vertical integration could be used to increase market power.

Resale Price Maintenance.   As Chapter 16 shows, a manufacturer may want to set the retail price at which its product is sold. The setting of retail price by a manufacturer is called **resale price maintenance.**

---

[70] *United States v. Yellow Cab Co.,* 332 U.S. 218 (1947).

[71] *United States v. Columbia Steel Company,* 334 U.S. 495 (1940).

[72] *United States v. E.I. du Pont de Nemours & Company,* 353 U.S. 586 (1957).

In 1911, the Court addressed the question of the pricing restrictions that a manufacturer could place on a distributor that sells its product. In the *Dr. Miles* case, John D. Park, a distributor, refused to enter into a contract that established minimum prices at which Dr. Miles' drug products could be sold.[73] The Court ruled that this pricing agreement suppressed competition among dealers and was equivalent to the fixing of price; therefore it was illegal. This ruling was unpopular, and the antitrust laws were eventually amended to allow resale price maintenance. In 1937, Congress passed the Miller-Tydings Resale Price Maintenance Act and in 1951 the McGuire Act. These acts gave manufacturers the right to set retail prices free of any antitrust liability provided the states had a *fair-trade* statute that allowed resale price maintenance (which would allow products to be sold at a "fair" price). Most states passed such fair-trade laws, although some did not. These states without fair trade laws became places where it was easier for one distributor to "free ride" on the promotional efforts of other distributors, because, as seen in Chapter 16, resale price maintenance is one way to control free riding. The resale price maintenance laws were repealed, and resale price maintenance again became per se illegal in 1976.

The procompetitive logic of resale price maintenance was explained in Chapter 16: resale price maintenance is one way for a manufacturer to induce its distributors to promote its products. This logic was not understood by most economists prior to the 1960s. Since the 1960s, a large literature has developed showing the competitive benefits of restraints that manufacturers can place on the distributors of their products. As explained in Chapter 16, economists make no distinction between pricing restrictions and other restrictions that manufacturers might want to place on their distributors. Both can promote competition and prevent free riding (Posner 1981). Resale price maintenance can also be anticompetitive if it facilitates a cartel.

The repeal of the laws on resale price maintenance appears to forbid control of prices by manufacturers. However, a recent decision by the Supreme Court seems to indicate a shift in direction. In *Business Electronics Corporation v. Sharp Electronics Corporation,* the Court analyzed a case in which a retailer that had cut prices had its supply terminated.[74] The retailer claimed that termination occurred because of the price-cutting and that the termination constituted a violation of the antitrust laws. Although the Court stated that vertical agreements on resale prices are illegal per se, it ruled that because there was no agreement on price among the other competing retailers and the manufacturer, there was no violation of the antitrust laws. However, the Court emphasized that in vertical cases, it is not the literal characterization of a restraint that matters, but rather whether the agreement promotes or restricts competition. The Court concluded, "There has been no showing here that an agreement between a manufacturer and a dealer to terminate a price cutter, without a further agreement on the price or price levels to be charged by the remaining dealer, tends to restrict competition and reduce output." Therefore, although the Court appears not to have overruled its per se prohibition on vertical price fixing, its decision in this case reaches the correct economic conclusion that a manufacturer's control of pricing should not necessarily create an antitrust problem.

---

[73] *Dr. Miles Medical Company v. John D. Park & Sons Company,* 220 U.S. 373 (1911).

[74] *Business Electronics Corporation v. Sharp Electronics Corporation,* No. 85-1910, 54 BNA 797 (5 May 1988). This citation refers to the BNA Reporter, another standard legal reference.

Exclusive Territories.   Chapter 16 presented situations in which a manufacturer would find it profitable to assign a geographic area to one of its dealers and not allow its other dealers to locate in that area. Such an area, called an **exclusive territory,** provides dealers with incentives to promote the product and prevents one dealer from free riding on the promotional efforts of another. Exclusive territories can also adversely affect competition if they facilitate a cartel. Obviously, a territorial restriction on the ability of a manufacturer's dealers to compete literally restricts competition, even though the purpose of the territorial restriction may be to promote competition and the sale of the product. In 1963, the Court addressed the issue of territorial restrictions in the *White Motor* case.[75] In that case, a truck manufacturer limited the territory in which its distributors could sell the product. The Court ruled that such territorial restrictions do not necessarily violate the antitrust laws and their legality should be determined only after examining their effects.

In the *General Motors* case, the Court investigated General Motors' behavior toward its dealers.[76] General Motors had location clauses in its dealers' contracts that prevented them from moving from one territory to another. General Motors also tried to prevent its dealers from reselling cars to discount dealers, who sold them without the same promotional activities as other dealers. The Court ruled that the efforts of General Motors "to eliminate sales of new Chevrolet cars by discounters was to protect franchise dealers from real or apparent price competition." Accordingly, the Court ruled that this behavior violated the antitrust laws.

In the *Schwinn* case, the Court took a hard line on exclusive territories.[77] It ruled that "under the Sherman Act, it is unreasonable without more for a manufacturer to seek to restrict and confine areas or persons with whom an article may be traded after the manufacturer has parted with dominion over it. . . . Such restraints are so obviously destructive of competition that their mere existence is enough." This important case made the use of exclusive territories a per se violation of the antitrust laws.

In 1977, the Court overruled the *Schwinn* case. In the *GTE Sylvania* case, Sylvania imposed restrictions on where its distributors could operate.[78] The Court recognized that vertical restrictions improved the ability of a manufacturer to sell its product and provided a way to get around certain free-rider problems, such as those discussed in Chapter 16. Therefore, the Court overruled *Schwinn*'s per se prohibition against territorial restrictions and instead instituted a rule of reason under which vertical restrictions should be judged.

The Court's reasoning was based on the promotion of interbrand competition (competition among different products) at the expense of restricting intrabrand competition (competition among dealers of the same product). This distinction is a bit misleading. Vertical restrictions can indeed promote interbrand competition by making it profitable for dealers to promote and service each product, but it is not at all obvious that there is an undesirable effect on intrabrand competition. Although it is true in the literal sense

---

[75] *White Motor Company v. United States,* 372 U.S. 253 (1963).

[76] *United States v. General Motors Corp.,* 384 U.S. 127 (1966).

[77] *United States v. Arnold, Schwinn & Company,* 388 U.S. 365 (1967).

[78] *Continental TV Inc. v. GTE Sylvania Inc.,* 433 U.S. 36 (1977).

that exclusive territories restrict the ability of one distributor to compete with another distributor, it is not true, as discussed in Chapter 16, that a single manufacturer uses exclusive territories to restrict competition solely to raise the retail price. If a manufacturer wants to, it can raise the retail price (assuming no constraint from other products) by raising the wholesale price even without vertical restrictions. In this way, the manufacturer affects the retail price everywhere its product is sold. Therefore, vertical restrictions should not be viewed as giving a single manufacturer the ability to control price better but rather as giving it the ability to control promotion and service better. The manufacturer can already influence retail price through the wholesale price. The important feature of the GTE decision for the economist is the Supreme Court's recognition that vertical restraints can indeed promote competition.

Exclusive Dealing.   The Court has also analyzed **exclusive dealing** in which a manufacturer prevents its distributors from selling competing brands. As Chapter 16 shows, exclusive dealing allows manufacturers to overcome a free-riding problem of a slightly different type than that overcome by exclusive territories. Exclusive territories address free riding of one dealer on the efforts of another; exclusive dealing addresses free riding of one manufacturer on the efforts of another. Exclusive dealing can also be used to raise entry barriers.

In 1922, the Supreme Court refused to enforce a manufacturer's contract with a retailer that forbade the retailer to sell brands of other manufacturer's. In 1949, in the *Standard Stations* case, the Court again addressed the problem of exclusive dealing.[80] In that case, Standard Oil of California required its independent dealers to purchase petroleum products and automobile accessories only from it. Rather than applying a rule of reason, the Supreme Court concluded that it would be too great a burden to show that competition had actually been diminished by the exclusive dealing and therefore it ruled that "Section 3 [of the Clayton Act, which forbids exclusive dealing] is satisfied by proof that competition has been foreclosed and a substantial share of the line of commerce affected." Justice Jackson recognized that the Court was making an economic error and stated, "I cannot agree that the requirements contract is per se an illegal one under the antitrust law, and that is the substance of what the Court seems to hold. I am not convinced that the requirements contract as here used is a device for suppressing competition instead of a device for waging competition." Justice Jackson recognized the economic insight that vertical restraints, like exclusive dealing, can promote competition.

In the *Tampa Electric* case, the Court returned to the question of exclusive dealing, though not in the context described in Chapter 16.[81] In the *Tampa Electric* case, a utility had signed a large contract to obtain coal over a period of 20 years from a coal supplier. After the contract was signed, the coal supplier claimed that the contract amounted to a requirements contract that would result in the lessening of competition. The Court ruled that such contracts did not violate the law, and said, "the competition foreclosed by the

---

[79] *Standard Fashion Company v. Magraine-Houston Co.,* 258 U.S. 346 (1922).

[80] *Standard Oil Company of California v. United States,* 337 U.S. 293 (1949).

[81] *Tampa Electric Company v. Nashville Coal Company,* 365 U.S. 320 (1961).

contract must be found to constitute a substantial share of the relevant market." It pointed out that in the *Standard Stations* case, 16 percent of the retail outlets were affected, while in this case, only a tiny fraction of all coal in the area was affected, approximately 1 percent. This focus on contracts foreclosing the market is troubling from an economic viewpoint. As long as contracts come up for renewal, and as long as there is competition at the time of renewal, it is hard to see the harm to competition unless the contracts somehow prevent a rival from acquiring a size critical to its survival. Even in this case, one would also want to consider the benefits from the long-term relationship.

The Court's future treatment of exclusive dealing will presumably incorporate its *Sylvania* decision, in which it recognized the value of vertical restrictions in dealing with the free-rider problem.

Antitrust Policy toward Vertical Relations

Recall from Chapter 16 that, in general, vertical integration and vertical restrictions are not necessarily anticompetitive. Even when a manufacturer is a monopolist, it is not at all clear that the vertical restrictions it may impose on a distributor reduce consumer welfare. As pointed out in Chapter 16, it is not possible to prove definitively that vertical integration or restrictions always improve society's welfare, but neither is it possible to prove that a monopolist's choice of quality or any other product dimension always improves consumer welfare. Moreover, it is typically costly to examine a particular case of a vertical relation or quality choice, and even after lengthy examination it may still be difficult to reliably predict the effect of the vertical relation or quality choice on consumer welfare. Few would ever suggest that the antitrust laws should be used to interfere with how a monopolist chooses quality or manufactures its product, yet there is usually no greater justification for interfering in the monopolist's choice of distribution than for interfering in its choice of production. In some situations, however, vertical integration or restrictions do result in a diminution in competition and create harm to society, and those are the ones the antitrust laws should try to prevent. We now discuss those situations.

A vertical restriction involving exclusive dealing can harm society if it is used as a means to prevent or impede rivals from obtaining distribution of their product. The same is true for vertical integration into distribution. However, as long as other efficient methods of distribution are available to rivals, neither exclusive dealing nor vertical integration can restrain the entry of rivals.

Other vertical restrictions, like exclusive territories, can have anticompetitive effects if they are forced upon a manufacturer by a dealer cartel. That is, the exclusive territories could be part of an agreement among competing dealers on how to allocate territories.[82] Only if the dealers have market power can such a claim make sense, as already shown in Chapter 16. No manufacturer would willingly take part in such a conspiracy of its dealers, because it would raise the manufacturer's distribution costs.

In *Sealy* and *Topco,* the Supreme Court interpreted territorial restrictions as agreements

---

[82] Vertical integration and vertical restrictions can also be used by manufacturers to facilitate collusion by making it easier to detect cheating on a cartel of manufacturers (see Chapters 9 and 16).

to limit competition among rivals.[83] In both these cases, groups of firms combined and agreed to territorial restrictions as part of an effort to promote their product, avoid the free-rider problem, and promote a common trademark. The Court held that in both cases, these agreements were per se violations of Section 1 of the Sherman Act. However, to the extent that in both cases the territorial restrictions were necessary to develop a new trademarked product, it would seem that the subsequent ruling in the *BMI* case (agreements among firms are acceptable if they are necessary to provide the product) would mean that the *Sealy* and *Topco* cases would, if examined now, be analyzed under the rule of reason, not as per se violations.

It is a common characteristic of distributors' complaints against vertical relationships that the complaint is characterized as an agreement between some distributors and a manufacturer to eliminate or prevent competition by other distributors. Plaintiffs phrase the complaint in this way so as to characterize the behavior as a conspiracy involving price-fixing or output restrictions. The reason for this is that plaintiffs hope to apply the per se rules of the antitrust laws against price and output agreements. They plead that there is an antitrust violation rather than just a breach of contract because they receive treble damages under the antitrust laws but only single damages under contract law. For example, a terminated dealer claims that the termination violates the antitrust laws rather than contract law in order to recover greater damages.

One example of an attempt to turn a vertical restriction case into a conspiracy case is the *Klor's* case.[84] In that case, the Court addressed the issue of the inability of an appliance store to obtain supplies from the same sources as its competitors. Klor's was an appliance store located close to a Broadway Hale store, a department store that also distributed appliances. Many well-known brands of appliances were sold to Broadway Hale but not to Klor's. Klor's claimed that there was a conspiracy among Broadway Hale and the appliance manufacturers to drive it out of business. Klor's claimed that Broadway Hale used its market power to prevent manufacturers from selling to Klor's. Broadway Hale's defense indicated that numerous other retailers located close to Broadway Hale also sold the appliances of major manufacturers. The important economic question is whether Broadway Hale had sufficient buying power over the manufacturers to prevent them from selling to Klor's. If it did not, then the likely alternative explanation for the manufacturers' behavior is to control free-rider problems, as discussed in Chapter 16.

Antitrust policy toward vertical relationships has implications for the ability of a firm to price discriminate. Chapter 16 explained how vertical integration and restrictions might enable price discrimination to take place. For example, a manufacturer that wanted to charge two different prices, one in New York and one in California, could do so if it prevented resale between the states and required distributors to sell only in their territories. Because it is unclear whether society is, in general, harmed or helped by price discrimination (Chapter 14), it seems unwise to make any general policy prescriptions based on this effect of vertical integration and restrictions. Moreover, to examine every instance of

---

[83] *United States v. Sealy, Inc.,* 388 U.S. 350 (1967) and *United States v. Topco Associates Inc.,* 405 U.S. 596 (1972).

[84] *Klor's, Inc. v. Broadway Hale Stores Inc.,* 359 U.S. 207 (1959).

TABLE 22.1   Horizontal and Vertical Preliminary Investigations of the Antitrust Division of the Department of Justice 1968-1984

	Number of Preliminary Investigations			
Year	Horizontal	Vertical	Total	Ratio of Horizontal to Vertical
1968	51	441	492	.11
1969	26	460	486	.06
1970	12	239	251	.05
1971	22	236	258	.09
1972	47	204	251	.23
1973	49	124	173	.39
1974	37	88	125	.42
1975	41	23	64	1.78
1976	55	24	79	2.29
1977	70	8	78	8.75
1978	94	2	96	47.00
1979	129	5	134	25.80
1980	71	25	96	2.84
1981	60	8	68	7.50
1982	79	11	90	7.18
1983	74	7	81	10.57
1984	108	7	115	15.43

SOURCE: Johnson and Smith (1986), Table 3.

---

price discrimination would be unwise because it would be costly, and even after the analysis, it typically can be difficult to reliably predict the welfare effects of the discrimination.

Current government policy of the FTC and Department of Justice toward vertical mergers seems to recognize that it is wrong to regard vertical integration as an evil in itself. For example, the recent Vertical Merger Guidelines of the Department of Justice emphasize that only vertical arrangements that adversely affect competition should be challenged. Table 22.1 shows how the Department of Justice's enforcement policy toward vertical mergers has shifted since 1973, when the Economic Policy Office of the Department of Justice was created, whose function it is to evaluate the economic merits of potential cases. The table documents the dramatic decline in the number of preliminary investigations into vertical mergers. (The Department of Justice conducts a preliminary investigation of a merger when it feels that it may create potential competitive problems.)

Altough the FTC and Department of Justice appear to understand the consequences of vertical integration, the same cannot always be said for the courts. In several relatively recent cases, a court has misunderstood the purpose of the vertical relationship between firms. For example, in the *Fotomat* case, the Court of Appeals for the Seventh Circuit ruled against a franchisor that sought to open outlets in competition with its own franchisee.[85] It is a mistake of economic logic to believe vertical integration forward into distribution is necessarily an antitrust violation because independent dealers face additional competition.

---

[85] *Photovest v. Fotomat Corp.*, 606 F.2d 704 (7th Cir. 1979).

Tie-In Sales

Obscurity often brings safety. — AESOP

The antitrust laws have been used to prevent a firm from using **tie-in sales** in which the sale of one product is conditioned upon the purchase of another. The courts often characterize tie-in sales as a way of denying competitors the opportunity to make sales. Chapter 15 examines in detail some of the reasons for tie-in sales. Some of the reasons arise because a firm has some market power in one market and by the use of tie-in sales is able to earn higher profits than if it could only charge for one product. Tie-in sales, then, can be a variant of price discrimination. That is, they raise the return to being a monopolist in an industry. They do not necessarily create greater inefficiency losses and could result in output expansion. Despite the apparent lack of any strong economic argument based on price discrimination against tie-in sales, the law has not treated tie-in sales favorably. As already discussed in Chapter 15, aside from the price discrimination motive, many products are naturally and efficiently tied together. For example, a car consists of its component parts, as does a radio. It would be improper to prohibit efficient bundling of components. There may be some cases where tie-ins are anticompetitive. For example, tie-in sales could be used to raise entry costs (by tying repair to a machine, no independent repair shops arise, and entrants are disadvantaged). However, the courts have not focused solely on these types of cases in their decisions to prohibit tie-in sales.

In early cases involving patented products, the Supreme Court ruled that tie-in sales were indeed legal. For example, in *Henry v. A. B. Dick Company,* the Court did not find fault with A. B. Dick's practice of selling its patented mimeograph machines with a requirement that only ink purchased from A. B. Dick Company, as well as other supplies made by A. B. Dick, could be used.[86] As Chapter 15 explains, this tie-in could enable A. B. Dick to identify and extract more money from those who used the machine most intensively.

The Clayton Act, passed in 1914, contained a section outlawing tie-in sales that had the effect of reducing competition. Soon thereafter, the Court overruled the *A. B. Dick* case in *Motion Picture Patents v. Universal Film Manufacturing Co.*[87] In two subsequent cases, the Supreme Court refused to alter its prohibition against tie-ins. In the *IBM* case, the United States attacked the practice whereby IBM's sale of certain machines required that the purchaser use only IBM tabulating cards.[88] IBM granted a special exception to the government that allowed it to use tabulating cards of its own manufacture provided the government paid an extra 15 percent rent. The Supreme Court used the government's experience to reject IBM's claim that its reputation would be damaged unless its tabulating cards were used because otherwise its machines might malfunction.

---

[86] *Henry v. A. B. Dick Company,* 224 U.S. 1 (1912).

[87] *Motion Picture Patents v. Universal Film Manufacturing Co.,* 243 U.S. 502 (1917).

[88] *IBM Corporation v. United States,* 298 U.S. 131 (1936).

In the *International Salt* case, the Court investigated the requirement by International Salt Company that its purchasers use salt provided by International Salt in some machines that International Salt provided.[89] As in the *IBM* case, the Court rejected International Salt's claim that its reputation would be damaged if low-quality salt were used with resulting damage to its machines. The Court ruled that since a substantial amount of the salt market was "foreclosed" to competitors, the tie-in was per se illegal.

In the *Northern Pacific Case,* the Court ruled that Northern Pacific's requirements that lessees of certain lands be required to ship over its railway under certain conditions was a per se violation.[90] "Tying agreements serve hardly any purpose beyond the suppression of competition. They deny competitors free access to the market for the tied product, not because the party imposing the tying requirement has a better product or a lower price, but because it has power leverage in another market." The Court found that the defendant possessed substantial economic power and concluded that the tie-in was illegal. In *Fortner II,* the Court stated that "for a tie-in to be illegal, the seller must have some advantage not shared by his competitors in the market for the tie-in product."[91]

An important case involving tie-ins is the *Hyde*[92] case. In that case, a hospital had contracted for the provision of anesthesiology services from a private firm. The hospital agreed to use only that firm in the provision of anesthesiology services to its patients. An anesthesiologist sued and charged the hospital with tying anesthesiology to its other hospital services. The Court's decision is a bit murky. The Court states that the requirements for an illegal tie are (1) the existence of two products, (2) market power in one product, and (3) forcing. By *forcing,* the Court means that products get sold together that would not be sold together without the tie. The Court said, "It is far too late in the history of our antitrust jurisprudence to question the proposition that certain tying arrangements pose an unacceptable risk of stifling competition. . ." The Court did not find that the questioned conduct was illegal, apparently because the hospital lacked market power.

The courts' rulings regarding tie-in sales, especially in regard to the relationship between franchisors and franchisees, have been particularly troublesome and inconsistent with the economic theory of Chapter 16. As that chapter points out, there are many types of restrictions that a franchisor may place on a franchisee in order to obtain the desired economic performance. The franchisor also needs to be compensated for its efforts. One method by which a franchisee can compensate the franchisor is through various tie-in sales. For example, the franchisor could require that it be the sole supplier of napkins to the franchisee as a rough way of charging a franchise fee based on sales. This conduct has been attacked under our antitrust laws under the ban on tie-in sales.[93] The proper way to view such tie-in sales between a franchisor and a franchisee is not necessarily as a

---

[89] *International Salt Company v. United States,* 332 U.S. 392 (1947). See Peterman (1979) for an economic analysis of this case.

[90] *Northern Pacific Railway Company v. United States,* 356 U.S. 1 (1958).

[91] *United States Steel Corporation v. Fortner Enterprises, Inc.,* 429 U.S. 610 (1977).

[92] *Jefferson Parish Hospital District No. 2 v. Hyde,* 466 U.S. 2 (1984).

[93] See, for example, *Siegel v. Chicken Delight Inc.,* 448 F.2d (9th Cir. 1971) cert. denied, 405 U.S. 955.

method to foreclose competition in napkins, but rather as a method by which the franchisor and franchisee together can reach a compensation arrangement under which the franchisor gets compensated and the franchisee produces the desired product.

Litigation under Section 2 of the Sherman Act

Section 2 of the Sherman Act deals with a firm's exclusionary conduct (bad acts) that is deemed to adversely affect competition. The problem with Section 2 cases is that the Court has left unclear exactly how vigorously a dominant firm can respond to new competition. Moreover, as shown in Chapter 13, economists cannot usually say with certainty which types of strategic behavior lead to benefits for consumers when competitors are harmed. For example, the case of strategic investment in advance is a good example of a policy that can benefit consumers even if it prevents competition from entering the field. It is precisely this difficulty of distinguishing competitive responses designed to benefit consumers from competitive responses whose only purpose is to destroy competition that makes Section 2 litigation so difficult.

Section 2 litigation can be costly (as can all complicated litigation). One example of costly litigation is the IBM case in which the government sought to force IBM to break itself up into several firms. The government claimed that IBM practiced numerous predatory policies designed to exclude competition. The legal fees as well as the time of IBM and government employees probably put the litigation cost in the area of hundreds of millions of dollars. The government eventually dropped the case.[94]

In striking a balance as to how vigorously to pursue Section 2 cases, it is wise to keep the following in mind. Where entry can occur, market power may be short lived and will be eliminated over time. Overvigorous enforcement of Section 2 not only could reduce market power but also could dissuade firms from ever pursuing certain efficient policies that would benefit consumers. This efficiency loss could be large and would not diminish over time. Striking the right balance in Section 2 cases will continue to be difficult.

■ OTHER ANTITRUST VIOLATIONS

This section briefly examines two additional areas where the antitrust laws have been applied. The first is price discrimination under the Robinson-Patman Act. The second is antitrust in regulated industries. Each area contains numerous complications, and the reader is referred to Posner and Easterbrook (1980) for greater details.

Price Discrimination under the Robinson-Patman Act

As already explained, the antitrust laws can attack price discrimination if a firm uses it to harm rivals and create or maintain market power (for example, *Utah Pie*). The antitrust

---

[94] See Fisher, McGowan, and Greenwood (1983) for a description of this lengthy litigation. See Houthakker (1985) for a different view.

laws also forbid price discrimination that is judged to harm competition among the customers of the seller.[95] The **Robinson-Patman Act** prohibits both types of price discrimination. A concern with the effect of price discrimination on competition among customers was the primary reason for the passage of the Robinson-Patman Act (which amended Section 2 of the Clayton Act in 1936). The Robinson-Patman Act was passed in response to political pressure from small retail stores (for example, grocery stores) which complained that larger chains were able to purchase supplies on more favorable terms and thereby charge lower prices. Many economists view the Robinson-Patman Act as special-interest legislation designed to protect small firms from competition from larger, more efficient firms that would be able to purchase supplies at low cost in the absence of the Act (Ross 1984).

One consequence of the Robinson-Patman Act is higher prices to consumers, who are deprived of the benefits of economies of scale in purchasing that the chain stores would otherwise be forced by competition (amongst themselves) to pass along (Ross 1984). The Robinson-Patman Act has led to substantial litigation (though government litigation has waned recently) and has also distorted pricing in many markets (Elzinga and Hogarty 1978). It is a law that often results in harm to consumers.

Regulated Industries

Suppose a firm is regulated by a government agency that oversees the firm's actions. Can such a firm be sued under the antitrust laws? The answer is yes. Regulation does not provide an absolute defense against antitrust prosecution. One example of the application of the antitrust laws to a regulated entity involves AT&T. In many private suits as well as in a case brought by the government, AT&T was charged with engaging in numerous predatory acts, such as improper pricing, denial of hookups to competitors, and requiring rivals to install costly and unnecessary interconnection devices.[96] The private suits resulted in some of the largest damage awards in history. The result of the government's case against AT&T was the divestiture of the phone company into seven independent local operating companies plus a long-distance carrier.

■ THE EFFECTS OF ANTITRUST RULINGS ON THE ORGANIZATION OF ECONOMIC ACTIVITY

Whenever laws prohibit actions that firms want to take, firms seek alternate routes to accomplish their objectives. If the antitrust laws inhibit agreements between independent firms, both horizontally and vertically, then one response would be for firms to merge or

---

[95] Such price discrimination is called *secondary-line discrimination*. Price discrimination that harms competition in the market of the firm practicing the discrimination (for example, as alleged in *Utah Pie*) is called *primary-line price discrimination*.

[96] *Litton Systems v. American Telephone and Telegraph Co.*, 746 F.2d 168 (2d Cir. 1984); *MCI Communications v. American Telephone and Telegraph Co.*, 708 F.2d 1081 (7th Cir. 1983); *United States v. Western Electric (AT&T)*, 552 F. Supp. 131 (1982).

simply grow large and do everything themselves. It is peculiar that the antitrust laws encourage firms to merge or grow larger than would otherwise occur. Some of the decisions of the Supreme Court to forbid certain types of contractual vertical restrictions creates an incentive for vertical integration.[97] Several states have responded by adopting statutes that prevent certain manufacturers from integrating forward into distribution. For example, several states prevent oil companies from owning and operating their own gasoline stations.

The antitrust laws, as already mentioned, affect how a franchisor can deal with a franchisee. The effect of the antitrust laws (and several state franchise laws) is to transfer certain rights from franchisors to franchisees and to make the franchise arrangement less attractive as a method of distribution (Smith 1982). If laws make it difficult for franchisors to control franchisees' actions, the incentive to use this mode of organization is diminished.

■ SUMMARY

The major federal antitrust statutes are the Sherman Act, the Clayton Act, and the Federal Trade Commission Act. The interpretation of these statutes has varied considerably over time. Recently there has been an increasing emphasis on the use of economic analysis in deciding what the antitrust laws should prohibit.

It is a common mistake to think that the antitrust laws prohibit monopoly. They do not. However, they do prohibit certain actions that could allow a firm to acquire or maintain monopoly power. Many antitrust cases revolve around whether a firm has market power, which is the ability to set price above the competitive price. It is often difficult to assess directly whether a firm has market power. Courts and economists often use market share as a rough guide to whether a firm has market power. For this calculation of market share to be meaningful, the market must be properly defined. The market definition should include all those products whose presence significantly constrains the price of the product under analysis.

The courts use both per se rules and rules of reason. A per se rule prohibits certain acts without regard to the effect of the acts. For example, a price-fixing conspiracy whose sole purpose is to raise price is a per se violation. A rule of reason requires an investigation of the effect of the challenged conduct. Vertical restraints, other than on price, are now judged under a rule of reason.

The antitrust laws severely limit the types of cooperative behavior that competitors can engage in. For example, any attempt to fix price or limit output so as to harm consumers is a per se violation. This means that even unsuccessful attempts to fix price violate the law. There are some instances where the courts allow cooperative behavior if the cooperative behavior is essential to producing a new, more desirable product. Mergers among

---

[97] Alternatively, firms could use devices whose legality turns on legal technicalities. For example, a distributor may sell a good on consignment (which means that the manufacturer, not the distributor, owns the good) rather than owning the good and reselling it. The restrictions that can be placed on consignment sales can differ from those on nonconsignment sales.

competitors can be prevented if the effect of the merger is to create additional market power. Curiously, two firms with no market power are allowed to merge even though those same two firms would violate the law if they remained independent but spoke to each other and set price together.

The antitrust laws also constrain the actions of a firm designed to hamper its rivals. For example, strategic behavior designed to drive a rival out of business through, for example, predatory pricing, is illegal. The difficulty with antitrust enforcement in this area is that it is difficult to distinguish vigorous competition from strategic behavior that harms consumers. Overzealous enforcement could deprive consumers of the benefits of competition.

An important application of the antitrust laws has been to vertical relations between firms. The Court's reasoning has often been confused and has relied on a foreclosure of competition doctrine in which one firm that, say, vertically integrates into steel production is said to foreclose other steel producers from selling steel to the first firm. There are a variety of reasons why a firm vertically integrates or imposes vertical restraints on its distributors. Many, but not all, of these reasons promote competition. Recently, the Court has recognized the possible procompetitive effect of nonprice vertical restrictions but still regards vertical restrictions on price as a per se violation. It is impossible to prove that vertical restrictions always benefit each consumer. The welfare effect of some vertical restrictions is ambiguous. Even after careful study, an analyst may be unable to decide whether a particular vertical restriction harms consumers. They help some consumers and harm others. But the same could be said of the choice of product quality. There often is no greater justification for interfering with how a manufacturer distributes its product than there is in interfering with the quality of product that the monopolist produces. However, there are a few cases where vertical integration or restrictions can only harm consumers. Where the vertical integration or restrictions harm rivals by significantly impeding or foreclosing entry or where they allow distributors or manufacturers to act like a cartel, they harm consumers.

The welfare effects of price discrimination and tie-in sales are generally ambiguous, and, as in the case of certain vertical restrictions, it is often costly and difficult to determine conclusively whether consumers are harmed in a particular situation. Pursuing strenuous general antitrust enforcement in areas with ambiguous welfare effects is unwise.

■ Key Terms

antitrust laws	exclusive dealing	resale price maintenance
Celler-Kefauver Act	exclusive territory	Robinson-Patman Act
Clayton Act	Federal Trade Commission Act	rule of reason
contribution	legal standing	Sherman Act
cross-elasticity of demand	market definition	tie-in sales
essential facilities	per se	treble damages
exclusionary actions		

■ Discussion Questions

1. Suppose a firm sells a computer and a printer. The firm is a monopolist of computers. The printer must be compatible and interconnect with the computer to work. Suppose the firm refuses to release the interconnection requirements and is therefore the only firm that can sell the printers. Discuss the effects of the firm's actions. (Consider in your answer the effort used to develop interconnection standards, the theory of tie-in sales [computer plus printer is a package tie], and the creation of entry barriers.) Discuss the facts that would have to be proven to establish bad conduct, and assess whether you think such litigation is feasible.

2. The retail market definition in *Brown Shoe* included shoes sold through shoe stores but not through department stores. Comment.

3. If Firm A is located in Europe and ships goods to the United States, should only the U.S. sales of Firm A be considered as a constraint on U.S. price, or should the entire capacity of Firm A be considered as the constraint?

4. Explain why a franchisor might want to own some outlets and compete with its franchisees. Can you think of any way in which consumers could be harmed by such conduct?

5. How will the comparison of efficiency to deadweight loss in Figure 22.1 change if the resources devoted to becoming the monopolist are included as part of the deadweight loss? (Review Chapter 5.)

■ Problems

1. In the United Shoe case, the Court ruled that the 10-year leases adversely affected competition, in part because they prevented other competitors from selling to a customer who was still on a United Shoe lease. Such a claim can be made of any contract. Identify circumstances where a long-term lease would impede competition and where it would not.

2. Suppose Firm A is the only one that can sell in New York. Firm A faces competition elsewhere in the country. If Firm A can price discriminate, will the prices in New York differ from those elsewhere? Will there be a high correlation of price movements between New York and elsewhere? Are there one or two geographic markets?

3. Suppose there are some industries in which the competitive equilibrium does not exist (the core does not exist—see Chapter 4). Should firms in these industries be allowed to collude under the antitrust laws?

4. Economic theory can establish that

$$\frac{\partial Q_j}{\partial p_i} = \frac{\partial Q_i}{\partial p_j},$$

where Q stands for quantity demanded, p for price, and subscripts indicate the products i or j. (Technically, the demand curves should be "compensated," that is, corrected for an income effect.) Suppose $p_i = p_j$, but $Q_i = 100 \, Q_j$. What will be true about the relative size of the two relevant cross-elasticities of demand? Why does it matters which one is used in the analysis of market definition?

5. Another relation from economic theory is that

$$\frac{p_i}{Q_i} \frac{\partial Q_i}{\partial p_i} = -\sum_{\substack{j \\ j \neq i}} \frac{p_j}{Q_i} \frac{\partial Q_i}{\partial p_j},$$

where Σ is a summation sign. (Again, the Q's are compensated demands). Explain how this relation can be used to relate the elasticity of demand to cross-elasticities of demand. Use the formula to determine which cross-elasticity an analyst investigating market power in Product A should examine to determine whether Product B constrains the pricing of Product A.

Answers to the odd-numbered problems are given at the back of the book.

■ Recommended Readings

For an economic analysis of some recent antitrust cases, see Kwoka and White (1989).

■ References

Aghion, Philippe, and Patrick Bolton. 1987. "Contracts as a Barrier to Entry. *American Economic Review* 77:338–401.

Areeda, Phillip. 1986. *Antitrust Law, vols. 6 and 7*. Boston: Little, Brown and Co.

Areeda, Phillip, and Donald Turner. 1978, 1980. *Antitrust Law, vols. 1-5*. Boston: Little, Brown and Co.

Audretsch, David. 1987. "The Effects of Legalized Cartels in West Germany." Berlin: International Institute of Management.

Baker, Jonathan B., and Timothy F. Bresnahan. 1985. "The Gains from Merger or Collusion in Product Differentiated Industries." *Journal of Industrial Economics* 33:427–44.

Bittlingmayer, George. 1982. "Decreasing Average Cost and Competition: A New Look at the Addyston Pipe Case." *Journal of Law and Economics* 25:201–29.

———. 1985. "Did Antitrust Policy Cause the Great Merger Wave?" *Journal of Law and Economics* 28:77–118.

Bork, Robert H. 1978. *The Antitrust Paradox: A Policy at War with Itself*. New York: Basic Books.

Carlton, Dennis W., and Mark J. Klamer. 1983. "The Need for Coordination Among Firms with Special Reference to Network Industries." *Univ. of Chicago Law Review* 50:446–65.

Easterbrook, Frank H.; William M. Landes; and Richard A. Posner. 1980. "Contributions Among Antitrust Defendants: A Legal and Economic Analysis." *Journal of Law and Economics* 23:331–70.

Elzinga, Kenneth G., and Thomas F. Hogarty. 1978. "*Utah Pie* and the Consequences of Robinson-Patman." *Journal of Law and Economics* 21:427–34.

Fisher, Franklin M.; John J. McGowan; and Joen E. Greenwood. 1983. *Folded, Spindled and Mutilated: Economic Analysis and U.S. v. IBM*. Cambridge: The MIT Press.

Halverson, James T. 1988. "The Future of Horizontal Restraints Analysis." *Antitrust Law Journal* 57:33–48.

Henderson, James J., and Richard E. Quandt. 1980. *Microeconomic Theory*. New York: McGraw-Hill.

Houthakker, Hendrik. 1985. "Book Review" of Fisher et al. (1983). *Journal of Political Economy* 93:618–21.

Johnson, Richard L., and David D. Smith. 1986. "Antitrust Division Merger Procedures and Policy, 1968–1984." Department of Justice Discussion Paper.

Kwoka, John E., Jr., and Lawrence J. White. 1989. *The Antitrust Revolution*. Glenview, Ill.: Scott, Foresman.

Landes, William M. 1983. "Optimal Sanctions for Antitrust Violations." *University of Chicago Law Review* 50:652–78.

Landes, William M., and Richard A. Posner. 1979. "Should Indirect Purchasers Have Standing to Sue Under the Antitrust Laws? An Economic Analysis of the Rule of Illinois Brick." *University of Chicago Law Review* 46:602–35.

———. 1981. "Market Power in Antitrust Cases." *Harvard Law Review* 95:937–96.

Marshall, Alfred. 1920. *Principles of Economics*. Philadelphia: Porcupine Press.

McGee, John. 1958. "Predatory Price Cutting: The Standard Oil (N.J.) Case." *Journal of Law and Economics* 1:137–69.

Nicholls, William. 1951. *Price Policies in the Cigarette Industry*. Nashville: Vanderbilt University Press.

Peterman, John. 1975. "The Federal Trade Commission v. The Brown Shoe Company." *Journal of Law and Economics* 18:361–421.

———. 1979. "The International Salt Case." *Journal of Law and Economics* 22:351–64.

Posner, Richard A. 1976. *Antitrust Law, An Economic Perspective*. Chicago: University of Chicago Press.

———. 1981. "The Next Step in the Antitrust Treatment of Restricted Distribution: Per Se Legality." *University of Chicago Law Review* 48:6–26.

Posner, Richard A., and Frank H. Easterbrook. 1980. *Antitrust Cases, Economic Notes, and Other Materials*. St. Paul, Minn.: West Publishing Co.

Ross, Thomas W. 1984. "Winners and Losers Under the Robinson-Patman Act." *Journal of Law and Economics* 27:243–71.

Scheffman, David, and Pablo Spiller. 1987. "Geographic Market Definition Under the U.S. Department of Justice Merger Guidelines." *Journal of Law and Economics* 30:123–48.

Scherer, Frederic M. 1980. *Industrial Market Structure and Economic Performance*. Skokie, Ill.: Rand McNally College Publishing.

Schmalensee, Richard. 1978. "Entry Deterrence in the Ready-to-Eat Breakfast Cereal Industry." *Bell Journal of Economics* 9:305–27.

Smith, Richard. 1982. "Franchise Regulation: An Economic Analysis of State Restrictions on Automobile Distribution." *Journal of Law and Economics* 25:125–57.

Stigler, George J., and Robert A. Sherwin. 1985. "The Extent of the Market." *Journal of Law and Economics* 29:555–85.

Swann, Dennis D.; Dennis O'Brien; W. Peter Maunder; and W. Stewart Howe. 1974. *Competition in British Industry; Restrictive Practices Legislation in Theory and Practice*. London: Allen & Unwin.

Telser, Lester G. 1972. *Competition, Collusion, and Game Theory*. New York: Macmillan.

Tennant, Richard B. 1950. *The American Cigarette Industry: A Study in Economic Analysis and Public Policy*. New Haven: Yale University Press.

White, Lawrence J., ed. 1989. *Private Antitrust Litigation: New Evidence, New Learning*. Cambridge: The MIT Press.

Williamson, Oliver E. 1968–69. "Economies as an Antitrust Defense: The Welfare Trade-offs." *American Economic Review* 58:18–36; 58:1372–76; and 59:954–69.

CHAPTER 23

REGULATION

There is no human problem which could not be solved if people would simply do as I advise.

GORE VIDAL

One of the greatest delusions in the world is the hope that the evils in this world are to be cured by legislation.

THOMAS B. REED

Government regulation of firms' behavior may increase welfare in markets that are not perfectly competitive. Unfortunately, actual regulation often deviates considerably from optimal regulation and exacerbates market inefficiencies. A prime example of an inefficient market is a monopolized industry, which charges too high a price. Optimal regulation can force a monopoly to set the competitive price. If a monopoly is badly regulated, however, shortages occur, or the monopoly is encouraged to produce inefficiently. Even where regulations are properly applied, the cost of administering them may exceed the benefits. This chapter examines the causes and effects of both good and bad regulation.

Regulation of monopolies is only one type of regulation commonly seen in Western economies. For example, in some countries, such as West Germany, the hours that firms may stay open are strictly limited. The major U.S. regulatory agencies are listed in Table 23.1 on p. 782. As discussed in Chapter 6, some government agencies, such as the Environmental Protection Agency (EPA), control pollution. Other agencies protect workers (for example, the Occupational Safety and Health Agency [OSHA]) or consumers (for example, the Consumer Product Safety Commission and the Federal Trade Commission [FTC]), as discussed in Example 23.1. The regulation of advertising and disclosure laws is discussed in Chapter 18, and the regulation of oligopolistic and monopolistically competitive industries is discussed in Chapters 9 and 11. In Chapter 14, government-imposed marketing orders are shown to allow otherwise competitive firms to collectively price discriminate and restrict output.

EXAMPLE 23.1

PIZZA PROTECTION

On average, each American adult and child eats seven pizzas a year. To protect these consumers, 310 separate rules govern what goes on a pizza and how these toppings may be described on labels and menus and fill over 40 pages of federal documents. The following are a few of these rules:

- *Crust:* There must be 2.9 milligrams of thiamine, 24 milligrams of niacin, and at least 13 (but not more than 16) milligrams of iron in each pound of flour.
- *Mozzarella cheese:* The cheese must contain at least 30 percent but no more than 45 percent fat and be made from pasteurized cow's milk.
- *Anchovies:* Imports from Spain, Portugal, and Morocco must be packed in oil and in a solution of at least 12 percent salt.
- *Green peppers:* Salt preservatives, such as calcium chloride, in canned green peppers must not exceed 0.26 percent of the food's weight.
- *Onions:* Only if the onions come from the bulb of the plant rather than the stalk may canned onions be used.
- *Beef:* Fat must constitute no more than 30 percent of ground beef.
- *Italian sausage:* To be called that, sausage must be uncured, unsmoked and contain at least 85 percent meat. If more than 13 percent extenders are used, sausage must carry the notice, "texturized soy flour added."

These regulations affect the final product in many ways. For example, the labeling division of the U.S. Department of Agriculture (USDA) initially concluded that the frozen trendy pizza of famous Los Angeles chef Wolfgang Puck could not be called a *pizza* since it did not have tomatoes on it. Puck said, "I think it's ridiculous that some bureaucrat in Washington thinks they are going to tell us what a pizza is. Tomato sauce has a cheap image on pizza and we decided to have fresh ingredients." Nonetheless, Puck agreed to add some tomato chunks to the basil-pesto sauce. The USDA also discovered that the "country sausage" on the label was made in the City of Commerce, which is not a rural area. Puck agreed to change the label to "Spago's Original Sausage and Herbs."

SOURCES: "The Pizza Principles." 1982. *San Francisco Examiner,* June 6, "This World" section, 15. Garchik, Leah. 1987. "Federal Ruling on Pizza Without Tomatoes." *San Francisco Chronicle,* November 11, A10.

This chapter focuses on regulations that directly affect price, quantity, quality, or entry. We begin by considering the objectives of the regulators and then consider the regulations that make monopolistic industries more competitive and those that make competitive industries more monopolistic. Finally, the chapter examines the effects of recent deregulation efforts.

TABLE 23.1   Major U.S. Regulatory Agencies

Agency	Year Established	Jurisdiction[a]
Economic Regulation		
Interstate Commerce Commission (ICC)	1887	Interstate railroads (1887)
		Interstate trucks (1935)
		Interstate water carriers (1940)
		Interstate telephone (1910–34)
		Interstate oil pipelines (1906–77)
State Regulatory Commissions	35 states 1907–20; 50 states by 1973	Local electricity (46 states by 1973)
		Local gas (47 states in 1973)
		Local telephone (48 states in 1973)
Federal Communications Commission (FCC)	1934	Interstate telephone (1934)
		Broadcasting (1934)
		Cable television (1968)
Federal Power Commission (FPC)	1935	Interstate wholesale electricity (1935)
Federal Energy Regulatory Commission (FERC)	1977	Interstate natural gas pipelines (1938)
		Field price of natural gas sold in interstate commerce (1954)
		Oil pipelines (1977)
		Intrastate gas and gas pipelines (1978)
Federal Maritime Commission (FMC)	1936	Ocean shipping (1936)
Civil Aeronautics Board (CAB)	1938	Interstate airlines (1938)
Postal Rate Commission	1970	Establishes classes of mail and rates for these classes; sets fees for other services (1970)
Federal Energy Administration (FEA)	1973	Petroleum prices and allocation (1973)
Energy Regulatory Administration (ERA)	1974	
Copyright Royalty Tribunal	1976	Copyright material (1976)
Environmental, Safety, and Health Regulation		
Food and Drug Administration (FDA)	1906	Safety of food, drugs (1906), and cosmetics (1938)
		Effectiveness of drugs (1962)

■ THE OBJECTIVES OF REGULATORS

> *Still one thing more, fellow citizens—a wise and frugal government, which shall restrain men from injuring one another, which shall leave them otherwise free to regulate their own pursuits of industry and improvement, and shall not take from the mouth of labor the bread it has earned. This is the sum of good government, and this is necessary to close the circle of our felicities.*
> —THOMAS JEFFERSON

> *But who would guard the guards themselves?*—JUVENAL

There are two contradictory views about regulation and its effects. One view holds that government should and can regulate to correct market inefficiencies. The opposing view

TABLE 23.1   Major U.S. Regulatory Agencies   continued

Agency	Year Established	Jurisdiction[a]
Animal and Plant Health Inspection Service	1907	Meat and poultry packing plants (1907)
Federal Trade Commission (FTC)	1914	False and misleading advertising (mainly after 1938), antitrust
Securities and Exchange Commission (SEC)	1934	Public security issues and security exchanges (1934) Public utility holding companies (1935)
CAB Federal Aviation Administration (FAA)	1938 1958	Airline safety (1938) (flight standards program only)
Atomic Energy Commission (AEC) Nuclear Regulatory Commission (NRC)	1947 1975	Licensing of nuclear power plants (1947)
National Highway Traffic Safety Administration (NHTSA)	1970	Automobile safety (1970), automobile fuel economy (1975)
Occupational Safety and Health Administration (OSHA)	1971	Industrial safety and health (1971)
Environmental Protection Agency (EPA)	1972	Air, water, and noise pollution (various environmental laws were enforced by several agencies 1963–72)
Consumer Product Safety Commission	1972	Safety of consumer products (1972)
Mine Enforcement Safety Administration (MESA)	1973	Safety and health in mining, especially coal mines (1973)
Mine Safety and Health Administration	1978	

[a]Beginning year and ending year if applicable.

SOURCES: Weiss (1981a, Table 1), MacAvoy (1979, Table A.1).

is that either the government lacks the information necessary to regulate optimally or that special-interest groups pressure legislatures and regulators so that regulations create market inefficiencies. Presumably, most economists do not subscribe strictly to either extreme view, but take some intermediate position.

Correcting Market Inefficiencies

As discussed at length throughout this book, there are many causes of deviations from perfect competition or market inefficiencies. Commonly observed causes of market inefficiencies include externalities such as pollution, monopoly power, uncertainty, and various forms of opportunistic behavior. Williamson (1975, Ch. 1) contends that market imperfections are caused by human and environmental factors. Human factors likely to lead to market inefficiencies include *bounded rationality* and *opportunism*. Environmental factors include small numbers of firms and uncertainty. For example, bounded rationality limits people's ability to analyze and deal with uncertain or complex situations. Thus, market inefficiencies are likely where there is a great deal of complexity or uncertainty. Opportunism leads to problems when there are few buyers or sellers (market power) or asymmetric information. Unfortunately, the same factors that make market inefficiencies likely make correcting the inefficiencies difficult.[1]

Consumer advocates, such as Ralph Nader, argue for regulations that are designed to promote or protect the public welfare.[2] Many legislators pass such laws believing that government can increase welfare. Although these optimists recognize the fallibility of humanity (for example, self-interested regulators), they believe that with eternal vigilence useful and desirable regulations can be enacted and enforced.

Of course, even such people of goodwill differ as to the appropriate objectives for government actions. Many, if not most, economists argue that the chief objective of government regulation should be economic efficiency (Schmalensee 1979; Kahn 1970, 1975); that is, the correction of market inefficiencies. Some economists and consumer advocates, however, argue that regulation should be used to redistribute income. Although economists recognize that regulations can be used to redistribute income (Feldstein 1972a, 1972b) many believe that trying to use regulation to redistribute income is difficult, and possibly counterproductive (Kahn 1975, Peltzman 1976). As Schmalensee (1979, 23) concludes, evaluating distributional issues may be possible in principle, but it is extremely difficult, and it is unlikely that legislatures would ever empower regulators to do so. Thus, for the rest of this chapter, we concentrate on the use of regulations to promote economic efficiency.

Capture Theory and Interest Group Theory

Man is the only animal that laughs and has a state legislature.
—SAMUEL BUTLER

An alternative, more cynical—or more realistic—explanation (depending on your viewpoint) is the **capture theory** of the Chicago school of economics. It holds that the firms in an industry want to be regulated because they can then "capture" (persuade, bribe, or threaten) the regulators, so that the regulators do what the industry wants. Regulation, according to this theory, protects firms from competition. Although these economists typically believe that the appropriate objective of regulation is to correct market inefficiencies, they believe that even if an appropriate law were passed, the affected industry would subvert the purpose of the law by capturing the regulators.

---

[1] Although the economics literature tends to call all deviations from perfect competition inefficiencies, this term can be misleading. Not all inefficiencies can or should be corrected. For example, if the inefficiency stems from limited information, the government may not be able to obtain and disseminate the relevant information cost effectively. That is, the world might be better off with full and costlessly disseminated information, but that is not a viable option.

[2] See Joskow (1974) on the efforts environmentalists direct at electric utility regulation.

EXAMPLE 23.2

CROSS-SUBSIDIZATION

Many public utilities cross-subsidize rates. For example, they price discriminate, charging one group higher rates than another for identical services. The high-price users are said to be cross-subsidizing the low-price users. In another common form of price discrimination, two groups pay the same rate, even though the cost of providing the service is more to the subsidized group. For example, urban and rural phone rates are often the same, even though the costs of providing the service in rural areas are higher.

Regulators often force a public utility to cross-subsidize. Why? One explanation is that a powerful group of consumers takes advantage of a less powerful group through pressuring the regulators to subsidize them.

The hypothesis that regulators impose cross-subsidies can be tested using data from a period when there are both regulated and unregulated states. Industrial users consume larger amounts of electricity than residential customers and are relatively few in number, so they can more effectively lobby regulators. Thus, under this hypothesis, the ratio of the residential price to the industrial price is higher in regulated states. Presumably any cost differences in providing the services to the two groups are not substantial across regulated and unregulated states.

As predicted, in 1917, the average ratio of the residential price to the industrial price was 1.616 in regulated states and 1.445 in unregulated states. Thus, the relative price residential consumers paid was 12 percent higher in regulated states. The corresponding ratios in 1937 were 2.459 in regulated states and 2.047 in unregulated states, so that the relative price for residential customers was 20 percent higher. In short, regulators forced residential users to subsidize industrial users.

SOURCE: Stigler and Friedland (1962).

A generalization of this theory is that various interest groups are affected differently by regulation. Interest groups compete to influence legislation; those that are the best organized and most affected by regulation spend the most money attempting to promote their own interest through legislation and sympathetic regulators. In this more general **interest group theory,** either firms or consumers can capture a regulatory body (Stigler 1971; Posner 1971, 1974; Peltzman 1976; Becker 1983). In some cases, one consumer group benefits at the expense of another; see Example 23.2.

A prime example of this self-interest theory is occupational licensing. Here, the regulated occupations—such as plumbers, electricians, doctors, lawyers, and beauticians—lobby for licensing laws and set the rules themselves (Chapter 17). Not surprisingly, the regulations typically make entry into these occupations difficult, thereby raising the wages in regulated occupations. Another example of this theory is building codes (see Example 23.3).

Industries may capture regulatory bodies directly or indirectly. First, firms in an industry may lobby legislatures as to how to be regulated. Occupational licensing, and

EXAMPLE 23.3

BUILDING CODES

Many studies show that outmoded building codes that regulate residential construction impede technical progress in the construction industry. Although the stated purpose of these regulations is to protect consumers from unsafe buildings, the regulations prevent the use of new and less expensive materials and construction practices. Various studies conclude that if the 10 most "wasteful practices" required by building codes were eliminated, the average cost saving for a single family house would range from 5 to 15 percent. (Oster and Quigley 1977).

Why do building codes penalize society in this way? Several explanations have been offered. Oster and Quigley (1977) hypothesize that the probability of an innovation in material, design, or organization being permitted by a local building code depends on the professional background of the chief building official and the perceived level of conflict caused by permitting the proposed change. In turn, the conflict is a function of the actual or potential interference by firms, organized labor, or housing consumers.

These interest groups engage in informational or persuasive activities if their potential benefits exceed their lobbying costs. For example, if nonmetallic sheathed cables for wiring are cheaper and easier to install than metal conduit and can be installed by less-skilled electricians, both manufacturers of metal conduit and electricians (especially unionized electricians) may oppose their use.

Their study of four innovations shows that these factors do determine the rate of adoption. For example, if the chief building official has two more years of education (they average 14 years), then the probability that preassembled plumbing and wider placement of studs (both of which reduce the demand for local labor) are permitted rises by 5–6 percent. The higher the percentage of local workers who are unionized, the less likely that innovations reducing the demand for local labor are adopted. Similarly, as the average size of local construction firms increases (and hence their average fixed costs of lobbying decrease), it is less likely that innovations will be permitted.

the regulation of railroads, trucking, and inland water shipping are often presented as examples. Second, firms in an industry may capture the staff of the regulatory agency.

There are at least three reasons why regulatory agencies are likely to become captured (Asch and Seneca, 1985, 316–17). First, regulatory commissions are usually staffed by experts on the regulated industry who have typically worked in the industry or related government agencies and hence are sympathetic to the interests of firms within the industry. Second, regulatory staff members often expect to receive attractive jobs in the industry after leaving the regulatory agency. After all, their services are valuable to firms because they are experts on regulations. Job prospects may increase their sympathy for the industry. Third, because regulatory commissions often have limited resources, they may rely on well-financed regulated firms to cover many of their expenses. These expenses may then be "reimbursed" in the form of higher allowed profits to the regulated firms.

Of 174 people appointed and confirmed to the Civil Aeronautics Board (CAB), Federal

Communications Commission (FCC), or Interstate Commerce Commission (ICC) by the end of 1977, 48 percent had some precommission experience in a related public sector, whereas 21 percent previously held related private-sector jobs (Eckert 1981). Of the 142 ex-commissioners whose postcommission jobs are known, 51 percent took private-sector jobs in the regulated industry, and 11 percent of ex-commissioners took related public-sector jobs. These jobs, deaths in office, and retirements, account for 70 percent of all commissioners. In short, commissioners were twice as likely to come from the related public sector as the related private sector. They were, however, nearly five times as likely to leave their jobs for related private-sector jobs than for related public-sector jobs. Nearly half (49 percent) of the commissioners who were patronage appointees went to work for the regulated industry, whereas only a third of the regulators who came from the private sector did so (Spiller 1988).

A spectacular example of the capture of a regulatory body occurred when trucks first started competing with railroads for long-distance freight moving business in the early 1930s (Stigler 1971, 8). Texas and Louisiana placed a 7000-pound payload limit on trucks serving two or more railroad stations (and hence competing with railroads), but applied a 14,000-pound limit to trucks serving only one station (and hence not competing directly with railroads).

Often, however, several agencies regulate a single industry, so that capturing regulators may be difficult. For example, many agencies have jurisdiction over genetically altered products created by the new biotechnology industry: the Environmental Protection Agency (EPA), U.S. Department of Agriculture (USDA), Food and Drug Administration (FDA), Occupational Safety and Health Administration (OSHA), and the National Institute of Health (NIH). Any of these may decide that certain risks are unacceptable and ban a product.[3] In addition, the National Environmental Policy Act (NEPA) of 1969 empowers courts to review agency actions that will have a "significant impact" on the environment. Moreover, in some industries both federal and state agencies may regulate.

The rest of this chapter ignores the original or declared intent of the enabling legislation and the objectives of individual regulators and concentrates on the market effects of specific types of regulations. We start with regulations designed to create competition and then examine regulations that decrease competition.

■ MAKING MONOPOLIES MORE COMPETITIVE

As a monopoly created by a barrier to entry can be a particularly serious market inefficiency, the case for regulation is strong if the government chooses to allow only one firm in an industry (Kahn 1970, 1975; Schmalensee 1979; and Joskow and Noll 1981). The problem of monopoly is inherent in industries in which it is efficient for only one firm to provide all the output because of economies of scale. When a single firm can produce industry output at lower cost than two or more firms it is called a **natural monopoly.** Competition

---

[3] Huber, Peter W. 1987. "Biotechnology and the Regulation HYDRA." *Technology Review,* November/December: 57–65. Following a study by the White House Office of Science and Technology in June 1986, some order in the system emerged. Where one agency has statutory authority, the report establishes a lead agency and provides for coordinated regulatory review. At least one interagency group was also established.

among several firms is inefficient in such a market, but an unregulated natural monopoly sets the price too high—above marginal cost. Concern over the pricing of (possible) natural monopolies provides one justification for the regulation of many public utilities such as telephone service, electricity, and gas. There are several approaches to regulating such monopolies. One approach is direct government ownership. Alternatively, a variety of price or rate-of-return regulations have been used to lower the price in such markets. After examining these types of regulations, we consider some of their unintended side effects.

Whenever a monopoly exists, resources are not efficiently allocated. This static view is often used to justify regulating all monopolies, whether natural or not. The danger in this reasoning is the failure to understand how a firm becomes a monopolist. If it does so by developing a new product, making a new discovery, or having a more efficient technology than anyone else, then regulation that removes these incentives for dynamic efficiencies without replacing them with other incentives is harmful (see Chapter 20). Moreover, the fear of being regulated could have a chilling effect on firms' incentives to innovate.

If a market is contestable (Baumol, Panzar, and Willig 1982), so that entry and exit can occur costlessly, there is little or no need to regulate because market pressures eliminate monopoly power. If a monopoly is created through the merger of many firms, then the appropriate response is to restore competition (prevent monopoly through mergers) rather than to regulate. In general, the antitrust laws are designed to prevent actions that reduce competition, whereas regulation should be aimed at controlling natural monopolies. In general, firms in the United States are not subject to government regulation just because they have monopoly power. Let us now discuss the various types of regulations of natural and other monopolies.

Government Ownership

One approach to regulating a natural monopoly is to have the government own it and set prices to maximize welfare rather than profits. Many governments have tried this approach.

Public ownership of utilities is common in the United States. Today three-quarters of the population is served by publicly owned water supplies, and one-fifth of the electricity is provided by publicly run firms. In the United States, 28 percent of the employees in the utility sectors (electricity, gas, water, and sanitation) are public employees, compared to 20 percent in Japan, 43 percent in West Germany, and 60 percent in Switzerland (Schmalensee 1979, 85). In most countries, postal services are publicly owned. In Great Britain, many industries have been owned by the government at one time or another in the post–World War II period.

There appears to be little evidence, however, that government monopoly results in welfare maximization. Typically, government-owned firms are less efficient than privately-owned firms (Example 23.4). Williamson (1967) points out that managers have less of an incentive to maximize profits under public ownership. Indeed, Pashigian (1976) finds that public urban transit systems have lower profit rates than private ones and contends that public ownership subsidizes firms to compensate them for their lower profit rates.

---

[4] See, however, DeAlessi (1974), who surveys much of the literature. DeAlessi also suggests that rates to various classes of customers vary between publicly and privately owned utilities.

EXAMPLE 23.4

PUBLIC, MONOPOLISTIC, AND COMPETITIVE REFUSE COLLECTION

The type of firm that collects household refuse varies across cities. Some cities use public monopolies, others use private monopolies, and still others use unregulated firms that compete with each other. All three market organizations are common. New York City has a public monopoly. Boston pays a private firm to collect refuse. Portland, Oregon has private firms collect from some, but not all, households in an area.

If there are scale economies in collecting refuse, then a monopoly can collect refuse at lower unit cost, so that refuse collection is a natural monopoly. If there are no scale economies, then competition among many firms keeps the competitive price as low as possible. Some scale economies are expected in collecting refuse because it should be cheaper for one firm to collect from all the houses on a block than for two firms to collect from, say, every other house.

Using data from 340 public and private firms in as many cities across the United States, Stevens (1978) estimates cost functions, holding service levels constant and taking market structure as given. She draws four chief conclusions.

First, there are economies of scale for cities with populations of less than 20,000 (or cities served by less than four trucks). Second, in all cities, the competitive arrangement is from 26 to 48 percent more costly than the private monopoly arrangement. This difference may be due to billing expenses and the extra costs due to nonexclusivity within a market area.

Third, for cities with populations less than 50,000, the price charged by the private monopoly is equivalent to the price of the public monopoly. Fourth, for larger cities, public monopoly or the competitive arrangement are from 27 to 37 percent more expensive than the private monopoly. One reason is that labor productivity in a public monopoly is lower than that of the private monopoly, and this difference increases with city size. The mean crew size for the public monopolist is 3.26 compared to 2.15 for the private monopolist. Similarly, the public monopolist uses trucks with smaller capacity: 20.63 cubic yards compared to 27.14.

SOURCE: Stevens (1978).

Peltzman (1971) finds that although municipal utilities charge lower prices on average than regulated privately owned utilities, there is little evidence that government-owned firms set prices to maximize welfare.[4]

Franchise Bidding

Alternatives to direct ownership also have been tried. In some cases, **franchise bidding** is used: the government sells the right to a monopoly to the highest bidder.[5] Thus, instead of having the government give monopoly rights to firms (as in the assignment of television

---

[5] According to Schmalensee (1979, 68–73), this proposal dates back to John Stuart Mill in 1848.

and radio station rights in the United States), the government captures the monopoly rents. The government may require, as a condition of bidding, that the firm operate so as to increase welfare over the monopoly level. There was franchise bidding for water supply and funeral services in France over 100 years. Indeed, railroad franchises were awarded to firms offering to charge the lowest rates (Chadwick 1859). Bidding was also used in New York City around the turn of the century (Schmalensee 1979, 71).

One school of thought holds that awarding a monopoly franchise to the firm that offers to supply the product on the best terms for consumers can eliminate monopoly profits (Demsetz 1968; Posner 1972; Baumol, Panzar, and Willig 1982).[6] That is, instead of awarding the franchise to the highest bidder, which allows the government to capture the expected monopoly profits, the franchise is awarded to the firm that offers to produce in the manner that is best for consumers (see Example 23.5).

Such bidding, although it may eliminate monopoly profits, does not necessarily result in efficient pricing (Telser 1969, Williamson 1976, 1985, Schmalensee 1979). As the following discussion shows, efficiency requires that a firm set price equal to marginal cost, but if the firm is a natural monopoly, it loses money at that price. As a result, none of the bidders for a natural monopoly are willing to price efficiently (unless they are allowed to price discriminate). Moreover, this approach does not eliminate the need for regulation: the government may need to confirm regularly that the winning firm is keeping its agreement and not raising prices or reducing service. A further problem is that the economic environment changes over time, so that the initial agreement may not be desirable in the future. Thus, repeated bidding may be required, and the incumbent may gain an advantage in subsequent bidding because of its experience (Williamson 1976, 1985).

Price Controls

It makes a difference whose ox is gored. —MARTIN LUTHER

Governments frequently use **price controls** to attempt to control inflation or to keep prices in a particular industry low. The discussion here concentrates on the effects of price regulation on a monopoly.

Many methods are used to control prices. In countries such as Great Britain, Sweden, and various Eastern-block countries, the government owns many monopolies and hence can control prices directly. Most countries use direct controls, taxes, or subsidies that affect the prices that monopolies charge. Most Western countries have special agencies that control the prices set by regulated monopolies. Typically, a regulatory board sets the price explicitly or must approve a rate proposed by a monopoly.

In the following example, the board mandates the maximum price that the monopoly may charge. We start by examining the effect of price regulation on a monopoly with increasing marginal costs, and then examine the effect of regulation on one with constant or decreasing marginal costs. As previously discussed, only if market forces will not

---

[6] Spiller (1988) discusses allowing potential regulators to bid for jobs, as they eventually will be rewarded or "bribed" by the regulated industry.

EXAMPLE 23.5

FRANCHISE BIDDING FOR A CABLE TV MONOPOLY

A 1969 Oakland, California city ordinance called for bids for a community-antenna television (CATV) franchise to provide cable television for residents. The award was to be nonexclusive and not to exceed 20 years. The city was authorized to inspect the franchisee's property and books and to terminate a franchise for noncompliance after thirty days' notice and a public hearing. The city also retained the right to buy the CATV system at the cost of reproducing it.

Rather than soliciting bids immediately, a city agency engaged in preliminary discussions with prospective franchisees and community groups. After 10 months, the city told five applicants that it would receive their bids. These bids had to cover providing various television and radio services, serving all areas of the city, paying the city the greater of 8 percent of gross receipts or $125,000, and providing the city with certain free connections and services (including studio facilities for originating programming). The city set time limits for providing the service and allowed requests for rate increases annually. The franchise contract was to last for 15 years.

The lowest bid, by a local company, Focus Cable, was for a monthly connection fee of $1.70. The next lowest bid was for $3.48, and Tele Promp Ter Corporation bid $5.95. Tele Promp Ter eventually entered a joint venture with Focus, which lacked financial resources. In exchange for providing the financing, Tele Promp Ter obtained an equal partnership, which it could convert to a majority interest immediately and exercise options to obtain 80 percent of the stock. Presumably Tele Promp Ter became involved in supplying basic services for 30 percent of its initial bid, because it expected to make profits from providing special programming and other services at a higher rate.

Within 18 months of the initial city ordinance calling for CATV, the franchise was awarded. Focus requested and had approved a rate of $4.45 per month for the special programming, so that the combined rate for both services was $6.15 per month. Focus soon requested a reduction in the penalties for not completing construction in time, not connecting all households, and providing only a single cable instead of the dual cable originally specified. The city negotiated with the company instead of trying to find another firm or shifting the franchise to public ownership.

Probably the most serious problem with the bidding system was that bidders only had to specify the rate for the basic service and not for the "futuristic" special programming services. Over 90 percent of subscribers took both services and thereby paid 3½ times more than the specified basic rate. The wide spread in bids for the basic service raises the question of whether Focus's bid of $1.70 was even close to per-unit production costs. Sufficient complaints about quality were received that an outside firm was engaged to test the degree of compliance of the service with technical requirements. Thus, the uncertainty and enforcement difficulties resulted in a system providing lower levels of service at possibly higher prices than initially envisioned—but at least bidding occurred. In Manhattan, in contrast, two companies were awarded noncompetitive, 20-year CATV franchises.

SOURCE: Williamson (1985, 352–64).

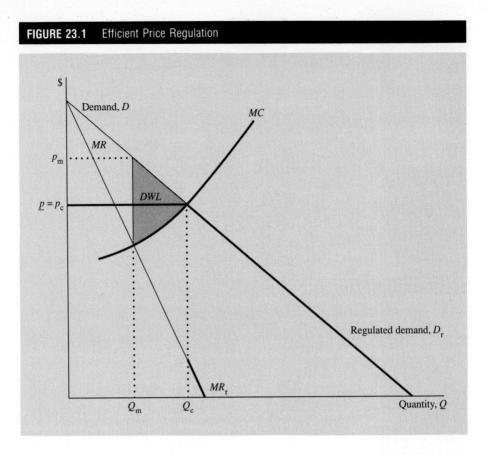

FIGURE 23.1 Efficient Price Regulation

eventually eliminate a monopoly's market power, for example, because of a barrier to entry, is there a case for regulation, and even there, the regulation could adversely affect dynamic incentives of firms. Generally only some natural monopolies and monopolies created by government barriers to entry need not fear competition from potential entrants.

Price Regulation of a Monopoly with Increasing Marginal Costs. Price regulation of a monopolist has both efficiency and redistribution effects. Moderate reductions in a monopolist's price increase the quantity sold and raise efficiency. An excessive reduction in price creates shortages and can actually decrease the quantity sold. Lowering prices also redistributes wealth from the monopolist to consumers. As a result, monopolists dislike price regulations and consumers generally applaud them.

Figure 23.1 shows the demand and marginal revenue curves facing a monopolist and its upward sloping marginal cost curve. In the absence of regulation, the monopolist (profitably) charges price p_m and sells Q_m units of output, which is determined by the intersection of the marginal revenue and marginal cost curves. The deadweight loss to society is the shaded triangle labelled *DWL*, which is below the demand curve and above the marginal cost curve to the right of Q_m. This deadweight loss reflects the loss in both consumer and producer surplus due to the relatively few units of output sold. That is, consumers are willing to purchase more units at a price equal to the marginal cost of production. Indeed, the inefficiency of monopoly is due to setting the price above the marginal cost.

If the regulatory board sets the maximum price that the monopolist may charge, $\underline{p}$, above p_m, so that the monopolist is not constrained, the regulation has no effect.[7] We first show that if $\underline{p}$ is set equal to marginal cost (the competitive or efficient price), welfare is maximized. Then we show that if a lower $\underline{p}$ is set, shortages may occur.

Efficient Price Regulation.   If the regulatory board sets $\underline{p} = p_c$, the deadweight loss is eliminated, as we now show. The monopoly faces a new effective demand curve. Because it can no longer charge a price higher than p_c, its (regulated) demand curve (thick line) D_r, is horizontal at $\underline{p} = p_c$ until it hits the original demand curve, at Q_c, and is downward sloping thereafter.

The monopolist's regulated marginal revenue curve, MR_r, corresponding to this new demand curve is horizontal and equal to the new demand curve, where the new demand curve is horizontal.[8] Where the demand curve slopes down, the marginal revenue curve also slopes down. Indeed, for this portion of the demand curve, the marginal revenue curve is the same as in the unregulated case, as shown by the thickened line on the relevant portion of the downward sloping marginal revenue curve. At Q_c, the marginal revenue curve is discontinuous.

The regulated monopolist sets marginal revenue equal to marginal cost to determine its optimal price. With regulation, the marginal revenue (thick lines) equals marginal cost at Q_c rather than at Q_m as in the unregulated case. If the monopoly sells one less unit, it loses profits because its marginal revenues fall by more than its marginal costs. If it sells one more unit, its marginal revenues increase by less than its marginal costs. Its profits are lower than without regulation, but the monopoly is still maximizing its (regulated) profits.

In summary, if $\underline{p}$ is set at p_c, the efficient (competitive) solution is obtained, and there is no deadweight loss because price equals marginal cost. Most economists, as a result, praise such a result. As Kahn (1970, 65) says, "The central policy prescription of microeconomics is the equation of price and marginal cost."

Even in this static model, this type of regulation is not desirable or feasible, however, unless two other conditions are also met. First, the monopoly must make positive profits, or else it refuses to produce. Second, the cost of running the regulatory board should be less than the social gain (the elimination of the deadweight loss). Unfortunately, the cost

---

[7] A price control set above the current price has no effect in a static model; however, in an intertemporal model it can have an effect by distorting incentives over time. See Lee (1978).

[8] Its marginal revenue curve is horizontal for the same reason that a competitive firm's marginal revenue is horizontal: its demand curve is horizontal. Along a horizontal demand curve, additional units can be sold without lowering price, so the marginal revenue equals the average revenue or price. Mathematically, marginal revenue equals $d[p(Q)Q]/dQ = p'(Q)Q + p(Q)$, where $p(Q)$ is the inverse demand curve, $p(Q)Q$ is total revenue, and $p'(Q)$ is the slope of the inverse demand curve. If the demand curve is horizontal at $\underline{p}$, $p(Q) = \underline{p}$ and $p'(Q) = 0$, so marginal revenue equals $p(Q) = \underline{p}$.

of administration is often high. For example, Gerwig (1962) finds that the cost of regulating natural gas prices in interstate commerce was about 7 percent of the base price of the gas.

Inefficient Price Regulation.   Often, the regulatory board has trouble setting $\underline{p}$ at p_c. The board may not know either costs or demand exactly. Thus, even if the board wants to set $\underline{p} = p_c$, it may set $\underline{p}$ too high or too low.[9] If the board chooses a p between p_m and p_c, the monopoly sells at that price, by the same reasoning as above.[10] Consumers are better off than in the unregulated case: they buy more units at a lower price. Their welfare increases, however, if $\underline{p}$ is lowered to p_c.

If the board sets too low a price, the price regulation introduces a new problem: if the price is so low that the firm shuts down, then consumers can buy nothing, so all consumer surplus is lost. A less extreme case, where the monopoly does not shut-down, is illustrated in Figure 23.2: the same demand and cost curves are shown as in Figure 23.1, but $\underline{p}$ is set well below p_c. The monopoly's new effective demand curve is horizontal at $\underline{p}$, and thereafter downward sloping. Where the demand curve is horizontal, the marginal revenue curve is horizontal and is the same as the demand curve.

Thus, the monopoly charges $\underline{p}$. Consumers want to purchase Q_h units at this price, but the monopoly only sells $\underline{Q}$ units. If the monopoly sells any more units, it loses money on each unit. As a result, there is a shortage of $Q_h - \underline{Q}$ units. Which consumers are lucky enough to buy at these very low prices depends on how the monopoly chooses to allocate its output. Discrimination on some basis other than price may occur. Some consumers are better off than in the unregulated case, because they buy the good at a very low price. Other consumers are worse off, however, because they are unable to buy the good at all.

As drawn, there is greater deadweight loss here than in the unregulated case. The deadweight loss from unregulated monopoly pricing is Area *A* in Figure 23.2 (the same area as shown in Figure 23.1). The deadweight loss from this regulation is Area *A* plus Area *B*. In Figure 23.2, $\underline{p}$ is much lower than p_c. If it were only slightly below p_c, only small shortages would occur, and the deadweight loss would be less than in the unregulated case.

The regulatory board should consider raising $\underline{p}$ if shortages occur.[11] It also should consider raising $\underline{p}$ if the monopoly chooses to shut down rather than operate at that price.

The Effects of Price Regulation.   This analysis has four main results:

- If $\underline{p} \geqq p_m$, the regulation has no effect in a static model: price $= p_m$ and quantity $= Q_m$.

---

[9] A number of methods to induce firms to truthfully reveal the relevant information have been devised, however. See, for example, Baron and Meyerson (1982) and Riordan (1984).

[10] The regulated demand curve is a horizontal line at $\underline{p}$ until it hits the original demand curve at $\underline{Q}$, and is then downward sloping. The corresponding marginal revenue curve is horizontal up to $\underline{Q}$ and then has a vertical section and a downward sloping section, as in Figure 23.1. The marginal cost curve intersects the marginal revenue curve in its vertical section, so the monopoly sets price equal to $\underline{p}$. See Problem 2.

[11] Of course, the board must be sure that the monopoly is not trying to trick it by causing a shortage even though $\underline{p} \geqq p_c$.

FIGURE 23.2   Price Regulation that Causes a Shortage

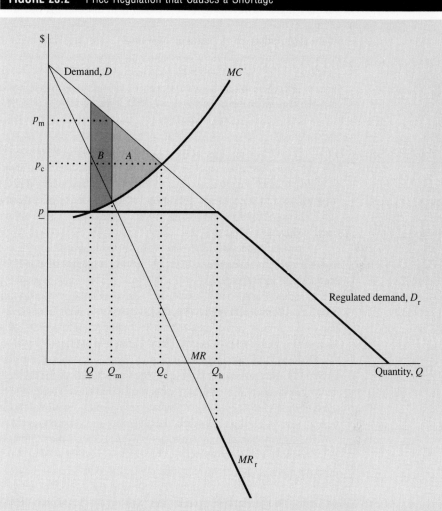

- If $p_m > \underline{p} > p_c$, then price $= \underline{p}$, output lies between Q_m and Q_c, and consumers are better off than in the unregulated case, but not as well off as if $\underline{p} = p_c$.
- If $\underline{p} = p_c$, then price $= \underline{p}$, quantity $= Q_c$, and there is no deadweight loss.
- If $\underline{p} < p_c$, then price $= \underline{p}$, quantity demanded is greater than Q_c, but quantity supplied is less than Q_c. The deadweight loss may be greater or smaller than in the unregulated case.

Thus, the regulatory board should set $\underline{p} = p_c$. If it guesses wrong and sets a $\underline{p}$ so low that shortages occur and persist, it should raise $\underline{p}$. The harm to society from setting too high a $\underline{p}$ may be less serious than setting too low a $\underline{p}$. If the cost of running the board is very high, however, the best solution is to disband the board and not to regulate.

Price Regulation of a Natural Monopoly. A firm is a natural monopoly if it can produce industry output more efficiently (at lower cost) than two or more firms. Formally, let $q_1, \ldots, q_k$ be the output of k firms such that $q_1 + \ldots + q_k = Q$, total industry output. If each firm has a cost function $C(q_i)$, and one firm can produce Q at lower cost than the sum of the k firms for any $k \geq 2$, then

$$C(Q) < C(q_1) + C(q_2) + \ldots + C(q_k), \qquad (23.1)$$

and the least expensive (most efficient) way to produce is to have one firm produce all Q units. A cost function is said to be **subadditive** at Q if this inequality holds, so **subadditivity** is a necessary condition for the existence of a natural monopoly (Sharkey 1982; Baumol, Panzar, and Willig 1982). Equation 23.1 also applies if the firm produces many products.

A natural monopoly often has constant or falling marginal and average costs in the region in which it operates. Figure 23.3 shows a natural monopoly with constant marginal cost and falling average cost.

It is often argued that electrical, gas, telephone and other utilities are natural monopolies. There is a relatively high fixed cost for running an electric power line or a phone line to a home or firm, but constant or falling marginal costs of supplying the service. As a result, marginal cost is constant or falls, and average cost falls as output increases.[12]

If the natural monopoly is not regulated, it charges p_m, sells Q_m units, and makes large profits (because price is well above average cost). If the regulatory board sets $\underline{p} = p_a$, the price determined by the intersection of the average cost curve and the demand curve, the monopoly sells Q_a units and makes zero profits, as shown in Figure 23.3. Consumers benefit from such regulation because they buy more output at a lower price.

Regulatory boards may try to set $\underline{p} = p_a$ because they know that if they set $\underline{p}$ lower, the monopoly will stop operating. Nonetheless, setting $\underline{p} = p_a$ leads to inefficient pricing because p_a is greater than marginal cost. The consumer is paying more than it costs to produce the last unit of output. The efficient solution is to set $\underline{p} = p^* = MC$ and sell Q^* units. A competitive equilibrium with many actual producers is not possible here. Because average costs are always falling with larger scale, there is only room for one firm in this industry.

If $\underline{p} = p^*$, price is below average cost, so the monopoly loses money. Its lost profits equal Area A + Area B in Figure 23.3.[13] The monopoly prefers to shut down rather than

---

[12] The empirical literature, however, leaves some doubt as to whether any utilities exhibit increasing returns to scale, which implies downward sloping marginal and average cost curves. In any case, showing that there are scale economies in one range of output is not always sufficient to demonstrate that a firm is a natural monopoly (that is, the cost function is subadditive). See, for example, Fuss and Waverman (1981) and Evans and Heckman (1982a, 1982b).

[13] The monopolist is covering its variable costs, since $p^* =$ average variable costs, but not its fixed costs, F. As drawn, its costs are $C(Q) = mQ + F$, where m is its constant marginal costs and average variable costs. At $p^* = m$, its profits are $\pi (Q^*) = p^*Q^* - mQ^* - F = -F$.

FIGURE 23.3 Price Regulation of a Natural Monopoly

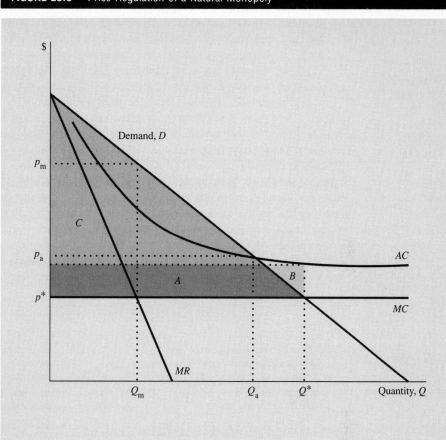

make losses. One way to keep the monopoly operating, and operating efficiently is to allow it to price discriminate. Of course, some consumers dislike this solution because it transfers income from them to the monopoly and treats different consumers unequally.[14]

Alternatively, society could keep the monopoly operating at p^* by subsidizing it by an amount equal to the lost profits, $A + B$. Suppose welfare is defined as consumer surplus plus firm profits (or losses) minus the regulatory board's administrative costs. At $\underline{p} = p^*$, consumer surplus, $C + A$, minus firm losses, $A + B$, *equals* $C - B$. Welfare is maximized at p^*.[15]

---

[14] Economists started advocating time-of-day pricing around the turn of the century (Hausman and Neufeld 1984). Since the 1970s, time-of-day (*peak-load pricing*) and seasonal pricing have been widely used in regulating U.S. public utilities such as electrical power and telephones (Weiss 1981b). California, New York, and Wisconsin have gone the furthest in incorporating differential rates over time (Weiss 1981b). This type of pricing is different from price discrimination because the costs consumers impose upon the system vary.

[15] At any higher price, the increase in profits is less than the loss of consumer surplus. See Problem 1 for an example.

If the monopolist is subsidized using efficiently raised tax revenues, then society is better off with price equal to marginal cost and a subsidy.[16] The subsidy is a transfer of wealth from the monopolist and nonusers to consumers of the product and, as such, has no efficiency implications. Thus, setting price equal to marginal cost and subsidizing the monopolist leads to efficiency. Unless the government owns the monopoly, as with postal services in most countries, it is often politically infeasible to subsidize a monopoly. Thus, we commonly see second-best regulations that set price at p_a rather than $p*$.[17]

If a firm produces many products, the analysis of optimal regulation is more complicated. The regulatory prices that maximize consumer welfare subject to the requirement that revenues cover costs are called **Ramsey pricing,** after Frank P. Ramsey (1927), who first derived this result. This solution is similar to optimal monopoly price discrimination. Essentially, the optimal prices are the monopoly prices scaled down so that total revenue exactly equals costs (Baumol and Bradford 1970, Sharkey 1982).[18] Using the idea of Ramsey pricing, Ross (1984) shows that regulators' preferences can be determined by observing the relative regulated prices.

Sustainability of Natural Monopolies. Strangely, a natural monopoly may not be immune to profit-seeking entry (Faulhaber 1975; Baumol, Bailey, and Willig 1977; Panzar and Willig 1977; Sharkey 1982). Even if it is most efficient for one firm to produce the

---

[16] Unfortunately, governments rarely, if ever, raise taxes efficiently. Most commonly used taxes, such as income and sales taxes, are distorting. Thus, subsidies typically have a real resource cost. Moreover, it does not pay to subsidize all unprofitable firms (Coase 1946).

[17] The need for price regulation and other objectives for regulation, such as redistributing income are discussed in Demsetz (1968), Bailey and Panzar (1981), and Baumol, Panzar, and Willig (1982), and are well-summarized in Sharkey (1982, 147–51). With other objectives, the appropriate form of regulation differs from that discussed here.

[18] For simplicity, suppose that inverse demand functions for the n goods ($q_1, q_2, \ldots, q_n$) are independent:

$$q_i = D_i(p_i), \, i = 1, 2, \ldots, n.$$

The total revenue is

$$R(q_1, \ldots, q_n) = p_1(q_1)q_1 + \ldots + p_n(q_n)q_n.$$

The cost of producing these goods is $C(q_1, \ldots, q_n)$. The regulator wants to choose outputs so as to maximize the consumer surplus

$$\sum_{i=1}^{n} \int_0^{q_i} p_i(t) \, dt - C(q_1, \ldots, q_n),$$

subject to the constraint (with a Lagrangian multiplier, λ) that revenues exactly equal costs (or that profits are a given constant). The first-order conditions are

$$p_i - C_i = -\lambda(R_i - C_i),$$

where C_i and R_i are the partial derivatives of C and R with respect to q_i. This condition may be rewritten as

$$(p_i - C_i)/p_i = -k/\epsilon_i,$$

where $k = \lambda/(1 + \lambda)$ and ϵ_i is the elasticity of demand for q_i. That is, the price markup over marginal cost, $(p_i - C_i)/p_i$, is inversely proportional to the elasticity of demand for that good. If $k = 1$, this condition is essentially the standard monopoly price-discrimination condition. At $k = 0$, this condition is the same as in competition.

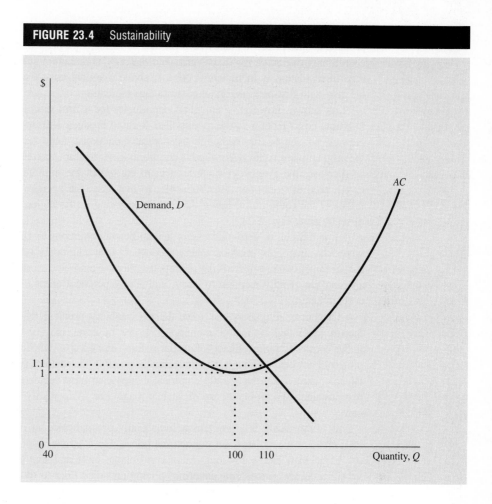

FIGURE 23.4   Sustainability

entire industry output, such a firm may not be able to simultaneously prevent entry, satisfy consumer demand, and cover its costs. A natural monopoly that can prevent entry is said to be **sustainable.**[19]

A single-product natural monopoly is sustainable at every output if and only if there are economies of scale at all outputs (Sharkey 1982, 88–90). That is, a natural monopoly with increasing returns to scale (see Figure 23.3) that has a strictly falling average cost curve, is immune to entry. A natural monopoly with a U-shaped average cost curve need not be immune.

To illustrate the problem of sustainability, consider a monopoly with a U-shaped average cost function as shown in Figure 23.4. The demand curve crosses the average

---

[19] A natural monopoly is sustainable if, given a cost function C and a demand function D, there is a price p and an output $q = D(p)$ such that (Baumol, Bailey, and Willig 1977; Sharkey 1982) $pq = C(q)$ and $p^*q^* < C(q^*)$ for all $p^* < p$ and all $q^* \leq D(p^*)$. This definition also applies if q is a vector of different outputs.

cost curve at a price of $1.10 and 110 units of output. If the monopolist is regulated to produce at that price, it makes zero profits. In this second-best regulation, the firm can charge only one price for its product, and the regulators cannot subsidize the firm. This type of regulation is inefficient—price is above marginal cost—so society is less well off than with first-best (marginal-cost pricing) regulation.

As shown, however, there is an opportunity for a firm to enter profitably if it has the same cost function as the monopolist. It could produce 100 units and charge a price between $1 and $1.10. Although the natural monopolist could respond, it is clear that the original point is not a *sustainable* equilibrium. If, instead, the demand curve in Figure 23.4 crosses the average cost curve at or to the left of the minimum point ($1 and 100 units), then the monopoly is sustainable. In that case, the average cost curve is strictly falling at the equilibrium; hence the firm is operating in the region of increasing returns to scale, as in Figure 23.3.

It is difficult to derive necessary and sufficient conditions to guarantee sustainability where the monopoly produces many products.[20] It is commonly believed, however, that sustainability is more likely if the monopolist may use a nonlinear pricing scheme (Chapter 15) and can rapidly respond to entry, and if any potential entrant must sink substantial costs to enter.

Of course, regulators can solve the sustainability problem by forbidding entry and thereby protecting the natural monopolist. Entry, however, may be desirable—especially if the entrant is more efficient than the natural monopolist, who may become lax in a protected market. Although it is theoretically possible that natural monopolies are unsustainable, there is currently little empirical evidence in most regulated industries showing that sustainability problems are of such a magnitude as to justify regulators forbidding entry.

If sustainability is a problem at the socially optimal price, it is even more likely to be a problem if regulators set nonoptimal prices. For example, suppose regulators decide to charge high prices for long-distance telephone calls and use the extra revenues to subsidize local service. This pattern of pricing prevailed prior to the breakup (divestiture) of AT&T. Given this cross-subsidy, where the revenues earned from one product are used to pay for the cost of providing another, there is an incentive for alternative providers of long-distance service to enter the market, even if they have higher costs than the natural monopolist. Indeed, before the breakup of AT&T, firms offering only long-distance service entered the market and underpriced AT&T.

If regulators insist on cross-subsidizing, they must prevent entry.[21] In the telephone case, entry was eventually permitted under deregulation, and the cross-subsidization was reduced. Of course, if the monopoly is protected against entry and its prices or profits are regulated, its incentives to hold down prices and produce efficiently are reduced.

---

[20] The problem is even more difficult when there are several competing firms producing differentiated products (Braeutigam 1984).

[21] For a variety of views, see Baseman (1981), comments by Baumol (1981, 361–64), Panzar (1981, 365–69), and Brock and Sheinkman (1983).

Regulatory Lag. Inducing regulated firms to produce efficiently may be a problem. Regulated firms are not rewarded when they achieve lower costs because their regulated price is lowered accordingly. For this reason a number of economists argue that **regulatory lag,** a delay in instituting and enforcing regulations, is desirable (Baumol 1967, Williamson 1971, Bailey 1973, and Wendel 1976). They reason that if regulators are slow to react, then regulated monopolies earn increased profits in the interim, and the short-term gains give them an incentive to cut costs. In the 1960s, intervals between electric power rate cases were long, although possibly for other reasons (Joskow 1974).

Obviously, there are mechanical problems in determining the best interval of time between setting new prices because there is a trade-off between lower costs in the long run and the lowest possible price at any given time. Insisting on the lowest possible price in the short run could so deprive a firm of incentives to behave efficiently that consumers are harmed.

Regulatory lag may also be unattractive during periods of rapid increases in the costs of factors of production, as with energy costs in the 1970s. Under those conditions, delays in allowing prices to rise cause regulated firms to lose money for long periods of time. When regulators finally act, they may be tempted to grant extremely large price increases to make up for these lost profits, which would result in prices that were too high in some periods and too low in others.

Price Regulation May Not Lower Price. Although we have just argued that lowering the price set by a monopolist is desirable, there is considerable doubt that regulatory boards do lower prices. The regulation of electrical rates provides an example (Stigler and Friedland 1962). Today most states have commissions to regulate rates of electric utilities, but only 6 states had such commissions prior to 1910, and only 29 adopted commissions between 1910 and 1920. By 1937, 39 states had regulating commissions. Thus, using historical data, we can test whether regulatory boards lower prices.

The average price per kilowatt-hour (kwh) was 1.88¢ in regulated states and 3.20¢ in unregulated states in 1917, or 41 percent lower in the regulated states. This comparison is not terribly informative, however, because the rates were relatively low in the regulated states *before* regulation went into effect.

Stigler and Friedland's statistical analyses separate the effects of regulation from those of other factors such as urban population, per capita income, and the proportion of energy from hydroelectric sources. For the years 1912, 1922, 1932, and 1937, these factors explain between 50 and 65 percent of the variation in average price for all customers of the electric utilities. Only in 1937, after controlling for other factors, did regulation have a statistically significant effect on price, lowering it by a third. Possibly, the reason that more dramatic effects are not found when the average price is examined is that regulation only helps certain classes of consumers (Example 23.2). For example, in 1937, regulation did not statistically significantly lower price to domestic customers, but did so for commercial and industrial customers. Apparently regulation cross-subsidized commercial industrial users at the expense of households.

Thus, it appears that regulations did not lower average prices in the first several decades they were in place, with the exception of lowering prices for businesses in 1937.

Of course, it is possible that utilities in nonregulated states kept their prices down to prevent regulation. Unless that explanation is valid, however, there is substantial question whether regulatory authorities substantially reduced average prices.

If regulation does lower price, it must lower the profitability of the monopoly. Thus, an alternative test of the effect of regulation is whether the stock values of the electric companies in regulated states are adversely affected by regulation. Statistical analyses that control for the growth in sales do not show a statistically significant effect of regulation on stock prices.[22]

One other explanation of regulation's effects is that boards act slowly, and this regulatory lag keeps prices from rising as rapidly as costs in some period (though prices eventually catch up). If that is true, however, regulated firms should have lower earnings. Again, the case for lower earnings appears weak.

Although the Stigler-Friedland study has been criticized on methodological grounds, few if any later studies, so far as we know, find evidence that direct price regulations lowered prices during this early period. Moreover, some studies of electrical utilities in later periods do find statistically significant effects of other types of regulations, such as rate-of-return regulation. We now turn to this very common form of nonoptimal, indirect price regulation.

Rate-of-Return Regulation

Don't get the idea that I'm knocking the American system. — AL CAPONE

In the United States, regulatory boards generally use **rate-of-return regulation** to limit the rate of return (ROR) to capital of utility monopolies, such as electric and gas companies, instead of controlling prices directly. Although ROR regulation may help consumers, it does not encourage firms to behave efficiently. One commonly cited inefficiency is the tendency to overinvest in capital (Averch and Johnson 1962). This phenomenon is called the **Averch-Johnson effect.** Thus, better types of regulation theoretically exist.

The effects of ROR regulation can be illustrated using a model of a public utility that uses labor, L, and capital, K, as inputs to produce electric power.[23] If unregulated, this monopoly uses labor and capital so as to produce as efficiently and profitably as possible. That is, the firm hires workers up to the point where the last dollar spent on labor adds \$1 to revenues, and similarly for capital. The firm chooses its output level through its choice of labor and capital so as to maximize its profits at the monopoly level.[24]

---

[22] Schwert (1981) criticizes this approach for failing to control for changes in risk.

[23] The mathematical analysis in Appendix 23A is based on Takayama (1969). The corresponding graphic analysis follows Zajac (1970) and Baumol and Klevorick (1970). In our graphs, however, the firm is assumed to be a natural monopoly, whereas in their diagrams, a decreasing-returns to scale production function is implicitly assumed.

[24] The relation between output and labor and capital is described by a production function: $Q = f(L,K)$. Profits are a function of output, so that profits are also a function of labor and capital: $\pi(Q) = \pi(f(L,K))$. By choosing L_m units of labor services and K_m units of capital services, the firm maximizes its profits at the monopoly level, $\pi_m(f(L_m, K_m))$.

TABLE 23.2 Rates of Return (%) in Regulated Industries, 1974–77		
Industry	On Book Value of Assets[a]	On Investors' Value[b]
Electricity	8.3	5.8
Gas transportation	9.7	5.7
Gas utilities	10.9	6.1
Telephone	8.7	5.8
Railroad transportation	6.0	4.2
Airline transportation	5.0	3.7
Motor-freight transportation	7.9	6.1
Market return	5.8	
Unregulated service industries		6.6

[a] The rate of return is the book-value weighted average of retained earnings plus dividends plus interest payments divided by the book value of assets.

[b] The rate of return on investors' value is the market-value weighted average of all interest and dividends plus price appreciation divided by the market value of all securities (such as stocks and bonds) for that industry.

SOURCE: MacAvoy (1979; Table 2.13 and Appendix C).

A firm whose ROR is regulated behaves differently. The firm's rate of return is defined as the profits, π, as a ratio of the value of the capital stock, $p_k K$:

$$ROR = \frac{pQ - wL - uK}{p_k K},\qquad(23.2)$$

where w is the wage the firm pays to hire one unit of labor, L; u is the user cost of capital (the cost of using or renting the capital for 1 period; see Chapter 3); and p_k is the purchase price of a unit of the capital stock, K.[25] One reason for the use of the ROR is to facilitate comparisons of profits across different-sized firms. For example, a firm with a big factory may have a higher profit level than one with a smaller factory, but they may have identical RORs if their profits per dollar of factory are equal.

An unregulated monopoly generally has a much higher ROR than competitive firms. Many regulatory boards limit the ROR of monopolists to a fair rate of return. For example, the rate may be set at the average ROR in the unregulated sectors of the economy.[26] Table 23.2 shows the rates of return in a number of regulated industries in the late 1970s, before the recent deregulation movement.

[25] Some analysts alternatively define the ROR by replacing u in Equation 23.2 with the depreciation rate of capital; for example, see Table 23.2. With the definition in Equation 23.2, an ROR of zero is a normal rate of return (that is, no unusual economic profits).

[26] This description of the regulatory process, however, has been criticized as being over simplistic (Joskow 1973, 1974).

A regulated firm must lower its ROR from the monopoly level. It can do that in two ways: either it can lower its profits or increase its capital, or both. Thus, Averch and Johnson point out that a regulated firm has an incentive to increase its capital relative to the amount of labor it uses so as to produce inefficiently. That is, it could produce at lower cost, using a lower capital-labor ratio. Normally a firm buys labor and capital in proportions that minimize the cost of producing a given level of output. Now, however, capital has an additional value to the firm. The more capital, all else the same, the lower the ROR (see Equation 23.2), so that the firm can have higher profits without violating any given restriction on the rate of return. This overcapitalization result is illustrated in the following numerical example.

An Example.   The People's Power Company produces electricity using labor and capital. The inverse demand curve facing the firm is

$$p(Q) = 100 - Q, \tag{23.3}$$

where p is the price and Q is the quantity of electricity sold.

The wage, w, and the user cost of capital, u, are \$168.[27] The interest rate is $r = 10$ percent, and there is no depreciation. The price of capital is \$1680. The quantity of electricity that the firm can produce is a function of the labor and capital inputs it uses:

$$Q = f(L,K) = LK. \tag{23.4}$$

This production function exhibits increasing returns to scale. If both labor and capital are doubled, output, instead of doubling, rises four-fold: $(2L)(2K) = 4LK = 4Q$. That is, this firm is a natural monopoly, with downward sloping average and marginal cost curves, as shown in Figure 23.5.

Table 23.3 shows how much output the firm can produce with various levels of labor and capital. If the monopoly is unregulated, it maximizes its profits at \$288 by using 6 units of labor and 6 units of capital to produce 36 units of output.

Since the wage of labor equals the per unit cost of capital, and the production function is symmetric in L and K, the least expensive way for the firm to produce is to use labor and capital in equal proportions. For example, at the profit-maximizing level of 36 units of output, the firm uses 6 units each of labor and capital. If the firm uses equal amounts of labor and capital to produce 36 units of output, its factor costs are \$2016 $= wL + uK = (168 \times 6) + (168 \times 6)$. As Table 23.3 shows, 36 units of output could also be produced using 4 units of labor and 9 units of capital. If the firm produces that way, however, its costs are \$2184 $= (168 \times 4) + (168 \times 9)$, or 8.33 percent higher.

Profits are maximized, in this example, where the ratio of capital to labor equals one $(K/L = 1)$. Table 23.3 shows that the levels of capital and labor that maximize profits

---

[27] As discussed in Chapter 3, the user cost of capital is

$$u = (r + \delta - \Delta p_k/p_k)p_k,$$

where p_K is the price of the capital asset, r is the interest rate, δ is the depreciation rate of the capital (the rate at which the capital stock is used up), and $\Delta p_k/p_k$ is the appreciation rate of the price of capital (the percentage change in the price of capital over the period).

FIGURE 23.5   Rate-of-Return Regulation

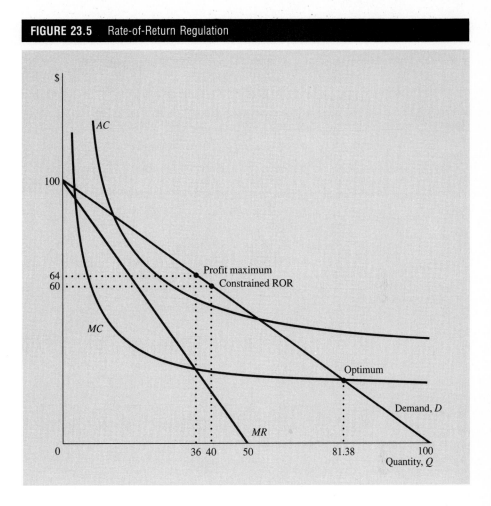

do not maximize ROR. For example, at the profit maximizing levels, $K = 6$, $L = 6$, the ROR is 2.86 percent, whereas at $K = 5$ and $L = 7$, the ROR is 3.08 percent, although profits are only $259. That is, the rate of return per unit of capital is raised by producing labor-intensively ($K/L = 0.71$).

If the regulatory board sets the fair rate of return at 1.61 percent, the monopoly tries to maximize its profits subject to the constraint that its ROR is less than or equal to the fair rate. It changes its behavior by lowering π or raising K or both. By inspecting the table, the monopoly can achieve this regulatory constraint by choosing $L = 5$ and $K = 8$. The regulated firm increases its output by 11.1 percent (from 36 to 40 units of output). Its profits fall 33 percent to $216, and its capital rises by 33 percent. Thus, by lowering profits and raising capital, the firm lowers its rate of return by 56 percent. The firm also lowers its labor by 20 percent. As a result, its capital-to-labor ratio increases 61 percent to 1.61.

TABLE 23.3   Rate-of-Return (ROR) Regulation

Capital	Labor	Output	Price	Profits	Capital / Labor	Rate of Return	Consumer Surplus	Welfare
K	L	Q	p	π	K/L	ROR	CS	W
5	4	20	80	88	1.25	1.05%	200.0	288.0
5	5	25	75	195	1.00	2.32	312.5	507.5
5	6	30	70	252	0.83	3.00	450.0	702.0
5	7	35	65	259	0.71	3.08	612.5	871.5
5	8	40	60	216	0.62	2.57	800.0	1016.0
5	9	45	55	123	0.56	1.46	1012.5	1135.5
6	4	24	76	144	1.50	1.43	288.0	432.0
6	5	30	70	252	1.20	2.50	450.0	702.0
6	**6**	**36**	**64**	**288**	**1.00**	**2.86**	**648.0**	**936.0**
6	7	42	58	252	0.86	2.50	882.0	1134.0
6	8	48	52	144	0.75	1.43	1152.0	1296.0
6	9	54	46	−36	0.67		1458.0	1422.0
7	4	28	72	168	1.75	1.43	392.0	560.0
7	5	35	65	259	1.40	2.20	612.5	871.5
7	6	42	58	252	1.17	2.14	882.0	1134.0
7	7	49	51	147	1.00	1.25	1200.5	1347.5
7	8	56	44	−56	0.87		1568.0	1512.0
7	9	63	37	−357	0.78		1984.5	1627.5
8	4	32	68	160	2.00	1.19	512.0	672.0
8	**5**	**40**	**60**	**216**	**1.60**	**1.61**	**800.0**	**1016.0**
8	6	48	52	144	1.33	1.07	1152.0	1296.0
8	7	56	44	−56	0.87		1568.0	1512.0
8	8	64	36	−384	1.00		2048.0	1664.0
8	9	72	28	−840	0.89		1592.0	1752.0
9	4	36	64	120	2.25	0.79	648.0	768.0
9	5	45	55	123	1.80	0.81	1012.5	1135.5
9	6	54	46	−36	1.50		1458.0	1422.0
9	7	63	37	−357	1.29		1984.5	1627.5
9	8	72	28	−840	1.12		2592.0	1752.0
9	9	81	19	−1485	1.00		3280.5	1795.5
9.02	**9.02**	**81.38**	**18.62**	**−1515.4**	**1.00**		**3311.4**	**1796.0**
10	10	100	0	−3360	1.00		5000.0	1640.0

NOTES: The ROR is not shown if it is negative.

w = u = 168.

r = interest rate = 10 percent.

The regulated firm is producing inefficiently because it is not using equal quantities of capital and labor. It costs the firm $2184 to produce 40 units of output using $L = 5$ and $K = 8$. It only costs the firm $2125 (2.8 percent less) to produce 40 units of output using 6.32 units each of labor and capital.

Thus, as predicted, the firm responds to the regulation by *overcapitalizing*. It is now producing inefficiently, has lowered its profits, and, to sell its 11.1 percent extra output it must lower its price by 7 percent. Consumers are better off. Consumer surplus rises by 23 percent and welfare (defined as consumer surplus plus producer surplus [profits]) rises by 8.5 percent. If the board's administrative costs are low, this inefficient form of regulation increases welfare.

The board can achieve a higher level of welfare if it regulates so that the firm produces efficiently. As discussed earlier, welfare is maximized when quantity is set so that price equals marginal cost and where the least-cost mix of labor and capital is used to produce that level of output, as is the case when optimal direct price regulation is used.[28]

Graphic Analysis.   Figure 23.5 shows three equilibria. The unregulated profit-maximizing equilibrium ($Q = 36$) occurs where the profits are maximized. The ROR regulated equilibrium has more output ($Q = 40$), so consumers are better off. The best solution, however, occurs where price equals marginal cost ($Q = 81.38$). The least-cost way to produce 81.38 units is to use 9.02 units each of capital and labor. Although production and consumption are efficient in the best solution, the firm must be subsidized because, as shown in the figure, the price is below average cost at that point.

Thus, in this example, the best type of regulation more than doubles output (81.38) obtained under the fair rate of return regulation (40). Could the fair rate of return type of regulation achieve close to the optimal level of output? No, it cannot, so long as a positive fair rate is set. As Table 23.3 and Figure 23.5 show, profits are negative at the welfare maximum; hence the rate of return is negative as well.

An alternative graphic analysis is presented in Figures 23.6 and 23.7. Figure 23.6 shows a three-dimensional view of the profit "hill." The hill reaches its peak at $K = 6$ and $L = 6$. If we put rubber bands around the hill at various heights (profit levels) and then viewed the hill from above, these rubber bands look like contour lines, as shown in Figure 23.7. These oval contour lines are called *isoprofit curves*. Each point along an isoprofit curve represents various combinations of capital and labor that lead to the same profit level. The point in the middle ($K = 6$, $L = 6$) is the maximum profit, $288, that an unregulated firm can achieve. It is a point rather than a curve, because there is only one combination of labor and capital that can produce the maximum profit.

Moving away from that point, we reach a relatively small isoprofit curve where profits are $270. The next isoprofit curve shown, moving outward, has a profit level of $216. The largest isoprofit curve shown corresponds to a profit level of $0.

Also shown in the figure is a line labeled *efficient points*. These are the combinations of capital and labor that allow the firm to produce any given level of output at minimum

---

[28] Klevorick (1971), Bailey and Coleman (1971), and Sheshinski (1971) discuss how to set the ROR to maximize social welfare.

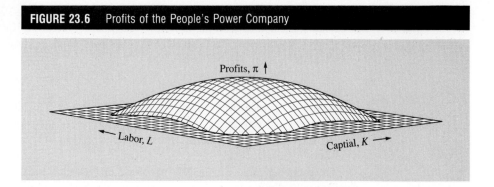

FIGURE 23.6   Profits of the People's Power Company

cost. In our example, the lowest cost method to produce any given output level is to use equal proportions of capital and labor. The maximum profit level is an efficient point ($K = 6$, $L = 6$). If it were not an efficient point, the same output could be produced at a lower cost, so it would not be the maximum profit level.

The dashed line in the figure, labeled *regulated points,* shows capital-labor combinations that a regulated firm chooses. The points in this line are those furthest to the right on any isoprofit curve. That is, these points are the input combinations requiring the greatest use of capital for any given profit level, so the rate of return is lowest. On the $216 isoprofit curve, the right-most point ($K = 8$ and $L = 5$) is the combination that the ROR regulated utility chooses if the fair rate of return is set at 1.61 percent.

The line of efficient points lies *above* the dotted line of regulated points. That is, it is more efficient to produce with a lower capital/labor ratio than a regulated utility chooses. Thus, ROR regulation leads to overcapitalization and inefficient production if the fair rate of return is positive.

Despite its inefficiency, ROR regulation may increase welfare because the loss from inefficiency in production is offset by the gain from greater output and lower prices. Optimal direct price regulation, however, can lower the price without inducing production inefficiencies, so optimal direct price regulation is preferable theoretically. Determining the optimal regulation is a difficult task, and setting rates badly may be harmful.

Firms May Undercapitalize.   Recently, several economists have argued that rate-of-return regulation may lead to undercapitalization rather than overcapitalization. For example, if firms maximize sales revenue instead of profits, an Averch-Johnson type of model predicts undercapitalization (Bailey 1973, Chap. 5).

Using dynamic considerations, underinvestment in capital also becomes more likely. Gilbert and Newbery (1988) argue that firms may undercapitalize because of fears that their sunk capital will be "expropriated" by tighter (more proconsumer) regulation. Dechert (1984) shows that there is underinvestment—not overinvestment—in capital when a regulated natural monopoly adjusts its production slowly over time. A firm may adjust its capital slowly over time if the faster it adjusts, the higher the adjustment costs. Dechert shows that even for a firm with decreasing returns to scale, overinvestment occurs only for some ranges of ROR, where there is a costly adjustment process.

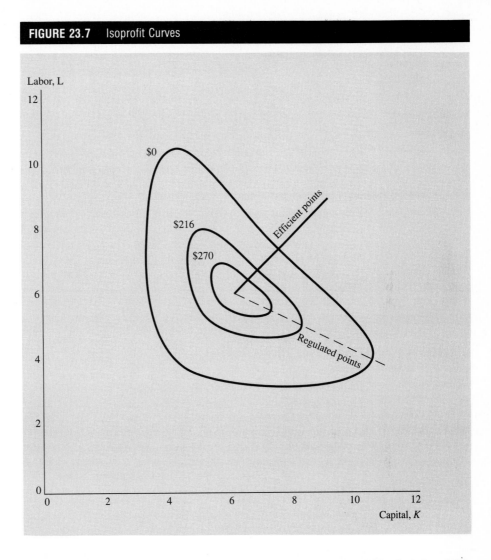

FIGURE 23.7   Isoprofit Curves

Empirical Evidence.   Three empirical studies from the early 1970s find that ROR regulation has substantial effects on electric utilities (Courville 1974, Peterson 1975, and Spann 1974). Courville (1974), for example, estimates overcapitalization at nearly 12 percent, on average, in the electric utility industry. These studies have been criticized on technical grounds (McKay 1977). A number of recent studies (such as Smithson 1978) fail to find evidence of overcapitalization, and Baron and Taggart (1977) find evidence of undercapitalization. In short, the empirical evidence on overcapitalization is mixed. There is a general consensus, however, that production under ROR regulation is likely to be inefficient.

Regulators often only intervene when pressured by the firm or consumers (Joskow 1974). From 1963 to 1967, when declining fuel prices and improvement in technology

EXAMPLE 23.6

DRUG BUSTING

Congress passed the 1962 Kefauver-Harris Amendment to the Food, Drug, and Cosmetics Act to prevent economic loss by regulating pharmaceuticals. In part, it was a response to the belief that many new drugs of dubious efficacy were sold at unusually high prices. The thalidomide tragedy of 1961–62 was another motivating factor. Thalidomide had been kept off the U.S. market by the Food and Drug Administration (FDA), but was distributed by some physicians for experimental purposes. The deformed babies of European mothers exposed to the drug led many to conclude that not enough controls were placed on drug companies in the United States.

Two key provisions of the amendment are a *proof-of-efficacy* requirement and new testing procedures. The proof-of-efficacy requirement requires drug companies to show that a drug fulfills the manufacturer's claims. Thus, this law requires that no new drug can be marketed until the FDA determines that the drug is both safe and effective in its intended use. Recently, however, this rule was weakened for certain experimental drugs.

The law also makes the testing procedures used by manufacturers subject to FDA regulation. The manufacturer must submit a plan for any clinical test to the FDA along with information from preclinical tests. Thus, the FDA can terminate or order changes in clinical investigation if the tests are deemed to be unsafe or ineffective.

The lawmakers reasoned that the FDA could now collect sufficient information to evaluate claims and then block ineffective drugs, thus protecting ignorant consumers from wasting money. Further, humans are not exposed to dangerous drugs during premarket evaluations.

It is hard to argue with the intent of this law, but it is reasonable to ask: Did consumers obtain a more useful flow of new drugs under these regulations? The rules cut the flow of new drugs in half, but if the new drugs are safer and more effective, consumer welfare may have risen.

The regulations reduce the flow by eliminating some drugs outright and by increasing the costs of bringing new drugs to market. Manufacturers now must subject

---

reduced costs for electric utilities, there were only 17 electric utility rate cases, so that prices did not fall quickly. During the rapid inflation of 1973–77, however, there were 119 rate cases (Braeutigam and Quirk 1984). Many utilities, however, reported that they reduced rates in the 1960s, so the asymmetry in regulation may not be quite as extreme as it appears at first. Fitzpatrick (1987) uses a statistical model to show that the utilities "voluntarily" lowered their prices to keep consumers from organizing and complaining to rate commissions, thereby causing even greater rate reductions.

drugs to more costly testing and wait longer before marketing them. As a result, they are less inclined to try to develop new drugs—especially risky ones. The flow of new drugs in the United States was 1.13 times that in Great Britain in 1960–61, but only 0.52 as much in 1966–71.

Are consumers helped or harmed by this reduced flow? If only worthless drugs are kept off the market, they are helped; however, if potentially valuable drugs are not developed and sold, they are harmed. Peltzman (1973) calculates that as of 1970, about $300 to $400 million per year of consumer surplus was lost due to reduced innovation. He estimates a $100 to $150 million upper bound on the annual gain from eliminating worthless drugs. He expects a further loss of $50 million annually due to reduced price competition resulting from lower levels of innovation. There are also additional FDA administration costs of perhaps $15 million. On net, he concludes, the effect of the amendments on consumers is comparable to a 5 to 10 percent tax on their $5 billion annual drug purchases.

These figures do not reflect fully the benefit from avoiding Thalidomide-type disasters. Nonetheless, if Peltzman is even approximately correct, these regulations harm some of the consumers they were intended to help.

In November 1988, apparently in response to pressure from AIDS patients and others, the FDA announced that U.S. citizens may order foreign pharmaceuticals by mail for personal use, even though the drugs are not approved in the United States, on a trial basis. The only exceptions are 40 kinds of drugs proscribed by the FDA as fraudulent or dangerous. A licensed U.S. doctor must oversee the treatment. At least one consumer group has objected that this policy violates the 1962 law. If, however, this new policy is allowed to continue, it may reduce some of the costs Peltzman describes.

SOURCES: Peltzman (1973) and Grady, Denise, and Doug M. Podolsky. 1988. "FDA Allows Mail-Order of Foreign Drugs." *San Francisco Chronicle*, November 29, B5.

Quality Effects

There we were, one foot on a bar of soap and the other in the gutter.
—COMMANDER PURSEY, M. P. (attributed)

Although price cone controls and ROR regulation may lower prices, they may cause some vexing problems (see Example 23.6). For example, they may alter the quality of the product regulated or reduce the variety of products from which a consumer may choose (Archibald 1964, Stigler 1968, White 1972). Unless more sophisticated regulations than pure price and entry controls are used, society must choose between two unattractive alternatives: high price and optimal quality versus low price and nonoptimal quality.

For the purposes of this discussion, based on White (1972), suppose that quality is a secondary output of a firm. For example, if a firm's primary output is air transportation, the secondary output could be in-flight meals or in-flight movies.

The quality output of the firm influences the demand for the firm's primary output and may be jointly produced and consumed. For example, a consumer may be more likely to fly on a given airline, all else the same, if a meal is served on board. Moreover, an in-flight meal can be consumed only while simultaneously flying, by definition.

Price and entry restrictions affect the number or tastiness of meals (or other quality measures).[29] Suppose, initially, that airlines are unregulated and that travel and meals can be purchased separately. The number of flights demanded, Q_T, and the quantity of meals demanded per passenger per trip, Q_M, vary with the price of a flight, p_T, and the price of a meal, p_M:

$$Q_T = Q_T(p_T, p_M) \qquad (23.5)$$
$$Q_M = Q_M(p_T, p_M). \qquad (23.6)$$

The total quantity of meals demanded is $Q_M Q_T$. Assume, also, that the average (marginal) cost of producing a trip, C_T, or a meal, C_M, are constants.

If there are a substantial number of airline firms, then the industry is competitive. The price of basic transportation and of meals equals the corresponding marginal costs: $p_T = C_T$ and $p_M = C_M$. If each industry is monopolized, prices are higher than the corresponding marginal costs: $p_T > C_T$ and $p_M > C_M$.

A competitive industry provides a wide choice of quality levels. Flights with 1, 2, 3, or more meals are offered, where flights with more meals cost more. For example, first class costs more than coach because first class provides better meals, bigger seats, and so forth. A monopolist may provide a different choice of qualities than a competitive industry offers (see Chapter 15).

If regulating authorities forbid new entry and set a single price, p^*_T, that must be charged regardless of the level of quality provided, the demand for flights depends only on the fixed price and the level of services:

$$Q_T = Q_T(p^*_T, Q_M) \qquad (23.7)$$

Firms can only attract business from their competitors by providing higher quality flights; they cannot compete on price. If an extra meal generates positive profits, then the firm increases the number of meals. Each firm adds meals until the added profits made on

---

[29] White (1972) shows that analogous results are obtained for other quality variables such as advertising, luxurious waiting rooms, or in-flight films, which are not directly tied to the quantity of the primary output as are meals. Schmalensee (1977) and Panzar (1979) discuss other quality measures of airlines, such as load factors and flight frequencies.

each customer are driven to zero. That is, the net revenue from each passenger, $p^*_\mp - C_T$, from basic transportation just equals the marginal cost of providing that number of meals, $Q_M C_M$.

Thus, regulated competitive firms increase quality so long as they can profitably take customers from their competitors. This competition drives profits to zero because meals are provided at constant marginal cost. Because only one price, $p^*_\mp$ is charged, each firm chooses the same quality level: $Q_M = (p^*_\mp - C_T)/C_M$. In contrast to the unregulated case, no variability in quality is observed across flights within a given market.

A regulated monopolist offers a lower level of quality per passenger than a regulated competitive industry holding the regulated price constant. Each regulated competitive firm believes that the increase in the number of seats sold as the number of meals is increased is infinite: the demand curve facing the competitive firm is horizontal. In contrast, the regulated monopolist knows that the industry demand curve slopes downward, so that increasing meals increases seat sales by a limited amount. As a result, the regulated competitive firm has a greater incentive to increase quality than the monopolist.[30]

There are five main results of this analysis. First, a regulated competitive industry offers more quality per passenger than does a regulated monopolist holding the regulated price fixed. Second, as a result, a regulated competitive industry sells more seats than a regulated monopoly. Third, the higher the regulated price, $p^*_\mp$, the higher the quality provided by the competitive industry, because the rewards to attracting more business are higher. Fourth, regulation of a competitive industry harms most fliers by providing only one quality level. Regulation of a monopoly may help or hurt fliers because the loss of variety in quality may be offset by a lower price. Fifth, raising the price of a regulated competitive industry does not increase profitability, because firms increase quality to compete until all extra profits are dissipated.[31]

With the Airline Deregulation Act of 1978, some of these hypotheses can be tested. There should, for example, be more variety in quality level and probably a lower overall level now than before deregulation. The empirical evidence, discussed later in the section on airline deregulation, supports these hypotheses.

---

[30] The profits of a regulated firm, if its price per seat is regulated and it cannot charge for meals is:

$$\pi = (p^*_\mp - C_T)Q_T - C_M Q_M Q_T.$$

The firm determines the optimal number of meals by differentiating π with respect to Q_M and setting this first derivative equal to zero:

$$d\pi/dQ_M = (p^*_\mp - C_T)(\partial Q_T/\partial Q_M) - C_M Q_M(\partial Q_T/\partial Q_M) - C_M Q_T = 0.$$

Rearranging terms, the profit-maximizing number of meals is

$$Q_M = (p^*_\mp - C_T)/C_M - Q_T/(\partial Q_T/\partial Q_M).$$

This expression holds for both regulated competitive and monopolistic firms. Competitive firms, however, believe that $\partial Q_T/\partial Q_M = \infty$, while the regulated monopolist faces a finite $\partial Q_T/\partial Q_M$. As a result, Q_M is bigger for a regulated competitive firm, all else the same.

[31] Several authors argue that regulated firms often have strong incentives to provide high-quality products, especially if quality is capital-intensive. See Schmalensee (1979, 33), Kahn (1970, 21–26), and Spence (1975). See Crew and Kleindorfer (1978) and Telson (1975) on utilities choosing excessive levels of reliability. See Panzar (1979) on regulating monopolistically competitive markets.

■ MAKING COMPETITIVE INDUSTRIES MORE MONOPOLISTIC

Governments often regulate competitive industries, making them less competitive and lowering welfare. Governments may regulate poorly because of mistakes or because legislatures or regulators are captured by special interest groups.

Earlier chapters present several examples in which regulations make markets more monopolistic. Many occupations—such as electricians, realtors, lawyers, and doctors—are or have been enpowered by governments to establish barriers to entry, fix prices, and in other ways convert competitive industries into monopolies (see Examples 5.3 and 9.4 and Chapter 17). Agricultural marketing orders (Appendix 14A) allow farmers to act collectively to reduce the total crop and to price discriminate. In some industries, governments forbade advertising about prices (Example 18.3), which gave firms information-based monopoly power and resulted in higher prices. Example 23.7 discusses how rent control can create inefficiencies as well as redistribute income. This section examines two types of government intervention that harm consumers and reduce efficiency: restrictions on the number of firms in an industry, and agricultural regulations, such as price supports and quantity controls.

Limiting Entry

> *Every decent man is ashamed of the government he lives under.*
> —H. L. MENCKEN

In many industries, governments create barriers to entry. For example, occupational licensing laws often allow current, licensed members of an occupation to write the licensing exam (Example 23.8 on p. 816). If they write a difficult exam, or grade unreasonably, potential entrants can be denied licenses. Similarly, potential competitors to the U.S. Postal Service are not allowed to deliver mail to individuals' mailboxes. There are also restrictions on entry in the international air travel industry, banking, health care, insurance, and public utilities. This section concentrates on government control of the number of business licenses (rights to operate in an industry), which restricts entry.

By restricting entry into an industry, a government creates artificial scarcity and raises prices to consumers. The higher prices cause a transfer of wealth from consumers to firms in the industry. That is, the government creates property rights—the rights to operate a firm in the industry—and transfers these rights to a few, lucky individuals.

When the barriers to entry are first created, governments often provide these rights or business licenses to all the firms already in the industry, which are said to be *grand-fathered*. New firms are prohibited from entering the industry without business licenses. Unless the government creates additional licenses, a potential entrant can only obtain a license from a license-holder who is willing to leave the industry. As a result, the number of firms in the industry stays constant.

Any rents from these licenses go to the original owners. That is, an owner sells a license for the present discounted value of the future stream of profits. Thus, new entrants do not make excess profits on their investments, although consumers continue to pay high prices. Only those lucky enough to get the original licenses benefit.

Presumably, lobbying by firms leads to legislatures limiting business licenses. Econ-

EXAMPLE 23.7

RENT CONTROL

Regulation can reduce the efficiency of competitive markets. In many cities around the world, government agencies regulate apartment rental rates, using *rent controls* to keep rental rates below the competitive level. As a result, the demand for housing exceeds the supply.

Rent control transfers wealth from owners to renters. It also reduces the incentive to build new rental housing, exacerbating the shortage in the long run. Similarly, owners have less of an incentive to maintain rental housing, so it deteriorates faster than otherwise.

Rent control is common throughout much of the world. Large percentages of housing in Britain, Sweden, Mexico City, New York City, Berkeley, and San Francisco have been covered by rent control. In the United States, some 200 cities, including nearly 50 in California, have some type of rent control.

Olsen's (1972) empirical study finds that in New York City in 1968, occupants of controlled housing consumed 4.4 percent less housing services and 9.9 percent more nonhousing goods than they would have consumed in the absence of rent control. As a result, their real income was 3.4 percent higher, and poorer families received larger benefits than richer ones. The cost of rent control to landlords, however, was twice its benefit to the tenants.

Which communities adopt rent control and why? Epple (1987), using data for New Jersey communities between 1973 and 1976, shows that, controlling for other factors, rent control is more likely in communities where households view the cost of leaving the community as relatively low. For example, people who work outside their community of residence typically view the cost of not being able to find housing where they work as lower than those who work in the community of residence.

Controlling for a number of other factors, he finds that the greater the rate of population increase, the more likely a community is to have rent control. Long-time renters are more likely to obtain rent-control units, so they benefit more from rent control than new arrivals. He also concludes that rent control is more likely in communities with more durable rental structures, which allow wealth to be more successfully transferred to renters when suppliers' ability to reduce supply is limited.

SOURCES: Olsen (1972), Epple (1987), and Tessler, Ray. 1988. "Rent Control Wins Decision in High Court." *San Francisco Chronicle*, February 25, 1.

omists often refer to such lobbying efforts as **rent seeking:** the use of resources to obtain government-created monopoly profits. It is worth lobbying for additional profits (rents) up to the point where the marginal cost from more lobbying equals the expected marginal gain.[32]

There are many examples of governments restricting entry by limiting business licenses. In California, a law allowing only one salmon fish farm resulted in that firm

---

[32] Pittman (1988) shows that rent seeking is most likely in concentrated industries.

EXAMPLE 23.8

LEGAL MONOPOLIES

Lawyers throughout the world obtain market power by restricting entry into the profession and fixing prices. In virtually all of the member countries (most European and Scandinavian countries, Australia, Canada, Japan, New Zealand, and the United States) of the Organization for Economic Cooperation and Development (OECD), lawyers must earn a degree from a recognized law school and obtain a license in order to practice their trade. They are often also required to join the bar association or law society, as in the Netherlands.

As an OECD (1985, 35) report notes, "Control of the licensing process by Bar Associations may in most countries operate, directly or indirectly, to limit the numbers of new entrants to the legal profession. Requirements that candidates be of 'good conduct' allow for subjective decisions as to who will be permitted to practice."

In the United States and other countries, bar associations have authority over the writing and grading of exams. Since practicing lawyers make up the bar association, it is not surprising that, although applicants for the bar exam are graduates of accredited law schools, the average failure rate is 25–30 percent.

Many countries also have quotas for entrance to law schools. For example, there are only 150 places annually for solicitors in Ireland. Some countries, such as Belgium and France, have quotas on the number of entrants and practitioners of certain public legal functions.

The geographic mobility of lawyers is limited in most OECD countries. These limits allegedly ensure that lawyers are familiar with local laws and regulations. In the United States, lawyers must be licensed in each state in which they practice. Reciprocity between states is limited. In the United Kingdom, there is reciprocity, after three years of practice, between Scotland, Northern Ireland, and England and Wales. Canada has restrictions on practicing in other provinces. Indeed, in Alberta, provincial regulations prevent local lawyers from practicing with lawyers from other provinces.

Traditionally, most OECD countries have barred lawyers from advertising (which increases price competition), seeking free publicity in the media, and other means of attracting new business. In recent years, several countries, including Denmark, Sweden, and the United States, have modified or rescinded advertising restrictions, however. Other countries still have restrictive rules, such as Belgium, England and Wales, Finland, Germany, Japan, Norway, and Spain.

Fee schedules, otherwise known as price-fixing, are common in OECD countries. Typically the fees are set by the bar association, often under government authority. Ireland sets fees by statute and association rules. Fees are set locally or regionally in Canada. Germany sets upper limits. The courts or other authorized bodies in Australia set fee schedules. Some countries, such as England and Wales, however, do not set fees. Government officials challenged fee scales in Denmark and France. Court decisions have sharply restricted fee setting by lawyers in the United States. Thus, in some countries, lawyers' most monopolistic practices are gradually eroding.

EXAMPLE 23.9

BREWING TROUBLE

The California Legislature overwhelmingly passed a bill to grant monopolies to beer distributors. The bill required breweries to sell beer to only a single wholesaler in any given area. Ninety percent of the beer sold by breweries to California wholesalers is under exclusive dealer contracts. Nonetheless, wholesalers wanted to make the practice state law to prevent major retailers from buying directly from breweries. Wholesalers also feared that the courts would use antitrust laws to reject exclusive distribution contracts.

Consumer groups, large store chains, and the state attorney general opposed the bill. Common Cause and the Consumers Union branded the bill as the worst special-interest measure of the year. They claimed that when Indiana, New Jersey, and New York adopted similar laws, beer prices increased 10 to 20 percent, or 25¢ to 50¢ per six-pack.

Why did it pass easily? Although we don't know for sure, wholesalers were extremely generous in their campaign contributions to Republicans and Democrats alike. Of the 120 members of the state Assembly and Senate, 116 reported receiving in excess of $530,000 collectively. The governor vetoed the bill.

SOURCES: Wiegand, Steve. 1987. "Beer Distributors' Monopoly Bill OKd." *San Francisco Chronicle,* August 28, A-10. "Veto the Beer Bill." 1987. *San Francisco Examiner,* August 30, A-18.

earning a 1200 percent return on capital. Another proposed law in California reflected an attempt to monopolize beer wholesaling (Example 23.9). In some states, to sell liquor, one must have a liquor license; licenses are restricted, driving their free market value to over $100,000.

One other well-known example of an industry with entry restrictions is taxicabs; in many cities, governments limit the number of taxicab licenses. Partially offsetting the anticompetitive effects of these barriers to entry are price controls on cabs.

Entry into the taxicab market is often restricted by requiring each cab to have a business license, a *medallion,* and then limiting the number of medallions. In most years, new cabs cannot enter the market unless they buy a medallion from an existing owner. As a result, the original owners capture the present value of future excess profits by charging high prices for their medallions. In some cities, medallions have sold for $30,000 to $100,000 or more. In Chicago in the 1960s the market price for medallions was $15,000, and there were 2739 medallions operated full-time, so that the rents were $41,085,000 (Kitch, Isaacson, and Kaspar 1971). The loss to consumers must be well in excess of that figure, unless there are offsetting benefits.

Other regulations are sometimes used to offset, at least partially, the bad effect of the entry barrier and to justify this entry barrier. Typically a medallion owner is subject to a number of restrictions, including price and safety regulations, which may benefit consumers.

Local market power of cabs can be kept in check, at least partially, by the threat of losing a medallion. Imagine that you arrive in a strange city and there is only one cab within sight. You are tired and hungry and the rain is coming down hard. The cab driver says, "I'll take you to your hotel for five times the amount on the meter." As angry as that makes you, you may still take the cab. If, however, your report of this incident could cause the driver to lose the medallion at least for a while, the driver would be hesitant to make such a demand.

Most of these justifications for regulation, however, fail to explain why the number of cabs must be limited to the point where a medallion is worth tens of thousands of dollars. One justification for entry limitation is that, given search costs associated with matching cabs to riders, there is excessive entry, as in fisheries (Gallick and Sisk 1984). It is difficult to believe, however, even if some regulation is required, that most cities operate optimally, given the high values of medallions. Presumably the main purpose of these regulations is to transfer wealth from riders to cab drivers. One explanation for why wealth is transferred in this way is the interest group theory: cab owners lobby strongly for these restrictions.

An alternative explanation is that the type of regulation is in large part determined by the incentives facing regulators (Eckert 1973). The taxi industry tends to be regulated by either municipal agencies or independent commissions. Municipal agencies are run by bureaucrats who impose rules and require supervision of the industry so as to justify large salaries and staffs. Independent commissioners, in contrast, have part-time appointments. Supervising large staffs and dealing with exceptions would require more of their time. Moreover, as they tend to be appointed for a limited term, long-run returns in higher salaries to more regulations would aid only their successors.

Commissioners often find that they can reduce their level of regulatory effort if they only have to deal with a single "responsible" firm. Equivalently, the market may be divided into exclusive territories through regulation, creating local monopolies. Thus, according to this hypothesis, commissions prefer monopolies or market divisions more than do agency bureaucrats. Of 33 cities that Eckert studied, 5 of the 6 cities with commissions (83.3 percent) had monopolies or market divisions. Of the 27 cities with agencies, only 5 (18.5 percent) had monopolies or market divisions.

Regardless of commissioners' motives, cab riders probably lose and cab drivers gain from entry restrictions in most cities. Surely there is a more efficient way to transfer wealth to cab drivers if that is society's purpose. These transfers, however, are trivial compared to those in agriculture.

Agricultural Regulations: Price Supports and Quantity Controls

U.S. Agricultural programs have resulted in enormous budgetary costs, benefits that do not reach those most in need, huge surpluses of farm products, major trade disputes with other countries, and great harm to well-functioning international markets. Programs instituted at the federal level have distorted economic incentives sufficiently to create serious long-term problems. Programs for some commodities have imposed substantial losses on consumers. Chronic surpluses of major commodities exist throughout the world, largely because of

high U.S. Government target prices and heavy subsidization of agricultural production by most other developed countries.
—ECONOMIC REPORT OF THE PRESIDENT, 1987

Most standard microeconomic textbooks point to agricultural markets as examples, possibly the only examples, of perfectly competitive markets. After all, agricultural markets are typified by a large number of small firms. Unfortunately, in virtually every country in the world, governments intervene in these markets and reduce their efficiency, driving them from the competitive equilibrium.

Why do governments engage in policies that promote inefficiency and harm consumers? One common explanation is that the government wants to transfer income to the agricultural sector but does not want to do so openly and directly by simply giving farmers money. To accomplish this transfer of income, price supports and quantity controls are used.

Price Supports.   In the United States during the Great Depression, farmers were struck early and hard. In response, the Federal Farm Board was established in 1929 to buy and sell farm output in order to ensure "orderly agricultural marketing."[33] The board used **price supports**: by buying when prices would otherwise be low, it prevented prices from falling below certain levels, called *support prices*. By buying large quantities at high prices, it created large stockpiles and exhausted its available funds.

Figure 23.8 shows why. Farm price supports induce individual farmers and hence the market as a whole to produce more than would be produced by a competitive market.[34] The competitive equilibrium is determined by the intersection of the demand curve and the supply curve, S. The competitive price is p_c, and the competitive quantity is Q_c. If the government guarantees farmers a support price of $p_s > p_c$, farmers do not sell for less. At that higher price, consumers are only willing to buy $\underline{Q}$ units. Thus, the government must buy the rest of the total amount supplied, $Q_s - \underline{Q}$, and store it. The government cannot sell it domestically as long as the price remains at p_s.

This program is a very inefficient way to transfer income to farmers. It costs consumers and taxpayers much more than farmers receive. Under this program, farmers' incomes rise by areas $A + B + C$ in Figure 23.8. This total area represents the extra income from selling more units (Q_s rather than Q_c) at a higher price (p_s rather than p_c) less the cost of producing the extra units (the area under the supply curve from Q_c to Q_s). At the

---

[33] Apologists for our agricultural policy usually justify it on the grounds that it stabilizes prices. By maintaining a support price, prices are more stable (fluctuate less from year to year) than they would be otherwise. By eliminating uncertainty, proponents of such stabilization maintain, farmers' welfare is increased. It is unclear why this market needs stabilizing more than other markets, and why this type of stabilization should be achieved through government intervention. For example, farmers can use futures markets to reduce risk.

[34] Technically, during most of the history of U.S. farm supports, explicit price supports have not been used. Rather, the Commodity Credit Corporation (CCC) makes "nonrecourse" loans with the farmer's potential crop as collateral. That is, if the farmer does not pay back the loan, the agency keeps the crop used as collateral, but has no further recourse to the farmer's assets if the crop does not cover the loan. If agricultural prices are below the implicit rate set by the loan, the farmer defaults on the loan and the CCC claims the crop. This technique is equivalent to a formal price support, but involves more paperwork.

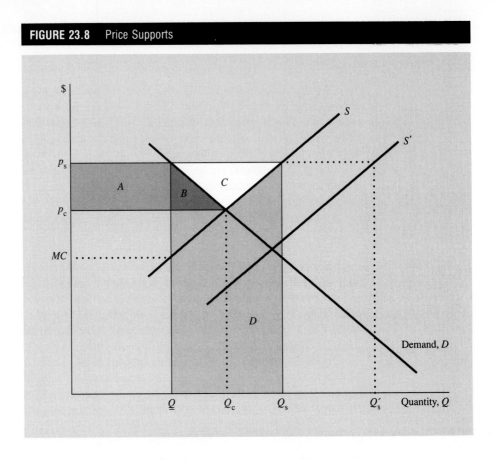

FIGURE 23.8   Price Supports

higher price, consumer surplus falls by $A + B$. The government pays $p_s(Q_s - \underline{Q})$, which equals $B + C + D$, for the extra crop and then pays to store the surplus. Thus, the net loss to society is $B + D$ plus the cost of storage.

There are three chief sources of this loss. First, there is *excess production:* too much output is produced. Instead of producing Q_c units when the competitive price is p_c, farmers produce Q_s units. We know this output is excessive, since consumers do not want to consume it at the price p_s. Second, there is *suboptimal consumption:* consumers pay p_s for $\underline{Q}$ units of output. The marginal cost of producing that output is MC. Thus, the consumer is paying a price above marginal cost: $p_s > MC$. Third, the government is paying to *store* the excessive output.

The losses are greater if there is technological progress, which has been spectacular in American agriculture. Technological advances (better fertilizers, higher-quality tractors, new seeds) shift the supply curve out, to S' in Figure 23.8. If the support program is unchanged, the government must buy all the extra output. The government now buys and stores $Q'_s - \underline{Q}$ output at cost $P_s(Q'_s - \underline{Q})$. Consumers do not gain from the technological progress because the price they pay, p_s, does not change due to the support program. All else the same, the relatively high support prices induce more technological progress than

FIGURE 23.9   Quota and Price Support

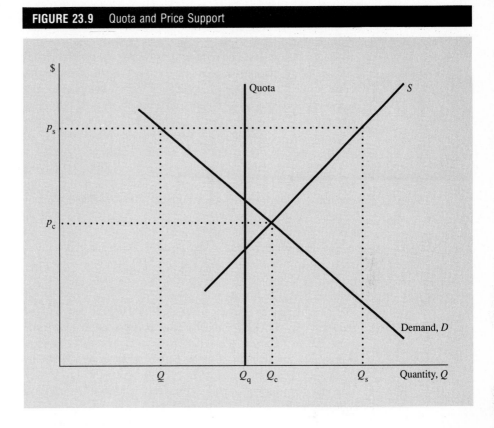

would otherwise occur, because the returns to research and development are higher than in a competitive market (see Chapter 20).

Franklin D. Roosevelt's New Deal farm policy was designed to keep farmers' incomes in a fixed ratio to incomes of the rest of the nation (maintain *parity*) without large surpluses. The target of the parity policy was to reestablish the relative price ratio between agricultural commodities and other goods of the World War I era. Because productivity had grown relatively rapidly in agriculture while demand had not, the free-market relative prices of agricultural products dropped substantially by the end of the Great Depression, and substantial subsidies were necessary to raise the relative prices to their earlier levels.

Quantity Controls.   To keep these high price supports from leading to large stockpiles, farmers were *paid not to produce* as well as for their actual production. Further, quotas were used to limit acreage.[35] In other words, to offset problems from the first type of regulation—the expense and the embarrassment from storing enormous quantities of unused food—additional regulations were added.

The effects of an output quota are shown in Figure 23.9. Here, we suppose that the

---

[35] For a discussion of the government programs see Johnson (1973) and *Economic Report of the President* (1987, Ch. 5).

(arbitrary) output quota is Q_q. Thus, consumers still buy Q units at price p_s, but now the government buys only $Q_q - Q$ units, instead of $Q_s - \bar{Q}$ units, at price p_s. As a result, it buys and stores less food.

Rather than restrict output directly, however, the government usually restricts acreage. Presumably the reason for restricting acreage is that weather fluctuations make output harder to predict. A quota on acreage, however, complicates the analysis. Farmers can increase their output on a restricted number of acres by using more fertilizer, labor, and other inputs. That is, they can use labor-, capital-, and fertilizer-intensive farming techniques similar to those of Japanese farmers, who have relatively small farms. As a result, cutting acreage by 25 percent does not cut output by 25 percent.

Although an output quota can reduce the required subsidy, acreage quotas add two new distortions to the ones previously discussed with respect to price support alone. First, *production is inefficient:* farmers use too little land and too much fertilizer and other factors. Thus, the cost of producing a given output is higher than in the absence of acreage quotas. Second, there are *inefficiencies across farms.* Some farms are more limited by acreage quotas than others, so that costs of production vary across farms. Thus, relatively inefficient farms are producing at higher cost than efficient farms.

Changes in Agricultural Policy over Time.   Since World War II, our basic agricultural policy has remained relatively unchanged, although the details of the program have changed frequently. By the 1950s, the base for parity was no longer the World War I relative prices, but an average of prices during the previous decade. Moreover, prices were allowed to drop to some fraction of parity before price supports were instituted. These changes allowed relative farm prices to drop, but much more slowly than in a free market. Soil bank and other programs paid substantial amounts to farmers to leave millions of acres unplanted.

In the 1970s, shifts in the value of the dollar, crop failures in much of the rest of the world, and increasing world population led to increased exports. Stockpiles were depleted. At the peak of the world-wide drought that led to mass starvation in 1971–72, grain prices shot up by 70 percent. Farmers' income similarly rose.

Farmers' relative success led to a restructuring of agricultural support programs in 1973. The government no longer purchased and stored crops. Under the new policy, the government supplemented the market price with direct cash, or *deficiency* payments to farmers only if market prices dropped below *target prices.* That is, consumers bought commodities at the market clearing price, and the government made deficiency payments on the output actually sold, but did not buy any output itself. Thus, if the farmers sold Q_c units at a price, p_c, that was below the target price, the government gave farmers $(p_s - p_c)Q_c$. Depending on how p_s is set, the cost of this approach may be more or less than the older price support program.

In practice, because the target prices covered most but not all production costs, farmers were no longer guaranteed a profit, but were protected against large losses. Farmers stored the crops and decided when to sell them. Indeed, the government made low-interest loans so that farmers could purchase their own storage facilities. Many of the earlier distortions—high consumer costs, inefficient production, excessive production, and unnecessary storage—were eliminated or reduced.

U.S. agricultural policy was revised in 1981 and 1985. Under these laws, deficiency payments are based on the difference between the target price and the higher of the basic loan rate (the price set under the loan program) or the average price received by farmers over the first five months of the marketing year. Loan rates are set by the Secretary of Agriculture prior to the marketing year. The effective loan rate is set at world market prices for cotton and rice. Cotton and rice farmers who participate in government programs can pledge their output as collateral for a loan at the basic rate and then repay the loan at maturity at the world market price if it is lower than the basic rate.

In theory, our agricultural policy was designed to maintain the living standards of poor, single-family farms. Historically, however, large farms benefited disproportionately. As a result, the current laws place upper limits on deficiency payments. Such limits may induce corporations to break up large farms into smaller ones, at least on paper. Nonetheless, large farms still receive a disproportionate share of all support.

The Cost of U.S. Agricultural Programs.   The new agricultural programs are designed to reduce government costs in three ways. First, farmers who accept deficiency payments must idle some portion of their land. Second, under the new laws, government stocks can be placed on the market even when prices are below loan rates. Third, income supports have been lowered substantially for some (but not all) commodities. Still, the federal government spent about $60 billion on farm price and income-support programs between 1981 and 1985 and $25.9 billion in 1986.

The severe recession in agriculture in the mid-1980s propelled many farms, especially family-size ones (sales between $40,000 and $250,000, representing a quarter of all farms), into financial stress and some into bankruptcy. Effectively, the government made loans to farms when commercial banks did not. Thus, supply was kept artificially high by keeping some farms from exiting the industry. Moreover, when some of these farms (typically the riskiest) went under, the government was left with the bad debts. The federal Farm Credit System (FCS) had delinquent loans in 1987 estimated at $7.1 billion. The federal government subsidized 55.2 percent of all farm credit.

The United States also uses import quotas and tariffs to protect domestic farmers, thereby raising prices to consumers. For example, due to import quotas, U.S. sugar prices are three to four times the world price. This distortion is so large that it is profitable to produce high-fructose corn syrup, which is a costly substitute for sugar, and to extract sugar from imported processed goods that contain sugar, such as cakes and pancake mixes. In 1985 import quotas were placed on processed goods that contain sugar to protect U.S. producers who face high domestic prices.

Table 23.4 shows the annual gains and losses from income-support programs under the 1985 Food Security Act and trade restrictions for several major crops. In all cases estimated consumer losses and taxpayer costs exceed producer gains by up to several billion dollars per year. For example, for milk, the estimated cost to consumers of $1.6–$3.1 billion plus the taxpayers' expense of $1.0 billion exceed producer gains of $1.5–$2.4 billion by $1.1–$1.7 billion. These losses are over 70 percent of the amount transferred to producers. In tobacco, the losses may be between 3 and 4 times as much as the total transfer to farmers. Thus, we could subsidize farmers by direct transfer payments at much lower cost than the current system.

TABLE 23.4 Annual Gains and Losses from Income-Support Programs Under the 1985 Food Security Act and Trade Restrictions (billions of dollars)

Commodity	Consumer Loss	Taxpayer Cost[a]	Producer Gain	Net Loss
Corn	0.5 –1.1	10.5	10.4 –10.9	0.6 –0.7
Sugar I[b]	1.8 –2.5	0	1.5 – 1.7	.3 – .7
Sugar II[b]	1.1 –1.8	0	1.0 – 1.4	.1 – .4
Milk	1.6 –3.1	1.0	1.5 – 2.4	1.1 –1.7
Cotton	([c])	2.1	1.2 – 1.6	.5 – .9
Wheat	.1 – .3	4.7	3.3 – 3.6	1.4 –1.5
Rice	.02– .06	1.1	.8 – 1.1	.06– .32
Peanuts	.2 – .4	0	.15– .40	.0 – .05
Tobacco	.4 – .7	.1	.1 – .2	.4 – .6

NOTE: All figures reflect Gramm-Rudman-Hollings.

[a] Includes CCC expenses after cost recovery.

[b] Case I assumes U.S. policies do not affect world sugar prices. Case II takes into account the fact that U.S. policies reduce world sugar prices. The value of sugar import restrictions to those exporters who have access to the U.S. market (that is, value of quota rents) is $250 million.

[c] Less than $50 million.

SOURCE: Compiled by the Council of Economic Advisors from various sources.

The Cost of Agricultural Programs in Other Countries. Other countries also use price supports and tariffs to keep prices high domestically. The European Community (EC) uses price supports for grains, dairy, livestock, and sugar; deficiency payments for oilseeds; production quotas for sugar; export refunds for grains, dairy, and livestock; and various import tariffs and quotas. The cost of the EC's "common agricultural policies" is about the same budgetary cost as in the United States. The EC's direct subsidy costs during 1986 were estimated to be $23 billion, of which, perhaps, $3 billion was spent on surplus disposal. The EC's subsidy of taxpayers and consumers to farmers was up to $40 billion during 1984 and is rising (*Economic Report of the President* 1987, 164–65).

Japan uses deficiency payments for oilseeds; price supports and deficiency payments for dairy; price stabilization programs for sugar; and quotas and tariffs for rice, beef, pork, poultry, sugar, and other commodities. Japan's GNP is about half that of the United States or the EC, but its farm subsidies were about $10.5 billion in 1984. The food prices paid by Japanese consumers are estimated to be at least 60 percent above competitive levels, so that Japanese consumers' losses are probably multiples of the direct government outlays (*Economic Report of the President* 1987, 165).

The proportion of the costs of these support programs that fell on consumers of the subsidized products rather than on taxpayers was higher in Japan and the EC than in the United States, except for dairy products. In the United States, consumers bore 29 percent of the cost of supports for wheat, 42 percent for beef, and 95 percent for dairy. The comparable figures in Japan were 67, 92, and 77 percent; in the EC they were 63, 76, and 58 percent (*Economic Report of the President* 1987, 167).

A World Bank study estimates that if all the subsidies and protectionism throughout the industrialized world had been eliminated, taxpayers and consumers would have saved $100 billion a year in the early 1980s, while farmer incomes would have fallen by about half that amount.[36] In some developing nations, such as India and Nigeria, however, subsidies go to consumers rather than farmers.

■ DEREGULATION

To insure Peace of Mind, ignore the Rules and Regulations. —GEORGE ADE

In markets in which regulation is harmful rather than helpful, deregulation makes sense. In the last two decades, many industries have been deregulated (Table 23.5), especially during the Carter and Reagan administrations. Industries that were partially or totally deregulated include airlines, interstate trucking, railroads, banking and savings and loans (limits on interest-rates), television, and telephones. Unfortunately, there has been little deregulation in agriculture.

Typically, there are strong supporters and opponents of any proposal to deregulate an industry. Indeed, deregulation campaigns create some strange bedfellows. Supporters of deregulation typically include many, but certainly not all, economists, some regulators, and some consumer groups. Opponents typically include some economists, most regulators, some consumer groups, the regulated firms, and unions that work for those firms.

Supporters of deregulation want to remove regulations that set prices and restrict entry. They claim that deregulation increases efficiency and lowers prices. They point to two types of efficiency gains from removing the distortions created by price regulations. The first is a result of letting the market set relative prices rather than regulators. For example, many transportation and telephone regulations cross-subsidized people and firms in rural areas at the expense of other consumers. Deregulation, by allowing these rates to adjust, increases consumption along major transportation routes or phone usage in urban areas and decreases it on minor routes and in the boondocks, increasing efficiency. Some consumers gain and others lose from these adjustments.

Second, proponents claim that deregulation lowers prices overall. In many industries, regulated prices are set well above marginal costs. Because prices are regulated but service levels typically are not, regulated firms compete by increasing product quality or the frequency of their service, thereby driving their costs up to the level of the regulated prices, rather than allowing prices to fall to low-cost levels. Moreover, to the degree that regulated prices are cost-based, firms have little incentive to cut costs. Further, because regulators restrict entry, deregulation leads to lower prices due to increased competition from new entrants. Thus, proponents believe that deregulation lowers prices by ceasing to prop up prices artificially, allowing quality or service levels to fall from their high levels and increasing the number of firms.

Opponents argue that most regulated industries are inherently oligopolistic. As a result, they claim, deregulation eventually causes prices to rise because firms will collude. They also argue that, without controls, service and quality fall. In particular, small communities lose service under deregulation, since, without the cross-subsidization, it is

---

[36] Cited in *Economic Report of the President* (1987).

TABLE 23.5	Major Deregulation Decisions

Year	Decision
1968	The Supreme Court permits non-AT&T equipment to be connected to the Bell System.
1969	MCI is permitted to connect its long-distance network to local phone systems.
1970	Interest rates are deregulated on bank deposits of $100,000 or more.
1972	The Federal Communications Commission (FCC) establishes a domestic satellite open skies policy.
1975	The Securities and Exchange Commission ends fixed brokerage fees for stock market transactions.
	Rate bureaus for railroads and trucking firms are prohibited from protesting independent rate filings.
1976	The Railroad Revitalization and Regulatory Reform Act of 1976 partially deregulates railroads and makes rate-setting more cost-based.
1977	Deregulation of air cargo gives airlines more freedom in pricing.
1978	Congress partially decontrols natural gas.
	The Occupational Safety and Health Administration revokes 928 "nit-picking" rules.
	The Civil Aeronautics Board is phased out, eliminating controls over airline entry and prices.
	The Environmental Protection Agency permits trading in property rights to emit pollutants.
1980	The FCC removes most federal regulation of cable TV and of equipment in consumers' premises.
	The Motor Carrier Act eliminates barriers to entry into trucking and permits operators to establish fares and routes with little oversight by the Interstate Commerce Commission.
	The Depository Institutions law phases out interest rate ceilings and permits savings and loans to offer interest-bearing checking accounts
	The Staggers Rail Act enables railroads to adjust rates without government approval and enter into contracts with shippers.
1981	President Reagan decontrols crude oil prices and petroleum allocations.
	The FCC removes many radio regulations.
1982	A new bus regulatory statute allows intercity bus companies to change routes and fares.
	The Garn-St. Germain Act allows savings and loans to make more commercial and consumer loans and removes interest-rate differentials between banks and savings and loans.
1984	As part of an antitrust settlement, AT&T agrees to divest local operating companies.
	Individual ocean-shipping companies are allowed to offer lower rates and better service than those set by shipping associations.

SOURCES: Weidenbaum (1987) and Lee, Baumel, and Harris (1987).

unprofitable to provide the same level of service as under regulation. The deregulators counter that if it is unprofitable to serve these areas, they should not be served.

In most industries, deregulation has occurred slowly over time. Slow deregulation has created inequities and inefficiencies in some markets. For example, under the 1978 National Gas Policy Act, prices on natural gas wells differed by the time of discovery, with "old" gas still controlled and "new" uncontrolled.

In other industries, partial deregulation caused other problems. For example, many controls on savings and loans and banks were removed in 1980, and federal insurance limits on accounts more than doubled. The insurance is provided by two federal entities: the Federal Deposit Insurance Corporation (FDIC) and the Federal Savings and Loan Insurance Corporation (FSLIC). These insurers were exposed to risks by bank and savings and loan owners and managers (White 1988). These individuals could take extremely high risks, knowing that the insurers would bail them out if they failed but that they could keep the high returns if they succeeded. Without adequate regulations on risk-taking and with higher insurance protection, many banks and savings and loan institutions became insolvent. According to the Federal Home Loan Bank Board, 520 savings and loans were insolvent in 1987, and 434 in 1988, compared to 43 in 1980.

Nonetheless, in several major industries, decontrol was rapid and fairly complete. Although all evidence is not in yet, many early studies of deregulation in these industries find overall efficiency gains. The following sections examine deregulation in three transportation industries—airlines, trucking, and railroads—in more detail.

Airlines

In 1938, Congress established the Civil Aeronautics Administration, which later became the Civil Aeronautics Board (CAB). The CAB controlled the interstate airlines industry, including entry by airline companies, air routes, rates, and agreements between airlines and provided subsidies to promote air transportation. Entry was often limited to only one or two carriers between many cities. The CAB would not give approval for airlines to compete on fares for most first-class and regular coach passengers, though it did allow price discrimination, such as lower rates for children. As a result, airlines competed on the quality of service (such as better meals, free movies, and empty seats) and the frequency of service (Spiller 1983). Putting more seats in airplanes (using all-coach seating configurations) and filling the planes to 70 percent capacity could have cut the cost of a transcontinental ticket roughly in half in the mid-1970s (Breyer 1982).

The combination of barriers to entry and rates high enough to allow firms to supply extensive services led many economists to conclude that the pricing was near cartel levels. Indeed, in the early 1970s, intrastate flights in California, which were not regulated, had prices that were about 40 percent less than fares in comparable eastern interstate markets. (Breyer 1982).

President Carter's chairman of the Civil Aeronautics Board (CAB), Alfred Kahn, an economist who is an expert on regulation, was a forceful advocate of airline deregulation. When airlines were first deregulated, he observed, "I have more faith in greed than in regulation."[37]

Deregulators argued that prices would fall. Some claimed that a deregulated airline travel market is *contestable*. That is, since planes can be moved easily to different locations, there are many potential entrants on each route, even though the number of actual com-

---

[37] *New York Times*, October 7, 1980.

petitors is small. Indeed, since regulators prevented entry, entry should be facilitated by deregulation. They also claimed that deregulated firms would offer better mixes of quality and be more responsive to the fluctuating desires of the public.

Opponents included the major airlines and their unions.[38] They feared economic harm. Some opponents argued that the airlines would become unsafe. Despite these objections, President Carter signed the Airline Deregulation Act in 1978, which took pricing and route decisions from the CAB and allowed airlines to make these decisions. Indeed, the CAB reduced entry barriers and permitted considerable pricing freedom starting in 1977. The CAB rapidly implemented the Airline Deregulation Act, permitting entry routinely. The Act eliminated the CAB at the end of 1984.

To deal with one of the largest fears about deregulation, however, service to smaller communities was guaranteed for 10 years. The Essential Air Service Program, designed to cover a 10-year "phased transition" to a completely unregulated and unsubsidized market, cost $71 million to subsidize 202 communities in the continental United States in its first year of operation. By 1987, only 102 communities were being subsidized at a cost of $21 million.[39] The smallest nonhub cities, as a group, experienced practically no change in their average weekly departures from 1978 to 1987; whereas small hub cities (where an airline has flights to several other cities) had a 42 percent increase (Kahn 1988).

The actions of the CAB before deregulation and soon after led to an increase in firms and flights. The number of passenger and freight air carriers tripled between 1976 and 1983, and the number of passenger carriers alone more than doubled. A Herfindahl index of concentration fell 12.5 percent in the long-haul market and 14 percent in small-city markets over the same period (Moore 1986).

A study by Bailey and Williams (1988) indicates that a full continuum of price-quality choices are now available. In particular, in contrast to the regulated period, low-price, low-quality service is now offered. Improved service is also available for higher fares (Moore 1986). Overall, however, service has declined—there are greater travel delays, longer travel times, and more lost luggage. Many, if not most of these problems stem from greater congestion in hub cities and relatively fewer air traffic controllers, due to lack of action by Congress and the Department of Transportation (Moses and Savage 1987).

---

[38] Spiller (1983) points out that, based on history during the regulatory period, some airlines could be predicted to profit from deregulation and others to lose. Moreover, potential entrants expected to gain from deregulation. As a result, some firms favored deregulation.

[39] Anderson, Jack. 1987. "The High Cost of Air Travel." *San Francisco Chronicle*, December 1, A23: According to a Department of Transportation (DOT) analysis, without the subsidies, about 70 of the 102 communities would not have air service. Of the 70, however, 43 serve fewer than five passengers a day and 33 are within 75 highway miles of airports with scheduled, unsubsidized flights. At the end of 1987, Congress voted to extend the subsidy for another 10 years. "Subsidy Cuts Threaten Rural Air Service." 1989. *San Francisco Chronicle*, January 4, p A10: In fiscal 1989, Congress appropriated $25 million for the program—$6.6 million less than necessary to maintain the 1988 level of support. DOT announced cutbacks eliminating service to up to 56 communities in as many as 39 states, but exempting Alaska and Hawaii because air service is often the only feasible transportation mode in those states.

Bailey and Williams (1988) also conclude that, initially, new entrants had a cost advantage. Most of the firms that operated during regulation signed high union wage contracts containing strong work-rule clauses that left them with higher costs than new entrants. In the first seven years after deregulation, however, the change in the value of the stock and profit margins of the largest domestic carriers were greater than those of smaller firms, probably due to scale-based advantages (which, for example, let them offer more attractive frequent-flier benefits).

Medium-sized firms, lacking the scale economies of larger firms, merged to achieve these economies. Thus, the initial influx of new carriers after deregulation was offset by exits and mergers, so that the industry is becoming more concentrated, especially along routes that are not heavily traveled. From 1979 through 1987, there were at least 14 mergers (Congressional Budget Office [CBO] 1988, 14). Of the 22 firms that entered during 1979–85, by 1987, 6 were acquired (merged into) other airlines, and 11 failed (CBO 1988, 12). Thus, only 23 percent continued to operate independently. As a result, the industry is now more concentrated. In 1978, the top 4 firms had 57.7 percent of revenue passenger miles, and the top 8 had 80.4 percent, whereas in 1987 the top 4 had 66.0 percent and the top 8 had 91.7 percent (CBO 1988, 15).

In the first 10 years since deregulation, the Department of Transportation presided over and approved 21 mergers, two of which were over Department of Justice objections.[40] Since January 1, 1989, authority over airline mergers has shifted to the Justice Department, which may be less likely to permit mergers.

Brueckner and Spiller (1988) argue that there are significant potential benefits of mergers among airlines that lead to larger hub networks. They point out that if mergers increase traffic and hence fill planes on feeder routes, marginal costs for both local and pass-through passengers fall. These efficiency gains are greater the larger the economies of scale and the higher the demand. As an example, they point to the TWA-Ozark merger, after which TWA increased the number of direct routes out of St. Louis from 85 in June 1986 to 91 in June 1987, and increased the number of cities served by jets from 72 to 74. At the same time, other carriers serving St. Louis reduced the number of direct routes from 83 to 66 and the number of cities served by jets from 62 to 60. This evidence is consistent with the hypothesis that the merger increased the efficiency of the combined airline, but is not sufficient to show that welfare increased.

Two studies, Call and Keeler (1985) and Moore (1986), show that entry lowers prices.[41] Call and Keeler (1985) conclude, based on a statistical analysis of the first few years after deregulation, that fares fell on high-density routes, but that the fall was gradual and resulted from entry. They find that the entry of a major carrier into a new market reduces the lowest unrestricted fare by 23 percent and reduces revenues by 7.5 percent

---

[40] "Justice Department to Oversee Mergers in Airline Industry." *San Francisco Chronicle*, December 23, 1988, C4.

[41] Entry is especially likely to lower prices where there is significant market power. Bailey and Williams (1988) show that in certain local markets, one or a few airlines have virtual monopolies. Bailey, Graham, and Kaplan (1985) and Hurdle et al. (1988) conclude that not all city pairs are perfectly contestable (price is above marginal cost).

compared to the Standard Industry Fare Level (SIFL) regulated rates. They also calculate that a shift from monopoly to four equal-size firms would reduce the fare by 10.5 percent.

Moore (1986), using a statistical analysis, concludes that the CAB regulations led to pricing based on a fixed rate plus a per-mile cost. Just before deregulation, the CAB members felt that short-distance flights were underpriced relative to cost. Indeed, since deregulation, short-flight prices have increased more than for long flights. There is now increased variance in prices over routes, apparently reflecting market conditions and structure. For example, in 1983, though not in 1976, rates were lower if there were five or more carriers in a market than in markets with fewer firms. For long-haul flights of an average distance of 1955 miles, having five or more carriers lowers the price by nearly 30 percent. In large metropolitan markets, for a flight of 368 miles, fares are 41 percent lower with four or more carriers.

Kahn (1988) concludes that overall prices have fallen and that the industry is more competitive.[42] He roughly calculates that the gains represented savings of $11 billion to airline passengers in 1986 alone. He believes, however, that price discrimination has intensified: passengers on "thinner" routes are paying more relative to costs than those on frequently traveled routes.

Not only do fares differ across routes, but they are changed more frequently. Under regulation, there were relatively few rates, and they changed infrequently. Even in the early 1980s, the Airline Traffic Publishing Co., a cooperative venture owned by the airlines to process changes in ticket prices, considered 25,000 daily fare changes a large number. By 1988, 40,000 to 60,000 changes were not unusual, and in one week, nearly 600,000 were processed. Indeed, United alone files about 30,000 fare changes a day.[43]

Deregulation also led to greater efficiency, which helped lower prices. The regulated fares, SIFL, did not reflect true costs, at least in part because they changed too infrequently and hence resulted in a nonoptimal mix of services being consumed. Moreover, because airlines could pass on inefficient costs through higher rates, they did not minimize costs. Sickles, Good, and Johnson (1986) show that allocative distortions were large in 1970, but were essentially eliminated by 1981. Most of the reduction in allocative distortions, however, occurred towards the end of the regulatory period, as firms were allowed to raise prices by 10 percent above or lower them 70 percent below SIFL without approval, and greater entry was allowed.

Sickles, Good, and Johnson contend that the elimination of service to small communities led to more appropriate overall matching of equipment type and route density. They also find that the product mix (passengers versus cargo) was nonoptimal in some periods, such as the early 1970s. They find little evidence of overcapitalization or other factor-mix distortions, at least towards the end of regulation, though there was a substantial overuse of labor in the early 1970s.

A comparison of U.S. airlines to those in other countries also reveals a substantial increase in efficiency from deregulation (Caves et al. 1987). In the postregulation period, the rate of growth in productive efficiency for U.S. airlines was at least as high as before deregulation, whereas the rate of growth for non-U.S. airlines declined by nearly 40

---

[42] Many of his results are based on Meyer, Oster, and Strong (1987a, 1987b).

[43] Hamilton, Martha M. 1988. "Airline Pricing: Highly Complex, Hotly Competitive." *Washington Post,* November 20, H1, H16.

percent. Assuming the United States would have had the non-U.S. experience had deregulation not occurred, deregulation lowered U.S. airline unit costs by 10 percent by 1983, a saving of over $4 billion.

Despite the failure to expand airports, provide traffic-controller support at the level of the previous era, or to increase the number of Federal Aviation Administration (FAA) inspectors, the long-term trend in improvement in airline safety continued after deregulation.[44] During the 1972–78 period, there were 2.35 accidents per 100,000 flight hours, whereas from 1979–86, there were 1.73 per 100,000 hours (Weidenbaum 1987). Rose (1988), however, using a statistical study that controls for a number of factors, finds that lower profitability is correlated with higher accident and incident rates, particularly for smaller carriers. Thus, the safety record after deregulation may be more uneven across airlines as variability in profitability increases. Kanafani and Keeler's (1989) statistical analysis, however, shows no difference between the safety of new entrants and established carriers.

The long-term fall in prices lowered the profits of airlines. The Civil Aeronautics Board used to consider a 12 percent rate of return standard; however, the industry earned a 4.9 percent rate of return in 1986 and a 7.3 percent rate of return in 1987.[45]

To summarize, recent research shows seven major effects of airline deregulation. First, airline fares fell. Second, many of the initial entrants failed, and many firms merged, resulting in higher concentration rates in the industry. Third, airline markets are not perfectly contestable, so fares do vary with the number and relative size of actual competitors. Fourth, a greater variety of services are now offered, though average quality fell. Fifth, productivity, output, and other measures of efficiency increased. Sixth, although the safety record may be more uneven across firms, on average deregulation did not reduce safety. Seventh, profits of airlines fell. Thus, overall, in the first decade after deregulation, consumers benefited. Whether the trend towards mergers and greater concentration will continue and reduce these gains remains to be seen.

Ground Transportation: Trucking and Railroads

The Act to Regulate Commerce in 1887 created the Interstate Commerce Commission (ICC), an independent agency of the U.S. government. It was the first regulatory commission in the United States. Over time, it was given jurisdiction over freight-service transportation, now including railroads, trucking companies, bus lines, freight forwarders, water carriers, oil pipelines, transportation brokers, express agencies, telegraph, telephone, wireless, and cable companies.

The Transportation Act of 1920 gave the ICC the power to fix rates that would yield "a fair return upon the aggregate value of the railway property of the country." The ICC's price regulations led to more uniform pricing by railroads and essentially eliminated price wars. The ICC also has power to approve or block mergers. Indeed it was supposed to

---

[44] Although the number of FAA-certified airlines increased 50 percent since deregulation, the number of FAA inspectors has increased by only 2, according to the FAA (cited in Lapham, Lewis H., Michael Pollan, and Eric Etheridge. 1987. *The Harper's Index Book*. New York: Henry Holt and Company).

[45] Hamilton, Martha M. 1988. "Airline Pricing: Highly Complex, Hotly Competitive." *Washington Post*, November 20, H1, H16.

plan the consolidation of railroads into a small number of integrated systems. The Motor Carriers Act of 1935 gave the ICC control over pricing and entry into the bus and trucking industries. The licenses required to operate were valuable, indicating significant restraints on entry. The ICC certified general freight carriers could discuss and agree on rates, which were then presented to the ICC for approval (Moses and Savage 1987). As a result, firms competed only on quality. There was also substantial cross-subsidization. The Motor Carrier Act of 1980 (trucking) and the Staggers Act of 1980 (railroads) continued the movement towards deregulation of surface transport, which began in the late 1970s.

Trucking. Trucking deregulation led to entry, improved safety, greater efficiency, a drop in union drivers' wages, and lowered trucking rates. Keeler (forthcoming) finds that deregulating trucking allows efficient firms to expand, where before their routes were limited. As a result, efficient firms now expand to optimal size, taking advantage of economies of scale. The largest firms (those with over 5 percent of the market) increased their collective share of the market from 11.6 percent to 20.8 percent of the market from 1980 to 1984.

Keeler (forthcoming) calculates that deregulation reduced trucking rates from the start and that the effect grew stronger over time, presumably as entry occurred and firms became more efficient, so that rates were ultimately reduced by 22 percent from what they would have been with regulation. Boyer (1987), however, does not find that deregulation had a statistically significant effect on real trucking rates, but his data are more aggregated than Keeler's.

Boyer does show that deregulation had a statistically significant effect on how freight was shipped. In the first four years of deregulation, the for-hire (regulated) trucking industry's share rose 5.6 points, and the private (unregulated) carriers lost 7.1 points (Boyer, 1987, 412–14).

Rose (1987) shows that, before deregulation, union drivers captured up to 75 percent of total industry rents (profits in excess of the usual rate of return), but nonunion drivers did not capture a significant share of regulatory rents. After deregulation, there were substantial reductions in union wages. The union markup over nonunion wages fell from 50 percent to less than 30 percent, implying that union workers lost, in aggregate, between $950 million and $1.6 billion. The individual union driver's compensation fell by between 10–20 percent of what it would have been if the 50 percent wage differential had been maintained. Apparently nonunion drivers and truck drivers outside the regulated trucking industry were little affected. Between 1970 and 1980, real wages in trucking increased by 0.5 percent a year, whereas between 1980 and 1985, real wages fell by 3 percent per year (Moses and Savage 1987).

Safety improved under deregulation (Moses and Savage 1987). Adjusting for changes in the quality of goods carried, an accidents index fell substantially from 100 in 1978 to 69 in 1985. An index of auto fatalities in truck-related accidents per mile of automobile usage also fell by 21 percent from 1978 to 1985. These reductions occurred despite the higher accident rate of new firms. New firms in 1985 had 0.246 accidents per million miles, whereas firms established in 1980–81 had an accident rate of 0.167 in 1985.

Railroads. Deregulation of the railroads started with the Railroad Revitalization and Regulatory Reform Act of 1976 (4-R Act), which called for more competition and cost-based rate setting, which was at least partially reflected in the way that the ICC behaved. The Staggers Rail Act of 1980 further deregulated the industry, giving firms substantial freedom to set rates. In combination with administrative actions by the ICC, this legislation gives railroads virtually unlimited rights to lower rates, and railroads that are not "market dominant" can raise them. In practice, the ICC only exercises rate-setting powers over certain bulk commodities where railroads are not subject to truck competition. Trucking competition is taken as evidence that railroads are not dominant in a market (Boyer 1987). Although Boyer (1987) does not find a statistically significant effect on overall rail rates, Lee, Baumel, and Harris (1987) show a statistically significant decrease in the rate per ton-mile for Class I (large) railroads of 18 percent during the 4-R years and 23 percent in the first four years after the Staggers Act.

Because more than one-third of total railroad costs are fixed (including tracks, right-of-ways, and locomotive power), railroad lines are often natural monopolies (Willig and Baumol 1987, 29). If during regulation prices had been set equal to marginal costs, railroads would have suffered losses. Willig and Baumol (1987, 30-31) argue that, prior to deregulating, the ICC "undermined competition through protectionist rules, froze rail business into inefficient and out-dated patterns, interfered with and delayed private decisions, and, ironically, virtually precluded the financial viability of railroads. . . . The commission protected rival transport modes from price competition by setting inflated floors below which individual rates were not permitted to fall. . . . The railroads were generally unable to abandon services—even services with such limited demand that there was no prospect of profitable operation."

Thus, many of the gains from deregulation are likely to come from letting more efficient firms expand, by allowing firms to abandon unused track, and by eliminating cross-subsidization. The studies to date typically find that deregulation had modest to large positive efficiency effects. Boyer (1987) calculates gains of at most $93 million, whereas Barnekov and Kleit (1988) estimate that deregulation created billions of dollars worth of efficiency gains. Stansell and Hollas (1988) also find a significant drop in industry costs in the postregulation period. Lee, Baumel, and Harris (1987) find that operating expenses per ton-mile fell by 17 percent during the 4-R years and 29 percent during the first four years of the Staggers Act. McFarland (1989) concludes that the annual rate of growth in labor productivity increased by about 0.9 percent annually after deregulation. Deregulation also had dramatic effects on the mode of transit used. Deregulation statistically significantly decreased rail's share (compared to that of motor vehicles) by 5.2 points during the first four years of deregulation (Boyer 1987).

The chief fear about deregulating railroads was that monopoly prices would be charged, at least in some markets. Although the 1980 Staggers Rail Act allows higher rates in less competitive markets as long as they are "reasonable," some carriers may be charging monopolistic rates. For example, an Interior Department study finds that rates charged utility buyers by the one railroad serving much of the Wyoming and Montana coalfields were "monopolistic"—a charge denied by the railroad. Yet when a competitor ran a spur line to one section, rates there fell by 20 percent.[46]

One test of whether railroads earn unusual profits is to compare the ratio of a railroad's

---

[46] Welles, Chris, with Seth Payne, France Seghers, and Tom Ichniowksi. 1986. "Is Deregulation Working?" *Business Week*, December 22, 50–55.

market value to the replacement cost of its assets, a measure called *Tobin's q* (see Chapter 12), to that of other nonfinancial firms (McFarland 1987). This test finds that railroads do not earn supracompetitive profits, and that their Tobin's *q* is lower than for other nonfinancial firms.

In summary, deregulation has changed the trucking and railroad industries. Deregulation has eliminated many of the harms resulting from previous regulation and has resulted in more efficient and lower-price industries.

■ SUMMARY

How many economists does it take to screw in a light bulb?
Economist: *None, the market will do it.*
Consumer Advocate: *None, the regulators will do it.*

Optimal regulation, if feasible, can eliminate market inefficiencies and increase welfare. Nonetheless, due to problems of limited information, uncertainty, unsustainability, human frailties, and institutional weakness, regulators often badly apply regulations or use regulations that create harmful distortions in order to help special interest groups. It is difficult to find an example of optimal regulation, though there are many examples of markets in which nonoptimal regulations help.

Particularly disturbing are regulations that convert efficient, competitive markets into inefficient monopolistic markets. In some examples, the regulations appear designed to redistribute wealth from consumers to special interest groups that have successfully pressured or captured legislators or regulators. In some of these examples, such as agriculture, the social losses are enormous.

The recent trend toward deregulation is an attempt to remove particularly harmful regulations and "let markets work." In recent years, regulators and legislators who recognized these harms have improved or eliminated regulations in several markets. The subsequent deregulation of these industries has generally improved efficiency. As a result, in many, if not most, of these deregulated markets, cross-subsidization ended, the rate of entry increased, concentration fell in major markets and rose in minor ones, efficiency in production and allocation increased, safety levels were relatively unchanged, and overall prices fell while output increased.

■ Key Terms

Averch-Johnson effect
capture theory
franchise bidding
interest-group theory
natural monopoly

price controls
price supports
Ramsey pricing
rate-of-return regulation

regulatory lag
rent seeking
subadditive, subadditivity
sustainable

■ Discussion Questions

1. What are the major arguments for and against regulations?
2. What have been the major effects of deregulation in the last decade?
3. For which market inefficiencies would franchise bidding be likely to be superior to regulation? For which markets are regulations likely to be better?

4. Suggest a method to prevent regulators from being captured by special interest groups. Is it practical?
5. How would you identify natural monopolies? What evidence might you collect to determine if the U.S. Postal Service or your local utilities are natural monopolies?

■ Problems

1. In Figure 23.3, prove that welfare, defined as consumer surplus plus profits, is higher at $p = p^* =$ marginal cost than at $p = p_a =$ average cost, even though it is necessary to subsidize the monopolist. *Hint:* At p_a, profits are zero, so that $(p_a - p^*)Q^* =$ fixed costs = Area A + Area B, because $p^* =$ average variable costs. You should show that welfare increases by a triangular area in the figure.
2. In a figure like 23.1 or 23.2, show the effect of regulating a monopolist's price at a level strictly between p_m and p_c.
3. What is the effect of an acreage quota on the supply curve shown in Figure 23.7?
4. Which of the following two agricultural policies will cost the government (taxpayers) more? (a) A program with price supported at p_s ($> p_c$, the competitive price) and with a quota equal to the competitive output level, Q_c. (b) A target-price program under which farmers sell Q_c units at the competitive price, p_c, and the government gives them a subsidy equal to $(p_s - p_c)Q_c$. (*Note:* the elasticity of demand for most agricultural goods is inelastic.)
5. Suggest an alternative agricultural policy that eliminates the inefficiencies in price-support/quota programs and yet transfers an equivalent amount of income to farmers. Why is your program better?
6. Several years ago, MCI started competing with Bell

Telephone by offering lower rates on long-distance calls. Many people thought that Bell's long-distance service was a natural monopoly. Nonetheless, MCI may have been able to cover its costs. Is that possible? Should MCI's entry have been encouraged or prohibited by regulators? Why or why not? (When MCI started, it only provided service to a limited number of areas. Although MCI's pricing was not constrained, Bell's rates were regulated.)

7. Under rate-of-return regulation, a firm that earns too high a rate of return must give some of it back to ratepayers, but a firm that fails to earn the target rate of return bears the shortfall itself. Explain how this affects a firm's incentive to innovate. Is rate-of-return regulation more or less appropriate for an industry undergoing technological change?

8. Compute an example of the effects of rate-of-return regulation (similar to Table 23.3) where the production function is Leontief: $Q = \min (L,K)$ and labor and capital cost the same. (This production function implies that efficient production involves equal amounts of labor and capital. It takes 1 unit of each to produce 1 unit of output, and 2 units of each to produce 2 units of output.) What effect does rate-of-return regulation have on output, profits, consumer surplus, and capital/labor ratio? *Note:* This question can be answered without using mathematical analysis or calculating a table.

Answers to odd-numbered problems are given at the back of the book.

■ Recommended Readings

This chapter has only scratched the surface of the economics of regulation. Two recent, excellent textbooks are Asch and Seneca (1985) and Spulber (1989). For an alternative, case approach, see Weiss and Strickland (1982). Schmalensee (1979) and Sharkey (1982) have technical and nontechnical sections on natural monopoly. Waterson (1987) surveys the recent developments in natural monopoly theory. A good, nontechnical, empirical overview is MacAvoy (1979). Caves and Roberts (1975), Phillips (1975), Weiss and Klass (1981) and Fromm (1981) are interesting collections of case studies. Ontario Economic Council (1978) has Canadian case studies. For the theory of contestable markets, see Baumol, Panzar, and Willig (1982).

■ References

Archibald, G. C. 1964. "Profit-Maximizing and Non-Price Competition." *Economica* 31:13–22.

Asch, Peter, and Rosalind Seneca. 1985. *Government and the Marketplace*. New York: The Dryden Press.

Averch, Harvey, and Leland L. Johnson. 1962. "Behavior of the Firm Under Regulatory Constraint." *American Economic Review* 52:1052–69.

Bailey, Elizabeth E. 1973. *Economic Theory of Regulatory Constraint*. Lexington, Mass. D. C. Heath.

Bailey, Elizabeth E., and John C. Panzar. 1981. "The Contestability of Airline Markets During the Transition to Deregulation." *Law and Contemporary Problems* 44:125–46.

Bailey, Elizabeth E.; David R. Graham; and Daniel P. Kaplan. 1985. *Deregulating the Airlines*. Cambridge: The MIT Press.

Bailey, Elizabeth E., and Jeffrey R. Williams. 1988. "Sources of Economic Rent in the Deregulated Airline Industry." *Journal of Law and Economics* 31:173–202.

Bailey, Elizabeth E., and Roger D. Coleman. 1971. "The Effect of Lagged Regulation in an Averch-Johnson Model." *The Bell Journal of Economics* 2:278–92.

Barnekov, Christopher C., and Andrew N. Kleit. 1988. "The Costs of Railroad Regulation: A Further Analysis." Bureau of Economics Working Paper no. 164. Washington, D.C.: Federal Trade Commission.

Baron, David P., and Robert A. Taggart, Jr. 1977. "A Model of Regulation Under Uncertainty and a Test of Regulatory Bias." *The Bell Journal of Economics* 8:151–67.

Baron, David P., and Roger B. Myerson. 1982. "Regulating a Monopolist with Unknown Costs." *Econometrica* 50:911–30.

Baseman, Kenneth C. 1981. "Open Entry and Cross-Subsidization in Regulated Markets," in Gary Fromm, ed., *Studies in Public Regulation*. Cambridge: The MIT Press.

Baumol, William J. 1967. "Reasonable Rules for Rate Regulation: Plausible Policies for an Imperfect World," in Almarin Phillips and Oliver E. Williamson, eds., *Prices: Issues in Theory, Practice, and Public Policy*. Philadelphia: University of Pennsylvania Press.

———. 1981. "Comments," in Gary Fromm, ed., *Studies in Public Regulation*. Cambridge: The MIT Press, 361–64.

Baumol, William J., and David F. Bradford. 1970. "Optimal Departures from Marginal Cost Pricing." *American Economic Review* 60:265–83.

Baumol, William J., and Alvin K. Klevorick. 1970. "Input Choices and Rate-of-Return Regulation: An Overview of the Discussion." *The Bell Journal of Economics* 1:162–90.

Baumol, William J.; Elizabeth E. Bailey; and Robert D. Willig. 1977. "Weak Invisible-Hand Theorems on the Sustainability of Prices in a Multiproduct Monopoly." *American Economic Review* 67:350–65.

Baumol, William J.; John C. Panzar; and Robert D. Willig. 1982. *Contestable Markets and the Theory of Industrial Structure*. New York: Harcourt Brace Jovanovich.

Becker, Gary S. 1983. "A Theory of Competition Among Pressure Groups for Political Influence." *Quarterly Journal of Economics* 98:371–400.

Boyer, Kenneth D. 1987. "The Costs of Price Regulation: Lessons from Railroad Deregulation." *The Rand Journal of Economics* 18:408–16.

Braeutigam, Ronald R. 1984. "Socially Optimal Pricing with Rivalry and Economies of Scale." *The Rand Journal of Economics* 15:127–34.

Braeutigam, Ronald R., and James P. Quirk. 1984. "Demand Uncertainty and the Regulated Firm." *International Economic Review* 25:45–60.

Breyer, Stephen. 1982. *Regulation and Its Reform*. Cambridge, Mass: Harvard University Press.

Brock, William A., and José A. Sheinkman. 1983. "Free Entry and the Sustainability of Natural Monopoly: Bertrand Revisited by Cournot," in David S. Evans, ed., *Breaking Up Bell*. New York: Elsevier Science Publishing.

Brueckner, Jan K., and Pablo T. Spiller. 1988. "Competition and Mergers in Airline Networks." Bureau of Economic and Business Research, Working Paper no. 1523, Urbana-Champaign-Ill.: University of Illinois.

Call, Gregory D., and Theodore E. Keeler. 1985. "Airline Deregulation, Fares, and Market Behavior: Some Empirical Evidence," in Andrew F. Daughety, ed., *Analytical Studies in Transport Economics*. New York: Cambridge University Press.

Caves, Richard E., and Marc J. Roberts. 1975. *Regulating the Product: Quality and Variety*. Cambridge, Mass. Ballinger.

Caves, Douglas W.; Laurits R. Christensen; Michael W. Tretheway; and Robert J. Windle. 1987. "An Assessment of the Efficiency Effects of U.S. Airline Deregulation via an International Comparison," in Elizabeth E. Bailey, ed., *Public Regulation: New Perspectives on Institutions and Policies*. Cambridge: The MIT Press.

Chadwick, E. 1859. "Results of Different Principles of Legislation and Administration in Europe; of Competition for the Field, as Compared with Competition within the Field, of Service." *Journal of the Royal Statistical Society*. Series A, 22:381–20.

Coase, Ronald H. 1946. "The Marginal Cost Controversy." *Economica* 14:169-82.

Congressional Budget Office. 1988. *Policies for the Deregulated Airline Industry*. Washington, D.C.: U.S. Government Printing Office.

Courville, Leon. 1974. "Regulation and Efficiency in the Electric Utility Industry." *The Bell Journal of Economics* 5:53–74.

Crew, Michael A., and Paul R. Kleindorfer. 1978. "Reliability and Public Utility Pricing." *American Economic Review* 68:263–53.

DeAlessi, Louis. 1974. "An Economic Analysis of Government Ownership and Regulation: Theory and Evidence from the Electric Power Industry." *Public Choice* 19:1-42.

Dechert, W. Davis. 1984. "Has the Averch-Johnson Effect been Theoretically Justified?" *Journal of Economic Dynamics and Control* 8:1–17.

Demsetz, Harold. 1968. "Why Regulate Utilities?" *Journal of Law and Economics* 11:55–65.

Economic Report of the President. 1987. Washington, D.C.: U.S. Government Printing Office, Ch. 5.

Eckert, Ross D. 1973. "On the Incentives of Regulators: The Case of Taxicabs." *Public Choice* 14:83–100.

———. 1981. "The Life Cycle of Regulatory Commissioners." *Journal of Law and Economics* 24:113–20.

Epple, Dennis. 1987. "Rent Control with Reputation: Theory and Evidence." Working Paper, Graduate School of Industrial Administration. Pittsburgh: Carnegie-Mellon University.

Evans, David S., and James J. Heckman. 1982a. "Natural Monopoly," in David S. Evans, ed., *Breaking Up Bell*. New York: Elsevier Science Publishing.

———. 1982b."Multiproduct Cost-Function Estimates and Natural Monopoly Tests for the Bell System," in David S. Evans, ed., *Breaking Up Bell*. New York: Elsevier Science Publishing.

Faulhaber, Gerald R. 1975. "Cross-Subsidization: Pricing in Public Enterprises." *American Economic Review* 65:966–77.

Feldstein, Martin. 1972a. "Distributional Equity and the Optimal Structure of Public Prices." *American Economic Review* 62:32–36.

———. 1972b. "Equity and Efficiency in Public Pricing." *Quarterly Journal of Economics* 86:175–87.

Fitzpatrick, Mary E. 1987. "A Test of Passive Regulation Using an Endogenous Switching Regression." Economic Analysis Group Discussion Paper 87-5. Washington, D.C.: Antitrust Division, U.S. Department of Justice.

Fromm, Gary. 1981. *Studies in Public Regulation*. Cambridge: The MIT Press.

Fuss, Melvyn A., and Leonard Waverman. 1981. "Regulation and the Multiproduct Firm: The Case of Telecommunications in Canada," in Gary Fromm, ed., *Studies in Public Regulation*. Cambridge: The MIT Press.

Gallick, Edward C., and David E. Sisk. 1984. "Specialized Assets and Taxi Regulation: An Inquiry into the Possible Efficiency Motivation of Regulation." Bureau of Economics Working Paper no. 119. Washington, D.C.: Federal Trade Commission.

Gerwig, Robert W. 1962. "Natural Gas Production: A Study of Costs of Regulation." *Journal of Law and Economics* 5:69–92.

Gilbert, Richard J., and David M. Newbery. 1988. "Regulation Games." Department of Economics Working Paper no. 8879. Berkeley: University of California, Berkeley.

Hausman, William J., and John L. Neufeld. 1984. "Time-of-Day Pricing in the U.S. Electric Power Industry at the Turn of the Century." *The Rand Journal of Economics* 15:116–26.

Hurdle, Gloria J.; Richard L. Johnson; Andrew S. Joskow; Gregory J. Werden; and Michael A. Williams. 1988. "Concentration, Potential Entry, and Performance in the Airline Industry." Economic Analysis Group Discussion Paper. Washington, D.C.: Antitrust Division, U.S. Department of Justice.

Johnson, D. Gale. 1973. *Farm commodity programs*. Washington, D.C.: American Enterprise Institute.

Joskow, Paul L. 1973. "Pricing Decisions of Regulated Firms: A Behavioral Approach." *The Bell Journal of Economics* 4:118–40.

———. 1974. "Inflation and Environmental Concern: Structural Change in the Process of Public Utility Price Regulation." *Journal of Law and Economics* 17:291–328.

Joskow, Paul L., and Roger C. Noll. 1981. "Regulation in Theory and Practice: An Overview," in Gary Fromm, ed., *Studies in Public Regulation*. Cambridge: The MIT Press.

Kahn, Alfred E. 1970. *The Economics of Regulation*. vol. 1. New York: John Wiley and Sons.

———. 1975. *The Economics of Regulation*. vol. 2. New York: John Wiley and Sons.

———. 1988. "Surprises of Airline Deregulation." *American Economic Review* 78:316–21.

Kanafani, A., and Theodore E. Keeler. 1989. "New Entrants and Safety: Some Statistical Evidence on the Effects of Airline Deregulation," in Leon N. Moses and Ian Savage, eds., *Safety Performance Under Deregulation*. Oxford: Oxford University Press.

Keeler, Theodore E. Forthcoming. "Deregulation and Scale Economies in the U.S. Trucking Industry: An Econometric Extension of the Survivor Principle." *Journal of Law and Economics*.

Kitch, Edmund W.; Marc Isaacson; and Daniel Kaspar. 1971. "The Regulation of Taxicabs in Chicago." *Journal of Law and Economics* 14:285–350.

Klevorick, Alvin K. 1971. "The 'Optimal' Fair Rate of Return." *The Bell Journal of Economics* 2:122–53.

Lee, Dwight R. 1978. "Price Controls, Binding Constraints, and Intertemporal Economic Decision Making." *Journal of Political Economy* 86:293–301.

Lee, Tenpao; C. Phillip Baumel; and Patricia Harris. 1987. "Market Structure, Conduct, and Performance of the Class I Railroad Industry, 1971–1984." *Transportation Journal* 26:54–66.

MacAvoy, Paul W. 1979. *The Regulated Industries and the Economy*. New York: W.W. Norton.

McFarland, Henry. 1987. "Did Railroad Deregulation Lead to Monopoly Pricing? An Application of Q." *Journal of Business* 60:385–400.

———. 1989. "The Effect of U.S. Railroad Deregulation on Shippers, Labor, and Capital." Economic Analysis Group Discussion Paper EAG 89-4. Washington, D.C.: Antitrust Division. U.S. Department of Justice.

McKay, D. J. 1977. "Two Essays on the Economics of Electricity Supply." Ph.D. diss. Pasadena, Calif.: California Institute of Technology.

Meyer, John R.; Clinton J. Oster, Jr.; and John S. Strong. 1987a. "Airline Financial Performance Since Deregulation," in John R. Meyer and Clinton V. Oster, Jr. et al., eds., *Deregulation and the Future of Intercity Passenger Travel*. Cambridge: The MIT Press.

———. 1987b. "The Effect on Travelers: Fares and Service," in John R. Meyer and Clinton V. Oster, Jr. et al. eds., *Deregulation and the Future of Intercity Passenger Travel*. Cambridge: The MIT Press.

Moore, Thomas Gale. 1986. "U.S. Airline Deregulation: Its Effect on Passengers, Capital, and Labor." *Journal of Law and Economics* 29:1–28.

Moses, Leon N., and Ian Savage. 1987. "Transportation Deregulation and Safety: Summary Report on a Conference." *Transportation Deregulation and Safety*. Evanston, Ill.: Northwestern University Transportation Center.

Olsen, Edgar O. 1972. "An Econometric Analysis of Rent Control." *Journal of Political Economy*. 80:1081–1100.

Ontario Economic Council. 1978. *Government Regulation:Issues and Alternatives*. Toronto: Ontario Economic Council.

Organization for Economic Cooperation and Development. 1985. *Competition Policy and the Professions*. Paris: OECD.

Oster, Sharon M., and John M. Quigley. 1977. "Regulatory Barriers to the Diffusion of Innovation: Some Evidence from Building Codes." *The Bell Journal of Economics* 8:361–77.

Panzar, John C. 1979. "Equilibrium and Welfare in Unregulated Airline Markets." *American Economic Review* 69:92–95.

———. 1981. "Comments," in Gary Fromm, ed., *Studies in Public Regulation*. Cambridge: The MIT Press, 365–69.

Panzar, John C., and Robert D. Willig. 1977. "Free entry

and the Sustainability of Natural Monopoly." *The Bell Journal of Economics* 8:1–22.

Pashigian, B. Peter. 1976. "Consequences and Causes of Public Ownership of Urban Transit Facilities." *Journal of Political Economy* 84:1239–60.

Peltzman, Sam. 1971. "Pricing in Public Enterprises: Electric Utilities in the United States." *Journal of Law and Economics* 14:109–48.

———. 1973. "An Evaluation of Consumer Protection Legislation: The 1962 Drug Amendments." *Journal of Political Economy* 81:1049–91.

———. 1976. "Toward a More General Theory of Regulation." *Journal of Law and Economics* 19:211–40.

Petersen, H. Craig. 1975. "An Empirical Test of Regulatory Effects." *The Bell Journal of Economics* 6: 111–26.

Phillips, Almarin, ed. 1975. *Promoting Competition in Regulated Markets*. Washington, D.C.: The Brookings Institution.

Pittman, Russell. 1988. "Rent-Seeking and Market Structure: Comment." *Public Choice* 58:173-85.

Posner, Richard. 1971. "Taxation by Regulation." *The Bell Journal of Economics* 2:22–50.

———. 1972. "The Appropriate Scope of Regulation in the Cable Television Industry." *The Bell Journal of Economics* 3:98–129.

———. 1974. "Theories of Economic Regulation." *The Bell Journal of Economics* 5:335–58.

Ramsey, Frank P. 1927. "A Contribution to the Theory of Taxation." *Economic Journal* 37:47–61.

Riordan, Michael H. 1984. "On Delegating Price Authority to a Regulated Firm." *The Rand Journal of Economics* 15:108–15.

Rose, Nancy L. 1987. "Labor Rent Sharing and Regulation: Evidence from the Trucking Industry." *Journal of Political Economy* 95:1146–78.

———. 1988. "Profitability and Product Quality: Financial Indicators and Airline Safety Performance." Sloan School of Management Working Paper. Cambridge: Massachusetts Institute of Technology.

Ross, Thomas W. 1984. "Uncovering Regulators' Social Welfare Weights." *Rand Journal* 15:152–55.

Schmalensee, Richard. 1977. "Comparative Static Properties of Regulated Airline Oligopolies." *The Bell Journal of Economics* 8:565–76.

———. 1979. *The Control of Natural Monopolies*. Lexington, Mass. Lexington Books.

Schwert, G. William. 1981. "Using Financial Data to Measure Effects of Regulation." *Journal of Law and Economics* 24:121–58.

Sharkey, William W. 1982. *The Theory of Natural Monopoly*. New York: Cambridge University Press.

Sheshinski, Eytan. 1971. "Welfare Aspects of a Regulatory Constraint: Note." *American Economic Review* 61: 175–78.

Sickles, Robin C., David Good, and Richard L. Johnson. 1986. "Allocative Distortions and the Regulatory Transition of the U.S. Airline Industry." *Journal of Econometrics* 33:143–63.

Smithson Charles W. 1978. "The Degree of Regulation and the Monopoly Firm: Further Empirical Evidence." *Southern Economic Journal* 44:568–80.

Spann, Robert M. 1974. "Rate-of-Return Regulation and Efficiency in Production: An Empirical Test of the Averch-Johnson Thesis." *The Bell Journal of Economics* 5:38–52.

Spence, A. Michael. 1975. "Monopoly, Quality, and Regulation." *The Bell Journal of Economics* 6:407–14.

Spiller, Pablo T. 1983. "The Differential Impact of Airline Regulation on Individual Firms and Markets: An Empirical Analysis." *Journal of Law and Economics* 26:655-89.

———. 1988. "Politicians, Interest Groups, and Regulators: A Multiple-Principals Agency Theory of Regulation (or 'Let Them be Bribed')." Bureau of Economic and Business Research Faculty Working Paper no. 1436. Urbana-Champaign: University of Illinois.

Spulber, Daniel F. 1989. Regulation and Markets. Cambridge, Mass.: MIT Press.

Stansell, Stanely R., and Daniel R. Hollas. 1988. "An Examination of the Economic Efficiency of Class I Railroads: A Profit-Function Analysis." *Review of Industrial Organization* 3:93–117.

Stevens, Barbara J. 1978. "Scale, Market Structure, and the Cost of Refuse Collection." *Review of Economics and Statistics* 60:438–48.

Stigler, George J. 1968. "Price and Non-Price Competition." *Journal of Political Economy* 76:149–54.

———. 1971. "The Theory of Economic Regulation." *The Bell Journal of Economics* 2:3–21.

Stigler, George J., and Claire Friedland. 1962. "What Can Regulators Regulate? The Case of Electricity." *Journal of Law and Economics* 5:1–16.

Takayama, Akira. 1969. "Behavior of the Firm Under Regulatory Constraint." *American Economic Review* 59:255-60.

Telser, Lester. 1969. "On the Regulation of Industry: A Note." *Journal of Political Economy* 77:937–52.

Telson, Michael L. 1975. "The Economics of Alternative

Levels of Reliability for Electric Power Generation Systems." *The Bell Journal of Economics* 6:679–94.

Waterson, Michael. 1987. "Recent Developments in the Theory of Natural Monopoly." *Journal of Economic Surveys* 1:59–80.

Weidenbaum, Murray. 1987. *The Benefits of Deregulation*. Contemporary Issues Series, no. 25. Center for the Study of American Business. St. Louis: Washington University.

Weiss, Leonard W. 1981a. "Introduction: The Regulatory Reform Movement," in Leonard W. Weiss and Michael W. Klass, eds., *Case Studies in Regulation: Revolution and Reform*. Boston: Little, Brown.

———. 1981b. "State Regulation of Public Utilities and Marginal-cost Pricing," in Leonard W. Weiss and Michael W. Klass, eds., *Case Studies in Regulation: Revolution and Reform*. Boston: Little, Brown.

Weiss, Leonard W., and Michael W. Klass, eds., 1981. *Case Studies in Regulation: Revolution and Reform*. Boston: Little, Brown.

Weiss, Leonard W., and Allyn D. Strickland. 1982. *Regulation: A Case Approach*. New York: McGraw-Hill.

Wendel, Jeanne. 1976. "Firm-Regulator Interaction with Respect to Firm Cost-Reduction Activities." *The Bell Journal of Economics* 7:631–40.

White, Lawrence J. 1972. "Quality Variation When Prices are Regulated." *The Bell Journal of Economics* 3: 425–36.

———. 1988. "Litan's *What Should Banks Do?*: A Review Essay." *The Rand Journal of Economics* 19:305–15.

Williamson, Oliver E. 1967. "The Economics of Defense Contracting: Incentives and Performance," in R. N. McKean, ed., *Issues in Defense Economics*. New York: Columbia University Press.

———. 1971. "Administrative Controls and Regulatory Behavior," in H. M. Trebling, ed., *Essays on Public Utility Pricing and Regulation*. Institute of Public Utilities. East Lansing Mich.: Michigan State University.

———. 1975. *Markets and Hierarchies: Analysis and Antitrust Implications*. New York: The Free Press.

———. 1976. "Franchise Bidding for Natural Monopolies—In General and with Respect to CATV." *The Bell Journal of Economics* 7:73–104.

———. 1985. *The Economic Institutions of Capitalism*. New York: The Free Press.

Willig, Robert D., and William J. Baumol. 1987. "Railroad Deregulation: Using Competition as a Guide." *Regulation* 11:28-35.

Zajac, E. E. 1970. "A Geometric Treatment of Averch-Johnson's Behavior of the Firm Model." *American Economic Review* 60:117–25.

RATE-OF-RETURN REGULATION

The Averch-Johnson effect of overcapitalization under rate of return (ROR) regulation can be shown using a mathematical model. This presentation follows Takayama (1969) closely. Suppose a monopolist produces output using labor, L, and capital, K, according to the following production function:

$$Q = f(L,K). \qquad (23\text{A}.1)$$

Its profits are

$$\pi = p(Q)Q - wL - uK = R(L,K) - wL - uK, \qquad (23\text{A}.2)$$

where $p(Q)$ is the inverse demand curve, w is the wage rate, u is the user cost of capital, and $R(L,K)$ is the revenue function:

$$R(L,K) = p(Q)Q = p(f(L,K))f(L,K).$$

Suppose the board decides the fair rate of return is v, so that, using Equation 23A.2,

$$\frac{\pi}{p_k K}; \frac{R(L,K) - wL - uK}{p_k K} \leqq v, \qquad (23\text{A}.3)$$

We can rewrite this constraint as

$$\frac{R(L,K) - wL}{p_k K} \leqq v + u = s. \qquad (23\text{A}.4)$$

That is, this type of regulation requires that revenues left over after covering labor expenses per unit of capital cannot exceed s, where s is the user cost of capital per dollar of capital stock plus the fair rate of return. For simplicity, we now assume $p_k = 1$. If s is less than u ($v < 0$), then the firm will not produce. We assume in the following that $v > 0$, so that $s > u$.[1]

---

[1] It is not necessary for v to be positive. If $v = 0$, $\pi = 0$, and the firm covers costs because the user cost already incorporates a normal rate of return to capital. If $v = 0$, this solution resembles that of Ramsey pricing in which price equals average cost.

The regulated firm's objective is to maximize profits, Equation 23A.2, subject to the rate-of-return restriction implied by Equation 23A.4. The firm's optimal behavior is determined by finding the saddle point of the following Lagrangian:

$$R(L,K) - wL - uK - \lambda [R(L,K) - wL - sK], \tag{23A.5}$$

where λ is the Lagrangian multiplier, and the term in parentheses is obtained by multiplying Equation 23A.4 through by K and rearranging terms.

If the L and K at the saddlepoint of 23A.5 are positive, and the constraint binds, then the following conditions,[2]

$$R_L = w, \tag{23A.6}$$

$$R_K = u - \left(\frac{s - u}{1 - \lambda}\right) \lambda, \tag{23A.7}$$

$$R - wL - sK = 0, \tag{23A.8}$$

$$\lambda > 0, \tag{23A.9}$$

determine the optimal values of L, K, and λ. Equation 23A.6 says that the value of the marginal product of labor equals the wage. Equation 23A.7 equates the value of the marginal product of capital to the user cost of capital less an adjustment factor that depends on the fair rate of return ($v = s - u$) and the Lagrangian multiplier. Equation 23A.8 is the rewritten constraint, Equation 23A.4.

If the constraint does not bind ($\lambda = 0$), Equations 23A.6 and 23A.7 are the usual profit-maximizing equations of the unregulated monopolist:

$$R_L = w \tag{23A.6'}$$

$$R_K = u. \tag{23A.7'}$$

That is, the value of the marginal product of labor equals the wage, and the value of the marginal product of capital equals the user cost of capital. The unconstrained ROR, then is (where the subscript 0 indicates unconstrained)

$$u_0 = \frac{R_0 - wL_0}{K_0}. \tag{23A.10}$$

---

[2] See Takayama (1969) for the full set of conditions where L or K may be zero, and the constraint may be inactive ($\lambda = 0$).

Where the constraint binds, $\lambda > 0$. From Equation 23A.7, we obtain an expression for λ (assuming $R_K \neq s$)[3]:

$$\lambda = \frac{R_K - u}{R_K - s}. \tag{23A.11}$$

So long as R_K is a continuous function of L and K, λ is a continuous function of s. Differentiating Equation 23A.8 with respect to s, we obtain

$$\frac{dL}{ds} (R_L - w) + \frac{dK}{ds} (R_K - s) = K. \tag{23A.12}$$

Evaluating at $s = u_0$ (the unconstrained, profit-maximizing rate of return) and substituting using Equations 23A.6 and 23A.7 this equation may be rewritten as:

$$\frac{dK}{ds} = \frac{-K_0}{u_0 - u} < 0. \tag{23A.13}$$

Thus, since $u_0 > u$, introducing an active fair-rate-of-return constraint (that is, lowering s from u_0) must increase capital: the Averch-Johnson effect. By similar reasoning, so long as $R_{LL} < 0$ and $R_{LK} > 0$, then $dL/ds < 0$.

---

[3] If $R_K - s = 0$, Equation 23A.7 implies that $(1 - \lambda)s = u - \lambda s$ or $s = u$, but we have already assumed that $s > u$, so $R_K - s \neq 0$.

Answers to Odd-Numbered Problems

I was gratified to be able to answer promptly. I said I don't know.

Mark Twain

Chapter 2

1. Although some monitoring problems increase with size, large firms exist because some benefits also increase with size, and other monitoring problems fall as size increases. For example, the average cost of monitoring quality may fall with size if the firm can obtain reliable results by checking a small percentage of a large output.

3. Transaction costs are likely to be relatively high in (a), (b), and (c). In these three cases, there is likely to be only one firm.

5. The president is likely to make decision (a) because its consequences would be hard to reverse.

Chapter 3

1. No. Even if all costs are fixed, marginal cost need not be zero. For example, if a firm is operating at full capacity and is unable to produce more output, its marginal costs are effectively infinitely large (at no finite cost can an extra unit of output be produced).

3. The marginal cost of cars is 70. Producing 100 cars and 200 trucks in the same plant costs $33,000 ($10,000 + 70 \times 100 + 80 \times 200$). Producing them in two separate plants costs $17,000 for cars and $26,000 for trucks. Thus the savings from jointly producing them is $10,000 (the extra fixed cost). The measure of scope economies is $10,000/33,000$ or about 0.3.

5. If all plants are in the same area, they face similar costs. If the industry is in equilibrium, then a wide range of plant sizes indicates that the AC curve has a flat section over a wide range of output. If plants are located in different countries, they probably face different costs. All one can conclude in this case is that the efficient-scale plant may vary considerably depending on cost conditions.

Chapter 4

1. No, a tax of $1 per unit of output raises the AC and MC curves of the firm by the same amount. As a result, the output at which the AC curve reaches its minimum is unchanged by the tax. Where all competitive firms are identical and there are an unlimited number of firms ready to produce, then each firm operates at the minimum of its AC curve in the long run.

3. (a) The supply curve is horizontal at $p = \$10$. The supply and demand curves intersect at $p = \$10$, $Q = 990$.

   (b) If the one firm with a fixed capacity of 10 enters, that firm's entry leaves unchanged the supply curve beyond 10 units. Supply and demand intersect at the same p and Q as in (a).

   (c) Positive economic profits for some firms are not inconsistent with long-run competitive equilibrium. The new firm in (b) earns a profit of $10.

(d) The marginal cost of the last unit supplied is $10. If demand expands or contracts, it is the firms whose marginal costs are $10 that vary their output.

(e) The less efficient firms earn 0.

(f) Yes. Otherwise additional entry or exit would occur.

5. When there are no shutdown costs, the AC curve coincides with the AVC curve, and the shutdown point becomes the minimum point of the AC curve.

Chapter 5

1. The monopolist's profits equal $(p - 4)(10 - p)$. The p that maximizes profits equals $7. If $p = 7$, $Q = 3$. Since $dQ/dp = -1$, the elasticity, $\dfrac{dQ}{dp}\dfrac{p}{Q}$, is $-7/3$.

3. Since $dQ/dp = (-5/p^2)$ and $Q = 5/p$, the elasticity equals $(dQ/dp)(p/Q)$ or $(-5/p^2)[p/(5/p)] = -1$. Total revenue equals pQ which always equals 5. Since revenue always equals $5, profits are maximized when costs are minimized. The monopolist should produce as little as possible to maximize profits.

5. Under competition, all 5 units are always sold, so that the supply curve is vertical at $Q = 5$. Supply equals demand at $Q = 5$, $p = 5$. The monopolist wants to maximize profits. If it sells fewer than 5 units, profits fall. The reason is that marginal revenue is positive if output is less than 5. If the monopolist sells 5 units, price equals 5. Hence, monopoly and competition produce identical results.

Chapter 6

1. A monopolist that is taxed at a rate equal to the social marginal cost of pollution internalizes the externality. That is, its private marginal cost equals the social marginal cost, MC_s in Figure 6.1, which takes full account of the harm of pollution. Making the monopolist bear the full social costs, however, does not lead to the social optimum. The monopolist equates its marginal revenue with MC_s. As shown in Figure 6.1, it will produce even less than Q_m, the amount it would produce if it were not taxed. As a result, its price rises. Society gains because of lower pollution levels, but loses because too small a Q is produced. If feasible, a better solution is to force the monopolist

to produce the socially optimal quantity, Q^*, at a price, p^*, equal to the marginal social cost.

3. There are three equilibria shown in the diagram: X, Y, and Z. Equilibria X and Z are stable, and Y is unstable. If a price less than p_X, the price at equilibrium X, were charged, there would be excess demand resulting in upward pressure on the price. The price rises until it reaches p_X (where there is no excess demand). Similarly, if the price were slightly too high, excess supply would force the price down. Thus, equilibrium X is a stable equilibrium. By similar reasoning, equilibrium Z is also stable. If, however, the price is slightly less than p_Y, the price at equilibrium Y, excess supply puts downward pressure on the price. The price falls until a new equilibrium at X is established. Similarly, if the price is slightly above p_Y, excess demand drives the price up until it reaches p_Z. Thus, Y is an equilibrium (demand equals supply), but it is unstable. Any shock will cause the market to shift to either equilibrium X or Z.

5. A tax of t per fish may actually reduce the price

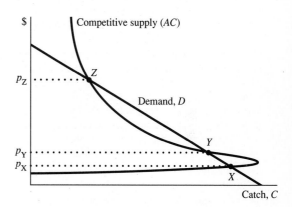

consumers pay. There is excessive fishing activity in a competitive fishery because fishermen's private marginal costs are less than the social marginal costs. A properly set tax causes the fishermen to internalize the externality. To show how the tax can help, consider Figure 6.3a. A tax of t shifts the effective demand for fish down by t. For a small t, this tax increases output from C_c and reduces the price from p_c, so consumers benefit from the tax. In addition the government collects tax revenues. In Figure 6.3b, a tax would reduce the output, and the price would rise from the optimal tax.

Chapter 7

1. As long as the new entrant can duplicate Firm A's success, it need not face a long-run entry barrier. However, the entrant may be concerned that if it enters, it may not recoup its specialized R&D costs, and this fact could deter entry.

3. High rates of entry are found in industries with high rates of exit even when overall industry demand is relatively stable. This result can occur only if firms are heterogeneous and if their relative efficiencies are constantly changing.

5. Aggregate concentration can change if the importance of individual industries changes. For example, if Industry 1 has a CR4 of .50 and Industry 2 has a CR4 of .30, aggregate concentration rises as Industry 1 becomes larger relative to Industry 2.

Chapter 8

1. In Figure 8.2, the dominant firm sells Q_d, whereas the monopolist sells Q_m. Since the monopolist could have sold Q_d and chose not to, it must make higher profits at Q_m. The monopolist's costs to produce the extra output are the area under the MC curve between Q_d and Q_m. Its extra revenues are the area under the marginal revenue curve, MR_m, between Q_d and Q_m. Thus, by producing Q_m instead of Q_d, its profits increase by the area between the MR_m and the MC curve between Q_d and Q_m. On the first Q_d units, the monopolist's costs are the same as the dominant firm's (by assumption), and it receives a higher price, p_m instead of p. Thus, the monopolist makes more on the first Q_d units as well, and hence must make higher profits overall.

3. If the n fringe firms have U-shaped average cost curves with a minimum cost c at quantity q, the fringe's supply curve is horizontal at c up to quantity nq and then is upward sloping and equal to n times a single firm's marginal cost curve. As a result, the dominant firm's residual demand curve has three sections. The first section of the residual demand curve, which corresponds to the upward sloping section of the fringe's supply curve, is similar to the higher section in Figure 8.1b. The next section, corresponding to the flat section of the fringe's supply curve, is flat at c. The last section, as in Figure 8.1b, shows that the residual demand curve equals the market demand at prices less than c. There may be equilibria

in each of these three sections, with equilibria in the first and third sections similar to those shown in Figure 8.1b. Equilibria in the flat section may lead to some of the fringe firms exiting the industry.

5. In Figure 8.2, if the MC curve crosses the MR_r and MR_m curves below the point where these two curves cross, a dominant firm produces more than a monopolist.

Chapter 9

1. Your drawing should look like Figure 8.1b if you assume no entry, where the cartel acts as though it is a dominant firm. If you assume free entry, your drawing should look like Figure 8.3b. If the cartel's marginal costs are low enough so that it maximizes its profits at a price below the noncartel member's shut-down price, the cartel drives the fringe out of business.

3. Your graph should show that as the demand curve becomes flatter at a given point (that is, its elasticity increases), the cartel's residual demand curve also becomes flatter. As a result, the intersection of MC and residual MR occurs at a lower quantity and a lower price.

5. Because noncartel members produce more than cartel members, shifting one of the n firms from the cartel to the noncartel group increases output, all else the same. Increasing the number of noncartel firms, m, by Equation 9A.11, causes the cartel's quantity to fall:

$$\frac{\partial Q_c}{\partial m} = -\frac{(a - bd)(be + n)}{(be + 2n - m)^2} < 0,$$

because $(a - bd)$ is positive (or else Q_c is negative). Total output, Q, is the sum of the fringe supply, $m(p - d)/e$ (from Equation 9A.4), and Q_c (Equation 9A.11). After substituting for p from Equation 9A.1 and rearranging terms:

$$Q = (nbe + 2nm - m^2)(a - bd)/D,$$

where $D = (be + 2n - m)(be + m)$. Differentiating this expression for Q with respect to m, we obtain

$$\partial Q/\partial m = 2(n - m)b^2e^2(a - bd)/D^2 > 0.$$

Because total output increases, price must fall.

Chapter 10

1. A sufficient condition for the Cournot and Bertrand equilibria to be identical is for the market demand curve to be horizontal (perfectly elastic). Another sufficient condition is for there to be an infinite number of firms, so that the elasticity facing any one firm is infinite.

3. Given this new payoff table, it pays for both firms to cooperate and charge the high price. Neither firm has an incentive to deviate from this strategy.

5. The modified table is:

Number of Firms	Market Elasticity, ϵ	Lerner's Measure	Consumer Surplus	Welfare	Dead-weight Loss
2	−1.0833	.4615	115.2	230.4	28.8
5	−.6666	.3	180	252	7.2
10	−.5271	.1884	214.4	257.2	2.0
50	−.4166	.048	249.1	259.1	.1
1,000	−.3903	.0026	258.7	259.2	.0

Note that in confirming that Lerner's measures equals $1/(n\epsilon)$, the outputs prices for 10 or more firms in Table 10.3 are rounded.

Chapter 11

1. A franchise or lump-sum tax shifts up a firm's average cost, but not its marginal cost curve. As a result, a franchise tax has no effect on a monopoly unless it causes it to shut down. The quantity that maximizes the before-tax profits maximizes the after-tax profits as well.

The tax does affect individual competitive firms. If all competitive firms are identical and there is free entry, then after the tax, firms still in the industry are producing at a higher minimum average cost (reflecting the tax) and a higher quantity. Because the price is higher, less total quantity is consumed, thus because each firm produces more than without the tax, there are fewer competitive firms.

The tax also affects monopolistically competitive firms, but the effects are complex and depend on the shapes of the demand and cost curves. Table 11.2 shows what happens with a linear demand curve and a cost function $= mq + F$. For example, if $F = \$1.60$ and a franchise tax of $4.80 is applied, the equilibrium number of firms drops from 17 to 8, output per firm doubles from 40 to 80, and the price rises from 32¢ to 36¢. See the answer to Problem 5 below for a more formal approach.

3. Table 11.2 shows three monopolistically competitive equilibria (for $F = \$6.40$, $1.60, and $0). In the third of these equilibria ($F = \$0$), there are an infinite number of firms; the competitive price, 28¢, is charged; and output equals 720 (using the demand curve: $Q = 1000 - 1000p$). Where $F = \$160$, there are 17 firms in equilibrium; the price, 32¢, is above the competitive level; and total output is only 680. Suppose, however, that one more firm were to produce at the same level (40 units) as the existing firms. Output would equal 720, and price equals MC, 28¢. Similarly, at the equilibrium with $F = \$6.40$, industry output is 640, and price is 36¢. Yet, if one more firm were to produce at the same level as these firms, industry output would equal 720, where price equals MC. Indeed, it is positive fixed costs that keep the Cournot, monopolistically competitive equilibrium from being efficient. Where fixed costs are positive, there is only room for one less firm than would make industry output equal the competitive output at $F = 0$. There is only room in the sense that if one more firm were to enter, all firms would lose money.

5. A technological innovation that lowers fixed costs has the opposite effect of a franchise tax, discussed in the answer to Problem 1 above. A technological change that lowers marginal cost would tend to increase output, but the exact effects depend on the shapes of the demand and cost curves.

Formally, suppose the market demand curve is linear, $P = a - bnq$, where there are n identical firms, each of which produces q units of output with total costs $mq + F$. Each firm's profits are

$$\pi_i = (a - bnq)q - mq - F.$$

If the firms play Cournot, each firm's profit-maximizing, first-order condition ($MR - MC = 0$) is

$$(a - bnq) - b - m = 0,$$

where the third term is b instead of bn because of the Cournot assumption. Free entry implies that firms enter until price equals average cost:

$$a - bnq = m + F/q.$$

Combining the last two equations to eliminate m and rearranging terms yields $q = F/b$. Thus, $dq/dF = 1/b > 0$. So as F falls, q falls in equilibrium, as shown in Table 11.2 and discussed in the answer to Problem 1 above. Using $q = F/b$ and the free-entry equation,

$$n = (a - b - m)/F$$

Differentiating this expression with respect to F, we obtain $dn/dF = -(a - b - m)/F^2 < 0$. Thus, technological progress that lowers F increases the number of firms. The change in total output is

$$dnq/dF = ndq/dF + qdn/dF$$
$$= (nF - a + b + m)/bF < 0,$$

and the change in price is $dp/dF = -b(dnq/dF) > 0$. Similarly, $dn/dm = -1/F < 0$, $dq/dm = 0$, $dnq/dm < 0$, and $dp/dm = 1$.

Chapter 12

1. The commonly used price-cost margin typically excludes capital and advertising costs. Moreover, even when costs include advertising, the cost measure typically expenses advertising rather than depreciating it, as is proper if advertising effects are long-lasting. These sources of bias can sometimes be mitigated by including A/Q and K/Q ratios on the right side of the regression. Both ratios are probably endogenous variables and are chosen simultaneously with price. Therefore, appropriate simultaneous equation econometric techniques should be used. Moreover, it is not always true that including these ratios linearly is appropriate. For example, if advertising depreciation is nonlinear, including A/Q won't remove the bias. Moreover, if rental rates on capital are not constant over time, including K/Q with a single coefficient is wrong.

3. The domestic concentration ratio based on data from only domestic firms is an upper bound on the relevant concentration ratio if international trade is important. An increase in imports in an industry could explain why high concentration ratios are less correlated with high price-cost margins, since those industries are now increasingly competitive.

5. In a perfectly competitive world, each firm's price equals marginal cost even in the short run. With entry, profits of the last firm to enter equal zero. Firms that are relatively efficient earn profits. In a noncompetitive world, (for example, one with monopolistic competition) price can exceed marginal cost. With entry, price can remain in excess of marginal cost, but the profits of the last firm to enter typically are driven to zero in the long run.

Chapter 13

1. Swaps can save transportation costs. If the paper firm in New York had to ship to its California customer, and the paper firm in California had to ship to its New York customer, freight costs would be higher than if the firms shipped to the customers located in their own states. Swaps can also facilitate collusion. Suppose two firms collude by assigning customers to each other. This division of the market may make collusion simple because it may be easy to detect a rival's sales to another rival's assigned customers. In the absence of swaps, the assignment of customers to firms may be too costly because of transportation costs.

3. If all firms have a high debt/equity ratio, and if going bankrupt is a blot on a manager's record, then the incentive to cut price is reduced. If firms differ widely in their debt/equity ratios, if new firms can enter, or if the interest rates on debt vary widely across firms, the price level is not likely to be affected by whether a few firms have high debt/equity ratios.

5. The discounted present value of the annual loss of $1 million is $8.51 million, using the formula given in the question. The discounted present value of the annual gain of $1 million from Year 21 onward is $1.49m$, using the formula given in the question. In order for the gain to exceed the loss, m must exceed $5.7 million.

Chapter 14

1. No producers of aluminum wire can survive. The price of aluminum ingot is so high that there is not enough profit left between the price of aluminum wire and the price of aluminum ingot.

3. Senior citizens may be less costly to serve than others. For example, they may litter the theater less, and their preferences for movies may be easier to predict

than those of teenagers so that there are fewer unsold seats.

5. The demand curve forms a rectangle. It is horizontal from zero to 1 unit at $10 and then drops to zero at 1 unit. The maximum consumer surplus that can be captured is the entire area under the demand curve, which occurs if price is set equal to $10. When there are two consumers, there is no consumption inefficiency because there are no further transactions that would improve at least one consumer's welfare.

Chapter 15

1. Suppose the coupon entitles the consumer to a 10¢ price reduction, and the consumer has 20 coupons. The firm may want to lower the price to the consumer on 20 units by 10¢ rather than lowering the price on 1 unit by $2.

3. The consumer's budget constraint is $Y + X^2 = 100$, so that $Y = 100 - X^2$. Utility equals $100 - X^2 + 10X$. The X that maximizes utility is 5.

5. Monopolist 1 maximizes $p_1(10 - 2p_1 + p_2)$ and Monopolist 2 maximizes $p_2(10 + p_1 - 2p_2)$. The two first-order conditions are $10 - 4p_1 + p_2 = 0$ and $10 + p_1 - 4p_2 = 0$. Solving yields $p_1 = p_2 = 10/3$. A monopolist of both products chooses p_1 and p_2 to maximize $p_1(10 - 2p_1 + p_2) + p_2(10 + p_1 - 2p_2)$. The two first-order conditions are $10 - 4p_1 + p_2 + p_2 = 0$ and $p_1 + 10 + p_1 - 4p_2 = 0$. Solving yields $p_1 = p_2 = 5$.

Chapter 16

1. The profits of a franchisee are $\pi = R(q)(1 - \alpha) - C(q)$, where $R(q)$ are sales and $C(q)$ are costs, if royalties are α times sales or revenues. The franchisee bears all costs but receives only part of the revenues. Therefore, the franchisee sells less than is optimal. If royalties are β share of (preroyalty) profits, then $\pi = [R(q) - C(q)](1 - \beta)$. Whichever q maximizes preroyalty profits also maximizes postroyalty profits. Thus, the franchisee sells the optimal amount. Presumably, franchisors collect royalties as a percent of sales, in spite of this reasoning, because observing profits is more difficult than observing revenues. That is, franchisees may be better able to lie about costs than revenues (see also the answer to Problem 5).

3. Example 16.3 provides an analogous example. If a pure profits tax is only collected at the retail level, there is a greater incentive to vertically integrate, even with fixed-proportions production. For example, an integrated firm could charge its own retailer a very high price for the factor it supplies. As a result, profits at the downstream level are relatively low (and hence relatively untaxed), and profits at the upstream level are relatively high. If the tax were collected both upstream and downstream, this incentive is removed. A sales tax at the retail level does not provide a similar incentive to integrate.

5. The franchisor (Kentucky Fried Chicken) uses the number of barrels to check the veracity of its retailers (Gino's) so as to insure they pay all the royalties they owe. The only obvious way to avoid this monitoring device is to sell chicken in other containers. Spot checks by the franchisor may discourage this avoidance technique. The argument for allowing this approach is that it facilitates vertical relations.

Chapter 17

1. If consumers who are most price-sensitive are more likely to read a certain magazine than other consumers, manufacturers can *target* the former by only providing discount coupons in that magazine. That way, the manufacturer can give a price discount to price-sensitive consumers and charge other consumers a higher price. This approach only increases the manufacturer's profits if it does not have to worry about resale between the two groups of consumers, if the two consumer groups have different elasticities, and if not too many of the other group of consumers read the magazine (or otherwise obtain the discount coupons).

3. Many authors (including us) agree to royalties that are a percent of revenues rather than profits. Such a royalty system gives the publisher the incentive to produce too few books, since the publisher incurs the full marginal cost of printing the last book but only gets a fraction of the revenues, $1 - \alpha$. As a result, joint profits are lower than they would be under the other two systems, where the publisher has the incentive to produce the optimal number of books. One possible reason that authors do not want royalties that are a percent of profits is that they are afraid that the

publisher may lie about its costs. Even without lying, authors and publishers could differ about appropriate costs because many costs of publishing are joint costs, and it is hard to allocate costs between various books. You may have read in newspapers that movie actors entitled to a percent of profits are constantly suing producers who tell them that their hit movie produced no profits because of large costs. Publishers may be hesitant to pay authors lump-sum royalties because authors would then have little incentive to produce products that will sell well. See also the answer to problem 16.1.

5. Suppose a consumer's estimate of the price in store i is

$$s_i = p_i + \beta\epsilon_i,$$

where β is a constant and ϵ_i is a random variable drawn from a distribution with a mean of zero. That is, the consumer's expectation of the price is unbiased: $E(s_i) = p_i + \beta E(\epsilon_i) = p_i$. If $\beta = 0$, the consumer knows the true price. As β becomes larger, the consumer's estimate of the true price, although unbiased, could be very inaccurate. A consumer then buys from the store that he or she believes has the lowest price. That is, the consumer goes to store 1 if $s_1 < s_2$. By using the reasoning discussed in Appendix 11C, one can show that the markup of price over marginal cost increases as β becomes larger. That is, stores have more market power, the less accurately consumers know the prices charged by each store.

Chapter 18

1. Shapiro (1980)[1] illustrates his point using an example with two consumers in which each consumer's demand is $q(p)$, and the monopolist produces with constant marginal cost, c. By assumption, before advertising, only one consumer knows about the product, and after advertising, both know it exists. Advertising does not change tastes; it merely informs the unaware consumer that the product exists. The preadvertising demand curve, $q(p)$, is half of the postadvertising demand curve, $2q(p)$, which is the horizontal sum of the demand of the two consumers.

[1] See Chapter 18 references.

The monopolist charges p^* in either case, where p^* maximizes $(p - c)q(p)$ and $(p - c)2q(p)$, since c is constant. In the preadvertising equilibrium, point E in the figure, output is $q^* = q(p^*)$. In the postadvertising equilibrium, E', output is $2q^*$.

In the preadvertising equilibrium, E, only one potential consumer purchases the good, so welfare is the area under the $q(p)$ demand curve between 0 and q^* above c. Advertising has a distributive gain, shown in the accompanying figure by the shaded triangle, which reflects the gain in consumer surplus from informing the other consumer. That is, consumer surplus is the area under the $2q(p)$ demand curve if the two consumers each consume half of the output, instead of having one consumer consume it all and the other, none. Since the monopolist does not capture this gain, it has *too little* incentive to advertise.

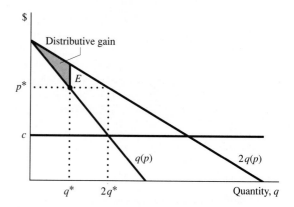

3. See Butters (1977)[1] for an analysis of this problem. If firms are advertising that they have low prices, then the analysis is similar to that of the tourist-native model in Chapter 17. It is possible that, in equilibrium, some stores charge high prices and other stores charge low prices.

5. The monopolist's problem is

$$\max_{Q,\alpha} \pi = pQ - cQ - \alpha$$

$$= (a + \alpha - bQ)Q - cQ - \alpha.$$

The two first-order conditions are

$$\frac{\partial \pi}{\partial Q} = a + \alpha - 2bQ - c = 0$$

$$\frac{\partial \pi}{\partial \alpha} = Q - 1 = 0.$$

That is, $Q = 1$ and $\alpha = 2b + c - a$.

Chapter 19

1. Let the demand for tractor services be $D(R)$, where R is the rental rate of tractors, and let the elasticity of demand for tractor services be ϵ. The demand for tractors facing the monopolist, $D^*(R)$, is $D(R) - 20$. The elasticity of demand for tractors, ϵ^*, is then

$$\frac{dD^*}{dR} \frac{R}{D^*} = \frac{dD}{dR} \frac{R}{D(R) - 20}$$
$$= \frac{dD}{dR} \frac{R}{D(R)} \frac{D(R)}{D(R) - 20}$$
$$= \epsilon \frac{D(R)}{D(R) - 20},$$

since $dD^*/dR = d(D(R) - 20)/dR = dD/dR$. That is, $\epsilon^* = \epsilon(N + O)/N$, where N is the number of new tractors, $D(R) - 20$, and O is the number of old tractors, 20. Holding the elasticity for tractor services, ϵ, constant, then as the ratio of old to new machines, O/N, rises, so does the elasticity for new tractors, ϵ^*.

3. If transaction costs are high, the demand for new tractors is not affected by the stock of old tractors if the farmers who currently need tractors are not the same ones who already own old tractors. If, on the other hand, the same farmers that need tractors today may already own old tractors from before, the analysis is the same as in (1).

5. If many other firms make tractors that are close substitutes for the four-wheel-drive tractor produced by a monopolist, then the elasticity for tractor services, ϵ (defined in the answer to (1) above), is high and thus the monopolist has little market power: ϵ^* is high.

Chapter 20

1. A sales tax reduces the profits from a monopoly without affecting the costs of research. Because the ben-

efits fall and the costs do not, research effort falls.

3. In Figure 20.1a, a longer patent life does not affect the cost curve, but shifts up the expected benefit curve, reflecting the longer time that the patent winner receives monopoly rents. As a result, the expected benefit and cost curves intersect further to the right (larger number of firms). Typically, the number of firms competing increases with patent life.

5. Suppose that each firm that races to make a discovery must incur a fixed cost to enter the race (for example, the expense of setting up a research lab). If there is a constant marginal cost of additional research effort, than each research firm is operating in a region of falling average costs. These fixed costs give society an incentive to reduce the number of research firms if one research firm can conduct many independent projects.

Chapter 21

1. If the bakery produces 50, it always can sell them at $5 each. Costs are $50, so the bakery's profits are $200. If the bakery produces 100, it incurs costs of $100 and earns revenues of either $500 or $250, or $375 on average. Hence, its average profits are $275, and producing 100 is optimal. If the price is $1.50, then when the bakery produces 50, its profits are $25. When the bakery produces 100, its revenues are either $150 or $75, or $112.50 on average; its costs are $100; and average profits are $12.50. Hence producing 50 is optimal. (Readers should convince themselves that the optimal output can only be 0, 50, or 100.)

3. A competitive firm chooses quantity so that price equals marginal cost. As price rises above the shutdown point, the price-average cost margin increases.

5. If it is costly to use the price system, the variability of a customer's demand affects the supplier's cost, and so customers with different demand variabilities pay different prices. There is no price discrimination when prices vary according to costs.

Chapter 22

1. If a customer has signed a contract of fixed duration, rival suppliers are precluded from obtaining (at least some of) the customer's business. If there is competition initially to sign up the customer, the fact that

contracts last for 10 years does not necessarily prevent the customer from paying a competitive price. If the contracts prevent rivals from reaching a scale required for efficiency, competition could be reduced.

3. Unclear. In some industries, collusion could lead to efficiency gains that outweigh any harm caused by elevated collusive pricing. It may be a difficult task for an enforcement agency to identify such industries.

5. The formula says that the direct price elasticity of good i equals (in absolute value) the sum of all cross-elasticities of good i with respect to the price of good j. If a cross-elasticity is large and positive, the price elasticity tends to be large, and market power tends to be low. The relevant cross-elasticity, according to the formula, is the one relating the quantity of Product A to the price of Product B.

Chapter 23

1. In Figure 23.3, at $p = p_a$, the profits are zero, so $(p_a - p^*)Q_a$ = fixed costs = Areas $A + B$. The consumer surplus, and hence welfare, is the area under the demand curve and above p_a between 0 and Q_a. At $p = p^*$, the firm's lost profits equal Areas $A + B$. The consumer surplus is the area under the demand curve and above p^* between 0 and Q^*. That is, consumer surplus equals Areas $A + C$. But, since the lost profits equal $(p_a - p^*)Q_a$, total welfare equals Areas $A + C$ minus $(p_a - p^*)Q_a$. That is, at

$p = p^*$, total welfare is equal to two triangles, a triangle equal to the consumer surplus at $p = p_a$ and a second triangle that lies under the demand curve and above p^* between Q_a and Q^*. Thus, welfare must be higher at $p = p^*$ than at $p = p_a$.

3. An acreage quota causes farmers to use more of other inputs, such as labor and fertilizer, so that output does not fall as much as acreage. This inefficiency in production leads to deadweight loss. It also causes the supply curve to shift to the left, but by a smaller percentage than acreage falls. Holding the support price constant, the government buys less excessive crops than without acreage controls.

5. One alternative is to give farmers cash. Such a program improves farmers' well-being at lower cost than existing programs. It does not cause the production and distribution inefficiencies described in the chapter.

7. Because of the asymmetry in returns, rate-of-return regulation provides limited incentives to invent. If a firm makes an important discovery that, say, lowers its costs of production, its profits rise less than in proportion to the social gain. If it is unsuccessful in making the discovery, the firm bears the expense and has lower profits. This problem in an industry with rapid innovation can be reduced if regulators are slow to change the cost basis in calculating the rate of return.

Legal Case Index

Author Index

SUBJECT INDEX